Western Civilizations

Their History & Their Culture

Western Civilizations
Their History & Their Culture

BRIEF SIXTH EDITION
VOLUME TWO

> **JOSHUA COLE**
University of Michigan, Ann Arbor

> **CAROL SYMES**
University of Illinois, Urbana-Champaign

W. W. NORTON & COMPANY
Independent Publishers Since 1923

W. W. NORTON & COMPANY has been independent since its founding in 1923, when William Warder Norton and Mary D. Herter Norton first published lectures delivered at the People's Institute, the adult education division of New York City's Cooper Union. The firm soon expanded its program beyond the Institute, publishing books by celebrated academics from America and abroad. By midcentury, the two major pillars of Norton's publishing program—trade books and college texts—were firmly established. In the 1950s, the Norton family transferred control of the company to its employees, and today—with a staff of four hundred and a comparable number of trade, college, and professional titles published each year—W. W. Norton & Company stands as the largest and oldest publishing house owned wholly by its employees.

Printed in Canada

Editor: Justin Cahill
Senior Associate Editor: Anna Olcott
Project Editor: Linda Feldman
Managing Editor, College: Marian Johnson
Production Manager: Sean Mintus
Media Editor: Betsy Twitchell
Associate Media Editor: Hillary Roegelein
Media Project Editor: Rachel Mayer
Media Editorial Assistant: Jennifer Jussell
Managing Editor, College Digital Media: Kim Yi

Ebook Producer: Kate Brayton
Marketing Manager: Sarah England Bartley
Design Director: Rubina Yeh
Director of College Permissions: Megan Schindel
Permissions Specialist: Elizabeth Trammell
Photo Editor: Mike Cullen
Composition: KW Global
Illustrations Studio: Mapping Specialists
Manufacturing: Transcontinental

The Library of Congress has cataloged a previous edition as follows:

Names: Cole, Joshua, 1961- author. | Symes, Carol, author.
Title: Western civilizations : their history & their culture / Joshua Cole,
  Carol Symes.
Description: 20th edition. | New York : W. W. Norton & Company, [2020] |
  Includes index.
Identifiers: LCCN 2019030137 | ISBN 9780393418750 (cloth)
Subjects: LCSH: Civilization, Western—Textbooks. |
  Europe—Civilization—Textbooks.
Classification: LCC CB245 .C56 2020 | DDC 909/.09821—dc23
LC record available at https://lccn.loc.gov/2019030137

This edition: ISBN 978-1-324-04305-8 (pbk)

W. W. Norton & Company, Inc., 500 Fifth Avenue, New York, NY 10110
wwnorton.com

W. W. Norton & Company Ltd., 15 Carlisle Street, London W1D 3BS
1 2 3 4 5 6 7 8 9 0

About the Authors

JOSHUA COLE (PhD, University of California, Berkeley) is professor of history at the University of Michigan, Ann Arbor. He has published work on gender and the history of population sciences, colonial violence, and the politics of memory in nineteenth- and twentieth-century France, Germany, and Algeria. His first book was *The Power of Large Numbers: Population, Politics, and Gender in Nineteenth-Century France* (2000), and he recently published a second book, *Lethal Provocation: The Constantine Murders and the Politics of French Algeria* (2019), that won three national awards.

CAROL SYMES (PhD, Harvard University) is associate professor of history and University Scholar at the University of Illinois, Urbana-Champaign, where she has served as director of undergraduate studies in history and won numerous teaching awards. Her main areas of study include the history of medieval Europe in its global context, cultural history, and the history of media and communication technologies. Her first book, *A Common Stage: Theater and Public Life in Medieval Arras* (Cornell University Press, 2007), won four national awards. She is the founding executive editor of *The Medieval Globe*, the first academic journal to promote a global approach to medieval studies.

Brief Contents

Contents

Chapter 21 › REVOLUTIONS AND NATION BUILDING, 1848–1871   722

Chapter 22 › IMPERIALISM AND COLONIALISM, 1870–1914   764

Chapter 29 › A WORLD WITHOUT WALLS? GLOBALIZATION AND THE WEST   1042

Maps

Primary Sources

Preface

THIS BRIEF SIXTH EDITION of *Western Civilizations* is a landmark in a long and continuing journey. Since the original publication of the Full Edition in 1941, this book has been assiduously updated by succeeding generations of historians who have kept it at the forefront of the field in both scholarship and pedagogical innovation. Our newest edition carries this legacy forward, further honing the tools we have developed to empower students—our own and yours—to engage effectively with the themes, sources, and challenges of history. It presents a clear and concise narrative of events that unfolded over many thousands of years, supplemented by a compelling selection of primary sources and striking images. At the same time, it features a unified program of pedagogical elements that guide students from understanding core content to reading and analyzing historical sources and, finally, to developing a sophisticated sense of the ways that historians reconstruct the past on the basis of those sources. This framework, and a brand-new set of activities built around select sources from each chapter, helps students to read and interpret historical evidence on their own, encouraging them to become active participants in the learning process and helping them to think historically.

The wide chronological and geographical scope of this book offers an unusual opportunity to trace historical trends across several interrelated regions—western Asia, the Middle East, North Africa, and Europe—whose cultural diversity has been constantly reinvigorated and renewed. Our increasing awareness that no region's history can be isolated from global processes and connections has merely heightened the need for a richly contextualized and broad-based history such as that represented in *Western Civilizations*. In this edition, we have added an attention to the changing meanings of ethnicity and race in human societies. This focus adds a further dimension to our already rich treatment of human mobility. The study of human mobility—and the corresponding evolution of ideas about human differences—have emerged as a vital field of study in recent years. Today's students are deeply interested and invested in the relationship between globalization and population movements, and the ways that this mobility is related to social conflict, environmental changes, and contemporary disagreements about race, ethnicity, and national identity. It is important that students be able to put these contemporary discussions in historical context and to see their own concerns and aspirations reflected in the historical curriculum.

As in previous editions, we have continued to balance the coverage of political, social, economic, and cultural phenomena with extensive treatment of gender, race, sexuality, daily life, material culture, art, science, and popular culture. Our history is also attentive to the latest developments in historical scholarship. The title of this book asserts that there is no single and enduring "Western civilization" whose inevitable march to domination can be traced chapter by chapter through time. This older paradigm, strongly associated with the curriculum of early twentieth-century American colleges and universities, no longer conforms to what we know about the human past. It was also overly reliant on the nationalist histories of only a few countries, notably England, France, and Germany. In this book, we therefore pay much closer attention to central and eastern Europe, as well as to Europeans' near neighbors in Asia, Africa, and the Atlantic world, with a particular focus on European and Muslim relations throughout the Mediterranean and Middle East. No history of Western civilizations can be coherent if it leaves out the intense conflicts, extraordinary ruptures, and dynamic changes that took place within and across all of these territories. Indeed, smoothing out the rough edges of the past does students no favors. Even an introductory text such as this one should present the past as it appears to the historians who study it: as a complex panorama of human effort, filled with possibility and achievement but also fraught with discord, uncertainty, accident, and tragedy.

Pedagogical Features

In our continuing effort to promote the active study of history, we've designed this book to reinforce your course objectives by helping your students to master core content while challenging them to think critically about the past. Those familiar with the previous Brief Edition of *Western Civilizations* will find here refined pedagogical tools inspired by instructor and student feedback, including bolded key terms with definitions in the margins as well as marginal review flags that offer guidance for students as they review. As we know from long experience, many students in introductory survey courses find the sheer quantity of information overwhelming, and so we have provided guidance to help them navigate through the material and to read in meaningful ways.

At the outset of each chapter, the *Before You Read This Chapter* feature offers two key windows into the material to be covered: *Story Lines*, which allow the student to become familiar with the primary narrative threads that tie the chapter's elements together, and *Core Objectives*, which alert the student to the primary teaching points in the chapter. The student is then reminded of these teaching points upon completing the chapter, in the *After You Read This Chapter* section, which revisits the material in four key ways. First, the *Chronology* presents a brief timeline of major developments in the period under study. The second, *Reviewing the Objectives*, asks the reader to reconsider the *Core Objectives* by answering a pointed question about each one. Third, *Peoples, Ideas, and Events in Context* summarizes some of the particulars that students should retain from their reading, through questions that allow them to relate individual terms to the major objectives and story lines. These key terms appear in bold type in the body of the chapter along with the marginal definitions mentioned above. Finally, *Thinking About Connections* allows for more open-ended reflection on the significance of the chapter's main themes, drawing students' attention to issues that connect it to previous chapters and to their own historical present. Together, these pedagogical features serve to enhance the student's learning experience by breaking down the process of reading and analysis into manageable tasks.

A second package of pedagogical features is designed to capture students' interest and to compel them to think about what is at stake in the construction and use of historical narratives. Each chapter opens with a vignette that showcases a particular person or event representative of the era as a whole. Within each chapter, an expanded program of illustrations and maps are enhanced by the addition of *Questions for Analysis* that urge the reader to explore the historical contexts and significance of these images in a more analytical way. The historical value of visual artifacts is further emphasized in another feature: **Interpreting Visual Evidence.** This section provides a provocative departure point for analytical discussions about the key issues raised by visual sources, which students often find more approachable than texts. Once this conversation has begun, students can further develop their skills with the **Analyzing Primary Sources** feature, which offers close readings of primary texts accompanied by thought-provoking interpretive questions. The diversity of Western civilizations is also illuminated through a look at **Competing Viewpoints** in each chapter, in which specific debates are presented through paired primary source texts. In the new Norton Illumine Ebook, the **Competing Viewpoints** features have been transformed into engaging interactive activities that marry audio, pop-ups providing definitions and analysis of sources, and clickable assessments graded on completion. These interactive activities are paired with two new Check Your Understanding questions with rich answer-specific feedback at the end of each chapter section that motivate students and give them opportunities to practice their learning. The bibliographical Further Readings, located at the end of the book, has also been brought up to date.

A Tour of Chapters and the Newest Revisions

Our previous edition of *Western Civilizations* updated and reorganized the presentation of material on central and eastern Europe in order to provide a richer account of Europe's diverse political and social histories. We also developed a theme on environmental history in both volumes, with special attention to the ways that human society has been shaped by—and affected—the physical world. For this Sixth Edition we paid particular attention to the ways that evolving notions of "race" and other forms of human difference have intersected with the rise of Western concepts of democracy, liberalism, and equal citizenship.

In the Full Twenty-First Edition, we made a number of exciting updates, many of which were imported into this Brief Sixth Edition. Highlights include the following:

Chapter 1 takes account of recent scholarship challenging the traditional narrative of civilizational development as a straight line from settlements to urban centers. Though changes in the climate allowed for increased sedentary food production and regional trade, these practices did not entirely replace hunting and foraging or temporary settlements, as previously thought. In keeping with the new theme of this volume, which traces emerging ideas of human difference, this chapter explains how some early societies resisted developments in managed food production to avoid accumulating wealth or establishing the hierarchical structures characteristic of many civilizations. The chapter includes attention to new research on the role of ritual architecture in early settlements, such as Gobekli Tepe in Turkey. A new *Competing Viewpoints* feature examines how forms of inequality and unfree labor emerged in early societies, featuring excerpts from Exodus and an inscription from the Sumerian city of Lagash. A new *Analyzing Primary Sources* excerpt is taken from a ritual incantation performed at the entombment ceremony of an Egyptian pharaoh.

Chapter 2 has been updated with rich new research that adds nuance to our understanding of the various peoples who came to prominence during the Bronze Age, including the Hyksos and Phoenicians. A new *Analyzing Primary Sources* feature includes an excerpt from the Hebrew book of Samuel that depicts Samuel's ambivalence about choosing a human king to rule over the Israelites. A new section, "Climate Change and Civilizational Collapse," considers new research indicating that the fall of the Neo-Assyrian Empire can be partially attributed to a decades-long drought induced by climate change and over-farming. A new *Thinking About Connections* question asks students to consider how climatic changes have contributed to the success or failure of early civilizations.

Chapter 3 explores how Hellenic group identity was formed to exclude "barbarians": foreigners whom the Greeks considered to be culturally inferior. The *Story Lines* have been revised to reflect this focus, and a new section, "Hellenic Expansion and Identity," discusses the development of *ethnos*, or the Hellenic idea of group identity. A new *Interpreting Visual Evidence* feature reveals how recent discoveries add nuance to our own notions of Hellenic identity by demonstrating that classical Greek sculptures and buildings were brilliantly painted at the time of their creation: not starkly white, as once believed. The section titled "The Daily Life of Athens: Men, Women, and Slaves" includes a revised discussion of the role of slavery in ancient civilizations, emphasizing how any person could become enslaved, most often by warfare or poverty. A new *Thinking About Connections* question invites students to consider how modern anachronisms and assumptions have made it challenging to look for evidence of "race thinking" in pre-modern societies.

Chapter 4 continues with the investigation of slavery in antiquity through a new *Analyzing Primary Sources* excerpt in which Aristotle justifies the subjugation of humans by arguing that some people are naturally "free," namely Greek men, while others are not. The *Competing Viewpoints* feature includes a revised selection from Plato's *Republic* to better highlight Plato's argument about the participation of women in Hellenic society. Chapter 5 has been generally revised to underscore the presence of slavery in Roman society and the roles that enslaved individuals played in everyday life.

In Chapter 6, a new section on the narrowing pathway to Roman citizenship helps to explain the tensions between new waves of migrants and the imperial government, as well as the Goth's remarkable transition from refugees to rulers. A new *Analyzing Primary Sources* feature highlights an excerpt from the *Getica*, a history of the Gothic tribes that describes the career of Theodoric, who ruled the Eastern Gothic Kingdom of Italy. This excerpt further contributes to the theme of "difference" by revealing how Theodoric was able to rule successfully by maintaining and blending both Gothic and Roman cultural and identities. A new *Thinking About Connections* question prompts students to consider why women were excluded from leadership roles in the Christian Church.

The *Story Lines, Core Objectives*, and *Chronology* of Chapter 7 have been revised to account for new evidence on the effects of the Justinianic Plague, based on advances in ancient DNA research and archaeological evidence that have revealed the devastating effects of this first (semi-global) pandemic. A new map fully depicting the Arab world's relationships with the Roman Empire's heirs helps to demonstrate the complex political and cultural dynamics undergirding Islam's expansion, while a new section on the emergence of Islam more accurately captures the circumstances that enabled the proliferation of this new religion, including the varying levels of religious tolerance among neighboring civilizations. A brand-new discussion of the Iconoclast Controversy now emphasizes the role of wealthy monasteries in Byzantine society, as well considering how both Rabbinic Judaism and Islam affected Christian religious practices during this era.

Chapters 8 and 9 continue to elaborate on the many cultural, political, and economic changes of the Middle Ages, as the focus of the book shifts to northern and western Europe for the first time. Chapter 8 includes a new map of Paris that demonstrates how medieval cities were constructed and evolved over time, and how religious and urban life were intertwined. Chapter 9 includes a more extended discussion of developments in the Islamic world, considering how elite women were afforded opportunities and freedoms there as well as in Christian Europe and Byzantium.

Chapter 10 includes several new primary sources that offer insights on the ways that various forms of "difference" were understood in medieval Europe. A new *Analyzing Primary Sources* features a remarkable verse romance that complicates conventional understandings of premodern gender roles. A new *Competing Viewpoints* compares two documents describing antisemitic attacks on Jewish communities and the responses of Christian officials to those attacks. New research on the origins and spread of the Black Death has been included, since evidence now indicates that the plague had begun devastating communities in Asia by the end of the twelfth century.

In Chapter 11, a new section titled "Later Medieval Ideas of Religious and Physical Difference" engages in a nuanced discussion of how, over time, European Christians came to associate certain physical characteristics with Jews and Muslims. A new *Competing Viewpoints* includes two excerpts that reflect starkly different views on interreligious marriages and the meanings attached to dark skin. Finally, a *Thinking About Connections* question prompts students to consider how ideas about race were constructed before the modern era.

Chapter 12 has been revised to better capture the forced conversion or expulsion of Muslims from Iberia that accompanied the "reconquest" of Christian Spain. The discussion of encounters between European conquistadors and the Indigenous peoples of the Americas takes account of recent scholarship and clarifies what we know about the new arrivals' reliance on native interpreters like La Malinche, without whom Cortes would have been unable to challenge the Aztec empire. In Chapter 13, a revised discussion of the Christian reformers who preceded Martin Luther helps to contextualize the shifting landscape of a divided Christian Europe during the sixteenth century. A new *Thinking About Connections* question prompts students to consider whether a revolutionary break within the Roman Church was inevitable.

In Chapter 14, key sections have been revised to emphasize the destructive consequences of European colonial projects in the Americas, including emergence of a new, racially based idea of slavery in the Atlantic World. A new *Analyzing Primary Sources* reveals how the ruler of Ethiopia responded to the growing traffic in enslaved Africans by outlawing the capture or sale of his Christian subjects. Chapter 15 elaborates on the kidnap and sale of African men and women into slavery, noting that racial justifications for slavery came in later years. A careful discussion of the Code noir has been added, which examines how rules for enslaved people in the French colonies contributed to the emergence of modern ideas about racial difference. The description of John Locke's critique of absolutism has been revised to contextualize his complicated views on hereditary slavery.

Chapter 16 has been revised to account for the emergence of scientific theories about human races. A new section titled "From Geology to Geography and the Human Sciences" draws connections from the study of geology to the study of human populations, citing François Bernier, whose work categorizing humans by physical traits was an early example of what would become a general consensus about the existence of distinct human races. A new *Analyzing Primary Sources* includes an excerpt from Bernier's work where he puts forth his theory of different "races" or "species" of human. A new *Thinking About Connections* question asks students to consider the role of science and progress for natural philosophers and its implication for the future.

We have revised Chapter 17 to focus on the divergence between Enlightenment ideals and the treatment of enslaved African peoples. This chapter also includes a more in-depth discussion of slavery in the United States at the time of the Revolution. Chapter 18 explores these ideas further with a newly detailed discussion of the Haitian revolution and its radical application of Enlightenment ideals to enslaved populations.

Chapter 19's revisions focus on how industrialization and new technologies allowed for the further proliferation and profitability of slavery. Chapter 20 maintains its focus on the spread of nationalism, with a new emphasis on who was routinely excluded from the nationalist imagination. Threaded throughout the chapter is a new discussion of how racial hierarchy excluded enslaved Africans from citizenship and other "inalienable" rights.

Chapter 21 continues with concerns brought up in Chapter 20 regarding the exclusion of minority groups from national identity. Special attention is paid in this chapter to the deportation of Native Americans from their lands as the United States expanded westward, accompanied by a new map that shows the deported groups. The discussion of the American Civil War has been revised to include a depiction of Reconstruction and the implementation of so-called Black codes. A new *Competing Viewpoints* includes an excerpt from Frederick Douglass and an excerpt from an Italian nationalist, both invoking slavery as a lens to view national identity and freedom. A new *Analyzing Primary Sources* criticizes earlier writers who purported human populations could be divided into distinct races.

Chapter 22 defines, with greater specificity, kinds of imperialism and colonialism, and the resistance of colonized peoples, including indigenous peoples, enslaved peoples, and settlers themselves. Greater detail has been added to the discussion of the dynamics of settlers in Africa and the colonized population. A more nuanced discussion of Darwin's work has also been added and clarifies Darwin's stance on the delineation of human "races." A new *Analyzing Primary Sources* engages with the work of Arthur de Gobineau, which popularized a view of history where the major turning points could be explained by the relationships between "strong" and "weak" races. A new *Thinking About Connections* prompts students to consider how beliefs about race influenced the support of European colonialism in the nineteenth century.

In Chapter 23, we continue to examine how the idea of race emerged with a new *Analyzing Primary Sources* featuring work from Madison Grant, an American who embraced scientific definitions of race. The section on Social Darwinism has been revised to emphasize how the concept deviates from Darwin's original theories. A new *Thinking About Connections* question asks students to consider how scientific racism continues to resonate in the present. Chapter 24 has been revised to discuss how non-Turkish minorities came to be persecuted as nationalism grew, with particular focus on the American genocide.

Chapter 25 includes revisions to the section on Hitler's economic plan for Nazi Germany, accompanied by a new image showing Nazi propaganda promising economic recovery. The section titled "Nazi Racism" has been revised to connect the threads of conversation in earlier chapters about the long tradition of European racism with Hitler's own ideas of racial hierarchy and antisemitism. More details have been added to the sections on Jim Crow laws in the American South, the origins of the Great Depression, and the developments in physics that led to the development of the atomic bomb. Chapter 26 emphasizes the role of the French colonies in Africa as the roots of resistance against the Vichy government.

Chapter 27 has been revised with greater focus on the precarious position of the former European colonies after decolonization, including their vulnerability to extractive industries and the wealth inequality among Europeans and the diverse African populations. A new *Thinking About Connections* question asks students to consider the role of the United States and Europe in eastern European affairs during the Cold War and today. Revisions to Chapter 28 expand on the condition of Europe's colonies after decolonization, with particular focus on the legacy of colonial racism. A new *Competing Viewpoints* feature compares an article from German magazine *Der Spiegel* and bell hooks, both of whom invoked race in discussions of American popular music's social resonance in the second half of the 20th century, albeit in very different ways.

Chapter 29 brings both volumes to a close in a wide-ranging discussion that connects current events in Europe and the world to the deeper past. The *Core Objectives*, *Story Lines*, and *Chronology* have been updated to account for major world events including Brexit, the COVID-19 pandemic, and Russia's war in Ukraine. This final chapter discusses the economic and political turbulence of the first decades of the twenty-first century—the threat of terrorism, the global financial crisis of 2008, and the rise of populist political parties in Europe that challenge the goal of European integration—as an indication that the global order that emerged in the aftermath of the Second World War is now being transformed into something else whose contours remain as yet unclear. Political polarization and a weakening of democratic institutions in the United States has aggravated this uncertainty, and Russia's invasion of Ukraine in 2022 threatens to upend it altogether. The conclusion invites students to place these contemporary debates within the context of Europe's broader history, allowing them to connect what they have learned from the past to the world in which they themselves live.

Media Resources for Instructors and Students

History becomes an immersive experience for students using Norton's digital resources with *Western Civilizations*. The comprehensive ancillary package includes tools for teaching and learning that reinforce the *Core Objectives* from the narrative while building on the history skills introduced in the pedagogy throughout the book. This Brief Sixth Edition features a groundbreaking suite of resources, including a Norton Illumine Ebook that shines light on student learning through engaging and motivational features that illuminate core concepts for students in a supportive, low-stakes environment; InQuizitive, Norton's award-winning formative adaptive system; and an extensive library of History Skills Tutorials to guide students in analysis and interpretation. Norton is unique in partnering exclusively with subject matter experts who teach the course to author these and other resources listed below. As a result, instructors have all the course materials they need to successfully manage their Western Civilizations course, whether they are teaching face-to-face, online, or in a hybrid setting.

Student Resources

Norton Illumine Ebook Norton's high-quality content shines brighter through engaging and motivational features that illuminate core concepts for all students in a supportive, accessible, and low-stakes environment. Embedded interactives engage students with applications and explorations of important course content, and Check Your Understanding questions with rich feedback motivate students and build confidence in their learning. The active reading experience also includes the ability to highlight, take notes, search, read offline, and more. Instructors can promote student accountability by adding their own content and notes and through easy-to-use assignment tools in their LMS. Norton Ebooks can be viewed on—and synced among—all computers and mobile devices. Norton Ebooks are born accessible, which means we keep all learners in mind during the entire production process. The assignable *Western Civilizations* Norton Illumine Ebook includes the following enhanced features:

+ **NEW** Check Your Understanding questions with rich answer-specific feedback that motivates students and builds confidence in their learning. Multiple-choice questions appear at the end of each chapter section and provide students the opportunity to test their understanding of important material immediately after they first encounter it within the reading.

+ **NEW** Competing Viewpoints interactives transform the popular primary source document feature in each chapter into an engaging integrative activity, including embedded interactive questions and feedback. One interactive in each chapter includes an embedded audio reading of each document excerpt to help students engage with sources that may seem dense and unfamiliar, as well as embedded, pop-up annotations to provide reading support to students and help them better understand the trickier elements of the source excerpt. Interactive questions about each passage with rich answer-specific feedback prompt students to think critically about each primary source.

+ Embedded author videos with the textbook authors give students a closer look at each chapter's essential developments, difficult concepts, and primary source documents. All videos are available with transcripts and closed captioning.

+ Tool-tip key term definitions.

+ Expandable images and maps.

InQuizitive is a groundbreaking, formative adaptive learning tool that improves student understanding of the core objectives in each chapter. Students receive personalized quiz questions on the topics with which they need the most help. Questions range from vocabulary and concepts to interactive maps and primary sources that challenge students to begin developing the skills necessary to do the work of a historian. Engaging, gamelike elements motivate students as they learn. As a result, students come to class better prepared to participate in discussions and activities.

History Skills Tutorials combine video and interactive assessments to teach students how to analyze sources. Three overview tutorials provide start-of-the-semester introductions to "Analyzing Primary Sources," "Analyzing Images," and "Analyzing Maps." Developed by Stacey Davis (Evergreen State), a library of tutorials for each chapter asks students to interpret a document, image, or map from their reading—with guided questions and explanatory author videos—and then relate that source to a key chapter theme. These tutorials give students the opportunity to practice and hone their critical analysis skills every week of the semester, and because each tutorial builds from a source, image, or map in each chapter, students can get the most from their textbooks.

Instructor Resources

RESOURCES FOR YOUR LMS

Easily add high-quality Norton digital resources to your online, hybrid, or lecture course. Get started building your course with our easy-to-use coursepack files; all activities can be accessed right within your existing learning management system, and many components are customizable.

+ **NEW Norton Illumine Ebook** is an engaging and motivational digital version of the textbook that supports instructors and students by bringing learning to light.

+ **InQuizitive** is Norton's award-winning, easy-to-use adaptive learning tool that personalizes the learning experience for students and helps them master—and retain—key learning objectives.

- **History Skills Tutorials** are interactive, online modules that provide practice and a framework for analyzing primary source documents, images, and maps.
- **Author Videos** on both *Core Objectives* and *Past and Present* feature topics from the reading.
- **Online Reader** offers hundreds of additional Primary Sources and supplemental Media Analysis Worksheets.
- **Flashcards** for each chapter, which can be flipped, printed, or downloaded, align key terms and events with brief descriptions and definitions.
- **Chapter Outlines** provide students with an opportunity to see at a glance what will be covered in the chapter.

OTHER INSTRUCTOR RESOURCES

- **Instructor's Manual** is designed to help instructors prepare lectures and exams and contains detailed chapter outlines, general discussion questions, document discussion questions, lecture objectives, interdisciplinary discussion topics, and recommended reading and film lists.
- **Test Bank** contains more than 2,000 multiple-choice, true/false, and essay questions. This edition of the Test Bank has been completely revised for content and accuracy. All test questions are now aligned with Bloom's Taxonomy for greater ease of assessment.
- **Lecture PowerPoint Slides** are ready-made presentations that provide comprehensive outlines of each chapter, as well as discussion prompts to encourage student comprehension and engagement. They can easily be customized to meet your presentation needs.
- **Graphic content** includes all of the art from the book available in JPEG and PowerPoint format for instructor use. Alt-text is provided for each item.

Acknowledgments

In working on this Brief Sixth Edition, we continue to be very grateful for the expert assistance and support of the Norton team, especially that of our editor, Justin Cahill and senior associate editor Anna Olcott. Linda Feldman, our fabulous project editor, has driven the book beautifully through the manuscript process. Meanwhile, Mike Cullen and Julie Tesser did an excellent job of clearing many of the exact images we specified. Sean Mintus has efficiently marched us through the production process, masterfully orchestrating the many permutations of this text, both print and electronic. The wonderful Betsy Twitchell has been tirelessly developing the book's fantastic e-media, particularly in developing, with Julia Gossard (Utah State University), the exciting new interactive feature and Check Your Understanding questions in the Norton Illumine Ebook. Hillary Roegelein and Jennifer Jussell have ably managed many other electronic ancillary materials. Finally, we want to thank Sarah England Bartley and social science specialists Julie Sindel, Alison Hodges, Susan Hood, and Carrie Polvino for spearheading the marketing and sales campaign for the revision.

We are also indebted to the numerous expert readers who commented on various chapters, thereby strengthening the book as a whole. We are thankful to our families for their patience and advice, and to our students, whose questions and comments over the years have been essential to the framing of this book. And we extend a special thanks to, and hope to hear from, all the teachers and students we might never meet: their engagement with this book will frame new understandings of our shared past and its bearing on our future.

REVIEWERS

Full Nineteenth Edition Consultants

Dawn L. Gilley, Northwest Missouri State University

Andrzej S. Kamiński, Georgetown University

Adam Kożuchowski, University of Warsaw

Peter Kracht, University of Pittsburgh Press

Eulalia Łazarska, Łazarski University

Krzysztof Łazarski, Łazarski University

John Merriman, Yale University

Daria Nałęcz, Łazarski University

Andrzej Novak, Jagiellonian University

Nicoletta Pellegrino, Regis College

Endre Sashalmi, University of Pécs

Robert Schneider, Indiana University

Full Nineteenth Edition Reviewers

Ken Bartlett, University of Toronto

Keith Chu, Bergen Community College

Bruce Delfini, SUNY Rockland Community College

Paul Fessler, Dordt College

Peter Goddard, University of Guelph

Bonnie Harris, San Diego State University

Anthony Heideman, Front Range Community College

Justin Horton, Thomas Nelson Community College

Catherine Humes, John Abbott College

Leslie Johnson, Hudson Valley Community College

Megan Myers, Howard Community College

Craig W. Pilant, County College of Morris

Christopher Thomas, J. Sargeant Reynolds Community College

Rebecca Woodham, Wallace Community College

Brief Fifth and Full Twentieth Edition Reviewers

Antonio Acevedo, Hudson County Community College

Seth Armus, St. Joseph's College

Ben Beshwate, Cerro Coso College

Robert S. Boggs, North Greenville University

Vivian Bouchard, Vanier College

Edward Boyden, Nassau Community College

Jan Bulman, Auburn University at Montgomery

Julien Charest, Cegep John Abbott College

Keith Chu, Bergen Community College

Eric Cimino, Molloy College

Emily Dawes, Midlands Technical College

Patrice Laurent Diaz, Montgomery County Community College

John Diffley, Springfield Technical Community College

Nicole Eaton, Boston College

Greg Eghigian, Pennsylvania State University

Daniel Ferris, Miles Community College

Bryan Givens, Pepperdine University

Abbie Grubb, San Jacinto College

Ingo Heidbrink, Old Dominion University

Ke-chin Hsia, Indiana University Bloomington

Nicole Jacoberger, Nassau Community College

Leslie Johnson, Leslie C. Johnson

Stephen Julias, Rockland Community College

Lisa Keller, Purchase College

Andrew Keitt, University of Alabama at Birmingham

Deborah Kruger, Butler County Community College

John P. Lomax, Ohio Northern University

Anthonette McDaniel, Pellissippi State Community College, Knoxville, Tennessee

Stan Mendenhall, Illinois Central College

Alexander Mikaberidze, Louisiana State University Shreveport

Marisa Balsamo Nicholson, Long Island University Post

Thomas Ort, Queens College, City University of New York

David Parnell, Indiana University Northwest

Betsy Pease, Concordia University Wisconsin

Hannah C. Powers, Thomas Nelson Community College

Nicole Rudolph, Adelphi University

Shannan Schoemaker-Mason, Lincoln Land Community College

Michael Shanshala, Trident Technical College

Jennifer Sovde, State University of New York at Canton

Chris Vicknair, Brother Martin Highschool

Kevin Wolfe, Trident Technical College

Dirk Yarker, Texas Southmost College

Margarita Youngo, Pima Community College

Brief Sixth and Full Twenty-First Edition Reviewers

Robert Bast, The University of Tennessee Knoxville

Jacob Baum, Texas Tech University

Edward A. Boyden, Nassau Community College

Robert Brown, SUNY Finger Lakes

Heather Bryson, Valencia College

Kirsten L. Cooper, United States Military Academy, West Point

Carl Creasman, Valencia College

Dane Daniel, Wright State University

Greg Eghigian, Pennsylvania State University

Daniel Hutchinson, Belmont Abbey College

Adrien Ivan, Vernon College

Sam Klein, Horry-Georgetown Technical College

Christian Knudsen, Sheridan College

Jason Linn, California Polytechnic State University, San Luis Obispo

Mike Long, Front Range Community College

Patricia McFarland, Clackamas Community College

Richard R. Moore, Metropolitan Community College

Christopher M. Paulin, Manchester Community College

John D. Poling, Parkland College

Alex Popovich, Kwantlen Polytechnic University

Erika Rappaport, University of California, Santa Barbara

Adam Schor, University of South Carolina

Evan P. Sullivan, SUNY Adirondack

Bonnie White, Memorial University of Newfoundland

Brandon Williams, Community College of Aurora

Bradley Woodworth, University of New Haven

William D. Young, Metropolitan Community College

Margarita Youngo, Pima Community College

Matthew A. Zembo, Hudson Valley Community College

Tiffany A. Ziegler, Midwestern State University

Western Civilizations
Their History & Their Culture

10

The Medieval World, 1250–1350

WHEN CHRISTOPHER COLUMBUS set out to find a new trade route to the East, he carried with him two influential books written centuries before his voyage. One was *The Book of Marvels*, composed around 1350 and attributed to John de Mandeville, an English adventurer (writing in French) who claimed to have reached the far horizons of the globe. The other was Marco Polo's *Description of the World*, an account of that Venetian merchant's journey through the vast Eurasian realm of the Mongols to the court of the Great Khan in China. He had dictated it to an author of popular romances in 1298, when both men were in prison—coincidentally, in Columbus's own city of Genoa. Both books reflect an extraordinary era of unprecedented interactions among the peoples of Europe, Asia, and the interconnected Mediterranean world. This was a time when ease of communication and commercial exchange made Western civilizations part of an interlocking network that had the potential to span the globe. Although this network would prove fragile in the face of a large-scale demographic crisis, the Black Death, it created a lasting impression of infinite possibilities. Indeed, it was only *because* of this network's connective channels that the Black Death wreaked such devastation beginning in Asia at least a century before arriving in Europe in 1347. Looking back, we can see the century leading up to this near-worldwide crisis as the beginning of a new global age.

Europeans' integration with this widening world not only put them into contact with unfamiliar cultures and commodities; it also

BEFORE YOU READ THIS CHAPTER ❯

STORY LINES

> The Mongol Empire widened channels of communication, commerce, and cultural exchange between Europe and the Far East. At the same time, Europeans were extending their reach into the Atlantic Ocean.

> Western civilizations' integration with this wider medieval world led to new ways of mapping, measuring, and describing that world.

> Despite these broadening horizons, most Europeans' lives were bounded by their communities and focused on the parish church.

> Meanwhile, the growing strength of the kings of France and England drew them into territorial disputes that led to the Hundred Years' War.

> As global climate change affected the ecosystems of Europe and caused years of famine, the integrated networks of the medieval world facilitated the rapid transmission of the Black Death.

CORE OBJECTIVES

> **DESCRIBE** the effects of the Mongol conquests.

> **IDENTIFY** the key characteristics of the medieval world system.

> **UNDERSTAND** the reasons for the papacy's loss of prestige and the rise of strong secular monarchs.

> **DEFINE** the concept of sovereignty and its importance.

> **EXPLAIN** the rapid spread of the Black Death in this historical context.

changed the world they already knew and inspired novel artistic and intellectual responses. At the same time, involvement in this wider world placed new pressures on long-term developments within Europe, notably the growing tensions among territorial monarchies and between these secular powers and the papacy. The ensuing struggles for sovereignty would have a profound impact on the balance of power and further complicate Europeans' relationships with one another.

The Mongol Empire and the Reorientation of the West

Links between the Mediterranean world and the Far East reach back into antiquity, as we have often noted. But it was not until the mid-thirteenth century that Europeans were able to establish direct connections with India, China, and the so-called Spice Islands of the Indonesian archipelago. These connections would prove profoundly important, as much for their impact on the European imagination as for their economic significance. For the peoples of Asia, however, the more frequent appearance of Europeans was less consequential than the events that made their journeys possible: the rise of a new empire that encompassed the continent.

THE EXPANSION OF THE MONGOL EMPIRE

Although closely connected with the Turkish peoples of the central Asian steppes, the Mongols were herdsmen who spoke their own distinctive language and had their own homeland, in what is now known as Mongolia. They were also highly accomplished horsemen and raiders; indeed, it was to curtail the Mongols' raids that the Chinese had fortified their Great Wall many centuries before. Primarily, though, China defended itself from the Mongols by ensuring that the various tribes turned their energies against each other.

In the late twelfth century, however, a Mongol chief named Temujin (c. 1162–1227) began to assert dominance over other tribal chiefs by incorporating their warriors into his own army. In 1206, his supremacy was reflected in a new title, **Genghis Khan** or "universal ruler," which revealed his wider ambitions. Taking advantage of China's division into three warring states, Genghis Khan launched an attack on the northern Chin Empire and penetrated deep into its interior by 1211. These initial attacks were probably looting expeditions rather than deliberate attempts at conquest, but their aims were soon sharpened under Genghis Khan's successors. Shortly after his death in 1227, a full-scale invasion of both northern and western China was under way. In 1234, these fell to the Mongols. By 1279, one of Genghis Khan's numerous grandsons, Kublai Khan, would complete the conquest of southern China, too.

For the first time in centuries, China was connected to western and central Asia in ways unprecedented in its long history, as Genghis Khan had brought crucial commercial cities and Silk Road trading posts into his empire. Building on these achievements, one of his sons, Ögedei (*EHRG-uh-day*), conquered the Rus' capital at Kyiv between 1237 and 1240, and then launched a two-pronged assault on the

Mongolian conquest under Ögedei spreads from China into central Asia and eastern Europe

Map labels:

EUROPE

Moscow
Kyiv
Kazan
CUMANS

KHANATE OF THE GOLDEN HORDE

Danube River
Volga R.
BLACK SEA
Constantinople
GEORGIA
CAUCASUS MTS.
Trebizond
SELJUKS
CASPIAN SEA
KHWARIZM
ARAL SEA
KARA-KHITAI
Lake Balkhash
ALTAI MTS.
TIEN SHAN

Lake Baikal

SEA OF JAPAN
JAPAN

Karakorum
GOBI

CHAGATAI EMPIRE
Tashkent
Samarkand
Bukhara
Turfan
Yellow River

EMPIRE OF THE GREAT KHAN
Kaifeng

MEDITERRANEAN SEA
Tabriz
Euphrates R.
Tigris R.
Jerusalem
MAMLUKS
Baghdad
Gurgan
Heràt
Kabul
HINDU KUSH
ILKHANATE
Persian Gulf
Ormuz
Nile R.
RED SEA
ARABIA

SULTANATE OF DELHI
Indus R.
Delhi
HIMALAYAS
TIBET

Hangzhou
EAST CHINA SEA

SONG EMPIRE
(conquered 1279)

Yangtze R.
Guangzhou

Ganges R.
INDIA
BURMA (MYANMAR)
ANNAM
CHAMPA

Bay of Bengal
ARABIAN SEA

SOUTH CHINA SEA

CEYLON

INDIAN OCEAN

to Java

Legend:
→ Mongol campaigns post-1259
— The Silk Road

0   500   1000 Miles
0   500   1000 Kilometers

THE STATES OF THE MONGOL EMPIRE. Like Alexander's, Genghis Khan's empire was swiftly assembled and encompassed vast portions of Europe and Asia. **› How many different Mongol khanates were there after 1260, when Kublai Khan came to power? Were these domains mapped onto older divisions within Western civilizations? › How might the Mongol occupation of the Islamic world have aided the expansion of European trade? › At the same time, why would it have complicated the efforts of crusader armies in the Holy Land?**

rich lands of the European frontier. The smaller of two Mongol armies swept through Poland toward Germany; the larger went southwest toward Hungary. In April 1241, the smaller force met a hastily assembled army of Germans and Poles at the Battle of Legnica in southern Poland, where the Mongols were driven back. Two days later, the larger Mongol army annihilated a Hungarian army at the river Sajó. Its further advance into Europe was halted only when Ögedei Khan died in December of that year.

MUSCOVY AND THE MONGOL KHANATE

Kyiv had long been a hub of diplomatic and trading relations with western Europe, Byzantium, and the Islamic caliphate at Baghdad. But with the arrival of the Mongols, the locus of power in Rus' moved from Kyiv to their own settlement on the lower Volga River. From there, the Mongols extended their dominion over terrain stretching from the Black Sea to central Asia. It became known as the Khanate of the Golden Horde, a name that captures the striking impression made by Mongol tents hung with cloth of gold. (The word *horde* derives from the Mongol word meaning "encampment" and the related Turkish word *ordu*, "army.")

Initially, the Mongols ruled the lands of Rus' directly, installing their own officials and requiring local princes to show their obedience by traveling in person to the Mongol court of the Great Khan in China. But after Kublai Khan's death in 1294, the Mongols began to tolerate the existence of several semi-independent principalities. Kyiv did not recover its dominant position, but one of these principalities, the duchy of Moscow, gained prominence due to its strategic geographical location. Moscow became the tribute-collecting center for the Mongol Khanate, and its dukes were even encouraged to extend their lordship into neighboring territories. Eventually, the Muscovite dukes came to control the khanate's tax-collecting mechanisms. As a reflection of these extended powers, Duke Ivan I (r. 1325–1340) gained the title Grand Prince of Rus'. When the Mongol Empire began to disintegrate, the Muscovites were therefore in a strong position to succeed their former overlords.

> *Moscow becomes important financial and political center* ❯

THE MAKING OF THE MONGOL ILKHANATE

As Ögedei Khan moved into the lands of Rus' and eastern Europe, Mongol armies also subdued the vast territory that had been encompassed by the former Persian Empire and its Roman successors. Indeed, the strongest state in this region was known as the sultanate of Rûm (the Arabic word for "Rome"), which had been founded by the Seljuk Turks in 1077 and consisted of Anatolian provinces formerly belonging to the eastern Roman Empire. It had successfully withstood waves of European crusading ventures while capitalizing on the misfortunes of Byzantium, taking over several key ports on the Mediterranean and Black Seas.

But in 1243, the Seljuks of Rûm surrendered to the Mongols, who had already occupied what is now Iraq, Iran, portions of Pakistan and Afghanistan, and the Christian kingdoms of Georgia and Armenia. Thereafter, the Mongols easily found their way into regions weakened by centuries of Muslim infighting and Christian crusading movements. The capitulation of Rûm left remaining Byzantine possessions in Anatolia open to the Mongols. In 1261, however, Emperor Michael VIII Palaeologus (r. 1259–1282) managed to regain control of Constantinople and its immediate hinterland from the Venetians. And although the crusader principality of Antioch succumbed to the Mongols in 1268, their advance into Palestine was halted by the Mamluk Sultanate of Egypt, established in 1250 and ruled by a powerful military caste.

All of these disparate territories came to be called the *Ilkhanate*, the "subordinate khanate," meaning that its Mongol rulers paid deference to the Great Khan. The first Ilkhan was Hulagu, a brother of China's Kublai Khan. His descendants would rule this realm for another eighty years, eventually converting to Islam.

THE MONGOL RULER OF ISLAMIC PERSIA, HIS CHRISTIAN QUEEN, AND HIS JEWISH HISTORIAN. Hulagu Khan (1217–1265) was a grandson of Genghis and a brother of Kublai. He consolidated Persia and its neighboring regions into the Ilkhanate. This image shows him with his wife, Dokuz Khatun, who was a Turkic princess and a Christian. The image comes from the *Compendium of Chronicles* by Rashid al-Din (1247–1318), a Jewish convert to Islam, whose work exemplifies the pluralistic culture encouraged by Mongol rule: written in Persian and often translated into Arabic, it embeds the achievements of the Mongol ruler within the long history of Islam. **›** Why would Rashid al-Din have wanted to place the new Mongol dynasty in this historical context?

THE *PAX MONGOLICA* AND ITS PRICE

Although the Mongols' expansion into Europe had been checked, their combined conquests stretched from the Black Sea to the Pacific: one-fifth of the earth's surface, the largest land empire in history. Yet no single Mongol ruler's power was absolute within this domain, and the distribution of authority made Mongol rule flexible and adaptable to local conditions. The Mongol khans were also highly tolerant of all religious beliefs, which was a further advantage in governing peoples who observed an array of Buddhist, Christian, and Islamic practices, not to mention Hindus, Jews, and many itinerant groups whose beliefs reflected a melding of many cultures.

This acceptance of cultural and religious difference, alongside the Mongols' encouragement of trade and love of rich things, created ideal conditions for some merchants and artists. Hence, the term *Pax Mongolica* ("Mongol Peace") is often used to describe the century from 1250 to 1350, a period analogous to the one fostered by the Roman Empire at its greatest extent (Chapter 5). However, this peace was bought at a great price. The artists whose varied talents created the gorgeous textiles, utensils, and illuminated books prized by the Mongols were not all willing participants. Many were captives or slaves subject to ruthless relocation. The Mongols would often transfer entire families and communities of craftsmen

> Mongol's massive empire was characterized by religious toleration and cultural diversity

THE MEDIEVAL WORLD SYSTEM, c. 1300. At the turn of the fourteenth century, Western civilizations were more closely connected to each other and to the rest of the world than ever before: waterways and overland routes stretched from Greenland to the Pacific coast of Southeast Asia and down to West Africa. The interlocking regions and contact zones of this system are represented on this map. › **How did Europe's relationship with its neighbors change as a result of its integration into this wider world?** › **How were seemingly marginal territories (such as Rus' or Hungary, Scotland, or Norway) central to one or more interlocking components of this system?**

Pax Mongolica In imitation of the *Pax Romana* ("The Roman Peace," see Chapter 5), this phrase is used to describe the relatively peaceful century after the Mongol conquests, 1250–1350, which enabled an intensified period of trade, travel, and communication within the Eurasian landmass.

from one part of the empire to another, to encourage a fantastic blend of techniques, materials, and motifs. The result was an intensive period of cultural exchange that might combine Chinese, Persian, Venetian, and Hungarian influences (among many others) in a single work of art.

The Mongol Peace was also achieved at the expense of many flourishing Muslim cities that were devastated or crippled during the bloody process of Mongol expansion—cities that preserved the heritage of even older civilizations. The city of Heràt, situated in one of Afghanistan's few fertile valleys and described by a Persian poet as the "pearl in the oyster," was entirely destroyed by Genghis Khan in 1221. Baghdad, the splendid capital of the Abbasid caliphate and a haven for artists and intellectuals since the eighth century (Chapter 8), was savagely besieged and sacked in 1258. Amid many other atrocities, this destroyed the House of Wisdom, the library and research center where Muslim scientists, philosophers, and translators had preserved classical knowledge and advanced cutting-edge scholarship in mathematics, astronomy, and medicine.

BRIDGING EAST AND WEST

To facilitate the movement of peoples and goods within their empire, the Mongols took control of caravan routes, policing bandits and making conditions safer for travelers. They also streamlined trade by funneling many exchanges through the Persian city of Tabriz, on which both land and sea routes from China converged. These measures accelerated and intensified the possible contacts between the Far East and the West. Prior to Mongol dominance, such networks had been inaccessible to most European merchants. The Silk Road was not a highway, but a tangle of trails and trading posts which few outsiders could navigate. Now travelers at all points of the route found their way smoothed.

Among the first travelers were Franciscan missionaries whose journeys were bankrolled by European rulers. In 1253, the friar William of Rubruck was sent by King Louis IX of France as his ambassador to the Mongol court, with letters of introduction and instructions to make a full report of his findings. Merchants quickly followed. The most famous are three Venetians: the brothers Niccolò and Matteo Polo, and Niccolò's son, Marco (1254–1324). **Marco Polo**'s account of his travels, which began when he was seventeen, reflects his twenty-four-year sojourn in the service of the Great Khan,

Mongols make long-distance trade easier, leading to increased cultural exchange

Marco Polo (1254–1324) Venetian merchant who traveled through Asia for twenty years and published his observations in a widely read memoir.

VENETIAN AMBASSADORS TO THE GREAT KHAN. Around 1270, the Venetian merchant brothers Niccolò and Matteo Polo returned to Europe after their first prolonged journey through the empire of the Great Khan, bearing with them an official letter to the Roman pope. This image, from a manuscript of Marco Polo's *Description of the World*, shows his father and uncle at the moment of their arrival in the Great Khan's court, to which they have seemingly brought a Christian cross and a Bible. › Knowing what you've learned about the Mongols and the medieval world, do you think it is plausible that the Polo brothers would have carried these items with them?

Two Travel Accounts

Two of the books that influenced Christopher Columbus and his contemporaries were travel narratives describing the exotic worlds that lay beyond Europe—worlds that may or may not have existed as they are described. The first excerpt here is taken from the account dictated by Marco Polo of Venice in 1298. The young Marco had traveled overland from Constantinople to the court of Kublai Khan in the early 1270s, together with his father and uncle. He became a gifted linguist and remained at the Mongol court until the early 1290s, when he returned to Europe after a journey through Southeast Asia and Indonesia, and across the Indian Ocean. The second excerpt is from the Book of Marvels, attributed to John de Mandeville. This is an almost entirely fictional account of wonders that also became a source for European ideas about Southeast Asia. This particular passage concerns a legendary Christian figure named Prester ("Priest") John, who is alleged to have traveled to the East and become a great ruler.

Marco Polo's Description of Java

Now know that when one leaves Champa[1] and went between south and southeast 1,500 miles, then one comes up to a very large island called Java which, according to what good sailors say who know it well, is the largest island in the world, for it is more than three thousand miles around. It has a great king; they are idolators and pay tribute to no man in the world. This island is one of very great wealth: they have pepper, nutmeg, spikenard, galangal, cubeb, cloves, and all the expensive spices you can find in the world. To this island come great numbers of ships and merchants who buy many commodities and make great profit and great gain there. On this island, there is such great treasure that no man in the world could recount or describe it. I tell you the Great Khan could never have it on account of the long and fearsome way in sailing there. Merchants from Zaytun[2] and Mangi[3] have already extracted very great treasure from this island, and continue to do so today.

[1] A collective name for the kingdoms of central Vietnam.
[2] The major port city of Quanzhou on southeastern coast of China.
[3] The kingdom of the Southern Song in China, south of the Huai River. The word *mangi* (or *manzi*) means "barbarians," which is what the northern Chinese called the people of the southern realm. When Marco Polo was in the service of the Great Khan, the Mongol conquest of the kingdom was still ongoing. It was completed in 1279.

Source: Marco Polo, *The Description of the World*, trans. Sharon Kinoshita, (Indianapolis/Cambridge, 2016), p. 149.

John de Mandeville's Description of Prester John

This emperor Prester John has great lands and has many noble cities and good towns in his realm and many great, large islands. For all the country of India is separated into islands by the great floods that come from Paradise, that divide the land into many parts. And also in the sea he has many islands. . . .

and the story of his journey home through the Spice Islands, India, and Persia (see *Competing Viewpoints* above). As we noted on page 334, this book had an enormous effect on the European imagination; Christopher Columbus's copy still survives.

Even more impressive in scope than Marco's travels are those of the Muslim adventurer Ibn Battuta (1304–1368), who left his native Morocco in 1326 to go on the sacred pilgrimage to Mecca—but then kept going. By the time he returned home

This Prester John has under him many kings and many islands and many varied people of various conditions. And this land is full good and rich, but not so rich as is the land of the Great Khan. For the merchants do not come there so commonly to buy merchandise as they do in the land of the Great Khan, for it is too far to travel to. . . .

[Mandeville then goes on to describe the difficulties of reaching Prester John's lands by sea.]

This emperor Prester John always takes as his wife the daughter of the Great Khan, and the Great Khan in the same way takes to wife the daughter of Prester John. For these two are the greatest lords under the heavens.

In the land of Prester John there are many diverse things, and many precious stones so great and so large that men make them into vessels such as platters, dishes, and cups. And there are many other marvels there that it would be too cumbrous and too long to put into the writing of books. But of the principal islands and of his estate and of his law I shall tell you some part.

This emperor Prester John is Christian and a great part of his country is Christian also, although they do not hold to all the articles of our faith as we do. . . .

And he has under him 72 provinces, and in every province there is a king. And these kings have kings under them, and all are tributaries to Prester John.

And he has in his lordships many great marvels. For in his country is the sea that men call the Gravelly Sea, that is all gravel and sand without any drop of water. And it ebbs and flows in great waves as other seas do, and it is never still. . . . And a three-day journey from that sea there are great mountains out of which flows a great flood that comes out of Paradise. And it is full of precious stones without any drop of water. . . .

He dwells usually in the city of Susa [in Persia]. And there is his principal palace, which is so rich and so noble that no one will believe the report unless he has seen it. And above the chief tower of the palace there are two round pommels of gold and in each of them are two great, large rubies that shine full brightly upon the night. And the principal gates of his palace are of a precious stone that men call sardonyxes [a type of onyx], and the frames and the bars are made of ivory. And the windows of the halls and chambers are of crystal. And the tables upon which men eat, some are made of emeralds, some of amethyst, and some of gold full of precious stones. And the legs that hold up the tables are made of the same precious stones. . . .

Source: Sir John Mandeville, *Mandeville's Travels*, ed. M. C. Seymour (Oxford: 1967), pp. 195–99 (language modernized from Middle English by R. C. Stacey).

Questions for Analysis

1. What does Marco Polo want his readers to know about Java, and why? What does this suggest about the interests of these intended readers?

2. What does Mandeville want his readers to know about Prester John and his domains? Why are these details so important?

3. Which of these accounts seems more trustworthy, and why? Even if we cannot accept one or both at face value, what insight do they give us into the expectations of Columbus and the other European adventurers who relied on these accounts?

in 1354, he had been to China and sub-Saharan Africa, as well as to the ends of both the Islamic and Mongolian worlds: a journey of over 75,000 miles.

The window of opportunity that made such journeys possible was relatively narrow, however. By the middle of the fourteenth century, hostilities among various components of the Mongol Empire were making travel more perilous. The Mongols of the Ilkhanate came into conflict with merchants from Genoa who were finally forced to abandon their settlement in Tabriz, breaking one of the major links in the commercial chain. In 1346, the Mongols of the Golden Horde besieged the Genoese colony at Caffa on the Black Sea, providing a conduit for the transmission of the Black Death (see pages 360–65). When the last Mongol rulers of China were overthrown in 1368, most foreigners were now denied access to its borders and the remaining Mongol warriors were restricted to cavalry service in the imperial armies of the new Ming dynasty. The conditions that had fostered an integrated trans-Eurasian cultural and commercial network were no longer sustainable.

Mongol rule disintegrates

The Extension of European Commerce and Settlement

The increased access of Western civilizations to the riches of the Far East ran parallel to a number of ventures that were extending the European presence in the Mediterranean and beyond. These endeavors were both mercantile and colonial, and in many cases resulted in the control of strategic trade routes that connected North Africa to the Silk Road as well as to the conduits of the sub-Saharan gold trade.

THE QUEST FOR AFRICAN GOLD

European commerce in African gold was not new. It had been going on for centuries, facilitated by Muslim traders whose caravans brought a steady supply from the Niger River to the North African ports of Algiers and Tunis. In the early thirteenth century, rival bands of merchants from Catalonia and Genoa had established trading colonies in Tunis to expedite this process, exchanging woolen cloth from northern Europe for both North African grain and sub-Saharan gold.

Gold—portable and newly plentiful— was used for new currencies

But the medieval demand for gold accelerated during the late thirteenth and fourteenth centuries, because the luxuries coveted by Europeans were now too costly to be bought solely with bulk goods. Although precious textiles (usually silk) were a form of wealth the Mongols valued, the burgeoning economy of the medieval world demanded a reliable and abundant supply of more portable currency. Gold was therefore an obvious alternative currency for large transactions, and in the thirteenth century some European rulers began minting gold coins. But Europe itself had few natural gold reserves, and so maintaining and expanding these currencies required the exploitation of new sources.

The most obvious were in West Africa, especially Mali and Ghana. The sultan and emperor of that region, Mansa Musa (d. 1337), was the richest man in the world—and may have been the richest person in history. His sub-Saharan realm was also famed for its ivory, since the tusks of African elephants were especially prized by European artists, like the one who crafted the statue of the Virgin on page 312.

Genoa Maritime city on Italy's northwestern coast; the Genoese were active in trading ventures along the Silk Road and in the establishment of trading colonies in the Mediterranean.

Catalonia Maritime region in northeastern Spain; during the thirteenth century, Catalan adventurers conquered and colonized a series of western Mediterranean islands.

MODELS OF MEDITERRANEAN COLONIZATION: CATALONIA, GENOA, AND VENICE

The heightened European interest in the African gold trade, by the seafaring merchants of **Genoa** and **Catalonia** in particular, coincided with these merchants' creation of entrepreneurial empires in the western Mediterranean. During the thirteenth century, Catalan adventurers conquered and colonized a series of western Mediterranean islands, including Majorca, Ibiza, Minorca, Sardinia, and Sicily.

MANSA MUSA. Musa I was the ruler of the wealthy West African empire of Mali. His title, Mansa, means both "sultan" and "emperor," capturing the breadth of his power as a conqueror, king, and religious leader. He is depicted prominently in an important cartographic manuscript known as the Catalan Atlas, created in 1375. In keeping with Mansa Musa's reputation as the richest man on earth—at that time, and maybe for all time—he wears a crown of real gold leaf and holds up a gold coin. He is also shown enthroned and holding a scepter, just like a European monarch. **› How does this image, and the making of such an atlas, reflect the developments we are studying in this chapter?**

Except in Sicily, which already had a large and diverse population that included many Christians (Chapter 8), the pattern of Catalan conquest was largely the same: expulsion or extermination of the existing population, usually Muslim; the encouragement of new settlers; and a heavy reliance on slave labor.

These Catalan colonial efforts were mainly carried out by private individuals or companies operating under royal charters. They therefore contrast strongly with the state-sponsored colonial practices of the maritime empire controlled by **Venice** in the eastern Mediterranean, where the Venetians dominated the trade in spices and silks. Venetian colonies were administered directly by the city's rulers or by their appointed colonial governors. These colonies included long-settled civilizations such as Greece and Cyprus, meaning that Venetian administration laid just another layer on top of many older structures.

The Genoese, to take yet another case, also had extensive interests in the western Mediterranean, where they traded bulk goods such as cloth, hides, grain, timber, and sugar. They also established trading colonies, but these tended to consist of family networks that were closely integrated with the peoples of North Africa, Spain, and the shores of the Black Sea.

Venice An ancient city on Italy's Adriatic coast, it became the capital of a maritime trading empire during the thirteenth century.

FROM THE MEDITERRANEAN TO THE ATLANTIC

For centuries, European maritime commerce had been divided between the Mediterranean and the northeastern Atlantic seaboard of northern France, the Low Countries, the British Isles, and Scandinavia. Starting around 1270, however, Italian merchants began to sail through the Straits of Gibraltar and up to the wool-producing regions of England and the Low Countries. This was a step toward the extension of Mediterranean commerce into the Atlantic. Another step was the European discovery of Atlantic island chains known as the Canaries and the Azores, which Genoese sailors reached in the fourteenth century.

Efforts to colonize the Canary Islands, and to convert and enslave their inhabitants, began almost immediately. Eventually, the Canaries would become the base for Portuguese voyages down the west coast of Africa. They would also be the point from which Christopher Columbus would sail westward across the Atlantic Ocean in the hope of reaching Asia (see Chapter 12).

There was also a significant European colonial presence in the northern Atlantic, and there had been for centuries. Norse voyagers from Iceland had begun to colonize Greenland in the late tenth century and had established a settlement in a place they called Vinland (the coast of Newfoundland in present-day Canada) around 1000. While North America did not become home to a permanent European population at this time, the Norse did build a viable community on Greenland, which eventually formed part of the kingdom of Norway. This settlement was facilitated by the warming of the earth's climate between 800 and 1300 (Chapter 8). For several centuries, favorable conditions made it possible to sustain some farming activities on the southern coastline of that huge island, supplemented by fishing, hunting, and foraging. But with the gradual cooling of the climate in the fourteenth century, which caused famines even in the rich farmlands of Europe, this fragile ecosystem was eroded and the Greenlanders died of starvation.

Ways of Knowing and Describing the World

European commercial expansion in this era both drove and depended on significant innovations in measuring and mapping. It also coincided with intellectual, literary, and artistic initiatives that aimed to capture and describe the workings of this wider world.

Europe–Asia contact, a legacy of Mongol expansion, leads to new innovations

BALANCE SHEETS, BANKS, CHARTS, AND CLOCKS

The closer integration of European and Asian commerce called for the refinement of existing business models and accounting techniques. New forms of partnership and the development of insurance contracts helped to minimize the risks associated with long-distance trading (see *Interpreting Visual Evidence* on pages 350–51). Double-entry bookkeeping, widely used in Italy by the mid-fourteenth century, gave merchants a much clearer picture of their profits and losses by ensuring that both credits and debits were clearly laid out in parallel columns. The Medici family of Florence established branches of its bank in each of the major cities of Europe and were careful that the failure of one would not bankrupt the entire firm. Banks also experimented with advanced credit techniques borrowed from Muslim and Jewish financiers, allowing their clients to transfer funds without any real money changing hands. Such transfers were carried out by written receipts, the direct ancestors of the check.

Other late medieval technologies kept pace in different ways with the demands for increased efficiency. Eyeglasses, first invented in the 1280s, were perfected in the fourteenth century. The use of the magnetic compass helped ships to sail farther away from land, making longer-distance Atlantic voyages possible for the first time. And as more and more mariners began to sail waters less familiar to them, pilots began to make and use special charts that mapped the locations of ports; called *portolani* (**portolan charts**), they took note of prevailing winds, good harbors, and known perils.

Among the many implements of modern daily life invented in this era, the most familiar are clocks, which came into use shortly before 1300. They were too large and expensive for private purchase, but towns vied with each other to install them in prominent public buildings, thus advertising municipal wealth and good governance. Mechanical timekeeping had a profound effect on the regulation of daily life. Until the advent of clocks, time was flexible. Although days had been *theoretically* divided into hours, minutes, and seconds since the time of the Sumerians (Chapter 1), there was no way to map these temporal measurements onto an actual day. Now, clocks relentlessly divided time into exact units, giving rise to new expectations about labor and productivity. People were expected to start and end work "on time," and even to equate time with money. Like the improvements in bookkeeping, timekeeping made some kinds of work more efficient, but it also created new tensions and anxieties.

PORTOLAN CHART. The chart shown here is the oldest surviving example of a map used by mariners to navigate between Mediterranean ports: the word *portolan* is the term for such charts. It dates from the end of the thirteenth century, and its shape clearly indicates that it was made from an animal hide. Although parchment was extremely durable, it would slowly have worn away due to prolonged exposure to salt water and other elements—hence the rarity of this early example.

KNOWLEDGE OF THE WORLD AND OF GOD

In the mid-thirteenth century, Thomas Aquinas had argued that God's workings in the world are comprehensible to the inquiring human mind (Chapter 9). But a later philosopher, William of Ockham (d. c. 1348), an English Franciscan, denied that human reason could prove fundamental theological truths. Instead, he urged humans to investigate the natural world and better understand its laws—without positing any necessary connection between nature and divinity.

This philosophical position, known as *nominalism*, has had an enormous impact on modern thought. The distinction between the rational comprehensibility of the real world and the spiritual incomprehensibility of God encourages scientific investigation without reference to supernatural explanations. As such, it encourages empirical observation, since knowledge of the world should rest on sensory experience rather than abstract theories. These are the medieval foundations of the scientific method (see Chapter 16).

REPRESENTING GOD'S CREATION THROUGH ART

The artists of this era were also paying close attention to empirical evidence and creating realistic representations of the world. Carvings of plants and flowers are clearly recognizable to botanists as distinct species. Statues of

portolani (**portolan charts**) These special charts were invented by medieval mariners during the fourteenth century and were used to map the locations of ports and sea routes, while also taking note of prevailing winds and other conditions at sea.

humans are realistic in their portrayals of facial expressions and bodily proportions. This trend toward naturalism extended to manuscript illumination and painting, as well. Indeed, painting itself was becoming realistically portable: while humans have been decorating walls since before the Neolithic Revolution, artists in the thirteenth century began to adapt the techniques used by icon painters in Byzantium, making freestanding pictures on pieces of wood or canvas using tempera (pigments mixed with water and natural gums) or oil paints. Because these devotional images and portraits were mobile, they were also more commercial. As long as artists could afford the necessary materials, they did not have to wait for specific commissions and could choose their own subject matter, putting an individual stamp on their work—one of the reasons why we know the names of many more artists from this era.

One of these artists, Giotto di Bondone of Florence (c. 1267–1337), painted both walls and portable wooden panels. **Giotto** (*gee-OHT-toh*) was an especially keen observer of nature: not only do his human beings and animals look lifelike, they do natural things. When Christ enters Jerusalem on Palm Sunday, boys climb trees to get a better view; when the Virgin's parents meet after a long separation, they embrace and kiss one another tenderly. Although many of the artists who came after Giotto moved away from naturalism, this style would become the norm by 1400. For this reason, Giotto is often regarded as a painter who inspired the Italian Renaissance (see Chapter 11).

A VISION OF THE WORLD WE CANNOT SEE

An exact contemporary of Giotto's had a different way of capturing the spiritual world in a naturalistic way, and in a different medium. **Dante Alighieri** (1265–1321) of Florence pioneered what he called a "sweet new style" of poetry in his native Italian, which was now so different from Latin that it had become a new language. Yet, Dante also strove to make this Italian vernacular an instrument for serious political and social critique. His great work, known in his own day as the *Comedy* (called the *Divine Comedy* by later admirers), was composed during the years he spent in exile from his beloved city, after the political party he supported was ousted from power in 1301.

The *Comedy* describes the poet's imaginary journey through hell, purgatory, and paradise; a journey that begins in a "dark wood," a metaphor for the personal and political crises that threatened Dante's faith and livelihood. In the poem, the narrator is led out of this forest and through the first two realms by the Roman poet Virgil

Dante's Comedy elevates vernacular Italian from an everyday language to a literary one

>

(Chapter 5), who represents the best of classical culture. But Dante can only be guided toward knowledge of the divine by his deceased beloved, Beatrice, who symbolizes Christian wisdom. In the course of this visionary pilgrimage, Dante's narrator meets the souls of many historical personages and contemporaries, inviting them to explain why they met their fates. This was Dante's ingenious way of commenting on current events and passing judgment on his enemies. In many ways, this monumental poem is a fusion of classical and Christian cultures, Latin learning, and vernacular artistry.

Papal Power and Popular Piety

Dante's *Comedy* was a creative response to the political turmoil that engulfed Italy during his lifetime, a situation that was transforming the papacy, too. Indeed, many of the men whom Dante placed in Hell were popes. Yet despite the weakening authority of the papal office, which caused violent divisions within the Church, popular piety arguably achieved its strongest expressions during this era.

THE LIMITS OF PAPAL POWER

As we saw in Chapter 9, the papacy reached new heights of power at the beginning of the thirteenth century, as holders of the office continued to centralize the government of the Church. But they extended their influence into the secular sphere, which led to protracted political struggles and the ultimate weakening of the papacy's credibility.

For example, the Italian territories under papal lordship shared a border with the kingdom of Sicily, which comprised all of southern Italy as well as Sicily itself. The ruler of these territories was also the German emperor Frederick II, who proved a formidable opponent. The reigning pope, therefore, called a crusade against him. But in order to implement this crusade, the pope needed to find a military champion willing to lead an army against a fellow Christian ruler: someone with little to lose and everything to gain.

This turned out to be Charles of Anjou, the youngest brother of the French king, and who was eventually crowned king of Sicily. But he made matters in southern Italy worse by antagonizing his own subjects, who instead offered their allegiance to the king of Aragon. The papacy then made Aragon the target of yet another crusade, resulting in a disastrous war among Christian princes and their armies on European soil. In the wake of this debacle, the French king **Philip IV** (r. 1286–1314) resolved to punish the papacy for abusing its powers.

In 1300, Pope **Boniface VIII** (r. 1294–1303) called for the celebration of a papal jubilee, asserting that the Roman pope was the arbiter of all power. But just a few years later, there was no longer a Roman pope: the new capital of Christendom had moved to France, because Philip IV had challenged Boniface to prove that he could exercise real power—not just the power of propaganda. Following a heated dispute about the king's intervention in papal affairs, Philip sent thugs to the papal residence, where Boniface (then in his seventies) was so mistreated that he died a month later. Philip then pressed his advantage, forcing the new pope, Clement V, to thank him for his zealous defense of the faith; then, in 1309, he moved the entire papal court to **Avignon** (*AH-vee-nyon*), a city in his own realm.

Giotto (c. 1266–1377) Florentine painter and architect who is often considered a forerunner of the Renaissance.

Dante Alighieri (c. 1265–1321) Florentine poet and intellectual whose *Divine Comedy* was a pioneering work in the Italian vernacular and a vehicle for political and religious critique.

Philip IV King of France from 1285 until his death, Philip's conflict with Pope Boniface VIII led to the transfer of the papal court to Avignon from 1309 to 1378.

Boniface VIII (r. 1294–1303) Pope whose repeated claims to papal authority were challenged by King Philip IV of France.

Avignon City in southeastern France that became the seat of the papacy between 1305 and 1377, a period known as the "Babylonian Captivity" of the Roman Church.

Seals: Signs of Identity and Authority

For much of human history, applying a seal to a document was the way to certify its legality and identify the people who had ratified it. During antiquity and the early Middle Ages, those people were only powerful men—kings, bishops, heads of monasteries—and occasionally powerful women. But as participation in documentary practices became more and more common, seals were increasingly used by corporations (such as universities and crusading orders), towns, and many individuals. The devices (images) and legends (writing) on these seals were carefully chosen to capture central attributes of their owners' personalities or status. A seal was made by pressing a deeply incised lead matrix onto hot wax or resin, which would quickly dry to form a durable impression. The images reproduced here are later engravings that make the features of the original seals easier to see.

A. Seal of the town of Dover, 1281. Dover has long been one of the busiest and most important port cities of England because of its strategic proximity to France; indeed, the Dover Strait that separates this town from Calais, just across the English Channel, is only twenty-one miles wide. In 1281, when this seal was used, ferries and other ships like the one depicted here made this crossing several times a day. The legend around the edges of the seal reads (in Latin) "Seal of the commune of barons of Dover." It reflects the high status accorded to the free men of Dover by the English crown: because of their crucial role in the economy and defense of the kingdom, they were considered a corporate body and entitled to representation in Parliament alongside individual barons.

B. Personal seal of Simon de Montfort, earl of Leicester, 1258. Simon de Montfort (c. 1208–1265) was a French nobleman who rose to a position of great power in England. In 1238, he married Eleanor, sister of King Henry III: a match that was opposed by England's great lords because it gave this foreigner a great deal of power. Indeed, Simon would later use that power to lead a rebellion against his royal brother-in-law, dying on the battlefield in 1265. This image was appended to a document made when Simon was fifty, but it shows him as a courtly youth, riding out with his favorite hound and blowing on a hunting horn. This means that Simon had continued to use a seal made for him when he was a much younger man, probably at the time when he was knighted, many years before, in France. The Latin legend, indeed, makes no mention of his English title: "Seal of Simon de Montfort."

Questions for Analysis

1. Medieval towns represented themselves in a variety of ways on their seals: sometimes showing a group portrait of town councilors, sometimes a local saint, sometimes a heraldic beast, and sometimes distinctive architectural features. Why would Dover choose this image (A)? What messages does this seal convey?

2. Think carefully about the mystery of Simon de Montfort's seal (B). Usually, powerful men and women had new seals made to reflect their elevated status. What are all the possible reasons that the English earl would have continued to use a seal made for him so many years earlier, in France? What are the possible ramifications of this choice?

3. The seals of medieval women were almost always shaped like almonds (pointed ovals; the technical term is *vesica-shaped*). Yet Helwig's seal is round, like the seals of men and corporations (C). Why might that be the case?

4. In general, what is the value of seals for the study of history? What are the various ways in which they function as sources?

C. Seal of Helwig von Ysenburg, countess of Büdingen, 1274. Unlike the engravings of seals pictured on the facing page, this is an original wax impression of Helwig's seal and includes the silken cords that were used to fasten it to a document in 1274. It shows a slim young lady in a long, elegant gown and cape, pointed shoes, and an elaborate headdress. The falcon on her fist suggests that she is dressed to go hunting, but she is depicted against an interior background of diamond-shaped tiles—like her dress, a sign of wealth and status. The legend is difficult to decipher, but reads "Seal of Helwig von Ysen[burg]."

Philip IV's legacy: political control over papacy ❯

THE BABYLONIAN CAPTIVITY OF THE PAPACY

The papacy's capitulation to French royal power illustrates the enormous gap between rhetoric and reality. Although Boniface was merely repeating the old claim that kings ruled by divine approval as recognized by the Church, the Church now exercised its authority only by bowing to the power of a king. The papacy would remain in Avignon for nearly seventy years (see Chapter 11): a period called the "**Babylonian Captivity**" of the papacy, recalling the Jews' exile in Babylon during the sixth century B.C.E. (Chapter 2). Even though the move was probably supposed to be temporary, it was not reversed after Philip IV's death in 1314. Perhaps many suppliants found that doing business in Avignon was easier than in Rome. Not only was Avignon closer to the major centers of power in northwestern Europe, it was removed from the tumultuous politics of Italy. Moreover, all the popes elected there were natives of the region, as were nearly all the cardinals whom they appointed. This further cemented their loyalty to the French king.

Although the Avignon popes never abandoned claims to the lordship of Rome and the Papal States, making good on these claims required a great deal of money. The Avignon popes accordingly imposed new taxes and obligations on the wealthy dioceses of France, England, Germany, and Spain. Judicial cases from ecclesiastical courts also brought large revenues into the papal coffers. Most controversially, the Avignon popes claimed the right to appoint bishops and priests to vacant offices anywhere in Christendom, bypassing the rights of individual dioceses and collecting huge fees from successful appointees.

By these and other measures, the Avignon popes further strengthened administrative control while further weakening the papacy's moral authority. Stories of the

THE PAPAL PALACE AT AVIGNON. The work on this great fortified palace was begun in 1339 and symbolizes the apparent permanence of the papal residence in Avignon. ❯ Why was it constructed as a fortress as well as a palace?

court's unseemly luxury circulated widely, especially during the reign of the notoriously corrupt Clement VI (r. 1342–1352), who openly sold spiritual benefits for money (he would appoint a jackass to a bishopric if it would turn a profit, he boasted) and who insisted that his sexual transgressions were therapeutic. His reign also coincided with the Black Death, which did not improve his reputation for leadership.

MANIFESTING FAITH: THE POWER OF SACRAMENTS

Despite the centralizing power of the papacy, most medieval Christians experienced the Church at a local level, within their community's parish. In these churches, parish priests not only taught the elements of Christian doctrine but also administered the **sacraments**: rituals that conveyed the grace of God by marking significant moments in the life cycle of every person and significant times in the Christian calendar.

Medieval piety came to revolve around these sacraments, which included baptism, confession of sins (also known as Penance), Extreme Unction (last rites for the dying), the ordination of priests, and the Eucharist or Mass. Baptism, which had been administered to adults in the early centuries of Christianity (Chapter 6), had become a sacrament given to infants as soon as possible after birth, to safeguard their souls in case of an early death. Periodic confession of sins to a priest was thought to guarantee God's forgiveness, for if a sinner did not perform appropriate acts of penance, he or she would have to complete atonement in Purgatory—the netherworld between Paradise and Hell, whose existence was confirmed as a doctrine for the first time in 1274. Another sacrament, marriage, was very seldom practiced as a formal ceremony; in reality, it required only the exchange of promises and was often formed simply by an act of sexual intercourse.

"THIS IS MY BODY": THE ELEVATION OF THE HOST. This fresco from a chapel in Assisi was painted by Simone Martini in the 1320s. It shows the moment in the Mass when the priest raises the eucharistic host so that it can be seen by the faithful. The Latin phrase spoken at this moment, *Hoc est enim corpus meum* ("This is my body"), was regarded as transforming the substance of bread into the divine substance of Christ's body. › Since medieval Christians believed that the sight of the host was just as powerful as ingesting it, how would they have responded to this life-size image of the elevation? › What does the appearance of angels (above the altar) signify?

THE MIRACLE OF THE EUCHARIST

Of these sacraments, the one most central to the religious lives of medieval Christians was the Eucharist, or Mass. As we noted in Chapter 9, the ritual power of the Mass was greatly enhanced in the twelfth century, when the Church began promoting the doctrine of transubstantiation. Christians attending Mass were taught that when the priest spoke Christ's ritual words "This is my body" and "This is my blood," the substances of bread and wine on the altar were miraculously transformed into the body and blood of Jesus.

To consume one or both of these substances was to ingest holiness. So powerful was this idea that most Christians received the sacramental bread just once a year, at Easter.

But to share in the miracle of the Eucharist, one did not even have to consume it. One had only to witness the elevation of the Host: the wafer of bread raised up by the priest, which "hosted" the real presence of Jesus Christ. Daily attendance at Mass simply to view the consecration of the Host was a common form of devotion, as was the practice of displaying a consecrated wafer in a special reliquary called a monstrance ("showcase") set up on an altar or carried through the streets.

THE PURSUIT OF HOLINESS

The fundamental theme of preachers in this era, that salvation lay open to any Christian who strove for it, helps to explain the central place of the Mass and other sacraments in daily life. It also compelled many to seek out new paths that could lead to God. But, as we noted in Chapter 9, some believers who sought to achieve a mystical union with God were ultimately condemned for heresy because they did not subordinate themselves to Church authority. Even less radical figures might find themselves on dangerous ground, especially if they published their ideas.

For example, the German preacher Master Eckhart (c. 1260–1327), a Dominican friar, taught that there is a "spark" deep within every human soul, and that God lives in this spark. Through prayer and self-renunciation, any person could retreat into this inner recess of his or her being, and access divinity. This conveyed the message that laypeople could attain salvation through their own efforts, without the intervention of a priest or any of the sacraments he alone could perform. As a result, many of Eckhart's teachings were condemned. But very similar views continued to find support in the teachings of popular preachers.

Struggles for Sovereignty

When the French king Philip IV transplanted the papal court to Avignon, he was not just responding to papal abuses of power; he was bolstering his own. By the middle of the thirteenth century, the growth of strong territorial monarchies, combined with the increasing sophistication of royal justice, taxation, and propaganda, had given some secular rulers greater power than any European ruler had wielded since the time of Charlemagne. Although a king still needed to be anointed with holy oil at the time of his coronation—a rite that required a bishop and, by extension, papal support—a king's authority in his own realm rested on the consent of the aristocracy and the popular perception of his reputation for justice, piety, and regard for his subjects' prosperity. On the wider stage of the medieval world, it also rested on his successful assertion of his kingdom's sovereignty.

THE PROBLEM OF SOVEREIGNTY

sovereignty An inviolable authority over a defined territory.

Sovereignty can be defined as an inviolable authority over a defined territory. In Chapter 9, we learned that Philip Augustus was the first monarch to call himself "king of France" and not "king of the Franks." In other words, he was defining his kingship in geographical terms, claiming that there was an entity called France and that he was king within that area.

But what was France? Was it the tiny "island" (Île-de-France) around Paris, which had been Philip's father's domain? If so, France was very small—and very vulnerable, lacking in sovereignty. Or did France include any region, such as Champagne or Normandy, whose lord was willing to do homage to the French king? In that case, the king would need to enforce his rights of lordship constantly and, if necessary, exert his rule directly.

But what if some of France's neighboring lords ruled in their own right, as did the independent counts of Flanders, thus threatening the security of France's borders? In that case, the king would need either to forge an alliance with these borderlands or deny their independence. He would need to assert his sovereignty by absorbing these regions into an ever-growing kingdom.

The problem of sovereignty, then, is a zero-sum game: one state's sovereignty is won and maintained by diminishing that of other states. Although many French citizens today would assert that France has, in some mystical way, always existed in its present form, in fact, France and many other European states were being cobbled together during the medieval period through a process of annexation and colonization—just as the United States was assembled at the expense of the empires that had colonized North America and through the killing or displacement of autonomous native peoples.

Sovereignty as a "zero-sum game": one state asserts authority at expense of others

The process of achieving sovereignty is thus an aggressive and often violent one. In Spain, the "reconquest" of Muslim lands, which had accelerated in the twelfth century, continued apace in the thirteenth and fourteenth centuries, to the detriment of these regions' Muslim and Jewish inhabitants. German princes continued to push northward into the Baltic, where they responded with brutal force to native resistance. Meanwhile, the Scandinavian kingdoms that had been forming in the eleventh and twelfth centuries fought among themselves and their neighbors for the control of contested regions and resources. Italy and the Mediterranean became a constant battleground, as we have observed.

Among these emerging states, the two most strident in their assertion of sovereignty were France and England.

THE PRESTIGE OF FRANCE: THE SAINTLY KINGSHIP OF LOUIS IX

After the death of Philip Augustus, the heirs to the French throne continued to pursue an expansionist policy, pushing the boundaries of the kingdom to the east and south. There were significant pockets of resistance, though, notably from the independent towns of Flanders. In 1302, citizen militias from several of these towns, fighting on foot with farming implements and other unconventional weapons, managed to defeat the heavily armed French cavalry. This victory at the Battle of Courtrai (Kortrijk in Flemish) is still celebrated as a national holiday by Flemish-speaking Belgians.

This defeat was a setback for Philip IV of France, much of whose power derived from his grandfather, **Louis IX** (r. 1226–1270). Louis was famous for his piety and his conscientious exercise of kingship. Unlike most princes, Louis not only pledged to go on a crusade—he actually went. And although both of his campaigns were notorious failures (he died on the second, in 1270), they cemented his saintly reputation and political clout.

Louis IX King of France from 1226 to his death on crusade in 1270, Louis was renowned for his piety and for his close attention to the administration of law and justice in his realm.

BLANCHE OF CASTILE AND HER SON, KING LOUIS IX. Blanche was a granddaughter of Eleanor of Aquitaine and daughter of King Alfonso VII of Castile and his queen, Eleanor of England. Well-educated and politically savvy, Blanche became the *de facto* ruler of France when her husband, King Louis VIII, died—leaving her with to raise her children and secure the throne for her son, Louis IX, who was only 12 years old at the time. That fact that she did so successfully would pave the way for Louis' successful reign. Here, in a contemporary illumination, mother and soon sit enthroned as equals in their palace in Paris. Their gestures show that Blanche is offering her son advice and instruction, which he gladly receives.

First, Louis's willingness to risk his life (and those of his brothers) in the service of the Church would give him tremendous influence in papal affairs—a key factor in making his youngest brother, Charles of Anjou, the king of Naples and Sicily. Second, ensuring the good administration of his kingdom during his years of absence prompted Louis to invent or reform many key aspects of royal governance, which made France the bureaucratic rival of England for the first time. Third, Louis's crusading ventures were seen as confirmation that the king of France had inherited the mantle of Charlemagne as the protector of the Church.

The prestige of the French monarchy found artistic expression in the Sainte-Chapelle (Holy Chapel), a gorgeous jewel box of a church that Louis built in Paris for his collection of relics thought to have been used for the torture and crucifixion of Christ. The most important of these was the Crown of Thorns, intended by Pilate as a mocking reference to "the king of the Jews" (see Chapter 6). Now that this holy crown belonged to Louis and was housed in Paris, it was a sign that Paris was the new Jerusalem.

Widely regarded as a saint in his lifetime, Louis was formally canonized in 1297 by the same Pope Boniface VIII who was brought down by Philip IV, Louis's grandson. Indeed, Boniface partly intended this gesture as a rebuke, but Philip turned it to his advantage. He even used his grandfather's pious reputation as a cloak for his frankly rapacious treatment of the Knights Templar, whose military order he suppressed in 1314 so that he could confiscate its wealth and dissolve his own debts. He had expelled the Jews from his realm in 1306 for similar reasons.

CASTLES AND CONTROL: EDWARD I AND THE EXPANSION OF ENGLISH RULE

The expulsion of Jews who depended on a king's personal protection had been a precedent set by Philip's contemporary and kinsman, **Edward I** of England (r. 1272–1307). Unlike Philip, Edward had to build up the sovereignty of his state

Edward I King of England from 1272 to his death in 1307, Edward presided over the creation of new legal and bureaucratic institutions in his realm, violently subjugated the Welsh, and attempted to colonize Scotland. He expelled English Jews from his domain in 1290.

almost from scratch—for his father, Henry III (r. 1216–1272), had a long but troubled reign. Henry inherited the throne as a young boy, shortly after his father John's loss of Normandy and capitulation to Magna Carta (Chapter 9), and he had to contend with rebellions among the restive barons of his realm. When Edward himself became king in 1272, he took steps to ensure that there would be no further revolts by tightening his control on the aristocracy's lands, diffusing their power by strengthening that of Parliament and reforming the administration of the realm.

Edward then looked to England's borders. Since Welsh chieftains had been major backers of the rebel barons, he was determined to bring "wild Wales" within the orbit of English sovereignty. Edward accordingly embarked on an ambitious and ruthless campaign of castle building, ringing the hilly country with enormous fortifications on a scale not seen in most of Europe—these were, in fact, crusader castles—and treating the Welsh (his fellow Christians) as infidels. Indeed, he treated Wales like a conquered state, making it a settler colony and subjecting the Welsh to the lordship of his own men. When his son, the future Edward II, was born in 1284 at the great castle he had built at Caernarvon, he gave the infant the title "Prince of Wales": a title usually borne by a Welsh chieftain.

Edward then turned to England's final frontier. Until now, control of Scotland had not been an English concern. The Scottish border had been peaceful for many years, and the Scottish kings did homage to the English king for some of their lands. In 1290, however, the succession to the Scottish throne was disputed among rival claimants,

CAERNARVON CASTLE. One of many massive fortifications built by Edward I, this castle was the birthplace of the first English Prince of Wales and the site where the current Prince of Wales, Charles, was formally invested with that title in 1969. › **Castles of this size and strength had been constructed in the Crusader States and on the disputed frontiers of Muslim and Christian Spain, but never before in Britain (see the photo on page 304). What does their construction reveal about Edward's attitude toward the Welsh?**

A Girl Raised as a Boy: The Story of Silence

Surviving in a single illustrated manuscript, the Roman de Silence, *the "romance" or story about Silence, is a remarkable literary artifact testifying to the complexity of medieval gender roles, as well as conflicting attitudes toward disguise and deception, sexuality, women's social and legal status, and the factors that affect a person's identity and destiny. Composed in the first half of the thirteenth century, it is attributed to a pseudonymous author called Heldris of Cornwall, written in a dialect of Old French from northeastern France. Its protagonist is the daughter of a nobleman and his wife who decide to raise the child as a boy because the fictional king of England has outlawed female inheritance. They choose the name "Silence" to indicate that their deception must remain a secret. In the following passage, Silence has realized that they are female. This scene is immediately followed by a debate between Nature and Nurture over Silence's true gender. The changing pronouns are original to the text.*

And when this child was of an age
to understand he was a maid,
his father gave the reason why,
explaining how they came to lie,
that his true sex might be concealed. [. . .] 5
"My sweet, fair son: it was for you
that we did this, not for us two.
Now that you know, my son, be sure
to keep this secret thing secure.
Upon your honor: tell no one." 10
And he replied, like a good son:
"Don't fear, when all is said and done,
With God's help, I will do my best
To hide myself from all the rest." [. . .]
The seneschal, to make him fit 15
and to improve his horsemanship
through woods and streams took him to ride,

and all throughout that countryside:
in frost and heat, bright day and dim,
in quest to make a man of him. 20
To such men's ways he was so used,
and those of women so refused,
that he lacked nothing of a male:
no one could see he wasn't male.
Yet all's not what it seems to be: 25
beneath the clothes, he is a she. [. . .]
And by the time of his twelfth year
there was no one he could not beat
when challenged to a wrestling meet,
in jousting, or in skirmishing. 30
Alone he kept his peers trembling.
Silence was disturbed by this,
for in their heart they knew that it
had happened through deceitful means.

and Edward intervened to press his own claim and threatened to take Scotland by force. To avoid this, the Scots forged an alliance with the French, but could not prevent Edward's army from fighting its way through to Scone Abbey in 1296.

Scone was a symbolic target: the site of the Stone of Destiny on which Scottish kings were traditionally enthroned. So Edward seized this potent symbol, brought it back to Westminster Abbey in London, and embedded it in the coronation chair of his namesake, Edward the Confessor, the last Anglo-Saxon king of England (Chapter 8). Save for a brief hiatus in 1950, when the stone was stolen from the abbey by students at the University of Glasgow, it would remain there until 1996,

And just when they had reached their teens,
Nature came and, grumbling,
said, "Look, this is the strangest thing,
that you behave now like a male,
going about in wind and hail,
when with my very special brand   40
I formed you with my own two hands,
and all the pretty tricks I knew
I laid on thick when I made you!
A thousand people now curse me
for wasting on you such beauty   45
because away from them I took
such loveliness to make your looks." [. . .]
So Nature said, "Get going, go!
Get to your chamber, learn to sew—
for that's what Nature's law demands!   50
You are not Silence, not a man!" [. . .]
Now who should enter but Nurture,
who saw what went on with Nature,
and said to him, "What's going on?"
And he said, "Nature says I'm wrong,   55
and maybe after all it's true
that I've not done what I should do,
that this is not what I should be,
that I've behaved unnaturally."[. . .]
Now, do you think, when Nurture heard,   60
that she was happy with these words?
No way! Instead, she shook with rage
toward Nature while she held her gaze
and glared with great ferocity.
And then she said, oh so sweetly,   65
"Just let go of my protégé
or I will curse you. Go away." [. . .]

Then Reason came to make her case
and did it with such strength and grace
That Silence understood indeed
what folly it would be to heed—
or think of taking—bad advice
and give up on his good old life
and take up feminine habits.
For now that he remembered it,
he'd heard about a woman's ways,
when shut up in her room all day.
When he compared that lot to his,
the choice was clear as day. That is,
a man has all a woman lacks:
his life is better, that's a fact.

Source: Translated by Carol Symes, based on the edition of Lewis Thorpe, *Le Roman de Silence* (Cambridge: 1972), first published in Nottingham Medieval Studies 5–8 (1961–64) and 10–11 (1966–67); and revised by Sarah Roche-Mahdi, *Silence: A Thirteenth-Century French Romance* (East Lansing, MI: 1992–2007), vv. 2329–2656 (excerpts).

Questions for Analysis

1. How does this source reveal the ambiguity of Silence's gender identity? How does Reason intervene in the debate between Nature and Nurture?

2. Many medieval tales survive in single manuscript copies, so it is often hard to tell how popular they were. But based on your reading of this excerpt and what you have learned about medieval gender roles, do you think that the story of Silence would have found a wide audience? Why or why not?

after which it was returned to Scotland. (It will be temporarily loaned to London when the next British monarch is crowned.)

Edward considered the subjugation of Scotland to be England's manifest destiny. He called himself the "Hammer of the Scots" and, before he died, he charged his son Edward II (r. 1307–1327) with the completion of his task. But the younger Edward was not a ruthless advocate of English expansion; he had to contend, instead, with a rebellion led by his own queen, Isabella of France, who eventually engineered his abdication and murder. Their son, Edward III (r. 1327–1377), did renew his grandfather's expansionist policies, but his main target was not Scotland—it was France.

A Declaration of Scottish Independence

In April 1320, a group of powerful Scottish lords gathered at the abbey of Arbroath to draft a letter to Pope John XXII in Avignon. The resulting Declaration of Arbroath petitioned the exiled pope (a Frenchman loyal to the French king) to recognize the Scots as a sovereign nation and to support their right to an independent kingdom that would be free from encroachment by the English. The Scots' elected king, Robert the Bruce, had been excommunicated by a previous pope who had upheld English claims to lordship in Scotland. The letter therefore makes a number of different arguments for the recognition of the Scots' right to self-governance.

We know, most Holy Father and lord, and have gathered from the deeds and books about men in the past, that . . . the nation of the Scots has been outstanding for its many distinctions. It journeyed from the lands of Greece and Egypt by the Tyrrhenian Sea and the Pillars of Hercules, . . . but could not be subdued anywhere by any peoples however barbaric. . . . It took possession of the settlements in the west which it now desires, after first driving out the Britons and totally destroying the Picts, and although often attacked by the Norwegians, Danes and English. Many were its victories and innumerable its efforts. It has held these places always free of all servitude, as the old histories testify. One hundred and thirteen kings of their royal lineage have reigned in their kingdom, with no intrusion by a foreigner.

If the noble qualities and merits of these men were not obvious for other reasons, they shine forth clearly enough in that they were almost the first to be called to his most holy faith by the King of Kings and Lord of Lords, our Lord Jesus Christ, after his Passion and Resurrection, even though they were settled on the most distant boundaries of the earth. . . .

Thus our people lived until now in freedom and peace . . . , until that mighty prince Edward [I] king of England (the father of the present king) in the guise of a friend and ally attacked our kingdom in hostile fashion, when it had no head and the people were not harbouring any evil treachery, nor were they accustomed to wars or attacks. His unjust acts, killings, acts of violence, pillagings, burnings, imprisonments of prelates, burnings of monasteries, robbings and killings of regular clergy, and also innumerable other outrages, which he committed against the said people, sparing none on account of age or sex, religion or order—no one could write about them or fully comprehend them who had not been instructed by experience.

From these countless ills we have been set free, with the help of Him who follows up wounds with healing and cures, by our most energetic prince, king and lord Sir Robert [the Bruce; r. 1306–1329]. . . . By divine

THE OUTBREAK OF THE HUNDRED YEARS' WAR

Hundred Years' War
(1337-1453) Series of wars between England and France, fought mostly on French soil and prompted by the territorial and political claims of English monarchs.

The **Hundred Years' War** was the longest and widest-ranging military conflict since Rome's wars with Carthage in the third and second centuries B.C.E. (Chapter 5). Although England and France were its principal antagonists, almost all major European powers became involved at some stage. Active hostilities began in 1337 and lasted until 1453, interrupted by truces of varying lengths. We will continue tracing its developments in Chapter 11.

The most fundamental source of conflict was the fact that the kings of England held the duchy of Gascony as vassals of the French king; this had been part of Eleanor of Aquitaine's domain, added to the Anglo-Norman Empire in 1154 (Chapter 9).

providence his succession to his right according to our laws and customs which we intend to maintain to the death, together with the due consent and assent of us all, have made him our prince and king. . . . But if he should give up what he has begun, seeking to subject us or our kingdom to the king of the English, . . . we would immediately strive to expel him as our enemy and a subverter of his right and ours, and we would make someone else our king, who is capable of seeing to our defence. For as long as a hundred of us remain alive, we intend never to be subjected to the lordship of the English, in any way. For it is not for glory in war, riches or honours that we fight, but only for the laws of our fathers and for freedom, which no good man loses except along with his life.

Therefore, most Holy Father and lord, we implore your holiness with all vehemence in our prayers that you . . . look with paternal eyes on the troubles and difficulties brought upon us and the Church of God by the English. And that you deign to admonish and exhort the king of the English, who ought to be satisfied with what he has (since England was formerly enough for seven kings or more), to leave us Scots in peace, living as we do in the poor country of Scotland beyond which there is no dwelling place, and desiring nothing but our own. . . .

It is important for you, Holy Father, to do this, since you see the savagery of the heathen raging against Christians (as the sins of Christians require), and the frontiers of Christendom are being curtailed day by day, and you have seen how much it detracts from your holiness's reputation if (God forbid!) the Church suffers eclipse or scandal in any part of it during your time. Let it then rouse the Christian princes who are covering up their true motivation when they pretend that they cannot go to the assistance of the Holy Land on account of wars with their neighbours. The real reason that holds them back is that in warring with their smaller neighbours they anticipate greater advantage to themselves and weaker resistance. . . .

But if your Holiness too credulously trusts the tales of the English fully, or does not leave off favouring the English to our confusion, then we believe that the Most High will blame you for the slaughter of bodies. . . . Dated at our monastery at Arbroath in Scotland 6 April 1320 in the fifteenth year of our said king's reign.

Source: Walter Bower. *Scotichronicon*, vol. 7, ed. A. B. Scott and D. E. R. Watt (Aberdeen, Scotland: 1996).

Questions for Analysis

1. On what grounds does this letter justify the political independence of the Scots? What different arguments does it make? Which in your view is the most compelling?

2. Why does this letter mention crusading? What are the Scottish lords implying about the relationship between Europe's internal conflicts and the ongoing wars with external adversaries?

3. Imagine that you are an adviser to the pope. Applying your knowledge of the papacy's situation at this time, would you advise him to do as this letter asks? Why or why not?

In the thirteenth century, when the French kings had not yet absorbed this region into their domain, this fact had seemed less of an anomaly. But as the French monarchy began to claim sovereignty within the "natural" boundaries of their domains, the English presence in Gascony became more and more problematic. The fact that England also had close commercial and cultural ties to Flanders—which consistently resisted annexation by France—added fuel to the fire, as did the French alliance with the Scots.

Complicating this volatile situation was the disputed French succession. In 1328, the last of Philip IV's three sons died without leaving a son to succeed him: the Capetian dynasty, founded by the Frankish warlord Hugh Capet in 987 (Chapter 8),

THE DISPUTED FRENCH SUCCESSION IN 1328

(1) Isabella == Philip III == Mary (2)
(r. 1270–1285)

Philip IV, The Fair == Joan
(r. 1285–1314)

Charles, Count of Valois

Philip VI of Valois
(r. 1328–1350)

Louis X
(r. 1314–1316)

Philip V
(r. 1316–1322)

Charles IV
(r. 1322–1328)

Isabella == Edward II,
King of England
(r. 1307–1327)

John II
(r. 1350–1364)

[Daughter]

[Daughters]

[Daughters]

Edward III,
King of England
(r. 1327–1377)

Charles V
(r. 1364–1380)

had finally exhausted itself. A new dynasty, the Valois, came to the throne—but only by insisting that women could neither inherit royal power nor pass it on. For otherwise, the heir to France was Edward III of England, whose ambitious mother, Isabella, was Philip IV's only daughter. Initially, when his mother's claim was passed over, Edward was only fifteen and in no position to protest. In 1337, however, when the disputes over Gascony and Scotland erupted into war, Edward raised the stakes by claiming to be the rightful king of France.

Although France was richer and more populous than England by a ratio of at least three to one, the English crown was more effective in mobilizing the entire population, for reasons we discussed in Chapter 9. Edward III was therefore able to levy an army of seasoned and well-disciplined soldiers, cavalrymen, and archers. The huge but virtually leaderless armies assembled by the French proved no match for the tactical superiority of these smaller English forces. English armies pillaged the French countryside at will, while civil wars broke out between embattled French lords. A decade after the declaration of war, French knights were defeated in two humiliating battles at Crécy (1346) and Calais (1347). The English seemed invincible—but they were no match for a new and unexpected adversary approaching from the East.

From the Great Famine to the Black Death

By 1300, Europe was connected to Asia by an intricate network that fostered connections of all kinds. At the same time, Europe was reaching its own ecological limits. Between 1000 and 1300, the population had tripled; a sea of grain fields stretched, almost unbroken, from Ireland to Ukraine; forests had been cleared, marshes drained, and pastureland reduced by generations of peasants performing lifetimes of labor. But still, Europe was barely able to feed its people. At the same time, the Medieval Warm Period (Chapter 8) was ending, and with it the favorable climatic conditions that had enabled the agricultural revolution of the previous three centuries. Even a reduction of 1 or 2° C is enough to cause substantial changes in rainfall patterns, shorten growing seasons, and decrease agricultural productivity. So it did in Europe, with disastrous consequences.

EVIL TIMES: THE SEVEN YEARS' FAMINE

Between the years 1315 and 1322, the cooling global climate caused continuous adverse weather conditions in northern Europe. Winters were extraordinarily severe: in 1316, the Baltic Sea froze over and ships were trapped in the ice. Rains prevented planting in spring or summer; when a crop did struggle through, it would be dashed by rain and hail in autumn. Amid these natural calamities, dynastic warfare continued in the sodden farmland, as the princes of Scandinavia and the Holy Roman Empire fought for supremacy and succession. In the once-fertile fields of Flanders, French armies slogged through mud in continued efforts to subdue the Flemish population. On the Scottish and Welsh borders, uprisings were ruthlessly suppressed and the peasantry pillaged to feed the English raiders.

The result was human suffering more devastating than that caused by any European famine since that time; hence the name "**Great Famine**" to describe this terrible crisis. Weakened by malnutrition, between 10 and 15 percent of the northern population perished. Many starved, while others fell victim to epidemic diseases. In southern Europe, around the shores of the Mediterranean, the effects of climate change were more muted, and food could be distributed through different channels. Nonetheless, the overall health of this region also suffered from the disruption of trade and the shortage of staple goods, as well as from the highly unstable political situation we have discussed.

As food grew scarcer, prices climbed unpredictably, making most goods unobtainable by the poor. Plans for future crops, which kept hope alive, would be dashed when flooded fields prevented seeds from germinating. People then spent cold summers and autumns foraging for food. Hunting was restricted to the nobility (Chapter 9), but even those who risked the death penalty for poaching found little game. Wages did not keep pace with rising costs, so those who lived in towns and depended on markets had less to spend on scarce provisions. Only a year after the famine began, townspeople were dying of ailments that would not have been fatal in good years.

The effects of the famine were especially devastating for children, since even those who survived were highly susceptible to disease, owing to the severe impairment of their immune systems. It may have been the Great Famine, then, that paved the way for the even more horrific destruction of the Black Death.

A CRISIS OF CONNECTIVITY: TRACKING THE BLACK DEATH

The **Black Death** is the name given to a global plague pandemic that spread from central Asia to China, northern India, and western Asia with the Mongol conquests, and then to Africa and Europe. Research has led to the realization that this outbreak

Great Famine Period of terrible hunger and deprivation in Europe that peaked between 1315 and 1317, caused by a cooling of the climate and by environmental degradation due to overfarming. It is estimated to have reduced the population of Europe by 10 to 15 percent.

Black Death The plague pandemic that ravaged Europe, Asia, and North Africa during the fourteenth century, killing at least one-third to half of the population.

was caused by the same microbe responsible for the Justinianic plague of the sixth century and may have been active as early as the end of the twelfth century. By 1346, the plague had reached the Black Sea, where it was transmitted to the Genoese colonists at Caffa and transported by their ships to North Africa, Sicily, and northern Italy. From there, it spread rapidly along global trade routes By 1350, it had reached Scandinavia and northern Russia, then spread southward again until it linked up with the original waves of infection in its breeding grounds in central Asia. In Europe, it continued to erupt in local epidemics until the eighteenth century. In Asia and Africa, it was still causing devastating losses of life into the nineteenth century.

Although the *absolute* (total) mortality caused by other global pandemics has been greater—including the influenza pandemic of 1918–1919 and the ongoing HIV/AIDS pandemic—the *percentage* of the population affected by the Black Death was higher. In the space of a few decades, 40 to 70 percent of all people in these affected areas had died. The tremendous consequences of this catastrophe and the survivors' responses to the world left behind will be explored in Chapter 11. But what made this pandemic so deadly?

The *Yersinia pestis* genome was sequenced in 2013 using aDNA from the teeth of Black Death victims buried in London. Epidemiologists have since been able to show that it morphed rapidly into multiple strains after the Justinianic plague. Its bubonic form, which attacks the lymph nodes and produces painful pus-filled buboes in the groin, neck, and armpits, had probably developed in antiquity, and this was the form in which it spread during the sixth century. Thereafter, however, it morphed into more virulent septicemic and pneumonic variants.

In its *bubonic* form, the plague microbe is carried by fleas that can live and travel in the fur or feathers of many different animals, including rats, marmots, hamsters, rabbits, camels, dogs, and birds. Humans contract it through flea bites or contact with an animal host. *Septicemic* plague occurs when an infected flea introduces the microbe directly into the human bloodstream, causing death within hours, usually before any symptoms of disease are obvious. *Pneumonic* plague, perhaps the most frightening variation, results when particles of *Y. pestis* are inhaled and infect the lungs, allowing the contagion to spread silently and invisibly, in the same ways as the common cold. Other forms of plague can be contracted by eating an infected animal, and many of its animal hosts were common dietary staples in medieval societies.

One of the things that made the Black Death so terrifying, therefore, was that it was mysteriously inconsistent. Those afflicted by the hideous bubonic plague might actually recover, whereas others—seemingly untouched—might die suddenly, from no apparent cause. Observers quickly realized that the plague was contagious, but precisely how it spread remained unknown. Some believed that it was caused by breathing "bad air" and so urged people to flee from stricken areas, which caused the disease to spread even faster. Another response was the flagellant movement, so called because of the whips (*flagella*) with which traveling bands of penitents lashed themselves in order to appease the wrath of God. The unruly and sometimes hysterical mobs that gathered around the flagellants aroused the concern of both ecclesiastical and secular authorities, and the movement was suppressed by papal order.

Still others looked for scapegoats and revived old conspiracy theories that implicated Jews in the poisoning of communal water sources. Scores of Jewish communities were attacked and thousands of their inhabitants massacred in parts of the Rhineland, southern France, and the Christian kingdoms of Spain. For example,

Map labels:
ATLANTIC OCEAN
NORTH SEA
BALTIC SEA
BLACK SEA
ADRIATIC SEA
MEDITERRANEAN SEA
EUROPE
AFRICA
Area of detail

Elbe R.
Vistula R.
Dnieper R.
Rhine R.
Loire R.
Po R.
Danube R.
Ebro R.
PYRENEES MTS.
ALPS MTS.

June 30, 1350
December 31, 1350
December 31, 1349
June 30, 1349
December 31, 1348
December 31, 1348
June 30, 1348
June 30, 1347
December 31, 1347

Towns: Bergen, Wisby, Moscow, Durham, Drogheda, Lancaster, Preston, York, Dublin, Kilkenny, Chester, Lincoln, Nottingham, Lübeck, Rostock, Danzig, Frankfurt an der Oder, Thorn, Norwich, Yarmouth, Bremen, Hamburg, Oxford, Cambridge, Bristol, London, Canterbury, Osnabrück, Magdeburg, Weymouth, Southampton, Calais, Bruges, Ghent, Cologne, Erfurt, Amiens, Liège, Frankfurt, Würzburg, Nuremberg, Paris, Strasbourg, Colmar, Mühldorf, Vienna, Basel, Zurich, Lucerne, St. Gall, Angers, Bordeaux, Milan, Verona, Venice, Po R., Toulouse, Montpellier, Genoa, Bologna, Florence, Ancona, Sebenico, Huesca, Narbonne, Marseilles, Pisa, Perugia, Ragusa, Saragossa, Lérida, Siena, Teruel, Barcelona, Rome, Caffa, Constantinople, Valencia, Naples, Seville, Almería, Messina, Agrigento, Catania, Syracuse

Legend:
• Plague-stricken towns and areas
— Progress of plague at certain dates
▪ Towns and areas not stricken by the plague

0   100   200   300 Miles
0 100 200 300 Kilometers

EUROPEAN OUTBREAKS OF THE BLACK DEATH, 1347–1350. › What trajectories did the Black Death follow once it arrived in Europe? › How might the growth of towns, trade, and travel have contributed to the spread of the Black Death? › Would such a rapid advance have been likely during the early Middle Ages or even in the ancient world? Why or why not?

an important archaeological and forensic study published in 2014 reveals that hundreds of Jews—including children, the elderly, and the disabled—were brutally clubbed and hacked to death by their Christian neighbors in the small Catalonian town of Tàrrega (see **Competing Viewpoints** on page 364). The papacy and some local authorities tried to halt such attacks, but these efforts usually came too late.

The Black Death and the Jews: Christian Responses to Antisemitic Violence

When the Black Death began to devastate Europe after 1347, it fueled a wave of violence against Jews. Jews were often accused of being the catalysts for the plague, for allegedly poisoning water supplies or through other nefarious means, or by taking undue advantage of the Christians who were dependent on them for financial reasons. In the small Catalonian town of Tàrrega, a massacre of Jews by their Christian neighbors is documented both in the royal inquest that condemned it and in a series of mass graves, dug by survivors, in which their slaughtered loved ones were carefully buried. In the German cities of the Rhineland, where Jews had also thrived for centuries under the protection of local rulers or municipal authorities, attempts were made to preempt such massacres by spreading the news of their occurrence in other parts of Europe, as we see in a letter from the town council of Cologne to their counterparts in nearby Strasbourg.

The Slaughter Of The Jews Of Tàrrega By Their Christian Neighbors, July 1348

In the year just passed [i.e. 1348], some individuals of this town strongly aroused its people to put aside the fear of God and our authority, not hesitating to offend our majesty. Incited by a diabolical spirit, with armed hand and deliberate intent, they came maliciously to the *call* of the Jewish community [*aljama*] and with unwarranted recklessness they violently broke down and destroyed the gates of this *call* with axes and other types of weapons, and they even destroyed the *call* itself, entering into it all together and shouting loudly with raised voices, "Kill the traitors" [*Muyren los traydors*]. And not satisfied with that, but rivaling terrible acts with even worse things, they ruthlessly raided Jewish homes with spears, stones, and arrows. And, finally entering the said houses, they took away all the goods and property of the Jews, just as if they were thieves, and lawlessly they tore and burned many legal instruments and various written contracts of the Jews and they senselessly murdered many Jews in this community, and others were beaten mercilessly and were wounded, and they inflicted many terrible evils, grave injuries, offenses, robberies, harms, and atrocities and on these Jews.

Source: Anna Colet, et al. "The Black Death and Its Consequences for the Jewish Community in Tàrrega: Lessons from History and Archeology," *The Medieval Globe*. Latin text trans. Monica H. Green and Carol Symes (Yorkshire, UK: 2014): pp. 71–2.

Conclusion

The century between 1250 and 1350 was a time of significant change within all Western civilizations. The growing power of some monarchies led to encroachments on territories and cities that had once been independent, fueling resistance. The papacy, whose power had seemed so secure at the turn of the thirteenth century, would itself become a pawn in the keeping of the French king by the beginning of the fourteenth. Rome thereby lost its last source of authority while the New Rome, Constantinople, struggled to rebuild its prestige in the face of Mongol expansion. Yet for the Mongol khans and the merchants they favored, for seafaring cities such

A Letter from the Town Council of Cologne to the Town Council of Strasbourg (Germany), 12 January 1349

Very dear friends, all sorts of rumours are now flying about against Judaism and the Jews prompted by this unexpected and unparalleled mortality of Christians. . . . Throughout our city, as in yours, many-winged Fame clamours that this mortality was initially caused, and is still being spread, by the poisoning of springs and wells, and that the Jews must have dropped poisonous substances into them. When it came to our knowledge that serious charges had been made against the Jews in several small towns and villages on the basis of this mortality, we sent numerous letters to you and to other cities and towns to uncover the truth behind these rumours, and set a thorough investigation in train. . . .

If a massacre of the Jews were to be allowed in the major cities (something which we are determined to prevent in our city, if we can, as long as the Jews are found to be innocent of these or similar actions) it could lead to the sort of outrages and disturbances which would whip up a popular revolt among the common people—and such revolts have in the past brought cities to misery and desolation. In any case we are still of the opinion that this mortality and its attendant circumstances are caused by divine vengeance and nothing else. Accordingly we intend to forbid any harassment of the Jews in our city because of these flying rumours, but to defend them faithfully and keep them safe, as our predecessors did—and we are convinced that you ought to do the same. . . .

Source: From Rosemary Horrox, ed. and trans., *The Black Death* (Manchester, 1994), pp. 219–20.

Questions for Analysis

1. How does the report of the massacre in Tàrrega describe the motives of the Christian murders? What are their apparent grievances against their Jewish neighbors?

2. Why does the Council of Cologne wish to quell violence against the city's Jews? How does this reasoning complement or challenge what we have learned so far about the treatment of Jews in medieval Europe?

3. In your view, do these two perspectives display a rational approach to the horrors of the Black Death? Why or why not? What are their wider implications for our understanding of antisemitic tropes and forms of violence?

as Venice and Genoa, for ambitious students at the universities, and for men on the make, the opportunities for advancement and mobility were great.

But even in good times, Europe's population had outgrown its capacity to produce food; and when the climate grew cooler, years of cold summers and heavy rainfall took an enormous toll. Those regions most closely tied to the new global networks were densely settled and urban, which made the shortage of food and the spread of disease more acute there. In short, the benefits and drawbacks of increased globalization were already beginning to manifest themselves in the early fourteenth century—700 years ago. The Black Death can be understood as the ultimate example of such connectivity.

The scale of mortality caused by this pandemic is almost unimaginable, to us as to those who survived it; in Europe alone, at least a third, and probably over half, of the population died between 1347 and 1353. In the countryside, thousands of villages disappeared. Cities and towns, overcrowded and unsanitary, were particularly vulnerable to plague and, thereafter, to outbreaks of violence. The immediate social consequences were profound, as were the economic ones. Crops rotted in the fields, manufacturing ceased, and trade came to a standstill in affected areas. Basic commodities became scarcer and prices rose

AFTER YOU READ THIS CHAPTER ⌄

CHRONOLOGY

1206–1279	Rapid expansion of the Mongol Empire under Genghis Khan and his heirs
1240	The territory of Rus' is dominated by the Mongols; Mongol Khanate of the Golden Horde established
1260–1294	Reign of Kublai Khan, Great Khan, and emperor of China
1271–1295	Travels of Marco Polo
1309	"Babylonian Captivity" of the papacy in Avignon begins
1315–1322	The Great Famine in Europe
1320	The Declaration of Arbroath proclaims Scotland's independence from England
1326–1354	The travels of Ibn Battuta
1337	Beginning of the Hundred Years' War
1347–1353	Spread of the Black Death in Europe
1350	Circulation of Mandeville's *Book of Marvels*

REVIEWING THE OBJECTIVES

❯ How did the conquests of the Mongols significantly impact Europe?

❯ The expansion of commerce and communication between Eastern and Western civilizations created a new world system. What were some key characteristics of this system? What kinds of exchange did it enable?

❯ What is *sovereignty*? What were the effects of competition for sovereignty among European rulers?

❯ What were the short- and long-term causes for the papacy's loss of prestige? Why was the papal court moved to Avignon?

❯ What caused the Black Death? In what sense can it be seen as a product of the new world system that began with the Mongol conquests?

higher, prompting ineffectual efforts to control prices and to force the remaining able-bodied laborers to work.

These were the short-term effects. How did the Black Death matter to those who survived it—including us? According to Ibn Khaldun (1332–1406), a Muslim historian who is considered one of the founders of modern historical methods, it marked the end of the old world and the beginning of a new one that would require new systems of government, bodies of knowledge, and forms of art. Was he right? We will begin to answer that question in Chapter 11.

Go to INQUIZITIVE to see what you've learned—and learn what you've missed—with personalized feedback along the way.

PEOPLE, IDEAS, AND EVENTS IN CONTEXT

> What accounts for the success of **GENGHIS KHAN** and his successors? What circumstances enabled **MARCO POLO**'s travels to China? To what extent does the term *PAX MONGOLICA* describe this era in history?

> How did seafaring communities such as **GENOA**, **VENICE**, and **CATALONIA** rise to prominence in this era? Why were new navigational aids such as **PORTOLAN CHARTS** necessary?

> How do the paintings of **GIOTTO** capture contemporary attitudes toward the world? How does **DANTE**'s artistry respond to the religious and political trends of his day?

> What was at stake in the controversy between **BONIFACE VIII** and **PHILIP IV**? Why was the papacy's residency at **AVIGNON** called the **BABYLONIAN CAPTIVITY**? What is a **SACRAMENT**? Why were these rites so important?

> In what different ways did **LOUIS IX** of France and **EDWARD I** of England contribute to the **SOVEREIGNTY** of their respective kingdoms? What was the relationship between claims to sovereignty and the causes of the **HUNDRED YEARS' WAR**?

> How did climate change contribute to the outbreak of the **GREAT FAMINE**?

> What were the long- and short-term causes of the **BLACK DEATH**?

THINKING ABOUT CONNECTIONS

> If the Mongol khan Ögedei had not died in 1241, the Mongols could conceivably have continued their westward movement into Europe. Knowing what you have learned about Mongol rule, how do you think this might have changed the history of the world?

> How do the patterns of conquest and colonization discussed in this chapter compare with those of earlier periods, particularly those of antiquity? How many of these developments were new in 1250–1350?

> We live in a world in which the global circulation of people, information, goods, and bacteria is rapid— hence the dangers of emerging viruses such as COVID-19. How does the medieval system compare with ours? What features seem familiar? What are the differences?

11

Rebirth and Unrest, 1350–1453

BEFORE YOU READ THIS CHAPTER ❯

IN JUNE 1381, thousands of laborers from rural England rose up in rebellion against local authorities. Most were peasants or village artisans who were dismissed as ignorant by contemporary chroniclers. Yet the revolt was carefully coordinated. Plans were spread in coded messages circulated by word of mouth and by the followers of a renegade Oxford professor, John Wycliffe, who had called for the redistribution of Church property and taught that common people should be able to read the Bible in their own language.

The rebellion's immediate catalyst had been a series of exorbitant taxes levied by Parliament for the support of the ongoing war with France. But its more fundamental cause was an epidemic that had occurred thirty years earlier. The Black Death had reduced the entire population of Europe by 60 to 70 percent and drastically altered the world of those who survived it. In this new world, workers were valuable and could stand up to those who paid them poorly or treated them like slaves. Indeed, Parliament had immediately responded to this new reality by enacting the Statute of Laborers in 1351, in a futile attempt to prohibit the movement of workers and their demands for higher wages.

During that fateful summer of 1381, the peasants of England even vowed to kill representatives of both the Church and the government and destroy all the documents that had been used to keep them in subjugation. It was a revolution, and it partly succeeded. Although the leaders were eventually captured and executed, the rebellion had made the strength of the common people known to all.

STORY LINES

> The Black Death altered Europe in profound ways and the surviving population was confronted by an array of new opportunities and challenges.

> Some of these developments were associated with a burgeoning artistic and cultural movement known as the Renaissance, which began in Italy.

> This movement was characterized by a renewed appreciation of classical arts and the ancient Greek language, whose instruction was facilitated by the flight of Greek-speaking intellectuals from Byzantium, as the Ottoman Empire absorbed the remaining lands of the eastern Roman Empire.

> Meanwhile, the competing territorial claims of Europe's sovereign powers led to large-scale warfare and the development of new military tactics and technologies.

> Even after the papacy's return to Rome from Avignon, the failure of internal reform efforts led to the further decline of papal credibility. Consequently, a number of influential religious leaders sought more radical reforms.

CORE OBJECTIVES

> **TRACE** the economic and social effects of the Black Death.

> **EXPLAIN** the relationship between the concepts of the Middle Ages and the Renaissance.

> **DESCRIBE** the intellectual, cultural, and technological innovations of this era.

> **DEFINE** the concept of national monarchy and summarize its implications.

> **UNDERSTAND** the significance of the conciliar movement and its defeat by the papacy.

The fourteenth century is often seen as a time of crisis: famine and plague cut fearful swaths through the population; war was a brutally recurrent fact of life; and the papacy spent seventy years in continuous exile from Italy, only to see its prestige decline further after its return to Rome. But this was also a time of extraordinary opportunity and achievement. The exhausted land of Europe recovered from centuries of overfarming. Workers gained the economic edge; and eventually, some even gained social and political power. Meanwhile, popular and intellectual movements sought to reform the Church. A host of intellectual, artistic, and scientific innovations contributed to all of these phenomena.

This era of rebirth and unrest has often been called by two different names: the later Middle Ages and the Renaissance. But these are not two separate historical periods; rather, these two terms reflect two different ways of naming an era that is the immediate precursor of modernity. To understand it, we need to study it holistically.

Life after the Black Death

By 1353, when the **Black Death** began to loosen its death grip on Europe, the Continent had lost at least half its population from famine and disease in the space of two generations (see Chapter 10). In the following century, recurring outbreaks of the plague and frequent warfare resulted in further reductions. Life was therefore radically different for those who survived, because massive depopulation affected every aspect of existence, from nutrition to spirituality.

THE ENVIRONMENTAL IMPACT OF THE PLAGUE

This devastating mortality had significant environmental implications. In central Europe, some 400 towns and villages became depopulated and disappeared. Around Paris, more than half the farmland became wasteland or pasture due to the absence of workers and decreased demand for food. In many regions, fields returned to woodland, increasing forested areas for the first time in centuries. This reestablished a healthier ecological balance, replenishing nutrients in the exhausted soil and providing habitats for animals in danger of extinction. Meanwhile, the smaller population reduced demand for grain, so farmers began to diversify their crops and establish livestock herds.

At the same time, the environment continued to be affected by the plague because *Yersinia pestis* became endemic (that is, permanently embedded) in some locales. This bacterium thrives in cool, upland climates, where it can lie dormant for many years. But a sudden change in temperature can activate it, as can intensified interactions between humans and the animals who act as hosts. To take one example, remote villages in the Alps suffered repeated outbreaks of the plague harbored by local fauna, including marmots and other rodent species. The plague would spread still farther if a villager exposed to plague traveled to a city or brought animal skins there for sale.

Smaller population in wake of Black Death leads to better nourishment and wages

THE SOCIAL IMPACT OF THE PLAGUE

The relative abundance of food meant that the price of bread—the staple of the medieval diet—fell. At the same time, the scarcity of workers made labor more valuable, and so some peasants and artisans could negotiate higher wages. Ordinary people could now afford a better diet, including dairy products, meat, fish, and vegetables. As a result, Europeans became better nourished than they had ever been—better than many are today. The improved health of the population also caused improved fertility and birthrates.

Survivors of the Black Death also experienced tremendous social and economic changes—even small farmers, who were able to increase the size of their holdings and achieve a higher social status. However, large landholders often responded to the labor shortage by forcing their peasants to perform additional, unpaid labor; in parts of eastern Europe, formerly free workers became serfs for the first time.

In France and the Low Countries, by contrast, peasants were able to exercise more freedoms than in the past. In England, where peasant bondage had been more common than in France, serfdom disappeared altogether. Although the Peasants' Revolt of 1381 was unsuccessful, increased economic opportunity led to increased geographic mobility, as workers moved either to towns or to the lands of a lord who offered lower rents, fewer work requirements, and greater freedoms. As we have often noted, geographical mobility and social mobility are intertwined. In the cities affected by the plague, mortality rates were high; but some populations recovered relatively quickly due to emigration from the countryside. In Florence, for example, the population rebounded rapidly but was eventually depleted by civil unrest (see page 374).

As a result, a far larger number of people were living in towns by 1500: approximately 20 percent, as opposed to about 5 percent prior to the Black Death. Also fueling this growth was the increasing specialization of the economy. With farmers under less pressure to produce grain in bulk, they could diversify their crops and sell produce more efficiently on the open market. Towns with links to trading networks grew exponentially. In northern Europe, a group of cities formed a coalition called the Hanseatic League, which came to control commerce from Britain and Scandinavia to the Baltic. In northern Italy, the increased demand for luxury goods brought renewed wealth to the spice- and silk-trading city of Venice. Milan's armaments industry also prospered, supplying its warring neighbors and the large armies of Europe's growing monarchies.

THE PLAGUE CLAIMS A VICTIM. A priest gives the last rites to a bedridden plague victim as a smiling devil pierces the dying man with a spear and Christ looks mercifully down from heaven. **›** **What are the possible meanings of this image? ›** **What does it reveal about contemporary attitudes toward death by the plague?**

POPULAR REVOLTS AND REBELLIONS

Europeans did not adjust easily to these changes. Established elites, in particular, resisted the demands of newly powerful workers; as a result, hundreds of popular rebellions challenged the status quo in many regions. In 1358, peasants in northeastern France rose up against their lords, destroying property and even murdering targeted individuals. This incident is known as the Jacquerie Rebellion, because peasants were caricatured by the aristocracy as "Jacques" ("Jack"). As we have already noted, the **English Peasants' Revolt** involved thousands of people marching on London, targeting the royal bureaucracy, killing the archbishop of Canterbury, and meeting with the fourteen-year-old king, Richard II, to demand an end to serfdom and call for the redistribution of property. It ended with the arrest and execution of the ringleaders.

In Florence, workers in the cloth industry, known as the Ciompi (*chee-OHM-pee*), were more successful in the short term. Their rebellion began in 1378, when guild members protested high unemployment and mistreatment by the manufacturers, who also ran the Florentine government. They seized control of the city, demanding tax relief, full employment, and political representation. Remarkably, the Ciompi regime remained in power for nearly four years, before it was suppressed by the urban elite.

The local circumstances behind each of these revolts were unique, but there are certain common features. Those who took part were empowered by the new economy and wanted to leverage their position to enact larger changes. Some rebellions were touched off by resistance to higher taxes; others targeted unpopular governments weakened by factionalism. In all cases, rural and urban laborers were taking advantage of their new status and importance.

ARISTOCRATIC LIFE IN THE WAKE OF THE PLAGUE

The rural aristocracies of Europe did not adapt easily to this "world turned upside down." Although many great families became wealthier, they now had to compete with an upwardly mobile population and enriched urban elites. Noble families traditionally derived revenue from vast land holdings, but some now tried to increase their income through investment in trading ventures. In Catalonia, Italy, Germany, and England, this became common. In France and Castile, however, involvement in commerce was regarded as socially demeaning and avoided by established families. Commerce could be a route to higher status in these kingdoms, but once a merchant achieved wealth he was expected to adopt an appropriate lifestyle: living in a rural castle or urban palace surrounded by a lavish household, embracing the values and conventions of chivalry, and serving his ruler at court and in warfare.

What it meant to be "noble" became, as a result, even more difficult to define than during the twelfth and thirteenth centuries. In regions where noble rank entailed certain legal privileges, proven descent from aristocratic ancestors might be necessary. Fundamentally, however, nobility was expressed and epitomized by land ownership, political influence, deference from social inferiors, courtly manners, and ostentatious display. This means that, in practice, distinctions between noble and non-noble families were very hard to discern. Even on the battlefield, where the mark of nobility was to fight on horseback, the supremacy of the mounted knight was being threatened by the growing importance of professional soldiers, archers, crossbowmen, and artillery experts. There were even hints of a more radical critique of the aristocracy's claims to superiority. As the English rebels put it in 1381, "When Adam dug and Eve spun, who then was a gentleman?" In other words, social distinctions are not innate but artificial.

In the Ciompi rebellion, cloth workers seize control of Florence, demanding economic and political reforms

Social distinctions between nobles and non-nobles become increasingly blurry

English Peasants' Revolt
In this violent 1381 uprising, thousands of people marched on London to demand an end to serfdom and called for the redistribution of property. It ended with the arrest and execution of the ringleaders.

Precisely because nobility was contested, those who claimed it took elaborate measures to assert their right to this status through what we would call conspicuous consumption. This helps to explain the extraordinary number, variety, and richness of the artifacts and artworks that survive from this period. Aristocrats, or those who wanted to be classed as such, vied with each other in hosting lavish banquets that required numerous costly utensils, specially decorated chambers, legions of servants, and the most exotic foods. They also dressed in rich and extravagant clothing—close-fitting doublets and hose with long, pointed shoes for men; multilayered silk dresses with ornate headdresses for women. Some noble households were enormous: in France, for example, the Duke of Berry had 400 matched pairs of hunting dogs and 1,000 servants. Aristocrats also took part in elaborately staged tournaments, in which participants dressed as the heroes of chivalric romances. All of these activities supported a growing number of artists and artisans.

Across Europe, kings and princes also competed for status by founding chivalric orders, such as the Knights of the Garter in England. These orders exalted the nobility as a special class, strengthening the links that bound powerful families to their sovereign lords. These bonds were further strengthened by the gifts, offices, and marriage prospects that rulers could bestow. Indeed, the alliance forged in the fifteenth century between kings and their noble supporters would become one of the most characteristic features of Europe's ruling class.

CAPTURING THE NEW REALITY IN WRITING

The writings of those who survived the Black Death or grew up in the decades following it are characterized by intense observations of the world—and these works were read by a larger and more diverse audience than ever before. The vernacular languages that were becoming powerful vehicles for literary expression (Chapter 9) were now being used to advance critical perspectives on changing social norms, political developments, and religious beliefs. We can see these innovations at work in the writings of three major authors: Giovanni Boccaccio, Geoffrey Chaucer, and Christine de Pizan.

Giovanni Boccaccio (*bohk-KAHT-chee-oh*; 1313–1375) is best known for *The Decameron*, a collection of stories about sex, adventure, and trickery told over a period of ten days (hence the title of the book: "ten days") by a sophisticated party of young women and men who have taken residence in a country villa outside Florence to escape the Black Death. Whereas Dante had used the Florentine dialect to evoke the awesome landscape of sacred history in the *Divine Comedy* (Chapter 10), Boccaccio used it to capture in plain-spoken prose the foibles of human beings.

The poet **Geoffrey Chaucer** (c. 1340–1400) was among the first to pioneer a form of English that readers today can understand with just a little effort. Known as Middle English, it blended Anglo-Saxon (Old English) with the French dialect of the Norman conquerors to create a new language. Chaucer's masterpiece, *The Canterbury Tales*, was influenced by Boccaccio's *Decameron*: it, too, is a collection of stories held together by a framing narrative. In this case, the stories are in verse and are told by a diverse group of people traveling together on a pilgrimage to the shrine of Saint Thomas Becket at Canterbury. Each character tells a story that is particularly suited to his or her own occupation and outlook, forming a kaleidoscopic human comedy.

Vernacular languages are now common vehicles for social and political commentary

Giovanni Boccaccio (c. 1313–1375) Italian writer best known for *The Decameron*.

Geoffrey Chaucer (c. 1340–1400) English poet and author who was among the first to pioneer Middle English, which blended Anglo-Saxon (Old English) with the French dialect of the Norman conquerors to create a new language.

CHRISTINE DE PIZAN. One of the most prolific authors of the Middle Ages, Christine used her influence to uphold the dignity of women and to celebrate their history and achievements. Here, we see her presenting and discussing her work with a group of noblemen at the French court of King Charles VI.

In the generation or so after the Black Death, we find professional authors who could make their living through aristocratic patronage and broader publication networks. One of the first was a woman, **Christine de Pizan** (c. 1365–c. 1430). Born in northern Italy, Christine spent her adult life in France, where her husband was a member of the king's household. When he died, Christine wrote to support herself and her children, mastering a wide variety of genres that include treatises on chivalry and warfare as well as many works celebrating the capacities and history of women (see *Analyzing Primary Sources* on page 377). Indeed, Christine took part in a vigorous pamphlet campaign that condemned the misogynistic claims made by male authors such as Boccaccio. This debate became so famous that it was given a name: the *querelle des femmes* ("the debate over women"). Remarkably, Christine even wrote a song in praise of Joan of Arc—though she did not live long enough to see her younger contemporary put to death for behaving too much like a man (see page 392).

VISUALIZING THE NEW REALITY

The desire to capture real experiences was also a dominant trait of the visual arts produced after the Black Death. This is evident both in the older arts of manuscript illumination and in the new kinds of painting and sculpture we discussed in Chapter 10. A further innovation was the technique of painting in oils: a medium pioneered in Flanders, where artists found a ready market for their works among wealthy merchants. Oil paints were revolutionary because they do not dry so quickly as water-based pigments, so a painter can work more slowly, taking time with more difficult techniques and making corrections. Masterly practitioners included Rogier van der Weyden (c. 1400–1464), who communicated deep spiritual messages against a backdrop of everyday life (see *Interpreting Visual Evidence* on page 381). This conveyed the message that Biblical events are constantly present, here and now.

The same immediacy is also evident in drama, because medieval plays were often devotional exercises that involved the entire community. In the English city of York, for example, an annual series of pageants reenacted the history of human salvation from the Creation to the Last Judgment in a single summer day, beginning at

Christine de Pizan
(c. 1365–c. 1430) The first laywoman to earn her living by writing. She is the author of treatises in warfare and chivalry, as well as of books and pamphlets that challenge long-standing misogynistic claims.

Why a Woman Can Write about Warfare

Christine de Pizan (c. 1365–c. 1434) was one of the West's first professional writers, best known today for her Book of the City of Ladies *and* The Treasure of the City of Ladies, *works that aimed to provide women with an honorable and rich history and to combat generations of institutionalized misogyny. But in her own time, Christine was probably best known for the work excerpted here,* The Book of Deeds of Arms and of Chivalry, *a manual of military strategy and conduct written in 1410, at the height of the Hundred Years' War.*

As boldness is essential for great undertakings, and without it nothing should be risked, I think it is proper in this present work to set forth my unworthiness to treat such exalted matter. I should not have dared even to think about it, but although boldness is blameworthy when it is foolhardy, I should state that I have not been inspired by arrogance or foolish presumption, but rather by true affection and a genuine desire for the welfare of noble men engaging in the profession of arms. I am encouraged, in the light of my other writings, to undertake to speak in this book of the most honorable office of arms and chivalry. . . . So to this end I have gathered together facts and subject matter from various books to produce this present volume. But inasmuch as it is fitting for this matter to be discussed factually, diligently, and sensibly . . . and also in consideration of the fact that military and lay experts in the aforesaid art of chivalry are not usually clerks or writers who are expert in language, I intend to treat the matter in the plainest possible language. . . .

As this is unusual for women, who generally are occupied in weaving, spinning, and household duties, I humbly invoke . . . the wise lady Minerva [Athena], born in the land of Greece, whom the ancients esteemed highly for her great wisdom. Likewise the poet Boccaccio praises her in his *Book of Famous Women*, as do other writers praise her art and manner of making trappings of iron and steel, so let it not be held against me if I, as a woman, take it upon myself to treat of military matters. . . .

O Minerva! goddess of arms and of chivalry, who, by understanding beyond that of other women, did find and initiate among the other noble arts and sciences the custom of forging iron and steel armaments and harness both proper and suitable for covering and protecting men's bodies against arrows slung in battle—helmets, shields, and protective covering having come first from you—you instituted and gave directions for drawing up a battle order, how to begin an assault and to engage in proper combat. . . . In the aforementioned country of Greece, you provided the usage of this office, and insofar as it may please you to be favorably disposed, and I in no way appear to be against the nation from which you came, the country beyond the Alps that is now called Apulia and Calabria in Italy, where you were born, let me say that like you I am an Italian woman.

Source: From Christine de Pizan, *The Book of Deeds of Arms and of Chivalry*, ed. Charity Cannon Willard and trans. Sumner Willard (University Park, PA: 1999), pp. 11–13.

Questions for Analysis

1. Christine very cleverly deflects potential criticism for her "boldness" in writing about warfare. What tactics does she use?

2. The Greco-Roman goddess Athena (Minerva) was the goddess of wisdom, weaving, and warfare. Why does Christine invoke her aid? What parallels does she draw between her own attributes and those of Minerva?

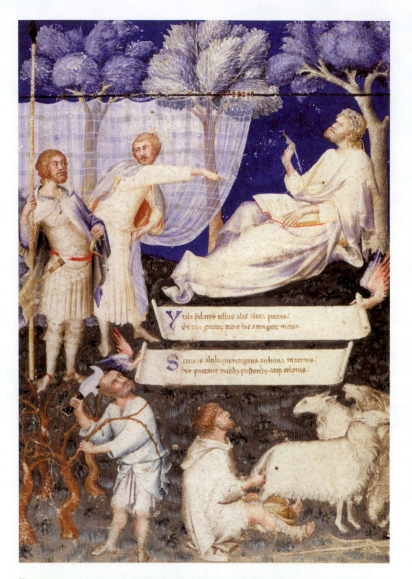

PETRARCH'S COPY OF VIRGIL. Petrarch's devotion to the classics of Roman literature prompted him to commission this new frontispiece for his treasured volume of Virgil's poetry. It was painted by the Sienese artist Simone Martini, who (like Petrarch) was attached to the papal court at Avignon. It is an allegorical depiction of Virgil (top right) and his poetic creations: the hero Aeneas, wearing armor (top left); and the farmer and shepherd, whose humble labors are celebrated in Virgil's lesser-known works. The figure next to Aeneas is the fourth-century scholar Servius, who wrote a famous commentary on Virgil. He is shown drawing aside a curtain to reveal the poet in a creative trance. The two scrolls proclaim (in Latin) that Italy was the country that nourished famous poets, and that Virgil helped it to achieve the glories of classical Greece. **› How does this image encapsulate and express Petrarch's devotion to the classical past?**

dawn and ending late at night. Each pageant was produced by a particular craft guild and showcased that guild's special talents: "The Last Supper" was performed by the bakers, whose bread became the first Eucharist, whereas "The Crucifixion" was performed by the nail makers and painters, whose wares were instrumental in Christ's bloody death on the cross.

In Italy, guilds and confraternities (brotherhoods) competed to honor local saints with songs and processions. In many regions of Spain, there were elaborate dramas celebrating the life and miracles of the Virgin. One of these is still performed every year in the Basque town of Elche, making it the oldest European play in continuous production. In northern France, the Low Countries, and German-speaking lands, civic spectacles were performed over a period of several days, celebrating the community's connection to the sacred history of the Bible. But not all plays were pious; some honored visiting kings, while others celebrated the flouting of social conventions through cross-dressing and the reversal of hierarchies: appropriate for the topsy-turvy world after the Black Death.

The Beginnings of the Renaissance in Italy

Rummaging through the books in a cathedral library, an Italian bureaucrat at the papal court in Avignon was surprised to find a manuscript of Cicero's letters, which he had not known to exist. They had probably been copied in the time of Charlemagne and then forgotten for centuries. How many other great works of antiquity had been lost to posterity? Clearly, thought Francesco Petrarca (1304–1374), he was living in an age of ignorance. A great gulf seemed to open up between his own time and that of the ancients.

For centuries, Christian intellectuals had regarded the "dark ages" as the time between Adam's expulsion from Eden and the birth of Christ. But now, Petrarch (the anglicized form of Petrarca) redefined that concept. According to him, this "dark age" was not the pagan past but the time that separated him from direct communion with the classics. "I would have written to you long ago," he said in a Latin letter to the Greek poet Homer (dead for over 2,000 years), "had it not been for the fact that we lack a common language." Petrarch was famous in his own day as an Italian poet, a Latin stylist, and a tireless advocate for the resuscitation of antiquity. The values that he and his followers espoused would give rise to a new intellectual and artistic movement in Italy, a movement strongly critical of the present and admiring of a past that had disappeared with the fragmentation of Rome's empire and Italy's greatness.

We know this movement as the **Renaissance**, from the French word for *rebirth*: a term invented in the eighteenth century and popularized in the nineteenth, when the term *medieval* was also invented. It has since become shorthand for the epoch *following* the Middle Ages—but it was actually part of that same era.

RENAISSANCE CLASSICISM

Talking about "the Renaissance," then, is a way of talking about some significant changes in education and artistic outlook that began in northern Italy during the late fourteenth century—and that eventually influenced the rest of Europe, too. Yet the term should not be taken literally, as though antiquity had ceased to be appreciated in earlier centuries: we have been tracing the enduring influence of classical civilization through many chapters, and have constantly noted the reverence accorded to the heritage of antiquity, not to mention the persistence of Roman law and institutions.

That said, the concept of "renaissance" does help to explain some new developments. For example, the ancient texts that had long been preserved in monastic libraries now came to be more widely available to secular scholars such as Petrarch. Their "discovery" of works by Livy, Tacitus, and Lucretius expanded the classical canon considerably, supplementing the well-studied works of Virgil, Ovid, and Cicero.

Even more important was scholars' expanded access to ancient Greek literature. As we noted in Chapters 8 and 9, Greek scientific and philosophical works became available to Europeans in the twelfth and thirteenth centuries thanks to increased contact with scholars of the Islamicate world, via Latin translations of Arabic translations of the original Greek. However, no Greek poems or plays were yet available in Latin translations, and neither were the major dialogues of Plato. Moreover, only a handful of Europeans could read the language of classical Greece. But as the Mongols and, after them, the Ottoman Turks put increasing pressure on the shrinking borders of Byzantium (see page 384), more and more Greek-speaking intellectuals fled to Italy, bringing their books and knowledge with them.

Some Italian scholars not only had increased access to more classical texts but they also used these texts in new ways. For centuries, Christian teachers had worked to bring ancient writings and values into line with their own beliefs (Chapter 6). But the new reading methods of Petrarch and his circle fostered an increased awareness of the conceptual gap that separated their contemporary world from that of antiquity. This awareness awakened a determination to recapture truly ancient worldviews. In the second half of the fifteenth century, especially, classical models

Renaissance From the French word *rebirth*, this term came to be used in the nineteenth century to describe the artistic, intellectual, and cultural movement that emerged in Italy after 1300, and which sought to recover and emulate the heritage of the classical past.

Contact with the Islamicate world enables more Europeans access to ancient Greek literature

humanism A program of study associated with the movement known as the Renaissance, humanism aimed to replace the scholastic emphasis on logic and philosophy with the study of ancient languages, literature, history, and ethics.

also shaped the distinctive artistic style that is most strongly associated with the Renaissance, which we will address in Chapter 12.

Another distinguishing feature of this new perspective on the classical past was in its commercialization. Competition among and within Italian states fostered a culture that used the symbols and artifacts of ancient Rome as pawns in an endless power game. Meanwhile, the relative weakness of the Church contributed to the growth of claims to power based on classical models—even by Italian bishops and Church-sponsored universities. When the papacy eventually returned to Rome, it also had to compete in this Renaissance arena.

RENAISSANCE HUMANISM

A crucial feature of this new intellectual and cultural movement is summarized in the term *humanism*. This was a program of study that aimed to replace the scholastic emphasis on logic and theology—central to the curriculum of universities—with the study of ancient literature, rhetoric, history, and ethics. The goal of a humanist education was the understanding of the human experience through the lens of the classical past. In contrast, a scholastic education filtered human experience through the teachings of scripture and the Church Fathers, with human salvation as the ultimate goal.

Humanists accordingly preferred ancient writings to those of more recent authors. And although some humanists wrote in Italian as well as Latin, most regarded vernacular literature as a lesser diversion; serious scholarship and praise-worthy poetry could be written only in Latin or Greek. Proper Latin, moreover, had to be the classical Latin of Cicero and Virgil, not the evolving language common to universities, international diplomacy, law, and the Church. Renaissance humanists therefore condemned the living Latin of their day as a barbarous departure from "correct" standards. And ironically, their determination to revive this older language eventually killed the lively Latin that had continued to flourish: for by insisting on outmoded standards of grammar, syntax, and diction, they turned Latin into a fossilized discourse that ceased to have any relevance to daily life. They thus contributed, unwittingly, to the ultimate triumph of Europe's vernaculars and the demise of Latin as a common medium of communication.

Because humanism was an educational program designed to produce virtuous citizens and able public officials, it also excluded women, who were largely denied any role in Italian public life—at least in theory. In practice, they frequently showed themselves more capable than their male counterparts. In a political context, humanism could be made to serve either the ideals of citizenship as exemplified by the Roman Republic, or the authoritarian agendas of autocratic rulers who wanted to emulate Roman imperial power.

WHY ITALY?

These new attitudes toward education and the ancient past were fostered in northern Italy for historically specific reasons. After the Black Death, this was the most densely populated part of Europe; other urban areas, notably northeastern France and Flanders, had been decimated by the Great Famine as well as by the plague. Northern Italy also differed from the rest of urbanized Europe because aristocratic families lived in cities rather than in rural castles; consequently, they became more

Realizing Devotion

These two paintings by the Flemish artist Rogier van der Weyden (*FAN der VIE-den*; c. 1400–1464) capture some of the most compelling characteristics of late medieval art, particularly the trend toward realistic representations of holy figures and sacred stories. In image A, the artist depicts himself as the evangelist Luke, regarded in Christian tradition as a painter of portraits. He is sketching the Virgin nursing the infant Jesus in a townhouse overlooking a Flemish city. In image B, van der Weyden imagines the entombment of the body of Christ by his followers, including the Virgin (left), Mary Magdalene (kneeling), and the disciple John (right). Here he makes use of a motif that became increasingly prominent in the later Middle Ages: Christ as the Man of Sorrows, displaying his wounds and inviting the viewer to share in his suffering. In both paintings, van der Weyden emphasizes the humanity of his subjects rather than their iconic status (see Chapter 7), and places them in the urban and rural landscapes of his own world.

Questions for Analysis

1. How are these paintings different from the sacred images of the earlier Middle Ages (see, for example, page 348)? What messages does the artist convey by setting these events in his own immediate present?

2. In what ways do these paintings reflect broad changes in popular piety and medieval devotional practices? Why, for example, would the artist display the dead body of Christ, covered with wounds, rather than depicting him as resurrected and triumphant, or as an all-seeing creator and judge?

3. In general, how would you interpret these images as evidence of the worldview of the fifteenth century? What do they tell us about people's attitudes, emotions, and values?

A. *Saint Luke Drawing the Virgin.*

B. *The Lamentation of Christ.*

fully involved in public affairs. Moreover, many town-dwelling aristocrats were engaged in banking or mercantile enterprises, while many rich mercantile families imitated the aristocracy: a prime example of the latter is the Florentine ruling family, the Medici, who originally made their fortune in commerce.

These developments help to explain the emergence of humanist education. Newly wealthy families were not content to have their sons learn only the skills necessary for business; they sought teachers who would impart the knowledge and finesse that would enable them to cut a figure in society, mix with their noble neighbors, and speak with authority on public affairs. Consequently, Italy produced and attracted a large number of independent intellectuals who were not affiliated with monasteries, cathedral schools, or universities. Many served as schoolmasters for wealthy young men while acting as cultural consultants and secretaries for their families. And they advertised their learning by producing political and ethical treatises and works of literature that would attract the attention of wealthy patrons. As a result, Italian schools and private tutors turned out the best-educated laymen in Europe, men who constituted a new generation of wealthy, knowledgeable patrons ready to invest in new forms of literary and artistic expression.

A second reason was that late-medieval Italy was politically disjunctive and competitive. Unlike France and England, or the kingdoms of Spain, Scandinavia, and eastern Europe, Italy had no unifying political institutions. Italians therefore looked to the classical past for their time of glory, dreaming of a day when Rome would be, again, the center of the world. They boasted that ancient Roman monuments were omnipresent in their landscape and that classical Latin literature referred to cities and sites they recognized as their own. By reappropriating their classical heritage, Italians particularly sought to establish an independent cultural identity that could oppose the intellectual and political supremacy of France. The removal of the papacy to Avignon had heightened antagonism toward the powerful monarchy beyond the Alps. This also explains humanists' rejection of scholasticism, since ancient Roman models were an intellectual alternative to the dominant university in Paris.

Finally, this Italian Renaissance could not have occurred without the underpinning of Italian wealth gained through the commercial ventures described in Chapter 10. This wealth meant that talented men seeking employment and patronage also fueled the artistic and intellectual competition that arose from the intensification of urban pride and the concentration of individual and family wealth in urban areas. Cities themselves became among the primary patrons of art and learning.

> *In ancient Roman past, Italians find a source of heritage and pride*

FLORENTINE CIVIC IDEALS

Petrarch's personal goal was a solitary life of contemplation. But for subsequent Italian intellectuals, especially those of Florence, the goal of classical education was civic enrichment. Humanists such as Leonardo Bruni (c. 1370–1444) and Leon Battista Alberti (1404–1472) taught that man's nature equips him for action, for usefulness to his family, and for serving the state. In their view, worldly ambitions were noble impulses that ought to be encouraged and channeled toward these ends. They also refused to condemn the accumulation of material possessions, arguing that the history of human progress is inseparable from the human dominion of the earth and its resources.

Many of the Florentine humanists' civic ideals are expressed in Alberti's treatise *On the Family* (1443), in which he presents the nuclear family as the fundamental unit of the city-state. Alberti accordingly argued that women—who, in reality, governed the household—should be relegated to childbearing, child rearing, and subservience to men even within this domestic realm. He asserted, furthermore, that women should play no role whatsoever in the public sphere. Although actual women fiercely resisted such dismissals of their abilities, Renaissance humanism was characterized by a pervasive denigration of them—a misogyny often mirrored in the works of classical literature that the humanists so much admired.

NEW WAYS OF READING ANCIENT TEXTS

The humanists were aided by a number of Byzantine immigrants to northern Italy who gave instruction in the ancient form of their own language. Wealthy, well-connected men increasingly aspired to acquire Greek masterpieces, which often involved journeys back to Constantinople. In 1423, one adventurous bibliophile managed to bring back 238 manuscript books, among them rare works of Sophocles, Euripides, and Thucydides. These were quickly paraphrased in Latin and so made accessible to medieval Europeans for the first time.

Byzantine immigrants bring knowledge of ancient Greek texts to Italy

This influx of classical texts spurred a new interest in the critical reading of ancient sources. A pioneer in this activity was Lorenzo Valla (1407–1457). Born in Rome and active as a secretary to the king of Naples, Valla had no allegiance to the civic ideals of the Florentine humanists. Instead, he turned his skills to the painstaking analysis of Greek and Latin writings to show how the historical study of language could discredit old assumptions and even unmask some texts as forgeries. For example, papal propagandists were arguing that the papacy's claim to secular power in Europe derived from rights granted to the bishop of Rome by Constantine in the fourth century, as enshrined in a document known as the "Donation of Constantine." By analyzing the language of this text, Valla proved that it could not have been written in the time of Constantine because it contained more recent Latin usages and vocabulary.

This demonstration not only threatened to discredit more traditional scholarly methods but also alerted scholars to the necessity of avoiding anachronism in the study of history—that is, the intellectual vigilance needed to avoid projecting present values and expectations onto the past. Valla even applied his expert knowledge of Greek to elucidate the meaning of Saint Paul's letters, which he believed had been mangled by Jerome's Latin translation (Chapter 6). Valla's work was to prove an important link between Renaissance humanism and the Christian humanism that fueled the Reformation (see Chapter 13).

The Consolidation of the Ottoman Empire

The Greek-speaking refugees who arrived in Italy after the Black Death were responding to a succession of calamities that had reduced the once-proud eastern Roman Empire to a scattering of provinces. When Constantinople fell to papal crusaders in 1204, the surrounding territories of Byzantium were severed from the capital (Chapter 9). When the Latin presence in Constantinople was finally expelled, in 1261, imperial power had been so weakened that it extended only into the immediate hinterlands of the city and to parts of the Greek Peloponnese. The rest of the empire had become a collection of small principalities in precarious alliance with the Mongols, on whom they depended for survival (Chapter 10).

Then, with the coming of the Black Death, the imperial capital suffered a loss of population and shrank still further. Meanwhile, the disintegration of the Mongol Empire laid the larger region open to a new set of conquerors.

THE RISE OF THE OTTOMAN TURKS

When the Mongols arrived in northwestern Anatolia, the Turks—originally a nomadic people—were already being converted to Islam by the resident Muslim powers of the region: the Seljuk sultanate of Rûm and the Abbasid caliphate of Baghdad. But when the Mongols toppled these older powers, they eliminated the two traditional authorities that had kept the Turkish chieftains in check. So now the Turks were free to raid, unhindered, along the soft frontiers of Byzantium. At the same time, the Turks remained far enough from the centers of Mongol power to avoid being destroyed themselves. One of their chieftains, Osman Gazi (1258–1326), even managed to establish his own kingdom; over time, his name became that of the Turkish dynasty known as the **Ottomans**.

By the mid-fourteenth century, Osman's successors had solidified their preeminence by capturing a number of important cities. These successes brought the Ottomans to the attention of the Byzantine emperor, who hired a contingent as mercenaries in 1345. They were extraordinarily successful, but the eastern Roman Empire could not control them. The Turks struck out on their own and began to extend their control westward. By 1370, their holdings stretched all the way to the Danube. In 1389, they defeated a powerful coalition of Serbian forces at the Battle of Kosovo and began subduing Bulgaria, the Balkans, and eventually Greece. In 1396, the Ottoman army attacked Constantinople itself, although it withdrew to repel an ineffectual crusading force that had been hastily sent by the papacy.

In 1402, another attack on Constantinople was deflected—this time, by a more potent foe. Timur the Lame (Tamerlane, as he was called by European admirers) was born to a family of small landholders in the Mongol Khanate of Chagatai. While still a young man, he rose to prominence as a military leader and gained a reputation for tactical genius. He never officially assumed the title of khan in any of the territories he dominated, but instead moved ceaselessly from conquest to conquest, becoming the master of lands stretching from the Caspian Sea to the Volga River, as well as most of Persia. For a time, it looked briefly as if the Mongol Empire might be reunited under his reign. But Timur died in 1405, on his way to invade China, and his various conquests fell to local rulers. In Anatolia, the Ottoman Turks were able to regain their dominant position.

THE CAPTURE OF CONSTANTINOPLE

As Ottoman pressure increased on Constantinople during the 1420s and 1430s, monasteries and schools that had been established since the time of Constantine found themselves in the path of an advancing army. A steady stream of scholars fled westward, carrying a millennium's worth of books preserving the heritage of ancient Greece and the Hellenistic world. Then, in 1451, the Ottoman sultan Mehmet II turned his full attention to the conquest of the imperial city. In 1453, after a brilliantly executed siege, his army succeeded in breaching its walls. The Byzantine emperor was killed in the assault, the city was violently plundered, and its remaining population killed or sold into slavery.

Ottoman Empire
(c. 1300–1923) During the thirteenth century, the Ottoman dynasty established itself as leader of the Turks. From the fourteenth to sixteenth centuries, they conquered Anatolia, Armenia, Syria, and North Africa as well as parts of southeastern Europe, the Crimea, and areas along the Red Sea.

The Ottoman conquest of Constantinople administered an enormous intellectual shock to Europeans, yet its wider political and economic impact was minor. Ottoman control may have reduced European access to the Black Sea, but Europeans got most of their spices and silks through Venice, from Alexandria and Beirut, which did not fall to the Ottomans until the 1520s. Moreover, as we saw in Chapter 10, Europeans already had colonial settlements in West Africa and the eastern Atlantic that connected them to far-reaching networks.

But if the practical effects on Europe were modest, the effects on the Turks themselves were transformative. Vast new wealth poured into Anatolia, which the Ottomans increased by carefully tending the industrial and commercial interests of their new capital city, which they called Istanbul: the Turkish pronunciation of the Greek phrase *eis tan polin* ("in the city"). Trade routes were redirected to feed the capital, and the Ottomans became a naval power in the eastern Mediterranean as well as in the Black Sea. As a result, Istanbul's population grew from fewer than a hundred thousand in 1453 to more than half a million. By 1600, it was the largest city in the world outside of China.

This growth also reflects the fact that tens of thousands of Jews found a welcome refuge from the persecutions and expulsions that had become frequent in Christian Europe. The Ottoman sultans were Sunni Muslims who often dealt harshly with other Muslim sects, but they legally recognized the Christian and Jewish communities and permitted them some rights of self-government. When the Christian monarchs of Iberia completed their "reconquest" of the peninsula in 1492 (see Chapter 12), many refugees found their way to Ottoman territories.

SYSTEMATIZED SLAVERY IN THE OTTOMAN EMPIRE

To manage its continual expansion, the Ottoman army and imperial administration grew exponentially, drawing manpower from conquered territories. And because both army and bureaucracy were largely composed of enslaved men, the demand for more soldiers and administrators could best be met through further conquests that would yield yet more slaves. This cycle mirrors, in many respects, the dilemma of the Roman Empire in the centuries of its rapid expansion (Chapter 5).

Not only were enslaved people the backbone of the Ottoman state but they also were critical to the lives of Ottoman elites. An important measure of status was the number of slaves in one's household, with some powerful families maintaining households in the thousands. By the sixteenth century, the sultan alone possessed more than 20,000 enslaved attendants, not including his bodyguard and elite infantry units.

SULTAN MEHMET II, "THE CONQUEROR" (r. 1451–1481). This portrait, executed by the Ottoman artist Siblizade Ahmed, exhibits stylistic features characteristic of both central Asia and Europe. The sultan's pose—his aesthetic appreciation of the rose, his elegant handkerchief—are indicative of the former, as is the fact that he wears the white turban of a scholar and the thumb ring of an archer. But the subdued coloring and three-quarter profile may reflect the influence of Italian portraits. › **What did the artist achieve through this blending of styles and symbols?** › **What messages does this portrait convey?**

MOSCOW

HOLY
ROMAN
EMPIRE

AUSTRIA

Kyiv

ATLANTIC
OCEAN

FRANCE

Vienna 1529 ✳Pressburg
Budapest 1526, 1528, 1541 ✳
Venice Mohacs 1526 ✳

HUNGARY

MOLDAVIA

Azov

KHANATE
OF CRIMEA

ARAL
SEA

Belgrade 1521 ✳

BOSNIA
SERBIA
Kosovo 1389 ✳

Nish 1393 ✳

BULGARIA

Nicopolis 1396 ✳

BLACK SEA

Constantinople
1453

Sinope

CASPIAN
SEA

SPAIN

Adrianople 1361 ✳
Gallipoli
1354 ✳

Angora
1402

Chaldiran 1514 ✳

Algiers
1529, 1541 ✳

NAPLES

Prevesa 1538 ✳

Lepanto 1571 ✳

Athens

MOREA

ANATOLIA

Smyrna
1424

CARAMANIA

ARMENIA

Erzerum 1552 ✳

Tabriz
1534,
1538 ✳

Oran

ALGERIA

Tunis 1534, ✳
1535

TUNIS

Marjdabik 1516 ✳

Aleppo

Hamadan 1553 ✳

MOROCCO

MEDITERRANEAN SEA

SYRIA

Damascus

MESOPOTAMIA

Baghdad 1534 ✳

PERSIA

TRIPOLI

Jerusalem

BARBARY

Cairo
1517

EGYPT

RED SEA

Medina

HEJAZ

Persian Gulf

ARABIA

Mecca

Power base 1326
Expansion to 1451
Expansion to 1481
Expansion to 1520
Expansion to 1566
✳ Battle site

0   250   500   750   1000 Miles

0   500   1000 Kilometers

ARABIAN
SEA

YEMEN

THE GROWTH OF THE OTTOMAN EMPIRE. Consider the patterns of Ottoman expansion revealed in this map. › **Where is Constantinople (Istanbul), and how might its capture in 1453 have facilitated further conquests?** › Compare the extent of the Ottoman Empire in 1566 with that of the Byzantine Empire under Justinian (see the map on page 220). How would you account for their similarities?

Where did all of these slaves come from? Many were captured in war and many others were taken during raiding forays into eastern Europe, then sold to merchants who shipped them from the Black Sea to the markets of Istanbul. But slaves were also recruited from rural areas of the Ottoman Empire itself. In the Balkans, especially, many Christians were enslaved as children, handed over by their families to pay the "child tax" imposed on areas too poor to pay a monetary tribute.

LATER MEDIEVAL IDEAS OF RELIGIOUS AND PHYSICAL DIFFERENCE

Although the followers of all three major cohabitating religions forbade the sale or ownership of individuals who shared the same faith, slave traders and potential buyers throughout the Mediterranean world found many ways to work around these prohibitions. And while certain physical characteristics came to be associated with certain groups of people, including tattoos or piercings, there is little evidence that skin color or phenotype were becoming markers of racial identity.

However, there is evidence, especially from northern Christendom, that Jews and Muslims were becoming associated with certain physical stereotypes: Jews were depicted with reddish hair and hooked noses, Muslims as dark-skinned or swarthy. The latter reflects the fact that medieval Christians were constantly exposed to imagery that associated "blackness" with sin and "whiteness" with virtue. For example, Psalm 51:7 depicts a sinner pleading to be cleansed from sin: "wash me and I will be made whiter even than snow." At the same time, however, medieval theologians frequently quoted the female lover's exclamation in the Song of Songs, "I am black but beautiful, O daughters of Jerusalem," interpreting it as a reference to the human condition: all people are black and beautiful, because we are all sinners hoping for salvation.

For this reason, popular stories and images of religious conversion or intermarriage suggest that the color of an individual's skin could reflect their spiritual status, even changing if their status changed (see **Competing Viewpoints**, pages 388–89). Over time, such descriptions could provide a vocabulary for talking about racial constructs. But it is important to remember that the ideas about difference expressed in literary or theological texts, in any era, do not always match the facts on the ground, or determine the dynamics of real and complex human interactions.

Warfare and Nation Building

War has always been an engine for the development of new technologies. But in the era after the Black Death, the pace and scale of warfare escalated to an unprecedented degree—as did the deployment of new weapons. Explosives had been invented in China, for use in fireworks displays as well as in warfare, and they were now used to destructive effect in Europe. Although the earliest cannons were as dangerous to those who fired them as to those they targeted, these weapons revolutionized the nature of warfare. In 1453, heavy artillery played a leading role in the outcomes of two crucial conflicts: the Ottoman Turks' breach of Constantinople's ancient defenses and the French capture of the English-held city of Bordeaux, which brought an end to the **Hundred Years' War**.

Thereafter, cannons made it more difficult for rebellious aristocrats to hole up in their stone castles, and this artillery consequently aided in the consolidation of monarchies. Cannons placed aboard ships made Europe's developing navies more effective agents of empire. A handheld firearm, the pistol, was also invented during the fourteenth century; and around 1500, the musket ended forever the military dominance of armored cavalry, giving the advantage to foot soldiers recruited from the ranks of average citizens.

Indeed, there is a symbiotic relationship between warfare and nation building, as well as between warfare and technology. Because Europeans were almost constantly at war from the fourteenth century to the middle of the twentieth, governments claimed new powers to tax their subjects and to recruit them as soldiers. Armies became larger and military technology deadlier. Wars became more destructive and society more militarized. As a result, the most successful European states were aggressively expansionist, and they aggressively engaged in creating an idea of national identity that would bind their peoples together against a common enemy.

Hundred Years' War
(1337–1453) A series of wars between England and France, fought mostly on French soil and prompted by the territorial and political claims of English monarchs.

Prevalence of warfare leads to new relationship between governments and citizens

Skin Color, Religious Difference, and Intermarriage

The two medieval romances excerpted here describe their protagonists' skin colors in various ways and assign different meanings to the intermarriage of Christians with Muslims. The first text comes from Wolfram von Eschenbach's Parzival, *composed in the German vernacular during the early thirteenth century. It opens with the story of the Christian prince Gahmuret, heir to the French "kingdom" of Anjou, and Queen Belacane, the beautiful, dark-skinned ruler of the fictional African kingdom of Zazamanc. The pair fall passionately in love and marry after Gahmuret and his men help the queen to rout her enemies on the battlefield. Their son will grow up to be a famous knight. The second text is a selection from an early Middle English romance called* The King of Tars, *composed more than a hundred years later, around 1330. Here, the unnamed daughter of the Christian king of Tars is reluctantly given in marriage to the heathen Sultan of Damscus, and the birth of their son is attended with great difficulties.*

From *Parzival*

So that proud warrior sojourned there
until he found it hard to bear:
there were no knightly deeds to try,
and so a sadness dimmed his joy.
And yet he held his black-skinned wife
more dear to him than his own life.
No wife was ever so well made,
nor woman's heart more constant, staid,
so full of true sincerity
and gentle, wifely modesty.

The lady bore, when time fell due
a son whose skin was of two hues.

God's wonder-working showed in him:
whiter and darker seemed his skin.
The Queen would often kiss the lighter
places where his skin showed whiter.
The mother named her boy "Proud Son":
Fierefiz the Angevin.
Like magpies he was black and white
of hair and skin, a wondrous sight.

Translated from the Middle High German text by Carol Symes.

From *The King of Tars*

And now, we let her parents mourn
and tell about that maiden young
    sent to the sultan's care.
He came with many great lordings
to welcome home that sweetest thing
    when she came to him there.
He kissed her well, time and again—
could not describe his joy to men—
    away went every care!
Into his chamber she was led,
and in rich clothing she was clad,
    as heathen women wear.
And when she came into the hall,

before the highest lordings all,
    they sat her by the sultan's side.
Great sadness was it now to see
That fairest maiden, whereas he
    was foul mate for such a bride.

On their wedding night, the sultan demands that his wife convert to his religion. A few months later, when she becomes pregnant, she prays to Jesus and the Blessed Virgin for help.

And when the child was finally born,
the women sorrowed at its form,
    for no limbs had it, none:

but like a shapeless lump of flesh
it lay there in the chamber's crèche,
    without nor blood nor bone.
For grief the lady wished to die,
for it had neither nose nor eyes,
    but lay there dead as stone.
The sultan, when he saw the babe,
upon his wife the blame he laid:
    it was her fault alone.

"Madame," he said to her with scorn,
"against my gods you are foresworn—
    and here is proof in brief!
That child which from you is born
of limbs and features is forlorn:
    all through your false belief!"

The lady answered and said, "No,"
for all she lay there in such woe,
    "Leave sir, let be that thought;
the child was made by both of us,
and for thy faith it now fares thus,
    by Him that us hath wrought!
Take now this flesh and blood of ours
into thy temple, to thy gods,
    and do just as you ought:
pray to all your gods above,
as they to you have given love,
    that it to life be brought."

When the sultan's gods do not respond to his prayers, his wife insists that a priest be found to baptize the child.

And just as it had been baptized
it took on life, and limbs, and eyes,
    and cried without delay.
Both skin and bone that flesh took on,
as just to every child belongs,
    as I tell you today. [. . .]

The sultan then knew well by sight
that Jesus was of much more might
    than was his own false law.
"Lady," he said, "because of this
I will forsake my gods' worship:
    they shall be burned and fall.

But tell me how, for charity
and for the love you have for me,
    to see now as you saw.
My own gods I will now forsake:
Tell me the truth about your faith—
    I will believe it all."

The lady teaches him about Jesus, and then arranges for her husband to be baptized.

The Christian priest, named Cleophas,
called the Sultan of Damascus
    after his own name.[1]
His skin, that black and loathsome was,
all white became, through God's good grace,
    and clear, washed clean of blame.
And when the sultan saw that sight,
he believed in God's great might,
    so joy replaced his shame.
And when the priest all prayers had said
And holy water on him laid,
    they home together came.

1. Cleophas was one of the first disciples to meet and recognize Jesus after his resurrection. Here, the priest also acts as the sultan's godfather by giving him his own name.

Source: From John H. Chandler, ed. *The King of Tars*. Medieval Institute Publications (Kalamazoo, MI: 2015), vv. 370–393; vv. 574–609; vv. 823–834; vv. 919–930. Translated from the early Middle English text by Carol Symes.

Questions for Analysis

1. What messages do these two texts convey about the relationship between physical and spiritual differences? Does gender seem to a play a role?

2. How does *The King of Tars* reveal anxieties about intermarriage, social status, religion, and childbirth? Does the story of Fierefiz's birth betray the same anxieties? What conclusions might you draw from the contrast between these two depictions?

3. Given that *The King of Tars* dates from the 1330s, and *Parzival* from around the year 1200 (see Chapter 10), can we conclude that attitudes have changed in the intervening century? Why or why not? Given that both texts continued to be read for centuries, how might their meanings have changed along with the historical contexts in which they were received?

THE HUNDRED YEARS' WAR RESUMES

The Hundred Years' War can be divided into three main phases (see the map on page 391). The first phase dates from the initial declaration of war in 1337 (see Chapter 10), after which the English won a series of startling military victories before the Black Death put a temporary halt to hostilities. The war then resumed in 1356, with another English victory at Poitiers. Four years later, in 1360, Edward III decided to leverage his strong position and renounced his larger claim to the French throne, in return for full sovereignty over a greatly enlarged duchy in southwestern France.

But the terms of that treaty were never honored, nor did the treaty resolve the underlying issues that had led to war: namely, the problem of making any claim to sovereignty in contested territory and the question of the English king's place in the French royal succession. The French king continued to treat the English king as his vassal, while Edward and his heirs quickly renewed their claim to the throne of France.

Although there were no pitched battles in France itself for two decades after 1360, a destabilizing proxy war developed during the 1360s and 1370s, which spread violence to neighboring regions. Both English and French soldiers organized themselves into "Free Companies" of mercenaries and hired themselves out in the service of hostile factions in Castile and competing city-states in northern Italy. By 1376, when the conflict reignited, the Hundred Years' War had become a Europe-wide phenomenon.

THE BRIEF VICTORY OF HENRY V

During this second phase, the tide quickly shifted in favor of France. The new king, Charles V (r. 1364–1380), imposed a series of taxes to fund an army, restored order by disbanding the Free Companies, and hired the leader of one as the commander of his army. He thereby created a professional military that could match the English in discipline and tactics. By 1380, English territories in France had been reduced to a core area around the southwestern city of Bordeaux and the port of Calais in the extreme northeast.

Meanwhile, the aging Edward III had been succeeded by his nine-year-old grandson, Richard II (r. 1377–1399), who was too young to resume armed conflict. This was problematic because the war had been extremely popular in England. Moreover, mismanagement by Richard's advisers had triggered the Peasants' Revolt in 1381. But when Richard came of age and showed no signs of warlike ambition, many of his own relatives turned against him. Richard retaliated against the ringleader of this faction, his cousin Henry of Lancaster, sending him into exile and confiscating his property. Henry's supporters rebelled and, in 1399, Richard was deposed and eventually murdered.

As a usurper whose legitimacy was always in doubt, Henry IV (r. 1399–1413) struggled to maintain his authority in the face of further rebellions and challenges to his kingship. The best way to unite the country would have been to renew the war against France, but Henry was frequently ill. However, when his son Henry V succeeded him in 1413, the young king immediately began to prepare for an invasion. His timing was excellent: the French royal government was foundering, owing to the mental illness of the reigning king, Charles VI (r. 1380–1422). A brilliant diplomat as well as a capable soldier, Henry V sealed an alliance with the powerful Duke of Burgundy, who was nominally loyal to France but stood to gain from its defeat. Henry also made a treaty with the German emperor, who agreed not to come to France's aid.

When he crossed the English Channel with his troops in the autumn of 1415, Henry thus faced a much-depleted French army that could not rely on reinforcements.

THE PHASES OF THE HUNDRED YEARS' WAR. Here we see three snapshots of the political geography of France during the Hundred Years' War. › **In what areas of France did England make its greatest territorial gains before 1360?** › **How and why did this change in the period leading up to 1429?** › **What geographic and strategic advantages did the French monarchy enjoy after 1429 that might help explain its success in recapturing the French kingdom from the English?**

Although it was still vastly larger, with hundreds of mounted knights, it was undisciplined. It was also severely hampered by bad weather and deep mud when the two armies clashed at Agincourt on October 25 of that year—conditions that favored the lighter English infantry. Henry's men managed to win a crushing victory. Then, over the next five years, Henry conquered most of northern France. In 1420, the ailing Charles VI was forced to recognize him as heir to the throne, thereby disinheriting his own son, the Dauphin (*DOE-fah*, "dolphin"), a ceremonial title derived from the heraldic symbol of the borderland province he controlled. Henry sealed the deal by marrying the French princess, Catherine, and fathering an heir to the joint kingdom of England and France.

JOAN OF ARC'S TRIUMPH AND BETRAYAL

Unlike his great-grandfather Edward III, who had claimed the French throne largely as a bargaining chip, Henry V honestly believed himself to be the rightful king of France. And his astonishing success in capturing the kingdom seemed to put the stamp of divine approval on that claim. But Henry's successes in France also transformed the nature of the conflict, turning it from a profitable war of conquest and plunder into an extended and expensive military occupation. It might have been sustainable had Henry been as long-lived as his predecessors, but he died early in 1422, just short of his thirty-sixth birthday. King Charles VI died only a few months later, leaving the infant Henry VI (r. 1422–1461) to be crowned the first—and last—king of both realms.

The Dauphin was now determined to win back his inheritance. Yet French confidence in his right to the throne had been shattered by his own mother's declaration that he was illegitimate. It began to look as though England would once again rule an empire comprising much of France, as it had for a century and a half after the Norman Conquest.

But in 1429, a peasant girl from Lorraine (a territory only marginally part of France) made her way to the Dauphin's court and announced that an angel had told her that he, Charles, was the rightful king, and that she, Joan, should drive the English out of France. The very fact that **Joan of Arc** even got a hearing underscores the hopelessness of the Dauphin's position—as does the extraordinary fact that he gave her a contingent of troops. With this force, Joan liberated the strategic city of Orléans (*or-lay-ah*), then under siege by the English. She then led her army to a series of victories that culminated in the coronation of the Dauphin as King Charles VII in the cathedral of Reims, where French kings had been crowned for nearly a thousand years.

Despite her miraculous successes, Charles and his aristocratic generals regarded Joan as an embarrassment: a peasant leading nobles, a woman dominating men, and a commoner who claimed divine inspiration. Her very charisma made her dangerous. So when the Burgundians captured her in battle a few months later, and handed her over to the English as a prisoner of war, the king she had helped to crown did nothing to save her. Accused of witchcraft, condemned by the theologians of Paris, and tried for heresy by an English ecclesiastical court, Joan was burned to death in the market square at Rouen in 1431 (see *Analyzing Primary Sources* on page 393). She was nineteen years old.

The French forces whom Joan had inspired, however, continued on the offensive. In 1435, the duke of Burgundy withdrew his alliance with the English, whose young king,

JOAN OF ARC. A contemporary sketch of Joan was drawn in the margin of this register, documenting official proceedings at the Parlement of Paris in 1429.

The Condemnation of Joan of Arc by the University of Paris, 1431

After Joan's capture by the Burgundians, she was handed over to the English and tried for heresy at an ecclesiastical court set up in Rouen. It was on this occasion that the theology faculty of Paris pronounced the following verdict on her actions.

You, Joan, have said that, since the age of thirteen, you have experienced revelations and the appearance of angels, of St. Catherine and St. Margaret, and that you have very often seen them with your bodily eyes, and that they have spoken to you. As for the first point, the clerks of the University of Paris have considered the manner of the said revelations and appearances. . . . Having considered all . . . they have declared that all the things mentioned above are lies, falsenesses, misleading and pernicious things and that such revelations are superstitions, proceeding from wicked and diabolical spirits.

Item: You have said that your king had a sign by which he knew that you were sent by God, for St. Michael, accompanied by several angels, some of which having wings, the others crowns, with St. Catherine and St. Margaret, came to you at the chateau of Chinon. All the company ascended through the floors of the castle until they came to the room of your king, before whom the angel bearing the crown bowed. . . . As for this matter, the clerks say that it is not in the least probable, but it is rather a presumptuous lie, misleading and pernicious, a false statement, derogatory of the dignity of the Church and of the angels. . . .

Item: You have said that, at God's command, you have continually worn men's clothes, and that you have put on a short robe, doublet, shoes attached by points, also that you have had short hair, cut around above the ears, without retaining anything on your person which shows that you are a woman, and that several times you have received the body of Our Lord dressed in this fashion, despite having been admonished to give it up

several times, the which you would not do. You have said that you would rather die than abandon the said clothing, if it were not at God's command, and that if you were wearing those clothes and were with the king, and those of your party, it would be one of the greatest benefits for the kingdom of France. You have also said that not for anything would you swear an oath not to wear the said clothing and carry arms any longer. And all these things you say you have done for the good and at the command of God. As for these things, the clerics say that you blaspheme God and hold him in contempt in his sacraments; you transgress Divine Law, Holy Scripture, and canon law. You err in the faith. You boast in vanity. You are suspected of idolatry and you have condemned yourself in not wishing to wear clothing suitable to your sex, but you follow the custom of Gentiles and Saracens.

Source: Carolyne Larrington, ed. and trans., *Women and Writing in Medieval Europe* (New York: 1995), pp. 183–84.

Questions for Analysis

1. Paris was in the hands of the English when this condemnation was issued. Is there any evidence that its authors were coerced into making this pronouncement?

2. On what grounds was Joan condemned for heresy?

3. In what ways does Joan's behavior highlight larger trends in late medieval spirituality and popular piety?

Henry VI, proved to be first incompetent and then insane. Finally, a series of French victories culminated in the capture of Bordeaux. After 1453, English control over French territory was limited to the port of Calais on the French coast of the English Channel.

THE LONG SHADOW OF THE HUNDRED YEARS' WAR

The Hundred Years' War challenged the very existence of France. The disintegration of that kingdom—first during the 1350s and 1360s, and again between 1415 and 1435—glaringly revealed the fragility of the bonds that tied the king to his people and the royal capital to the kingdom's outlying regions. Yet the king's power had increased by the war's end, laying the foundations on which the power of the French state would be built.

The Hundred Years' War also had dramatic effects on the English monarchy. When English armies in France were successful, the king rode a wave of popularity that fueled an emerging sense of English identity. When the war turned against them, defeats abroad undermined support for the monarch at home. This was a consequence of England's peculiar form of kingship, whose strength depended on the king's ability to mobilize popular support through Parliament while maintaining the support of his nobility through successful wars. Failure to maintain this balance was even more destabilizing in England than it would have been elsewhere, precisely because royal power was so centralized.

In France, the nobility could endure the insanity of Charles VI because his government was not powerful enough to threaten them. In England, by contrast, neither the nobility nor the nation could afford the weak kingship of Henry VI. The result was an aristocratic rebellion that led to a full-blown civil war: the Wars of the Roses, so called because of the floral emblems (red and white) adopted by the two competing noble families, Lancaster and York. It ended only when a Lancastrian claimant, Henry Tudor (r. 1485–1509), resolved the dynastic feud by marrying Elizabeth of York and ruling as Henry VII, establishing a new dynasty whose symbol was a rose with both white and red petals. His second son would become Henry VIII (see Chapter 13).

In spite of England's ultimate defeat, the Hundred Years' War strengthened English identity in several ways. First, it equated national belonging with the power of the state and its king. Second, it fomented a strong anti-French sentiment that led to the triumph of the English language over French for the first time since the Norman Conquest, over 300 years earlier; the first royal court to speak English was that of Richard II, a patron of Geoffrey Chaucer. And having lost its continental possessions, England became a self-contained island nation that looked to the sea for defense and opportunity—not to the Continent.

> *An emerging sense of English identity built on (1) power of state and king and (2) dominance of English language*

CONFLICT IN ITALY AND THE HOLY ROMAN EMPIRE

Elsewhere, the perpetual warfare that began to characterize the history of Europe during this period was even more destructive. In northern and central Italy, the second half of the fourteenth century was marked by incessant conflict. With the papacy based in Avignon, Rome was torn by factional violence. Warfare among northern Italian city-states was constant. Finally, around 1400, Venice, Milan, and Florence succeeded in stabilizing their differing forms of government: Venice was now ruled by an oligarchy of merchants; Milan by a family of despots; and Florence was ruled as a republic but dominated by the influence of a few wealthy clans, especially the Medici banking family. These three cities then began to expand their influence by subordinating other cities to their rule.

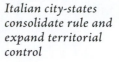

Italian city-states consolidate rule and expand territorial control

Eventually, almost all the towns of northern Italy were allied with one or another of these powers. An exception was Genoa, which had its own trading empire in the Mediterranean and Atlantic (Chapter 10). The papacy, meanwhile, reasserted its control over central Italy after its return to Rome in 1377. The southern kingdom of Naples persisted as a separate entity, but a constantly unstable one. After 1453, when the Hundred Years' War had ended and Ottoman expansion had temporarily halted, an uneasy peace was achieved.

In the lands of the Holy Roman Empire, meanwhile, armed conflict among territorial princes significantly weakened all combatants. Periodically, a powerful emperor would emerge to play a role, but the dominant trend was toward the continuing disintegration of power, with German princes dividing their territories among their heirs while free cities and local lords strove to shake off the princes' rule. Only in the eastern regions of the empire were the rulers of Bavaria, Austria, and Brandenburg-Prussia able to strengthen their authority, by supporting the nobility's efforts to subjugate the peasants and colonizing new territories on their eastern frontiers.

In German lands, political power is mostly fragmentary

THE FLOURISHING OF EASTERN EUROPE

During the thirteenth century (Chapter 9), Poland had been culturally and economically enriched by its willingness to welcome the Jewish communities that were being expelled from other parts of Europe. In the fourteenth century, Polish towns also benefited from a wave of German immigrants, mostly merchants, with ties to the Hanseatic League and to independent cities in the Holy Roman Empire. In order to attract and accommodate these newcomers, the rulers of Poland and other eastern European kingdoms granted special charters to the towns in which they settled. These charters granted citizens the rights of self-governance, collectively known as Magdeburg Law (named after a major German city).

In the centuries after the Black Death, more and more towns and villages were able to take advantage of these privileges, promoting the rapid urbanization of the once rural region of eastern Europe and creating a web of prosperous and diverse cities that generated enormous wealth. Lviv, now in western Ukraine, is a splendid example: ruled by Polish kings and governed by German town law, it fostered a large population of Armenians, Jews, Serbians, and Hungarians, among many others.

Alongside the commercial benefits of these burgeoning towns were the intellectual benefits. Just as medieval universities flourished in western Europe during the economic boom of the twelfth century, they now came to be established in central and eastern Europe, too. The first was founded in the Bohemian capital of Prague in 1347, by Emperor Charles IV. The Polish king Casimir III (r. 1333–1370) followed his lead by establishing a fledgling university in Kraków in 1364. Universities in Vienna and Pécs (Hungary) were also established in the next few years. The university at Kraków soon came to be known as the Jagiellonian University, after the new dynasty that endowed it as a permanent institution.

KING JADWIGA OF POLAND AND THE JAGIELLONIAN DYNASTY

The Jagiellonian dynasty was formed when the young female ruler of Poland, Jadwiga (*yahd-VEE-gah*), married the Grand Duke of Lithuania, Jagiello (*yahg-ee-EL-oh*). It was an extraordinary match. Jadwiga had been crowned king (not queen) in 1384, when she was barely ten years old. The Polish lords who acted as her advisers had insisted on the title because they did not want to see her eventual husband ruling over them. In search of a suitable match, they turned their gaze to the neighboring northern territory of Lithuania, which would give Poland more access to the Baltic Sea and more support against ongoing encroachments from the east by the Teutonic Knights of Prussia. Jadwiga agreed to the match, even though Duke Jagiello was thirty years her senior—and the last pagan ruler in Europe. They were married after Jagiello's acceptance into the Roman Church in 1386, when he received the baptismal name Wladyslaw (*VWAD-is-laff*).

Jadwiga and Wladyslaw II Jagiello ruled their realms jointly, tripling the size of Poland-Lithuania and making it the largest and most powerful state in central Europe. Their patronage of the new university at Kraków turned it into one of Europe's intellectual powerhouses: it would later nurture such great Polish scholars as Nicolaus Copernicus (1473–1543) (see Chapter 16). Jadwiga also promoted Polish as a literary language, encouraging the translation of the Bible into the vernacular. When she died in 1399, in the course of a difficult childbirth, her husband married the wife she had chosen for him. In 1997, she was canonized as a saint of the Catholic Church.

THE EMERGENCE OF NATIONAL MONARCHIES

In France, England, Poland, Hungary, and in smaller kingdoms such as Scotland and Portugal, the later Middle Ages saw the growth of more cohesive states than any that had existed before. The political patterns established in the formative twelfth and thirteenth centuries had made this possible, yet the active construction of a sense of shared identity in these territories, and the fusion of that identity with kingship, were new phenomena. Fueled by the growing cultural importance of vernacular languages, this fusion produced a new type of political organization: the national monarchy.

The advantages of a national monarchy over older forms of political organization—such as the empire, the principality, or the city-state—are significant. But the new national monarchies brought significant disadvantages, too. They guaranteed the prevalence of warfare in Europe as they continued their

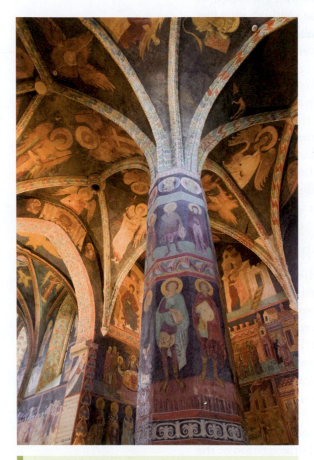

THE ROYAL CHAPEL OF KING WLADYSLAW II JAGIELLO. This image captures only some of the hundreds of magnificent paintings that decorate the walls of the chapel in Lublin (Poland). This cycle of frescoes, which depict scenes from the Bible, was commissioned by King Jagiello after the death of his royal wife Jadwiga. The paintings, completed in 1418, were executed by a team of master artists from Ukraine, who combined Eastern Orthodox imagery and styles with those of western Europe. › **Based on what you have learned about Jagiello, why would he have chosen to decorate his chapel in this way?**

struggles for sovereignty and territory. Eventually, they would export their rivalry through imperial ventures in Africa and the New World. While a shared feeling of belonging to a nation can be extremely positive, it can also be poisoned or undermined if one ethnic group, or one region, claims superiority over others.

Challenges of the Roman Church

The century after the Black Death witnessed the papacy's return to Rome, but it also witnessed changes that would have far-reaching consequences. After almost seventy years of exile, the Church was now riven by a debilitating forty-year schism and faced a protracted battle with reformers who sought to reduce the pope's role in Church governance. While the papacy won this battle in the short term, the renewed abuse of papal power would, in the long run, bring about the permanent schism of the Reformation (see Chapter 13).

THE GREAT WESTERN SCHISM

In the decades after the plague, calls for the papacy's return to Rome grew more insistent. It was eventually brought about by the letter-writing campaign of the nun and mystic Catherine of Siena (1347–1380), whose teasing but pious missives to Gregory XI (r. 1370–1378) alternately shamed and coerced him. In 1377, he was persuaded to make the move.

But the papacy's restoration in Rome was short-lived. A year after Gregory's return, he died. His cardinals—many of them Frenchmen—then struggled to interpret the wishes of the volatile Romans, whose habit of expressing themselves through violence was unsettling to outsiders. Later, the cardinals would claim that they had unwillingly capitulated to the Roman mob when they elected an Italian candidate, Urban VI. When Urban fell out with them, the cardinals fled the city and, from a safe distance, declared his reign invalid because they had elected him under duress. They then elected a new pope, a Frenchman who took the name Clement VII. Urban retaliated by naming a new and entirely Italian College of Cardinals. The French pope and his cardinals withdrew ignominiously to the papal palace in Avignon, while the Italian pope remained in Rome.

The resulting rift is known as the **Great Schism** (or, more specifically, the Great Western Schism, to distinguish it from the East–West Schism between the Roman and Orthodox Churches). Between 1378 and 1417, the Roman Church was divided between two—and, ultimately, three—competing papacies, each claiming to be legitimate and each denouncing the heresy of the others. Europe's religious allegiances largely fractured along political lines drawn by the ongoing Hundred Years' War: France and its allies Scotland, Castile, Aragon, and Naples recognized the pope in Avignon; England, Germany, northern Italy, Scandinavia, Bohemia, Poland, and Hungary recognized the Roman pope.

There was no obvious way to end this impasse, and the two rival Colleges of Cardinals continued to elect successors every time a pope died, perpetuating the problem. Finally, in 1409, some cardinals from both camps met at Pisa, where they ceremonially declared the deposition of both popes and named a new one from among their number. But neither of the popes reigning in Rome and Avignon accepted that decision, and there were now three rival popes excommunicating each other instead of two.

Great Schism (1378–1417) Also known as the Great Western Schism, to distinguish it from the long-standing rupture between the Greek East and Latin West. During the schism, the Roman Church was divided between two (and, ultimately, three) competing popes. Each pope claimed to be legitimate, and each denounced the heresy of the others.

Legend:
- Allegiance to Rome
- Allegiance to Avignon
- Eastern Orthodox
- Islamic territories
- Shifting allegiances
- ■ Council cities

Scale: 0 250 500 Miles / 0 250 500 Kilometers

THE GREAT SCHISM, 1378–1417. During the Great Western Schism, the various territories of Europe were divided in their allegiances. › **According to the map key, what choices were the peoples of these regions making?** › **What common interests would have united the supporters of the Avignon pope or of the Roman pope?** › **Why would areas such as Portugal and Austria waver in their support?**

THE COUNCIL OF CONSTANCE AND THE FAILURE OF THE CONCILIAR MOVEMENT

This debacle was ultimately addressed between 1414 and 1418 at the **Council of Constance**, the largest and longest ecclesiastical gathering since the Council of Nicaea more than a thousand years before (Chapter 6). Its chief mission was to remove all rival claimants for papal office before agreeing on the election of a new pope, an Italian who took the name Martin V. But many of the council's delegates had even farther-reaching plans for the reform of the Church, ambitions that stemmed from the legal doctrine that gave the council the power to depose and elect popes in the first place.

This doctrine, known as **conciliarism**, holds that supreme authority within the Church rests not with the pope but with a representative general council. The delegates at Constance thus decreed that general councils should meet regularly to oversee the governance of the Church and to act as a check on the unbridled abuse of papal power. Had conciliarism triumphed, the Reformation of the following century might not have occurred.

But, perhaps predictably, Martin V and his successors did everything they could to undermine this doctrine, precisely because it limited their power. When the next general council met at Siena in 1423, Pope Martin duly sent representatives—who then turned around and went back to Rome. (The Council of Constance had specified that councils must meet frequently, but had not specified how long they should last.) A lengthy struggle for power ensued between the advocates of papal monarchy and the conciliarists. Twenty-five years later, in 1449, the Council of Basel dissolved itself, bringing an end to a radical experiment in conciliar government—and dashing the hopes of an internal reformation that would keep the Roman Church intact.

SPIRITUAL CHALLENGES

The spiritual and social lives of medieval Christians were inextricably intertwined; indeed, any distinction between the two would have made little sense to most people of the time. The parish church stood literally at the center of their lives. Churchyards were communal meeting places, sometimes even the sites of markets; church buildings were a refuge from attack and a gathering place for parish business; church's holidays marked the passage of the year; and church's bells marked the hours of the day. The church was holy, but it was also essential to daily life.

Yet, in the wake of the Black Death, many parishes ceased to exist because so many communities were decimated. And increasingly, medieval Christians were not satisfied with the conventional practices and forms of piety. As Joan of Arc's predicament reveals, medieval women found it particularly challenging to find outlets for their faith that would not earn them the condemnation of the Church. Executed as a heretic, Joan was officially exonerated a generation later; but she would not be canonized as a saint until 1920.

Many women therefore internalized their devotional practices or confined them to the domestic sphere—sometimes to the inconvenience of their families and communities. The young Catherine of Siena, the one who later convinced the pope to return to Rome, refused to help with the housework or to support her working-class family; instead, she took over one of the house's two rooms for her private prayers, confining her parents and a dozen siblings to the remaining room. Julian of Norwich (1342–1416) withdrew from the world into a small cell built next to her local church, where she spent the rest of her life in prayer and contemplation. Her younger contemporary, the housewife Margery Kempe (c. 1372–c. 1439), resented the fact that she could not take such a step because she had a husband, numerous children, and a household to support. In later life, she renounced her domestic duties and devoted her life to performing acts of histrionic piety that alienated many of those who came into contact with her. For example, she was so

In medieval Europe, the church was an engine of holy life

Pope over Council: The Condemnation of Conciliarism

The Great Schism spurred a fundamental and far-reaching debate about the nature of authority within the Church. Arguments for papal supremacy rested on traditional claims that the popes were the successors of Saint Peter, to whom Jesus Christ had delegated his own authority. Arguments for the supremacy of a general council had been advanced by many intellectuals throughout the fourteenth century, but it was only during the circumstances of the schism that these arguments found a wide audience. However, the papacy's short-lived subordination to conciliar supremacy, which had been established at the Council of Constance in 1415, was quickly challenged by a succession of popes and finally condemned in 1460, in the following papal bull.

Execrabilis (1460)

An execrable abuse, unheard of in earlier times, has sprung up in our period. Some men, imbued with a spirit of rebellion and moved not by a desire for sound decisions but rather by a desire to escape the punishment for sin, suppose that they can appeal from the Pope, Vicar of Jesus Christ—from the Pope, to whom in the person of blessed Peter it was said, "Feed my sheep" and "whatever you bind on earth will be bound in heaven"—from this Pope to a future council. How harmful this is to the Christian republic, as well as how contrary to canon law, anyone who is not ignorant of the law can understand. For . . . who would not consider it ridiculous to appeal to something which does not now exist anywhere nor does anyone know when it will exist? The poor are heavily oppressed by the powerful, offenses remain unpunished, rebellion against the Holy See is encouraged, license for sin is granted, and all ecclesiastical discipline and hierarchical ranking of the Church are turned upside down.

Wishing therefore to expel this deadly poison from the Church of Christ, and concerned with the salvation of the sheep committed to us . . . with the counsel and assent of our venerable brothers, the Cardinals of the Holy Roman Church, together with the counsel and assent of all those prelates who have been trained in canon and civil law who follow our Court, and with our own certain knowledge, we condemn appeals of this kind, reject them as erroneous and abominable, and declare them to be completely null and void. And we lay down that from now on, no one should dare . . . to make such an appeal from our decisions, be they legal or theological, or from any commands at all from us or our successors.

Source: Reprinted by permission of the publisher from Gabriel Biel, *Defensorium Obedientiae Apostolicae et Alia Documenta*, ed. and trans. Heiko A. Oberman, Daniel E. Zerfoss, and William J. Courtenay (Cambridge, MA: 1968), pp. 224–27. Copyright © 1968 by the President and Fellows of Harvard College.

Questions for Analysis

1. Why did the Council of Constance consider it necessary for councils to meet regularly? What might have been the logical consequences of such regular meetings, and why would the papacy have wanted to challenge them?

2. On what grounds does *Execrabilis* condemn the authority of future councils that have no specified meeting date? Why would it not have condemned the conciliar movement altogether?

moved by the contemplation of Jesus' sufferings on the cross that she would cry hysterically for hours, disrupting the Mass; and when on a pilgrimage in Rome, she cried at the sight of babies that reminded her of the infant Jesus or young men whom she thought resembled him.

The extraordinary piety of such individuals could be inspiring, but it could also threaten the Church's control and the links that bound individuals to their communities. It could, therefore, be regarded as dangerous. More safely orthodox was the practical mysticism preached by Thomas à Kempis, whose *Imitation of Christ* (c. 1427) taught readers how to appreciate aspects of the divine in their everyday lives. Originally written in Latin, it was quickly translated into many vernacular languages and is now more widely read than any other Christian book except the Bible.

POPULAR AND INTELLECTUAL REFORMERS

For the most part, the threat of dissenting movements was less dangerous to the Church than the corruption of the papacy. But in the kingdoms of England, Bohemia (the modern Czech Republic), and Poland, some reform movements posed serious challenges because they were galvanized by respected intellectuals. In Poland, a professor at the new Jagiellonian University in Kraków, Paulus Vladimiri (Pawel Wlodkowic; c. 1370–1435), wrote a treatise that criticized papal and imperial efforts to convert the peoples of eastern Europe and the Baltic by force, through their support of the Teutonic Knights. He argued that the violence could not be justified, and that pagans and Christians could coexist in peace. He advanced these radical arguments as the Polish representative to the Council of Constance.

The Oxford theologian **John Wycliffe** (c. 1330–1384) was a central figure in both the English and Bohemian reform movements. A survivor of the Black Death and an outspoken critic of the papacy, he asserted that the empty sacraments of a corrupt Church could not save anyone, and therefore urged the English king to confiscate ecclesiastical wealth and to replace decadent priests and bishops with men who would live according to apostolic standards of poverty and piety.

Some of Wycliffe's followers went even further, dismissing the sacraments as fraudulent attempts to extort money from the faithful. These preachers advocated for direct access to the scriptures and promoted an English translation of the Bible sponsored by Wycliffe himself. Wycliffe's teachings also played an important role in the Peasants' Revolt of 1381, and his movement was even supported by a number of aristocratic families. But after a failed uprising in 1414, both the movement and its supporters went underground.

In Bohemia and other regions of central Europe, Wycliffe's ideas lived on and put down even deeper roots. They were powerfully adopted by **Jan Hus** (c. 1373–1415), a charismatic teacher at the Charles University in Prague. In contrast to English followers of Wycliffe, Hus emphasized the centrality of the Eucharist to Christian piety. Indeed, he demanded that the laity be allowed to receive not only the consecrated bread but also the consecrated wine, which was usually reserved for priests. This demand became a rallying cry for the Hussite movement. Influential nobles also supported Hus, partly in the hope that reforms might restore revenues they had lost to the Church over the previous century.

John Wycliffe (c. 1330–1384) A professor of theology at the University of Oxford, Wycliffe urged the English king to confiscate ecclesiastical wealth and to replace corrupt priests and bishops with men who would live according to the apostolic standards of poverty and piety. He advocated direct access to the Scriptures and promoted an English translation of the Bible.

Jan Hus (c. 1373–1415) A Czech reformer who adopted many of the teachings of the English theologian John Wycliffe, and who also demanded that the laity be allowed to receive both the consecrated bread and wine of the Eucharist.

WYCLIFFE'S ENGLISH BIBLE. Although John Wycliffe was not directly responsible for this translation of the Bible, it was made in the later fourteenth century by his followers. Written in the same Middle English vernacular that Geoffrey Chaucer used for his popular works, it was designed to be accessible to lay readers who did not understand Latin. This page shows the beginning of the Gospel of Mark: "The byg*yn*-/nyng of Þe gos-/pel of Ih*e*su Crist/Þe sone of god. . . ." (Note that the old English letter Þ stands for *th*.) › **What might have been the impact of this translation on readers and listeners in the late fourteenth century?** › **How would this English Bible have helped to further the reforming efforts of Wycliffe and his disciples?**

Accordingly, most of Bohemia was behind him when Hus traveled to the Council of Constance to publish his views and urge the assembled delegates to undertake sweeping reforms. But instead, the other delegates convicted Hus of heresy and had him burned at the stake. Back home, Hus's supporters raised the banner of open revolt, and the aristocracy took advantage of the situation to seize Church property. Between 1420 and 1424, armed bands of fervent Hussites resoundingly defeated several armies, as priests, artisans, and peasants rallied to pursue Hus's goals of religious reform and social justice.

These victories increased popular fervor, but they also made radical reformers increasingly volatile. Accordingly, in 1434, a more conservative arm of the Hussite movement was able to negotiate a settlement with the Bohemian church. By the terms of this settlement, Bohemians could receive both the bread and the wine of the Mass, which thus placed them beyond the pale of Latin orthodoxy and effectively separated the Bohemian national church from the Church of Rome.

English and Czech reforming efforts exhibit a number of striking similarities. Both began in universities and then spread to the countryside, both called for the clergy to live in simplicity and poverty, and both attracted noble support. Both movements also employed their own vernacular languages (English and Czech), and both relied on vernacular preaching and social activism. In all these respects, they established patterns that would emerge again in the vastly larger currents of the Protestant Reformation (see Chapter 13).

Conclusion

The century after the Black Death was a period of tremendous creativity and revolutionary change. The effects of the plague were catastrophic, but the resulting food surpluses, opportunities, and experimentation opened up broad avenues for advancement. Europe's economy diversified and expanded, while increasing wealth and access to education produced new forms of art and new ways of looking at the world. Women were still excluded from formal schooling, but nevertheless they became active—and in many cases dominant—participants in literary endeavors, cultural life, and religious movements. Average men and women not only became more active in cultivating their own worldly goals; they also took control of their spiritual destinies at a time when the institutional Church provided little inspiring leadership.

Meanwhile, some states were growing stronger and more competitive, whereas other regions remained deeply divided. The rising Ottoman Empire eventually absorbed many of the oldest territories of Western civilizations, including the venerable Muslim caliphate at Baghdad, the western portions of the former Mongolian Empire, the Christian Balkans and Greece, and—above all—the surviving core of the eastern Roman Empire at Constantinople. As a result, Greek-speaking refugees streamed into Italy, many bringing with them classic works of Greek philosophy and literature hitherto unknown in western Europe. Fueled by new ideas and a fervid nostalgia for the ancient past, Italians began to experiment with new ways of reading ancient texts, advocating a return to classical

THE TEACHINGS OF JAN HUS. An eloquent religious reformer, Jan Hus was burned at the stake in 1415 after he was found guilty of heresy at the Council of Constance. This woodcut portrait was featured in a booklet printed in German and circulating widely in Protestant realms, including Hus's native Bohemia, after 1587—more than 170 years after his death. › *What does Hus's commemoration in this booklet suggest about how his image and theology were put to use during the later Protestant Reformation?*

models while at the same time trying to counter the political and cultural authority of the more powerful kingdoms north of the Alps.

In contrast to Italy, these emerging national monarchies cultivated shared identity through the promotion of a common vernacular language and allegiance to a strong, more centralized state. These tactics allowed kingdoms such as Poland and Scotland to increase their territories and influence, and also led France and England into an epic battle for sovereignty and hegemony. The result, in all cases, was the escalation of armed conflict as incessant warfare

AFTER YOU READ THIS CHAPTER ⌄

CHRONOLOGY

1304–1374	Lifetime of Petrarch
1351	The Black Death at its most virulent in Europe
	The English Parliament passes the Statute of Laborers
1377	The papacy returns to Rome from Avignon
1378	The Great Schism within the Roman Church begins
1381	Rebellions culminate in the English Peasants' Revolt
1414–1418	The Council of Constance is convened to end the Great Schism
	Jan Hus burned at the stake in 1415
1429–1431	The career of Joan of Arc
1431–1449	The Council of Basel fails to check papal power
1440	Lorenzo Valla debunks the "Donation of Constantine"
1453	The Hundred Years' War ends
	Constantinople falls to the Ottoman Turks

REVIEWING THE OBJECTIVES

❯ The Black Death had short- and long-term effects on the economy and societies of Europe. What were some of the most important changes?

❯ The later "Middle Ages" and the "Renaissance" are often perceived to be two different periods, but the latter was actually part of the former. Explain why.

❯ What were some of the intellectual, cultural, and artistic innovations of this era in Italy and elsewhere in Europe?

❯ How did some European kingdoms become stronger and more centralized during this period? What were some examples of national monarchies?

❯ How did the conciliar movement seek to limit the power of the papacy? Why was this movement unsuccessful?

drove more powerful governments to harvest a larger percentage of their subjects' wealth through taxation, which they proceeded to invest in ships, guns, and the standing armies made possible by new technologies and more-effective administration.

In short, the generations that survived the calamities of famine, plague, and warfare seized the opportunities their new world presented. In the latter half of the fifteenth century, they stood on the verge of an extraordinary period of expansion and conquest that enabled them to dominate the globe.

Go to **INQUIZITIVE** to see what you've learned—and learn what you've missed—with personalized feedback along the way.

PEOPLE, IDEAS, AND EVENTS IN CONTEXT

❱ Compare and contrast the **BLACK DEATH**'s effects on rural and urban areas.

❱ In what ways do rebellions such as the **ENGLISH PEASANTS' REVOLT** reflect the changes brought about by the plague? How do the works of **GIOVANNI BOCCACCIO, GEOFFREY CHAUCER**, and **CHRISTINE DE PIZAN** exemplify the culture of this era?

❱ What was **HUMANISM**? How was it related to the artistic and intellectual movement known as the **RENAISSANCE**?

❱ How did the **OTTOMAN EMPIRE** come to power? What were some of the consequences of its consolidation in the territories of the eastern Roman Empire?

❱ What new military technologies were deployed during the **HUNDRED YEARS' WAR**? How did this conflict affect other parts of Europe, beyond England and France? What role did **JOAN OF ARC** play?

❱ How did the **COUNCIL OF CONSTANCE** respond to the crisis of the **GREAT SCHISM**?

❱ Why did **CONCILIARISM** fail? How did **JOHN WYCLIFFE** and **JAN HUS** seek to reform the Church?

THINKING ABOUT CONNECTIONS

❱ In the year 2000, a group of historians was asked to identify the most significant historical figure of the past millennium. Rather than selecting a person (e.g., Martin Luther, Shakespeare, Napoleon, Adolf Hitler), they chose the microbe *Yersinia pestis,* which caused the Black Death. Do you agree with this assessment? Why or why not?

❱ Given what we have learned about the history of the Roman Church, do you think the conciliar movement was doomed to fail? Why or why not? How far back do we need to go to trace the development of disputes over ecclesiastical governance?

❱ Scholars of the ancient and medieval world are just beginning to explore how ideas about race were constructed before the modern era. What are the benefits and challenges of trying to understand premodern ideas of race? How would you, in your role as historian, go about gathering and interpreting evidence for such ideas?

Innovation and Exploration, 1453–1533

WHAT IF EXACT COPIES of an idea could circulate quickly, all over the world? What if the same could be done for the latest news, the most beautiful poems, or the most exciting discoveries? It would do for knowledge what the invention of coinage did for wealth, making it portable and easier to disseminate. Indeed, it's no accident that the man who developed such a technology, **Johannes Gutenberg** of Mainz (c. 1398–1468), was the son of a goldsmith who made coins: metal disks stamped with identical words and images impressed by a reusable matrix. In similar fashion, the pages of the first printed books were stamped with ink spread on rows of movable type (lead or cast-iron letter forms and punctuation marks) slotted into frames to form lines of words. Once a set of pages was ready, a **printing press** could make hundreds of copies in a matter of hours, many hundreds of times faster than the same page being copied by hand.

A major stimulus for this invention was the availability of paper, which became more widespread in Europe during the late thirteenth century. Made from rags turned into pulp by mills, paper was both cheaper and far easier to use than parchment. Accordingly, books became cheaper and written communication even more common. Growing levels of literacy then led to a growing demand for books, which in turn led to Gutenberg's breakthrough of the 1450s. By 1455, his workshop had printed multiple copies of the Latin Bible (of which forty-eight complete or partial volumes survive).

BEFORE YOU READ THIS CHAPTER

❯

❯ The invention of the printing press enabled the widespread dissemination of information, including reports on the riches of the New World.

❯ Competition for power in Italy led to increased violence as well as to increased patronage, providing opportunities to a new breed of humanist artists and intellectuals associated with the Renaissance.

❯ Meanwhile, the humanist approach to education that had developed in Italy spread to other parts of Europe, influencing new approaches to biblical scholarship and new political philosophies.

❯ Spain, the newest and most powerful European state, completed its "reconquest" of the Iberian Peninsula in 1492 and then looked to counter the successful colonial ventures of the Portuguese. This led to the early beginnings of a Spanish Empire in the Americas.

CORE OBJECTIVES

❯ **UNDERSTAND** the relationship between Renaissance ideals and the political and economic realities of Italy.

❯ **IDENTIFY** the key characteristics of Renaissance arts and learning during this period.

❯ **DEFINE** the term *reconquista* and its implications.

❯ **DESCRIBE** the methods and motives of European colonization during this period.

❯ **EXPLAIN** the factors that allowed Europeans to subjugate the peoples of the New World.

Johannes Gutenberg of Mainz European inventor of the printing press. His shop in Mainz produced the first printed book—a Bible—between the years 1453 and 1455.

printing press This new technology quickly revolutionized communication and played a significant role in political, religious, and intellectual movements.

Niccolò Machiavelli (1469–1527) As the author of *The Prince* and the *Discourses on Livy*, he looked to the Roman past for paradigms of greatness, at the same time hoping to win the patronage of contemporary rulers who would restore Italy's political independence.

Refugees from Ottoman conquest bring ancient Greek texts to Europe ❯

Although printing never entirely replaced traditional modes of manuscript publication, it revolutionized the spread of information.

In fact, the printing press played a crucial role in many of the developments that we will study in this chapter. The artistic and intellectual experiments of the Italian Renaissance were rapidly exported to other parts of Europe. Plans for innovative weapons were printed on the same presses that churned out humanist writings. News of Columbus's first voyage and the subsequent conquests of the Americas would spread via the same medium. Printing not only increased the volume and rapidity of communication—it also made it more difficult for those in power to censor dissenting opinions. The printing press also made it possible for rulers to govern growing empires abroad and increasingly centralized states at home. The "reconquest" of Spain and the extension of Spanish imperialism to the New World were both facilitated by printed propaganda. Printing even helped standardize languages by enabling governments to promote one official dialect over others: hence "the king's English," the language spoken around London, was imposed throughout the English realm and contributed to the growth of a common linguistic and national identity.

Renaissance Ideals—and Realities

The intellectual movement that began in Italy during the fourteenth century was, as we noted in Chapter 11, characterized by an intense interest in the classical past and a new type of educational program known as humanism. This movement was extended and diversified in the later fifteenth century: by the time the Ottoman conquest of Constantinople was complete, just a year or so before Gutenberg's invention, hundreds of refugees had brought precious manuscripts of Greek texts to Europe, such as the epics of Homer and the dialogues of Plato. Prior to the invention of print, such manuscripts could be owned and studied by only a very few. Now, printers in Venice and other cities rushed to produce cheap editions of classical texts, as well as Greek grammars and glossaries that could facilitate reading them.

Within a few decades, an informal "Platonic Academy" had formed in Florence, fostered by the patronage of the wealthy Cosimo de' Medici. Based on his reading of Plato, the philosopher Marsilio Ficino (1433–1499) moved away from the focus on civic life that had been such a feature of earlier humanist thought. Instead, he taught that the individual man should work to free his immortal soul from its "always miserable" mortal body—a Platonic idea very compatible with late-medieval Christian piety. Ficino's translation of Plato's works into Latin made them widely accessible—again, thanks to the medium of print. His disciple, Giovanni Pico della Mirandola (1463–1494), also rejected the everyday world of public affairs and took an even more exalted view of man's intellectual and artistic capacities, arguing that man (but not woman) could aspire to union with God through the exercise of his unique talents.

THE POLITICS OF ITALY AND THE PHILOSOPHY OF MACHIAVELLI

But not all Florentines were galvanized by Platonic ideals. The most influential author of this era was a thoroughgoing realist who spent more time studying ancient Roman history than Greek philosophy: **Niccolò Machiavelli** (1469–1527).

THE SPREAD OF PRINTING

| Up until 1470 |
| 1471–1500 |
| 1501–1600 |

THE SPREAD OF PRINTING. This map shows how quickly the technology of printing spread throughout Europe between 1470 and 1600. › In what regions were printing presses most heavily concentrated? › What factors may have led to their proliferation in the Low Countries, northern Italy, and central Europe—compared with France, Spain, and England? › Why would so many presses have been located along waterways?

Printing, Patriotism, and the Past

The printing press helped create new communities of readers by standardizing national languages and even promoting patriotism. And as it enabled authors of new works to reach larger audiences, it also allowed printers to popularize older writings that had previously circulated only in manuscript. The two sources presented here exemplify two aspects of this trend. The first is a preface by William Caxton of London, a printer who specialized in publishing books that glorified England's history and heritage. The preface is to a version of the legend of King Arthur, originally written by the English soldier Sir Thomas Malory, who completed it in 1470. It was printed for the first time in 1485 and quickly became a bestseller. The second excerpt is from the concluding chapter of Machiavelli's treatise The Prince. *Like the book itself, these remarks were originally addressed to Lorenzo de' Medici, head of Florence's most powerful family. But when* The Prince *was printed in 1532, five years after Machiavelli's death, the author's passionate denunciation of foreign "barbarians" and his lament for Italy's lost glory resonated with a wider Italian-speaking public.*

William Caxton's preface to Thomas Malory's *Le Morte d'Arthur* ("The Death of Arthur"; printed 1485)

After I had accomplished and finished diverse histories, both of contemplation and of other historical and worldly acts of great conquerors and princes, . . . many noble and diverse gentlemen of this realm of England came and demanded why I had not made and imprinted the noble history of the Holy Grail, and of the most renowned Christian king and worthy, King Arthur, which ought most to be remembered among us Englishmen before all other Christian kings. . . . The said noble gentlemen instantly required me to imprint the history of the said noble king and conqueror King Arthur, and of his knights, with the history of the Holy Grail . . . considering that he was a man born within this realm, and king and emperor of the same: and that there be, in French, diverse and many noble volumes of his acts, and also of his knights. To whom I answered that diverse men hold opinion that there was no such Arthur, and that all such books as have been made of him be feigned and fables, because some chronicles make of him no mention. . . . Whereto they answered, and one in special said, that in him that should say or think that there was never such a king called Arthur might well be accounted great folly and blindness. . . . For in all places, Christian and heathen, he is reputed and taken for one of the Nine Worthies, and the first of the three Christian

men. And also, he is more spoken of beyond the sea, and there are more books made of his noble acts than there be in England, as well in Dutch, Italian, Spanish, and Greek, as in French. . . . Wherefore it is a marvel why he is no more renowned in his own country. . . .

Then all these things aforesaid alleged, I could not well deny but that there was such a noble king named Arthur, reputed one of the Nine Worthies, and first and chief of the Christian men. And many noble volumes be made of him and of his noble knights in French, which I have seen and read beyond the sea, which be not had in our maternal tongue. . . . Wherefore, among all such [manuscript] books as have late been drawn out briefly into English I have . . . undertaken to imprint a book of the noble histories of the said King Arthur, and of certain of his knights, after a copy unto me delivered—which copy Sir Thomas Malory did take out of certain books of French, and reduced it into English. And I, according to my copy, have done set it in print, to the intent that noble men may see and learn the noble acts of chivalry, the gentle and virtuous deeds that some knights used in those days, by which they came to honor, and how they that were vicious were punished and oft put to shame and rebuke; humbly beseeching all noble lords and ladies (with all other estates of what estate or degree they be) that shall see and read in this said book and work, that they take the good and honest acts to their remembrance, and follow the same. . . . For herein may be seen noble chivalry, courtesy, humanity, friendliness, hardiness, love, friendship, cowardice, murder, hate, virtue, and sin. Do after the good and leave the evil, and it shall bring you to good fame and renown.

Source: Sir Thomas Malory, *Le Morte d'Arthur* (London: 1485) (text and spelling slightly modernized).

From the conclusion of Niccolò Machiavelli, *The Prince* (completed 1513; printed 1532)

Reflecting in the matters set forth above and considering within myself where the times were propitious in Italy at present to honor a new prince and whether there is at hand the matter suitable for a prudent and virtuous leader to mold in a new form, giving honor to himself and benefit to the citizens of the country, I have arrived at the opinion that all circumstances now favor such a prince, and I cannot think of a time more propitious for him than the present. If, as I said, it was necessary in order to make apparent the virtue of Moses, that the people of Israel should be enslaved in Egypt, and that the Persians should be oppressed by the Medes to provide an opportunity to illustrate the greatness and the spirit of Cyrus, and that the Athenians should be scattered in order to show the excellence of Theseus, thus at the present time, in order to reveal the valor of an Italian spirit, it was essential that Italy should fall to her present low estate, more enslaved than the Hebrews, more servile than the Persians, more disunited than the Athenians, leaderless and lawless, beaten, despoiled, lacerated, overrun and crushed under every kind of misfortune. . . . So Italy now, left almost lifeless, awaits the coming of one who will heal her wounds, putting an end to the sacking and looting in Lombardy and the spoliation and extortions in the Realm of Naples and Tuscany, and cleanse her sores that have been so long festering. Behold how she prays God to send her someone to redeem her from the cruelty and insolence of the barbarians. See how she is ready and willing to follow any banner so long as there be someone to take it up. Nor has she at present any hope of finding her redeemer save only in your illustrious house [the Medici] which has been so highly exalted both by its own merits and by fortune and which has been favored by God and the church, of which it is now ruler. . . .

This opportunity, therefore, should not be allowed to pass, and Italy, after such a long wait, must be allowed to behold her redeemer. I cannot describe the joy with which he will be received in all these provinces which have suffered so much from the foreign deluge, nor with what thirst for vengeance, nor with what firm devotion, what solemn delight, what tears! What gates could be closed to him, what people could deny him obedience, what envy could withstand him, what Italian could withhold allegiance from him? THIS BARBARIAN OCCUPATION STINKS IN THE NOSTRILS OF ALL OF US. Let your illustrious house then take up this cause with the spirit and the hope with which one undertakes a truly just enterprise. . . .

Source: Niccolò Machiavelli, *The Prince*, ed. and trans. Thomas G. Bergin (Arlington Heights, IL: 1947), pp. 75–76, 78.

Questions for Analysis

1. What do these two sources reveal about the relationship between patriotism and the awareness of a nation's past? Why do you think Caxton looks back to a legendary medieval king, whereas Machiavelli's references are all to ancient examples? What do both excerpts reveal about the value placed on history in the popular imagination?

2. How does Caxton describe the process of printing a book? What larger conclusions can we draw from this about the market for printed books in general?

3. Why might Machiavelli's treatise have been made available in a printed version nearly twenty years after its original appearance in manuscript? How might his new audience have responded to its message?

Machiavelli's writings reflect the unstable politics of his home city, as well as his aspirations for a unified Italy that could revive the glory of Rome. We have observed that Italy had been in political disarray for centuries, a situation exacerbated by the "Babylonian Captivity" of the papacy and the controversies raging after its return to Rome (Chapters 10 and 11). Now, Italy was becoming the arena where bloody international struggles were being played out: the kings of France and Spain both had claims to territory there, and both sent invading armies into the peninsula while busily competing for the allegiance of various city-states, which in turn were torn by internal dissension.

In 1498, Machiavelli became a prominent official in a new Florentine republic, founded after a French invasion led to the expulsion of the ruling Medici family. His duties largely involved diplomatic missions to other Italian city-states. He became fascinated by the career of Cesare Borgia (1475–1507), illegitimate son of Pope Alexander VI, who was attempting to create his own principality in central Italy. Machiavelli noted Borgia's ruthlessness and his complete subordination of personal ethics to political ends. In 1512, when the Medici returned to overthrow the Florentine republic, Machiavelli was imprisoned, tortured, and exiled. He thereafter devoted his energies to the articulation of a political philosophy suited to the times and the tactics of the family that had ousted him.

On the surface, Machiavelli's two great works of political analysis appear to contradict each other. In his *Discourses on Livy*, which drew on the works of that Roman historian (Chapter 5), he praised the Roman Republic as a model for his own contemporaries, lauding constitutional government and equality among citizens. There is little doubt, in fact, that Machiavelli was a committed believer in the free city-state as the ideal form of human government. Yet Machiavelli also wrote *The Prince*, a "handbook for tyrants" in the eyes of his critics, and dedicated this work to Lorenzo, the son of Piero de' Medici, whose family had overthrown the Florentine republic.

Because *The Prince* has been much more widely read, it has often been interpreted as an endorsement of power for its own sake. But Machiavelli's real position was quite different: in the political chaos of his time, he saw the likes of Cesare Borgia as the only hope for revitalizing the spirit of independence and thus making Italy fit, eventually, for self-governance. Machiavelli never ceased to hope that his contemporaries would rise up, expel the French and Spanish, and restore ancient traditions of liberty and equality. He regarded a period

THE STATES OF ITALY, c. 1494. This map shows the divisions of Italy on the eve of the French invasion in 1494. Contemporary observers often described Italy as being divided among five great powers: Milan, Venice, Florence, the Papal States, and the united kingdoms of Naples and Sicily. **› Which of these powers seems most capable of expanding their territories? › Which neighboring states would be most threatened by such attempts at expansion? › Why would Florence and the Papal States so often find themselves in conflict with each other?**

of despotism as a necessary step toward that end, not as a permanently desirable form of government. Accordingly, Machiavelli insisted that a prince's actions must be judged by their consequences and not by their intrinsic moral quality. He argued that the "necessity of preserving the state will often compel a prince to take actions which are opposed to loyalty, charity, humanity, and religion." As we shall see in later chapters, many subsequent political philosophers would go even further than Machiavelli in arguing that the avoidance of political chaos does indeed warrant the exercise of absolute power (see Chapters 14 and 15).

◄ *Machiavelli argues rulers can justify absolute power to preserve the state*

THE IDEAL OF THE COURTIER

Machiavelli's political theories were informed by years of diplomatic service in the courts of Italy, and so was his engaging literary style. Indeed, he never ceased writing courtly poems and plays. In this he resembled another poet-courtier, Ludovico Ariosto (1474–1533), who undertook diplomatic missions for the Duke of Ferrara and some of Rome's most powerful prelates. Ariosto's lengthy verse narrative, *Orlando Furioso* ("The Madness of Roland"), was a retelling of the heroic exploits celebrated in the French *Song of Roland* (Chapter 8)—but without the heroism. Although very different in form and tone from *The Prince*, it shared that work's skepticism of political or chivalric ideals. It emphasized the comedy of its lovers' passionate exploits and sought to charm an audience that found consolation in pleasure and beauty.

Thus a new Renaissance ideal was born: the ideal of the courtier, personified by the diplomat and nobleman Baldassare Castiglione (*bahl-dahs-SAH-re kah-stig-lee-OH-neh*; 1478–1529). His handbook, *The Book of the Courtier*, stands in sharp contrast to the treatises on public virtue composed in the previous century. Whereas Bruni and Alberti (Chapter 11) had lauded the sober virtues of service to the city-state, Castiglione taught how to attain the elegant and seemingly effortless skills necessary for advancement in princely courts. Many of these talents are still associated with the "Renaissance man": accomplished in many different pursuits, witty, cultured, and stylish. But in many ways, Castiglione's courtiers—women as well as men—represent a *rejection* of the older ideals associated with humanism's emphasis on classical education for public men. Castiglione also rejected the misogyny of the humanists by showing how court ladies could rise to influence and prominence through the graceful and wily exercise of their womanly powers.

THE DILEMMA OF THE ARTIST

Without question, the most enduring legacy of the Italian Renaissance has been the contributions of its artists, particularly those who embraced new media and new attitudes toward the human body. The creative and economic opportunities afforded by painting on canvas or wood panels freed artists from having to work on site and entirely on commission. We have also noted (Chapter 11) that the increased use of oil-based paints, as pioneered by the artists of Flanders, further revolutionized painting styles. To these benefits, the artists of Italy added an important technical ingredient: mastery of a vanishing (one-point) perspective, which gave an illusion of three-dimensional space. They also experimented with effects of light and shade, and intently studied anatomy and bodily proportions: techniques that also influenced sculptors. Just as Petrarch and other early humanists had urged a return to classical poetry and rhetoric, artists now recaptured the symmetry of classical art and placed the human subject at the center of artistic experience.

But behind all their beautiful artworks lie some harsh realities. Increasing private wealth and political jockeying had created a huge demand for commodities that could increase the status of men grappling for prestige. The development of portraiture was a direct result because princes and merchants alike sought to glorify themselves and their families—and to compete with neighbors and rivals. An artist therefore had to study the techniques of the courtier, and not just the new artistic techniques, in order to win patrons. He also had to perform services for which he needed other talents: overseeing the building and decoration of palaces; designing tableware, furniture, and liveries (uniforms) for servants and soldiers; even decorating firearms. Some artists were prized as much for their capacity to invent deadly weapons as for their paintings.

Renaissance artists drawn into intense political and social competition of era ❯

THE CAREER OF LEONARDO

The most adventurous and versatile artist of this period was **Leonardo da Vinci** (1452–1519). Leonardo personifies the Renaissance ideal: he was a painter, architect, musician, mathematician, engineer, and inventor. The illegitimate son of a notary, he had set up an artist's shop in Florence by the time he was twenty-five and gained the patronage of the Medici ruler Lorenzo the Magnificent. Yet Leonardo had a weakness: he worked slowly and had difficulty finishing anything. This naturally displeased Lorenzo and other Florentine patrons, who regarded artists as craftsmen who worked on their patrons' time, not their own. Leonardo, however, strongly objected to this view, considering himself to be an inspired, independent innovator. He therefore left Florence in 1482 and went to work for the Sforza dictators of Milan, whose favor he courted by emphasizing his skills as a maker of bombs, cannons, and siege engines. He remained there until the second French invasion of 1499, and then wandered about until finally accepting the patronage of the French king.

THE VIRGIN OF THE ROCKS. This painting reveals Leonardo's interest in the variety of human faces and facial expressions, and in natural settings.

Paradoxically, considering his skill in fashioning weapons, Leonardo believed in the essential divinity of all living things. He was a vegetarian—unusual at the time—and went to the marketplace to buy caged birds only to release them once he had finished observing them. He made careful drawings of grass, cloud formations, a waterfall; he obtained human corpses for dissection to study the minutest features of the body. This knowledge he poured into his paintings: *The Virgin of the Rocks* typifies not only his technical skill but also his passion for nature. In *The Last Supper*, Leonardo displayed his equally keen studies of human psychology. In this image, a serene Christ has just announced that one of his gathered disciples will betray him. Leonardo succeeds in portraying the mingled emotions of surprise, horror, and guilt on their faces. He also implicates the painting's viewers in this dramatic scene, since they, too, dine alongside Christ in the very same room.

THE LAST SUPPER. This fresco on the refectory wall of the monastery of Santa Maria delle Grazie in Milan is a testament to both the powers and the limitations of Leonardo's artistry. It skillfully employs the techniques of one-point perspective to create the illusion that Jesus and his disciples are actually dining at the monastery's head table; but because Leonardo had not mastered the techniques of fresco painting, he applied tempera pigments onto a dry wall that had been coated with a sealing agent. As a result, the painting's colors began to fade just years after its completion. By the middle of the sixteenth century, it had seriously deteriorated, and large portions of it became invisible. It was the object of a major restoration campaign in the 1990s.

ARTISTS AND PATRONS

The innovations of Florentine artists were widely imitated by Venetian painters, whose sumptuous portraits of the rich and powerful mirrored the tastes of the patrons for whom they worked. Rome, too, became a major artistic center in this era. Among its eminent painters was Raffaello Sanzio, or Raphael (1483–1520). Although influenced by Leonardo, Raphael cultivated a more philosophical approach: as we noted in Chapter 4, his fresco *The School of Athens* depicts both the harmony and the differences of Platonic and Aristotelian thought (see page 122). It also includes a number of Raphael's contemporaries as models: the image of Plato is actually a portrait of Leonardo, the architect Donato Bramante (c. 1444–1514) stands in for Euclid, and Michelangelo for the philosopher Heraclitus.

Michelangelo Buonarroti (1475–1564), who spent many decades in the service of the papacy, was another native of Florence. Like Leonardo, he was a polymath: painter, sculptor, architect, and poet. But whereas Leonardo was a naturalist, Michelangelo was an idealist. At the center of all his work, as at the center of Renaissance humanism, is the male figure: the embodied masculine mind. Michelangelo's greatest achievements in painting appear in a single location: the Sistine Chapel of the Vatican palace. As products of two different periods in the artist's life, they exemplify two different artistic styles and outlooks on the human condition. More famous are the extraordinary frescoes painted on the ceiling

Leonardo da Vinci (1452–1519) Florentine inventor, sculptor, architect, and painter whose breadth of interests typifies the ideal of the "Renaissance man."

Michelangelo Buonarroti (1475–1564) A virtuoso Florentine sculptor, painter, and poet who spent much of his career in the service of the papacy. He is best known for the decoration of the Sistine Chapel and for his monumental sculptures.

during the years between 1508 and 1512, depicting scenes from the book of Genesis. Of all the panels in this series, *The Creation of Adam* exemplifies the young artist's commitment to classical artistic principles and affirms the heroic qualities of mankind.

But a quarter of a century later, when Michelangelo returned to work in the Sistine Chapel, both his style and mood had changed dramatically. In the enormous *Last Judgment*, a fresco completed on the chapel's altar wall in 1536, Michelangelo repudiated classical restraint and represented humans racked with fear, guilt, and frailty. He even included himself in it via a grotesque self-portrait on the flayed flesh of Saint Bartholomew, who was martyred by being skinned alive. One wonders whether Michelangelo intended this as a reflection on the challenges of working for the papal court.

SELF-PORTRAIT OF THE ARTIST AS A YOUNG MAN: DETAIL FROM *THE SCHOOL OF ATHENS*. We already analyzed aspects of Raphael's famous group portrait of the Greek philosophers, with Plato and Aristotle at the center (see page 122). In addition to featuring his own contemporaries as models—including the artists Leonardo and Michelangelo and the architect Bramante—Raphael put himself in the picture. › **What messages does this choice convey?**

THE RENAISSANCE OF SCULPTURE

Although sculpture was not a new medium for artists, as oil painting was, it became an important area of Renaissance innovation. For the first time since late antiquity, monumental statues became figures "in the round" rather than sculptural elements incorporated into buildings or featured on tombs. By freeing sculpture from its bondage to architecture, the Renaissance reestablished it as a separate art form.

THE CREATION OF ADAM. This is one of a series of frescoes Michelangelo painted on the ceiling of the Sistine Chapel in the Vatican palace in Rome. He executed them over a period of many years and under circumstances of extreme physical hardship. It has since become an iconic image. › **How might it be said to capture Renaissance ideals?**

Leonardo da Vinci Applies for a Job

Few sources illuminate the tensions between Renaissance ideals and realities better than the résumé of accomplishments submitted by Leonardo da Vinci to a prospective employer, Ludovico Sforza of Milan. In the following letter, Leonardo explains why he deserves to be appointed chief architect and military engineer in the duke's household administration. He got the job and moved to Milan in 1481.

1. I have the kind of bridges that are extremely light and strong, made to be carried with great ease, and with them you may pursue, and, at any time, flee from the enemy; . . . and also methods of burning and destroying those of the enemy.

2. I know how, when a place is under attack, to eliminate the water from the trenches, and make endless variety of bridges . . . and other machines. . . .

3. . . . I have methods for destroying every rock or other fortress, even if it were built on rock, etc.

4. I also have other kinds of mortars [bombs] that are most convenient and easy to carry. . . .

5. And if it should be a sea battle, I have many kinds of machines that are most efficient for offense and defense. . . .

6. I also have means that are noiseless to reach a designated area by secret and tortuous mines. . . .

7. I will make covered chariots, safe and unattackable, which can penetrate the enemy with their artillery. . . .

8. In case of need I will make big guns, mortars, and light ordnance of fine and useful forms that are out of the ordinary.

9. If the operation of bombardment should fail, I would contrive catapults, mangonels, trabocchi [trebuchets], and other machines of marvelous efficacy and unusualness. In short, I can, according to each case in question, contrive various and endless means of offense and defense.

10. In time of peace I believe I can give perfect satisfaction that is equal to any other in the field of architecture and the construction of buildings. . . . I can execute sculpture in marble, bronze, or clay, and also in painting I do the best that can be done, and as well as any other, whoever he may be.

Having now, most illustrious Lord, sufficiently seen the specimens of all those who consider themselves master craftsmen of instruments of war, and that the invention and operation of such instruments are no different from those in common use, I shall now endeavor . . . to explain myself to your Excellency by revealing to your Lordship my secrets.

Source: Excerpted from Leonardo da Vinci, *The Notebooks*, in *The Italian Renaissance Reader*, eds. Julia Conaway Bondanella and Mark Musa (Harmondsworth, UK: 1987), pp. 195–96.

Questions for Analysis

1. Judging from the qualifications Leonardo highlights in this letter, what can you conclude about the political situation in Milan and the priorities of its duke? What can you conclude about the state of military technologies during this period and the conduct of warfare?

2. What do you make of the fact that Leonardo mentions his artistic endeavors only at the end of the letter? Does this fact alter your opinion or impression of him? Why or why not?

THE POWER AND VULNERABILITY OF THE MALE BODY. Donatello's *David* (left) was the first freestanding nude executed since antiquity. It shows the Hebrew leader as an adolescent youth and is a little over five feet tall. In contrast, Michelangelo's *David* (center) stands thirteen feet high and was placed prominently in front of Florence's city hall to proclaim the city's power and humanistic values. Michelangelo's *Descent from the Cross* (right), which shows Christ's broken body in the arms of the elderly Nicodemus (the sculptor himself), was made for Michelangelo's own tomb. (The Gospels describe Nicodemus as a Pharisee who became a follower of Jesus, and who was present at his death.) **› Why would Michelangelo choose to represent himself as Nicodemus? › How does his representation of David, and the context in which this figure was displayed, compare with that of Donatello's sculpture?**

The first acclaimed master of Renaissance sculpture was the Florentine known as Donatello (c. 1386–1466). His bronze statue of David, triumphant over the head of the slain Goliath, is the first freestanding nude of the period. Yet this *David* is clearly an agile adolescent rather than the muscular Greek athlete of Michelangelo's *David*, which was executed in 1501 as a public expression of Florentine civic life. Michelangelo regarded sculpture as the most exalted of the arts because it allowed the artist to imitate God most fully in re-creating human forms. He also insisted on working in marble—the "noblest" sculptural material—and creating figures twice as large as life.

By sculpting a serenely confident young man at the peak of physical fitness, Michelangelo celebrated the Florentine republic's own determination to resist tyrants and uphold ideals of civic justice. Yet in the sculptures of Michelangelo's later life, as in his painting, he began to explore the use of anatomical distortion to create emotional intensity. The culmination of this trend is his unfinished but intensely moving *Descent from the Cross*, a depiction of an old man (the sculptor himself) grieving over the distorted, slumping body of the dead Christ.

RENAISSANCE ARCHITECTURE

Renaissance architecture had its roots in the classical past to an even greater extent than either sculpture or painting. The Gothic style pioneered in northern France (see Chapter 9) had not found a welcome reception in Italy. Most of the buildings constructed there were Romanesque, and the great architects generally adopted their building plans from these structures. They also copied decorative devices from the authentic ruins of ancient Rome and studied the writings of Vitruvius (fl. c. 60–15 B.C.E.), the Roman architect and engineer. The principles laid out by Vitruvius were popularized by Leon Battista Alberti in his book *On the Art of Building*, which began to circulate in manuscript around 1450.

In keeping with these classical models, Renaissance buildings emphasized geometrical proportion inspired by Platonic philosophy, which taught that certain mathematical ratios reflect the harmony of the universe. For example, the proportions of the human body are the basis for the proportions of the quintessential Renaissance building: St. Peter's Basilica in Rome. Designed by some of the most celebrated architects of the time, including Bramante and Michelangelo, it is still one of the largest buildings in the world. Yet it seems smaller than a Gothic cathedral because it is built to human scale. The same artful proportions are evident in smaller-scale buildings too, as in the aristocratic country houses later designed by the northern Italian architect Andrea Palladio (1508–1580), who created secular miniatures of ancient temples to glorify his patrons.

The Renaissance North of the Alps

It was not until the very end of the fifteenth century that the innovative artistry and learning of Italy began to be exported across the Alps into northern Europe and across the Mediterranean into Spain. For beyond Italy, intellectual life was dominated by universities such as those of Paris, Oxford, Kraków, and Prague, whose scholastic curricula still focused on logic, dialectic, and theology. Universities in Italy, by contrast, were more often professional schools specializing in law and medicine, and were more integrally tied to the interests of urban elites. In northern Europe, scholars who *were* influenced by Italian ideas usually worked outside the university system, under the private patronage of kings and princes.

In Italy, as we have seen, such patronage was an important arena for competition between political rivals. Elsewhere in Europe, however, political units were larger and political rivals fewer; it was therefore less necessary to promote art for political purposes than in the small principalities and city-states of Italy. But as royal courts became more firmly established in royal capitals—and so became showcases for royal power—kings increasingly needed to impress their own subjects and to display their power to foreign courtiers and visitors. Consequently, they relied more and more on artists and intellectuals to advertise their wealth and taste.

In northern Europe, art was used less frequently for political purposes

ERASMUS, **BY HANS HOLBEIN THE YOUNGER.** This is generally regarded as the most evocative portrait of the preeminent Christian humanist.

CHRISTIAN HUMANISM AND THE CAREER OF ERASMUS

In general, then, the Renaissance movement in northern Europe differed from that of Italy because it grafted certain Italian ideals onto preexisting traditions, rather than sweeping away older forms of knowledge and artistry. This can be seen very clearly in the case of a hybrid development known as Christian humanism. Although Christian humanists shared the Italian humanists' scorn for scholasticism's limitations and applied new critical methods to ancient texts, these northern scholars were more committed to seeking ethical guidance from biblical and religious precepts, as well as from Cicero or Virgil. Like their Italian counterparts, these scholars embraced the wisdom of antiquity, but the antiquity they favored was Christian as well as classical: the antiquity of the New Testament and the early Church.

Chief among them was **Desiderius Erasmus** (c. 1469–1536). The illegitimate son of a priest, Erasmus was born near Rotterdam in the Netherlands. Forced to enter a monastery when he was a teenager, the young Erasmus found little useful instruction there—but plenty of freedom to read widely. He devoured all the classics he could get his hands on, alongside the writings of the Church Fathers (Chapter 6). When he was about thirty years old, he obtained permission to leave the monastery and to enroll in the University of Paris, where he completed the requirements for a bachelor's degree in divinity.

But Erasmus subsequently rebelled against what he regarded as the arid learning of Parisian scholasticism, and he never served actively as a priest. Instead, he made his living from teaching, writing, and the proceeds of various ecclesiastical offices that required no pastoral duties. Ever on the lookout for new patrons, he traveled often to England, stayed for three years in Italy, and resided in several different cities in Germany and the Low Countries before settling, toward the end of his life, in Basel (Switzerland). Through these travels, as well as a voluminous correspondence with learned friends, Erasmus became the humanist leader of northern Europe.

As a Latin prose stylist, Erasmus was often compared to Cicero. Extraordinarily eloquent and witty, he reveled in tailoring his mode of discourse to fit his subject, creating dazzling verbal effects and coining puns that took on added meaning if the reader knew Greek as well. Although Erasmus's urbane style and humor earned him a wide audience, he intended everything he wrote to promote the "philosophy of Christ." He believed that the society of his day had lost sight of the Gospels' teachings. Accordingly, he offered his contemporaries three different kinds of writings: clever satires in which people could recognize their own foibles, serious moral treatises meant to offer guidance toward proper Christian behavior, and new editions of basic Christian texts.

In the first category belong works that are still widely read today: *The Praise of Folly* (1511), in which Erasmus ridiculed pedantry, ignorance, and gullibility—even within the Church; and the *Colloquies* (1518), in which he subjected contemporary religious practices to keen examination, couching a serious message in an ironic tone. In these books, Erasmus let fictional characters do the talking, so his own views on any given topic can only be determined by inference. But in his second category of writings, Erasmus spoke clearly in his own voice. In *Handbook of the Christian Knight* (1503), he used the language of chivalry to encourage a life of inward piety; in *Complaint of Peace* (1517), he argued movingly for Christian pacifism.

The third set of writings, which Erasmus himself considered his greatest achievement, were critical editions of works by Augustine, Jerome, and Ambrose. He also used his extraordinary command of Latin and Greek to produce a more accurate edition of the New Testament. After reading Lorenzo Valla's *Notes on the New Testament* in 1504, Erasmus became convinced that nothing was more imperative than divesting the Christian scriptures of the myriad errors in transcription and translation that had piled up over the course of preceding centuries. He therefore spent ten years comparing all the early Greek biblical manuscripts he could find in order to establish an authoritative text. When it finally appeared in 1516, Erasmus's Greek New Testament—published together with explanatory notes and his own new Latin translation—became one of the most important scholarly landmarks of all time. It would play a critical role in the early stages of the Reformation (see Chapter 13).

THE INFLUENCE OF ERASMUS

One of Erasmus's closest friends was another prominent Christian humanist, Sir **Thomas More** (1478–1535). In later life, following a successful career as a lawyer and speaker of the House of Commons in Parliament, More was appointed lord chancellor of England in 1529. However, he lost that post when he opposed King Henry VIII's plan to establish a national church under royal control, in order to deny the supremacy of the pope (see Chapter 13). He was executed in 1535 and is now revered as a Catholic martyr.

In 1516, More published his most famous book, *Utopia* (Greek for *No Place*). Written in Latin and purporting to describe an ideal community on an imaginary island, the book is really a satirical critique of contemporary culture. In contrast to Europeans, the inhabitants of the fictional Utopia hold all their goods in common; work only six hours a day (so that all may have leisure for intellectual pursuits); and practice the virtues of wisdom, moderation, fortitude, and justice. Although More did not advance explicit arguments in favor of Christianity, he may have meant to imply that if the Utopians could manage their society so well without the benefit of Christian revelation, Europeans who knew the Gospels ought to be able to do even better.

Erasmus and More head a long list of energetic and eloquent northern humanists who made signal contributions to the collective enterprise of revolutionizing the study of early Christianity, and their achievements had a direct influence on

Thomas More (1478–1535) Christian, humanist, English statesman, and author of *Utopia*. In 1529, he was appointed lord chancellor of England but resigned because he opposed King Henry VIII's plans to establish a national church under royal control.

SIR THOMAS MORE, BY HANS HOLBEIN THE YOUNGER. Holbein's skill in rendering the gravity and interiority of his subject is matched by his masterful representation of the sumptuous chain of office, furred mantle, and velvet sleeves that indicate the political and professional status of Henry VIII's lord chancellor.

Protestant reformers (as we will see in the next chapter). Yet very few of these men were willing to join Luther and other Protestant leaders in rejecting the fundamental principles on which the power of the Roman Church was based. Most tried to remain within its fold while still espousing an ideal of inward piety and scholarly inquiry. But as the leaders of the Church grew less and less tolerant of dissent, even mild criticism came to seem like heresy. Erasmus died early enough to escape persecution, but several of his less fortunate followers did not.

THE LITERATURE OF THE NORTHERN RENAISSANCE

Alongside Christian humanism, a literary Renaissance also flourished in northern Europe. Poets in France and England vied with one another to adapt the elegant lyric forms pioneered by Petrarch and popularized by many subsequent poets, including Michelangelo. The sonnet was particularly influential and would become one of the verse forms embraced by William Shakespeare (1564–1616) (see Chapter 14). Another English poet, Edmund Spenser (c. 1552–1599), drew on the literary innovation of Ariosto's *Orlando Furioso*: his *Faerie Queene* is a similarly long chivalric romance that revels in sensuous imagery.

Meanwhile, the more satirical side of humanism was embraced by the French writer François Rabelais (*RAH-beh-lay*; c. 1494–1553). Like Erasmus, Rabelais began his career in the Church but soon left the cloister to study medicine. A practicing physician, Rabelais interspersed his professional activities with literary endeavors, the most enduring of which are the twin books *Gargantua* and *Pantagruel*: a series of "chronicles" describing the lives and times of giants whose fabulous size and gross appetites serve as vehicles for much lusty humor. Like Erasmus, too, Rabelais also satirized religious hypocrisy, pedantry, superstition, and bigotry. But unlike Erasmus, who wrote in a highly cultivated Latin style comprehensible only to very learned readers, Rabelais addressed a wider audience by writing in extremely crude French and glorifying human foibles as natural and healthy.

NORTHERN ARCHITECTURE AND ART

Although many architects in northern Europe continued to build in the flamboyant Gothic style of the later Middle Ages, the classical values of Italian architects can be seen in some of the splendid new castles constructed in France's Loire valley—châteaux too elegant to be defensible—and in the royal palace of the Louvre in Paris (now the museum), which replaced an old twelfth-century fortress. The influence of Renaissance ideals is also visible in the work of the German artist Albrecht Dürer (*DIRR-er*; 1471–1528). Dürer was the first northerner to master the techniques of proportion and perspective, and he shared with contemporary Italians a fascination with nature and the human body. He also took advantage of the printing press to circulate his work to a wide audience, making his delicate pencil drawings into engravings that could be mass produced.

But Dürer never really embraced classical subjects, as his Italian counterparts did; instead, he drew inspiration from Christian legends and the humanism of Erasmus.

For example, Dürer's serenely radiant engraving of Saint Jerome seems to express the scholarly absorption that Erasmus himself would have enjoyed while working in his study. Indeed, Dürer aspired to immortalize Erasmus himself in a major portrait, but the paths of the two men crossed only once. Instead, the accomplishment of capturing Erasmus's pensive spirit in art was left to another northern artist, the German Hans Holbein the Younger (1497–1543). Holbein also painted an acute portrait of Erasmus's friend, Sir Thomas More. These two portraits, in themselves, exemplify a Renaissance emphasis on the making of naturalistic likenesses that express human individuality.

TRADITION AND INNOVATION IN MUSIC

Like the visual arts, the lovely music produced during this era was nourished by patrons' desire to surround themselves with beauty. Yet unlike painting and sculpture, musical practice did not reach back to classical antiquity, but instead drew on well-established medieval conventions. Even before the Black Death, a musical movement called *ars nova* ("new art") was already flourishing in France and spread to Italy during the lifetime of Petrarch; its outstanding composers were Guillaume de Machaut (*mah-SHOH*; c. 1300–1377) and Francesco Landini (c. 1325–1397).

The part-songs and ballads composed by these musicians and their successors expanded on earlier genres of secular music, but their greatest achievement was a highly complicated yet delicate contrapuntal style adapted for the liturgy of the Church. Machaut's polyphonic (multivoiced and harmonized) setting of the major sections of the Mass is the earliest by a single composer. In the fifteenth century, the dissemination of this new musical aesthetic combined with a host of French, Flemish, and Italian elements in the multicultural courts of Europe, particularly that of Burgundy. By the beginning of the sixteenth century, Franco-Flemish composers dominated many important cathedrals, too, creating a variety of new forms and styles that bear a close affinity to Renaissance art and poetry.

Throughout Europe, the general level of musical proficiency during this era was very high. The singing of part-songs was a popular pastime in homes and at informal social gatherings, and the ability to read a part at sight was considered part of an elite education. Aristocratic women, in particular, were expected to display mastery of the new musical instruments that had been developed to add nuance and texture to existing musical forms, including the lute, the viol, the violin, and a variety of woodwind and keyboard instruments such as the harpsichord.

Although most composers of this period were men trained in the service of the Church, they rarely made sharp distinctions between sacred and secular music. Like

SAINT JEROME IN HIS STUDY, BY DÜRER. Jerome, the biblical translator of the fourth century (Chapter 6), was a hero to both Dürer and Erasmus, and the paragon of inspired Christian scholarship. Note how the scene exudes contentment, even down to the sleeping lion, which seems more like an overgrown tabby cat than a symbol of Christ.

sculpture, music was coming into its own as a serious, independent art. As such, it would become an important medium for the expression of both Catholic and Protestant ideals during the Reformation, and also one of the few art forms equally acceptable to all.

The Politics of Christian Europe

We have already observed how the intellectual and artistic activity of the Renaissance was both fueled and hindered by the political developments of the later fifteenth century—within Italy, and throughout Europe. In 1453, France had emerged victorious in the Hundred Years' War, whereas England plunged into three decades of bloody civil conflict that touched every corner of that kingdom. The French monarchy, therefore, was able to rebuild its power and prestige while at the same time extending its control over regions once controlled by the English, but now part of an enlarged French kingdom.

In 1494, the French king Charles VIII expanded his reach even farther, into Italy. Leading an army of thirty thousand well-trained troops across the Alps, and aided by an alliance with the duchy of Milan, he intended to press his ancestral claim to the kingdom of Naples. This effort solidified Italian opposition to French occupation—as we noted in our discussion of Machiavelli.

The rulers of Spain, whose territorial claims on Sicily also extended to Naples, were spurred by Charles's expansionism to forge an uneasy alliance with the Papal States, some principalities of the Holy Roman Empire, Milan, and Venice. But the respite was brief, for Charles's successor, Louis XII, launched a second French invasion in 1499. For more than a generation, until 1529, warfare in Italy was virtually uninterrupted. Alliances and counter alliances among city-states became further catalysts for violence and made Italy a magnet for mercenaries who could barely be kept in check by the generals who employed them.

Meanwhile, the northern Italian city-states' virtual monopoly on trade with Asia, which had been one of the chief economic underpinnings of artistic and intellectual patronage, was being gradually eroded by the shifting of trade routes from the Mediterranean to the Atlantic (Chapters 10 and 11). It was also hampered by the increasing power of the Ottoman Empire, and even by the imperial pretensions of a new Russian ruler.

THE POWER OF IVAN THE GREAT

In Chapter 10, we saw that Moscow had emerged as an administrative capital under the Mongols, and had then become the center of an independent principality, the Grand Duchy of Muscovy. In the fifteenth century, its exponential growth was driven by its ruler Ivan III (r. 1462–1505), also known as **Ivan the Great**, the first Muscovite prince to adopt a distinctive imperial agenda.

Ivan launched a series of conquests that annexed all the independent principalities between Moscow and the border of Poland–Lithuania. After invading Lithuania in 1492 and 1501, he also succeeded in bringing parts of that domain (portions of modern Belarus and Ukraine) under his control, although this did not sever the region's strong cultural ties to Poland or its religious allegiance to Rome.

Ivan the Great (1440–1505) Russian ruler who annexed neighboring territories and consolidated his empire's position as a European power.

THE EXPANSION OF MUSCOVITE TERRITORY TO 1505. The Grand
Duchy of Moscow (also known as Muscovy) was the heart of what would
become an empire. › With what other empires and polities did the Muscovites
have to compete during this period of expansion?

Meanwhile, Ivan married the niece of the last Byzantine emperor: an alliance that
inspired later Russian rulers to claim that Moscow was the "third Rome" while they
were heirs of the Caesars—hence the title *czar* or **tsar**. Ivan also rebuilt his fortified
Moscow residence, known as the Kremlin, in magnificent Italianate style. By the
time of his death in 1505, Muscovy was firmly established as a dominant power on
the frontier of Europe.

THE GROWTH OF NATIONAL CHURCHES

At the same time that Muscovy laid claim to the mantle of Roman imperial power,
the papacy was pouring resources into the glorification of the original Rome
and the aggrandizement of the papal office. But neither the city nor its rulers
could keep pace with their political and religious rivals. Following the Council of

tsar Russian word for
"emperor," derived from the
Latin *caesar* and similar to
the German word *Kaiser*.
This was the title claimed
by the rulers of medieval
Muscovy and of the later
Russian Empire.

In a series of concordat treaties, popes cede political power and revenues to kings and princes

Constance (Chapter 11), the papacy's victory over the conciliar movement was a costly one. To win the support of Europe's kings and princes, various popes negotiated a series of religious treaties known as "concordats," which granted these rulers extensive authority over churches within their domains. Under the terms of these concordats, kings now received many of the revenues that had previously gone to the papacy and acquired new powers to appoint candidates to Church offices. The papacy thus secured its theoretical supremacy at the expense of its real power, and strengthened the national monarchies that were emerging during this era. Such changes were, in many ways, a drastic reversal of the hard-won reforms of the eleventh and twelfth centuries that had created such a powerful papacy in the first place.

Having given away so many sources of revenue and authority, the popes of the late fifteenth century became even more dependent on their own territories in central Italy. But to tighten their hold on the Papal States, they had to rule like other Italian princes: leading armies, jockeying for alliances, and undermining their opponents by every possible means—including covert operations and assassinations. By the secular standards of the day, these efforts paid off: the Papal States became one of the better-governed and wealthier principalities in Italy. But such methods did nothing to enhance the popes' reputation for piety, and disillusionment with the papacy as a force for the advancement of spirituality became even more widespread.

AN ITALIAN RENAISSANCE CATHEDRAL IN MUSCOVITE RUS'. Ivan the Great commissioned the Italian architect Aristotele Fioravanti to build this cathedral, dedicated to the Blessed Virgin and honoring her Assumption into heaven. It is now part of the Kremlin palace complex in Moscow. **> Why would Ivan choose to build this cathedral and commission this particular architect? > What messages might he have been trying to convey?**

With papal authority and Rome's spiritual prestige in decline, kings and princes became the primary figures to whom both clergy and laity looked for religious and moral guidance. Many secular rulers responded to such expectations aggressively, closing scandal-ridden monasteries, suppressing alleged heretics, and prohibiting the lower classes from dressing like the nobility. By these and other such measures, rulers could present themselves as champions of moral reform even as they strengthened their political power. The result was an increasingly close link between national monarchies and national churches, a link that would become even stronger after the Reformation.

THE TRIUMPH OF THE *RECONQUISTA*

The Christian kingdoms of the Iberian Peninsula were also in constant conflict during this period. In Castile, civil war and incompetent governance allowed the Castilian nobility to gain greater control over the peasantry and greater independence from the monarchy. In Aragon, royal government benefited from the extended commercial influence of Catalonia, which was under Aragonese rule. But after 1458, Aragon also became enmeshed in a civil war that involved both France and Castile.

The solution to the disputed succession that had caused this war ultimately lay in the blending of two powerful royal families. In 1469, Prince **Ferdinand of Aragon** was recognized as the undisputed heir to that throne and, in the same year, secured this position by marrying **Isabella**, the heiress of **Castile**. Isabella became queen in 1474 and Ferdinand became king in 1479. Although Castile and Aragon continued to be ruled as separate kingdoms until 1714—there are tensions between the two former kingdoms even now—their marriage enabled Isabella and Ferdinand to pursue several ambitious policies. In particular, their combined resources went to the creation of Europe's most powerful army, which was employed to conquer the last remaining Muslim principality of what had been al-Andalus, Islamic Spain. That principality, Granada, fell in 1492.

THE END OF THE *CONVIVENCIA* AND THE EXPULSION OF THE MUSLIMS AND JEWS

For more than seven centuries, many of Iberia's Jewish communities had enjoyed certain privileges extended by their Muslim rulers, who were also relatively tolerant of their Christian subjects. Scholars often refer to this period of history as a time of *convivencia*, "living together" or "coexistence." Although relations among various religious and ethnic groups were not always peaceful or positive, the policies of Muslim rulers in al-Andalus had enabled an extraordinary hybrid culture to flourish.

The aims of the Spanish *reconquista* were diametrically opposed to those of "living together." The "reconquest" sought to forge a single, homogeneous community based on the fiction that Spain had once been entirely Christian and should be restored to its former purity. The year 1492, therefore, marks not only the end of Islamic rule in medieval Iberia and the forced conversion or expulsion of all Muslims but also the culmination of Jewish exclusion, a process that had accelerated in the late thirteenth century (Chapter 9). Within this history, the Spanish expulsion of the Jews stands

Ferdinand of Aragon (1452–1516) In 1469, he married the heiress to Castile, Isabella. Their union allowed them to pursue several ambitious policies, including the conquest of Granada, the last Muslim principality in Spain, and the expulsion of Spain's large Jewish community.

Isabella of Castile (1451–1504) The heiress to Castile, she married Ferdinand of Aragon. In 1492, she granted three ships to Christopher Columbus of Genoa (Italy), who went on to claim portions of the New World for Spain.

reconquista A period of "reconquest" in medieval Spain that sought to forge a single, homogeneous community based on the fiction that Spain had once been entirely Christian and should be restored to its former purity.

FERDINAND AND ISABELLA HONORING THE VIRGIN. In this contemporary Spanish painting, the royal couple are shown with two of their children and two household chaplains, in the company of the Blessed Virgin, the Christ Child, and saints from the Dominican order. (The Dominicans were instrumental in conducting the affairs of the Spanish Inquisition.) › How clear is the distinction between these holy figures and the royal family? › What message is conveyed by their proximity?

out for the staggering scope of the displacements and destruction it entailed: at least 100,000 (and possibly as many as 200,000) men, women, and children were forced from their homes as refugees.

The Christian monarchs' motives for ordering these expulsions are still debated. Tens of thousands of Spanish Jews had already converted to Christianity between 1391 and 1420, many as a result of coercion. And for a generation or so, it seemed possible that these converts, known as *conversos*, might successfully assimilate into Christian society. But the same civil wars that led to the union of Ferdinand and Isabella made the *conversos* targets of discrimination. Conflicts may also have fueled popular suspicions that these converts remained Jews in secret. To make "proper" Christians out of the *conversos*, the "Most Catholic" monarchs (as they were now called) may have concluded that they needed to remove any potentially seditious influences that might stem from the continuing presence of a Jewish community in Spain.

Most of the Spanish Muslims who refused conversion initially moved to North Africa. But what became of the Jews? Some traveled north, to the towns of Germany and the Low Countries, or to Poland and eastern Europe. Most settled in Muslim regions of the Mediterranean, where many found a haven in the Ottoman Empire. As we already noted, there were many opportunities for advancement in the Ottoman imperial bureaucracy, while the Ottoman economy benefited from the highly skilled labor of Jewish artisans and the vast trading networks of Jewish merchants. In time, new forms and expressions of Jewish culture would emerge, but the descendants of these Spanish Jews—known as Sephardic Jews, or Sephardim—still treasured the traditions and customs formed in Spain over a thousand years.

THE EXTENSION OF THE *RECONQUISTA*

The Christian conquest of Granada and the expulsion of the Jews in 1492 were watershed events. They mark the beginning of a sweeping initiative to construct a unified kingdom that could transcend rival regional identities. Like other contemporary monarchs, Ferdinand and Isabella strengthened their emerging nation-state by constructing an exclusively Christian identity for its people, attaching that new identity to the crown, and promoting a single national language: Castilian Spanish. They also succeeded in capturing and redirecting another language: the rhetoric of crusade.

The crusading ethos, as we have seen, always seeks new outlets. With the creation of a new Christian kingdom through the defeat of all external enemies and internal threats, where could the energies harnessed by the *reconquista* be directed? The answer came from an unexpected quarter. Just a few months after Ferdinand and Isabella marched victoriously into Granada, the queen granted three ships to a Genoese adventurer who promised to reach India by sailing westward across the Atlantic Ocean, and to claim any new lands he found for Spain. Columbus never reached India, but he did help to extend the traditions of reconquest and crusading to the New World—with far-reaching consequences.

New Targets and Technologies of Conquest

The Spanish monarchs' decision to underwrite a voyage of exploration was spurred by their desire to counter the successful Portuguese ventures of the past half century. It was becoming clear that the tiny kingdom on the northwestern tip of the Iberian Peninsula would soon dominate the sea lanes if rivals did not find alternate routes and establish equally lucrative colonies. This competition with Portugal was another reason that Isabella turned to a Genoese sea captain—not to a Portuguese one—when she sought to expand Spain's wealth and global influence.

PRINCE HENRY THE NAVIGATOR AND PORTUGUESE COLONIAL INITIATIVES

Although Portugal had been an independent Christian kingdom since the twelfth century (Chapter 9), it was never able to compete effectively with its more powerful neighbors on land. But when the focus of European economic expansion began to shift toward the Atlantic (Chapter 10), Portuguese mariners were well placed to take advantage of this trend.

A central figure in this maritime history is **Prince Henry** (1394–1460), later called "**the Navigator**," a son of King João I of Portugal and his English queen Philippa, the sister of England's Henry IV. Prince Henry was fascinated by the sciences of cartography and navigation, and he helped to ensure that Portuguese sailors had access to the latest charts and technologies. He was also inspired by the stories told by Marco Polo and other travel writers—particularly the legend of Prester John, the mythical Christian king whom Europeans believed would be their ally against the Muslims (if only they could find him). Indeed, Prince Henry was Grand Master of a new crusading order, the Order of Christ, whose mission was to drive the Muslims out of Africa. He also had ambitions to extend Portuguese control into the Atlantic, to tap into the burgeoning market for slaves in the Ottoman Empire, and to establish direct links with sources of African gold.

Prince Henry played an important part in organizing the Portuguese colonization of Madeira, the Canary Islands, and the Azores. He also pioneered the Portuguese slave trade, which almost entirely eradicated the population of the Canaries before targeting **West Africa**. By the 1440s, Portuguese explorers had reached the Cape Verde Islands. In 1444, they landed on the African mainland, in the area that became known as the Gold Coast, where they began to collect cargoes of gold and enslaved captives for export.

Prince Henry the Navigator (1394-1460) A member of the Portuguese royal family, Henry encouraged the exploration and conquest of western Africa and the trade in gold and slaves.

West Africa The western coastal region of the African continent which had long been linked to Western civilization by trading networks, but which became, in the fifteenth century, a source of enslaved humans for trafficking.

Prince Henry personally directed eight of the thirty-five Portuguese voyages to Africa that took place during his lifetime. Also, in order to outflank the cross-Saharan gold trade, largely controlled by the Muslims of North Africa and mediated by the Genoese (Chapter 10), he decided to intercept this trade at its source by building a series of forts along the African coastline, manned by armed soldiers. By establishing these many permanent outposts, the Portuguese were also poised to dominate the global trade in enslaved Africans that would become the engine of European colonialism after 1492.

> *Under leadership of Henry, Portuguese establish permanent trading outposts in Africa*

FROM AFRICA TO INDIA AND BEYOND: AN EMPIRE OF SPICES

By the 1470s, Portuguese sailors had also rounded the western coast of Africa and were exploring the Gulf of Guinea. In 1483, they reached the mouth of the Congo River. In 1488, the Portuguese captain Bartolomeu Dias was inadvertently blown around the southern tip of Africa by a gale, after which he named the point Cape of Storms. But King João II (r. 1481–1495), taking a more optimistic view, renamed it the Cape of Good Hope and began planning a naval expedition to India. In 1497–1498, Vasco da Gama rounded the cape and then, with the help of a Muslim navigator named Ibn Majid, crossed the Indian Ocean to Calicut, on the southwestern coast of India.

This voyage opened a viable sea route between Europe and the Far Eastern spice trade for the first time. Although da Gama lost half his fleet and one-third of his men on this two-year voyage, his cargo of spices was so valuable that these losses were deemed insignificant. His heroism became the basis for the Portuguese national epic, the *Lusiads*.

Now masters of the quickest route to riches in the world, the Portuguese swiftly capitalized on their decades of accomplishment. Not only did their trading fleets sail regularly to India, they attempted to monopolize the entire spice trade. In 1509, the Portuguese defeated an Ottoman fleet and blockaded the mouth of the Red Sea, attempting to cut off one of the traditional routes by which spices traveled to Alexandria. By 1510, Portuguese forces had established a series of forts along the western Indian coastline, with headquarters at Goa. In 1511, Portuguese ships seized Malacca, a center of the spice trade on the Malay Peninsula. By 1515, they had reached the Spice Islands (Indonesia) and the coast of China.

NAVAL TECHNOLOGY AND NAVIGATION

The Portuguese caravel—the workhorse ship of those first voyages to Africa—was based on ship and sail designs that had been in use among Portuguese fishermen since the thirteenth century. Starting in the 1440s, however, Portuguese shipwrights began building larger caravels of about 50-tons' displacement and equipped with two masts, each carrying a triangular (lateen) sail. Columbus's *Niña* was a ship of this design, although it was refitted with two square sails in the Portuguese Canary Islands, to help it sail more efficiently before the Atlantic wind. Such ships required much smaller crews than did the multi-oared galleys still commonly used in the Mediterranean. By the end of the fifteenth century, even larger caravels of around 200 tons were being constructed, with a third mast and a combination of square and lateen sails.

New navigational instruments also made these voyages possible. Quadrants, which could be used to calculate latitude by the height of the North Star above the horizon, were in widespread use by the 1450s. As sailors approached the equator, however, the quadrant became less and less useful, so navigators instead used astrolabes to reckon latitude by the height of the sun. Although both of these techniques had been in use for centuries, it was not until the 1480s that they became practical instruments for seaborne navigation, thanks to the preparation of standardized tables for the calculation of latitude. Compasses, too, were coming into more widespread use. The accurate calculation of longitude, however, remained impossible until the eighteenth century, when the invention of the marine chronometer made it possible to keep accurate time at sea. In this prior age, sailors had to rely on their skill at dead reckoning to determine how far east or west they were.

These sailors also benefited from new maps and navigational charts. Printed books known as rutters or *routiers* contained detailed sailing instructions and descriptions of the coastal landmarks a pilot could expect to encounter en route to a variety of destinations. Mediterranean sailors had relied on similar information recorded on portolan charts since the thirteenth century (see Chapter 10). During the fifteenth century, mapmaking was extended to the Atlantic Ocean. By the end of the sixteenth, rutters spanned the globe.

New technologies enable surge of long-distance naval exploration

ARTILLERY AND EMPIRE

Larger, more maneuverable ships and improved navigational aids enabled Europeans to reach West Africa, Southeast Asia, and—eventually—the Americas. But fundamentally, the lasting empires established in these regions were military achievements that extended what Europeans had learned in their wars against each other. Perhaps the most critical military advance was the increasing sophistication of artillery, a development made possible not only by gunpowder but also by improved metallurgical techniques for casting cannon barrels. By the middle of the fifteenth century, as we observed in Chapter 11, the use of artillery pieces had rendered the stone walls of medieval castles and towns obsolete, a fact brought home in 1453 by the successful French siege of Bordeaux (which ended the Hundred Years' War), and by the Ottoman siege of Constantinople (which ended the Byzantine Empire).

Indeed, the new ship designs were important in part because their larger size made it possible to carry effective artillery pieces: scores of guns mounted in fixed positions along their sides and swivel guns mounted fore and aft. These guns and ships were vastly expensive, but they made it possible to back mercantile ventures with military power. Although Vasco da Gama had sailed to the Indian Ocean in 1498, the Portuguese did not control that ocean until 1509, when they defeated Ottoman and Indian naval forces. Without this essential military component, the European maritime empires that were emerging in this period could not have existed.

A NEW KIND OF RACIALIZED SLAVERY

Although chattel slavery is rarely documented in much of northwestern Europe by the early twelfth century, it continued in parts of the Mediterranean world and was actually increasing in many regions of central and eastern Europe after the Black Death. In general, medieval slavery existed on a very small scale; there were no slave-powered factories or large-scale agricultural systems in this period. The only major slave economies were in the Ottoman Empire, where slaves ran the vast bureaucracy and staffed the army. In all these cases, as in antiquity, no aspect of slavery was racially based. Most Ottoman slaves were European Christians. In the early Middle Ages, Germanic and Celtic peoples had been widely enslaved. In antiquity, slaves had come from every part of the known (and unknown) world.

What was new about the slavery of the late fifteenth century was its increasing racialization. To Europeans, West African slaves were visible in ways that other slaves were not, and it became convenient for those who dealt in them to justify the mass deportation of entire populations by claiming their racial inferiority and their "natural" fitness for a life of bondage. This nefarious ideology has had long-lasting and tragic consequences that still afflict the civilizations of our own world.

Europeans justify slavery by claiming racial superiority over Africans

In Lisbon, which became a significant market for enslaved West Africans during Prince Henry's lifetime, something on the order of 15,000 to 20,000 captives were sold within a twenty-year period. In the following half century, by about 1505, the numbers amounted to 150,000. For the most part, the purchasers of these enslaved individuals regarded them as status symbols; it became fashionable to have African footmen, pageboys, and ladies' maids. In the Atlantic colonies—Madeira, the Canaries, the Azores—land was still worked mainly by European settlers or native sharecroppers. Slave labor, if employed at all, was generally used only in sugar mills. On Madeira and the Canaries, where sugar became the predominant cash crop during the last quarter of the fifteenth century, some enslaved workers were introduced as agricultural laborers. But even sugar production did not lead to the widespread use of slavery on these islands.

However, a new kind of slave-based sugar plantation began to emerge in Portugal's Cape Verde Islands in the 1560s, and then extended southward into the Gulf of Guinea. These islands were not populated when the Portuguese began to settle them, and their climate generally discouraged Europeans from living there. They were ideally located, however, along the routes of slave traders venturing outward from the nearby West African coast. It is this plantation model that would be exported to Brazil by the Portuguese and to the Caribbean islands of the Americas by their Spanish conquerors, with incalculable human and environmental costs (see Chapter 14).

Europeans in a New World

Like his contemporaries, **Christopher Columbus** (1451–1506) understood that the world was a sphere; but he also thought it was much smaller. (As we saw in Chapter 4, the accurate calculation of the globe's circumference, done in ancient Alexandria, had been later suppressed by Roman geographers.) Furthermore, it had long been accepted that there were only three continents: Europe, Asia, and Africa; hence the hypothesis that one could reach Asia by sailing west.

The "discovery" of the Canary Islands and the Azores further suggested that the Atlantic was dotted with similar lands all the way to Japan. This emboldened Columbus's royal patrons, who were convinced that the Genoese mariner could reach China in about a month, after a stop for provisions on the Canaries. So when Columbus reached the Bahamas and the island of Hispaniola after only a month, he thought that he had reached the outer islands of Asia.

THE SHOCK OF DISCOVERY

Of course, Columbus was not the first European to set foot on an American continent. Viking sailors had briefly settled present-day Newfoundland, Labrador, and perhaps even portions of New England around the year 1000 (Chapter 8).

Christopher Columbus
(1451–1506) A Genoese sailor who persuaded King Ferdinand and Queen Isabella of Spain to fund his expedition across the Atlantic, with the purpose of discovering a new trade route to Asia. His miscalculation landed him in the Bahamas and the island of Hispaniola in 1492.

But knowledge of these landings had been forgotten or unknown outside of Iceland for hundreds of years. It wasn't until the 1960s that the stories of these expeditions were corroborated by archaeological evidence. (In 2016, a new site of Norse settlement was identified on the coast of Baffin Island.) Moreover, the tiny Norwegian colony on Greenland—technically part of the North American landmass—had been abandoned in the fifteenth century, when the cooling of the climate (Chapter 10) destroyed the fragile ecosystems that barely sustained the lives of settlers there.

Although Columbus did not return with spices to prove that he had found an alternate route to Asia, he did return with some small samples of gold and a few Indigenous people—whose existence gave promise of entire tribes that might be enslaved or "saved" by conversion to Christianity, and whose lands could provide homes for Spanish settlers seeking new frontiers after the *reconquista*. This provided sufficient incentive for the "Most Catholic" monarchs to finance three more expeditions by Columbus and many more by adventurers, missionaries, and colonists.

> *Gold, land, and Indigenous peoples (to enslave or convert) justify further Spanish exploration*

Meanwhile, the Portuguese, who had already obtained a papal decree granting them (theoretical) ownership of all lands south of the Canaries, rushed to establish their own claims. After two years of wrangling and conflicting papal pronouncements, the Treaty of Tordesillas (1494) sought to demarcate Spanish and Portuguese possession of as-yet-undiscovered lands. The Spanish would ultimately emerge as the big winners in this game of blindman's bluff: within a decade, the coasts of two hitherto unknown continents were identified, as were clusters of new islands, most on the Spanish side of the meridian.

Gradually, Europeans reached the conclusion that the voyages of Columbus and his successors had revealed an entirely "New World." And, shocking to Europeans, this world had not been foretold by either the teachings of Christianity or the wisdom of the ancients. Among the first to champion the fact of two new continents' existence was the Italian explorer and geographer Amerigo Vespucci (1454–1512), whose name was soon adopted as a descriptor for them. Eventually, those who came to accept this fact were forced to question the reliability of the key sources of knowledge on which Western civilizations had hitherto hinged (see Chapter 14).

At first, the realization that the **Americas** were not an outpost of Asia came as a disappointment to the Spanish, because it meant that two major land masses and two vast oceans disrupted their plans to beat the Portuguese to the Spice Islands. But new possibilities quickly became clear. In 1513, the Spanish explorer Vasco Núñez de Balboa first viewed the Pacific Ocean from the Isthmus of Panama, and news of the narrow divide between two vast oceans prompted Ferdinand and Isabella's grandson to renew their dream. This young monarch, Charles V (1500–1556), ruled not only Spain but also a huge patchwork of territories encompassed by the Holy Roman Empire. In 1519, he accepted Ferdinand Magellan's proposal to see whether a route to Asia could be found by sailing around South America.

Americas The name given to the two great landmasses of the New World, derived from the name of the Italian geographer Amerigo Vespucci.

Yet Magellan's voyage demonstrated beyond question that the world was simply too large for any such plan to be feasible at that time. Of the five ships that left Spain under his command, only one returned, three years later, having been forced to circumnavigate the globe. Out of a crew of 265 sailors, only 18 survived, most having died of scurvy or starvation. Magellan himself had been killed in a skirmish with native peoples in the Philippines. This fiasco ended all hope of discovering an

America as an Object of Desire

Under the influence of popular travel narratives that had circulated in Europe for centuries, Columbus and his fellow voyagers were prepared to find the New World full of cannibals. They also assumed that the Indigenous peoples' custom of wearing little or no clothing—not to mention their "savagery"—would render their women sexually available. In a letter sent back home in 1495, one of Columbus's men recounted a troubling encounter with a "cannibal girl" whom he had taken captive in his tent. He was surprised to find that she resisted his "advances"—that is, rape—so fiercely that he had to tie her up—which of course made it easier for him to "subdue" her. In the end, he cheerfully reports, the girl's sexual performance was so satisfying that she might have been trained, as he put it, in a "school for whores."

The Flemish artist Jan van der Straet (1523–1605) would have heard many such reports of the encounters between (mostly male) Europeans and the peoples of the New World. This engraving, based on one of his drawings, is among the thousands of mass-produced images that circulated widely in Europe, thanks to the invention of printing. It imagines the first encounter between a male "Americus" (such as Columbus or Amerigo Vespucci himself) and the New World "America," depicted as a voluptuous, available woman. The Latin caption reads: "America rises to meet Americus; and whenever he calls her, she will always be aroused."

Questions for Analysis

1. Study the details of this image carefully. What does each detail symbolize? How do they work together as an allegory of conquest and colonization?

2. On what stereotypes of Indigenous peoples does this image draw? Notice, for example, the cannibalistic campfire of the group in the background and the posture of "America."

3. Why is the New World itself ("America") imagined as female in this image? What messages might this—and the suggestive caption—have conveyed to a European viewer?

Americen Americus retexit, & AMERICA. *Semel vocauit inde semper excitam.*

"America rises to meet Americus; and whenever he calls her, she will always be aroused."

easy southwest passage to Asia—although the deadly dream of a northwest passage survived and motivated many European explorers of North America into the twentieth century. It has been revived today, in our age of global warming. The retreat of Arctic pack ice has led to the opening of new shipping lanes and, in 2019, a meeting of the Arctic Council in Finland revealed competing plans for a new round of colonial ventures.

THE DREAM OF GOLD AND THE DOWNFALL OF EMPIRES

Europeans were quick to capitalize on the sources of wealth that the New World could offer. What chiefly fired the imagination were those small samples of gold that Columbus had initially brought back to Spain. Although rather paltry in themselves, they nurtured hopes that gold might lie piled in ingots somewhere in these vast new lands. Rumor fed rumor, until a few freelance Spanish soldiers really did strike it rich beyond their most avaricious imaginings.

Their success, though, had little to do with their own efforts. After Columbus's first landing, European diseases had spread rapidly among the Indigenous peoples of the Caribbean and the American coastlines. These diseases—especially measles and smallpox—were not fatal to those who carried them, because Europeans had developed immunities over many generations. But to the peoples of this New World, these viruses were extremely deadly: of the 250,000 people living on Hispaniola when Columbus arrived, 70 percent had perished from disease within a generation.

Disease and brutality decimate Indigenous population in Central and South America

The ambitions of Spanish *conquistadors* (conquerors) were also assisted by the complex political, economic, and military rivalries that already existed among the sophisticated societies they encountered. The Aztec Empire of Mexico rivaled any European state in its power, culture, and wealth—and like any successful empire it had subsumed many neighboring territories in the course of its own conquests. Its capital, Tenochtitlán (*ten-och-tit-LAN*; now Mexico City), amazed its European assailants, who had never seen anything like the height and grandeur of its buildings or the splendor of its public works. This splendor was itself evidence of the Aztecs' imperial might, which was resisted by many of the peoples from whom they demanded tribute.

The Aztecs' eventual conqueror, Hernán Cortés (1485–1547), arrived in Hispaniola as a young man, in the wake of Columbus's first landing. He had received a land grant from the Spanish crown and acted as magistrate in one of the new towns established there. In 1519, he headed an expedition to the mainland, which had been the target of some earlier exploratory missions rebuffed by the Aztecs. But Cortés had the advantage, based on local knowledge provided by a native woman known as La Malinche. She became his interpreter in the Nahua language, the lingua franca among the many different ethnic groups within the empire. With her help, he discovered that some subjugated peoples were rebellious, and so he began to form alliances with their leaders.

These alliances were crucial. Although Cortés and his small force had potentially superior weapons—guns and horses—these were more effective for their novelty than their utility: gunpowder dampened by the humid climate had a tendency to misfire or fail to ignite. So Cortés adopted the tactics and weaponry of

THE AZTEC CITY OF TENOCHTITLÁN. The Spanish conquistador Bernal Díaz del Castillo (1492–1585) took part in Hernán Cortés's conquest of the Aztec Empire and later wrote an account of his adventures. His admiring description of the Aztec capital at Tenochtitlán records that the Spaniards were amazed to see such a huge city built in the midst of a vast lake, with gigantic buildings arranged in a meticulous urban plan around a central square, and broad causeways linking the city to the mainland. This hand-colored woodcut was included in an early edition of Cortés's letters to Emperor Charles V, printed at Nuremberg (Germany) in 1524.

his native allies in his dealings with the Aztec king Montezuma II (r. 1502–1520) and in his assaults on the fortifications of Tenochtitlán. In the end, though, it was European bacteria, not European technology, that secured his victory: the Aztecs were devastated by an outbreak of the plague that had arrived with Cortés and his men. In 1521, the Aztec Empire fell.

In 1533, another lucky conquistador, Francisco Pizarro, would manage to topple the highly centralized empire of the Incas, based in what is now Peru, by similar means. In this case, he took advantage of an ongoing civil war that had weakened the reigning dynasty; he was also assisted by an epidemic of smallpox. Like Cortés, Pizarro promised his native allies liberation from an oppressive regime. But the former subjects of the Aztecs and Incas would soon be able to judge how sincere these promises were.

A Spanish Critique of New World Conquest

Not all Europeans approved of European imperialism or its "civilizing" effects on the peoples of the New World. One of the most influential contemporary critics was Bartolomé de las Casas (1484–1566) of Spain. In 1502, when Bartolomé was eighteen years old, he and his father joined an expedition to Hispaniola. In 1510, he became the first ordained priest in the Americas and eventually bishop of Chiapas (Mexico). Although he was a product of his times—he owned many slaves—he was also prescient in discerning the devastating impact of European settlement in the West Indies and Central America, and he particularly deplored the exploitation and extermination of Indigenous peoples. The following excerpt is from one of the many eloquent manifestos he published in an attempt to gain the sympathies of the Spanish crown and to reach a wide readership. It was printed in 1542, but it draws on the impressions and opinions he had formed since his arrival in New Spain as a young man.

God made all the peoples of this area, many and varied as they are, as open and as innocent as can be imagined. The simplest people in the world—unassuming, long-suffering, unassertive, and submissive—they are without malice or guile, and are utterly faithful and obedient both to their own native lords and to the Spaniards in whose service they now find themselves. . . . They are innocent and pure in mind and have a lively intelligence, all of which makes them particularly receptive to learning and understanding the truths of our Catholic faith and to being instructed in virtue; indeed, God has invested them with fewer impediments in this regard than any other people on earth. . . .

It was upon these gentle lambs . . . that from the very first day they clapped eyes on them the Spanish fell like ravening wolves upon the fold, or like tigers and savage lions who have not eaten meat for days. The pattern established at the outset has remained unchanged to this day, and the Spaniards still do nothing save tear the natives to shreds, murder them and inflict upon them untold misery, suffering and distress, tormenting, harrying and persecuting them mercilessly. . . .

When the Spanish first journeyed there, the indigenous population of the island of Hispaniola stood at some three million; today only two hundred survive.

THE PRICE OF CONQUEST

In Mexico and Peru, the *conquistadors* had access to hoards of gold and silver that had been accumulated for centuries by Aztec and Inca rulers. And almost immediately, a search for the sources of these metals was launched by agents of the Spanish crown. The first gold deposits were discovered in Hispaniola, where surface mines were speedily established using enforced Indigenous laborers who were already dying in appalling numbers from disease, and who were now further decimated by brutality. The population soon dwindled to a mere 10 percent of its pre-Columbian strength.

The loss of so many workers made the mines of Hispaniola uneconomical to operate, so European colonists turned instead to livestock and sugar production. Modeling their sugarcane plantations on those of the Cape Verde Islands and St. Thomas (São Tomé) in the Gulf of Guinea, colonists began to import thousands of West African slaves to labor in the new industry. Sugar production was, by its

The island of Cuba, which extends for a distance almost as great as that separating Valladolid from Rome, is now to all intents and purposes uninhabited; and two other large, beautiful and fertile islands, Puerto Rico and Jamaica, have been similarly devastated. Not a living soul remains today on any of the islands of the Bahamas . . . even though every single one of the sixty or so islands in the group . . . is more fertile and more beautiful than the Royal Gardens in Seville and the climate is as healthy as anywhere on earth. The native population, which once numbered some five hundred thousand, was wiped out by forcible expatriation to the island of Hispaniola, a policy adopted by the Spaniards in an endeavour to make up losses among the indigenous population of that island. . . .

At a conservative estimate, the despotic and diabolical behaviour of the Christians has, over the last forty years, led to the unjust and totally unwarranted deaths of more than twelve million souls, women and children among them. . . .

The reason the Christians have murdered on such a vast scale and killed anyone and everyone in their way is purely and simply greed. . . . The Spaniards have shown not the slightest consideration for these people, treating them (and I speak from first-hand experience, having been there from the outset) not as brute animals—indeed, I would to God they had done and had shown them the consideration they afford their animals—so much as piles of dung in the middle of the road. They

have had as little concern for their souls as for their bodies, all the millions that have perished having gone to their deaths with no knowledge of God and without the benefit of the Sacraments. One fact in all this is widely known and beyond dispute, for even the tyrannical murderers themselves acknowledge the truth of it: the indigenous peoples never did the Europeans any harm whatever.

Source: Bartolomé de las Casas, *A Short Account of the Destruction of the Indies*, trans. Nigel Griffin (Harmondsworth, UK: 1992), pp. 9–12.

Questions for Analysis

1. Given his perspective on the behavior of his countrymen, how might Bartolomé de las Casas have justified his own presence in New Spain (Mexico)? What do you think he may have hoped to achieve by publishing this account?

2. What comparisons does Bartolomé make between New Spain (Mexico) and the Old, and between Indigenous peoples and Europeans? What is he trying to convey?

3. Compare this account with its contemporary print on page 435. What new light does this excerpt shine on that visual allegory? How might a reader-viewer of the time have reconciled these two very different pictures of European imperialism?

nature, a capital-intensive undertaking, and the need to import slave labor added further to its costs. This guaranteed that control over the new industry would fall into the hands of a few extremely wealthy planters and financiers.

Despite the establishment of Caribbean plantations and Mexican cattle and sheep ranching—whose devastating effects on the fragile ecosystem of Central America will be discussed in Chapter 14—it was mining that would shape the Spanish colonies most fundamentally in this period. If gold was the lure that had inspired the conquest, silver became its most lucrative export. Even before the discovery of vast silver deposits, the Spanish crown had assumed direct control over all colonial exports. It was therefore to the Spanish crown that the profits of the empire were channeled. Europe's silver shortage, which had been acute for centuries, came to an end.

Yet this massive infusion of silver created more problems than it solved, because it accelerated the monetary inflation that had already begun in the late fifteenth century. Initially, it had been driven by the renewed growth of the European population, an expanding economy, and a relatively fixed supply of food. Thereafter, thanks to the influx of New World silver, inflation was driven by the vastly increased supply of coinage, which led to the doubling and quadrupling of prices in the course of the sixteenth century and the collapse of the European economy—which paradoxically drove a wave of impoverished refugees to settle in the New World in ever greater numbers.

Conclusion

The intensified connections between the Mediterranean and the Atlantic worlds, which had accelerated in the thirteenth century, were essential to the rise of European empires in West Africa, India, and the Americas. Other events and innovations we have surveyed in this chapter played a key role, too: the rapid communications fueled by the printing press; the struggles for power that led to the development of ever deadlier weapons; the navigational and colonial initiatives of the Portuguese; and the Spanish *reconquista*, which drove Spanish rulers and adventurers to seek their fortunes overseas.

AFTER YOU READ THIS CHAPTER ⌄

CHRONOLOGY

1453–1455	Gutenberg's printed Bible completed
1488	Bartolomeu Dias rounds the Cape of Good Hope (Africa)
1492	Christopher Columbus reaches the West Indies
1494	Treaty of Tordesillas divides the New World Charles VIII of France invades Italy
1498	Vasco da Gama reaches India
1511	Erasmus publishes *The Praise of Folly*
1511	The Portuguese venture to Indonesia
1512	Michelangelo completes painting the ceiling of the Sistine Chapel
1513	Niccolò Machiavelli completes *The Prince* Vasco Núñez de Balboa reaches the Pacific Ocean
1516	Thomas More publishes *Utopia*
1519–1521	Aztec wars enable Cortés's conquest of Mexico
1519–1522	Magellan's fleet circumnavigates the globe
1531–1533	Pizarro's conquest of the Inca Empire

REVIEWING THE OBJECTIVES

❯ The artists of Italy were closely tied to those with political and military power. How did this relationship affect the kinds of work these artists produced?

❯ Which aspects of Renaissance artistry and learning were adopted in northern Europe?

❯ What was the *reconquista*, and how did it impact the Muslim and Jewish communities of the Iberian Peninsula?

❯ Europeans, especially the Portuguese, developed new technologies and techniques that enabled exploration and colonial ventures in this period. What were they? How did older ideas of slavery begin to change with the increased enslavement of peoples from West Africa?

❯ The "discovery" of the New World had profound effects on the Indigenous peoples and the environment of the Americas. Describe some of these effects.

For the enslaved West Africans and Indigenous peoples of Africa and the Americas, the results were cataclysmic. Within a century of Europeans' arrival, between 50 and 90 percent of some native populations had perished from disease, massacre, and enslavement. Moreover, competing imperial ventures profoundly destabilized Europe's already warring territories.

The ideals of the humanists and the artistry associated with the Renaissance therefore stand in sharp contrast to the harsh realities in which they were rooted. Artists could thrive in the atmosphere of competition and one-upmanship that characterized this period, but they were also compelled to subordinate their artistry to the demands of warfare, espionage, and slavery. Some humanists may have wanted to revive the principles of the Roman Republic, but many of them worked for ambitious despots who modeled themselves on Rome's dictators. Meanwhile, the theories that undergirded European politics and colonial expansion were being used to legitimize a newly racialized industry of enslavement. All of these trends would be carried forward into the sixteenth century, and would play a role in the upheaval that shattered Europe's fragile religious unity. It is to this upheaval—the Reformation—that we turn in Chapter 13.

Go to INQUIZITIVE to see what you've learned—and learn what you've missed—with personalized feedback along the way.

PEOPLE, IDEAS, AND EVENTS IN CONTEXT

❯ Why was **GUTENBERG**'s invention of the **PRINTING PRESS** such a significant development?

❯ How did **NICCOLÒ MACHIAVELLI** respond to Italy's political situation within Europe? In what ways do artists such as **LEONARDO DA VINCI** and **MICHELANGELO BUONARROTI** exemplify the ideals and realities of the Renaissance?

❯ How did northern European scholars such as **DESIDERIUS ERASMUS** and **THOMAS MORE** apply humanist ideas to Christianity? How were these ideas expressed in art?

❯ What is significant about **IVAN THE GREAT**'s use of the title **TSAR**?

❯ How did **ISABELLA OF CASTILE** and **FERDINAND OF ARAGON** succeed in creating a unified Spain through the *RECONQUISTA*?

❯ How does **PRINCE HENRY THE NAVIGATOR** exemplify the motives for pursuing overseas expansion? Why were Portuguese colonies off the coast of **WEST AFRICA** important?

❯ What were the expectations that launched **COLUMBUS**'s voyage? What enabled the Spanish **CONQUISTADORS** to subjugate the peoples of the **AMERICAS**?

THINKING ABOUT CONNECTIONS

❯ Phrases such as "Renaissance man" and "Renaissance education" are still part of our common vocabulary. Given what you have learned in this chapter, how has your understanding of such phrases changed? How would you explain their true meaning to others?

❯ How do the patterns of conquest and colonization discussed in this chapter compare with those of earlier periods, such as the era of the crusades or the empires of antiquity? How many of these developments were new?

❯ Although the growth of the West African slave trade resulted in a new racialization of slavery, the justifications for slavery had very old roots. How might Europeans have used Greek and Roman precedents to defend these new ventures (see Chapters 4 and 5)?

13

The Age of Dissent and Division, 1500–1564

IN 1517, ON THE NIGHT before the Feast of All Saints—All Hallows' Eve (or Halloween)—a professor of theology at a small university in northern Germany nailed a list of debating points to the door of Wittenberg's Castle Church. The building was part of the princely palace of the local ruler, the elector of Saxony, and it also served as the university's chapel. Despite its timing, the professor's action was not a prank; it was the usual method of announcing a scholarly disputation. Yet Martin Luther's choice of an evening associated with mischief making was appropriate, because the posting of these Ninety-Five Theses was a highly subversive act. For one thing, the sheer number of propositions that Dr. Luther offered to debate was unusual. But what really caught the attention of fellow scholars was their unifying theme: the corruption of the Roman Church and, in particular, the office of the pope. It was a topic very much in vogue at the time, but it had seldom been dissected so clearly by a licensed theologian who was also a monk, an ordained priest, and a charismatic teacher.

This document, and the wider controversy it stimulated, soon spread far beyond Wittenberg. By the time the papacy formally retaliated in 1520, religious dissent was mounting—and not only among academics. Many of Europe's rulers saw the political advantages of either defying or defending the pope, and they chose sides accordingly. Luther's own lord, Frederick III of Saxony, would spend the rest of his life shielding the man who had first expounded those theses in his own church.

BEFORE YOU READ THIS CHAPTER

>

> The movement catalyzed by Martin Luther's challenge to the Roman Church grew out of much earlier attempts at reform, but it was also a response to more recent religious and political developments.

> Within a decade of Luther's excommunication, religious dissent was widespread and a number of different Protestant faiths were taking hold in various regions of Europe.

> Forms of Protestantism transformed not only the religious and political landscape of Europe, but also basic structures of the family and attitudes toward marriage and sexuality that still shape our lives today.

> These changes also affected the structures and doctrine of the Roman Catholic ("universal") Church, which reemerged as an institution different in many ways from the medieval Church, and more similar to that of today.

CORE OBJECTIVES

> **DEFINE** the main premises of Luther's teachings.

> **EXPLAIN** why some rulers and/or regions embraced forms of Protestant Christianity and why others did not.

> **UNDERSTAND** the reasons behind England's unusual Protestant faith.

> **DESCRIBE** how the Roman Catholic Church was restructured to challenge the spread of Protestantism.

> **IDENTIFY** the ways in which family structures and values changed during the Reformation and the Catholic response to it.

Martin Luther (1483–1546) had grown up in a largely peaceful Europe. The population was rebounding, cities were growing, and warfare among the major monarchies was contained. Finally, the Roman Church had weathered the storms of the Avignon captivity and the Great Schism, and the papacy avoided being held accountable to a Church council. And yet generations of reformers prior to Luther (Chapters 11 and 12) had been loud in their condemnations of priests who were ignorant or neglectful of their spiritual duties. In the wake of the Black Death, their calls to stamp out corruption in the Church and to redistribute Church property had been eliciting passionate—and even rebellious—responses from the laity.

The debate ignited by Martin Luther set off a chain reaction we know as the Reformation. These long-festering problems were hammered home in Luther's debating points. Although initially intended as a call for another phase in the Church's long history of internal reforms, Luther's teachings instead launched a religious revolution, the **Reformation,** which splintered most of Europe into a variety of Protestant ("dissenting") faiths and prompted the Roman Church to reaffirm its status as the only true Catholic ("universal") faith. The result was also a profound transformation of the social, cultural, and political landscape that affected the lives of everyone in Europe—and many in the new European colonies.

Martin Luther and the Reformation in Germany

Although Luther began as a reformer seeking to change the Church from within, he quickly became an uncompromising opponent of it, and many of his followers were even more radical. The movement that began with Luther therefore went beyond "reformation" and instead dismantled religious, political, and social institutions that had been in place for a thousand years.

MARTIN LUTHER. This portrait by Lucas Cranach the Elder (1472–1553), the court painter to the electors of Brandenburg and a friend of Luther, was made late in Luther's life.

LUTHER'S UNDERSTANDING OF GOD'S JUSTICE

Martin Luther was the son of a German peasant who had prospered through business ventures. Eager to see his clever son rise in the world, he sent Martin to the University of Erfurt to study law. In 1505, however, Martin shattered his father's hopes by becoming a monk of the Augustinian order. But he never lost touch with his peasant roots and, indeed, his later literary successes owed a great deal to the earthy German dialect he had learned from the cradle.

As a monk, Luther zealously pursued all the traditional means for achieving holiness. Not only did he fast and pray continually, he also confessed his sins so often that his exhausted confessor reportedly joked that he should wait until he did something really bad. Still, Luther regarded himself as deeply sinful and feared that he could never perform enough good deeds to deserve salvation.

To Luther, it seemed unfair for God to issue commandments he knew humans could not observe, and to then punish them with eternal damnation. But then he had an insight that led to a new understanding of God's justice and his critique of the Church's teaching on sin. Studying the Bible, he realized that God's justice lay not in his power to punish, but in his mercy. As Luther later wrote, "I began to understand the justice of God as that by which God makes *us* just . . . and at this I felt as though I had been born again, and had gone through open gates into paradise."

Lecturing at Wittenberg in the years immediately following this realization, which occurred around 1515, Luther reached his central doctrine of "justification by faith" as he pondered a passage in Paul's letter to the Romans: "[T]he just shall live by faith" (1:17). He concluded that God's justice does not demand endless pious works and religious rituals, because humans can never attain salvation through their own weak efforts. Rather, humans are saved by God's grace—that is, by the unconditional and benevolent love of the divine being, manifested on earth by the sacrifice of Jesus Christ. God offers this grace as an utterly undeserved gift to those whom he has predestined (selected) for salvation. Men and women are therefore "justified"—made worthy of salvation—by their faith in God's grace. Works of piety and charity are signs of that faith, but they are not what saves the soul. They are merely visible signs of each believer's invisible spiritual state, which is known to God alone.

GRACE *VERSUS* INDULGENCE

The essence of Luther's doctrine was not new. In fact, it had been central to the thought of Augustine (see Chapter 6), the patron saint of Luther's own monastic order. During the twelfth and thirteenth centuries, however, theologians such as Peter Lombard and Thomas Aquinas (see Chapter 9) had developed a very different understanding of salvation. Though not discounting the importance of faith, they had emphasized the crucial role that the Church and its sacraments played in the process of salvation. In subsequent centuries, the Church had increasingly represented the process of salvation in quantitative terms. It taught that a believer could reduce the penance owed for sins—and thus the soul's time in Purgatory (Chapter 10)—by a specific number of days through performing specific actions, such as making a pilgrimage or a pious donation. These actions earned the "indulgence" of God to the degree merited by the piety of the action.

When **indulgences** were first conceptualized in the late eleventh century, they could be earned only through performing demanding spiritual exercises, such as joining a crusade. But by the end of the fourteenth century, indulgences were for sale. And a

LUTHER'S TRANSLATION OF THE BIBLE. The printing press was instrumental to the rapid dissemination of Luther's messages, as well as those of his supporters and challengers. It enabled pamphlets and vernacular Bibles such as this one to be rapidly and cheaply mass produced. Also essential was the fact that Luther addressed his audience in plain language, in their native German.

century later, when Luther was a child, the papacy had begun to claim that the purchase of indulgences could even benefit the dead, meaning that faithful men and women could purchase multiple indulgences for deceased family members or friends to reduce the number of days or years they spent in purgatory.

Long before Luther, critics of this practice argued that the sale of indulgences was scandalous, even heretical. The sin of exchanging God's grace for cash was a heresy known as simony, which had been loudly condemned by Wycliffe and his followers (Chapter 11) and later by Erasmus (Chapter 12). But Luther's objections to indulgences had much more radical consequences because they rested on a set of theological premises that, taken to their logical conclusion, resulted in dismantling much of contemporary religious practice—not to mention the authority of the Church. Luther himself does not appear to have realized this at first, but as the implications of his ideas became clear, he did not withdraw them. Instead, he pressed on.

> *Luther's central doctrine: salvation through personal faith, not ritual, doctrine, or indulgences*

THE SCANDAL OF SALVATION FOR SALE

In 1517, Luther was provoked to public action by a local abuse of spiritual power. The worldly Bishop Albert of Hohenzollern had paid a large sum for papal permission to hold the lucrative bishoprics of Magdeburg and Halberstadt concurrently—even though, at twenty-three, he was not old enough to be a bishop. When the prestigious archbishopric of Mainz fell vacant the following year, Albert bought that, too, by taking out loans from a German banking firm. He then struck a bargain with Pope Leo X (r. 1513–1521): Leo would authorize the sale of indulgences in Albert's ecclesiastical territories—where Luther lived—with the understanding that half of the income would go to Rome, where it would finance the building of the new St. Peter's Basilica; the other half would go to Albert.

Luther did not know the sordid details of this bargain, but he did know that a Dominican friar named Tetzel was soon hawking indulgences throughout the region, deliberately giving people the impression that an indulgence was an automatic ticket to heaven for oneself or one's loved ones in purgatory. Not only was Tetzel violating Luther's conviction that people are saved by God's grace alone, he was also misleading people into thinking that they no longer needed to confess their sins to a priest. In short, Tetzel was putting innocent souls at risk and extorting them.

Luther therefore focused his Ninety-Five Theses on dismantling the doctrine of indulgences. He originally wrote up these points for debate in Latin, but they were soon translated into German and published more widely. As this hitherto obscure academic gained widespread notoriety, Tetzel and his allies demanded that Luther withdraw his charges against the Church. But Luther grew bolder. In 1519, at a public disputation in Leipzig attended by throngs of people, he defiantly maintained that all clerics, even the pope, were merely fallible men and that the highest authority was the truth of scripture.

ST. PETER'S BASILICA, ROME. The construction of a new papal palace and monumental church began in 1506. This enormous complex replaced a modest, dilapidated Romanesque basilica that had replaced an even older church built on the site of the apostle Peter's tomb. **› How might contemporaries have interpreted this building project depending on their attitudes toward the papacy?**

PUBLISHING PROTESTANT TEACHINGS

In 1520, building on this argument, Luther published a series of pamphlets setting forth his three primary teachings: justification by faith, the authority of scripture, and the "priesthood of all believers." We have already examined the meaning of the first premise. His second premise meant that the Bible took precedence over all other Church traditions, including the teachings of theologians and the sacraments, and that any beliefs (such as the existence of Purgatory) or practices (such as the veneration of the saints) that were not explicitly grounded in scripture should be rejected as human inventions. Finally, Luther declared that Christian believers were spiritually equal before God, which meant that priests, monks, and nuns had no special authority—hence the "priesthood of all believers."

From these premises, a host of practical consequences logically followed. Because works could not lead to salvation, fasting, pilgrimages, and the veneration of relics were spiritually valueless, and the veneration of relics could be blasphemous. Luther thus called for the dissolution of all monasteries and convents, and advocated that religious rites be simplified, proposing the substitution of German (and other vernacular languages) for Latin and calling for a reduction in the number of sacraments from seven to two. In his view, the only true sacraments were Baptism and the Eucharist, both of which had been instituted by Christ. (He included Penance later.) Although Luther continued to believe that Christ was really present in the consecrated bread and wine, he insisted that it was only through the faith of the individual believer that this sacrament could lead to God; it was not a miraculous act performed by a priest.

To further emphasize that those who served the Church had no supernatural authority, Luther insisted on calling them ministers or pastors, rather than priests. He also proposed to abolish the entire ecclesiastical hierarchy, from pope to bishops on down. Finally, on the principle that no distinction existed between clergy and laity, he argued that ministers could and should marry. In 1525, he himself took a wife, Katharina von Bora, one of a dozen nuns whom he had helped to escape from a convent.

LUTHER'S BREAK WITH ROME

Widely disseminated in Latin and German through use of the printing press, Luther's polemical pamphlets gained him passionate popular support and touched off a religious revolt against the papacy. Whereas the average press run of a printed book before 1520 had been 1,000 copies, the first run of Luther's letter *To the Christian Nobility* (1520) was 4,000—and it sold out in a few days; many thousands of copies quickly followed. Even more popular were woodcut illustrations mocking the papacy and exalting Luther; these sold in the tens of thousands and could be readily understood even by those who could not read. (See *Interpreting Visual Evidence* on pages 448–49.)

Luther's denunciations took hold because they reflected widespread public dissatisfaction with the corruption of the papacy. Pope Alexander VI (r. 1492–1503) had bribed cardinals to gain his office and then used the money raised from the papal jubilee of 1500 to support the military campaigns of his illegitimate son, Cesare Borgia (1475–1507). His successor, Julius II (r. 1503–1513), devoted his reign to enlarging the Papal States in a series of wars. Leo X (r. 1513–1521) was a self-indulgent member of the Medici family of Florence.

In *The Praise of Folly*, first printed in 1511 and frequently reprinted (Chapter 12), Erasmus had declared that the popes of his day were incapable of leading Christlike lives. But his Latin writings reached only a select audience.

Split into principalities, Germany has weaker influence over the papacy than some other regions

Decoding Printed Propaganda

The printing press has been credited with helping to spread the teachings of Martin Luther and thus securing the success of the Protestant Reformation. But even before Luther's critiques were published, reformers were using the new technology to disseminate images that attacked the corruption of the Church. After Luther rose to prominence, both his supporters and detractors vied to disseminate propaganda that appealed visually to a lay audience and could be understood even by those who could not read.

The first pair of images below is really a single printed artifact dated to around 1500, an early example of a "pop-up" card. It shows Pope Alexander VI (r. 1492–1503) as a stately pontiff (image A) whose true identity is concealed by a flap, but when the flap is raised, he is revealed as a devil (image B). The Latin texts read: "Alexander VI, *pontifex maximus*" and "I am the pope," respectively.

The other two examples represent both sides of the debate as it had developed by 1530, and they do so with

A. Pope Alexander VI as pontiff.

B. Pope Alexander VI as a devil.

reference to the same image: the seven-headed beast mentioned in the Book of Revelation. Image C, a Lutheran engraving, shows the papacy as the beast with seven heads, representing seven orders of Catholic clergy. The sign on the cross (referring to the sign hung over the head of the crucified Christ) is in German, and reads: "For money, a sack full of indulgences"; the Latin words on either side say: "Reign of the Devil." By contrast, image D, a Catholic engraving produced in Germany, shows Luther as Revelation's beast, with its seven heads labeled: "Doctor–Martin–Luther–Heretic–Hypocrite–Fanatic–Barabbas," the last alluding to the thief who should have been executed instead of Jesus, according to the Gospels.

Questions for Analysis

1. Given that the attack on Pope Alexander VI precedes Martin Luther's critique of the Church by nearly two decades, what can you conclude about its intended audience? To what extent can it be read as a barometer of popular disapproval? What might have been the reason(s) for using the concealing flap?

2. What do you make of the fact that both Catholic and Protestant propagandists used the same imagery? What do you make of the key differences, such as the fact that the seven-headed papal beast sprouts out of an altar on which a eucharistic chalice is displayed, while the seven-headed Martin Luther is reading a book?

3. All of these printed images make use of words. Would the message of each image be clear without the texts? Why or why not?

C. The seven-headed papal beast.

D. The seven-headed Martin Luther.

Luther's doctrines (personal salvation and the importance of the Bible over traditions) lead to argument for Church simplification ❯

In Germany, resentment of the papacy ran especially high because there were no special agreements (concordats) limiting papal authority in its principalities, as there were in Spain, France, Bohemia, and England (Chapter 12). German princes complained that papal taxes were draining the country of its wealth, and yet Germans had almost no influence over papal policy. Frenchmen, Spaniards, and Italians dominated the College of Cardinals and the papal bureaucracy, and the popes were almost invariably Italian (as they would continue to be until 1978, when the Polish John Paul II was elected). As a result, graduates from the rapidly growing German and central European universities almost never found employment in Rome; instead, many joined the throngs of Luther's supporters, to become leaders of the new religious movement.

EMPEROR CHARLES V AND THE CONDEMNATION AT WORMS

In 1520, Pope Leo X issued a papal edict condemning Luther's publications as heretical and threatening him with excommunication. Luther was defiant: rather than acquiescing to the pope, he staged a public burning of the edict. As a confirmed heretic, he was formally given over to his overlord, Frederick III "the Wise" of Saxony, for punishment. Frederick, however, proved a critic of the papacy, too. Rather than burning him at the stake, he declared that Luther had not yet received a fair hearing. Early in 1521, he therefore brought Luther to the city of Worms (*VORMS*) to be examined by a select assembly known as a "diet."

THE EMPEROR CHARLES V. This portrait by the Venetian painter Titian depicts Europe's most powerful ruler sitting quietly in a chair, dressed in simple clothing of the kind worn by judges or bureaucrats. **❯ Why might Charles have chosen to represent himself this way, rather than in the regalia of his many royal, imperial, and princely offices?**

At Worms, the diet's presiding officer was the newly elected Holy Roman Emperor Charles V, a member of the Habsburg family who had been born and bred in his ancestral holding of Flanders. By 1521, through the unpredictable workings of dynastic inheritance, marriage, and election, he had become not only the ruler of the Netherlands but also the king of Germany, Holy Roman emperor, duke of Austria, duke of Milan, and ruler of the Franche-Comté. And as the grandson of Ferdinand and Isabella on his mother's side, he was also the king of Spain; king of Naples, Sicily, and Sardinia; and ruler of all the Spanish possessions in the New World.

Governing such an extraordinary combination of territories posed enormous challenges, especially since this empire had no centralized administrative institutions and shared no common language or geographically contiguous borders. Because of this diversity, Charles could not tolerate threats to the fundamental force that held it together: Catholicism, as the religion of Rome was coming to be called.

There was, therefore, little doubt that the **Diet of Worms** would condemn Martin Luther for heresy. And when Luther refused to back down, Frederick the Wise intervened once more, arranging for him to be "kidnapped" and hidden for a year at the elector's castle of the Wartburg. Although Charles proclaimed Luther an outlaw, this edict was never enforced.

THE EUROPEAN EMPIRE OF CHARLES V, c. 1526. Charles V ruled a variety of widely dispersed territories in Europe and the New World, and as Holy Roman emperor he was also the titular ruler of Germany. **› What were the main countries and kingdoms under his control? › Which regions were most threatened by Charles's extraordinary power, and where might the rulers of these regions turn to for allies? › How might the expansion of the Ottoman Empire have complicated the political and religious struggles within Christian Europe?**

A year later, in 1522, Luther returned in triumph to Wittenberg, where the changes he had called for had already been put into practice by his supporters. When several German princes formally converted to Lutheranism, they brought their territories with them. In a little over a decade, a new form of Christianity had been established.

THE GERMAN PRINCES AND THE LUTHERAN CHURCH

Ensconced in Wittenberg under princely protection, Luther began to express his political and social views more vehemently. In a treatise of 1523, he insisted that "godly" (Protestant) rulers must be obeyed in all things and that even "ungodly" ones should never be targets of dissent, because tyranny "is not to be resisted but endured." In 1524–1525, when peasants throughout Germany rebelled against

> *Spread of Lutheran religion depends on support of German princes*

Diet of Worms The select council of the Church that convened in the German city of Worms and condemned Martin Luther on a charge of heresy in 1521.

their landlords, Luther initially called for a peaceful resolution; but when the rebellion turned violent, he responded with intense hostility. In his vituperative pamphlet *Against the Thievish, Murderous Hordes of Peasants*, he urged readers to hunt the rebels down as though they were mad dogs. After the ruthless suppression of this revolt, which may have cost as many as 100,000 lives, the firm alliance of Lutheranism with state power helped preserve and sanction the existing social order. The decision of some German princes to embrace Lutheran religious practices is an important development, because popular support for Luther would not have been enough to ensure the success of his teachings. Indeed, it was only in those territories where Lutheranism was formally established that the new religion prevailed. Elsewhere in Germany, Luther's sympathizers were forced to flee, face death, or conform to Catholicism.

A long tradition of political control over religious practice >

The power of individual lords to control the practice of religion in their lands reflects developments we have noted in previous chapters. Rulers had long sought to control appointments to Church offices, to restrict the flow of money to Rome, and to limit the reach of ecclesiastical courts. But in Germany, neither the emperor nor the princes had been strong enough to secure such privileges—until Luther provided a new justification for their independence: in one of the pamphlets published in 1520, Luther explicitly encouraged German princes to confiscate the wealth of the Church. Personal convictions surely played a role in individual cases of conversion, but political and economic considerations were generally more decisive. Protestant princes could consolidate authority by naming their own religious officials, cutting off fees to Rome, and curtailing the jurisdiction of Church courts. No longer would a rival ecclesiastical prince (such as a bishop or archbishop) be able to use his spiritual office to undermine a secular prince's sovereignty.

Similar considerations also moved a number of free cities to adopt Lutheranism. Acting independently, town councils could establish themselves as the supreme governing authorities within their jurisdictions, cutting out local bishops or powerful monasteries. Given the added fact that, under Lutheranism, monasteries and convents could be shut down and their lands appropriated by the newly sovereign secular authorities, the practical advantages of the new faith were overwhelming.

The Many Forms of Protestantism

Originating as a term applied to Lutherans who "protested" Catholic rule, the word **Protestant** was soon applied to a much wider range of dissenting forms of Christianity. Lutheranism planted lasting roots in northern Germany and Scandinavia, where it became the state religion of Denmark, Norway, and Sweden as early as the 1520s. Elsewhere in Europe, competing forms of Protestantism soon emerged from the seeds Luther had sown.

Protestantism The name given to the many dissenting varieties of Christianity that emerged during the Reformation in sixteenth-century western Europe.

A LABORATORY OF DISSENT: PROTESTANTISM IN SWITZERLAND

Switzerland offers a particularly useful case study because religious affiliations differed from one independent city to another, with three main forms of Protestantism emerging between 1520 and 1550: Zwinglianism, Anabaptism, and Calvinism.

Legend:
- Church of England
- Calvinist
- Eastern Orthodox
- Lutheran
- Roman Catholic
- Hussite
- Anabaptist
- Islamic
- Boundary of the Holy Roman Empire

CONFESSIONAL DIFFERENCES, c. 1560. The religious affiliations (confessions) of Europe's territories had become very complicated by the year 1560, roughly a generation after the adoption of Lutheranism in some areas. › Which major countries and kingdoms had embraced a form of Protestantism by 1560? › To what extent do these divisions conform to political boundaries? › To what extent did the divisions complicate the political situation? › Why might Lutheranism have spread north into Scandinavia, but not south into Bavaria or west across the Rhine?

Ulrich Zwingli (1484–1531)
A former priest from the Swiss city of Zurich, Zwingli joined Luther and Calvin in attacking the authority of the Roman Catholic Church.

Anabaptists Adherents to the Protestant movement, Anabaptism, that emerged in Switzerland in 1521. They insisted that only adults could be baptized Christians.

Zwinglianism, founded in Zurich by **Ulrich Zwingli** (*TSVING-lee*; 1484–1531), was the most theologically moderate form. Zwingli had begun his career as a Catholic priest, but his humanist study of the Bible convinced him that Catholic theology conflicted with the Gospels. This eventually led him to condemn religious images and hierarchical authority. In 1522, Zwingli began attacking Rome directly, and soon some northern Swiss communities had accepted his religious leadership.

Although his reforms closely resembled those of Luther, Zwingli differed regarding the theology of the Eucharist. Whereas Luther believed in the real presence of Christ's body in the sacrament, Zwingli taught that the Eucharist was simply a reminder and celebration of Christ's historic sacrifice on the cross. This fundamental disagreement prevented Lutherans and Zwinglians from uniting in a common Protestant front.

A more radical form of Protestantism was embraced by the **Anabaptists**. Initially, these were members of Zwingli's circle in Zurich, but they broke from him on the issue of infant baptism: Anabaptists were convinced that the sacrament of Baptism was effective only when administered to willing adults who understood its significance. They accordingly required those who had been baptized as infants to be baptized again as adults (the term *Anabaptism* means "rebaptism"). This doctrine reflects the Anabaptists' fundamental belief that the true church was a small community of believers whose members had to make a deliberate, inspired decision to join it.

THE ANABAPTISTS' CAGES, THEN AND NOW. After the three Anabaptist leaders of Münster were executed in 1535, their corpses were prominently displayed in cages hung from a tower of the marketplace church. As can be seen from the photo on the right, their bones are gone, but the iron cages remain. › **What would be the purpose of keeping these cages on display?** › **What different messages might this sight convey?**

No other Protestant groups went so far in rejecting the medieval view of the Church as a single vast body to which all Christian members of society belonged from birth. And because almost everyone assumed that religious and secular authority were inextricably connected, Anabaptism was rejected by all established powers, both Protestant and Catholic. It was a movement that appealed to sincere religious piety in calling for strict personal morality and extreme simplicity of worship.

This changed when a group of Anabaptist extremists managed to gain control of the German city of Münster in 1534. These zealots were driven by millenarianism: the belief that God intends to institute a completely new order throughout the world before the end of time. Determined to help God bring about this goal, the extremists attempted to turn Münster into a new Jerusalem. A former tailor named John of Leyden assumed the title "king of the New Temple" and proclaimed himself the successor of the Hebrew king David. Under his leadership, Anabaptist religious practices were made obligatory, private property was abolished, and even polygamy was permitted, based on Old Testament precedents. Such practices were deeply shocking to Protestants and Catholics alike. Accordingly, Münster was besieged and captured by Catholic forces little more than a year after the Anabaptist takeover. The new "David," together with two of his lieutenants, was put to death by torture, and the three bodies were displayed in iron cages in the town square.

Thereafter, even moderate Anabaptists throughout Europe were ruthlessly persecuted on all sides. The few who survived banded together in the Mennonite sect, named after its founder, the Dutchman Menno Simons (c. 1496–1561). This sect, dedicated to pacifism and the simple "religion of the heart" of original Anabaptism, is still particularly strong in the central United States.

JOHN CALVIN'S REFORMED THEOLOGY

A year after the events in Münster, a twenty-six-year-old Frenchman, **John Calvin** (1509–1564), published the first version of his *Institutes of the Christian Religion*, the most influential formulation of Protestant theology ever written. Born in northern France, Calvin had originally trained for the law; by 1533, he was studying the Greek and Latin classics while living off the income from a priestly benefice. As he later wrote, he was "obstinately devoted to the superstitions of popery" until he experienced a miraculous conversion. He became a Protestant theologian and propagandist, eventually fleeing to the Swiss city of Basel to escape persecution.

Although some aspects of Calvin's early career resemble those of Luther, the two men were very different. Luther was a volatile personality and a lover of controversy. He responded to theological problems as they arose, or as the impulse struck him, and never attempted to systematize his beliefs. Calvin, however, was a cool-headed legal analyst who resolved to set forth Protestant principles comprehensively, logically, and systematically. After several revisions and enlargements, the definitive edition of *Institutes* appeared in 1559.

Calvin's austere and stoical theology starts with the omnipotence of God: the entire universe depends on the will of the Almighty, who knows all things present and to come. Because of man's original fall from grace, all human beings are sinners by nature, yet God (for reasons of his own) predestines some for eternal salvation and damns the rest. There is nothing, then, that individuals can do to alter their fate. And yet Christians cannot be indifferent to their conduct, for if they are among

John (Jean) Calvin (1509–1564) French-born theologian and reformer whose radical form of Protestantism was adopted in many Swiss cities, notably Geneva.

Calvin's essential doctrine: predestination

the elect God will implant in them the desire to live according to his laws. Upright conduct is thus a sign that an individual has been chosen, as is membership in the Reformed Church (as Calvinist churches are known). Most of all, true Christians will show themselves to be chosen instruments of God, actively fulfilling his purposes on earth and doing all that they can to prevent sin.

Calvin's religious teachings therefore diverged from those of Luther in several essentials. For Luther, a Christian should endure the trials of life through suffering; for Calvin, the world was to be mastered through unceasing labor. Calvin's religion was also more controlling: although Luther insisted that his followers attend church on Sunday, he did not demand that they refrain from all pleasure or work during the remainder of the day. Calvin, however, issued stern strictures against worldliness of any sort on the Sabbath and forbade all sorts of minor self-indulgences even on non-Sabbath days.

The two men also differed on fundamental matters of church governance and worship. Although Luther broke from the Catholic system of hierarchical church government, Lutheran district superintendents exercised some of the same powers as bishops. Luther also retained many features of traditional Christian worship, including music and ritual. Calvin, however, rejected everything that smacked of "popery" and argued for the elimination of all traces of hierarchy; each congregation should elect its own ministers, and assemblies of ministers and "elders" should govern the Reformed Church as a whole. He also insisted on the utmost simplicity in worship, prohibiting (among much else) vestments, processions, instrumental

JOHN CALVIN. This recently discovered portrait by an anonymous artist shows the young Protestant reformer as a serene and authoritative figure. It places the grotesque caricature of Calvin (right) in perspective.

CALVIN AS SEEN BY HIS ENEMIES. In this image, which circulated among Calvin's Catholic detractors, the reformer's facial features are a disturbing composite of a fish, toad, and chicken. Instead of a collar, his head rises from the pages of a heretical book.

music, and religious images of any sort. He also dispensed with all remaining vestiges of Catholic sacramental theology by making the sermon, rather than the Eucharist, the centerpiece of reformed worship. As a sign of this change, pulpits were frequently moved to the center of the church sanctuary.

CALVINISM IN GENEVA

Calvin was intent on putting his religious teachings into practice. Sensing an opportunity in the French-speaking Swiss city of Geneva—then in the throes of political and religious upheaval—he moved there in 1536 and immediately began to preach and organize. In 1538, his activities caused him to be expelled by the city council, but he returned in 1541.

With Calvin's guidance, Geneva's government became a theocracy: a society under the "rule of God." Supreme authority was vested in a "consistory," or assembly composed of twelve lay elders and between ten and twenty pastors whose weekly meetings Calvin dominated. In addition to passing legislation, the consistory's main function was to supervise morality, public and private. To this end, Geneva was divided into districts and a committee of the consistory visited every household, without prior warning, to check on the behavior of its members. Dancing, card playing, attending the theater, and working or playing on the Sabbath were all outlawed as works of the devil. Innkeepers were forbidden to allow anyone to consume food or drink without first saying grace, or to permit any patron to stay up after nine o'clock. Adultery, blasphemy, and heresy all became capital crimes, and even penalties for lesser crimes were severe. During the first four years after Calvin gained control, there were fifty-eight executions in a city whose total population was only 16,000.

As rigid as such a regime may seem today, Geneva was a beacon of light to thousands of Protestants throughout Europe. Calvin's disciple John Knox (c. 1514–1572), who brought the reformed religion to Scotland, declared Geneva the "most perfect school of Christ that ever was on earth since the days of the apostles." Converts such as Knox flocked to Geneva for refuge or instruction, and then returned home to become ardent proselytizers. Geneva thus became the center of an international movement dedicated to spreading reformed religion to the rest of Europe.

By the end of the sixteenth century, Calvinists were a majority in Scotland (where they were known as Presbyterians) and Holland (where they founded the Dutch Reformed Church). They were also influential in England, where the Church of England adopted aspects of reformed theology but not reformed worship. (Calvinists who sought further reforms were known as Puritans.) There were also substantial Calvinist minorities in France (where they were called Huguenots), Germany, Hungary, Lithuania, and Poland. By the end of the sixteenth century, Calvinism had spread to the New World.

THE BEGINNINGS OF RELIGIOUS WARFARE IN DIVIDED EUROPE

Less than a generation after Luther's challenge to the Church, wars between Catholic and Protestant rulers began. In Germany, Charles V launched a military campaign against several German princes who had instituted Lutheran worship; but despite

With Calvin's influence, Geneva's laws make Protestant ideals into law

several notable victories, his efforts to defeat the Protestant princes failed because their Catholic counterparts worked against him, fearing that any suppression of Protestant princes might diminish their own independence. Meanwhile, the French were also at war with Charles and looked beyond Christian Europe to form a powerful alliance with the Muslim sultan Suleiman the Magnificent (r. 1520–1566), who brought the Ottoman Empire into the military and diplomatic sphere of Europe.

Religious warfare in various regions was intermittent until a compromise settlement was reached via the Peace of Augsburg in 1555. Its governing principle was *cuius regio, eius religio* ("as the ruler, so the religion"). This meant that, in those principalities where Lutherans ruled, Lutheranism would be the sole state religion; where Catholic princes ruled, the people of their territories would be Catholic. In some regions, this rule was not needed or enforced, because local rulers permitted religious diversity. In Transylvania, a province under the overlordship of Hungary (now in Romania), Catholics lived alongside three different Protestant groups in relative peace. In Poland, Lithuania, and Ukraine, Eastern Orthodox Christianity expanded its influence alongside Catholicism and was eventually tolerated. But these were rare exceptions.

For better and for worse, the Peace of Augsburg was a historical milestone. For the first time since Luther had been excommunicated, Catholic rulers were forced to acknowledge the legality of Protestantism. Yet the peace set a dangerous precedent, because it seemed to establish the premise that no sovereign state can tolerate religious diversity. Moreover, it excluded Calvinism entirely and thus spurred German and Scottish Calvinists to become aggressive opponents of the status quo. As a result, Europe was riven by religious warfare for another century and exported that sectarian violence to the New World (see Chapter 14).

Peace of Augsburg guarantees political rulers could determine state religion

The Domestication of Reform

Within two decades, Protestantism had become a diverse revolutionary movement whose underlying claims for the spiritual equality of all Christians had the potential to undermine the political, social, and even gender hierarchies on which European society rested. Luther himself did not anticipate that his ideas might have such implications, and most other prominent Protestant leaders were also reluctant to relinquish the support of existing elites by embracing more radical reforms. As a result, the Reformation movement was speedily "domesticated" in two senses: its revolutionary potential was toned down, and there was an increasing emphasis on the patriarchal family as the central institution of Protestant life.

REFORM AND DISCIPLINE

As we have seen, injunctions to lead a more disciplined and godly life had been a frequent message of previous religious reform movements, especially after the Black Death (Chapter 11). Many of these efforts had been actively promoted by princes and town councils, most famously perhaps in Florence, where the Dominican preacher Girolamo Savonarola led the city on an extraordinary but short-lived campaign of puritanism and moral reform between 1494 and 1498. And there are numerous other examples of rulers legislating against sin. When Erasmus called on secular authorities to think of their territories as giant monasteries, he was sounding an already familiar theme.

Protestant rulers, however, took the need to enforce godly discipline with particular seriousness because the depravity of human nature was a fundamental tenet of Protestant belief. Like Saint Augustine at the end of the fourth century (Chapter 6), they believed that people would inevitably turn out to be bad unless they were compelled to be good. It was therefore the responsibility of secular and religious leaders to control and punish the misbehavior of their people, because otherwise their evil deeds would anger God and destroy human society.

Protestant godliness began with the discipline of children. Luther himself wrote two catechisms (instructional tracts) designed to teach children the tenets of their faith and the obligations—toward parents, masters, and rulers—that God imposed on them. Luther also insisted that all children, boys and girls alike, be taught to read the Bible in their own languages. Schooling thus became a characteristically Protestant preoccupation and rallying cry. Even the Protestant family was designated a "school of godliness," in which fathers were expected to instruct and discipline their wives, children, and household servants.

But family life in the early sixteenth century still left much to be desired in the eyes of Protestant reformers. Drunkenness, domestic violence, illicit sexual relations, dancing, and blasphemous swearing were frequent topics of reforming discourse. Various methods of discipline were attempted, including public confessions of wrongdoing, public penance and shaming, exclusion from church services, and even imprisonment. All of these efforts met with varying, but generally modest, success. Creating godly Protestant families and enforcing discipline within entire communities were going to require the active cooperation of the authorities.

> *Protestant reformers target family life in moral crusade to create godly discipline*

NEW REGIMES OF RELIGIOUS DISCIPLINE

The domestication of the Reformation took place principally in the free towns of Germany, Switzerland, and the Netherlands. Here, Protestant attacks on monasticism and clerical celibacy also found a receptive audience because citizens resented the immunity of monastic houses from taxation and regarded clerical celibacy as a subterfuge for the seduction of their own wives and children. Protestant emphasis on the depravity of the human will also resonated powerfully with guilds and town governments, which were anxious to maintain and increase the control exercised by urban elites (merchants and master craftsmen) over the apprentices and journeymen who made up the majority of the male population. Protestant town governments could thus consolidate all public authority into their own hands.

Meanwhile, Protestant authorities reinforced the domestic power of men by emphasizing the family as the basic unit of religious education. In place of a priest, an all-powerful father figure was expected to assume responsibility for instructing and disciplining his household according to the precepts of reformed religion. At the same time, Protestant regimes introduced a new religious ideal for women. No longer was the virginal nun the exemplar of female holiness; in her place stood the obedient Protestant "goodwife." As one Lutheran prince wrote in 1527, "Those who bear children please God better than all the monks and nuns singing and praying." To some extent, then, Protestantism resolved the tensions between piety and sexuality that had long characterized Christian teachings, by declaring the holiness of marital sex.

But this did not promote a progressive view of women's spiritual potential or elevate their social and political status. Quite the contrary: Luther regarded women

Marriage and Celibacy: Two Views

These two selections illustrate strong contrasting views on the spiritual value of marriage versus celibacy as embraced by Protestant and Catholic religious authorities. The first selection is part of Martin Luther's more general attack on monasticism, which emphasizes his contention that marriage is the natural and divinely intended state for all human beings. The second selection, from the canons of the Council of Trent (1545–1563), restates traditional Church teaching on the holiness of marriage but also emphasizes the spiritual superiority of virginity to marriage and the necessity of clerical celibacy. Celibacy for all clergy (not only monks and nuns) had been instituted for the first time in the eleventh century (Chapter 8), but it had never been fully accepted, especially in Britain and Scandinavia, or universally practiced.

Luther's Views on the Impossibility of Celibacy (1535)

Listen! In all my days I have not heard the confession of a nun, but in the light of Scripture I shall hit upon how matters fare with her and know I shall not be lying. If a girl is not sustained by great and exceptional grace, she can live without a man as little as she can without eating, drinking, sleeping, and other natural necessities. Nor, on the other hand, can a man dispense with a wife. The reason for this is that procreating children is an urge planted as deeply in human nature as eating and drinking. That is why God has given and put into the body the organs, arteries, fluxes, and everything that serves it. Therefore what is he doing who would check this process and keep nature from running its desired and intended course? He is attempting to keep nature from being nature, fire from burning, water from wetting, and a man from eating, drinking, and sleeping.

Source: E. M. Plass, ed., *What Luther Says*, vol. 2 (St. Louis, MO: 1959), pp. 888–89.

Church Canons on the Sacrament of Matrimony (1563)

CANON 1: If anyone says that matrimony is not truly and properly one of the seven sacraments . . . instituted by Christ the Lord, but has been devised by men in the Church and does not confer grace, let him be anathema [cursed]. . . .

CANON 9: If anyone says that clerics constituted in sacred orders or regulars [monks and nuns] who have made solemn profession of chastity can contract marriage . . . and that all who feel that they have not the gift of chastity, even though they have made such a vow, can contract marriage, let him be anathema, since God does not refuse that gift to those who ask for it rightly, neither does he suffer us to be tempted above that which we are able.

CANON 10: If anyone says that the married state excels the state of virginity or celibacy, and that it is better and happier to be united in matrimony than to remain in virginity or celibacy, let him be anathema.

Source: H. J. Schroeder, *Canons and Decrees of the Council of Trent* (St. Louis, MO: 1941), pp. 181–82.

Questions for Analysis

1. On what grounds does Luther attack the practice of celibacy? Do you agree with his basic premise? Why or why not?

2. How do the canons of the Catholic Church respond to Protestant views such as Luther's? What appears to be at stake in this defense of marriage and celibacy?

as even more sexually depraved than men, and less capable of controlling their desires. His opposition to convents rested on his belief that it was impossible for women to remain chaste, so sequestering them simply made illicit behavior inevitable. To prevent sin, it was necessary that all women be married, preferably at a young age, and placed under the governance of a godly husband.

For the most part, Protestant town governments were happy to cooperate in shutting down female monasteries, since a convent's property then went to the town. But conflicts did arise between Protestant reformers and town fathers over marriage and sexuality, especially over the reformers' insistence that both men and women should marry young as a restraint on lust. In many towns, men were traditionally expected to delay marriage until they had achieved the status of master craftsman—an expectation that had become increasingly difficult to meet, as guilds sought to restrict the number of journeymen permitted to become masters. In theory, then, apprentices and journeymen were not supposed to marry, but instead were expected to frequent brothels and taverns—a legally sanctioned outlet for extramarital sexuality long viewed as necessary to men's physical well-being—which Protestant reformers now deemed morally abhorrent.

Towns responded to these opposing pressures in various ways. Some instituted special committees to police public morals, as in Calvin's Geneva. Some abandoned the legislation of Protestant reforms altogether. And others, such as the German town of Augsburg, alternated between Protestant and Catholic governance for several decades. Yet regardless of a town's religious allegiance, a revolution had taken place with respect to public morality by the end of the sixteenth century. For in their competition with each other, neither Catholics nor Protestants wished to be seen as soft on sin. The result was the widespread closing of publicly licensed brothels, the outlawing of prostitution, and far stricter supervision of many other aspects of private life than had ever been the case in any Western civilization.

THE CONTROL OF MARRIAGE

Protestant reforming movements also increased parents' control over their children's choice of marital partners. The medieval Church had defined marriage as a sacrament, but one that did not require the involvement of a priest: the mutual consent of two individuals, even if exchanged without witnesses or parental approval, was enough to constitute a legally valid marriage. Opposition to this doctrine had long come from wealthy families, because marriage involved rights of inheritance to property; it was regarded as too important to be left to the choice of unsupervised adolescents. Instead, elite parents wanted the power to prevent unsuitable matches and, in some cases, to force their children to accept the marriage arrangements their families might negotiate on their behalf. For such elites, Protestantism offered an opportunity to obtain this control. Luther had declared marriage to be a purely secular matter, not a sacrament at all, and one that could be regulated however governing authorities thought best. Calvin largely followed suit.

Even the Catholic Church was eventually forced to give way. Although it never abandoned its insistence that both members of a couple must freely consent, the Church's new doctrine required formal public notice of intent to marry and insisted on the presence of a priest at the wedding ceremony. Both rules were efforts to prevent clandestine marriages and to allow families time to intervene before an unsuitable match was concluded. Individual Catholic countries sometimes went even further in asserting parental control: in France, for example, couples who married without parental consent forfeited their rights to inherit property.

In somewhat different ways then, both Protestantism and Catholicism moved to strengthen the control parents could exercise over their children, and husbands over their wives. Both confessions also empowered the state to exercise an unprecedented degree of control over the bodies and individual choices of all people.

The Reformation in England

In England, the Reformation took a rather different course than it did in continental Europe. Although a long tradition of popular dissent paved the way for Protestant ideas, England was not particularly oppressed by the papal abuses that roiled Germany, and English monarchs already exercised a great deal of control over Church appointments and received the lion's share of papal taxes. Even the power of ecclesiastical courts did not inspire any particular resentments; on the contrary, these courts would continue to function in Protestant England until the eighteenth century. Why, then, did England become a Protestant country at all?

"THE KING'S GREAT MATTER"

HENRY VIII OF ENGLAND. Hans Holbein the Younger executed several portraits of the English king. This one depicts him in middle age, confident of his powers.

In 1527, King **Henry VIII** of England (r. 1509–1547) had been married to Ferdinand and Isabella's daughter, Catherine of Aragon, for eighteen years. Yet all the offspring of this union had died in infancy, with the exception of a daughter, Mary. Because Catherine was now past childbearing age and Henry needed a male heir to preserve the peaceful succession to the throne, he had political reasons to propose a change of wife. He also had a more personal motive, having become infatuated with a courtier named Anne Boleyn.

Henry therefore appealed to Rome to annul his marriage to Catherine, arguing that because she had previously been married to his older brother Arthur, who had died in adolescence, his marriage to Catherine had been invalid from the beginning. As Henry's representatives pointed out, the Bible pronounced it "an unclean thing" for a man to marry his brother's wife and cursed such a marriage with childlessness (Leviticus 20:21). Even a papal dispensation, which Henry and Catherine had obtained, could not exempt them from such a clear prohibition—as their childless marriage proved.

Henry's petition put Pope Clement VII (r. 1523–1534) in an awkward position. Popes had long granted annulments to reigning monarchs on far weaker grounds. But if the pope granted Henry's annulment, he would cast doubt on the validity of all papal dispensations. More seriously, he would provoke the wrath of Emperor Charles V, Catherine of Aragon's nephew, whose armies were in firm command of Rome and who at that moment held the pope himself in captivity. Clement was trapped; all he could do was procrastinate and hope that the matter would resolve itself. For two years, he allowed Henry's case to proceed in England without reaching a verdict. Then, suddenly, he transferred the case to Rome, where the legal process began all over again.

Exasperated by these delays, Henry began to increase pressure on the pope. In 1531, he compelled an assembly of English clergy to declare him "protector and only supreme head" of the Church in England. In 1532, he encouraged Parliament to produce an inflammatory list of grievances against the English clergy and used this threat to force their concession to his right, as king, to approve or deny all Church legislation. In January 1533, Henry married Anne Boleyn (already pregnant) even though his marriage to Catherine had still not been annulled. The new archbishop of Canterbury, Thomas Cranmer, later provided the required annulment in May, acting on his own authority.

In September, Princess Elizabeth was born; her father, disappointed again in his hopes for a son, refused to attend her christening. Nevertheless, Parliament settled the succession to the throne on the children of Henry and Anne, redirected all papal revenues from England into the king's hands, prohibited appeals to the papal court, and formally declared the "King's Highness to be Supreme Head of the Church of England" in 1534. In 1535, Henry executed his former tutor and chancellor, Sir Thomas More (Chapter 12), for his refusal to endorse this declaration of supremacy, and he took steps toward dissolving England's many monasteries. By the end of 1539, these monasteries and convents were emptied and their lands and wealth confiscated by the king, who distributed their properties and revenues to reward his supporters and appease his potential enemies.

These measures, masterminded and engineered by Henry's Protestant adviser Thomas Cromwell (c. 1485–1540), broke the bonds that linked the English Church to Rome. But they did not make England a wholly Protestant country. Although certain traditional practices (such as pilgrimages and the veneration of relics) were prohibited, the **Church of England** remained overwhelmingly Catholic in organization, doctrine, ritual, and language. The Six Articles promulgated by Parliament in 1539 at Henry VIII's behest left no room for doubt as to the official orthodoxy: confession to priests, masses for the dead, and clerical celibacy were all confirmed; the Latin Mass continued; and Catholic eucharistic doctrine was not only confirmed but its denial was made punishable by death. To most English people, only the disappearance of the monasteries and the king's own continuing matrimonial adventures (he married six women in all) were evidence that their Church was no longer in communion with Rome.

THE BRIEF REIGN OF EDWARD VI AND THE RETURN TO CATHOLIC RULE UNDER MARY

For truly committed Protestants, the changes Henry VIII enforced on the English Church did not go nearly far enough. And in 1547, the accession of the nine-year-old king Edward VI (Henry's son by his third wife, Jane Seymour) gave them the opportunity to finish the task of reform. Henry's last wife, Catherine Parr, was a Lutheran sympathizer and, as the teacher of the royal children, contributed greatly to further reforms that stripped many Roman practices from the English Church. Edward's government permitted priests to marry; English services replaced Latin ones; the veneration of images was discouraged and the images themselves were defaced or destroyed; prayers for the dead were declared useless, and endowments for such prayers confiscated; and new articles of belief repudiated all sacraments

> *Henry declares a new Church of England with himself as spiritual leader*

Church of England
Founded by Henry VIII in the 1530s as a consequence of his break with the authority of the Roman pope.

The Six Articles of the English Church

Although Henry VIII withdrew the Church of England from obedience to the papacy, he continued to reject most Protestant theology. Some of his advisers, most notably Thomas Cromwell, were committed Protestants, and the king allowed his son and heir, Edward VI, to be raised as a Protestant. But even after several years of rapid (and mostly Protestant) change in the English Church, Henry reasserted a set of traditional Catholic doctrines in the Six Articles of 1539. These remained binding on the Church of England until the king's death in 1547.

First, that in the most blessed sacrament of the altar, by the strength and efficacy of Christ's mighty word, it being spoken by the priest, is present really, under the form of bread and wine, the natural body and blood of our Savior Jesus Christ, conceived of the Virgin Mary, and that after the consecration there remains no substance of bread or wine, nor any other substance but the substance of Christ, God and man;

Secondly, that communion in both kinds is not necessary for salvation, by the law of God, to all persons, and that it is to be believed and not doubted . . . that in the flesh, under the form of bread, is the very blood, and with the blood, under the form of wine, is the very flesh, as well apart as though they were both together;

Thirdly, that priests, after the order of priesthood received as afore, may not marry by the law of God;

Fourthly, that vows of chastity or widowhood by man or woman made to God advisedly ought to be observed by the law of God;

Fifthly, that it is right and necessary that private masses be continued and admitted in this the king's English Church and congregation . . . whereby good Christian people . . . do receive both godly and goodly consolations and benefits; and it is agreeable also to God's law;

Sixthly, that oral, private confession is expedient and necessary to be retained and continued, used and frequented in the church of God.

Source: *Statutes of the Realm*, vol. 3 (London: 1810–1828), p. 739 (modernized).

Questions for Analysis

1. Three of these six articles focus on the sacrament of the Eucharist (the Mass). Given what you have learned in this chapter, why would Henry have been so concerned about this sacrament? What does this reveal about his values and those of his contemporaries?

2. Given Henry's insistence on these articles, why might he have allowed his son to be raised a Protestant? What does this suggest about the political situation in England?

except Baptism and Communion, affirming the Protestant creed of justification by faith alone. Most important, *The Book of Common Prayer* by Archbishop Cranmer, considered one of the great landmarks of English literature, defined precisely how the new English-language services of the church were to be conducted.

Yet Edward's reign was brief and his successor was his much older half sister Mary (r. 1553–1558): a committed Catholic and granddaughter of the "Most Catholic" Ferdinand and Isabella. Mary speedily reversed her half brother's religious policies, restoring the Latin Mass and requiring married priests to give up their wives. She even prevailed on Parliament to vote for England's return to papal allegiance. Hundreds of Protestant leaders fled abroad, many to Geneva; others, including Archbishop Cranmer, were burned at the stake for refusing to abjure their

QUEEN MARY AND QUEEN ELIZABETH. The two daughters of Henry VIII, Queen Mary (left) and Queen Elizabeth (right), were the first two queens regnant of England; that is, the first women to rule in their own right. Despite the similar challenges they faced, they had strikingly different fates and have been treated very differently in popular histories. **› How do these two portraits suggest differences in the queens' personalities and their self-representation as rulers?**

Protestantism. News of the martyrdoms shocked Protestant Europe, but Mary's policies sparked relatively little resistance in England. After two decades of religious upheaval, most English men and women were probably hoping that Mary's reign would bring some stability to their lives.

This, however, Mary could not do. The executions she ordered were insufficient to wipe out religious resistance; instead, Protestant propaganda about "Bloody Mary" caused widespread unease, even among those who welcomed the return of traditional religious forms. She also could not restore monasticism, because too many leading families had profited from Henry VIII's dissolution for her to reverse this policy. Mary's marriage to her cousin Philip, Charles V's son and heir to the Spanish throne, was another miscalculation. Although the marriage treaty stipulated that Philip could not succeed her, in the event of her death, her English subjects never trusted him. When she allowed herself to be drawn by Philip into a war with France on Spain's behalf—in which England lost Calais, its last foothold on the European continent—many became highly disaffected.

Ultimately, however, what doomed Mary's policies was an accident of biology: she was unable to conceive an heir. When she died after only five years of rule, her throne passed to her Protestant half sister, Elizabeth.

THE ELIZABETHAN SETTLEMENT

The daughter of Henry VIII and Anne Boleyn, Elizabeth (r. 1558–1603) was predisposed in favor of Protestantism by the circumstances of her parents' marriage as well as by her upbringing. But Elizabeth also recognized that supporting radical Protestantism in England might provoke bitter sectarian strife. Accordingly, she presided over what is often known as the "Elizabethan settlement" or compromise. By a new Act of Supremacy (1559), she repealed Mary's Catholic legislation, prohibiting foreign religious powers (the pope) from exercising any authority within England and declaring herself "supreme governor" of the English Church—a more Protestant title than Henry VIII's "supreme head," since most Protestants believed that Christ alone was the head of the Church. She also adopted many of the Protestant liturgical reforms instituted by her half brother Edward, including Cranmer's revised version of *The Book of Common Prayer*.

In Act of Supremacy, Elizabeth brings back Anglican Church in a slightly more Protestant form

But Elizabeth retained vestiges of Catholic practice, too, including the hierarchy of bishops, church courts, and many liturgical rites. Still, religious tensions persisted, not only between Protestants and Catholics but also between moderate and more extreme Protestants. On the one hand, the queen was obliged to continue Mary's practice of persecuting notorious heretics—in this case, Catholics who refused to practice their faith discreetly—and executing them for treason. On the other hand, her attempts to promote a "middle way" among competing forms of Christianity caused dissatisfaction among hard-liners of all stripes.

In the long run, what preserved the "Elizabethan settlement" was the extraordinary length of the queen's reign and the fact that, for much of that time, Protestant England was at war with Catholic Spain. Under Elizabeth, Protestantism and English forms of nationalism gradually fused into a potent conviction that God himself had chosen England for greatness. After 1588, when English naval forces won an improbable victory over the Spanish Armada (see Chapter 14), Protestantism and Englishness became nearly indistinguishable. Laws against Catholic practices became increasingly severe, and although an English Catholic tradition survived, its adherents were a small minority. In Ireland, where the vast majority of people remained Catholic despite the government's efforts to impose Protestantism, Irishness would be as firmly identified with Catholicism as was Englishness with Protestantism—but it was the Protestants who were in power in both countries.

The Rebirth of the Roman Catholic Church

So far, our account of Protestantism has cast the spotlight on dissident reformers such as Luther and Calvin. But there was also a powerful reform movement within the Church during the same decades, which resulted in the birth (or rebirth) of a Catholic ("universal") faith. For some, this movement is the "Catholic Reformation"; for others, it is the "**Counter-Reformation**." Those who prefer the former term emphasize that the Church was continuing significant reforming movements that can be traced back to the eleventh century (Chapter 8) and that gained new

Counter-Reformation The movement to counter the Protestant Reformation, initiated by the Catholic Church at the Council of Trent in 1545.

momentum in the wake of the Great Schism (Chapter 11). Others insist that most Catholic reformers of this period were reactionaries, inspired primarily by the urgent need to resist Protestantism and strengthen the power of the Roman Church in opposition.

CATHOLIC REFORMS

Even before Luther's challenge, there was a strong movement for moral and institutional reform within the Church, as we have seen. And while the papacy showed little interest in these efforts, they were receiving new support from several secular rulers. In Spain, for example, reforming activities directed by Cardinal Francisco Jiménez de Cisneros (1436–1517) were designed to eliminate abuses prevalent among the clergy. Jiménez (*he-MEN-ez*) also helped to regenerate the spiritual life of the Spanish Church. In Italy, earnest clerics labored to make the Italian Church more worthy of its prominent position despite the poor example set by the papal court. Some new religious orders, dedicated to high ideals of piety and social service, were also emerging. In northern Europe, Christian humanists such as Erasmus and Thomas More played a role in this Catholic reform movement (Chapter 12).

These internal measures were inadequate, however, as a response to the concerted challenges of Protestantism. Starting in the 1530s, therefore, a more aggressive phase of reform began to gather momentum under a new style of vigorous papal leadership. The Counter-Reformation popes Paul III (r. 1534–1549), Paul IV (r. 1555–1559), Pius V (r. 1566–1572), and Sixtus V (r. 1585–1590) were the most zealous reformers of the Church since the eleventh century. All led upright lives; some, indeed, were so grimly ascetic that contemporaries longed for the bad old days. And these Counter-Reformation popes were not merely holy men but also accomplished administrators, reorganizing papal finances and filling ecclesiastical offices with bishops and abbots who were no less renowned for austerity and holiness than the popes themselves.

Papal reform efforts were consolidated at the **Council of Trent**, a general meeting of the entire Church convened in 1545 and continuing at intervals until 1563. The decisions made at Trent, a provincial capital of the Holy Roman Empire (Trento in modern-day Italy), provided the foundations on which a new Roman Catholic Church would be erected. Although the council began by debating some form of compromise with Protestantism, it ended by reaffirming all the Catholic tenets challenged by Protestant critics. "Good works" were affirmed as necessary for salvation and all seven sacraments were declared indispensable, without which salvation was impossible. Transubstantiation, purgatory, the invocation of saints, and the discipline of

THE INSPIRATION OF SAINT JEROME, BY GUIDO RENI (1635). The Council of Trent declared Saint Jerome's Latin translation of the Bible, the Vulgate, to be the Catholic Church's official version. Biblical scholars had known since the early sixteenth century that Saint Jerome's translation contained numerous mistakes, so Catholic defenders of the Vulgate insisted that even his mistakes had been divinely inspired. **› How does this painting attempt to make this point?**

celibacy for the clergy were all confirmed as dogmas—essential elements—of the Catholic faith. The Bible, in its imperfect Vulgate translation (not the critical edition of Erasmus, Chapter 12), and the traditions of apostolic teaching were held to be of equal authority. Papal supremacy over every bishop and priest was expressly maintained, and the supremacy of the pope over any Church council was declared outright, signaling a final defeat of the still-active conciliar movement (Chapter 11). The Council of Trent even reaffirmed the doctrine of indulgences that had touched off the Lutheran revolt, although it condemned the worst abuses connected with their sale.

The decrees issued at Trent were not confined to matters of doctrine. To improve pastoral care of the laity, bishops and priests were forbidden to hold more than one spiritual office. To address concerns that priests were not sufficiently prepared for their tasks, a theological seminary was to be established in every diocese. The council also suppressed a variety of local religious practices and saints' cults, replacing them with new cults authorized and approved by Rome. To prevent heretical ideas from corrupting the faithful, the council further decided to censor or suppress dangerous books.

Seeking to maintain purity of Catholic doctrine, Council of Trent turns to censorship

In 1564, a specially appointed commission published the first *Index of Prohibited Books*, an official list of writings forbidden to Catholics. It is ironic that all of Erasmus's works were immediately placed in the *Index*, even though he had been a champion of the Church against Martin Luther only forty years before. A permanent agency known as the Sacred Congregation of the Index was later set up to revise the list, which was maintained until 1966, when it was abolished after the Second Vatican Council (1962–1965). For centuries, it symbolized the doctrinal intolerance that characterized much of sixteenth-century Christianity, in both Catholic and Protestant varieties.

IGNATIUS LOYOLA AND THE SOCIETY OF JESUS

Another force propelling the Counter-Reformation was the foundation of the **Society of Jesus** (commonly known as the Jesuits) by **Ignatius Loyola** (1491–1556). In the midst of a career as a mercenary, this young Spanish nobleman had been wounded in battle in 1521: the same year in which Luther defied authority at the Diet of Worms. While recuperating, he turned from the reading of chivalric romances to a romantic retelling of the life of Jesus. The impact of this experience convinced him to become a spiritual soldier of Christ.

For ten months, Ignatius lived as a hermit in a cave near the town of Manresa, where he experienced ecstatic visions and worked out the principles of his subsequent guidebook, the *Spiritual Exercises*. This manual, completed in 1535 and first published in 1541, offered practical advice on how to master one's will and serve God through a systematic program of meditations on sin and on the life of Christ. It eventually became the basic handbook for all Jesuits and has been widely studied by Catholic laypeople, as well. Indeed, Loyola's *Spiritual Exercises* ranks alongside Calvin's *Institutes* as the most influential religious text of the sixteenth century.

The Jesuit order originated as a group of six disciples who gathered around Loyola during his belated career as a student in Paris. Vowing to serve God in

Society of Jesus The religious order commonly known as the Jesuits, founded in 1540 by Ignatius Loyola to combat the spread of Protestantism.

Ignatius Loyola (1491-1556) Founder of the Society of Jesus (commonly known as the Jesuits), whose members vowed to serve God through poverty, chastity, and missionary work.

The Demands of Obedience

*The necessity of obedience in the spiritual formation of monks and nuns can be traced back to the **Rule of Saint Benedict** in the early sixth century. In keeping with the mission of its founder, Ignatius of Loyola (1491–1556), the Society of Jesus brought renewed fervor to this old ideal, dedicating its members to superior intellectual achievements, teaching, and missionary work. Below are excerpts from two of the order's founding texts, the **Spiritual Exercises of Ignatius** and the Jesuit Constitutions.*

Rules for Thinking with the Church

1. Always to be ready to obey with mind and heart, setting aside all judgment of one's own, the true spouse of Jesus Christ, our holy mother, our infallible and orthodox mistress, the Catholic Church, whose authority is exercised over us by the hierarchy.

2. To commend the confession of sins to a priest as it is practised in the Church; the reception of the Holy Eucharist once a year, or better still every week, or at least every month, with the necessary preparation. . . .

* * *

4. To have a great esteem for the religious orders, and to give the preference to celibacy or virginity over the married state. . . .

* * *

6. To praise relics, the veneration and invocation of Saints: also the stations, and pious pilgrimages, indulgences, jubilees, the custom of lighting candles in the churches, and other such aids to piety and devotion. . . .

* * *

9. To uphold especially all the precepts of the Church, and not censure them in any manner; but, on the contrary, to defend them promptly, with reasons drawn from all sources, against those who criticize them.

10. To be eager to commend the decrees, mandates, traditions, rites, and customs of the Fathers in the Faith or our superiors. . . .

11. That we may be altogether of the same mind and in conformity with the Church herself, if she shall have defined anything to be black which to our eyes appears to be white, we ought in like manner to pronounce it to be black. For we must undoubtingly believe, that the Spirit of our Lord Jesus Christ, and the Spirit of the Orthodox Church His Spouse, by which Spirit we are governed and directed to salvation, is the same. . . .

From the Constitutions of the Jesuit Order

Let us with the utmost pains strain every nerve of our strength to exhibit this virtue of obedience, firstly to the Highest Pontiff, then to the Superiors of the Society; so that in all things . . . we may be most ready to obey his voice, just as if it issued from Christ our Lord . . . leaving any work, even a letter, that we have begun and have not yet finished; by directing to this goal all our strength and intention in the Lord, that holy obedience may be made perfect in us in every respect, in performance, in will, in intellect; by submitting to whatever may be enjoined on us with great readiness, with spiritual joy and perseverance; by persuading ourselves that all things [commanded] are just; by rejecting with a kind of blind obedience all opposing opinion or judgment of our own.

Source: Henry Bettenson, ed., *Documents of the Christian Church*, 2nd ed. (Oxford: 1967), pp. 259–61.

Questions for Analysis

1. How might Loyola's career as a soldier have inspired the language used in his "Rules for Thinking with the Church"?

2. In what ways do these Jesuit principles respond directly to the challenges of Protestant reformers?

poverty, chastity, and missionary work, they were formally constituted by Pope Paul III in 1540. By the time of Loyola's death, the Society of Jesus already numbered some 1,500 members. It was by far the most militant of the religious orders fostered by the Catholic reform movements of the sixteenth century: not merely a monastic society but a company of soldiers sworn to defend the faith through eloquence, persuasion, and correct instruction. Their activities consisted primarily of proselytizing and establishing schools, which meant that they were ideal emissaries for the Counter-Reformation. Accordingly, Jesuits were soon dispatched to preach and teach in India, China, and the Spanish colonies in the Americas. One of Loyola's closest associates, Francis Xavier (*ZAY-vyer*; 1506–1552), baptized thousands of people and traveled thousands of miles in South and East Asia.

After Loyola's death, his Society of Jesus has global impact ▶

Although Loyola had not conceived of his society as a battalion of "shock troops" in the fight against Protestantism, that is what it became. Through preaching and diplomacy—sometimes at the risk of their lives—Jesuits in the second half of the sixteenth century helped to colonize the world. In many places, they were instrumental in keeping rulers and their subjects loyal to Catholicism; in others, they met martyrdom; and in still others, notably Poland and parts of Germany and France, they succeeded in regaining territory previously lost to followers of Luther and Calvin. Wherever they were allowed to settle, they set up schools and colleges on the grounds that only a vigorous Catholicism nurtured by widespread literacy and education could combat Protestantism.

A NEW CATHOLIC CHRISTIANITY

The greatest achievement of these reform movements was the revitalization of the Roman Church. Had it not been for such determined efforts, Catholicism would not have swept over the globe during the seventeenth and eighteenth centuries—or reemerged in Europe as a vigorous spiritual force.

The reforms had other consequences, such as the rapid advancement of lay literacy in Catholic countries and the growth of intense concern for acts of charity. Because Catholicism continued to emphasize good works as well as faith, charitable activities took on an extremely important role.

There was also a renewed emphasis on the role of religious women. While Catholicism did not exalt marriage as a route to holiness to the same degree as Protestantism, it did encourage the piety of female religious elites. For example, it embraced the mysticism of Saint Teresa of Ávila (1515–1582) and her renewal of religious women's spirituality through new orders of nuns, such as the Ursulines and the Sisters of Charity. Both Protestants and Catholics continued to exclude women from the priesthood or ministry, but Catholic women could pursue religious lives with at least some degree of independence; the convent thus continued to be a route toward spiritual and even political advancement.

The reformed Catholic Church did not, however, embrace the tolerant Christianity of Erasmus. Instead, Christian humanists lost favor with the papacy, and even scientists such as Galileo were regarded with suspicion (see Chapter 16). Yet contemporary Protestantism was just as intolerant and sometimes even more hostile to the cause of rational thought. Indeed, because Catholic theologians turned for guidance to the scholasticism of Thomas Aquinas (Chapter 9), they tended to be much more committed to the dignity of human reason than some of their Protestant counterparts, who emphasized the literal interpretation of the Bible and the importance of unquestioning faith. It is no coincidence that René Descartes, one of the pioneers of rational philosophy ("I think, therefore I am"), was educated by Jesuits.

It would be wrong, therefore, to claim that the Protestantism of this era was more forward-looking or progressive than Catholicism. Both were, in fact, products of the same troubled time. Each variety of Protestantism responded to specific historical conditions and the needs of specific peoples in specific places, while carrying forward certain aspects of the Christian tradition considered valuable by those communities. The Catholic Church also responded to new spiritual, political, and social realities—to such an extent that it must be regarded as distinct from either the early Church of the later Roman Empire or the ever-evolving Church of the Middle Ages. That is why the phrase "Roman Catholic Church" has not appeared in this book prior to this chapter; the Roman Catholic Church as we know it emerged in the sixteenth century.

Conclusion

The Reformation grew out of the complex historical processes that we have been tracing in the last few chapters. Foremost among these was the increasing power of Europe's sovereign states. As we have seen, the German princes who embraced Protestantism were moved to do so by their desire for sovereignty. The kings of Denmark, Sweden, and England followed suit for many of the same reasons. Protestantism bolstered state power because Protestant leaders preached absolute obedience to godly rulers, and the state in Protestant countries assumed direct control of its churches. Yet the power of the state had been growing for a long time prior to the Reformation, especially in such countries as France and Spain, where Catholic kings already exercised most of the same rights that were seized by Lutheran authorities and by Henry VIII of England. Those rulers who aligned themselves with Catholicism, then, had the same need to bolster their sovereignty and power.

Ideas of national identity, too, were already influential and available for manipulation by Protestants and Catholics alike. Religion thus became a new source of both identity and disunity. Prior to the Reformation, peoples in different regions of Germany spoke such different dialects that they had difficulty understanding each other. But Luther's Bible gained such currency that it eventually became the linguistic standard for all these disparate regions, which began to conceive of themselves as part of a single nation. Yet religion alone could not achieve the political unification of Germany, which did not occur for another 300 years (see Chapter 21); and, indeed, it contributed to existing divisions by cementing the opposition of Catholic princes and peoples. Elsewhere in Europe—as in the Netherlands, where Protestants fought successfully against a foreign, Catholic overlord—religion created a shared identity where politics could not. In England, where it is arguable that a certain sense of nationalism had already been fostered before the Reformation (Chapter 12), membership in the Church of England became a new, if not uncontested, attribute of "Englishness."

Renaissance ideals also contributed something to the Reformation and the Catholic responses to it. The criticisms of Christian humanists helped to prepare Europe for the challenges of Lutheranism, and close textual study of the Bible led to the publication of the newer, more accurate editions used by Protestant reformers. For example, Erasmus's improved edition of the Latin New Testament enabled Luther to reach some crucial theological conclusions and became the foundation for Luther's own translation of the Bible. However, Erasmus was not a supporter of Lutheran principles, and most other Christian humanists shunned Protestantism as soon as it became clear to them what Luther was actually teaching. Indeed, in certain basic respects, Protestant doctrine was completely at odds with the principles, politics, and beliefs of most humanists, who mostly became staunch supporters of the Catholic Church.

AFTER YOU READ THIS CHAPTER

CHRONOLOGY

1517	Luther posts his Ninety-Five Theses
1521	Luther is excommunicated
1520s	Lutheranism becomes the official religion of Scandinavian countries
1524–1525	German peasants' revolt
1529	Luther breaks with Zwingli
1534	Henry VIII establishes the Church of England
1534	Ignatius Loyola founds the Society of Jesus (the Jesuits)
1541	Geneva adopts a theocratic government based on Calvinism
1545–1563	Council of Trent is convened
1553–1558	Mary Tudor attempts to restore the Catholic faith in England
1555	Peace of Augsburg attempts to quell religious violence in Europe
1559	Elizabeth reestablishes Protestantism in England
1564	Papal *Index of Forbidden Books* is published for the first time

REVIEWING THE OBJECTIVES

❯ The main premises of Luther's theology had religious, political, and social implications. What were they?

❯ Switzerland fostered a number of different Protestant movements. Why was this the case?

❯ The Reformation had a profound effect on the basic structures of family life and on the attitudes toward marriage and morality. Describe these changes.

❯ The Church of England was established in response to what specific political situation?

❯ How did the Catholic Church respond to the challenge of Protestantism?

In the Americas and Asia, both Protestantism and Catholicism became forces of imperialism and new catalysts for competition. The race to secure colonies and resources now became a race for converts, too, as missionaries of both faiths fanned out over the globe. In the process, the confessional divisions of Europe were mapped onto these regions, often with violent results. Over the course of the ensuing century, newly sovereign nation-states would struggle for hegemony at home and abroad, setting off a series of religious wars that would cause as much destruction as any plague. Meanwhile, Western civilizations' extension into the Atlantic would create new ecosystems, forms of wealth, and types of bondage.

Go to INQUIZITIVE to see what you've learned—and learn what you've missed—with personalized feedback along the way.

PEOPLE, IDEAS, AND EVENTS IN CONTEXT

> How did **MARTIN LUTHER**'s attack on **INDULGENCES** tap into a more widespread criticism of the papacy? What role did the printing press and the German vernacular play in the dissemination of his ideas?

> Why did many German principalities and cities rally to Luther's cause? Why did his condemnation at the **DIET OF WORMS** not lead to his execution on charges of heresy?

> How did the Protestant teachings of **ULRICH ZWINGLI**, **JOHN CALVIN**, and the **ANABAPTISTS** differ from one another and from those of Luther?

> What factors made some of Europe's territories more receptive to **PROTESTANTISM** than others? What was the meaning of the principle *CUIUS REGIO, EIUS RELIGIO*, established by the Peace of Augsburg?

> How did the **REFORMATION** alter the status and lives of women in Europe? Why did it strengthen male authority in the family?

> Why did **HENRY VIII** break with Rome? How did the **CHURCH OF ENGLAND** differ from other Protestant churches in Europe?

> What decisions were made at the **COUNCIL OF TRENT**? What were the founding principles of **IGNATIUS LOYOLA**'s **SOCIETY OF JESUS**, and what was its role in the **COUNTER-REFORMATION** of the Catholic Church?

THINKING ABOUT CONNECTIONS

> Our study of Western civilizations has shown that reforming movements are nothing new, and Christianity has been continually reformed throughout its long history. What made this Reformation so different?

> Was a Protestant break from the Catholic Church inevitable? Why or why not?

> The political, social, and religious structures put in place during this era continue to shape our lives in such profound ways that we scarcely notice them—or we assume them to be inevitable and natural. In your view, what is the farthest-reaching consequence of this age of dissent and division? Why? In what ways has it formed your own values and assumptions?

Europe in the Atlantic World, 1550–1660

THE ATLANTIC OCEAN THRASHES the western shores of Europe and Africa with waves that have traveled thousands of miles from the American coasts. It links continents shaped by a wide variety of climates and ecologies. For most of human history, the limited movement of peoples across this ocean meant that each region had long nurtured its distinctive cultures, its own forms of plant and animal life, and its own unique microbes and pathogens.

But in the sixteenth century, the Atlantic world became an arena of cultural and economic exchange that broke down the isolation of these societies and ecosystems. Populations of humans, animals, and plants on once-remote shores came into frequent and intense contact. Europeans brought diseases that devastated the peoples of the Americas, along with gunpowder and a hotly divided Christianity. Meanwhile, the huge influx of silver from South America transformed (and eventually exploded) the cash-starved European economy, along with the arrival of American commodities such as tobacco, sugar, and chocolate. The need for workers to power the plantations that supplied these consumer products fostered a vast industry of human trafficking and caused the violent removal and enslavement of nearly 11 million people from Africa over the course of three centuries. The Indigenous peoples of the Americas were confronted with the invasive and destructive presence of newly arrived immigrants and were subjected to forms of coerced labor. Colonial settlement in North and South America also created new social hierarchies and new forms of inequality among Europeans, too. And

BEFORE YOU READ THIS CHAPTER

STORY LINES

❯ By the middle of the sixteenth century, the Atlantic Ocean had become a central space for colonization, migration, and settlement, as the peoples of this widening Atlantic world confronted each other.

❯ In the wake of the Reformation, Europe itself remained politically unstable, and devastating religious wars were waged on the Continent. In England, mounting pressures caused a crisis that resulted in civil war and the execution of the reigning king.

❯ At the same time, competition among Western powers had global impact, as Europeans exported their political and religious conflicts to the new American colonies.

❯ This widening world and its pervasive violence and unrest caused many Europeans to question the beliefs of earlier generations. Intellectuals and artists sought new sources of authority and new ways of explaining the complex circumstances of their time.

CORE OBJECTIVES

❯ **TRACE** the new linkages between Western civilizations and the wider Atlantic world.

❯ **DESCRIBE** the various forms of unfree labor that developed in European colonies during this period.

❯ **IDENTIFY** the monarchies that dominated Europe and the Atlantic world and the newer powers whose influence was expanding.

❯ **EXPLAIN** the reasons for Europe's religious and political instability and its consequences for Europe's monarchies and the Atlantic world.

❯ **UNDERSTAND** how artists and intellectuals responded to the crises and uncertainties of this era.

together, Indigenous peoples and colonial settlers were enmeshed in the meddling interference of distant imperial bureaucracies.

Meanwhile, European states were riven by dissent and deadly competitions among themselves. Galvanized by the crisis of the Reformation (Chapter 13), the Roman Catholic Church sought to spread its influence to the Americas and Asia through the work of new missionary orders. Attempts by the Catholic Habsburg monarchy to enforce religious uniformity among their varied territories in central Europe led to the Thirty Years' War, one of the longest and bloodiest conflicts in history. These deadly disputes pushed persecuted minorities to emigrate, replanting and propagating religious rivalries throughout the Atlantic world.

Religion was not the only cause of conflict. Tension was growing between powerful monarchs and landowning elites who disputed the rights of rulers to raise revenues through increased taxation. As notions of kingship were strained, political and moral philosophers struggled to redefine the role of government in a world of religious pluralism and to articulate new ideologies that did not necessitate violence among peoples of different faiths. Intellectuals and artists also strove to reassess the place of Europeans in an expanding world, and to make sense of the profound changes that were occurring in daily life.

The Emergence of the Atlantic World

By the middle of the sixteenth century, Spanish and Portuguese ventures into Africa, the Caribbean, and South America were galvanizing other European kingdoms to launch imperial experiments of their own. In 1497–1498, the Italian-born explorer John Cabot was hired by the English crown to explore the mouth of the St. Lawrence River; but it was nearly a century later, in 1585, that Walter Raleigh attempted to start an English colony just north of Spanish Florida. The settlement at Roanoke Island (present-day North Carolina) was intended to solidify English claims to the territory of Virginia, named for the "Virgin Queen" Elizabeth. It originally encompassed the North American seaboard from South Carolina to Maine, including Bermuda.

However, this bold experiment ended with the disappearance of the first colonists. It was followed by Christopher Newport's expedition to the Chesapeake Bay in 1606: a voyage funded by a private London firm, the Virginia Company. Newport and his followers did not conceive of themselves as empire builders. They were "gentleman planters" whose goal was to provide agricultural goods for the European market and so make their fortunes before returning home. Nevertheless, Newport's band reserved the right to "subdue" any Indigenous peoples who proved unwelcoming or uncooperative. Any sign of Indigenous violence or resistance could be a catalyst for the murder or enslavement of Native Americans.

Chief motivations for English colonists: fortune from trade

For decades thereafter, the native populations of North America remained capable of both threatening and nurturing the fragile European settlements on the coast. Especially in the early years of colonization, when the number of European immigrants was small, some Native American peoples sought to take advantage of these contacts to trade for goods otherwise unavailable to them. European settlers, for their part, often behaved with a combination of paternalism and contempt for the peoples they encountered. Some hoped to make converts to Christianity, others sought laborers. Ultimately, however, the balance was tipped by environmental, biological, and demographic factors.

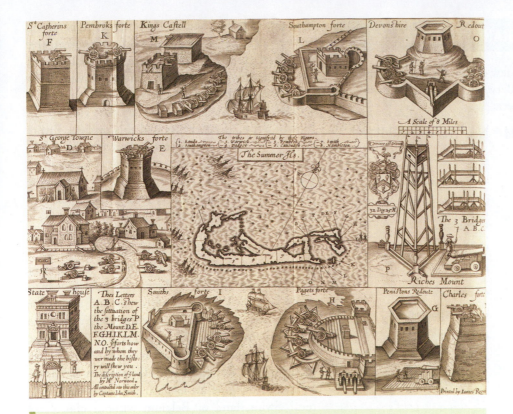

THE ISLAND OF BERMUDA. This map of the "Summer Isle" of Bermuda and the accompanying images of its major fortifications and sites were drawn by Captain John Smith and published in *The Generall Historie of Virginia, New-England, and the Summer Isles* (1624). **› Why would such features be of interest to readers of this pamphlet?**

THE COLUMBIAN EXCHANGE AND ITS ENVIRONMENTAL IMPACTS

The accelerating rate of global connections in the sixteenth century precipitated the unprecedented movement of peoples, plants, animals, and bacteria. This movement is known as the **Columbian exchange**, and it soon came to encompass lands that lay far beyond the purview of Columbus and his contemporaries, even reaching Australia and the Pacific Islands.

Because of its profound consequences, the Columbian exchange is a fundamental turning point in both human history and the history of the earth's ecology. It put new agricultural products into circulation, introduced new species of domesticated animals, and accidentally encouraged the spread of diseases and the devastating invasions of non-native plants and animals. For example, the introduction of pigs and other domesticated European animal species to islands in the Caribbean resulted in the extinction of indigenous animals and birds. The landscapes of Central America and southwestern North America were denuded of vegetation after Spanish settlers attempted large-scale herding and ranching operations. European honeybees displaced native insect populations and fostered harmful plant species. Gray squirrels and raccoons from North America found

Columbian exchange The widespread exchange of peoples, plants, animals, diseases, goods, and culture between the African and Eurasian landmasses (on the one hand) and the region that encompasses the Americas, Australia, and the Pacific Islands (on the other); precipitated by Christopher Columbus.

THE COLUMBIAN EXCHANGE

The following are just a few of the commodities and contagions that moved between the Old World and the New World in this era.

Old World → New World	New World → Old World
• Wheat	• Corn
• Sugar	• Potatoes
• Bananas	• Beans
• Rice	• Squash
• Wine grapes	• Pumpkins
• Horses	• Tomatoes
• Pigs	• Avocados
• Chickens	• Chili peppers
• Sheep	• Pineapples
• Cattle	• Cocoa
• *Smallpox*	• Tobacco
• *Measles*	
• *Typhus*	

their way to Britain and the European Continent, and brown rats and even some species of earthworms were transported to the Americas. Insects from all over the world traveled to new environments and spread unfamiliar forms of bacteria and pollen.

The mass transfer—voluntary or violent—of human populations accelerated this process. Entire peoples were wiped out by force, resettlement, or disease. As much as 90 percent of the pre-Columbian population of the Americas died of smallpox, cholera, influenza, typhoid, measles, malaria, and bubonic plague—all brought from Europe.

Meanwhile, the importation of foodstuffs from one part of the world to another, and their cultivation in new habitats, revolutionized the diets of local populations. The American potato, which could be grown in substandard soil and stored for long periods, eventually became the staple diet of the European poor. Indeed, the foods and flavors that characterize today's iconic cuisines are, to an extraordinary degree, the result of the Columbian exchange. Who can imagine an English meal without potatoes? Switzerland or Belgium without chocolate? Thai food without chili peppers? On the other side of the Atlantic, Florida without oranges? Colombia without coffee? Hawaii without pineapples? Of the ingredients that make up the quintessential American hamburger—ground-beef patties on a bun with lettuce, tomato, pickles, onion, and (if you like) cheese—only one component is indigenous to America: tomato. Everything else is Old World. Even the name is European, a reference to Hamburg in Germany.

EARLY COLONIAL POPULATIONS COMPARED

Most newcomers to the Americas are Africans forced into enslavement

Compared to the 7 million Africans forced to labor and die on plantations across the Atlantic, only about 1.5 million Europeans immigrated to the Americas in the sixteenth and seventeenth centuries. Most of them were men, and they were subject to high mortality rates. Rulers did what they could to encourage fresh waves of settlement, but the number of those who chose to seek their fortunes abroad remained relatively small during this period.

In the Spanish colonies, by 1570, some 150,000 settlers were largely concentrated in the military and administrative centers of the empire. Even the owners of plantations lived in cities, with foremen to manage their estates. Only those who had been granted *encomiendas* tended to live on the lands entrusted to them by the crown (the Spanish verb *encomendar* means "to entrust"). The *encomienda* system was an extension of the earlier *reconquista* of Spain (Chapter 12), originally set up to manage Muslim populations in territories captured by Christian crusaders. In the American version of the system, the lands overseen by *encomenderos* (agents) were still technically owned by native peoples; but in practice, settlers exploited these lands for their own profit, treating native workers like serfs. Some *encomenderos* were descendants of the first conquistadors. Others were drawn from Aztec and Inca elites, many of whom were women—including the daughters of the Aztec emperor Montezuma.

In North America, by contrast, English colonies in New England and the Chesapeake Bay were tiny and rural. Yet they grew more quickly, with settlers numbering about a quarter of a million by 1700. Part of the reason for this growth was the greater impetus for overseas emigration caused by overpopulation in the British Isles. The persecution of radical Protestant groups also played an important role in driving immigration, especially to the New England colonies, with the relocation of entire families and even communities being common. The colonies in Virginia offered additional incentives by granting 100 acres to each settler.

The number of migrants was also swelled by indentured servitude, a practice that brought thousands of "free" European laborers across the Atlantic under terms that made them temporarily enslaved. The term *indenture* refers to the contract that bound a servant to a master for a set period of time: copied in duplicate on a single sheet of paper or parchment, the two halves of the agreement would be cut apart in such a way as to leave jagged edges that looked like teeth (in Latin, *dentes*), which could be fitted together to prove the contract's validity. As much as 80 percent of the people who arrived in the Chesapeake colony were indentured servants, and nearly a quarter of those, women.

Indentured servitude: a different form of unfree labor

NEW SOCIAL HIERARCHIES IN NEW SPAIN

After the conquests of the Aztec and Inca Empires (Chapter 12), the Spanish established colonial governments known as viceroyalties in Mexico and Peru. Overseen by a bureaucracy in Madrid, these colonies were highly centralized—but only because they built on the administrative structures of Indigenous governments. For the most part, native peoples already lived in large, well-regulated villages and towns, so the Spanish government worked closely with local elites to maintain order. Indeed, the *encomienda* system was so effective because it built on these established structures and did not attempt to uproot or eliminate existing societies. The Spanish also co-opted the Inca's system of mandatory service on public works projects, which the colonists then used to control and exploit native labor, especially for aggressive mining operations (see *Analyzing Primary Sources* on page 480).

Spanish colonizers partner with Aztec and Inca elites in efficient, yet exploitative, rule

While the Spanish worked to convert native peoples to Catholicism, they did not attempt to change basic patterns of life. The result was widespread cultural assimilation by the relatively small numbers of (usually male) European settlers, who mostly intermarried with their colonial subjects. This pattern gave rise to a complex and distinctive caste system in New Spain, with a few "pure-blooded" immigrants, a larger number of creoles (American-born individuals of mostly European descent) and *mestizos* (those with mixed European, African, and Native American ancestry), with a still larger group of Native Americans forming the bottom of the hierarchy. In theory, these emerging racial categories also corresponded to class distinctions; but in practice, race and class did not always coincide. Racial concepts were still extremely flexible, and prosperous families of mixed descent often found ways to establish their "pure" Spanish ancestry by adopting the social practices of colonial elites. The lingering effects of this complicated stratification can still be seen in Latin America today.

Conscripted Native Laborers at Potosí

The Spanish crown received one-fifth of all revenues from the mines of its American colonies. It also maintained a monopoly over the mercury used to refine the ore from these mines into silver. Thus, it had an important stake in ensuring the mines' productivity. To this end, the crown granted colonial mine owners the right to conscript native peoples, allowing them considerable freedom over the (mis)treatment of their workers. This account, dated to about 1620, describes the conditions endured by these native laborers at Potosí (discussed in Chapter 12), a productive but highly dangerous mine in the Viceroyalty of Peru.

According to His Majesty's warrant, the mine owners on this massive range [at Potosí] have a right to the conscripted labor of 13,300 Indians in the working and exploitation of the mines, both those [mines] which have been discovered, those now discovered, and those which shall be discovered. It is the duty of the *Corregidor* [municipal governor] of Potosí to have them rounded up and to see that they come in from all the provinces between Cuzco . . . and as far as the frontiers of Tarija and Tomina. . . .

The conscripted Indians go up every Monday morning to the . . . foot of the range; the *Corregidor* arrives with all the provincial captains or chiefs who have charge of the Indians assigned him for his miner or smelter; that keeps him busy till 1 P.M., by which time the Indians are already turned over to these mine and smelter owners.

After each has eaten his ration, they climb up the hill, each to his mine, and go in, staying there from that hour until Saturday evening without coming out of the mine; their wives bring them food, but they stay constantly underground, excavating and carrying out the ore from which they get the silver. They all have tallow candles, lighted day and night; that is the light they work with, for as they are underground, they have need for it all the time. . . .

These Indians have different functions in the handling of the silver ore; some break it up with bar or pick, and dig down in, following the vein in the mine; others bring it up; others up above keep separating the good and the poor in piles; others are occupied in taking it down from the range to the mills on herds of llamas; every day they bring up more than 8,000 of these native beasts of burden for this task. These teamsters who carry the metal are not conscripted, but are hired.

Source: Antonio Vázquez de Espinosa, *Compendium and Description of the West Indies*, trans. Charles Upson Clark (Washington, DC: 1968), p. 62.

Questions for Analysis

1. From the tone of this account, what do you think was the narrator's purpose in writing it? Who is his intended audience?

2. Reconstruct the conditions in which these laborers worked. What would you estimate to be the human costs of a week's labor? Why, for example, would a fresh workforce be needed every Monday?

SUGAR, SLAVERY, AND THE TRANSATLANTIC TRIANGLE

The European settlers in the Americas faced a major problem: a shortage of labor. Mining and agriculture required many workers, and the Indigenous labor supply had already been decimated by disease. Indeed, the recurrence of plague in Europe, along with the loss of life in wars of religion, meant that Europe could not satisfy labor needs either. Colonial agents thus began the systematic capture and trafficking of people from West Africa to bolster the labor force and produce the wealth they

The following text labels appear on the map:

GREENLAND

ARCTIC OCEAN

HUDSON BAY COMPANY

NEWFOUNDLAND

BRITAIN
Bristol

NETHERLANDS
Amsterdam

NEW FRANCE

Québec
ACADIA

TOBACCO, FURS

FRANCE
Bordeaux

Boston
New York

SUGAR

PORTUGAL
Lisbon

SPAIN
Cadiz

LOUISIANA

Jamestown
VIRGINIA

ATLANTIC OCEAN

Charleston

NEW SPAIN

FLORIDA
Gulf of Mexico

AFRICA

Mexico

CARIBBEAN SEA

SLAVES

SUGAR

St. Louis

Panama

SLAVES

GAMBIA

GUINEA

SURINAME
FRENCH GUYANA

SLAVES

GOLD COAST

Inset area

NEW GRANADA

KENYA

Lima

BRAZIL

TOBACCO, SUGAR

ANGOLA

MOZAMBIQUE

MADAGASCAR

PACIFIC OCEAN

Rio de Janeiro

PERU

Buenos Aires

CAPE OF GOOD HOPE

Legend:
- Spanish
- Portuguese
- French
- British
- Dutch

0   1000   2000 Miles
0   1000   2000 Kilometers

Inset map labels:

Havana

SLAVES

BRITISH BAHAMAS

0   200   400 Miles
0   200   400 Kilometers

CUBA

SLAVES

SAINT-DOMINGUE (Fr.)

PUERTO RICO

ATLANTIC OCEAN

JAMAICA (Br.)

HISPANIOLA

BELIZE (Br.)

CARIBBEAN SEA

SLAVES

GUADELOUPE (Fr.)
MARTINIQUE (Fr.)

SLAVES

NEW SPAIN

SLAVES

BARBADOS (Br.)

CURAÇAO (Dutch)
TOBAGO (Fr.)
TRINIDAD (Sp.)

SLAVES

PACIFIC OCEAN

NEW GRANADA

THE ATLANTIC WORLD AND THE TRIANGULAR TRADE. › Trace the routes of the triangular trade. What products did French and British colonies in North America provide to the European market? › Which colonies were most dependent on slave labor and what products did they produce? › How did these products enter into the triangle?

triangular trade The commercial Atlantic shipping pattern that took rum from New England to Africa, traded it for enslaved captives taken to the West Indies, and brought sugar back to New England to be processed into rum.

so avidly sought. And overwhelmingly, that wealth was not gold or silver but a new commodity for which Europeans had an insatiable appetite: sugar.

Sugar was at the center of the "**triangular trade**" pattern that linked markets in Africa, the Americas, and Europe—all of which were driven by enslaved labor. For example, ships that transported enslaved Africans to the Caribbean might trade their human cargo for molasses made on sugar plantations. These ships would proceed to New England, where the molasses would be traded to make rum. Rum made in the colonies would be loaded onto the slaver ships, which would return to Africa and repeat the process. An alternative trade triangle brought manufactured goods from England to Africa, trading those goods for enslaved humans who were then shipped to Virginia. The human cargo was offloaded and exchanged for tobacco, which was then exported to England.

Many other branches of the Atlantic world economy were tied to the slave trade: investors in Amsterdam, London, and Lisbon financed the slave ships; insurance brokers negotiated complex formulas for protecting investments in human flesh; bankers offered a range of credit options to new slave traders. And in myriad ways, the everyday lives of average people were also bound to slavery: all who bought the commodities produced by enslaved labor, or who manufactured the implements and weapons that enabled it, were implicated. The enslavement of Africans created wealth and prestige for every sector of European society, not merely for those who had direct contact with it. It was the engine that created the modern globalized, capitalist economy.

THE HUMAN COST OF THE SLAVE TRADE

The Portuguese were the first to bring enslaved Africans to sugarcane plantations in Brazil, in the 1540s. By this time, systemic and racialized slavery was becoming crucial to the domestic economies of West African kingdoms. In the following decades, as a result, the demand for slaves would cause the disintegration of political order in these regions—fomenting war and raiding among rival groups. Moreover, the increased traffic in human beings called for more systematized methods for corralling, sorting, and shipping them. By the end of the sixteenth century, the Portuguese government established a fortified trading outpost on an island off the central West African coast (near what is now Angola). Additional posts were established along that coast to assist with processing captives.

On board ships, enslaved humans were shackled below decks in spaces barely wider than their own bodies, without sanitary facilities of any kind. The mortality rate on these voyages was relatively low, probably 10 percent, but this was only because those chosen for transport were healthy to begin with, and already the toughened survivors of unimaginable hardships. To place that statistic in a larger context, we need to consider that of 100 people captured in the African interior, 36 would perish in the six-month-long forced march to the coast, and another dozen or so would die in prisons there. Eventually, perhaps 57 of the original 100 would be taken aboard ship, and some 51 would survive the journey and be sold into slavery. If the destination was Brazil's sugar plantations, only 40 would still be alive after two years. Put plainly, the actual mortality rate of enslaved people was closer to 60 percent—and this doesn't begin to account for their shortened life expectancy in bondage.

The people consigned to this fate were those who shaped the emerging Atlantic world. When opportunity arose, enslaved individuals banded together in revolt—a

An Ethiopian Royal Ban on the Enslavement of Christians, 12 February 1548

The ancient African kingdom of Ethiopia was one of the first polities to embrace Christianity. It continued to be a rich and vibrant source of literary, artistic, and religious innovation, as well as a dynamic participant in economic and cultural exchanges with the other civilizations of Afro-Eurasia. In the sixteenth century, however, its sovereignty and the freedom of its peoples were threatened by Islamic political expansion into the Horn of Africa and the growing reliance on enslaved labor in the Americas, which resulted in the increasingly aggressive trafficking of captives from Africa. Fearing that his people would be caught up in the escalation of human trafficking, King Gälawdéwos of Ethiopia (r. 1540–1559) issued an edict that banned the sale or ownership of his fellow Christians, on pain of death. The edict was promulgated in Ge'ez, an ancient Semitic language related to Hebrew and Arabic, which is still the language of the Ethiopian Orthodox Church.

I, King Gälawdéwos, son of Wänag Sägäd,[1] have ordered that from now onwards any merchant [traveling with slaves], whether he be Muslim or Christian, shall not proceed to the sea, to [the Islamic sultanate of Adal][2] and to other market places visited by merchants, without coming to my gate [for inspection]. Let him bring both female and male slaves before me. Let him write down the number of slaves [he is traveling with] and report them to the *mäkwanent* [local nobility], *mäsafent* [princes], and *seyuman* [administrators] of the district along the route they pass through. When any captive who is not on the list reported to the [these officials] is discovered, let them take him into custody. If the captive turns out to be Christian and the one [who knowingly bought him] is an Arab, let them deprive him of all his merchandise and send him to me. Let them kill the seller who [knowingly] puts up for market and sale [to the Arab merchant] the Christian slave. If the seller who [knowingly] sold a Christian is a merchant, whether he be Muslim or a Christian Ethiopian compatriot, let them kill him. If an Arab [merchant] knowingly purchases a Christian, let them confiscate all his property. Any *azaj* [official], whether he be *fätahit* (judge), or *mäkonnen*, or *seyum* of the district, who [slacks on his obligation] and does not follow our commands, deserves to be killed without mercy and his house ransacked; and let him be damned by the mouth of the Father, the Son, and the Holy Ghost, and by the mouth of all Church Fathers.

I, King Gälawdéwos, legislated this law and sanctioned this writing. Let it be the established law and regulation of the land of Ethiopia forever and ever. Anyone who violates my decree, whether they be future kings, or judges, is under perpetual anathema [damnation] both in his life and after his death.

1. Gälawdéwos's father.
2. Adal was a Sunni Muslim principality established in the Horn of Africa, across from the Arabian Peninsula, around 1415. It reached the height of its power at the time of this edict, and its expansion during these centuries posed a threat to the Christian kingdom of Ethiopia.

Source: Habtamu Mengistie Tegegne, "The Edict of King Gälawdéwos against the Illegal Slave Trade in Christians: Ethiopia, 1548," *Medieval Globe* 2.2 (2016): 89–90.

Questions for Analysis

1. During the Middle Ages, laws about who could or could not be enslaved relied on the shared doctrine that no one should buy or sell individuals of the same religion. How does the edict of King Gälawdéwos reflect this shared understanding?

2. Carefully trace the legal process that is outlined in the edict. How does King Gälawdéwos rely on existing administrative structures in order to enforce this ban? What picture emerges of the larger bureaucratic structures of the Ethiopian state?

price revolution An unprecedented inflation in prices during the latter half of the sixteenth century, resulting in part from the enormous influx of silver bullion from Spanish America.

perpetual possibility that led to draconian regimes of violence and punishment. They also resorted to other forms of resistance, among them suicide and infanticide. Above all, they sought to liberate themselves, and communities of fugitives sprang up throughout the Americas. Some were large enough to assert and defend their autonomy. One such community, founded in 1603 in the hinterlands of Brazil, persisted for more than a century and had as many as 20,000 inhabitants. Most others were much smaller and more ephemeral, but their existence testifies to the limits of imperial authority and the power of human ingenuity.

Conflict and Competition in Europe and the Atlantic World

Most of Europe had enjoyed steady economic growth since the middle of the fifteenth century, and colonization of the Americas seemed to promise further prosperity. But the prolonged political, religious, and economic crises of the sixteenth century were devastating. And inevitably, these European conflicts spread to European colonies.

NEW WORLD SILVER AND OLD WORLD ECONOMIES

In the latter half of the sixteenth century, unprecedented price inflation profoundly destabilized the European economy and caused widespread panic. There were two underlying developments for what historians have termed a *price revolution*. The first was demographic: after the Black Death (Chapter 11), Europe's population had grown from roughly 50 million people in 1450 to 90 million in 1600: an increase of nearly 80 percent in a short span of time. Yet Europe's food supply remained nearly constant, causing food prices to rise steeply due to the high demand for basic commodities. Second, the enormous influx of silver and gold from Spanish America flooded a previously cash-poor economy (Chapter 12), and the sudden availability of ready coin drove prices higher still.

Causes of rapid inflation: (1) explosive population growth outstrips limited food supply

Causes of rapid inflation: (2) an influx of gold and silver from the Americas lowers real value of currency

About 10 million ducats' worth of silver, roughly equivalent to 10 billion U.S. dollars in today's currency, passed through the Spanish port of Seville in just four years, from 1556 to 1560. Yet the high worth of these coins was quickly downgraded due to the large amount of money in circulation; and as more silver poured in, the value of coinage decreased even more. By 1580, the amount of imported silver doubled; by 1595, it more than quadrupled. And because most of this money was used by the Spanish crown to pay its armies and its many creditors, this huge volume of debased coinage was circulated through European banks, making inflation even more widespread. Since some people suddenly had more money to pay for goods and services, those who supplied these commodities charged higher and higher prices. But at the same time, the value of the coinage itself was plummeting. "I learned a proverb here," said a French traveler in Spain in 1603. "Everything costs a lot, except silver."

THE NEW EUROPEAN POOR

In this economic climate, aggressive entrepreneurs profited from financial speculation, landholders from the rising prices of agricultural produce, and merchants from the demand for luxury goods. But workers were caught in a vise: wages were not keeping pace with rising prices because the population boom kept labor cheap. As the cost of food rose, poor people had to spend an ever-greater percentage of their

POPULATION DENSITY, c. 1600. › In what regions was the population most dense? › The largest gains in population were on the coasts; why might that be? › How would urbanization affect patterns of life and trade?

incomes on necessities. The overall cost of living in England, for example, more than doubled in William Shakespeare's lifetime. When disasters such as wars or bad harvests drove grain prices higher still, the poor starved to death.

The price revolution also placed new pressures on European states. Inflation depressed the value of money, so income derived from fixed taxes and rents yielded less actual wealth. Governments were forced to raise taxes just to keep revenues constant; yet most states needed even more revenue because they were engaging in more wars, and warfare was increasingly expensive. When taxes rose, governments also faced continuous threats of defiance and even armed resistance from citizens.

Although population growth and the flood of silver began to slow after 1600, the ensuing decades were a time of economic stagnation. A few areas—notably the Netherlands (see pages 487–88)—still thrived, and the rich were usually able to hold their own, but the laboring poor made no advances. Indeed, the plight of the poor deteriorated further, as helpless civilians were plundered by tax collectors, looting soldiers, or sometimes both. Peasants who had been dispossessed of property or driven off once-common lands were branded as vagrants, and vagrancy itself became a criminal offense. It was this population of newly impoverished men and women who became the indentured servants or deported criminals of Europe's colonies.

> *Many of Europe's peasants, dispossessed and sometimes criminalized, find new lives in colonies*

WARS OF RELIGION IN FRANCE

Compounding these economic problems were the wars that erupted within many European states. As we began to observe in Chapter 9, most medieval kingdoms were created through the colonization of smaller, traditionally autonomous territories—either by conquest or through marriage alliances with ruling families. Now these enlarged but disunited states began to make ever-greater claims on their citizens while at the same time demanding religious uniformity. The result was regional and civil conflict, as local populations and even elites rebelled against the centralizing demands of monarchs who often embraced a different religion than their subjects.

France was the first to be enflamed by religious warfare. Calvinist missionaries from Geneva had made significant headway there, assisted by the conversion of many aristocratic Frenchwomen who in turn converted their husbands. By the 1560s, French Calvinists, known as Huguenots (*HEW-guh-nohz*), made up between 10 and 20 percent of the population. Although there was no open warfare, political rivalries led factions within the government to break down along religious lines, pitting the (mostly southern) Huguenots against the (mostly northern) Catholic aristocracy. While the Huguenots were not strong enough to threaten Catholic dominance, they were too many to be ignored.

In 1572 the two sides almost brokered a truce: the presumptive heir to the throne, Prince Henry of Navarre—who had become a Protestant—was to marry the Catholic sister of the reigning king, Charles IX. But this compromise was undone by the Queen Mother, Catherine de' Medici, whose faction plotted to kill all the Huguenot leaders assembled in Paris for her daughter's wedding. In the early morning of Saint Bartholomew's Day (August 24), most of these Protestant aristocrats were murdered in their beds and thousands of humble Protestants were slaughtered in the streets or drowned in the river Seine. When word of the massacre spread to the provinces, local massacres proliferated.

Henry of Navarre escaped, along with his bride, but the war continued for more than two decades. In 1589, when Catherine's death was followed by that of her son, who had

HENRY IV OF FRANCE. Henry of Navarre (r. 1589–1610) founded the Bourbon dynasty that would rule France until 1792 and ended the bitter civil war that had been waged between Catholic and Huguenot factions. This somewhat satirical image shows the king in the guise of the classical hero Hercules, vanquishing a many-headed hydra representing the Catholic League, a major proponent of religious violence.

produced no heir, Henry of Navarre became **Henry IV** and renounced his Protestant faith to placate the Catholic majority. In 1598, Henry made a landmark effort to end the conflict by issuing the Edict of Nantes, which recognized Catholicism as the official religion of the realm but permitted Protestants to practice their religion in specified places.

This was an important step toward a policy of religious tolerance. For the first time, Protestants in France were allowed to hold public office and enroll in universities. And because the religious divide was also a regional one, the edict reinforced a tradition of local autonomy in southwestern France, countering the monarchy's centralized power. The success of this effort can be measured by the fact that peace was maintained even after Henry IV was assassinated by a Catholic in 1610.

With Edict of Nantes, France retains official Catholic religion but tolerates Protestants

THE REVOLT OF THE NETHERLANDS AND THE DUTCH TRADING EMPIRE

Warfare between Catholics and Protestants also broke out in the Netherlands during this period. Controlled for almost a century by the same Habsburg family that ruled Spain and its overseas empire, the Netherlands had prospered through intense involvement with Atlantic world trade. The Dutch had the highest per capita wealth in Europe, and the city of Antwerp (now in Belgium) was northern Europe's leading financial center. So when the Spanish king **Philip II** (r. 1556–1598) attempted to tighten his hold there in the 1560s, the fiercely independent Dutch cities resented his imperial intrusion and were ready to fight it.

This conflict became a religious one because Calvinism had spread to the Netherlands from France, whereas Philip was an ardent Catholic. When crowds began ransacking and desecrating Catholic churches throughout the country, Philip dispatched an army of 10,000 Spanish soldiers to wipe out Protestantism in his Dutch territories. A reign of terror ensued, which further catalyzed the Protestant opposition.

In 1572, a Dutch aristocrat, William of Orange, emerged as the anti-Spanish leader and sought help from religious allies in France, Germany, and England. Organized fleets of Protestant privateers (privately owned ships) began harassing the Spanish navy in the North Atlantic. William's Protestant army then seized control of the Netherlands' northern provinces. Although William was assassinated in 1584, his efforts were instrumental in forcing the Spanish crown to recognize the independence of a northern Dutch Republic in 1609. Once united, these seven provinces became wholly Calvinist; the southern region, still largely Catholic, remained under Spanish rule.

This new Dutch Republic emerged as the most prosperous European commercial empire of the seventeenth century, extending beyond the Atlantic to the Indian Ocean and East Asia. The Dutch colonial project owed more to the strategic "fort and factory" model favored by the Portuguese than to the Spanish model of conquest and settlement. Many early initiatives were spurred by the establishment of the Dutch East India Company, a private mercantile corporation that came to control Sumatra, Borneo, and the Moluccas (the so-called Spice Islands). The company also secured an exclusive right to trade with Japan, and maintained military and trading outposts in China and India.

The Dutch also established a North American colonial outpost known as New Amsterdam until it was surrendered to the English in 1667 and renamed New York. Their remaining territorial holdings in the Atlantic were Dutch Guyana (present-day Surinam) on the coast of South America and the islands of Curaçao and Tobago

Henry of Navarre (1553–1610) Crowned King Henry IV of France, he renounced his Protestantism but granted limited toleration to Huguenots (French Protestants) through the Edict of Nantes in 1598.

Philip II King of Spain from 1556 to 1598 and briefly king of England and Ireland during his marriage to Queen Mary I of England.

PROTESTANTS RANSACKING A CHURCH. The destruction of medieval religious images was widespread in Protestant regions of Europe, including the Netherlands, where it provoked a stern response from Emperor Philip II. This contemporary depiction of iconoclasm shows the removal and burning of paintings and statuary in Zurich, where Protestants controlled the city. › **Why would such acts have been seen to advance the Protestant cause?** › **How would they have been understood by Catholics?**

in the Caribbean. The establishment of a second mercantile enterprise, the Dutch West India Company, allowed them to dominate the African slave trade after 1621.

In constructing this transoceanic trading empire the Dutch pioneered a new investment mechanism: the joint-stock company. The Dutch East and West India Companies raised cash by selling shares to individual investors whose liability was limited to the sum of their investments. While not part of the company's management, these investors were entitled to a proportionate share in the profits. Originally, the Dutch East India Company had intended to pay off its investors within ten years; but when that period was up, it convinced those investors who wanted to realize their profits immediately to sell their shares on the open market. The creation of a market in shares of stock, which we now call a stock market, was a major innovation. Stock markets now control the world's economy.

The joint-stock company, a Dutch invention, drives a surge in investment

THE PROTESTANT SETTLEMENT OF IRELAND AND STRUGGLE BETWEEN ENGLAND AND SPAIN

Religious strife could spark civil war (as in France) or political rebellion (as in the Netherlands), and could also provoke warfare between sovereign states, as in the struggle between England and Spain. In this case, religious conflict was entangled with both dynastic claims and economic competition in the Atlantic world.

The dynastic competition came from the English royal family's division along confessional lines. The Catholic queen Mary (r. 1553–1558), eldest daughter of

Henry VIII and granddaughter of Ferdinand and Isabella of Spain (Chapter 13), had married her cousin Philip II of Spain in 1554, and she ruled at a time of great strife between Catholics and Protestants in England. After Mary's death, her Protestant half-sister Elizabeth (r. 1558–1603) came to the throne, and relations with Spain rapidly declined. They deteriorated further when Catholic Ireland—an English colony—rebelled in 1569 with Spain's support. Although it took almost thirty bloody years, English forces eventually suppressed the Irish. Elizabeth then cemented the defeat by encouraging Protestant occupation of their lands. She did so in conscious imitation of Spanish colonial policy in the Americas, in hopes of creating a new state with a largely English identity. Instead, these measures created the deep ethnic and religious conflicts that trouble Ireland to this day.

England's conflict with Spain was worsened by the fact that English economic interests were directly opposed to those of Spain. English traders were making steady inroads into Spanish commercial networks in the Atlantic, as English sea captains such as Sir Francis Drake and Sir John Hawkins plundered Spanish vessels on the high seas. In a particularly dramatic exploit lasting from 1577 to 1580, prevailing winds and a lust for booty propelled Drake all the way around the world, to return with stolen Spanish treasure worth twice as much as Queen Elizabeth's annual revenue.

After suffering numerous such attacks over a period of two decades—and after Elizabeth's government openly supported the Dutch revolt in 1585—King Philip finally resolved to fight back. In 1588, he dispatched an enormous fleet, confidently called the "Invincible Armada," whose mission was to invade England. But after an indecisive initial encounter between the two fleets, a fierce storm—hailed as a "Protestant wind" by the lucky English—drove the Spanish galleons off course, wrecking many off the Irish coast. Elizabeth took credit for her country's miraculous escape.

ENGLAND'S COLONIAL AMBITIONS

Unlike New Spain, England's North American colonies had no significant mineral wealth; instead, English colonists sought to profit from the establishment of large-scale plantations in North America and the Caribbean. The first permanent colony was founded at Jamestown, Virginia, in 1607. Over the next forty years, about 80,000 immigrants established more than twenty autonomous settlements.

Many were religious refugees—hence the name given to the Pilgrims who landed at Plymouth, Massachusetts, in 1620. These radical Calvinists, known as Puritans, were also

THE NETHERLANDS AFTER 1609. › What were the two main divisions of the Netherlands? › Which was Protestant and which was Catholic? › How could William of Orange and his allies use the geography of the northern Netherlands against the Spanish?

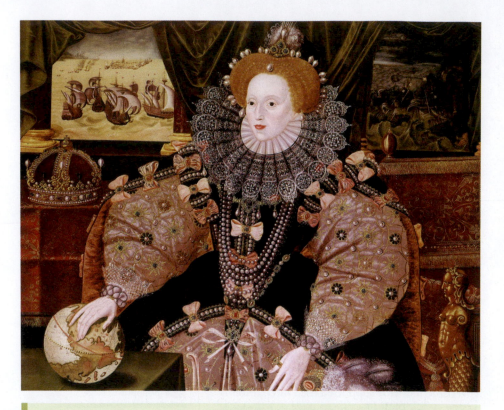

THE "ARMADA PORTRAIT" OF ELIZABETH. This is one of several royal portraits that commemorated the defeat of the Spanish Armada in 1588. Through the window on the left, an English flotilla sails serenely on sunny seas; on the right, Spanish ships are wrecked by a "Protestant wind." Elizabeth's right hand rests protectively—and commandingly—on the globe. › **How would you interpret this image?**

political dissidents and were almost as unwelcome as Catholics in England. Yet even these committed Christians showed little interest in converting Native American peoples. Missionizing played a much larger role in Spanish Central and South America, and in French efforts to penetrate the North American wilderness.

Another difference between Spanish and English colonialism is the fact that English colonies did not begin as royal enterprises. They were private ventures, either by individual landholders (as in Maryland and Pennsylvania) or managed by joint-stock companies (as in Virginia and the Massachusetts Bay Colony). Because most land in Europe was owned by royal and aristocratic families, the accumulation of wealth through the control of land was a new and exciting prospect for small- and medium-scale landholders in the new English colonies. This helps to explain the colonies' rural, agricultural character—in contrast to the great cities of New Spain. But the focus on agriculture was also due to the demographic catastrophe that had decimated the native population; a great deal of rich land had been abandoned by Native American farmers because there were so few of them to till it. As more colonists arrived, and competition for land increased, Indigenous peoples who had survived European diseases were now under threat from Europeans who wanted complete and exclusive control over these lands.

To this end, the English soon set out to eliminate, through expulsion and massacre, the former inhabitants of the region. There were a few exceptions, such as in the Quaker colony of Pennsylvania, where colonists and Native Americans maintained friendly relations for more than half a century. In the Carolinas, by contrast, there was widespread enslavement of native peoples, either for sale to the West Indies or for work on the rice plantations along the coast. In another contrast to the Spanish and French colonies, intermarriage between English colonists and native populations was rare, which also created the sense of an unbridgeable racial divide in North America.

English colonists expel and massacre Native Americans in fierce competition over land

The Thirty Years' War and Its Outcomes

With the promulgation of the Edict of Nantes in France, the end of open hostilities between England and Spain, and the truce between Spain and the Dutch Republic, religious warfare in Europe came briefly to an end. In 1618, however, a new series of wars broke out in central Europe, in the German-speaking lands that had felt the first divisive effects of the Reformation. This period of warfare was one of the longest in history, and one of the bloodiest, engulfing most of the Continent before it ended thirty years later, in 1648. Although it began as a religious conflict, it quickly became an international struggle for dominance that claimed some 8 million lives, with entire regions devastated by the rapacity of crisscrossing armies.

THE BEGINNINGS OF THE THIRTY YEARS' WAR AND THE DOWNFALL OF BOHEMIA

Like the variety of combatants involved, the causes of the **Thirty Years' War** are complicated. On one level, it was an outlet for aggressions and tensions that had been building up since the Peace of Augsburg in 1555. On another level, it grew out of longer-standing disputes among rulers and territories in the patchwork of

Thirty Years' War
(1618–1648) Beginning as a conflict between Protestants and Catholics in Germany, the series of skirmishes escalated into a general European war fought on German soil by armies from Sweden, France, and the Holy Roman Empire.

provinces that made up the Holy Roman Empire. On still another level, it was an opportunity for players on the fringes of power to rise to prominence.

The catalyst came in 1618, when the Austrian Habsburg (Catholic) prince Ferdinand, who also ruled Hungary and the united Polish-Lithuanian Commonwealth, was named heir to the throne of Protestant Bohemia. This prompted a rebellion among the Bohemian aristocracy. A year later, the complex dynastic politics of Europe also resulted in Ferdinand's election as Holy Roman emperor, a title that gave him access to an imperial (Catholic) army, which he sent to crush the Protestant revolt. The Bohemians, meanwhile, were bolstered by the support of some Austrian nobility—many also Protestant—who saw a way to recover power from the ruling Habsburg family.

In 1620, the war escalated when the Ottomans threw their support behind the Protestants and touched off a war with staunchly Catholic Poland, whose borders the Muslim army needed to cross. The Poles won, and the Ottomans retreated. Meanwhile, Ferdinand's Habsburg cousin, the Spanish king Philip IV, had renewed his war against the Dutch Republic—thus forming an alliance between the two Habsburg rulers. This led to a major pitched battle between united Protestant forces and the Spanish-led Catholic army just outside of Prague. The Habsburgs were victorious, and the Czechs of Bohemia were forced to accept Ferdinand's Catholic rule. As a result, the kingdom of Bohemia, a powerful force in the region and an early cradle of Protestant reform (Chapter 12), ceased to exist.

> *An alliance of two Catholic Habsburg rulers*

THE TANGLED POLITICS AND PRICE OF WAR

The conflict should have ended there, but it did not. Instead, it metastasized when tensions between Catholics and Protestants in other parts of central Europe erupted into war. French Catholics and Protestants, who had enjoyed relatively peaceful relations since 1598, came into violent contact once again. Protestant Denmark, fearing that Catholic victories in neighboring parts of the Holy Roman Empire might threaten its sovereignty, was also drawn in.

In this new phase of the war, political expediency soon outweighed either religious or dynastic allegiances. When a confederation of Catholic princes seemed close to uprooting Protestantism in Germany in 1630, other German Catholic princes allied with Protestants to preserve their autonomy. Joining them was the Protestant king of Sweden, Gustavus Adolphus (r. 1611–1632), who championed both the German Lutheran states and his own nation's sovereignty in the wake of Denmark's territorial losses. Yet his Protestant army was secretly subsidized by Catholic France, which sought to avoid being surrounded by a strong Habsburg alliance on its borders.

Gustavus, who had become king at age seventeen, was one of the great military commanders of all time. Like another young general, Alexander the Great (Chapter 4), he was not only an expert tactician but also a charismatic leader. His army became the best-trained and best-equipped fighting force of the era—the first modern army. By the time he died in battle, in 1632, a month before his thirty-eighth birthday, Sweden had become a global power rivaling Spain and Russia in size and prestige.

In 1635, with Gustavus dead, France was compelled to join Sweden in declaring war on the Spanish and Austrian Habsburgs. In the middle lay central Europe,

EUROPE AT THE END OF THE THIRTY YEARS' WAR. This map shows the complex political checkerboard that resulted from the Peace of Westphalia in 1648. › When you compare this map with the one on page 451, what are the most significant territorial changes between c. 1526 and 1648? › Which regions were weakened or endangered by this arrangement? › Which were in a strong position to dominate Europe?

already weakened by seventeen years of war and now a helpless battleground. In the next thirteen years, this region suffered more from warfare than at any other time until the twentieth century (see *Analyzing Primary Sources* on page 494). Several cities were besieged and sacked nine or ten times over. Soldiers from all nations, who had to sustain themselves by plunder, gave no quarter to defenseless civilians. With plague and disease adding to the toll of butchery, some towns were nearly eradicated. The carnage continued into the war's final years, even after peace negotiators arrived at broad areas of agreement.

The Devastation of the Thirty Years' War

The author of the following excerpt, Hans Jakob Christoffel von Grimmelshausen (GRIM-mill-show-sen; 1621–1676), barely survived the horrors of the Thirty Years' War. His parents were killed, probably when he was thirteen years old, and he himself was kidnapped the following year and forced into the army. By age fifteen, he was a soldier. His darkly satiric masterpiece, Simplicissimus ("The Simpleton"), drew heavily on these experiences and, although technically a fictional memoir, portrays with brutal accuracy the terrible realities of this era.

Although it was not my intention to take the peaceloving reader with these troopers to my dad's house and farm, seeing that matters will go ill therein, yet the course of my history demands that I should leave to kind posterity an account of what manner of cruelties were now and again practised in this our German war: yes, and moreover testify by my own example that such evils must often have been sent to us by the goodness of Almighty God for our profit. For, gentle reader, who would ever have taught me that there was a God in Heaven if these soldiers had not destroyed my dad's house, and by such a deed driven me out among folk who gave me all fitting instruction thereupon? . . .

The first thing these troopers did was, that they stabled their horses: thereafter each fell to his appointed task: which task was neither more nor less than ruin and destruction. For though some began to slaughter and to boil and to roast so that it looked as if there should be a merry banquet forward, yet others there were who did but storm through the house above and below stairs. Others stowed together great parcels of cloth and apparel and all manner of household stuff, as if they would set up a frippery market. All that they had no mind to take with them they cut in pieces. Some thrust their swords through the hay and straw as if they had not enough sheep and swine to slaughter: and some shook the feathers out of the beds and in their stead stuffed in bacon and other dried meat and provisions as if such were better and softer to sleep upon. Others broke the stove and the windows as if they had a never-ending summer to promise. Houseware of copper and tin they beat flat, and packed such vessels, all bent and spoiled, in with the rest. Bedsteads, tables, chairs, and benches they burned, though there lay many cords of dry wood in the yard. Pots and pipkins must all go to pieces, either because they would eat none but roast flesh, or because their purpose was to make there but a single meal.

Our maid was so handled in the stable that she could not come out, which is a shame to tell of. Our man they laid bound upon the ground, thrust a gag into his mouth, and poured a pailful of filthy water into his body: and by this, which they called a Swedish draught, they forced him to lead a party of them to another place where they captured men and beasts, and brought them back to our farm, in which company were my dad, my mother, and our Ursula.

And now they began: first to take the flints out of their pistols and in place of them to jam the peasants' thumbs in and so to torture the poor rogues as if they had been about the burning of witches: for one of them they had taken they thrust into the baking oven and there lit a fire under him, although he had as yet confessed no crime: as for another, they put a cord round his head and so twisted it tight with a piece of wood that the blood gushed from his mouth and nose and ears. In a word each had his own device to torture the peasants, and each peasant his several tortures.

Source: Hans Jakob Christoph von Grimmelshausen, *Simplicissimus*, trans. S. Goodrich (New York: 1995), pp. 1–3, 8–10, 32–35.

Questions for Analysis

1. The first-person narrator here recounts the atrocities committed "in this our German war," in which both perpetrators and victims are German. How believable is this description? What lends it credibility?

2. Why would Grimmelshausen have chosen to publish his account as a satirical fiction rather than as a straightforward historical narrative or an autobiography? How would this choice have affected readers' response to scenes such as he describes?

THE PEACE OF WESTPHALIA AND THE DECLINE OF SPAIN

The adoption of the Peace of Westphalia in 1648 was a watershed in European history. It marked the emergence of a new Swedish empire and the rise of France as the predominant power on the Continent, a position it would hold for the next two centuries. The greatest losers in the conflict (aside from the millions of victims) were the Austrian Habsburgs, who were forced to surrender all the territory they had gained and to abandon their hopes of dominating central Europe. The Spanish Habsburgs were also substantially weakened, and no longer able to fall back on the wealth of their empire. Large portions of the Atlantic trade had been infiltrated by merchants from other countries, while the expansion of colonial economies made them less dependent on trade with Spain itself. In 1600, the Spanish Empire had been the mightiest power in the world; a half-century later, it had begun to fall apart.

Moreover, as we have noted, New Spain's great wealth had proven a liability when the infusion of silver spiked inflation and slowed economic development at home. Lacking both agricultural and mineral resources of its own, Spain could have developed its own industries and built a balanced trading pattern, as some of its Atlantic rivals were doing. But instead, it used imperial silver to buy manufactured goods from other parts of Europe, offering no incentives to develop exports of its own. So when the river of silver abated, Spain was plunged into debt.

Meanwhile, the Spanish crown's commitment to supporting the Catholic Church involved it in costly wars, as did attempts to maintain Spain's international dominance. The Thirty Years' War was the last straw: the strains of warfare drove the kingdom, with its power base in Castile, to raise more money and soldiers from the other Iberian provinces. This led to revolts in Catalonia and Portugal (incorporated into Spain in 1580), followed by the southern Italians' rebellion against their viceroys in Naples and Sicily. It was only by chance that Spain's greatest external enemies, France and England, could not act to take advantage of its plight. By 1652, the Castilian government had brought Catalonia to heel, but Portugal regained its independence. After the Peace of Westphalia, Spain was isolated, weakened, and without European allies.

The Peace of Westphalia favors France and Sweden, with Spanish and Austrian Hapsburgs markedly weakened

THE SWEDISH EMPIRE AND THE INVASION OF POLAND-LITHUANIA

In the decades after 1648, the power of Sweden continued to rise. With its mighty and disciplined army, Sweden colonized the Baltic in the course of the Thirty Years' War. But a richer prize lay to the south: the wealthy Polish-Lithuanian Commonwealth, with its prosperous commercial centers, rich agricultural lands, and mineral deposits. As Sweden's fortunes rose, Poland-Lithuania was in conflict with Russia for dominance of Ukraine, while also struggling to put down rebellions by Cossacks and Ukrainian peasants along its eastern frontier. Moreover, the reigning king, John II Casimir (r. 1648–1668), was unpopular with many factions within the Polish aristocracy, some of whom urged Charles Gustav of Sweden, the king's cousin, to claim the Polish crown.

In the summer of 1655, two Swedish armies marched into Poland from the north, supported by forces from Transylvania and Brandenburg-Prussia. Over the next five years, the formerly peaceful commonwealth suffered losses nearly as devastating as those later experienced in World War II (see Chapter 26), fighting on multiple fronts with only shaky support from its allies and more harm than help from the Russians. By 1660, when a peace treaty was negotiated, the capital of Warsaw had been destroyed, cities looted or torched, castles razed, and churches desecrated.

FRENCH POWER IN EUROPE AND NORTH AMERICA

France emerged from the crisis of the Thirty Years' War with a stronger state, more dynamic economy, and increased influence. Like Spain, France had grown over the course of previous centuries by absorbing formerly independent principalities whose inhabitants cherished traditions of local independence. The fact that France became more powerful as a result of this process, whereas Spain did not, can be attributed in part to France's more significant natural resources and in part to the greater prestige of the French monarchy. Most subjects of the French king, including the Protestants whose welfare had been cultivated by Henry IV, were loyal to the crown. Moreover, France had enormous economic resiliency, thanks to its rich and varied agricultural productivity. Unlike Spain, which had to import food, France was able to feed itself. Furthermore, Henry IV's ministers had financed the construction of roads, bridges, and canals to facilitate the flow of goods, supporting royal factories that manufactured luxury goods such as crystal, glass, and tapestries. Henry also supported the production of silk, linen, and wool throughout the kingdom.

Henry's patronage had enabled the explorer Samuel de Champlain to claim parts of Canada as France's first foothold in the New World. In 1608, Champlain founded the colony of Québec in the Saint Lawrence River Valley. Whereas the English had limited their colonial settlements to regions along the Atlantic coastline, the French set out to dominate the interior of the continent. French traders ranged far up and down the Canadian rivers that led inland, exchanging furs and goods with the Native American groups they encountered; French missionaries, meanwhile, used the same arteries to spread Catholic Christianity from Québec to Louisiana. Eventually, French imperial ventures spread via the Great Lakes and the great river systems along the Mississippi to the prairies of America's Midwest.

Unlike English and Dutch private ventures, French colonies administered by the crown

These far-flung French colonies were established and administered as royal enterprises, like those of Spain, a fact that distinguished them from the private commercial ventures of the English and the Dutch. Also, like New Spain, the colonies of New France were overwhelmingly populated by men. The elite of French colonial society were military officers and administrators sent from Paris; below their ranks were fishermen, traders, small farmers, and commoners. Because the fishing and fur trades relied on cooperative relationships with native peoples, a mutual economic interdependence grew up between the French colonists and the peoples of the surrounding regions; intermarriage between French traders and native women was common.

Yet in contrast to both Spanish and English colonies, these French colonies remained dependent on the wages and supplies sent to them from the mother country; only rarely did they become truly self-sustaining. Indeed, their financial rewards were modest: only furs, fish, and tobacco were exported to European markets. It was not until the late seventeenth century that some French colonists began to realize large profits by establishing sugar plantations on the Caribbean islands of Hispaniola (the French portion of this large island, now Haiti, was known as Saint-Domingue), Guadeloupe, and Martinique. By 1750, half a million enslaved individuals were laboring on Saint-Domingue under extraordinarily harsh conditions to produce 40 percent of the world's sugar and 50 percent of its coffee (see Chapter 15).

ILLINOIS INDIANS TRADING WITH FRENCH SETTLERS. This engraving from Nicolas de Fer's 1705 map of the Western Hemisphere illustrates the economic interdependence that developed between the early French colonists and the native peoples of the surrounding region. **> How did this situation differ from relations between Native Americans and English agricultural communities on the Atlantic coast?**

THE POLICIES OF CARDINAL RICHELIEU

This expansion of French power can be credited, in part, to Henry IV's de facto successor: Armand Jean du Plessis, **Cardinal Richelieu** (*REESH-eh-lyuh*). The real king of France, Henry's son Louis XIII (r. 1610–1643), had come to the throne at the age of nine. Richelieu, as his chief minister of state, dominated his reign, centralizing royal bureaucracy while exploiting opportunities to foster French influence abroad.

Within France, Richelieu amended the Edict of Nantes so that it no longer supported the military and political rights of Huguenots. He also prohibited French Protestants from settling in Québec. Yet the fact that he allowed the edict to stand at all reflects his larger interest in fostering a sense of French identity centered on the monarchy. In keeping with this policy, he imposed direct taxation on powerful provinces that had long retained their financial autonomy. Later, to ensure that taxes were efficiently collected, Richelieu instituted a new system of local government that empowered royal officials to put down provincial resistance.

These measures made the French royal government more powerful than any in Europe. It also doubled the crown's income. But this increased centralization of royal authority also provoked challenges from aristocratic elites and popular factions in the years after Richelieu's death—eventually leading to the French Revolution (see Chapter 18).

THE CHALLENGE OF THE FRONDE

An immediate response to these policies was a series of revolts known collectively as the *Fronde* (from the French for "slingshot"). In 1643, just after the death of Richelieu, Louis XIII was succeeded by his five-year-old son, Louis XIV. The young king's regents were his mother, Anne of Austria, and her alleged lover, Cardinal Jules Raymond Mazarin. Both were foreigners—Anne was a Habsburg and Mazarin an Italian—and

Cardinal Richelieu
(1585–1642) First minister to King Louis XIII, he is considered by many to have ruled France in all but name, centralizing political power and suppressing dissent.

both were despised by many powerful nobles, who also hated the way that Richelieu's government had curtailed their authority in their own ancestral provinces. Popular resentments were aroused as well, because the costs of the ongoing Thirty Years' War had combined with several consecutive years of bad harvests. So when the nobles expressed their disgust for Mazarin, they found much popular support.

In 1648, the levy of a new tax sent protesters out on the streets of Paris, armed with slings and projectiles. Neither the aristocratic leaders of the Fronde nor the commoners who joined them claimed to be resisting the young king; their targets were the corruption and mismanagement of Mazarin. But years later, when Louis XIV began to rule in his own right, the memory of these early turbulent years haunted him, and he resolved never to let the aristocracy or their provinces get out of hand. With this aim, he became the most effective absolute monarch in Europe (see Chapter 15).

The Crisis of Kingship in England

Of all the crises that shook Europe in this era, the most radical in its consequences was the English Civil War. The causes of this conflict were similar to those that had sparked trouble in other countries: regional hostilities, religious animosities, struggles among competing aristocratic factions, and a fiscal system that could not keep pace with the increasing costs of government. But in England, these developments led to the unprecedented criminal trial and execution of a king: an event that sent shock waves throughout the world.

THE ORIGINS OF THE CIVIL WAR

The chain of events that led to civil war can be traced to the last decades of Queen Elizabeth's reign. The expenses of England's defense against Spain, rebellion in Ireland, widespread crop failures, and the inadequacies of the antiquated English taxation system drove the queen's government deeply into debt. In 1603, when Elizabeth died and was succeeded by her cousin, James Stuart—King James VI of Scotland, James I of England—bitter disputes at court were complicated by the financial crisis. When the English Parliament rejected James's demands for more taxes, he raised what revenues he could without parliamentary approval, imposing new tolls and selling trading monopolies to favored courtiers. These measures aroused resentment against the king and made voluntary grants of taxation from Parliament even less likely.

James also struggled with religious divisions among his subjects. His own kingdom of Scotland had been firmly Calvinist since the 1560s. England, too, was Protestant—but of a very different kind, because the Church of England retained many of the rituals, hierarchies, and doctrines of the medieval Church (Chapter 13). Indeed, a significant number of English Protestants, the Puritans, wanted to bring this church more firmly into line with Calvinist principles. Although James was largely successful in mediating these conflicts, he stirred up trouble in staunchly Catholic Ireland by encouraging thousands of Scottish Calvinists to settle in the northern Irish province of Ulster, exacerbating a situation that had already become violent under Elizabeth.

PARLIAMENT VERSUS THE KING

The situation became more volatile in 1625, when James was succeeded by his surviving son, **Charles I**. Charles alarmed his Protestant subjects by marrying the Catholic sister of France's Louis XIII; he then launched a new war with Spain,

Charles I (r. 1625–1649)
The second Stuart king of England, Ireland, and Scotland, Charles attempted to rule without the support of Parliament, sparking a controversy that erupted into civil war in 1642.

straining his already slender financial resources. When Parliament refused to grant him funds, he demanded forced loans from his subjects and punished those who refused by lodging soldiers in their homes and imprisoning others without trial. Parliament responded in 1628 by imposing the Petition of Right, which declared that taxes not voted by Parliament were illegal, condemned arbitrary imprisonment, and prohibited the quartering of soldiers in private houses. Thereafter, Charles tried to rule England without Parliament—something that had not been attempted since the establishment of that body 400 years earlier (Chapter 9). He also ran into trouble with his Calvinist subjects in Scotland because he began to favor the most Catholic-leaning elements in the English Church. The Scots rebelled in 1640, and a Scottish army marched south into England to demand the withdrawal of Charles's "Catholicizing" measures.

Conflict sparks as Charles declares war without the financial support of Parliament

To meet the Scottish threat, Charles was forced to summon Parliament, whose members were determined to impose radical reforms on the king's government before they would consider granting him funds for an army. The Scottish Calvinists even found support among some Puritans in Parliament. To avoid dealing with this difficult political situation, Charles tried to arrest Parliament's leaders and force his own agenda. When this failed, he withdrew from London to raise his own army. Parliament responded by mustering a separate military force and voting itself the taxation to pay for it. By the end of 1642, open warfare had erupted between the English king and the English government: something inconceivable in neighboring France, where king and government were inseparable.

Arrayed on the king's side were most of England's aristocrats and largest landowners, many of whom owned lands in the Atlantic colonies as well. The parliamentary forces were made up of smaller landholders, tradesmen, and artisans, many of whom were Puritan sympathizers. The king's royalist supporters were commonly known by the aristocratic name of Cavaliers. They derisively called their opponents, who cut their hair short in contempt for the fashionable custom of wearing long curls, Roundheads. After 1644, when the parliamentary army was efficiently reorganized, the royalist forces were badly beaten; and in 1646, the king was compelled to surrender. Soon thereafter, the episcopal hierarchy of the Church of England was abolished and a Calvinist-style church was mandated throughout England and Wales.

The struggle might have ended here had not a quarrel developed within the parliamentary party (see **Competing Viewpoints** on pages 502–3). The majority of its members were ready to restore Charles to the throne as a limited monarch, under an arrangement whereby a uniformly Calvinist faith would be imposed on both Scotland and England as the state religion. But a radical minority of Puritans, known as Independents, insisted on religious freedom for themselves and all other Protestants. Their leader was Oliver Cromwell (1599–1658), who had risen to command the Roundhead army, which he reconstituted as the "New Model Army."

Charles 1ª b 1600.

CHARLES I. King Charles I of England was a connoisseur of the arts and a patron of artists. He was adept at using portraiture to convey the magnificence of his tastes and the grandeur of his conception of kingship. **› How does this portrait by Anthony van Dyck compare with the engravings of the "martyred" king in Interpreting Visual Evidence on page 505?**

THE FALL OF CHARLES STUART AND THE ESTABLISHMENT OF OLIVER CROMWELL'S COMMONWEALTH

Taking advantage of the dissension within the ranks of his opponents, Charles renewed the war in 1648. But he was forced to surrender after a brief campaign, and Cromwell seized control of the government. To ensure that the Puritan agenda would be carried out, Cromwell ejected all the moderates from Parliament by force. This "Rump" (remaining) Parliament then proceeded to put the king on trial and eventually to condemn him to death for treason against his own subjects.

Charles Stuart was publicly beheaded on January 30, 1649—marking the first time in history that a reigning king had been legally deposed and executed. Europeans reacted to his death with horror, astonishment, or rejoicing, depending on their political convictions (see *Interpreting Visual Evidence* on page 505).

After the king's execution, his son Charles and his royalist supporters fled to France. Cromwell and his supporters then abolished Parliament's hereditary House of Lords and declared England a Commonwealth: an English translation of the Latin *res publica*. Technically, the Rump Parliament continued as the legislative body; but Cromwell, with the army at his command, possessed the real power. By 1653 the "Commonwealth" had become the "Protectorate," a thinly disguised autocracy established under a constitution drafted by officers of the army. Called the *Instrument of Government*, this text is the nearest approximation to a written constitution that England has ever had. Extensive powers were given to Cromwell as Lord Protector for life, and his office was made hereditary.

THE RESTORATION OF THE MONARCHY

By this time, though, Cromwell's Puritan military dictatorship was growing unpopular, not least because it prohibited public recreation on Sundays and closed London's theaters. Many became nostalgic for the milder and more tolerant Church of England and began to hope for the restoration of a royalist regime.

The opportunity came with Cromwell's death in 1658. His son Richard had no sooner succeeded to the office of Lord Protector when a faction within the army removed him from power. As groups of royalists plotted an uprising, a new Parliament was organized. In April 1660, it declared that King Charles II had been the ruler of England since his father's execution in 1649. Almost overnight, England became a monarchy again.

Charles II (r. 1660–1685) revived the Church of England but was careful not to revive the provocative

OLIVER CROMWELL AS PROTECTOR OF THE COMMONWEALTH. This coin, minted in 1658, shows the Lord Protector wreathed with laurel garlands like a classical hero or a Roman consul. It also proclaims him to be "by the Grace of God Protector of the Commonwealth." › **What mixed messages does this imagery convey?**

policies of his father. Quipping that he did not wish to "resume his travels," he agreed to respect Parliament and to observe the Petition of Right. He also accepted all the legislation passed by Parliament immediately before the outbreak of civil war in 1642, including the requirement that Parliament be summoned at least once every three years. England thus emerged from its civil war as a limited monarchy, in which power was exercised by "the king in Parliament." It remains a constitutional monarchy to this day.

Under Charles II monarchy is restored, but with new powers for Parliament

THE ENGLISH CIVIL WAR AND THE ATLANTIC WORLD

These tumultuous events had a significant influence on the development of a new political sensibility within England's Atlantic colonies. The landed aristocracy had sided with the king during this conflict, but many in the colonies had sympathized with Parliament and its claims to protect the liberties of small landowners. Even after the Restoration of the monarchy in 1660, many colonial leaders maintained an antimonarchist and antiaristocratic bias. Moreover, twelve years of civil war had given the colonies a large degree of independence. As a result, efforts to extend royal control over the colonies caused increasing friction (see Chapter 15). The bitter religious conflicts that had divided the more radical Puritans from the Church of England also forced the colonies to come to grips with the problem of religious diversity. Some colonies, like Massachusetts, took the opportunity to impose their own brand of Puritanism on settlers, while others experimented with forms of religious toleration that went beyond the freedoms that existed in England.

After independence during civil war, English colonies resent growing authority

Paradoxically, though, the spread of ideas about the protection of liberties and citizens' rights coincided with a rapid and considerable expansion of unfree labor in the colonies. Prior to the 1640s, English colonies in North America and the Caribbean had been assured of a steady stream of immigrants. But the civil war and subsequent triumph of the Puritans under Cromwell caused a drop in migration. In the colonies, the decline was so sudden that it caused a depression in local economies: the demand for labor was increasing rapidly owing to the expansion of tobacco plantations in Virginia and sugar plantations in Barbados and Jamaica, which the British captured from the Spanish in 1655. These plantations, with their punishing conditions and high mortality rates, were insatiable in their demand for workers. Plantation owners thus sought to meet this demand by investing ever more heavily in indentured servants and enslaved Africans. The social and political crisis unleashed by the English Civil War also led to the forced migration of paupers and political prisoners, especially from Scotland, Wales, and Ireland.

These immigrants, many without resources, swelled the ranks of the unfree and the very poor in England's Atlantic colonies. As earlier arrivals sought to distance themselves from more-recent immigrants, whom they regarded as inferiors, new social hierarchies formed. The crisis of kingship in England thus led to a substantial increase in the African slave trade and a sharpening of social and economic divisions in the colonies.

Debating the English Civil War

The English Civil War raised fundamental questions about political rights and responsibilities, many of which are addressed in the following two excerpts. The first comes from a lengthy debate held within the General Council of Cromwell's army in October 1647. The second is taken from the speech given by King Charles I, moments before his execution in 1649.

The Army Debates, 1647

COLONEL RAINSBOROUGH: Really, I think that the poorest man that is in England has a life to live as the greatest man, and therefore truly, sir, I think it's clear, that every man that is to live under a government ought first by his own consent to put himself under that government, and I do think that the poorest man in England is not at all bound in a strict sense to that government that he has not had a voice to put himself under . . . insomuch that I should doubt whether I was an Englishman or not, that should doubt of these things.

GENERAL IRETON: Give me leave to tell you, that if you make this the rule, I think you must fly for refuge to an absolute natural right, and you must deny all civil rights, and I am sure it will come to that in the consequence. . . . For my part, I think it is no right at all. I think that no person has a right to an interest or share in the disposing of the affairs of the kingdom, and in determining or choosing those that shall determine what laws we shall be ruled by here, no person has a right to this that has not a permanent fixed interest in this kingdom, and those persons together are properly the represented of this kingdom who, taken together, and consequently are to make up the representers of this kingdom. . . .

We talk of birthright. Truly, birthright there is. . . . [M]en may justly have by birthright, by their very being born in England, that we should not seclude them out of England. That we should not refuse to give them air and place and ground, and the freedom of the highways and other things, to live amongst us, not any man that is born here, though he in birth or by his birth there come nothing at all that is part of the permanent interest of this kingdom to him. That I think is due to a man by birth. But that by a man's being born here he shall have a share in that power that shall dispose of the lands here, and of all things here, I do not think it is a sufficient ground.

Source: David Wootton, ed., *Divine Right and Democracy: An Anthology of Political Writing in Stuart England* (New York: 1986), pp. 286–87 (language modernized).

An Age of Doubt and the Art of Being Human

On the first day of November in 1611, a new play by **William Shakespeare** premiered in London. *The Tempest* takes place on a remote island, where an exiled duke from the Italian city of Milan has used his magical arts to subjugate the island's inhabitants. The plot drew on reports from the Caribbean, where slaves were called Caribans—hence the name of the play's rebellious Caliban, who seeks revenge on the magician Prospero, his oppressive master. Reminded that he owes his knowledge of English to the teaching of Prospero's daughter, Miranda, Caliban retorts, "You taught me language, and my profit on't is, I know how to curse." The benefits

William Shakespeare
(1564–1616) An English playwright who flourished during the reigns of Elizabeth I and James I.

Charles I on the Scaffold, 1649

I think it is my duty, to God first, and to my country, for to clear myself both as an honest man, a good king, and a good Christian.

I shall begin first with my innocence. In truth I think it not very needful for me to insist long upon this, for all the world knows that I never did begin a war with the two Houses of Parliament, and I call God to witness, to whom I must shortly make an account, that I never did intend to incroach upon their privileges. . . .

As for the people—truly I desire their liberty and freedom as much as anybody whatsoever. But I must tell you that their liberty and freedom consists in having of government those laws by which their lives and goods may be most their own. It is not for having share in government. That is nothing pertaining to them. A subject and a sovereign are clean different things, and therefore, until they do that—I mean that you do put the people in that liberty as I say—certainly they will never enjoy themselves.

Sirs, it was for this that now I am come here. If I would have given way to an arbitrary way, for to have all laws changed according to the power of the sword, I needed not to have come here. And therefore I tell you (and I pray God it be not laid to your charge) that I am the martyr of the people.

Source: Brian Tierney, Donald Kagan, and L. Pearce Williams, eds., *Great Issues in Western Civilization* (New York: 1967), pp. 46–47.

Questions for Analysis

1. What fundamental issues are at stake in both excerpts? How do the debaters within the parliamentary army (first excerpt) define "natural" and "civil" rights?

2. How does Charles defend his position? What is his theory of kingship? How does it compare with that of Cardinal Richelieu (see page 497)? How does it conflict with the ideas expressed in the army's debate?

3. It is interesting that none of the participants in these debates seems to have recognized the implications that their arguments might have for the political rights of women. Why would that have been the case?

---

of a European education could not outweigh the evils of colonization—but could be used to resist it.

The doubt and uncertainty caused by Europe's extension into the Atlantic world were primary themes and motivators of this era's creative arts, which both documented and critiqued contemporary trends. Another artistic response is the novel *Don Quixote*, which Miguel de Cervantes (*sehr-VAHN-tehs*; 1547–1616) composed largely in prison. It recounts the adventures of an idealistic Spanish gentleman, Don Quixote of La Mancha, who becomes deranged by his reading of chivalric romances and sets out to have delusional adventures of his own. His sidekick, Sancho Panza, is his exact opposite: a plain, practical man content with modest pleasures. *Don Quixote* is both a devastating satire of Spain's decline and a sincere celebration of human optimism.

Throughout the long century between 1550 and 1660, Europeans confronted a world in which all that they had once taken for granted was cast into confusion. Vast continents had been discovered, populated by millions of people whose very existence challenged Western civilizations' former parameters and Europeans' most basic assumptions. Not even religion seemed an adequate foundation on which to build new certainties, for European Christians now disagreed about the fundamental truths of their faith. Political allegiances were similarly under threat, as intellectuals and common people alike asserted the right to resist princes with whom they disagreed. The very notions of morality and custom were beginning to seem arbitrary. There was a sometimes desperate search for new bases on which to construct some measure of certainty.

WITCHCRAFT AND THE POWER OF THE STATE

Contributing to the anxiety was the widespread conviction that witchcraft was an increasing threat. Although belief in magic was not new, it was not until the late fifteenth century that authorities began to insist that such powers could derive only from some kind of satanic bargain. In 1484, Pope Innocent VIII had ordered papal inquisitors to use all means at their disposal to detect and eliminate witchcraft. Predictably, torture increased the number of accused witches who "confessed" to their alleged crimes; and as more accused witches "confessed," more witches were "discovered," tried, and executed—even in places such as England and Scotland, where torture was not legal and the Catholic Church had no influence. For both Luther and Calvin had urged that accused witches be tried and sentenced with less leniency than ordinary criminals.

It was through this fundamental agreement between Catholics and Protestants, and with the complicity of secular states, that an early modern "**witch craze**" claimed tens of thousands of victims. The final death toll will never be known, but the vast majority of the victims were women. When accusations of witchcraft diminished in Europe they became endemic in some European colonies, such as at the English settlement of Salem in the Massachusetts Bay Colony.

The obsession with witches resulted in part from fears that traditional religious remedies (prayer, the sacraments) were no longer adequate to guard against evil. It also reflected Europeans' growing conviction that only the state had the power to protect them. Even in Catholic countries, where witchcraft prosecutions began in Church courts, these cases were transferred to the state for final judgment and punishment because Church courts could not carry out capital penalties. In most Protestant countries, the entire process of identifying, prosecuting, and punishing suspected witches was carried out under state supervision.

THE SEARCH FOR A SOURCE OF AUTHORITY

The crisis of religious and political authority in Europe also spurred more rational approaches to the problem of uncertainty. The French nobleman **Michel de Montaigne** (*mohn-TEHN-yeh*; 1533–1592), the son of a Catholic father and a Huguenot mother of Jewish ancestry, applied a searching skepticism to all traditional ways of knowing and adopted a practice of profound introspection (see *Analyzing Primary Sources* on page 508). His *Essays* (from the French for "attempts") were composed during the French wars of religion and proceed from one basic question: *Que sais-je?* ("What do I know?"). Their first premise is that every human perspective is

Obsession with witchcraft comes from the anxieties of the age: religious change and growing state power >

witch craze The rash of prosecutions that took place in both Catholic and Protestant countries of early modern Europe and their colonies, facilitated by secular governments and religious authorities.

Michel de Montaigne (1533–1592) French philosopher and social commentator, best known for his *Essays*.

The Execution of a King

This allegorical engraving (image A) accompanied a pamphlet called *Eikon Basilike* ("The Kingly Image"), which began to circulate in Britain just weeks after the execution of King Charles I. It was purported to be an autobiographical account of the king's last days, and a justification of his royal policies. It was intended to arouse widespread sympathy for the king and his exiled heir, Charles II; and it succeeded admirably, as the cult of Charles "King and Martyr" became increasingly popular. Here, the Latin inscription on the shaft of light suggests that Charles's piety will beam "brighter through the shadows," while the scrolls on the left proclaim "virtue grows beneath weight" and "unmoved, triumphant." Charles's earthly crown (on the floor at his side) is "splendid and heavy," whereas the crown of thorns he grasps is "bitter and light"; this heavenly crown is "blessed and eternal." Even people who could not read these and the other Latin mottoes would have known that Charles's last words were: "I shall go from a corruptible to an incorruptible Crown, where no disturbance can be."

At the same time, broadsides showing the moment of execution (image B) circulated in various European countries with explanatory captions. This one was printed in Germany, with almost identical versions surviving from the Netherlands. It shows members of the crowd fainting and turning away at the sight of blood spurting from the king's neck while the executioner holds up the severed head.

Questions for Analysis

1. How would you interpret the message of image A? How might it have been read differently by Catholics and Protestants within Britain and Europe?

2. What might have been the political motives underlying the publication and display of these images? For example, would you expect the depiction of the king's execution to be supportive of monarchy or antiroyalist? Why?

3. Given what you have learned about the political and religious divisions in Europe at the time of the king's execution, where do you think image A would have found the most sympathetic audiences? Why might it be significant that image B circulated more widely in Germany and the Netherlands than in France or Spain?

A. King Charles I as a martyr.

B. The execution of King Charles I.

limited: what may seem true and moral to one group of people may seem absolutely false to another. From this follows Montaigne's second main premise: the need for moderation. Because all people think they follow the true religion or have the best form of government, he concludes that no religion or government is really perfect, and consequently no belief is worth fighting or dying for.

Another French philosopher, **Blaise Pascal** (*pahs-KAHL*; 1623–1662), confronted the problem of doubt by embracing an extreme form of puritanical Catholicism known as Jansenism, named after its Flemish founder, Cornelius Jansen. Until his death, he worked on a highly ambitious philosophical–religious project meant to establish the truth of Christianity by appealing simultaneously to the intellect and the emotions. In his posthumous work, *Pensées* ("Thoughts"), Pascal argued that only faith could resolve the contradictions of the world because "the heart has its reasons, of which reason itself knows nothing." Pascal's own awe in the face of evil and uncertainty is presented as evidence for the existence of God. His hope was that some measure of confidence in humanity and its capacity for self-knowledge could be rediscovered through faith.

THE SCIENCE OF POLITICS

The French jurist **Jean Bodin** (*boh-DAN*; 1530–1596) found a solution to uncertainty in the power of the state. Like Montaigne, Bodin was troubled by the upheavals of the religious wars. He had witnessed the Saint Bartholomew's Day Massacre of 1572 and, in response, developed a theory of absolute sovereignty that would (he surmised) put an end to such catastrophes. In his monumental *Six Books of the Commonwealth* (1576), he argued that the state has its origins in the needs of family-oriented communities, and its paramount duty is to maintain order.

Bodin defined sovereignty as the "most high, absolute, and perpetual power over all subjects," meaning that a sovereign head of state could make and enforce laws without the consent of those governed: precisely what King Charles of England later argued when he tried to dispense with Parliament—and precisely what his subjects ultimately rejected. Even if the ruler proved a tyrant, Bodin insisted that subjects had no right to resist, for any resistance would open the door to anarchy, "which is worse than the harshest tyranny in the world."

In England, experience of civil war led **Thomas Hobbes** (1588–1679) to propose a different theory of sovereignty in his treatise *Leviathan* (1651). Whereas Bodin assumed that sovereign power should be vested in a monarch, Hobbes argued that any form of government capable of protecting its subjects' lives and property might act as an all-powerful sovereign. Hobbes's conviction of the need for a strong state arose from his view of human nature. The "state of nature" before government, he wrote, was "war of all against all." Because any man naturally behaves as "a wolf" toward other men, life without government is "solitary, poor, nasty, brutish, and short." To escape such consequences, people must surrender their liberties to a sovereign state, in exchange for the state's obligation to keep the peace.

Hobbes and Bodin developed such theories in response to their firsthand experience of political and social upheavals. Their different philosophies thus reflect a practical preoccupation with the observation and analysis of actual occurrences (empirical knowledge) rather than abstract or theological arguments. Because of this practical bent, they are seen as early examples of a new kind of discipline: what we now call political science.

POETRY AND THEATER

In the late sixteenth century, the construction of public playhouses (enclosed theaters) made drama an especially effective mass medium for the formation of public opinion and the dissemination of ideas. Theater was an especially influential artform in England during the last two decades of Elizabeth's reign and that of her successor, James, and it fostered the very different talents of three particularly innovative playwrights.

Christopher Marlowe (1564–1593), who may have been a spy for Elizabeth's government and who was mysteriously murdered in a tavern brawl, was extremely popular in his day. In plays such as *Tamburlaine*, about the life of the Mongolian warlord Timur the Lame (Chapter 12), and *Doctor Faustus*, he created heroes who pursue larger-than-life ambitions only to be felled by their limitations. In contrast to the heroic tragedies of Marlowe, Ben Jonson (c. 1572–1637) wrote dark comedies that expose human vices and foibles. In *The Alchemist*, he balanced an attack on pseudoscientific quackery with admiration for resourceful lower-class characters who take advantage of their supposed betters.

William Shakespeare (1564–1616) was born into a family of a tradesman in the provincial town of Stratford-upon-Avon, where he attained a modest education before moving to London around the age of twenty. There, he composed or collaborated on an unknown number of plays, of which some forty survive in whole or in part. They owe their longevity to the author's unrivaled gifts of verbal expression, humor, and psychological insight. Those written during the playwright's early years reflect the upheavals of the late sixteenth century, including many history plays that recount episodes from England's medieval past and the struggles that established the Tudor dynasty. They also include the lyrical tragedy *Romeo and Juliet* and a number of comedies that explore fundamental problems of identity, honor and ambition, love, and friendship. The plays from Shakespeare's second period, like other contemporary artworks, are characterized by a troubled search for the mysteries and meaning of human existence; they showcase the perils of indecisive idealism (*Hamlet*) and the abuse of power (*Macbeth* and *King Lear*). The plays composed toward the end of his career emphasize the possibilities of reconciliation and peace, even after years of misunderstanding and violence: *The Tempest* is one of these.

THE ARTISTS OF SOUTHERN EUROPE

The ironies and tensions inherent in this age also found expression in the visual arts. In Italy and Spain, many painters cultivated a highly dramatic style sometimes known as Mannerism. The most unusual of these artists was

***VIEW OF TOLEDO*, BY EL GRECO.** This is one of El Greco's many landscape paintings depicting the hilltop city that became his home in later life. Its supple style almost defies historical periodization.

Montaigne on Cannibals

The Essays of Michel de Montaigne (1533–1592) reflect his attempts to grapple with the contradictions of his own time. In this famous passage, he contrasts the barbarism of the European wars of religion and conquest with the reported behavior of peoples in the New World.

I had with me for a long time a man who had lived ten or twelve years in that other world which has been discovered in our time. . . . This discovery of so vast a country seems to me worth reflecting on. I should not care to pledge myself that another may not be discovered in the future, since so many greater men than we have been wrong about this one. . . .

[And] I do not believe, from what I have been told about [the] people [of this land] that there is anything barbarous or savage about them, except that we call barbarous anything that is contrary to our own habits. Indeed we seem to have no other criterion of truth and reason than the type and kind of opinions and customs current in the land where we live. . . . These people are wild in the same way . . . that fruits are wild, when nature has produced them by herself and in her ordinary way; whereas, in fact, it is those that we have artificially modified, and removed from the common order, that we ought to call wild. . . .

These [people], then, seem to me barbarous in the sense that they have received very little moulding from the human intelligence, and are still very close to their original simplicity. . . . They are in such a state of purity that it sometimes saddens me to think that we did not learn of them earlier . . . when there were men who were better able to appreciate them than we. . . .

[For example,] they have their wars against the people who live further inland, on the other side of the mountains; and they go to them quite naked, with no other arms but their bows or their wooden swords, pointed at one end. . . . [And after] treating a prisoner well for a long time, and giving him every attention he can think of, his captor assembles a great company of his acquaintances.

He then ties a rope to the prisoner's arms, holding him by the other end, at some yards' distance for fear of being hit, and gives his best friend the man's other arm, to be held in the same way; and these two, in front of the whole assembly, dispatch him with their swords. This done, they roast him, eat him all together, and send portions to their absent friends. . . .

I am not so anxious that we should note the horrible savagery of these acts as concerned that, whilst judging their faults so correctly, we should be so blind to our own. I consider it more barbarous to eat a man alive than to eat him dead; to tear by rack and torture a body still full of feeling, to roast it by degrees, and then give it to be trampled and eaten by dogs and swine—a practice which we have not only read about but seen within recent memory, not between ancient enemies, but between neighbours and fellow-citizens and, what is worse, under the cloak of piety and religion—than to roast and eat a man after he is dead.

Source: Michel de Montaigne, *Essays*, trans. J. M. Cohen (Harmondsworth: 1958), pp. 105–13.

Questions for Analysis

1. How does Montaigne regard the "barbarous" people of the New World? How does he (re)define that concept?

2. How does Montaigne critique the assumptions and values of his own time in this passage?

3. Montaigne compares the reported behavior of cannibals with the behavior of Europeans during the ongoing wars of religion. What is he trying to achieve by making this comparison?

El Greco ("the Greek"; c. 1541–1614), a pupil of the Venetian master Tintoretto (1518–1594). Born Doménikos Theotokópoulos on the island of Crete, El Greco absorbed some of the stylized elongation characteristic of Byzantine icon painting (Chapter 7) before traveling to Italy and then settling in Spain. Many of his paintings were too strange to be truly appreciated in his day, and even now appear so avant-garde as to be almost surreal. His *View of Toledo*, for example, is a transfigured landscape, mysteriously lit from within.

In the seventeenth century, the dominant artistic style of southern Europe was the Baroque, whose name has become a synonym for elaborate, highly wrought sculpture and architectural details. This style originated in Rome during the Counter-Reformation and promoted a glorified Catholic worldview. Its most imaginative and influential figure was the architect and sculptor Gianlorenzo Bernini (1598–1680), a frequent employee of the papacy who created a magnificent celebration of papal grandeur in the sweeping colonnades leading up to St. Peter's Basilica. Breaking with the more serene classicism of Renaissance styles (Chapter 12), Bernini's work drew inspiration from the restless motion and artistic bravado of Hellenistic statuary (Chapter 4).

Characteristics of this Baroque style can also be found in paintings, such as those of the great Spanish master Diego Velázquez (*vay-LAH-skez*; 1599–1660), who served the Spanish Habsburg court in Madrid. Although many of his canvases display a Baroque attention to motion and drama, those most characteristic are more conceptually thoughtful and daring. An example is *The Maids of Honor (Las Meniñas)*, a masterpiece of self-referentiality, completed around 1656. It shows the artist himself at work on a double portrait of the Spanish king and queen, but the scene is dominated by the children and servants of the royal family.

THE MAIDS OF HONOR (LAS MENIÑAS), BY DIEGO VELÁZQUEZ. The artist himself (standing on the left) is shown working at his easel and gazing out at the viewer—or at the subjects of his double portrait, the Spanish king and queen, depicted in the distant mirror. The real focus of the painting is the delicate, impish princess in the center, flanked by two young ladies-in-waiting, a dwarf, and another royal child, as courtiers in the background look on.

***THE MASSACRE OF THE INNOCENTS,* BY PIETER BRUEGEL THE ELDER.** This painting shows how effective art can be as a means of political and social commentary. Here, Bruegel depicts the suffering of the Netherlands at the hands of the Spanish in his own day, with reference to the biblical story of Herod's slaughter of Jewish children after the birth of Jesus—thereby collapsing the two historical incidents.

DUTCH PAINTING IN THE GOLDEN AGE

Southern Europe's main rival in the visual arts was the Netherlands. Pieter Bruegel the Elder (*BROO-ghul*; c. 1525–1569) exulted in portraying the busy, elemental life of the peasantry. But late in his career, Bruegel became appalled by the intolerance and bloodshed he witnessed during the Calvinist riots and the Spanish repression of the Netherlands. He expressed his criticism in works such as *The Massacre of the Innocents*: from a distance, this painting looks like a snug scene of village life; but, in fact, soldiers are methodically breaking into homes and slaughtering helpless infants—as Herod's soldiers allegedly did after the birth of Jesus, and as warring armies did in Bruegel's own day.

Another Dutch painter, Peter Paul Rubens (1577–1640), was inspired by very different politics. A native of Antwerp, part of the Spanish Netherlands, Rubens was a staunch Catholic who glorified the Roman Church and the local aristocrats who supported the Habsburg regime. Even when his intent was not propagandistic, Rubens reveled in the sumptuous extravagance of the Baroque style. (He is most famous today for the pink and rounded flesh of his well-nourished nudes.) Although he celebrated martial valor for most of his career, his late painting *The Horrors of War* movingly captures what he called "the grief of unfortunate Europe, which, for so many years now, has suffered plunder, outrage, and misery."

In some ways a blend of Bruegel and Rubens, Rembrandt van Rijn (*vahn REEN;* 1606–1669) defies all attempts at easy characterization. Living in the staunchly Calvinist Dutch Republic, Rembrandt managed to put both realistic and Baroque

SELF-PORTRAITS. Self-portraits became common during the sixteenth and seventeenth centuries, reflecting the intense introspection of the period. Rembrandt painted more than sixty self-portraits; this one on the left, dating from around 1660, captures the artist's creativity, theatricality (note the costume), and honesty of self-examination. Judith Leyster, shown on the right, was a contemporary of Rembrandt who pursued a successful career during her early twenties before she married. Respected in her own day, she was all but forgotten for centuries thereafter, but is once again the object of much attention.

traits to new uses. Early in his career, he gained fame and fortune as a painter of biblical scenes and portraits for wealthy patrons. But as personal tragedies mounted in middle age, his art gained dignity, subtlety, and mystery. His later self-portraits are highly introspective and suggest that only part of the story is being told. Equally frank and fearless is the gaze of Rembrandt's slightly younger contemporary, Judith Leyster (1609–1660), who looks out of her own self-portrait with a refreshingly good-humored expression.

Conclusion

It would take centuries for Europeans to adapt themselves to the changes brought about by their integration into the Atlantic world. Finding new lands and cultures unknown to the ancients and unmentioned in the Bible had exposed the limitations

AFTER YOU READ THIS CHAPTER ⌄

CHRONOLOGY

1562–1598	French wars of religion
1566–1609	Dutch wars with Spain
1588	Destruction of the Spanish Armada
1598	Henry IV issues the Edict of Nantes
1607	English colony of Jamestown founded
1608	French colony in Québec founded
1611	William Shakespeare's play *The Tempest* performed in London
1618	Thirty Years' War begins
1621	Dutch West India Company founded
1642–1649	English Civil War
1648	Beginning of the Fronde rebellions
	Thirty Years' War ends
1660	Restoration of the English monarchy

REVIEWING THE OBJECTIVES

❯ How were the peoples and ecosystems of the Americas, Africa, and Europe intertwined during this period? What were some of the consequences of these new linkages?

❯ Why did the colonies of the Spanish, the English, and the Dutch differ from each other? How did these differences affect the lives and labor of colonists, both free and unfree?

❯ Which European powers came to dominate the Atlantic world? What factors led to the decline of Spain and the rise of France?

❯ What forms did religious and political conflict take in France, the Netherlands, and Germany? What were the causes of the English Civil War? What impact did this event have on the English colonies?

❯ How do the arts and the political philosophies of this period reflect the turmoil of Europe and the Atlantic world?

of Western civilizations' accumulated knowledge and called for new ways of knowing and explaining the world. The Columbian exchange of people, plants, animals, and pathogens that had previously been isolated from each other had a profound and lasting effect on populations and ecosystems throughout the globe. The transatlantic slave trade, which made all this possible, brought Africans and their cultures into a world of growing global connections under the worst possible circumstances—yet this did not prevent them from actively shaping this new world.

Meanwhile, the influx of silver from New Spain precipitated the great price revolution of the sixteenth and seventeenth centuries, which contributed to the atmosphere of crisis in a post-Reformation Europe already riven by religious and civil warfare. The response was a trend toward stronger centralized states, justified by theories of absolute government. Led by the French monarchy of Louis XIV, these absolutist regimes would reach their apogee in the coming century.

Go to **INQUIZITIVE** to see what you've learned—and learn what you've missed—with personalized feedback along the way.

PEOPLE, IDEAS, AND EVENTS IN CONTEXT

> What was the **COLUMBIAN EXCHANGE**? How did it affect relations among the peoples of the Americas, Africa, and Europe during this period?

> What circumstances led to the development of the **TRIANGULAR TRADE**?

> What were the main sources of instability in Europe during the sixteenth century? How did the **PRICE REVOLUTION** exacerbate this instability?

> How did **HENRY IV** of France and **PHILIP II** of Spain deal with the religious conflict that beset Europe during these years?

> What were the origins of the **THIRTY YEARS' WAR**? Was it primarily a religious conflict? Why or why not?

> How did the policies of **CARDINAL RICHELIEU** strengthen the power of the French monarchy?

> What policies of England's **CHARLES I** were most detested by his subjects? Why was his execution so momentous?

> In what ways did the **WITCH CRAZE** of early modern Europe reveal the religious and social tensions of the sixteenth and seventeenth centuries?

> What were the differences between **JEAN BODIN**'s theory of absolute sovereignty and that of **THOMAS HOBBES**?

> How did philosophers such as **MICHEL DE MONTAIGNE** and **BLAISE PASCAL** respond to the uncertainties of the age? How were contemporary trends reflected in the works of **WILLIAM SHAKESPEARE** and in the visual arts?

THINKING ABOUT CONNECTIONS

> The emergence of the Atlantic world can be seen as the *cause* of new developments as well as the *result* of historical processes. What long-term political, economic, and demographic circumstances drove the expansion of European influence into the Atlantic? What subsequent historical developments can be attributed to the creation of this interconnected world?

> The political crises of this era reveal the tensions produced by sectarian religious disputes as well as by a growing rift between powerful centralizing monarchies and landholding elites who are unwilling to surrender their authority and independence. What other periods in history are marked by similar tensions? How do those periods compare with the one we have studied in this chapter?

> The intellectual currents of this era reveal that a new generation was challenging the assumptions of its predecessors. In what other historical eras do we find similar phenomena? What social and political circumstances tend to produce consensus, and what tend to produce dissent, skepticism, and doubt?

15

European Monarchies and Absolutism, 1660–1725

IN THE MOUNTAINOUS REGION of central France known as the Auvergne, the Marquis of Canillac had a notorious reputation. His noble title gave him the right to collect minor taxes on special occasions, but he insisted that these privileges be converted into annual tributes. To collect these payments, he housed twelve accomplices in his castle whom he called his apostles. Their other nicknames—one was known as Break Everything—gave a more accurate sense of their activities in local villages. The marquis imprisoned those who resisted and forced their families to buy their freedom. In an earlier age, the marquis might have gotten away with this profitable arrangement. In 1662, however, he ran up against the authority of a king, **Louis XIV**, who was determined to demonstrate that the power of the central monarch was absolute. The marquis was brought up on charges before a special court of judges from Paris, was found guilty, and was forced to pay a large fine. The king then confiscated his property and had his castle destroyed.

Louis XIV's special court in the Auvergne heard nearly 1,000 civil cases over four months in 1662. It convicted 692 people, many of whom, like the Marquis of Canillac, were nobles. The verdicts were an extraordinary example of Louis XIV's ability to project his authority into the remote corners of his realm. During his long reign (1643–1715), Louis XIV systematically asserted his power over the nobility, the clergy, and the provincial courts. These elites were forced to look to the crown to guarantee their

> After 1660, many European rulers invoked an absolutist definition of sovereignty to expand the power of the monarchy. The most successful absolutist kings, such as Louis XIV of France or Peter the Great of Russia, limited the power of aristocratic elites and the independence of religious institutions.

> Absolutism was not universally successful. Efforts by English monarchs to create an absolutist regime in England after the civil war were resisted by political opponents of the Crown in Parliament. Other regimes in Europe that found alternatives to absolutism included the Dutch Republic and the Polish-Lithuanian Commonwealth.

> Absolutism reinforced the imperial ambitions of European monarchies and led to frequent wars that were fought both in Europe and in colonial territories in other parts of the world. The pressures of war favored dynasties capable of building strong centralized states with reliable sources of revenue from trade and taxation.

CORE OBJECTIVES

> **DEFINE** *absolutism,* **UNDERSTAND** its central principles as a theory of government, and **IDENTIFY** the major absolutist rulers in Europe during this period.

> **DEFINE** *mercantilism* and its relation to absolutist rule.

> **EXPLAIN** the alternatives to absolutism that emerged, most notably in England, the Dutch Republic, and Poland-Lithuania.

> **DESCRIBE** how the wars between 1661 and 1715 changed the balance of power in Europe and in the colonial spheres of the Atlantic world.

> **UNDERSTAND** the reforms undertaken by Peter the Great in Russia and **COMPARE** his regime with the absolutist kingdoms of western and central Europe.

interests, and their own power became closely connected with the monarchy. Louis XIV's model of kingship was known as *absolute monarchy*—a system of government that invested all authority in the king. In recognition of the influence of Louis XIV's political system, the period from around 1660 (when the English monarchy was restored and Louis XIV began his personal rule in France) to 1789 (when the French Revolution erupted) is traditionally known as the age of absolutism. This is a crucial period in the development of modern, centralized, bureaucratic states in Europe.

Absolutism was a political theory that encouraged rulers to claim complete sovereignty within their territories. An absolute monarch could make law, dispense justice, create and direct a bureaucracy, declare war, and levy taxation without the approval of any other governing body. Absolutist rulers claimed to govern by divine right, just as fathers ruled over their households (see **Competing Viewpoints** on pages 522–23). After the chaos and religious wars of the previous century, many Europeans believed that only absolute rulers could bring order to European life.

European monarchs also projected their power abroad. By 1660, the French, Spanish, Portuguese, English, and Dutch had established colonies in the Americas and Asia. These colonies brought profitable new consumer goods such as sugar, tobacco, and coffee to a wide public in Europe, and significant tax revenues to absolutist monarchs. They also relied on slavery to produce these goods. Rivalry among colonial powers to control the trade in human cargo and consumer goods was intense, leading to wars fought both in Europe and in contested colonies. These wars, in turn, drove absolutist rulers to extract more revenue from their subjects and to develop the armies, navies, tax systems, and trade controls that enhanced their power.

Absolutism was not universally successful. The English monarchy, restored in 1660 after the turbulent years of the civil war, attempted to impose absolutist rule but met resistance from parliamentary leaders. After 1688, England, Scotland, the Dutch Republic, Switzerland, Venice, Sweden, and Poland-Lithuania were all either limited monarchies or republics. In Russia, on the other hand, an extreme autocracy emerged that gave the tsar a degree of political control far beyond anything imagined by western European absolutists. Even in Russia, however, absolutism was never unlimited in practice. Absolute monarchs could rule effectively only with the consent of their subjects, particularly the nobility. When serious opposition erupted, even powerful kings were forced to back down. King George III of Britain discovered this when his North American colonies declared their independence in 1776, forming the United States of America. In 1789, a more sweeping revolution began in France, and the entire structure of absolutism came crashing to the ground (see Chapter 18).

Population and Climate in the Absolutist Age

A period of disorder and war drives European states to seek stability and order

Absolutism's promise of stability was in part a response to the disorder of the previous century. Religious persecution and war put large populations on the move before 1650 as religious minorities were expelled from many regions of Europe. The expulsion of Jews from Spain (between 1420 and 1520) was followed by similar expulsions of Jews from Geneva, areas of southern France, southern Italy, and some

German cities. Many French Protestants, known as Huguenots, emigrated in the last decades of the sixteenth century during France's wars of religion.

These population movements were dwarfed by the catastrophe of the Thirty Years' War (1618–1648), which killed one-third of the town dwellers in German territories of central Europe, and 40 percent of the rural population from hunger, disease, and murder. Many Europeans scrambled to meet basic security and subsistence needs. This problem was magnified by the Little Ice Age, a period of much lower temperatures in Europe and North America in the mid-seventeenth century that brought colder winters, a shorter growing season, and more- frequent crop failures. For populations living on the edge of subsistence—most people in Europe—famine was an ever-present threat.

Even in times of peace, European populations were highly mobile. This movement of people challenges myths of a "traditional" Europe where people were born and died in a single village. Regions that could not support their own population sent laborers annually to more fertile areas where larger farms paid higher wages. Tens of thousands of migrant workers went every summer to eastern England, to the farms of the Paris basin in northern France, and to Castile and Galicia in Spain to harvest grain. Similar numbers moved annually to southern France to pick grapes and to northern Italy to harvest rice.

Itinerant traders accompanied labor migrants. Commercial travelers built enduring networks: by the 1700s, for example, forty villages on the border between the Netherlands and present-day Belgium sent 500 to 800 traders every year on routes that reached from the Atlantic coast to western Russia, selling textiles, copper products, and women's hair for the wig industry along the way. Other mobile trades included chimney sweeps, stonemasons, and construction workers who moved seasonally from rural areas to cities to seek work. This mobility of people within Europe was just as important for economic development as the broader movement of peoples in the Atlantic world (see Chapter 14).

WINTER LANDSCAPE WITH ICE SKATERS, c. 1608, HENDRICK AVERCAMP. During the "Little Ice Age" more-frequent cold winters regularly froze rivers and canals in northern Europe. Dutch painters frequently depicted winter village scenes, which provide a vivid portrait of daily life, work, and leisure during this period.

Absolutism's Goals and Opponents

Absolutist monarchs sought control of the state's armed forces and its legal system, and demanded the right to collect and spend the state's financial resources at will. To do this, they needed an efficient bureaucracy that owed its allegiance to the monarch. Creating such a bureaucracy was expensive but necessary to weaken the authority of other bodies that hindered the free exercise of royal power. The nobility and the clergy, with their traditional legal privileges; the political authority of semiautonomous regions; and representative assemblies such as parliaments, diets, or Estates General were all obstacles—in the eyes of absolutists—to strong, centralized monarchical government. The history of absolutism is the history of kings who attempted to bring such institutions to heel.

By expanding royal bureaucracy, absolutist rulers diminish financial and legal power of nobility and clergy

In most Protestant countries, the church had already been subordinated to the state when the age of absolutism began. Even where Roman Catholicism remained the state religion, such as in France, Spain, and Austria, absolutist monarchs worked to bring the Church under royal control. Louis XIV took an active role in religious matters, appointing his own bishops and encouraging the repression of religious dissidents. Unlike his predecessors, however, he rarely appointed members of the clergy to offices within his administration.

The most important opponents of royal absolutism were nobles. Louis XIV deprived the French nobility of political power but increased their social prestige by making them live at his court at Versailles (*vuhr-SY*). **Peter the Great** of Russia forced his nobles into lifelong government service. Successive monarchs in Brandenburg-Prussia co-opted the aristocracy by granting them immunity to taxation and giving them the right to enserf their peasants; in exchange, they ceded administrative control to the Prussian state. In most European monarchies, including Spain, France, Prussia, and England, the nobility retained their role within the military. Absolutist monarchies of the eighteenth century continued to trade privileges for allegiance, so that nobles came to see their own interests as tied to those of the crown. For this reason, wary cooperation between kings and nobles was more common than open conflict during the eighteenth century.

The Absolutism of Louis XIV

In Louis XIV's state portrait, it is almost impossible to discern the human being behind the facade of the absolute monarch dressed in his coronation robes and surrounded by the symbols of his authority. Louis and his successors staged theatrical demonstrations of their sovereignty to enhance their position as rulers endowed with godlike powers.

PERFORMING ROYALTY AT VERSAILLES

Louis's most elaborate staging of his authority took place at his palace at Versailles, outside Paris. The building's front was a third of a mile in length. Inside, tapestries and paintings celebrated French military victories, and mirrors reflected light throughout the building. In the vast gardens outside, statues of the Greek god of the sun, Apollo, recalled Louis's claim to be the "Sun King" of France. Noblemen vied to attend him when he arose from bed, ate his meals (usually stone-cold after having traveled the distance of several city blocks from kitchen to table), strolled in his gardens (even the way the king walked was choreographed by the royal dancing master), or rode to the hunt. France's leading nobles were required to reside with Louis at Versailles for a portion of the year; the splendor of Louis's court was calculated to blind them to the possibility of disobedience (see *Interpreting Visual Evidence* on pages 520–21).

But the nobility did not surrender all their power. They retained enormous privileges and rights over local peasants within their jurisdiction. The absolutist system forced the nobility to depend on the crown, but it did not seek to undermine their superior place in a deeply hierarchical society. The relationship between Louis XIV and the nobility was more a negotiated settlement than a complete victory of the king. In their own way, absolutists still depended on the consent of other powerful elites in their kingdom.

ADMINISTRATION AND FINANCE

Absolutist rulers concentrated power in fewer hands, thus diminishing the ability of local elites to shape policy. Under Louis, the royal administration was run by thirty-three royal attendants appointed to each of France's regions. Members of regional *parlements* (law courts) that refused to approve his laws were exiled. The Estates General, the French representative assembly that met at the king's pleasure, was last summoned in 1614 and did not meet at all in Louis's long reign. It was not convened again until 1789.

Louis's most able official was Jean-Baptiste Colbert, finance minister from 1664 to 1683. Before Louis XIV's reign, the tax system was notoriously inefficient: the nobility was exempt from the land tax (*taille*), and collection of indirect taxes on salt, wine, tobacco, and other goods was difficult. Colbert eliminated the practice of tax farming, which permitted collection agents to retain a percentage of taxes they gathered for the king. When Colbert assumed office, only about 25 percent of collected taxes reached the treasury. By the time he died, this figure reached 80 percent. Colbert raised additional funds through the sale of public offices, including judgeships and mayoralties, and he forced guilds to pay for the enforcement of trade regulations.

Colbert was a **mercantilist**—he believed that the state must organize the economy to increase its power. The monarchy's wealth would grow if the realm reduced its imports and increased its exports. He imposed tariffs on foreign goods and used state money to promote the domestic manufacture of imports like silk, lace, tapestries, and glass. To encourage trade he improved France's roads, bridges, and waterways. But Colbert's efforts to increase royal revenues fell short of the insatiable demands of Louis XIV's wars (see pages 520–21). By the end of Louis's reign, his aggressive foreign policy lay in ruins, and his country's finances had been shattered by the unsustainable costs of war.

> **mercantilism** A theory and policy for directing the economy of monarchial states between 1600 and 1800, based on the assumption that wealth and power depended on a favorable balance of trade and the accumulation of precious metals.

> *Colbert's mercantilist policy: protecting domestic industries through tariffs and favorable trade policies*

LOUIS XIV'S RELIGIOUS POLICIES

Louis was determined to impose religious unity on France. The majority of the French population was Roman Catholic, but Louis vigorously persecuted dissenting movements within the Church, especially the Quietists and the Jansenists. Quietists emphasized a personal mysticism that believed in a direct relationship between God and the individual. Louis and the Church hierarchy disliked Quietism because it implied that believers did not need the intermediary services of the clergy. Jansenism—a movement named for its founder, Cornelius Jansen, a seventeenth-century bishop of Ypres—held to an Augustinian doctrine of predestination that sounded like a kind of Catholic Calvinism. Louis offered Quietists and Jansenists a stark choice between recanting and prison, or exile. At the same time, he supported the Jesuits in their efforts to create a Counter-Reformation Catholic Church in France. Louis's support for the Jesuits upset the traditional Gallican Catholics of France, however, who desired a French church independent of papal, Jesuit, and Spanish influence. As a result of this dissension among Catholics, the religious aura of Louis's kingship diminished during his reign.

Against the Protestant Huguenots Louis waged unrelenting war. Protestant churches and schools were destroyed, and Protestants were banned from many professions. In 1685, Louis revoked the Edict of Nantes, the legal foundation of the toleration the Huguenots had enjoyed since 1598. Protestant clerics were exiled, laymen were sent to the galleys as slaves, and their children were forcibly

The Performance and Display of Absolute Power at the Court of Louis XIV

Historians studying the history of absolutism and the court of Louis XIV in particular have emphasized the Sun King's brilliant use of symbols and display to demonstrate his personal embodiment of sovereignty. Royal portraits, such as that painted by Hyacinthe Rigaud in 1701 (image A), vividly illustrate the degree to which Louis's power was based on a studied performance. His pose, with his exposed and shapely calf, was an important indication of power and virility, necessary elements of legitimacy for a hereditary monarch. In the elaborate rituals of court life at Versailles, Louis often placed his own body at the center of attention, performing in one instance as the god Apollo in a ballet before his assembled courtiers. His movements through the countryside, accompanied by a retinue of soldiers, servants, and aristocrats, were another occasion for highly stylized ritual demonstrations of his quasi-divine status. Finally, of course, the construction of his palace at Versailles, with its symmetrical architecture and sculpted gardens, was a demonstration that his power extended over the natural world as easily as it did over the lives of his subjects.

Questions for Analysis

1. Who was the intended audience for the king's performance of absolute sovereignty?

2. Who were Louis's primary competitors in this contest for eminence through the performance of power?

3. What possible political dangers might lie in wait for a regime that invested so heavily in the sumptuous display of semidivine authority?

A. Hyacinthe Rigaud's 1701 portrait of Louis XIV.

B. Louis XIV as the Sun King (1653).

C. *A Cavalcade*, by Adam Frans van der Meulen (1664).

D. *The Palace of Versailles*, by Pierre Patel (c. 1668).

Absolutism and Patriarchy

These selections show how two political theorists justified royal absolutism by deriving it from the absolute authority of a father over his household. Bishop Jacques-Bénigne Bossuet (1627–1704) was a famous French preacher and the tutor to the son of King Louis XIV of France before becoming bishop of Meaux. Sir Robert Filmer (1588–1653) was an English political theorist. Filmer's works attracted particular attention in the 1680s, when John Locke directed the first of his Two Treatises of Government *to refute Filmer's views on the patriarchal nature of royal authority.*

Bossuet on the Nature of Monarchical Authority

There are four characteristics or qualities essential to royal authority. First, royal authority is sacred; Secondly, it is paternal; Thirdly, it is absolute; Fourthly, it is subject to reason.... All power comes from God.... Thus princes act as ministers of God, and his lieutenants on earth. It is through them that he exercises his empire.... In this way ... the royal throne is not the throne of a man, but the throne of God himself....

We have seen that kings hold the place of God, who is the true Father of the human race. We have also seen that the first idea of power that there was among men, is that of paternal power; and that kings were fashioned on the model of fathers. Moreover, all the world agrees that obedience, which is due to public power, is only found ... in the precept which obliges one to honor his parents. From all this it appears that the name "king" is a father's name, and that goodness is the most natural quality in kings....

Royal authority is absolute. In order to make this term odious and insupportable, many pretend to confuse absolute government and arbitrary government. But nothing is more distinct, as we shall make clear when we speak of justice.... The prince need account to no one for what he ordains.... Without this absolute authority, he can neither do good nor suppress evil: his power must be such that no one can hope to escape him.... [T]he sole defense of individuals against the public power must be their innocence....

One must, then, obey princes as if they were justice itself, without which there is neither order nor justice in affairs. They are gods, and share in some way in divine independence.... It follows from this that he who does not want to obey the prince ... is condemned irremissibly to death as an enemy of public peace and of human society.... The prince can correct himself when he knows that he has done badly; but against his authority there can be no remedy....

Source: Jacques-Bénigne Bossuet, *Politics Drawn from the Very Words of Holy Scripture*, trans. Patrick Riley (Cambridge: 1990), pp. 46–69, 81–83.

> *Religious persecution causes massive migration, with human and economic effects* ❯

baptized as Catholics. Many families converted, but 200,000 Protestant refugees fled to England, Holland, Germany, and America, taking with them their professional and artisanal skills. This emigration was an enormous loss to France. Huguenots fleeing Louis XIV's persecution, for example, established the silk industries of Berlin and London.

FRENCH COLONIALISM UNDER LOUIS XIV

Colbert regarded overseas expansion as an integral part of the monarchy's economic policy, and with his guidance, France emerged as a major colonial power. Colbert encouraged the development of sugar-producing colonies in the West Indies, the largest of which was Saint-Domingue (present-day Haiti). Sugar, virtually unknown

Filmer on the Patriarchal Origins of Royal Authority

The first government in the world was monarchical, in the father of all flesh, Adam being commanded to multiply, and people the earth, and to subdue it, and having dominion given him over all creatures, was thereby the monarch of the whole world; none of his posterity had any right to possess anything, but by his grant or permission, or by succession from him. . . . Adam was the father, king and lord over his family: a son, a subject, and a servant or a slave were one and the same thing at first. . . .

I cannot find any one place or text in the Bible where any power . . . is given to a people either to govern themselves, or to choose themselves governors, or to alter the manner of government at their pleasure. The power of government is settled and fixed by the commandment of "honour thy father"; if there were a higher power than the fatherly, then this commandment could not stand and be observed. . . .

All power on earth is either derived or usurped from the fatherly power, there being no other original to be found of any power whatsoever. For if there should be granted two sorts of power without any subordination of one to the other, they would be in perpetual strife which should be the supreme, for two supremes cannot agree. If the fatherly power be supreme, then the power of the people must be subordinate and depend on it. If the power of the people be supreme, then the fatherly power must submit to it, and cannot be exercised without the licence of the people, which must quite destroy the frame and course of nature. Even the power which God himself exercises over mankind is by right of fatherhood: he is both the king and father of us all. As God has exalted the dignity of earthly kings . . . by saying they are gods, so . . . he has been pleased . . . [t]o humble himself by assuming the title of a king to express his power, and not the title of any popular government.

Source: Robert Filmer, "Observations upon Aristotle's Politiques," in *Divine Right and Democracy: An Anthology of Political Writing in Stuart England*, ed. David Wootton (Harmondsworth, UK: 1986), pp. 110–18. First published 1652.

Questions for Analysis

1. Bossuet's definition of *absolutism* connected the sacred power of kings with the paternal authority of fathers within the household. What consequences does he draw from defining the relationship between king and subjects in this way?

2. What does Filmer mean when he says, "All power on earth is either derived or usurped from the fatherly power"? How many examples does he give of paternal or monarchical power?

3. Bossuet and Filmer make obedience the basis for order and justice in the world. What alternative political systems did they most fear?

---

in Christian Europe during the Middle Ages, became a popular luxury item in the late fifteenth century (see Chapter 14). It took the establishment of slavery in the Caribbean to turn sugar into a mass-market product.

The enslavement of Indigenous populations of the Caribbean and indentured servants from Europe demonstrated the profits to be made from unfree labor but could not satisfy the demand for more workers. It was in this context that the kidnapping and sale of African men and women as forced laborers developed in the Caribbean. Once the African coast was recognized as the most profitable source of unfree labor, the observed physical differences between African people and Europeans began to be cited as justifications for the practice, even as intermarriage and migration produced a diverse population made up of whites and free people of color alongside the growing number of enslaved people.

In 1685, Louis XIV established a legal framework for slavery in French colonies with an edict known as the *Code noir* (Black Code). The Code barred non-Catholics from owning enslaved people, banned slave markets or slave labor on Sundays, and prohibited enslaved persons from engaging in economic activity on their own. At the same time, the meanings attached to skin color remained complex: the Code accorded free people of color the same rights as whites, and free women of color who owned property attracted offers of marriage from ambitious whites seeking their fortune. In this context, the meanings attributed to "race"—understood as skin color—were both fluid and mutable.

By 1750, enslaved Africans in Saint-Domingue produced 40 percent of the world's sugar (and 50 percent of its coffee), exporting more sugar than Jamaica, Cuba, and Brazil combined. The sugar plantations of the Caribbean had their own social structure, with enslaved people at the bottom, people of mixed African and European descent forming the middle layer, and wealthy European plantation owners at the top. Well over half of the sugar and coffee sent to France was resold to markets throughout Europe. Historians estimate that as many as 1 million of the 25 million inhabitants of France in the eighteenth century lived off the money flowing through this colonial trade, making the slave colonies of the Caribbean a powerful force for economic change in France. The wealth generated from these colonies added to the prestige of France's absolutist government.

By 1700, France also dominated the interior of the North American continent, where French traders exchanged with Native Americans and missionaries preached Christianity in a vast territory that stretched from Québec to Louisiana. Like the earlier Spanish colonies (see Chapter 14), the French colonies were established and administered as direct crown enterprises. French colonial settlements in North America served as military outposts and trading centers, and they were overwhelmingly populated by men. The elite were military officers and administrators sent from Paris. Below their ranks were fishermen, fur traders, small farmers, and common soldiers who constituted the majority of French settlers in North America. Because the fishing and the fur trades relied on cooperative relationships with native peoples, a mutual economic interdependence grew between the French colonies and the peoples of the surrounding region. Intermarriage, especially between French traders and Native American women, was common. The financial returns from North America were never large, however. Furs, fish, and tobacco were exported to European markets but never matched the profits from the Caribbean sugar colonies or from trading posts in India.

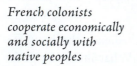

Colbert's mercantilist financial policy drives growth of colonial expansion

French colonists cooperate economically and socially with native peoples

Alternatives to Absolutism

Absolutism did not take root everywhere in Europe. A republican oligarchy continued to rule in Venice. In the Polish-Lithuanian Commonwealth, the monarch was elected by the nobility and governed alongside a parliament that met every two years. England, which had suffered through violent civil war between 1642 and 1651, followed by Oliver Cromwell's Commonwealth and the Protectorate (see Chapter 14), arrived at a constitutional settlement that gave a larger role to Parliament and allowed the participation of non-nobles in the affairs of state. Arriving at this settlement was not easy, however. The end of the civil wars had made it clear that England would be a monarchy and not a republic, but what sort of monarchy England would be remained an open question. Two issues were paramount: religion and the relationship between Parliament and the king.

THE RESTORATION MONARCHY IN ENGLAND

Following the restoration of the Stuarts in 1660, **Charles II** (r. 1660–1685) showed his affinity for Catholicism by bringing bishops back to the Church of England, but he also declared limited religious freedom for Protestant "dissenters." He promised to observe the Magna Carta and he accepted legislation stating that Parliament be summoned at least once every three years. England thus emerged from its civil war as a limited monarchy, with power exercised by the "king in Parliament." During the 1670s, however, Charles began openly to model his kingship on the absolutism of Louis XIV. England's elites became divided between Charles's supporters (known as "Tories," a nickname for Irish Catholic bandits) and his opponents (called "Whigs," a nickname for Scottish Presbyterian rebels). Both sides feared absolutism and the prospect of renewed civil war, but they could not agree which possibility frightened them more.

Charles's known sympathy for Roman Catholicism and his claim that he had the right to ignore parliamentary legislation worked to the advantage of his Whig opponents, who won a series of electoral victories between 1679 and 1681. Charles responded by moving aggressively against Whig leadership, executing several on charges of treason. Charles died in 1685 with his power enhanced, but his divisive legacy was the undoing of his less able successor, his Roman Catholic brother **James II**.

James's admiration of the French monarchy's Gallican Catholicism led him to look for ways to develop an absolutist state in England. His commitment to absolutism led him to build up the English army and navy, which required increased taxation and generated resentment in towns required to quarter troops. He took control over the country's new post office, making domestic surveillance routine, and prosecutions of seditious speech frequent. For the Whigs, James's policies were all that they had feared. The Tories, meanwhile, remained loyal to the Church of England and were alienated by James's Catholicism. When a son was unexpectedly born to the royal couple, and it was announced that he was to be raised a Catholic, events moved swiftly to a climax. A delegation of Whigs and Tories crossed the channel to Holland to invite James's Protestant daughter Mary Stuart and her Protestant husband, William of Orange, to sail to England with an invading army to preserve English Protestantism, the Church of England, and English liberties by summoning a new Parliament.

THE GLORIOUS REVOLUTION

Following the invasion, James fled for exile in France. Parliament declared the throne vacant, allowing William and Mary to succeed him as joint sovereigns in 1688. Parliament passed a Bill of Rights, which reaffirmed civil liberties, such as trial by jury, *habeas corpus* (a guarantee that no one could be imprisoned unless charged with a crime), and the right to petition the monarch through Parliament. The Bill of Rights also declared that

CHARLES II OF ENGLAND (R. 1660–1685) *IN HIS CORONATION ROBES.* This full-frontal portrait of the monarch, holding the symbols of his rule, seems to confront the viewer personally with the overwhelming authority of the sovereign's gaze. Compare this classic image of the absolutist monarch with the very different portraits of William and Mary, who ruled after the Glorious Revolution of 1688 (page 526). › **What had changed between 1660, when Charles II came to the throne, and 1688, when the more popular William and Mary became the rulers of England?**

the monarchy was subject to the law. The Act of Toleration granted Protestant dissenters the right to worship freely. In 1701, the Act of Settlement ordained that every future English monarch must be a member of the Church of England.

The English referred to the events of 1688–1689 as the "**Glorious Revolution**" because it established England as a mixed monarchy governed by the "king in Parliament" according to the rule of law. After 1688, no English monarch attempted to govern without Parliament, which has met annually ever since. The House of Commons also strengthened its control over taxation and expenditure. Although Parliament never codified the legal provisions of this form of monarchy into one constitutional document, historians consider the settlement of 1688 as a founding moment in the development of a constitutional monarchy in Britain.

Yet the revolution of 1688 was not all glory. It was accompanied by violence in many parts of England, Scotland, and Ireland. The revolution consolidated the position of large property holders, whose control over local government had been threatened by the absolutist policies of Charles II and James II. It reinforced the power of a wealthy class of English elites who would soon become even wealthier from government patronage and the profits of war. It also brought misery to the Catholic minority in Scotland and to the Catholic majority in Ireland. After 1690, power in Ireland would lie firmly in the hands of a "Protestant Ascendancy," whose dominance over Irish society would last until modern times.

The Glorious Revolution nevertheless favored the growth and political power of the English commercial classes, especially the urban populations whose livelihood depended on trade with the Atlantic world and beyond. In the decades to come, trade became a political issue, and merchants' associations began to lobby Parliament for favorable legislation. Whigs in Parliament became the voice of this newly influential pressure group of commercial entrepreneurs, and they called for revisions to the tax code that would benefit those engaged in manufacturing and trade. In 1694, the Whigs succeeded in establishing the Bank of England, inaugurating a financial revolution that would make London the center of a vast network of international banking and investment in the eighteenth century.

WILLIAM AND MARY. In 1688, William of Orange and his wife, Mary Stuart, became Protestant joint rulers of England in a coup that took power from her father, the Catholic James II. Compare this contemporary print with the portraits of Louis XIV (page 520) and Charles II (page 525). › What relationship does this portrait seem to depict between the royal couple and their subjects? › What is the significance of the gathered crowd in the public square in the background? › How is this different from the spectacle of divine authority projected by Louis XIV or the image of Charles II looking straight at the viewer?

JOHN LOCKE'S CRITIQUE OF ABSOLUTISM

The Glorious Revolution was the product of unique circumstances, but it also reflected antiabsolutist theories of politics that were taking shape in the late seventeenth century. Chief among these opponents of absolutism was **John Locke** (1632–1704), whose *Two Treatises of Government* were written before the Glorious Revolution but published for the first time in 1690.

Locke's **contract theory of government** was based on a parable about the origins of human society. According to Locke's story, humans had originally lived in a state of nature characterized by absolute freedom and equality, with no government of any kind. The only law was the law of nature, by which individuals enforced for themselves their natural rights to life, liberty, and property. Soon, however, humans perceived that the inconveniences of the state of nature outweighed its advantages. Accordingly, they agreed to establish a civil society based on absolute equality, and then to set up a government to arbitrate the disputes that might arise within this civil society. Locke considered this agreement to be the founding contract that gave government its legitimacy through the consent of the people. The contract did not make government's powers absolute. All powers not expressly surrendered to the government were reserved to the people themselves; as a result, governmental authority was conditional. If a government exceeded or abused the authority granted to it, the people had the right to dissolve it and create another.

What about slavery? Was the absolute power of the owner over the enslaved as illegitimate as the absolute power of the king? Locke's *Two Treatises* explicitly suggested that those who supported absolutist government were in fact endorsing slavery. Locke had not always been so outspoken in his opposition to this "vile and miserable" practice earlier in his career. He was an investor in the West African slave trade as early as 1663 and was secretary to a group working to enshrine the practice of slavery in British colonial territory. Toward the end of his life, Locke appears to have disapproved of the system of hereditary slavery that took root, but his opposition did not prevent the establishment of a racialized and hereditary slavery in British colonial property law.

In the late eighteenth century, Locke's ideas would resurface as part of the intellectual background of both the American and French Revolutions. Between 1690 and 1720, however, they served a far less radical purpose. The landed gentry who replaced James II with William and Mary read Locke as a defense of their conservative revolution. Rather than protecting their liberty and property, James II had threatened both; hence, the magnates were entitled to overthrow the king and replace him with a government that would preserve their "natural rights." English government after 1689 was dominated by Parliament; Parliament in turn was controlled by a landed aristocracy that perpetuated its control by limiting the right to vote or run for office to men who possessed substantial property. During the beginning of the eighteenth century, then, both France and Britain had solved the problem of political dissent and social disorder in their own way. The emergence of a limited monarchy in England after 1688 contrasted vividly with the absolutist system developed by Louis XIV, but both systems, in fact, worked well enough to balance the competing interests of royal authority and powerful landed nobles. At the same time, both systems appeared equally compatible with the expansion of the African slave trade, which remained extremely profitable for both British and French merchants.

THE DUTCH REPUBLIC

The Dutch Republic of the United Provinces, which had gained its independence from Spanish rule in 1648, also rejected absolutism (see Chapter 14). The seven provinces of the Dutch Republic preserved their autonomy with a federal legislature known as the States General, with delegations from each province. This flexible structure was intended to prevent the reestablishment of hereditary monarchy. Instead of a king, the republic delegated the title of *stadtholder*, or steward, to the princes of the House of Orange. The *stadtholder* had no power to make laws, though they had some military authority.

contract theory of government Posits that government authority is both contractual and conditional; therefore, if a government has abused its given authority, society has the right to dissolve it and create another.

Through a global
trade network and
tolerant policies,
the Dutch Republic
becomes home to
diverse population—
with some limits

By 1670, the prosperity of the Dutch Republic was strongly linked to trade: grain and fish from eastern Europe and the Baltic Sea; spices, silks, porcelains, and tea from the Indian Ocean and Japan; and enslaved people, silver, coffee, sugar, and tobacco from the Atlantic world. With a population of nearly 2 million and a capital, Amsterdam, that was an international hub for goods and finance, the Dutch Republic's commercial network was global (see Chapter 14). Trade brought with it an extraordinary diversity of peoples and religions, as Spanish and Portuguese Jews, French Huguenots, English Quakers, and Protestant dissidents all sought to take advantage of the spirit of relative toleration that existed in the Netherlands. This toleration had limits. The few enslaved people brought to the Republic rarely gained their freedom, though there was no legalized slavery in the European territory. Jews were not segregated, as in many other European capitals, but they were prohibited from joining guilds or trade associations. Tensions between Calvinists and Catholics were also a perennial issue.

Dutch power declined by the end of the seventeenth century. In 1672, the French king, Louis XIV, put together a coalition that quickly overran all but two of the Dutch provinces. Popular anger at the failures of Dutch leadership turned violent, and the panicked assemblies named William of Orange the new stadtholder of Holland. William opened the dikes that held back the sea from the republic's low-lying territories, and the French armies were forced to retreat in the face of rising waters. After the Glorious Revolution of 1688 in England brought William of Orange to the English throne, the Dutch allied with the English against the French.

English alliance draws
Dutch into costly wars

This alliance protected the republic from France, but it also forced the Dutch into heavy expenditures on fortifications and involved them in a series of costly wars (see the next section). As a result, the flexible political institutions that had been part of the strength of the Dutch Republic became more rigid and inflexible over time. In the eighteenth century, the Dutch no longer exercised the same influence abroad.

THE POLISH-LITHUANIAN COMMONWEALTH

The Commonwealth of Poland and Lithuania ruled over much of present-day Poland, Lithuania, Latvia, Estonia, Belarus, and Ukraine between 1569 and 1795. At its greatest extent, in the early seventeenth century, the Commonwealth reached from the Baltic coast nearly to the Black Sea. The Commonwealth had a tradition of limits to royal authority, making it an important exception to the trend toward absolutist rule.

The limits to the king's power in Poland-Lithuania were enforced by the relatively numerous landowning gentry. These nobles elected members to smaller provincial assemblies and to a parliament known as the Sejm (SAY-m). It was generally accepted that the king could not outfit an army or raise taxes without consulting the Sejm. After 1569, the Chamber and the Senate met for a six-week session at least every two years. When the king died, the Sejm supervised the process by which the landowning aristocracy elected a new ruler. Parliamentary authority was not at all complete, however, and the crown retained considerable power. One-sixth of the land in the Commonwealth remained under the direct control of the king.

Therefore, in the Restoration monarchy of England after 1688, the Dutch Republic, and the Polish-Lithuanian Commonwealth, circumstances allowed for greater power to remain in the hands of the gentry. In France, Prussia, and Russia (see page 531), on the other hand, absolutist rulers eventually succeeded in imposing their will on the aristocrats who remained their most powerful rivals for authority.

War and the Balance of Power, 1661–1715

By the beginning of the eighteenth century, Europe was being reshaped by wars whose effects were global. These wars were caused by the French monarch's efforts to challenge his European rivals: the Habsburg powers in Spain, the Spanish Netherlands, and the Holy Roman Empire. Louis XIV's personal rule began in 1661 (he had come to the throne as a child in 1643), and he first invaded the Spanish Netherlands in 1667. In successive campaigns, he expanded his territory, eventually taking Strasbourg (1681), Luxembourg (1684), and Cologne (1688). In response, William of Orange organized the League of Augsburg, which eventually included Holland, England, Spain, Sweden, Bavaria, Saxony, the Rhine Palatinate, and the Austrian Habsburgs. The resulting Nine Years' War between France and the League extended from Ireland to India to North America (where it was known as King William's War), demonstrating the broadening imperial reach of European dynastic regimes and the significance of French and English competition in the Atlantic world.

These wars demonstrated both the power of Europe's absolutist regimes and their vulnerability. Financing costly wars was a central challenge faced by all of Europe's absolutist monarchs, and the pressure to raise revenues from their subjects through taxation strained European society to a breaking point. By the end of the eighteenth century, popular unrest and political challenges to absolutist and imperial states were widespread, both on the European continent and in the colonies of the Atlantic world.

FROM THE LEAGUE OF AUGSBURG TO THE WAR OF THE SPANISH SUCCESSION

The League of Augsburg reflected a new diplomatic goal in western and central Europe: preserving the **balance of power**. This goal animated European diplomacy for 200 years, until the balance-of-power system collapsed with the outbreak of the First World War. The main proponents of balance-of-power diplomacy were England, the United Provinces (Holland), Prussia, and Austria. By 1697, the League forced Louis XIV to make peace, because France was exhausted by war and famine. Louis returned many of his gains but sought a bigger prize: a French claim to the throne of Spain and its empire in the Americas, Italy, the Netherlands, and the Philippines.

In the 1690s, both Louis XIV of France and Leopold I of Austria (r. 1658–1705) pushed for their own relatives to succeed King Charles II of Spain, threatening the balance of power in Europe. When Charles II died, Louis XIV's grandson Philip (r. 1700–1746) was proclaimed King Philip V of Spain, and Louis XIV rushed troops into the Spanish Netherlands while also sending French merchants into the Spanish Americas to challenge Spain's monopoly on trade. Immediately the War of the Spanish Succession broke out, pitting England, the United Provinces, Austria, and Prussia against France, Bavaria, and Spain. English generals marched their armies deep into the European continent, inflicting a devastating defeat on the French and their Bavarian allies at Blenheim (1704). Soon after, the English captured Gibraltar, establishing a commercial foothold in the Mediterranean. The costs of the campaign nevertheless created a chorus of complaints from English and Dutch merchants, who feared the damage that was being done to trade and commerce. Queen Anne of England (Mary's sister and William's successor) grew disillusioned with the war, and her government sent out peace feelers to France.

In 1713, the war finally came to an end with the **Treaty of Utrecht**. Its terms were reasonably fair to all sides. Philip V remained on the throne of Spain and

balance of powers The principle that no one country should be powerful enough to destabilize international relations.

Treaty of Utrecht (1713) Resolution to the War of the Spanish Succession that reestablished a balance of power in Europe, to the benefit of Britain and in ways that disadvantaged Spain, Holland, and France.

France's motivation to control Spanish succession is tied to its colonial holdings

THE TREATY OF UTRECHT, 1713. This illustration from a French royal almanac depicts the treaty that ended the War of the Spanish Succession and reshaped the balance of power in western Europe in favor of Britain and France.

After the Treaty of Utrecht, Britain emerges as the dominant power in slave trade ❯

kept Spain's colonial empire intact. In return, Louis agreed that France and Spain would never be united under the same ruler. Austria gained territories in the Spanish Netherlands and Italy, including Milan and Naples. The Dutch were guaranteed protection of their borders against future invasions by France, but the French retained both Lille and Strasbourg. The most significant consequences of the settlement, however, were played out in the Atlantic world, as the balance of powers among Europe's colonial empires underwent a profound shift.

IMPERIAL RIVALRIES AFTER THE TREATY OF UTRECHT

The fortunes of Europe's colonial empires changed dramatically owing to the wars of the late seventeenth and early eighteenth centuries. Habsburg Spain proved unable to defend its early monopoly over colonial trade, and by 1700, although Spain still possessed a substantial empire, it lay at the mercy of its more dynamic rivals. Portugal, too, found it impossible to prevent foreign penetration of its colonial empire. In 1703, the English signed a treaty with Portugal allowing English merchants to export woolens duty free into Portugal and allowing Portugal to ship its wines duty free into England. Access to Portugal also led British merchants to trade with the Portuguese colony of Brazil, an important sugar producer and the largest of all the American markets for enslaved Africans.

The 1713 Treaty of Utrecht opened a new era of colonial rivalries. The French retained Québec and other territories in North America, as well as their small foothold in India. The biggest winner by far was Great Britain, as the combined kingdoms of England and Scotland were known after 1707. The British kept Gibraltar and Minorca in the Mediterranean and also acquired large chunks of French territory in the New World, including Newfoundland, mainland Nova Scotia, the Hudson Bay, and the Caribbean island of St. Kitts. Britain also gained the right to transport and sell enslaved Africans in Spanish America. As a result, the British were now poised to become the principal merchants of human cargo and the dominant colonial and commercial power of the eighteenth-century world.

The Treaty of Utrecht thus reshaped the balance of power in the Atlantic world in fundamental ways. Spain's collapse was already precipitous, and by 1713 it was complete. Spain would remain the "sick man of Europe" for the next two centuries. The Dutch decline was more gradual, but by 1713, the inability of Dutch merchants to compete with the British in the slave trade diminished their economic clout. In the Atlantic, Britain and France were now the dominant powers. Although they would duel for another half century for control of North America, the balance of colonial power tilted decisively in Britain's favor after Utrecht. Within Europe, the myth of French military supremacy had been shattered. Britain's navy, not France's army, would rule the new imperial and commercial world of the eighteenth century.

The Remaking of Central and Eastern Europe

The decades between 1680 and 1720 were decisive in reshaping the balance of power in central and eastern Europe. As Ottoman power waned, the Austro-Hungarian Empire of the Habsburgs emerged as the dominant power in central and southeastern Europe. To the north, Brandenburg-Prussia was also a rising power. The most dramatic changes occurred in Russia, which emerged from a long war with Sweden as the dominant realm in the Baltic Sea and would soon threaten the combined kingdom of Poland-Lithuania. Within these regimes, the main tension came from ambitious monarchs who sought to increase the power of the centralized state at the expense the aristocracy and the Church. In Brandenburg-Prussia and in tsarist Russia, these efforts were largely successful, whereas in Habsburg Austria, regional nobilities retained much of their influence.

THE AUSTRIAN HABSBURG EMPIRE

In the second half of the seventeenth century, as Louis XIV of France demonstrated the power of absolutism in western Europe, the Austrian Habsburg Empire, with its capital in Vienna, must have seemed like a holdover from a previous age. Habsburg Austria was the largest state within what remained of the medieval Holy Roman Empire, a complex federal association of nearly 300 nominally autonomous dynastic kingdoms, principalities, duchies, and archbishoprics that had been created to protect and defend the papacy. Each Holy Roman emperor was chosen by seven "electors" who were either of noble rank or archbishops—but in practice, the emperor was always from the Habsburg family. Through strategic marriages with other royal lines, earlier generations of Habsburg rulers had consolidated their control over a substantial part of Europe, including Austria, Bohemia, Moravia, and Hungary in central Europe; the Netherlands and Burgundy in the west; and, if one included the Spanish branch of the Habsburg family, Spain and its vast colonial empire as well. After 1648, when the Treaty of Westphalia granted individual member states within the Holy Roman Empire the right to conduct their own foreign policy, the influence of the Austrian Habsburgs waned, at precisely the moment when they faced challenges from France to the west and the Ottoman Empire to the east.

The complicated structure of the Holy Roman Empire limited the extent to which a ruler such as Leopold I of Austria could emulate the absolutist rule of Louis XIV in France. Every state within the empire had its own political institutions and its own entrenched nobilities. Each state had a strong incentive to resist the centralization of tax collection or the raising of armies. Even if direct assertion of absolutist control was impossible, Habsburg rulers found ways to increase their authority. In Bohemia and Moravia, the Habsburgs encouraged landlords to produce crops for export by forcing peasants to provide three days of unpaid work per week to their lords. In return, the landed elites of these territories permitted the emperors to reduce the political independence of their traditional legislative estates. In Hungary, however, the powerful and independent nobility resisted such compromises. In 1679, when the Habsburgs began a campaign against Hungarian Protestants, an insurrection broke out that forced Leopold to grant concessions to Hungarian nobles in exchange for their assistance in restoring order. When the Ottoman Empire sought

Limitations to absolutist rule within Habsburg states

to take advantage of this disorder to press an attack against Austria from the east, the Habsburgs survived only by enlisting the help of a Catholic coalition led by the Polish king John Sobieski (r. 1674–1696).

In 1683, the Ottomans launched their last assault on Vienna, but after their failure to capture the Habsburg capital, Ottoman power in southeastern Europe declined. By 1699, Austria had reconquered most of Hungary from the Ottomans, and by 1718, it controlled Hungary, Transylvania, and Serbia. With these victories, Austria became one of the arbiters of the European balance of power. Obstacles to centralized absolutist rule persisted, however, and Austria was increasingly overshadowed in central Europe by the rise of another German-speaking state: Prussia.

EUROPE AFTER THE TREATY OF UTRECHT (1713). ▸ **What were the major Habsburg dominions?** ▸ **What geographical disadvantage faced the kingdom of Poland as Brandenburg-Prussia grew in influence and ambition?** ▸ **How did the balance of power change in Europe as a result of the Treaty of Utrecht?**

THE RISE OF BRANDENBURG-PRUSSIA

After the Ottoman defeat, the main threat to Austria came from Brandenburg-Prussia. Like Austria, Prussia was a composite state made up of geographically divided territories acquired through inheritance by a single royal family, the Hohenzollerns. Their main holdings were Brandenburg, centered on its capital city, Berlin, and the duchy of East Prussia. Between these territories lay Pomerania (claimed by Sweden) and an important part of the kingdom of Poland, including the port of Gdansk (Danzig). The Hohenzollerns sought to unite their state by acquiring these intervening territories. Over the course of more than a century of steady state building, they finally succeeded. In the process, Brandenburg-Prussia became a dominant military power and a key player in European balance-of-power diplomacy.

The foundations for Prussian expansion were laid by Frederick William, the "Great Elector" (r. 1640–1688). He obtained East Prussia from Poland in exchange for help in a war against Sweden. Behind the elector's diplomatic triumphs lay his

THE CITY OF STETTIN UNDER SIEGE BY THE GREAT ELECTOR FREDERICK WILLIAM IN THE WINTER OF 1677–1678 (C. 1680). This painting depicts the growing sophistication and organization of military operations under the Prussian monarchy. Improvements in artillery and siege tactics forced cities to adopt new defensive strategies, especially the zones of battlements and protective walls that became ubiquitous in central Europe during this period. › How might these defensive developments have shaped the layout of Europe's growing towns and cities? › How might this emphasis on the military and its attendant bureaucracy have affected the relationship between the monarchy and the nobility, or between the king and his subjects?

The Siege of Vienna (1683)

In 1683, the armies of the Ottoman Empire besieged the city of Vienna, the capital of the Austrian Habsburg monarchy, which was defended by forces of the Holy Roman Empire of the German Nations, led by King John III Sobieski of the Polish-Lithuanian Commonwealth. The battle marked the high point of Ottoman expansion into southeastern Europe, and the Ottoman defeat was celebrated by many in Europe as a victory of Christianity over Islam. The reality was more complicated, however, as Protestant armies in Hungary that allied with anti-Habsburg forces had received arms and support from the Ottoman Empire in the years before the battle, apparently in exchange for a promise that Hungary would control Vienna in the event of an Ottoman victory. This source, published in 1684 in English in Cologne and London, contains enough details to allow one to assume that it was, at least in part, informed by eyewitnesses of the events.

Emperor Leopold I Flees Vienna for Passau

The Emperor who had receiv'd a fierce alarm by the suddain irruption of the Infidels, and who consider'd that after the revolt of the Hungarians, he could no longer remain at Vienna in surety, bethought himself at the same time of leaving it. But first augmented the privileges of the Scholars, which were already very great, and considerable, that having receiv'd them as a recompence of their Courage which they shew'd heretofore against Solyman [the Ottoman Emperor Suleiman the Magnificent], when he besieg'd the City [in 1529] this should be a fresh incitement to defend it with the same resolution. He gave also to the Shoomakers Apprentices their Freedom, who were to the number of about 1500, in case they took Arms, and did any thing considerable for the Country.

* * *

Every one wept at his departure, and this Prince had much ado to forbear himself. So greatly was he afflicted to be thus constrained to abandon his people to the mercy of the Infidels. In the mean time each one endeavor'd to follow him, to avoid the being expos'd to those mischiefs which they represented. In fine, there being not Coaches enough to carry all those that offer'd 'emselves, several Women of Quality got behind like Lacques [servants]; so that one might have seen the first Prince in the World, follow'd by all the flower of the German Nobility, to go as an exul [exile] amidst the screeches and lamentations of his people, who presented 'emselves in his passage with showr's of tears. . . .

* * *

The Emperor all this while marched with a countenance sad and dejected like his fortune. Others kept a mournful silence, and although each had left their estates behind 'em 'twas not known whether their own mishap or that

---

> *Frederick William gains support of Junker nobles in exchange for financial privileges and wealth*

success in building an army and mobilizing the resources to pay for it. He gave the powerful nobles of his territories, known as "Junkers" (*YUN-kurs*), the right to enserf their peasants and immunity from taxation. In exchange, they staffed the officer corps of his army and supported his autocratic taxation system. Secure in their estates and made wealthy from the grain trade, the Junkers surrendered management of the Prussian state to the elector's reformed bureaucracy, whose main task was increasing the size and strength of the Prussian army.

By supporting Austria in the War of the Spanish Succession, the Great Elector's son, Frederick I (r. 1688–1713), earned the right to call himself king of Prussia of the Prince was to be most lamented. In fine, this march much resembled a Funeral Pomp, when another spectacle encreas'd the dolour and compassion. For they beheld the other side of the *Danube* all in fire, and the Emperor having caused his Coach to stop, knowing not at first what it was, soon perceived 'twas the *Turks*, who shew'd there new testimonies of their barbarous cruelty. He could not withhold his tears at the sight of a thing so much needing his compassion, and although he did all he could to refrain his grief, he could not effect it.

Disease Afflicts the Defenders of Vienna

And having made his retreat, and taken great care of the wounded, [Stahrenberg, the military commander of Vienna] made a review of those Forces he had left him; which he found diminish'd by a third part, not so much by Sallies, and in this last occasion, as by the Dysentery or Flux which began to rage in the Town, as well amongst the Citizens and Soldiers. In effect the fatigues together with the bad food they eat, had so heated the bloud of most of 'em, that they fell sick every day. And it being impossible for 'em after this to do service, the rest, whose weariness increased as fast as the number of the others diminish'd, were soon in the same condition, or at least so tir'd out with labour and watching, that they were all ready to drop down as they march'd. . . .

* * *

But that which contributed to render this malady more incurable was the Airs being so infected by the stench of the dead Bodies which lay unburied, that it could not be more dangerous in a time of Plague. The cause of this stench was that Stahrenberg would not yield to any terms of a Truce propos'd by the Visier [Vizier], to take away those of his party, who had been kild in so many several skirmishes, hoping that besides the displeasure he would receive thereby, this would be a spectacle to damp the Courage of the Soldiers, when in marching up to the Charge, they should see before their Eyes the fortune of their Companions, which would be a presage to them of the like. Howsoever whether 'twas this infection or something else, which brought this grievous sickness into the Town, they were so greatly incommodated [*sic*] by it, that they would willingly have been deliver'd from of it at the cost of a greater danger from the enemy. Yet did this distemper rage as well in the Camp of the Turks, of which there dyed every day near 300, but which was scarce perceivable, because they continually receiv'd fresh supplies, which made up their losses.

Source: Anonymous, *The History of the late war with the Turks, during the siege of Vienna, and the great victory obtain'd against them at the raising of the siege* (Cologne and London, 1684), pp. 33–86.

Questions for Analysis

1. How did Emperor Leopold encourage the people of the city to defend themselves even as he retreated to a safer location?

2. What is the significance of the term *Infidels*, which the author uses to describe the Ottomans?

3. What does this description tell us about the effects of the siege on military and civilian populations? What explanation does the author give for the spread of disease in the city and among the attacking armies?

from the Austrian emperor. He too was a crafty diplomat, but his main attention was devoted to developing the cultural life of his new royal capital, Berlin. His son, Frederick William I (r. 1713–1740), however, focused on building the army as his grandfather had done. During his reign, the Prussian army grew from 30,000 to 83,000 men, becoming the fourth largest army in Europe, after those of France, Austria, and Russia. To support his army, Frederick William I increased taxes and shunned the luxuries of court life. For him, the theater of absolutism was not the palace but the office, where he personally supervised his army and the growing bureaucracy that sustained it. Frederick William's son, known as Frederick the

Great, would use this Prussian army and the bureaucracy that sustained it to transform the kingdom into a major power in central Europe after 1740 (see Chapter 17).

Thus, in both Prussia and Habsburg Austria, the divided nature of the respective realms and the entrenched strength of local nobilities forced the rulers of each to grant significant concessions to noble landowners in exchange for increases in the power of the centralized state. The nobility in France sought to maximize their power by participating in the system of absolutist rule at the court of Louis XIV, and wealthy landowners in England sought to exercise their influence through Parliament. The nobilities of Prussia and Habsburg Austria had more leverage to demand something in return for their cooperation, most often the right to enserf or coerce labor from the peasantry in their domains. In both eastern and western Europe, therefore, the state became stronger. In eastern Europe, however, this increase in state power came at the expense of intensified feudal obligations that the peasantry owed to their local lords.

> *In Prussia and Habsburg Austria, nobles defer to growing state power in exchange for tightened grip over peasantry*

Autocracy in Russia

An even more dramatic transformation took place in Russia under Tsar Peter I (r. 1682–1725). Peter's official title was "autocrat of all the Russias," but he was soon known as Peter the Great. His imposing height (six feet, eight inches tall) and his mercurial personality (jesting one moment, raging the next) added to the outsize impression he made on his contemporaries. Peter was not the first tsar to bring his country into contact with western Europe, but his policies were decisive in making Russia a great European power.

THE EARLY YEARS OF PETER'S REIGN

Like Louis XIV of France, Peter came to the throne as a young boy, and his minority was marked by political dissension and court intrigue. In 1689, however, at the age of seventeen, he overthrew the regency of his half sister Sophia and assumed personal control of the state. Determined to make Russia into a great military power, the young tsar traveled to Holland and England to study shipbuilding and recruit skilled workers to help him build a navy. But while he was abroad, his elite palace guard (the *streltsy*) rebelled, attempting to restore Sophia to the throne. Peter returned home and crushed the rebellion with striking savagery. About 1,200 suspected conspirators were summarily executed, many of them gibbeted outside the walls of the Kremlin, where their bodies rotted for months as a graphic reminder of the fate awaiting those who challenged the tsar's authority.

THE TRANSFORMATION OF THE TSARIST STATE

Peter is most famous as the tsar who attempted to westernize Russia by imposing a series of social and cultural reforms on the traditional Russian nobility: ordering noblemen to cut off their long beards and flowing sleeves; publishing a book of manners that forbade spitting on the floor and eating with one's fingers; encouraging polite conversation between the sexes; and requiring noblewomen to appear, together with men, in western garb at weddings, banquets, and other public occasions. The children of Russian nobles were sent to western European courts for their education. Thousands of western European experts were brought to Russia to staff the new schools and academies Peter built; to design the new buildings he constructed; and to serve in the tsar's army, navy, and administration.

These measures were important, but the tsar was not motivated primarily by a desire to modernize or westernize Russia. Peter's policies transformed Russian life in fundamental ways, but his real goal was to make Russia a great military power, not to remake Russian society. For example, while his new taxation system (1724), which assessed taxes on individuals rather than on households, rendered many of the traditional divisions of Russian peasant society obsolete, it was created to raise more money for war. His Table of Ranks, imposed in 1722, had similar impact on the nobility. By insisting that all nobles must work their way up from the (lower) landlord class to the (higher) administrative class and to the (highest) military class, Peter reversed the traditional hierarchy of Russian noble society, which had valued landlords by birth above administrators and soldiers who had risen by merit. This created a powerful new incentive to lure his nobility into administrative and military service to the tsar.

As "autocrat of all the Russias," Peter the Great was the absolute master of his empire to a degree unmatched elsewhere in Europe. After 1649, Russian peasants were legally the property of their landlords; by 1750, half were serfs and the other half were state peasants who lived on lands owned by the tsar himself. (In contrast, many peasants in western Europe owned their own land, and very few were serfs.) State peasants could be conscripted to serve as soldiers in the tsar's army, as workers in his factories (whose productive capacity increased enormously during Peter's reign), or as forced laborers in his building projects. Serfs could also be taxed by the tsar and summoned for military service, as could their lords. All Russians, of whatever rank, were expected to serve the tsar, and all Russia was considered in some sense to belong to him. Russia's autocracy thus went even further than the absolutism of Louis XIV.

To consolidate his power further, Peter replaced the Duma—the tsar's handpicked council of noble elites—with a smaller handpicked senate, a group of nine administrators who supervised military and civilian affairs. In religious matters, he took direct control over the Russian Orthodox Church by appointing an imperial official to manage its affairs. To cope with the demands of war, he also fashioned a new, larger, and more efficient administration, for which he recruited both nobles

PETER THE GREAT CUTS THE BEARD OF AN OLD BELIEVER. This woodcut depicts the Russian emperor's enthusiastic policy of westernization, as he pushed everybody in Russia who was not a peasant to adopt western styles of clothes and grooming. The Old Believer (a member of a religious sect in Russia) protests that he has paid the beard tax and should therefore be exempt. › Why would an individual's choices about personal appearance be so politically significant in Peter's Russia? › What customs were the target of Peter's reforms?

The Revolt of the *Streltsy* and Peter the Great

The streltsy were four regiments of Moscow guards involved in a conspiracy in support of Peter the Great's older sister Sophia, who had earlier made claim to the throne while Peter was still a child. Approximately 4,000 of the rebels were defeated in June 1698 by troops loyal to Peter. Peter himself was abroad during the fighting, and although his officers had already tortured many of the streltsy *to determine the involvement of other nobles, he ordered further-reaching investigation on his return. One thousand of the* streltsy *were executed after being tortured again. Afterward, their bodies were put on display in the capital. Johann Georg Korb, an Austrian diplomat in Moscow, recorded his observations of the power wielded by the Russian autocrat.*

How sharp was the pain, how great the indignation to which the Czar's Majesty was mightily moved, when he knew of the rebellion of the Strelitz [*streltsy*], betrayed openly a mind panting for vengeance. [*sic*] . . . Going immediately to Lefort (the only person almost that he condescended to treat with intimate familiarity), he thus indignantly broke out: "Tell me, Francis, son of James, how I can reach Moscow, by the shortest way, in a brief space, so that I may wreak vengeance on this great perfidy of my people, with punishments worthy of their flagitious crime. Not one of them shall escape with impunity. Around my royal city, of which, with their impious efforts, they meditated the destruction, I will have gibbets and gallows set upon the walls and ramparts, and each and every of them will I put to a direful death." . . .

His first anxiety, after his arrival [in Moscow] was about the rebellion. In what it consisted? What the insurgents meant? Who had dared to instigate such a crime? And as nobody could answer accurately upon all points, and some pleaded their own ignorance, others the obstinacy of the Strelitz, he began to have suspicions of everybody's loyalty, and began to cogitate about a fresh investigation. The rebels that were kept in custody . . . were all brought in by four regiments of the guards, to a fresh investigation and fresh tortures. Prison, tribunal, and rack, for those that were brought in, was in Bebraschentsko. No day, holy, or profane, were the inquisitors idle; every day was deemed fit and lawful for torturing. As many as there were accused there were knouts, and every inquisitor was a butcher. Prince Feodor Jurowicz Romadonowski showed himself by so much more fitted for his inquiry, as he surpassed the rest in cruelty. He put the interrogatories, he examined the criminals, he urged those that were not confessing, he ordered such Strelitz as were more pertinaciously silent, to be subjected to more cruel tortures; those that had already confessed about many things were questioned about more; those who were bereft of strength and reason, and almost of their senses, by excess of torment, were handed over to the skill of the doctors, who were compelled to restore them to strength, in order that they might be broken down by fresh excruciations. The whole month of October was spent in butchering the backs of the culprits with knout and with flames: no day were those that were left alive exempt from scourging or scorching, or else they were broken upon the wheel, or driven to the gibbet, or slain with the axe—the penalties which were inflicted upon them as soon as their confessions had sufficiently revealed the heads of the rebellion.

Source: Johann Georg Korb, *Diary of an Austrian Secretary of Legation at the Court of Czar Peter the Great*, trans. Count MacDonnell (London: 1863), vol. 2, pp. 85–87.

Questions for Analysis

1. Why was it important for Korb to begin this account with a description of the monarch's pain?

2. What does this episode reveal about Peter's conception of his own person and of the loyalty that his subjects owed him? Does it show that his power was fragile, immense, or both?

3. What does it mean to describe torture as an "investigation" even while also describing it as "vengeance"?

and non-nobles. The rank in the new bureaucracy did not depend on birth. One of his principal advisers, Alexander Menshikov, began his career as a cook and finished as a prince. This degree of social mobility would have been impossible in any contemporary western European country. In Russia, more so than in western Europe, noble status depended on government service, with all nobles expected to participate in Peter's army or administration. Peter was not entirely successful in enforcing this requirement, but the administrative machinery he devised furnished Russia with its ruling class for the next 200 years.

Peter creates new noble hierarchy with emphasis on military merit and government service

RUSSIAN IMPERIAL EXPANSION

The goal of Peter's foreign policy was to secure year-round ports for Russia on the Black Sea and the Baltic Sea. In the Black Sea, his enemy was the Ottoman Empire. Here, however, he had little success, and Russia would not secure its position in the Black Sea until the end of the eighteenth century. Nevertheless, Peter continued to push against the Ottoman Empire in the northern Caucasus region throughout his reign. This mountainous area on Russia's southern flank became an important site for Russia's experiments in colonial expansion into central Asia, which began during the sixteenth century and would later mirror the process of colonial conquest undertaken by European powers and the United States in North and South America. Like those of France and Britain, the Russian state bureaucracy was built during a period of ambitious colonialism; and as in Spain, the monarchy's identity was shaped by a long contest with Muslim power on its borders.

Since the late sixteenth century, successive Russian leaders had extended their control over bordering territories of central Asia. Although merchants helped fund early expeditions into Siberia, this expansion was primarily motivated by geopolitical concerns; the tsar sought to gain access to the populations of Russia's border areas and bring them into the service of the expanding Russian state. In this sense, Russian colonialism during this period differed from western European expansion into the Atlantic world, which had primarily been motivated by hopes of commercial gain.

In its early stages, as successive Russian emperors moved Russian troops eastward into Asia, they relied on a process of indirect rule, often seeking to co-opt local elites. Later in the eighteenth century, they had more success settling Russians in border regions to rule directly over local populations. Religion also provided a cover for expansion, and Peter and his successors funded missionary work by Georgian Christians among Muslims in the Caucasus. Efforts to convert Muslim populations to Orthodox Christianity had little effect, and in fact the opposite occurred: the region's commitment to Islam was continuously renewed through contact with different strains of Islamic practice coming from neighboring Ottoman lands and Persia.

Peter could point to more concrete success to the north. In 1700, he began what would become a twenty-one-year war with Sweden, then the dominant power in the Baltic Sea. By 1703, Peter had secured a foothold on the Gulf of Finland and immediately began to build a new capital city there, which he named St. Petersburg. After 1709, when Russian armies decisively defeated the Swedes at the battle of Poltava, work on Peter's new capital city accelerated. An army of serfs was now conscripted to build the new city, whose centerpiece was a royal palace designed to imitate and rival Louis XIV's Versailles. Conditions for the laborers were grueling and Peter's building sites required armed guards to maintain order. In 1714, he forced

The following labels appear on the map:

ARCTIC OCEAN

BARENTS SEA

SIBERIA

FINLAND
KARELIA
• Archangel

Ob R.

Okhotsk
1649

BERING SEA

ESTONIA
• St. Petersburg
• Narva 1700
LIVONIA
• Pskov
LITH.
• Moscow
• Minsk
• Smolensk • Kazan
• Warsaw
POLAND
• Poltava
Kyiv 1709
URAL MOUNTAINS
Volga R.
Ural R.
Irtysh R.
Tomsk
1604
Lake Baikal
SEA OF OKHOTSK

• Odessa
• Azov
• Sevastopol • Astrakhan
ARAL SEA
Lake Balkhash
QING EMPIRE
SEA OF JAPAN (EAST SEA)
JAPAN

Danube R.
BLACK SEA
CASPIAN SEA

PACIFIC OCEAN

OTTOMAN
Tigris R.
Euphrates R.

EMPIRE
Nile R.
Indus R.
HIMALAYAN MTS
Ganges R.
Yellow R.
Yangtze R.

ARABIAN SEA

Legend:
- Russia in 1584
- Acquisitions, 1584–1700
- Acquisitions, 1700–1772 (primarily by Peter the Great)
- Acquisitions, 1772–1796 (by Catherine the Great)
- Area of Pugachev rebellion, 1773–1775
- Ottoman Empire, c. 1800
- Qing Empire, c. 1850
- ✳ Battle sites

Scale: 0 — 1000 — 2000 Miles
0 — 1000 — 2000 Kilometers

THE GROWTH OF THE RUSSIAN EMPIRE. › How did Peter the Great expand the territory controlled by Russia? › What neighboring dynasties were most affected by Russian expansion? › How did the emergence of a bigger, more powerful Russia affect the European balance of power?

1,000 aristocrats to move into the new capital with their families, ignoring their protests. Peter's model city was equipped with remarkable amenities: street lighting, regular waste collection, and a fire brigade. But resentment at his autocratic methods remained for generations afterwards.

The Great Northern War with Sweden ended in 1721 with the Peace of Nystad. This treaty marked a realignment of power in eastern Europe comparable to the Treaty of Utrecht in the West. Sweden lost its North Sea territories to Hanover, and its Baltic German territories to Prussia. Its eastern territories, including the entire Gulf of Finland, Livonia, and Estonia, passed to Russia. Poland-Lithuania survived but only as a declining power. By the end of the eighteenth century, this kingdom would disappear altogether, its territories swallowed up by its more powerful neighbors (see Chapter 17). The victors at Nystad were the Prussians and the Russians.

Peter's accomplishments came at enormous cost. Direct taxation in Russia increased 500 percent during his reign, and in the 1720s, his army numbered more than 300,000 men. Peter made Russia a force to be reckoned with on the European scene, but in so doing, he aroused great resentment, especially among his nobility. Peter's only son and heir, Alexis, became the focus for conspiracies against the tsar, and Peter had him arrested and executed in 1718. As a result, when Peter died in 1725, he left no son to succeed him. A series of ineffective tsars followed, and resentful nobles reversed many of Peter the Great's reforms. In 1762, however, the crown passed to Catherine the Great, a ruler whose ambitions and determination were equal to those of her great predecessor (see Chapter 17).

Conclusion

By the time Peter the Great died in Russia in 1725, the power of Europe's absolutist realms was visible to all. Government was more bureaucratic; state service was more professionalized; and administrators loyal to kings had become more numerous, more efficient, and more demanding. Despite the increasing scope of government, the principles of royal authority changed relatively little. Apart from Great Britain, the Dutch Republic, and Poland-Lithuania, the great powers of eighteenth-century Europe were still governed by rulers who styled themselves as absolutist monarchs in the mold of Louis XIV, claiming authority from God and ruling over a society in which social hierarchies based on birth were taken for granted.

These absolutist regimes could not hide the fact that their rule depended on a negotiated settlement with other powerful elites within European society, in particular with landed aristocrats and religious leaders. Louis XIV used his power to curb the worst excesses of nobles who abused their position, and to defend Catholic orthodoxy against dissident Catholics and Protestants. This power depended on a delicate exchange of favors: French aristocrats surrendered their political authority to the state in exchange for social and legal privileges and immunity from many (but not all) forms of taxation. The Church made a similar bargain. Peter the Great's autocratic rule in Russia worked out a different balance of powers between his state and the Russian aristocracy, tying aristocrats more closely to an ideal of state service. This model also worked for the rulers of Brandenburg-Prussia. Even in England, the establishment of a limited constitutional monarchy and a king who ruled alongside Parliament was not really a radical departure from the European absolutist model. It was merely a different institutional answer to the same problem: What relationship should the monarchical state have with other elites within society?

The demands of state building during this period required kings to raise enormous revenues—for the sumptuous displays of their sovereignty in royal residences such as Louis XIV's palace at Versailles, for the sponsorship of royal academies and the patronage of artists, but most of all, for war. Expanding territory within Europe and holding on to colonial empires in the Atlantic world were costly. Distributing the burden of taxation to pay for these endeavors became an intensely fraught political issue for European monarchs and the financing of royal debt became a sophisticated art. Colbert's mercantilism attempted to harness the power of the economy for the benefit of royal government, and Spain, Holland, England, and France competed for the revenue from the Atlantic world. The balance of power was increasingly played on a global stage.

These themes—the expansion of state powers; conflicts between the monarchy and the aristocracy or with religious dissidents; the intensification of the tax burden on the population; and the opening up of Europe to interactions with peoples in the Atlantic world, the Indian Ocean, and eventually, the Pacific—prompted many in eighteenth-century Europe to reflect on the consequences of absolutism. What were the limits to state power? How should the actions of rulers be judged? What was the proper measure of economic prosperity, and who was it for? Could a well-ordered society tolerate religious diversity? Given Europe's growing awareness of cultures in other parts of the world with different religions, different political systems, and different ways of expressing their moral and ethical

AFTER YOU READ THIS CHAPTER

CHRONOLOGY

1643–1715	Reign of Louis XIV of France
1660	Restoration of the Stuart kings in England
1682–1725	Reign of Peter the Great of Russia
1683	Ottoman siege of Vienna
1685	Revocation of the Edict of Nantes
1688	Glorious Revolution in England
1688–1697	War of the League of Augsburg
1690	Publication of John Locke's *Two Treatises of Government*
1702–1713	War of the Spanish Succession
1713	Treaty of Utrecht

REVIEWING THE OBJECTIVES

❯ Absolutist rulers claimed a monopoly of power and authority within their realms. What was absolutism? Who were the most successful absolutist monarchs?

❯ Mercantilism was an economic doctrine that guided the policies of absolutist rulers. What did mercantilists believe?

❯ Alternatives to absolutist government emerged in England, Holland, and Poland-Lithuania. What forms of government did these regimes develop? How did they differ from the absolutist and autocratic regimes of France, Prussia, and Russia?

❯ The wars begun by Louis XIV after 1680 drove his opponents to ally with each other to achieve a balance of power. What was the result of these conflicts in Europe and in the Atlantic world?

❯ Peter the Great embarked on an ambitious program of reform and territorial expansion in Russia. How did his autocratic government compare with absolutist regimes in western and central Europe?

values, how might Europeans justify or measure their own beliefs and customs? The intellectuals who looked for answers to these questions were similar to earlier generations of scientific researchers in their respect for reason and rational thought, but they turned their attention beyond problems of natural philosophy and science to the messy world of politics and culture. Their movement—known as the Enlightenment—reached its peak in the middle decades of the eighteenth century and created the basis for a powerful critique of Europe's absolutist regimes. The Enlightenment itself emerged slowly from a revolution in scientific thinking that had begun earlier in the early modern period, and it is to this history that we now turn.

Go to **INQUIZITIVE** to see what you've learned—and learn what you've missed—with personalized feedback along the way.

PEOPLE, IDEAS, AND EVENTS IN CONTEXT

› What did the absolutism of **LOUIS XIV** of France and **PETER THE GREAT** of Russia have in common? How did they deal with those who resisted their attempts to impose absolutist rule?

› Compare the religious policies of **LOUIS XIV** of France with the religious policies of the English Stuart kings **CHARLES II** and **JAMES II**. In what way did religious disagreements limit their ability to rule effectively?

› How did European monarchies apply the economic theory known as **MERCANTILISM** to strengthen the power and wealth of their kingdoms? How did this theory influence French colonialism?

› What was the **CONTRACT THEORY OF GOVERNMENT** according to the English political thinker **JOHN LOCKE** and what was the basis for his critique of absolute monarchies?

› How were the tensions between landed elites and the monarchy resolved in Great Britain as a result of the **GLORIOUS REVOLUTION**?

› What was significant about the new **BALANCE OF POWER** that developed in Europe as a result of **LOUIS XIV**'s wars?

› What does the **TREATY OF UTRECHT** (1713) tell us about the diminished influence of Spain and the corresponding rise of Britain and France as European and colonial powers?

› What was different about the attempts by rulers in Habsburg Austria and Brandenburg-Prussia to impose **ABSOLUTISM** in central Europe?

› What innovations did **PETER THE GREAT** bring to Russia?

THINKING ABOUT CONNECTIONS

› What makes absolutism different from older models of kingship in earlier periods?

› Was the absolutist monarchs' emphasis on sumptuous displays of their authority something new? Explain how the display of power under absolutism is different from the way that political power is represented in democratic societies today.

The New Science of the Seventeenth Century

Doubt thou the stars are fire,
Doubt that the sun doth move,
Doubt truth to be a liar,
But never doubt I love.

SHAKESPEARE, *HAMLET*, II.2

BEFORE YOU READ THIS CHAPTER ❯

"DOUBT THOU THE STARS ARE FIRE" and "that the sun doth move." Was Shakespeare alluding to controversial ideas about the cosmos that contradicted the teachings of medieval scholars? *Hamlet* (c. 1600) was written more than fifty years after the Polish astronomer Nicolaus Copernicus suggested that the earth revolved around the sun. Shakespeare probably knew of such theories, although they circulated only among small groups of learned Europeans. As Hamlet's speech to Ophelia makes clear, they were considered conjecture—or strange mathematical hypotheses. These theories were not exactly new: a heliocentric (sun-centered) universe had been proposed as early as the second century B.C.E. by ancient Greek astronomers. But they contradicted the consensus that had set in after Ptolemy proposed an earth-centered universe in the second century C.E. To Shakespeare's contemporaries, they defied common sense.

Still, a small handful of thinkers did doubt. Shakespeare was born in 1564, the same year as Galileo. By the time they were adults, scientific observers were discovering a new set of rules that explained how the

› After about 1550, new sciences in Europe questioned older beliefs about the physical universe. New methods of inquiry led to the development of astronomy, physics, biology, chemistry, geology, and new institutions that supported scientific research and education.

› The scientific revolution gave rise to theoretical breakthroughs in explaining the physical universe as well as advances in the practical knowledge of artisans who built mechanical devices such as telescopes or microscopes. This combination of scientific inquisitiveness and craft techniques encouraged technological developments that would later be useful in industrialization.

› The new sciences did not mark a clean rupture with older traditions of religious thinking. Most scientists of the 1600s remained essentially religious in their worldview. In any case, their work was accessible only to a small, literate minority who had access to books.

CORE OBJECTIVES

› **DEFINE** *scientific revolution* and **EXPLAIN** what is meant by *science* in this historical context.

› **UNDERSTAND** the older philosophical traditions that were important for the development of new methods of scientific investigation during the seventeenth century.

› **IDENTIFY** the sciences that made important advances during this period and **UNDERSTAND** what technological innovations encouraged a new spirit of investigation.

› **EXPLAIN** the differences between the Ptolemaic view of the universe and the new vision of the universe proposed by Nicolaus Copernicus.

› **UNDERSTAND** the different definitions of *scientific method* that emerged from the work of Francis Bacon and René Descartes.

Science: a body of knowledge, a method of inquiry, and a community of practitioners.

universe worked. A hundred years later, the building blocks of the new view had been put in place. This intellectual transformation brought sweeping changes to European philosophy and to Western views of the natural world and of humans' place in it.

Science entails at least three things: a body of knowledge, a method or system of inquiry, and a community of practitioners and the institutions that support their work. The *scientific revolution* of the seventeenth century involved each of these three realms. First, the scientific revolution saw the confirmation of a heliocentric view of the planetary system, which displaced the earth—and humans—from the center of the universe. Even more fundamental, it brought a new mathematical physics that gave precision to this view. Second, the scientific revolution established a method of inquiry for understanding the natural world, a method that emphasized the role of observation, experimentation, and the testing of hypotheses. Third, *science* emerged as a distinctive branch of knowledge. During the period covered in this chapter, people referred to the study of matter, motion, optics, or the circulation of blood as natural philosophy (the more theoretical term), experimental philosophy, medicine, and—increasingly—science. The growth of institutions dedicated to what we now commonly call scientific research was central to the changes at issue here. Science required not only brilliant thinkers but also patrons, states, and communities of researchers; the scientific revolution was thus embedded in other social, religious, and cultural transformations.

The scientific revolution was not an organized effort. Brilliant hypotheses sometimes led to dead ends, discoveries were often accidental, and artisans grinding lenses for telescopes played as big a role as did great abstract thinkers. Educated women also claimed the right to participate in scientific debate, but their efforts were met with opposition or indifference. Old and new worldviews often overlapped as individual thinkers struggled to make their theories—about the movement of bodies in the heavens, or the age of the earth, for instance—consistent with their faith or received wisdom. It did not necessarily undermine religion, and it certainly did not intend to (figures such as Isaac Newton thought their work confirmed and deepened their religious beliefs). Science worked its way into popular understanding slowly. But as the new method started to produce radical new insights into the workings of nature, it eventually came to be accepted beyond the small circles of experimenters and philosophers with whom it had begun.

The Intellectual Origins of the Scientific Revolution

The scientific breakthroughs of the sixteenth and seventeenth centuries were rooted in earlier developments. Artists and intellectuals had been observing the natural world with great precision since at least the twelfth century. Medieval sculptors accurately carved plants, animals, and human forms. The link among observation, experimentation, and invention was not new. The magnetic compass had been known in Europe since the thirteenth century; gunpowder since the early fourteenth; and printing—which opened new possibilities for disseminating ideas quickly and building libraries—since the middle of the fifteenth. A fascination with light encouraged the study of optics. Lens grinders laid the groundwork for the invention of the telescope and microscope, creating reading glasses along the way. Astrologers were also active in the later Middle Ages, charting the heavens in the firm belief that the stars controlled the fates of human beings.

Behind these efforts to understand the natural world lay a nearly universal conviction that the natural world had been created by God. Religious belief spurred scientific study. One school of thinkers, the **Neoplatonists**, argued that nature was a book written by its creator to reveal the ways of God to humanity. Convinced that God's perfection must be reflected in nature, Neoplatonists searched for the perfect structures they believed must lie behind the "shadows" of the everyday world. Mathematics, particularly geometry, were important tools in this quest.

Renaissance humanism provided a foundation for the scientific revolution. Humanists revered the authority of the ancients. The energies the humanists poured into recovering and translating classical texts about the natural world made many of those important works available for the first time to a wider audience. Previously, Arabic sources had provided Europeans with the main route to ancient Greek learning. Greek authors such as Ptolemy were translated into Arabic by Islamic scholars, who often knew them better than Europeans did. Later these texts returned to Europe through the work of late-medieval scholars in Spain and Sicily. The humanists' return to the original texts—and the fact that they could be printed and circulated in larger numbers—encouraged study and debate. The humanist rediscovery of works by Archimedes—the great Greek mathematician who had proposed that the natural world operated on the basis of mechanical forces, like a great machine, and that these forces could be described mathematically—profoundly impressed important late-sixteenth- and seventeenth-century thinkers.

The Renaissance also encouraged collaboration between artisans and intellectuals. Twelfth- and thirteenth-century thinkers had observed the natural world, but they had little contact with the artisans who constructed machines for practical use. During the fifteenth century, however, these two worlds began to come together. Renaissance artists such as Leonardo da Vinci were accomplished craftsmen; they investigated the laws of perspective and optics, they worked out geometric methods for supporting the weight of enormous architectural domes, they studied the human body, and they devised new and more-effective weapons for war. Wealthy amateurs built observatories, measured the courses of the stars, and published work in astrology and alchemy. This fusion of intellectual curiosity and skilled handiwork created new possibilities for research and encouraged the creation of new fields of knowledge.

Sixteenth-century observers often linked the exploration of the globe to new knowledge of the cosmos. An admirer wrote to Galileo that he had kept the spirit of exploration alive: "The memory of Columbus and Vespucci will be renewed through you, and with even greater nobility, as the sky is more worthy than the earth." The parallel does not work quite so neatly, however. Columbus had not been driven by an interest in science. Moreover, it took centuries for European thinkers to realize the New World's implications for different fields of study, and the links between the voyages of discovery and breakthroughs in science were largely indirect. The discoveries of new lands made the most immediate impact in the field of natural history, which was vastly enriched by travelers' detailed accounts of the peoples, animal life, and plants of the Americas. Finding new lands and cultures in Africa and Asia and the revelation of the Americas—a world unknown to the ancients and unmentioned

Neoplatonism A school of thought based on the teachings of Plato, which had a profound effect on the formation of Christian theology. Believing the natural world was a divine creation, Neoplatonists searched nature for proof of God's perfection.

Renaissance humanism An intellectual movement that stressed the study and debate of ancient Greek and Roman texts.

Renaissance legacies: (1) increased circulation of classical texts, including those by ancient scientists and mathematicians

(2) closer relationship between intellectual curiosity and skilled handiwork

in the Bible—also laid bare gaps in Europeans' inherited body of knowledge. In this sense, the exploration of the New World dealt a blow to the authority of the ancients.

In sum, the late medieval recovery of ancient texts, the expansion of print culture and reading, turmoil in the Church after the Reformation, and the encounter with the Americas all shook the authority of older ways of thinking in Europe. What we call the scientific revolution was part of the intellectual excitement that surrounded these challenges to established beliefs.

PTOLEMAIC ASTRONOMICAL INSTRUMENT. Armillary sphere, 1560s, built to facilitate the observation of planetary positions relative to the earth, in support of Ptolemy's theory of an earth-centered universe. In the sphere, seven concentric rings rotated about different axes. When the outermost ring was set to align with a north–south meridian, and the next ring was set to align with the celestial pole (the North Star, or the point around which the stars seem to rotate), the user could determine the latitude where the instrument was located. The inner rings were used to track the angular movements of the planets, key measurements in validating the Ptolemaic system. › **What forms of knowledge were necessary to construct such an instrument? › How do they relate to the breakthrough that is known as the scientific revolution?**

The Copernican Revolution

Medieval cosmologists, like their ancient predecessors, wrestled with the contradictions between older texts and the evidence of their own observations. Their view of an earth-centered universe was influenced by the teachings of Aristotle (384–322 B.C.E.) and by Ptolemy of Alexandria (100–170 C.E.). Ptolemy's vision of an earth-centered universe contradicted an earlier proposal by Aristarchus of Samos (310–230 B.C.E.), who had deduced that the earth and other planets revolve around the sun. Ptolemy's medieval followers used astronomical observations to support their theory, but the persuasiveness of this model for medieval scholars also derived from the ways that it fitted with their Christian beliefs (see Chapter 4). According to Ptolemy, the heavens orbited the earth in a hierarchy of spheres. Earth and the heavens were made of fundamentally different matter and subject to different laws of motion. The sun, moon, stars, and planets were formed of a perfect unchanging ether. The earth, by contrast, was composed of four elements (earth, water, fire, and air), and each of these elements had its natural place: the heavy elements (earth and water) toward the center and the lighter ones farther out. The heavens—first the planets, then the stars—traced perfect circular paths around the stationary earth. The motion of these celestial bodies was produced by a prime mover, whom Christians identified as God. The view fitted Aristotelian physics, according to which objects could move only if acted on by an external force. The Ptolemaic view confirmed the belief in the purposefulness of God's universe.

By the late Middle Ages, astronomers knew that this "**Ptolemaic system**" did not correspond exactly to what many had observed. Orbits did not conform to the Aristotelian ideal of perfect circles. Certain planets, Mars in particular, sometimes appeared to loop backward. Ptolemy accounted for these irregularities with complicated mathematics, but efforts to make the observed motions of the planets fit into the model of perfect circles in an earth-centered cosmos produced bewildering complexity. Most importantly, the Ptolemaic system also proved unable to solve serious difficulties with the calendar. That practical crisis precipitated Nicolaus Copernicus's intellectual leap forward.

By the early sixteenth century, the old Roman calendar was significantly out of alignment with the movements of the heavenly bodies. The major saints' days, Easter, and the other holy days were sometimes weeks off from where they should have been according to the stars. Catholic authorities tried to correct this problem, consulting mathematicians and astronomers all over Europe. One of these was a Polish church official and astronomer, **Nicolaus Copernicus** (1473–1543), a devout Catholic who did not believe that God's universe could be as messy as Ptolemy's model. His proposed solution, based on mathematical calculations, was simple and radical: Ptolemy was mistaken. The earth was not stationary; it rotated on its axis and orbited with the other planets around the sun. Reordering the Ptolemaic system simplified the geometry of astronomy and made the orbits of the planets comprehensible.

Copernicus was in many ways a conservative thinker. He did not consider his work to be a break with either the Church or the authority of ancient texts. He believed, rather, that he had restored a pure understanding of God's design. Still, the implications of his theory troubled him. His ideas contradicted centuries of astronomical thought, and they were hard to reconcile with the observed behavior of objects on earth. If the earth moved, why was that movement imperceptible? Copernicus calculated the distance from the earth to the sun to be at least 6 million miles. Even by Copernicus's very low estimate, the earth was hurtling around the sun at the dizzying rate of many thousands of miles an hour. How did people and objects remain standing? (The earth is actually about 93 million miles from the sun, moving through space at 67,000 miles an hour and spinning on its axis at about 1,000 miles an hour!)

Copernicus was not a physicist. He tried to refine, rather than overturn, traditional Aristotelian physics, but his effort to reconcile that physics with his new model of a sun-centered universe created new problems that he could not resolve. These frustrations dogged Copernicus's later years, and he hesitated to publish his findings. Just before his death, he consented to the release of his major treatise, *On the Revolutions of the Heavenly Spheres* (*De Revolutionibus Orbium Coelestium*), in 1543. To fend off scandal, the Lutheran scholar who saw his manuscript through its printing added an introduction to the book declaring that Copernicus's system should be understood as an abstraction, a set of mathematical tools for doing astronomy and not a dangerous claim about the nature of heaven and earth. For decades

NICOLAUS COPERNICUS. This anonymous portrait of Copernicus characteristically blends his devotion and his scientific achievements. His scholarly work (behind him in the form of an early planetarium) is driven by his faith (as he turns toward the image of Christ triumphant over death). **› What relationship between science and religion is evoked by this image?**

Ptolemaic system In Ptolemy's vision of cosmology, influenced by Aristotle, the heavens orbit the earth in an organized hierarchy of spheres. The earth and the heavens are made of different matter and subject to different laws of motion. A prime mover (usually understood to be God) produces the motion of the celestial bodies.

after 1543, Copernicus's ideas were taken in just that sense—as useful but not realistic mathematical hypotheses. In the long run, however, Copernicanism represented a serious challenge to the Ptolemaic conception of the universe.

Tycho's Observations and Kepler's Laws

Within fifty years, Copernicus's cosmology was modified by two astronomers: **Tycho Brahe** (*TI-koh BRAH-hee*; 1546–1601) and **Johannes Kepler** (1571–1630). Tycho was born into the Danish nobility, but he abandoned his family's military and political legacy to pursue his passion for astronomy. Like Copernicus, he sought to correct the contradictions in traditional astronomy. But unlike Copernicus, who was a theoretician, Tycho championed observation. He first made a name for himself by observing a completely new star, a "nova," that flared into sight in 1572. The Danish king Frederick II granted him the use of a small island, where Brahe built a castle specially designed to house an observatory. For over twenty years, Tycho meticulously charted the movements of each significant object in the night sky, compiling the finest set of astronomical data in Europe.

Tycho suggested that the planets orbited the sun and that the whole system orbited a stationary earth. This picture of cosmic order, though clumsy, seemed to fit the observed evidence better than the Ptolemaic system, and avoided the upsetting physical and theological implications of the Copernican model. In the late 1590s, Tycho moved his work and his huge collection of data to Prague, where he became the court astronomer to the Holy Roman emperor Rudolf II. In Prague, he was assisted by a young mathematician from a troubled family, Johannes Kepler. Kepler was more impressed with the

Nicolaus Copernicus (1473–1543) Polish astronomer who advanced the idea that the earth revolves around the sun.

Tycho Brahe (1546–1601) Danish astronomer who believed that the careful study of the heavens would unlock the secrets of the universe.

Johannes Kepler (1571–1630) Mathematician and astronomer who elaborated on and corrected Copernicus's theory and is chiefly remembered for his discovery of the three laws of planetary motion that bear his name.

TYCHO BRAHE'S EARTH-CENTERED UNIVERSE. This image of Tycho's heliocentric (earth-centered) vision is from a 1660 star atlas published by a Dutch-German cartographer. Note the geometric renderings of planetary orbits accompanied by astrological symbols on the outer ring of the image. In the foreground are images of people using instruments to make astronomical observations alongside young people being taught about the physical characteristics of the terrestrial globe. Tycho himself is portrayed in the lower right corner.

Copernican model than was Tycho, and he combined the study of Copernicus's work with his own interest in mysticism, astrology, and the religious power of mathematics.

Kepler published his revolutionary work on planetary motion, *Astronomia Nova*, in 1609. He believed that everything in creation, from human souls to the orbits of the planets, had been created according to mathematical laws. Understanding those laws would allow humans to share God's wisdom and penetrate the inner secrets of the universe. Mathematics was God's language. After Tycho's death, Kepler had inherited Tycho's position in Prague as well as his trove of observations and calculations. Those data demonstrated to Kepler that two of Copernicus's assumptions about planetary motion simply did not match observations. Copernicus, in keeping with Aristotelian notions of perfection, had believed that planetary orbits were circular. Kepler, however, calculated that the planets traveled in elliptical orbits around the sun (this finding became the first of Kepler's three laws of planetary motion). Copernicus held that planetary motion was uniform. But Kepler stated that the speed of the planets varied with their distance from the sun (consequences of his second and third laws). Kepler also argued that magnetic forces between the sun and the planets kept the planets in orbital motion, an insight that paved the way for Newton's law of universal gravitation nearly eighty years later. Kepler's version of Copernicanism fitted with remarkable accuracy the best observations of the time (which were Tycho's). Kepler's search for rules of motion that could account for the earth's movements in its new position was also significant. More than Copernicus, Kepler broke down the distinction between the heavens and the earth that had been at the heart of Aristotelian physics. In his view, the earth and the heavens were subject to the same physical laws.

Drawing on Tycho's data, Kepler corrects Copernican model and develops laws of planetary motion

New Heavens, New Earth, and Worldly Politics: Galileo

Kepler had a friend deliver a copy of *Cosmographic Mystery* to the "mathematician named Galileus Galileus," then teaching mathematics and astronomy at Padua, near Venice. **Galileo Galilei** (1564–1642) thanked Kepler in a letter that nicely illustrates the Italian's views at the time (1597):

> So far I have only perused the preface of your work, but from this I gained some notion of its intent, and I indeed congratulate myself of having an associate in the study of Truth who is a friend of Truth. . . . I adopted the teaching of Copernicus many years ago, and his point of view enables me to explain many phenomena of nature which certainly remain inexplicable according to the more current hypotheses. I have written many arguments in support of him and in refutation of the opposite view—which, however, so far I have not dared to bring into the public light. . . . I would certainly dare to publish my reflections at once if more people like you existed; as they don't, I shall refrain from doing so.

Kepler replied, urging Galileo to "come forward!" Galileo did not answer.

At Padua, Galileo could not teach what he believed; Ptolemaic astronomy and Aristotelian cosmology were the established curriculum (see **Interpreting Visual Evidence** on pages 552–53). By the end of his career, however, Galileo provided powerful

Galileo Galilei (1564-1642) Italian physicist and inventor; the implications of his ideas raised the ire of the Catholic church, and he was forced to retract most of his findings.

Astronomical Observations and the Mapping of the Heavens

One (often-repeated) narrative about the scientific revolution is that it marked a crucial break, separating modern science from an earlier period permeated by an atmosphere of superstition and theological speculation. But, in fact, medieval scholars tried hard to come up with empirical evidence for beliefs that their faith told them must be true, and without these traditions of observation, scientists like Copernicus would never have been led to propose alternative cosmologies (see "Ptolemaic Astronomical Instrument" on page 548).

The assumption that the "new" sciences of the seventeenth century marked an extraordinary rupture with a more ignorant or superstitious past is thus not entirely correct. It would be closer to the truth to suggest that works such as that of Copernicus or Galileo provided a new context for assessing the relationship between observations and knowledge that came from other sources. Printed materials provided opportunities for early modern scientists to learn as much from each other as from more ancient sources.

A. The Ptolemaic universe, as depicted in Peter Apian, *Cosmographia* (1524).

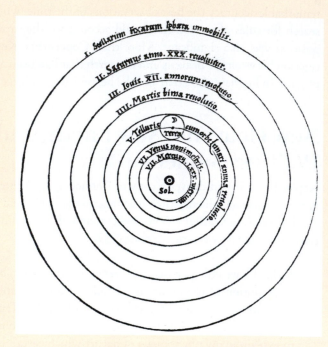

B. The Copernican universe (1543).

evidence in support of the Copernican model and laid the foundation for a new physics. What was more, he wrote in the vernacular (Italian) as well as in Latin, and his writings were widely translated and read, raising awareness of changes in natural philosophy across Europe. His discoveries made him the most famous scientific figure of his time, but his work put him on a collision course with Aristotelian philosophy and the authority of the Catholic Church.

The illustrations here are from scientific works on astronomy both before and after the appearance of Copernicus's work. All of them were based on some form of observation and claimed to be descriptive of the existing universe. Compare the abstract illustrations of the Ptolemaic (image A) and Copernican (image B) universes with Tycho Brahe's (image C) attempt to reconcile heliocentric observations with geocentric assumptions, or with Galileo's illustration of sunspots (image D) observed through a telescope.

Questions for Analysis

1. What do these illustrations tell us about the relationship between knowledge and observation in sixteenth- and seventeenth-century science? What kinds of knowledge were necessary to produce these images?

2. Are the illustrations A and B intended to be visually accurate, in the sense that they represent what the eye sees? Can we say the same of illustration D? What makes Galileo's illustration of sunspots different from the others?

3. Are the assumptions about observation in Galileo's drawing of sunspots (image D) applicable to other sciences such as biology or chemistry? If yes, how so?

C. Tycho Brahe's universe (c. 1572). A, earth; B, moon; C, sun.

D. Galileo's sunspots, as observed through a telescope (1612).

In 1609, Galileo heard reports from Holland of a lens grinder who had made a spyglass that could magnify very distant objects. Excited, Galileo quickly devised his own telescope. He trained it first on earthly objects to demonstrate that it worked, and then dramatically pointed it at the night sky. Galileo studied the moon, finding features of an earthlike landscape containing mountains, valleys, and plains. His observations suggested that celestial bodies resembled the earth, a view at odds with the concept of the heavens as an unchanging sphere of heavenly perfection, inherently and necessarily different from the earth. He saw moons orbiting Jupiter, evidence that earth was not at the center of all orbits. And he saw spots on the sun. Galileo published these results, first in *The Starry Messenger* (1610) and then in *Letters on Sunspots* (1613). *The Starry Messenger*, with its amazing reports of Jupiter's moons, was short, aimed at a wide reading audience, and bold. It only hinted at Galileo's Copernicanism, however. The *Letters on Sunspots* declared it openly.

Galileo provides proof for Copernicus's theoretical model

As a professor of mathematics, Galileo chafed at the power of university authorities who were subject to Church control. Princely courts offered an inviting alternative. The Medici family of Tuscany, like others, burnished its reputation and bolstered its power by surrounding itself with intellectuals as well as artists. Persuaded he would be freer at its court than in Padua, Galileo took a position as tutor to the Medicis and flattered and successfully cultivated the family. He addressed *The Starry Messenger* to them and named the newly discovered moons of Jupiter the "Medicean stars." He was rewarded with the title of chief mathematician and philosopher to Cosimo II de' Medici, the grand duke of Tuscany. Now well positioned in Italy's networks of power and patronage, Galileo was able to pursue his goal of demonstrating that Copernicus's heliocentric (sun-centered) model of the planetary system was correct.

This pursuit, however, was a high-wire act, for he could not afford to antagonize the Catholic Church. In 1614, an ambitious and outspoken Dominican monk denounced Galileo's ideas as dangerous deviations from biblical teachings. Disturbed by the murmurings against Copernicanism, Galileo defended himself in a series of letters. He addressed the relationship between natural philosophy and religion, and argued that one could be both a sincere Copernican and a sincere Catholic (see **Analyzing Primary Sources** on page 556). The Church, Galileo said, did the sacred work of teaching scripture and saving souls, but accounting for the workings of the physical world was a task better left to natural philosophy, grounded in observation and mathematics. For the Church to take a side in controversies over natural science might compromise its spiritual authority and credibility. Galileo envisioned natural philosophers and theologians as partners in a search for truth, but with very different roles: the purpose of the Bible, he said, was to "teach us how to go to heaven, not how heaven goes."

For Galileo, scientific and theological inquiry are not mutually exclusive

In 1616, the Church moved against Galileo. The Inquisition ruled that Copernicanism was "foolish and absurd in philosophy and formally heretical." Copernicus's *De Revolutionibus Orbium Coelestium* was placed on the Index of Prohibited Books, and Galileo was warned not to teach Copernicanism.

For a while, he did as he was asked. But when his Florentine friend and admirer Maffeo Barberini was elected pope as Urban VIII in 1623, Galileo believed the door to Copernicanism was (at least half) open. He drafted one of his most famous works, *A Dialogue Concerning the Two Chief World Systems*, which was published in 1632. The *Dialogue* was a hypothetical debate between supporters of the old Ptolemaic system, represented by a character he named Simplicio (simpleton) on the one hand, and proponents of the new astronomy on the other. Galileo gave the best lines to the Copernicans throughout. However, at the very end, to satisfy the letter of the Inquisition's decree, he had them capitulate to Simplicio.

The Inquisition banned the *Dialogue* and ordered Galileo to stand trial in 1633. Pope Urban, provoked by Galileo's scorn and needing support from Church conservatives during a difficult stretch of the Thirty Years' War, refused to protect his former friend. The verdict of the secret trial shocked Europe. The Inquisition forced Galileo to repent his Copernican position, banned him from working on or even discussing Copernican ideas, and placed him under house arrest for life. According to a story that began to circulate shortly afterward, as he left the court for house arrest he stamped his foot and muttered defiantly, looking down at the earth, "Still, it moves."

The Inquisition could not put Galileo off his life's work. He proposed an early version of the theory of inertia, which held that an object's motion stays the same until an outside force changes it. He calculated that objects of different weights fall at almost the same speed and with a uniform acceleration. He argued that the motion of objects follows regular mathematical laws. The same laws that govern the motions of objects on earth (which could be observed in experiments) could also be observed in the heavens—an important step toward a coherent physics based on a sun-centered model of the universe. Compiled under the title *Two New Sciences* (1638), this work was smuggled out of Italy and published in Protestant Holland.

Galileo believed that Copernicanism and natural philosophy in general need not subvert theological truths, religious belief, or the authority of the Church. But his trial seemed to show the contrary: that natural philosophy and Church authority could not coexist. Galileo's trial silenced Copernican voices in southern Europe, and the Church's leadership retreated into conservative reaction. It was therefore in northwest Europe that the new philosophy Galileo had championed would flourish.

Despite the Inquisition's house arrest, Galileo continued to make breakthrough discoveries in physics

From Geology to Geography and the Human Sciences

It is not surprising that the Church perceived Galileo's teachings to be a threat. This split between religion and new sciences was not absolute, however. The modern science of geology, for example, emerged out of a long debate that juxtaposed evidence from religious texts on the one hand, and data gathered by those who made observations about the physical landscape of the earth's surface. The debate that fostered this discussion revolved around a fundamental question that had long provoked theologians: How old was the earth?

In 1654, **James Ussher** (1581–1656), the archbishop of Armagh in Ireland, published an account of the earth's creation, using both biblical and secular sources. Ussher declared that the world had been created on Saturday, October 22, 4004 B.C.E. Often ridiculed as an extreme example of biblical literalism, his estimate differed little from other writers at the time. Ussher's chronology simply tried to construct a time line for world history that combined observations of the appearance of comets, volcanic eruptions, and solar and lunar eclipses alongside sacred dates. His decision to treat the Bible as one source among many was in fact a significant departure from a purely religious approach, and his desire to divide the history of the earth into "epochs" or "eras" marked an important step toward a more historical approach to the earth's past.

James Ussher (1581-1656) An Irish archbishop who attempted to reconcile natural and biblical events in a later discredited chronology of the world.

Galileo on Nature, Scripture, and Truth

One of the clearest statements of Galileo's convictions about religion and science comes from his 1615 letter to the grand duchess Christina, the mother of Galileo's patron, Cosimo II de' Medici, and a powerful figure in her own right. Galileo knew that others objected to his work. The Church had warned him that Copernicanism was inaccurate and impious, that it could be disproved scientifically, and that it contradicted the authority of those who interpreted the Bible. Thoroughly dependent on the Medicis for support, he wrote to the grand duchess to explain his position. In this section of the letter, Galileo sets out his understanding of the parallel but distinct roles of the Church and natural philosophers. He walks a fine line between acknowledging the authority of the Church and standing firm in his convictions.

Possibly because they are disturbed by the known truth of other propositions of mine which differ from those commonly held, and therefore mistrusting their defense so long as they confine themselves to the field of philosophy, these men have resolved to fabricate a shield for their fallacies out of the mantle of pretended religion and the authority of the Bible. . . .

Copernicus never discusses matters of religion or faith, nor does he use arguments that depend in any way upon the authority of sacred writings which he might have interpreted erroneously. He stands always upon physical conclusions pertaining to the celestial motions, and deals with them by astronomical and geometrical demonstrations, founded primarily upon sense experiences and very exact observations. He did not ignore the Bible, but he knew very well that if his doctrine were proved, then it could not contradict the Scriptures when they were rightly understood. . . .

I think that in discussions of physical problems we ought to begin not from the authority of scriptural passages, but from sense-experiences and necessary demonstrations; for the holy Bible and the phenomena of nature proceed alike from the divine Word, the former as the dictate of the Holy Ghost and the latter as the observant executrix of God's commands. It is necessary for the Bible, in order to be accommodated to the understanding of every man, to speak many things which appear to differ from the absolute truth so far as the bare meaning of the words is concerned. But Nature, on the other hand, is inexorable and immutable; she never transgresses the laws imposed upon her, or cares a whit whether her abstruse reasons and methods of operation are understandable to men. For that reason it appears that nothing physical which sense-experience sets before our eyes, or which necessary demonstrations prove to us, ought to be called in question (much less condemned) upon the testimony of biblical passages which may have some different meaning beneath their words. For the Bible is not chained in every expression to conditions as strict as those which govern all physical effects; nor is God any less excellently revealed in Nature's actions than in the sacred statements of the Bible. . . .

Source: Galileo, "Letter to the Grand Duchess Christina," in *Discoveries and Opinions of Galileo*, ed. Stillman Drake (Garden City, NY: 1957), pp. 177–83.

Questions for Analysis

1. How does Galileo deal with the contradictions between the evidence of his senses and biblical teachings?

2. For Galileo, what is the relationship between God, man, and nature?

3. Why did Galileo need to defend his views in a letter to Christina de' Medici?

Ussher, like other early seventeenth-century writers, assumed that the earth's history and human history covered roughly the same length of time: following the story of Genesis, they assumed that humans appeared on earth soon after its creation. They also assumed that the stories told in the Bible—including the story of Noah and the Flood—had some basis in historical fact. A German Jesuit, Athanasius Kircher (1602–1680), suggested that the Flood story could be analyzed historically, and he attempted to calculate the amount of water that would have been required to cover the earth's mountains. He assumed that the physical landscape of the earth would have been transformed as the floodwaters drained away. Only later did natural philosophers realize the vast expanse of earth's history that predated human society, but they were already beginning to imagine that this history was accessible to human knowledge through observation.

Such speculation was fueled by natural philosophers who wondered about the fossils found in the European countryside. As interest in natural philosophy developed, scholars assembled collections of what they called "curiosities"—forms of animals and plants found in stones and seashells collected on mountaintops far from the ocean, as well as the bones of animals both recognizable and unknown. A Danish physician, Niels Stensen (Latin name: **Nicolas Steno**), compiled this evidence in ways that lay the foundation for the science of geology. In 1667 Steno demonstrated that shark's teeth, obtained from a recently caught animal, were structurally similar, though smaller in size, to petrified teeth encased in stone on land far from the sea. Steno believed that the physical landscape of Tuscany (where he was living at the time) constituted a visible record of a historical sequence that could be reconstructed through observation. He noted a tendency of broken hillsides to reveal strata of

Nicolas Steno Danish scientist whose studies of rock layers and fossils was foundational to the development of geological sciences.

Human Diversity during the Scientific Revolution

François Bernier (1620–1688) was a French doctor who served as a physician at the court of the Mughal ruler Aurangzeb in Agra, a city in northern India, for eight years before returning to Paris and reporting on Indian society to the French royal government. In this essay, published in the journal of the French Academy of Sciences, he suggested that the human populations of the earth could be subdivided into four or five "races" or "species." Historians now recognize this as the first attempt to define the word race in European history according to the standards of scientific practice that were emerging in Europe in the seventeenth century. Although this use of the term did not immediately replace older usages of race to describe the lineage of prized animals or aristocratic families, Bernier's idea was subsequently picked up by other authors who helped to develop the human and social sciences during the Enlightenment (see Ch. 18).

Up to now, geographers have only divided the Earth by different countries or regions [. . .]. Observations that I have made about men during my long and frequent Voyages have led me to divide the Earth differently. Although men are almost all different from one another according to the exterior form of the body and the face, [. . .] I have nevertheless remarked that there are above all four or five Species or Races of men whose differences are so notable that they may be used to create a new division of the Earth.

I include in the first species [the residents of] France, Spain, England, Denmark, Sweden, Germany, Poland, and generally all of Europe. One could also add a small part of Africa, including the Realms of Fez and Morocco, Algiers, Tunis and Tripoli, up to the Nile, and also a good portion of Asia, such as the Empire of the Great Sultan [the Ottoman Empire] with the three Arabys, all of Persia, the Mughal Empire, the Kingdom of Golconda, that of Visapur, the Maldives and a part of the Kingdoms of Arakan, Pegu, Siam, Sumatra, Banten and Borneo. Because though the Egyptians, for example, and the Indians are very black, or rather brown, this color is only accidental to them, coming only from their exposure to the Sun; since those who protect themselves from it, and who are not obliged to expose themselves are not more black than many Spaniards. It is true that the majority of Indians have something rather different from us in the shape of the face and in their color which tends toward yellow, but that does not seem sufficient to make of them a particular species, because we would

different stones, as if one layer had been laid down over the previous one. An English natural philosopher, Robert Hooke, writing at the same time in England, came to the same conclusion, asserting that the rocks and fossils were "documents" to be read in the book of nature.

These new secular claims about the history of the earth and the origins of fossils were soon followed by claims about the secular history of human populations. In 1684, a doctor named François Bernier published an article based on observations he made during twelve years of travel to Egypt, the Arabian peninsula, and northern India (see *Analyzing Primary Sources* on pages 558–59). This article included the first scientific use of the term *race* to describe distinct groups among human populations according to their physical characteristics. Bernier's article proposed a then also have to do the same with Spaniards, Germans, and several other Peoples of Europe.

In the second species I put all of Africa except for the coasts that I have already mentioned. We call them a different species because of (1) their thick lips and their flat nose, few of them possessing an aquiline nose and lips of a medium thickness. (2) their blackness which is essential to them, and which is not caused by the Sun, as some think, because when one transports a black man and a black woman to a colder country their children remain black unless they marry with a white woman. We must thus see the cause [of their color] in some particular aspect of their bodies, in their semen or blood, which are nevertheless the same color as everywhere else. (3) Their skin which is oily, smooth, and polished except in places that are roasted by the Sun. (4) Their thin beards. (5) Their hair which is not really hair but rather a kind of wool [...] and finally their whiter teeth, their tongues and the inside of their mouths which are as red as Coral.

The third species includes a part of the Kingdoms of Arakan and of Siam, of the Island of Sumatra and Borneo, the Philippines, Japan, and the Kingdom of Pegu, Tonkin, Cochinchina, China, Tartary which lies between China, the Ganges, and Muscovy, Uzbekistan, Turkistan [...]. The inhabitants of all these countries are veritably white; but they have large shoulders, flat faces, little flat noses, small eyes like pigs, and very thin beards.

The Lapps compose the 4th species. These are little people with thick legs, large shoulders, short necks, a face I cannot describe except as extremely frightening, and which resembles a Bear. I have only seen two in Danzig, but according to the portraits I have seen, and the description given to me by people who have been in this country, they are nasty animals.

As for the Americans, they are in truth in large part olive, and their faces are shaped in a different manner than our own, but I do not find here a large enough difference to call them a particular species or different from our own.

Source: François Bernier, "Nouvelle division de la terre par les différentes espèces ou races d'hommes qui l'habitent, envoyée par un fameux Voyageur à M. l'Abbé de la ***** à peu près en ces termes," *Journal des sçavans*, 24 April 1684, pp. 133–36. Translated from the original by Joshua Cole.

Questions for Analysis

1. Does Bernier offer a clear definition of what he means by "race" in these passages?

2. Who does Bernier include alongside the Europeans in his first racial category? What distinguishes this first group from Africans or Asians? Is he consistent in his arguments about the connections between skin color and his racial classifications?

3. Bernier admitted that he had only seen two individual Lapps. In what way can we understand his claim that the Lapps constitute a separate "race" as a "scientific" argument? What does his essay reveal about the kinds of arguments that were acceptable in a scientific publication in seventeenth-century France?

"New Division of the Earth" into four or five "races of men": Europeans, Africans, Asians, and the Samoed people of Lapland (a region of northern Finland). Bernier's criteria for distinguishing between races were subjective, but he presented these new categories of people as a scientific innovation. In the next century, Bernier's use of "race" as a synonym for *species* was picked up by other influential authors (see Ch. 18). The word *race* in French had already been in use for over 200 years to describe desirable traits in breeding animals, and it was also adopted to speak about the perceived superior qualities of high-ranking aristocratic families, but it did not refer to a division of humans into distinct groups.

The line from Steno and Hooke to modern geological research is direct, but the connections between Bernier's work to modern claims about the existence of human "races" is more complicated. Nevertheless, the natural philosophers' decision to extend the realm of their scientific observations from material objects (stones, planets, and stars) to human beings was significant. The evolution of natural philosophy in the seventeenth century indicated new possibilities for a scientific understanding of the terrestrial environment, but it also contained powerful ideas about the allegedly "natural" division of humanity into distinct groups, with different capacities and roles.

Methods for a New Philosophy: Bacon and Descartes

Advances in the new sciences eventually became concentrated in northwest Europe. Sir **Francis Bacon** (1561–1626) and **René Descartes** (*deh-KAHRT*) loom especially large in this development, setting out the methods or the rules that should govern modern science.

"Knowledge is power." This phrase is Bacon's and captures the new confidence in the potential of human thinking. Bacon trained as a lawyer, served in Parliament, and was briefly the lord chancellor to James I of England. His abiding concern was with the assumptions, methods, and practices of natural philosophy. The authority of the ancients should not constrain modern thinkers, and deference to accepted doctrines could block innovation or obstruct understanding. Pursuing knowledge did not mean thinking abstractly and leaping to conclusions; it meant observing, experimenting, and confirming ideas. If thinkers will be "content to begin with doubts," Bacon wrote, "they shall end with certainties." We thus associate Bacon with the gradual separation of scientific investigation from philosophical argument.

Bacon advocated an *inductive* approach to knowledge: amassing evidence from many discrete observations to draw general conclusions. In Bacon's view, many philosophical errors arose from beginning with assumed first principles (see **Competing Viewpoints** on pages 562–63). The traditional view of the cosmos, for instance, rested on the principles of a prime mover and the perfection of circular motion for the planets and the stars. The inductive method required accumulating data (as Tycho had done) and then, after careful review and experiment, drawing appropriate conclusions about the motions of heavenly bodies. Bacon argued that scientific knowledge was best tested through the cooperative efforts of scientists performing experiments that could be repeated and verified. In this practical sense, his work anticipated the modern research university. At the same time, he also connected the new science with the expansion of European colonialism. The title page of his work *Novum Organum* (1620), depicts bold ships sailing beyond the Straits of Gibraltar, formerly the limits of the West, into the open sea. Through such imagery, Bacon's vision of science as "discovery" also became incorporated into a political vision of expanding European power.

In René Descartes's (1596–1650) *Discourse on Method* (1637), for which he is best known, he recounted his dismay at the "strange and unbelievable" theories he encountered in his traditional education. His first response, as he described it, was to doubt everything he had ever known or been taught. His rule was "never to receive anything as a truth which [he] did not clearly know to be such." He took the human ability to think as his point of departure, summed up in his famous and enigmatic *Je pense, donc je suis*, later translated into Latin as *Cogito, ergo sum* and into English as "I think, therefore I am." As the phrase suggests, Descartes's doubting led (quickly, by our standards) to self-assurance and truth: the thinking individual existed, reason existed, God existed. For Descartes, then, doubt was a ploy, a strategy that he used to defeat skepticism. Certainty, not doubt, was the centerpiece of the philosophy he bequeathed to his followers.

Unlike Bacon, however, Descartes emphasized *deductive* reasoning, proceeding logically from one known certainty to another. "So long as we avoid accepting as true what is not so," he wrote in *Discourse on Method*, "and always preserve the right order of deduction of one thing from another, there can be nothing too remote to be reached in the end, or too well hidden to be discovered." For Descartes, mathematical thought expressed the highest standards of reason, and his work contributed greatly to the authority of mathematics as a model for scientific reasoning.

Descartes made a particularly forceful statement for *mechanism*, a view of the world shared by Bacon and Galileo and one that came to dominate seventeenth-century scientific thought. As the name suggests, mechanical philosophy proposed to consider nature as a machine. It rejected the traditional Aristotelian distinction between the works of humans and those of nature, and the view that nature, as God's creation, necessarily belonged to a different—and higher—order. In the new picture of the universe that was emerging from the discoveries and writings of the early seventeenth century, it seemed that all matter was composed of the same material and that all motion obeyed the same laws. Descartes sought to explain everything, including the human body, mechanically. As he put it firmly, "There is no difference between the machines built by artisans and the diverse bodies that nature alone composes." Nature operated according to regular and predictable laws and thus was accessible to human reason. This belief guided and inspired the scientific work of the seventeenth century.

In inductive reasoning, the scientist amasses many observations and then draws general conclusions or proposes theories on the basis of these data

In deductive reasoning, the scientist begins with one self-evident principle and uses reason to derive other truths from this foundation

Descartes's mechanical philosophy

The New Science and the Foundations of Certainty

Francis Bacon (1561–1626) and René Descartes (1596–1650) were both enthusiastic supporters of science in the seventeenth century, but they differed in their opinions regarding the basis for certainty in scientific argumentation. Bacon's inductive method emphasized the gathering of particular observations about natural phenomena, which he believed could be used as evidence to support more-general conclusions about causes, regularity, and order in the natural world. Descartes, on the other hand, defended a deductive method. He believed that certainty could be built only by reasoning from first principles that one knew to be true, and he was less certain of the value of evidence that came from the senses alone.

Aphorisms from *Novum Organum*

XXXI It is idle to expect any advancement in science from the super-inducing and engrafting of new things upon old. We must begin anew from the very foundations, unless we would revolve forever in a circle with mean and contemptible progress. . . .

XXXVI One method of delivery alone remains to us which is simply this: we must lead men to the particulars themselves, and their series and order; while men on their side must force themselves for a while to lay their notions by and begin to familiarize themselves with facts. . . .

XLV The human understanding of its own nature is prone to suppose the existence of more order and regularity in the world than it finds. And though there be many things in nature which are singular and unmatched, yet it devises for them parallels and conjugates and relatives which do not exist. Hence the fiction that all celestial bodies move in perfect circles. . . . Hence too the element of fire with its orb is brought in, to make up the square with the other three which the sense perceives. . . . And so on of other dreams. And these fancies affect not dogmas only, but simple notions also. . . .

XCV Those who have handled sciences have been either men of experiment or men of dogmas. The men of experiment are like the ant, they only collect and use; the reasoners resemble spiders, who make cobwebs out of their own substance. But the bee takes a middle course: it gathers its material from the flowers of the garden and of the field, but transforms and digests it by a power of its own. Not unlike this is the true business of philosophy; for it neither relies solely or chiefly on the powers of the mind, nor does it take the matter which it gathers from natural history and mechanical experiments and lay it up in the memory whole . . . but lays it up in the understanding altered and digested. Therefore, from a closer and purer league between these two faculties, the experimental and the rational (such as has never yet been made), much may be hoped. . . .

Source: Michael R. Matthews, ed., *The Scientific Background to Modern Philosophy: Selected Readings* (Indianapolis, IN: 1989), pp. 47–48, 50–52.

From *Discourse on Method*

Just as a great number of laws is often a pretext for wrong-doing, with the result that a state is much better governed when, having only a few, they are strictly observed; so also I came to believe that in the place of the great number of precepts that go to make up logic, the following four would be sufficient for my purposes, provided that I took a firm but unshakeable decision never once to depart from them.

The first was never to accept anything as true that I did not *incontrovertibly* know to be so; that is to say, carefully to avoid both *prejudice* and premature conclusions; and to include nothing in my judgments other than that which presented itself to my mind so *clearly* and *distinctly*, that I would have no occasion to doubt it.

The second was to divide all the difficulties under examination into as many parts as possible, and as many as were required to solve them in the best way.

The third was to conduct my thoughts in a given order, beginning with the *simplest* and most easily understood objects, and gradually ascending, as it were step by step, to the knowledge of the most *complex*; and *positing* an order even on those which do not have a natural order of precedence.

The last was to undertake such complete enumerations and such general surveys that I would be sure to have left nothing out.

The long chain of reasonings, every one simple and easy, which geometers habitually employ to reach their most difficult proofs had given me cause to suppose that all those things which fall within the domain of human understanding follow on from each other in the same way, and that as long as one stops oneself taking anything to be true that is not true and sticks to the right order so as to deduce one thing from another, there can be nothing so remote that one cannot eventually reach it, nor so hidden that one cannot discover it. . . .

[B]ecause I wished . . . to concentrate on the pursuit of truth, I came to think that I should . . . reject as completely false everything in which I could detect the least doubt, in order to see if anything thereafter remained in my belief that was completely indubitable. And so, because our senses sometimes deceive us, I decided to suppose that nothing was such as they lead us to imagine it to be. And because there are men who make mistakes in reasoning, even about the simplest elements of geometry, and commit logical fallacies, I judged that I was as prone to error as anyone else, and I rejected as false all the reasoning I had hitherto accepted as valid proof. Finally, considering that all the same thoughts which we have while awake can come to us while asleep without any one of them then being true, I resolved to pretend that everything that had ever entered my head was no more true than the illusions of my dreams. But immediately afterwards I noted that, while I was trying to think of all things being false in this way, it was necessarily the case that I, who was thinking them, had to be something; and observing this truth: *I am thinking therefore I exist*, was so secure and certain that it could not be shaken by any of the most extravagant suppositions of the sceptics, I judged that I could accept it without scruple, as the first principle of the philosophy I was seeking.

Source: René Descartes, *A Discourse on the Method*, trans. Ian Maclean (New York: 2006), pp. 17–18, 28.

Questions for Analysis

1. Descartes's idea of certainty depended on a "long chain of reasonings" that departed from certain axioms that could not be doubted, and rejected evidence from the senses. What science provided him with the model for this idea of certainty? What was the first thing that he felt he could be certain about? Did he trust his senses?

2. Bacon's idea of certainty pragmatically sought to combine the benefits of sensory knowledge and experience (gathered by "ants") with the understandings arrived at through reason (cobwebs constructed by "spiders"). How would Descartes have responded to Bacon's claims? According to Bacon, was Descartes an ant or a spider?

3. What do these two thinkers have in common?

FROM RENÉ DESCARTES, *L'HOMME* **(1729; ORIGINALLY PUBLISHED AS** *DE HOMINE,* **1662).**
Descartes's interest in the body as a mechanism led him to suppose that physics and mathematics could be used to understand all aspects of human physiology, and his work had an important influence on subsequent generations of medical researchers. In this illustration, Descartes depicts the optical properties of the human eye. **› How might such a mechanistic approach to human perception have been received by proponents of Baconian science who depended so much on the reliability of human observations?**

THE POWER OF METHOD AND THE FORCE OF CURIOSITY: SEVENTEENTH-CENTURY EXPERIMENTERS

For nearly a century after Bacon and Descartes, most of England's natural philosophers were Baconian, and most of their colleagues in France, Holland, and elsewhere in northern Europe were Cartesians (followers of Descartes). The Cartesians turned toward mathematics and logic. Descartes himself pioneered analytical geometry. Blaise Pascal (1623–1662) worked on probability theory and invented a calculating machine before applying his intellectual skills to theology. A Dutch Cartesian, Baruch Spinoza (1632–1677), applied geometry to ethics and believed he had proved that the universe was composed of a single substance that was both God and nature.

English experimenters pursued a different course. They began with practical research, putting the alchemist's tool, the laboratory, to new uses. They also sought a different kind of conclusion: empirical laws or provisional generalizations based on evidence rather than absolute statements of deductive truth. Among the many English laboratory scientists of this era were the physician William Harvey (1578–1657), the chemist Robert Boyle (1627–1691), and the inventor and experimenter Robert Hooke (1635–1703).

Harvey observed human and animal bodies and explained that blood circulated through the arteries, heart, and veins. Boyle's experiments established a law (known as Boyle's law) showing that at a constant temperature the volume of a gas decreases in proportion to the pressure placed on it. Hooke introduced the microscope to the experimenter's tool kit. The compound microscope had been invented in Holland early in the seventeenth century, but it was not until the 1660s that Hooke and others demonstrated its potential by using it to study the cellular structure of plants. Like the telescope before it, the microscope revealed an unexpected dimension of material phenomena. Examining even the most ordinary objects revealed detailed structures of perfectly connected smaller parts, and this persuaded many that with improved instruments they would uncover even more of the world's intricacies.

The microscope also provided what many regarded as new evidence of God's existence. The minute structure of a living organism, when viewed under a microscope, corresponded to its purpose and testified not only to God's existence but also to God's wisdom. The mechanical philosophy did not exclude God but in fact could be used to confirm his presence. If the universe was a clock, there must be a clockmaker. Hooke himself declared that only imbeciles would believe that what they saw under the microscope was "the production of chance" rather than of God's creation.

ROBERT HOOKE'S *MICROGRAPHIA*.
Hooke's diagram of a fly's eye as seen through a microscope seemed to reveal just the sort of intricate universe the mechanists predicted.
› **Compare this image with that of Galileo's sunspots (page 553). What do these two images have in common?**

THE STATE, SCIENTIFIC ACADEMIES, AND WOMEN SCIENTISTS

Seventeenth-century state building (see Chapter 14) helped secure the rise of science. In 1660, the newly crowned King Charles II granted a group of natural philosophers a royal charter to establish the **Royal Society** of London, for the "improvement of natural knowledge." The Royal Society would pursue Bacon's goal of collective research, in which members would conduct formal experiments, record the results, and share them with other members. These members would in turn study the methods and attempt to reproduce the experiment. This enterprise would give England's natural philosophers a common sense of purpose and a system to reach reasoned, gentlemanly agreement on "matters of fact." By separating systematic scientific research from the dangerous language of politics and religion that had marked the English Civil War, the Royal Society could help restore a sense of order and invite rational discussion in intellectual life.

The French **Academy of Sciences** was founded in 1666, and it was also tied to seventeenth-century state building, in this case, Bourbon absolutism (see Chapter 15). Royal societies, devoted to natural philosophy as a collective enterprise, provided a state- (or prince-) sponsored framework for science, and an alternative to the important but uncertain patronage of religious (and largely conservative, Aristotelian) universities. Scientific societies reached rough agreements about what constituted legitimate research; they established the modern scientific custom of

Royal Society British society founded to pursue collective research, giving English scientists a sense of common purpose as well as a system for reaching a consensus on facts.

Academy of Sciences French institute of scientific industry founded in 1666 by Louis XIV. France's statesmen exerted control over the academy and sought to share in the rewards of any discoveries its members made.

crediting discoveries to those who were the first to publish results; and they enabled the easier exchange of information and theories across national boundaries. Science began to take shape as a discipline.

The early scientific academies did not have explicit rules barring women, but with few exceptions they consisted only of men. This did not mean that women did not practice science, though their participation in scientific research and debate remained controversial. In some cases, the new science could itself become a justification for women's inclusion, as when the Cartesian philosopher François Poullain de la Barre used anatomy to declare in 1673 that "the mind has no sex." Since women possessed the same physical senses as men and the same nervous systems and brains, Poullain asserted that they might occupy the same roles in society as men. In fact, historians have discovered more than a few women who taught at European universities in the sixteenth and seventeenth centuries, above all in Italy. Elena Cornaro Piscopia received her doctorate in philosophy in Padua in 1678, the first woman to do so. **Laura Bassi** became a professor of physics at the University of Bologna after receiving her doctorate there in 1733, and on the merits of her exceptional contributions to mathematics, she became a member of the Academy of Science in Bologna. Her papers—such as "On the Compression of Air" (1746), "On the Bubbles Observed in Freely Flowing Fluid" (1747), and "On Bubbles of Air That Escape from Fluids" (1748)—gained her a stipend from the academy.

Italy appears to have been an exception in allowing women to win formal recognition for their education and research in established institutions. Elsewhere, elite women could educate themselves by associating with learned men. The aristocrat **Margaret Cavendish** (1623–1673), a natural philosopher in England, gleaned the information necessary to start her career from her family and their friends, a network

that included Thomas Hobbes and René Descartes. These connections were not enough to overcome the isolation she felt working in a world of letters that was still largely the preserve of men, but this did not prevent her from developing her own speculative natural philosophy and using it to critique those who would exclude her from scientific debate. The "tyrannical government" of men over women, she wrote, "hath so dejected our spirits, that we are become so stupid, that beasts being but a degree below us, men use us but a degree above beasts. Whereas in nature we have as clear an understanding as men, if we are bred in schools to mature our brains."

The construction of observatories in private residences enabled some women living in such homes to work their way into the growing field of astronomy. Between 1650 and 1710, some 14 percent of German astronomers were women, the most famous of whom was **Maria Winkelmann** (1670–1720). Winkelmann had collaborated with her husband, Gottfried Kirch, in his observatory; by the time of his death, she had already done significant work, including discovering a comet and preparing calendars for the Berlin

Academy of Sciences. As Kirch's widow, she petitioned the academy to allow her to take her husband's place in that prestigious body—but she was rejected. Gottfried Leibniz, the academy's president, explained, "Already during her husband's lifetime the society was burdened with ridicule because its calendar was prepared by a woman. If she were now to be kept on in such capacity, mouths would gape even wider." In spite of this rejection, Winkelmann continued to work as an astronomer, training both her son and two daughters in the discipline.

Like Winkelmann, the entomologist **Maria Sibylla Merian** (1647–1717) was able to carve out a space for her scientific work by exploiting the precedent of guild women who learned their trades in family workshops. Merian was a daughter of an engraver and illustrator in Frankfurt and served as his informal apprentice before beginning her own career as a scientific illustrator, specializing in detailed engravings of insects and plants. Traveling to the Dutch colony of Surinam, Merian supported herself and her two daughters by selling exotic insects and animals she collected and brought back to Europe. She fought the colony's sweltering climate and malaria to publish her most important scientific work, *Metamorphosis of the Insects of Surinam*, which detailed the life cycles of Surinam's insects in sixty ornate illustrations. Merian's *Metamorphosis* was well received in her time; in fact, Peter I of Russia proudly displayed her portrait and books in his study.

"And All Was Light": Isaac Newton

Sir Isaac Newton's work marks the culmination of the scientific revolution. Galileo had come to believe that the earth and the heavens were made of the same material, and he proposed theories of inertia. But it was Newton who articulated the laws of motion and presented a coherent, unified vision of how the universe worked. One set of forces, which could be expressed mathematically, explained why planets orbited in ellipses and why (and at what speed) apples fell from trees. There was only one universe, and Newton claimed to have discovered its laws.

Isaac Newton (1642–1727) entered Trinity College in Cambridge University in 1661, where he would remain for the next thirty-five years, first as a student and then as the Lucasian Professor of Mathematics. His first great burst of creativity came at Cambridge from 1664 to 1666, where he broke new ground in three areas. The first was optics. Using prisms he had purchased at a local fair, Newton showed that white light was composed of different-colored rays (see image on page 568). Newton's work on the composite nature of white light led him to make a reflecting telescope, which used a curved mirror rather than lenses. The telescope earned him election to the Royal Society in 1672. The second area was in mathematics. In a series of brilliant insights, Newton invented both integral calculus and differential calculus, providing mathematical tools to model motion in space. The third area of his creative genius involved his early work on gravity. Newton later told different versions of the same story: the idea about gravity had come to him when he was in a "contemplative mood" and was "occasioned by the fall of an apple." Why did the apple "not go sideways or upwards, but constantly to the earth's center? . . . Assuredly the reason is, that the earth draws it. There must be a drawing power in matter." His theory of gravity rested on mathematical formulations, and Newton did not work it out fully until the *Principia*, more than twenty years later.

Margaret Cavendish (1623–1673) English natural philosopher who developed her own speculative natural philosophy. She used this philosophy to critique those who excluded her from scientific debate.

Maria Winkelmann (1670–1720) German astronomer who discovered a comet and prepared calendars for the Berlin Academy of Sciences

Maria Sibylla Merian (1647–1717) A scientific illustrator and an important early entomologist.

Isaac Newton (1642–1727) An English mathematician and physicist; he is noted for his development of calculus, work on the properties of light, and theory of gravitation.

NEWTON'S EXPERIMENTS WITH LIGHT (1672). Earlier scientists had explained the color spectrum, which they produced by shining sunlight through a prism, by insisting that the colors were a by-product of contaminating elements within the prism's glass. Newton disproved this theory by shining the sunlight through two consecutive prisms. The first produced the characteristic division of light into a color spectrum. When one of these colored beams passed through a second prism, however, it emerged on the other side unchanged, demonstrating that the glass itself was not the cause of the dispersal.

Newton's *Principia Mathematica* (Mathematical Principles of Natural Philosophy) was published in 1687. It was prompted by a question being discussed at the Royal Society: Was there a mathematical basis for the elliptical orbits of the planets? This question inspired Newton to expand his earlier calculations into an all-encompassing theory of celestial—and terrestrial—dynamics. *Principia* was long and difficult—purposefully so, for Newton said he did not want to be "baited by little smatterers in mathematics." Its central proposition was that gravitation was a universal force that could be expressed mathematically. Newton built on Galileo's work on inertia, Kepler's findings concerning the elliptical orbits of planets, the work of Boyle and Descartes, and even on his rival Robert Hooke's work on gravity. But Newton's theory of gravity formulated something entirely new, offering a single, descriptive, and mathematical account of mass and motion. His theory was, literally, universal.

By 1713, pirated editions of *Principia* were being published in Amsterdam for distribution throughout Europe. And by the time Newton died, in 1727, he had become an English national hero and was given a funeral at Westminster Abbey. The poet Alexander Pope expressed the awe that Newton inspired in some of his contemporaries in a famous couplet:

> Nature and nature's law lay hid in night;
>
> God said, "Let Newton be!" and all was light.

Voltaire, the French champion of the Enlightenment (discussed in the next chapter), was largely responsible for Newton's reputation in France. In this, he was helped by a woman who was a brilliant mathematician in her own right, Emilie du Châtelet. She coauthored a book with Voltaire introducing Newton to a French audience; and she translated *Principia*, a daunting scientific and mathematical task and one well beyond Voltaire's mathematical abilities. Newton's French admirers and publicists disseminated Newton's findings. In their eyes, Newton exemplified a cultural transformation, a turning point in the history of knowledge.

SCIENCE AND CULTURAL CHANGE

From the seventeenth century on, science stood at the heart of what it meant to be "modern." It grew increasingly central to the self-understanding of Western culture, and scientific and technological power became one of the justifications for the expansion of Western empires and the subjugation of other peoples. At the same time, however, the break was not as sudden as the idea of a scientific "revolution" seems to indicate. To begin with, the transformation we have considered in this chapter involved elite knowledge. Ordinary people inhabited a very different cultural world. Second, natural philosophers' discoveries—Tycho's mathematics and Galileo's observations, for instance—did not undo the authority of the ancients in one blow, nor did they seek to do so. Third, science did not subvert religion. Even when traditional concepts collapsed in the face of new discoveries, natural philosophers seldom gave up on the project of restoring a picture of a divinely ordered universe. Science was thoroughly compatible with belief in God's providential design, at least through the seventeenth century.

Like his predecessors, Newton saw the world as God's message to humanity, a text to be deciphered, and close reading and study would unlock its mysteries. This same impulse led Newton to read accounts of magic, investigate alchemy's claims that base metals could be turned into gold, and immerse himself in the writings of the Church Fathers and the Bible, which he knew in intimate detail. If these activities sound unscientific from the perspective of the present, it is because the strict distinction between rational inquiry and belief in the occult or religious traditions simply did not exist in Newton's time. Such a distinction is a product of a long history of scientific developments after the eighteenth century.

Conclusion

What, then, did the scientific revolution change? Knowledge itself was reconceived. In the older model, to learn was to absorb a finite body of knowledge. In the newer one, to learn was to discover something new. Seventeenth-century natural philosophers sought and produced new answers to fundamental questions about the physical world. This process brought about a new approach to amassing and integrating information in a systematic way, an approach that helped yield more insights into the workings of nature as time went on. During this period, the most innovative scientific work moved out of the restrictive environment of the Church and the universities. Natural philosophers began talking to and working with each other in lay organizations that developed standards of research. England's Royal Society spawned imitators in Florence and Berlin, and later, in Russia. The French Academy of Sciences had a particularly direct relationship with the monarchy and the French state. France's statesmen exerted control over the academy and sought to share in the rewards of any discoveries made by its members.

The pioneering natural philosophers remained circumspect about their abilities. Some sought to lay bare the workings of the universe, while others believed humans could only catalog and describe the regularities observed in nature. By unspoken but seemingly mutual agreement, the question of first causes was left aside. The new science did not say "why," but "how." Newton, for one, worked toward explanations that would reveal the logic of creation laid out in mathematics. Yet, in the end, he settled for theories explaining motions and relationships that could be observed and tested.

But the step from scientific theory to practice would prove both awe-inspiring and consequential. As Kepler wrote to Galileo, "How great a difference there is between theoretical speculation and visual experience, between Ptolemy's discussion of the Antipodes and Columbus's discovery of the New World." Kepler's use of a metaphor

AFTER YOU READ THIS CHAPTER ⌄

CHRONOLOGY

1543	Nicolaus Copernicus (1473–1543) publishes *On the Revolutions of the Heavenly Spheres*
1576	Tycho Brahe sets up Uraniborg observatory
1609	Johannes Kepler (1571–1630) publishes *Astronomia Nova*
1610	Galileo (1564–1642) publishes *The Starry Messenger*
1620	Francis Bacon (1561–1626) publishes *Novum Organum*
1632	Galileo publishes *Dialogue Concerning the Two Chief World Systems*
1633	Galileo's trial
1637	René Descartes (1596–1650) publishes *Discourse on Method*
1660	Royal Society of London founded
1666	French Academy of Sciences founded
1687	Isaac Newton (1642–1727) publishes *Principia Mathematica*

REVIEWING THE OBJECTIVES

❯ The scientific revolution marked a shift toward new forms of explanation in descriptions of the natural world. What made the work of scientists during this period different from earlier forms of knowledge or research?

❯ The scientific revolution nevertheless depended on earlier traditions of philosophical thought. What earlier traditions proved important in fostering a spirit of scientific investigation?

❯ Observations of natural processes both in the heavens and on the earth played a central role in the scientific revolution. What technological innovations made new astronomical work possible? What questions led to the development of geology and the earth sciences?

❯ Central to the scientific revolution was the rejection of the Ptolemaic view of the universe and its replacement by the Copernican model. What was this controversy about?

❯ Francis Bacon and René Descartes held contrasting ideas about scientific method. What approach to science did each of these natural philosophers defend?

about "Columbus's discovery" to characterize the new science was not completely innocent, however, since it also associated the new science with the power and violence that European empires brought to other parts of the world. When scientific observations were turned to human populations, as in François Bernier's theories of race, the prestige of science became available for other, potentially more dangerous uses. Society, technology, government, religion, even the individual human mind seemed to be mechanisms or parts of a larger nature waiting for study. As we will see in the next chapter, the natural philosophers who began investigating the human sciences cast aside some of their predecessors' caution.

Go to **INQUIZITIVE** to see what you've learned—and learn what you've missed—with personalized feedback along the way.

PEOPLE, IDEAS, AND EVENTS IN CONTEXT

> How did the traditions of **NEOPLATONISM** and **RENAISSANCE HUMANISM** contribute to a vision of the physical world that encouraged scientific investigation and explanation?

> In what way did the work of **NICOLAUS COPERNICUS, TYCHO BRAHE, JOHANNES KEPLER**, and **GALILEO GALILEI** undermine the intellectual foundations of the **PTOLEMAIC SYSTEM**? Why did their work largely take place outside the traditional centers of learning in Europe, such as universities?

> What was the significance of **JAMES USSHER**'s claim that the earth was created in 4004 B.C.E.? How did **NICOLAS STENO** demonstrate that the different layers of the earth's surface were visible signs of the earth's history? What new division of human populations did François Bernier suggest?

> What differences in scientific practice arose from **FRANCIS BACON**'s emphasis on observation and **RENÉ DESCARTES**'s insistence that knowledge could be derived only from unquestionable first principles?

> What were **ISAAC NEWTON**'s major contributions to the scientific revolution? Why have some suggested that Newton's interests and thinking were not all compatible with modern conceptions of scientific understanding?

> What was important about the establishment of institutions such as the British **ROYAL SOCIETY** or the French **ACADEMY OF SCIENCES** for the development of scientific methods and research?

> What prevented women from entering most of Europe's scientific academies? How did educated women such as **LAURA BASSI**, **MARGARET CAVENDISH**, **MARIA WINKELMANN**, and **MARIA SIBYLLA MERIAN** gain the skills necessary to participate in scientific work?

THINKING ABOUT CONNECTIONS

> What possible connections might be made between the intellectual developments in scientific thinking during the seventeenth century and the Reformation of the sixteenth century? Was the new science incompatible with religious faith?

> Did the search for new forms of knowledge by seventeenth-century natural philosophers have implications for their vision of the future? What might an association between science and progress have meant for their understandings of human history and the role that science might play in creating new ways of understanding and living in the world?

Europe during the Enlightenment

IN 1762, THE *PARLEMENT* (LAW COURT) of Toulouse, in France, convicted Jean Calas of murdering his son. Calas was a Protestant in a region where Catholic–Protestant tensions ran high. Witnesses claimed that the father had murdered his son to prevent him from converting to Catholicism. Jean Calas was tortured to force a confession and to identify his alleged accomplices. His arms and legs were slowly pulled apart, gallons of water were poured down his throat, his body was broken on a wheel before the executioner cut off his head. Throughout the trial and torture, Calas had maintained his innocence. Two years later, the parlement reversed its verdict, declaring Calas not guilty and offering the family payment in compensation.

François-Marie Arouet, also known as Voltaire, was appalled by this case. Voltaire was the most famous personality in the European intellectual movement known as the Enlightenment and he set out to clear Calas's name. He hired lawyers for the family and wrote briefs, letters, and essays to bring the case to the public eye. These writings circulated widely among an increasingly literate middle-class audience. For Voltaire, Calas's case exemplified nearly everything he found backward in European culture: intolerance, ignorance, and religious "fanaticism." Torture demonstrated the power of the courts but could not uncover the truth. Secret interrogations, trials behind closed doors, summary judgment (Calas was executed the day after being convicted, with no review by a

BEFORE YOU READ THIS CHAPTER

❯

STORY LINES

> During the eighteenth century, intellectuals in Europe sought to answer questions about the nature of good government, morality, and the social order by applying principles of rational argument. They questioned the value of traditional institutions and insisted that "enlightened" reason could solve social problems better than age-old customs.

> Population growth, economic development, and colonial expansion created prosperity for some regions in western Europe and greater economic vulnerability in others. Aggregate increases in wealth fueled the beginnings of a consumer society, and global trade fostered a new awareness of the world's diverse cultures and peoples.

> Absolutist rulers used Enlightenment ideals to justify the centralization of authority and bureaucratic rule. Enlightenment authors also criticized the eighteenth-century social and political order and questioned religious institutions.

CORE OBJECTIVES

> **DESCRIBE** the eighteenth-century consumer revolution in Europe and its relationship to the Enlightenment.

> **DEFINE** the term *Enlightenment* as eighteenth-century thinkers used it, and **IDENTIFY** the figures most closely associated with this intellectual movement.

> **EXPLAIN** how the ideas associated with the Enlightenment spread and the consequences of this expanded world of public discussion.

> **EXPLORE** the ways that the Enlightenment was linked to imperial expansion as larger numbers of Europeans became more aware of the globe's diverse cultures and peoples.

> **UNDERSTAND** how Enlightenment thought challenged central tenets of eighteenth-century culture and politics.

THE CRUEL DEATH OF CALAS. This print, reproduced in a pamphlet that circulated in Britain in the late eighteenth century, portrayed the French Protestant Jean Calas as a martyr to his beliefs, and directly implicated the Roman Catholic Church in the cruelty of his execution by placing an enthusiastic priest prominently at the scene. The pamphlet may also have sought to reinforce anti-French sentiments among an increasingly nationalistic British population. **> How might Enlightenment authors have used such a scene to promote their message of toleration? > How might Church officials have responded to such attacks?**

higher court), and barbaric punishments defied reason, morality, and human dignity. Any criminal, however wretched, "is a man," wrote Voltaire, "and you are accountable for his blood."

Voltaire's writings on the Calas case illustrate the central concerns of the Enlightenment: the dangers of arbitrary and unchecked authority, the value of religious toleration, and the overriding importance of law, reason, and human dignity. He borrowed most of his arguments from others—from his predecessor the Baron de Montesquieu and from the Italian writer Cesare Beccaria, whose *On Crimes and Punishments* appeared in 1764. Voltaire's reputation did not rest on his originality as a philosopher; it came from his effectiveness as a writer and advocate, and his ability to reach a wide audience in print.

The emergence of this audience for Voltaire's writings was just as significant as his arguments. Urban growth and the spread of literacy helped fuel the Enlightenment's atmosphere of critical reflection on religion, law, the power of the state, and the dignity of the individual. Voltaire's celebrity showed that a new kind of literate, reading public had developed in Europe. The growing numbers of people who had income to spare on printed material created a market for newspapers and novels. The works of Voltaire and his peers were discussed in coffeehouses, where ordinary people gathered to debate the issues of the day. The coffee, sugar, and tobacco that people consumed as they debated all came from the Atlantic colonial trade, produced by the labor of enslaved people. The Enlightenment was not only an intellectual movement but a cultural phenomenon, exposing an increasingly broad part of the population to new forms of consumption and goods as well as ideas.

Population, Commerce, and Consumption

The Enlightenment's audience of urban readers and consumers were receptive to new cultural forms: the essay, the political tract, the satirical engraving, the novel, the newspaper, theatrical spectacles, and even musical performances. Such an audience could only develop in a society where significant numbers of people had achieved a level of wealth that freed them from the immediate cares of daily sustenance. By the beginning of the eighteenth century, this level of wealth had been achieved in the cities of northwestern Europe, especially in France and Britain.

Economic development that favored cities during the eighteenth century did not change the fundamental balance of population between town and country. Europe remained primarily a rural society during the Enlightenment, but the nature of the rural economy changed. Wealth became more concentrated in towns and in rural areas where forms of preindustrial production took root. These concentrations of wealth became magnets for those seeking opportunity, and intensified the pressures associated with labor migration and itinerant trade (Chapter 15). Population growth also encouraged mobility, as poorer regions increasingly became exporters of laborers in search of work and livelihood.

POPULATION AND ECONOMY IN EIGHTEENTH-CENTURY EUROPE

By 1750, then, population growth was changing older patterns of migration in western Europe. Germany's population increased by a third between 1750 and 1800, from 18.4 to 24.5 million. France's 18 percent increase in the same period was slower but similar in its effects: creating more pressure for internal migration, and providing a supply of laborers for the manufacture of goods in the countryside and in growing towns.

Demographic growth in western Europe was made possible by cheaper food and declines in mortality from disease. Intensive agriculture produced more food per acre, and improved transportation resulted in fewer famines. The importation of corn and potatoes from the Americas provided new and cheaper staple crops. Half the population continued to die before the age of twenty from infectious disease, but plague outbreaks became less frequent, and better diet and sanitation reduced mortality caused by typhoid, cholera, smallpox, and measles. Under these conditions, cities in western Europe experienced rapid growth, especially those connected with the Atlantic trade such as Amsterdam, Hamburg, and Liverpool. Spectacular population growth also occurred in Europe's capital cities: London grew from

Growth in population enabled by (1) more-intensive agriculture and new staple crops from the Americas

(2) improved diet and sanitation, reducing mortality rates

POPULATION GROWTH, c. 1600. › Where did the population grow more rapidly? › Why were the largest gains in population on the coasts? › How did urbanization affect patterns of life and trade?

674,000 in 1700 to 860,000 a century later; Paris's population went from 180,000 in 1600 to more than 500,000 in 1800; and Berlin's population grew from 6,500 in 1661 to 140,000 in 1783.

The prosperity of northwestern Europe was linked to developments in trade, manufacturing, and consumption that had begun in the late medieval period, culminating in a **commercial revolution** by the eighteenth century. The growing production and trade in textiles provides a good example of how changes in labor, commerce, and consumption were interrelated. Improvements in transportation led entrepreneurs to produce textiles in the countryside. They distributed, or "put out," wool and flax to rural workers who spun and wove it into cloth on a piece-rate basis. The entrepreneur sold the finished cloth in a market that extended from local towns

commercial revolution
A period of economic development in Europe lasting from c. 1500 to c. 1800.

to international exporters. This system (sometimes called protoindustrialization) sustained rural employment during slack seasons. Economic development in rural areas increased the proportion of the population who depended on wage labor for their survival, rather than working their own fields.

New inventions changed patterns of work in some crafts. Knitting frames quickened the manufacture of textiles. Wire-drawing machines for nail production spread from Germany into Britain. Techniques for printing colored designs directly on calico cloth were imported from Asia. More-efficient printing presses appeared, first in Holland and then elsewhere. But workers did not readily accept innovations of this kind. Labor-saving machines left people out of work. Governments intervened to block the use of machines if they increased unemployment or created unrest, and states protected their powerful commercial and financial backers. Both Britain and France outlawed calico printing for a time to protect local textile manufacturers. The pressures for economic innovation were nevertheless irresistible, because behind them lay an insatiable eighteenth-century appetite for goods.

Rural population increasingly relies on wage labor tied to production of goods, not subsistence farming

A WORLD OF GOODS

By the mid-eighteenth century, the commercial revolution produced a mass market for consumer goods, concentrated in northwestern Europe. Houses became larger, particularly in towns, and were now stocked with sugar, tobacco, tea, coffee, chocolate, newspapers, books, pictures, clocks, toys, china, glassware, pewter, silver plate, soap, razors, furniture (including beds with mattresses, chairs, and chests of drawers), shoes, cotton cloth, and spare clothing. Demand for such products consistently outstripped the supply, causing prices for these items to rise faster than the price of foodstuffs. But the demand for them continued unabated.

TOPSY-TURVY WORLD, **BY JAN STEEN.** This Dutch painting depicts a household in the throes of the exploding consumer economy that hit Europe in the eighteenth century. Consumer goods ranging from silver and china to clothing and furniture cluttered the houses of ordinary people as never before.

The result of all these developments was a European economy more complex, more specialized, more integrated, more commercialized, and more productive than anything the world had seen before. During the Enlightenment—the name historians give to a period of intellectual dynamism in eighteenth-century Europe—people shared a sense of living in a time marked by change. Many Enlightenment thinkers defended such changes as "progress," but others were more critical, fearing that valued traditions were being lost. Such debates lay at the heart of Enlightenment thought.

The Foundations of the Enlightenment

Enlightenment thinkers did not agree on everything, but most shared a belief that they lived at a moment in history in which human **reason** would prevail over the superstitions and traditions of the past. Enlightenment authors believed themselves to be the defenders of a new ideal, the "party of humanity."

The confidence that Enlightenment thinkers placed in the powers of human reason stemmed from the accomplishments of the scientific revolution. Newton's physics provided a model for scientific inquiry into other phenomena. If Nature operated according to laws that could be grasped by study, observation, and thought, perhaps the same could be said of human society and history. The work of the Scottish writer **David Hume** (*A Treatise of Human Nature*, 1739–1740; and *An Enquiry Concerning Human Understanding*, 1748) provided the most direct bridge from science to the Enlightenment. Newton had refused speculation about ultimate causes, arguing instead for a precise description of natural phenomena (Chapter 16). Hume applied this same rigor and skepticism to the study of morality, the mind, and government. Hume criticized the "passion for hypotheses and systems" that dominated earlier philosophical thinking. Experience and careful observation, he argued, usually did not support the premises on which those systems rested.

Embracing human reason meant confronting the power of Europe's traditional monarchies and the religious institutions that supported them. The German philosopher Immanuel Kant challenged his contemporaries in his classic 1784 essay "What Is Enlightenment?" writing "Dare to know!" Kant likened the intellectual history of humanity to the growth of a child: The Enlightenment was

DIVINE LIGHT. The frontispiece for Voltaire's book on the science of Isaac Newton portrays Newton as the source of a divine light that is reflected onto Voltaire's desk through a mirror held by Émilie du Châtelet, the French translator of Newton who was also Voltaire's lover. Newton's clouded throne and the adoring angels holding du Châtelet aloft were familiar motifs from earlier generations of religious paintings, but the significance of the carefully portrayed ray of light is recast by the books, inkwell, and precise scientific measuring tools surrounding Voltaire. **› What does this image say about the relationship between religious thought and Enlightenment science?**

an escape from humanity's "self-imposed immaturity" and a break with humanity's self-imposed parental figure, the Catholic Church. Coming of age meant that individuals must have the "determination and courage to think without the guidance of someone else." Reason required autonomy and freedom from tradition.

Enlightenment thinkers nevertheless recognized a great debt to their predecessors, especially **John Locke**, **Francis Bacon**, and **Isaac Newton**. They drew heavily on Locke's studies of human knowledge, especially his *Essay Concerning Human Understanding* (1690). Locke's theories of how humans acquire knowledge gave education and environment a critical role in shaping human character. All knowledge, he argued, originates from sense perception. The human mind at birth is a "blank tablet" (in Latin, *tabula rasa*). Only when an infant begins to perceive the external world with its senses does anything register in its mind. Education, then, was essential to the creation of a good and moral individual. Locke believed that humans were both naturally good and capable of improvement. Building on Locke's theories, eighteenth-century thinkers believed that social progress could be achieved by making education more accessible. Locke's theories had potentially radical implications for eighteenth-century society: if all humans were capable of reason, education might also challenge hierarchies associated with status, sex, or race. As we will see, only a few Enlightenment thinkers embraced radical ideas of equality.

Enlightenment thinkers often incorporated ideas of human diversity into their project of organizing all knowledge. The *scientific method*, by which they meant the empirical observation of particular phenomena to arrive at general laws, offered a way to pursue research in all areas—to study human affairs as well as natural ones. They collected evidence to learn the laws governing the rise and fall of nations, the distribution of peoples and cultures, and compared forms of government to arrive at an ideal universal political system. They took up a strikingly wide array of subjects in this systematic manner: knowledge and the mind, natural history, economics, government, religious beliefs, customs of Indigenous peoples of the New World, human nature, and sexual (or what we would call gender) and racial differences.

The World of the Philosophes

The culture of Enlightenment thinkers was European in a broad sense. French was their common language, but "French" books were often published in Switzerland, Germany, and Russia. Enlightenment thinkers admired British institutions and British scholarship, and Great Britain produced important Enlightenment thinkers: the historian Edward Gibbon and the Scottish philosophers David Hume and Adam Smith. Americans Thomas Jefferson and Benjamin Franklin were also recognized as part of the Enlightenment world. Smaller networks of educated elites also flourished across central and southern Europe. Enlightenment thinkers, regardless of where they lived, are often called by the French word *philosophes*. *Philosophe*, in eighteenth-century French, simply meant "a free thinker," a person whose reflections were unhampered by the constraints of religion or dogma in any form.

reason The human capacity to solve problems and discover truth in ways that can be verified intellectually.

David Hume (1711–1776) Scottish writer who applied Newton's method of scientific inquiry and skepticism to the study of morality, the mind, and government.

John Locke (1632–1704) English philosopher and political theorist known for his contributions to liberalism.

Francis Bacon (1561–1626) British philosopher and scientist who pioneered the scientific method and inductive reasoning.

Isaac Newton (1642–1727) One of the foremost scientists of all time, Newton was an English mathematician and physicist; he is noted for his development of calculus, work on the properties of light, and theory of gravitation.

philosophe During the enlightenment, this word referred to a person whose reflections were unhampered by the constraints of religion or dogma.

VOLTAIRE

The best-known philosophe was **Voltaire**, born François-Marie Arouet (1694–1778). Voltaire essentially personified the Enlightenment, commenting on an enormous range of subjects in a variety of literary forms. Voltaire became an admirer of British political institutions and the ideas of Newton, Bacon, and Locke. He popularized Newton's work in France and championed British empiricism against French thinkers influenced by Descartes and deductive reasoning (Chapter 16).

Voltaire's *Philosophical Letters* (or *Letters on the English Nation*), published in 1734, was an immediate sensation. Voltaire's themes were religion and political liberty, and his weapons were comparisons. His admiration for British culture and politics became a stinging critique of France—and other absolutist European countries. He praised British open-mindedness and the country's respect for scientists and their research. He considered the relative weakness of the British aristocracy to be a sign of Britain's political health. Unlike the French, the British respected commerce and people who engaged in it, Voltaire wrote. The British House of Commons represented the middle classes and, in contrast with French absolutism, brought balance to British government. In one of the book's more incendiary passages, he argued that in Britain, violent revolution had actually produced political moderation and stability by limiting the power of the king.

Voltaire also admired the religious pluralism and toleration of British society, which brought together citizens of different religions in a harmonious and productive culture. In this and other instances, Voltaire oversimplified: British Catholics, Dissenters, and Jews did not have equal civil rights. Yet the British policy of "toleration" did contrast with Louis XIV's intolerance of Protestants. The revocation of the Edict of Nantes (1685) had stripped French Protestants of civil rights and helped create the atmosphere in which Jean Calas and others were persecuted.

Of all forms of intolerance, Voltaire opposed religious bigotry most. He passionately denounced religious fraud, faith in miracles, fanaticism, and superstition. He did not oppose religion per se; rather, he sought to rescue morality (which he believed came from God) from dogma and Church bureaucracy. He argued for common sense and simplicity, contending that these would bring out the goodness in humanity and establish stable authority. "The simpler the laws are, the more the magistrates are respected; the simpler the religion will be, the more one will revere its ministers."

Voltaire relished his position as a critic. He was regularly exiled from France and other countries, and his books were banned and burned. As long as his plays attracted large audiences, however, the French king felt he had to tolerate the author. Voltaire had an attentive international public,

VOLTAIRE'S *CANDIDE*. Voltaire's best-selling novel gently mocked the optimism of some Enlightenment thinkers. The young Candide's tutor, Pangloss, insisted on repeating that "this is the best of all possible worlds," even as he, Candide, and Candide's love, the beautiful Cunégonde, suffered terrible accidents and misfortune. In the scene shown here, Candide is thrown out of the castle by Cunégonde's father, with "great kicks in the rear," after they have been caught kissing behind a screen. This mix of serious message and humorous delivery was quite common in Enlightenment literature. **› How might this combination of humor and philosophical meditation have been received by the educated middle-class audience that made up the readership of works such as *Candide*?**

including Frederick II of Prussia, who invited him to his court at Berlin, and Catherine of Russia, with whom he corresponded about reforms she might introduce in Russia. When he died in 1778, a few months after a triumphant return to Paris, Voltaire was possibly the best-known writer in Europe.

MONTESQUIEU

The baron de **Montesquieu** (*mahn-tuhs-KYOO*; 1689–1755) was a very different kind of Enlightenment figure. Montesquieu was a nobleman, and a magistrate in Bordeaux. He was not a provocateur like Voltaire but a cautious jurist, though he did write a satirical novel, *The Persian Letters* (1721), as a young man. The novel, composed as letters from two Persian visitors to France, compared manners at the French court with those in Turkish harems, and likened French absolutism to despotism. *The Persian Letters* was an immediate bestseller.

Montesquieu's treatise *The Spirit of Laws* (1748) may have been the most influential work of the Enlightenment. Montesquieu asked about the structures that shaped law in human societies. How had different environments, histories, and religious traditions come together to create the variety of governmental institutions in the world? What were the different forms of government? What spirit characterized each, and what were their respective virtues and shortcomings?

Montesquieu suggested that there were three forms of government: republics, monarchies, and despotisms. A republic was governed by many individuals—either an elite aristocracy of citizens or the people as a whole. The soul of a republic was virtue, which allowed individual citizens to transcend their particular interests and rule in accordance with the common good. In a monarchy, on the other hand, one person ruled in accordance with the law. The soul of a monarchy, wrote Montesquieu, was honor, which gave individuals an incentive to behave with loyalty toward their sovereign. The third form of government, despotism, was rule by a single person unchecked by law or other powers. The soul of despotism was fear, since no citizen could feel secure, and punishment took the place of education. Montesquieu devoted two chapters to the French monarchy, spelling out what he saw as a dangerous drift toward despotism. Montesquieu admired the British system and its separation of the executive, legislative, and judicial functions of government. Such a balance of powers preserved liberty by avoiding a concentration of authority in a single individual or group. His idealization of "checks and balances" helped to guide the authors of the U.S. Constitution in 1787.

DIDEROT AND THE *ENCYCLOPEDIA*

The most remarkable Enlightenment project was a collective one: the *Encyclopedia*. The *Encyclopedia* claimed to summarize all human knowledge, making it available to any reader. It demonstrated how scientific analysis could be applied in all realms of thought and aimed to encourage critical reflection on an enormous range of traditions and institutions. The *Encyclopedia*'s editor was **Denis Diderot** (1713–1784), who was helped by the mathematician Jean Le Rond d'Alembert (1717–1783) and other leading men of letters, including Voltaire and Montesquieu. Published in installments between 1751 and 1772, the *Encyclopedia* ran to seventeen large volumes of text and eleven more of illustrations, with more than 70,000 articles.

Montesquieu (1689–1755) An enlightenment philosophe whose most influential work was *The Spirit of Laws*. In this work, he analyzed the structures that shaped law and categorized governments into three types: republics, monarchies, and despotisms.

Encyclopedia Joint venture of French philosophe writers, led by Denis Diderot, which proposed to summarize all modern knowledge in a multivolume illustrated work with over 70,000 articles.

Denis Diderot (1713–1784) French philosophe and author who was the guiding force behind the publication of the first encyclopedia.

TECHNOLOGY AND INDUSTRY. This engraving, from the Mining section, is characteristic of Diderot's *Encyclopedia*. The project aimed to detail technological changes, manufacturing processes, and forms of labor—all in the name of advancing human knowledge.

Diderot commissioned articles on science and technology, to demonstrate how science could promote progress and alleviate human misery. Diderot turned the same methods to politics and the social order, including articles on economics, taxes, and the slave trade. Censorship made it difficult to write openly anti-religious articles, but Diderot thumbed his nose at religion in oblique ways. At the entry on the Eucharist, for example, the reader found a terse cross-reference: "See *cannibalism*." At one point, the French government revoked the publishing permit for the *Encyclopedia*, declaring in 1759 that the encyclopedists were trying to "propagate materialism" (by which they meant atheism). The volumes sold remarkably well despite such bans and their hefty price. Purchasers belonged to Europe's elite: aristocrats, government officials, prosperous merchants, and a scattering of members of the higher clergy.

Major Themes of Enlightenment Thought

Enlightenment thinkers across Europe raised similar themes: humanitarianism, or the dignity and worth of all individuals; religious toleration; and liberty. These ideals inspired important debates about three issues in particular: law and punishment, the place of religious minorities, and the state's relationship to society and the economy.

LAW AND PUNISHMENT

The Enlightenment beliefs about education and the perfectibility of human society led many thinkers to question the harsh treatment of criminals by European courts. An influential work by the Italian jurist **Cesare Beccaria** (1738–1794), *On Crimes and Punishments* (1764), provided Voltaire with most of his arguments in the Calas case. Beccaria criticized the prevalent view that punishments should be society's vengeance on the criminal. The only legitimate rationale for punishment instead should be to maintain social order and to prevent other crimes. Beccaria argued for the greatest possible leniency compatible with deterrence; respect for individual dignity dictated that humans should punish other humans no more than absolutely necessary.

Above all, Beccaria's book eloquently opposed torture and the death penalty. Public execution, he argued, was intended to dramatize the power of the state and the horrors of hell, but it dehumanized the victim, judge, and spectators. In 1766, a few years after the Calas case, another French trial provided an example of what horrified Beccaria and the philosophes. A nineteen-year-old French nobleman, convicted of blasphemy, had his tongue cut out and his hands cut off before he was burned at the stake. The court discovered the blasphemer had read Voltaire and ordered his *Philosophical Dictionary* burned along with the body. Sensational cases such as this helped publicize Beccaria's work. *On Crimes and Punishments* was quickly translated into a dozen languages. Owing primarily to its influence, by around 1800 most

European countries had eliminated torture, branding, whipping, and mutilation from their penal codes, and reserved the death penalty for capital crimes. Nevertheless, in places where slavery remained legal, such practices remained routine for decades longer, reinforced by racist assumptions about social hierarchy.

HUMANITARIANISM AND RELIGIOUS TOLERATION

Humanitarianism and reason also counseled religious toleration. Enlightenment thinkers spoke almost as one on the need to end religious warfare and the persecution of heretics and religious minorities. Most Enlightenment authors distinguished between religious belief (which they accepted) and the Church as an institution and dogma (which they rebelled against). It was in this sense that Voltaire opposed the Church's influence over society. Few Enlightenment authors were atheists—a notable exception was Paul-Henri d'Holbach (1723–1789)—and only a few more were agnostics. Many, including Voltaire, were deists, believers in a God who, acting as a "divine watchmaker" at the beginning of time, constructed a perfect universe and then left it to run with predictable regularity. Enlightenment inquiry proved compatible with very different stances on religion.

Nevertheless, Enlightenment support for toleration was sometimes limited. Most Christians saw Jews as heretics and Christ killers. Enlightenment thinkers commonly viewed Judaism and Islam as backward, superstitious religions. One of the few Enlightenment figures to treat Jews sympathetically was the German philosophe Gotthold Lessing (1729–1781). Lessing's play *Nathan the Wise* (1779) took place in Jerusalem during the Fourth Crusade and begins with a pogrom—a violent, orchestrated attack on Jews—in which the wife and children of Nathan, a Jewish merchant, are murdered. Nathan survives to become a sympathetic and wise father figure. He adopts a Christian-born daughter and raises her with three religions:

> *For most Enlightenment thinkers, individual religious belief was distinct from harms of institutionalized Church*

Christianity, Islam, and Judaism. At several points, authorities ask him to choose the one true religion, but Nathan showed that none exists. The three great monotheistic religions are, he argued, three versions of the truth. Religion is authentic, or true, only insofar as it makes the believer virtuous.

Lessing modeled his hero on his friend Moses Mendelssohn (1729–1786), a self-educated rabbi and bookkeeper (and the grandfather of the composer Felix Mendelssohn). Moses Mendelssohn moved—though with some difficulty—between the Enlightenment circles of Frederick II and the Jewish community of Berlin. Repeatedly attacked and invited to convert to Christianity, he defended Jewish communities against antisemitic policies and Judaism against Enlightenment criticism. At the same time, he promoted reform within the Jewish community, arguing that his community had special reason to embrace the broad Enlightenment project: religious faith should be voluntary, states should promote tolerance, and humanitarianism would bring progress to all.

LESSING AND FRIEND VISIT MENDELSSOHN. This painting of a meeting between the philosophe Gotthold Lessing (shown standing), a Christian, and his friend Moses Mendelssohn (seated right), a Jewish rabbi, emphasizes the personal nature of their intellectual relationship, which transcended their religious backgrounds. The Enlightenment's atmosphere of earnest discussion is invoked both by the open book before them and the shelf of reading material behind Lessing. Compare this image of masculine discussion (note the role of the one woman in the painting) with the image of the aristocratic salon (page 599) and the coffeehouse (page 600). **› What similarities and differences might you point to in these various illustrations of the Enlightenment public sphere?**

GOVERNMENT, ADMINISTRATION, AND THE ECONOMY

Enlightenment ideas had a very real influence over government institutions. The philosophes defended reason and knowledge for humanitarian reasons. But they also promised to make nations stronger and more efficient and prosperous. In other words, the Enlightenment spoke not only to individuals but also to states. The philosophes also took up matters of administration, tax collection, and economic policy.

The rising fiscal demands of eighteenth-century states and empires made these issues newly urgent. Which economic resources were most valuable to states? During the seventeenth century, mercantilists had argued that regulation of trade was necessary to maximize government revenues (Chapter 15). During the eighteenth century, Enlightenment economic thinkers, known as the physiocrats, argued that real wealth came from the land and agricultural production, which prospered with less government interference. They advocated simplifying the tax system and following a policy of laissez-faire, which comes from the French expression *laissez faire la nature* ("let nature take its course"), letting wealth and goods circulate without government interference. Their innovation was to suggest the economy was a kind of natural order that could be studied scientifically.

The classic expression of Enlightenment political economy came from **Adam Smith** (1723–1790) in his landmark treatise *Inquiry into the Nature and Causes of the*

Adam Smith (1723–1790) Scottish economist and liberal philosopher who proposed that competition between self-interested individuals led naturally to a healthy economy.

Wealth of Nations (1776). Observing the beginnings of industrialization in Britain, Smith argued that the division of labor into discrete and organized tasks led to enormous increases in productive capacity. Smith argued that markets functioned like a self-regulating mechanism, balanced between the opposing forces of supply and demand. If the cost of manufacturing and bringing goods to market fell below the price that buyers were willing to pay, more manufacturers would enter the market with goods for sale. This in turn would create competition between sellers, who would be forced to lower their prices to retain their market share. On the other hand, if the cost of bringing goods to market was higher than buyers were willing to pay, manufacturers would stop selling. This would create competition between buyers, who could then only purchase goods if they paid higher prices. In both cases, an imbalance in the market would lead naturally to a counter reaction that restored equilibrium. Smith's work made him the most influential of the eighteenth-century economic thinkers. Later, his work became the target of reformers and critics who had less faith in the power of markets to generate wealth and prosperity for all.

Empire and Enlightenment

The colonial world loomed large in Enlightenment thinking. Some Enlightenment thinkers saw the Americas as an unblemished territory where humanity's natural simplicity was expressed in the lives of native peoples. In comparison, Europe and Europeans appeared decadent or corrupt. At the same time, European colonial activities—especially the slave trade—raised pressing issues about humanitarianism, individual rights, and natural law. The effects of colonialism on Europe were a central Enlightenment theme.

One of the most widely read treatises of the Enlightenment was the *Philosophical and Political History of European Settlements and Trade in the Two Indies* (1770), produced and edited by the abbé Guillaume Raynal. Raynal drew his inspiration from the *Encyclopedia* and aimed at nothing less than a total history of colonization: customs and civilizations of Indigenous peoples, natural history, exploration, and commerce in the Atlantic world and India. Raynal asked whether colonization had made humanity happier, more peaceful, or better. The question was fully in the spirit of the Enlightenment, as was the answer: Raynal believed that industry and trade brought improvement and progress. Like other Enlightenment writers, however, he and his coauthors considered natural simplicity an antidote to the corruptions of their culture. They sought out and idealized what they considered examples of "natural" humanity, many of them in the New World. They condemned the tactics of the Spanish in Mexico and Peru, of the Portuguese in Brazil, and of the British in North America. They echoed Montesquieu's theme that good government required checks and balances against arbitrary authority. In the New World, they argued, Europeans found themselves with virtually unlimited power, which encouraged them to be arrogant, cruel, and despotic. In a later edition, after the outbreak of the American Revolution, the book went even further, drawing parallels between exploitation in the colonial world and inequality in Europe. Eighteenth-century radicals repeatedly warned that overextended empires sowed seeds of decadence and corruption at home.

Slavery and the Enlightenment

The encyclopedists made an exhaustive and deliberate effort to comment on every institution, trade, and custom in Western culture. The project was conceived of as an effort to catalog, analyze, and improve each facet of society. Writing in an age of burgeoning maritime trade and expanding overseas empires, they could not, and did not wish to, avoid the subject of slavery. These were their thoughts on plantation slavery, the African slaves who bore its brunt, and broader questions of law and liberty posed by the whole system.

Thus there is not a single one of these hapless souls—who, we maintain, are but slaves—who does not have the right to be declared free, since he has never lost his freedom; since it was impossible for him to lose it; and since neither his ruler nor his father nor anyone else had the right to dispose of his freedom; consequently, the sale of his person is null and void in and of itself: this Negro does not divest himself, indeed cannot under any condition divest himself of his natural rights; he carries them everywhere with him, and he has the right to demand that others allow him to enjoy those rights. Therefore, it is a clear case of inhumanity on the part of the judges in those free countries to which the slave is shipped, not to free the slave instantly by legal declaration, since he is their brother, having a soul like theirs.

Source: From *Encyclopédie*, vol. 16 (1765), as cited in David Brion Davis, *The Problem of Slavery in Western Culture* (Ithaca, NY: 1966), p. 416.

Questions for Analysis

1. What arguments against slavery does this *Encyclopedia* article present? What "natural rights" were violated by the practice of slavery, according to this view?

2. The enslavement of conquered peoples was an ancient and well-established custom, approved by civil and religious authorities. Some Enlightenment figures, such as Thomas Jefferson, were slave owners. How did some Enlightenment philosophes use universal ideas of freedom to argue against custom in regard to slavery and other questions?

SLAVERY AND THE ATLANTIC WORLD

As colonial trade grew in importance, no issue challenged Enlightenment thinkers as much as the institution of slavery. The Atlantic trade in enslaved people (Chapter 14) reached its peak in the eighteenth century. European traders sent at least 1 million Africans into New World slavery in the late seventeenth century, and at least 6 million in the eighteenth century. Control of the slave trade became fundamental to great power politics in Europe.

Even thinkers as radical as Raynal and Diderot hesitated to criticize human trafficking, and their hesitations reveal the tensions in Enlightenment thought. Enlightenment thinking began with the premise that individuals could reason for and govern themselves. Individual moral freedom lay at the heart of what the Enlightenment considered to be a just, stable, and harmonious society, and slavery defied natural law and natural freedom. Nearly all Enlightenment thinkers condemned slavery in the metaphorical sense (see *Analyzing Primary Sources* above). That the "mind should break free of its chains" and that "despotism enslaved the king's subjects" were phrases that echoed through much of eighteenth-century writing. Writers dealt more gingerly, however, with the actual enslavement and forced labor of Africans.

Adam Smith condemned slavery as uneconomical. Voltaire wondered whether Europeans would look away if Europeans—rather than Africans—were enslaved. Voltaire, however, did not question his belief that Africans were inferior peoples. Montesquieu, who came from Bordeaux, one of the central ports for the Atlantic trade, believed that slavery debased owner and enslaved alike. But he also argued that all societies balanced their systems of labor in accordance with their different needs, and the forced labor of enslaved people was one such system. Like many Enlightenment thinkers, he defended property rights, including those of slaveholders.

The *Encyclopedia* condemned the slave trade in the clearest possible terms as a violation of self-government. Humanitarian antislavery movements, which emerged in the 1760s, advanced similar arguments. However, from deploring slavery to imagining freedom for enslaved people proved a very long step. When a group of Enlightenment figures founded the Society for the Friends of Blacks in France, their leader, Jacques Brissot de Warville timidly called for a gradual emancipation of enslaved people in the French Empire. Brissot was influenced by the Enlightenment's faith in environmental determinism—the belief that environment shaped character. According to this view, slavery corrupted its victims, destroyed their natural virtue, and crushed their natural love of liberty. Enslaved people, by this logic, were not ready for freedom. Enslaved African men and women proved this assumption false on countless occasions by defending their personhood and relationships and seizing opportunities to create their own free communities. The debate about slavery in Europe rarely addressed the reality of enslaved people's lives, and Enlightenment claims about the universal rights of individuals coexisted uneasily with acceptance of the racist assumptions about social hierarchy that underlay the organized human trafficking.

For most Enlightenment thinkers, slavery was a corrupting force—on both society and enslaved people themselves

EXPLORATION AND THE PACIFIC WORLD

The Pacific world figured prominently in Enlightenment thinking. While Pacific Islanders had traveled this vast ocean for thousands of years, European voyagers arrived in the eighteenth century as part of a wave of imperial expansion that attracted the attention of the wider public. These voyages were also scientific missions, connecting the Enlightenment project of expanding scientific knowledge and the politics of European empires. In 1767, the French government sent Louis-Antoine de Bougainville (1729–1811) to the South Pacific in search of a new route to China, new lands suitable for colonization, and new spices for the ever-lucrative trade. The French public avidly consumed Bougainville's travel accounts. The British captain James Cook (1728–1779), who followed Bougainville, made two trips into the South Pacific (1768–1771 and 1772–1775), charting the coasts of New Zealand and New Holland and visiting the New Hebrides and Hawaii. He explored the outer limits of the Antarctic continent, the shores of the Bering Sea, and the Arctic Ocean.

The artists and scientists who accompanied Cook and Bougainville expanded the boundaries of European botany, zoology, and geology; and their drawings—

Enlightenment mission of expanding scientific understanding of world drives increase in overseas exploration

The Europeans Encounter the Peoples of the Pacific in the Eighteenth Century

When European explorers set out to map the Pacific, they brought with them artists to paint the landscapes and peoples they encountered. Later, other artists produced engravings of the original paintings, and these engravings were made available to a wider public. In this way, even people of modest means or only limited literacy could learn something about the different cultures and peoples elsewhere in the world.

These artists documented what they saw, but their vision was also shaped by the ideas that they brought with them and by European styles of portraiture and landscape painting. On the one hand, their images sometimes emphasized the exotic or essentially different quality of life in the Pacific. On the other hand, the use of conventional poses in the portraiture or in the depiction of human forms suggests hints of a developing understanding of the extent to which Europeans and people elsewhere in the world shared essential human characteristics. This ambiguity was typical of Enlightenment political and social thought, which sought to uncover universal human truths, while at the same time remaining deeply interested and invested in exploring the differences they observed in peoples from various parts of the globe.

A. A preliminary sketch for *Portrait of Omai* by Joshua Reynolds (c. 1773).

B. *Omiah [sic] the Indian from Otaheite, presented to their Majesties at Kew* (1774).

such as Sydney Parkinson's portraits of the Maori and William Hodge's depictions of Tahitians—became well known (see *Interpreting Visual Evidence* on pages 588–89). Large numbers of people in Europe read travel accounts of these voyages, and when Cook and Bougainville brought Pacific Islanders back to Europe, they attracted large crowds. (In late January 1779, a misguided attempt to communicate with South Pacific Islanders, perhaps with the intention of conveying them to Europe, ended in the deaths of Cook and four royal marines in Hawaii.)

The first two images depict a Tahitian named Omai, who came to Britain as a crew member on a naval vessel in July 1774. Taken three days later to meet King George III and Queen Charlotte at Kew (image B), he became a celebrity in England and had his portrait drawn by Joshua Reynolds, a famous painter of the period (image A). The third image is an engraving by two Florentine artists after a drawing by Sydney Parkinson, who was with James Cook on his first voyage to the Pacific in 1768 (image C). The two artists had never visited the South Pacific, and their image is noteworthy for the way that the bodies of the islanders are rendered according to the classical styles of European art.

Questions for Analysis

1. Does the Reynolds portrait, in its choice of posture and expression, imply that Europeans and the peoples of the Pacific might share essential traits? What uses might Enlightenment thinkers have made of such a universalist implication?

2. How might a contemporary person in Britain have reacted to the portrait of Omai kneeling before the king?

3. Do you think image C is an accurate representation of life in the South Pacific? What purpose did such imaginary and idyllic scenes serve for their audience in Europe?

C. *View of the Inside of a House in the Island of Ulietea, with the Representation of a Dance to the Music of the Country*, engraving after Sydney Parkinson (1773).

THE IMPACT OF THE SCIENTIFIC MISSIONS

Back in Europe, Enlightenment thinkers drew freely on reports of scientific missions. In 1772, Diderot published his own reflections on the significance of Bougainville's accounts in *Supplément au Voyage de Bougainville*. For Diderot, the Tahitians were the original human beings and he believed they represented humanity in its natural state, uninhibited about sexuality, free of religious dogma, and untainted by European influence. Their alleged simplicity, he believed, exposed the hypocrisy and rigidity of overcivilized Europeans. Others considered the Indigenous peoples of the Pacific akin to the classical civilizations of Greeks and Romans, associating Tahitian women, for instance, with Venus, the Roman goddess of love.

Such views said more about Europe and European utopias than about the Indigenous cultures in the Pacific. Enlightenment thinkers usually found it impossible to see other peoples as anything other than primitive versions of themselves. Even these views, however, marked a change from former times. In earlier periods, Europeans had understood the world as divided between Christendom and heathen others. Increasingly, all peoples were seen to be part of a shared humanity, with cultures and beliefs that reflected their own experiences. In sum, during the eighteenth century, religious understandings of European identity were giving way to more-secular and historical explanations for human diversity.

The Radical Enlightenment

How revolutionary was the Enlightenment? Enlightenment thought challenged central tenets of eighteenth-century culture and politics. Yet Enlightenment thinkers did not hold to any single political position. Even the most radical among them disagreed on the implications of their thought. Jean-Jacques Rousseau and Mary Wollstonecraft provide good examples of such radical thinkers.

THE WORLD OF ROUSSEAU

Jean-Jacques Rousseau (*roo-SOH*; 1712–1778) was an "outsider" who quarreled with the other philosophes. He shared the philosophes' search for intellectual and political freedom and attacked inherited privilege, yet he introduced other strains into Enlightenment thought, especially what was then called "sensibility," or the cult of feeling. Rousseau's interest in emotions led him to develop a more complicated portrait of human psychology than other Enlightenment writers, who emphasized reason as the most important attribute of human beings. He was also considerably more politically radical than his counterparts, being one of the first to talk about popular sovereignty and democracy.

Rousseau's milestone and difficult treatise on politics, *The Social Contract*, began with a now famous paradox: "Man was born free, and everywhere he is in chains." Rousseau's account of how this happened was historical: in the state of nature all men had been both free and equal. (On women, men, and nature, see **Competing Viewpoints** on page 596.) Over time, however, both their freedom and their equality had been eroded by the imposition of authority, or government. For Rousseau, the question was if such authority was legitimate, and if it was not, to explain how it could become so.

Rousseau stated that legitimate governments could be formed, but only as the result of "a form of association . . . in which each, while uniting himself with all, may still obey himself alone, and remain as free as before." This form of association could only come from consent, what Rousseau called "the social contract." Agreeing to the social contract meant that equal citizens obeyed laws they had made themselves. Social inequality, anchored in private property, profoundly corrupted the "social contract" if it led to a situation in which governments and laws represented only the rich and privileged. They became instruments of repression and enslavement. Rousseau did not advocate social leveling; by *equality* he meant only that no one would be "rich enough to buy another, nor poor enough to have to sell oneself."

Rousseau's argument on legitimate authority has three parts. First, sovereignty belonged to the people alone. This meant sovereignty should not be divided among different branches of government (as suggested by Montesquieu), nor could it be usurped by a king. Second, exercising sovereignty transformed the nation. Rousseau argued that when individual citizens formed a "body politic," that body became more than just the sum of its parts. He offered an appealing image of the nation in which citizens were bound by mutual obligation rather than by coercive laws, and united in equality rather than divided by privilege. Third, this national community would be united by what Rousseau called the *general will*. This term is notoriously difficult. Rousseau proposed it as a way to understand the common interest, which rose above the needs of individuals. The general will favored equality because, in principle at least, equality guaranteed that citizens' common interests would be represented in the whole.

Rousseau's lack of concern for balancing private interests against the general will leads some political theorists to consider him authoritarian, coercive, or moralistic. Others interpret the general will as one expression of his utopianism. During the eighteenth century, *The Social Contract* was the least understood of Rousseau's works (see **Analyzing Primary Sources** on page 593). Yet it provided influential radical

Jean-Jacques Rousseau (1712–1778) Philosopher and radical political theorist whose *Social Contract* attacked privilege and inequality. One of the primary principles of Rousseau's political philosophy is that politics and morality should not be separated.

Rousseau's concept of the general will

arguments and, more important, extraordinarily powerful images and phrases, which were widely cited during the French Revolution.

Rousseau was also well known for his writing on education. His novel *Émile* (1762) tells the story of a young man who learns virtue and moral autonomy in the school of nature rather than in the academy. Rousseau disagreed with other philosophes' emphasis on reason, insisting instead that "the first impulses of nature are always right," and children should not be forced to reason early in life. Books, which "teach us only to talk about things we do not know," should not be central to learning until adolescence. Émile's tutor thus walked him through the woods, where Émile studied nature and its simple precepts, cultivated his conscience, and, above all, his sense of independence.

Such an education aimed to give men moral autonomy and make them good citizens. Rousseau argued that women should have very different educations: "All education of women must be relative to men, pleasing them, being useful to them, raising them when they are young and caring for them when they are old, advising them, consoling them, making their lives pleasant and agreeable, these have been the duties of women since time began." Women were to be useful socially as mothers and wives. In *Émile*, Rousseau laid out just such an education for Émile's wife-to-be, Sophie. At times, Rousseau seemed convinced that women "naturally" sought out such a role: "Dependence is a natural state for women, girls feel themselves made to obey."

Rousseau's assumptions about women's "natural state" were controversial. Already, before *Émile* was published, female authors such as Émilie du Châtelet had begun to call for the education of women. Nevertheless, Rousseau's conflicting views on female nature provide a good example of the shifting meaning of nature, a concept central to Enlightenment thought. Enlightenment thinkers used nature as a yardstick against which to measure society's shortcomings. "Natural" was better, simpler, uncorrupted. What, though, was nature? It could refer to the physical world or it could refer to allegedly primitive societies. Often, it was a useful invention.

Rousseau's novels sold exceptionally well, especially among women, and became part of a larger cult of *sensibilité* ("feeling") in middle-class and aristocratic circles,

ROUSSEAU ON EDUCATION. Jean-Jacques Rousseau believed that the accumulated wisdom of human civilization was full of error. "Everything good as it leaves the hands of the Author of things," he wrote, and "everything degenerates in the hands of man." Education, therefore, should be less about the book learning and more about the individual's interaction with the God-given world. Learning should take place outside, where the individual's natural abilities and virtues could blossom free from the contamination of mistaken ideas. His ideal applied only to male students, however. He believed that women should only receive enough education to become capable mothers of their children. This image is from an early edition of Rousseau's treatise on education, *Émile* (1762) (see **Competing Viewpoints**, pages 596–97).

Rousseau's *Social Contract* (1762)

Jean-Jacques Rousseau (1712–1778) was one of the most radical Enlightenment thinkers. In his works, he suggested that humans needed not only a clearer understanding of natural laws but also a much closer relationship with nature itself and a thorough reorganization of society. He believed that a sovereign society, formed by free association of equal citizens without patrons or factions, was the clearest expression of natural law. This society would make laws and order itself by the genuine collective wisdom of its citizens. Rousseau sets out the definition of his sovereign society and its authority in the passages reprinted here.

Book I, Chapter 6

"To find a form of association that defends and protects the person and possessions of each associate with all the common strength, and by means of which each person, joining forces with all, nevertheless obeys only himself, and remains as free as before." Such is the fundamental problem to which the social contract furnishes the solution.

Book II, Chapter 4

What in fact is an act of sovereignty? It is not an agreement between a superior and an inferior, but an agreement between the body and each of its members, a legitimate agreement, because it is based upon the social contract; equitable, because it is common to all; useful, because it can have no other purpose than the general good; and reliable, because it is guaranteed by the public force and the supreme power. As long as the subjects are only bound by agreements of this sort, they obey no one but their own will, and to ask how far the respective rights of the sovereign and citizens extend is to ask to what point the latter can commit themselves to each other, one towards all and all towards one.

Source: Jean-Jacques Rousseau, *Rousseau's Political Writings*, trans. Julia Conaway Bondanella, eds. Alan Ritter and Julia Conaway Bondanella (New York: 1988), pp. 92–103.

Questions for Analysis

1. What was the goal of political association, according to Rousseau?

2. How did Rousseau claim to overcome the tension between the need for some form of social constraint and the desire to preserve liberty?

3. Which was more important for Rousseau: equality or liberty?

which emphasized spontaneous expressions of emotion and a belief that sentiment was an expression of authentic humanity. This thematic aspect of Rousseau's work contradicted much of the Enlightenment's cult of reason and is more closely related to the concerns of nineteenth-century Romanticism.

THE WORLD OF WOLLSTONECRAFT

Rousseau's sharpest critic was the British writer Mary Wollstonecraft (1759–1797). Wollstonecraft published her best-known work, *A Vindication of the Rights of Woman*, in 1792, during the French Revolution. Wollstonecraft shared Rousseau's

IMAGE OF A WOMAN READING. Female literacy increased in the eighteenth century, as middle-class women became consumers of printed matter and were more likely to be educated. Images of women reading could be both powerful and unsettling, because the idea of women as independent thinkers capable of coming to their own conclusions about the world challenged entrenched notions of female dependency. The image is a 1769 painting by Jean-Honoré Fragonard of a young girl reading; it creates an idealized vision of a sight that became much more common in middle-class households in eighteenth-century Europe.

political views and admired his writing and influence. She called monarchy "the pestiferous purple which renders the progress of civilization a curse, and warps the understanding." She spoke even more forcefully than Rousseau against inequality and the artificial distinctions of rank, birth, and wealth. Believing that equality laid the basis for virtue, she contended, in classic Enlightenment language, that the society should seek "the perfection of our nature and capability of happiness." She argued more forcefully than any other Enlightenment thinker that (1) women had the same innate capacity for reason and self-government as men, (2) *virtue* should mean the same thing for men and women, and (3) relations between the sexes should be based on equality.

Wollstonecraft did what few of her contemporaries even imagined. She applied the radical Enlightenment critique of monarchy and inequality to the family. The legal inequalities of marriage law, which among other things deprived married women of property rights, gave husbands "despotic" power over their wives. Just as kings cultivated their subjects' deference, so culture, she argued, cultivated women's weakness. "Civilized women are . . . so weakened by false refinement, that, respecting morals, their condition is much below what it would be were they left in a state nearer to nature." Middle-class girls learned manners, grace, and seductiveness to win a husband, and trained to be dependent creatures. "My own sex, I hope, will excuse me, if I treat them like rational creatures instead of flattering their *fascinating* graces, and viewing them as if they were in a state of perpetual childhood, unable to stand alone. I earnestly wish to point out in what true dignity and human happiness consists—I wish to persuade women to endeavor to acquire strength, both of mind and body." A culture that encouraged feminine weakness produced women who were childish, cunning, cruel—and vulnerable. To Rousseau's specific prescriptions for female education, which included teaching women timidity, chasteness, and modesty, Wollstonecraft replied that Rousseau wanted women to use their reason to "burnish their chains rather than to snap them." Instead, education for women had to promote liberty and self-reliance. She was considered scandalously radical for merely hinting that women might have political rights.

The Enlightenment left a mixed legacy on gender, one that closely paralleled that on slavery. Enlightenment writers developed and popularized arguments about natural rights, but they also elevated natural differences to a higher plane by suggesting that nature should dictate different, and quite possibly unequal, social roles. Mary Wollstonecraft and Jean-Jacques Rousseau shared a radical opposition to despotism and slavery, a moralist's vision of a corrupt society, and a concern with virtue and community. Their divergence on gender is characteristic of Enlightenment disagreements about nature and its imperatives, and is a good example of the different directions in which the logic of Enlightenment thinking could lead.

The Enlightenment and Eighteenth-Century Culture

THE BOOK TRADE

The Enlightenment owed a great deal to the expansion of printing and print culture. During the early eighteenth century, book publishing flourished, especially in western Europe. National borders mattered little, and much of the book trade was both international and clandestine. Readers bought books from stores, through subscription, and by mail from book distributors abroad. Cheaper printing and better distribution multiplied the numbers of scientific and literary journals, and brought daily newspapers, which first appeared in London in 1702, to Moscow, Rome, and cities and towns throughout Europe. By 1780, Britons could read 150 different magazines, and thirty-seven English towns had local newspapers. These changes have been called a "revolution in communication," and they form a crucial part of the Enlightenment.

Governments did little to check this revolutionary transformation. In Britain, the press encountered few restrictions, although the government did use a stamp tax on printed goods to raise the price of newspapers and books. Elsewhere, laws required publishers to apply in advance for the license to print and sell any given work. In practice, though, publishers frequently printed books without advance permission. Russian, Prussian, and Austrian censors tolerated much less dissent, but those governments also sought to stimulate publishing and, to a certain degree, permitted public discussion. In the smaller states of Germany and Italy, it was easier to find progressive local patrons, and English and French works circulated widely through those regions.

Censorship only made banned books expensive, keeping them out of the hands of the poor. Clandestine booksellers, most near the French border in Switzerland and the Rhineland, smuggled thousands of books across the border. What did readers want, and what does this tell us about the reception of the Enlightenment? Many clandestine dealers specialized in what they called "philosophical books," which meant subversive literature of all kinds: stories of languishing in prison, gossipy memoirs of life at the court, pornographic fantasies (often about religious and political figures), and tales of crime and criminals. Much of this flourishing eighteenth-century "literary underground" echoed the radical Enlightenment's themes, especially the corruption of the aristocracy and the monarchy's degeneration into despotism.

> *Explosive growth in the variety and circulation of printed material*

HIGH CULTURE, NEW ELITES, AND THE PUBLIC SPHERE

The Enlightenment was not simply embodied in books; it was produced in networks of readers and new forms of sociability and discussion. These networks included people of diverse backgrounds. Eighteenth-century elite, or "high," culture was small in scale but cosmopolitan and very literate, and it took literary and scientific discussion seriously. Middle-class men and women also became consumers of literature. Meanwhile, popular discussions of Enlightenment themes developed in the coffeehouses and taverns of European cities, where printed material might be read

Rousseau and His Readers

Jean-Jacques Rousseau's writings provoked very different responses from eighteenth-century readers—women as well as men. Many women readers loved his fiction and found his views on women's character and pre-scriptions for their education inspiring. But other women disagreed vehemently with his conclusions. In the first excerpt here, from Rousseau's novel Émile *(1762), the author sets out his views on a woman's education. He argues that her education should fit with what he considers her intellectual capacity and social role. It should also complement the education and role of a man. The second selection is an admiring response to* Émile *by Anne-Louise-Germaine Necker, or Madame de Staël (1766–1817), a well-known French writer and literary critic. Although she acknowledged that Rousseau sought to keep women from participating in political discussion, she also thought that he had granted women a new role in matters of emotion and domesticity. The third excerpt is by Mary Wollstonecraft, who shared many of Rousseau's philosophical principles but sharply disagreed with his assertion that women and men should have different virtues and values. She believed that women such as Madame de Staël were misguided in embracing Rousseau's ideas on women.*

Rousseau's *Émile*

Researches into abstract and speculative truths, the principles and axioms of sciences—in short, everything which tends to generalize our ideas—is not the proper province of women; their studies should be relative to points of practice; it belongs to them to apply those principles which men have discovered. . . . All the ideas of women, which have not the immediate tendency to points of duty, should be directed to the study of men, and to the attainment of those agreeable accomplish-ments which have taste for their object; for as to works of genius, they are beyond their capacity; neither have they sufficient precision or power of attention to succeed in sciences which require accuracy; and as to physical knowledge, it belongs to those only who are most active, most inquisitive, who comprehend the greatest variety of objects. . . .

She must have the skill to incline us to do everything which her sex will not enable her to do herself, and which is necessary or agreeable to her; therefore she ought to study the mind of man thoroughly, not the mind of man in general, abstractedly, but the dispositions of those men to whom she is subject either by the laws of her country or by the force of opinion. She should learn to penetrate into the real sentiments from their conversa-tion, their actions, their looks and gestures. She should also have the art, by her own conversation, actions, looks, and gestures, to communicate those sentiments which are agreeable to them without seeming to intend it. Men will argue more philosophically about the human heart; but women will read the heart of men better than they. . . . Women have most wit, men have most genius; women observe, men reason. From the concurrence of both we derive the clearest light and the most perfect knowledge which the human mind is of itself capable of attaining.

Source: Jean-Jacques Rousseau, *Émile* (1762), as cited in Mary Wollstonecraft, *A Vindication of the Rights of Woman*, ed. Miriam Brody (New York: 1992), pp. 124–25.

Madame de Staël

Though Rousseau has endeavoured to prevent women from interfering in public affairs, and acting a brilliant part in the theatre of politics; yet in speaking of them, how much has he done it to their satisfaction! If he wished to deprive them of some rights foreign to their sex, how has he for ever restored to them all those to which it has a claim! And in attempting to diminish their influence over the deliberations of men, how sacredly has he established the empire they have over their happiness! In aiding them to descend from an usurped throne, he has firmly seated them upon that to which they were destined by nature; and though he be full of indignation against them when they endeavour to resemble men, yet when they come before him with all the *charms, weaknesses, virtues,* and *errors* of their sex, his respect for their *persons* amounts almost to adoration.

Source: Cited in Mary Wollstonecraft, *A Vindication of the Rights of Woman,* ed. Miriam Brody (New York: 1992), pp. 203–4.

Mary Wollstonecraft

Rousseau declares that a woman should never, for a moment, feel herself independent, that she should be governed by fear to exercise her *natural* cunning, and made a coquettish slave in order to render her a more alluring object of desire, a *sweeter* companion to man, whenever he chooses to relax himself. He carries the arguments, which he pretends to draw from the indications of nature, still further, and insinuates that truth and fortitude, the corner stones of all human virtue, should be cultivated with certain restrictions, because, with respect to the female character, obedience is the grand lesson which ought to be impressed with unrelenting rigour.

What nonsense! When will a great man arise with sufficient strength of mind to puff away the fumes which pride and sensuality have thus spread over the subject! If women are by nature inferior to men, their virtues must be the same in quality, if not in degree, or virtue is a relative idea; consequently, their conduct should be founded on the same principles, and have the same aim.

Source: Cited in Susan Groag Bell and Karen M. Offen, eds., *Women, the Family, and Freedom: The Debate in Documents,* vol. 1, *1750–1880* (Stanford, CA: 1983), p. 58.

Questions for Analysis

1. Why did Rousseau seek to limit the sphere of activities open to women in society? What capacities did he feel they lacked? What areas of social life did he feel women were most suited for?

2. Did Madame de Staël agree with Rousseau that women's social roles were essentially different from those of men? What power do women exercise over men in society according to Staël?

3. What was the basis for Mary Wollstonecraft's disagreement with Rousseau?

4. Why did gender matter to Enlightenment figures such as Rousseau, Staël, and Wollstonecraft?

aloud, allowing even illiterate people to have access to the debates of the day. This atmosphere of discussion among people of different social positions led to the development of a new idea: "public opinion."

Among the institutions that produced the new elite were learned societies: the American Philosophical Society of Philadelphia, British literary and philosophical societies, and the Select Society of Edinburgh. Such groups organized intellectual life outside the universities. They provided libraries, published journals, and organized debates on issues from literature and history to economics and ethics. Elites also met in "academies," financed by governments to advance knowledge, researching into the natural sciences. These included the Royal Society of London and the French Academy of Sciences, both founded in the 1660s; the Royal Prussian Academy of Sciences, founded in 1701; and the French Academy of Literature (1635). In smaller cities, provincial academies played much the same role, providing a way for Enlightenment discussions to spread beyond European capitals.

Salons, an important venue for intellectual exchange among elite in society

Salons provided an alternative venue for discussion but operated informally. They were organized usually by well-connected and learned aristocratic women who invited local personalities to their homes to meet with authors and discuss their latest works. The prominent role of women distinguished the salons from the academies and universities. Salons brought together men and women of letters with members of the aristocracy for conversation, debate, drink, and food. Rousseau loathed this kind of ritual and viewed salons as a sign of superficiality in a privileged and overcivilized world. Thomas Jefferson thought the influence of women in salons had put France in a "desperate state." Some of the salons reveled in parlor games. Others, such as the one organized in Paris by Madame Necker, the wife of the future French reform minister, lay quite close to the halls of power and were testing ground for new policy ideas. Madame Marie-Thérèse Geoffrin, another celebrated French *salonnière*, became an important patron of the *Encyclopedia* and exercised influence in placing scholars in academies. Moses Mendelssohn held an open house for intellectuals in Berlin. Salons in London, Vienna, Rome, and Berlin worked the same way, and like academies, they promoted among their participants a sense of belonging to an active, learned elite.

Scores of similar societies emerged in the eighteenth century, eventually breaking the hold of elites over public debate and literate discussion. Masonic lodges, organizations with elaborate secret rituals whose members pledged themselves to the regeneration of society, attracted a remarkable array of aristocrats and middle-class men. The composer Wolfgang Amadeus Mozart, Emperor Frederick II, and Montesquieu were Masons. Behind their closed doors, the lodges were egalitarian. They pledged themselves to a common project of rational thought and benevolent action and to banishing religion and social distinction—at least from their ranks. Other networks of sociability were even less exclusive. Coffeehouses multiplied with the colonial trade in sugar, coffee, and tea, and they occupied a central spot in the circulation of ideas. A group of merchants gathering to discuss trade, for instance, could turn to politics; and the many newspapers lying about the café tables provided a ready-to-hand link between their smaller discussions and news and debates elsewhere.

Eighteenth-century cultural changes—expanding networks of sociability, flourishing book trade, new genres of literature, and circulation of Enlightenment ideas—

A READING IN THE SALON OF MADAME GEOFFRIN, 1755. Enlightenment salons encouraged a spirit of intellectual inquiry and civil debate, at least among educated elites. Such salon discussions were notable for the extent to which women helped organize and participated in the conversations. This fact led Rousseau to attack the salons for encouraging unseemly posturing and promiscuity between the sexes, which he believed were the antithesis of rational pursuits. In this painting, Madame Geoffrin, a famed hostess (at left in gray), presides over a discussion of a learned work. Note in the background the bust of Voltaire, the patron saint of rationalist discourse. › What developments were required for this notion of free public discussion among elites to become more general in society? › Would Enlightenment thinkers favor such developments? (Compare this image with the ones on pages 584 and 600.)

widened the circles of reading and discussion, expanding what some historians and political theorists call the "**public sphere**." That, in turn, began to change politics. Few thought the "public" involved more than the elite. Yet, by the late eighteenth century, European governments recognized the existence of a new arena for debate and discussion that stretched from salons to coffeehouses, academies, and circles of government, to which they needed in some measure to respond.

MIDDLE-CLASS CULTURE AND READING

Lower on the social scale, shopkeepers, small merchants, lawyers, and professionals read more and chose books from a broad variety of subjects. Instead of owning one well-thumbed Bible to read aloud, a middle-class family would buy and borrow books to read casually, pass on, and discuss. This literature consisted of science, history, biography, travel literature, and fiction. A great deal of it was aimed at middle-class women, among the fastest-growing groups of readers in the eighteenth century. Etiquette books sold very well; so did how-to manuals for the household. Scores of books about the manners, morals, and education of daughters, and popular versions of Enlightenment

public sphere Between the official realm of state activities and the private realm of the household and individual lies the public sphere.

Growth in reading
all sorts of books,
especially among
middle-class women

treatises on education and the mind, illustrate close parallels between the intellectual life of the high Enlightenment and the everyday middle-class reading matter.

The rise of a middle-class reading public, much of it female, helps account for the soaring popularity and production of novels, especially in Britain. Novels were the single most-popular new form of literature in the eighteenth century. A survey of library borrowing in late-eighteenth-century Britain, Germany, and North America showed that 70 percent of books taken out were novels. For centuries, Europeans had read romances such as tales of the Knights of the Round Table, but the setting of popular novels was closer to home. The novel's more recognizable, non-aristocratic characters seemed more relevant to common middle-class experience. Moreover, examining emotion and inner feeling also linked novel writing with a larger eighteenth-century concern with personhood and humanity. As we have seen, classic Enlightenment writers such as Voltaire, Goethe, and Rousseau wrote very successful novels; and those should be understood alongside *Pamela* or *Clarissa* by Samuel Richardson (1689–1761), *Moll Flanders* or *Robinson Crusoe* by Daniel Defoe (1660–1731), and *Tom Jones* by Henry Fielding (1707–1754).

Many historians have noted that women figured prominently among fiction writers. The works of Jane Austen (1775–1817), to many readers, especially *Pride*

A COFFEEHOUSE IN LONDON, 1798. Coffeehouses were centers of social networks and hubs of opinion, contributing to a public consciousness that was new to society and brought about by the Enlightenment. This coffeehouse scene illustrates a mixing of classes, lively debate, and a burgeoning culture of reading. Compare this image with that of the aristocratic salon (page 599) and the meeting of Lessing and Mendelssohn (page 584). › **How were coffeehouses different from aristocratic salons or the middle-class drawing room discussion between two German thinkers?** › **Can they all be seen as expressions of a new kind of "public sphere" in eighteenth-century Europe?**

and Prejudice and *Emma*, are the height of the novelist's craft. Women, however, were not the only ones to write novels, nor were they alone in paying close attention to the domestic or private sphere. Their work took up central eighteenth-century themes of human nature, morality, virtue, and reputation. Their novels, like much of the nonfiction of the period, explored those themes in domestic as well as in public settings.

POPULAR CULTURE: URBAN AND RURAL

How much did books and print culture touch the lives of the common people? Literacy rates varied dramatically by gender, social class, and region, but were generally higher in northern than in southern and eastern Europe. It is not surprising that literacy ran highest in cities and towns—higher, in fact, than we might expect. In early eighteenth-century Paris, 85 percent of men and 60 percent of women could read. Well over half the residents of poorer Parisian neighborhoods, especially small shopkeepers, domestic servants and valets, and artisans, could read and sign their names. Even the illiterate lived in a culture of print, though they had few books on their own shelves. They saw one-page newspapers and broadsides or fly sheets posted on streets and tavern walls and regularly heard them read aloud. Moreover, visual material—inexpensive woodcuts especially, but also prints, drawings, and satirical cartoons—figured as prominently as text in much popular reading material. By many measures, the circles of reading and discussion were even larger than literacy rates might suggest, especially in cities.

Neither England nor France required any primary schooling, leaving education to haphazard local initiatives. In central Europe, some regimes made efforts to develop state-sponsored education. Catherine of Russia summoned an Austrian consultant to set up a system of primary schools, but by the end of the eighteenth century, only 22,000 out of a population of 40 million had attended any kind of school. In the absence of primary schooling, most Europeans were self-taught.

Apart from scattered local initiatives for public education, most Europeans are self-taught

Like its middle-class counterpart, popular culture rested on networks of sociability. Guild organizations offered discussion and companionship. Street theater and singers mocking local political figures offered culture to people of different social classes. In the countryside, market days and village festivals brought social classes together, and popular entertainments reached a wide social audience. Folktales and traditional songs resist pigeonholing as elite, middle-class, or popular culture, because they passed from one cultural world to another, being revised and reinterpreted in the process. Second, oral and literate culture overlapped. In other words, even people who could not read often had a great deal of "book knowledge," arguing seriously about points from books, and they believed that books conferred authority.

It remains true that the countryside was desperately poor. Life there was far more isolated than in towns. A yawning chasm separated peasants from the world of the high Enlightenment. The philosophes, well established in the summits of European society, looked at popular culture with distrust and ignorance. They saw the common people of Europe much as they did Indigenous peoples of other continents. The philosophes were humanitarians, critical thinkers, and reformers—but they were not democrats. The Enlightenment, though well entrenched in eighteenth-century elite culture, nonetheless involved changes that reached far beyond elite society.

War and Politics in Enlightenment Europe

WAR AND EMPIRE IN THE EIGHTEENTH-CENTURY WORLD

After 1713, western Europe remained largely at peace for a generation. In 1740, however, that peace was shattered when Frederick the Great of Prussia seized the Austrian province of Silesia. In the resulting War of the Austrian Succession, France and Spain fought on the side of Prussia, hoping to reverse some of the losses they had suffered in the Treaty of Utrecht; whereas Britain and the Dutch Republic sided with Austria. The war quickly spread beyond the frontiers of Europe. In India, the British East India Company lost control over the coastal area of Madras to its French rival. But in North America, British colonists from New England captured the important French fortress of Louisbourg on Cape Breton Island. When the war finally ended in 1748, Britain recovered Madras and returned Louisbourg to France.

Eight years later, these colonial conflicts reignited when Prussia once again attacked Austria. This time, however, Prussia allied itself with Great Britain, and Austria found support from both France and Russia. In Europe, the Seven Years'

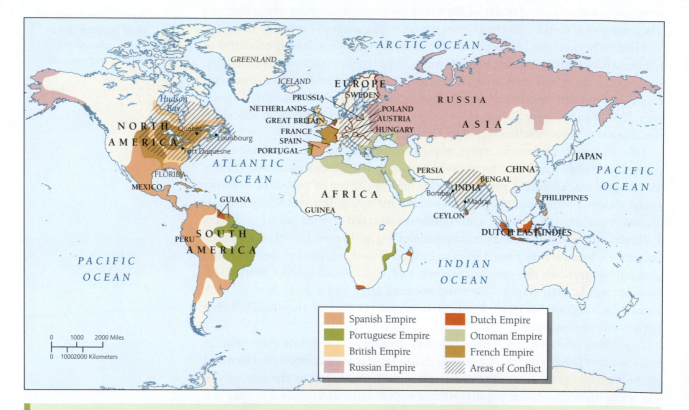

THE SEVEN YEARS' WAR, 1756–1763. › Which continents were involved in the Seven Years' War? › What was the impact of naval power on the outcome of the war? › What were the consequences for the colonies involved in the conflict?

War (1756–1763) ended in a stalemate, while in India and North America, the war had decisive consequences. In India, mercenary troops employed by the British East India Company joined with native allies to eliminate their French competitors. In North America (where the conflict was known as the French and Indian War), British troops captured both Louisbourg and Québec and drove French forces from the Ohio River Valley and the Great Lakes. By the Treaty of Paris in 1763, which brought the Seven Years' War to an end, France formally surrendered both Canada and India to the British; six years later, the French East India Company was dissolved.

ENLIGHTENED ABSOLUTISM IN EASTERN EUROPE

The rulers of Prussia, Austria, and Russia, who initiated these wars on the Continent, were among the pioneers of a new style of "enlightened absolutism" within their realms. They demonstrated their commitment to absolutist rule by centralizing their administrations, increasing taxation, creating a professional army, and tightening their control of the Church. And they justified this expansion of powers in the name of the Enlightenment ideal of reason—as rational solutions to the problems of government.

Rulers influenced by the spirit of enlightened absolutism included Empress Maria Theresa (r. 1740–1780) of Austria and her son Joseph II (r. 1765–1790); from 1765 until 1780, the two were co-rulers. They created statewide systems of primary education, relaxed censorship, and instituted a more-liberal criminal code for the Habsburg Empire. Joseph II was particularly energetic in challenging the power of the Church: he closed hundreds of monasteries, limited the number of monks and nuns permitted to live in contemplative orders, and ordered that the education of priests be placed under government supervision (Chapter 15).

The most emblematic enlightened absolutist, however, was Frederick II (1740–1786) of Prussia. As a young man, Frederick devoted himself to the flute and admired French culture, exasperating his military-minded father, Frederick William I. When Frederick rebelled by running away from the court with a friend, his father had them apprehended and the friend executed before Frederick's eyes. This grisly lesson took. Although Frederick never gave up his love of music and literature, he applied himself energetically to his royal duties, earning himself the title Frederick the Great.

Frederick raised Prussia to the status of a major power. In 1740, as soon as he became king, he mobilized his army and occupied the Austrian province of Silesia. Eventually, Frederick consolidated his gains over all the Polish territories that lay between East Prussia and Brandenburg, transforming Prussia into a powerful, contiguous kingdom by 1786. Frederick was careful to cultivate support from the Prussian nobility, known as the Junkers. His father had recruited civil servants according to merit rather than birth, but Frederick relied on the Junkers to staff the army and his expanding administration. His strategy worked. His nobility remained loyal, and he fashioned the most professional and efficient bureaucracy in Europe.

Frederick supervised a series of "enlightened" social reforms. He prohibited the judicial torture of accused criminals, abolished the bribing of judges, and

In so-called enlightened absolutism, rulers seek efficient and rational rule

Frederick's "enlightened" social reforms

MARIA THERESA OF AUSTRIA AND HER FAMILY. A formidable and capable ruler who fought to maintain Austria's dominance in central Europe against the claims of Frederick the Great of Prussia, Maria Theresa had sixteen children, including Marie Antoinette, later the queen of France as wife of Louis XVI. › **Why did Maria Theresa emphasize her role as mother in a royal portrait such as this one rather than her undeniable political skills? › How does this portrait compare with those of Louis XIV (page 520) or William and Mary (page 526)?**

established a system of elementary schools. Although strongly antisemitic, he encouraged religious toleration toward Jews, and declared that he would happily build a mosque in Berlin if he could find enough Muslims to fill it. On his own royal estates, he abolished capital punishment, curtailed the forced labor services of his peasantry, and granted the peasants long leases on the land they worked. He encouraged scientific forestry and the cultivation of new crops. He cleared new lands in Silesia and brought in thousands of immigrants to cultivate them. When wars ruined their farms, he supplied his peasants with new livestock and tools. However, he never attempted to extend these reforms to the estates of the Prussian nobility. To have done so would have alienated the very group on whom Frederick's rule depended.

Like Frederick, Catherine the Great of Russia (r. 1762–1796) thought of herself as an enlightened ruler and she corresponded with French philosophes. Also like Frederick, she could not afford to lose the support of the nobles, who had placed her on the throne after executing her husband, the weak and possibly mad Peter III. Under her reign, the nobility were exempted from taxation and corporal punishment, and their property rights over their estates were enhanced. Catherine's efforts at enlightened reform were limited: she founded hospitals and orphanages, and created an elementary school system for the children of the provincial nobility. Plans to reform the legal system were set aside after a massive peasant revolt in 1773–1775 (led by a Cossack, Yemelyan Pugachev) briefly threatened Moscow itself. Catherine gained her greatest achievements through war and diplomacy. In 1774, she won control over the northern coast of the Black Sea after a war with the Ottoman Empire. Russia thus obtained a long-sought goal: a warm-water port for the Russian navy.

In addition, Catherine succeeded in expanding Russian territory in the west, at the expense of the weaker kingdom of Poland. The plan for Russia, Austria, and Prussia to divide the Polish-Lithuanian Commonwealth among them was originally proposed by Frederick the Great: Russia would abandon its Danubian provinces and receive in exchange the grain fields of eastern Poland (population, between 1 and 2 million Poles); Austria would take Galicia (population, 2.5 million); and Prussia would consolidate the divided lands of its kingdom by taking Poland's coastal regions on the Baltic Sea. In fact, Russia had long hoped to absorb the

Commonwealth for itself. When the agreement was finalized in 1772, Poland had lost 30 percent of its territory and half its population.

The Polish state tried to reassert itself by writing a new constitution that would strengthen the kingdom's political institutions. The Constitution of 1791 gave the urban middle classes a greater voice to help counteract the influence of the more privileged nobility, and the state declared its intention to protect peasants from abuses linked to serfdom. The new constitution, however, angered conservative elements among the Polish aristocracy and Poland's more powerful neighbors. In a renewed war in 1792, the Polish state proved no match for the three major regional powers—Russia, Austria, and Prussia; and after a second partition in 1793, Poland was reduced further, so that only one-third of the population before 1772 remained in Polish territory. In 1794, a Polish uprising partially inspired by the French Revolution attempted to free Poland and Lithuania from Russian control (see Chapter 19), but its failure led Russia, Austria, and Prussia to erase Poland from the map altogether, and its territories and population were divided among the victors in a third and final partition. Poland, which along with Lithuania had been an independent commonwealth since 1569 and bound even longer by an informal union of the Polish and Lithuanian royal families, would not reappear as an autonomous nation-state until after World War I.

As a political program, therefore, enlightened absolutism clearly had its limits. Catherine the Great of Russia, Frederick the Great of Prussia, and Joseph II of Austria were ready to abandon the humanitarian impulse of Enlightenment thought and the ideal of self-government when it came to preserving their own power and the social hierarchies that sustained it.

THE AMERICAN REVOLUTION

The **American Revolution** of 1776 provided a more fruitful opportunity for putting Enlightenment ideals into practice—especially the rule of law and the importance of representative government, but it also exposed the limits of these ideals. Along the Atlantic seaboard, the rapidly growing British colonies chafed at the rule from London. To recover some of the costs of the Seven Years' War, the British Parliament imposed a series of new taxes on its American colonies. These taxes were immediately unpopular, and colonists complained that because they had no representatives in Parliament, they were being taxed without their consent. They also argued that British restrictions on colonial trade were strangling American livelihoods and making it impossible to pay even the king's legitimate taxes.

DIVIDING THE ROYAL SPOILS. A contemporary cartoon showing the monarchs of Europe at work carving up a hapless Poland. Note there is little reference here to the people who lived in the Polish territories that were being divided up among Russia, Prussia, and the Habsburg Empire. All three of these realms already contained people who spoke different languages and practiced different religions. The result of such expansion was to increase the linguistic and cultural diversity of these kingdoms. › **How might the redistribution of Polish territories have complicated the internal politics of these monarchies?** › **What long-term consequences might we expect from such multiethnic or multireligious societies?**

American Revolution
(1775–1783) A period of insurrection and war in which thirteen British colonies in North America won their independence from the British king and founded a new nation, the United States of America.

The British government, led since 1760 by the young and inexperienced King George III, responded to these oppositions with a badly calculated mixture of vacillation and force: various taxes were imposed and then withdrawn in the face of colonial resistance. In 1773, however, when East India Company tea was dumped into Boston Harbor by rebellious colonials objecting to the customs duties that had been imposed on it, the British government closed the port of Boston and curtailed the colony's representative institutions. These "Coercive Acts" galvanized the support of the other American colonies for Massachusetts, and in 1774, representatives from all the American colonies met at Philadelphia to form the Continental Congress, to negotiate with the Crown over their grievances. In April 1775, however, local militiamen at Lexington and Concord clashed with regular British troops sent to disarm them. Soon thereafter, the Continental Congress began raising an army, and an outright rebellion erupted against the British government.

The debate about slavery in Britain's North American colonies revealed the limits of the Continental Congress's claims to represent the cause of freedom for all. In November 1775, the royal governor of Virginia, the Earl of Dunmore, issued a proclamation that emancipated enslaved Africans and indentured servants in Virginia if they rallied to the British side and took up arms against the rebels. Around 800 formerly enslaved people joined the British army, and many thousands more were inspired to seek freedom in territory controlled by British troops. Writing in 1786, Thomas Jefferson criticized the Earl of Dunmore's actions as "exciting the savages against us" and encouraging "the insurrection of our slaves."

When the thirteen colonies formally declared their independence from Great Britain on July 4, 1776, their language showed their debt to Enlightenment writers. The Declaration of Independence declared that "all men are created equal" but the existence of slavery in the colonies went unmentioned. Refusing to address the question of slavery allowed the Continental Congress to preserve its unity against the British, but independence seemed unlikely during the first two years of the war. In 1778, however, France, hoping to challenge Britain's imperial hegemony, joined the war on the side of the Americans. Spain also entered the war in support of France, hoping to recover Gibraltar and Florida (the latter lost in 1763 to Britain). In 1780, Britain declared war on the Dutch Republic for continuing to trade with the rebellious colonies. Now facing a coalition of its colonial rivals, Great Britain saw the war turn against it. In 1781, combined land and sea operations by French and American troops forced the surrender of the main British army at Yorktown in Virginia.

Negotiations for peace were not concluded until September 1783. The Treaty of Paris left Great Britain in control of Canada and Gibraltar. Spain retained its possessions west of the Mississippi River and recovered Florida. The United States gained its independence with a western border fixed on the Mississippi River, but the new nation's commitment to political liberty was limited to free whites. The U.S. Constitution of 1788 did not contain the word "slave," but it stated that people who were not free would be counted as three-fifths of a person in the apportionment of congressional representatives from each state. This measure increased the number of representatives from states that permitted slavery without giving enslaved people a vote.

Finally, the American Revolution upset the balance of power in the Atlantic world. France gained the satisfaction of defeating its colonial rival, Britain, but that satisfaction was short-lived. Six years later, the massive debts France had incurred in supporting the American Revolution helped bring about another, very different kind of revolution in France, one that would permanently alter the history of Europe.

Conclusion

The Enlightenment arose from the scientific revolution, the new sense of power and possibility that rational thinking made possible, and the rush of enthusiasm for new forms of inquiry. Enlightenment thinkers scrutinized a remarkably wide range of topics: human nature, reason, understanding, religion, belief, law, the origins of government, economics, and new forms of technology. They also examined social practices such as marriage, child rearing, and education. Enlightenment ideas about social improvement and progress could and did occasionally serve the interests of European rulers, who saw in them a means both to rationalize their administrations and to challenge social groups or institutions that resisted the centralization of authority. Maria Theresa in Austria, Frederick the Great in Prussia, and Catherine the Great in Russia all found ways to harness aspects of Enlightenment thought to their strategies of government.

At the same time, however, the radical implications of the Enlightenment critique of tradition made many people uncomfortable. Ideas with subversive implications circulated in popular forms, from pamphlets and journalism to plays and operas. The intellectual movement that lay behind the Enlightenment thus had broad consequences for the creation of a new kind of elite based not on birth but on the acquisition of knowledge and the encouragement of open expression and debate. A new sphere of public opinion had come into existence, one which was difficult for the state to monitor and control, and one that would have profound consequences in the nineteenth and twentieth centuries.

The prosperity that had made the Enlightenment possible remained very unevenly distributed in late eighteenth-century Europe. In the cities, rich and poor lived separate lives in separate neighborhoods. In the countryside, regions bypassed by the developing commercial economy of the period continued to suffer from hunger and famine, just as they had done in the sixteenth and seventeenth centuries. In eastern Europe, the contrasts between rich and poor were even more extreme, as many peasants fell into a new style of serfdom that would last until the end of the nineteenth century. War, too, remained a fact of European life, bringing death and destruction to hundreds of thousands of people across the Continent and around the world—yet another consequence of the worldwide reach of these European colonial empires.

The Atlantic revolutions (the American Revolution of 1776, the French Revolution of 1789, and the Latin American upheavals of the 1830s)

WARS OF THE SEVENTEENTH AND EIGHTEENTH CENTURIES	
Glorious Revolution	1688–1689
War of the League of Augsburg	1689–1697
War of the Spanish Succession	1702–1713
Seven Years' War	1756–1763
American Revolution	1775–1783
The Russo-Turkish War	1787–1792

were steeped in the language of the Enlightenment. The constitutions of the new nations formed by these revolutions made reference to the fundamental assumptions of Enlightenment liberalism: the liberty of the individual conscience and the freedom from the constraints imposed by religious or government institutions. Government authority could not be arbitrary; equality and freedom were natural; and humans sought happiness, prosperity, and the expansion of their potential. Even after the Atlantic revolutions, these aspirations were only partially realized.

AFTER YOU READ THIS CHAPTER ⌄

CHRONOLOGY

1734	Voltaire (1694–1778), *Philosophical Letters*
1740–1780	Maria Theresa of Austria
1740–1786	Frederick II of Prussia
1748	Baron Montesquieu (1689–1755), *The Spirit of Laws*
1748	David Hume (1711–1776), *An Enquiry Concerning Human Understanding*
1751–1772	Denis Diderot (1713–1784), *Encyclopedia*
1756–1763	The Seven Years' War
1762	Jean-Jacques Rousseau (1712–1778), *The Social Contract*
r. 1762–1796	Catherine the Great of Russia
1776	The American Revolution begins
1776	Adam Smith (1723–1790), *Inquiry into the Nature and Causes of the Wealth of Nations*
1792	Mary Wollstonecraft (1759–1797), *A Vindication of the Rights of Woman*

REVIEWING THE OBJECTIVES

❯ Many eighteenth-century thinkers used the term *Enlightenment* to describe what their work offered to European society. Who were they, and what did they mean by this term?

❯ Enlightenment ideas spread rapidly throughout Europe and in European colonies. How did this expanded arena for public discussion shape the development of Enlightenment thought?

❯ Enlightenment debates were shaped by the availability of new information about peoples and cultures in different parts of the globe. How did Enlightenment thinkers incorporate this new information into their thought?

❯ Enlightenment thinkers were often critical of widely held cultural and political beliefs. What was radical about the Enlightenment?

When the North American colonists declared their independence from Britain in 1776, they called such ideas "self-evident truths." That bold declaration marked the self-confidence that was the Enlightenment's hallmark, but the fact that slavery endured in the Americas and the Caribbean for decades after these revolutions showed the very real limits of such ideals in practice. The Enlightenment's legacy was at best unevenly applied, and its universal reach remained an aspiration rather than an accomplishment.

Go to INQUIZITIVE to see what you've learned—and learn what you've missed—with personalized feedback along the way.

PEOPLE, IDEAS, AND EVENTS IN CONTEXT

❯ How did the **COMMERCIAL REVOLUTION** change social life in Europe?

❯ Who were the **PHILOSOPHES**? What gave them such confidence in **REASON**?

❯ What did **DAVID HUME** owe to **ISAAC NEWTON**? What made his work different from that of the famous physicist?

❯ What did **VOLTAIRE** admire about the works of **FRANCIS BACON** and **JOHN LOCKE**? What irritated Voltaire about French society?

❯ What was **MONTESQUIEU**'s contribution to theories of government?

❯ What made **DENIS DIDEROT**'s *ENCYCLOPEDIA* such a definitive statement of the Enlightenment's goals?

❯ What influence did **CESARE BECCARIA** have over legal practices in Europe?

❯ What contributions did **ADAM SMITH** make to economic theory?

❯ What was radical about **JEAN-JACQUES ROUSSEAU**'s views on education and politics?

❯ What does the expansion of the **PUBLIC SPHERE** in the eighteenth century tell us about the effects of the Enlightenment?

❯ What aspects of the **AMERICAN REVOLUTION** are related to central themes of Enlightenment thought?

THINKING ABOUT CONNECTIONS

❯ Compare the Enlightenment as an intellectual movement with the Reformation of the sixteenth century. What is similar about the two movements? What is distinctive?

❯ Did increases in literacy, the rise of print culture, and the emergence of new forms of intellectual sociability such as salons, reading societies, and coffeehouses really make public opinion more rational? How has our understanding of public opinion changed since the eighteenth century?

18

The French Revolution

A CROWD OF PARISIANS ATTACKED the nearly empty royal prison known as the **Bastille** on July 14, 1789. The revolt was a popular expression of support for a newly created National Assembly. Just weeks earlier, this representative body had declared its intention to put an end to absolutism in France by writing a constitution that made the nation, rather than the king, the sovereign authority in the land. Members of the National Assembly spoke the language of the Enlightenment, but the revolutionary crowd expressed itself with violent anger directed at the king's soldiers, who they feared might turn their guns on the city. When the governor of the Bastille prison opened fire on the attackers, killing as many as a hundred, the crowd responded with redoubled fury. By the end of the day, the prison had fallen, and the governor was dragged to a public square and beheaded.

This tension between noble political aspirations and cruel violence lies at the heart of the French Revolution.

Other kingdoms were not immune from the same social and political tensions that divided the French. Aristocrats across Europe and the colonies resented monarchical inroads on their ancient freedoms. The middle classes chafed under a system of official privilege that they saw as unjust and outmoded. Peasants resented the demands of government on their limited resources. And anger was not aimed just at kings—bitter resentments and tensions existed between country and city dwellers, rich and

**BEFORE
YOU
READ
THIS
CHAPTER**

❯

STORY LINES

> The French Revolution of 1789–1799 overthrew Louis XVI and created a government that was committed in principle to the rule of law, the liberty of the individual, and an idea of the nation as a sovereign body of citizens. These political changes also opened the way for the expression of a wide variety of social grievances by peasants, laborers, and women, as well as enslaved people in the French Empire.

> The French Revolution encouraged the spread of democratic ideas, but it also led to an increase in the power of centralized nation-states in Europe. The pressures of the revolutionary wars led governments to develop larger national bureaucracies, modern professional armies, new legal codes, and new tax structures.

> The French Revolution was part of a broader set of changes that rocked the Atlantic world at the end of the eighteenth century. Along with the Haitian Revolution and the American Revolution, this wave of cataclysmic change reshaped the political order of Europe and the Americas.

CORE OBJECTIVES

> **UNDERSTAND** the origins of the French Revolution in 1789.

> **EXPLAIN** the goals of French revolutionaries and the reactions of people elsewhere in Europe and the Atlantic world.

> **DESCRIBE** the events that made the revolution more radical in 1792–1794.

> **IDENTIFY** the connections between the revolution and Napoleon's regime after 1799, and the effects of Napoleon's conquests on Europe.

> **CONSIDER** the links between the French Revolution and the Atlantic world, which also saw revolutions in the Americas and in the Caribbean during these decades.

THE ATLANTIC REVOLUTIONS. The Atlantic revolutions shook nations and empires on both sides of the ocean, challenging the legitimacy of Europe's dynastic realms, lending further support to the notions of popular sovereignty, and forcing contemporaries to rethink the meanings of citizenship in a context of intense political and economic struggle. › How many of these struggles took place in Europe? › How many appear to have taken place on the periphery of the Atlantic world? › What circumstances may have made it more difficult for such revolutionary movements to develop in Europe?

poor, overprivileged and underprivileged, enslaved and free. The French Revolution was the tumultuous expression of all of these conflicts.

This age of revolution began on the other side of the Atlantic Ocean. The American Revolution of 1776 was a crisis of the British Empire, linked to conflicts between England and France over control of North America. It led to a major crisis of the Old Regime in France. "Enlightened" Europeans saw the success of the American Revolution as a source of optimism that reform was possible.

Change did come in Europe, but the conflicts that ensued were anything but modest. The revolution proved that the subjects of an old European monarchy could come together to constitute themselves as citizens of a new political idea: the nation.

Bastille The Bastille was a royal fortress and prison in Paris.

The revolutionaries in France posed new questions about the role of women in public life, the separation of church and state, and the rights of Jews and other minorities. A slave revolt in the French colonies forced revolutionaries to admit that the new liberties they defended also belonged to enslaved Africans, though few had suggested this at the outset. Meanwhile, the European wars precipitated by the revolution marked the first time that entire populations were mobilized as part of a new kind of devastating international conflict—the first "total war." In spite of the optimism of those who began the revolution in 1789, it quickly became something much more costly, complex, and violent. Its effects were to resonate throughout Europe for the next half century.

The French Revolution: An Overview

The term *French Revolution* refers to a complex series of events that took place in three stages between 1789 and 1799. Because of the French Revolution's broad impact, it is also closely related to the period that follows, 1799–1815, when Napoleon Bonaparte ruled in France and conquered much of Europe.

The first stage of the revolution was a struggle over the idea of a constitutional monarchy in France, and lasted from 1789 to 1792. This stage was relatively peaceful, and came about as social elites challenged the power of the king. Like the American revolutionaries, the early French revolutionaries refused taxation without representation, attacked despotism, and offered an Enlightenment-inspired program to rejuvenate the nation. Reforms, many of them breathtakingly wide ranging, were instituted—some accepted or even offered by the king, while others passed despite his objections. This peaceful, constitutional phase did not last, however. Unlike the American Revolution, the French Revolution did not stabilize around one constitution or one set of political leaders.

> Stage 1: From 1789 to 1792, a mostly peaceful struggle over constitutional reforms

The threat of dramatic change within one of the most powerful countries in Europe created international tensions. In 1792, these tensions exploded into war, as counterrevolutionary armies invaded France, instigating a crisis that brought about the end of the Bourbon monarchy and the establishment of a republic. This second stage of the revolution, which lasted from 1792 to 1794, was one of acute crisis, consolidation, and repression. A ruthlessly centralized government mobilized all the country's resources to fight the foreign enemy and the counterrevolutionaries at home.

> Stage 2: From 1792 to 1794, a radical and violent phase

The **Terror**, as this policy was called, saved the republic, but it exhausted itself in factions and collapsed in 1794. In the third stage, from 1794 to 1799, the government drifted. France remained a republic, and continued to fight with Europe; but, undermined by corruption and division, the state fell prey to the ambitions of a military leader, Napoleon Bonaparte. Napoleon's rule, punctuated by equally astonishing victories and catastrophes, stretched from 1799 to 1815. It began as a republic but became an empire, and ended—after a last hurrah—in the muddy fields outside the Belgian village of Waterloo. After Napoleon's final defeat, the other European monarchs restored the Bourbons to the throne. That restoration, however, was short lived, and the cycle of revolution and reaction continued into the nineteenth century.

> Stage 3: From 1794 to 1799, the French republic persists, but is divided by infighting

The Coming of the Revolution

What were the long-term causes of the revolution in France? Historians long ago argued that the causes and outcomes should be understood in terms of class conflict. According to this interpretation, a rising bourgeoisie, or middle class, inspired by Enlightenment ideas and its own self-interest, overthrew what was left of the aristocratic order. This interpretation drew on the writings of the nineteenth-century philosopher Karl Marx.

Historians have substantially modified this bold thesis. French society was not simply divided between a bourgeois class and the aristocracy. Instead, it was increasingly dominated by a new elite or social group that brought together aristocrats, officeholders, professionals, and—to a lesser degree—merchants and businessmen. To understand the revolution, we need to understand this new social group and its conflicts with the government of Louis XVI.

Legally, French society was divided into three estates. (An individual's *estate* marked his or her standing, or status, and it determined legal rights, taxes, and so on.) The First Estate comprised the clergy; the Second Estate, the nobility; and the **Third Estate**, by far the largest, included everyone else, from wealthy lawyers and businessmen to urban laborers and poor peasants. These legal distinctions often seemed artificial. To begin with, the social boundaries between nobles and wealthy commoners were ill defined. A noble title was accessible to anyone who could afford to buy an ennobling office. Close to 50,000 new nobles were created between 1700 and 1789. The nobility depended on a constant infusion of talent and economic power from the wealthy social groups of the Third Estate.

Most noble wealth was proprietary—that is, tied to land, urban properties, purchased offices, and the like. Yet noble families did not disdain trade or commerce. In fact, noblemen financed most industry and invested heavily in banking and such enterprises as the slave trade, ship owning, mining, and metallurgy. Moreover, the very wealthy members of the Third Estate also preferred to invest in secure, proprietary holdings. Thus, throughout the century, much middle-class wealth was transformed into noble wealth, and a significant number of rich bourgeois became noblemen. Wealthy members of the bourgeoisie did not see themselves as a separate class. They thought of themselves as different from—and often opposed to—the common people who worked with their hands, and identified with the values of the nobility.

There were, nonetheless, important social tensions. Less prosperous lawyers—whose numbers were increasing—were jealous of the privileged position of a favored few in their profession. Over the course of the century, the prices of offices rose, making it more difficult to buy into the nobility, and creating tensions between middling members of the Third Estate and the very rich in trade and commerce who, by and large, were the only group able to afford to climb the social ladder. Less wealthy nobles resented the success of rich, upstart commoners whose income allowed them to live in luxury. In sum, several fault lines ran through the elite and the middle classes. All these social groups could nonetheless join together in attacking a government and an economy that were not serving their interests.

Enlightenment ideas did not cause the revolution, but they played a critical role in articulating grievances. Voltaire was popular because of his attacks on noble privileges, and Locke and Montesquieu gained widespread followings because of their

PREREVOLUTIONARY PROPAGANDA. Political cartoons in late-eighteenth-century France commonly portrayed the Third Estate as bearing the burden of taxation while performing the bulk of the nation's productive work. In the image on the left, a peasant bears the burden of his tools and his harvest as a cleric and a nobleman look on. In the image on the right, the commoner is literally carrying his social superiors. › **What visual cues indicate the status of individuals in these images?** › **Would we expect the nobility or the clergy to defend their status on the basis of their usefulness to society?** › **Can we detect the power of certain Enlightenment ideas behind these forms of social critique? Which ones?** › **How might an opponent of Enlightenment thought have confronted such arguments?**

defense of private property and limited sovereignty. Montesquieu's ideas appealed to the officeholders who dominated France's powerful law courts, the *parlements.* They read his doctrine of checks and balances as support for their argument that the parlements could provide a check on the power of the king. When conflicts arose, noble leaders presented themselves as defenders of a nation that was threatened by the king and his ministers. The campaign for change was also fueled by economic reformers. The physiocrats (Chapter 17) urged the government to simplify the tax system and free the economy from mercantilist regulations.

In the countryside, peasants were caught in a web of obligations to landlords (fees for the use of the landlord's mill or wine press), the Church (a tithe, or levy, on farm produce), and state (fees when land changed hands). In addition, peasants paid a disproportionate share of both direct and indirect taxes. Further grievances stemmed from the requirement to maintain public roads (the *corvée*) and from hunting privileges that gave nobles the right to trample farmers' crops.

Social and economic conditions deteriorated on the eve of the revolution. A general price increase during much of the eighteenth century created hardship for the peasantry and urban laborers. Their plight deteriorated further at the end of the 1780s, when poor harvests sent bread prices sharply higher. High costs for food reduced demand for manufactured goods, and contracting markets in turn created unemployment. Many peasants left the countryside for the cities, hoping to find

Locke, Voltaire, and Montesquieu's political theories appeal to discontented nobles and members of the middle class

LOUIS XVI. Shown here in an official portrait, Louis XVI was committed to the forms of spectacular display that were so useful to Louis XIV in shoring up the monarchy. Louis XVI's attachment to the monarchy's absolutist powers and his inability to solve his regime's financial crisis led to his downfall. He was executed by the government of the French Republic on January 21, 1793, as the more radical phase of the revolution was just beginning.
› **What made absolutism less convincing in the late eighteenth century?** › **What caused the monarchy to lose its sacred aura?**

work there, only to discover that urban unemployment was far worse than in rural areas. Evidence indicates that between 1787 and 1789, the unemployment rate in many parts of urban France was as high as 50 percent.

FAILURE AND REFORM

An inefficient tax system, which varied widely from region to region, further weakened the country's financial position. The financial system nearly broke down under the costs incurred during France's participation in the American Revolution. The cost of servicing the national debt in the 1780s consumed 50 percent of the nation's budget. France's absolutist monarch, **Louis XVI** (r. 1774–1792), wished to shift the burden of taxation onto the richer classes, but lacked the support needed to accomplish this task.

The king appointed reformers such as Anne-Robert-Jacques Turgot (a physiocrat) and Jacques Necker (a Swiss Protestant banker) as finance ministers, arousing the opposition of traditionalists at court. His proposal for new taxes to be paid by the nobility was rejected by parlements, which defended the aristocracy's immunity from taxation. Louis allowed his wife, the young but strong-willed Marie Antoinette, daughter of Austria's Maria Theresa, a free hand in dispensing patronage among her friends, which resulted in constant intrigue at Versailles. By 1788, a weak monarch, together with a chaotic financial situation and severe social tensions, brought absolutist France to the edge of political disaster.

The Destruction of the Old Regime

The fiscal crisis precipitated the revolution. In 1787 and 1788, the king's ministers proposed new taxes to meet the growing deficit. Hoping to persuade the nobility to agree to these reforms, the king summoned an Assembly of Notables from among the aristocracy. This assembly insisted that any new tax policies must be approved by the **Estates General**, a representative body of the three estates of the realm that had not met since 1614.

Faced with economic crisis and financial chaos, Louis XVI agreed to summon the Estates General to meet in 1789. To many, his action appeared to be the only solution to France's deepening problems. As bread riots spread across the country in the spring of 1789, the three estates elected their deputies. Assemblies of these representatives were charged with the responsibility of drawing up lists of grievances to present to the king (*cahiers des doléances*), further heightening the general populations' expectations of fundamental reform. The delegates of the Third Estate,

> *At the Estates General in 1789, representatives of three estates compile a list of grievances, expecting reform* ›

elected by assemblies in which artisans and peasants participated, were far from commoners: 13 percent were men of business, about 25 percent were lawyers, and 43 percent were government officeholders of some sort.

By tradition, each estate met separately and voted as a body. In the past, this generally had meant that the First Estate (the clergy) combined with the Second (the nobility) to defeat the Third. In 1789, the members of the Third Estate made it clear that they would not tolerate such an arrangement. Instead, they proposed doubling the membership of the Third Estate to equal the size of the nobility and clergy combined, and that the entire body should vote together as individuals. The Third Estate's position was articulated most memorably by the **Abbé Emmanuel-Joseph Sieyès**, a radical member of the clergy. "What is the Third Estate?" asked Sieyès, in his famous pamphlet of January 1789 (see *Analyzing Primary Sources* on page 620). "Everything," he answered, and pointed to eighteenth-century social changes to bolster his point. In early 1789, Sieyès's views were unusually radical.

The king's unwillingness to take a strong stand on voting procedures cost him support he might have obtained from the Third Estate. Shortly after the Estates General opened at Versailles in May 1789, the Third Estate, angered by the king's attitude, took the revolutionary step of leaving the body and declaring itself the National Assembly. Locked out of the Estates General meeting hall on June 20, the Third Estate and a handful of sympathetic nobles and clergymen moved to a nearby indoor tennis court.

Here, under the leadership of the volatile, maverick aristocrat the Comte de Mirabeau and the radical clergyman Sieyès, they renamed themselves the National Assembly and bound themselves by a solemn oath not to separate until they had drafted a constitution for France. This **Tennis Court Oath**, sworn on June 20, 1789, can be seen as the beginning of the French Revolution. By claiming the authority to remake the government in the name of the people, the National Assembly was asserting its right to act as the highest sovereign power in the nation. On June 27, the king virtually conceded this right by ordering all delegates to join the National Assembly.

FIRST STAGES OF THE FRENCH REVOLUTION

The first stage of the French Revolution extended from June 1789 to August 1792. In the main, this stage was moderate, with its actions dominated by the leadership of liberal nobles and men of the Third Estate. Yet three events in the summer and fall of 1789 furnished evidence that their leadership would be challenged.

POPULAR REVOLTS From the beginning of the crisis, public attention was roused both by interest in political reform and by the economic crisis. Rumors spread that the aristocracy and the king were conspiring to punish the Third Estate by encouraging high prices. The artisans and shopkeepers who had voted for the Third Estate feared not only the king but also the Parisian poor, who had been threatening violence. This urban working population would soon be referred to as *sans-culottes* (*sahn koo-LAWT*), a term referring to the full-length trousers worn by laborers, which contrasted with the short breeches, stockings, and gold-buckled shoes worn by aristocrats. Fearful of spreading social unrest, supporters of the National Assembly formed a provisional municipal government

When Louis XVI doesn't support the Third Estate's demands, they abandon the Estates General and declare a new body, the National Assembly

Louis XVI (1754–1793) Well-meaning but ineffectual king of France from 1774 to 1792. He was executed during the French Revolution.

Estates General The representative body of the three estates of France.

Abbé Emmanuel-Joseph Sieyès (1748–1836) In 1789, he wrote the pamphlet *What Is the Third Estate?* in which he posed fundamental questions about the rights of the Third Estate and helped provoke its secession from the Estates General.

Tennis Court Oath (1789) Oath taken by representatives of the Third Estate, pledging to form a National Assembly and write a constitution limiting the powers of the king.

THE TENNIS COURT OATH, BY JACQUES-LOUIS DAVID (1748–1825). In June 1789, members of the Third Estate, now calling themselves the National Assembly, swore an oath not to disband until France had a constitution. In the center of this painting stands Jean Bailly, president of the new assembly. The Abbé Sieyès is seated at the table. In the foreground, a clergyman, an aristocrat, and a member of the Third Estate embrace in a symbol of national unity. The single deputy who refused to take the oath sits at far right, with his arms clasped against his chest. › **What is the significance of this near unanimity expressed in defiance of the king?** › **What options were available to those who did not support this move?**

Great Fear (1789) Following the outbreak of revolution in Paris, fear spread throughout the French countryside, as rumors circulated that royal troops were coming.

October Days (1789) The high price of bread and the rumor that the king was unwilling to cooperate with the National Assembly caused women who worked in Paris's large central market to march to Versailles along with their supporters to address the king.

and organized a militia of volunteers to maintain order that was necessary for reforms to succeed. On July 14, when rumors spread that the king's troops were mobilizing to march on the city, crowds of Parisians sought to arm themselves. They made their way to the Bastille, an ancient medieval fortress that symbolized royal authority. After crowds demanded arms from its governor, he ordered his troops to open fire, killing ninety-eight of the attackers. The crowd of *sans-culottes* took their revenge, capturing the fortress (which held only seven prisoners) and killing the governor. The fall of the Bastille was the first instance of the people's role in revolutionary change.

A second popular revolt occurred in the countryside. Peasants, too, expected and feared a monarchical and aristocratic counterrevolution. Rumors flew that the king's armies were on their way, that Austrians, Prussians, or "brigands" were invading. Frightened peasants organized militias, and attacked and burned manor houses. This "**Great Fear**," as historians have labeled it, compounded the confusion in rural areas. The news, when it reached Paris, convinced deputies at Versailles that the administration of rural France had simply collapsed.

A third instance of popular uprising, the "**October Days**" of 1789, was brought on by economic crisis. Parisian women from the market district, angered by the soaring price of bread and rumors of the king's apparent lack of cooperation with the assembly, marched to Versailles on October 5 and demanded to be heard. Not satisfied with its reception by the assembly, the crowd broke through the gates to the palace, calling for the king to return to Paris from Versailles. On the afternoon of the following day the king yielded and accompanied the crowd and the National Guard back to Paris. From this point on, the king's ability to act independently was much reduced.

In the face of these popular uprisings the king reluctantly agreed to let the National Assembly proceed with reforms. Even before the October Days, the assembly reacted to the Great Fear by abolishing all forms of privilege in an all-night session on August 4. It eliminated the Church tithe (tax on the harvest), the labor requirement known as the corvée, the nobility's hunting privileges, and a wide variety of tax exemptions and monopolies. In effect, these reforms obliterated the remnants of feudalism. A week later, the assembly abolished the sale of offices, thereby sweeping away one of the fundamental institutions of the Old Regime. These drastic changes were among the most fundamental of the revolutionary period.

THE NATIONAL ASSEMBLY AND THE RIGHTS OF MAN The assembly issued the **Declaration of the Rights of Man and of the Citizen** in August 1789, a statement of fundamental political beliefs. Strongly indebted to the

After a series of popular revolts, the king concedes the National Assembly's ability to make reforms

Declaration of the Rights of Man and of the Citizen (1789) French charter of liberties formulated by the National Assembly during the French Revolution.

What Is the Third Estate? (1789)

The Abbé Emmanuel-Joseph Sieyès (1748–1836) was, by virtue of his office in the Church, a member of the First Estate of the Estates General. Nevertheless, his political savvy led him to be elected as a representative of the Third Estate from the district of Chartres. Sieyès was a formidable politician as well as a writer. His career during the revolution, which he ended by assisting Napoleon's seizure of power, began with one of the most important radical pamphlets of 1789. In What Is the Third Estate? *Sieyès posed fundamental questions about the rights of this estate, which comprised the great majority of the population, and helped provoke its secession from the Estates General.*

The plan of this book is fairly simple. We must ask ourselves three questions.

1. What is the Third Estate? *Everything.*

2. What has it been until now in the political order? *Nothing.*

3. What does it want to be? *Something.*

* * *

It suffices to have made the point that the so-called usefulness of a privileged order to the public service is a fallacy; that without help from this order, all the arduous tasks in the service are performed by the Third Estate; that without this order the higher posts could be infinitely better filled; that they ought to be the natural prize and reward of recognized ability and service; and that if the privileged have succeeded in usurping all well-paid and honorific posts, this is both a hateful iniquity towards the generality of citizens and an act of treason to the commonwealth.

Who is bold enough to maintain that the Third Estate does not contain within itself everything needful to constitute a complete nation? It is like a strong and robust man with one arm still in chains. If the privileged order were removed, the nation would not be something less but something more. What then is the Third Estate? All; but an "all" that is fettered and oppressed. What would it be without the privileged order? It would be all; but free and flourishing. Nothing will go well without the Third Estate; everything would go considerably better without the two others.

Source: Emmanuel-Joseph Sieyès, *What Is the Third Estate?* ed. S. E. Finer, trans. M. Blondel (London: 1964), pp. 53, 65.

Questions for Analysis

1. How might contemporaries have viewed Sieyès's argument that the three estates should be evaluated according to their usefulness to the "commonwealth"?

2. Was Sieyès's language—accusing the privileged orders of "treason" and arguing for their "removal"—an incitement to violence?

3. What did Sieyès mean by the term *nation*? Could one speak of France as a nation in these terms before 1789?

Enlightenment, the Declaration proclaimed liberty, security, property, and "resistance to oppression" to be natural rights, along with freedom of speech, religious toleration, and liberty of the press. All citizens were equal before the law, and none could be imprisoned or punished without due process. Sovereignty resided in the people, who could depose officers of the government if they abused their powers. The Declaration became the preamble to the new constitution, which the assembly finished in 1791.

Whom did the Declaration mean by "man and the citizen"? The constitution distinguished between "passive" citizens, who had guaranteed rights under the law, and "active" citizens, who paid a certain amount in taxes and could thus vote and hold office. About half the adult men in France qualified as active citizens, but even their power was curtailed, because they could vote only for "electors," men whose property ownership qualified them to hold office. In 1792, the more radical republic abolished the distinction between active and passive, but conservative postrevolutionary regimes reinstated it.

Which men could be trusted to participate in politics and on what terms was a hotly contested issue. The revolution gave full civil rights to Protestants and, hesitantly, to Jews. Religious toleration, a central theme of the Enlightenment, meant ending persecution; it did not mean that the regime was prepared to accommodate religious differences. The assembly abolished serfdom and banned slavery in France's European territory. It remained silent on colonial slavery, however; and although delegations pressed the assembly on political rights for free people of color, the assembly exempted the colonies from the constitution's provisions.

The rights and roles of women also became the focus of sharp debate, as revolutionaries confronted demands that working women participate in guilds or trade organizations, and that laws on marriage, divorce, relief for the poor, and education be reconsidered. The Englishwoman Mary Wollstonecraft penned her milestone book *A Vindication of the Rights of Woman* (Chapter 17) during the revolutionary debate over national education. Should girls be educated? To what end? Wollstonecraft, as we have seen, argued strongly that reforming education required forging a new concept of independent and equal womanhood. Even Wollstonecraft, however, only hinted at political representation, aware that such an idea would "excite laughter."

Only a handful of thinkers broached the subject of women in politics: the aristocratic Enlightenment thinker the Marquis de Condorcet and Marie Gouze, the self-educated daughter of a butcher. The revolution gave Gouze the opportunity to publicize her views. She renamed herself Olympe de Gouges and composed her own manifesto, the *Declaration of the Rights of Woman and the Female Citizen* (1791). Arguing that "social distinctions can only be based on the common utility," she declared that women had the same rights as men, including resistance to authority, and participation in government. She also claimed a woman's right to name the fathers of illegitimate children. This last demand offers a glimpse of the shame, isolation, and hardship faced by unmarried women.

De Gouges's demand for equal rights was unusual, but many women participated in the everyday activities of the revolution, joining clubs, debating societies, and demonstrations. Women artisans' organizations asserted their rights to produce and sell goods. Market women were often central to the circulation of news and spontaneous popular demonstrations. (The October Days are a good example.) When the revolution became more radical, some revolutionaries saw political activity by women's organizations as a threat to public order, and in 1793 the revolutionaries shut down the women's political clubs. Even so, many ordinary women were able to make use of the revolution's new legislation on marriage (divorce was legalized in 1792) and inheritance to support claims for relief from abusive husbands or absent fathers, claims that would have been impossible under prerevolutionary legislation.

Many nonelite women participate in revolutionary activities

Declaration of the Rights of Man and of the Citizen

One of the first important pronouncements of the National Assembly after the Tennis Court Oath was the Declaration of the Rights of Man and of the Citizen. The authors drew inspiration from the American Declaration of Independence, but the language is even more heavily influenced by the ideals of French Enlightenment philosophers, particularly Rousseau. Following are the Declaration's preamble and some of its most important principles.

The representatives of the French people, constituted as the National Assembly, considering that ignorance, disregard, or contempt for the rights of man are the sole causes of public misfortunes and the corruption of governments, have resolved to set forth, in a solemn declaration, the natural, inalienable, and sacred rights of man, so that the constant presence of this declaration may ceaselessly remind all members of the social body of their rights and duties; so that the acts of legislative power and those of the executive power may be more respected . . . and so that the demands of the citizens, grounded henceforth on simple and incontestable principles, may always be directed to the maintenance of the constitution and to the welfare of all. . . .

Article 1. Men are born and remain free and equal in rights. Social distinctions can be based only on public utility.

Article 2. The aim of every political association is the preservation of the natural and imprescriptible rights of man. These rights are liberty, property, security, and resistance to oppression.

Article 3. The source of all sovereignty resides essentially in the nation. No body, no individual can exercise authority that does not explicitly proceed from it.

Article 4. Liberty consists in being able to do anything that does not injure another; thus the only limits upon each man's exercise of his natural laws are those that guarantee enjoyment of these same rights to the other members of society.

Article 5. The law has the right to forbid only actions harmful to society. No action may be prevented that is not forbidden by law, and no one may be constrained to do what the law does not order.

Article 6. The law is the expression of the general will. All citizens have the right to participate personally, or through representatives, in its formation. It must be the same for all, whether it protects or punishes. All citizens, being equal in its eyes, are equally admissible to all public dignities, positions, and employments, according to their ability, and on the basis of no other distinction than that of their virtues and talents. . . .

Article 16. A society in which the guarantee of rights is not secured, or the separation of powers is not clearly established, has no constitution.

Source: Declaration of the Rights of Man and of the Citizen, as cited in K. M. Baker, ed., *University of Chicago Readings in Western Civilization*, vol. 7: *The Old Regime and the French Revolution* (Chicago: 1987), pp. 238–39.

Questions for Analysis

1. To whom is the Declaration addressed? Is it only about the rights of the French, or do these ideas apply to all people?

2. What gave a group of deputies elected to advise Louis XVI on constitutional reforms the right to proclaim themselves a National Assembly? What was revolutionary about this claim to represent the French nation?

3. Article 6, which states that "law is the expression of general will," is adapted from Rousseau's *Social Contract*. Does the Declaration give any indication of how the "general will" can be known?

THE NATIONAL ASSEMBLY AND THE CHURCH The new government inherited the Old Regime's fiscal crisis, and this influenced their religious policy. In November 1789, the National Assembly decided to confiscate all Church lands and use them as collateral for issuing interest-bearing notes, known as *assignats*. The assembly hoped that this action would help to curb price inflation, and eventually, these notes circulated widely as paper money. To enforce the Church's loyalty, the assembly enacted the **Civil Constitution of the Clergy** in July 1790, bringing the Church under state authority. This new law forced all bishops and priests to swear allegiance to the state, which henceforth paid their salaries. The aim was to make the Catholic Church of France a national institution, free from interference by Rome.

Civil Constitution of the Clergy Issued by the French National Assembly in 1790, the Civil Constitution of the Clergy decreed that all bishops and priests should be subject to the authority of the state.

These reforms were bitterly divisive. On the one hand, many people resented the privileged status of the Church, with its vast monastic land holdings. On the other hand, for centuries, the parish church had been a central institution in small towns and villages, providing relief for the poor and other services, in addition to baptisms and marriages. The Civil Constitution of the Clergy sparked fierce resistance in some parts of rural France. When the pope threatened to excommunicate priests who signed the Civil Constitution, he raised the stakes: allegiance to the new French state meant damnation. Many people, especially peasants in the deeply Catholic areas of western France, were driven to open revolt.

The National Assembly's policy toward the Church was part of its larger attempt to transform the institutions of the Old Regime. To raise money, it sold off Church lands. To encourage economic growth, it abolished guilds. To diminish the power of the aristocracy, it reorganized local government and divided France into eighty-three equal departments. These measures all aimed to dismantle the customary privileges of local elites. The principal beneficiaries, however, were people who were already wealthy enough to take advantage of the opportunities, such as buying land or being elected to office. In this realm as elsewhere, the social changes of the revolution endorsed changes already under way during the eighteenth century.

A New Stage: Popular Revolution

In the summer of 1792, the revolution's moderate leaders were toppled and replaced by republicans, who repudiated the monarchy and claimed to rule on behalf of a sovereign people. Historians have focused on three factors to explain the revolution's radical turn: changes in popular politics, a crisis of leadership, and international polarization.

First, the revolution politicized the common people, especially in cities. Newspapers multiplied, freed from censorship. A wide variety of clubs became part of political life. Some were almost like political parties, gathering members of the elite to debate issues and influence decisions. Other clubs opened their doors to those excluded from formal politics. Political awareness was heightened by the economic crisis. Rising prices exasperated the working people of Paris. Urban demonstrations, often led by women, demanded cheaper bread; political leaders in clubs and newspapers called for the government to control inflation. These radical voices criticized the constitution of 1791 for giving the vote only to the propertied.

A second major reason for radical change, of course, was a lack of effective leadership. Louis XVI remained a weak monarch. He grudgingly supported

Reasons for radical turn in revolution: (1) heightened political awareness among common people

(2) Ineffective royal leadership, with Louis XVI fleeing

measures he detested, such as the Civil Constitution of the Clergy. He was sympathetic to the plottings of the queen, who was in contact with her brother Leopold II of Austria. Urged on by Marie Antoinette, Louis tried to escape from France in June 1791, hoping to rally foreign support for a counterrevolution. The members of the royal family were apprehended near Varennes, on the border, and brought back to the capital. The constitution of September 1791 declared France a monarchy, but by then Louis was little more than a prisoner of the assembly.

The third reason for the radical turn was war. From the outset, men and women across Europe had been compelled to take sides in the revolution. Initially the changes in France won the enthusiastic support of a wide range of thinkers. In Britain, the Low Countries, western Germany, and Italy, "patriots" proclaimed their allegiance to the new revolution. Others opposed the revolution from the start. Exiled nobles, who fled France for sympathetic royal courts in Germany and elsewhere, did all they could to stir up counterrevolutionary sentiment. In Britain, the conservative cause was strengthened by the publication of Edmund Burke's *Reflections on the Revolution in France* in 1790. A Whig politician who had sympathized with the American revolutionaries, Burke deemed the revolution in France a monstrous crime against the social order (see **Competing Viewpoints** on pages 626–27).

THE COUNTERREVOLUTION

Opposition to the revolution came both from within France and from other European monarchies. In 1791, Austria and Prussia declared that order and the rights of the king of France were matters of "common interest to all sovereigns of Europe." The leaders of the French assembly pronounced the declaration an affront to national sovereignty. As tensions worsened, both supporters and opponents of the revolution in France believed war would serve their cause. The National Assembly's radicals believed that war would shore up the people's loyalty and bring freedom to the rest of Europe. Counterrevolutionaries hoped the intervention of Austria and Prussia would undo all that had happened since 1789. On April 20, 1792, the assembly declared war against Austria and Prussia. Thus began the war that would keep the Continent in arms for a generation.

By August 1792, the allied armies of Austria and Prussia had crossed the frontier and were threatening to capture Paris. Many revolutionaries believed that the military disasters were evidence of the king's treason. On August 10, Parisian crowds, organized by their radical leaders, attacked the royal palace. The king was imprisoned, and a second and far more radical revolution began.

THE FRENCH REPUBLIC

The country's leadership passed into the hands of a group of radicals known as **Jacobins**, the name of a political club to which many of them belonged. Based in Paris, their membership extended throughout France. Their members included large numbers of professionals, government officeholders, and lawyers, but they proclaimed themselves representatives of the entire nation. An increasing number of artisans joined Jacobin clubs as the movement grew.

The **National Convention**, an assembly elected by free white men, became the effective governing body of the country for the next three years. It was elected in

Reasons for radical turn in revolution: (3) War, as sympathizers to both revolutionaries and establishment from nearby states spur action

Jacobins French radical political group during the French Revolution that took power after 1792, executed the French king, and sought to remake French culture.

National Convention The governing body of France from September 1792 to October 1795. It declared France a republic and then tried and executed King Louis XVI.

September 1792, at a time when enemy troops were advancing and spreading panic. Rumors flew that counterrevolutionary prisoners in Paris were plotting to aid the invaders. The prisoners were hauled from their cells, dragged before hastily convened tribunals, and executed. In the "September Massacres," more than 1,000 "enemies of the Revolution" were killed in less than a week. Similar riots engulfed Lyon, Orléans, and other French cities.

The newly elected National Convention was far more radical than the National Assembly, and its leadership was determined to end the monarchy. On September 21, the Convention declared France a republic. In December, it placed the king on trial; and in January 1793, it condemned the king to death. The heir to the grand tradition of French absolutism met his end bravely as "citizen Louis Capet," beheaded by the guillotine. Introduced as a swifter and more humane form of execution, this frightful mechanism came to symbolize revolutionary fervor.

The Convention took other radical measures. It confiscated the properties of the enemies of the revolution, breaking up large estates and selling them to less wealthy citizens. It canceled the policy of compensating nobles for their lost privileges. It repealed primogeniture, so that property would be divided equally among all immediate heirs. It abolished slavery in French colonies (see pages 641–43). It set maximum prices for grain and other necessities. In an astonishing effort to root

> The Convention's radical reforms extend beyond politics into many corners of social life

THE EXECUTION OF LOUIS XVI. The execution of Louis XVI shocked Europe. Even committed revolutionaries in France debated the necessity of such a dramatic act. The entire National Convention (more than 700 members) acted as jury, and although the assembly was nearly unanimous in finding the king guilty of treason, a majority of only one approved the final death sentence. Those who voted for Louis XVI's execution were known forever after as "regicides." **› What made this act necessary from the point of view of the most radical of revolutionaries? › What made it repugnant from the point of view of the revolution's most heated enemies?**

Debating the French Revolution: Edmund Burke and Thomas Paine

The best-known debate on the French Revolution set the Irish-born conservative Edmund Burke against the British radical Thomas Paine. Burke opposed the French Revolution from the beginning. His Reflections on the Revolution in France *was published early, in 1790, when the French king was still securely on the throne. Burke disagreed with the premises of the revolution. Rights, he argued, were not abstract and "natural" but the results of specific historical traditions. Remodeling the French government without reference to the past and failing to pay proper respect to tradition and custom had, in his eyes, destroyed the fabric of French civilization.*

Thomas Paine was one of many to respond to Burke. In The Rights of Man *(1791–1792), he defended the revolution and, more generally, conceptions of human rights. In the polarized atmosphere of the revolutionary wars, simply possessing Paine's pamphlet was cause for imprisonment in Britain.*

Edmund Burke

You will observe, that from the Magna Carta to the Declaration of Rights, it has been the uniform policy of our constitution to claim and assert our liberties, as an entailed inheritance derived to us from our forefathers. . . . We have an inheritable crown; an inheritable peerage; and a house of commons and a people inheriting privileges, franchises, and liberties, from a long line of ancestors. . . .

You had all these advantages in your ancient states, but you chose to act as if you had never been moulded into civil society, and had every thing to begin anew. You began ill, because you began by despising every thing that belonged to you. . . . If the last generations of your country appeared without much luster in your eyes, you might have passed them by, and derived your claims from a more early race of ancestors. . . . Respecting your forefathers, you would have been taught to respect yourselves. You would not have chosen to consider the French as a people of yesterday, as a nation of low-born servile wretches until the emancipating year of 1789. . . . [Y]ou would not have been content to be represented as a gang of Maroon slaves, suddenly broke loose from the house of bondage, and therefore to be pardoned for your abuse of liberty to which you were not accustomed and ill fitted. . . .

. . . The fresh ruins of France, which shock our feelings wherever we can turn our eyes, are not the devastation of civil war; they are the sad but instructive monuments of rash and ignorant counsel in time of profound peace. They are the display of inconsiderate and presumptuous, because unresisted and irresistible authority. . . .

Nothing is more certain, than that of our manners, our civilization, and all the good things which are connected out Christianity from everyday life, the Convention adopted a new calendar. The calendar year began with the birth of the republic (September 22, 1792) and divided the weeks and months in such a way as to eliminate the Catholic Sunday.

Most of these programs were a hastily improvised response to crisis and political pressure from the common people in the cities and their leaders. In the three years after 1790, prices had risen staggeringly: wheat by 27 percent, beef by 136 percent, and potatoes by 700 percent. While the government imposed its maximums in with manners, and with civilization, have, in this European world of ours, depended upon two principles; and were indeed the result of both combined; I mean the spirit of a gentleman, and the spirit of religion. The nobility and the clergy, the one by profession, the other by patronage, kept learning in existence, even in the midst of arms and confusions. . . . Learning paid back what it received to nobility and priesthood. . . . Happy if they had all continued to know their indissoluble union, and their proper place. Happy if learning, not debauched by ambition, had been satisfied to continue the instructor, and not aspired to be the master! Along with its natural protectors and guardians, learning will be cast into the mire, and trodden down under the hoofs of a swinish multitude.

Source: Edmund Burke, *Reflections on the Revolution in France* (1790; New York: 1973), pp. 45, 48, 49, 52, 92.

Thomas Paine

Mr. Burke, with his usual outrage, abuses the *Declaration of the Rights of Man*. . . . Does Mr. Burke mean to deny that man has any rights? If he does, then he must mean that there are no such things as rights any where, and that he has none himself; for who is there in the world but man? But if Mr. Burke means to admit that man has rights, the question will then be, what are those rights, and how came man by them originally?

The error of those who reason by precedents drawn from antiquity, respecting the rights of man, is that they do not go far enough into antiquity. They stop in some of the intermediate stages of an hundred or a thousand years, and produce what was then a rule for the present day. This is no authority at all. . . .

To possess ourselves of a clear idea of what government is, or ought to be, we must trace its origin. In doing this, we shall easily discover that governments must have arisen either *out* of the people, or *over* the people. Mr. Burke has made no distinction. . . .

What were formerly called revolutions, were little more than a change of persons, or an alteration of local circumstances. They rose and fell like things of course, and had nothing in their existence or their fate that could influence beyond the spot that produced them. But what we now see in the world, from the revolutions of America and France, is a renovation of the natural order of things, a system of principles as universal as truth and the existence of man, and combining moral with political happiness and national prosperity.

Source: Thomas Paine, *The Rights of Man* (1791; New York: 1973), pp. 302, 308, 383.

Questions for Analysis

1. How does Burke define liberty? Why does he criticize the revolutionaries for representing themselves as slaves freed from bondage?

2. What does Paine criticize about Burke's emphasis on history? According to Paine, what makes the French Revolution different from previous changes of regime in Europe?

3. How do these two authors' attitudes about the origins of human freedoms shape their understandings of the revolution?

Paris, small vigilante militias, representing the sans-culottes, attacked those they considered hoarders and profiteers.

The Convention also reorganized its armies, with astonishing success. By February 1793, Britain, Holland, Spain, and Austria were in the field against the French. Britain came into the war for strategic and economic reasons: it feared a French threat to Britain's growing global power. The allied coalition was a formidable force. To counter it, the revolutionary government mustered all men capable of bearing arms. The revolution flung fourteen hastily drafted armies into battle under the leadership of newly promoted young and inexperienced officers. What they lacked in training and discipline they made up for in organization, mobility, flexibility, courage, and morale. In 1793–1794, the French armies preserved their homeland. In 1794–1795, they occupied the Low Countries, the Rhineland, and parts of Spain, Switzerland, and Savoy. In 1796, they invaded and occupied key parts of Italy and broke the coalition that had arrayed itself against them.

THE REIGN OF TERROR

In 1793, those victories lay in a hard-to-imagine future. France was in crisis. The National Convention drafted a new democratic constitution based on male suffrage, but it never took effect—suspended indefinitely by wartime emergency. Instead, the Convention prolonged its own life year after year and increasingly delegated its responsibilities to a group of twelve leaders, the Committee of Public Safety, created in April 1793. The Committee's ruthlessness had two purposes: to seize control of the revolution and to prosecute all the revolution's enemies—"to make terror the order of the day." The Committee's reign lasted less than two years, but the **Terror** left a bloody and authoritarian legacy.

The three best-known leaders of the radical revolution were Jean-Paul Marat, Georges Danton, and Maximilien Robespierre (the latter two, members of the Committee of Public Safety). Marat was educated as a physician, and well known as the editor of the popular newspaper *The Friend of the People*. He opposed the revolution's moderates, including their admiration for Great Britain, which he considered corrupt and despotic. Persecuted by powerful factions in the constituent assembly who feared his radicalism, Marat was forced to take refuge in sewers and dungeons. Exposure to infection left him with a chronic and painful skin disease, from which baths provided the only relief. In July 1793, at the height of the crisis of the revolution, he was stabbed in his bath by Charlotte Corday, a young royalist, and became a revolutionary martyr.

Danton, like Marat, was a popular political leader, well known in the more plebeian clubs of Paris. Elected a member of the Committee of Public Safety in 1793, he had much to do with organizing the Terror. As time went on, however, he wearied of ruthlessness and displayed a tendency to compromise, which gave his opponents in the Convention their opportunity. In April 1794, Danton was sent to the guillotine. He is reported to have said, upon mounting the scaffold, "Show my head to the people; they do not see the like every day."

The most famous of the radical leaders was Maximilien Robespierre, known as the "Incorruptible." He trained in law before 1789 and became a modestly successful lawyer. His eloquence and his ruthless insistence that leaders respect the "will of the people" won him a following in the Jacobin club. Later, he became president of the National Convention and a member of the Committee of Public Safety. Though he had little to do with starting the Terror, he was nevertheless responsible for enlarging its scope.

The two years of the radical republic (August 1792–July 1794) brought dictatorship, centralization, suspension of liberties, and war. The government faced foreign enemies and opposition from both the political right and left at home. In June 1793, in response to an escalating crisis, leaders of the "Mountain," a party of radicals allied with Parisian artisans, purged moderates from the National Convention. Rebellions broke out in the provincial cities of Lyon, Bordeaux, and Marseilles, and were mercilessly repressed. The government also faced counterrevolution in the western region known as the Vendée, where peasants and artisans who believed their local areas were being invaded rebelled against the revolutionary government. By the summer, forces in the Vendée posed a serious threat to the Convention. The Committee of Public Safety, determined to stabilize France, redeployed its forces, and launched murderous campaigns of pacification—torching villages, farms, and fields; and killing all who dared oppose them, and many who did not.

In September 1793, the Convention passed the Law of Suspects, which allowed the revolutionary authorities to arrest and detain individuals seen as enemies of the state. During the next ten months the Terror reached its climax. The most reliable estimates place the number of deaths at close to 40,000; about 16,500 deaths resulted from official executions, and the rest from extrajudicial killings in prison. Approximately 300,000 people were incarcerated between March 1793 and August 1794. These numbers, however, do not include the pacification of the Vendée and rebellious cities in the Rhône Valley, which cost more than 100,000 lives. Few victims of the Terror were aristocrats; many more were peasants or laborers accused of hoarding, treason, or counterrevolutionary activity. Anyone who appeared to threaten the republic, no matter what his or her social or economic position, was at risk.

At the Terror's height, enemies of the state are executed or imprisoned by the thousands

THE LEGACY OF THE SECOND FRENCH REVOLUTION

The "second" French Revolution affected the everyday life of French men, women, and children in a remarkably direct way. Workers' trousers replaced the breeches that had been a sartorial badge of the middle classes and the nobility. A red cap, said to symbolize freedom from slavery, became popular headgear, and wigs vanished. Men and women addressed each other as "citizen" and "citizeness." Public life was marked by ceremonies designed to dramatize the break from the Old Regime and celebrate new forms of fraternity. In the early stages of the revolution, these festivals seem to have captured genuine popular enthusiasm. Under the Committee of Public Safety, they became didactic and hollow.

The radical revolution of 1792–1793 also dramatically reversed the trend toward decentralization and democracy. The assembly replaced local officials, some of them still royalist in sympathy, with "deputies on mission," whose task was to conscript troops and generate patriotic fervor. When these deputies appeared too eager to act independently, they were replaced by "national agents," with instructions to report directly to the Committee. In another effort to

PATRIOTIC WOMEN'S CLUB. The members of this patriotic club wear constitutional bonnets to show their support for the revolution and the reforms of the Convention. › What can we conclude about the atmosphere in Paris during the revolution from the existence of such associations?

stabilize authority, the assembly closed down all the women's political clubs, decreeing them a political and social danger. It was ironic that those who claimed to govern in the name of the people found the popular movement threatening.

Finally, the revolution eroded the strength of those traditional institutions—church, guild, parish—that had for centuries given people a common bond. In their place now stood patriotic organizations and a culture that insisted on loyalty to one national cause. These organizations included political clubs and local assemblies, which at the height of the revolution (1792–1793) met every day of the week and offered an apprenticeship in politics. The army of the republic became the premier national institution.

On the one hand, the revolution divided France, mobilizing counterrevolutionaries as well as revolutionaries. At the same time, the revolution, war, and culture of sacrifice forged new bonds. The sense that the rest of Europe, carrying what the verses of the "Marseillaise," the most famous anthem of the revolution, called the "blood-stained flag of tyranny," sought to crush the new nation and its citizens unquestionably strengthened French national identity.

From the Terror to Bonaparte: The Directory

The Committee of Public Safety might have saved France from enemy armies, but it could not save itself. Inflation became catastrophic. The long string of military victories convinced growing numbers that the Committee's demands for continuing self-sacrifice and terror were no longer justified. By July 1794, the Committee was virtually without allies. On July 27 (9 Thermidor, according to the new calendar), Robespierre was shouted down while attempting to speak on the floor of the Convention. The following day, along with twenty-one other conspirators, he met his death by guillotine.

Ending the Terror did not immediately bring moderation. Vigilante groups of royalists hunted down Jacobins. The repeal of price controls, combined with the worst winter in a century, caused widespread misery. Gradually, other measures that had constituted the Terror were repealed. In 1795, the National Convention adopted a new and more conservative constitution. It granted suffrage to adult male citizens who paid a certain amount of taxes and it set up indirect elections: citizens voted for electors, who in turn chose the legislative body. Wealthy citizens thus held authority. Eager to avoid personal dictatorship, the Convention vested executive authority in a board of five men chosen by the legislative body, known as the Directory. The new constitution included not only a bill of rights but also a declaration of the duties of the citizen.

A more moderate legislative body, the Directory, is established ❯

The Directory still faced discontent on both the radical left and the conservative right, but lasted longer than its revolutionary predecessors. On the left, the Directory repressed radical movements to abolish private property and parliamentary-style government. Dispatching threats from the right proved more challenging, however. In 1797, the first free elections held in France as a republic returned a large number of monarchists to the councils of government, alarming the politicians who had voted to execute Louis XVI. Backed by the army, the Directory annulled most of the election results. After two years of more uprisings and purges, and with the country still plagued by severe inflation, the Directory grew desperate. This time they called for help from a brilliant young general named **Napoleon Bonaparte**.

Bonaparte's first military victory had come in 1793, with the recapture of Toulon from royalist and British forces, which had earned him promotion from captain to brigadier general at the age of twenty-four. After the Terror, he was briefly arrested for his Jacobin associations. But he proved his usefulness to the Directory in October 1795 when he put down an uprising with "a whiff of grapeshot," saving the new regime from its opponents. Promoted, he won a string of victories in Italy, forcing Austria to withdraw (temporarily) from the war. He attempted to challenge Britain's global empire by invading Egypt and attempting to seize control of the Middle East. When the French fleet was defeated at Abukir Bay by the British navy, Bonaparte found himself trapped in Egypt and was unable to win a decisive victory.

It was at this point that the call came from the Directory. Bonaparte slipped away from Egypt and appeared in Paris, already having agreed to participate in a coup d'état with the leading Director, the former revolutionary champion of the Third Estate, Abbé Sieyès. On November 9, 1799 (18 Brumaire), Bonaparte was declared a "temporary consul." He was the answer to the Directory's prayers: a strong, popular leader who was not a king. Sieyès declared that Bonaparte would provide "[c]onfidence from below, authority from above." With these words, Sieyès pronounced the end of the revolutionary period.

FRANCE AND ITS SISTER REPUBLICS. › The French revolutionaries, fighting against the conservative monarchs of Europe, conquered and annexed large sections of which three countries? › Who were the potential supporters of the French Revolution in areas outside France during the Napoleonic era? › Who was most likely to oppose it in these areas?

Napoleon and Imperial France

Few figures in Western history have compelled the attention of the world as Napoleon Bonaparte did during the fifteen years of his rule in France. For the great majority of ordinary Europeans, memories of the French Revolution were dominated by those of the Napoleonic Wars, which devastated Europe, convulsed its politics, and traumatized its peoples for a generation.

Yet Bonaparte's relationship to the revolution was not simple. His regime consolidated some of the revolution's political and social changes but sharply repudiated others. He presented himself as the son of the revolution, but he also borrowed freely from very different regimes, fashioning himself as the heir to Charlemagne

Napoleon Bonaparte
(1769–1821) Corsican-born French general who seized power and ruled as dictator and emperor from 1799 to 1814.

or to the Roman Empire. His regime left a legacy of conflict and legends of French glory that lingered in the dreams, or nightmares, of Europe's statesmen and citizens for more than a century.

CONSOLIDATING AUTHORITY: 1799–1804

Bonaparte owed his career to the revolution. The son of a provincial Corsican nobleman, he attended the École Militaire in Paris. In prerevolutionary France he would have been unable to rise beyond the rank of major, which required buying a regimental command. The revolution, however, abolished the purchase of military office, and Bonaparte quickly became a general. Here, then, was a man who had risen from obscurity because of his own gifts, which he lent happily to the service of France's revolution.

Once in power, however, Bonaparte showed less respect for revolutionary principles. After the coup of 1799, he assumed the title of first consul. A new constitution established universal white male suffrage and set up two legislative bodies. Elections, however, were indirect, and the power of the legislative bodies was sharply curbed. "The government?" said one observer. "There is Bonaparte." Bonaparte instituted what has since become a common authoritarian device, the plebiscite, which puts a question directly to popular vote. This allowed the head of state to bypass politicians or legislative bodies that might disagree with him—and permitted local officials to tamper with ballot boxes. In 1802, flush with victory abroad, Bonaparte asked the legislature to proclaim him consul for life. When the Senate refused, Bonaparte's Council of State stepped in, offering him the title and having it ratified by plebiscite. His regime retained the appearance of consulting with the people, but its most important feature was the centralization of authority.

Bonaparte's accomplishments were extraordinary and lasting. He confirmed the abolition of privilege, thereby promising "careers open to talent." Centralizing administrative departments, he created a more orderly system of taxation. Better fiscal management also helped halt the inflationary spiral that had crippled the revolutionary governments, although Bonaparte's regime relied heavily on resources from areas he had conquered to fund his military ventures. Earlier revolutionary regimes reorganized France's administration and Bonaparte continued that work, emphasizing the centralization of authority. He replaced elected officials with centrally appointed prefects, who answered directly to the Council of State in Paris. The prefects wielded considerable power: they were in charge of everything from collecting statistics and reporting on the economy, to education, roads, and public works. With a more integrated administration in which the different branches were coordinated from above and a more professional bureaucracy, Napoleon's rule marked the transition from Bourbon absolutism to the modern state.

LAW, EDUCATION, AND A NEW ELITE

Napoleon's most significant contribution to modern state building was the promulgation of a new legal code in 1804. The Napoleonic Code, as the civil code came to be called, pivoted on two principles: uniformity and individualism. It cleared through the thicket of contradictory legal traditions that governed the ancient provinces of France, creating one uniform law. It confirmed the abolition of feudal privileges of

Napoleon uses plebiscite, a new process of putting a question directly to popular vote, to bypass legislative concerns

Two key ideas of Napoleonic Code: uniformity and individualism

all kinds, not only noble and clerical privileges but the special rights of craft guilds, municipalities, and so on. It set the conditions for exercising property rights, such as the drafting of contracts, leases, and stock companies. The code's provisions on the family, which Napoleon developed personally, insisted on the importance of paternal authority and the subordination of women and children. In 1793, during the most radical period of the revolution, men and women had been declared "equal in marriage"; now, Napoleon's code affirmed the "natural supremacy" of the husband. Married women could not sell property, run a business, or practice a profession without their husbands' permission. Fathers had the sole right to control their children's financial affairs, consent to their marriages, and (under the ancient right to correction) imprison them for up to six months without showing cause. Divorce remained legal, but under unequal conditions: a man could sue for divorce on the grounds of adultery, but a woman could do so only if her husband moved his "concubine" into the family's house. Most important to the common people, the code prohibited paternity suits for illegitimate children.

Napoleonic Code emphasizes paternal authority over women and children

In all, Napoleon developed seven legal codes covering commercial law, civil law and procedures, crime, and punishment. Like the civil code, the new criminal code consolidated some of the gains of the revolution, treating citizens as equals before the law and outlawing arbitrary arrest and imprisonment. Yet, it also reinstated brutal measures that the revolutionaries had abolished, such as branding and cutting off the hands of parricides. The Napoleonic legal regime was more egalitarian than the law under the Old Regime, but it was no less concerned with authority.

Napoleon also rationalized the educational system. He ordered the establishment of *lycées* (high schools) in every major town to train civil servants and army officers, and a school in Paris to train teachers. To supplement these changes, Napoleon brought the military and technical schools under state control and founded a national university to supervise the entire system. It is not surprising that he built up a new military academy. He reorganized and established solid financing for the premier schools of higher education: the polytechnic (for engineers) and the normal (for teachers), to which students would be admitted based on examinations and from which the technical, educational, and political elites of the country would emerge. Napoleon also embraced the burgeoning social and physical sciences of the Enlightenment. He sponsored the Institute of France, divided into four sections, or academies: fine arts, sciences, humanities, and language (the famous Académie Française). These academies dated back to the age of absolutism, but now they were coordinated and put on a new footing. Under Napoleon, they acquired the character they have preserved to this day: centralized, meritocratic, and geared to serving the state.

Educational reform

To win support for his ambitious measures, Napoleon made allies without regard to their past loyalties. His two fellow consuls were a regicide of the Terror and a bureaucrat of the Old Regime. His minister of police had been an extreme radical republican, and his minister of foreign affairs was the aristocrat and opportunist Charles Talleyrand. The most remarkable act of political reconciliation came in 1801, with his concordat with the pope, an agreement that put an end to more than a decade of hostility between the French state and the Catholic Church. Although it shocked anticlerical revolutionaries, Napoleon, ever the pragmatist, believed that reconciliation would create domestic harmony and international support. The agreement gave the pope the right to depose French bishops and discipline the

Representing the People during the French Revolution

From the moment the population of Paris came to the assistance of the beleaguered National Assembly in July 1789, representations of "the people" in the French Revolution took on an overwhelming significance. Building a new government that was committed to the idea of popular sovereignty meant that both the revolution's supporters and its opponents were deeply invested in shaping perceptions of the people. And of course, Article 3 of the Declaration of the Rights of Man ("The source of all sovereignty resides essentially in the nation") meant that any individual, group, or institution that could successfully claim to represent the will of the people could wield tremendous power, as long as others accepted that claim.

The revolutionary crowds, however, did not always conform to the images of them that circulated so widely in prints and paintings during the period 1789–1799. Some were spontaneous, and others were organized; some were made up of recognizable social and professional groups with clear political goals, and others were a hodgepodge of conflicting and even inarticulate aspirations; many were nonviolent, but some were exceedingly threatening and murderous. Regardless, all politicians sought to use them to support their political programs, and many learned to fear their unpredictable behavior.

These four images give a sense of the competing visions of the people that appeared in the public realm during the French Revolution. The first (image A) shows the killing of Foulon, a royal official who was lynched and beheaded by an enthusiastic crowd barely a week after the fall of the Bastille, because he was suspected

A. The punishment of Foulon (anonymous print, 1789).

B. *The Festival of Federation* by Charles Thévenin, 1790.

of conspiring to starve the Parisian population as punishment for their rebellion against the king. The second (image B) shows a more carefully choreographed representation of the people during the Festival of Federation, organized in July 1790 by the revolutionary government to commemorate the first anniversary of the fall of the Bastille. Finally, the last two illustrations show contrasting images of the revolutionary sans-culottes, the working-class revolutionaries who supported the government during the Terror in 1792–1794. The first (image C) is a sympathetic portrait of sans-culottes as a virtuous and self-sacrificing working man, standing with an eye to the future. Completely incongruous is the British satirist James Gillray's portrait of a cannibalistic sans-culottes family (image D), drawn literally "without pants," feasting on the bodies of their victims after a hard day's work.

Questions for Analysis

1. Image A depicts an event from July 1789, before the August publication of the Declaration of the Rights of Man. How does this image portray the crowd's vengeance on Foulon? What possible political messages are contained in this image?

2. Image B, on the other hand, chooses to display the people celebrating their own birth as a political body, by convening on the anniversary of the fall of the Bastille. What emotions is this painting designed to invoke? How does it relate to the more disturbing images such as image A?

3. How are the positive and negative portrayals of sans-culottes as political actors (images C and D) constructed? Can we imagine a painting of a worker such as in image C being produced before 1789? What does image D tell us about how the revolution was viewed from Britain?

C. An idealized sans-culotte painting by Louis-Léopold Boilly, 1792.

D. A British satirical cartoon of "a family of sans-culottes refreshing after the fatigues of the day" by James Gillray, 1792.

French clergy. In return, the Vatican agreed to forgo any claims to Church lands expropriated by the revolution. That property would remain in the hands of its new middle-class rural and urban proprietors. The concordat did not revoke the principle of religious freedom established by the revolution, but it did win Napoleon the support of conservatives who had feared for France's future as a godless state.

Such political balancing acts increased Napoleon's general popularity, and, combined with early military successes (peace with Austria in 1801 and with Britain in 1802), they muffled any opposition to his personal ambitions. In December of 1804, he finally cast aside any traces of republicanism. In a ceremony that evoked the splendor of medieval kingship and Bourbon absolutism, he crowned himself Emperor Napoleon I in the Cathedral of Notre Dame in Paris. Napoleon did much to create the modern state, but he did not hesitate to proclaim his links to the past.

Dispensing with republicanism, Napoleon crowns himself as emperor

IN EUROPE AS IN FRANCE: NAPOLEON'S EMPIRE

The nations of Europe had looked on—some in admiration, others in horror, and all in astonishment—at the phenomenon that was Napoleon. Austria, Prussia, and Britain led two coalitions against revolutionary France in 1792–1795 and in 1798; both were defeated. After Napoleon came to power in 1799, the alliance split. Russia and Austria withdrew from the fray in 1801, and even the intransigent British were forced to make peace the following year.

By 1805, the Russians, Austrians, and Swedes had joined the British in an attempt to contain France. Even after Prussia joined the coalition in 1806, Napoleon's military superiority prevailed. Napoleon was a master of well-timed, well-directed shock attacks on the battlefield. His army transformed European warfare. First raised as a revolutionary militia, it was now a trained conscript army—loyal, well supplied by a nation whose economy was committed to serving the war effort, and led by generals promoted on the basis of talent. This new kind of army inflicted crushing defeats on his enemies. The Battle of Austerlitz, in December 1805, was a triumph for the French against the combined forces of Austria and Russia, and it became a symbol of the emperor's apparent invincibility. His subsequent victories against the Prussians at Jena and against the Russians at Friedland in 1807 only added to his reputation.

Out of these victories, Napoleon created his new empire and affiliated states. To the southeast, the empire included Rome and the pope's dominions, Tuscany, and the Dalmatian territories of Austria (now the coastline of Croatia). To the east, Napoleon's rule extended over a federation of German states known as the Confederation of the Rhine and a section of Poland. These new states were presented as France's gift of independence to patriots elsewhere in Europe, but in practice, they were a military buffer against renewed expansion by Austria. The empire itself was ringed by the allied kingdoms of Italy, Naples, Spain, and Holland. Napoleon himself was King of Italy, and his brothers, brothers-in-law, and trusted generals ruled in the other kingdoms.

Napoleon exported French revolutionary reforms to other parts of Europe

The empire brought the French Revolution's practical consequences—a powerful, centralizing state and an end to old systems of privilege—to Europe's doorstep, applying to the conquered European territories the principles that had already transformed France. The empire changed the terms of government service and ended the nobility's monopoly on the officer corps. The new branches of government hired engineers, mapmakers, surveyors, and legal consultants. Public works and

EUROPE IN 1812
- French territory
- French dependencies
- Allied with Napoleon
- Ottoman Empire
- Independent states

NAPOLEON'S INVASION OF RUSSIA, 1812
- → Advance
- ◄- - Retreat
- ✳ Battle sites

EUROPE

AFRICA

Area of detail

NORWAY
SWEDEN
FINLAND (to Russia 1809)
NORTH SEA
BALTIC SEA
UNITED KINGDOM
DENMARK
Copenhagen
London
ATLANTIC OCEAN
English Channel
HOLLAND
Amsterdam
Brussels
Waterloo
Auerstadt
Paris
FRENCH EMPIRE
Bordeaux
CONFEDERATION OF THE RHINE
Jena
Ulm
HELVETIC REPUBLIC
Marengo
Rivoli
Arcole
Marseilles
KING OF ITALY
ILLYRIAN PROVINCES
SPAIN
Vimeiro
Madrid
Zaragoza
Lisbon
Talavera
Badajoz
Valencia
Bailén
Trafalgar
CORSICA
KINGDOM OF SARDINIA
PAPAL STATES
Rome
Naples
KINGDOM OF NAPLES
CORFU
KINGDOM OF SICILY
PRUSSIA
Berlin
Tilsit
Friedland
Eylau
Leipzig
DUCHY OF WARSAW
Warsaw
Austerlitz
Wagram
Vienna
AUSTRIAN EMPIRE
Danube R.
Borodino
Moscow
Napoleon, 1812
RUSSIA
BLACK SEA
OTTOMAN EMPIRE
AEGEAN SEA
MEDITERRANEAN SEA

0   200   400   600 Miles
0   200   400   600 Kilometers

NAPOLEON'S EUROPEAN EMPIRE AT ITS HEIGHT. At the height of his power in 1812, Napoleon controlled most of Europe, ruling either directly or through dependent states and allies. **› Compare this map with the one on page 631. By what means had Napoleon expanded French control on continental Europe? › Which major countries remained outside of French control? › Which areas felt the longest-lasting impact of Napoleon's reign?**

education were reorganized. Prefects in the outer reaches of the empire, as in France, built roads, bridges, hospitals, and prisons; and reorganized universities. New tax districts were created, and the taxes collected went to support the new state.

The Napoleonic Code was often introduced in the satellite kingdoms, but not always or entirely. In southern Italy, measures against the Catholic Church were deemed too controversial. The Duchy of Warsaw in Poland ended serfdom but offered no land reform, so former serfs became impoverished tenants. In most areas, the empire gave civil rights to Protestants and Jews. In Rome, the conquering French opened the gates of the Jewish ghetto—and made Jews subject to conscription.

***NAPOLEON ON HORSEBACK AT THE ST. BERNARD PASS*, BY JACQUES-LOUIS DAVID (1801), AND *LITTLE BONEY GONE TO POT*, BY GEORGE CRUIKSHANK (1814).** The depth of Napoleon's celebrity in Europe can be measured in the equal shares of adulation and hatred that he stirred up within Europe among his supporters and his enemies. Jacques-Louis David's portrait, painted before Napoleon became emperor of France, captures the ardent hopes that many attached to his person. The painting explicitly compared Napoleon with two previous European conquerors, Charlemagne and the ancient Carthaginian general Hannibal, by evoking their names in the stones at the base of the painting. In George Cruikshank's bitter caricature, published after Napoleon's exile to Elba, the devil offers him a pistol to commit suicide, and the former emperor, seated on a chamber pot, says he might, but only if the firing mechanism is disabled. Both images use assumptions about virility and masculine authority to make their point. **›Who are the intended audiences for these images? › How do they convey their respective arguments?**

In some areas, Catholic monasteries, convents, and other landholdings were broken up and sold, almost always to wealthy buyers. In the empire as during the revolution, many who benefited were the elite: people and groups already on their way up and with the resources to take advantage of the opportunities.

How did others see him? Some countries and social groups collaborated enthusiastically, some negotiated, and some resisted. Napoleon's image as a military hero genuinely inspired young men from the elite, raised in a culture that prized military honor. By contrast, Catholic peasants in Spain fought him from the beginning. In many small principalities previously ruled by princes—the patchwork states of Germany, for example, and the repressive kingdom of Naples—reforms that provided for more efficient and less corrupt administration were welcomed by most of the local population. Yet the Napoleonic presence proved a mixed blessing. Vassal states contributed heavily to the maintenance of the emperor's military power. The French levied taxes, drafted men, and required states to support occupying armies. The Italians, Germans, and Dutch paid an especially high price for reforms, in terms of economic cost and numbers of men recruited. From the point of view of the common people, the local lord and priest had been replaced by the French tax collector and army recruiting board.

It is telling that even Napoleon's enemies came to believe that the upstart emperor represented the wave of the future, particularly regarding the reorganization of the state. Though they fought Napoleon, Prussian and Austrian administrators set about instituting reforms that resembled his: centralizing the bureaucracy, imposing uniform law codes, eliminating privileges, and so on. Many who came of age under Napoleon's empire believed that, for better or worse, his empire was modern.

◀ Napoleon's enemies embrace his reforms as modern and institute versions of their own

The Return to War and Napoleon's Defeat: 1806–1815

Napoleon's boldest attempt at consolidation, a policy banning British goods from the Continent, was a dangerous failure. Britain had bitterly opposed each of France's revolutionary regimes. Napoleon's Continental System, established in 1806, sought to starve Britain's trade and force its surrender. The system failed for several reasons. The British naval blockade of the Continent, begun in 1807, effectively countered Napoleon's system, and the British successfully developed a lively trade with South America. A second reason for the failure was its internal tariffs. Europe became divided into economic camps that were at odds with each other as they tried to subsist on what the Continent alone could produce and manufacture. Finally, the system hurt the Continent more than Britain. Stagnant trade in Europe's ports and unemployment in its manufacturing centers eroded public faith in Napoleon's regime.

The Continental System was Napoleon's first serious mistake. His second was his attempt to create a European empire, ruled from Paris. The symbols of his empire—reflected in painting, architecture, and the design of furniture and clothing—were deliberate imitations of Roman style. Where early revolutionaries referred to the Roman Republic for their imagery, Napoleon looked to the more ostentatious style of the Roman emperors. In 1809, he divorced the empress Josephine and ensured himself a successor of royal blood by marrying a Habsburg princess, Marie Louise—the great-niece of Marie Antoinette. Such actions lost Napoleon the support of revolutionaries, former Enlightenment thinkers, and liberals across the Continent.

A crucial moment in Napoleon's undoing came with his invasion of Spain in 1808. Napoleon overthrew the Spanish king, installed his own brother on the throne, and imposed reforms similar to those he had instituted elsewhere in Europe. Napoleon's victory weakened Spain's hold on its colonies across the Atlantic, and the Spanish crown never fully regained its grip (see Chapter 20). But in Spain itself, two factors led to the ultimate failure of Napoleon's mission: the presence of British forces and the determined resistance of the Spanish people, who detested Napoleon's interference in the affairs of the Church. The Peninsular War, as the Spanish conflicts were called, was long and bitter. The smaller British force learned how to concentrate a devastating volume of gunfire on the French pinpoint attacks on the open battlefield, and laid siege to the French garrison towns. The Spanish wore down the French invaders through guerrilla warfare. Terrible atrocities were committed by both sides; the French military's torture and execution of Spanish guerrillas and civilians was immortalized by the Spanish

THE DISASTERS OF WAR, BY FRANCISCO GOYA (1746–1828). Goya was a Spanish painter and political liberal who had initially supported the French Revolution. After Napoleon invaded Spain in 1807, Spaniards rose up in revolt, leading to the Peninsular War of 1808–1814. Between 1810 and 1820, Goya documented the war's violence in a series of black-and-white prints containing stark images of atrocity, rape, and the aftermath of famine. Note the absence of political imagery and the pointed and bitter irony of Goya's caption: "A great heroic feat! With dead people!" **› Who or what is the target of Goya's sarcasm here?**

artist Francisco Goya (1746–1828) with sickening accuracy in his prints and paintings. Napoleon himself took charge of his army, but he only achieved a temporary victory. The Spanish campaign was the first indication that Napoleon could be beaten, and it encouraged resistance elsewhere.

The second, and most dramatic, stage in Napoleon's downfall began with the disruption of his alliance with Russia. Russia had suffered a severe economic crisis when it was no longer able to trade its surplus grain for British manufactures. Tsar Alexander I began to wink at trade with Britain and ignored the protests from Paris. By 1811, Napoleon decided that he could no longer tolerate this betrayal. He collected an army of 600,000 and set out for Russia in the spring of 1812. Only a third of the soldiers in this "Grande Armée" were French; nearly as many were Polish or German, joined by soldiers and adventurers from the rest of France's client states. It was the grandest of Napoleon's imperial expeditions: an army raised from across Europe and sent to punish the autocratic tsar. The invasion ended in disaster. The Russians refused to make a stand, drawing the French farther and farther into the heart of their country. As Napoleon neared Moscow, in the narrow streets of a town called Borodino, the Russian army drew the French forces into a bloody battle. Both sides suffered terrible losses of men, a result that was harder on the French, who were so far from home. After the battle, the Russians permitted Napoleon to occupy Moscow. But on the night of his entry, Russian partisans put the city to the torch, leaving little but the blackened walls of the Kremlin palaces to shelter the French troops.

Hoping that the tsar would eventually surrender, Napoleon lingered amid the ruins for more than a month. On October 19, he finally ordered the homeward march, but the delay was a fatal blunder. Long before he had reached the border, the terrible Russian winter was on his troops; temperatures dropped to –27° F. Frozen streams, mountainous drifts of snow, and bottomless mud slowed the retreat almost to a halt. Adding to the miseries of frostbite, disease, and starvation, mounted Cossacks rode out of the blizzard to harry the exhausted army. On December 13, a few thousand broken soldiers crossed the frontier into Germany—a fragment of the once proud Grande Armée. Nearly 300,000 of its soldiers and untold thousands of Russians lost their lives in Napoleon's Russian adventure.

After the French army's retreat from Russia, Prussia, Russia, Austria, Sweden, and Britain renewed their attack, united in their opposition to Napoleon. The climax of the campaign occurred in October 1813 when the allies defeated the French near Leipzig at the Battle of the Nations. By the beginning of 1814, the allies crossed the Rhine into France. Left with an army of inexperienced youths, Napoleon retreated to Paris, but on March 31, Tsar Alexander I of Russia and King Frederick William III of Prussia made their triumphant entry into Paris. Napoleon was forced to abdicate unconditionally and was sent into exile on the island of Elba, off the Italian coast.

Napoleon would be back on French soil in less than a year. But in the interim, the allies restored the Bourbon dynasty to the throne, in the person of Louis XVIII, brother of Louis XVI. The new king could not fill the void left by Napoleon's abdication. When the former emperor escaped from Elba, his fellow countrymen once more rallied to his side. By the time Napoleon's army reached Paris, Louis had fled the country. The allies, meeting in Vienna to conclude peace treaties with the French, were stunned by the news of Napoleon's return. They dispatched a hastily organized army to meet the emperor's typically bold offensive push into the Low Countries. At the Battle of Waterloo, fought over three bloody days from June 15–18, 1815, Napoleon was stopped by British and Prussian forces, and suffered his final defeat. This time, the allies took no chances and shipped their prisoner off to the bleak island of St. Helena in the South Atlantic. The once-mighty emperor, now the exile Bonaparte, lived out a dreary existence, writing self-serving memoirs until his death in 1821.

At Battle of Waterloo, Napoleon's forces were defeated by British and Prussians

LIBERTY, POLITICS, AND SLAVERY: THE HAITIAN REVOLUTION

In the French colonies across the Atlantic, the revolution took a different course, with wide-ranging ramifications. The Caribbean islands of Guadeloupe, Martinique, and Saint-Domingue occupied a central role in the eighteenth-century French economy because of the sugar trade. Sugar production depended on slavery, and planter elites

Saint-Domingue (1791–1804)
In September of 1791, the largest slave rebellion in history broke out in Saint-Domingue, an important French colony in the Caribbean.

On brink of war, France wanted newly freed slaves to join the army and fight the British and Spanish

Toussaint L'Ouverture

had powerful influence in Paris. The French National Assembly (like its American counterpart) declined to discuss the matter of slavery in the colonies, unwilling to encroach on the property rights of slave owners and fearful of losing the lucrative sugar islands to Britain and Spain. French men in the National Assembly also had to consider the question of rights for free men of color, a group that included a significant number of wealthy owners of property (and enslaved people).

Saint-Domingue had about 40,000 whites of different social classes, 30,000 free people of color, and half a million slaves, most of them recently enslaved from West Africa. In 1790, free people of color from Saint-Domingue sent a delegation to Paris, asking to be seated by the assembly, underscoring that they were men of property and, in many cases, of European ancestry. The assembly refused, and it sparked a rebellion among free people of color in Saint-Domingue. The French colonial authorities repressed the movement quickly—and brutally. They captured one of the leaders of the rebellion, Vincent Ogé, and publicly tortured him before executing him along with dozens of his supporters in February 1791. Radical deputies in Paris, including Robespierre, expressed outrage but could do little to change the assembly's policy.

In August 1791, the largest slave rebellion in history broke out in Saint-Domingue. How much that rebellion owed to revolutionary propaganda is unclear, because like many rebellions during the period, it had its own roots. The British and the Spanish invaded, confident that they could crush the rebellion and take the island. But in the spring of 1792, the French government, on the verge of collapse and war with Europe, scrambled to win allies in Saint-Domingue by offering citizenship to former slaves who had largely freed themselves already through revolt. A few months later (after the revolution of August 1792), the new French Republic dispatched commissioners to Saint-Domingue with troops and instructions to hold the island. There they faced a combination of different forces: Spanish and British troops, defiant Saint-Domingue planters, and slaves in rebellion. In this context, the local French commissioners reconsidered their commitment to slavery. In 1793, they promised freedom to slaves who would join the French. A year later, the assembly in Paris extended to slaves in all the colonies a liberty that the slave rebellion had accomplished in Saint-Domingue.

Emancipation and war brought new leaders to the fore, chief among them a former enslaved man, Toussaint Bréda, later Toussaint L'Ouverture (*too-SAN LOO-vehr-tur*), meaning "the one who opened the way." Toussaint and his soldiers, allied with the French army, defeated successively the French planters, the British (in 1798), and the Spanish (in 1801). Toussaint also broke the power of rival generals in the different armies composed of the formerly enslaved and free people of color, becoming the statesman of the revolution. In 1801, Toussaint set up a constitution, swearing allegiance to France but denying France any right to interfere in Saint-Domingue affairs. The constitution abolished slavery, reorganized the military, established Christianity as the state religion (entailing a rejection of vodoun, a blend of Christian and various West and Central African traditions), and made Toussaint governor for life. It was an extraordinary moment in the revolutionary period: a symbol of the universal potential of revolutionary ideas.

Toussaint's accomplishments, however, put him on a collision course with the other French general he admired and whose career was remarkably like his own: Napoleon Bonaparte. Saint-Domingue stood at the center of Bonaparte's vision of an expanded empire in the New World, an empire that would recoup the lucrative North American territories that France had lost under the Old Regime and the sugar and slave colonies of the Caribbean. In January 1802, Bonaparte dispatched 20,000 troops to bring the island under control; the expedition included both French soldiers and Polish legionnaires who had joined Napoleon's armies because of their enthusiasm for his recent victories over Austria.

The French troops captured Toussaint and shipped him under heavy guard to a prison in the mountains of eastern France, where he died in 1803. Fighting continued in Saint-Domingue, however, with fires now fueled by Bonaparte's decree reestablishing slavery where the Convention had abolished it. The war turned into a nightmare for the French. Yellow fever killed thousands of French and Polish troops, including one of Napoleon's best generals and his brother-in-law. Armies on both sides committed atrocities, and by December 1803, the French army had collapsed. Napoleon scaled back his vision of an American empire and sold the Louisiana territories to Thomas Jefferson. In Saint-Domingue, a general in the army of former slaves, Jean-Jacques Dessalines, declared the independent state of Haiti in 1804.

The **Haitian Revolution** was the most radical of the revolutions that occurred in this age because it abolished slavery and declared that the emancipatory ideas of the French Revolution and Enlightenment applied to non-Europeans and enslaved peoples. It contributed to the British decision to end slavery in 1838, and it cast a long shadow over nineteenth-century slave societies from the southern United States to Brazil. Napoleon's failed effort to reestablish slavery in the French Empire thus had wide-ranging effects across the Atlantic: in North America, the Louisiana Purchase; in the Caribbean, the Haitian Revolution; in Latin America, the weakening of Spain and Portugal's colonial empires.

Haitian Revolution (1802–1804) In 1802, Napoleon sought to reassert French control of Saint-Domingue, but stiff resistance and yellow fever crushed the French arm

TOUSSAINT L'OUVERTURE. A portrait of L'Ouverture, leader of what would become the Haitian Revolution, as a general.

Conclusion

The tumultuous events in France formed part of a broad pattern of late-eighteenth-century democratic upheaval. The French Revolution was the most violent and protracted of the era's revolutions, but the dynamics of revolution were similar everywhere. One of the most important developments of the French Revolution in Europe was the emergence of a popular movement, which included political clubs for people previously excluded from politics, newspapers read by and to the common people, and political leaders who spoke for the sans-culottes. In the French Revolution, as in other revolutions, the popular movement challenged the early and moderate revolutionary leadership, pressing for more radical and democratic measures. And, as in other revolutions, the popular movement in France was defeated, and authority was reestablished by a quasi-military figure. The revolutionary ideas of liberty, equality, and fraternity were not specifically French; their roots lay in the social structures of the eighteenth century and in the ideas and culture of the Enlightenment. Yet French armies brought them, literally, to the doorsteps of many Europeans during the revolutionary wars, and the former slaves of Saint Domingue claimed them for themselves in the Haitian Revolution.

What was the larger impact of the revolution and the Napoleonic era? Its legacy is partly summed up in three key concepts: liberty, equality, and nation. Liberty meant individual rights and responsibilities and, more specifically, freedom from arbitrary authority. By equality, as we have seen, the revolutionaries meant the abolition of legal distinctions of rank among European men. Though their concept of equality was limited, it became a powerful mobilizing force in the nineteenth century. An important legacy of the revolution was contained in the new term *nation*. Nationhood was a political concept. A nation was formed

AFTER YOU READ THIS CHAPTER ⌄

CHRONOLOGY

May 1789	The Estates General meets
June 1789	The Tennis Court Oath
July 1789	The Fall of the Bastille
September 1792	First French Republic
January 1793	Execution of King Louis XVI
September 1793– July 1794	The Terror
1798–1799	Napoleon's invasion of Egypt
January 1804	Haitian independence
1804	Napoleon crowned emperor
1804	Civil code
1808	Invasion of Spain
1812	Invasion of Russia
1814–1815	Napoleon's abdication and defeat

REVIEWING THE OBJECTIVES

> The French Revolution resulted from both an immediate political crisis and long-term social tensions. What was this crisis, and how did it lead to popular revolt against the monarchy?

> The revolutionaries in the National Assembly in 1789 set out to produce a constitution for France. What were their political goals, and what was the reaction of monarchs and peoples elsewhere in Europe?

> After 1792, a more radical group of revolutionaries seized control of the French state. How did they come to power, and how were their political goals different from those of their predecessors?

> Napoleon's career began during the revolution. What did he owe to the revolution, and what was different about his regime?

> Three major revolutions took place in the Atlantic world at the end of the eighteenth century: the American Revolution, the French Revolution, and the Haitian Revolution. What was similar about these revolutions? What was different?

of citizens, not of a king's subjects; it was ruled by law and treated its citizens as equal before the law; and sovereignty did not lie in dynasties or historic fiefdoms but in the nation of citizens. This new form of nation gained legitimacy when citizen armies repelled attacks against their newly won freedoms; the victories of "citizens in arms" lived on in myth and history and provided the most powerful images of the period. As the revolutionary wars continued, however, military nationhood began to overshadow its political cousin. And by the Napoleonic period, this shift became decisive. A new political body of freely associated citizens was most powerfully embodied in a centralized state, its army, and a kind of citizenship defined by individual commitment to the needs of the nation at war. This understanding of national identity spread throughout Europe in the coming decades.

Go to **INQUIZITIVE** to see what you've learned—and learn what you've missed—with personalized feedback along the way.

PEOPLE, IDEAS, AND EVENTS IN CONTEXT

❭ Why was **LOUIS XVI** forced to convene the **ESTATES GENERAL** in 1789?

❭ What argument did **ABBÉ SIEYÈS** make about the role of the **THIRD ESTATE**?

❭ What made the **TENNIS COURT OATH** a revolutionary act?

❭ What was the role of popular revolts (the attack on the **BASTILLE**, the **GREAT FEAR**, the **OCTOBER DAYS**) in the revolutionary movements of 1789?

❭ What was the connection between the French Revolution with the slave revolt in **SAINT-DOMINGUE** that began in 1791?

❭ What was the **DECLARATION OF THE RIGHTS OF MAN AND OF THE CITIZEN**?

❭ What was the **CIVIL CONSTITUTION OF THE CLERGY**?

❭ What circumstances led to the abolition of the monarchy in 1792?

❭ Why did the **JACOBINS** in the **NATIONAL CONVENTION** support a policy of the **TERROR**?

❭ What were **NAPOLEON BONAPARTE**'s most significant domestic accomplishments in France? What significance did Napoleon's military campaigns have for other parts of Europe and for the French Empire?

❭ What was the significance of the **HAITIAN REVOLUTION** of 1791–1804?

THINKING ABOUT CONNECTIONS

❭ Popular movements in favor of democracy, social justice, or national self-determination in the more than two centuries since 1789 have often used the French Revolution as a point of reference or comparison. Obvious comparisons are those movements that saw themselves as "revolutionary," such as the Russian Revolution of 1917 or the Chinese Revolution of 1949. More recent comparisons might be the civil rights movement in the United States in the twentieth century, popular movements for democratic change in Eastern Europe that resulted in the end of the Cold War in 1989, or the Arab Spring of 2011.

❭ Make a list of factors or circumstances that you might want to compare in considering the outcome of such movements. You might consider the degree to which elites support the current regime or situation, the degree of consensus within society about the need for chance, the goals of those who are protesting the status quo, economic circumstances, or the global context and international support for either the regime or for revolutionaries. What other factors might determine the outcome of revolutionary situations?

19

The Industrial Revolution and Nineteenth-Century Society

JAMES WATT, A SCOTTISH MECHANIC and instrument maker, changed the course of human history when he took the primitive steam engine designed by Thomas Newcomen around 1712 and added a separate condenser, which allowed it to generate more power while using less coal as fuel. Watt marketed his engine in 1775, and it was soon adapted to produce a rotary motion that could be used industrially in a multitude of ways, including grinding, milling, sawing, and weaving. Among its first uses was in pumps used to eliminate water from coal mines, allowing for deeper shafts, which effectively increased production and lowered prices for fuel. The spread of Watt's steam technology throughout the north of England at the end of the eighteenth century transformed the manufacturing world, reshaped the landscape of the English countryside, and began a revolution in the way that people lived and worked.

Watt's engine could have such influence only in a world where foresters, cotton merchants, and landowners could see profits in the purchase of expensive industrial sawmills, mechanical looms, and steam-driven threshers. Watt's invention depended on the labor of men and women, some enslaved, who produced raw materials like coal, copper, and cotton. The profits of industrial entrepreneurs in Europe depended on their ability to hire sawyers, weavers, and field-workers who were forced to accept a new way of working, where they no longer owned their own tools but rather worked as wage laborers for men of business seeking returns on

BEFORE YOU READ THIS CHAPTER

>

> Industrialization in Europe drove a new form of economic development based on the concentration of labor and production in areas with easy access to energy sources. This led to rapid growth of new industrial cities and to the development of new transport networks connecting industrial centers to growing markets.

> Industrialization created new social groups in society, defined less by their status at birth than by their place in the new economy. Workers faced new kinds of discipline in the workplace, and women and children entered the new industrial workforce in large numbers. A new elite composed of businessmen, entrepreneurs, bankers, engineers, and merchants emerged as the primary beneficiaries of industrialization.

> Population growth in rural areas spurred migration to cities, where laborers and the middle classes did not mix socially; they adopted different dress, speech, and leisure activities and had significantly different opportunities when it came to marriage, sex, and children.

CORE OBJECTIVES

> **UNDERSTAND** the local and global circumstances that allowed for industrialization to begin in Great Britain.

> **IDENTIFY** the industries that were the first to adopt new systems for mechanical production and the regions in Europe in which they thrived.

> **DESCRIBE** the changes in the nature of work, production, and employment that occurred as a result of the mechanization of industry.

> **EXPLAIN** the effects of industrialization on the environment and social life in Europe, especially in the new urban centers associated with industrial development.

> **IDENTIFY** the essential characteristics of the new "middle classes" in nineteenth-century Europe and their differences from the property-owning groups prior to the Industrial Revolution.

their investment. Business owners also needed customers for the larger amounts of finished timber, woven cloth, and grain that they were now bringing to market. Technology such as Watt's was an important part of the changes historians call the *Industrial Revolution*, but technology alone cannot explain the complicated social and economic transformation contained in the phrase.

The Industrial Revolution led to the proliferation of more capital-intensive enterprises, new ways of organizing human labor, and the rapid growth of cities. These developments triggered social and cultural changes with revolutionary consequences for Europeans and their relationship to the rest of the world. Of all the changes, perhaps the most revolutionary came at the very root of human endeavor: new forms of energy. Over the space of two or three generations, a society and an economy that had drawn on water, wind, and wood for most of its energy needs came to depend on machines driven by steam engines and coal. In 1800, the world produced 10 million tons of coal. In 1900, it produced 1 billion—a hundred times more. The Industrial Revolution brought the beginning of the fossil-fuel age, altering as it did so the equilibrium between human populations and their natural environment.

A dramatic increase in use of fossil fuels >

Mechanization made enormous gains in productivity in some sectors of the economy, but technology did not dispense with human toil; in fact, historians emphasize that the Industrial Revolution intensified human labor—mining for coal with picks and shovels, digging trenches, harvesting cotton, sewing by hand, or pounding hides—much more often than it eased it. One historian suggested that we would do better to speak of the "industrious revolution." This revolution did not lie solely in machines but in a new economic system based on mobilizing capital and labor on a much larger scale. The industrious economy redistributed wealth and power, creating new social classes and producing new social tensions.

It also prompted deep-seated cultural shifts. The English critic Raymond Williams has pointed out that during the eighteenth century, *industry* referred to a human quality: a hardworking woman was "industrious," or an ambitious clerk showed "industry." By the middle of the nineteenth century, *industry* had come to mean an economic system, one that followed its own logic and worked on its own—seemingly independent of humans. This modern understanding of the term was born in the early nineteenth century. The Industrial Revolution changed people's assumptions about economics and the role played by human beings in society.

The dramatic changes of the late eighteenth and early nineteenth centuries emerged out of earlier developments. Overseas commercial exploration opened new territories for trade. Asia, Africa, and the Americas were brought into the web of the European economy in ways that encouraged the exploitation of unfree labor, leading to the development of racial slavery. Expanding trade networks created new markets for goods and human trafficking, and sources for raw materials. The need to organize commerce over long distances fostered financial innovations and sophisticated credit schemes for managing risk. These developments paved the way for industrialization. Within Europe, the commercialization of agriculture and the spread of handicraft manufacturing in rural areas anticipated later industrial developments. A final factor seems to have been **population growth**, which began to accelerate in the eighteenth century. Because these earlier developments did not affect all areas in Europe the same way, industrialization did not always follow the same pattern across the Continent. Due to local circumstances and its place in an emerging global economic order, Britain began industrializing first.

population growth In the nineteenth century, Europe experienced a dynamic increase in population. During this period, the spread of rural manufacturing allowed men and women to marry younger and raise families earlier, which increased the size of the average family.

The Industrial Revolution in Britain, 1760–1850

The development of industry in Great Britain in the eighteenth century depended on a combination of natural, economic, and cultural resources. It was a small and secure island nation with a global empire and control over crucial ocean trade networks. It had ample accessible coal deposits, and rivers and canals to transport goods.

Agriculture in Britain was already more thoroughly commercialized than elsewhere, a result of new techniques, new crops, and the "**enclosure**" of fields and pastures into larger privately owned tracts. The British Parliament encouraged enclosure in the second half of the eighteenth century, believing that commercialized agriculture would produce higher profits and create wealth to be invested in industry, and yield more food for a growing and increasingly urban population At the same time, the concentration of property in fewer hands created enormous hardship, driving small farmers off the land, forcing them to look for work in other sectors of the economy.

A key precondition for industrialization was Britain's growing supply of form from both private wealth and well-developed banking and credit institutions. This capital was readily available to underwrite new economic enterprises and eased the transfer of money and goods—for instance, importing silks from the East or cottons from Egypt and North America. Even before industrialization, London had become a leading center for international trade, and the city was a primary distribution point for the transfer of raw materials, capital, and manufactured products throughout the world.

enclosure Long process of privatizing what had been public agricultural land in eighteenth-century Britain.

Preconditions for industrialization in Britain: (1) agriculture is privatized and modernized, making it more profitable

(2) Growing supply of capital and easily available credit

ENCLOSED FIELDS IN CENTRAL BRITAIN. The large, uniform square fields in the background of this photograph are fields that were enclosed from smaller holdings and common lands in the 1830s; they contrast with the smaller and older strip fields in the foreground. The larger enclosed fields were more profitable for their owners, who benefited from legislation that encouraged enclosure, but created hardship for the village communities that depended on the use of these lands for survival. › **What circumstances made enclosure possible?** › **What connections have historians made between enclosure and early industrialization?**

Social and cultural conditions also encouraged investment in enterprises. In Britain, far more than on the Continent, the pursuit of wealth was perceived to be a worthy goal. European nobility believed commerce to be beneath them. British aristocrats had less prejudice against business and did not hesitate to invest in new commercial opportunities. Their scramble to enclose their lands reflected a keen interest in commercial opportunities. Outside the aristocracy, an even lower barrier separated merchants from the rural gentry. Many of the entrepreneurs of the early Industrial Revolution came from the small gentry or independent farmer class. Eighteenth-century Britain was not free of social snobbery: lords looked down on bankers, and bankers looked down on craft workers. But a lord's disdain might well be tempered by the fact that his own grandfather had worked in the counting house.

POPULATION DENSITY, 1801

- 390–800 people per square mile
- 260–389 people per square mile
- 150–259 people per square mile
- Under 150 people per square mile
- ◉ Major town
- ⚓ Major port
- Principal canal, 1801
- Principal railway, 1851
- Coalfield
- I Iron ore mining
- C Copper mining
- L Lead mining
- T Tin mining

THE FIRST INDUSTRIAL NATION. Large-scale mechanization of industry developed first in Britain. › Large deposits of what two natural resources caused urban growth outside of London? › What new forms of transportation were critical for moving natural resources to market? › What else was necessary for industrialization to develop as it did?

Growing domestic and international markets made eighteenth-century Britain prosperous and the British voracious consumers. The court elite followed and bought up yearly fashions, as did most of Britain's landed and professional society. The country's small size and access to trade encouraged the development of a well-integrated domestic market. Unlike continental Europe, Britain did not have a system of internal tolls and tariffs, so goods could be moved freely to wherever they might fetch the best price. Moreover, a constantly improving transportation system boosted that freedom of movement, as did a favorable political climate.

British foreign policy responded to the nation's commercial needs, because foreign markets promised even greater returns than domestic ones, though with greater risks. At the end of every major eighteenth-century war, Britain wrested overseas territories from its enemies. At the same time, it gained access to markets in India and South America. In 1759, over one-third of all British exports went to the colonies; by 1784, if we include the former colonies in North America, that figure increased to one-half. Production for export rose by 80 percent between 1750 and 1770, while production for domestic consumption gained just 7 percent. The British merchant marine was capable of transporting goods around the world, and by the 1780s, British entrepreneurs possessed an unrivaled position at the center of world commerce.

(4) *Few barriers to domestic transport or trade of manufactured goods*

INNOVATION IN THE TEXTILE INDUSTRIES

The Industrial Revolution began with dramatic technological leaps in a few industries, the first of which was cotton textiles. Tariffs prohibiting imports of East Indian cottons, which Parliament had imposed to protect British woolen goods, had spurred the manufacture of British cotton. British textile manufacturers imported raw materials from India and the American South, and borrowed patterns from Indian spinners and weavers. What, then, were the revolutionary breakthroughs?

In 1733, John Kay's invention of the flying shuttle speeded the process of weaving, but spinning thread was still a laborious manual process. A series of comparatively simple mechanical devices eliminated this spinning-to-weaving bottleneck. The most important device was the **spinning jenny**, invented by James Hargreaves in 1764, which could produce sixteen threads at once. The invention of the water frame in 1769 by Richard Arkwright, a barber, made it possible to produce even more threads simultaneously. In 1799, Samuel Crompton invented the spinning mule, which combined the features of both the jenny and the frame.

A jenny could spin from 6 to 24 times more yarn than a hand spinner in the same amount of time; and by the end of the eighteenth century, a mule could produce 200 to 300 times more. Just as important, the new machines made better-quality—stronger and finer—thread. These machines revolutionized production across the textile industry. Last, the **cotton gin**, invented by the American Eli Whitney in 1793, mechanized the process of separating cotton seeds from the fiber, thereby speeding up the production of cotton and reducing its price. The cotton gin had many effects, including raising profits for slave owners in the United States, creating incentives for the expansion of slavery, and providing economic arguments for the defenders of slavery when challenged by

spinning jenny Invention of James Hargreaves (c. 1720–1778) that revolutionized the British textile industry by allowing a worker to spin much more thread than was possible on a hand spinner.

cotton gin Invented by Eli Whitney in 1793, the device mechanized the process of separating cotton seeds from cotton fibers, which helped speed up the production of cotton and reduced its price.

Cotton gin leads to growth in textile industry—and slave trade

abolitionists. The cotton-producing plantations in the American South were an essential part of the lucrative trade with cotton manufacturers in the northern United States and England.

As these machines grew in size and complexity, they were housed in workshops or mills located near sources of water power. The development of steam-driven equipment allowed manufacturers to build mills wherever they wished. The first industrial mills were built in towns in the north of England, near the coal fields that provided fuel for the new machines. From 1780 on, British cotton textiles flooded the world market. In 1760, Britain imported 2.5 million pounds of raw cotton; 22 million pounds in 1787; and 366 million pounds in 1837. By 1815, the export of cotton textiles amounted to 40 percent of the value of all domestic goods exported from Great Britain. Although the price of manufactured cotton goods fell dramatically, the market expanded so rapidly that profits continued to increase.

The explosive growth of textiles also prompted a debate about the benefits and tyranny of the new industries. By the 1830s, the British House of Commons was holding hearings on employment and working conditions in factories, testimonies about working days that stretched from 3:00 A.M. to 10:00 P.M., employment of very young children, and workers who lost hair and fingers in the mills' machinery. Women and children counted for roughly two-thirds of the labor force in textiles. The principle of regulating any labor (and emphatically that of adult men), however, was controversial. Only gradually did a series of factory acts prohibit hiring children under age nine and limit the labor of workers under age eighteen to ten hours a day.

COAL AND IRON

Meanwhile, decisive changes were transforming the production of iron. A series of eighteenth-century innovations—coke smelting, rolling, and puddling—enabled the British to substitute coal (which they had in abundance) for wood (which was scarce and inefficient) to heat molten metal and make iron. The new higher quality "pig iron" could be used to make the machines, engines, railway tracks, agricultural implements, and hardware that became, literally, the infrastructure of industrialization. Britain exported both coal and iron goods to rapidly expanding markets around the industrializing regions of the world. Between 1814 and 1852, exports of British iron doubled, to over 1 million tons, more than half of the world's total production.

Rising demand for coal required deeper mines. In 1711, Thomas Newcomen's steam engine proved immensely useful to the coal industry for pumping water from mines. After 1763, as we have seen, James Watt improved on Newcomen's

COTTON SPINNING, 1861. An illustration from a series showing spinning at Walter Evans and Company, cotton manufacturers in Derby, England. **› Why did textile factories prefer female employees?**

NED LUDD AND THE LUDDITES. In 1811 and 1812, in northern England, bands of workmen who resented the adoption of new mechanical devices in the weaving industries attacked several establishments and destroyed the frames used to weave cloth. The movement took the name "Luddites" from Ned Ludd, who had broken the frames belonging to his employer in 1779. His mythological presence in the movement is depicted in the illustration on the right. Although the anger was directed at the machines, the real target of resentment may have been the new pricing scheme imposed by the merchants who bought the finished work. The debate about prices is a central part of the poster on the left, which offers a reward for information leading to the conviction of the frame breakers. The poster is signed by several workers of the establishment who published the price they received for each piece of clothing and their lack of complaints about their employer. **› How might weavers, accustomed to getting fixed prices for their goods, have perceived the need to adjust to the price fluctuations of a market economy?**

machine; and by 1800, Watt and his partner Matthew Boulton had sold 289 engines for use in factories and mines. Watt and Boulton made their fortune from their invention's efficiency, earning a regular percentage of the increased profits from each mine that operated the engine.

Steam power was still energy consuming and expensive, so it only gradually replaced traditional water power. Even in its early form, however, the steam engine decisively transformed the nineteenth-century world with one application: the steam-driven locomotive. Railroads revolutionized industry, markets, public and private financing, and ordinary people's conceptions of space and time.

The Coming of Railways

Transportation had improved during the years before 1830, but moving heavy materials, particularly coal, remained a problem. The first modern railway, built in England in 1825, ran from the coalfield in Stockton to Darlington, near the coast. The locomotives on the Stockton–Darlington line traveled at fifteen miles per hour, the fastest rate at which machines had yet moved goods overland. Soon they would move people as well, transforming transportation in the process.

Building railways became a massive enterprise and a risky but potentially profitable opportunity for investment. No sooner did the first combined passenger and goods service open in 1830, operating between Liverpool and Manchester, England, than plans were formulated and money pledged to extend rail systems throughout Europe, the Americas, and beyond. In 1830, there were no more than a few dozen miles of railway in the world. By 1840, there were more than 4,500 miles; and by 1850, more than 23,000.

Throughout the world, a veritable army of construction workers built the railways. In Britain, they were called "navvies" (derived from *navigator*), a term first used for the construction workers on Britain's eighteenth-century canals. Navvies were a rough lot, living with a few women in temporary encampments as they migrated across the countryside. They were often immigrant workers who faced local hostility. Later in the century, railway-building projects in Africa and the Americas were lined with camps of immigrant Indian and Chinese laborers, who also became targets of *nativist* (a term that means "opposed to foreigners") anger.

The magnitude of the navvies' accomplishment was extraordinary. In Britain and in much of the rest of the world, mid-nineteenth-century railways were constructed almost entirely without the aid of machinery. An assistant engineer on the

BARRY DOCK AND ISLAND, WALES, 1895. The convergence of coal, steam power, railways, and maritime shipping were at the center of industrialization in Britain. **›** **In what way did the circular relationship among coal and iron production, the larger transportation revolution associated with the construction of railroads, and later, steamships, help sustain the initial growth associated with industrial development?**

London-to-Birmingham line calculated that the labor involved was the equivalent of lifting 25 billion cubic feet of earth and stone 1 foot high. He compared this feat with building the Great Pyramid, a task he estimated involved the hoisting of some 16 billion tons. The building of the pyramid, however, required more than 200,000 men and twenty years. The construction of the London-to-Birmingham railway was accomplished by 20,000 men in less than five years. Translated into individual terms, a navvy was expected to move an average of 20 tons of earth per day. Railways were produced by toil as much as by technology; they illustrate why some historians prefer to use the term *industrious revolution*.

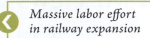

Massive labor effort in railway expansion

Steam engines, textile machines, new ways of making iron, and railways were all interconnected. Pumps run by steam engines made it possible to mine deeper veins of coal, and steam-powered railways made it possible to transport coal. Mechanization fueled the production of iron for machines and the mining of coal to run the steam engines. The railway boom multiplied the demand for iron products: rails, locomotives, carriages, signals, and switches. The scale of production expanded and the tempo of economic activity quickened, spurring the search for more coal, the production of more iron, the mobilization of more capital, and the recruitment of more labor. Steam and speed were becoming the foundation of the economy and a new way of life.

The Industrial Revolution on the Continent

Continental Europe followed a different path. Eighteenth-century France, Belgium, and Germany had manufacturing districts in regions with raw materials, access to markets, and long-standing traditions of craft and skill. Yet for a variety of reasons, changes along the lines seen in Britain did not occur until the 1830s. Britain's transportation system was highly developed, whereas those of France and Germany were not. France was far larger than England; its rivers more difficult to navigate and its seaports, cities, and coal deposits farther apart. Much of central Europe was divided into small principalities, each with its own tolls and tariffs, which complicated the transportation of goods over any considerable distance. The Continent had fewer raw materials, coal in particular, than Britain. The abundance and cheapness of wood discouraged exploration that might have resulted in new discoveries of coal, which also meant that coal-run steam engines were less economical on the Continent. Capital, too, was less readily available. Early British industrialization was underwritten by private wealth, but this was less feasible elsewhere. Different patterns of landholding formed obstacles to the commercialization of agriculture. In the east, serfdom was a powerful disincentive to labor-saving innovations. In the west, especially in France, the large number of small peasants—as farmers of humble origin were called in Europe—stayed put on the land.

The wars of the French Revolution and Napoleon disrupted economies. During the eighteenth century, the population had grown and mechanization had begun in a few key industries. The ensuing political upheaval and the financial strains of warfare hurt commerce badly. Napoleon's ban on British-shipped cotton stalled the growth of cotton textiles for decades, though the armies' greater demand for woolen cloth kept that sector of textiles humming. Iron processing increased to satisfy the

The Factory System, Science, and Morality: Two Views

Reactions to the Industrial Revolution and the factory system it produced ranged from celebration to horror. Dr. Andrew Ure, a Scottish professor of chemistry, was fascinated with these nineteenth-century applications of Enlightenment science. He believed that the new machinery and its products would create a new society of wealth, abundance, and, ultimately, stability through the useful regimentation of production.

Friedrich Engels (1820–1895) was one of the many socialists to criticize Dr. Ure as shortsighted and complacent in his outlook. Engels was part of a factory-owning family and so was able to examine the new industrial cities at close range. He provides a classic nineteenth-century analysis of industrialization. The Condition of the Working Class in England is compellingly written, angry, and revealing about middle-class concerns of the time, including women workers.

Dr. Andrew Ure (1835)

This island [Britain] is preeminent among civilized nations for the prodigious development of its factory wealth, and has been therefore long viewed with a jealous admiration by foreign powers. This very pre-eminence, however, has been contemplated in a very different light by many influential members of our own community, and has even been denounced by them as the certain origin of innumerable evils to the people, and of revolutionary convulsions to the state. . . .

The blessings which physico-mechanical science has bestowed on society, and the means it has still in store for ameliorating the lot of mankind, has [sic] been too little dwelt upon; while, on the other hand, it has been accused of lending itself to the rich capitalists as an instrument for harassing the poor, and of exacting from the operative an accelerated rate of work. It has been said, for example, that the steam-engine now drives the power-looms with such velocity as to urge on their attendant weavers at the same rapid pace; but that the hand-weaver, not being subjected to this restless agent, can throw his shuttle and move his treddles at his convenience. There is, however, this difference in the two cases, that in the factory, every member of the loom is so adjusted, that the driving force leaves the attendant nearly nothing at all to do, certainly no muscular fatigue to sustain, while it produces for him good, unfailing wages, besides a healthy workshop *gratis*: whereas the non-factory weaver, having everything to execute by muscular exertion, finds the labour irksome, makes in consequence innumerable short pauses, separately of little account, but great when added together; earns therefore proportionally low wages, while he loses his health by poor diet and the dampness of his hovel.

Source: Andrew Ure, *The Philosophy of Manufactures: Or, An Exposition of the Scientific, Moral, and Commercial Economy of the Factory System of Great Britain*, 1835, as cited in J. T. Ward, *The Factory System*, vol. 1 (New York: 1970), pp. 140–41.

military's rising needs, but techniques for making iron remained largely unchanged. Probably the revolutionary change most beneficial to industrial advance in Europe was the removal of previous restraints on the movement of capital and labor—for example, the abolition of craft guilds and the reduction of tariff barriers across the Continent.

After 1815, a number of factors combined to change the economic climate. In regions with a well-established commercial and industrial base—northeastern

Friedrich Engels (1844)

Histories of the modern development of the cotton industry, such as those of Ure, Baines, and others, tell on every page of technical innovations. . . . In a well-ordered society such improvements would indeed be welcome, but social war rages unchecked and the benefits derived from these improvements are ruthlessly monopolized by a few persons. . . . Every improvement in machinery leads to unemployment, and the greater the technical improvement the greater the unemployment. Every improvement in machinery affects a number of workers in the same way as a commercial crisis and leads to want, distress, and crime. . . .

Let us examine a little more closely the process whereby machine-labour continually supersedes hand-labour. When spinning or weaving machinery is installed practically all that is left to be done by the hand is the piecing together of broken threads, and the machine does the rest. This task calls for nimble fingers rather than muscular strength. The labour of grown men is not merely unnecessary but actually unsuitable. . . . The greater the degree to which physical labour is displaced by the introduction of machines worked by water- or steam-power, the fewer grown men need be employed. In any case women and children will work for lower wages than men and, as has already been observed, they are more skillful at piecing than grown men. Consequently it is women and children who are employed to do this work. . . . When women work in factories, the most important result is the dissolution of family ties. If a woman works for twelve or thirteen hours a day in a factory and her husband is employed either in the same establishment or in some other works, what is the fate of the children? They lack parental care and control. . . . It is not difficult to imagine that they are left to run wild.

Source: Friedrich Engels, *The Condition of the Working Class in England in 1844*, ed. and trans. W. O. Henderson and W. H. Chaloner (New York: 1958), pp. 150–51, 158, 160.

Questions for Analysis

1. According to Dr. Andrew Ure, why was industrialization good for Britain? How can the blessings of "physico-mechanical science" lead to the improvement of humanity?

2. What criticism did Engels level at Ure and other industrialization optimists? Why did Engels think conditions for workers were getting worse, not better?

3. What consequences do these two writers see for society in the wake of technological change? What assumptions do they make about the relationship between economic development and the social order?

France, Belgium, the Rhineland, Saxony, Silesia, and northern Bohemia (see map on page 660)—population growth boosted economic development. Rising population did not by itself produce industrialization. In Ireland, where other necessary factors were absent, more people meant less food.

Transportation improved: the Austrian Empire added more than 30,000 miles of roads between 1830 and 1847; Belgium almost doubled its road network in the same period; and France built new roads and 2,000 miles of canals. These improvements, combined with the construction of railroads, opened up new markets and encouraged new methods of manufacturing. In many of the Continent's manufacturing regions, however, industrialists continued to tap large pools of skilled but inexpensive labor, and older methods of handwork persisted alongside new-model factories longer than they did in Britain.

In what other ways was the Continental model of industrialization different? Governments played a more direct role in industrialization. France and Prussia granted subsidies to private companies that built railroads as did Belgium and, later, Russia. In Prussia, the state operated a large proportion of that country's mines. Governments on the Continent provided incentives for industrialization; limited-liability laws, to take the most important example, allowed investors to own shares in a corporation or company without becoming liable for the company's debts—and enabled enterprises to recruit investors to put together the capital for railroads, other forms of industry, and commerce. In this way, latecomers to industrialization used the state to catch up with earlier industrializers.

Mobilizing capital for industry was a challenge. Britain's well-organized financial markets contrasted with the Continent, where capital was dispersed and in short supply. New joint-stock investment banks, unlike private banks, were created that could sell bonds to and take deposits from individuals and smaller companies, and offer aspiring entrepreneurs start-up capital in the form of long-term commercial loans. The French Crédit Mobilier, for instance, founded in 1852 by the wealthy and well-connected Péreire brothers, assembled enough capital to finance insurance companies, the Parisian bus system, six municipal gas companies, transatlantic shipping, enterprises in other European countries, and, with the patronage of the state, the massive railroad-building spree of the 1850s. The French Crédit Mobilier collapsed in controversy, but the revolution in banking was well under way.

Industrialization on European continent spurred by governmental incentives

INDUSTRIALIZATION AFTER 1850

Until 1850, Britain remained the preeminent industrial power. Between 1850 and 1870, however, France, Germany, Belgium, and the United States emerged as challengers to the power and place of British manufacturers. Most of continental Europe's gains came as a result of continuing changes in transport, commerce, and government policy. International monetary unions were established and restrictions removed on international waterways such as the Danube. Free trade went hand in hand with removing guild barriers to entering trades. Guild control over artisanal production was abolished in Austria in 1859, and in most of Germany by the mid-1860s. Laws against usury, most of which had ceased to be enforced, were officially abandoned in Britain, Holland, Belgium, and in many parts of Germany. Investment banks continued to form, encouraged by an increase in the money supply and an easing of credit after the California gold fields opened in 1849.

A push to end barriers to free trade, including monetary policy and guild restrictions

The second half of the century brought changes further afield and in areas where Great Britain's early advantages were no longer decisive. Transatlantic cable (starting in 1865) and the telephone (invented in 1876) laid the ground for a revolution in communications. New chemical processes, dyestuffs, and pharmaceuticals emerged,

as did new sources of energy: electricity, in which the United States and Germany led both invention and commercial development. and oil, which was being refined in the 1850s and widely used by 1900 (Chapter 23).

In eastern Europe, the nineteenth century brought different patterns of economic development. Spurred by the ever-growing demand for food and grain, large sections of eastern Europe developed into concentrated, commercialized agriculture regions that played a specific role in exporting food to the West. Many of those large agricultural enterprises were based on serfdom and remained so in the face of increasing pressure for reform until 1850. Peasant protests and liberal demands for reform only gradually chipped away at the nobility's determination to hold on to its privilege and system of labor. The emancipation of Prussian peasants from serfdom was largely accomplished as early as 1810, as part of the reforms that followed Prussia's defeat by Napoleon's armies in 1807. Serfdom was abolished in the Habsburg Empire in 1848, and in Russia (and the Polish territories controlled by Russia) in the 1860s.

By 1870, the core industrial nations of Europe included Great Britain, France, Germany, Italy, the Netherlands, and Switzerland; Austria-Hungary stood at the margins; and Russia, Spain, Greece, Romania, and the western Ottoman Empire (which still included Serbia and Bulgaria in 1870) formed the industrial periphery—although some regions of these nations seemed virtually untouched by the advance of industry. What was more, even in Great Britain, the most fully industrialized nation, agricultural laborers still constituted the single largest occupational category in 1860, although they formed only 9 percent of the overall population. In Belgium, the Netherlands, Switzerland, Germany, France, Scandinavia, and Ireland, 25 to 50 percent of the population still worked on the land; and in Russia, the number was 80 percent. *Industry*, moreover, did not mean automation or machine production, which long remained confined to a few sectors of the economy. As machines were introduced in some sectors to do specific tasks, they usually intensified the tempo of handwork in other sectors. Thus, even in the industrialized regions, much work was still accomplished in tiny workshops—or at home.

> *Amid industrialization, agricultural work still most common*

INDUSTRY AND EMPIRE

From an international perspective, nineteenth-century Europe was the most industrial region of the world. And Europeans, particularly the British, jealously guarded their international advantages. They preferred to do so through financial leverage. Britain, France, and other European nations gained control of the national debts of China, the Ottoman Empire, Egypt, Brazil, Argentina, and other non-European powers. They also supplied large loans to other states, which bound those nations to their European investors. If the debtor nations expressed discontent, as Egypt did in the 1830s when it attempted to establish its own cotton textile industry, they confronted financial pressure and shows of force. Exerting power over other rulers was a form of **empire** building and led to the conquest of territory in Ottoman Algeria and Egypt (Chapter 22). Coercion, however, was not always necessary or even one-sided. Social change in other empires—China, Persia, and the Mughal Empire of India, for example—made those empires vulnerable and created new opportunities for the European powers and their local partners. Ambitious local elites often reached agreements with Western governments or groups such as the British East India Company. These trade agreements

empire Centralized political entity consolidated through the conquest and colonization of other nations or people in order to benefit the ruler and/or his homeland.

THE INDUSTRIAL REVOLUTION. Rapid industrial growth depended on a circular network of relationships. **> According to the map key, what elements made up the circular networks of relationships? > How were these elements connected, and how might they have reinforced each other, contributing to rapid growth? > Why do you think the percentage of populations living in cities was so much greater in the United Kingdom?**

For the most part, Europe dominates global production of manufactured goods, using colonies for raw materials and as dependent markets

transformed regional economies on terms that sent the greatest profits to Europe after a substantial gratuity to the Europeans' local partners. Where agreements could not be made, force prevailed, and Europe took territory and trade by conquest.

Industrialization tightened global links between Europe and the rest of the world, creating new networks of trade and interdependence. To a certain extent, the world economy divided between the producers of manufactured goods (Europe itself) and suppliers of the necessary raw materials and buyers of finished goods (everyone else). Cotton growers in the southern United States, sugar growers in the Caribbean, and wheat growers in Ukraine accepted arrangements with the industrialized West and typically profited from them. If there were disputes, however, those suppliers often found that Europe could look elsewhere for the same goods—or dictate the terms of trade down the business end of a bank ledger or a cannon barrel.

In 1811, Britain imported 3 percent of the wheat it consumed. By 1891, that portion had risen to 79 percent. Why? In an increasingly urban society, fewer people lived off the land. The commercialization of agriculture, which began early in Britain, had taken even firmer hold elsewhere, turning new regions—Australia, Argentina, and North America (Canada and the United States)—into centers of grain and wheat production. And new forms of transportation, finance, and communication made it easier to shuttle commodities and capital through international networks. These simple percentages dramatize the new interdependence of the nineteenth century. They illustrate, as well as any statistics can, how ordinary Britons' lives, like those of their counterparts in other nations, were embedded in an increasingly global economy.

The Social Consequences of Industrialization

We have mentioned population growth as one factor in industrial development, but it deserves treatment on its own terms. By any measure, the nineteenth century constituted a turning point in European demographic history. In 1800, the population of Europe as a whole was estimated roughly at 205 million. By 1850, it had risen to 274 million; to 414 million by 1900; and on the eve of the First World War, it was 480 million. (Over the same span of time, the world population went from about 900 million to 1.6 billion.) Britain, with its comparatively high standard of living, saw its population nearly triple, from 16 to 45 million. The territory that was eventually included in a united Germany after 1870 (Chapter 21) saw a similar increase, from about 22 million in 1801 to 67 million in 1913. Population increases came in the largely rural regions as well. In Russia, the population rose from 36 to 160 million during the same period. Growth was less pronounced in France, which only grew from about 27 million in 1801 to 40 million in 1910.

POPULATION GROWTH AND THE DEMOGRAPHIC TRANSITION

Across nineteenth-century Europe, populations began a gradual shift from high fertility and mortality to lower death rates and fewer births. Social scientists refer to this as the "demographic transition." The causes of this population shift are complex, and the same pattern is not observable everywhere in Europe. A gradual decline in death rates seems to have begun in northwestern Europe at the end of the eighteenth century and spread across the Continent south and eastward over the next 100 years. Birthrates remained high during the same period, and it is the conjunction between these two tendencies—slowly falling death rates and continued high birthrates—that probably accounts for much of the population growth in the nineteenth century. The general decline in mortality did not occur because of medical breakthroughs but appears to be largely the result of improved food supplies and clean water. Declines in mortality due to improved medicine and public health did not have a significant impact on the number of people who survived childhood to

Learning to Live in a Global Economy

The commercial networks of the Atlantic world were already well established before the Industrial Revolution, and Europeans were also trading widely with South and East Asia before the end of the eighteenth century. Nevertheless, the advent of an industrial economy in Europe at the beginning of the nineteenth century created such a demand for raw materials and for new markets abroad that it became profitable for manufacturers and merchants to ship much larger amounts of goods over longer distances than ever before. As various industrialized regions in Europe became increasingly dependent on overseas markets, people in Europe came to be aware of the extent to which their own activities linked them to other parts of the world. Awareness of

A. John Bull and cotton merchants.

reach adulthood until the late nineteenth century. In spite of these general improvements, mortality remained high in many areas, especially in the poorer neighborhoods of Europe's cities. Even in 1880, the average male life expectancy at birth in Berlin was no more than thirty years (in rural districts nearby, it was forty-three).

Population growth in the nineteenth century also resulted from increases in fertility. The spread of rural manufacturing allowed couples to marry and set up these linkages did not always mean that they possessed complete or accurate information about the people who produced the cotton that they wore or purchased the manufactured goods that they made; although it did stimulate their imagination and changed their consciousness of their place in the world.

This awareness is well illustrated in the cartoons shown here, which come from the British illustrated news in the 1850s and 1860s. The first (image A) depicts

POOR CONSOLATION.

Parisian. "COURAGE, MON AMI; 'AM I NOT A MAN AND A BROTHER?'"

B. Increasing global awareness in France.

John Bull, representing British textile manufacturers, looking on as U.S. cotton suppliers fight one another during the Civil War in the United States. He states, "Oh! If you two like fighting better than business, I shall deal at the other shop." In the background, an Indian cotton merchant is happy to have him as a customer.

The second cartoon (image B) depicts the ways that the increasingly interconnected global economy might stimulate a new kind of political awareness. A French worker, who Emperor Napoleon III placed in irons for participating in a revolutionary movement, compares his situation to that of an African slave seated next to him, saying, "Courage, my friend! Am I not a man and a brother?" A poster on the wall behind the two men refers to the Portuguese slave trade. Napoleon III himself came to power by overthrowing the Second Republic in France, a government that had abolished the slave trade in French territories.

Questions for Analysis

1. What constellation of private and national interests were at play in the relationships portrayed in image A? What significance might contemporaries have attached to the possibility that the British might have chosen to buy their cotton from an Asian source "over the way" rather than from North America?

2. In image B, what is the message of the cartoon's suggestion that the slave and the worker might find equality only in the fact that they are both in chains? What was at stake in comparing a worker with a slave in mid-nineteenth-century Europe? Why does the caption read "Poor Consolation?"

3. How does the racial imagery of these cartoons relate to their intended message?

households at a younger age, even before they inherited any land, raising the average number of children born to each woman and increasing the size of families. Not only did the age of marriage fall but also more people married. And because population growth increased the proportion of young and fertile people, the process reinforced itself in the next generation, setting the stage for a period of prolonged growth. In the early years of the nineteenth century, population growth was often feared as a social calamity. **Thomas Malthus**, an English political economist, suggested in 1798 that population growth would inevitably push a society beyond its capacity to support itself, leading to food shortages, malnutrition, disease, and political instability. After the 1850s, however, social theorists began to see population growth as a sign of dynamism, a stimulant to economic growth.

By the early twentieth century this pattern of demographic growth in Europe subsided. Families began to limit the number of children born, and population growth slowed markedly. Here, too, a range of contributing factors were involved, including the spread of female literacy and women's employment, as well as an increase in the relative proportion of the population that lived in cities and so no longer saw the same need for large families. (Contraception was not widely available in Europe until the twentieth century, and it is only then that demographers begin to see a strong correlation between contraceptive use and fertility.)

RURAL POPULATIONS IN MOTION

Even as the West grew more industrial, the majority of people continued to live on the land. Conditions in the countryside were harsh. Peasants still sowed and harvested by hand. Millions of tiny farms produced a subsistence living; and families wove, spun, and sold butter to make ends meet. The average daily diet for an *entire* family might amount to no more than two or three pounds of bread—a total of about 3,000 calories daily. By many measures, living conditions for rural inhabitants of many areas in Europe grew worse in the first half of the nineteenth century, a fact of considerable political importance in the 1840s. Rising populations put more pressure on the land, and small-sized holdings and indebtedness were chronic problems in regions where farmers scraped by on their own lands.

Over the course of the century, some 37 million people (most of them peasants) left Europe—an eloquent testimony to the bleakness of rural life—and settled in the

DINNERTIME AT ST. PANCRAS WORKHOUSE, LONDON. The British system of assistance to the poor was designed to be severe to discourage the able-bodied from seeking relief. In a system of municipal workhouses, people were given accommodations in exchange for labor, often involving tedious and painful tasks. After the economic downturn following the Napoleonic Wars, the number of poor in the workhouses grew rapidly; larger ones, such as St. Pancras Workhouse in London, shown here, housed and fed male and female populations separately.

United States, South America, northern Africa, New Zealand, Australia, and Siberia. In many cases, governments encouraged emigration to ease overcrowding, sometimes forcibly deporting populations they deemed undesirable. In the United States, the policy of Indian removal—the forced resettlement of Native American groups from their ancestral lands—is linked to these European migrations. This policy made land available for European settlers in the Southeast at enormous human cost by forcing Native American tribes to exchange land east of the Mississippi for territory in the West after 1830. This policy also is evidence of the continued importance of agricultural land even as industrialization grew increasingly central to national economies.

A tragic combination of poverty, hunger, and migration in nineteenth-century Europe was the **Irish potato famine** of 1845–1849. Potatoes, which had come to Europe from the New World, fundamentally transformed the diets of European peasants, providing more nutrition for less money than corn and grain. They also grew more densely, an advantage for peasants scraping a living from small plots of land. Nowhere did they become more important than in Ireland, where the climate and soil made growing grain difficult. When a fungus hit the potato crop—first in 1845 and again, fatally, in 1846 and 1847—no alternative foods were at hand, and at least 1 million Irish died of starvation; dysentery from spoiled foods; or fever, which spread through villages and the overcrowded workhouses (poorhouses), state-run institutions that housed poverty-stricken populations. Before the famine, tens of thousands of Irish were already crossing the Atlantic to North America; they accounted for one-third of all voluntary migration to the New World. In the ten years after 1845, one and a half million people left Ireland for good.

Changes in the land depended partly on particular governments. States sympathetic to commercial agriculture made it easier to transfer land, eliminate small farms, and create larger estates. In Britain, over half the total area of the country, excluding wasteland, was composed of estates of 1,000 acres or more. In Russia, some of the largest landowners possessed over half a million acres. Until the emancipation of the serfs in the 1860s, landowners claimed the labor of dependent peasant

IRISH POTATO FAMINE, 1845–1849. The Irish potato famine had human as well as natural causes. Historians have noted that food exports from Ireland continued and may have even increased for some products during the famine, as merchants sought higher prices abroad. The cartoon depicts armed soldiers keeping starving Irish Catholic families at bay as sacks of potatoes are loaded onto a ship owned by a prosperous Irish Protestant trader.

Laborers in Motion in the Industrial Era

During the Industrial Revolution, patterns of labor migration intensified, as economic development reinforced the inequalities among different regions in Europe, and laborers continued to move from areas that lacked resources to those that offered a greater chance of employment. Earlier generations had accepted such movement as normal, and workers' associations, like the blacksmiths' brotherhood in France described here by Agricol Perdiguier, incorporated this expectation of mobility into their rituals. Perdiguier (1805–1875) was a woodworker who joined a workers' confraternity after his apprenticeship, and wrote about the experience in his autobiography. These brotherhoods were organized by trade and operated as both professional and social organizations, with connections in many cities.

Later in the century, workers were more likely to face the uncertainties of labor migration without the help of such associations. Franz Rehbein (1867–1909), a farmworker from Pomerania in eastern Germany, describes the difficult life of a migrant day laborer some decades after Perdiguier's career. Rehbein followed the harvest as part of a crew operating a threshing machine. The machine allowed estate owners to bring in their crop with fewer workers, and created opportunities for migrant crews that moved from farm to farm. At the same time, it created an intense new pace for agricultural labor, now determined by the capacity of the machine.

Agricol Perdiguier, *Memoirs of a Compagnon* (1854)

The blacksmiths have created one of the strongest associations; they have spread themselves everywhere and one finds them in cities and in villages. But they are hard and tough! They won't put up with mockery. Their wrists can twist iron and they know it; they are all too ready to fight. Amongst themselves they have their own unique customs. Here is one I have seen:

They were in a field by the side of the road. They were performing what they called their duty. It was an outdoor ceremony, a required ritual for the benefit of one who was leaving.

Their walking sticks were stuck in the earth. Fluttering from their buttonholes were red, white, and green ribbons. Standing shoulder to shoulder they made a large circle and looked toward the center. One of them, holding in his right hand a glass filled with deeply colored wine, began to run, making his way around the exterior of this circle, shouting and crying until he came back to his place, where a companion waited for him, also with a glass in his hand. They faced one another, made some signs, stepped forward and leaned to one side, interlocked their right arms and carried their glasses to their lips, drinking at the same time. The one who had shouted and ran returned to his place and his neighbor stepped out and imitated him, and finally all of them, one after another did the same, down to the last man. They also performed some shouts all together.

The one who was leaving stepped away, with his goatskin sack on his back and his long walking stick in his hand, and his drinking gourd hanging to one side, two bright rings of gold shone at his ears. Each man called to him, and called to him again. But the temptation had no hold on him: he set off without turning his head, without showing any sign of weakness. They tried again, berating him, pleading with him, but nothing had an effect: He marched proudly before them. All at once he took his hat in his hands, threw it over his head far behind his back and took off. His brothers ran and picked it up, pursuing him, finally reaching him and stuffing the hat firmly back on his head. The one leaving remained insensible and did not acknowledge the one who had returned his head covering. He walked with a firm step, without looking to the right or to the left. He was a statue, nothing surprised him, nothing moved him, nothing could force him to step aside. The other companions returned the way they had come, the ritual was complete. He had proved his determination to leave.

Source: Agricol Perdiguier, *Memoires d'un Compagnon* (Geneva: Duchamp, 1853), vol. 2, pp. 8–10. Excerpt translated by Joshua Cole.

Franz Rehbein, *The Life of a Farmworker* (1911)

Not every farm has a threshing machine, and there are no cooperatives like in other places. The threshing machine operators are independent businessmen who buy their own machine with cash or loans. They hire their own crews and move with them from farm to farm where they have contracts. Threshers are paid hourly wages. To operate a threshing machine you need 25–30 men. [. . .]

Working the threshing machine is the most demanding and exhausting work that one can think of. Hour after hour you work like an animal. The more hours in a day, the quicker the farmer will be done with the team, and the fewer meals the farmer will have to feed them. The more hours the machine operator works, the more grain he can process and the higher his profit. The more hours the crew put in, the higher their weekly wage. You get up at 4 A.M. at the latest, sometimes already at 3, and then you work all day long without rest until 8 in the evening at the earliest, and often until 9 or 10, or even 11 and 12. The only rest is the time it takes you to eat your food, which amounts to no more than an hour total for the day. And even supper is not a break because you only eat it when work has stopped, no matter how late.

The work goes as fast as the thresher's "sweat box" can swallow the grain. The worker must keep up with the machine, he is a slave and becomes part of the machine. Imagine the nonstop howling and groaning of the thresher, and the impenetrable dust that surrounds you, and then you can understand what the threshing machine means for the worker. The dust collects almost a centimeter thick on people, especially if the grain has soaked up a lot of rain, and they can see nothing out of their swollen and burning eyes. Your nose is completely stuffed from inhaling dust, and when you spit big gobs of black slime come up your throat and out. The dust sticks fast to your sweaty skin causing an unpleasant itching and burning, as if your whole body was covered with ants.

When you've put in 15, 16, or 18 hours in such circumstances you are dead tired, in the truest sense of the word. You can barely get your supper down and you'd like nothing more than to go to bed. But sleep is only possible after work if the machine is going to stay several days at the same farm. Often you have to travel late or even in the middle of the night to the next farm, sometimes to a village hours away, and as luck would have it, under drenching rain. If the machine gets stuck in a country ditch then you can't think about rest. The thresher and the engine have to be lifted with levers, and the whole crew has to haul on the chains to help the horses pull. When you are finally there, the machine has to be set up by lantern light and only then can you go find a spot to get a couple hours rest.

Because there are never enough beds in one farm for so many people, only the master, the fireman, and the two packers get a bed. Most of the crew look for a bit of straw, hay or chaff wherever they can find it.

Source: Franz Rehbein, *Das Leben eines Landarbeiters* (Jena: 1911), pp. 238–40. Excerpt translated by Joshua Cole.

Questions for Analysis

1. What do these two passages tell us about the attitudes toward labor mobility among the workers themselves? Where does the impulse to move come from in each account?

2. What aspects of workers' experience do these two authors seek to show to their readers? What is different about the way workers think about their relation to each other?

3. In what way do you think industrialization shaped the lives of workers like those who appear in these accounts?

populations for as much as several days per week. But the system of serfdom gave neither landowners nor serfs much incentive to improve farming techniques.

European serfdom, which bound hundreds of thousands of men, women, and children to particular estates for generations, made it difficult to buy and sell land freely and was an obstacle to the commercialization of agriculture. Yet the opposite was also the case. In France, peasant landholders who had benefited from the French Revolution's sale of lands and the laws on inheritance stayed in the countryside, continuing to work their small farms. Although French peasants were poor, they were able to sustain themselves on the land. This had important consequences: France suffered less agricultural distress, even in the 1840s, than did other European countries; migration from country to city was slower than in the other nations; and far fewer peasants left France for other countries.

Industrialization also transformed rural areas. Improved communication networks gave rural populations a sense of events and opportunities elsewhere but also made it possible for governments to intrude into the lives of people in the countryside. Central bureaucracies found it easier to collect taxes from the **peasantry** and to conscript sons of peasant families into armies. Some rural cottage industries faced direct competition from factory-produced goods, which meant less work or lower piece rates and falling incomes for families, especially during the winter months. In other sectors of the economy, industry spread out into the countryside, with whole regions becoming specialized producers of shoes, shirts, ribbons, cutlery, and so on, in small shops and workers' homes. Changes in the market could usher in prosperity or bring entire regions to the verge of starvation.

Many onlookers considered the nineteenth-century cities dangerous seedbeds of sedition. Yet conditions in the countryside and frequent flare-ups of rural protest remained the greatest source of trouble for governments. In England in the late 1820s, small farmers marched under the banner of the mythical "Captain Swing" to protest the introduction of threshing machines, a symbol of agricultural capitalism. In southwest France, peasants attacked local authorities who barred them from collecting wood in the forest because the wood was in demand for new furnaces. Similar rural disturbances broke out across Europe in the 1830s and 1840s. Peasants were poor, deep in debt, and precariously dependent on markets. More important, a government's inability to contend with rural misery made it look autocratic, indifferent, or inept—all political failings.

URBAN MIGRATION

The growth of cities was one of the most important facts of nineteenth-century social history, and one with significant cultural reverberations. During the nineteenth century the overall population of Europe doubled, and **urban populations** increased sixfold. Cities such as Manchester, Birmingham, and Essen seemed to spring up from nowhere. Between 1750 and 1850, London—Europe's largest city—grew from 676,000 to 2.3 million. The population of Paris went from 560,000 to 1.3 million, and Berlin nearly tripled in size during the first half of the century. Such rapid expansion brought in its wake new social problems.

Almost all nineteenth-century cities were overcrowded and unhealthy, their largely medieval infrastructures strained under the burden of new population and the demands of industry. Construction lagged far behind population growth, and the poorest workers dwelled in wretched basements or attic rooms, often without any light or drainage. Such conditions bred misery and epidemic disease.

* Norwich, York, Salisbury, Chester, Worcester, Exeter, Cambridge, Coventry, Shrewsbury, Gloucester
** Bristol, Hull, Colchester, Newcastle, Ipswich, Great Yarmouth, King's Lynn, Southampton
*** Birmingham, Manchester, Leeds, Sheffield
Source: E. A. Wrigley, *People, Cities, and Wealth* (New York: 1987), p. 166.

URBAN GROWTH IN EARLY MODERN ENGLAND. This figure shows the percentage increases in population in England as a whole, as well as in several distinct groups of population centers. London had its greatest percentage increases in the periods 1520–1600 and 1600–1700, *before* the period of industrial expansion. The historic regional centers—cathedral and market towns—had steady but unspectacular growth across these years, as did English port cities. The most remarkable growth, however, was in the new industrial areas of the north in the second half of the eighteenth century. **› What can we conclude about the nature of population growth in England from this figure? › What other sorts of information would allow you to draw more certain conclusions about the nature of these demographic shifts?**

Governments gradually adopted measures in an attempt to cure the worst of these ills, if only to prevent the spread of catastrophic epidemics. Legislation was designed to rid cities of their worst slums by tearing them down and to improve sanitary conditions by supplying both water and drainage. Yet by 1850, these projects had only just begun. Paris, perhaps better supplied with water than any other European city, had enough for no more than two baths per person per year. In London, human waste remained uncollected in 250,000 domestic cesspools. And in Manchester, fewer than one-third of the dwellings were equipped with toilets of any sort.

THE SOCIAL QUESTION

Against the backdrop of the French Revolution of 1789 and subsequent revolutions (as we will see in the following chapters), the new "shock" cities of the nineteenth century and their swelling multitudes posed urgent questions. Political leaders, social scientists, and public health officials across all of Europe issued thousands of reports on criminality, water supply, sewers, prostitution, tuberculosis and cholera, alcoholism, wet nursing, wages, and unemployment. Radicals and reformers grouped all these issues under a broad heading known as the "social question." Governments felt they had to address these issues before complaints swelled into revolution, and they responded with new measures: police forces, public health offices, sewers and new water supplies, inoculations, elementary schools, Factory Acts (regulating work hours), Poor Laws (outlining the conditions for receiving relief), and new urban regulations and city planning. Central Paris, for instance, was almost entirely redesigned in the nineteenth century—the crowded, medieval, and revolutionary poor neighborhoods were gutted, markets were rebuilt, and

PROSTITUTION IN NINETEENTH-CENTURY EUROPEAN CITIES. This sketch by Constantin Guys (1802–1892) captures the moment when *grisettes* (slang for flirtatious working-class women) entertain a proposition from two men. Guys's portrayal of the men's indistinct facial features and the saucy posture of the women captured the impersonal nature of the exchange, as well as the mercenary intentions of all parties. **›** **How did the construction of new cities, with expanded streets designed to facilitate the efficient mixing and movement of people, change the way individuals interacted with each other?**

streets were widened and lit (Chapter 21). From the 1820s on, the social question hung over Europe like a cloud, and it formed part of the backdrop to the revolutions of 1848 (discussed in Chapter 21).

SEX IN THE CITY

Prostitution flourished in nineteenth-century cities; in fact, it offers a microcosm of the nineteenth-century urban economy. At midcentury, the number of prostitutes in Vienna was estimated to be 15,600; in Paris, where prostitution was a licensed trade, 50,000; and in London, 80,000. London newspaper reports of the 1850s cataloged the elaborate hierarchies of the vast underworld of prostitutes and their customers, and included entrepreneurs with names like Swindling Sal who ran lodging houses; the pimps and "fancy men" who managed the trade of prostitutes on the street; and the relatively few "prima donnas," courtesans who enjoyed the protection of rich, upper-middle-class lovers who entertained lavishly and whose wealth allowed them to move on the fringes of more respectable high society. The heroines in Alexandre Dumas's novel *La Dame aux Camélias (The Lady of the Camellias)* and in Giuseppe Verdi's opera *La Traviata (The Fallen Woman)* were modeled on these women. Yet the vast majority of prostitutes were not courtesans, but rather women (and some men) who worked long and dangerous hours in port districts of cities or at lodging houses in the overwhelmingly male working-class neighborhoods. Most prostitutes were young women who had just arrived in the city or working women trying to manage during periods of unemployment. Single women in the cities were very vulnerable to sexual exploitation. Many were abandoned by their partners if they became pregnant, and others faced the danger of rape by their employers. Such experiences—abandonment and rape—could lead to prostitution, because women in these circumstances were unlikely to secure "respectable" employment.

Industry and the Environment

Wherever industrial development occurred, contemporary observers were quick to note the significant impact that new methods of production and transport, and new sources of energy had on local environments. Coal mines produced mountains of slag, iron smelting plants belched smoke into the air, and industrial establishments flushed their waste into rivers and streams that were the main source of water for the towns and villages on the banks. When studying the broad scope of environmental change in the nineteenth century, it is useful to consider these most visible changes against the background of longer-term shifts that were already well under way the moment industrialization began at the end of the eighteenth century.

LAND AND WATER

Population growth and the development of commercial agriculture made arable land increasingly valuable and encouraged the draining of fens, swamps, and salt marshes throughout Europe. Farmers developed techniques for irrigating their meadows to increase hay yields, and, in turn, these activities led to more ambitious projects: the construction of dams, millponds, and canals in areas where rivers had previously meandered according to the season, overflowing their banks and even changing their course occasionally. The construction of dams had an impact on fish and animal populations, leaving river villages that depended in part on fishing to watch their livelihoods disappear, while farmers had better access to markets on newly constructed waterways. Canal construction was an essential part of early industrial development in northern England before the era of railways, and a network of narrow waterways connected Yorkshire, Lancashire, and Birmingham with the larger metropolis of London.

One of the most ambitious projects of river engineering was undertaken by the German authorities after 1812. Their goal was to "rectify" the course of the Rhine River as it flowed from the Swiss Alps between France and the western German states to the Netherlands and the North Sea. By the time the project was completed in the 1870s, the Rhine had been shortened from 220 to 170 miles by dozens of cuts that also removed more than 2,000 islands from the waterway. For each cut, a wide channel had to be excavated along the new course of the river, a process that took years of digging; and eventually, the ends were cut out and the river flowed swiftly along its new banks. The environmental transformation of the region was significant. River marshes gave way to cultivated fields, and communities that had previously survived on fish and bird populations or from harvesting reeds from the Rhine's banks now devoted themselves to the cultivation of beets and potatoes. In the space of only a few generations, the landscape had been irrevocably changed, and the human populations that lived in the region were forced to adapt to new circumstances.

AIR AND THE URBAN ENVIRONMENT

The most notorious environmental change associated with industrialization was that of the air itself. Charles Dickens's description of the choking air and polluted water of "Coketown," the fictional city in *Hard Times* (1854), is deservedly well known:

> It was a town of red brick, or of brick that would have been red if the smoke and ashes had allowed it. . . . It was a town of machines and tall chimneys, out of which interminable serpents of smoke trailed themselves forever and ever, and never got uncoiled.

Wood-fired manufacturing and heating for homes had long spewed smoke across the skies, but the new concentration of industrial activity and the transition to coal made the air measurably worse. Early iron furnaces, for example, burned 250 bushels of charcoal for every ton of iron produced, and each bushel of charcoal was made by burning the equivalent of a pile of wood that measured 4 by 4 by 48 feet. Since a single furnace could produce 500 tons of iron a year, the demand for wood became enormous. In this way, the amount of particulate matter in the atmosphere was directly related to the disappearance of forested land.

In London, where even homes switched to coal early, smoke from factories, railroads, and domestic chimneys hung heavily over the city; and the last third of the century brought the most intense pollution in its history. Over all of England, air pollution took an enormous toll on health, contributing to the bronchitis and tuberculosis that accounted for 25 percent of British deaths. The coal-rich and industrial regions of North America (especially Pittsburgh) and central Europe also had concentrations of pollution; the Ruhr, in particular, had the most polluted air in Europe by the end of the century.

Toxic water, caused by industrial pollution and human waste, posed the second critical environmental hazard in urban areas. London and Paris led the way in building municipal sewage systems, though those emptied into the Thames and the Seine. Cholera, typhus, and tuberculosis were natural predators in areas without adequate sewage facilities or fresh water. The Rhine River, which flowed through central Europe's industrial heartland and intersected with the Ruhr, was thick with

VIEW OF LONDON WITH SAINT PAUL'S CATHEDRAL IN THE DISTANCE, BY WILLIAM HENRY CROME. Despite the smog-filled skies and intense pollution, many entrepreneurs and politicians celebrated the new prosperity of the Industrial Revolution. As W. P. Rend, a Chicago businessman, wrote in 1892, "Smoke is the incense burning on the altars of industry. It is beautiful to me. It shows that men are changing the merely potential forces of nature into articles of comfort for humanity."

detritus from coal mining, iron processing, and the chemical industry. In the late nineteenth century, spurred by several epidemics of cholera, major cities began to purify their water supplies—but conditions in the air, rivers, and land continued to worsen until at least the mid-twentieth century.

The Middle Classes

Novelists such as Charles Dickens and William Makepeace Thackeray in Britain, Victor Hugo and Honoré Balzac in France, and Theodor Fontane in Germany painted a sweeping portrait of middle-class society in the nineteenth century, with characters from all walks of life: journalists, courtesans, small-town mayors, mill owners, shopkeepers, aristocrats, farmers, laborers, and students. The plots explored the ways the older hierarchies of rank, status, and privilege gradually gave way to a new set of gradations based on wealth and social class. In this new world, money trumped birth, and social mobility was an accepted fact rather than something to be hidden. Works of literature need to be approached cautiously, but they nevertheless offer an extraordinary source of social historical detail and insight, and we can safely say that the rising visibility of the middle classes and their new political and social power—lamented by some writers but hailed by others—were central facts of nineteenth-century society.

Who were the middle classes? (Another common term for this social group, the *bourgeoisie*, originally meant "city dweller.") Its ranks included shopkeepers and their households; the families of lawyers, doctors, and other professionals; and well-off factory owners who might aspire to marry their daughters to titled aristocrats. At the lower end of the social scale, the middle classes included families of salaried clerks and office workers for whom white-collar employment offered hope of a rise in status.

Movement within the middle-class ranks was possible in the course of one or two generations. Very few, however, moved from the working class into the middle class. Most middle-class success stories began in the middle class itself, with the children of relatively well-off farmers, skilled artisans, or professionals. Upward mobility was almost impossible without education, and education was a rare, though not unattainable, luxury for working-class children. Careers open to talents (a goal achieved by the French Revolution) frequently meant opening jobs to middle-class young men who could pass exams. The examination system was an important path upward within government bureaucracies.

Equally difficult was the journey from the middle class to the aristocratic, landed society. In Britain, mobility of this sort was easier to achieve than on the Continent. The sons of wealthy, upper-middle-class families might actually move up, if they were sent to elite schools and universities and if they left the commercial or industrial world for a career in politics. William Gladstone, son of a Liverpool merchant, attended the exclusive educational preserves of Eton (a private boarding school) and Oxford University, married into an aristocratic family, and became the prime minister of England. Yet Gladstone was an exception to the rule, even in Britain—and most upward mobility was much less spectacular.

Nevertheless, the European middle class helped sustain itself with the belief that it was possible to get ahead by means of intelligence, pluck, and serious devotion to work. The middle class's claim to political power and cultural influence rested on arguments that they constituted a new and deserving social elite, superior to the common people yet sharply different from the older aristocracy, and the rightful custodians of the nation's future. Middle-class respectability stood for

The middle classes, representing professionals and white-collar workers, grow

Despite new possibilities of social mobility within social classes, it is still difficult to move between them

THE *LEGISLATIVE BELLY*, BY HONORÉ DAUMIER, 1834. Daumier's caricatures of prosperous middle-class politicians drew attention to the political reforms that allowed men of property—no matter their background—to replace the aristocratic elites that had dominated political life before the nineteenth century. His harsh depictions of these politicians' facial features may also have contained a reference to the Jewish origins of some politicians. The accession of Jews to citizenship in 1791 paved the way for political assimilation, and the presence of Jews in parliament would have been noteworthy to contemporaries.

financial independence, providing responsibly for one's family, and avoiding gambling and debt. It suggested merit and character as opposed to aristocratic privilege, and hard work as opposed to living off noble estates. Respectable middle-class gentlemen might be wealthy, but they should live modestly and soberly, avoiding conspicuous consumption, lavish dress, womanizing, and forms of dandyish behavior associated with the aristocracy. Of course, these were aspirations and codes, not social realities. They nonetheless remained key to the middle-class sense of self and understanding of the world.

PRIVATE LIFE, GENDER, AND MIDDLE-CLASS IDENTITY

Family and home played a central role in forming middle-class identity, with distinct roles for both men and women. According to advice manuals, poetry, and middle-class journals, wives and mothers were supposed to occupy a "separate sphere" of life, in which they lived in subordination to their spouses. Boys were educated in secondary schools, girls at home. This nineteenth-century conception of separate spheres needs to be understood in relation to the much longer-standing traditions of paternal authority, which were codified in law. Throughout Europe, laws subjected women to their husbands' authority. The Napoleonic Code, a model for other countries after 1815, classified women, children, and the mentally ill together as legally incompetent. In Britain, a woman transferred all her property rights to her husband on marriage. Although unmarried women did enjoy a degree of legal independence in France and Austria, laws generally assigned them to the "protection" of their fathers. Gender relations in the nineteenth century rested on this foundation of legal inequality. Yet the idea or doctrine of separate spheres was meant to underscore that men's and women's spheres complemented each other. Thus, for instance, middle-class writings were full of references to spiritual equality between men and women; and middle-class people wrote, proudly, of marriages in which the wife was a "companion" and "helpmate."

Members of the middle class articulated their values in opposition to aristocratic customs, on the one hand, and the lives of the common people, on the other. They argued, for instance, that middle-class marriages did not aim to found aristocratic dynasties and were not arranged to accumulate power and privilege; instead, they were to be based on mutual respect and division of responsibilities. A respectable middle-class woman should be free from the unrelenting toil that was the lot of a woman of the people. Called the "angel in the house" in Victorian Britain, a middle-class woman was responsible for the moral education of her children. This "cult of domesticity" was central to middle-class Victorian thinking about women.

As a housewife, a middle-class woman had the task of keeping the household functioning smoothly and harmoniously. Having at least one servant was a mark of middle-class status; in wealthier families, governesses and nannies cared for children, idealized views of motherhood notwithstanding. The middle classes included many gradations of wealth, from a well-housed banker with a governess and five servants to a village preacher with one. Moreover, the work of running and maintaining a home was enormous. Linens and clothes had to be made and mended. Only the wealthy had the luxury of running water, and servants had to carry and heat water for cooking, laundry, and cleaning. Heating with coal and lighting with kerosene involved hours of cleaning. If the "angel in the house" was a cultural ideal, it was partly because she had real economic value.

Outside the home, women had very few respectable options for earning a living. But nineteenth-century convictions about women's moral nature, combined as they were with middle-class aspirations to political leadership, encouraged middle-class wives to undertake voluntary charitable work or to campaign for social reform. In Britain and the United States, women played an important role in the struggle to abolish the slave trade and slavery in the British Empire and the American South. Many of these movements also drew on the energies of religious, especially Protestant, organizations, committed to the eradication of social evils and moral improvement. Throughout Europe, a wide range of movements to improve conditions for the poor in schools and hospitals, for temperance, against prostitution, or for legislation on factory hours were often run by women.

Middle-class women campaign for social and moral reform

Queen Victoria, who came to the British throne in 1837, labored to make her solemn public image reflect contemporary feminine virtues of moral probity and dutiful domesticity. She was a successful queen because she embodied the traits important to the middle class, whose triumph she seemed to epitomize and whose habits of mind we have come to call Victorian. Nineteenth-century ideas about gender had an impact on masculinity as well: soon after the revolutionary and Napoleonic periods, men began to dress in sober, practical clothing, and to see as effeminate or dandyish the wigs, ruffled collars, and tight breeches that had earlier been the pride of aristocratic masculinity.

"PASSIONLESSNESS": GENDER AND SEXUALITY

Victorian ideas about sexuality are among the most remarked-on features of nineteenth-century culture. They have become virtually synonymous with anxiety, prudishness, and ignorance. An English mother counseling her daughter about her wedding night is said to have told her to "lie back and think of the empire." Etiquette apparently required that piano legs be covered. Many of these anxieties and prohibitions, however, have been caricatured. More recently, historians have tried to disentangle the teachings or prescriptions of etiquette books and marriage manuals from the actual beliefs of men and women. One of the defining aspects of nineteenth-century ideas about men and women is the extent to which they rested on scientific arguments about nature. Codes of morality and methods of science combined to reinforce the certainty that specific characteristics were inherent to each sex. Men and women had different social roles, and those differences were rooted in their bodies. Women were unsuited for higher education because their brains were smaller or because their bodies were fragile. "Fifteen or 20 days of 28 (we may say nearly always) a woman is not only an invalid, but a wounded one. She ceaselessly suffers from love's eternal wound," wrote the well-known French author Jules Michelet about menstruation.

Differences in the social roles of men and women believed to be rooted in biology

Finally, scientists and doctors considered women's alleged moral superiority to be literally embodied in an absence of sexual feeling, or "passionlessness." Scientists and doctors considered male sexual desire as natural, if not admirable, an unruly force that had to be channeled. Many governments legalized and regulated prostitution (which included the compulsory examination of women for venereal disease)

Marriage, Sexuality, and the Facts of Life

In the nineteenth century, sexuality became the subject of much anxious debate, largely because it raised other issues: the roles of men and women, morality, and social respectability. Doctors threw themselves into the discussion, offering their expert opinions on the health (including the sexual lives) of the population; yet they did not dictate people's private lives. Nineteenth-century men and women responded to what they experienced as the facts of life more than to expert advice. The first document provides an example of medical knowledge and opinion in 1870. The second offers a glimpse of the daily realities of family life in 1830.

A French Doctor Denounces Contraception (1870)

One of the most powerful instincts nature has placed in the heart of man is that which has for its object the perpetuation of the human race. But this instinct, this inclination, so active, which attracts one sex towards the other, is liable to be perverted, to deviate from the path nature has laid out. From this arises a number of fatal aberrations which exercise a deplorable influence upon the individual, upon the family and upon society. . . .

We hear constantly that marriages are less fruitful, that the increase of population does not follow its former ratio. I believe that this is mainly attributable to genesiac frauds. It might naturally be supposed that these odious calculations of egotism, these shameful refinements of debauchery, are met with almost entirely in large cities, and among the luxurious classes, and that small towns and country places yet preserve that simplicity of manners attributed to primitive society, when the *pater familias* was proud of exhibiting his numerous offspring. Such, however, is not the case, and I shall show that those who have an unlimited confidence in the patriarchal habits of our country people are deeply in error. At the present time frauds are practiced by all classes. . . .

The laboring classes are generally satisfied with the practice of Onan [withdrawal]. . . . They are seldom familiar with the sheath invented by Dr. Condom, and bearing his name.

Among the wealthy, on the other hand, the use of this preservative is generally known. It favors frauds by rendering them easier; but it does not afford complete security. . . .

Case X.—This couple belongs to two respectable families of vintners. They are both pale, emaciated, downcast, sickly. . . .

They have been married for ten years; they first had two children, one immediately after the other, but in order to avoid an increase of family, they have had recourse to conjugal frauds. Being both very amorous, they have found this practice very convenient to satisfy their inclinations. They have employed it to such an extent, that up to a few months ago, when their health began to fail, the husband had intercourse with his wife habitually two and three times in twenty-four hours.

The following is the condition of the woman: She complains of continual pains in the lower part of the

precisely because it provided an outlet for male sexual desire. Doctors disagreed about female sexuality, but the British doctor William Acton stood among those who asserted that women functioned differently:

> I have taken pains to obtain and compare abundant evidence on this subject, and the result of my inquiries I may briefly epitomize as follows:—I should say that the majority of women (happily for society) are not very much troubled with sexual feeling of any kind. What men are habitually, women are only exceptionally.

abdomen and kidneys. These pains disturb the functions of the stomach and render her nervous. . . . By the touch we find a very intense heat, great sensibility to pressure, and all the signs of a chronic metritis [inflammation of the uterus]. The patient attributes positively her present state to the too frequent approaches of her husband.

The husband does not attempt to exculpate himself, as he also is in a state of extreme suffering. It is not in the genital organs, however, that we find his disorder, but in the whole general nervous system; his history will find its place in the part of this work relative to general disturbances. . . .

Source: Louis-François-Etienne Bergeret, *The Preventive Obstacle, or Conjugal Onanism*, trans. P. de Marmon (New York: 1870), pp. 3–4, 12, 20–22, 25, 56–57, 100–01, 111–13. Originally published in Paris in 1868.

Death in Childbirth (1830)

Mrs. Ann B. Pettigrew was taken in Labour after returning from a walk in the garden, at 7 o'clock in the evening of June 30, 1830. At 40 minutes after 11 o'clock, she was delivered of a daughter. A short time after, I was informed that the Placenta was not removed, and, at 10 minutes after 12 was asked into the room. I advanced to my dear wife, and kissing her, asked her how she was, to which she replied, I feel very badly. I went out of the room, and sent for Dr. Warren.

I then returned, and inquired if there was much hemorrhage, and was answered that there was. I then asked the midwife (Mrs. Brickhouse) if she ever used manual exertion to remove the placenta. She said she had more than fifty times. I then, fearing the consequences of hemorrhage, observed, Do, my dear sweet wife, permit Mrs. Brickhouse to remove it: To which she assented. . . . After the second unsuccessful attempt, I desired the midwife to desist. In these two efforts, my dear Nancy suffered exceedingly and frequently exclaimed: "O Mrs. Brickhouse you will kill me," and to me, "O I shall die, send for the Doctor." To which I replied, "I have sent."

After this, my feelings were so agonizing that I had to retire from the room and lay down, or fall. Shortly after which, the midwife came to me and, falling upon her knees, prayed most fervently to God and to me to forgive her for saying that she could do what she could not. . . .

The placenta did not come away, and the hemorrhage continued with unabated violence until five o'clock in the morning, when the dear woman breathed her last 20 minutes before the Doctor arrived.

So agonizing a scene as that from one o'clock, I have no words to describe. O My God, My God! have mercy on me. I am undone forever. . . .

Source: Cited in Erna Olafson Hellerstein, Leslie Parker Hume, and Karen M. Offen, eds., *Victorian Women: A Documentary Account of Women's Lives in Nineteenth-Century England, France, and the United States* (Stanford, CA: 1981), pp. 193–94, 219–20.

Questions for Analysis

1. The French doctor states that the impulse to have sexual relations is "one of the most powerful instincts" given to humans by nature, while simultaneously claiming that this natural instinct is "liable to be perverted." What does this reveal about his attitude toward "nature"?

2. What does he mean by "genesiac frauds"? Who is being deceived by this fraud? What consequences for individuals and for society as a whole does the doctor fear from this deception?

3. What does the story of Mrs. Pettigrew's death reveal about the dangers of childbirth and the state of obstetric medicine in the nineteenth century?

Like other nineteenth-century men and women, Acton also believed that more-open expressions of sexuality were disreputable, and also that working-class women were less "feminine."

Convictions such as these reveal a great deal about Victorian science and medicine, but they did not necessarily dictate people's intimate lives. As far as sexuality was concerned, the absence of any reliable contraception mattered more in people's experiences and feelings than sociologists' or doctors' opinions. Abstinence and withdrawal were the only common techniques for preventing pregnancy, but their effectiveness was limited, since until the 1880s, doctors believed that a woman was most fertile during and around her menstrual period. Midwives and prostitutes knew of other forms of contraception and abortifacients (all of them dangerous and ineffective), and surely some middle-class women did as well, but such information was not respectable middle-class fare. In concrete terms, then, sexual intercourse was directly related to the very real dangers of frequent pregnancies. In England, 1 in 100 childbirths ended in the death of the mother; at a time when a woman might become pregnant eight or nine times in her life, this was a sobering prospect. Those dangers varied with social class, but even among wealthy and better-cared-for women, they took a real toll. It is not surprising that middle-class women's diaries and letters are full of their anticipations of childbirth, both joyful and anxious. Queen Victoria, who bore nine children, declared that childbirth was the "shadow side" of marriage—and she was a pioneer in using anesthesia!

WORKING-CLASS LIFE

Like the middle class, the working class was divided into various subgroups and categories, determined in this case by skill, wage, gender, and workplace. Workers' experiences varied, depending on where they worked, where they lived, and, above all, how much they earned. A skilled textile worker lived a life far different from that of a ditch digger, with the former able to afford the food, shelter, and clothing necessary for a decent existence, and the latter barely able to scrape by.

Some movement from the ranks of the unskilled to the skilled was possible, if children were provided, or provided themselves, with at least a rudimentary education. Yet education was considered by many parents a luxury, especially because children could be put to work at an early age to supplement the family's meager earnings. Downward mobility from skilled to unskilled was also possible, as technological change—the introduction of the power loom, for example—drove highly paid workers into the ranks of the unskilled and destitute.

Working-class housing was unhealthy and unregulated. In older cities, single-family dwellings were broken up into apartments, often with no more than one room per family. In new manufacturing centers, rows of tiny houses, located close to smoking factories, were built back to back, thereby eliminating garden spaces and any cross ventilation. Crowding was commonplace.

Household routines, demanding in the middle classes, were grinding for the poor. The family remained a survival network, in which everyone played a crucial role. In addition to working for wages, wives were expected to house, feed, and clothe the family on the small amounts of money earned by the various family members; a "good" wife was able to make ends meet even in bad times. Working women's daily lives involved constant rounds of carrying and boiling water, cleaning, cooking, and doing laundry in crowded, unventilated, and poorly lit one- and two-room apartments. Families could not rely on their own gardens to help supply them with food, so city markets catered to their needs for cheap foods. But this fare was regularly stale, nearly rotten,

APARTMENT LIVING IN PARIS. This print shows that on the Continent, rich and poor often lived in the same buildings—the rich on the lower floors and the poor on the top. This sort of residential mixing was less common in Britain.

or dangerously adulterated: formaldehyde was added to milk to prevent spoilage, pounded rice was mixed into sugar, and fine, brown earth was introduced into cocoa.

WORKING WOMEN IN THE INDUSTRIAL LANDSCAPE Few figures raised more public anxiety and outcry in the nineteenth century than the working woman. Contemporaries worried out loud about the "promiscuous mixing of the sexes" in crowded and humid workshops. Nineteenth-century writers, starting in England and France, chronicled what they considered to be the economic and moral horrors of female labor: unattended children running in the streets, small children caught in accidents at the mills or the mines, pregnant women hauling coal, or women laboring alongside men in shops.

Women's work was not new, but industrialization made it more visible. Both before and after the Industrial Revolution, labor was divided by gender, but as employers implemented new manufacturing processes, ideas about which jobs were appropriate for women shifted. In traditional textile production, for example, women spun and men operated the looms. In industrial textile factories, on the other hand, employers preferred women and children because they were considered more docile and less likely to make trouble and because it was believed that their smaller hands were better suited to the intricate job of tying threads on the power looms. Manufacturers sought to recruit women mill hands from neighboring villages, paying good wages compared with other jobs open to women. Most began working at the age of ten or eleven, and when they had children, they put their children out to a wet nurse, brought them to the mills, or continued to work by doing piecework at home. This transformation of the gendered structure of work caused intense anxiety in the first half of the nineteenth century, and it is one of the reasons that the emerging labor movement began to include calls for excluding women from the workplace in its programs.

Employers prefer women and children in textile factories

Most women did not work in factories, however, but continued to labor at home or in small workshops—"sweatshops," as they came to be called—for notoriously low wages that paid not by the hour but by the piece for each shirt stitched or each matchbox glued. The greatest number of unmarried working-class women worked less visibly in domestic service, a job that earned low wages and, judging by the testimony of many women, coercive sexual relationships with male employers or their sons. Domestic service, however, provided room and board. In a time when a single woman simply could not survive on her own wages, a young woman who had just arrived in the city had few choices: marriage, which was unlikely to happen right away; renting a room in a boardinghouse, many of which were often centers of prostitution; domestic service; or living with someone. How women balanced the demands for money and the time for household work varied with the number and age of their children. Mothers were actually more likely to work when their children were very small, because there were more mouths to feed and the children were not yet old enough to earn wages.

Poverty, the absence of privacy, and the particular vulnerabilities of working-class women made working-class sexuality very different from its middle-class counterpart. Illegitimacy rose dramatically between 1750 and 1850. In Frankfurt, Germany, for example, where the illegitimacy rate, which had been a mere 2 percent in the early 1700s, reached 25 percent in 1850. In Bordeaux, France, in 1840, one-third of the recorded births were illegitimate. Reasons for this increase are difficult to establish. Improved mobility and urbanization meant weaker family ties, more opportunities

CAPITAL AND LABOR. In its earliest years, the British magazine *Punch*, though primarily a humorous weekly, manifested a strong social conscience. This 1843 cartoon shows capitalists enjoying the rewards of their investments while hungry workers shiver in the cold. › **How would a defender of the new industrial order respond to this cartoon?**

for young men and women to meet without family supervision, and greater vulnerabilities for young women especially. Premarital sex was an accepted practice in preindustrial villages, but because of the social controls that dominated village life, it was almost always followed by marriage. These controls were weaker in the far more anonymous setting of a factory town or commercial city. The economic uncertainties of the early industrial age meant that a young workman's promise of marriage, based on his expectation of a job, might frequently be difficult to fulfill. Economic vulnerability drove many single women into temporary relationships that produced children and a continuing cycle of poverty and abandonment. Historians have shown, however, that in the city as in the countryside, many of these temporary relationships became enduring ones, and the parents of illegitimate children would marry later. Again, nineteenth-century writers dramatized what they considered the disreputable sexuality of the "dangerous classes" in the cities. Some of them attributed illegitimacy, prostitution, and so on, to the moral weakness of working-class people, others to the systematic changes wrought by industrialization. Both sides, however, overstated the collapse of the family and the destruction of traditional morality. Working-class families transmitted expectations about gender roles and sexual behavior: girls should expect to work, daughters were responsible for caring for their younger siblings as well as for earning wages, sexuality was a fact of life, midwives could help desperate pregnant girls going into labor (or even with information about birth control or ways to terminate a pregnancy), marriage was an avenue to respectability, and so on. The gulf that separated these expectations and codes from those of middle-class women was one of the most important factors in the development of nineteenth-century class identity.

A LIFE APART: "CLASS CONSCIOUSNESS"

The new demands of life in an industrial economy created common experiences and difficulties. The factory system denied skilled workers the pride in craft they had previously enjoyed. Stripped of the protections of guilds and apprenticeships and prevented from organizing by legislation in France, Germany, and Britain in the first half of the nineteenth century, workers felt vulnerable in the face of their socially and politically powerful employers. Workdays were long, usually twelve to fourteen hours. Textile mills were unventilated, and minute particles of lint lodged in the workers' lungs. Machines were unfenced and posed dangers to child workers. British physicians cataloged the toll that long hours tending machines took on children, including spinal curvature and bone malformations. Children were also employed in large numbers in mines—over 50,000 worked in British mines in 1841.

Factories also imposed new routines and disciplines. Artisans in earlier times also worked long hours for little pay, but they set their own schedules and controlled the pace of work, moving from their home workshops to their small garden plots as they wished. In a factory, all hands learned the discipline of the clock. To increase production, the factory system encouraged the breaking down of the manufacturing process into specialized steps, each with its own time. Workers began to see machinery itself as the tyrant that changed their lives and bound them to industrial slavery.

Yet the defining feature of working-class life was vulnerability—to unemployment, sickness, accidents in dangerous jobs, family problems, and spikes in the prices of food. Seasonal unemployment, high in almost all trades, made it impossible to collect regular wages. Markets for manufactured goods were small and unstable, producing cyclical economic depressions; when those came, thousands of workers found themselves laid off with no system of unemployment insurance to sustain them. The early decades of industrialization were also marked by several severe agricultural depressions and economic crises. During the crisis years of the 1840s, half the working population of Britain's industrial cities was unemployed. In 1840, some 85,000 went on relief in Paris. Families survived by working several small jobs, pawning their possessions, and getting credit from local wineshops and grocery stores. The chronic insecurity of working-class life helped fuel the creation of workers' self-help societies, fraternal associations, and early socialist organizations, which meant that economic crises could have explosive consequences (see Chapter 21).

By midcentury, various experiences were beginning to make working people conscious of their differences from and in opposition to the middle classes. Changes in the workplace were part of the picture—whether the introduction of machines and factory labor, demands for faster production, subcontracting to cheap labor, or the loss of guild protections. The social segregation of the rapidly expanding nineteenth-century cities also contributed to the sense that working people lived a life apart. Class differences seemed embedded in a very wide array of everyday experiences and beliefs: work, private life, expectations for children, the roles of men and women, and definitions of respectability. Over the course of the nineteenth century, all of these different experiences gave concrete, specific meaning to the word *class*.

Insecurities and difficulties of working-class life lead to growing sense of class identity

Conclusion

Why did the Industrial Revolution occur at this moment in human history? Why did it begin in Europe? Why did it not occur in other regions of the world with large populations and advanced technologies, such as China or India? These fundamental questions remain the subject of serious debate among historians. One argument focuses on the fact that the mechanization of industry occurred first in northern Europe, and seeks to explain the Industrial Revolution's origins in terms of this region's vibrant towns, its well-developed commercial markets, and the presence of a prosperous land-owning elite that had few prejudices against entrepreneurial activity. These historians have suggested that industrialization is best understood as a process rooted in European culture and history.

More recently, however, historians with a more global approach have argued that it may be incorrect to assert that industrialization developed as it did because of the advantages enjoyed by a central European core. Instead, they have explored the possibility that the world's economies constituted a larger interlocking system that had no definitive center until *after* the takeoff of European industrialization. Before that period, when it came to agricultural practices, ecological constraints, population densities, urbanization, and technological development, *many* global regions were not so different from the Western European model. So, in the end, Europe

AFTER YOU READ THIS CHAPTER ⌄

CHRONOLOGY

1780s	Industrialization begins in Britain
1825	First railroad in Britain
1830s	Industrialization begins in France and Belgium
1845–1849	Irish potato famine
1850s	Industrialization begins in Prussia and German states of central Europe
1861	Russian tsar emancipates the serfs

REVIEWING THE OBJECTIVES

❯ The Industrial Revolution in Europe began in northern England. What circumstances made this process of economic development begin there?

❯ Certain industries were particularly suitable for the kinds of technological developments that encouraged industrialization. What were these industries? Where did they exist in Europe?

❯ Industrial development changed the nature of work and production in significant ways. What were these changes? How did they change the relations between laborers and their employers, or between local producers and wider markets?

❯ Industrialization had social effects far beyond the factories. What larger changes in European society were associated with the Industrial Revolution?

❯ A large and diverse group of middle-class people emerged in Europe as a result of the social changes brought on by industrialization. What kinds of people qualified as middle class during the nineteenth century? How were they different from other social groups?

was able to move more quickly toward industrial production because its economies were better positioned to mobilize the resources available to them on the periphery of their trading sphere. The access European traders enjoyed to agricultural products from slave-owning societies in the Americas helped them escape the ecological constraints imposed by their own intensely farmed lands, making the move to an industrial economy possible. Contingent factors, such as patterns of disease and epidemic or the location of coal fields, may have also played a role.

There is less debate about the consequences of the Industrial Revolution within Europe. New forms of industrial production created a new economy and changed the nature of work for both men and women. Industrialization changed the landscape of Europe as well as the structures of families and the private lives of people in both the cities and the countryside. Industrialization created new forms of wealth along with new kinds of poverty, fostering an acute awareness of the disparity between social groups. In the eighteenth century, that disparity would have been described in terms of birth, rank, or privilege. In the nineteenth century, it was increasingly seen in terms of class. Both champions and critics of the new industrial order spoke of a "class society." The identities associated with class were formed in the crowded working-class districts of the new cities, in experiences of work, and in the new conditions of respectability that determined life in middle-class homes. These new identities would be sharpened in the political events to which we now turn.

Go to **INQUIZITIVE** to see what you've learned—and learn what you've missed—with personalized feedback along the way.

PEOPLE, IDEAS, AND EVENTS IN CONTEXT

❯ Why was **ENCLOSURE** an important factor in the Industrial Revolution?

❯ What was the **SPINNING JENNY**? What was the **COTTON GIN**? What effect did these machines have on industrial development?

❯ What was the significance of European **EMPIRES** and overseas expansion for industrialization?

❯ How did industrialization affect **POPULATION GROWTH** in Europe? What effects did it have on the **PEASANTRY** and on **URBAN POPULATIONS**?

❯ What environmental changes were associated with the development of commercial agriculture, the use of new sources of fuel, and the construction of large and concentrated centers of industrial manufacture?

❯ What was the **IRISH POTATO FAMINE**? How was it related to the economic developments of nineteenth-century Europe? What might **THOMAS MALTHUS** have thought about the potato famine?

THINKING ABOUT CONNECTIONS

❯ From modifications in the land to transformations of the built environment and the growth of cities, industrialization produced fundamental changes in the physical spaces occupied by society. How might these changes have affected people's conceptions of the spaces that provided the background to their lives and labor?

❯ Awareness that these changes made the present radically different from the recent past gave many people the sense that time was hurtling ever faster into a future with outlines that could only dimly be perceived. How might people have perceived their own lives against what they knew of their parents' generation or what they anticipated for their children? How might the perception of time itself have shifted?

❯ In the early twenty-first century, innovations in information technology are creating a similar sense of accelerated change and diminishing distances in a more interconnected globe. What are the similarities between our own period and the period between the 1780s and 1830s, when large numbers of people first began to think about the power of technology to change the way society was organized and to regard history as a head-long rush into the future? What are the differences?

20

The Age of Ideologies:

EUROPE IN THE AFTERMATH OF REVOLUTION, 1815–1848

BEFORE YOU READ THIS CHAPTER >

FOLLOWING NAPOLEON'S DEFEAT at Waterloo and exile on the rocky island of St. Helena in the South Atlantic in 1815, his European opponents hoped the age of revolution had ended. The Austrian foreign minister, **Klemens von Metternich**, perhaps the most influential conservative diplomat of the early nineteenth century, called revolution a "sickness," "plague," and "cancer," and set out to inoculate Europe against any outbreak. In his view, revolution produced war, and calls for national self-determination and representative government only created disorder. Peace depended on avoiding political turmoil and reinforcing the power of conservative monarchies in all corners of Europe. This project succeeded only in part.

The decades between 1815 and 1848 saw the legitimacy of these monarchies challenged on multiple fronts, and conservatives found the developments of the eighteenth century impossible to reverse. The expansion of an informed public, begun in the Enlightenment, continued. The word *citizen* (and the liberal political ideas contained within it) was controversial in the aftermath of the French Revolution, but conservatives found it difficult to banish this term from political debates. Liberalism's fundamental principles—equality before the law, freedom of expression, and the consent of the governed—were a potent threat to Europe's dynastic rulers, especially when coupled with the emotions stirred up by popular nationalism. Liberals believed that legitimate sovereignty could only be

❯ The conservative regimes that defeated Napoleon in 1815 set out to reverse the changes in Europe resulting from the French Revolution. They aimed for a balance of forces between European powers so that no single ruler could dominate Europe.

❯ Conservative rulers in Europe remained on the defensive as liberalism, republicanism, and nationalism continued to fuel resistance to the conservative order. Socialism provided Europe's laborers with a new vocabulary to express their unhappiness with industrialization.

❯ The conservative political reaction after 1815 found its cultural counterpart in Romanticism. This movement rejected the Enlightenment's rationalism and instead emphasized the power of nature and human emotions.

CORE OBJECTIVES

❯ **UNDERSTAND** the political goals of European leaders who met at the Congress of Vienna in 1815, and the challenges to the Concert of Europe in the decades between 1815 and 1848.

❯ **TRACE** the evolution of the debate about slavery after the French Revolution, and **UNDERSTAND** the reasons why an abolitionist movement developed even as slavery persisted in the United States, Latin America, and Cuba.

❯ **IDENTIFY** the core principles of conservatism, liberalism, republicanism, and socialism in Europe after 1815.

❯ **DEFINE** *nationalism* and understand how conservatives, liberals, republicans, and socialists were forced to grapple with this powerful political idea.

❯ **EXPLAIN** the ideas contained in the cultural movement known as Romanticism and its relationship to the Enlightenment.

(1773-1859) Austrian foreign minister whose primary goals were to bolster the legitimacy of monarchies and, after the defeat of Napoleon, to prevent another large-scale war in Europe.

exercised by citizens acting collectively as a nation, though their definitions for citizenship were often exclusive. Even the principle of national sovereignty was incompatible with the convictions of conservative monarchs, who believed their authority came not from the people but from God. Popular nationalism was especially threatening to the Austrian Habsburg Empire, which faced separate nationalist movements from Italians, Germans, Poles, Hungarians, Czechs, and others.

After Napoleon's downfall, opposition to the conservative order in Europe was infused with more radical political ideologies. Some liberals focused on limiting royal authority through constitutional law. Others believed that voting was a privilege that should be extended only to wealthy property owners. More radical were republicans who called for universal (male) suffrage and an end to monarchy altogether. Socialists went even further and argued that political reform was not enough to free the people from want and exploitation. To them, justice was possible only with a radical reordering of society that redistributed property equitably. Between 1815 and 1848, these more radical ideas circulated widely and occupied the attention of conservative monarchs (and their police spies) throughout Europe.

In culture as well as in politics, imagination and a sense of possibility were among the defining characteristics of the first half of the century. In painting and literature, romanticism broke from the formality of eighteenth-century art. Where the Enlightenment had championed reason, Romantics prized subjectivity, feeling, and spontaneity. The Romantics had no single political creed; some were revolutionaries and others were fervent traditionalists who looked to the past, religion, or history for inspiration. Their sensibility, however, infused politics and culture, and their collective search for new means of expression sent nineteenth-century art off in a new direction.

The Search for Order in Europe, 1815–1830

Near the end of 1814, the European powers met at the Congress of Vienna to settle pressing questions about the post-Napoleonic political order. The lavish celebrations of Louis XVIII's return to the throne in France could not hide the fact that twenty years of war, revolution, and political experimentation had changed Europe in fundamental ways. The task of the Congress of Vienna was to reinforce Europe's monarchical regimes against the powerful social and political forces that had been unleashed by the French Revolution and the Napoleonic Wars that followed.

THE CONGRESS OF VIENNA AND THE RESTORATION

The Russian tsar Alexander I (r. 1801–1825) and the Austrian diplomat Klemens von Metternich (1773–1859) dominated the Congress of Vienna. After Napoleon's fall, Russia became the most powerful state on the European continent. Alexander I presented himself as the "liberator" of Europe, and many feared that he would substitute an all-powerful Russia for an all-powerful France. The French were represented by prince Charles Maurice de Talleyrand (1754–1838), a canny

THE CONGRESS OF VIENNA. Note how the borders of European nations were established after the final defeat of Napoleon in 1815, and compare these boundaries with those formed in 1713 after the Peace of Utrecht (page 532). › What major changes had occurred in central Europe during the intervening years? › Which territorial powers played an active role in determining the balance of power at the Congress of Vienna? › What social or political developments might disrupt this balance?

survivor who had been a bishop and a revolutionary before becoming Napoleon's foreign minister.

Metternich's central concerns at the Congress of Vienna were to check Russian expansionism and prevent political change in Europe. He favored treating the defeated French with moderation, but he remained an archconservative who readily resorted to harsh repressive tactics, including secret police and spying. The peace he crafted helped prevent a major European war until 1914.

Metternich's chief goals at the Congress of Vienna

The Congress sought to restore order by insisting that Europe's dynastic rulers were the only legitimate political authorities. It recognized Louis XVIII as the sovereign of France and confirmed the restoration of Bourbon rulers in Spain and the Two Sicilies. Other European monarchs had no interest in undermining the French Restoration. After Napoleon's Hundred Days, the allies imposed an indemnity of 700 million francs and an occupying army for five years. France's borders remained the same as in 1789—less than the revolution's "greater France" but not so punitive as they might have been.

The guiding principle of the peace was the balance of power, according to which no country should be powerful enough to destabilize international relations. Metternich's immediate goal, therefore, was to build a barrier against renewed French expansion. The Dutch Republic, conquered by the French in 1795, was restored as the kingdom of the Netherlands, securing France's northern border. The Congress also ceded the left bank of the Rhine to Prussia, and Austria expanded into northern Italy. Britain received former Dutch and French territories in South Africa and South America, as well as the island of Ceylon (Sri Lanka).

In central Europe, the allied powers reorganized the German states, reducing them from more than 300 to 39 in number. Prussia and Habsburg Austria joined these German states in a loosely structured German Confederation, with Austria careful to reserve the presidency of this new body as a check against Prussia. Bavaria, Württemberg, and Saxony remained independent kingdoms.

Poland was also a major issue because Napoleon had established a client Polish state, the Duchy of Warsaw, in 1807. The Congress's 1815 compromise allowed for a nominally independent but much reduced kingdom of Poland that nevertheless had its own parliament (or *diet*), a relatively broad electorate, a constitution, and basic liberties of speech and the press. The Russian tsar, Alexander I, nevertheless retained control, and appointed his younger brother Constantine as viceroy and commander of the Polish army. The same agreement gave large slices of formerly Polish territory to Austria and Prussia. Constantine's autocratic rule soon alienated both the Polish officer corps and the Polish Parliament.

For the continent as a whole, the Congress of Vienna called for a balance of powers. Britain, Austria, Prussia, and Russia pledged to cooperate, and France joined this conservative alliance in 1818, which became known as the **Concert of Europe**. Alexander I pushed for what he called a Holy Alliance, dedicated to justice, Christian charity, and peace. The British foreign minister remained skeptical, calling the Holy Alliance "a piece of sublime mysticism and nonsense," but agreed that the European powers should defend a concept of authority founded on the principle of dynastic kingship. A ruler was legitimate if his power was guaranteed not only by claims of divine right but also by international treaties and the support of his recognized peers. The Concert of Europe's opposition to liberal notions of political representation and national self-determination could not have been clearer. Metternich and his fellow diplomats at Vienna dedicated their lives to ensuring that such innovations would never succeed. Their efforts ultimately failed, but the Congress's emphasis on a balance of powers was one reason that Europe had no continent-wide war between Napoleon's defeat and the outbreak of the First World War in 1914.

Balance of power, a key principle at the Congress of Vienna, holds that no single country should be powerful enough to threaten peace

Concert of Europe Series of diplomatic agreements, designed primarily by Austrian minister Klemens von Metternich, to maintain a balance of power on the Continent and to prevent destabilizing social and political change.

REVOLT AGAINST THE CONCERT OF EUROPE

Much of the resistance to the Restoration and the Concert of Europe was both clandestine and nationalist. On the Italian peninsula, the **Carbonari** (the name comes from the charcoal they used to blacken their faces) opposed the government in Vienna. Their political views varied: some called for constitutions and representative government, others praised Bonaparte. The Carbonari's influence spread through southern Europe and France in the 1820s, with members meeting in secret. Veterans of Napoleon's armies and military officers were prominent in their ranks.

In Naples and Piedmont, and in Spain and the Spanish Empire, opposition to Metternich's Concert of Europe turned into revolts when monarchs placed in power by the Congress of Vienna betrayed their promises of reform. Metternich responded by spurring Austria, Prussia, and Russia to take a strong stand against revolution. In the Troppau Protocol (1820), the conservative regimes pledged to assist one another in suppressing revolt. Austria dealt firmly with the Italian revolts; and France sent 200,000 troops to the Iberian Peninsula in 1823, crushing the Spanish revolutionaries and restoring King Ferdinand's authority.

> **Carbonari** An underground organization that opposed the Concert of Europe's restoration of monarchies.

REVOLUTION IN LATIN AMERICA

King Ferdinand's empire in Latin America, however, would not be restored. Napoleon's conquest of Spain (1807) had shaken Spain's once vast Atlantic empire. Local elites in the colonies resented Spanish imperial control and pushed for independence from the weakened monarchy. Río de la Plata (now Argentina) was the first to declare independence in 1816. Soon after, a monarchist general from Río de la Plata, José de San Martín (1778–1850), led an expedition to liberate Chile and Peru. At the same time, Simón Bolívar (1783–1830), a republican leader, sparked a series of uprisings from Venezuela to Bolivia. Bolívar envisioned mobilizing free people of color and slaves (who made up roughly a quarter of those fighting the Spanish) as well as Indians to fight against Spanish rule. Bolívar's goal was to create a Pan-American republic on the continent, along the lines of the United States. These political revolts unleashed violent social conflicts and civil war. Elite landowners who wanted only to free themselves from Spain opposed groups who wanted land reform and an end to slavery. In the end, the radical movements were suppressed, and the newly independent Latin American nations were dominated by an alliance of conservative landowners and military officers.

Britain and the newly ambitious United States prevented the European powers from intervening in the Latin American revolutions. In 1823, the U.S. president James Monroe issued the Monroe Doctrine, declaring that the United States would regard European meddling in the Americas as a hostile act. Without British support, however, the Monroe Doctrine was unenforceable. Britain saw the new South American republics as potential trading partners and used its navy to prevent Spain from intervening. By the 1820s, the Spanish Empire had vanished, ending an age that had begun in 1492. Brazil's independence in 1822 similarly ended the era of Portuguese colonialism in South America. Together, these revolutions demonstrated the circular relationships that bound the Atlantic world together. Latin American revolutionaries, encouraged by political movements associated with the French Revolution and Napoleon, in turn inspired nationalists in Europe who sought to overthrow Metternich's conservative Concert of Europe.

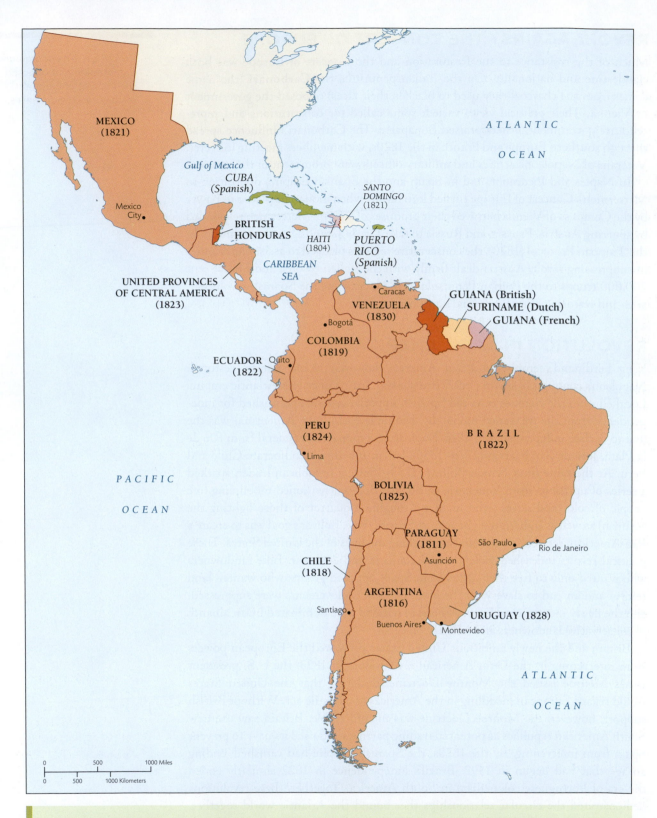

MEXICO
(1821)

Mexico City •

Gulf of Mexico

CUBA
(Spanish)

SANTO
DOMINGO
(1821)

HAITI
(1804)

PUERTO
RICO
(Spanish)

BRITISH
HONDURAS

*CARIBBEAN
SEA*

UNITED PROVINCES
OF CENTRAL AMERICA
(1823)

Caracas •

VENEZUELA
(1830)

GUIANA (British)
SURINAME (Dutch)
GUIANA (French)

Bogotá •

COLOMBIA
(1819)

ECUADOR
(1822)

Quito •

PERU
(1824)

Lima •

B R A Z I L
(1822)

*PACIFIC

OCEAN*

BOLIVIA
(1825)

PARAGUAY
(1811)

São Paulo •

Rio de Janeiro •

Asunción •

CHILE
(1818)

ARGENTINA
(1816)

Santiago •

Buenos Aires •

Montevideo •

URUGUAY (1828)

*ATLANTIC

OCEAN*

*ATLANTIC

OCEAN*

0   500   1000 Miles
0   500   1000 Kilometers

NEW NATIONS OF LATIN AMERICA. After Haiti became the second independent nation in the
Western Hemisphere, many areas of Central and South America also broke away from colonial rule.
› When did the nations of Latin America gain their independence? › What major events in Europe
contributed to this move toward independence? › What is the relationship between the events in Europe
and the Atlantic revolutions that occurred in the late eighteenth century?

RUSSIA: THE DECEMBRISTS

Revolt also broke out within conservative Russia. In 1825, Tsar Alexander I died, and a group of army officers known as the **Decembrists** led an uprising to push the pace of reform. Many were veterans of the Napoleonic Wars, and they feared that Russia could not be the "liberator of Europe" without changes in its conservative social and political order. Serfdom, for example, contradicted the promise of liberation; so did the tsar's monopoly on power and the lack of legal political opposition.

The Decembrists failed to gain support from rank-and-file soldiers, however, and without that support their revolt failed. The new tsar, Nicholas I (r. 1825–1855), had hundreds of mutinous soldiers interrogated, sentenced many to hard labor and exile in Siberia, and condemned their five primary leaders—all young and leading members of the aristocratic elite—to death. Fearing they would be seen as martyrs, Nicholas had them hanged at dawn behind the walls of a fortress in St. Petersburg and buried in secret graves.

Nicholas went on to rule in the manner of his predecessor, becoming Europe's most uncompromising conservative. Still, Russia was not immune to change. Bureaucracy became more centralized, more efficient, and less dependent on the nobility. Accomplishing this task required making Russia's complex legal system more systematic and uniform. He oversaw the publication of a new code of law, which recategorized every law passed since 1648 and codified them into forty-eight volumes, a measure comparable to Napoleon's Civil Code of 1804. Landowners responded to higher demand for Russian grain by reorganizing their estates to increase productivity, and the state began to build railroads to transport the grain to Western markets. Meanwhile, opponents of the regime, such as the writer Alexander Herzen, carried on the Decembrists' unresolved political legacy.

SOUTHEASTERN EUROPE: GREECE AND SERBIA

When the Greeks and Serbians revolted against the once powerful Ottoman Empire, the conservative European powers showed themselves to be more tolerant of rebellion. Serbs in the Balkans rebelled against the Ottomans as early as 1804 and, with the help of the Russians, succeeded in establishing hereditary rule by a Serbian prince in 1817. This Serbian quasi state persisted as an Orthodox Christian principality with a significant minority Muslim population, until finally achieving formal independence from the Ottoman Empire in 1878.

The Serb revolt and the subsequent Greek war for independence (1821–1827) were part of a new pattern in Ottoman history. Eighteenth-century revolts against Ottoman control in these regions usually had not sought outright separation and had generally been resolved within the imperial system by redistributing tax burdens or instituting legal reforms. After 1800, however, European powers were more likely to get involved, and the result was the establishment of new independent states and a weakening of Ottoman power. The French and the British hoped to expand their commercial networks in the eastern Mediterranean, while the Russian state sought greater influence over the Ottoman Empire's Balkan territories.

Greek nationalists eventually gained support from the British government, and sympathy for the Greeks was widespread in Europe. Christians in Europe cast the rebellion as part of an ongoing struggle between Christianity and Islam, and

Decembrists Nineteenth-century Russian army officers who were influenced by events in France and formed secret societies that espoused liberal governance.

◄ *Rather than seeking reform within the Ottoman Empire, discontented ethnic minorities increasingly push for independence* secular observers viewed the conflict as a contest between an ancient pre-Christian European heritage and the Ottoman Empire. Celebrating the Greeks went hand in hand with demonizing the Ottomans, despite the fact that the Ottoman Empire's imperial system had frequently proved more adaptable than European governments in preserving peace among diverse peoples and religions over many centuries of rule.

In the end, Greek independence depended on great-power politics, as it did in Serbia. In 1827, British, French, and Russian troops sided with the Greeks against the Ottomans, who were forced to concede and grant Greek independence. The new nations of Serbia and Greece were small and fragile. Only 800,000 Greeks actually lived in the new Greek state, and Serbia could not survive without Russian protection. Moreover, neither of the new nations broke their close links with the Ottomans, as Greek and Serbian merchants, bankers, and administrators were still very present in the Ottoman Empire. The region remained a borderland of Europe, where peoples alternated between tolerant coexistence and bitter conflict.

Leaders of independence movements were likely to succeed if they could take advantage of a conflict between great powers (as in Latin America), or if their movements aligned with Europe's competition with the Ottoman Empire (as in Greece and Serbia). Meanwhile, Metternich's ability to prevent the spread of nationalism and liberalism—ideologies associated with the French Revolution—increasingly depended on repressive political regimes that did not tolerate open expressions of dissent. Containing these movements for political and social change eventually became impossible.

Greece and Serbia win independence mostly as a result of balance-of-power politics

Citizenship and Sovereignty, 1830–1848

In the aftermath of the French Revolution, debates about citizenship, sovereignty, and social inequality remained divisive in many parts of Europe. In France, Belgium, and Poland, political movements challenging the post-Napoleonic settlement led to open revolt in the years 1830–1832, and a similar threat developed in the 1840s. During these same decades, conflicts over voting rights and the treatment of the poor threatened to lead to a similar crisis in Britain. Government leaders in Britain prevented open rebellion by implementing political reform, whereas the protest movements of the 1830s and 1840s on the Continent were followed by a wave of revolutions that swept across Europe in 1848 (see Chapter 21).

THE 1830 REVOLUTION IN FRANCE

The first decisive blow against the Concert of Europe came in 1830 in France. In 1815, the Congress of Vienna returned a Bourbon monarch to the throne, Louis XVIII. Louis claimed absolute power, but in the name of reconciliation he granted a "charter" and made some concessions: an end to the legal privileges accorded to the nobility, allowing non-nobles to hold office, and a two-chamber parliament. Property requirements excluded most citizens from voting, and Louis's narrow base of support, combined with the sting of military defeat, nostalgia for a glorious Napoleonic past, and memories of the revolution undermined the Restoration in France.

LIBERTY LEADING THE PEOPLE, BY EUGÈNE DELACROIX. This painting is among the best-known images of the revolutions of 1830. The allegorical female figure of liberty leads representatives of the united people: a middle-class man (identified by his top hat), a worker, and a boy of the streets wielding a pistol. This image of revolutionary unity is romanticized since neither middle-class people nor children fought on the barricades.
› What made this mix of social classes important for Delacroix's image of the French people in revolt? › Why did he portray this particular image of liberty, carrying a rifle, with exposed breasts?

In 1824, Louis XVIII was succeeded by his far more conservative brother, Charles X (r. 1824–1830). Charles pushed the parliament to compensate nobles whose land had been confiscated and sold during the revolution, antagonizing property holders. He restored the Catholic Church to its traditional place in French schools, provoking an oppositional movement in Parliament from French liberals. Economic troubles encouraged the opposition; in Paris and the provinces, police reports documented widespread unemployment, hunger, and anger. Confronted with alarming evidence of his regime's unpopularity, Charles called for new elections; when they went against him, he tried to overthrow the parliament with his so-called July Ordinances of 1830. He dissolved the new assembly before it had met, restricted suffrage even further, and announced strict press censorship.

In return, Charles got revolution. Parisian workers, artisans, and students took to the streets in three days of intense street battles. The press defied the censors and spread news of confrontations between protesters and the forces of order. In the end, the army was unwilling to fire into the crowd and, with his support evaporating, Charles was forced to abdicate. Many revolutionaries demanded a republic, but the leaders of the movement opted for stability by crowning the former king's cousin, the Duke of Orléans Louis-Philippe (r. 1830–1848), as the constitutional monarch. The July Monarchy, as it was called, doubled the number of voters, although voting was still based on steep property requirements. The propertied classes benefited most from the Revolution of 1830, but it also brought the common people back into politics, revived memories of 1789, and spurred movements elsewhere in Europe. For opponents of the Restoration, the year 1830 suggested that history was moving in a new direction and that the political landscape had changed since the Congress of Vienna.

BELGIUM AND POLAND IN 1830

In 1815, the Congress of Vienna joined Belgium (then called the Austrian Netherlands) with Holland to form a buffer against France; it came to be known as the United Provinces. The Belgians had never accepted this arrangement, and the 1830 revolution in France energized the Belgian opposition. The city of Brussels rebelled and forced Dutch troops to withdraw. Unwilling to intervene, the great powers agreed to guarantee Belgian independence and neutrality—a provision that remained in force until 1914. Although the economy of Belgian cities suffered by being separated from the Atlantic trade of the Dutch ports, religious divisions between the Catholic provinces of Belgium and Protestant Holland reinforced the separation. French-speaking elites in Belgium supported independence, although Flemish-speaking Belgians continue to cultivate a sense of cultural distinctiveness even today.

The years 1830–1832 thus brought full-fledged crises for the Concert of Europe. After France and Belgium, revolt spread to Poland, which was still governed by Constantine, the Russian tsar Nicholas's brother. Constantine increasingly ignored the liberties guaranteed to the Polish people, and news of the French Revolution of 1830 tipped Poland into revolt. Led by Polish officers in the army, the revolutionaries rallied supporters, including aristocrats, students, soldiers, and members of the Polish urban middle class. They took control of Warsaw, the Polish capital, and drove out Constantine (who died the next year in a cholera epidemic). With Austria and Prussia remaining neutral, Russia was given free rein to put down the rebellion by force; and within the year, the Polish rebellion was defeated.

Revolutions, Migration, and Political Refugees

In nineteenth-century Europe the spread of nationalism and the mobilization of large numbers of people and political conflicts intensified the pressures that created political migrations. Military operations during the Revolutionary and Napoleonic Wars (see Chapter 18) were a form of forced migration of their own. After peace was reestablished by the Congress of Vienna, cohorts of ex-soldiers, who often held strongly felt political ideals, were a destabilizing force in many parts of Europe.

Failed nationalist movements cause surge in political refugees

When the Greeks achieved independence from the Ottomans in 1829, other nationalist movements in Europe sought to follow their example, but few succeeded. When these attempts failed, further waves of political refugees spread across Europe. German republicans were chased out of central Europe by political police. The failed Polish insurrections of 1830–1831 against Russia led to three decades of Polish migration. Most Poles who fled went to France, but Polish colonies were also established in London, Brussels, and Switzerland. By the 1840s, the combination of failed insurrections in central Europe created a floating population of political exiles in western European cities. Their paths were not all the same. Giuseppe Mazzini, who had a future as a prominent voice for Italian unification, spent time in London in the 1830s and 1840s, where he set up a school for children of Italian migrants. Karl Marx, a German political exile, worked as a journalist in Paris and London in the 1840s before becoming prominent in the international socialist movement (see page 707). Carl Schurz, a nationalist revolutionary in western Prussia in the 1840s, migrated to the United States and served as a general in the Union army in the American Civil War before being elected to the Senate. Not all exiles became so well-known, but in many cases, their experience of defeat and police repression made them radical, and their frustration with Europe's conservative regimes made them impatient.

REFORM IN GREAT BRITAIN

The end of the Napoleonic Wars brought a major agricultural depression to Britain. Low wages, unemployment, and bad harvests provoked regular social unrest. In the new industrial towns of the north, radical members of the middle class joined with workers to demand increased representation in Parliament. In 1819, when 60,000 people gathered to demonstrate for political reform at St. Peter's Field in Manchester, the militia and soldiers on horseback charged the crowd, killing 11 and injuring 400. Radicals condemned "Peterloo" as a domestic Waterloo and criticized the nation's army for turning against its own citizens. Parliament quickly passed the Six Acts (1819), outlawing "seditious" literature, increasing the stamp tax on newspapers, allowing house searches, and restricting rights of assembly.

British political leaders reversed their opposition to reform in response to pressure from below. The crucial issue was parliamentary representation. About two-thirds of the House of Commons owed their seats to the patronage of the richest titled landowners in the country. In districts known as "rotten" or "pocket" boroughs, landowners used their power to return members of Parliament who would serve their interests. Defenders of this system argued that the interests of landed property coincided with those of the nation at large.

Liberals in the Whig Party, the new industrial middle class, and radical artisans argued passionately for reform. They were not necessarily democrats—liberals in particular wanted to enfranchise only responsible citizens—but they formed a common cause with organized middle-class and working-class radicals to push for reform. By July 1830, reform groups arose in several cities, some clashing with the army and police. Middle-class shopkeepers even announced they would withhold taxes and form a national guard. The country appeared to be on the verge of serious general disorder, if not outright revolution. Lord Grey, head of the Whig Party, seized the opportunity to push through reform.

The Reform Bill of 1832 eliminated the rotten boroughs and reallocated 143 parliamentary seats, mostly from the rural south to the industrial north. The bill expanded the franchise, but only one in six men could vote. Landed aristocrats saw their influence reduced but not destroyed. This modest reform brought British liberals and members of the middle class into a junior partnership with the landed elite that had ruled Britain for centuries. This more liberal Parliament abolished slavery in the British colonies in 1833 (Chapter 21).

A clear example of middle-class power came in the repeal of the Corn Laws in 1846. The Corn Laws (the British term for grain is *corn*) protected British land-owners and farmers from foreign competition by establishing tariffs for imports and keeping bread prices high. The middle class increasingly saw this as an unfair protection of the aristocracy and pushed for their repeal in the name of free trade. The **Anti–Corn Law League** held meetings throughout the north of England and lobbied Parliament, eventually resulting in a repeal of the law and a free-trade policy that lasted until the 1920s.

BRITISH RADICALISM AND THE CHARTIST MOVEMENT

Reformers disappointed with the narrow gains of 1832 pushed for expanded political reforms. They focused on a petition known as the "People's Charter," which contained six demands: universal male suffrage, a secret ballot, an end to property qualifications as a condition of public office, annual parliamentary elections, salaries for members of the House of Commons, and equal electoral districts. The **Chartists** organized committees across the country, and the People's Charter was eventually signed by millions of workers.

Women in the Anti–Corn Law League (1842)

Members of the Anti–Corn Law League sought to repeal the protectionist laws that prohibited foreign grain from entering the British market. The laws were seen as an interference in trade that kept bread prices artificially high, benefiting British landowners and grain producers at the expense of the working population. The campaign to repeal the Corn Laws enlisted many middle-class women, some of whom later campaigned for women's suffrage. This article, hostile to the reform, deplored women's participation in the reform movement.

We find that the council of the Manchester Anti-Corn Law Association had invited the inhabitants to "an *anti-Corn-law tea-party*, to be held on the 20th of May, 1841—gentlemen's tickets, 2s.; ladies 1s. 6d." . . . [L]adies were advertised as *stewardesses* of this assembly. So now the names of about 300 Ladies were pompously advertised as the *Patroness* and *Committee* of the *National Bazaar*. We exceedingly wonder and regret that the members of the Association . . . and still more that anybody else, should have chosen to exhibit their wives and daughters in the character of political agitators; and we most regret that so many ladies—modest, excellent, and amiable persons we have no doubt in their domestic circles—should have been persuaded to allow their names to be *placarded* on such occasions—for be it remembered, this Bazaar and these *Tea-parties* did not even pretend to be for any *charitable* object, but entirely for the purposes of *political agitation*. . . .

We have before us a letter from Mrs. Secretary Woolley to one body of workmen. . . . She "appeals to them to stand forth and denounce as *unholy*, unjust, and cruel all restrictions on the food of the people." She acquaints them that "the ladies are resolved to perform *their* arduous part in the attempt to *destroy a monopoly* which, for *selfishness* and its *deadly* effects, has no parallel in the history of the world." "We therefore," she adds, "ask you for contributions. . . ." Now surely . . . not only should the *poorer classes* have been exempt from such unreasonable solicitations, but whatever subscriptions might be obtainable from the wealthier orders should have been applied, not to *political agitation* throughout England, but to charitable relief at home.

Source: J. Croker, "Anti–Corn Law Agitation," *Quarterly Review* (December 1842), as cited in Patricia Hollis, ed., *Women in Public: The Women's Movement 1850–1900* (London: 1979), p. 287.

Questions for Analysis

1. Why does the article highlight the participation of women in the Anti–Corn Law Association? What does this argument tell us about attitudes toward women's political activity?

2. Does the article actually mention any of the arguments in favor of repealing the Corn Laws? What alternative to repeal does the article appear to support?

The Chartists presented massive petitions to Parliament in 1839 and 1842, but Parliament rejected them both times. Members of the movement resorted to strikes, trade union demonstrations, and attacks on factories and manufacturers who imposed low wages and long hours or who harassed unionists. The movement peaked in April 1848. Inspired by revolutions in Continental Europe (Chapter 21), the Chartists' leaders planned a major demonstration in London. Twenty-five thousand workers carried to Parliament a petition with

6 million signatures. With the specter of class conflict looming, the aging Duke of Wellington marshaled special constables and regular army units to resist any threat to public order. In the end, the Chartist leadership backed down and only a small delegation presented the petition to the government. A relieved liberal observer, Harriet Martineau, observed, "From that day it was a settled matter that England was safe from revolution."

The Politics of Slavery after 1815

These political conflicts about citizenship, sovereignty, and equality were also linked to a transnational debate about slavery. When the age of revolution opened in the 1770s, the enslavement of people of African descent was legal everywhere in the Atlantic world. French revolutionaries had abolished slavery in the French Empire, but Napoleon succeeded in reimposing the practice everywhere except Haiti, which gained its independence in 1804. By 1848, slavery remained legal in the southern United States, Brazil, and Cuba. (It endured, too, in most of Africa and parts of India and the Islamic world.) The debate about slavery was fundamental, both because of the significance of slavery for the Atlantic economy and because it challenged the defenders of liberty to live up to the claims of universality that had been a central part of Enlightenment political thought. If "all men" were "created equal," how could some be enslaved? Did only white people possess rights?

Issue of slavery exposes key contradiction in Enlightenment thinking

SLAVERY, ENLIGHTENMENT, AND REVOLUTION

The revolutions of the eighteenth century did not bring emancipation in their wake. Eighteenth-century Enlightenment thinkers persuaded many Europeans that slavery contradicted natural law and natural freedom (Chapter 17), a critique that allowed slavery to become a metaphor for any abuse of political authority. Virginia planters who helped lead the American Revolution angrily refused to be "slaves" to the English king, while at the same time defending plantation slavery. Such contradictions suggested that they did not believe enslaved Africans possessed legitimate rights. The planters' success in throwing off the British king expanded their power and strengthened slavery as an institution in North America.

Likewise, the French revolutionaries, while denouncing the tyranny of a king who would "enslave" them, refused to admit free people of color to the revolutionary assembly for fear of alienating planters in the lucrative colonies of Martinique, Guadeloupe, and Saint-Domingue. The insurrection of enslaved people in Saint-Domingue in 1791 forced the French revolutionaries to contend with the contradictions of revolutionary policy and reject a racial component to citizenship. Napoleon's failure to repress that rebellion allowed for the emergence of independent Haiti in 1804 (Chapter 18). The Haitian Revolution sent shock waves through the Americas, alarming slave owners while offering hope to enslaved and formerly enslaved people. In the words of a free Black sailmaker in Philadelphia, the Haitian nation signaled that Black people "could not always be detained in their present bondage."

Yet the revolution in Haiti had other, contradictory consequences. The "loss" of slavery-based sugar production in the former Saint-Domingue created an opportunity for its expansion elsewhere—in Brazil, where slavery expanded in the production of sugar, gold, and coffee—and in the American South. Slavery remained intact in the French, British, and Spanish colonial islands in the Caribbean, backed by the Congress of Vienna in 1815.

THE SLOW PATH TO ABOLITION

An abolitionist movement emerged in Britain, the nation that led the world in human trafficking. From the 1780s on, pamphlets and books—the best known is *The Interesting Narrative of the Life of Olaudah Equiano* (1789)—detailed the horrors of the slave ships to an increasingly sympathetic audience. Abolitionist leaders such as William Wilberforce believed that the slave trade was immoral, though like most abolitionists, Wilberforce did not want to foment revolt. In 1807, the reform movement compelled Parliament to pass a bill that prohibited British ships from participating in the slave trade. The United States joined in the agreement; and ten years later, the Portuguese agreed to a limited ban on traffic north of the equator. More treaties followed, which slowed but did not stop the trade. Nevertheless, ships carried 2.5 million slaves to markets in the Americas in the four decades *after* the abolition of the slave trade.

In England, and especially in the United States, religious revivals supplied much of the energy for the abolitionist movement. The hymn "Amazing Grace" was written by a former slave trader turned minister, John Newton, to describe his conversion experience and salvation. The moral and religious dimensions of the struggle made it acceptable for women to participate (they would move from the antislavery movement to the Anti–Corn Law League and, later, to the women's suffrage movement). Finally, the issue spoke to laborers, whose sometimes brutal working conditions and sharply limited political rights we have discussed in the previous chapters. To oppose slavery and to insist that labor be dignified, honorable, and minimally free resonated broadly in social classes accustomed to being

FEAR OF SLAVE VIOLENCE. This cartoon, published in Britain in 1789 in opposition to the movement to end slavery, played on public fears of the consequences of abolition. The former slaves, dressed in the fashionable attire of the landed gentry, dine at their former master's table and beat the master in retaliation for what they have suffered. In the background, other former slave owners are stooped in labor in the cane fields. According to the logic of this cartoon, such a reversal would be intolerable; and given the choice between "Abolition" and "Regulation" (the two heads at the bottom), the cartoonist would choose "Regulation" as the wiser course.

ABOLITION OF THE SLAVE TRADE, OR THE MAN THE MASTER.

treated as "servile." The issue, then, cut across material interests and class politics, and millions signed antislavery petitions during the 1820s and 1830s.

Rebellions by enslaved people also shook opinion, especially after the success of the Haitian Revolution (Chapter 19). In 1800, enslaved people rebelled in Virginia; in 1811, there was an uprising in Louisiana; and in 1822, an alleged conspiracy took hold in South Carolina. The British colonies saw significant rebellions in Barbados (1816) and in Demerara, just east of Venezuela (1823); and, most important, the month-long insurrection in Jamaica (1831). All of these were ferociously repressed. These rebellions had virtually no chance of succeeding and usually erupted only when some crack in the system opened up, such as divisions within the white elite or the (perceived) presence of a sympathetic outsider. Still, these rebellions had important consequences: they increased slaveowners' sense of vulnerability and isolation, and outsiders (in Britain or New England) often recoiled at the brutality of the repression.

Slave rebellions, though virtually guaranteed to fail, nonetheless have symbolic and political power

In Britain, the force of abolitionism wore down the defense of slavery. In the aftermath of the Great Reform Bill of 1832, Britain emancipated 800,000 enslaved people in its colonies—effective in 1838, after four years of "apprenticeship." In France, republicans took the strongest antislavery stance, and emancipation came to the French colonies when the revolution of 1848 brought republicans, however briefly, to power (Chapter 21).

In Latin America, slavery's fate was shaped by demographics, economics, and the politics of breaking away from the Spanish and Portuguese Empires. In most of mainland Spanish America (in other words, not Cuba or Brazil), slavery had been of secondary importance, owing to the relative ease of escape and the presence of other sources of labor. As the struggles for independence escalated, nationalist leaders recruited enslaved people and free people of color to fight against the Spanish, promising emancipation in return. Simón Bolívar's 1817 campaign to liberate Venezuela was fought in part by the enslaved and formerly enslaved, reinforced by 6,000 troops from Haiti. The new nations in Spanish America passed emancipation measures in stages, but they had eliminated slavery by the middle of the century.

Cuba was starkly different: with 40 percent of its population enslaved, the Spanish island colony had almost as many slaves as all of mainland Spanish America together. A Cuban independence movement would have detonated a revolution by enslaved people, providing a powerful incentive for Cuban elites to remain under the Spanish crown. Spain, for its part, depended on the revenues generated by the immensely profitable sugar industry and could not afford to alienate Cuban planters by pushing for an end to slavery. Only a combination of rebellion in Cuba and liberal revolution in Spain brought abolition, beginning in the 1870s. Brazil, too, was 40 percent enslaved and, like Cuba, had a large population of free people of color. Unlike Cuba, however, Brazil won national independence, breaking away from Portugal with relative ease (1822). Like the American South, Brazil came through the revolution for independence with slavery not only intact but expanding, and slavery endured in Brazil until 1888.

Taking Sides: New Ideologies in Politics

Debates about citizenship, sovereignty, and slavery made it clear that issues raised by the French Revolution were very much alive in Europe after 1815. The Congress of Vienna was able to place the Bourbon family back on the throne in

France, but it could not make debates about popular sovereignty, national independence, or the authority of conservative dynastic regimes go away. Throughout Europe, political actors increasingly understood they were facing fundamental choices about the legitimacy of different forms of government and the nature of the bonds that held societies together. Extremists in these debates viewed their opponents as intolerable and sought to impose their vision by any means necessary. Others sought a middle way, seeking areas of consensus about the goals of political association. It was within this context that modern political ideologies of conservatism, liberalism, socialism, and nationalism began to come into clearer focus.

Early nineteenth-century politics did not include parties as we know them today. But clearly defined groups and competing doctrines, or ideologies, took shape during this time. An ideology may be defined as a coherent system of thought that claims to represent the workings and structure of the social order and its relationship to political powers and institutions. Ideologies consciously compete with other views of how the world is or should be, and their defenders seek to establish their views as dominant. The roots of conservatism, liberalism, and nationalism lay in earlier times, but ongoing political battles over the legacy of the French Revolution and the social changes that accompanied the Industrial Revolution brought them to the fore.

> *Competing political ideologies emerge as Europeans debate the ideal structure of society*

CONSERVATISM

At the Congress of Vienna and during the Restoration generally, the most important guiding concept was legitimacy. Conservatives aimed to make legitimate—and thus to solidify—both the monarchy's authority and the hierarchical social order undermined by the French Revolution. They believed that the monarchy guaranteed political stability and that the nobility were the rightful leaders of the nation. They insisted that, as a matter of strategy, the nobility and the crown shared a common interest, despite their disagreements in the past. They also believed that change had to be slow, incremental, and managed so as to strengthen rather than weaken the structures of authority. Conserving the past and cultivating tradition would ensure an orderly future.

Edmund Burke's *Reflections on the Revolution in France* was more influential in this new context than it had been during the 1790s, when it was first published. Burke did not oppose all change. As a member of the British Parliament, he voiced support for constraints on royal power, and argued that the British should let go of the North American colonies. But he opposed talk of natural rights, which he considered pernicious abstractions. He believed enthusiasm for constitutions to be misguided and the Enlightenment's emphasis on what he called the "conquering power of reason" to be dangerous; instead, he counseled a much more cautious approach to social and political change, with deference to experience, tradition, and history. Other conservatives, such as the French writers Joseph de Maistre (1753–1851) and Louis-Gabriel-Ambroise Bonald (1754–1840), were even more resistant to change, believing that the monarchy, the aristocracy, and religion were the mainstays of social and political order. These institutions needed to stand together in the face of the challenges of the new century.

Edmund Burke (1729-1797) Conservative Anglo-Irish writer and member of the British Parliament who was critical of the French Revolution and its goal of radical political change.

Edmund Burke, *Reflections on the Revolution in France*

Edmund Burke's Reflections on the Revolution in France was first published in 1790, while the French Revolution was still under way. His opposition to revolutionary change had a profound influence on conservatives in the decades after the Congress of Vienna in 1815. The following passages contain Burke's defense of hereditary elites, his insistence on the power of tradition (which he refers to as "convention"), and his criticism of the doctrine of natural rights.

The power of perpetuating our property in our families is one of the most valuable and interesting circumstances belonging to it, and that which tends the most to the perpetuation of society itself. It makes our weakness subservient to our virtue; it grafts benevolence even upon avarice. The possessors of family wealth, and of the distinction which attends hereditary possession . . . are the natural securities for this transmission. With us, the house of peers is formed upon this principle. It is wholly composed of hereditary property and hereditary distinction; and made therefore the third of the legislature; and in the last event, the sole judge of all property in all its subdivisions. The house of commons too, though not necessarily, yet in fact, is always so composed in the far greater part. Let those large proprietors be what they will, and they have their chance of being amongst the best, they are at the very worst, the ballast in the vessel of the commonwealth. [. . .]

If civil society be the offspring of convention, that convention must be its law. That convention must limit and modify the descriptions of constitution which are formed under it. Every sort of legislative, judicial, or executor power are its creatures. They can have no being in any other state of things; and how can any man claim, under the conventions of civil society, rights which do not so much as suppose its existence? Rights which are

LIBERALISM

An underlying assumption of liberal thinking: humans act rationally

Liberalism's core was a commitment to human reason, which led liberals to define freedom in terms of individual autonomy. Human beings were rational, and freedom meant exercising this rationality without interference from anybody else. The most important function of government was to protect individual rights—doing so would benefit all, by promoting justice, knowledge, progress, and prosperity. The emphasis on individual rights led liberals to emphasize equality before the law, which meant ending aristocratic privileges and the arbitrary power of hereditary authority. Liberals held that government needed to be based on the consent of the governed. Finally, liberals believed that individuals should be free to engage in economic activities without interference from the state or the community.

The roots of legal and political liberalism lay in the work of John Locke in the late seventeenth century, who had defended the British Parliament's rebellion against absolutism and the "inalienable" rights of the British people (Chapter 15). Liberalism had been developed by the Enlightenment writers of the eighteenth century and was especially influenced by the founding texts of the American Revolution (the Declaration of Independence) and the French Revolution (the Declaration of absolutely repugnant to it? One of the first motives to civil society, and which becomes one of its fundamental rules, is *that no man should be judge in his own cause.* By this each person has at once divested himself of the first fundamental right of uncovenanted man, that is, to judge for himself, and to assert his own cause. He abdicates all right to be his own governor. He inclusively, in a great measure, abandons the right of self-defense, the first law of nature. Men cannot enjoy the rights of an uncivil and of a civil state together. That he may obtain justice he gives up his right of determining what it is in points the most essential to him. That he may secure some liberty, he makes a surrender in trust of the whole of it. [. . .]

Government is not made in virtue of natural rights, which may and do exist in total independence of it; and in a much greater degree of abstract perfection; but their abstract perfection is their practical defect. . . . The moment you abate anything from the full rights of men, each to govern himself, and suffer any artificial positive limitation upon those rights, from that moment the whole organization of government becomes a consideration of convenience. That is which makes the constitution of a state, and the due distribution of its powers, a matter of the most delicate and complicated skill. It requires a deep knowledge of human nature and human necessities, and of the things which facilitate or obstruct the various ends which are to be pursued by the mechanism of civil institutions. The state is to have recruits to its strength and remedies to its distempers. What is the use of discussing a man's abstract right to food or to medicine? The question is upon the method of procuring and administering them. In that deliberation I shall always advise to call in the aid of the farmer and the physician, rather than the professor of metaphysics.

Source: Edmund Burke, *Reflections on the Revolution in France*, 9th edition (London: 1791), pp. 75–76, 86–88, 89–90.

Questions for Analysis

1. Note that Burke does not defend hereditary elites with reference to God or a divinely inspired order. How does he justify the authority of the hereditary aristocracy?

2. What power does Burke grant to "convention" in the construction of the state and its laws?

3. What is Burke's principal complaint about revolutionaries who base their programs on "natural rights"?

the Rights of Man). The starting points for nineteenth-century liberalism were the principles of freedom from arbitrary authority, imprisonment, and censorship; freedom of the press; and the right to assemble and deliberate. Liberals believed that individual rights were inalienable, but they did not claim children, women, and enslaved people possessed these rights to equal degrees. They were committed to the rule of law and believed laws should be guaranteed in written constitutions. (Conservatives, as we saw earlier, considered constitutions abstract and dangerous.) Most liberals called for constitutional as opposed to hereditary monarchy; all agreed that a monarch who abused power could legitimately be overthrown.

Liberals advocated direct representation in government—at least for those who had property and public standing to be trusted with the responsibilities of power. But liberalism by no means required democracy. In the July Monarchy in France, established after the 1830 revolution, the property qualifications were so high that only 2 percent of the population could vote. Even after the Reform Bill of 1832 in England, only 18 percent of the population could vote for parliamentary representatives. Nineteenth-century liberals, with fresh memories of the French Revolution of 1789, were torn between their belief in rights and their fears of political turmoil.

Many liberals considered property and education essential prerequisites for participation in politics, and wealthy liberals opposed extending the vote to the common people. To demand universal male suffrage was too radical, and to speak of enfranchising women or people of color even more so. As far as gender and race were concerned, nineteenth-century liberalism inherited the contradictions of the Enlightenment, which reserved full citizenship only for males of European descent. Belief in individual liberty collided with vested economic interests, the determination to preserve order and property, and increasingly "scientific" theories of racial inequality (see Chapter 23).

The founding text of economic liberalism was **Adam Smith**'s *Wealth of Nations* (1776), which attacked mercantilism (the government practice of regulating manufacturing and trade to raise revenues) in the name of free markets. Smith's views were reinforced by a second generation of economists and popularized in journals such as the *Economist*, founded in 1838. The economists, or political economists as they were called, sought to identify basic economic laws—the law of supply and demand, the balance of trade, the law of diminishing returns, and so on—and argued that economic policy had to begin by recognizing these laws. David Ricardo (1772–1823) of Britain, for example, set out laws of wages and of rents, trying to determine the long-run outcomes of fluctuations in each.

Adam Smith believed that the economy had a natural equilibrium—between supply and demand, between producers and consumers, between foreign and domestic trade—that was best left untouched. This doctrine, known as *laissez-faire* (which translates, roughly, as "leave things to go on their own") held that governments should preserve order and protect property but not interfere with economic forces. Labor should be contracted freely, unhampered by guilds or unions, or state interference. Property should be unencumbered by feudal restrictions. Goods should circulate freely, which meant an end to government-granted monopolies, trade barriers, import tariffs, and traditional practices of regulating markets, especially in valuable commodities such as grain, flour, or corn. At the time of the Irish famine, for instance, their writings played a role in hardening the opposition to government intervention or relief (Chapter 19). Liberal economists believed that state interventions in the economy should be kept to a minimum, though they also argued that markets could not function without states to preserve the rule of law. This opposition to government intervention makes nineteenth-century liberalism different from common understandings of "liberalism" in the United States today.

One of the most influential British liberals was **Jeremy Bentham** (1748–1832). Bentham's major work, *The Principles of Morals and Legislation* (1789), illustrates how nineteenth-century liberalism continued the Enlightenment legacy as well as transformed it. Unlike Smith, for instance, Bentham did not believe that human interests were naturally harmonious or that a stable social order could emerge naturally from a body of self-interested individuals. Instead, he proposed that society adopt the organizing principle of **utilitarianism**. Social institutions and laws (an electoral system, for instance, or a tariff) should be measured according to their social usefulness—that is, whether they produced the "greatest happiness of the greatest number." If a law passed this test, it could remain on the books; but if it failed, it should be jettisoned. Utilitarians acknowledged the importance of the individual. Each individual best understood his or her own interests and was, therefore, best left free, whenever possible, to pursue those interests as he or she saw fit. Only when an individual's interests conflicted with the interests—the happiness—of the greatest number was individual freedom to be curtailed. The intensely practical spirit of utilitarianism

---

Adam Smith argues governments should protect—but not intervene in—the natural equilibrium of market forces

Adam Smith (1723–1790) Scottish economist and liberal philosopher who proposed that competition between self-interested individuals led naturally to a healthy economy.

Jeremy Bentham (1748–1832) Influential British liberal who proposed in his major work, *The Principles of Morals and Legislation* (1789), that society adopt the organizing principle of utilitarianism.

utilitarianism Theory based on the idea that social institutions and laws should be measured according to their social usefulness, which is equated to the amount of happiness it produced.

enhanced its influence as a creed for reform. In his personal political views, Bentham went further than many liberals—he befriended Jacobins and believed in equal rights for women. Nevertheless, his rationalist approach to measuring the "utility" of laws and reforms was an essential contribution to the liberal tradition.

RADICALISM, REPUBLICANISM, AND EARLY SOCIALISM

The liberals were flanked on their left by two radical groups: republicans and socialists. Republicans demanded a government by the people, an expanded franchise, and democratic participation in politics. The crucial distinction between the more moderate liberals and the radical republicans, therefore, depended on their criteria for defining citizenship. Both groups believed that government should have the consent of citizens, but liberals were more likely to support restricted qualifications for citizenship, such as property ownership or the amount of taxes paid. Nineteenth-century republicans were committed to political equality and advocated a more open definition of citizenship, one without regard to wealth or social standing. In thinking about the legacy of the French Revolution, liberals were likely to favor the attempts by the National Assembly to create a constitutional monarchy between 1789 and 1791, whereas Republicans sympathized more openly with the Jacobins of the French Republic after 1792. Liberals remained suspicious of direct democracy and "mob rule," while republicans supported civil militias, free public education, and civil liberties such as the free press and the right to assemble. Nevertheless, very few liberals or republicans supported allowing women to vote. Nearly all political thinkers of the period assumed that the virtues necessary for citizenship—rationality, sobriety, and independence of mind—were essentially masculine traits. Furthermore, citizenship continued to reflect presumptions about racial hierarchy even long after slavery was abolished.

QUADRILLE DANCING AT NEW LANARK, ROBERT OWEN'S MODEL COMMUNITY. Owen's Scottish experiment with cooperative production and community building, including schooling for infants, was only one of many utopian ventures in early nineteenth-century Europe and North America.

Socialism emerges
in response to
social and economic
problems created by
industrialization

>

Socialists distinguished themselves from both liberals and republicans by pointing out that giving men the vote would not necessarily eradicate other persistent forms of injustice and inequality. To put it in terms used at the time, socialists raised the "social question": How could the growing economic inequalities produced by industrialization and the miseries of working people be remedied? This "social" question, socialists insisted, was an urgent political matter, and they offered varied responses to this question and different ways of redistributing economic and social power. The solutions ranged from cooperation and new ways of organizing everyday life to collective ownership of the means of production; some were just speculative, others very concrete.

Socialism was a nineteenth-century system of thought and a response in large measure to the visible problems ushered in by industrialization: the intensification of labor, the poverty of working-class neighborhoods in industrial cities, and the widespread perception that a hierarchy based on rank and privilege had been replaced by one based on social class. For socialists, the problems of industrial society were not incidental, but arose from the core principles of competition, individualism, and private property. What socialists took from the Enlightenment was a commitment to reason and human progress. They did not oppose industry and economic development, but believed society could be both industrial and humane.

These radical thinkers were often explicitly utopian. **Robert Owen** (1771–1858), a wealthy industrialist turned reformer, bought a large cotton factory at New Lanark in Scotland and proceeded to organize the mill and the surrounding town according to the principles of cooperation rather than those of profitability. New Lanark organized decent housing and sanitation, good working conditions, child care, free schooling, and a system of social security for the factory's workers. Owen advocated a general reorganization of society on the basis of cooperation and mutual respect, and he tried to persuade other manufacturers of the rightness of his cause. The Frenchman **Charles Fourier** (1772–1837), too, tried to organize utopian communities based on the abolition of the wage system, division of work according to people's natural inclinations, complete equality of the sexes, and collectively organized child care and household labor. And the charismatic socialist Flora Tristan (1803–1844) toured France speaking to workers about the principles of cooperation and the equality of men and women. That so many men and women followed the teachings of **utopian socialists** and took their visions seriously is a measure of people's conviction that society could be organized along radically different lines.

Other socialists proposed simpler, practical reforms. Louis Blanc, a French politician and writer, campaigned for universal male suffrage with an eye to giving working-class men control of the state. Instead of protecting private property and the manufacturing class, the transformed state would become the "banker of the poor," extending credit to those who needed it and establishing "associations of production," a series of workshops governed by laborers that would guarantee jobs and security for all. Such workshops were established, fleetingly, during the French Revolution of 1848, as were clubs promoting women's rights. Pierre-Joseph Proudhon (1809–1865) proposed establishing producers' cooperatives, which would sell goods at a price workers could afford; working-class credit unions; and so on. Proudhon's *What Is Property?*—to which the famous answer was "Property is theft"—became one of the most widely read socialist pamphlets, familiar to artisans, laborers, and

Robert Owen (1771–1858)
Welsh industrialist and
reformer who made
efforts to improve factory
conditions for workers in
Scotland.

Charles Fourier (1772–1837)
French philosopher and
thinker who sought to
organize utopian societies.

utopian socialists A body
of writers and intellectuals
in western Europe who
supported social reforms
and economic planning
that would mitigate what
they saw as the devastating
effects of industrialization
on European society.

middle-class intellectuals, including Karl Marx. As we will see, a period of economic depression and widespread impoverishment in the 1840s brought the socialists many more working-class followers.

KARL MARX'S SOCIALISM

After 1848, a wave of revolutions and violent confrontations appeared to make the earlier socialists' emphasis on cooperation, experimental communities, and peaceful reorganization of industrial society seem naive. Out of these revolutions came a much more developed theory of social change, rooted in a broader view of history. The key figure in this development was **Karl Marx** (1818–1883).

Marx grew up in Trier, a city in the German Rhineland. His family was Jewish, but his father had converted to Protestantism to be able to work as a lawyer. Marx studied law briefly at the University of Berlin before turning instead to philosophy. His radicalism (and atheism, for he repudiated all his family's religious affiliations) made it impossible for him to get a post in a university. He became a journalist and from 1842 to 1843, he edited the liberal *Rheinische Zeitung (Rhineland Gazette)*. The paper's criticism of legal privilege and political repression put it on a collision course with the Prussian government, which closed it down and sent Marx into exile—first to Paris, then Brussels, and eventually London.

While in Paris, Marx studied early socialist theory, economics, and the history of the French Revolution. He also began a lifelong intellectual and political partnership with Friedrich Engels (1820–1895), the son of a German textile manufacturer. His parents had sent him to learn business with a merchant firm in Manchester, one of the centers of England's Industrial Revolution (Chapter 19). Engels worked in the family business until 1870, but this did not prevent him from taking up his pen to denounce the miserable working and living conditions in Manchester and what he saw as the systematic inequalities of capitalism. (He published *The Condition of the Working Class in England* in 1844.) Marx and Engels joined a small international group of radical artisans called the League of the Just, renamed the Communist League in 1847. The league asked Marx to draft a statement of its principles, which was published in 1848 as *The Communist Manifesto*, with Engels listed as coauthor.

The Communist Manifesto laid out Marx's theory of history in short form. From the conservative German philosopher Hegel, Marx imported the view of history as a dynamic process, with an inner logic, moving toward human freedom. (This is a good example of the larger influence of conservative historical thinking.) In Hegel's view, the historical process did not unfold in any simple and predictable way; instead, history proceeded "dialectically," or through conflict. He saw this conflict as one between ideas: a "thesis" produced an "antithesis," and the clash between the two created a distinctive and new "synthesis." In a classic example, Hegel posited that the natural but limited freedom of the savage (thesis) encountered its opposite (antithesis) in the constraints imposed on the individual by the family and the developing institutions of civil society. The result of this clash was a new and superior freedom (synthesis), the freedom of individuals within society, protected by moral customs, law, and the state.

Marx applied Hegel's dialectic, or theory of conflict, to history in a different way. He did not begin with ideas, as Hegel had, but rather with material, social, and economic forces. According to this materialist vision, world history had passed through three major stages, each characterized by conflict between social groups,

Hegel's "dialectic": a conflict between two opposing ideas

Karl Marx and Pierre-Joseph Proudhon, Correspondence

Karl Marx was both a prolific political and economic theorist as well as a political militant, who corresponded with socialists and other political radicals throughout Europe. He, with Friedrich Engels, was the author of The Communist Manifesto (1848), *a widely circulated polemical critique of the capitalist economic system, which predicted the emergence of a revolutionary movement led by Europe's industrial working classes. This exchange of letters with a prominent French socialist thinker, Pierre-Joseph Proudhon, reveals disagreements among socialists in Europe about the desirability of revolution, and Marx's ideas about how intellectuals such as himself might participate in the revolutionary movement.*

Brussels, 5 May 1846

My dear Proudhon, . . . I have made arrangements with the German communists and socialists for a constant interchange of letters which will be devoted to discussing scientific questions, and to keeping an eye on popular writings, and the socialist propaganda that can be carried on in Germany by this means. The chief aim of our correspondence, however, will be to put the German socialists in touch with the French and English socialists; to keep foreigners constantly informed of the socialist movements that occur in Germany and to inform the Germans in Germany of the progress of socialism in France and England. In this way differences of opinion can be brought to light and an exchange of ideas and impartial criticism can take place. It will be a step made by the social movement in its *literary* manifestation to rid itself of the barriers of *nationality*. And when the moment for action comes, it will clearly be much to everyone's advantage to be acquainted with the state of affairs abroad as well as at home.

Our correspondence will embrace not only the communists in Germany, but also the German socialists in Paris and London. Our relations with England have already been established. So far as France is concerned, we all of us believe that we could find no better correspondent than yourself. As you know, the English and Germans have hitherto estimated you more highly than have your own compatriots.

So it is, you see, simply a question of establishing a regular correspondence and ensuring that it has the means to keep abreast of the social movement in the different countries, and to acquire a rich and varied interest, such as could never be achieved by the work of one single person. . . .

Yours most sincerely

Karl Marx

Source: Karl Marx, Frederick Engels, *Collected Works*, vol. 38 (New York: 1982), pp. 38–40.

In Marx's conflict theory, struggles between social classes are the key driver of human history

or "classes," whose divisions were linked to the underlying economic order: master versus slave in ancient slavery, lord versus serf in feudalism, and bourgeois capitalist versus proletariat (industrial laborers) in capitalism. For Marx, this "class struggle" was the motor of human history. He believed that the feudal stage of history, where an aristocratic class dominated the enserfed peasantry, had ended in 1789, with the French Revolution. What followed was a new order, dominated by an entrepreneurial middle class—he called them "the bourgeoisie"—that built the world of industrial capitalism.

Lyon, 17 May 1846

My dear Monsieur Marx,

I am happy to become a recipient of your correspondence, whose goal and organization seem to me to be very useful. I cannot promise to write you at length or often, however, as my many occupations and my natural laziness will not permit such epistolary efforts. I would also like to take the liberty of expressing several reservations about a few of the passages in your letter.

First, [. . .] I believe that it is my duty, and the duty of all socialists, to maintain for the time being a skeptical or critical perspective, in a word, I claim [in matters of economics] an almost absolute anti-dogmatism.

Let us search together, if you wish, the laws of society, and the ways that these laws make themselves felt, and the process of development that allows us to discover them; but by God, after having demolished all the *a priori* dogmatisms, let us not dream of then indoctrinating the people ourselves, do not fall into the same contradiction faced by your compatriot Martin Luther, who after having overthrown Catholic theology, set about at once excommunicating others, in order to found a Protestant theology. [. . .] I applaud with all my heart your idea of bringing forth all possible opinions; let us therefore pursue a good and loyal argument; let us offer the world an example of a wise and perceptive toleration, but we should not, simply because we are the leaders of a movement, seek to pose as the apostles of a new religion, even if this religion is that of logic, of reason. Under these terms, I am happy to join your association, but if not—then No!

I would also like to comment on these words in your letter: *At the moment of action.* You may still think that no reform is possible at present without a bold stroke, without what was formerly called a revolution. [. . .] Having myself held this opinion for a long time, I confess now that my more recent works have made me revisit this idea completely. I believe that we do not need [a revolution] to succeed, because this alleged solution would simply be an appeal to force, to something arbitrary, in short, a contradiction. I see the problem like this: *to find a form of economic combination that would restore to society the wealth that has been taken from it by another form of economic combination.* In other words, [. . .] to turn Property against Property, in such a way as to establish what you German socialists call *community*, and which I limit myself to calling *liberty, equality.* [. . .] I prefer to burn Property with a slow fuse, rather than to give it new energy by massacring the property owners.

Your very devoted

Pierre-Joseph Proudhon

Source: P.-J. Proudhon, Amédée Jérôme Langlois, *Correspondance de P.-J. Proudhon* (Paris: 1875), pp. 198–200.

Questions for Analysis

1. What is the purpose of the network of correspondents that Marx was inviting Proudhon to join? Why did Marx believe it necessary to overcome "the barriers of nationality"?

2. Why does Proudhon compare Marx's analysis of "scientific questions" or "the laws of society" to religious dogmas?

3. Why does Proudhon reject Marx's assumption that a revolution is necessary? What alternative does he propose?

In *The Communist Manifesto*, Marx and Engels admired the revolutionary accomplishments of capitalism, saying that the bourgeoisie had "created more impressive and more colossal productive forces than had all preceding generations together." But, they argued, the revolutionary character of capitalism would also undermine the bourgeois economic order. As capital became more concentrated in the hands of the few, a growing army of wageworkers would become increasingly aware of its economic and political disenfranchisement, and this struggle between competing classes was central to industrial capitalism itself. Eventually, *The Communist Manifesto*

In The Communist Manifesto, *Marx predicts an egalitarian revolution will be society's final stage*

predicted, recurring economic crises, caused by capitalism's unending need for new markets and the cyclical instability of overproduction, would bring about the collapse of capitalism. Workers would seize the state, reorganize the means of production, abolish private property, and eventually create a communist society based on egalitarian principles. In other words, this ultimate revolution would abolish the division of labor altogether, ending the class conflict that had been the motor of history, and ushering in a future whose outlines Marx could only hesitantly describe.

CITIZENSHIP AND COMMUNITY: NATIONALISM

Of all the political ideologies of the early nineteenth century, nationalism is the most difficult to grasp. What, exactly, counted as a nation? Who demanded a nation, and what did that demand mean? In the early nineteenth century, nationalism was usually aligned with liberalism and against the conservative monarchies that dominated Europe after Napoleon's fall. As the century progressed, however, it became increasingly clear that nationalism could be molded to fit any doctrine.

The meaning of *nation* has changed over time. The term comes from the Latin verb *nasci* ("to be born") and suggests "common birth." In sixteenth-century England, *nation* designated the aristocracy, or those who shared a noble birthright; the French nobility also referred to itself as a nation—or "race"—both terms implying common descent. These earlier and unfamiliar usages are important, because they highlight the most significant development of the late eighteenth and early nineteenth centuries: the French Revolution redefined *nation* to mean the "sovereign people." The revolutionaries of 1789 boldly claimed that the nation, not the king, was the sovereign power. On a more concrete level, the revolutionaries built a national state, a national army, and a national legal system, whose jurisdiction trumped the older regional powers of the nobility and the local courts. In the aftermath of the French Revolution of 1789, the *nation* became what one historian calls the "collective image of modern citizenry."

In the early nineteenth century, then, *nation* symbolized the core values of liberalism: legal equality, constitutional government, and unity; or an end to feudal privileges and divisions. Conservatives disliked the term, because national unity and the creation of national political institutions threatened to erode the local power of aristocratic elites. New nations rested on constitutions, which, as we have seen, conservatives considered dangerous abstractions. But nationalism became an important rallying cry for liberals across Europe precisely because it was associated with political transformation. It celebrated the achievements and political awakening of the common people.

Nationalism also went hand in hand with liberal demands for economic modernity. Economists, such as the influential German Friedrich List (1789–1846), sought to develop national economies and national infrastructures: larger, stronger, better integrated, and more effective systems of banking, trade, transportation, production, and distribution. List linked the end of territorial fragmentation of the German states and the development of manufacturing to "culture, prosperity, and liberty."

Nationalism, however, did not always develop in tandem with liberalism. When liberals insisted on the importance of individual liberties, nationalists demanded that individuals be ready to sacrifice their freedom. The Napoleonic army, a particularly powerful symbol of nationhood, appealed to conservative proponents of military strength and authority. Eighteenth-century notions of race, or of communities defined by their climate or geography, also challenged liberalism's emphasis on

Inset map:
EUROPE
AFRICA
Area of detail

GAELIC
ERSE
WELSH
ENGLISH
CORNISH
DUTCH
FLEMISH
BRETON
WALLOON
GERMAN
FRENCH
BASQUE
PROVENÇAL
ITALIAN
PORTUGUESE
CATALAN
SPANISH
NORWEGIAN
SWEDISH
FINNISH
DANISH
ESTONIAN
LATVIAN
LITHUANIAN
WHITE RUSSIAN
GREAT RUSSIAN
POLISH
CZECH
SLOVAKIAN
UKRAINIAN
HUNGARIAN
SLOVENIAN
CROATIAN
SERBIAN
ROMANIAN
BULGARIAN
ALBANIAN
GREEK
TURKISH
ARABIC

NORTH SEA
BALTIC SEA
ATLANTIC OCEAN
BLACK SEA
MEDITERRANEAN SEA
Volga R.
Danube R.
CORSICA
SARDINIA
SICILY
BALEARIC ISLANDS
CRETE
CYPRUS

Legend:
Slavic
Hellenic
Germanic
Celtic
Baltic
Latin
Other
1848 boundaries

0   250   500 Miles
0   250   500 Kilometers

MAJOR EUROPEAN AND MEDITERRANEAN LANGUAGE GROUPS, c. 1850. Compare the distribution of language groups in Europe with the political boundaries of European nations in 1848. › **Do they line up?** › **Which political units were forced to deal with a multitude of languages within their borders?** › **How might this distribution of language groups be related to the history of European nationalism?**

individualism, and were used by nationalists as they sought to distinguish and define the apparent "nations" that peopled the earth.

Conceptions of national identity evolved everywhere in different ways. On the one hand, a sense of national belonging depended on common developments across Europe: rising literacy and the creation of strong national institutions. On the other hand, nationalists sought to distinguish themselves from their neighbors by claiming a uniqueness to their own history and culture. States saw the benefits of nationalist feeling, and they promoted new and distinct national rituals like the singing of anthems in national languages and the waving of unique national flags. State-supported educational systems attempted to eradicate regional dialects by teaching in a single national language. In this way, Italian became the official language of the Italian nation, despite the fact that only 2.5 percent of the population spoke it. In other words, even a minority could define a national culture. Textbooks and self-consciously nationalist theater, poetry, and painting helped elaborate and sometimes even invent a national heritage where no such allegiances had existed before.

The historical processes that make these "imagined communities" possible did not happen everywhere at the same time or in the same way. A sense of British distinctiveness emerged before the nineteenth century, in part because Britain was an island monarchy enriched by oceanic trade, but also because of its political traditions dating back to the Magna Carta. In central and eastern Europe, peoples without independent states, such as Poles and Hungarians, looked to the medieval past for historical precedents that could justify their claims for national independence against the powerful Russian, Austrian, or Prussian Empires that ruled over them. Among the oldest pedigrees claimed by nineteenth-century nationalists were those of Jewish and Armenian nationalists, who pointed to cultural, linguistic, and religious traditions dating back to antiquity. All of these nationalist movements, however, looked forward as well as backward, and the urgency that their adherents felt arose from a very modern idea: that peoples without nation-states to represent them could never be in control of their destiny.

In the nineteenth century, conservatives, liberals, and republicans in Europe all implicitly recognized the power of nationalism, and attempted to describe a vision of a nation that was compatible with their core principles. Conservatives linked dynastic ruling families and aristocratic elites to "national" traditions embodied in the history of territorially rooted peasant cultures and their traditional rulers. Liberals and republicans praised the nation as a body of free citizens who gave their consent to the laws that governed them. Marxist socialists, however, rejected the claims of nationalists, stating that the international solidary of social classes produced by the division of labor trumped national identity. The resolutely internationalist message of *The Communist Manifesto* was embodied in its concluding motto: "Workers of the world, unite!"

Conservatism, liberalism, republicanism, socialism, and nationalism were the principal political ideologies of the early nineteenth century. They were rooted in the eighteenth century but brought to the forefront by the political turmoil of the early nineteenth century. Some nineteenth-century ideologies were continuations of the French revolutionary trio: liberty (from arbitrary authority), equality (or the end of legal privilege), and fraternity (the creation of new communities of citizens). Others, like conservatism, were reactions against the French Revolution. But all could be reinterpreted, and all became increasingly common points of reference as the century unfolded.

Nationalists increasingly insist on a common sense of feeling and identity >

Cultural Revolt: Romanticism

Romanticism, the most significant cultural movement in the early nineteenth century, permeated politics and touched all the arts as well. It marked a reaction against the Classicism of the eighteenth century and the Enlightenment. Whereas Classicism aspired to reason, discipline, and harmony, Romanticism stressed emotion, freedom, and imagination. Romantic artists prized intense individual experiences and considered intuition and emotion to be better guides to truth and human happiness than reason and logic.

EARLY ROMANTIC LITERATURE

Romanticism developed first in England and Germany as a reaction against the Enlightenment. The German writer Johann Wolfgang von Goethe (1749–1832) had an enormous influence on the Romantic movement with his early novel *The Sorrows of Young Werther* (1774), which told the story of a young man's failure in love and eventual suicide. The significance of the novel lay in Goethe's ability to capture in prose the longing that many middle-class readers felt for something more meaningful than a life lived in strict conformity to social expectations. It also revealed that a new sense of self and aspirations for self-fulfillment might be emerging in Europe, alongside the narrower definitions of individualism that one might find in liberal political or economic theory. The English poet **William Wordsworth** (1770–1850) developed what became central themes of the Romantic movement— nature, simplicity, and feeling—in his *Lyrical Ballads* (1798). For Wordsworth, poetry was the "spontaneous overflow of powerful feelings," and he emphasized the ties of compassion that bind all humankind, regardless of social class. "We have all of us one human heart," he wrote. "[M]en who do not wear fine clothes can feel deeply." Wordsworth considered nature to be humanity's most trustworthy teacher and the source of true feeling, and his poems were inspired by the wild hills and tumbledown cottages of England's Lake District. In "The Ruined Cottage," he quotes from the Scottish Romantic poet Robert Burns (the last two lines):

> Give me a spark of Nature's fire,
> 'Tis the best learning I desire . . .
> My muse, though homely in attire,
> May touch the heart.

Wordsworth's poetry, along with that of his colleague Samuel Taylor Coleridge (1772–1834), offered a key theme of nineteenth-century Romanticism: a view of nature that rejected the abstract mechanism of eighteenth-century Enlightenment thought. Nature was not a system to be dissected by science but the source of sublime power that nourished the human soul.

The poet **William Blake** (1757–1827) sounded similar themes in his fierce critique of industrial society and the factories (which he called "dark satanic mills") that blighted the English landscape. He championed the individual imagination and poetic vision, seeing both as transcending the limits of the material world. He believed imagination could awaken human sensibilities and sustain belief in different values, breaking humanity's "mind-forged manacles." His poetry paralleled

Romanticism Beginning in Germany and England in the late eighteenth century and continuing until the end of the nineteenth century, Romanticism was a movement in art, music, and literature that countered the rationalism of the Enlightenment by placing greater value on human emotions and the power of nature to stimulate creativity.

William Wordsworth (1770–1850) Romantic poet whose central themes were nature, simplicity, and feeling.

William Blake (1752–1827) Romantic writer who criticized industrial society and factories.

NEWTON, **BY WILLIAM BLAKE (1795).** Blake was a brilliant graphic artist, as well as a poet. Here, he depicts Sir Isaac Newton shrouded in darkness, distracted by his scientific calculations from the higher sphere of the imagination. Blake's image is a Romantic critique of Enlightenment science, for which Newton had become a hero.

Lord Byron (1788-1824) Writer and poet whose life helped give the Romantics their reputation as rebels against conformity.

early socialist efforts to imagine a better world. And like many Romantics, he looked back to a past in which he thought society had been more organic and humane.

English Romanticism peaked with the next generation of poets: **Lord Byron** (1788–1824), Percy Bysshe Shelley (1792–1822), and John Keats (1795–1821). Their lives and loves often appealed to readers as much as their writings. Byron was an aristocrat, rich, handsome, and defiant of convention. Poetry, he wrote, was the "lava of the imagination, whose eruption prevents an earthquake." His love affairs helped give Romantics their reputation as rebels against conformity, but they were hardly carefree. Byron treated his wife cruelly and drove her away after a year. He also rebelled against Britain's political leaders, labeling them corrupt and repressive. A Romantic hero, he defended working-class movements and fought in the war for Greek independence, during which he died of tuberculosis. Byron's friend Shelley emphasized similar themes of individual audacity in his poem *Prometheus Unbound* (1820). In the poem, Prometheus defies an all-powerful god, Zeus, by stealing fire for humanity and is punished by being chained to a rock while an eagle tears out his liver, which regrows every night. The poem celebrates the title character as a selfless mythic hero, comparable to Christ in his willingness to sacrifice himself for others. Shelley, in his correspondence, described the poem as a parable about revolutionary change, and the need to overthrow tyranny in the name of a new political ideal of struggle and hope, a sentiment captured in the poem's closing lines:

> To suffer woes which Hope thinks infinite;
> To forgive wrongs darker than Death or Night;
> To defy Power, which seems omnipotent;

To love, and bear; to hope till Hope creates

From its own wreck the thing it contemplates;

Neither to change nor falter nor repent;

This, like thy glory, Titan! is to be

Good, great, and joyous, beautiful and free;

This is alone Life, Joy, Empire, and Victory.

WOMEN WRITERS, GENDER, AND ROMANTICISM

No Romantic work was more popular than Mary Shelley's *Frankenstein* (1818). Shelley (1797–1851) was the daughter of radical celebrities: the philosopher William Godwin and the feminist Mary Wollstonecraft (Chapter 17), who died just after her daughter was born. Mary Godwin met Percy Bysshe Shelley when she was sixteen and had three children by him before they were married, and published *Frankenstein* at twenty. The novel, which captures the Romantic critique of science and Enlightenment reason, tells the story of an eccentric doctor determined to find the secret of human life. Conducting his research on corpses and body parts retrieved from charnel houses, Dr. Frankenstein produces life in the form of a monster. The monster has human feelings and is overwhelmed by loneliness and self-hatred when his creator casts him out. Shelley tells the story as a twisted creation myth, a study of individual genius gone wrong. The novel remains one of the most memorable characterizations in literature of the limits of reason and the impossibility of controlling nature.

The Romantic belief in individuality and creativity ran in several directions. It became a cult of artistic genius—of the "inexplicably and uniquely creative individual" who could see things others could not. It led people to seek out experiences that would elicit intense emotions and spark their creativity, from foreign travel to opium use. The Romantic style encouraged the daring to defy convention, as did Lord Byron, the Shelleys, and the French writer George Sand (1804–1876).

MARY SHELLEY AT NINETEEN

MARY SHELLEY'S *FRANKENSTEIN.* Perhaps the best-known work of Romantic fiction, *Frankenstein* joined the Romantic critique of Enlightenment reason with early nineteenth-century ambivalence about science to create a striking horror story. Shelley (pictured left, around the time she published the book in 1818) was the daughter of the philosopher William Godwin and the feminist Mary Wollstonecraft; she married poet Percy Bysshe Shelley. On the right is an engraving from the first illustrated edition of *Frankenstein* (1831) by artist Theodor von Holst.

Sand, like Byron, cultivated a persona—in her case, by living as a woman writer, taking lovers at her pleasure, and wearing men's clothing.

Women played an important role in Romantic writing, and Romanticism stimulated new thinking about gender and creativity. It was common at the time to assert that men were rational and women emotional or intuitive. Many Romantics, like their contemporaries, accepted such gender differences as natural, and some exalted the superior moral virtues of women. Because Romanticism placed value on the emotions as an essential part of artistic creation, however, some female writers and painters were able to use these ideas to claim a place in the world of letters and the arts. Germaine de Staël (1766–1817), for example, emigrated from revolutionary France to Germany, and played a key part in popularizing German Romanticism in France. The language of Romanticism allowed Madame de Staël to describe herself as a genius, by way of explaining her own subversion of social norms. Romantics such as Madame de Staël suggested that men, too, could be emotional, and that feelings were a part of a common human nature shared by both sexes. For many literate middle-class people, the language of Romanticism was a way to express their own search for individual expression and feeling in writing—and in thinking—about love. In this way, Romanticism reached well beyond small circles of artists and writers into the everyday writing and thoughts of European men and women.

ROMANTIC PAINTING

Painters carried the Romantic themes of nature and imagination onto their canvases (see *Interpreting Visual Evidence* on pages 718–19). In Great Britain, John Constable (1776–1837) and Joseph Mallord William Turner (1775–1851) developed more emotional and poetic approaches to depicting nature. "It is the soul that sees," wrote Constable, echoing Wordsworth. Constable studied Isaac Newton and the properties of light but aimed to capture the "poetry" of a rainbow. Turner's intensely subjective paintings were even more unconventional; his experiments with brushstroke and color produced remarkable images. Critics assailed the paintings, calling them incomprehensible, to which Turner merely responded, "I did not paint it to be understood." In France, Théodore Géricault (1791–1824) and Eugène Delacroix (1798–1863) produced very different paintings from Turner's, but like the English painter, they, too, were preoccupied by subjectivity and the creative process. The poet Charles Baudelaire credited Delacroix with showing him new ways to see: "The whole visible universe is but a storehouse of images and signs. . . . All the faculties of the human soul must be subordinated to the imagination." These Romantic experiments prepared the way for the later development of modernism in the arts.

ROMANTIC POLITICS: LIBERTY, HISTORY, AND NATION

Victor Hugo (1802–1885) wrote that "Romanticism is only . . . liberalism in literature." Hugo's plays, poetry, and historical novels focused sympathetically on the experience of common people, especially *Notre-Dame de Paris* (1831) and *Les Misérables* (1862). Delacroix's painting *Liberty Leading the People* gave a revolutionary face to Romanticism, as did Shelley's and Byron's poetry. In works such as these, political life was no longer the preserve of social elites. Commoners in the street could embrace new freedoms with a violent passion that would have surprised the *philosophes*, with their emphasis on reasoned debate.

Yet Romantics also could be ardently conservative. The Frenchman François Chateaubriand's *Genius of Christianity* (1802) emphasized the primacy of religious emotions and feeling in his claim that religion was woven into the national past and could not be ignored without threatening French culture as a whole. This period, in fact, witnessed a broad and popular religious revival and a renewed interest in medieval literature, art, and architecture—all of which, as we have seen, drew heavily on religious themes. This fascination with the medieval past and its piety played an important part in the development of a new kind of Romantic nationalism, as writers and philosophers sought to ground their understanding of national belonging in something other than a rationalist approach to law and citizenship.

Early nineteenth-century nationalism took the Romantic emphasis on individuality and turned it into a faith in the uniqueness of individual cultures. Johann von Herder, among the most influential of nationalist thinkers, argued that civilization sprang from the culture of the common people, not from a learned or cultivated elite, as the *philosophes* had argued in the Enlightenment. Herder extolled the special creative genius of the German people, the *Volk*, and insisted that each nation be true to the common cultural and religious heritage of ordinary people.

Nationalists co-opt Romantic thinking in inventing common pasts

The Romantics' keen interest in history and the lives of commoners led to new kinds of literary and historical works. The brothers Jakob and Wilhelm Grimm, editors of the famous collection of fairy tales (1812–1815), traveled across Germany to study native dialects and folktales. The poet Friedrich Schiller retold the story of William Tell (1804) to promote German national consciousness, which the Italian composer Gioachino Rossini later turned into an opera that promoted Italian nationalism. In Britain, Sir Walter Scott retold the popular history of Scotland, and the Pole Adam Mickiewicz wrote a national epic *Pan Tadeusz* ("Lord Thaddeus"), a long poem in which he used the story of a love affair between the title character and a young woman to explore the theme of Polish unity under Russian rule. After 1848, these nationalist enthusiasms would overwhelm the political debates that divided conservatives from liberals and socialists in the first half of the nineteenth century (Chapter 21).

Conclusion

In 1848, with the fizzling of the Chartist movement, the British monarchy avoided an outbreak of revolution. But the monarchs on the Continent were not so lucky. As we will see in the next chapter, a wave of revolutionary activity, unprecedented since the 1790s, spread to nearly every capital in Europe. This resurgence of rebellion and revolt highlighted the powerful ways the French Revolution of 1789 polarized Europe during the first half of the nineteenth century. In the revolution's aftermath, the Congress of Vienna aimed to establish a new conservative, international system and to prevent further revolts. It succeeded in the first aim but only partially in the second. A combination of new political movements and economic hardship

Romantic Painting

Romantic painters shared with Romantic poets a fascination with the power of nature. To convey this vision of nature as both an overwhelming power and a source of creative energy, Romantic painters created new and poetic visions of the natural world, in which human beings and their activities were reduced in significance, sometimes nearly disappearing altogether. At times, these visions also were linked to a backward-looking perspective, as if the dramatic changes associated with industrialization provoked a longing for a premodern past, where Europeans sought and found their sense of place in the world from an awareness of a quasi-divine natural setting invested with powerful mysteries. John Martin's painting *The Bard* (1817) (image A) shows a highly romanticized vision of a medieval subject: a single Welsh bard strides across rocky peaks above a mountain river, after escaping a massacre ordered by the English king Edward I. Across the river, Edward's troops can barely be seen leaving the scene of the crime, which still glows with destructive fires. The emotional qualities of this early expression of Romantic nationalism are reinforced by the forbidding and dynamic sky above, where the clouds merge into the Welsh mountaintops as if they were stirred by the hand of God himself.

Other Romantic painters minimized the significance of human activity in their landscapes, and without reference to history. John Constable's *Weymouth Bay* (1816) (image B) contains a tiny, almost imperceptible human figure in the middle ground, a man walking on the beach near a thin stone wall that snakes up a hill in the background. These passing references to human lives are completely dominated by the sky and, in particular, the movement of the clouds, which seem to be the real subject of the painting.

Of all the Romantic painters, J. M. W. Turner may have tackled the tricky subject of the new industrialized

A. John Martin, *The Bard*, 1817.

undermined the conservative order. Social grievances and political disappointments gave rise to powerful movements for change, first in Latin America and the Balkans, and then in western Europe and Great Britain.

All the contesting ideologies of these postrevolutionary decades could look back to a longer history. Conservatives could point to traditional religious justifications for royal authority and the absolutist's conception of indivisible monarchical power. Liberals could point to the debates about the rule of law in the English revolution of the seventeenth century. Even socialists could point to age-old collective traditions landscape in the most novel way. His painting *Rain, Steam, and Speed—The Great Western Railway* (1844) (image C) boldly places the most modern technology of the period, the steam train, on an arched bridge in a glowing and radiant scenery, where both nature's forces and the tremendous new power unleashed by human activity seem to merge into one continuous burst of energy. To the left of the train, on the river's edge, a fire of indeterminate but evidently industrial origin burns, illuminating several small but ecstatic figures with its light. Most enigmatic of all, a tiny rabbit sprints ahead of the train between the rails (unfortunately invisible in this reproduction), highlighting the painting's complex message about nature and human creation. Are they heading in the same direction? Will one overtake the other and destroy it in the process?

Questions for Analysis

1. In Martin's *The Bard*, what vision of the individual emerges from the painting? How is it different from the rational, rights-bearing individual that political liberalism sought to protect?

2. Is Constable's painting concerned with nature as a source of nourishment for humans? Or is nature presented as a value in itself?

3. How are we to interpret Turner's explicit connection between the power of nature and the new force of industrial societies? Is he suggesting that contemplating the industrial landscape can be just as moving to a human observer as is the sight of nature's magnificence?

B. John Constable, *Weymouth Bay*, 1816.

C. J. M. W. Turner, *Rain, Steam, Speed—The Great Western Railway*, 1844.

among rural communities as precedents for their defense of communal property and egalitarianism. Nevertheless, all of these ideologies were shaped and brought into clearer focus during these decades by the combined effects of the French and Atlantic Revolution and industrialization. Conservatives may have disagreed among themselves as to why they preferred a government of monarchs and landed aristocrats, but they were united by their horror of revolutionary violence and dismayed by the social disruptions that attended industrialization. Liberals may have disagreed with each other about who qualified for citizenship, but they defended the revolution's insistence that the only legitimate government was one whose institutions and laws reflected the consent of at least some, if not all, of the governed. Many socialists, Marx included, celebrated the insurrectionary tradition of the French revolutionaries, even as they demanded a reordering of society that went far beyond the granting of new political rights to include an entire redistribution of society's wealth. Meanwhile, nationalists throughout Europe remained inspired by the collective achievements of the French nation that was forged in revolution in the 1790s.

The reemergence of social and political conflict in 1848 pitted the defenders of these ideologies against each other under the most dramatic of circumstances, making the revolutions of 1848 the opening act of a much larger drama. In France, as in 1792 and 1830, revolutionaries rallied around an expanded notion of representative government and the question of suffrage, though they were divided on

AFTER YOU READ THIS CHAPTER ⌄

CHRONOLOGY

1808	Slave trade prohibited by Britain and the United States but not slavery itself
1810–1825	South American revolutions
1814–1815	Congress of Vienna
1821–1827	Greek war for independence
1823	France restores King Ferdinand of Spain
1825	Decembrist revolt in Russia
1830	Revolutions in France and Belgium
1832	British Reform Bill
1833	Law abolishes slavery in the British Empire, with multiyear implementation plan
1840s	Chartist movement in Britain
1846	Corn Laws repealed
1848	Karl Marx's *The Communist Manifesto* published

REVIEWING THE OBJECTIVES

❯ The European leaders who met at the Congress of Vienna had a conservative vision for post-Napoleonic Europe. What were their goals? What challenges did their political system face between 1815 and 1848?

❯ Slavery persisted long after the French Revolution. What accounts for the development of an abolitionist movement? Why did slavery persist in the United States, Latin America, and Cuba?

❯ Conservatives, liberals, and republicans differed from each other about the lessons to be learned from the French Revolution, whereas socialists sought to address the inequalities produced by the Industrial Revolution. What were the core principles of conservatism, liberalism, republicanism, and socialism?

❯ Nationalism reshaped the political landscape in Europe between 1815 and 1848. How did conservatives, liberals, republicans, and socialists view the claims of nationalists?

❯ Romanticism was a cultural movement defined in opposition to the Enlightenment. Who were the Romantics? What did they believe?

how much responsibility their new government had for remedying social problems. In southern and central Europe, as we will see in the next chapter, the issues were framed differently, around new struggles for national identity. The eventual failure of these revolutions set a pattern that was observed elsewhere: exhilarating revolutionary successes were followed by a breakdown of revolutionary unity, and then by the emergence of new forms of conservative government. The crisis of 1848 became a turning point for all of Europe. The broad revolutionary alliances that had pushed for revolutionary change since 1789 were broken apart by class politics, and earlier forms of utopian socialism gave way to Marxism. In culture as in politics, Romanticism lost its appeal, with its expansive sense of possibility replaced by the more biting viewpoint of realism. No nationalist, conservative, liberal, or socialist was exempt from this bitter truth after the violent conflicts of 1848.

Go to **INQUIZITIVE** to see what you've learned—and learn what you've missed—with personalized feedback along the way.

PEOPLE, IDEAS, AND EVENTS IN CONTEXT

› Who was **KLEMENS VON METTERNICH**? What was the **CONCERT OF EUROPE**?

› How did the **CARBONARI** in Italy, the **DECEMBRISTS** in Russia, and Greek nationalists in the Balkans disturb the conservative order in Europe in the 1820s after Napoleon's defeat?

› Where did revolutions occur in 1830–1832? What were their outcomes?

› What political changes did movements such as the **CHARTISTS** or the **ANTI-CORN LAW LEAGUE** accomplish in Britain? Why was there no revolution in Britain?

› What beliefs made **EDMUND BURKE** a conservative?

› What beliefs made **ADAM SMITH** and **JEREMY BENTHAM** liberals? What was **UTILITARIANISM**?

› What beliefs did **UTOPIAN SOCIALISTS** such as **ROBERT OWEN** and **CHARLES FOURIER** share? What made **KARL MARX**'s brand of socialism different from that of his predecessors?

› How did the values of **ROMANTICISM** challenge Europeans to reconsider their assumptions about the differences between men and women?

› What beliefs led Romantic writers such as **WILLIAM WORDSWORTH, WILLIAM BLAKE**, and **LORD BYRON** to reject the rationalism of the Enlightenment and embrace emotion and imagination as the most essential and vital aspects of human experience?

THINKING ABOUT CONNECTIONS

› What new ideas about historical change made it possible to think of political conflict in terms of "conservatives" and "revolutionaries" during the decades immediately before and after 1800? Would such an opposition have been conceivable in earlier periods of history? Why or why not?

› Terms such as *conservative, liberal*, and *socialist* are still used today in contemporary political debates. Do they still mean the same thing as they did between 1815 and 1848?

21

Revolutions and Nation Building, 1848–1871

BEFORE YOU READ THIS CHAPTER

>

THE YEAR 1848 was a tumultuous one. From Paris to Berlin, and from Budapest to Rome, insurgents rushed toward hastily built barricades, forcing kings and princes to beat an equally hasty—though temporary—retreat. The aspirations of these revolutionaries were varied: some wanted more liberal democracy, others were motivated by nationalism or social-ism. Perhaps the most highly symbolic moment came on March 13, 1848, when Klemens von Metternich, the primary architect of the Concert of Europe, was forced to resign as minister of state in the Austrian capital of Vienna while a crowd of revolutionaries outside celebrated his departure. Metternich's balance of powers between traditional dynastic rulers was swept aside in a wave of enthusiasm for liberal political ideals mixed with popular anger. Metternich himself was forced to flee to England, which less than one month earlier had welcomed the French king Louis-Philippe, after another revolution in France.

Metternich's downfall and the collapse of the French monarchy made clear that the 1848 revolutions were strongly linked to powerful forces for change unleashed earlier by the French Revolution. At the same time, however, this was also the year that Karl Marx and Friedrich Engels pub-lished *The Communist Manifesto*, which announced as its goal an even more sweeping remaking of society. If 1848 was the last wave of the revolutionary movements that began in Europe and the Atlantic world at the end of the eighteenth century, it was also the first chapter in a new revolutionary move-ment that would have enormous consequences in the twentieth century.

> In 1848, a wave of liberal and national revolutions demanded but failed to achieve lasting constitutions and elected parliaments in many European kingdoms. Instead, Europe's conservative monarchs found ways to harness the popular nationalism expressed in the 1848 revolutions for their own ends.

> The emergence of Germany and Italy as unified nation-states upset the European balance of power, as did the increasing weakness of the Ottoman Empire. The resulting wars benefited Germany and diminished the power of Austria-Hungary in central Europe.

> Russia and the United States also went through an intense phase of nation building after 1850. Common to both were the conquest of native peoples, the acquisition of new territories, and economic development. As in Europe, the process of nation building unleashed sectional conflicts and intense debates about citizenship, slavery (or serfdom, in Russia), and the power of the nation-state.

CORE OBJECTIVES

> **EXPLAIN** why so many revolutions occurred nearly simultaneously in Europe in 1848.

> **UNDERSTAND** the causes and failures of the revolutions of 1848 in France.

> **DESCRIBE** the goals of revolutionaries in the German-speaking lands of central Europe and their attitudes toward the monarchies of Prussia and Austria.

> **IDENTIFY** the social groups that supported a process of national unification from below (by the people) in Italy and Germany and those that favored a process of national unification directed from the top (by the state).

> **DESCRIBE** the process of nation building in Russia and the United States in the nineteenth century, and the ensuing debates about slavery.

> **IDENTIFY** the powers involved in the Crimean War, the Austro-Prussian War, and the Franco-Prussian War, and understand how these wars changed the balance of power in Europe.

Revolutionary regime change, territorial expansion, economic development, and debates about who deserved citizenship were all issues in 1848. As we saw in the last chapter, the term *nation* had taken on a new meaning at the end of the eighteenth century, when it had come to mean "a sovereign people." *Nationalism* was a related political ideal, based on the assumption that governments could be legitimate only if they reflected the character, history, and customs of the nation—often understood to mean the "common people." This idea undermined Europe's dynastic rulers, who emphasized the differences between themselves and the people they ruled. Kings and aristocrats often did not even speak the same language as their subjects. Nobody would have thought this odd before 1789, because peasants often spoke regional dialects that were different from the language spoken in cities. But once the notion of national sovereignty emanating from the people became widespread, discrepancies in language and culture between elites and commoners loomed larger as political questions that needed to be solved. Intellectuals, revolutionaries, and governments all propagated the radical new idea that nations of like peoples and the states that ruled over them should be congruent with each other. This simple idea lay at the heart of all forms of nationalism, but there was often bitter debate about who best represented the nation and what the goals of a unified nationalist government should be.

Between 1789 and 1848, Europeans commonly associated nationalism with liberalism. Liberals saw constitutions, the rule of law, and representative government as necessary expressions of the people's will and sought to use popular enthusiasm for liberal forms of nationalism against the conservative monarchs of Europe. Liberals were aware of the threat to minority populations posed by new definitions of national identity and posited civic equality as a solution to the threat of discrimination against minorities. This commitment to equality had limits, however, and was confounded by emerging definitions of race in the nineteenth century. Some liberals argued that race had no scientific validity or bearing on national belonging (see *Analyzing Primary Sources* on page 726). In general, however, liberal definitions of national identity found it easier to apply the principle of civic equality to Europeans who were racialized as white than to enslaved Africans or Native Americans, and these latter groups were among the last to be recognized as citizens in states with liberal constitutions.

The upheavals of 1848 marked the high point of this period of liberal revolution, and their failure marked the end of that age. By the end of the nineteenth century, conservative governments also found ways to mobilize popular support by invoking nationalist themes. The only political movement to swim against the tide of nationalism was that of the socialists, who stressed the importance of class unity across national boundaries: Marx and his followers believed that German, French, and British workers had more in common with each other than with their middle-class employers. Even so, however, socialist movements in Europe developed in distinctly different national political contexts, making traditions of French socialism different from those of German socialism or Italian socialism.

The years following the 1848 revolutions witnessed a shift in the connections among liberalism, nationalism, and nation building. The construction of new nation-states in the heart of Europe happened simultaneously with the expansion of modern nation-states in North America and Asia. The treaty of Guadalupe Hidalgo transformed the boundaries between Mexico and the United States and added new states to the American republic. Equally significant was the American Civil War, which resulted in wrenching political change, the end of slavery, and new struggles about the rights of the formerly enslaved. During the same decades, the Russian tsar abolished serfdom and struggled with the nationalist aspirations of subject peoples in the massive lands that stretched between the Baltic and Black Seas. Finally, the well-established governments of France, Britain, and Austria undertook vast administrative reforms, overhauling their bureaucracies, expanding their electorates, and reorganizing relations among ethnic groups at home and in colonial territories abroad (see Chapter 22). These efforts at nation building helped to shift the balance of power in Europe toward states that were the earliest to industrialize and most successful in building strong, centralized states. Older imperial powers such as the Habsburg Empire in Austria-Hungary or the Ottoman Empire found their influence waning, in spite of their long history of successful rule over vast territories with diverse populations. At the heart of this nineteenth-century period of nation building lay changing relations between states and those they governed, which were hastened by reactions to the revolutionary upheavals of 1848.

The Revolutions of 1848

Throughout Europe, the spring of 1848 brought a dizzying sequence of revolution and repression. The roots of revolution lay in economic crisis, social antagonisms, and political grievances; but these revolutions were also shaped decisively by nationalism, especially in southern, central, and eastern Europe. Many reformers and revolutionaries had liberal goals—representative government, an end to aristocratic privilege, economic development, and so on. They also sought national unity, believing that their liberal goals could only be realized in a vigorous, "modern" nation-state. The 1848 revolutions demonstrated nationalism's power to mobilize opponents of the regime and its potential to override other allegiances entirely.

THE HUNGRY FORTIES

A deteriorating economic situation throughout Europe contributed to the outbreak of revolution in 1848, and helps to explain why revolutions occurred in so many places nearly simultaneously. Poor harvests in the early 1840s were followed by two years (1845–1846) when the grain harvest failed completely. A potato blight brought starvation in Ireland and hunger in Germany. Food prices doubled in 1846–1847, and bread riots broke out across Europe. Hungry people seized the grain and demanded that the merchants sell it at a "just" price. Compounding the problem was a cyclical industrial slowdown that spread across Europe, throwing thousands into unemployment. Public-relief organizations in many European cities were overwhelmed. In 1846 and 1847, these converging crises—food shortage, widespread misery, and public disorder—reached their apogee, and the decade was long remembered as the "Hungry Forties."

Poor harvests and grain shortages converge in the "Hungry Forties"

Hunger itself cannot cause revolution. It does, however, test governments' abilities to manage a crisis, and failure to solve food scarcity can make a ruler seem incompetent, and thus, illegitimate. When public relief foundered in France, troops repressed potato riots in Berlin, and regimes armed middle-class citizens to protect themselves against the poor, governments looked both authoritarian and inept. In the 1840s, European states already faced a host of political challenges: from liberals who sought constitutional government and limits on royal power, from republicans

The Human Species: Unity or Unequal "Races"?

Alexander von Humboldt (1769–1859) was a German geographer and naturalist. Humboldt's extensive voyages in the Americas and in Europe became the basis for his attempt to unify the many different branches of scientific research into a single universal science of the earth. In his multivolume work, Cosmos (1845–1847) he criticized earlier writers who believed that human populations could be divided into separate "species" or "races," arguing that this view was based on incomplete information about human diversity.

The most important questions of the civilization of mankind, are connected with the ideas of races, community of language, and adherence to one original direction of the intellectual and moral faculties.

As long as attention was directed solely to the extremes in varieties of colour and of form, and to the vividness of the first impression of the senses, the observer was naturally disposed to regard races rather as originally different species than as mere varieties. The permanence of certain types in the midst of the most hostile influences, especially of climate, appeared to favour such a view, not withstanding the shortness of the interval of time from which the historical evidence was derived. In my opinion, however, more powerful reasons can be advanced in support of the theory of the unity of the human race, as for instance, in the many intermediate gradations in the colour of the skin and in the form of the skull, which have been made known to us in recent times by the rapid progress of geographical knowledge—the analogies presented by the varieties in the species of many wild and domesticated animals—and the more correct observations collected regarding the limits of fecundity in hybrids. [. . .] On comparing the dark-coloured African nations [. . .] with the races inhabiting the islands of the South-Indian and West-Australian archipelago, and with the Papuas [. . .], we see that a black skin, woolly hair, and a negro-like cast of countenance are not necessarily connected together. So long as only a small portion of the earth was known to the Western nations, partial views necessarily predominated, and tropical heat and a black skin consequently appeared inseparable. [. . .]

The present races of animals have been produced by the combined action of many different internal, as well as external conditions, the nature of which cannot in all cases be defined, the most striking varieties being found in those families which are capable of the greatest distribution over the surface of the earth. The different races of mankind are forms of one sole species, by the union of two of whose members descendants are propagated. They are not different species of a genus, since in that case their hybrid descendants would remain unfruitful.

Source: Alexander von Humboldt, *Cosmos: A Sketch of a Physical Description of the Universe* (London: 1849), translated by E. C. Otté, pp. 361–64. https://babel.hathitrust.org/cgi/pt?id=inu.32000003195577&view=1up&seq=11&skin=2021

Questions for Analysis

1. What are the stakes of this discussion, according to von Humboldt? Why does he believe that it is important to understand whether humans all belong to the same species?

2. What explanation does von Humboldt offer for the widespread belief that human populations on earth could be divided up into different "species" or "races"?

3. What observations led Humboldt to suggest that this view is mistaken?

who campaigned for universal male suffrage, from nationalists who challenged the legitimacy of their hereditary rulers, and from socialists whose appeal lay in their claim to speak for the most economically vulnerable among the population. These political challenges were reinforced by the economic crisis of the 1840s, and the result was a wave of revolution that swept across Europe as one government after another lost the confidence of its people. The first of these revolutions came in France, but as elsewhere in 1848, it did not have the outcome the revolutionaries had hoped for.

THE FRENCH REVOLUTION OF 1848: A REPUBLICAN EXPERIMENT

The French monarchy after the revolution of 1830 (see Chapter 20) seemed little different from its predecessor. King **Louis-Philippe** gathered around him members of the banking and industrial elite, and refused demands to enlarge the franchise. Building projects, especially the railways, presented ample opportunities for graft, and the reputation of the government suffered. Republican associations proliferated in French cities, and in 1834, the government declared these organizations illegal. Rebellions broke out in Paris and Lyon, bringing a harsh repression that resulted in deaths and arrests. The government's refusal to compromise drove even moderates into opposition. In 1847, the opposition organized a campaign for electoral reform around repeated political "banquets" (an attempt to get around the laws against assembly). When they called for a giant banquet on February 22, 1848, the king responded by banning the meeting. A sudden and surprising popular revolution in the streets caused Louis-Philippe to abdicate his throne only days later, and a hastily assembled group of French political figures declared France a republic for the first time since 1792.

The provisional government of the new republic consisted of liberals, republicans, and—for the first time—socialists. They produced a new constitution, with elections based on universal male suffrage. Among their first acts was the abolition

Louis-Philippe (1773–1850) King of France from 1830 to 1848, during a period known as the July Monarchy, after the July Revolution of 1830 that brought him to the throne. Abdicated during the revolution of 1848.

THE BURNING OF THE THRONE (1848). A contemporary print shows revolutionaries burning the king's throne. Note the man with a top hat standing next to a man in a worker's smock on the left. Delacroix used similar images to depict cooperation between workers and middle-class revolutionaries (see page 693).

Two Views of the June Days, France, 1848

These two passages make for an interesting comparison. The socialist Karl Marx reported on the events of 1848 in France as a journalist for a German newspaper. For Marx, the bloodshed of the June Days shattered the "fraternal illusions" of February 1848, when the king had been overthrown and the provisional government established. That bloodshed symbolized a new stage in history—one of acute class conflict. For the socialist observer, the June Days represented a turning point: "The working class was knocking on the gates of history."

The French liberal politician Alexis de Tocqueville also wrote about his impressions of the revolution. However, for Tocqueville, a member of the government, the actions of the crowd sparked fear and conservative reaction. (Tocqueville's account is retrospective; he wrote his memoirs well after 1848.)

Karl Marx's Journalism (1848)

The last official remnant of the February Revolution, the Executive Commission, has melted away, like an apparition, before the seriousness of events. The fireworks of Lamartine [French Romantic poet and member of the provisional government] have turned into the war rockets of Cavaignac [French general, in charge of putting down the workers' insurrection]. *Fraternité*, the fraternity of antagonistic classes of which one exploits the other, this *fraternité*, proclaimed in February, on every prison, on every barracks—its true, unadulterated, its prosaic expression is civil war, civil war in its most fearful form, the war of labor and capital. This fraternity flamed in front of all the windows of Paris on the evening of June 25, when the Paris of the bourgeoisie was illuminated, whilst the Paris of the proletariat [Marxist term for the working people] burnt, bled, moaned. . . . The February Revolution was the beautiful revolution, the revolution of universal sympathy, because the antagonisms, which had flared up in it against the monarchy, slumbered peacefully side by side, still undeveloped, because the social struggle which formed its background had won only a joyous existence, an existence of phrases, of words. The June revolution is the ugly revolution, the repulsive revolution, because things have taken the place of phrases, because the republic uncovered the head of the monster itself, by striking off the crown that shielded and concealed it.—Order! was the battle cry of Guizot . . . Order! shouts Cavaignac, the brutal echo of the French National Assembly and of the republican bourgeoisie. Order! thundered his grape-shot, as

of slavery in France and French colonies (slavery had been abolished in 1794 during the revolution but reestablished by Napoleon in 1802). In spite of these accomplishments, tensions between propertied republicans and socialists shattered the unity of the coalition that toppled Louis-Philippe. Suffering because of the economic crisis, working men and women demanded the "right to work," or the right to earn a living wage. The provisional government responded by creating the National Workshops, a program of public works, to give jobs to the unemployed, headed by the socialist Louis Blanc. Initial plans were made to employ 10,000–12,000 workers, but unemployment was so high that 120,000 job seekers had gathered in the city by June 1848. Meanwhile, voters in rural areas resented the increase in it ripped up the body of the proletariat. None of the numerous revolutions of the French bourgeoisie since 1789 was an attack on order; for they allowed the rule of the class, they allowed the slavery of the workers, they allowed the bourgeois order to endure, however often the political form of this rule and of this slavery changed. June has attacked this order. Woe to June!

Source: *Neue Rheinische Zeitung* (New Rhineland Gazette), June 29, 1848, as cited in Karl Marx, *The Class Struggles in France (1848–1850)* (New York: 1964), pp. 57–58.

Alexis de Tocqueville Remembers the June Days (1893)

Now at last I have come to that insurrection in June which was the greatest and the strangest that had ever taken place in our history, or perhaps in that of any other nation: the greatest because for four days more than a hundred thousand men took part in it, and there were five generals killed; the strangest, because the insurgents were fighting without a battle cry, leaders, or flag, and yet they showed wonderful powers of coordination and a military expertise that astonished the most experienced officers.

Another point that distinguished it from all other events of the same type during the last sixty years was that its object was not to change the form of government, but to alter the organization of society. In truth it was not a political struggle (in the sense in which we have used the word "political" up to now), but a class struggle, a sort of "Servile War." . . . One should not see it only as a brutal and a blind, but as a powerful effort of the workers to escape from the necessities of their condition, which had been depicted to them as an illegitimate depression, and by the sword to open up a road towards that imaginary well-being that had been shown to them in the distance as a right. It was this mixture of greedy desires and false theories that engendered the insurrection and made it so formidable. These poor people had been assured that the goods of the wealthy were in some way the result of a theft committed against themselves. They had been assured that inequalities of fortune were as much opposed to morality and the interests of society as to nature. This obscure and mistaken conception of right, combined with brute force, imparted to it an energy, tenacity and strength it would never have had on its own.

Source: From Alexis de Tocqueville, *Recollections: The French Revolution of 1848*, ed. J. P. Mayer and A. P. Kerr, trans. George Lawrence (New Brunswick, NJ: 1987), pp. 136–37.

Questions for Analysis

1. Was Tocqueville sympathetic to the revolutionaries of June? Why or why not?

2. What was the historical significance of these events, according to Tocqueville?

3. Where did Tocqueville agree and disagree with Marx?

taxation required to pay for the public works program. When elections for Parliament were held—the first elections ever in France under a regime of universal male suffrage—the conservative voices won out, and a majority of moderate republicans and monarchists were elected.

A majority in the new assembly believed the National Workshops were a financial drain and a threat to order. In May, they closed the workshops to new enrollment, excluded recent arrivals to Paris, and sent members between the ages of eighteen and twenty-five into the army; on June 21, they abolished the workshops altogether. The workers of Paris—laborers, journeymen, the unemployed—rose in revolt, building barricades across Paris. For four days,

BARRICADE IN THE RUE DE LA MORTELLERIE, JUNE 1848, BY ERNEST MEISSONIER (1815–1891). A very different view of 1848: a depiction of the June Days.

June 23–26, they fought a hopeless battle against armed forces recruited from the provinces. The repression of the **June Days**, during which 3,000 were killed and 12,000 arrested, shocked the city's residents. Many of the prisoners were deported to labor camps in Algeria, then a French colony. Thereafter, support for the republic among the workers in Paris declined rapidly.

Subsequently, the government moved quickly to restore order. The parliament hoped for a strong leader in the next presidential election, and found one in the victor, Louis Napoleon Bonaparte, the nephew of the former emperor. Buoyed by enthusiastic support from rural voters, the upstart Louis Napoleon polled more than twice as many votes as the other three candidates combined. Louis Napoleon used his position to consolidate his power. He rallied the Catholics by restoring the Church to its former role in education and by sending an expedition to Rome to rescue the pope from revolutionaries. He banned radical activities and workers' associations, and suspended press freedoms. In 1851, he called for a plebiscite to give him the authority to change the constitution; and one year later, another plebiscite allowed him to establish the Second Empire, ending the republican experiment. He assumed the title of **Napoleon III** (r. 1852–1870), Emperor of the French.

The dynamics of the French Revolution of 1848—initial success, followed by divisions among the supporters of revolution, followed by a reassertion of authoritarian control—would be repeated elsewhere. Louis-Philippe's reign had alienated many of its middle-class supporters, leading them to join with the opposition and ally with radicals. Yet demands for reform soon led to fears of disorder and the desire for a strong state. This dynamic led to the collapse of the republic and to the rule of Napoleon III. The abandonment of the revolution's social goals—most visibly evident in the closing of the National Workshops—led to a stark polarization along class lines, with middle-class and working-class people demanding different things from the state. This political conflict would grow even more intense as socialism came into its own as an independent political force.

NATIONALISM, REVOLUTION, AND THE GERMAN QUESTION IN 1848

The revolutions of 1848 in the German-speaking lands of Europe shared some similarities with the revolutions in France. Like liberals in France, liberal Germans wanted a ruler who would abide by a constitution, allow for greater press freedoms, and accept some form of representative government, though not necessarily universal suffrage. As in France, artisans and urban laborers in German cities gravitated toward more-radical ideologies of republicanism and socialism, and protested against new methods of industrial production. The great difference between France and Germany in 1848, however, was that France already had a centralized state and a unified territory. In central Europe, a unified Germany did not exist. In 1815, the Congress of Vienna had created the German Confederation, a loose organization of thirty-nine states, including the German-speaking lands of Prussia and Habsburg Austria, but not the non-German-speaking lands under Prussian and Austrian control farther east. Because Prussia and Austria competed with each other to occupy the dominant position in German politics, revolutionaries in the German states were forced to reckon with these two powers as they struggled to find a path to national unity.

In 1806, Prussia had been defeated by the French under Napoleon. In response, Prussian officials passed a series of aggressive reforms. They reorganized the army, imitating Napoleon's policy of recruiting and promoting officers on the basis of merit rather than birth. In 1807, serfdom and the estate system were abolished. A year later, in a conscious attempt to increase middle-class Germans' sense of themselves as citizens, cities and towns were allowed to elect their councilmen and handle their own finances. (Justice and security continued to be administered by the central government in Berlin.) The Prussian reformers expanded facilities for both primary and secondary education and founded the University of Berlin, which numbered among its faculty several ardent nationalists.

Prussia aimed to establish itself as the leading German state and a counter to Austrian power in the region. Prussia's most significant victory in this respect came with the *Zollverein* (or customs union) in 1834, which established free trade among the German states and a uniform tariff against the rest of the world. By the 1840s, the union included almost all the German states, except German Austria, and offered manufacturers a market of almost 34 million people. Moreover, the spread of the railways after 1835 accelerated the exchange within this expanded internal market.

During the 1840s, political clubs of German students and other radicals joined with middle-class lawyers, doctors, and businessmen to demand representative government and reform. Newspapers multiplied,

> Unlike centralized France, Germany in 1848 is loosely unified, with Prussia and Austria competing for dominance

GERMAN CONFEDERATION, 1815. Compare this map with the one on page 747. › **Which major areas were left out of the German Confederation?** › **Why do you think they were left out?** › **What obstacles made it difficult to establish a unified German nation during this period?**

"EYES OPEN!" (c. 1845). This German cartoon from just before the 1848 revolution warns that aristocrats and clergy are conspiring to deny the German people their rights. The caption reads "Eyes Open! Neither the nobility nor the clergy shall oppress us any longer. For too long they have broken the backs of the people." › **Did supporters of the revolution consider the aristocracy or the clergy to be legitimate members of the nation? Compare this cartoon with the pamphlet that Abbé Sieyès wrote during the French Revolution (see page 620).**

defying censorship. Liberal reformers resented both Prussian domination of the German Confederation and the conservatism of the Habsburgs, who ruled the Austrian Empire. They attacked the combination of autocracy and bureaucratic authority that stifled political life in Prussia and Austria. German nationhood, they reasoned, would break Austrian or Prussian domination and end the sectional fragmentation that made reform so difficult.

When Frederick Wilhelm IV (r. 1840–1861) succeeded to the Prussian throne in 1840, hopes ran high. The new king gestured toward liberalizing reforms, but when economic troubles hit Frederick Wilhelm firmly asserted that his authority could not be questioned. He crushed a revolt among textile weavers in Silesia who protested against British imports, unemployment, falling wages, and hunger. The brutality of the regime's response shocked many. The king opposed constitutionalism and any representative participation in issues of legislation and budgets. Like the "enlightened" absolutists who preceded him, the Prussian king firmly believed that his leadership did not need assistance from elected legislatures or civil society as a whole.

When revolution came to France in the spring of 1848, unrest spread to the German states. In Catholic Bavaria, a student protest forced King Ludwig I to grant greater press freedoms, and when revolutionary movements appeared elsewhere in the smaller German states, the rulers yielded surprisingly quickly. The governments promised elections, expanded suffrage, jury trials, and other liberal reforms. In Prussia, Frederick Wilhelm was shaken by unrest in the countryside and stunned by a showdown in Berlin between the army and revolutionaries in which 250 were killed. He met with representatives of the protest movement and promised to grant a constitution.

THE FRANKFURT ASSEMBLY AND GERMAN NATIONHOOD

Frankfurt Assembly An elected assembly that met in Frankfurt in 1848 in order to prepare a constitution for a united Germany but failed to gain the support of the Prussian monarchy.

The reformers organized the election of 800 delegates to an all-German assembly in Frankfurt, where representatives from Prussia, Austria, and the small German states met to discuss the creation of a unified German nation. Most of the delegates came from the professional classes—lawyers, professors, administrators—and most were moderate liberals. They were not as radical as the workers and artisans who led the street protests against the king. The delegates assumed that the **Frankfurt Assembly** would draft a constitution for a liberal, unified Germany, much as an assembly of Frenchmen had done for their country in 1789. The comparison, however, was misguided. In 1789, a French nation-state and a centralized sovereign power already existed, needing only to be reformed and redirected by the assembled French delegates. In contrast, the Frankfurt Assembly had no resources, no sovereign power to take, no single legal code, and, of course, no army.

On the assembly floor, questions of nationality proved contentious and destructive. Which Germans would be in the new state? At first, a majority of the assembly's delegates supported a "Great Germany," arguing that the new nation should include as many Germans as possible. They were countered by a minority who called for a "Small Germany," one that left out all lands of the Habsburg Empire, including German Austria. After a long and difficult debate, the Austrian emperor withdrew his support, and the assembly retreated to the "Small Germany" solution. In April 1849, the Frankfurt Assembly offered the crown of a new German nation to the Prussian king, Frederick Wilhelm IV.

By this time, however, Frederick Wilhelm was negotiating from a position of greater strength. He used the military to repress radical revolutionaries in Berlin while delegates debated the constitutional question in Frankfurt. He was also encouraged by a backlash against revolutionary movements in Europe after the bloody repression of the June Days in Paris. He therefore refused to become a constitutional monarch on the terms offered by the Frankfurt Assembly. The Prussian monarch wanted both the crown and a larger German state, but on his own terms, and he therefore dissolved the Assembly before the delegates could approve the constitution with an official vote. After brief protests, summarily suppressed by the military, the Frankfurt delegates went home, disillusioned by the experience and convinced that their liberal and nationalist goals were incompatible. Some fled repression by immigrating to the United States; others decided to sacrifice their liberal views for the seemingly realistic goal of nationhood. In Prussia itself, the army dispatched what remained of the revolutionary forces.

Elsewhere in the German-speaking states, many moderate liberals began to have second thoughts about the pace of change. Peasants ransacked tax offices and burned castles; workers smashed machines in protests against industrialization. Citizen militias threatened the power of established elites. New daily newspapers multiplied, as did political clubs. For the first time, many of these clubs admitted women (although they were denied the right to speak), and newly founded women's clubs

"NO PIECE OF PAPER WILL COME BETWEEN MYSELF AND MY PEOPLE" (1848). In this cartoon, Frederick Wilhelm IV and a military officer refuse to accept the constitution for a new Germany offered to the king by the Frankfurt Assembly. Note that the caption refers to a conservative definition of the relationship between a monarch and "his people." Compare this autocratic vision of the nation-state with the liberal nationalist's demand for a government that reflects the will of the people. **› What contrasting visions of the nation and its relation to the state are contained in this cartoon?**

Frederick Wilhelm, refusing constitutional monarchy, dissolves Frankfurt Assembly

demanded political rights. This torrent of popular unrest made moderate reformers uneasy, and they considered universal male suffrage too radical. Throughout the German states, rulers took advantage of this shift in middle-class opinion to undo the concessions they had granted in 1848 and to push through counterrevolutionary measures in the name of order. After the failure of the Frankfurt Assembly, more-moderate German liberals increasingly looked to a strong Prussian state as the only possible route toward national unification.

PEOPLES AGAINST EMPIRE: THE HABSBURG LANDS

In the sprawling Habsburg (Austrian) Empire, nationalism played a different role. On the one hand, the Habsburg emperors could point to a remarkable record of political success. As heirs to the medieval Holy Roman Empire, Habsburg kings had ruled for centuries over a diverse array of ethnicities and language groups in central Europe that included Germans, Czechs, Hungarians, Poles, Slovaks, Serbs, and Italians, to name only the most prominent. In the sixteenth century, the empire had included Spain, parts of Burgundy, and the Netherlands. In the nineteenth century, however, the Habsburgs found it increasingly difficult to hold their empire together in the face of nationalist agitation after 1815. The greater ethnic and linguistic homogeneity of the German-speaking lands allowed for a convergence between liberal ideas of popular sovereignty and national unification, but no such program was possible in the Habsburg lands. Popular sovereignty for peoples defined in terms of their ethnic identity implied a breakup of the Habsburg Empire.

At the same time, the existence of nationalist movements did not imply unity, even within territories that spoke the same language. In the former Polish territories of the Habsburg Empire, nationalist sentiment was strong among landowners and the gentry. These elite groups were especially conscious of their historical role as leaders of the earlier Polish-Lithuanian Commonwealth, an example of an early modern political entity that was not solely defined by ethnic identity. Here, the Habsburg Empire successfully set serfs against their Polish landlords, ensuring that social grievances dampened the development of an ethnic Polish nationalism that could unite people of different social backgrounds.

In the Hungarian region, national claims were likewise advanced by the relatively small Magyar aristocracy. (*Magyar* is simply the Hungarian word for "Hungarian"; in English, it is sometimes used to describe Hungarian nationalists, whereas "Hungarian" might denote any citizen of Hungary, regardless of ethnic identity.) Yet **Magyar nationalism** gained an audience under the gifted and influential leadership of Lajos (Louis) Kossuth (*KAW-shut*; 1802–1894). A member of the minor nobility, Kossuth was by turns a lawyer, publicist, newspaper editor, and political leader. He campaigned for independence and a separate Hungarian parliament, and also (and more influentially) brought politics to the people. The Hungarian political leader combined aristocratic style with a populist's flare for mobilizing a crowd, a delicate balancing act but one that, when it worked, catapulted him to the center of Habsburg politics.

The other major nationalist movement that troubled the Habsburg Empire was **Pan-Slavism**. Slavs included Russians, Poles, Ukrainians, Czechs, Slovaks, Slovenes, Croats, Serbs, Macedonians, and Bulgarians. Before 1848, pan-Slavism

---

Magyar nationalism Lajos Kossuth led this national movement in the Hungarian region of the Habsburg Empire, calling for national independence for Hungary in 1848. With the support of Russia, the Habsburg army crushed the movement and all other revolutionary activities in the empire. Kossuth fled into exile.

Pan-Slavism Cultural movement that sought to unite native Slavic people within the Russian and Habsburg Empires under Russian leadership.

> *Nationalism increasingly demands a common ethnic identity, but Habsburg Empire notable for its ethnic diversity*

734   **Chapter 21** › Revolutions and Nation Building, 1848–1871

was primarily a cultural movement united by a general pro-Slavic sentiment. Internal divisions came from the competing claims of different Slavic languages and traditions. Poles, for example, tended to consider Pan-Slavism to be a cover for the expansion of Russian influence. The Polish Romantic poet Adam Mickiewicz (*mihtz-KYAY-vihch*) rejected it in favor of a Polish messianism that saw Poles championing the cause of oppressed nations everywhere. Pan-Slavism was much stronger among the Czechs and Slovaks, inspiring the works of the Czech historian and political leader František Palacký, the author of the *History of the Bohemian People*; and the Slovak Ján Kollár, whose book *Slávy Dcera* ("Slava's Daughter") mourned the loss of identity among Slavs in the Germanic world.

The fact that Russia and Austria were rivals made Pan-Slavism a volatile and unpredictable political force in the regions of eastern Europe, where the two nations vied for power and influence. Tsar Nicholas I of Russia sought to use Pan-Slavism to his advantage, but the tsar's efforts alienated Western-oriented Slavs who resented Russia's ambitions. Here, as elsewhere, nationalism created a tangled web of alliances and antagonisms.

AUSTRIA AND HUNGARY IN 1848: THE SPRINGTIME OF PEOPLES AND THE AUTUMN OF EMPIRE

Tensions in the Austro-Hungarian Empire exploded in 1848, with the opening salvo coming from Kossuth, who attacked the "Metternich system" of Habsburg autocracy and control and demanded autonomy for the Hungarian nation. The Hungarian Diet prepared to draft its own constitution. In Vienna, the Habsburg capital, a popular movement of students and artisans built barricades and attacked the imperial palace. A Central Committee of Citizens took shape, determined to maintain order and to press demands for reform. The Habsburg regime tried to shut the movement down by closing the university, but that only unleashed more popular anger, and the regime found itself forced to retreat. Metternich fled to Britain in disguise—a good indication of the political turmoil—leaving the emperor Ferdinand I in Vienna. The government conceded to radical demands for male suffrage and a single house of representatives, and agreed to withdraw troops from Vienna and to put forced labor and serfdom on a path to abolition. The government also agreed to Czech demands for a new diet (or parliament) in Bohemia. To the south, Italian

THE FIRST UNCENSORED NEWSPAPER AFTER THE REVOLUTION IN VIENNA, JANUARY 1848. This watercolor illustrates the power of public information during the 1848 revolution in the Austrian capital. An uncensored newspaper, wall posters, headgear with political insignia and slogans, and an armed citizenry are all evidence of a vibrant and impassioned public discussion on the events of the day. Note, too, the simple gown of the woman selling papers, the top hat and fashionable clothes of the middle-class man smoking a pipe, and the presence of military uniforms, all of which illustrate support for the revolution among a broad portion of the population. › **How does this vision of the public sphere in action compare with previous depictions of public debate in the Enlightenment (see page 599), in the French Revolution (see page 600), or elsewhere in Europe in 1848 (see page 740)?**

Lajos Kossuth on Democracy and Hungarian Nationalism

Lajos (Louis) Kossuth (1802–1894) was a lawyer and journalist who emerged as a leader of Hungarian nationalists in the Austrian Habsburg Empire during the 1848 revolution. He briefly became the governor of an independent Hungarian government but was forced to flee when Russian armies, supporting the Austrian Habsburgs, put an end to the Hungarian revolution. After a short stay in Turkey, the United States government invited Kossuth to visit. During his visit to the United States, he embarked on a successful speaking tour in which he was celebrated as a fervent supporter of democracy. This text comes from a speech he made before a banquet of journalists in New York City.

But happy art thou, free nation of America, founded on the only solid basis, —liberty! [. . .] Tyrants are not in the midst of you to throw the apple of discord and raise hatred in this national family, —hatred of *races*, that curse of humanity, that venomous ally of despotism. Glorious it is to see the oppressed of diverse countries, —diverse in language, history, habits, —wandering to these shores and becoming members of this great nation, regenerated by the principle of common liberty.

If language alone makes a nation, then there is no great nation on earth: for there is no country whose population is counted by millions, but speaks more than one language. No! It is not language only. Community of interests, of rights, of duties, of history, but chiefly community of institutions; by which a population, varying perhaps in tongue and race, is bound together through daily intercourse in the towns, which are the centers and home of commerce and industry: —besides these, the very mountain-ranges, the system of rivers and streams, —the soil, the dust of which is mingled with the mortal remains of those ancestors who bled on the same field, for the same interests, the common inheritance of glory and of woe, the community of laws and institutions, common freedom or

liberals and nationalists attacked the empire's territories in Venice; and in Milan, the forces of King Charles Albert of Piedmont-Sardinia routed the Austrians. Habsburg control of its various provinces seemed to be collapsing.

Yet the explosion of national sentiment that shook the empire also allowed the Habsburgs to recover. The paradox of nationalism in central Europe was that no cultural or ethnic majority could declare independence without prompting rebellion from other minority groups that inhabited the same area. In Bohemia, Czechs and Germans who lived side by side had worked together to pass reforms scuttling feudalism. Within a month, however, their alliance fractured: German Bohemians set off to attend the all-important Frankfurt Assembly, but the Czech majority refused to send representatives and countered by convening a confederation of Slavs in Prague. What did the delegates at the Slav confederation want? Some were hostile to the Austrian Empire, but the majority of delegates preferred to be ruled by the Habsburgs than to be dominated by either the Germans or the Russians.

This bundle of animosities allowed the Austrians to divide and conquer. In May 1848, during the Slav Congress, a student- and worker-led insurrection broke out

> *As nationalist sentiment surges, clashes between majority and minority ethnic groups create opening for Habsburgs to reassert control*

common oppression: —all this enters into the complex idea of Nationality.

That this is instinctively felt by the common sense of the people, nowhere is more manifestly shown than at this moment in my native land. Hungary was declared by Francis-Joseph of Austria *no more to exist* as a Nation, no more as a state. It was and is put under martial law. Strangers, aliens to our laws and history as well as to our tongue, rule now where our fathers lived and our brothers bled. To be a Hungarian is become [sic] almost a crime in our own native land. Well: to justify before the world the extinction of Hungary, the partition of its territory, and the reincorporating of the dissected limbs into the common body of servitude, the treacherous dynasty was anxious to show that the Hungarians are in a minority in their own land. They hoped that intimidation and terrorism would induce even the very Magyars to disavow their language and birth. They ordered a census of races to be made. They performed it with the iron rule of martial law; and dealt so arbitrarily that thousands of women and men, who professed to be Magyars, who professed not to know any other language than the Magyar, were, notwith-standing all their protestations, put down as Sclaves [sic], Serbs, Germans, or Wallachians, because their names had not quite a Hungarian sound. And still what was the issue of this malignant plot? That of the twelve millions of inhabitants of Hungary proper, the Magyars turned out to be more than eight millions, some two millions more than we know the case really is. The people instinctively felt that the tyrant had the design through the pretext of language to destroy the existence of the complex nation, and it met the tyrannic plot as if it answered, "We are, and must be, a nation; and if the tyrant takes language only for the mark of nationality, then we are all Magyars."

Source: Francis W. Newman, ed., *Speeches of Kossuth* (London: 1853), pp. 62–65.

Questions for Analysis

1. What does Kossuth admire about the political culture of the United States?

2. How does he define a "nation"? Why does he reject using language as the primary criterion for determining membership in a nation?

2. What does Kossuth's example of the national census taken by the Austrian government tell us about the new kinds of institutions that European states developed in response to the rise of nationalism?

in Prague. On the orders of the newly installed liberal government, Austrian troops entered the city to restore order, sent the Slav Congress packing, and reasserted control in Bohemia, rescinding the offer of a new parliament. For economic as well as political reasons, the new government was determined to keep the empire intact. The regime also sent troops to regain control in the Italian provinces of Lombardy and Venetia, where quarrels among the Italians helped the Austrians succeed.

Nationalism and counter-nationalism in Hungary set the stage for the final act of the drama. The Hungarian parliament had passed a series of laws, including new provisions for the union of Hungary and Austria. In the heat of 1848, Ferdinand I had little choice but to accept them. The Hungarian parliament abolished serfdom and ended noble privilege to prevent a peasant insurrection. It also established freedom of the press and religion and changed the suffrage requirements, enfranchising small property holders. Many of these measures (called the March laws) were hailed by Hungarian peasants, Jewish communities, and liberals. But other provisions—particularly the extension of Magyar control—provoked opposition from the Croats, Serbs, and Romanians within Hungary. On April 14, 1848,

LANGUAGES OF CENTRAL AND EASTERN EUROPE.
In Habsburg Austria-Hungary, the ethnic/linguistic boundaries did not conform to the political boundaries between states. › **How many languages were spoken in territories that were not contiguous with each other?** › **How did the diversity of peoples in the Habsburg Empire make uniting liberal revolution with nationalism more difficult to achieve?** › **What happens when you try to draw a border around the territories where German was spoken?** › **What tensions might you expect from the development of an expansionist German nationalism?**

Kossuth upped the ante, severing all ties between Hungary and Austria. The new Austrian emperor, Franz Josef, now played his last card: he asked for military support from Nicholas I of Russia. With the help of a Russian army of over 300,000, the Hungarian revolt was crushed by mid-August 1849. In Vienna, the liberal government capitulated. The Habsburg regime reestablished censorship, disbanded the national guard and student organizations, and put twenty-five revolutionary leaders to death in front of a firing squad. Kossuth went into hiding and lived the rest of his life in exile.

Paradoxically, then, the Habsburg Empire of Austria was in part saved by the very nationalist movements that threatened to tear it apart. Although nationalists in Habsburg lands, especially in Hungary, gained the support of significant numbers of people, different nationalist movements found it impossible to cooperate with one another. The new emperor, Franz Josef—with Russian help—was able to defeat the most significant challenges to his authority one by one, and consolidate his rule. Franz Josef would survive these crises and many others until his death in 1916 during World War I, a much larger conflict that finally overwhelmed and destroyed the Habsburg Empire for good.

THE EARLY STAGES OF ITALIAN UNIFICATION IN 1848

The Italian peninsula had not been united since the end of the Roman Empire. At the beginning of the nineteenth century, like the German-speaking lands of central Europe, the area that is now Italy was a patchwork of small states (see map on page 745). Austria occupied the northernmost states of Lombardy and Venetia, which were also the most urban and industrial. Habsburg dependents also ruled Tuscany, Parma, and Modena. The independent Italian states included the southern kingdom of the Two Sicilies, governed by members of the Bourbon family; the Papal States, ruled by Pope Gregory XVI (1831–1846); and most important, Piedmont-Sardinia, ruled by the reform-minded monarch Charles Albert (r. 1831–1849) of the House of Savoy. Charles Albert was not himself an enthusiastic nationalist, but by virtue of Piedmont-Sardinia's economic power, geographical location, and long tradition of opposition to the Habsburgs, his state played a central role in nationalist and anti-Austrian politics.

The leading Italian nationalist in this period was the republican Giuseppe Mazzini (1805–1872) from the city of Genoa, in Piedmont. Mazzini began his political career as a member of the Carbonari (see Chapter 20), an underground society pledged to resisting Austrian control of the region and establishing constitutional rule. In 1831, Mazzini founded his own society, Young Italy, dedicated to Italian unification under constitutional rule. Charismatic and persuasive, Mazzini was one of the best-known nationalists of his time. He spoke in characteristically Romantic tones about the awakening of the Italian people and of the common people's mission to bring republicanism to the world. Under his leadership, Young Italy clubs multiplied; yet the organization's favored tactics—plotting mutinies and armed rebellions—proved ineffective. In 1834, Mazzini launched an invasion of the kingdom of Sardinia, but without sufficient support it fizzled, driving him into exile in Britain.

Mazzini's republican vision of a united Italy clashed with the goals of his potential allies. Many liberals shared his commitment to creating a single Italian state but not his enthusiasm for the people and popular movements. They hoped instead to merge existing governments into some form of constitutional monarchy or, in a few cases, a government under the pope. Mazzini's insistence on a democratic republic committed to social and political transformation struck pragmatic liberals as utopian and well-to-do members of the middle classes as dangerous.

The turmoil that swept across Europe in 1848 raised hopes for political and social change and put Italian unification on the agenda. In March 1848, only a few weeks after revolution had toppled the French monarchy, popular revolts broke out in the northern provinces of Venetia and Lombardy, fueled by anger at the Austrian occupation. In Milan, the capital of Lombardy, thousands of people calling for reforms marched on the palace of the Austrian governor general, leading to pitched battles in the streets. In Venice, the revolutionaries forced the Austrian troops out of the city and declared it a republic. Charles Albert of Piedmont-Sardinia, seeing an opportunity to expand his own power, provided the rebels with military support and took up the banner of Italian nationalism as a way of challenging Austrian influence. At the same time, Charles Albert pleased Italian liberals by creating an elected legislature and relaxing press censorship in his kingdom.

In August 1848, an insurrection of laborers broke out in Bologna. Soon after, a popular uprising in Rome confronted the pope, and by February 1849, a new government in Rome had declared itself a republic. Mazzini returned from exile to join the revolutionary movement in Rome. These movements were neither coordinated nor ultimately successful. Charles Albert hesitated to confront the Austrians directly, and over the next few months the Austrians regained the upper hand in the north. French forces under Louis Napoleon intervened in Rome and the Papal States; although they met fierce resistance from the Roman republicans, they nonetheless restored the pope's power and defeated the Roman Republic. The short-lived Republic of San Marco in Venice was the last of the Italian revolutions

GIUSEPPE MAZZINI (1805–1872). Born in Genoa when it was ruled by Napoleon's France, Mazzini devoted his life to the cause of Italian unification and independence. Although his hopes for a republican Italy were blocked by Count Camillo Benso di Cavour's plans for unification under the leadership of Piedmont-Sardinia, Mazzini remained a hero to many Italians.

SIEGE OF VENICE, 1848. This image, designed to provoke anti-Austrian and nationalist sentiment among Italians, shows Venetian women and children donating their jewels to support their city while it was besieged by the Austrian army in 1848. › **What makes the image of women and children sacrificing their possessions for the larger good so powerful?** › **What does it say about the connections between nationalism and social obligations associated with gender?** › **Did nationalism depend on a vision of the family as well as of the nation?**

to fall, after a blockade and an artillery bombardment by the Austrian army in August 1849. Like most of the radical movements of 1848, these republican uprisings in Italy all failed. Still, they raised the hopes of nationalists who spoke of a *risorgimento* (or Italian resurgence) that would restore the nation to the position of leadership it had held in Roman times and during the Renaissance.

Building the Nation-State

Since the French Revolution of 1789, conservative politicians had associated nationhood with liberalism—constitutions, reforms, new political communities. In the wake of the revolutions of 1848, new nation-states were built or consolidated, often by former critics of nationalism. During the second half of the century, however, the political ground shifted dramatically. States and governments took the national initiative. Alarmed by revolutionary ferment, they promoted economic development, pressed social and political reforms, and sought to shore up their base of support. Rather than allow popular nationalist movements to emerge from below, statesmen consolidated their governments' powers and built nations from above.

FRANCE UNDER NAPOLEON III

Napoleon III, like his uncle, believed in personal rule and a centralized state. As emperor, he controlled the nation's finances, the army, and foreign affairs. The assembly, elected by universal male suffrage, could approve only legislation drafted at the emperor's direction. Napoleon's regime aimed to undermine France's traditional elites by expanding the bureaucracy and cultivating a new relationship with the people. "The confidence of our rough peasants can be won by an energetic authority," asserted one of the emperor's representatives.

Napoleon III also took steps to develop the French economy, believing that industrial expansion would bring prosperity and national glory. His government encouraged new forms of financing, passed new limited-liability laws, and signed a free-trade treaty with Britain in 1860. It also created the Crédit Mobilier, an investment banking institution that sold shares and financed railroad construction, coal mining, insurance and gas companies, and the building of the Suez Canal (see Chapter 22). Napoleon also reluctantly permitted the existence of trade unions and legalized strikes. By appealing to both the workers and the middle class, he sought to gain support for his goal of reestablishing France as a leading world power.

> *Napoleon III uses reforms to seek support from both workers and the middle class in France*

Most emblematic of the emperor's ambition was his transformation of the nation's capital. Paris's medieval infrastructure was buckling under the weight of population growth and industrial development. Cholera epidemics in 1832 and 1849 killed tens of thousands. In 1850, only one house in five had running water. Official concerns about public health were reinforced by political fears of crime and revolutionary militancy in working-class neighborhoods. A massive rebuilding project razed much of the medieval center of the city and erected 34,000 new buildings, including elegant hotels with the first elevators. The construction installed new water pipes and sewer lines, laid out 200 kilometers of new streets, and rationalized the traffic flow. The renovation did not benefit everyone. Rising rents drove working people from the city's center into increasingly segregated suburbs. Baron Georges-Eugène Haussmann, the prefect of Paris who presided over the project, considered the city a monument to "cleanliness and order." Others called Haussmann an "artist of demolition."

VICTORIAN BRITAIN AND THE SECOND REFORM BILL (1867)

Less affected by the revolutionary wave of 1848, Great Britain under Queen Victoria continued the changes that had begun in 1832 with the First Reform Bill. The government faced mounting demands to extend the franchise beyond the middle classes. Industrial expansion sustained a growing stratum of highly skilled and relatively well-paid workers (almost exclusively male), who turned away from the militant radicalism of the previous generation. They favored collective self-help through cooperative societies or trade unions, which accumulated funds for insurance against old age and unemployment. These prosperous workers saw education as a tool for advancement and patronized the mechanics' institutes and similar institutions founded by them or on their behalf, and their activities created real pressure for electoral reform.

Some workers argued for the vote in the name of democracy. Others borrowed arguments from earlier middle-class campaigns for electoral reform: they were responsible workers, respectable and upstanding members of society, with strong religious convictions and patriotic feelings. Unquestionably loyal to the state, the workers reasoned that they deserved the vote and direct representation just as much as the middle class. They were supported by many middle-class dissenting reformers in the Liberal party, whose religious beliefs (as dissenters from the Church of England) made them a target for discrimination. The dissenters were denied posts in the civil service and the military, and had been excluded from the nation's premier universities, Oxford and Cambridge, unless they renounced their faith and subscribed to the articles of the Anglican Church. Moreover, they resented paying taxes to support the Church of England, which was largely staffed by sons of the gentry and run in the interests of landed society. The fact that the community of dissent crossed class lines was vital to Liberal party politics and the campaign for reforming the vote.

Working-class leaders and middle-class dissenters joined in a countrywide campaign for a new reform bill. They were backed by some shrewd Conservatives, such as Benjamin Disraeli (1804–1881), who argued that political life would be improved, not disrupted, by including the "aristocrats of labor." In actuality, Disraeli was betting that the newly enfranchised demographic would vote Conservative; and in 1867, he steered through Parliament a bill that reached further than anything proposed by his political opponents. The 1867 Reform Bill doubled the franchise by extending the vote to any men who paid poor rates or rent of £10 or more a year in urban areas (this meant, in general, skilled workers) and rural tenants paying rent of £12 or more. The bill redistributed seats, with large northern cities gaining representation at the expense of the rural south. Although the Chartists' goal of universal male suffrage remained unfulfilled, the 1867 law allowed a portion of the working class to participate in the affairs of the state.

The reform bill was silent on women, but an important minority supported women's enfranchisement. These advocates mobilized a women's suffrage movement, building on the remarkable participation of women in earlier reform campaigns, especially the Anti–Corn Law League and the movement to abolish slavery. Their cause found a passionate supporter in **John Stuart Mill**, perhaps the century's most brilliant and influential defender of personal liberty. Influenced by the utilitarian philosopher Jeremy Bentham, Mill published *On Liberty* in 1859, a classic defense of individual freedom in the face of the "tyranny of the majority." He coauthored—with his lover and eventual wife, Harriet Taylor—essays on women's political rights and the law of marriage and divorce. At the time, Taylor was trapped in an unhappy marriage, but divorce required an act of

MILL'S LOGIC, OR FRANCHISE FOR FEMALES
" Pray clear the way, there, for these—ah—persons."

JOHN STUART MILL AND SUFFRAGETTES.
By 1860, when this cartoon was published, Mill had established a reputation as a liberal political philosopher and a supporter of women's right to vote. Mill argued that women's enfranchisement was essential from the standpoint of individual liberty as well as for the good of society as a whole. **> What is amusing about Mill's assertion in this cartoon that women should be considered persons in their own right?**

Parliament. Mill's *Subjection of Women* (1869), published after Taylor died, argued what few could even contemplate at the time: that women had to be considered individuals on the same plane as men and that women's freedom was a measure of social progress. *Subjection* was an international success and, with *On Liberty*, became one of the defining texts of Western liberalism. Mill's arguments, however, did not carry the day; it was the militant suffrage movements and the crisis of the First World War that brought women the vote.

The decade or so following the passage of the Reform Bill of 1867 marked the high point of British liberalism. By opening the doors to political participation, liberalism had accomplished a peaceful restructuring of political institutions and social life. It did so under considerable pressure from below, however, and in Britain, as elsewhere, liberal leaders made it clear that these doors were unquestionably not open to everyone. Their opposition to women's suffrage is interesting for what it reveals about their views on male and female nature. They insisted that female individuality—expressed in voting, education, or wage earning—would destabilize family life. Yet their opposition to women's suffrage reflected their conception of the vote; that is, casting a ballot was a privilege granted only to specific social groups in return for their contributions to and vested interest in society. Men of property championed the rule of law and representative government, but they balked at the prospect of truly democratic politics and did not shy away from heavy-handed law-and-order politics. Expanding the franchise created new constituencies with new ambitions, and paved the way for socialist and labor politics in the last quarter of the century.

GIUSEPPE GARIBALDI. Note the simple uniform Garibaldi wears in this commemorative portrait, with its iconic symbols of his nationalist movement: the red shirt and the flag of Italy in the background. Compare this image with the official portraits of absolutist rulers in previous chapters. › **What was significant about the absence of finery and precious materials in this painting?** › **What does this portrait say about images of masculine leadership in mid-nineteenth-century nationalist imagination? (Compare this painting with the drawing of Garibaldi and Victor Emmanuel on page 744.)**

ITALIAN UNIFICATION: CAVOUR AND GARIBALDI

After the failure of Italian unification in 1848, nationalists in Italy faced a choice between two strategies for achieving statehood. One group, supported by Mazzini and his follower Giuseppe Garibaldi, envisioned a republican Italy built from below by popular uprising. **Giuseppe Garibaldi** was a guerrilla fighter who had been exiled twice, first to Latin America, where he fought along with independence movements, and again to the United States. Like Mazzini, he was committed to achieving national unification through popular movements committed to democratic reforms.

A second group of nationalists, more conservative and suspicious of democracy, sought to unify Italy as a constitutional monarchy, under the leadership of the kingdom of Piedmont-Sardinia. The king of Piedmont-Sardinia, Charles Albert,

Giuseppe Garibaldi
(1807–1882) Italian revolutionary leader who led the fight to free Sicily and Naples from the Habsburg Empire.

had drawn the attention of Italian nationalists in 1848 when he took up the anti-Austrian cause. Charles Albert's son Victor Emmanuel II (r. 1849–1861) brought into his government a man who would embody the conservative vision of nationhood: the shrewd Sardinian nobleman **Count Camillo Benso di Cavour (1810–1861)**. Cavour pursued ambitious but pragmatic reforms guided by the state. As prime minister, he promoted economic expansion, encouraged the construction of a modern transportation infrastructure, reformed the currency, and sought to raise Piedmont-Sardinia's profile in international relations. Garibaldi and Cavour thus represented two different routes to Italian unification: Garibaldi stood for unification from below, Cavour for unification guided from above.

Cavour's plan depended on diplomacy, and he skillfully cultivated an alliance with one of Austria's traditional rivals: Napoleonic France. In 1858, Napoleon III agreed to help drive the Austrians from Italy if Piedmont ceded Savoy and Nice to France. Cavour provoked a war with Austria in 1859, but after some initial success Napoleon III suddenly withdrew, concerned that he might antagonize French Catholics, who were alienated by Cavour's hostility to the pope. Piedmont thus failed to expel the Austrians from Venetia, but the campaign made extensive gains in the north: Lombardy, Tuscany, Parma, and Modena all agreed by plebiscite to join Cavour's growing nation. By the end of this process in 1860, Piedmont-Sardinia had grown to more than twice its original size and was by far the most powerful state in Italy.

As Cavour's power increased, events in the southern states seemed to put those areas up for grabs as well. The unpopular Bourbon king of the Two Sicilies, Francis II (r. 1859–1860), faced a peasant revolt that rekindled the hopes of earlier insurrections of the 1820s and 1840s. The revolt got a much needed boost from Garibaldi, who landed in Sicily in May 1860. "The Thousand," as Garibaldi's volunteer fighters called themselves, embodied the widespread support for Italian unification. They came from the north as well as from the south and counted among them members of the middle class, workers, and artisans. Garibaldi's troops took Sicily and continued on to the mainland; and by November 1860,

"RIGHT LEG IN THE BOOT AT LAST." This image shows Garibaldi helping Victor Emmanuel, formerly the king of Piedmont-Sardinia and the newly crowned king of Italy, fit his foot in the Italian boot. What is the significance of their different forms of dress and postures? › Compare this image with the portrait of Garibaldi on page 743. How does this image portray the outcome of the contest between the conservative nationalism of Cavour and the more romantic and democratic nationalism of Garibaldi?

they, alongside local insurgents, had taken Naples and toppled the kingdom of Francis II. Emboldened by this success, Garibaldi looked to Rome, where French troops guarded the pope.

Garibaldi's rising popularity put him on a collision course with Cavour, who worried that Garibaldi's forces would bring French or Austrian intervention. Above all, Cavour preferred that Italian unification happen quickly, under Piedmont-Sardinia's stewardship. He dispatched Victor Emmanuel, king of Piedmont-Sardinia, to Rome with an army, and the king ordered Garibaldi to cede him military authority. Garibaldi obeyed, and Victor Emmanuel assumed the title of king of Italy (r. 1861–1878), unifying most of the peninsula under his rule. Cavour's vision of Italian nationhood had won the day.

The final steps of Italy's territorial nation building came indirectly. Venetia remained in the hands of the Austrians until 1866, when Austria's defeat in the Austro-Prussian War forced the Habsburg realm to relinquish its last Italian stronghold. Rome had resisted conquest largely because of the military protection Napoleon III accorded the pope. But in 1870, the outbreak of the Franco-Prussian War compelled Napoleon to withdraw his troops. That September, Italian soldiers occupied Rome; and in July 1871, Rome became the capital of the united Italian kingdom. The Italian Parliament passed the Law of Papal Guarantees to define and limit the pope's status, but Pius IX refused to have anything to do with a disrespectful secular government. His successors continued to close themselves off in the Vatican until 1929, when a series of agreements between the Italian government and Pius XI settled the dispute.

In 1871, Italy was a state, but nation building was hardly over. A minority of the "Italian" population spoke Italian, but the rest spoke local and regional dialects so diverse that schoolteachers sent from Rome to Sicily were mistaken for foreigners. As one politician remarked, "We have made Italy; now we must make Italians." This task proved to be difficult. The gap between an increasingly industrialized north and a poor and rural south remained wide. Banditry in the territory of the former kingdom of the Two Sicilies compelled the central administration to dispatch troops to quell serious uprisings, killing more people than in the war of unification. Regional differences and social tensions continued to challenge the Italian state into the twentieth century.

THE UNIFICATION OF ITALY. › How many phases were involved in Italian unification, according to the map key? › Why did it take an extra decade to incorporate Rome and Venetia into the Italian state? › Why was Italian unification incomplete until the early twentieth century?

THE UNIFICATION OF GERMANY: REALPOLITIK

Otto von Bismarck
(1815–1898) The prime minister of Prussia and later the first chancellor of a unified Germany.

After the failure of the 1848 revolutions, German liberalism persisted as a political force, but it no longer seemed capable of bringing about national unity. Those who sought a unified Germany focused their attention on pragmatic questions about political power: how to achieve it, and how to preserve it. This attitude—summed up in the expression *Realpolitik*, or practical, realistic policies—held that Enlightenment visions of rights and constitutions were less important than cold-eyed assessments of power and interests. This vision of Realpolitik became the watchword of Otto von Bismarck, the deeply conservative Prussian official whose leadership played an important role in German unification.

King Frederick Wilhelm granted a Prussian constitution in 1850 that established a two-house parliament, with the lower house elected by universal male suffrage. The electoral system nevertheless preserved the power of traditional elites by dividing voters into three classes based on the amount of taxes paid, and their votes were apportioned accordingly. The relatively small number of wealthy voters who paid one-third of Prussia's taxes elected one-third of the legislators in Parliament. In this way, a large landowner or a wealthy industrialist exercised perhaps seventeen times the voting power of a workingman. Voting took place in public, orally, so a secret ballot was impossible.

In 1861, Wilhelm I became king of Prussia. Under his rule, Prussia remained a notoriously conservative state, but a decade of industrial growth had also expanded the size and confidence of the middle classes. By the late 1850s, Prussia had an active liberal intelligentsia, a liberal civil service dedicated to political and economic modernization, and a thoughtful and engaged press. These forces helped forge a liberal political movement that won a majority in the lower house and thus could confidently confront the king.

Liberals in Prussia were especially opposed to the king's high levels of military spending. Wilhelm wanted to expand the standing army, and his opponents in Parliament suspected the king of wanting to make the military his own private force or a state within a state. Between 1859 and 1862, relations between the two deteriorated; and when liberals' protests went unanswered, they refused to approve the regular budget. Faced with a crisis, Wilhelm named **Otto von Bismarck** minister-president of Prussia in 1862. (A prime minister answers to Parliament; Bismarck did not.) This crucial moment in Prussian domestic politics became a decisive turning point in the history of German nationhood.

Born into the Junker class of conservative land-owning aristocrats, Bismarck had fiercely opposed the liberal movement of 1848–1849. He was not a nationalist; he was, before all else, a Prussian. When he maneuvered to bring other German states under Prussian domination, he did so not in pursuit of a grand German design but because he believed that union in some form was inevitable and so Prussia had to seize the initiative.

In Prussia, Bismarck defied parliamentary opposition. When the liberal majority refused to pass a budget, he dissolved Parliament, claiming that the constitution, whatever its purposes, had not been designed to subvert the state. His most decisive actions, however, were in foreign policy. Once opposed to nationalism, Bismarck skillfully played the national card to preempt his liberal opponents at home and to make German nation building an accomplishment—and an extension—of Prussian authority.

The other "German" power was Austria, which wielded considerable influence within the German Confederation and especially over the largely Catholic regions in the south. Bismarck saw a stark contrast between Austrian and Prussian interests and skillfully exploited Austria's economic disadvantages and the Habsburgs' internal ethnic struggles. He inflamed a long-smoldering dispute with Denmark over Schleswig (*SHLAYS-vihg*) and Holstein, two provinces peopled by Germans and Danes and claimed by both the German Confederation and Denmark. In 1864, the Danish king attempted to annex the provinces, prompting a German nationalist

Legend:

— German Confederation boundary (1815)

Prussian acquisitions

From Austria in 1763 — Prussia (1815)

From partitions of Poland in 1772, 1793, 1795 — Prussia (1815)

States annexed by Prussia in 1866

States joining Prussia in Confederation of 1867

— North German Confederation boundary

States added to form German Empire (1871)

Territories ceded by France (1871)

✳ Battle

■ Fortifications

TOWARD THE UNIFICATION OF GERMANY. Note the many elements that made up a unified Germany and the stages that brought them together. › Did this new nation have any resemblance to the unified Germany envisioned by the liberal revolutionaries of the Frankfurt Pre-Parliament in 1848 (see page 731)? › How many stages were involved in the unification of Germany? › How many years did it take to achieve unification? › What region filled with German-speaking peoples was not included in the new unified Germany? Why not?

outcry. Bismarck cast the conflict as a Prussian matter and persuaded Austria to join Prussia in a war against Denmark. The war was short, and it forced the Danish ruler to cede the two provinces to Austria and Prussia. As Bismarck hoped, the victorious alliance promptly fell apart. In 1866, casting Prussia as the defender of larger German interests, he declared war on Austria. The conflict, known as the Seven Weeks' War, ended in Prussian victory. Austria gave up all claims to Schleswig and Holstein, surrendered Venetia to the Italians, and agreed to dissolve the German Confederation. In its place, Bismarck created the North German Confederation, a union of all the German states north of the Main River.

Both wars had strong public support, and Prussian victories weakened liberal opposition to the king and his president-minister. In the aftermath of the Austrian defeat, Prussian liberals gave up their battle over budgets, the military, and constitutional provisions. Bismarck also sought support among ordinary citizens, and understood that Germans did not necessarily support business elites, the bureaucracies of their own small states, or the Austrian Habsburgs. The constitution of the North German Confederation gave the appearance of a more liberal political body, with a bicameral legislature, freedom of the press, and universal male suffrage in the lower house. Its structure, however, gave Prussia and the conservative emperor a decisive advantage in German politics.

The final step in the completion of German unity was the Franco-Prussian War of 1870–1871. Bismarck hoped that a conflict with France would arouse German nationalism in Bavaria, Württemberg, and other southern states still outside the confederation, and overcome their historical wariness of Prussia. A diplomatic tempest concerning the right of the Hohenzollerns (Prussia's ruling family) to occupy the Spanish throne created an opportunity to foment a Franco-German misunderstanding. King Wilhelm agreed to meet with the French ambassador at the resort spa of Ems in Prussia to discuss the Spanish succession. Wilhelm initially acquiesced to French demands, but when the French blundered by asking for "perpetual exclusion" of the Hohenzollern family from the Spanish throne, Bismarck seized his opportunity. He edited a telegraph from King Wilhelm so as to make it appear that the Prussian king had rebuffed the French ambassador. Once the redacted report reached France, the nation reacted with calls for war. Prussia echoed the call, and Bismarck published evidence that he claimed proved French designs on the Rhineland.

As soon as war was declared, the south German states rallied to Prussia's side. No European powers came to France's aid, however; Austria, the most likely candidate, was weakened by its recent war with Prussia. The Hungarians, meanwhile, welcomed a strengthened Prussia, for the weaker Austria was as a German power, the stronger would be the Magyar claims to power sharing in the empire. On the battlefield, France could not match Prussia's professionally trained and superbly equipped forces, and the conflict was quickly over. The war began in July and ended in September with the defeat of the French and the capture of Napoleon III at Sedan in France. Insurrectionary forces in Paris continued to hold out against the Germans through the winter of 1870–1871, but the French imperial government collapsed.

On January 18, 1871, in the Hall of Mirrors at Versailles, the German Empire was proclaimed. The remaining German states (except Austria) declared their allegiance to Wilhelm I, henceforth emperor, or kaiser, of Germany. Four months later, at Frankfurt, a treaty between the French and the Germans ceded the border region

Bismarck spurs war with France in hopes of stirring German nationalist feeling ❯

of Alsace to the new German Empire and forced the French to pay an indemnity of 5 billion francs. Prussia accounted for 60 percent of the new state's territory and population; and the Prussian kaiser, prime minister, army, and most of the bureaucracy remained intact, now reconfigured as the German nation-state. This was not the new nation for which Prussian liberals had hoped, for it marked a "revolution from above" rather than from below.

THE STATE AND NATIONALITY: CENTRIFUGAL FORCES IN THE AUSTRIAN EMPIRE

Germany emerged from the 1860s a stronger, unified nation. The Habsburg Empire, on the other hand, worked hard to preserve its precariously balanced, multiethnic dual monarchy, also called Austria-Hungary.

As we have seen, ethnic nationalism was a powerful force in the Habsburg monarchy in 1848. Yet the Habsburg state, with a combination of military repression and tactics that divided its enemies, had proved more powerful. It abolished serfdom and made few other concessions to its opponents. The Hungarians, who had nearly won independence in the spring of 1848, were essentially reconquered. Administrative reforms created a new and more uniform legal system and a rationalized taxation, and imposed a single-language policy that favored German.

Managing ethnic relations, however, only grew more difficult. Through the 1850s and 1860s, the subject nationalities bitterly protested the powerlessness of their local parliaments, military repression, and cultural disenfranchisement. The Czechs in Bohemia, for instance, grew increasingly alienated by policies that favored the German minority of the province. In response, they became more insistent on their Slavic identity—a movement welcomed by Russia, which became the sponsor of a broad Pan-Slavism. The Hungarians, or Magyars, the most powerful of the subject nationalities, sought to reclaim the autonomy they had glimpsed in 1848.

In this context, Austria's defeats at the hands of Piedmont-Sardinia in 1859 and Prussia in 1866 become especially significant. The 1866 war forced Emperor Francis Joseph (Franz Josef in German) to renegotiate the very structure of the empire. To forestall a revolution by the Hungarians, Francis Joseph agreed to a new federal structure in the form of the Dual Monarchy of Austria-Hungary. It had a common system of taxation and a common army, and made foreign and military policy together, with Francis Joseph as emperor of Austria and king of Hungary. But internal and constitutional affairs were separated. The *Ausgleich* (or Settlement) allowed the Hungarians to establish their own constitution, legislature, and capital, combining the cities of Buda and Pest.

The official policy of the Dual Monarchy stated that the smaller nationalities were not to be discriminated against and that they could use their own languages. This official policy was only loosely enforced. More important, elevating the Hungarians and conferring on them alone the benefits of political nationhood only worsened relations with other groups. Minority nationalities in Austria such as the Poles, Czechs, and Slovenes resented their second-class status. On the Hungarian side, the regime embarked on a project of Magyarization, attempting to make the state, the civil service, and the schools more thoroughly Hungarian—an effort that did not sit well with Serbs and Croats.

In spite of these divisions, the Austro-Hungarian Empire succeeded for a time in creating a different kind of political and cultural space within Europe, one that was

The New German Nation

In order to silence their critics at home and abroad, nationalists in Germany sought to create a vision of German history that made unification the natural outcome of a deep historical process that had begun hundreds of years before. Image A shows the family of a cavalry officer preparing to hang a portrait of King Wilhelm on the wall, next to the portraits of Martin Luther, Frederick the Great, and Field Marshal von Blücher, who commanded the Prussian forces at Waterloo. In the lower left corner, two boys are rolling up a portrait of the defeated French emperor, Napoleon III. The implication, of course, is that generations of German heroes all worked toward the same goal: the inevitable unification of Germany.

This unity, however, was controversial among German people. Image B, a pro-Bismarck cartoon, shows the German minister-president dragging the unwilling liberal members of the Prussian Parliament with him as he pulls a triumphal chariot toward his military confrontation with Austria in 1866. The caption reads, "And in this sense, too, we are in agreement with Count

A. *Homage to Kaiser Wilhelm [William] I*, by Paul Bürde (1871).

multinational rather than national. The Austrian capital of Vienna developed a reputation for intellectual and cultural refinement in part due to the many different peoples who made up the Habsburg lands, including Germans, Jews, Hungarians, Italians, Czechs, Poles, Serbs, Croats, and Balkan Muslims from lands that formerly belonged to the Ottoman Empire. This polyglot culture produced Béla Bartók (1881–1945), the great Hungarian composer and admirer of folk musical traditions; and Gustav Mahler (1860–1911), a German-Austrian composer whose Romantic symphonies and conducting prowess made him a global celebrity by the time of his death. From the same intellectual milieu came Sigmund Freud (1856–1939), a German-speaking

Bismarck, and we have pulled the same rope as him." Image C, on the other hand, expresses reservations about Prussian dominance in the new empire. The title reads "Germany's Future" and the caption, "Will it fit under one hat? I think it will only fit under a [Prussian] Pickelhaube." The *Pickelhaube* (the characteristic pointed helmet of the Prussian army) had already become a much-feared symbol of Prussian military force. Such an image may well have struck a chord with residents of the non-Prussian German states, who now paid taxes to the Prussian monarchy and served in an army dominated by Prussian officers.

Questions for Analysis

1. What is the significance of the familial setting in image A? Why was it important for nationalists to emphasize a multigenerational family as the repository of German national spirit?

2. How do images B and C treat the question of Prussia's role within the new German nation? Is German national identity seen as something built from below or defined from above by a strong monarchy?

3. What is the place of the individual citizen in these representations of the German nation?

C. "Germany's Future" (1870).

B. Prussian liberals and Bismarck after Königgrätz in the Austro-Prussian War (1866).

Jewish doctor from Vienna, whose writings helped shape modern psychology; and Gustav Klimt (1862–1918), a painter and founding member of the Viennese Secession movement, which rejected the reigning classicism of the Austrian art world and made the Austrian capital an important center for the birth of modern art.

The Austrian emperor's deep opposition to nationalism was not just geopolitical, but a defense of a different relationship between the nation-state and culture. Unlike the governments of France, England, Italy, or Germany, the Habsburgs did not seek to build a nation-state based on common cultural identity. It tried instead to build a state with an administrative structure that was strong enough to keep the pieces from spinning off, at times by playing different minorities against each other and, when necessary, conceding greater autonomy to different groups. As the nineteenth century unfolded, however, discontented subject nationalities began to appeal to other powers—Serbia, Russia, the Ottomans—and this balancing act became more difficult.

Nation and State Building in Russia and the United States

The challenges of nationalism and nation building also occupied Russia, the United States, and Canada. In all three countries, nation building entailed territorial and economic expansion, the incorporation or subjugation of new peoples, and—in Russia and the United States—contending with the enormous problems of slavery and serfdom.

RUSSIA'S NATIONALITY QUESTION AND THE EMANCIPATION OF THE SERFS

In the nineteenth century, Russia faced a nationality question every bit as complicated as that faced by the Habsburg Empire. Along the borders that separated Russia from the other European powers, the partitions of the Polish-Lithuanian Commonwealth had brought a culturally and linguistically diverse territory under Russian control, which extended from the Baltic coast to the area that is now western Ukraine. In this region, many of the nobility were Roman Catholic and spoke Polish, and Polish remained the language of high culture. The peasantry spoke dialects of Polish, Lithuanian, Belarusian, and, in the south, Ukrainian. A large portion of the urban population, meanwhile, were Jews who spoke Yiddish (the Polish partitions had brought the majority of the world's Jews under Russian control). After the Polish uprising of 1830–1831 (Chapter 20), the Russian government cracked down on languages that could become rallying points for distinctive "national" cultures within the Russian Empire.

Across the nineteenth century, Poles, Lithuanians, Belarusians, and Ukrainians perceived the advantages of a national culture and political independence from Russia, but each faced very different challenges. Polish nationalists looked for ways to attach their culture to a mass base in the countryside, and religion helped in this task, because both nobles and peasants in the territories around Warsaw were Roman Catholic. Lithuanians faced the opposite challenge: they had no problem claiming that their language and culture were rooted in the common people, because most of the peasantry in the area around Vilnius spoke Lithuanian; however, the absence of a long literary tradition in Lithuanian made it difficult to claim a rich and ancient cultural heritage. In Ukraine, a stumbling block was religion: both Polish-speaking and Ukrainian-speaking nobles had emerged from the Reformation firmly in the Roman Catholic camp, whereas the peasantry remained attached to the Orthodox Church. In general, nineteenth-century nationalisms encouraged people to look for a strong overlap between high and low culture, between urban and rural populations, and religious homogeneity. The complex history of central and eastern Europe made this an exceedingly difficult recipe to follow.

Debates about national culture in Russia and eastern Europe were also linked to debates within Russia about the **emancipation of the serfs**. Serfdom had developed over many centuries in Europe as a system for controlling agricultural labor. Serfs in Russia were bound to the land, prohibited from flight, and subject to corporal punishment by their owners. They also could be transferred from one landowner to another without their property or family members. After 1789, and especially after 1848, the abolition of serfdom elsewhere in Europe made the issue more urgent, as supporters for reform in Russia looked to Europe for examples. On this question, two schools of thought emerged. The "Slavophiles," or Romantic nationalists, sought to preserve Russia's distinctive features and rejected Western influence. In contrast, the "Westernizers" wished to see Russia adopt European developments in science, technology, and education, which they believed to be the foundation for Western liberalism and the protection of individual rights. Both groups were committed to expanding Russian power, and both agreed that serfdom must be abolished. The Russian nobility, however, tenaciously opposed emancipation. The Crimean War (see pages 759–61) broke the impasse: in its aftermath, **Tsar Alexander II** (r. 1855–1881) became convinced that the persistence of serfdom had contributed to its defeat in the war, so he ended serfdom in all of Russia by decree in 1861.

Before the reform could be fully carried out, the last and largest of the nineteenth-century Polish insurrections broke out in 1863 after a dispute about military conscription. The **January Rising** spread rapidly as thousands of men took to guerrilla warfare in the countryside. By April, the rebellion had spread eastward into Lithuania and Russia. As both sides competed to gain the support of the peasantry, the implementation of the tsar's emancipation decree became caught up in the struggle. Eventually, the Russian military prevailed; the leaders were caught and executed in 1864 and thousands of Poles were sent into permanent exile in Siberia. The violence of the Russian government's repression of the January Rising had an unintended consequence: the tradition of **Polish nationalism**, long associated with elite culture and the gentry, now took firm root among Polish-speaking peasants as well.

Elsewhere in Russia, the emancipation of the serfs produced only limited change at first. The Russian government granted legal rights to some 22 million serfs and granted them a portion of land, but it also agreed to compensate landowners. Large-scale landowners vastly inflated their compensation claims, however, and managed to retain much of the most profitable acreage for themselves. As a result, the land granted to peasants was often of poor quality and insufficient to sustain themselves and their families. Moreover, the newly liberated serfs had to pay in installments for their land, which was not granted to them individually but rather to a village commune, which collected their payments. As a result, the pattern of rural life in Russia did not change drastically, as the system of payment kept peasants in the villages—not as freehold farmers but as agricultural laborers for their former masters.

Russia also expanded its territory to the east and south, conquering several Islamic kingdoms in central Asia, and pushing into Siberia in search of natural resources. Concessions from the Chinese led to the founding of the Siberian city of Vladivostok in 1860. Competition with the British, who were active in Afghanistan, led the Russians to annex Tashkent, capital of present-day Uzbekistan, in 1865. The racial, ethnic, and religious differences made governing these territories a daunting task, and in most cases, the Russian state did not try

emancipation of the serfs (1861) The abolition of serfdom was central to Tsar Alexander II's program of modernization and reform, but it produced a limited amount of change. Former serfs now had legal rights.

Tsar Alexander II (1818–1881) After the Crimean War, Tsar Alexander embarked on a program of reform and modernization, which included the emancipation of the serfs.

January Rising Failed attempt by Polish nationalists to reestablish the Polish-Lithuanian Commonwealth in 1863–1864.

Polish nationalism Movement to reestablish an independent Polish nation after the partitions of the late eighteenth century divided the former Polish-Lithuanian Commonwealth between the Prussian, Austrian, and Russian Empires.

Russian serfs in debt and dependent on former masters after emancipation to assimilate the populations of the new territories. This acceptance of ethnic particularity was a pragmatic response to the difficulties of governing heterogeneous populations. Whether power was wielded by the nineteenth-century tsars or, later, by the Soviet Union, powerful centrifugal forces pulled against genuine unification. Expansion helped Russia create a vast empire that was geographically of one piece but by no means one nation.

TERRITORY AND THE NATION: THE UNITED STATES

The American Revolution had bequeathed to the United States a loose union of slave and free states. The Jeffersonian Revolution combined democratic aspirations with a drive to expand the nation's boundaries. The Democratic-Republican president Thomas Jefferson (president, 1801–1809) succeeded in his push to add the Bill of Rights to the Constitution while advocating for a smaller federal government. Though they supported, in principle, the separation of powers, they believed in the supremacy of the people's representatives, and viewed with alarm attempts by the executive and judicial branches to increase their power. The Jeffersonians claimed to support a political system based on an aristocracy of "virtue and talent," in which respect for personal liberty would be the guiding principle. Their vision of the republic rested on the independence of white yeoman farmers, and the prosperity of those farmers depended on the availability of new lands. This made territorial expansion, as exemplified by the Louisiana Purchase in 1803, central to Jeffersonian America.

Expansion had consequences. The Louisiana Purchase made land for farmers in the north and south at the expense of Native American peoples and extended the empire of slavery by adding millions of acres of prime cotton land. It also led

NATIVE AMERICAN DEPORTATION. This painting by Karl Bodmer depicts a Choctaw encampment on the Mississippi River during the deportation of Native Americans from the southeastern United States in 1833.

to the forcible deportation of Native Americans from the Old South to lands west of the Mississippi River. This process of expansion, extension of slavery, and violent expropriation continued from Jefferson's administration through the 1840s.

Under Andrew Jackson (president, 1829–1837), the Democrats transformed the circumscribed liberalism of the Jeffersonians. They campaigned to extend the suffrage to all white males, and sought the frequent rotation of men in positions of political power, a doctrine that permitted politicians to use patronage to build national political parties. Moreover, the Jacksonian vision of democracy and nationhood included westward expansion and the continued enslavement of African Americans. That policy brought Oregon and Washington into the Union through a compromise with the British, and brought Arizona, Texas, New Mexico, Utah, Nevada, and California through war with Mexico—and led to the wholesale expropriation of the remaining Native American lands and continued debates about slavery.

AMERICAN EXPANSION IN THE EARLY NINETEENTH CENTURY. › Which three European powers were involved in the division of North American territory as the United States expanded? › What was the U.S. policy toward Native American populations during the period of expansion?

National Independence and Slavery

In the middle decades of the nineteenth century, voices in Europe and North America debated the meaning of citizenship and national identity. Governments looked to nationalism as a way of mobilizing their populations, but this also made minority populations vulnerable. Individuals or groups who found themselves subject to discrimination or violence had a choice: they could demand definitions of national identity that might protect them, or they could declare that rule by states they saw as foreign was illegitimate and call for national independence. In these debates, key words like "liberty" or "freedom" could mean different things: individual rights, the rights of subject peoples, or freedom from centralized authority. In the United States, Frederick Douglass (1818–1895), a Black man born into slavery, gave a Fourth of July speech that questioned the nation's commitment to "liberty" while slavery persisted in the American South. Writing in the same decade, Italian nationalist Giuseppe La Farina (1815–1863) compared Austrian rule over Italians to "enslavement" while calling for Italian unification.

Frederick Douglass, "What to the Slave Is the Fourth of July?" (United States, 1852)

Fellow Citizens, I am not wanting in respect for the fathers of this republic. The signers of the Declaration of Independence were brave men; but they preferred revolution to peaceful submission to bondage. They were quiet men; but they did not shrink from agitating against oppression. They showed forbearance; but that they knew its limits. They believed in order; but not in the order of tyranny. With them, nothing was "*settled*" that was not right. With them, justice, liberty and humanity were "*final;*" not slavery and oppression.

Fellow-citizens, pardon me, allow me to ask, why am I called upon to speak here to-day? What have I, or those I represent, to do with your national independence? Are the great principles of political freedom and of natural justice, embodied in that Declaration of Independence, extended to us?

Would to God, both for your sakes and ours, that an affirmative answer could truthfully returned to these questions? Then would my task be light, and my burden easy and delightful.

But, such is not the state of the case. I say it with a sad sense of the disparity between us. I am not included within the pale of this glorious anniversary! Your high independence only reveals the immeasurable distance between us. The blessings in which you, this day, rejoice, are not enjoyed in common. —The rich inheritance of justice, liberty, prosperity and independence, bequeathed by your fathers, is shared by you, not by me. The sunlight that brought life and healing to you, has brought stripes and death to me. This Fourth [of] July is *yours*, not *mine*. *You* may rejoice, *I* must mourn. To drag a man in fetters into the grand illuminated temple of liberty, and call upon him to join you in joyous anthems, were inhuman mockery and sacrilegious irony. Do you mean, citizens, to mock me, by asking me to speak to-day?

Fellow-citizens; above your national, tumultuous joy, I hear the mournful wail of millions! whose chains, heavy and grievous yesterday, are, to-day, rendered more intolerable by the jubilee shouts that reach them. If I do forget, if I do not faithfully remember those bleeding children of sorrow this day, "may my right hand forget her cunning, and may tongue cleave to the roof of my mouth!" To forget them, to pass lightly over their wrongs, and to chime in with the popular theme, would be treason most scandalous and shocking, and would make me a reproach before God and the world. My subject, then, fellow-citizens is AMERICAN SLAVERY.

I shall see, this day, and its popular characteristics, from the slave's point of view. Standing, there, identified with the American bondman, making his wrongs mine, I do not hesitate to declare, with all my soul, that the character and conduct of this nation never looked blacker to me than on this 4th of July! Whether we turn to the declarations of the past, or to the professions of the present, the conduct of the nation seems equally hideous and revolting. America is false to the past, false to the present, and solemnly binds herself to be false to the future. Standing with God and the crushed and bleeding slave on this occasion, I will, in the name of humanity which is outraged, in the name of liberty which is fettered, in the name of the constitution and the Bible, which are disregarded and trampled upon, dare to call in question and to denounce, with all the emphasis I can command, everything that serves to perpetuate slavery—the great sin and shame of America!

Source: Source: Frederick Douglass, *Oration, Delivered in Corinthian Hall, Rochester, July 5th, 1832*, (Rochester, NY: Lee, Mann & Co., American Building, 1852), pp. 10, 11, 14–17.

The Political Creed of the National Society, February 1858

Italian independence should be the aim of every man of spirit and intelligence. Neither our educational system in Italy, nor our commerce and industry, can ever be flourishing or properly modernized while Austria keeps one foot on our neck. . . . What good is it to be born in the most fertile and beautiful country in the world, to lie midway between East and West with magnificent ports in both the Adriatic and Mediterranean, to be descended from the Genoese, the Pisans, the men of Amalfi, Sicily and Venice? What use is it to have invented the compass, to have discovered the New World and been the progenitor of two civilizations? . . .

To obtain political liberty we must expel the Austrians who keep us enslaved. To win freedom of conscience we must expel the Austrians who keep us slaves of the Pope. To create a national literature we must chase away the Austrians who keep us uneducated. . . .

Italy must become not only independent but politically united. Political unity alone can reconcile various interests and laws, can mobilize credit and put out collective energies to speeding up communications. Only thus will we find sufficient capital for large-scale industry. Only thus will we create new markets, suppress internal obstacles to the free flow of commerce, and find the strength and reputation needed for traffic in distant lands. . . .

Everything points irresistibly to political unification. Science, industry, commerce, and the arts all need it. No great enterprise is possible any longer if we do not first put together the skill, knowledge, capital and labor of the whole of our great nation. The spirit of the age is moving toward concentration, and woe betide any nation that holds back!

Source: A. Franchi, ed., *Scritti politici di Giuseppe La Farina*, vol. 2 (Milan: 1870), as cited in Denis Mack Smith, *The Making of Italy, 1796–1870* (New York: 1968), pp. 224–25.

Questions for Analysis

1. What principles of the liberal tradition contained in the American Declaration of Independence does Frederick Douglass endorse? Why does he refuse to celebrate the anniversary of this document in 1852? What claim is he making about the relationship between race and liberty in the United States at that moment?

2. What principles of the liberal political tradition does Giuseppe La Farina endorse in his defense of Italians living under Austrian rule? Whose freedom most interests him and what is his goal?

3. Note that in the 1850s, slavery existed in the United States but not on the Italian peninsula. How do these two documents invoke slavery to defend liberal definitions of national identity and freedom?

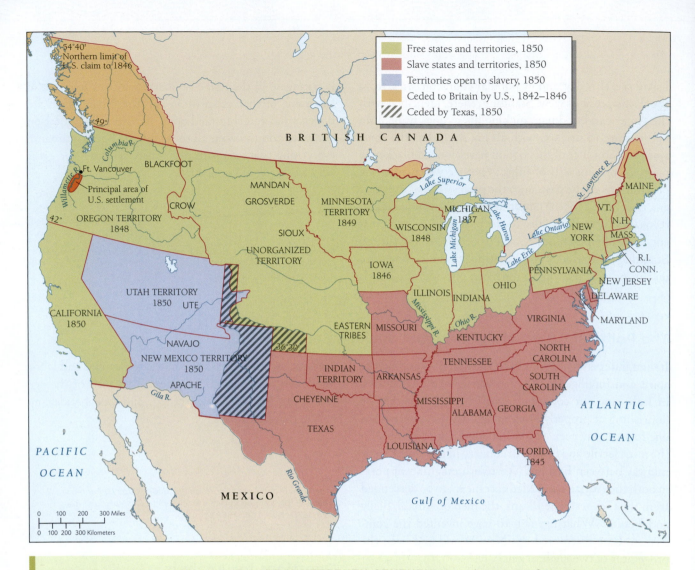

Free states and territories, 1850
Slave states and territories, 1850
Territories open to slavery, 1850
Ceded to Britain by U.S., 1842–1846
Ceded by Texas, 1850

AMERICAN EXPANSION IN THE LATE NINETEENTH CENTURY. Note the stages of American settlement across the North American continent, and the dates for the extension of slavery into new territories. **› How did the question of slavery shape the way the new territories were absorbed into the republic? › Compare American expansion with European colonialism in terms of military conquest, violent displacement of native peoples and their culture, absorption of territory into new states, and use of unfree labor. What are the long-term consequences of this European history on the development of political institutions in the United States?**

THE AMERICAN CIVIL WAR, 1861–1865

The politics of slavery already had led to its abolition in France and Britain (Chapter 20). In the United States, the combination of a growing abolitionist movement, a slave-owning class that feared the economic power of the North, and territorial expansion created deadlock and crisis. As the country expanded west, the North and South engaged in a protracted tug-of-war over whether the new states should be "free" or "slave." In the North, territorial expansion heightened calls for free labor; in the South, it deepened whites' commitment to an economy and society based on plantation slavery. Repeated failure to compromise pushed southern political leaders toward secession, leading to the outbreak of the **Civil War** in 1861.

This protracted and costly struggle proved a first experience of the horrors of modern war and decisively transformed the nation. In the aftermath, the U.S. government abolished slavery and passed the Fourteenth Amendment to the Constitution (1868), which granted full political rights to Black Americans and stated specifically that no citizen could be deprived of life, liberty, or property without due process of law. For a brief period known as Reconstruction, Black Americans voted in large numbers, and some were elected to Congress. By the 1870s, however, the former states of the Confederacy had passed so-called "Black codes" that restricted the employment and property rights of Black Americans. Those who violated these rules or who fell into debt could be imprisoned and fined, forced to pay back the money that they owed through labor contracts under conditions that resembled slavery. At the same time, the U.S. economy expanded at a stunning pace. Industrial and agricultural production rose, and American industrialists, bankers, and retailers introduced innovations in assembly-line manufacturing, corporate organization, and advertising that gave the United States new power in world politics. In these ways, the Civil War laid the foundations both for the accomplishments of the modern American nation-state and its persistent divisions along the lines of race, region, and social class.

> **Civil War** (1861–1865)
> Conflict between the northern and southern states of America that cost over 600,000 lives; this struggle led to the abolition of slavery in the United States.
>
> **Crimean War** (1853–1856)
> War waged by Russia against Great Britain and France.

"Eastern Questions": International Relations and the Decline of Ottoman Power

The rise of new powers in Europe, principally the German Empire, threatened the balance of power, and the waning power of older regimes made conflict more likely. The Crimean War, which lasted from 1853 to 1856, was a particularly gruesome attempt to cope with the most serious of such collapses: the decline of the Ottoman Empire. As the Ottoman Empire lost its grip on its provinces in southeastern Europe, other powers sought to benefit. And though the war occurred before the unification of the German and Italian states, it structured the system of Great Power politics that guided Europe until—and indeed toward—the First World War.

THE CRIMEAN WAR, 1853–1856

The root causes of the **Crimean War** lay in the decline of the Ottoman Empire. The crisis that provoked it, however, involved religion. In 1853, a three-way quarrel about the rights of religious minorities in Jerusalem broke out between France (on behalf of Roman Catholics), Russia (representing Eastern Orthodox Christians), and the Ottomans. The Russians moved troops into the Ottoman-governed territories of Moldavia and Walachia (see the map on page 760), confident that Turkey would be unable to resist. Turkey, persuaded that it would be supported by the British, declared

THE CRIMEAN WAR. Note the theater of operations and the major assaults of the Crimean War. › Which empires and nations were in a position to take advantage of Ottoman weakness? › Who benefited from the outcome of the war, and who was most harmed? › In what ways was the Crimean War the first modern war?

> *In Crimean War, Britain and France support the Ottoman Empire to check Russian expansion*

war on Russia in October 1853. This war became a disaster for the Turks, who lost their fleet at the Battle of Sinope in November. But Russia's success alarmed the British and the French, who considered Russian expansion a threat to their interests in the Balkans, the eastern Mediterranean, and, for the British, the route to India. Determined to check that expansion, France and Britain each declared war on Russia in March 1854. In September, French and British forces landed on the Russian peninsula of Crimea and headed toward the Russian naval base at Sevastopol, to which they laid siege. France, Britain, and the Ottomans were joined in 1855 by the small but ambitious Italian state of Piedmont-Sardinia. This was the closest Europe had come to a general war since 1815.

The war was relatively short, but its conduct was devastating. Disastrous mismanagement of supplies and hygiene by the British and French led to epidemics among the troops; at least as many soldiers died of typhus or cholera as from combat. Despite the disciplined toughness of the British and French troops, and their nations' dominance of the seas around Crimea, the Russians denied them a clear victory. Sevastopol, under siege for nearly a year, did not fall until September 1855; and the bitter, unsatisfying conflict was ended by a treaty in 1856.

For the French and Sardinians, the bravery of their soldiers bolstered positive national sentiment at home; for the British and Russians, however, the poorly managed war provoked waves of intense criticism. As far as international relations were concerned, the peace settlement dealt a blow to Russia, which had its influence in the Balkans drastically curbed. Austria's refusal to come to the aid of Russia cost Russia the support of its powerful former ally. The Crimean War embarrassed the British and left Russia and Austria considerably weaker, opening an advantage for Bismarck in the 1860s, as we saw earlier.

The Crimean War was covered by the first modern war correspondents and photojournalists, making it the most public war to date. Reports from the theater of war were sent "live" by telegraph to Britain and France with objective and sobering detail. The care and supply of the troops became national scandals in the popular press, prompting dramatic changes in the military's administrative and logistical systems, and making heroes of individual doctors and nurses such as Florence Nightingale. The British government and commercial publishers sent photographers to document the war's progress, and perhaps also to counter charges that troops were undersupplied and malnourished. These photographs introduced a new level of realism and immediacy to the public's conception of war.

With news and photojournalism coverage, Crimean War becomes a public war

Conclusion

The decades between 1848 and 1870 brought intense nation building in Europe and North America. The unification of Germany and Italy changed the map of Europe, with important consequences for the balance of power. The expansion of the Russian Empire and the emergence of the United States as a major power also had international ramifications. For old as well as new nation-states, economic development and political transformation—often on a very large scale—were important means of increasing and securing each state's power.

Prior to 1848, liberalism and nationalism had been closely linked. For many Europeans they had been nearly synonymous, just different ways of expressing similar ideas about the rights of different peoples to live under governments they had chosen for themselves. The liberal revolutionaries of 1848, however, did not achieve their goal of more representative government, and the states that defeated them found ways to tailor nationalism to their own ends. After 1848, nationalism proved to be a powerful force for rallying people in support of conservative governments as well as liberal ones. This new development revealed nationalism's power to exacerbate conflicts between states and the various peoples assembled within their borders. And the abolition of privilege and land reform still had to be reckoned with, as did the systems of slavery and serfdom. Trailing the banner of nationhood was an explosive set of questions about how to balance the power and interests of minorities and majorities, the wealthy and poor, and the powerful and the dispossessed, between majority populations and minorities defined by religion or ethnicity. Nation building not only changed states; it also transformed relations between states and their citizens, as well as relations between groups that were increasingly seen through the prism of race and social class.

The result of these many tensions was an age that seemed a contradictory mix of the old and the new: monarchies were beset with debates about nationality and citizenship, land-owning aristocratic elites were rubbing elbows with newly wealthy industrialists, and artisan handworkers were meeting up with factory laborers in

AFTER YOU READ THIS CHAPTER ⌄

CHRONOLOGY

1834–1870	Unification of Germany
1848	Revolutions of 1848
1848	France and Denmark abolish slavery
1848	Treaty of Guadalupe Hidalgo
1848–1870	Unification of Italy
1853–1856	Crimean War
1861	Emancipation of the serfs, Russia
1861–1865	American Civil War
1863	January Rising in Poland

REVIEWING THE OBJECTIVES

❯ Revolutions broke out in 1848 in almost every capital of Europe, except London and St. Petersburg. What accounted for this wave of simultaneous revolutionary movements?

❯ Liberal revolutionaries in France in 1848 did not have the same goals as their socialist allies. What were their goals, and why did they fail to achieve them?

❯ Liberal revolutionaries in the German-speaking lands of central Europe in 1848 were forced to reckon with Austrian and Prussian states in their bid for national unification. What did they want, and why did they fail?

❯ Nationalists in both Germany and Italy were divided between those who supported the creation of a new nation from below, through popular movements, and those who preferred it from above. How did these divisions work themselves out in the process of national unification?

❯ Creating a modern nation in Russia entailed the end of serfdom, whereas in the United States, political leaders from the North and South debated on the place of slavery in the modern nation-state. In what ways were national debates about citizenship in these countries shaped by their widespread practices of bondage?

❯ The three major European wars in this period were of relatively short duration, but they had profound effects on the international balance of power in Europe. Which countries emerged stronger from these conflicts? Which found their interests most damaged?

workers' associations, where debates about the proper path toward realizing social-ist goals were held. Remarkably, this period of intense nation building on the Continent ushered in an era of unprecedented capitalist and imperial expansion (see Chapters 22 and 23). The antagonisms unleashed by German unification and the crumbling of the Ottoman Empire would reemerge, however, in the Great Power politics that precipitated the First World War.

Go to INQUIZITIVE to see what you've learned—and learn what you've missed—with personalized feedback along the way.

PEOPLE, IDEAS, AND EVENTS IN CONTEXT

❯ What circumstances led to the downfall of **LOUIS-PHILIPPE**'s government in France? What divisions between supporters of the revolution led to the **JUNE DAYS** in Paris in 1848?

❯ What role did the *ZOLLVEREIN* and the **FRANKFURT ASSEMBLY** play in the creation of a unified Germany?

❯ How and why did **OTTO VON BISMARCK** aim for a policy of German national unification during his time in office?

❯ How did **GIUSEPPE GARIBALDI** and **COUNT CAMILLO BENSO DI CAVOUR** initially see the process of Italian unification? Whose vision came closest to reality?

❯ Who was **NAPOLEON III**? How did his policies contribute to nation building in France?

❯ What was the contribution of **JOHN STUART MILL** to the debates about citizenship in Britain?

❯ Why were nationalist movements such as **PAN-SLAVISM** or **MAGYAR NATIONALISM** a danger to the Austro-Hungarian Empire?

❯ What was the **JANUARY RISING** of 1863? How did **POLISH NATIONALISM** evolve after 1848?

❯ Why did **TSAR ALEXANDER II** decide to **EMANCIPATE THE SERFS**?

❯ What made the **CRIMEAN WAR** different from previous conflicts and more like the wars of the twentieth century?

❯ How did the circumstances of Black Americans change in the aftermath of the **CIVIL WAR** in the United States?

THINKING ABOUT CONNECTIONS

❯ Revolutionaries in 1848—whether in Paris, Rome, Berlin, or Vienna—must have been aware of the connections between their struggles and the historical example of the French Revolution of 1789–1799. Did they have goals at the end of the eighteenth century that were similar to the goals of the French revolutionaries?

❯ How might the failure of the 1848 revolutions have shaped the beliefs of European conservatives and liberals, or the beliefs of supporters of more radical ideologies such as republicanism and socialism?

22

Imperialism and Colonialism, 1870–1914

BEFORE YOU READ THIS CHAPTER

❯

IN 1869, THE SUEZ CANAL opened with a grand celebration. The imperial yacht *Eagle*, with Empress Eugénie of France on board, entered the canal on November 17, followed by sixty-eight steamships carrying the emperor of Austria, the crown prince of Prussia, the grand duke of Russia, and scores of other dignitaries. Flowery speeches flowed freely, as did the champagne. The ceremony cost a staggering £1.3 million (about $156 million today). Even so, the size of the celebration paled in comparison with the canal itself. The largest project of its kind, the canal sliced through 100 miles of Egyptian desert to link the Mediterranean Sea to the Red Sea, cutting the trip from London to Mumbai in half. The canal dramatically showcased the abilities of Western power and technology to transform the globe, but the human cost was high: 30,000 Egyptians worked on the canal as forced laborers, and thousands died during cholera epidemics in the work camps.

The building of the canal was the result of decades of European involvement in Egypt. French troops under Napoleon led the way, but Britain's bankers soon followed. European financial interests developed a close relationship with those who governed Egypt as a semi-independent state inside the Ottoman Empire. By 1875, the British controlled the canal, after purchasing 44 percent of the canal's shares from the Egyptian khedive (viceroy) when he was threatened with bankruptcy. By the late 1870s, these economic and political relationships had produced debt and instability

STORY LINES

> Industrialization, rapid technological development, and the concentration of economic wealth gave western European nations great power during this period, and they used that power to extend their control over land and peoples in other parts of the world through colonization and imperial rule.

> European imperialism developed simultaneously with the emergence of mass politics and the spread of consumer culture in Europe, a combination that made colonies and the power to control them an important part of national identity for many people in Europe, especially in Britain, France, and Germany.

> The new imperialism ushered in an era of conflict between European powers and the newly colonized peoples in Africa and Asia, as well as among the imperial nations themselves, as they competed with each other for global influence and resources.

CORE OBJECTIVES

> **DEFINE** *imperialism* and locate the major colonies established by European powers in Africa and Asia in the nineteenth century.

> **UNDERSTAND** the major reasons for European colonial expansion in the nineteenth century.

> **DESCRIBE** the choices confronting colonized peoples in the face of European power.

> **EXPLAIN** how imperialism shaped the culture of European nations at home.

> **UNDERSTAND** the nature of the crisis faced by European imperial powers at the end of the nineteenth century.

THE INAUGURATION OF THE SUEZ CANAL. This allegory illustrates the union of the Mediterranean Sea and the Red Sea, attended by Ismail Pasha, the khedive (viceroy) of Egypt; Abdul Aziz, the sultan of the Ottoman Empire; Ferdinand de Lesseps, the president of the Suez Canal Company; Empress Eugénie of France; and sea creatures of different races and genders. It also represents the nineteenth-century vision of imperialism as a bearer of global progress, promoting technological advancement and breaking down barriers between Europe and the peoples of the Middle East, Africa, and Asia. ❯ **Who was the audience for this image?** ❯ **How might contemporaries have interpreted the depiction of racial difference among the angels and sea creatures in the image?**

in Egypt. In 1882, in a bid for national independence, a group of Egyptian army officers led by 'Urabi Pasha took control of Egypt's government.

The British government, determined to protect its investments, decided to intervene. The Royal Navy shelled Egyptian forts along the canal into rubble, and a British task force landed near 'Urabi Pasha's central base, overwhelming the Egyptian lines. This striking success rallied popular support at home, and its political outcomes lasted for seventy years. Britain took effective control of Egypt, and a British lord, Evelyn Baring, assumed the role of proconsul in a power-sharing relationship with Egyptian authorities—but the real power rested with Britain. Britain demanded the repayment of loans and regulated the trade in Egyptian cotton, which helped supply Britain's textile mills. Most important, the intervention secured the route to India and the markets of the East.

The Suez Canal and the conquest of Egypt were made possible by the convergence of technology, money, politics, and a global strategy of imperial control. A similar interplay between economics and colonialism produced the stunning expansion of European empires in the late nineteenth century. The years 1870 to 1914 brought both rapid industrialization throughout the West and an intense push to expand the influence of Western power abroad. The "new imperialism" of the late nineteenth century was distinguished by its scope, intensity, and long-range consequences. It transformed cultures and states in Europe, Africa, and Asia. Projects such as the Suez Canal changed, literally, the landscape and the map of the world. They also embodied an ideology: the belief that European civilization was superior to other global cultures, and that Europeans were morally obligated to impose their ways on the local populations of their empires. Supporters of European imperialism also drew on emerging sciences of race in the nineteenth century to justify their claims about the superiority of the European race over others. In the minds of imperialists, the elimination of geographic barriers had opened the entire world—its lands and its peoples—to the power of the West.

In this new imperialism, the political and economic relationships between colonies and dependent states on one side, and the "metropole" (the colonizing power) on the other, ran both ways. The new imperialism was an expression of European strength, but it was also profoundly destabilizing, because fierce competition among nations upset the balance of power.

Imperialism

Imperialism is the process of extending one state's control over another. Sometimes control was exercised by *direct rule*, with the conquering nation annexing territories outright and subjugating the peoples who lived there to military occupation. Imperialism through direct rule is sometimes referred to as *colonialism*, and when accompanied by migration from Europe to the colony, we refer to *settler colonialism*. Imperialism can also work through *indirect rule*, as for example, when powerful European nations forced compliant local leaders to serve as intermediaries for European authority. Finally, *informal imperialism* could be a less visible exercise of state power, whereby stronger states allowed weaker states to maintain their independence while reducing their sovereignty by carving out zones of foreign influence and privilege.

Both formal and informal imperialism expanded dramatically in the nineteenth century. The "scramble for Africa" was the most startling case: from 1875 to 1902, Europeans seized up to 90 percent of the continent. The overall picture is no less remarkable: between 1870 and 1900, a small group of states (France, Britain, Germany, the Netherlands, Russia, and the United States) colonized about one-quarter of the world's land surface. In addition, these same states extended informal empires into China and Turkey, across South and East Asia, and into Central and South America. So striking was this expansion of European power that contemporaries spoke of the "new imperialism." Nevertheless, imperialism was not new; it is more helpful to think of these nineteenth-century developments as a new stage of European empire building, after the collapse of Europe's early modern empires in North and South America at the end of the eighteenth century.

The nineteenth-century empires developed against the backdrop of industrialization, liberal revolution, and the rise of nation-states. Industrialization produced greater demand for raw materials from distant locations. And many Europeans

Different forms of imperialism and colonialism

EUROPEAN EMPIRES IN 1914. › Where were Britain's major imperial interests? › Which trade routes did Britain have the most incentive to protect? › Where were France's most important imperial holdings? › Who was France's major competitor? › How substantial were German, Dutch, Portuguese, or U.S. colonies compared to British and French holdings?

Britain **France** **Germany** **Portugal** **Spain** **Netherlands** **Belgium** **Denmark** **Italy** **United States** **Ottoman** **Russia** **Japan** **Independent**

became convinced that their economic development, science, and technology would bring progress to the rest of the world. A problem arose, however, from the fact that European governments relied on the consent of the governed, especially in Britain and France. Liberal ideas such as civic equality made conquest difficult to justify and raised questions about the status of colonized peoples. Earlier European conquerors had claimed a missionary zeal and used converting Indigenous peoples to Christianity as justification for their actions. Nineteenth-century imperialists justified their projects by claiming that their investments in infrastructure—railroads, harbors, and roads—and social reforms would bring civilization to the rest of the world. Supporters of the French Empire spoke of this as their "civilizing mission." This vision of the "white man's burden," the title of a poem by Rudyard Kipling, explicitly connected assumptions about civilizational superiority to commonly held beliefs about racial difference (see **Competing Viewpoints** on pages 772–73).

"Civilizing mission" was used to justify imperial expansion

In spite of the power imbalances between Europe and other global regions, the resistance of colonized peoples did as much to shape the history of colonialism as did the ambitious plans of the colonizers. The Haitian revolution of 1804 compelled the British and the French to end slavery and the slave trade in their colonies in the 1830s and the 1840s. The American Revolution encouraged the British to grant self-government to white settler states in Canada (1867), Australia (1901), and New Zealand (1912). Rebellion in India in 1857 caused the British to place the colony under the direct control of the Crown, rather than that of the East India Company. In general, nineteenth-century imperialism involved less independent entrepreneurial activity by merchants and traders and more settlement and direct administrative control. All colonial regimes developed complex legal systems that excluded local populations from political, civil, and property rights and made further legal distinctions based on race or religion to organize relationships between Europeans and various Indigenous groups. (Apartheid in South Africa is but one example.) Defending such empires thus became a vast project, involving legions of soldiers, government officials, legal experts, schoolteachers, and engineers. Nineteenth-century imperialism produced new forms of government and management in the colonies; and as it did so, it forged new interactions between Europeans abroad and in the colonies, and the Indigenous peoples who confronted them.

Imperialism in South Asia

India was the center of the British Empire, the jewel of the British crown, secured well before the period of the new imperialism. The conquest of most of the subcontinent began in the 1750s and quickened during the age of revolution. By the mid-nineteenth century, India was the focal point of Britain's newly expanded global empire, which reached from southern Africa across South Asia and to Australia. Keeping this region involved changing tactics and forms of rule.

Until the mid-nineteenth century, British territories in India were under the control of the British **East India Company**. The company had its own military, divided into European and (far larger) Indian divisions, and held the right to collect taxes on land from Indian peasants. Until the early nineteenth century, the company had legal monopolies over trade in all goods, including indigo, textiles, salt, minerals, and—most lucrative of all—opium. Unlike North America, however, India never became a settler state. In the 1830s, Europeans were a tiny minority, numbering 45,000 in an Indian population

East India Company
(1600–1858) British charter company created to outperform Portuguese and Spanish traders in the Far East.

IMAGES OF WOMEN IN THE COLONIES. Photographs and engravings of women in Africa and Asia circulated widely in Europe during the nineteenth century, and these images shaped attitudes toward colonization. Many images—some openly pornographic—portrayed African or Asian women as attractive, exotic, and in postures that invited European fantasies of domination. "Reclining Jewess" (left) from French Algeria is a typical example of such imagery. Other images portrayed colonial women as victims of barbaric customs, such as *sati*, a social funeral practice in which a new widow burns herself during the cremation of her deceased husband (right). This image, which first appeared in a work by a missionary who had been to Calcutta, was widely reproduced later as an illustration of the need for the British to bring "civilization" to India. **› Could these images have the same impact without the emphasis on the subject's gender? Why or why not?**

of 150 million, but the company's rule was repressive and enforced by the military. Soldiers collected taxes, civil servants wore military uniforms, and British troops brashly commandeered peasants' oxen and carts for their own purposes. Typically, though, the company could not enforce its rule uniformly. It governed some areas directly, others through alliances with local leaders, and still others by simply controlling goods and money. Indirect rule, here as in other empires, meant finding Indigenous collaborators and maintaining their goodwill. Thus, the British cultivated groups that had provided administrators for earlier regimes: the Rajputs and Bhumihars of northern India, whom they considered especially effective soldiers; and merchants of big cities, such as Calcutta (present-day Kolkata). The British offered economic privileges, state offices, or military posts to either groups or entire nations that agreed to ally with them against others.

> *Indirect rule characterized by alliances between British and local elites*

British policy shifted between two poles: one group wanted to "westernize" India, while another group believed it safer and more practical to defer to local culture. Christian missionaries, whose numbers increased as the occupation expanded, were determined to replace "blind superstition" with the "genial influence of Christian light and truth." Indignant at such practices as child marriage and *sati* (in which a widow immolates herself on her husband's funeral pyre), missionaries sought support in England for a wide-ranging assault on Hindu culture. Secular reformers, many of them liberal, considered "Hindoos" and "Mahommedans" susceptible to forms of despotism—both in the family and in the state—and turned their reforming zeal to legal and political change. But other British administrators warned their countrymen not to meddle with Indian institutions; indirect rule, they argued, would work only with the cooperation of local powers. Conflicts such as these meant that the British never agreed on any single cultural policy.

FROM MUTINY TO REBELLION

In 1857–1858, the East India Company's rule was badly shaken by a revolt of Indian soldiers in the British army. The Great Mutiny of 1857, also known as the **Sepoy Mutiny**, began near Delhi, when the military disciplined a regiment of *sepoys* (the traditional term for Indian soldiers employed by the British) for refusing to use rifle cartridges greased with animal fat—unacceptable to either Hindus or Muslims. The causes of the mutiny were deeper, however, and involved social, economic, and political grievances. Indian peasants attacked law courts and burned tax rolls to protest debt and corruption. In areas that had recently been annexed, rebels defended their traditional leaders who had been ousted by the British. The mutiny spread through large areas of northwest India, and European troops—who numbered fewer than one-fifth of those in arms—found themselves losing control. Religious leaders, both Hindu and Muslim, seized the occasion to denounce Christian missionaries sent in by the British and their assault on local traditions.

The fighting lasted for more than a year, and the British matched the rebels' early massacres with a systematic campaign of repression. Whole rebel units were killed rather than being allowed to surrender or were tried on the spot and executed. Towns and villages that supported the rebels were burned, just as the rebels had burned European homes and outposts. Yet the defeat of the rebellion caught the British public's imagination. After the bloody, inconclusive mess of Crimea, the terrifying threat to British India and the rescue of European hostages and British territory by British troops were electrifying news. Pictures of the Scottish highland regiments (wearing wool kilts in the sweltering heat of India) liberating besieged white women and children went up in homes across the United Kingdom. British leaders were stunned by how close the revolt had brought them to disaster.

After the mutiny, the British were compelled to reorganize their Indian empire and develop new strategies of rule. The East India Company was abolished, replaced by the British Crown. The British *raj* (or rule) was now directly governed, although the British still sought out collaborators and cooperative interest groups. Princely India was left to the local rulers, who were subject to British advisers. The British reorganized the military and tried to change relations among soldiers; Indigenous troops were separated from each other to avoid the kind of fraternization that had proved subversive. Even more than before, the British sought to rule through the Indian upper classes rather than in opposition to them. Civil-service reform opened new positions to members of the Indian upper classes. The British also had to reconsider their relationship to Indian cultures. Missionary activity was no longer encouraged, and the British channeled their reforming impulses into the more secular projects of economic development, railways, roads, irrigation, and so on. Still, consensus on effective colonial strategies was lacking: some administrators counseled more reform, while others sought to support the princes. The British tried both policies, in fits and starts, until the end of British rule in 1947.

What did India do for Britain? By the eve of the First World War, India was Britain's largest export market. India mattered enormously to Britain's balance of payments; surpluses earned there compensated for the deficits in Europe and the United States. Equally important to Britain were the human resources of India.

Sepoy Mutiny (1857)
Violent insurrection against rule of the British East India Company in India that spread rapidly before being repressed.

A shift to direct rule, still with local collaboration

Indians and Migration in the British Empire

Lord George Nathaniel Curzon (1859–1925) served as viceroy of India from 1898 to 1905, and foreign secretary from 1919 to 1924. A prominent Tory politician, he was a vocal supporter of the new imperialism. In this passage, he defends British imperial policy in India by enumerating the ways in which Indians serve the needs of the entire British Empire, including in Africa and Southeast Asia. Curzon was correct that the British needed Indian labor—by the end of the nineteenth century, British India was sending 425,000 Indian laborers abroad every year, many of them to other parts of the British Empire in Africa and Southeast Asia.

If you want to save your Colony of Natal from being over-run by a formidable enemy, you ask India for help, and she gives it; if you want to rescue the white men's legations from massacres at Peking, and the need is urgent, you request the Government of India to despatch an expedition, and they despatch it; if you are fighting the Mad Mullah in Somaliland, you soon discover that Indian troops and an Indian general are best qualified for the task, and you ask the Government of India to send them; if you desire to defend any of your extreme out-posts or coaling stations of the Empire, Aden, Mauritius, Singapore, Hong-Kong, even Tien-tsin or Shan-haikwan, it is to the Indian Army that you turn; if you want to build a railway to Uganda or in the Soudan, you apply for Indian labour. When the late Mr. Rhodes was engaged in developing your recent acquisition of Rhodesia, he came to me for assistance. It is with Indian coolie labor that you exploit the plantations equally of Demerara and Natal; with Indian trained officers that you irrigate and dam the Nile; with Indian forest officers that you tap the resources of Central Africa and Siam; with Indian surveyors that you explore all the hidden places of the earth. . . . [Moreover,] India is a country where there will be much larger openings for the investment of capital in the future than has hitherto been the case, and where a great work of industrial and commercial exploitation lies before us.

Source: Andrew Porter, ed., *The Oxford History of the British Empire*, vol. 3, *The Nineteenth Century* (Oxford: 1999), p. 403.

Henry Polak (1882–1959) migrated to the British colony of Natal, in southeastern Africa, from England in 1903. He became a friend of Mohandas Gandhi, then a lawyer practicing in South Africa. In this passage, Polak describes the treatment of Indian migrants in East London, a British colonial city on the Indian Ocean in Natal. He compares their status to that of the African peoples of the colony, using a word (Kaffir) that is now considered extremely derogatory and dehumanizing. In contemporary South Africa, the term is inflammatory, often simply referred to as the "K-word."

In [East London], municipal regulations were promulgated ... by virtue whereof, British Indians, even though considerable merchants, registered voters, and large rate-payers, have been reduced to the status of the African aboriginal native. These regulations prohibit their using the side-walks in the public streets; being out in the streets after 8 P.M. without a pass; residing and carrying on their business, within certain limits of the municipal area, except upon securing a municipal certificate—literally a police pass ... Whilst the East London Indians are thus legally and practically deprived of their full individual liberty, and placed below the level of their own Kaffir servants, they have, as masters and employers, to grant permits allowing freedom of movement in the town to these very servants, who are also otherwise protected and whose interests are safeguarded by special legislation. Many other petty insults are put upon them, such as not being allowed the use of the benches in the public parks, which benches are marked "for Europeans only"; the ferry boats on the Buffalo River are barred to them, except with considerable trouble and inconvenience; in the public markets British Indians are relegated with the Kaffirs, whilst the white people are granted separate stands; and in the public tram-cars, Indians are not allowed inside. As these are municipal regulations, the Cape Government, though sympathetic, can do nothing to procure relief.

Source: Henry Polak, *The Indians of South Africa* (Madras: 1909), p. 86.

Questions for Analysis

1. What benefits does Britain gain from British India, according to Curzon? Does he express an interest in what British Indians themselves might want? Are there any risks to the British policy of relying on colonial troops to keep the peace throughout their empire?

2. Curzon mentions Natal, the British colony in South Africa that Polak describes. What value do Indians contribute to the colony in Natal, according to Curzon?

3. What does Polak's description of the situation faced by Indians in Natal reveal about the importance of race in the settler city of East London? What is the relationship between discrimination against British Indians and the treatment of African peoples in this colonial city, according to Polak? Does he appear to be equally concerned about discrimination against the local African population?

Indian laborers worked on tea plantations in Assam (near present-day Myanmar) and built railways and dams in southern Africa and Egypt. More than 1 million indentured Indian servants left their country during the second half of the century to work elsewhere in the empire. India also provided the British Empire with highly trained engineers, land surveyors, clerks, bureaucrats, schoolteachers, and merchants. The nationalist leader Mohandas Gandhi, for instance, first came into the public eye as a young lawyer in Pretoria, South Africa, where he worked for an Indian law firm. The British deployed Indian troops across the empire. (They would later call up roughly 1.2 million troops in the First World War.) Many British leaders found it impossible to imagine their empire, or even their nation, without India.

How did the British raj shape Indian society? The British practice of indirect rule sought to create an Indian elite that would serve British interests. As one British writer put it, a group "who may be the interpreters between us and the millions whom we govern—a class of persons Indian in colour and blood, but English in tastes, in opinion, in morals, and in intellect." Eventually, this practice created a class of British-educated Indian civil servants and businessmen, well trained for government but skeptical about British claims that they brought progress to the subcontinent. This group provided the leadership for the nationalist movement that challenged British rule in India; yet, at the same time, became increasingly distant from the rest of India. The overwhelming majority of Indians remained desperately poor peasants struggling to subsist on diminishing plots of land and, in many cases, in debt to British landlords.

Imperialism in China

In China, too, European imperialism began well before the period of the new imperialism—but there, it took a different form. Europeans did not conquer and annex whole regions; instead, they forced favorable trade agreements at gunpoint, set up treaty ports where Europeans lived and worked under their own jurisdiction, and established outposts of European missionary activity.

European trade with China focused on luxuries such as silk, porcelain, art objects, and tea. The Chinese government, however, was determined to exclude foreign trade and influence. By the early nineteenth century, Britain's global ambitions and rising power were setting the stage for a confrontation. The British demanded open harbors and special trading privileges, and another source of constant friction involved the harsh treatment of British subjects by Chinese law courts—including the summary execution of several Britons convicted of crimes. By the 1830s, these diplomatic conflicts intensified due to the opium trade.

THE OPIUM TRADE

Opium provided direct links among Britain, British India, and China. In fact, opium (derived from the poppy plant) was one of the very few commodities that Europeans could sell in China. When the British conquered northeast India, they annexed one of the world's richest opium-growing areas, and thus became deeply involved in the trade—so much so that historians have called the East India Company's rule a "narco-military empire." British agencies designated specific poppy-growing regions and gave cash advances to Indian peasants who cultivated the crop. Producing opium was a labor-intensive process: peasant cultivators collected sap from the poppy seed capsules, and then others cleaned the sap and formed it into opium balls that were dried before being weighed and shipped out. In the opium-producing areas northwest of Calcutta, each "factory" employed as many as 1,000 Indian workers.

The East India Company sold the opium to small fleets of British, Dutch, and Chinese shippers, who carried the drug from India to Southeast Asia and China. The company, in turn, used the silver it earned from the sale of opium to buy Chinese goods for the European market. The trade, therefore, was not only profitable—it was also a key to a triangular European-Indian-Chinese economic relationship. Production and export rose dramatically in the early nineteenth century, despite the Chinese emperor's attempts to discourage the trade. By the 1830s, when the British-Chinese confrontation was taking shape, opium provided British India with more revenues than any other source other than those amounts collected from taxes on land.

People all over the world consumed opium, for medicinal reasons as well as for pleasure, but the Chinese market was especially lucrative. A large, wealthy Chinese elite of merchants and government officials made up much of the market, but opium smoking and opium addiction also spread among soldiers, students, and

THE OPIUM TRADE, 1880s. A European merchant examines opium. At first, European traders were forced to carry silver to China to pay for the luxury goods they wanted. But the discovery that they could sell this highly addictive narcotic in China allowed them to correct this trade imbalance and increase their profits.

BRITISH OPIUM TRADE. Note the way that the British trade in opium linked the economies of India, China, and Europe. ❯ What were the major products involved in the trade among East Asia, South Asia, and Europe during this period? ❯ In what ways did the opium trade destabilize East Asia? ❯ What efforts did the Chinese government make to restrict the sale of opium? ❯ What was the response of European nations involved in this trade?

Chinese laborers. In the nineteenth century, opium imports followed Chinese labor all over the world, from Southeast Asia to San Francisco. In 1799, in an effort to control the problem, the Chinese government banned opium imports and began a full-scale campaign to purge the drug from China. That campaign set the Chinese emperor on a collision course with British opium traders. In one confrontation, the Chinese drug commissioner Lin confiscated 3 million pounds of raw opium from the British and washed it out to sea. In other instances, the Chinese authorities blockaded British ships in port, and local citizens demonstrated angrily in front of British residences.

THE OPIUM WARS In 1839, these simmering conflicts broke into what was called the first **Opium War**. The dispute over the drug trade highlighted larger issues of sovereignty and economic status. The Europeans claimed the right to trade with whomever they pleased, bypassing Chinese monopolies. In addition, they wished to set up zones of European residence in defiance of Chinese sovereignty, to proselytize,

Opium Wars (1839–1842; 1856–1860) Wars fought between the British and Qing China to protect the British trade of opium; resulted in the ceding of Hong Kong to the British.

IMPERIALISM IN SOUTH AND EAST ASIA, c. 1914. › Which imperial powers were most present in Asia? › Where were their primary zones of control and influence? › Why were European nations and the United States interested in establishing treaty ports in China? › How were the Chinese treaty ports different from the territorial conquests pursued by the British, French, and Dutch in their respective Asian colonies?

and to open schools. The Chinese government could not accept these challenges to its authority, and war flared up several times over the course of the century. After the first war of 1839–1842, in which British steam vessels and guns overpowered the Chinese fleet, the Treaty of Nanking (1842) compelled the Chinese to give the British trading privileges, the right to reside in five cities, and conceded the port of Hong Kong to the British government "in perpetuity." After a second war, the British secured still more treaty ports and privileges, including the right to send missionaries.

In the aftermath of those agreements between the Chinese and the British, other countries demanded similar rights and economic opportunities. By the end of the nineteenth century, the French, Germans, and Russians all had claimed mining rights and permissions to build railroads, to begin manufacturing with cheap Chinese labor, and to arm and police European communities in Chinese cities. The United States, not wanting to be shouldered aside, declared its own Open Door Policy. Japan was an equally active imperialist power in the Pacific, and the Sino-Japanese War of 1894–1895 was a decisive moment in the history of the region. The Japanese victory forced China to concede trading privileges, the independence of Korea, and the Liaotung Peninsula in Manchuria. It opened a scramble for spheres of influence and for mining and railway concessions.

British wrest from the Chinese trading privileges and ports, including Hong Kong

Surrendering privileges to Europeans, the United States, and the Japanese seriously undermined the authority of the Chinese Qing (*Ching*) emperor at home and heightened popular hostility to foreign intruders. Authority at the imperial center had been eroding for more than a century by 1900, hastened by the Opium Wars and the vast Taiping Rebellion (1852–1864), an enormous, bitter, and deadly conflict in which radical Christian rebels in south-central China challenged the authority of the emperors. On the defensive against the rebels, the dynasty hired foreign generals, including the British commander Charles Gordon, to lead its forces. The fight devastated China's agricultural heartland; and the death toll, never confirmed, may have reached 20 million. This ruinous conflict, together with the increasing inability of the emperor to keep order and collect the taxes necessary to repay foreign loans, led European countries to increase their direct control of the China trade.

THE BOXER REBELLION

From a Western perspective, the most important of the nineteenth-century rebellions against the corruptions of foreign rule was the **Boxer Rebellion** of 1900. The Boxers were a secret society of young men trained in Chinese martial arts who believed they possessed spiritual powers. Antiforeign and antimissionary, they provided the spark for a loosely organized but widespread uprising that included a march on Beijing in the spring of 1900. They laid siege to the foreign legations in the city, home to several thousand Western diplomats and merchants and their families. The legations' small garrison defended their walled compound with little more than rifles, bayonets, and improvised artillery, but they withstood the siege for fifty-five days until a large relief column arrived. The rebellion, particularly the siege at Beijing, mobilized a global response. Europe's Great Powers, rivals everywhere else in the world, drew together in response to this crisis to tear China apart. An expedition numbering 20,000 troops—combining the forces of Britain, France, the United States, Germany, Italy, Japan, and Russia—ferociously repressed the Boxer movement. The outside powers then demanded indemnities, new trading concessions, and reassurances from the Chinese government.

The Boxer Rebellion was one of several anti-imperialist movements at the end of the nineteenth century. The rebellion testified to the vulnerability of Europeans' imperial power and dramatized the resources Europeans would have to devote to maintaining their far-flung influence. In the process of repression, the Europeans became committed to propping up corrupt and fragile governments to protect their agreements and interests, and were drawn into putting down popular uprisings against local inequities and foreign rule.

In China, the age of the new imperialism capped a century of conflict and expansion. By 1900, virtually all of Asia had been divided up among the European powers; Japan, an active imperial power in its own right, maintained its independence. British rule extended from India across Burma, Malaya (part of present-day Malaysia), Australia, and New Zealand; the Dutch, Britain's long-standing trade rivals, secured Indonesia; and Thailand remained independent. In the 1880s, however, the French moved into Indochina. Driven by competition with each other, European powers pressed for more influence in Asia, which, in turn, encouraged the development of nationalist feeling among local populations. Imperial expansion was beginning to show its destabilizing effects.

Boxer Rebellion
(1899–1900) Chinese peasant movement that opposed foreign influence, especially that of Christian missionaries.

Faced with anti-imperialist movements, European imperialists put down popular movements and prop up local government partners, however fragile or corrupt

RUSSIAN IMPERIALISM

Throughout the nineteenth century, Russia championed a policy of annexation—by conquest, treaty, or both—of lands bordering on the existing Russian state. Beginning in 1801, with the acquisition of Georgia after a war with Persia, the tsars continued to pursue their expansionist dream. Bessarabia and Turkestan (taken from the Turks) and Armenia (from the Persians) vastly increased the empire's size. This southward colonization brought large Muslim populations in central Asia into the Russian Empire. It also brought the Russians close to war with the British twice: first in 1881, when Russian troops occupied territories in the trans-Caspian region; and again in 1884–1887, when the tsar's forces advanced to the frontier of Afghanistan. In both cases, the British feared incursions into areas they deemed within their sphere of influence in the Middle East, and were concerned about a possible threat to India. The maneuvering, spying, and support of friendly puppet governments by Russia and Britain became known to the news-reading public in Europe as the "Great Game," and foreshadowed Western countries' jockeying for the region's oil resources in the twentieth century.

Russian expansion also moved east. In 1875, the Japanese traded the southern half of Sakhalin Island for the previously Russian Kuril Islands. The tsars' eastward

BUILDING THE RUSSIAN EMPIRE. > In what directions did the Russian Empire primarily expand after 1795? > What drove Russian expansion? > Which areas were most contentious? Why?

advance finally halted in 1904, when Russian expansion in Mongolia and Manchuria came up against Japanese expansion. In the **Russo-Japanese War** of 1904, Russia's huge imperial army more than met its match. Russia's navy was sent halfway around the world to reinforce the beleaguered Russian troops but was ambushed and sunk by the better-trained and better-equipped Japanese fleet. This national humiliation helped provoke a revolt in Russia and led to an American-brokered peace treaty in 1905 (see Chapter 23). The defeat shook the already unsteady regime of the tsar, proving that European nations were not the only ones who could play the imperial game successfully.

The French Empire and the Civilizing Mission

Like British expansion into India, French colonialism in northern Africa began before the new imperialism of the late nineteenth century. By the 1830s, the French had created a general government of their possessions in Algeria, the most important of which were cities along the Mediterranean coast. From the outset, the Algerian conquest was different from most other colonial ventures in that Algeria became a settler state. The settlers were by no means all French; they included Italian, Spanish, and Maltese merchants and shopkeepers of modest means, as well as laborers and peasants. By the 1870s, in several of the coastal cities, the heterogeneous settler population outnumbered Indigenous Algerians; and within that community, other Europeans outnumbered the French. With the incorporation of Algeria into French civil territory, settlers were allowed to appropriate the most fertile land. French business concerns took cork forests and established mining works in copper, lead, and iron. Economic activity was for European benefit; the first railroads, for instance, did not carry passengers, instead hauling iron ore to the coast for export to France, where it would be smelted and sold.

The settlers and the French government did not necessarily pursue common goals. In the 1870s, in an effort to ensure the settlers' loyalty, the new and still-fragile Third Republic (founded after Napoleon III was defeated in 1870; see Chapter 21) made the colony a department of France, which gave the French settlers the full rights of republican citizenship. It also gave them the power to pass laws in Algeria that consolidated their privileges and community (naturalizing all Europeans, for instance), and further disenfranchised Indigenous Muslim populations, who had no voting rights at all. France's divide and rule strategy, which treated European settlers, Arabs, Berbers, and Jews very differently from one another, illustrates the contradictions of the **"civilizing mission"** in action.

Before the 1870s, there was relatively little interest in colonial activities among the French at home. But after the humiliating defeat in the Franco-Prussian War (1870–1871) and the establishment of the Third Republic, colonial lobby groups and politicians became increasingly adamant about the benefits of colonialism, which were not simply economic. Taking on the civilizing mission would reinforce the international influence of the French republic and the prestige of the French people. Jules Ferry, a republican leader, successfully argued for expanding the French presence in Indochina, saying, "the superior races have a right vis-à-vis the inferior races . . . they have a right to civilize them." In the French Empire, as in the British, the belief in the assumptions of racial superiority served an important function in legitimating the colonial system.

Russo-Japanese War (1904–1905) Collision of Japanese and Russian expansionist goals in Manchuria and Korea.

"civilizing mission" The basis of an argument made by Europeans to justify colonial expansion in the nineteenth century. Supporters of this idea believed that Europeans had a duty to impose Western ideals on Indigenous peoples they ruled over in their colonies.

***THE ENTRY OF THE CRUSADERS INTO CONSTANTINOPLE*, BY EUGÉNE DELACROIX (1840).** The invasion of Algeria in 1830 became an occasion for thinking about Europe's long historical relationship with Muslim civilizations in Africa and the Middle East. Delacroix's work, painted while the conquest of Algeria was going on, portrays these civilizations as exotic and subservient, and glorifies the figures of conquering Christian armies.
› **How might this long historical view have shaped European attitudes toward conquest in the nineteenth century?**

Under Ferry, the French acquired Tunisia (1881), northern and central Vietnam (Tonkin and Annam; 1883), and Laos and Cambodia (1893). The French also carried this civilizing mission into their colonies in West Africa. European and Atlantic trade with the west coast of Africa—in slaves, gold, and ivory—had been well established for centuries, but in the late nineteenth century, trade gave way to formal administration. In 1895, the French established the Federation of French West Africa, a loosely organized administration that governed an area nine times the size of France, including Guinea, Senegal, and the Ivory Coast.

French control remained uneven, and despite military campaigns of pacification, resistance persisted. The French dealt gingerly with tribal leaders, at times deferring to their authority and at others trying to break their power. They established French courts and law only in cities, leaving Islamic or tribal courts to run the other areas. The federation aimed to rationalize the economy by emphasizing a more careful management of resources. They embarked on an ambitious program of public works including the construction of railroads, harbors, and sanitation systems. The French called this "enhancing the value" of the region, which was part of the civilizing mission.

Such programs plainly served French interests; none of these measures aimed to give Indigenous peoples political rights. Furthermore, French projects were often not successful. The French government did not have the resources to carry out its plans, which proved much more expensive and complicated than anyone imagined. Transportation costs ran very high but labor posed the largest problems. Here, as elsewhere, Europeans faced massive resistance from the African peasants, whom they relied on to do everything from building railroads to working mines to carrying rubber. The Europeans therefore resorted to forced labor, signing agreements with local tribal leaders to deliver workers, and turned a blind eye to the continuing use of slave labor in the interior.

Colonists rely on forced labor and slavery for the project of "civilizing" African colonies

The "Scramble for Africa" and the Congo

The scope and speed with which the major European powers asserted formal control over Africa were astonishing. In 1875, about 11 percent of the continent was in European hands; by 1902, the figure was 90 percent. European powers mastered the logistical problems of transport and communication, and learned how to keep diseases at bay. They also had new weapons: the Maxim gun, adopted by the British army in 1889 and first used by British colonial troops, pelted out as many as 500 rounds a minute, turning encounters with Indigenous forces into bloodbaths and making armed resistance virtually impossible.

THE CONGO FREE STATE

Until the latter part of the nineteenth century, much of interior Africa had been out of bounds for Europeans, because the rapids downstream on such strategic rivers as the Congo and the Zambezi made it difficult to move inland and tropical diseases were lethal to most European explorers. But during the 1870s, a privately financed group of Belgian colonizers paid by their king, Leopold II (r. 1865–1909), began a new drive into the fertile valleys around the river Congo. They followed in the footsteps of Henry Morton Stanley, an American newspaperman and explorer who later became a British subject and a knight of the realm. His "scientific" journeys inspired the creation of a society of researchers and students of African culture in Brussels, which, in reality, was a front organization for the commercial company set up by Leopold. The ambitiously named International Association for the Exploration and Civilization of the Congo was set up in 1876, and soon signed treaties with local elites, opening the whole

Berlin Conference At this conference in 1884, the leading colonial powers met and established ground rules for the partition of Africa by European nations.

In wake of Berlin Conference agreement, Congo region opened to exploitation of natural resources and unfree labor

Congo River basin to commercial exploitation. The vast resources of palm oil and natural rubber, as well as the promise of minerals—including diamonds—were now within Europeans' reach.

The strongest resistance to Leopold's company came from other colonial powers. In 1884, a conference was called in Berlin to settle the matter of control over the Congo River basin. It was chaired by the master of European power politics, Otto von Bismarck, and attended by all the leading colonial nations and the United States. The **Berlin Conference** established ground rules for a new phase of imperial expansion. Europe's two great overseas empires, those of Britain and France, and the strongest emerging power inside Europe, Germany, joined forces in a settlement that seemed to be perfectly in line with nineteenth-century liberalism: the Congo valleys would be open to commerce; a slave trade, still run by some of the Islamic kingdoms in the region, would be suppressed; and a Congo Free State would be set up, denying the region to the formal control of any single European country.

In reality, however, the Congo Free State was run by Leopold's private company, and the region was opened up to unrestricted exploitation by a series of large European corporations. Huge tracts of land, larger than whole European countries, became diamond mines or plantations for the extraction of palm oil, rubber, or cocoa. The older slave trade was suppressed, but the European companies took the African labor guaranteed in Berlin and forced them to work in appalling conditions, with no medicine or sanitation and ruthless production quotas, hundreds of thousands of laborers died from disease and overwork. Moreover, because European managers did not respect the different season cycles in central Africa, whole crop years were lost, leading to repeated famines. Laborers working in the heat of the dry season often carried individual loads on their backs that would have been handled by heavy machinery in a European factory. Thousands of Africans were pressed into harvesting goods Europe wanted, and did so for little or no pay, under the threat of beatings and mutilations for dozens of petty offenses against the plantation companies that made the laws of the Free State. Eventually, the scandal in Congo became too great to go unquestioned. A whole generation of authors and journalists, most famously Joseph Conrad in his *Heart of Darkness*, publicized the arbitrary brutality and the vast scale of suffering, while simultaneously confirming European presumptions about the "primitive" state of African societies. In 1908, Belgium was forced to take direct control of the Congo, turning it into a Belgian colony. A few restrictions at least were imposed on the activities of the great plantation companies, which brought a vast new store of raw materials to European industry by using what was slavery in all but name.

THE PARTITION OF AFRICA

The occupation of Congo, and its promise of great material wealth, pressured other colonial powers into expanding their holdings. By the 1880s, the "scramble for Africa" was well underway. The guarantees made at the 1884 Berlin Conference allowed

SLAVES IN CHAINS, 1896. In Africa, native labor was exploited by Europeans and other Africans.

ATLANTIC OCEAN

MEDITERRANEAN SEA

Ceuta (Sp.)
Melilla (Sp.)
Algiers (Fr.)
ALGIERS
TUNIS
MOROCCO
TRIPOLI
RIO DE ORO
EGYPT
British occupied
(nominally Turkish
suzerainty)

RED SEA

SENEGAL
GAMBIA
PORT. GUINEA
SIERRA LEONE
LIBERIA
IVORY COAST
GOLD COAST
TOGO
Porto Novo (Fr.)
LAGOS
OIL RIVERS
FERNANDO PO (Sp.)
SÃO TOMÉ (Port.)
RIO MUNI (Sp.)

TUKOLOR EMPIRE
SAMORI'S STATE
ASHANTI
DAHOMEY
SOKOTO CALIPHATE
BORNU
Lake Chad
ROYAL NIGER COM. SPHERE
CAMEROON

MAHDIST STATE
ERITREA
OBOCK (Fr.)
ABYSSINIAN EMPIRE (ETHIOPIA)
BRITISH SOMALILAND

BUNYORO
BUGANDA KINGDOM
Lake Victoria
Witu (Ger.)
BRITISH EAST AFRICA SPHERE

ATLANTIC OCEAN

FRENCH CONGO
CONGO FREE STATE

Lake Tanganyika
SULTANATE OF ZANZIBAR
GERMAN EAST AFRICA CODEPENDENCY SPHERE

KATANGA
ANGOLA
TEKE
Lake Nyasa

MOZAMBIQUE
MADAGASCAR
INDIAN OCEAN

SOUTH-WEST AFRICA
HERERO
WALVIS BAY (Br.)
NAMA
BECHUANALAND PROTECTORATE
BRITISH BECHUANALAND
MATABELE LAND
TRANSVAAL REPUBLIC
SWAZILAND
ZULULAND
NATAL
BASUTOLAND
CAPE COLONY
ORANGE FREE STATE

0   500   1000 Miles
0   500   1000 Kilometers

Indigenous power
Turkish suzerainty
Portuguese
British
King Leopold's State
German
Boer
French
Italian
Spanish

AFRICA, c. 1886. › What is the single biggest difference in terms of rulership between this map and the one on the next page? › Who were the winners and losers in the "scramble for Africa" before the First World War? › What does the result of the "scramble for Africa" suggest about how European powers regarded each other?

the Europeans to take further steps. The French and Portuguese increased their holdings, and Italy moved into territories along the Red Sea, beside British-held land and the independent kingdom of Ethiopia.

Germany came relatively late to overseas empire. Bismarck was reluctant to engage in an enterprise he believed would yield few economic or political advantages; yet he did not want either Britain or France to dominate Africa, so Germany seized colonies in Cameroon and Tanzania. Though the Germans were not the most enthusiastic colonialists, they were fascinated by the imperial adventure and

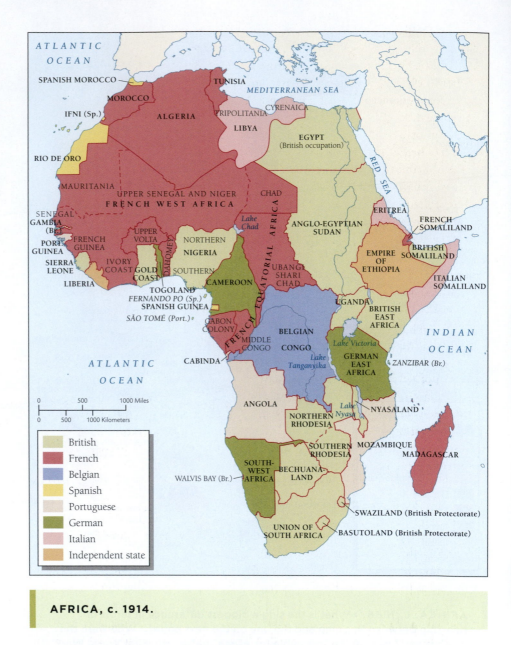

ATLANTIC OCEAN

SPANISH MOROCCO

MOROCCO

TUNISIA

MEDITERRANEAN SEA

IFNI (Sp.)

ALGERIA

TRIPOLITANIA

CYRENAICA

RIO DE ORO

LIBYA

EGYPT
(British occupation)

MAURITANIA

UPPER SENEGAL AND NIGER
FRENCH WEST AFRICA

CHAD

RED SEA

SENEGAL

ERITREA

FRENCH SOMALILAND

GAMBIA (Br.)

UPPER VOLTA

NORTHERN NIGERIA

ANGLO-EGYPTIAN SUDAN

PORT. GUINEA

FRENCH GUINEA

DAHOMEY

Lake Chad

EMPIRE OF ETHIOPIA

BRITISH SOMALILAND

SIERRA LEONE

IVORY COAST

GOLD COAST

SOUTHERN

UBANGI SHARI CHAD

ITALIAN SOMALILAND

LIBERIA

TOGOLAND

CAMEROON

FERNANDO PO (Sp.)

SPANISH GUINEA

SÃO TOMÉ (Port.)

GABON COLONY

MIDDLE CONGO

UGANDA

BRITISH EAST AFRICA

BELGIAN CONGO

Lake Victoria

CABINDA

Lake Tanganyika

GERMAN EAST AFRICA

INDIAN OCEAN

ZANZIBAR (Br.)

ATLANTIC OCEAN

ANGOLA

Lake Nyasa

NYASALAND

0   500   1000 Miles
0   500   1000 Kilometers

NORTHERN RHODESIA

MOZAMBIQUE

MADAGASCAR

SOUTHERN RHODESIA

SOUTH-WEST AFRICA

BECHUANA-LAND

WALVIS BAY (Br.)

SWAZILAND (British Protectorate)

UNION OF SOUTH AFRICA

BASUTOLAND (British Protectorate)

British
French
Belgian
Spanish
Portuguese
German
Italian
Independent state

AFRICA, c. 1914.

jealous of their territories. When the Herero people of German Southwest Africa (now Namibia) rebelled in 1904, the Germans responded with a vicious campaign of village burning and ethnic killing. The drive to exterminate the local populations resulted in the deaths of 80 percent of the Herero people, and over half of the Nama, in what is now recognized as the first genocide of the twentieth century.

Great Britain and France had their own ambitions. The French aimed to move from west to east across the continent, an important reason for the French expedition to Fashoda (in the Sudan) in 1898 (discussed on page 794). Britain's part in the "scramble" took place largely in southern and eastern Africa, and was encapsulated in the dreams and career of one man: Cecil Rhodes, the diamond tycoon, colonial politician, and imperial visionary. Rhodes, who made a fortune from the South African diamond mines in the 1870s and 1880s and founded the diamond-mining company DeBeers, became prime minister of Britain's Cape Colony in 1890. (He left part of this fortune for the creation of the Rhodes scholarships to educate future leaders of the empire at Oxford.) He pursued two great personal and imperial goals. The personal goal was to build a southern African empire that was founded on diamonds; "Rhodesia" would fly the Union Jack out of pride but send its profits into Rhodes's own companies. He helped carve out territories occupying the modern nations of Zambia, Zimbabwe, Malawi, and Botswana—most of the savannah of southern Africa—through bribery, double dealing, careful coalition politics with the British and Boer settlers, warfare, and outright theft. Rhodes also had a broader imperial vision: first, a British presence along the whole of eastern Africa, symbolized by the goal of a Cape-to-Cairo railway; second, that the empire should make Britain self-sufficient, with British industry able to run on the goods and raw materials shipped in from its colonies, then exporting many finished products back to those lands.

As each European power sought its "place in the sun" (famous phrase by the German kaiser Wilhelm II), they brought more and more of Africa under direct colonial control. African peoples thus faced a combination of direct European control and indirect rule, which allowed local elites friendly to European interests to lord it over those who resisted. The partition of Africa was the most striking case of the new imperialism, with broad consequences for the subject peoples of European colonies and for the international order as a whole.

"THE RHODES COLOSSUS." This cartoon, which appeared in *Punch* magazine, satirized the ambitions of Cecil Rhodes, the driving force behind British imperialism in South Africa.

Imperial Culture

Imperialism was thoroughly anchored in the culture of late nineteenth-century Europe and the United States. Images of empire were everywhere, not just in the propagandist literature of colonialism's supporters but on tins of tea and boxes of cocoa, and as background themes in posters advertising everything from dance halls to sewing machines. Museums and world's fairs displayed the products of empire and introduced spectators to "exotic peoples" (see *Interpreting Visual Evidence* on pages 792–93). Music halls rang to the sound of imperialist songs. Empire was present in novels of the period, sometimes appearing as a faraway setting for fantasy, adventure, or stories of self-discovery. The popular literature of empire showed a particular fascination with sexual practices in faraway places: photos and postcards of North African harems and unveiled Arab women were common in European pornography, as were colonial memoirs that chronicled the sexual adventures of the authors.

Empire thus played an important part in establishing European identity during these years. In France, the so-called civilizing mission demonstrated to French citizens the grandeur of their nation, and building railroads and "bringing progress to other lands" illustrated the vigor of the French republic. Many British writers spoke in similar tones; as one author wrote, "The British race may safely be called a missionary race. The command to go and teach all nations is one that the British people have, whether rightly or wrongly, regarded as specially laid upon themselves."

> *Empire as key to development of Europeans' sense of identity*

The first step towards lightening

The White Man's Burden

is through teaching the virtues of cleanliness.

Pears' Soap

is a potent factor in brightening the dark corners of the earth as civi zation advances, while amongst the cultured of all nations it holds highest place—it is the ideal toilet soap.

THE WHITE MAN'S BURDEN AND PEARS' SOAP. By the end of the nineteenth century, advertisers had begun to use images of empire to sell their products to consumers. This soap advertisement appeared in an 1899 magazine. The image of the white-uniformed officer washing his hands connects the theme of cleanliness and personal hygiene with the notions of racial superiority and the necessity of bringing civilization to the "dark corners of the earth."

This combination of high moral purpose with a sense of racial superiority was not restricted to male writers or to figures of authority. In England, the United States, Germany, and France, the speeches and projects of women's reform movements were full of references to empire and the civilizing mission. Britain's women's suffrage movement, for example, was fiercely critical of the government while also nationalist and imperialist. For British women reformers, women's participation in politics also meant the right to participate in imperial projects; they wrote about the oppression of Indian women by child marriage and *sati* and saw themselves shouldering the "white woman's burden" of reform. In France, the suffragist Hubertine Auclert criticized the colonial government in Algeria for its indifference to the condition of Muslim women in their domains; she used an image of women suffering in polygamous marriages abroad to dramatize the need for reform. Arguments such as these enabled European women in their home countries to see themselves as bearers of progress, as participants in a superior civilization. Similarly, John Stuart Mill often used Hindu or Muslim culture as a foil when he wanted to make a point of freedom of speech and religion. This contrast between colonial backwardness alongside European civility and cultural superiority shaped Western culture and political debate, and liberal ideas in particular.

IMPERIALISM AND RACIAL THOUGHT

Imperial culture gave new prominence to racial thinking. In the 1850s, Count Arthur de Gobineau (*GOH-bih-noh*; 1816– 1882) wrote a massive work, *Essay on the Inequality of the Races*, but it sparked little interest until the period of the new imperialism, when it was translated into English and widely discussed (see **Analyzing Primary Sources** on page 787). For Gobineau, race offered the "master key" for understanding human societies in the modern world. Gobineau's work followed from Enlightenment investigations of various cultures in the world, but unlike Enlightenment authors who attributed cultural differences to environmental factors, Gobineau claimed that humans were originally divided into three races—"black," "white," and "yellow"—and peoples of the present day were variously mixed from these original components. The white race, he argued, had preserved purer bloodlines and was therefore superior, while others suffered "adulteration" and were therefore degenerate and no longer capable of civilization. Gobineau's readers included some defenders of the Confederacy during the American Civil War and, later, Adolf Hitler.

Followers of Gobineau's racial thinking looked increasingly to the biological sciences and medicine to legitimize their theories. As biology and medicine became increasingly professionalized and prestigious in the nineteenth century, "scientific" claims about alleged differences among racial groups acquired a veneer of credibility. This prestige received a powerful boost when the natural scientist Charles Darwin published his influential work, *On the Origin of Species*, in 1859 (see also Chapter 23).

Human History, Race, and Degeneration

Arthur de Gobineau (1816–1882) was a French aristocrat and conservative supporter of the Bourbon dynasty in France with little scientific education who popularized a view of history in which major turning points could be explained by the relative power and evolution of strong and weak "races" over time. His work, Essay on the Inequality of Human Races *was first published in 1853–1854, translated into many languages, and influenced the supporters of white supremacy in the United States during and after the Civil War. In the first decades of the twentieth century, Gobineau's followers influenced the framing of immigration law in the United States, as well as Adolf Hitler's German Nazi Party.*

***

I had to give way to the evidence, that the ethnic question dominates all other problems in history, holding the key, and that the inequality of races whose competition shapes every nation is sufficient to explain every subsequent development of a people's destiny. There is not a single person, besides, who has not been struck with some presentiment of this striking idea.

***

After having recognized that there are strong races and weak races, I devoted myself to observing especially the first of these, in order to understand their aptitudes, and above all to trace back the line of their genealogies.

***

The periods that I trace are broad and long. I begin with the first peoples of times gone by, in order to understand those who no longer exist. I only calculate in terms of many centuries. I practice, in a word, moral geology. I speak rarely of man, even more rarely of the citizen or the subject, but often and always of different ethnic fractions, because what matters for me, on the high peaks which I have placed myself, are not fortunate nations or the existence of States, but only races, their societies, and their diverse civilizations.

***

How and why do [societies] lose their strength? That is what we must ask. How do they degenerate?

***

I think that the word degenerate, when applied to a people, must signify that this people no longer have the intrinsic value that they previously possessed, because they no longer have in their veins the same blood, whose value has been gradually modified through successive alliances; in other words, though they bear the same name, they have not preserved the race of their founders; to the point that the decadent man, which we call the degenerate man, is a different product, from the ethnic point of view, from the heroes of the grandiose past. I would be pleased if he possessed something of this essence; but the more he degenerates, the more something is lost. The heterogeneous elements which predominate henceforth within him compose a completely new nationality, unfortunate in its originality; he no longer belongs to those that he still calls his fathers, except in a very indirect sense.

Source: Joseph Arthur de Gobineau, *Essai sur l'inégalité des races humaines* (Paris: 1884), pp. 16, 66.

Questions for Analysis

1. What connection does Gobineau make between the existence of "races" and the "destiny of nations"? Does he mention evidence for this? What words reveal his assumptions about how he distinguishes between "strong" and "weak" races?

2. What is a "degenerate man," according to Gobineau? What measures does he imply would be necessary to prevent a population from "degenerating"? What do these views tell us about how Gobineau viewed the trajectory of human history?

3. Does Gobineau present his views as "political" opinions or "scientific" opinions?

theory of evolution A biological theory about the ways that different life forms change through time and across generations according to a natural process of selection, first proposed in its modern form by Charles Darwin in his work *The Origin of Species* (1859).

"Scientific" theories of racial difference gain prominence ❯

His influential **theory of evolution** was an attempt to explain the earth's tremendous biodiversity in scientific terms. Darwin theorized that some individuals possessed variations that gave them an advantage in the struggle for existence, and that when these individuals survived to reproductive age, they passed these fortunate variations to their offspring. The result of this process of "natural selection," he argued, was the gradual divergence of different species from common ancestors over time.

In a later work, *The Descent of Man* (1871), Darwin declared that the so-called human races were not separate species, but rather a result of a shared lineage that had been dispersed widely over the globe for millennia. At the same time, however, *The Descent of Man* contained passages that expressed the common racism that Darwin shared with many Europeans, especially when it came to generalizing about people from Africa. Nineteenth-century racial theorists borrowed Darwinian explanations about competition between individual living creatures and applied them to larger populations: races, social classes, and nations. Racial theorists and followers of Gobineau such as Houston Stewart Chamberlain (1855–1927) seized upon Darwin's arguments about the evolution of different species to bolster their claims that different human "races" existed, that they competed with one another, and that this competition was a fundamental aspect of human history. Popularized in the press, the increasingly "scientific" racism of late nineteenth-century Europe made it easier for many to reconcile their contempt for other peoples with the rhetoric of progress, individual freedom, and the civilizing mission. Biologists now know that the complexity of human genetic variation far surpasses what was imagined by Darwin and his nineteenth-century contemporaries, and this variation is not distributed in patterns that can be described as races.

OPPOSITION TO IMPERIALISM

Support for imperialism was not unanimous. Critics at home and abroad condemned the entire enterprise as an act of greed and arrogance. The Polish-born Joseph Conrad, a British novelist, shared much of the racism of his contemporaries but nevertheless believed that imperialism was an expression of deeply rooted pathologies in European culture. Other anti-imperialists were men and women from the colonies who took their case to the metropole. The British Committee of the Indian National Congress gathered together many members of London's Indian community to educate the British public about the exploitation of Indian peoples and resources. In the Arab world, the focus was on finding a way to respond to European imperialism that was consistent with Islam. In 1884, Jamal ad-Din al-Afghani, a political thinker from Iran, and Muhammad Abduh, an Egyptian religious scholar, founded an Arabic language newspaper in Paris, which criticized the British and their imperial policy in the Middle East.

RACIAL THINKING IN THE AGE OF EMPIRE. This plate was published in a German anthropology book, probably around 1850. It's a good example of how racial categories were given scientific legitimacy and disseminated in a way that lent them credibility in the popular imagination. Note how the map implies that the earth is divided into homogeneous "racial" zones. ❯ **Does this image contain any message of racial hierarchy, implying that some "races" were superior to other?** ❯ **Is the idea of "race" promoted in this illustration purely biological, or does it appear to contain references to culture as well—for example, in the hairstyles of the individuals shown?**

Perhaps the most defiant anti-imperialist action was the London **Pan-African Conference** of 1900, staged at the height of the "scramble for Africa" and during the Boer War (discussed on page 795). The conference grew out of an international tradition of African American, British, and American antislavery movements, and brought the rhetoric used earlier to abolish slavery to bear on the tactics of European imperialism. Attendees protested that forced labor in the mining compounds of South Africa was akin to slavery, and asked in very moderate tones for some autonomy and representation for African peoples. The conference was small, but it drew delegates from the Caribbean, West Africa, and North America, including the thirty-two-year-old Harvard PhD and leading African American intellectual W. E. B. Du Bois (1868–1963). The conference issued a proclamation "To the Nations of the World," with a famous introduction written by Du Bois: "In the metropolis of the modern world, in this closing year of the nineteenth century, there has been assembled a congress of men and women of African blood, to deliberate solemnly upon the present situation and outlook of the darker races of mankind." The British government ignored the conference, but Du Bois's prescient words set the stage both for the anti-racist activism of the twentieth century as well as the movements of anticolonial nationalism that ultimately brought the era of European colonial expansion to an end.

COLONIAL CULTURES

Imperialism created new colonial cultures in other parts of the world. Cities such as Bombay, Calcutta, and Shanghai boomed, more than tripling in size. Casablanca, Algiers, and Cairo developed new neighborhoods with French architectural styles. Treaty ports such as Hong Kong were transformed as Europeans built banks, shipping enterprises, schools, and religious missions. As Europeans and Indigenous peoples encountered and transformed each other, new hybrid cultures emerged. Elsewhere, new social instabilities grew as European demands for labor took men out of their villages and away from their families, and crowded them into shantytowns bordering sprawling new cities. Hopes that European rule would create a well-disciplined labor force were quickly dashed.

People on both sides of the colonial divide worried about preserving national traditions and identity in the face of these hybrid and changing colonial cultures. In China and India, suggestions that local populations adopt European models of education set off fierce controversies. Chinese elites, already divided over such customs as foot-binding and concubinage (the legal practice whereby men maintained formal sexual partners outside of marriage), found their dilemmas heightened as imperialism became a more powerful force. Should they defend such practices as integral to their culture? Should they argue for a Chinese path to reform? Proponents of change in China or India thus had to sort through their stance toward both Western culture and their traditional popular culture.

For their part, British, French, and Dutch authorities worried that too much familiarity between colonized and colonizer would weaken European prestige and authority. In Phnom Penh, Cambodia (part of French Indochina), French citizens lived apart, separated from the rest of the city by a moat, and authorities required "dressing appropriately and keeping a distance from the natives." Sexual relations provoked the most anxiety and the most contradictory responses. "In this hot climate, passions run higher," wrote a French administrator in Algeria. "French soldiers seek out Arab women due to their strangeness and newness." A British man stationed

Address to the Nations of the World by the Pan-African Conference in London (1900)

The Pan-African Conference that met in London in 1900 brought together a group of people of African heritage from many parts of the world. They were determined to add their voices to those discussing and debating the consequences of European imperialism in the last decades of the nineteenth century. The declaration they produced gives a clear picture of their vision of history, their sense of the injustices associated with colonial conquest, and their hopes for the future. The chair of the committee who wrote the address was W. E. B. Du Bois (1868–1963), an African American professor of history, sociology, and economics, who studied at Harvard and the University of Berlin. In 1909, he became a founding member of the National Association for the Advancement of Colored People (NAACP).

In the metropolis of the modern world, in this the closing year of the nineteenth century, there has been assembled a congress of men and women of African blood, to deliberate solemnly upon the present situation and outlook of the darker races of mankind. The problem of the twentieth century is the problem of the colour-line, the question as to how far differences of race—which show themselves chiefly in the colour of the skin and the texture of the hair—will hereafter be made the basis of denying to over half the world the right of sharing to their utmost ability the opportunities and privileges of modern civilization.

To be sure, the darker races are today the least advanced in culture according to European standards. This has not, however, always been the case in the past, and certainly the world's history, both ancient and modern, has given many instances of no despicable ability and capacity among the blackest races of men.

In any case, the modern world must remember that in this age when the ends of the world are being brought so near together the millions of black men in Africa, America, and the Islands of the Sea, not to speak of the brown and yellow myriads elsewhere, are bound to have a great influence upon the world in the future, by reason of sheer numbers and physical contact. If now the world of culture bends itself towards giving Negroes and other dark men the largest and broadest opportunity for education and self-development, then this contact and influence is bound to have a beneficial effect upon the world and hasten human progress. But if, by reason of carelessness, prejudice, greed and injustice, the black world is to be exploited and ravished and degraded, the results must be deplorable, if not fatal—not simply to them, but to the high ideals of justice, freedom and culture which a thousand years of Christian civilization have held before Europe.

And now, therefore, to these ideals of civilization, to the broader humanity of the followers of the Prince of Peace, we, the men and women of Africa in world congress assembled, do now solemnly appeal:

Let the world take no backward step in that slow but sure progress which has successively refused to let the spirit of class, of caste, of privilege, or of birth, debar from life, liberty and the pursuit of happiness a striving human soul.

Let not color or race be a feature of distinction between white and black men, regardless of worth or ability.

in Shanghai reported, "It was common practice for [an] unmarried Englishmen resident in China to keep a Chinese girl, and I did as the others did." He married an Englishwoman, however, and sent his Chinese mistress and their three children to Britain to avoid awkwardness. European administrators fitfully tried to prohibit liaisons between European men and local women, labeling such affairs "corrupting." But such prohibitions only drove these relations underground, increasing the gap between the public facade of colonial rule and the private reality of colonial lives.

Let not the natives of Africa be sacrificed to the greed of gold, their liberties taken away, their family life debauched, their just aspirations repressed, and avenues of advancement and culture taken from them.

Let not the cloak of Christian missionary enterprise be allowed in the future, as so often in the past, to hide the ruthless economic exploitation and political downfall of less developed nations, whose chief fault has been reliance on the plighted faith of the Christian Church.

Let the British nation, the first modern champion of Negro Freedom, hasten to crown the work of Wilberforce, and Clarkson, and Buxton, and Sharpe, Bishop Colenso, and Livingstone, and give, as soon as practicable, the rights of responsible government to the black colonies of Africa and the West Indies.

Let not the spirit of Garrison, Phillips, and Douglass wholly die out in America; may the conscience of a great nation rise and rebuke all dishonesty and unrighteous oppression toward the American Negro, and grant to him the right of franchise, security of person and property, and generous recognition of the great work he has accomplished in a generation toward raising nine millions of human beings from slavery to manhood.

Let the German Empire, and the French Republic, true to their great past, remember that the true worth of colonies lies in their prosperity and progress, and that justice, impartial alike to black and white, is the first element of prosperity.

Let the Congo Free State become a great central Negro State of the world, and let its prosperity be counted not simply in cash and commerce, but in the happiness and true advancement of its black people.

Let the nations of the World respect the integrity and independence of the first Negro States of Abyssinia, Liberia, Haiti, and the rest, and let the inhabitants of these States, the independent tribes of Africa, the Negroes of the West Indies and America, and the black subjects of all nations take courage, strive ceaselessly, and fight bravely, that they may prove to the world their incontestible right to be counted among the great brotherhood of mankind.

Thus we appeal with boldness and confidence to the Great Powers of the civilized world, trusting in the wide spirit of humanity, and the deep sense of justice of our age, for a generous recognition of the righteousness of our cause.

ALEXANDER WALTERS (Bishop)
President Pan-African Association
HENRY B. BROWN
Vice-President
H. SYLVESTER-WILLIAMS
General Secretary
W. E. BURGHARDT DU BOIS
Chairman Committee on Address

Source: J. Ayodele Langley, *Ideologies of Liberation in Black Africa 1856–1970* (London: 1979), pp. 738–39.

Questions for Analysis

1. What value do the authors ascribe to "race" as a description of human difference?

2. According to the authors, what choices do European powers have to make as they exercise their power in Africa? What are their hopes for Africans in a world shaped by European expansion?

3. What specific "ideals of civilization" do the authors of this declaration invoke? Do they share these ideals with peoples elsewhere?

4. Are there echoes of European liberalism or nationalism in its Pan-Africanism?

EUROPEAN IMPERIALISM AND THE MUSLIM WORLD

The new imperialism of the nineteenth century launched Europe into a new relationship with Muslim societies in Africa, the Middle East, and Asia. For centuries, Muslims had close connections with Europe through at least three different points of territorial involvement. First, the Arab cultures of Muslim North Africa had been in constant contact with the Spanish peninsula, France, and the Italian city-states since the medieval period. Second, the Ottoman Empire had long ruled

Displays of Imperial Culture: The Paris Exposition of 1889

The French colonies were very visible in 1889, during the celebration of the centenary of the French Revolution. In that year, the French government organized a "Universal Exposition" in the capital, which attracted more than 6 million visitors to the broad esplanade that was covered with exhibitions of French industry and culture, including the newly constructed Eiffel Tower, a symbol of modern French engineering.

At the base of the Eiffel Tower (image A), a colonial pavilion placed objects from France's overseas empire on display, and a collection of temporary architectural exhibits showed reproductions of buildings from French colonies in Asia and Africa, as well as samples of architecture from other parts of the world. The photographs here show a reproduction of a Cairo Street (image B); the Pagoda of Angkor, modeled after the Khmer temples of Angkor Wat in Cambodia, a French protectorate (image C); and examples of West African dwellings (image D). The Cairo Street was the second most popular tourist destination at the fair, after the Eiffel Tower. It contained twenty-five shops and restaurants, and employed dozens of Egyptian servers, shopkeepers, and artisans who had been brought

A. Eiffel Tower, 1889.

over areas of the Balkans and southeastern Europe. Third, Muslim groups from central Asia had periodically migrated westward, bringing them into frequent interaction with northern Europeans, particularly Russians. In all three cases, these points of contact between Muslims and the various peoples of Europe produced long periods of significant cultural exchange and trade, as well as moments of conflict.

As Europe established and expanded its colonial empires, many Muslim societies came under the direct or indirect rule of Europeans. By 1914, the French ruled directly over Algeria and much of Muslim West Africa, and had established protectorates in Morocco and Tunisia. The British established a protectorate in Egypt, and ruled over many Muslims in India and Malaysia. And the Dutch ruled over a large Muslim population in Indonesia. After World War I, with the collapse of the Ottoman Empire (see Chapter 23), the number of Muslim societies under European control grew further, as Palestine, Iraq, Lebanon, and Syria came under French and British control.

Prior to the nineteenth century, trade often brought goods from Muslim lands to Europe, such as grain from North Africa, cotton from Egypt and Syria, or

> *In imperial age, an increasing number of Muslim societies come under European rule*

to Paris to add authenticity to the exhibit. Other people on display in the colonial pavilion included Senegalese villagers and a Vietnamese theater troupe.

Questions for Analysis

1. What vision of history and social progress is celebrated in this link between France's colonial holdings and the industrial power displayed in the Eiffel Tower?

2. What might account for the popularity of the Cairo Street exhibit?

3. Why was it important for the exposition to place people from European colonies on display?

B. Reproduction of a Cairo Street at the Paris Exposition, 1889.

C. Pagoda of Angkor at the Paris Exposition, 1889.

D. West African dwellings at the Paris Exposition, 1889.

silks and other luxury goods from the Middle East. In the nineteenth century, however, Muslim societies began to import manufactured goods produced by European industry. This trade often benefited Christian minorities in Syria or Lebanon who had privileged relations with European merchants, but it threatened local artisans, whose craft traditions could not compete with cheaper imported European goods.

The political and social challenges posed to Muslim societies by European colonialism were substantial. Muslim states that retained their independence in the nineteenth century, such as the Ottoman Empire, looked for ways to reform and adapt to growing European influence and the reality of European power. Meanwhile, Islamic scholars and intellectuals throughout the Muslim world looked to their religious tradition for guidance, as they sought to understand the changing circumstances their societies faced (see *Analyzing Primary Sources* on pages 790–91). Muslims who came under direct control by European powers looked for ways to preserve their culture and independence from foreign attempts to impose new institutions and new ways of life on their populations.

Fashoda incident (1898)
Disagreements between
the French and the British
over land claims in North
Africa that led to a standoff
between armies of the two
nations at the Sudanese
town of Fashoda.

Crises of Empire at the Turn of the Twentieth Century

The turn of the twentieth century brought a series of crises to the Western empires. The crises did not end European rule, but they did create sharp tensions among Western nations and shook their confidence. The crises also drove imperial nations to expand their economic and military commitments into territories overseas. In these ways, they became central to Western culture in the years before the First World War.

FASHODA

In the fall of 1898, British and French armies nearly went to war at Fashoda, in the Egyptian Sudan. This crisis had complex causes. In the early 1880s, in an attempt to control the headwaters of the Nile River, the British had used a local uprising in the Sudan as an excuse to move southward from Egypt. In 1885, a project that began with Cecil Rhodes's grandiose dreams of connecting Cairo to the Cape of Good Hope ran into catastrophe when an army led by Britain's most flamboyant general, Charles Gordon, was massacred in Khartoum by the forces of the Mahdi, a Sufi religious leader who claimed to be the successor to the prophet Muhammad. Avenging Gordon's death preoccupied the British for more than a decade, and in 1898, a second large-scale rebellion gave them the opportunity: an Anglo-Egyptian army commanded by General Horatio Kitchener attacked Khartoum and defeated the Mahdi's army, using modern machine guns and artillery.

The victory brought complications, however, as France, which held territories in central Africa adjacent to the Sudan, saw the British victory as a threat. A French expedition was sent to the Sudanese town of Fashoda (now Kodok) to challenge the British claims in the area. They faced off against troops from Kitchener's army, and for a few weeks in September 1898 the situation teetered on the brink of war. The matter was resolved through diplomacy, however, and France ceded the southern Sudan to Britain in exchange for a halt to further expansion. The **Fashoda incident** was a sobering reminder of the extent to which imperial competition could tip the international tensions between European powers.

ETHIOPIA

During the 1880s and 1890s, Italy had been developing a small empire on the shores of the Red Sea. Italy annexed Eritrea and parts of Somalia, and shortly after the death of Gordon at Khartoum, it defeated an invasion of their territories by the Mahdi's forces. Bolstered by this success, the Italians set out to conquer Ethiopia in 1896. Ethiopia was the last major independent African kingdom, ruled by a shrewd and capable emperor, Menelik II. His largely Christian subjects engaged in profitable trade on the East African coast, and revenues

EMPEROR MENELIK II. Ethiopia was the last major independent African kingdom, its prosperity a counter to the European opinion of African cultures. In 1896, Menelik soundly defeated Italy's attempt to conquer his kingdom.

from this trade allowed Menelik to invest in the latest European artillery. When the Italian army—mostly Somali conscripts and a few thousand Italian troops—arrived, Menelik allowed it to penetrate into the mountain passes of Ethiopia. To keep to the roads, the army was forced to divide its forces into separate columns. Meanwhile, the Ethiopians moved over the mountains themselves; and in March 1896, at Adowa, Menelik's army attacked, destroying the Italian army completely and killing 6,000. The failed **Italian invasion of Ethiopia** was a national humiliation for Italy and an important symbol for African political radicals during the early twentieth century.

SOUTH AFRICA: THE BOER WAR

In the late 1800s, competition between Dutch settlers in South Africa, known as Afrikaners or Boers, and the British led to a shooting war between them. When the Boers (an appropriation of the Dutch word for farmer) arrived in South Africa in the early nineteenth century, they had a long troubled relationship with their British neighbors in the colony. In the 1830s, the Boers trekked inland from the cape and set up two republics away from British influence: the Transvaal and the Orange Free State. After gold reserves were found in the Transvaal in the 1880s, Cecil Rhodes, the British diamond magnate (discussed on pages 784–85), tried to provoke war between Britain and the Boers to gain control of the Afrikaners' diamond mines. War finally broke out in 1899, but the British were unprepared for the ferocity of Boer resistance. British columns were shot to pieces by Afrikaner forces that knew the territory, and the British towns of Ladysmith and Mafeking were besieged. Angered by these early failures, the British replaced their commanders and began to fight in earnest, using the railroads built to service the diamond mines to bring in modern military hardware.

The Afrikaners responded by taking to the hills and fighting a costly guerrilla war that lasted another three years. The British tactics became more brutal as the campaign went on; for example, they set up *concentration camps*—the first use of the term—where Afrikaner civilians were rounded up and forced to live in appalling conditions so that they would be unable to help the guerrillas. Over the course of two years, nearly 20,000 civilians died in the camps from disease and poor sanitation. Meanwhile, Black Africans, despised by both sides, also suffered the effects of famine and disease as the war destroyed valuable farmland.

These concentration camps aroused opposition in Britain and elsewhere, and protesters campaigned against such violations of "European" rights—without regard for the fate of Africans caught in the conflict. In the end, the Afrikaners ceded control of their republics to a new British Union of South Africa, which gave them a share of political power. In the aftermath of the **Boer War**, both the British and Afrikaners preserved their high standards of living by relying on cheap African labor and, eventually, a system of racial segregation known as apartheid.

A BRITISH CONCENTRATION CAMP DURING THE BOER WAR. In an attempt to block support to guerrilla fighters, the British forced Afrikaner civilians to live in camps where appalling conditions led to the death of nearly 20,000 people over two years.

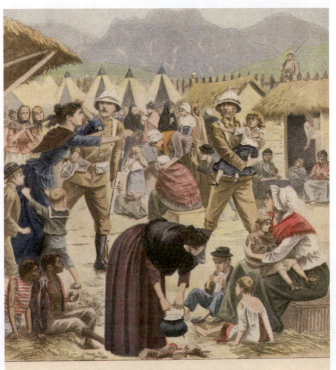

LA GUERRE AU TRANSVAAL
Les camps de reconcentration

U.S. IMPERIALISM: THE SPANISH-AMERICAN WAR OF 1898

In 1898, imperialism brought Spain and the United States to war. In the 1880s and 1890s, Spain's imperial powers were considerably weakened, and it faced rebellions in its colonies in the Caribbean and the Pacific. American economic interests had considerable investments in Cuba, and when an American battleship accidentally exploded at anchor in Havana, advocates of empire and the press in general clamored for revenge. President William McKinley, despite his misgivings, gave in to political necessity, and the government declared war on Spain in 1898, determined to protect U.S. economic interests in the Americas and the Pacific. The United States swiftly won.

In Spain, the **Spanish-American War** provoked an entire generation of writers, politicians, and intellectuals to national soul searching. The defeat undermined the Spanish monarchy, which managed to persist until 1931. The ensuing political tensions resurfaced in the Spanish Civil War of the 1930s—an important episode in the origins of the Second World War.

The United States followed up on their victory over Spain with the annexation of Puerto Rico, the establishment of a protectorate over Cuba, and a short but brutal war against Philippine rebels who liked American colonialism no better than that of the Spanish. In 1903, the United States intervened in a rebellion in Panama, backing the rebels and helping to establish a republic while building the Panama Canal on land leased from the new government. The Panama Canal opened in 1914, and, as the Suez Canal did for the British, it cemented U.S. dominance of the seas in the Western Hemisphere and the eastern Pacific. Later interventions in Hawaii and Santo Domingo gave further evidence of U.S. imperial power, and committed this former colony to a broad role in its new and greater sphere of influence.

IMPERIALISM IN THE BALANCE. This cartoon, titled "A Study—Imperialism," appeared in the United States in 1899 at the beginning of the Philippine-American War. The image shows the scale of justice weighing imperialism against the many victims of U.S. military action, which indicates that the peoples of colonial powers were divided about the virtues of imperial expansion and the "civilizing mission."

The Ecological Consequences of European Migrations

A period of mass migration coincided with the age of imperialism; more than 50 million Europeans migrated overseas between 1820 and 1930. This migration resulted in part from population growth (Chapter 19), changes in the economy and land ownership, political unrest, and the persecution of minority populations.

Germans and the British were among the first, and then the Irish accounted for a large part of the first wave, especially during the famine of the 1840s. An exodus of peasant populations from all corners of Europe soon followed, including Scandinavians escaping poverty; Italians, Poles, Hungarians, Czechs, and Slovaks uprooted by the 1848 revolutions; and Jews from the Pale of Settlement fleeing persecution. Along with Spaniards, Portuguese, Serbs, and Greeks from the Mediterranean basin, migrants traveled by foot and rail to European ports and purchased the cheapest passages they could find on steamships heading abroad.

Two-thirds of these migrants ended up in the United States, and smaller numbers went to Canada, Argentina, southern Brazil, Australia, and New Zealand. In these lands, the displacement of native populations had already been underway for several hundred years. Overwhelmed and in many cases annihilated by a combination of violence and diseases to which they had no immunity, the Indigenous peoples of the Americas, Australia, and New Zealand were replaced by European peoples, who became the majority population by seizing the land and its resources. In North and South America, this mass migration from Europe began as the institution of slavery ended. Slavery brought 11 million Africans to the Americas over four centuries, and former slaves and their descendants continued to shape the societies in which they lived, even as they frequently faced violent resistance against their full participation in social and political life. New migrants from Europe thus found themselves struggling to assimilate into societies that were already deeply conscious of racial and social identities; they faced discrimination in finding work or places to live, and in exercising their religions and expressing their political views.

Ecological transformations accompanied this demographic shift. The climate in European-settled areas of North and South America, Australia, and New Zealand was similar to that of Europe. So the crops that Europeans preferred could be grown with no greater trouble than at home, and the domesticated animals that provided meat, wool, leather, and transportation also thrived in the new environments. To increase agricultural profits, the new lands were cultivated and forests cleared for planting and pasturage. Wheat, rye, barley, turnips, cabbage, onions, fruit trees, cattle, sheep, pigs, and goats accompanied European settlers wherever they went, along with a flood of other biological newcomers, including ferns, thistles, nettles, and other weeds that spread rapidly. Nonnative plant life also proliferated from the seeds in the droppings and feed of herded animals. In 1769, only three plants of Eurasian origin grew in California; by 1900, an estimated 63 percent of the grasses in California were Eurasian in origin. Similar stories of massive biological replacement occurred in Canada, Mexico, Argentina, New Zealand, and even Australia, where the hot and dry climate of the interior preserved the older landscape to a greater degree than elsewhere.

The plants and animals Europeans brought with them during these years accelerated the Columbian exchange that had been already under way since the fifteenth century (Chapter 14). In the seventeenth and eighteenth centuries, pigs brought from Europe colonized the islands of the Caribbean, the forests of Virginia and the Carolinas, and the Brazilian grasslands. By 1800, the population of wild cattle on the Argentinian pampas was counted in the tens of millions. In New Zealand, where the only land mammal prior to the arrival of Europeans was a species of bat, there were 9 million sheep by 1870; meanwhile, in the century preceding that date, after exposure to pathogens brought by the English settlers, the human population of Maori New Zealanders had fallen from as many as 200,000 to fewer than 50,000. Deaths caused by disease and confiscation of land nearly wiped out the culture of the Maori people, and the population did not begin to recover until the 1930s.

As a result of these shifts in human, animal, and plant populations, San Francisco, Buenos Aires, Sydney, and Christchurch came to resemble the cities of Europe; and the planted and unplanted lands surrounding these cities began to take on the characteristics of European landscapes. Many of these "neo-Europes" became relatively wealthy societies, and in the twentieth century, the enormous productivity of commercial agriculture in these areas created surpluses that were exported at a profit to international markets. Europeans were slow to recognize the

Spanish-American War (1898) War between the United States and Spain in Cuba, Puerto Rico, and the Philippines. It ended with a treaty whereby the United States took over the Philippines, Guam, and Puerto Rico; Cuba won partial independence.

Imperial-age migrations accelerate exchange of plants, animals, and contagious diseases between continents

extent to which these processes created a new global balance of power and wealth, but these fundamental demographic and ecological changes intensified across the nineteenth century, shaping the emergence of a more globally connected world in the twentieth century.

Conclusion

In the last quarter of the nineteenth century, the long-standing relationship between Europe and the rest of the world entered a new stage distinguished by the stunningly rapid extension of formal Western control, new forms of economic exploitation, and new patterns of social discipline and settlement. It was driven by the rising economic

AFTER YOU READ THIS CHAPTER ⌄

CHRONOLOGY

1788	British establish colony in New South Wales, Australia
1797–1818	British expand foothold in India
1830	France invades Algeria
1839–1842	First Opium War in China
1840	British establish colony in New Zealand
1857	Sepoy Mutiny in India
1870–1900	European "scramble for Africa"
1875	Britain gains control of Suez Canal
1882	British occupation of Egypt begins
1883–1893	France moves into Vietnam, Laos, and Cambodia
1884–1885	Berlin West Africa Conference
1896	Ethiopians defeat Italian forces
1898	Fashoda incident
1898	Spanish-American War
1899–1902	Boer War
1900	London Pan-African Conference
1904–1905	Russo-Japanese War

REVIEWING THE OBJECTIVES

> European imperialism in the nineteenth century differed from earlier phases of colonial expansion. How was it different? Which parts of the globe were singled out by European imperial powers?

> European nations justified the cost and effort of their colonial policies in many ways. What were the major reasons for colonial expansion in the nineteenth century?

> The subjugated peoples of European colonies faced a choice between resistance and accommodation, though these choices were rarely exclusive. What examples of resistance or accommodation to colonialism can you identify?

> Imperialism shaped cultural developments within Europe in the nineteenth century. How did it change the lives of Europeans and their sense of their place in the world?

> Imperialism unleashed destabilizing competitive forces by the end of the nineteenth century, which drove European colonial powers into conflict with each other. Where were the flashpoints of these conflicts?

needs of the industrial West, territorial conflict, and nationalism, which, by the late nineteenth century, linked nationhood to empire. Among its immediate results was the creation of a self-consciously imperial culture in the West that, at the same time, clearly created unease and contributed powerfully to the sense of crisis that swept through the region.

For all its force, this Western expansion was never unchallenged; imperialism provoked resistance and required constantly changing strategies of rule. During the First World War, mobilizing the resources of empire would become crucial to victory. In the aftermath, reimposing the same conditions of the late nineteenth century would become nearly impossible. And over the longer term, the political structures, economic developments, and racial ideologies established in this period would be contested throughout the twentieth century.

Go to INQUIZITIVE to see what you've learned—and learn what you've missed—with personalized feedback along the way.

PEOPLE, IDEAS, AND EVENTS IN CONTEXT

> What was the **EAST INDIA COMPANY**? How did the British reorganize their rule in India after the **SEPOY MUTINY**?

> What did the French mean when they justified colonial expansion in the name of the **"CIVILIZING MISSION"**?

> How did the **OPIUM WARS** change the economic and political relationships between Europe and China?

> How did the **BERLIN CONFERENCE** of 1884 shape the subsequent colonization of Africa?

> What were the limits of colonial power revealed by the **BOXER REBELLION**, the failed **ITALIAN INVASION OF ETHIOPIA**, and the **RUSSO-JAPANESE WAR**?

> What expressions of anti-imperialism emerged from the London **PAN-AFRICAN CONFERENCE**?

> How did European scientists apply Darwin's **THEORY OF EVOLUTION** in order to defend scientific racism?

> How did the **BOER WAR** and the **FASHODA INCIDENT** contribute to a sense of crisis among European colonial powers?

> What effects did the **SPANISH-AMERICAN WAR** have on the attitudes toward imperialism in the United States, itself a former European colony?

> What were the demographic consequences of **MIGRATION FROM EUROPE** during the period of European imperial expansion, and how did the movement of nonnative animals, plants, and microbes affect landscape and human populations of the Americas or Oceania in the late nineteenth century?

THINKING ABOUT CONNECTIONS

> Compare the consequences of late nineteenth-century European colonial conquest with earlier episodes of imperial expansion such as the Roman Empire or the early modern colonization of the Atlantic world. What was similar? What was different?

> What challenges were faced by colonial regimes in the nineteenth century, such as France and Britain, which expanded their institutions of representative and elected government at home even as they subjugated the conquered peoples in their new colonies?

> The histories of colonial conquest in the nineteenth century helped to establish a network of political and cultural connections that shaped the history of the world in the next century. What was the legacy of these connections during the period of decolonization in the twentieth century?

> How is the history of industrialization connected to the history of colonialism?

> What role did older ideas about the alleged existence of human races play in the defense of European colonialism in the nineteenth century?

23

Modern Industry and Mass Politics, 1870–1914

WE ARE ON THE EXTREME PROMONTORY OF AGES!"
decreed the Italian poet F. T. Marinetti in 1909. In a bombastic manifesto printed on the front page of a Paris newspaper, Marinetti introduced Europe to an aggressive art movement called *futurism*. Rebelling against what he considered the impotent conservatism of Italian culture, Marinetti called for a radical renewal of civilization through "courage, audacity, and revolt." Enamored with the raw power of modern machinery and the dynamism of urban life, he trumpeted "a new form of beauty, the beauty of speed." Marinetti embraced the heroic violence of warfare and disparaged the cultural traditions that formed the bedrock of liberalism.

Few Europeans embraced the modern era with the unflinching abandon of the futurists, but many would have agreed with Marinetti's claim that modern life was characterized above all by flux, movement, and an accelerating rate of change. In the last decades of the nineteenth century, a second industrial revolution produced new manufacturing techniques and new sources of power, including electricity and petroleum-based fuels. These developments transformed European towns and cities, and people felt the immediate effects of the changes in their daily lives.

At the same time, European nation-states faced new political realities. Electorates expanded, and new blocs of voters began participating directly in politics. Mass-based political parties brought new demands to the political arena, and governments struggled to maintain order and legitimacy

BEFORE YOU READ THIS CHAPTER

❯

STORY LINES

> The second industrial revolution intensified the scope and effects of technological innovations, as new techniques for producing steel and chemicals became widespread and new sources of power—electricity and oil—provided alternatives to coal-burning machinery.

> The expansion of the electorate in many European nation-states created a different kind of politics, as workers and rural populations were given voting rights for the first time, even as women continued to be excluded from voting and running for office. New political parties on the right and the left engaged in partisan struggles to win the support of new voters.

> While the advances in technology and industry encouraged a sense of self-confidence about European society and progress, other scientific and cultural movements expressed doubt or anxiety about the effects of rapid modernization on European culture.

CORE OBJECTIVES

> **UNDERSTAND** the origins and consequences of the second industrial revolution.

> **DEFINE** *mass politics*, and **EXPLAIN** how the expansion of voting rights in European nations led to the development of organized political parties that sought the support of the working classes.

> **UNDERSTAND** the arguments both for and against women's suffrage during this period.

> **IDENTIFY** the ways that European liberalism and conservatism evolved as new social and political tensions emerged with the advent of mass politics and intensified industrial development.

> **EXPLAIN** the contributions made by scientists and other cultural figures who came to prominence in the final decades of the nineteenth century to the debates about human nature, modern society, and the natural world.

in the face of these challenges. Socialists mobilized growing numbers of industrial workers, while suffragists demanded the franchise for women. The ability of traditional elites to control the political life of nations was sorely tested.

Beyond politics, new theories in the arts and sciences challenged older notions of nature, society, truth, and beauty. Since the eighteenth century at least, science had been a frequent ally of political liberalism, because both liberals and scientists shared a common faith in human reason and an openness to rational inquiry into the laws of society and nature. In the late nineteenth century, however, this common agenda was strained by scientific investigations in new fields—such as biology and psychology—that challenged liberal assumptions about human nature. Meanwhile, in the arts, a new generation of artists and writers embraced innovation and rejected the established conventions in painting, sculpture, poetry, and literature. A period of intense experimentation in the arts followed, leading artists and writers to develop radically new forms of expression.

The nineteenth century, then, ended in a burst of energy as many Europeans embraced a vision of a society racing headlong into what they hoped was a more promising and better future; however, behind this self-confidence lay significant uncertainty about the eventual destination. What aspects of the European past would continue to be relevant in the modern age? In politics and social life, and in the culture as a whole, such questions produced more conflict than consensus.

New Technologies and Global Transformations

During the last third of the nineteenth century, new technologies transformed manufacturing in Europe, leading to economic growth and complex realignments among industry, labor, and national governments. Europe's first industrial revolution centered on coal, steam, and iron; but the key innovations in the second industrial revolution were in steel, electricity, and chemistry.

Steel had long been prized as a construction material, but before the mid-nineteenth century, producing steel cheaply and in large quantities was

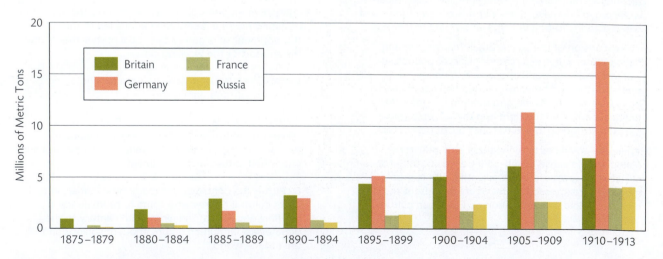

OUTPUT OF STEEL (IN MILLIONS OF METRIC TONS).

Source: Carlo Cipolla, *The Fontana Economic History of Europe*, vol. 3, pt. 2 (London: 1976), p. 775.

impossible. That changed after the 1850s, when different processes for refining and mass-producing alloy steel revolutionized the metallurgical industry. Britain's ship-builders made a quick and profitable switch to steel construction, and Germany and America dominated the rest of the steel industry. By 1905, Germany was producing 50 percent more steel than Britain, enabling Germany to build a massive national and industrial infrastructure.

In the 1880s, electricity was made available for commercial and domestic use, after the development of alternators and transformers capable of producing high-voltage alternating current. By the century's end, large power stations, which often used cheap water power, could send electric current over vast distances. After Thomas Edison invented the light bulb in 1879, the demand for electricity skyrocketed. Soon entire metropolitan areas were electrified, powering subways, tramways, and railroads, and dramatically altering daily life.

New technologies enable a surge in commercial and domestic electricity use

Advances in the chemical industry transformed the manufacture of consumer goods such as paper, soaps, textiles, and fertilizer. Britain—but particularly Germany—became leaders in the field. Heightened concerns for household hygiene and new techniques in mass marketing enabled the British entrepreneur William Lever to market his cleaners around the world. German chemical producers focused on industrial use and came to control roughly 90 percent of the world's chemical market.

The second industrial revolution also produced the liquid-fuel internal combustion engine. By 1914, most navies had converted from coal to oil, as had domestic steamship companies. The discovery of oil fields in Russia, Borneo, Persia, and

THE SECOND INDUSTRIAL REVOLUTION. A German electrical engineering factory illustrates the scale of production during the second industrial revolution. › **What changes in business practices and labor management made factories of this size possible?**

Texas around 1900 allowed such engines to become generally available—and protecting these oil reserves became vital for all states. The adoption of oil-powered machinery had another important consequence: industrialists who had previously depended on nearby rivers or coal mines for power were free to take their enterprises to regions bereft of natural resources. The potential for worldwide industrialization was now in place.

CHANGES IN SCOPE AND SCALE

These technological changes were part of a much larger process: the impressive increases in the scope and scale of industry. At the end of the nineteenth century, size mattered. Factories and cities grew hand in hand, while advances in media and mobility spurred the creation of national mass cultures. For the first time, ordinary people followed the news on national and global levels. They watched as European powers divided the globe and enlarged their empires with prodigious feats of engineering mastery, building railroads, dams, canals, and harbors to monumental proportions. Such projects embodied the ideals of modern European industry, and generated enormous income for builders, investors, bankers, entrepreneurs, and, of course, makers of steel and concrete.

The population continued to grow, particularly in central and eastern Europe. In the space of a generation, Russia's population increased by nearly a quarter and Germany's population by half. Britain's population, too, rose by nearly one-third between 1881 and 1911. Thanks to improvements in both crop yields and shipping, food shortages declined, rendering entire populations less susceptible to illness and infant mortality. Advances in medicine, nutrition, and personal hygiene diminished the prevalence of dangerous diseases, such as cholera and typhus. Improved conditions in housing and public sanitation transformed the urban environment.

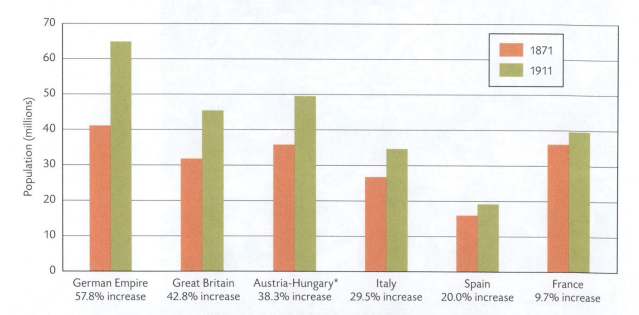

POPULATION GROWTH IN MAJOR STATES BETWEEN 1871 AND 1911 (POPULATION IN MILLIONS).

*Not including Bosnia-Herzegovina.

Source: Colin Dyer, *Population and Society in Twentieth-Century France* (New York: 1978), p. 5.

Railroad Development
— Lines completed by 1848
— Area of main railroad completed by 1870
— Lines after 1870

■ Steel
▬ Engineering
⬭ Chemicals
▼ Electrical industry
▲ Oil production

Mining
□ Low-grade coal
■ High-grade coal
■ Iron ore
■ Petroleum

Industrial Concentration
• Cities
▬ Industrial regions

0   100   200   300 Miles
0   100   200   300 Kilometers

THE INDUSTRIAL REGIONS OF EUROPE. This map shows the distribution of mineral resources, rail lines, and industrial activity. › Which nations enjoyed advantages in the development of industry? Why? › Which resources were most important for industrial growth in the second half of the nineteenth century? › Which resources in Britain became dominant as a result of industrialization?

CREDIT AND CONSUMERISM

Changes in the scale of industry also altered consumption. Department stores offering both practical and luxury goods to the middle class were a sign of the power of urban growth, economic expansion, and the new importance attached to merchandising. Advertising took off and retailers sought to attract working-class consumers by introducing credit payment. In earlier times, working-class families pawned watches, mattresses, or furniture to borrow money, but now they began to buy on credit. This change would eventually have seismic effects on both households and national economies.

These new late nineteenth-century patterns of consumption, however, were largely urban. In the countryside, peasants continued to save money under mattresses, and to make, launder, and mend their own clothes and linens. Mass consumption remained difficult to imagine in what was still a deeply stratified society.

THE RISE OF THE CORPORATION

Economic growth and mass consumption spurred the reorganization and regulation of capitalist institutions. Businesses had sold shares in joint-stock companies since the sixteenth century, but the modern corporation emerged during the second industrial revolution. To provide protection for investors, most European countries enacted limited-liability laws, which ensured that stockholders would lose only the value of their shares in the event of bankruptcy. Insured in this way, many thousands of middle-class men and women considered corporate investment a promising venture.

Limited liability was one part of a larger trend of incorporation as companies sought to expand as a strategy for growth and survival. Growth required outside investment, and control over corporations gradually shifted from company founders and local directors to distant bankers and financiers. Because financial institutions represented the interests of investors whose primary concern was the bottom line, bankers' control over industrial growth encouraged an ethos of impersonal finance capital. This development ran counter to older expectations about the ties of obligation between employers and employees.

Equally important, the second industrial revolution created a strong demand for technical expertise, which undercut traditional forms of family management. University degrees in engineering and chemistry became more valuable than on-the-job apprenticeships. The emergence of a white-collar class (middle-level salaried managers who were neither owners nor laborers) marked a significant change in work life and in society's evolving class structure.

The drive toward larger business enterprises was spurred by a belief that consolidation protected society against the hazards of boom-and-bust economic fluctuations. Some industries combined vertically, attempting to control every step of production from the acquisition of raw materials to the distribution of finished products. A second form of corporate self-protection was horizontal alignment: organized into cartels, companies in the same industry would band together to fix prices and control competition, if not eliminate it outright. Coal, oil, and steel companies were especially suited for this organization, because only a few major players could afford the huge expense of running mines, refineries, and foundries. Cartels were particularly strong in Germany and the United States, but they were less so in Britain, where dedication to free-trade policies made price-fixing difficult. In France, both family firms and laborers opposed cartels, and there was also less heavy industry.

Governments occasionally challenged the power of cartels, but the dominant trend of this period was increased cooperation between governments and industry. Contrary to the laissez-faire mentality of early capitalism, corporations developed close relationships with the states in the West—most noticeably in colonial industrial projects, such as the construction of railroads, harbors, and seafaring steamships. These efforts were so costly, or so unprofitable, that private enterprise could not have undertaken them alone, and because they served a larger political and

Increasingly impersonal relationship between financial investors and labor industry

Rise of cartels as companies attempt to protect themselves against market fluctuations

strategic interest, governments funded them willingly. Furthermore, because these new forms of business organization developed within nations that were expanding their colonial holdings in Africa and Asia, the rise of modern corporations had an impact around the globe.

GLOBAL ECONOMICS

Industrial development heightened competition between European empires and drove them to search for markets and goods abroad. The unevenness of this development also drove an unprecedented number of Europeans to migrate elsewhere. Between the 1840s and the 1940s, more than 55 million Europeans moved to North and South America (Chapter 22). To protect home markets from foreign competition, European powers created trade barriers and resorted to tariffs to raise the cost of imported goods. Because the demand for labor was insatiable in rapidly developing economies, there were few corresponding limitations on the mobility of people before the First World War.

The growth of international trade combined with population migrations to produce a worldwide system of interlocking relationships that linked manufacturing, labor, commerce, and finance. The near universal adoption of the gold standard in currency exchange greatly facilitated world trade. The British Empire was the first European nation to peg its currency to a fixed rate of gold, and other nations soon followed suit. The gold standard made currency exchange predictable and safe, a necessary condition for international trade. The gold standard also gave European nations a vehicle for mitigating the trade imbalances that were driven by industrial development. Almost all European countries were dependent on vast supplies of raw materials for their growing factories, leading them to import more than they exported. To alleviate these trade deficits, European economies relied on "invisible" exports: shipping, insurance, and banking services. The extent of Britain's exports in these areas was far greater than any other country, making London the money market of the world. By 1914, Britain had $20 billion invested overseas, compared with $8.7 billion for France and $6 billion for Germany.

FINANCING EMPIRE. This 1908 photograph shows two financial institutions in the center of London, and at the heart of an expanding global system of exchange and investment. Bankers would meet with merchants at the Royal Exchange (center, with pillars). The Bank of England (left) issued notes backed by gold, which made currency exchange predictable, but limited the government's ability to use monetary policy to influence the business cycle.

Booker T. Washington, *The Man Farthest Down* (1912)

Booker T. Washington (1856–1915), born into slavery in Alabama in the years before the Civil War, became an important educator and voice for reform in the United States during a period in which racial segregation was enshrined in law and defended by the threat of violence. The founding leader in 1881 of a new college for Black American students, the Tuskegee Institute, Washington worked tirelessly with other educators and community leaders to improve educational opportunities for African Americans. In 1910, he traveled to Europe for two months with the goal of understanding "the condition of the poorer and working classes in Europe, particularly in those regions from which an ever-increasing number of immigrants are coming to our country each year." The result of this trip was his book, The Man Farthest Down, which examined the proposition that the progress of human society could best be measured and understood by studying the lives and labors of the working class.

I had crossed Europe from north to south before I got my first glimpse of an emigrant bound for America. On the way from Vienna to Naples I stopped at midnight at Rome, and in the interval between trains I spent an hour in wandering about in the soft southern air—such air as I had not found anywhere since I left my home in Alabama.

In returning to the station my curiosity was aroused, as I was passing in the shadow of the building, by what seemed to me a large vacant room near the main entrance to the station. As I attempted to enter this room I stumbled over the figure of a man lying on the stone floor. Looking farther, I saw something like forty or fifty persons, men as well as women, lying on the floor, their faces turned toward the wall, asleep.

The room itself was apparently bare and empty of all furniture. There was neither a bench nor a table, so far as I could see, in any part of the room. It seems that, without any expectation of doing so, I had wandered into the room reserved for emigrants, and came accidentally upon one of the sights I most wanted to see in Italy—namely, a party of emigrants bound for America.

As near as I could learn, these people were, for the most part, peasants, who had come in from the surrounding country, carrying what little property they possessed on their backs or tied up in little bundles in their arms, and were awaiting the arrival of the train that was to take them to the port from which they could take ship for America.

I confess it struck me as rather pathetic that, in this splendid new and modern railway station, in which the foreign traveler and the native Italian of the upper classes were provided with every convenience and luxury, so little thought had been given to the comfort of these humble travelers, who represent the people in Italy who pay proportionately most of the taxes, and who, by their patient industry and thrift, have contributed more than any other class to such progress as Italy has made in recent years.

Later on I had an opportunity to pass through the country from which perhaps the majority of these emigrants

At moments of economic downturn, however, adherence to the gold standard prevented European nations from stimulating their economy through inflationary monetary policies. Without such monetary tools, competitiveness could only be reestablished by allowing unemployment to drive down wages. For these reasons, it was much easier to defend the gold standard when Europe's working-class populations did not yet vote. When universal male suffrage became the rule at the end of the nineteenth century, the connections between international trade, economic policy, and the fate of the working classes took on new political significance (see *Analyzing Primary Sources* above).

had come. I travelled through a long stretch of country where one sees only now and then a lonesome shepherd or a wretched hut with one low room and a cowstall. I also visited some of the little villages which one sees clinging to the barren hilltops, to escape the poisonous mists of the plains below. There I saw the peasants in their homes and learned something of the way in which the lowly people in the rural districts have been neglected and oppressed. After that I was able to understand that it was no special hardship that these emigrants suffered at Rome. Perhaps many of them had never before slept in a place so clean and sanitary as the room the railway provided them. [. . .]

I inquired why it was that I saw so many women in the fields in this part of the country, for I had understood that Italian women, as a rule, did not go so frequently into field work as the women do in Austria and Hungary. I learned that it was because so many of the men who formerly did this work had emigrated to America. As a matter of fact, three fourths of the emigration from Italy to America comes from Sicily and the other southern provinces. There are villages in lower Italy which have been practically deserted. There are others in which no one but women and old men are left behind, and the whole population is more than half supported by the earnings of Italian laborers in America. There are cities within twenty miles of Naples which have lost within ten years two thirds of their inhabitants. In fact, there is one little village not far from the city of which it is said that the entire male population is in America. [. . .]

From all that I can learn, public sentiment in Italy is rapidly being aroused to the evils which cling to the present system of dealing with the agricultural labourer and the poorer classes. But Italy has not done well by her lower classes in the past. She has oppressed them with heavy taxes; has maintained a land system that has worn out the soil at the same time that it has impoverished the labourer; has left the agricultural labourers in ignorance; has failed to protect them from the rapacity of the large landowners; and has finally driven them to seek their fortunes in a foreign land.

In return, these emigrants have repaid their native country by vastly increasing her foreign commerce, by pouring back into Italy the earnings they have made abroad, by themselves returning with new ideas and new ambitions and entering into the work of building up the country.

These returned emigrants have brought back to the mother country improved farming machinery, new methods of labour, and new capital. Italian emigrants abroad not only contribute to their mother country a sum estimated at between five and six million dollars annually, but Italian emigration has awakened Italy to the value of her laboring classes, and in doing this has laid the foundation for the prosperity of the whole country. In fact, Italy is another illustration that the condition of the man at the bottom affects the life of every class above him. It is to the class lowest down that Italy largely owes what prosperity she has as yet attained.

Source: Booker T. Washington, *The Man Farthest Down: A Record of Observation and Study in Europe* (London: 1912), pp. 105–108, 122.

Questions for Analysis

1. How does Washington's thinking about the migrants in the Rome train station change in the course of his anecdote?

2. What does this brief excerpt tell us about Washington's research methods as he seeks to understand the modern phenomenon of migration?

3. What are the goals of his research into the question of European migration?

Labor Politics, Mass Movements

The rapid expansion of late nineteenth-century industry brought a parallel growth in the size, cohesion, and activism of Europe's working classes. The men and women who worked as wage laborers resented corporate power. As corporations devised new methods of protecting and promoting their interests, workers did the same. Labor unions, which were traditionally limited to skilled male workers in small-scale enterprises, grew during the late nineteenth century into mass, centralized, nationwide organizations. This "new unionism" emphasized organization across entire industries and, for the first time, brought unskilled workers into their ranks, increasing their power to negotiate wages and job conditions. The creation of national unions provided a framework for a new type of political movement: the socialist mass party.

Why did socialism develop in Europe after 1870? Changing political institutions provide part of the answer. Parliamentary governments opened the political process to new voters, including socialists. Now part of the legislative process, socialists in national assemblies led efforts to expand voting rights in the 1860s and 1870s. Their success created new constituencies of working-class men. At the same time, traditional struggles between labor and management moved up to the national level: governments aligned with business interests, and legislators countered working-class agitation with antilabor and antisocialist laws. To radical leaders, the organization of national mass political movements seemed the only effective way to counter the industrialists' political strength. Socialist movements thus abandoned their earlier revolutionary traditions (exemplified by the romantic image of barricaded streets) in favor of legal, electoral competition within Europe's parliamentary systems.

THE SPREAD OF SOCIALIST PARTIES—AND ALTERNATIVES

The most influential socialist thinker was Karl Marx. Since the 1840s, Marx and his collaborator Friedrich Engels worked to organize fledgling socialist movements. Marx, in his three-volume study *Capital*, refused to be content with a moral critique of capitalism. He claimed to offer a systematic and scientific analysis of how capitalism forced workers to exchange their labor for subsistence wages while enabling their employers to amass both wealth and power. Followers of Marx called for workers everywhere to ally with each other to create an independent political force, and few other groups pushed as strongly to secure civil liberties, expand conceptions of citizenship, or build a welfare state. **Marxists** also made powerful claims for gender equality, although in practice women's suffrage took a backseat to class politics.

Not all working-class movements were Marxist. Differences among various left-wing groups remained strong, and the most divisive questions were the role of violence and whether socialists should cooperate with liberal governments. Some "gradualists" were willing to work with liberals for piecemeal reform, whereas other radical groups rejected parliamentary politics altogether. When European labor leaders met in 1864 at the first meeting of the International Working Men's Association, Marx argued strongly in favor of mass movements that would prepare the working classes for revolution. He was strongly opposed by anarchist Mikhail Bakunin, who rejected any form of state or party organization and instead called for terror and violence to destabilize society.

Between 1875 and 1905, Marxist socialists founded political parties in Germany, Belgium, France, Austria, and Russia. These parties were disciplined workers' organizations that aimed to seize control of the state and make revolutionary changes in the social order. The most successful was the German **Social Democratic party** (SPD). The SPD worked within Germany's parliamentary system but became more radical in the face of Bismarck's oppressive antisocialist laws. By the outbreak of the First World War, the SPD was the largest, best-organized workers' party in the world. Rapid and extensive industrialization, a large urban working class, and a national government hostile to organized labor made German workers particularly receptive to the goals and ideals of social democracy.

In Britain—the world's first and most industrialized economy—the socialist presence was much smaller and more moderate. Much of the socialist agenda was advanced by radical liberals in Britain, which forestalled the growth of an independent socialist party. Even when a separate **Labour party** was formed in 1901, it remained moderate, committed to reforming capitalism with measures such as support for public housing or welfare benefits, rather than a complete overhaul of the economy. For the Labour party, and for Britain's many trade unions, Parliament remained a legitimate vehicle for achieving social change, limiting the appeal of revolutionary Marxism.

Militant workers found alternatives to Marxism in **anarchism** and **syndicalism**. Anarchists agreed with Marx about capitalist exploitation, but they opposed centrally organized economies and the very existence of the state. Rather than participate in parliamentary politics, anarchists aimed to establish small-scale, localized, and self-sufficient democratic communities that could guarantee the maximum of individual sovereignty. Renouncing parties, unions, and any form of modern mass organization, anarchists fell back on the tradition of conspiratorial violence, which Marx had denounced. Anarchists assassinated Tsar Alexander II in 1881 and five other heads of state in the following years, believing that such "exemplary terror" would spark popular revolt. Syndicalists, meanwhile, did not call for terror but embraced a strategy of strikes and sabotage by workers against their employers. Their hope was that a general strike of all workers would bring down the capitalist state and replace it with workers' syndicates or trade associations. Anarchism's opposition to any form of organization kept it from making substantial gains as a movement. Likewise, the syndicalists' refusal to participate in politics limited their ability to command wide influence, but the tradition was kept alive, especially in France, through participation in trade unions.

By 1895, seven socialist parties in Europe had captured between a quarter and a third of the votes in their countries, but working-class movements never gained full worker support. Some workers remained loyal to older liberal traditions or to religious parties, while many others were excluded from socialist politics by its narrow definition of who constituted the working class—male industrial workers.

SOCIALIST PARTY PAMPHLET, c. 1895. Socialism emerged as a powerful political force throughout Europe in the late nineteenth century, although in different forms depending on the region. This German pamphlet quotes from Marx's *Communist Manifesto* of 1848, calling for workers in Asia, Africa, America, and Australia to unite under the banners of equality and brotherhood. › **What was the significance of this claim for equality, given the image's apparent references to racial difference?**

SANGLANTES ÉMEUTES A LIMOGES
Les manifestants essayent d'enfoncer les portes de la prison

"BLOODY RIOTS IN LIMOGES." Labor unions used strikes to draw attention to low wages and dangerous working conditions and to extract concessions from employers. Some militant groups, known as syndicalists, hoped that a general strike of all workers would lead to revolutionary change. Fear of labor militancy was a common theme in the popular press, as in this newspaper illustration from Limoges in France, where soldiers are depicted defending the gates of a prison from laborers brandishing the revolutionary red flag of socialism. › **What connection might this newspaper's readers have made between labor militancy and earlier revolutionary movements in Europe?**

women's suffrage movement Nineteenth- and early twentieth-century campaigns led by women to gain the right to vote and run for office.

Furthermore, some committed socialists began to question Marx's core assumptions. A German group of so-called revisionists, led by Eduard Bernstein, challenged Marx's belief in the inevitability of revolution and called for a shift to moderate and gradual reform through electoral politics. Orthodox Marxists were incensed by Bernstein's program, because they feared that the official reforms that favored laborers might make the status quo more acceptable to the working class.

Conflicts over strategy peaked just before the First World War. On the eve of the war, governments discreetly consulted with labor leaders about workers' willingness to enlist and fight. Having gained impressive organizational and political strength since the 1870s, working-class parties now affected the ability of nation-states to wage war. Much to the disappointment of socialist leaders, however, European laborers—many of whom had voted for socialist candidates in previous elections—nevertheless donned the uniforms of their respective nations and marched off to war in 1914, proving that national identities and class identities were not necessarily incompatible with one another.

Demanding Equality: Suffrage and the Women's Movement

After the 1860s, working-class activism and liberal constitutionalism expanded male suffrage across Europe, and by 1884, most men could vote in Germany, France, and Britain. Nowhere did women have the right to vote. Excluded from parliamentary politics, women pressed their interests through independent organizations and direct action. The new women's movement won crucial legal reforms during this period, including access to education, the right to control their own property, and to initiate divorce. The next step was the vote.

To the **women's suffrage movement**, enfranchisement meant not only political progress but also economic, spiritual, and moral advancement for women. Throughout western Europe, middle-class women founded clubs, published journals, organized petitions, and sponsored assemblies to press for the right to vote. These programs were largely compatible with liberalism, adding only the principle

FEMINIST PROTEST IN THE AGE OF MASS POLITICS. These two images demonstrate the ways in which supporters of the vote for women in Britain sought to use the public realm for political advantage. The left image shows Emily Davison being fatally struck by the king's horse at a racetrack. She sought to draw attention to the injustice of women's exclusion from political citizenship by disrupting the Epsom Derby, the richest race in Britain and an annual society event. Her death, widely seen by her supporters as a martyrdom in the cause of women's rights, led to a public funeral procession through London. The right image shows a woman reading the feminist paper *Suffragette* on a British tram. By the end of the nineteenth century, the penny press and growing literacy rates vastly increased the ability of organized political groups to get their message out.

of gender equality. Further to the left were feminist socialists such as Clara Zetkin and Lily Braun, who believed that only a socialist revolution would free women from exploitation.

In Britain, women's suffrage campaigns exploded in violence. In 1897, Millicent Fawcett, a distinguished middle-class woman with connections to the political establishment, brought together sixteen different organizations into the National Union of Women's Suffrage Societies, committed to peaceful, constitutional reform. But the movement lacked the political or economic clout to sway a male legislature dominated by two parties—the Liberals and the Conservatives—each party fearing that women's suffrage would benefit the other. Exasperated by this, Emmeline Pankhurst founded the Women's Social and Political Union (WSPU) in 1903, which adopted tactics of militancy and civil disobedience. WSPU women chained themselves to the visitors' gallery in the House of Commons, slashed paintings in museums, inscribed "Votes for Women" in acid on the greens of golf courses, disrupted political meetings, burned politicians' houses, and smashed department store windows. The government countered these violent activities with repression. When arrested women went on hunger strikes in prisons, wardens fed them by force: tying them down, holding their mouths open with wooden and metal clamps, and running tubes down their throats. In 1910, the suffragists' attempt to enter the House of Commons set off a six-hour riot with policemen and bystanders, shocking and outraging a nation unaccustomed to such violence from women. The intensity of the suffragists' moral claims was dramatically embodied by the 1913 martyrdom of Emily Wilding Davison, who, wearing a "Votes for Women" sash, threw herself in front of the king's horse on Derby Day and was trampled to death.

REDEFINING WOMANHOOD

The campaign for women's suffrage was the most visible aspect of a larger cultural shift in which the traditional Victorian gender roles were redefined. Economic and social changes during industrialization undermined the view that men and women should occupy distinctly different spheres. Women became increasingly visible in the workforce and took up a greater variety of jobs, including in industry. The expansion of government and corporate bureaucracies created employment for middle-class women as social workers and clerks. The increase in hospital services and the advent of national compulsory education required more nurses and teachers, and a shortage of male workers made women a logical choice. Thus, women, who had campaigned vigorously for access to education, began to see doors opening to them. The achievements of this generation of educated women were remarkable. Marie Skłodowska-Curie, the daughter of a Warsaw high school teacher, became a professor of physics in Paris in 1906 and by 1911 had won two Nobel Prizes, in physics and chemistry. These changes in women's employment and education began to deflate the myth of female domesticity.

Women also became more active in politics, following the precedent of reform movements in the early nineteenth century that had raised women's standing in public. Beginning with charity work in religious associations and later with hundreds of secular associations, women throughout Europe directed their energies toward poor relief, prison reform, Sunday school, temperance, ending slavery and prostitution, and expanding educational opportunities for women. Reform groups brought women together outside the home and encouraged them to speak their minds as free-thinking equals and to pursue political goals. Although some women in reform groups supported political emancipation, many others were drawn into reform politics by a belief that they had a special moral mission: they saw public activities as a logical extension of their feminine domestic duties. Eventually, the

CHANGES IN WHITE-COLLAR WORK. Clerical work was primarily male until the end of the nineteenth century, when cadres of women workers and the emergence of new industries and bureaucracies transformed employment. **› How might have these changing patterns of employment affected family life or attitudes toward marriage and child rearing?**

nineteenth-century reform movements opened up the world beyond the home, particularly for middle-class women, and widened the scope of possibilities for later generations.

These changes in women's roles were paralleled by the emergence of a new social type, dubbed the "new woman." A new woman demanded education and a job, refused to be escorted by chaperones when she went out, and rejected the restrictive corsets of midcentury fashion. In other words, she claimed the right to an active life, physically and intellectually, and refused to conform to the norms that defined nineteenth-century womanhood. The new woman was an image created in part by artists and journalists who filled newspapers, magazines, and advertising billboards with pictures of women riding bicycles in bloomers (voluminous trousers under a short skirt); smoking cigarettes; and enjoying the cafés, dance halls, tonic waters, soaps, and other emblems of consumption. Very few women actually fit this image, however, because, among other things, most were too poor. Still, middle- and working-class women demanded more social freedom, and redefined gender norms in the process. For supporters, these new women symbolized a welcome era of social emancipation. For some onlookers, however, women's newfound independence amounted to shirking domestic responsibilities, and they attacked women who defied convention as ugly "half-men," unfit and unable to marry.

Opposition was intense, sometimes violent, and not exclusively male. Men scorned women who threatened their elite preserves in universities, clubs, and public offices, but a wide array of female antisuffragists also denounced the movement. Octavia Hill, a noted social worker, stated that women should refrain from politics and, in

Opponents of women's suffrage

ORGANIZED ANTIFEMINISM. Male students demonstrate against admitting women to Cambridge University in England in 1881. A female figure is hung in effigy (on the right), and the suspended banner reads in part: "There's No Place for You Maids."

so doing, "temper this wild struggle . . . for place and power." Christian commentators criticized suffragists for causing moral decay through selfish individualism. Still others believed that feminism would dissolve the family, a theme that fed into a larger discussion on the decline of the West amid a growing sense of cultural crisis. Indeed, the struggle for women's rights provided a flashpoint for an array of European anxieties over labor, politics, gender, and biology—all of which suggested that an orderly political consensus, so ardently desired by middle-class society, was slipping out of reach.

Liberalism and Its Discontents: National Politics at the Turn of the Century

Having championed individual rights throughout the nineteenth century, middle-class liberals found themselves on the defensive after 1870. Previously, political power had rested on a balance between middle-class interests and traditional elites. The landed aristocracy shared power with industrial magnates, and monarchical rule coexisted with constitutional freedoms. During the late nineteenth century, the rise of mass politics upset this balance. Trade unions, socialists, and feminists all challenged Europe's governing classes by demanding that political participation be open to all. Political struggles became increasingly fierce, and by the First World War, the foundation of traditional parliamentary politics was crumbling in the face of a new kind of mass politics.

FRANCE: THE THIRD REPUBLIC AND THE PARIS COMMUNE

The Franco-Prussian War of 1870 resulted in a bruising defeat for France. The Second Empire collapsed, and the French proclaimed a republic, its third since 1792. Crafting a durable republican system proved difficult, however, and in the ensuing decades the Third Republic faced class conflicts, scandals, and the rise of new forms of right-wing politics that would poison French politics for decades to come.

The republic's first crisis was a direct result of military defeat. During the Franco-Prussian War, Paris had appointed its own municipal government, the Commune, and it not only refused to surrender to the Germans but proclaimed itself the true government of France. The capital was besieged by the Germans for four months, and the remaining population, hungry and radicalized, defied the national government that sat in Versailles and negotiated the terms of an armistice with the Germans. In March 1871, after long and fruitless negotiations, the government sent troops to disarm the capital. But because the Commune's strongest support came from the workers of Paris, the conflict became a class war. For a week, the communards battled against the government's troops, building barricades to stop the invaders, taking and shooting hostages, then retreating very slowly into the northern working-class neighborhoods of the city. The French government's repression was brutal: at least 25,000 Parisians were executed, killed in fighting, or consumed in the fires that raged through the city; and thousands more were deported to the penal colony of New Caledonia in the South Pacific. The Paris Commune was a brief episode, but it cast a long shadow and reopened old political wounds. For Marx, who wrote about the Commune, and other socialists, it illustrated the futility of an older insurrectionary tradition on the left and the need for more mass-based democratic politics.

THE DREYFUS AFFAIR AND ANTISEMITISM AS POLITICS

On the other side of the French political spectrum, new forms of radical right-wing politics emerged. Stung by the defeat of 1870 and critical of the republic and its premises, the new right was nationalist, anti-parliamentary, and had contempt for a liberalism that defended individual liberties and democratic rights. During the first half of the nineteenth century in France, nationalism had been associated with the left-wing traditions of the French revolutions. (Chapter 20). But now, it was more often invoked by the right and linked to xenophobia (fear of foreigners) in general, and **antisemitism** in particular.

The power of popular antisemitism in France was made clear by a public controversy that erupted in the 1890s, which became known as the **Dreyfus Affair**. In 1894, a group of monarchist officers in the army accused Alfred Dreyfus, a Jewish captain on the general staff, of selling military secrets to Germany. Dreyfus was convicted and deported for life to Devil's Island, a prison colony in French Guiana. Two years later, an intelligence officer named Georges Picquart discovered that the documents used to convict Dreyfus were forgeries. The War Department refused to grant Dreyfus a new trial, and the case became an enormous public scandal. Republicans, some socialists, liberals, and intellectuals backed Dreyfus, claiming that the case was about individual rights, and the rule of law. Nationalists, prominent Catholics, and other socialists opposed Dreyfus and refused to question the military's judgment. One Catholic newspaper insisted that the question was not whether Dreyfus was guilty or innocent but whether or not the Jews and unbelievers were the "secret masters of France."

The antisemitism of the anti-Dreyfus camp was a combination of three strands of anti-Jewish thinking in Europe: (1) long-standing currents of antisemitism within Christianity, which damned the Jewish people as Christ killers; (2) economic antisemitism, which insisted that the wealthy Rothschild banking family was representative of all Jews; and (3) late nineteenth-century racial thinking, which contrasted a so-called Aryan (Indo-European) race against an inferior Semitic race. Anti-Dreyfus supporters whipped these ideas into a potent form of propaganda in antisemitic newspapers whose circulation soared during the height of the Dreyfus Affair.

In 1899, Dreyfus was pardoned and freed by executive order. In 1906, the French Supreme Court declared him free of all guilt, and he was reinstated in the army as a major. The French Republic withstood the attacks of radical antisemites in the first decade of the twentieth century, but the same right-wing and nationalist forces made their voices heard elsewhere in Europe. In 1897, the mayor of Vienna was elected on an antisemitic platform. The Russian secret police forged and published the book *The Protocols of the Learned Elders of Zion* (1903 and 1905), which imagined a Jewish plot to dominate the world and held Jews responsible for the French Revolution and the dislocating effects of industrialization. Political antisemitism remained popular among a substantial number of Europeans who believed that social and political problems could be understood in racial terms.

Varieties of antisemitism

Zionism A political movement dating to the end of the nineteenth century, holding that Jews constitute a nation and are entitled to a national homeland.

ZIONISM

Theodor Herzl (1860–1904), a Hungarian-born journalist working in Paris, observed the Dreyfus Affair with alarm. The rise of virulent antisemitism in the land of the French Revolution troubled him deeply. Herzl came to believe that Jews might never be assimilated into Western culture and that staking the Jewish community's hopes on acceptance and tolerance was dangerous folly. He endorsed a different strategy called **Zionism**: the building of a separate Jewish homeland outside of Europe (though not necessarily in Palestine). A small movement of Jewish settlers, mainly refugees from Russia, had already begun to establish such settlements. Herzl was not the first to voice these goals, but he was the most effective advocate of the idea that Jews needed a modern nationalist movement of their own, capable of negotiating with other states. Throughout, Herzl was involved in high politics, meeting with British and Ottoman heads of state. In 1896, he published *The State of the Jews*, and a year later, convened the first Zionist Congress in Switzerland. His vision of a Jewish homeland had strong utopian elements, for he believed in building a new state based on a new and transformed society without inequality and with established rights. Although Herzl's writings met with much skepticism, they received an enthusiastic reception among Jews who lived in areas of eastern Europe, where antisemitism was especially violent.

Violence and hatred lead to waves of Jewish emigration from Europe

Beginning in the 1880s, after a period of violent pogroms in Russia, more than 2.5 million Jews left Europe. (*Pogrom* is a Russian term for violent attacks on civilians, which, in the late nineteenth century, were usually aimed at Jewish communities.) This Jewish migration from eastern Europe was part of the much broader "Great Departure" that brought millions of people from Europe to the Americas during these decades (see Chapter 22). Most Jewish migrants went to the United States, much to the consternation of Zionists. During the same period, much smaller numbers of eastern European Jews—about 30,000 by 1903—migrated to Palestine, which was then still part of the Ottoman Empire. During the turmoil of the First World War, competing demands for national sovereignty from Zionists and Palestinian Arabs caused conflicts in the region, in which the British also became involved, embroiling Zionism in international diplomacy (see Chapter 24).

GERMANY'S SEARCH FOR IMPERIAL UNITY

Through deft foreign policy, three short wars, and a groundswell of national sentiment, Otto von Bismarck created a united Germany between 1864 and 1871. Bismarck sought to safeguard the privileges of Germany's traditional elites, and preserve a dominant role for Prussia while also building a modern, centralized nation-state. Bismarck's constitution gave the emperor control of foreign and military affairs, while the elected parliament's lower house was checked by a conservative upper house whose members were appointed by the emperor. Three fault lines in Germany's political landscape nevertheless threatened to crack the national framework: the divide between Catholics and Protestants, the growing Social Democratic party, and the potentially divisive economic interests of agriculture and industry.

JEWISH MIGRATION IN THE LATE NINETEENTH CENTURY. › What drove Jews to migrate from Europe in the late nineteenth century? › From what parts of Europe did Jews primarily flee? › Where did those who decided to leave go?

Legend:
- The Pale of Settlement
- Other areas of large Jewish population
- Cities with a large Jewish population
- General routes of Jewish exodus

Between 1871 and 1878, Bismarck governed principally with liberal factions interested in promoting economic growth. To strengthen ties with this coalition, he unleashed an anti-Catholic campaign in Prussia, in what is known as the *Kulturkampf* (or "cultural struggle"). He passed laws that imprisoned priests for political sermons, banned Jesuits from Prussia, and curbed the Church's control over education and marriage. The campaign backfired, however, and public sympathy for the persecuted clergy helped the Catholic Center party win a full one-quarter of the seats in the Reichstag in 1874. In the Polish provinces, the campaign also strengthened the movement for national independence.

Bismarck responded by fashioning a new coalition of agricultural and industrial interests and conservative Catholics. This new alliance passed protectionist legislation (tariffs on grain, iron, and steel) that satisfied German producers but alienated free-trade liberals and Social Democrats whose voters faced higher prices. Bismarck responded by declaring the SPD as the enemy of the empire and passed antisocialist laws that prohibited the Social Democrats from public activities. The SPD became a clandestine party, and its members increasingly viewed socialism as the sole answer to their political persecution.

To split workers from their militant leadership, Bismarck offered a package of social reforms: old-age pensions, health and accident insurance, factory inspections, limited hours for women and children, and a maximum workday for men. By 1890, Germany's social legislation was unrivaled in Europe, but the reforms failed to win workers' loyalty, and the SPD became legal again after Bismarck's death. By 1912, the Social Democrats were the largest single bloc in parliament and the German government's standoff with the increasingly well-organized workers' party remained unresolved before the outbreak of the First World War.

BRITAIN: FROM MODERATION TO MILITANCY

The Second Reform Bill of 1867 extended the vote to more than a third of the nation's adult males, and further legislation in 1884 gave the vote to more than three-fourths of adult men. The two major political parties, Liberals and Conservatives, competed to win the support of this growing electorate, and Parliament passed legislation that recognized the legality of trade unions, provided education for all children, and commissioned large projects of urban rebuilding.

Two figures dominated the new parliamentary politics: the Conservative Benjamin Disraeli—a pragmatic figure from a converted Jewish family—and the Liberal William Gladstone, a devout Anglican with a strong moral sense. Despite their opposing sensibilities and bitter parliamentary clashes, both parties were drawn from the upper middle class and the landed gentry, and both parties offered moderate programs that appealed to the widening electorate.

Even Britain's working-class movements were notably moderate before 1900. A more strident voice appeared in 1901, when a coalition of trade unions and middle-class socialist societies created the Labour party. This new organization pressed the Liberal government to enact sickness, accident, old-age, and unemployment insurance paid for through progressive income and inheritance taxes. The bill provoked a rancorous showdown with the House of Lords, which was forced not only to pass the budget but also to surrender permanently its power to veto legislation passed by the Commons.

Outside of Parliament, more activist groups rejected legislative activity in favor of radical action. Coal and rail workers launched nationwide strikes against laboring conditions, city workers shut down transport networks in London and Dublin,

New Labour party pushes for social reforms

Antisemitism and the Popular Press in France

The Dreyfus Affair lasted twelve years: from 1894, when Captain Alfred Dreyfus was first arrested and convicted of treason by a military court, to 1906, when he was finally absolved of all guilt and reinstated in the army. Most people in France followed the events of the affair through the popular press, which had undergone rapid expansion as public schooling became more general and literacy spread through the population. The newspapers milked every episode of the case for all of its sensational drama, and editors openly took sides to increase their circulation and profits. The illustrated press was particularly popular, and images associated with antisemitism became ubiquitous in both the respectable and the more popular press. Image A is a caricature of Jakob Rothschild, a French Jewish banker. He is shown stretching his demonic hands around the globe. Image B shows Édouard Drumont, the antisemitic editor of *La Libre Parole*, who used the scandal to launch his own political career. His celebrity status is evident in this caricature of him that appeared in a competing paper,

Le Rire. Even illustrations that did not aim at caricature carried a powerful message about the intensity of popular antisemitism in France during the Dreyfus Affair, such as in image C, which depicts young people burning Alfred Dreyfus's brother Mathieu in effigy during a demonstration. Mathieu Dreyfus played a key role in the effort to establish his brother's innocence.

Questions for Analysis

1. What fears about the economy are exploited in image A? (Compare this image with the one of socialists circling the globe, hand in hand, on page 811.)

2. Is *Le Rire*'s portrait of Édouard Drumont (image B) antisemitic? Or is it critical of Drumont's antisemitism?

3. Taken together, what do these images tell us about the connections among antisemitism, the popular press, and the definitions of national identity that were current in France during the Dreyfus Affair?

A. Antisemitic French caricature of Jakob Rothschild, 1898.

B. "The Ogre's Meal," caricature of Édouard Drumont, editor of *La Libre Parole*, that appeared in the competing paper *Le Rire*, 1896.

C. "Antisemitic Agitation in Paris: Mathieu Dreyfus burned in effigy in Montmartre (Paris)."

and women's suffrage militants adopted violent forms of direct action. In Ireland, disagreements over Irish self-government threatened to produce armed confrontations between increasingly radical Irish nationalists and Protestants opposed to home rule.

The British Parliament had ruled Ireland directly since 1800, and previous efforts to regain Irish sovereignty had failed. After the 1880s, a modern nationalist party began to exert some influence, but more-radical organizers increasingly eclipsed its agenda. Newer groups promoted an interest in Irish history and culture and provided organizational support to militant organizations such as Sinn Fein and the Irish Republican Brotherhood. Firmly opposed to the nationalists was the Protestant Ulster Volunteer Force. In 1913, as the Liberal government once more discussed home rule, Britain seemed on the verge of a civil war. This prospect, however, was delayed by the outbreak of the First World War.

RUSSIA: THE ROAD TO REVOLUTION

The industrial and social changes that swept Europe proved especially unsettling in Russia, where an autocratic political system was ill equipped to handle conflict and the pressures of modern society. Western industrialization challenged Russia's military might, and its political doctrines—liberalism, democracy, and socialism—threatened Russia's internal political stability. Like other nations, tsarist Russia negotiated these challenges with a combination of repression and reform.

In the 1880s and 1890s, Russia launched a program of industrialization that made it the world's fifth largest economy by the early twentieth century. The state largely directed this industrial development because Russia simply did not possess an independent middle class that was capable of raising capital and stewarding industrial enterprises.

Rapid industrialization heightened social tensions. The transition from country to city life was sudden and harsh. Men and women left agriculture for industrial jobs in areas where workers lived in large barracks and were marched, military-style, to and from the factories. Working conditions were among the worst in Europe. They coped by leaving their villages only temporarily and returning to their farms for planting or the harvest. Social change strained Russia's legal system, which recognized neither trade unions nor employers' associations. Laws still distinguished among nobles, peasants, clergy, and town dwellers, categories that did not correspond to an industrializing society. Outdated banking and financial laws failed to serve the needs of a modern economy.

Real legal reform, however, would threaten the regime's stability. When in 1881 Alexander II (r. 1855–1881), the liberator of the serfs, was killed by a radical assassin, his successor, Alexander III (r. 1881–1894), steered the country sharply to the right. Alexander III claimed that Russia had nothing in common with western Europe. His people would be lost without a strong autocratic system. This principle guided stern repression: the regime curtailed all powers of local assemblies, increased the authority of the secret police, and subjected villages to the governmental authority of nobles appointed by the state. The press and schools also remained under strict censorship.

AUTOCRACY AND REPRESENTATIVE GOVERNMENT. In Russia, Tsar Nicholas II allowed for the creation of a new legislative body, a form of Parliament called the Duma, in response to the revolution of 1905. Although he later succeeded in limiting the powers of the Duma, its very existence indicated that even the autocratic and conservative Russian state was forced to pay lip service to the principle of representative government. In this photo, note the extent to which the opening ceremony evoked the traditional hierarchies of Russian society, exemplified in the presence of the tsar and members of his family, the military, the aristocracy, and the clergy.

Russification: Nicholas II imposes Russian culture on non-Russian subjects by force

Nicholas II (r. 1894–1917) continued these repressive policies. Like his father, he ardently advocated Russification: government programs to extend the language, religion, and culture of greater Russia over the empire's non-Russian subjects. Russification often amounted to coercion, expropriation, and physical oppression. Finns lost their constitution, Poles studied their own literature in Russian translation, and Jews perished in pogroms. The Russian government did not organize the pogroms, but it was openly antisemitic and made a point of looking the other way when villagers massacred Jews and destroyed their homes, businesses, and synagogues. Other groups whose repression by the state led to long-lasting undercurrents of anti-Russian nationalism included the Georgians, Armenians, and Azerbaijanis of the Caucasus Mountains.

The most important radical political group in late nineteenth-century Russia was a large, loosely knit group of men and women who called themselves Populists (Russian: *Narodniki*). The Populists believed that Russia needed to modernize on its own terms. They envisioned an egalitarian Russia based on the ancient institution of the village commune (*mir*). Advocates of Populism sprang primarily from the middle class, many of its adherents were young students, and women made up about 15 percent—a significantly large proportion for the period. They formed secret bands and plotted the overthrow of tsarism through anarchy and insurrection. Populism's emphasis on peasant socialism influenced the Social Revolutionary party, formed in 1901, which concentrated on increasing the political power of the peasantry and building a socialist society based on the agrarian communalism of the mir.

The emergence of industrial capitalism and a new working class gave rise to Russian Marxism. Organized as the Social Democratic party, Russian Marxists

Bolsheviks Former members of the Russian Social Democratic party who advocated for the destruction of capitalist political and economic institutions and started the Russian Revolution.

Mensheviks Within the Russian Social Democratic party, the Mensheviks advocated slow changes and a gradual move toward socialism.

Russian Revolution of 1905 After Russia's defeat in the Russo-Japanese War, Russians began clamoring for political reforms. Protests grew over the course of 1905, and the autocracy lost control of entire towns and regions as workers went on strike, soldiers mutinied, and peasants revolted.

concentrated their efforts on behalf of urban workers—which distinguished them from the Populists—and saw themselves as part of the international working-class movement. They made little headway in the peasant-dominated Russia before the First World War, but they provided disaffected urban factory workers and intellectuals alike with a powerful ideology that stressed the inevitability of a better future: autocracy would give way to capitalism and capitalism to an egalitarian, classless, socialist society.

In 1903, the Russian Social Democratic party leadership split over an important disagreement on revolutionary strategy. One group, temporarily in the majority and quick to name itself the **Bolsheviks** ("majority group"), believed that the Russian situation called for a strongly centralized party of active revolutionaries. They insisted that the rapid industrialization of Russia meant that they did not have to follow Marx's model for the West. Instead of working for liberal capitalist reforms, Russian revolutionaries could skip a stage and immediately begin to build a socialist state. The other group, the **Mensheviks** ("minority group"— though they outnumbered the Bolsheviks before 1917), was more cautious or "gradualist." They sought slow changes and were reluctant to depart from Marxist orthodoxy. When the Mensheviks regained control of the Social Democratic party, the Bolsheviks formed a splinter party under the leadership of a young, dedicated revolutionary, Vladimir Ilyich Ulyanov, who wrote under the pseudonym Lenin.

Lenin spent the years 1900–1917 in exile in western Europe. From abroad, Lenin preached unrelenting class struggle, the need for a coordinated revolutionary socialist movement throughout Europe, and, most important, the belief that Russia was passing into an economic stage that made it ripe for revolution. In his treatise *What Is to Be Done?* (1902), Lenin denounced gradualists, who had urged collaboration with moderate parties, and argued that only vanguard agents of the party, acting in the name of the working class, could bring about a revolution.

THE FIRST RUSSIAN REVOLUTION The **Russian Revolution of 1905** took all the radical movements by surprise. Its immediate cause was Russia's defeat in the Russo-Japanese War of 1904–1905, but this revolution had deeper roots. Rapid industrialization had transformed Russia unevenly, leaving certain regions heavily industrial and others less integrated into the market economy. Also, the economic boom of the 1880s and 1890s turned to bust in the early 1900s. The demand for goods tapered off, prices plummeted, and the nascent working class suffered high levels of unemployment. At the same time, low grain prices resulted in a series of peasant uprisings, which, combined with students' energetic radical organizing, became overtly political.

As dispatches reported the defeats of the tsar's army and navy by Japan in 1905, the Russian people grasped the full extent of the regime's inefficiency. Even middle-class subjects clamored for change, while radical workers organized strikes and held demonstrations in every important city. Trust in the benevolence of the tsar was severely shaken on January 22, 1905—"Bloody Sunday"—when a group of 200,000 workers and their families, led by a priest, Father Gapon, went to demonstrate their grievances at the tsar's Winter Palace in St. Petersburg. When troops killed 130 demonstrators and wounded several hundred others, the government seemed not only ineffective but arbitrary and brutal.

Over the course of 1905, general protest grew: merchants closed their stores, factory owners shut down their plants, lawyers refused to plead cases in court. The autocracy lost control of entire rural towns and regions as enraged peasants ejected and often killed local authorities. Forced to yield, Tsar Nicholas II issued the October Manifesto, pledging guarantees of individual liberties, a moderately liberal franchise for the election of a Duma ("house," or legislature), and genuine legislative veto powers for the Duma. Although the 1905 revolution brought the tsarist system perilously close to collapse, it failed to convince the tsar that fundamental political change was necessary. Between 1905 and 1907, Nicholas revoked most of the promises made in the October Manifesto and, above all, he deprived the Duma of its principal powers and decreed that it be elected indirectly on a class basis, which ensured a legislative body of obedient followers.

Nonetheless, the revolution of 1905 persuaded the tsar's more perceptive advisers that reform was urgent. Between 1906 and 1911, agricultural reforms granted peasants permission to withdraw from the mir and form independent farms, and canceled peasant property debts. Further decrees legalized labor unions, reduced the working day (to ten hours in most cases), and established sickness and accident insurance. Liberals could reasonably hope that Russia was moving toward becoming a progressive nation based on the Western model. The tsar, however, remained stubbornly autocratic and Russian industry remained behind that of western Europe.

NATIONALISM AND IMPERIAL POLITICS: THE OTTOMAN EMPIRE

Young Turks The 1908 Turkish reformist movement that aimed to modernize the Ottoman Empire, restore parliamentary rule, and depose Sultan Abdul Hamid II.

The Ottoman Empire gradually loses territories in the Balkans and North Africa

In the last decades of the nineteenth century, the Ottoman Empire's hold over the Balkan lands of southeastern Europe was challenged by many of the same nationalist movements that troubled the Habsburg Empire in the region. These internal problems were compounded by an external threat: the expansion of European imperialism into Ottoman territory in the Balkans and the Middle East.

The Ottoman Empire had been a major power in the Mediterranean for over 400 years. In the first half of the nineteenth century, as much as half of its population lived in the European provinces of the empire, but in the 1870s a series of catastrophes led to the loss of the Ottoman Empire's territories in the Balkans. When the sultan's government repressed uprisings in Bosnia, Herzegovina, and Bulgaria in 1875–1876, the Russians saw an opportunity to intercede following reports of atrocities committed against Christians in the region. After a Russian victory in the Russo-Turkish War (1877–1878), the tsar forced the sultan to surrender nearly all of his European territory, except for a remnant around Constantinople. In 1878, a congress of great powers convened in Berlin to divide the spoils: Bessarabia went to Russia, Thessaly to Greece, and Bosnia and Herzegovina fell under the control of the Austrian Empire. But Montenegro, Serbia, and Romania became independent states, launching the modern era of Balkan nationalism. In 1908, Bulgaria claimed independence from the Ottomans and the Austrians annexed Bosnia and Herzegovina outright. By this time, the proportion of the Ottoman Empire's population that lived in its European provinces had fallen to one-fifth. The Ottomans also lost territory in North Africa. The loss of Algeria to the French in 1830 was followed by the establishment of a French protectorate in Tunisia in 1881. The British occupied Egypt in 1882, and Tripoli was annexed by the Italians in 1912. The Ottoman Empire's loss of territory significantly strained Europe's imperial balance of power and discredited the Ottoman regime among many of its own subjects.

Educated Turks, grown impatient with the weakness of Sultan Abdul Hamid II (r. 1876–1909), began to call for national rejuvenation through the introduction of Western science and political reforms. In 1908, these reformers, calling themselves "**Young Turks**," forced the sultan to establish a constitutional government. The following year, they deposed the sultan and placed his brother, Mehmed V (r. 1909–1918), on the throne. The powers of government were entrusted to a grand vizier and ministers accountable to an elected parliament. (Non-Turkish inhabitants of the empire were not given the vote.) The Young Turks launched a vigorous effort to "Ottomanize" all the imperial subjects, and they tried to bring both Christian and Muslim communities under centralized Turkish control. The effort, intended to compensate for the loss of territories in Europe, undercut the popularity of the new reformist regime. At the same time, the Ottoman government began seriously to consider joining with a European power to prevent further encroachments on its territory. This calculation eventually led to an Ottoman alliance with Germany in 1914, at the outset of the First World War (see Chapter 24).

INDIAN OCEAN

CASPIAN SEA

ARAL SEA

RUSSIAN EMPIRE

PERSIA

Tehran

ARMENIA

GEORGIA
1878

Tiflis

Kars

Batum
1703

1859

1784
1783

SEA OF
AZOV

1739

1783

1791

1812

1699

Odessa

Sevastopol

BLACK SEA

Kuchuk-
Kainarji

Angora

Constantinople

TURKEY

MESOPOTAMIA

Baghdad

Basra

Tigris R.

Euphrates R.

ARABIA

HEJAZ

Mecca

RED SEA

Persian Gulf

ADEN

Damascus

Acre
HOLY LAND
Jerusalem

Suez Canal
SINAI

Tel-el-Kebir
Cairo

EGYPT
1882

Nile R.

SUDAN

AFRICA

CYPRUS
1878

AEGEAN
SEA

Athens

GREECE
1830

CRETE

Navarino

MEDITERRANEAN SEA

CYRENAICA

Benghazi

LIBYA
Conquered by Italy
1912

Tripoli

AUSTRIA

EUROPE

FRANCE

HUNGARY
1699
1716

1699

Budapest

Vienna
SWITZ. Turks defeated
1683

ITALY

Rome

ROMANIA
1878

SERBIA
1878

BOSNIA
1878

BULGARIA
1908
1886

MONTENEGRO

TURKEY IN
EUROPE

ADRIATIC SEA

IONIAN
SEA

TYRRHENIAN
SEA

SPAIN

Madrid

Bay of
Biscay

Algiers

Oran

Tunis

ALGERIA
1830

TUNISIA
1881

Benghazi

250 Miles

500 Miles

0

0

250

500 Kilometers

Boundary of Ottoman Empire 1699

Austria

Russia

Britain

France

Independent states (with date of independence)

Ottoman Empire 1912

THE DECLINE OF THE OTTOMAN EMPIRE, 1699–1912. › Where were the farthest points that the Ottoman Empire reached in Europe and Africa? › How do you explain the slow decline of Ottoman power in relationship to Europe and the emerging global economy? › Why did the decline of Ottoman power have enormous significance on the relations among European nations?

The Science and Soul of the Modern Age

Darwin's theory of evolution Darwin's theory linking biology to history. It purported that competition among various organisms and their struggle with the environment were fundamental and unavoidable facts of life.

Nineteenth-century liberals believed in human reason, individualism, progress, and science. By 1900, new scientific developments challenged these core liberal beliefs. Darwin's theory of evolution, psychology, and social science all introduced visions of humanity that were sharply at odds with the liberal assumptions about human rationality. At the same time, artists and intellectuals mounted their own revolt against nineteenth-century beliefs and values. These upheavals in the world of ideas unsettled older conceptions of individuality, culture, and consciousness. Rather than the rational and free agent emphasized by the Enlightenment, the modern individual seemed to be a product of irrational inner drives and uncontrollable external circumstances.

DARWIN'S REVOLUTIONARY THEORY

British naturalist Charles Darwin transformed the wider culture's ideas about nature itself. **Darwin's theory of evolution** (see also Chapter 22) introduced an unsettling new picture of human biology and behavior.

Theories of evolution did not originate with Darwin. Geologists in the nineteenth century had challenged the biblical account of creation with evidence showing that the world was formed by natural processes over millions of years, but they did not have a satisfactory explanation for the existence of different species. In the early nineteenth century, French biologist Jean Lamarck argued that behavioral changes could alter an animal's physical characteristics within a single generation, and that these new traits could be passed on to the offspring. Over time, Lamarck suggested, the inheritance of acquired characteristics would produce new species of animals.

In 1859, Darwin published *On the Origin of Species*, with a more convincing hypothesis of organic evolution (see *Competing Viewpoints* on pages 832–33). Darwin had traveled for five years around the world as a naturalist on the HMS *Beagle*, a ship that had been chartered for scientific exploration. After observing the diversity of species in different lands, he wondered about their origins. Darwin knew that particular traits could be selected through controlled breeding. Was a similar process of selection at work in nature?

His answer was yes. Darwin theorized that variations in traits within a population, such as longer beaks or protective coloring, made certain individual organisms better equipped for survival, increasing their chances of reproducing and passing their advantageous traits to the next generation. His theory drew on the work of Thomas Malthus, a political economist who argued that human populations grow faster than the available food supply, leading to a fatal competition for scarce resources (Chapter 19). For Darwin, this Malthusian competition was a general rule of nature, whereby the strong survived and the weak perished. Competition with other animals and struggle with the environment produced a "natural selection" of some traits over others, leading to a gradual evolution of different species over time. Darwin eventually applied this theory of evolution not only to plant and animal species but also to humans. In his view, the human race had evolved from an apelike ancestor, long since extinct.

Darwin's ideas influence religious and social thought ❯

DARWINIAN THEORY AND RELIGION The implications of Darwin's writings went far beyond evolutionary sciences. They challenged deeply held religious beliefs, sparking a public discussion on the existence and knowability of God. Popular critics denounced Darwin for contradicting the literal interpretations of the Bible, but these contradictions were not necessarily what made religious middle-class readers uncomfortable. People did not need to abandon either Christianity or faith simply because Darwin argued that the world and its life-forms had developed over millions of years rather than six days. What nineteenth-century religious readers found difficult to accept was the challenge to their belief in a benevolent God and a morally guided universe. According to Darwin, the world was governed not by order, harmony, and the divine will, but by random chance and constant, undirected struggle. The Darwinian worldview seemed to reduce the notions of good and bad to simply the ability to survive, robbing humanity of critical moral certainties. Although Darwin himself was able to reconcile his theory with a belief in God, others latched onto his work to fiercely attack Christian orthodoxy.

SOCIAL DARWINISM

The theory of natural selection also influenced the social sciences, which were just developing at the end of the nineteenth century. New disciplines such as sociology, psychology, anthropology, and economics aimed to apply scientific methods to the analysis of society, and introduced new ways of quantifying, measuring, and interpreting the human experience. Under the authoritative banner of "science," these disciplines often contributed to improving the health and well-being of European men and women. They were also enlisted to provide justification for forms of economic, imperial, and racial dominance.

The so-called Social Darwinists adapted Darwinian thought in ways that Darwin himself never considered: applying his concept of individual competition and survival to relationships among classes, races, and nations. Darwin believed that natural selection worked at the level of individuals, not larger human collectives like tribes, nations, or social classes, which he believed to be subject to a complex set of factors that the theory of evolution could not account for. Such issues did not prevent some social scientists from attempting to prove that Darwin's theory also could be used to explain the destinies of nations and races, or to argue that the biological struggle for existence was the same as economic competition in the capitalist marketplace. Nevertheless, English philosopher Herbert Spencer (1820–1903) coined the phrase "survival of the fittest," and he used evolutionary theory to expound on the virtues of free competition and to attack state welfare programs. As a champion of individualism, Spencer condemned all forms of collectivism as primitive, relics of an earlier stage of social evolution. In his view, government attempts to relieve economic and social hardships—or to place constraints on big business—were hindrances to the advancement of civilization, which could occur only through individual adaptation and competition. Particularly in America, such claims earned Spencer high praise from wealthy industrialists who counted themselves among the fittest.

Unlike the science of biological evolution, a popularized Social Darwinism was easy to reduce to political slogans. Proponents of laissez-faire capitalism and opponents of socialism used Darwinist rhetoric to justify marketplace competition and the "natural order" of the rich and poor, as if the inequalities in the social order did not also result from human actions. Nationalists and colonialists embraced Social Darwinism to rationalize imperialist expansion and conquest, though Darwin had never argued that evolution worked at the level of nations or larger collectivities. Spencer's doctrine became closely tied to theories of racial hierarchy and white superiority, which claimed that the white race had reached the height of evolutionary

"Scientific Racism" in the United States

A lawyer from a wealthy New York family, Madison Grant (1865–1937) was a eugenicist and an enthusiastic popularizer of "race science," a now discredited attempt to define race in scientific terms. A friend of President Theodore Roosevelt, he was also well-known for his work as a conservationist. Among other activities, he served as a vice-president of the Immigration Restriction League (founded 1894), which sought to prevent migrants from southern and central Europe (especially Italians and Jews) from coming to the United States because of their allegedly inferior "racial" attributes. In this passage he uses the contested concept of "race" to argue that social inequalities have a purely biological explanation.

In many countries the existing classes represent races that were once distinct. In the city of New York and elsewhere in the United States there is a native American aristocracy resting upon layer after layer of immigrants of lower races and these native Americans [. . .] have [. . .] up to this time supplied the leaders in thought and in the control of capital as well as of education and of the religious ideals [. . .] of the community.

In the democratic forms of government the operation of universal suffrage tends toward the selection of the average man for public office rather than the man qualified by birth, education and integrity. How this scheme of administration will ultimately work out remains to be seen but from a racial point of view it will inevitably increase the preponderance of the lower types and cause a corresponding loss of efficiency in the community as a whole. [. . .]

It must be borne in mind that the specializations which characterize the higher races are of relatively recent development, are highly unstable and when mixed with generalized or primitive characters tend to disappear. Whether we like to admit it or not, the result of the mixture of two races, in the long run, gives a race reverting to the more ancient, generalized and lower type. The cross between a white man and an Indian is an Indian; the cross between a white man and a Hindu is a Hindu; and the cross between any of the three European races and a Jew is a Jew. [. . .]

development and had thus earned the right to dominate and rule other races (see Chapter 25). Francis Galton (1822–1911) advocated improving a population's racial characteristics by selective breeding of "superior types." Galton and others, fearing that improvements in health care and hygiene might allow individuals with "inferior" traits to survive to reproductive age, promoted a system of population management called *eugenics*, which they claimed would save European populations from a decline in their vitality and biological fitness. In this way, a popularized and simplistic, Darwinism was used to advance a range of political objectives and to shore up an array of ingrained prejudices (see *Analyzing Primary Sources* above).

CHALLENGES TO RATIONALITY: PAVLOV, FREUD, AND NIETZSCHE

Although the new social scientists self-consciously relied on the use of rational, scientific principles, their findings often stressed the opposite: the irrational, even animalistic nature of human experience. Darwin had already called into question the notion that humanity was fundamentally superior to the rest of the animal kingdom, and similarly discomfiting conclusions came from the new field of psychology.

In defining race in Europe it is necessary not only to consider pure groups or pure types but also the distribution of characters belonging to each particular subspecies of man found there. The interbreeding of these populations has progressed to such an extent that in many cases such an analysis of physical characters is necessary to reconstruct the elements which have entered into their ethnic composition. To rely on averages alone leads to misunderstanding and to disregard of the relative proportion of pure, as contrasted with mixed types. [. . .]

In dealing with European populations the best method of determining race has been found to lie in a comparison of proportions of the skull, the so-called cephalic index. This is the ratio of maximum *width* taken at the widest part of the skull above the ears to maximum *length*. [. . .]

The use of this test, the cephalic index, enables us to divide the great bulk of the European populations into three distinct subspecies of man, one northern and one southern, both dolichocephalic or characterized by a long skull and a central subspecies which is brachycephalic or characterized by a round skull. [. . .]

In zoology, related species when grouped together constitute subgenera and genera and the term species implies the existence of a certain definite amount of divergence from the most closely related type but race does not require a similar amount of difference. In man, where all groups are more or less fertile when crossed, so many intermediate or mixed types occur that the word species has at the present day too extended a meaning.

For the sake of clearness the word race and not the word species or subspecies will be used [. . .] as far as possible.

Source: Madison Grant, *The Passing of the Great Race or The Racial Basis of European History* (New York: 1919), pp. 5, 15, 17–22.

Questions for Analysis:

1. Who is Grant referring to when he uses the phrase "native Americans"? How does he describe the origins of social hierarchies in the United States?

2. What is the basis of his critique of democracy? What do these arguments have to do with his beliefs about race?

3. Does Grant clearly distinguish between race and species? Compare his arguments to earlier writers on the subject in earlier chapters. Is he clear about how to distinguish between "pure" and "mixed" races?

The Russian physician Ivan Pavlov (1849–1936) asserted that animal behavior could be understood as a series of trained responses to physical stimuli. Pavlov's famous experiment showed that if dogs were fed after they heard the ringing of a bell, they would eventually salivate at the sound of the bell alone, exactly as if they had smelled and seen food. Pavlov insisted that such conditioning constituted a significant part of human behavior as well. Known as "behaviorism," this type of physiological psychology recast human activity as a bundle of physiological responses to stimuli in the environment. This was a significant departure from Enlightenment views of human rationality.

Like behaviorism, a second major school of psychology suggested that human behavior was largely motivated by unconscious and irrational forces. Founded by the Austrian physician **Sigmund Freud** (1856–1939), the discipline of psychoanalysis posited a new, dynamic, and unsettling theory of the mind, according to which various unconscious drives and desires conflict with a rational and moral conscience. Developed over many years of treating patients with nervous ailments, Freud's model of the psyche contained three elements: (1) the *id*, or undisciplined desires for pleasure, sexual gratification, aggression, and so on; (2) the *superego*, or conscience, which registers the prohibitions of morality and culture; and (3) the *ego*, or the arena in which the conflict between

Sigmund Freud (1856–1939) Austrian physician who founded the discipline of psychoanalysis and suggested that human behavior is largely motivated by unconscious and irrational forces.

Darwin and His Readers

Charles Darwin's On the Origin of Species *(1859) and his theory of natural selection transformed Western knowledge of natural history. The impact of Darwin's work, however, extended well beyond scientific circles, and assumed a cultural importance that exceeded even his scholarly contribution. How Darwinism was popularized is a complex question, for writers and readers could mold Darwin's ideas to fit a variety of political and cultural purposes. The first excerpt comes from the conclusion to* On the Origin of Species *and sets out the different laws that Darwin thought governed the natural world. The second excerpt comes from the autobiography of Nikolaus Osterroth (1875–1933), a clay miner from western Germany, who was ambitious and self-educated. The passage recounts his reaction to hearing about Darwin and conveys his enthusiasm for late nineteenth-century science.*

Charles Darwin, *On the Origin of Species*

The natural system is a genealogical arrangement, in which we have to discover the lines of descent by the most permanent characters, however slight their vital importance may be.

The framework of bones being the same in the hand of a man, wing of a bat, fin of the porpoise, and leg of the horse,—the same number of vertebrae forming the neck of the giraffe and of the elephant,—and innumerable other such facts, at once explain themselves on the theory of descent with slow and slight successive modifications. The similarity of pattern in the wing and leg of a bat, though used for such different purposes,—in the jaws and legs of a crab,—in the petals, stamens, and pistils of a flower, is likewise intelligible on the view of the gradual modification of parts or organs, which were alike in the early progenitor of each class. . . .

It is interesting to contemplate an entangled bank, clothed with many plants of many kinds, with birds singing on the bushes, with various insects flitting about, and with worms crawling through the damp earth, and to reflect that these elaborately constructed forms, so different from each other, and dependent on each other in so complex a manner, have all been produced by laws acting around us. These laws, taken in the largest sense, being Growth with Reproduction; Inheritance which is almost implied by reproduction; Variability from the indirect and direct action of the external conditions of life, and from use and disuse; a Ratio of Increase so high as to lead to a Struggle for Life, and as a consequence to Natural Selection, entailing Divergence of Character and the Extinction of less-improved forms. Thus, from the war of nature, from famine and death, the most exalted object which we are capable of conceiving, namely, the production of the higher animals, directly follows. There is grandeur in this view of life, with its several powers, having been originally breathed into a few forms or into one; and that, whilst this planet has gone cycling on according to the fixed law of gravity, from so simple a beginning endless forms most beautiful and most wonderful have been, and are being, evolved.

Source: Charles Darwin, *On the Origin of Species* (Harmondsworth, UK: 1968; original work published 1859), pp. 450–51, 458–60.

id and superego works itself out. In works such as *The Interpretation of Dreams* (1899), Freud argued that most cases of mental disorder result from an irreconcilable tension between the natural drives and the restraints placed on individuals. He believed that by studying such disorders, as well as dreams and slips of the tongue, scientists could catch a glimpse of the submerged areas of consciousness and thus understand seemingly irrational behavior. His search for an all-encompassing theory of the mind was deeply

Nikolaus Osterroth: A Miner's Reaction

The book was called *Moses or Darwin?* . . . Written in a very popular style, it compared the Mosaic story of creation with the natural evolutionary history, illuminated the contradictions of the biblical story, and gave a concise description of the evolution of organic and inorganic nature, interwoven with plenty of striking proofs.

What particularly impressed me was a fact that now became clear to me: that evolutionary natural history was monopolized by the institutions of higher learning; that Newton, Laplace, Kant, Darwin, and Haeckel brought enlightenment only to the students of the upper social classes; and that for the common people in the grammar school the old Moses with his six-day creation of the world still was the authoritative world view. For the upper classes there was evolution, for us creation; for them productive liberating knowledge, for us rigid faith; bread for those favored by fate, stones for those who hungered for truth!

Why do the people need science? Why do they need a so-called Weltanschauung [worldview]? The people must keep Moses, must keep religion; religion is the poor man's philosophy. Where would we end up if every miner and every farmhand had the opportunity to stick his nose into astronomy, geology, biology, and anatomy? Does it serve any purpose for the divine world order of the possessing and privileged classes to tell the worker that the Ptolemaic heavens have long since collapsed; that out there in the universe there is an eternal process of creation and destruction; that in the universe at large, as on our tiny earth, everything is in the grip of eternal evolution; that this evolution takes place according to inalterable natural laws that defy even the omnipotence of the old Mosaic Jehovah. . . . Why tell the dumb people

that Copernicus and his followers have overturned the old Mosaic creator, and that Darwin and modern science have dug the very ground out from under his feet of clay?

That would be suicide! Yes, the old religion is so convenient for the divine world order of the ruling class! As long as the worker hopes faithfully for the beyond, he won't think of plucking the blooming roses in this world. . . .

The possessing classes of all civilized nations need servants to make possible their godlike existence. So they cannot allow the servant to eat from the tree of knowledge.

Source: Alfred Kelly, ed., *The German Worker: Working-Class Autobiographies from the Age of Industrialization* (Berkeley, CA: 1987), pp. 185–86.

Questions for Analysis

1. Was the theory of evolution revolutionary? If so, how? Would it be fair to say that Darwin did for the nineteenth century what Newton had done for the seventeenth and eighteenth centuries? Why or why not?

2. Why did people think the natural world was governed by laws? Was this a religious belief or a scientific fact?

3. What aspects of Darwin's theory appealed to Osterroth? Why?

---

grounded in the tenets of nineteenth-century science. By stressing the irrational, however, Freud's theories fed a growing anxiety about the value and limits of human reason. Likewise, they brought to the fore a powerful critique of the constraints imposed by the moral and social codes of Western civilization.

No one provided a more sweeping or more influential assault on Western values of rationality than the German philosopher Friedrich Nietzsche (*NEE-chuh*; 1844–1900).

In a series of works that rejected rational argumentation in favor of an elliptical, suggestive prose style, Nietzsche argued that bourgeois faith in such concepts as science, progress, democracy, and religion represented a futile and reprehensible search for security and truth. He categorically denied the possibility of knowing truth or reality, because all knowledge comes filtered through linguistic, scientific, or artistic systems of representation. He famously ridiculed Judeo-Christian morality for instilling a repressive conformity that drained civilization of its vitality. Nietzsche's philosophy resounded with themes of personal liberation, especially freedom from the stranglehold of history and tradition. Indeed, Nietzsche's ideal individual, or "superman," was one who abandoned the burdens of cultural conformity and created an independent set of values based on artistic vision and strength of character. He forecast salvation for Western civilization only through individual struggle against the chaotic universe.

RELIGION AND ITS CRITICS

Faced with these challenges, the institutions responsible for the maintenance of traditional faith found themselves on the defensive. The Roman Catholic Church responded to the encroachments of secular society by appealing to its dogma and venerated traditions. In 1864, Pope Pius IX issued the *Syllabus of Errors*, condemning what he regarded as the principal religious and philosophical errors of the time, among them materialism, free thought, and indifferentism (the idea that one religion is as good as another). In 1871, the pope convoked the first Church council since the Catholic Reformation and pronounced the dogma of papal infallibility, which meant that in his capacity "as pastor and doctor of all Christians," the pope was infallible regarding all matters of faith and morals. Though generally accepted by pious Catholics, the claim of papal infallibility provoked a storm of protests and was denounced by the governments of several Catholic countries, including France, Spain, and Italy. The death of Pius IX in 1878 and the accession of Pope Leo XIII brought a more accommodating climate to the Church. The new pope acknowledged that there was good as well as evil in modern civilization, added a scientific staff to the Vatican, and opened archives and observatories; but made no further concessions to liberalism in the political sphere.

Protestants were also compelled to respond to a modernizing world. But because they were taught to understand God with the help of just the Bible and a willing conscience, Protestants, unlike Catholics, had little in the way of doctrine to help them defend their faith. Some fundamentalists chose to ignore the implications of scientific and philosophical inquiry altogether and continued to believe in the literal truth of the Bible. Others agreed with the school of American philosophers known as pragmatists, principally Charles S. Peirce and William James, who taught that "truth" was whatever produced useful, practical results; that is, if belief in God provided mental peace or spiritual satisfaction, then that belief was true. Still others

SIGMUND FREUD. Freud's theory of the mind and the unconscious broke from many of the basic human nature assumptions of his time. He remained, however, a committed nineteenth-century scientist and believed he had uncovered new laws that governed culture as well as individuals.

POPULAR RELIGION IN THE MODERN AGE. The political and social changes that accompanied the second industrial revolution and the advent of mass politics transformed European society in fundamental ways, but these events did not lead to a waning of traditional religious faith. Instead, practices of religious devotion changed with society as a whole. A good example of this is the emergence of new, popular destinations for Catholic pilgrimage, such as the Grotto of Lourdes, where a young girl had a series of visions of the Virgin Mary in 1858. After the vision was verified by a local bishop in 1860, the place became a pilgrimage site for the faithful. In 2012, it was estimated that 200 million people had visited the site since 1860. **› What developments during the second industrial revolution helped to make the pilgrimage to Lourdes a global phenomenon?**

sought solace from religious doubt by founding missions, laboring among the poor, and other good works; many adherents to this social gospel were also modernists who accepted the ethical teachings of Christianity but rejected beliefs in miracles and original sin.

The Culture of Modernity

NEW READERS AND THE POPULAR PRESS

The diffusion of new ideas about science and religion was facilitated by rising literacy rates and new forms of printed mass culture. Between 1750 and 1870, readership had expanded from the aristocracy to include middle-class circles and, thereafter, to an increasingly literate general population. In 1850, approximately half of Europe's population was literate. In subsequent decades, country after country introduced state-financed elementary and secondary education to provide opportunities for social advancement, to diffuse technical and scientific knowledge, and to inculcate civic and national pride. By 1900, approximately 85 percent of the population in Britain, France, Belgium, the Netherlands, Scandinavia, and Germany could read.

In countries where literacy rates were highest, commercial publishers, such as Alfred Harmsworth in Britain and William Randolph Hearst in the United States, hastened to serve the new reading public. Advertisements also drastically lowered the costs of the mass-market newspapers, enabling even workers to purchase one or two newspapers a day. Newspapers began to appeal to the newly literate with sensational journalism and spicy, easy-to-read serials. The "yellow journalism" of the penny presses merged entertainment and sensationalism with the news, aiming to increase circulation and thus securing more lucrative advertising sales. The era of mass readership had arrived, and writers, artists, activists, and, above all, governments increasingly focused their message for this mass audience.

THE NINETEENTH-CENTURY NOVEL

No literary form is more closely associated with nineteenth-century European culture than the **novel**. This relatively new form of writing flourished throughout Europe between the end of the Napoleonic Wars in 1815 and the First World War in 1914. The premise of the novel was that a work of fiction should focus on the lives of believable individuals whose predicaments were recognizable to the audience. The success of a novel depended on its ability to portray its protagonists in ways that allowed readers to identify with their struggles and understand their innermost thoughts and feelings.

The novel thus fused liberalism's emphasis on the individual with romanticism's attention to emotions and mental states. The novel's reliance on realistic narrative description freed literature from the constraints of older genres and allowed writers to move beyond plots borrowed from classical history or mythology. The brilliance of novelists in this period was matched only by the avidity with which a fascinated public—both men and women—consumed their works.

In France, Stendhal's *The Red and the Black* (1830), Honoré de Balzac's multivolume *Human Comedy* (ninety-one works published between 1830 and 1849), Gustave Flaubert's *Madame Bovary* (1856) and *Sentimental Education* (1869), and Émile Zola's twenty-volume *Rougon-Macquart* series (1871–1893) all displayed very different sensibilities, but the novelists shared a common concern with the fates of ordinary people. Their novels portrayed young men from unremarkable families attempting to make careers in the capital city, women trapped in loveless marriages, fathers blinded by their love for their unfaithful daughters, and working men and women struggling with back-breaking labor and poverty. Some literary critics were dismayed by the attention given to the lives of ordinary people, finding it vulgar; whereas others insisted that this was an appropriate subject for literature in a more democratic age.

Women made up a significant portion of the audience for novels, and they also produced them. Earlier in the century in England, Jane Austen had almost single-handedly defined a new genre of romantic fiction (Chapter 17). Her novels—among them *Sense and Sensibility* (1811) and *Pride and Prejudice* (1813)—were spiced with incisive social satire and ironic commentary on the foibles of upper-middle-class men and women as they looked for love, marriage, and (not incidentally) property. Her works were published anonymously during her lifetime, but she was recognized as the author after her nephew published a memoir in 1869; her fame and popularity continue into the present. In France, George Sand (the pseudonym of Amantine-Aurore-Lucile Dupin; 1804–1876) became a literary celebrity, as famous for her love affairs with artists and musicians as she was for her best-selling novels, such as *Indiana* (1832) and *Consuelo* (1842–1843).

Many novelists were as interested in describing society as they were in their characters, a preoccupation that was a natural outgrowth of their attempts to provide a realistic portrait of contemporary European life. Victor Hugo's *Les Misérables* (1862) follows the story of a good man who had been imprisoned for stealing food to feed his sister's hungry children, and recounts along the way the undercurrents of revolutionary activity in Paris across the century. Émile Zola's *Germinal* (1885) portrays a mining town in northern France in the throes of a violent strike, and his *L'Assommoir* (1877) contains an unflinching exploration of a working couple losing a struggle with alcoholism and poverty. Hugo's works, written in a romantic vein, celebrated the spirit of progress and the French Revolution, while Zola's more pessimistic novels were less confident about the future.

Perhaps the most famous of the great nineteenth-century novelists in the English-speaking world was Charles Dickens (1812–1870). In *Hard Times* (1854), he offered a cutting portrait of the effects of the Industrial Revolution in Britain. Dickens's favorite theme, however, was stories of young men struggling against disadvantages of birth and family, rendered in scenes that alternated between humor and sentimentality, such as in *Oliver Twist* (1837–1839), *David Copperfield* (1849–1850), and *Great Expectations* (1860–1861). Like many writers, Dickens published his novels in installments in the penny press. This publishing innovation was a crucial part of the mass appeal of his novels, because it vastly increased his audience. Here, too, we see the novel as the product of both an astonishingly creative mind and a keen awareness of the market—simultaneously a work of art and a consumer item.

By the end of the nineteenth century, the prestige of the novel led to an explosion of publishing and novel reading in every European language. Perhaps the most respected novelists of the nineteenth century were Russian. In *War and Peace* (1869), Leo Tolstoy (1828–1910)

LEO TOLSTOY. Although a wealthy landowner, Tolstoy often dressed as a peasant. He became increasingly ascetic, casting off the corruptions of the world, and a pacifist. In this picture, he is leaving his home for a hermitage.

tells the history of the Napoleonic Wars through the experiences of a group of interconnected families; interspersed within the massive narrative were philosophical digressions about religion and musings on the fate of individuals during a period of radical historical change. Tolstoy's *Anna Karenina* (1873–1877) is about an aristocratic woman's struggle to reconcile her social status as the wife of a senior government official with her passionate love for another man. In this novel, he not only creates a remarkable portrait of the title character, but also explores contemporary debates about religion and the reform of Russia's feudal system. Fyodor Dostoyevsky (1821–1881), meanwhile, was preoccupied with the internal mental anguish of Russian men and women struggling to reconcile religious faith with worldly desires. As a young man, Dostoyevsky had served four years of hard labor in a Siberian work camp for political activity of the mildest sort, and this experience produced *The House of the Dead* (1861). His *Crime and Punishment* (1866) offers a dark story of a young man driven by an interior compulsion to kill an elderly woman. Dostoyevsky's last work, *The Brothers Karamazov* (1880), is the culmination of his extended meditation on faith and religious doubt, delivered as a story about four brothers—including an illegitimate son brought up as a servant—and their conflicts with their unbearably uncouth and violent father. With Tolstoy and Dostoyevsky, the novel reached its apogee, proving itself to be a literary form capable of astonishing universality that is able to comprehend both the wide sweep of history and the profoundly interior universe of the human mind.

THE FIRST MODERNS: INNOVATIONS IN ART

While novelists explored the lives of individuals struggling with broader historical forces, visual artists across the Continent began to question the moral and cultural values of liberal, middle-class society. A few did so with grave hesitation, others with heedless abandon. In a dizzying array of experiments, innovations, ephemeral art movements, and bombastic manifestos, the pioneers of what would later be termed *modernism* developed the artistic forms and aesthetic values that came to dominate much of the twentieth century.

Modernism encompassed a diverse and often contradictory set of theories and practices that spanned the entire range of cultural production from painting, sculpture, literature, and architecture to theater, dance, and musical composition. Despite such diversity, however, modernist movements did share certain key characteristics. First, a sense that the world had radically changed and that this change should be embraced; hence the modernists' interest in science and technology. Second, a belief that traditional values and assumptions were outdated. Third, a new conception of what art could do, stressing expression over representation and insisting on experiment and freedom.

Early modernism was also distinguished by a new understanding of the relationship between art and society. Few artists remained interested in purely aesthetic questions, but many others embraced the notion that art could bring about profound social and spiritual change. The abstract painter Wassily Kandinsky (1866–1944) believed that the materialism of the nineteenth century was a source of social and moral corruption, and he looked toward a future in which artists would nourish the human spirit that was threatened by the onset of industrial society.

modernism A late nineteenth- and early twentieth-century aesthetic movement in the arts and literature that sought to break with traditional forms of representation and embrace innovative and experimental forms.

Other artists believed that they had a duty to document unflinchingly what they saw as the pathological aspects of life in modern cities or the inward chaos of the human mind. In the political arena, modernist hostility toward conventional values sometimes translated into support for antiliberal or revolutionary movements of the extreme right or left.

THE REVOLT ON CANVAS Like most artistic movements, modernism defined itself in opposition to a set of earlier principles. For painters, in particular, this meant a rejection of mainstream academic art, which affirmed the chaste and moral outlook of museumgoers, as well as of the socially conscious realist tradition, which strove for rigorous, scientific exactitude in representing material reality. The modern artists rebelled even further, however, by discarding the centuries-old tradition of realistic representation altogether. Since the Renaissance, Western art had sought to depict accurately three-dimensional visual reality, and paintings were considered to be mirrors of or windows on the world. But during the late nineteenth century, artists turned their backs to the visual world, focusing instead on the subjective, psychologically oriented, intensely emotional forms of self-expression. As the Norwegian painter Edvard Munch

Modernist painters reject tradition of realistic representation

claimed, "Art is the opposite of nature. A work of art can come only from the interior of man."

The first significant break from traditional representational art emerged with the French impressionists, who came to prominence as young artists during the 1870s. Strictly speaking, the impressionists were realists; steeped in scientific theories about sensory perception, they attempted to record natural phenomena objectively. Instead of painting objects, they captured the transitory play of light on surfaces, giving their works a sketchy, ephemeral quality that differed sharply from realist art. Although subsequent artists revolted against what they deemed the cold objectivity of this scientific approach, the impressionist painters, most famously Claude Monet (*moh-NAY*; 1840–1926) and Pierre-Auguste Renoir (1841–1919), left two important legacies to the European avant-garde. First, by developing new techniques without reference to past styles, the impressionists paved the way for younger artists to experiment more freely. Second, because the official salons rejected their work, the impressionists organized their own independent exhibitions from 1874 to 1886. These shows effectively undermined the French Academy's centuries-old monopoly on artistic display and aesthetic standards, and established a tradition of autonomous outsider exhibits that figures prominently in the history of modernism.

At the end of the nineteenth century, in the wake of impressionism, a handful of innovative artists laid the groundwork for an explosion of creative experimentation; chief among them, the Frenchman Paul Cézanne (1839–1906). Perhaps more than anyone, Cézanne shattered the window of representational art. Painting became a vehicle for an artist's self-expression rather than a reflection of the world. Dutchman Vincent van Gogh also explored art's expressive potential, with greater emotion and subjectivity. For van Gogh, painting was a labor of faith, a way to channel his violent passions. For another artist, Paul Gauguin, who fled to the Pacific Islands in 1891, art promised a utopian refuge from the corruption of Europe.

After the turn of the century, a diverse crop of avant-garde movements flowered across Europe. In Germany and Scandinavia, expressionists such as Emil Nolde (1867–1956) and Edvard Munch (1863–1944) turned to acid colors and violent figural distortions to express the interior consciousness of the human mind. The Austrian Egon Schiele (1890–1918) explored sexuality and the body with disturbingly raw, graphic imagery. In bohemian Paris, the Frenchman Henri Matisse (1869–1954) and Pablo Picasso (1881–1973), a Catalan Spaniard, pursued their groundbreaking aesthetic experiments in relative quiet. Clamoring for attention, however, were groups of artists who reveled in the energetic

SELF-PORTRAIT, **BY EGON SCHIELE (1912).** The Viennese artist Egon Schiele represents another side of early modernism that sought to portray raw psychological expression, instead of moving toward abstraction.

dynamism of modern life. The cubists in Paris, the vorticists in Britain, and the futurists in Italy all embraced a hard, angular aesthetic of the machine age. Other modernists, meanwhile, sought an antidote to end-of-the-century malaise by looking backward to the so-called primitive cultures. These new movements embraced the future in all its uncertainty, often with the kind of aggressive, hypermasculine language that later emerged as a hallmark of fascism. In *The Manifesto of Futurism*, for instance, Filippo Tommaso Marinetti proclaimed, "We will glorify war—the only true hygiene of the world— militarism, patriotism, the destructive gesture of anarchist, the beautiful ideas which kill." In Russia and Holland, a few intensely idealistic painters made perhaps the most revolutionary aesthetic leap of early modernism: the totally abstract, or "object-less" painting.

The breadth and diversity of modern art defy simple categories and explanations. Though they remained the province of a small group of artists and intellectuals before 1914, soon after the First World War these radical revisions of artistic values entered the cultural mainstream (see Chapter 25).

Conclusion

Many Europeans who had grown up in the period from 1870 to 1914, but lived through the hardships of the First World War, looked back on the prewar period as a golden age of European civilization. In one sense, this retrospective view is correct. After all, the Continental powers had successfully avoided major wars, enabling a second phase of industrialization that provided better living standards for the growing populations of mass society. An overall spirit of confidence and purpose fueled Europe's perceived mission to exercise political, economic, and cultural dominion in the far reaches of the world. Yet, European politics and culture also registered the presence of powerful—and destabilizing—forces of change. Industrial expansion, relative abundance, and rising literacy produced a political climate of escalating expectations. As the age of mass politics arrived, democrats, socialists, and feminists clamored for access to political life, all threatening violence, strikes, and revolution. Marxist socialism, in particular, changed radical politics and redefined the terms of debate for the next century. Western science, literature, and the arts

PORTRAIT OF AMBROISE VOLLARD, BY PABLO PICASSO (1909). In the early twentieth century, Pablo Picasso and Georges Braque radically transformed painting with their cubist constructions, which breaks the depiction of reality into fragmented planes. This image of Vollard, an important art dealer of the period, loses recognizable form in the lower part of the painting. › **Compare this portrait with Schiele's Self-Portrait on the left. What do these paintings say about the task of an artist?** › **What makes these paintings "modern"?**

explored new perspectives on the individual, undermining some of the cherished beliefs of nineteenth-century liberals. The competition and violence central to Darwin's theory of evolution, the subconscious urges in human behavior found in Freud's study, and the rebellion against representation in the arts all pointed toward new and baffling directions. These experiments, hypotheses, and nagging

AFTER YOU READ THIS CHAPTER

CHRONOLOGY

1850s–1870s	Production of steel alloys revolutionized
1859	Publication of Charles Darwin's *On the Origin of Species*
1861	Emancipation of the serfs in Russia
1871	Paris Commune
1871–1878	Bismarck's *Kulturkampf*
1880–1890s	Russia launches industrialization program
1890s	Electricity becomes available in many European cities
1894–1906	Dreyfus Affair
1899	Publication of Sigmund Freud's *The Interpretation of Dreams*
1901	Labour party founded in Britain
1903	Russian Marxists split into Bolsheviks and Mensheviks
1905	The First Russian Revolution

REVIEWING THE OBJECTIVES

❯ The second industrial revolution was made possible by technological innovations that stimulated the production of steel and created new energy sources. What were the consequences of this era of rapid growth for the European economy and society?

❯ Liberalism and nationalism were changed by the advent of mass politics. How did the expansion of the electorate change political life across Europe?

❯ Expanded electorates meant that more people were participating in politics, especially among the working classes. What parties and movements emerged to represent European workers? What were their goals?

❯ At the end of the nineteenth century, militant agitation in favor of women's suffrage increased. What obstacles did women who demanded the vote face?

❯ Technological innovations and scientific ideas about human nature and modern society changed the way people thought about their place in the world, inspiring artists and writers to new and revolutionary forms of creative expression. What were these scientific ideas? Why were they so controversial at the end of the nineteenth century?

questions accompanied Europe into the Great War of 1914, and they would help shape Europeans' responses to the devastation of that war. After the war, the political changes and cultural unease of the period from 1870 to 1914 would reemerge, in the form of mass movements and artistic developments that would define the twentieth century.

Go to INQUIZITIVE to see what you've learned—and learn what you've missed—with personalized feedback along the way.

PEOPLE, IDEAS, AND EVENTS IN CONTEXT

> Why was the British **LABOUR PARTY** more moderate in its goals than the German **SOCIAL DEMOCRATIC PARTY**?

> What disagreements about political strategy divided **ANARCHISTS** and **SYNDICALISTS** from **MARXISTS** in European labor movements?

> What legal reforms were successfully achieved by the **WOMEN'S SUFFRAGE MOVEMENT** in late nineteenth-century western European nations?

> What was the **DREYFUS AFFAIR**? How was it related to the spread of popular **ANTISEMITISM** and the emergence of **ZIONISM** in European Jewish communities?

> What were the goals of the **BOLSHEVIKS** and the **MENSHEVIKS** in the **RUSSIAN REVOLUTION OF 1905**?

> Who were the **YOUNG TURKS**? What circumstances in the Ottoman Empire brought them to power? What changes did they provoke?

> Why did **CHARLES DARWIN'S THEORY OF EVOLUTION** generate debate between religious and secular thinkers? What was Social Darwinism?

> Why was the psychology of **SIGMUND FREUD** so troubling for liberals in Europe?

> What made the **NOVEL** so popular among nineteenth-century readers?

> What common ideas did the artists and writers who came to be known as **MODERNISTS** share?

THINKING ABOUT CONNECTIONS

> How did the expansion of the electorate and the spread of representative political institutions in Europe at the end of the nineteenth century change the nature of debates about the power of public opinion and the responsibility of government for the people?

> Compare the age of mass politics at the end of the nineteenth century in Europe with earlier eras of rapid change, such as the Reformation of the sixteenth century or the period of the French Revolution. What was similar? What was different?

> Can you think of contemporary debates that draw upon the claims made by social Darwinists at the end of the nineteenth century? In what ways have the claims of scientific racism continued to resonate in the present?

The First World War

THE BATTLE OF THE SOMME began on June 24, 1916, with a fearsome British artillery barrage against German trenches along a twenty-five-mile front. Hour after hour, day and night, the British guns swept across the barbed wire and fortifications that faced their own lines, firing 1.5 million rounds over seven days. Mixing gas with explosive rounds, the gunners pulverized the landscape and poisoned the atmosphere. On the other side, deep in underground bunkers, the German defenders huddled in their gas masks. When the big guns fell silent, tens of thousands of British soldiers rose up out of the trenches, each bearing sixty pounds of equipment, and made their way into the cratered No Man's Land that separated the two armies. They had been told that wire-cutting explosives used during the barrage would have destroyed the labyrinth of barbed wire between the trenches, leaving them free to charge across and occupy the front trench before the stunned Germans could recover. But to their horror, they found the barbed wire intact. Instead of taking the German trench, they found themselves caught in the open when the German machine gunners manned the defensive parapets. The result proved, all too graphically, the efficiency of the First World War's mechanized methods of killing. On the first day of the Battle of the Somme, 29,000 British soldiers were killed and another 30,000 wounded. Because British units sometimes allowed volunteers to serve with their friends—the "pals battalions"—in some British neighborhoods and villages, every married woman became a

BEFORE YOU READ THIS CHAPTER >

STORY LINES

❯ In 1914, the balance of power in Europe collapsed in a war that mobilized the full resources of modern industrialized nations, their global empires, and their populations.

❯ The war transformed the relationship between state and society, as governments conscripted an entire generation of young men, encouraged women to work in industry, and took control of the economy to produce goods and matériel for the military.

❯ The war provoked the first successful socialist revolution in modern history when the Russian Empire collapsed and the Bolsheviks seized power in October 1917. The Russian Revolution set the stage for the major ideological confrontations of the twentieth century.

CORE OBJECTIVES

❯ EXPLAIN the origins of the First World War.

❯ DESCRIBE the circumstances that led to trench warfare on the Western Front and the consequences of the offensive strategy pursued by all sides.

❯ IDENTIFY the major effects of the war on civilian life.

❯ EXPLAIN the war's effects on territories beyond Europe's borders, in the Middle East, Africa, and Asia.

❯ UNDERSTAND the origins and goals of the Bolshevik movement in Russia and the circumstances that allowed the Bolsheviks to seize power in 1917.

❯ IDENTIFY the people responsible for the final terms of the Versailles peace treaty and UNDERSTAND its goals.

widow in the span of a few minutes. The British commanders pressed the offensive for nearly five more months, and the combined casualties climbed to more than 1 million; however, the German line never broke.

This contest between artillery and machine guns was a war that was possible only in an industrialized world. (Before beginning the assault, the British had stockpiled 2.9 million artillery shells; as a comparison, Napoleon had only 20,000 at Waterloo.) Although European armies marched off to war in 1914 with confidence and ambition bred by their imperial conquests, they soon confronted the ugly face of industrial warfare and the grim capacities of the modern world. In a catastrophic combination of old mentalities and new technologies, the war left 9 million dead soldiers in its wake.

And soldiers were not the only casualties. Four years of fighting destroyed many of the institutions and assumptions of the previous century, from monarchies and empires to European economic dominance. It disillusioned many, even among citizens of the victorious nations. As the British writer Virginia Woolf put it, "It was a shock . . . to see the faces of our rulers in the light of shell-fire." The war led European states to take over their national economies. The states set quotas for production and consumption, and took responsibility for sustaining the civilian population during the crisis. By toppling the Prussian and Austrian monarchies, the war banished older forms of authoritarianism. And by provoking the Russian Revolution of 1917, the war ushered in new forms of rule that bore the distinctive marks of the twentieth century. Finally, the war proved nearly impossible to settle; antagonisms bred in battle only intensified in the war's aftermath and, eventually, led to the Second World War. Postwar Europe faced more problems than peace could manage.

The July Crisis

In the decades before 1914, Europe had built a seemingly stable peace around two systems of alliance: the Triple Entente (later the Allied Powers) of Britain, France, and Russia faced the Triple Alliance (later the Central Powers) of Germany, Austria-Hungary, and Italy. Within this balance of power, the nations of Europe challenged each other for economic, military, and imperial advantage. The scramble for colonies abroad accompanied a fierce arms race at home, with military leaders assuming that superior technology and larger armies would result in a quick victory in a European war. Nobody expected that the Balkan crisis of July 1914 would touch off a conflict that would engulf all of Europe.

The Balkan Peninsula was a satellite of the Ottoman Empire. As Ottoman power diminished in the nineteenth century, Austria-Hungary and Russia competed to replace the Ottomans as the dominant force in the region. Meanwhile, Slavic nationalist movements in Serbia and Bulgaria pushed for independence in the same region. Russia, with its own Slavic traditions, encouraged these nationalist movements, while Austria-Hungary saw them as a threat to its multiethnic empire.

In multiethnic Balkan Peninsula, a vacuum of power is created as Ottoman power wanes

In 1912 and 1913, two wars pitted the Ottoman Empire against the independent Balkan states of Serbia, Greece, Bulgaria, and Montenegro. The Great Powers (Britain, France, Germany, Austria, and Russia) preserved European peace by remaining neutral. The alliance system could ensure stability only as long as this neutrality endured. If one Great Power became embroiled in the Balkans, their alliances could trigger a wider war.

The spark came from the Balkan province of Bosnia, a multiethnic region of Serbs, Croats, and Bosnian Muslims ruled by Austria since 1878. Bosnian Serbs longed to secede from Austrian rule and join the neighboring independent state of Serbia. On June 28, 1914, a group of Bosnian Serbs assassinated the heir to the Austro-Hungarian throne, Archduke **Franz Ferdinand** (1863–1914), and his wife, Sophie, as they paraded through Sarajevo, the capital of Bosnia.

Shocked by Ferdinand's death, the Austrians treated the assassination as a direct attack by the Serbian government. They sent an ultimatum to Serbia, demanding that they allow Austro-Hungarian officials to prosecute Serbian officials whom they

Franz Ferdinand (1863–1914) Archduke of Austria and heir to the Austro-Hungarian Empire; his assassination led to the beginning of the First World War.

THE BALKAN CRISIS, 1878–1914. › Which major empires were involved in the Balkans at the time? › According to the maps, what was the major change in the Balkans during this period? › What problems did nationalism, ethnicity, and race create in this region?

believed to be responsible for the assassination. The demands were designed to be rejected—the Austrians wanted war to crush Serbia. After agreeing to all but the most important demands, the Serbs mobilized their army and Austria responded with its own mobilization order on July 28, 1914. Shaken from their summer distractions, Europeans began to realize that the treaty system they relied on for stability was actually provoking a much larger confrontation: Austria and its ally Germany were facing a war with Serbia, Serbia's ally Russia, and, by extension, Russia's ally, France.

Diplomats tried but failed to prevent the outbreak of a wider war. When Russia announced a "partial mobilization" to defend Serbia against Austria, the German ministers telegraphed the French to find out if they intended to honor France's defensive treaty with Russia. The French responded that France would "act in accordance with her interests," meaning that it would immediately mobilize against Germany. Facing the threat from both sides it had long feared, Germany mobilized on August 1 and declared war on Russia—and two days later, on France. The next day, the German army invaded Belgium on its way to take Paris.

The invasion of neutral Belgium gave Britain a reason to honor its treaty obligations with France and enter the war against Germany. Other nations were quickly drawn into the struggle. On August 7, the Montenegrins joined the Serbs against Austria. Two weeks later, the Japanese declared war on Germany, mainly to attack German possessions in the Far East. On August 2, Turkey allied with Germany and, in October, began the bombardment of Russian ports on the Black Sea. Italy had been allied with Germany and Austria before the war, but at the outbreak of

FRANZ FERDINAND AND HIS WIFE, SOPHIE. The Austrian archduke and archduchess in Sarajevo on June 28, 1914. They are shown approaching their car minutes before they were assassinated. **›** What made their deaths the spark that unleashed a general war in Europe?

hostilities, it declared neutrality, insisting that because Germany had invaded neutral Belgium, it did not owe Germany protection.

The diplomatic maneuvers during the five weeks after the assassination at Sarajevo have been called a "tragedy of miscalculation." Austria's determination to punish Serbia, Germany's unwillingness to restrain its Austrian ally, and Russia's desire to use Serbia as an excuse to maintain its influence in the Balkans all made war more likely. Diplomats were constrained by rigid timetables set by their military leaders, and all sides felt that it was important to make a show of force. German officials argued that war was inevitable, and this sense of urgency characterized the strategies of all combatant countries. The lure of a bold, successful strike against one's enemies, and the fear that too much was at stake to risk losing the advantage, created a rolling tide of military mobilization that carried Europe into battle.

EUROPEAN ALLIANCES ON THE EVE OF THE FIRST WORLD WAR.
› Which major countries were part of the Triple Alliance and which were part of the Triple Entente? › As you examine the map, why do you think Germany declared war on France so quickly once Russia began to mobilize? › According to the map, why were the Balkan countries such a volatile region?

Toward the First World War: Diplomacy in the Summer of 1914

The assassination of Franz Ferdinand in Sarajevo on June 28, 1914, set off an increasingly desperate round of diplomatic negotiations. As the following exchanges show, diplomats and political leaders on both sides vacillated from trying to provoke war to attempting to avert or at least contain it. A week after his nephew, the heir to the throne, was shot, Emperor Franz Joseph set out his interpretation of the long-standing conflict with Serbia and its larger implications (reprinted here).

The second selection comes from an account of a meeting of the Council of Ministers of the Austro-Hungarian Empire on July 7, 1914. The ministers disagreed sharply about diplomatic strategies and how crucial decisions should be made.

Austria-Hungary's ultimatum to Serbia included the demands given in the final extract here. The British foreign secretary Sir Edward Grey, for one, was shocked by Austria's demands, especially its insistence that Austrian officials participate in Serbian judicial proceedings. The Serbian government's response was more conciliatory than most diplomats expected, but diplomatic efforts to avert war still failed.

Emperor Franz Joseph of Austria-Hungary to Kaiser Wilhelm II of Germany, July 5, 1914

The plot against my poor nephew was the direct result of an agitation carried on by the Russian and Serb Pan-Slavs, an agitation whose sole object is the weakening of the Triple Alliance and the destruction of my realm.

So far, all investigations have shown that the Sarajevo murder was not perpetrated by one individual, but grew out of a well-organized conspiracy, the threads of which can be traced to Belgrade. Even though it will probably be impossible to prove the complicity of the Serb government, there can be no doubt that its policy, aiming as it does at the unification of all Southern Slavs under the Serb banner, encourages such crimes, and that the continuation of such conditions constitutes a permanent threat to my dynasty and my lands. . . .

This will only be possible if Serbia, which is at present the pivot of Pan-Slav policies, is put out of action as a factor of political power in the Balkans.

You too are [surely] convinced after the recent frightful occurrence in Bosnia that it is no longer possible to contemplate a reconciliation of the antagonism between us and Serbia and that the [efforts] of all European monarchs to pursue policies that preserve the peace will be threatened if the nest of criminal activity in Belgrade remains unpunished.

Austro-Hungarian Disagreements over Strategy

[Count Leopold Berchtold, foreign minister of Austria-Hungary]: [B]oth Emperor Wilhelm and [chancellor] Bethmann Hollweg had assured us emphatically of Germany's unconditional support in the event of military complications with Serbia. . . . It was clear to him that a military conflict with Serbia might bring about war with Russia. . . .

[Count Istvan Tisza, prime minister of Hungary]: We should decide what our demands on Serbia will be [but] should only present an ultimatum if Serbia rejected them. These demands must be hard but not so that they cannot be complied with. If Serbia accepted them, we could register a noteworthy diplomatic success and our prestige in the Balkans would be enhanced.

If Serbia rejected our demands, then he too would favor military action. But he would already now go on record that we could aim at the down sizing but not the complete annihilation of Serbia because, first, this would provoke Russia to fight to the death and, second, he—as Hungarian premier—could never consent to the monarchy's annexation of a part of Serbia. Whether or not we ought to go to war with Serbia was not a matter for Germany to decide. . . .

[Count Berchtold] remarked that the history of the past years showed that diplomatic successes against Serbia might enhance the prestige of the monarchy temporarily, but that in reality the tension in our relations with Serbia had only increased.

[Count Karl Stürgkh, prime minister of Austria] . . . agreed with the Royal Hungarian Prime Minister that we and not the German government had to determine whether a war was necessary or not . . . [but] Count Tisza should take into account that in pursuing a hesitant and weak policy, we run the risk of not being so sure of Germany's unconditional support. . . .

[Leo von Bilinski, Austro-Hungarian finance minister]: . . . The Serb understands only force, a diplomatic success would make no impression at all in Bosnia and would be harmful rather than beneficial.

Source: Ralph Menning, *The Art of the Possible: Documents on Great Power Diplomacy, 1814–1914* (New York: 1996), pp. 400, 402–3, 414–15.

Austria-Hungary's Ultimatum to Serbia

The Royal Serb Government will publish the following declaration on the first page of its official *journal* of 26/13 July:

"The Royal Serb Government condemns the propaganda directed against Austria-Hungary, and regrets sincerely the horrible consequences of these criminal ambitions.

"The Royal Serb Government regrets that Serb officers and officials have taken part in the propaganda above-mentioned and thereby imperiled friendly and neighborly relations.

"The Royal Government . . . considers it a duty to warn officers, officials, and indeed all the inhabitants of the kingdom [of Serbia], that it will in future use great severity against such persons who may be guilty of similar doings.

The Royal Serb Government will moreover pledge itself to the following:

1. to suppress every publication likely to inspire hatred and contempt against the Monarchy;

2. to begin immediately dissolving the society called *Narodna Odbrana*,* to seize all its means of propaganda and to act in the same way against all the societies and associations in Serbia, which are busy with the propaganda against Austria-Hungary;

3. to eliminate without delay from public instruction everything that serves or might serve the propaganda against Austria-Hungary, both where teachers or books are concerned;

4. to remove from military service and from the administration all officers and officials who are guilty of having taken part in the propaganda against Austria-Hungary, whose names and proof of whose guilt the I. and R. Government [Imperial and Royal, that is, the Austro-Hungarian Empire] will communicate to the Royal Government;

5. to consent to the cooperation of I. and R. officials in Serbia in suppressing the subversive movement directed against the territorial integrity of the Monarchy;

6. to open a judicial inquest [*enquête judiciaire*] against all those who took part in the plot of 28 June, if they are to be found on Serbian territory; the I. and R. Government will delegate officials who will take an active part in these and associated inquiries.

The I. and R. Government expects the answer of the Royal Government to reach it not later than Saturday, the 25th, at six in the afternoon.

* *Narodna Odbrana*, or National Defense, was pro-Serbian and anti-Austrian but nonviolent. The Society of the Black Hand, to which Franz Ferdinand's assassin belonged, considered Narodna Odbrana too moderate.

continued on p. 852

(continued from p. 851)

Questions for Analysis

1. Emperor Franz Joseph's letter to Kaiser Wilhelm II tells of the Austrian investigation into the assassination of Archduke Franz Ferdinand. What did Franz Joseph seek from his German ally? What did the emperors understand by the phrase "if Serbia . . . is put out of action as a factor of political power in the Balkans"? Why might the Germans support a war against Serb-sponsored terrorism?

2. Could the Serbians have accepted the Austrian ultimatum without total loss of face and sacrifice of their independence? British and Russian foreign ministers were shocked by the demands on Serbia. Others thought that the Austrians were justified and that Britain would act similarly if threatened by terrorism. If, as Leo von Bilinski said, "The Serb understands only force," why didn't Austria declare war without an ultimatum?

1914: Mobilization and the Early Offensives

Declarations of war were met with a mix of public fanfare and private concern. Nationalists hoped the war would bring glory, but others recognized that war put decades of prosperity at risk. Bankers and financiers were among those most opposed to war, correctly predicting that a major war would create financial chaos. Many young men, however, enlisted with excitement. On the Continent, volunteer soldiers added to the strength of conscript armies, while in Britain—where conscription wasn't introduced until 1916—more than 700,000 men joined the army in the first eight weeks alone. Like many war enthusiasts, these men expected the fighting to be over by Christmas.

German military strategists had long foreseen the danger of a two-front war against France on one side and Russia on the other. The **Schlieffen Plan** sought to avoid a two-front war by attacking France first, before Russia could mobilize its larger army. The plan almost worked, but the French commander, Joseph Joffre, drew the Germans into a trap just thirty miles outside the French capital. Britain and France launched a successful counteroffensive at the **Battle of the Marne**, driving the Germans back to the Aisne River. The Schlieffen Plan had failed.

After the Marne, the armies were unable to advance and thus tried to outflank one another to the north, racing to the sea. After four months of swift charges across open ground, Germany set up a fortified, defensive position that the Allies could not break. Along an immovable front, stretching over 400 miles from the northern border of Switzerland to the English Channel, the Great Powers literally dug in for a protracted battle. By Christmas, trench warfare was born, and the war had just begun.

In the east, meanwhile, Russia had surprised the Germans and Austrians by moving quickly into East Prussia, threatening Berlin. At the same time, Russian forces moved to confront the Austrians through Polish Galicia just as the Austrians hoped to concentrate on Serbia. These initial Russian gains were obliterated, however, at the **Battle of Tannenberg** on August 26–30. Plagued with an array of problems, the Russian soldiers were tired and half starved. The Germans encircled them, taking 92,000 prisoners and virtually destroying the Russian Second Army. Two weeks later, the Germans won another victory at the Battle of the Masurian Lakes, forcing the Russians to retreat from German territory. But this time the

Schlieffen Plan Named for Count Alfred von Schlieffen (*SHLEE-fen*), who had foreseen the possibility of a two-front war, this offensive strategy called for Germany to achieve a quick victory over France before turning and facing the Russian threat.

Battle of the Marne A major battle of the First World War in September 1914; it halted the German invasion of France and led to protracted trench warfare on the Western Front.

Battle of Tannenberg German victory over Russian armies in August 1914, leading to the almost complete destruction of Russia's offensive capacity in the first months of the war.

THE SCHLIEFFEN PLAN AND THE GERMAN OFFENSIVE. The map on the left details the offensive strategy developed (and modified several times) by Alfred von Schlieffen, chief of the German general staff, and Helmuth von Moltke, his successor, in the decade after 1890. The map on the right shows the German offensive.
› **What strategy did the Schlieffen Plan propose, and why?** › **According to the map on the right, how was the plan modified, and why?** › **What were the consequences of this modified plan?** › **Why did the German offensive fail to achieve its ultimate goal?**

Russian armies were able to escape largely intact, and the continued threat forced the Germans to commit more troops to Russia.

The French victory at the Marne and the German victory at Tannenberg reversed the expectations of the Schlieffen Plan, and the consequences of this moment shaped the way Europe's powers thought about their chances for victory. In the west, the war of movement had stopped dead in its tracks, where it would remain for four years; thus dashing any remaining hope that the war would be over quickly. Politicians and generals sought to break the stalemate by seeking new allies, new theaters, and new weapons. But they also remained committed to offensive tactics on the Western Front. Whether through ignorance, stubbornness, callousness, or desperation, military leaders continued to order their men to go "over the top." In the east, the German victories of 1914 at Tannenberg and the Masurian Lakes were followed by devastating Austrian defeats in Galicia. Through 1915 and 1916, the Eastern Front remained bloody and indecisive, with neither side able to capitalize on its gains.

Stalemate, 1915

In the search for new points of attack, both the Allied and the Central Powers took advantage of new partners. The Ottoman Empire (Turkey) joined Germany and Austria at the start of the war. In May 1915, Italy joined the Allies, lured by promises of financial reparations, parts of Austrian territory, and pieces of Germany's African colonies when (and if) the Allies won the war. Bulgaria joined the war on the side of the Central Powers a few months later. The entry of these new belligerents introduced the possibility of breaking the stalemate in the west by waging offensives on other fronts.

OTTOMAN TURKEY, GALLIPOLI, AND THE ARMENIAN GENOCIDE

Ottoman Turkey faced an internal crisis even before the war began, as the absolutist rule of Sultan Abdul Hamid II (r. 1876–1909) was challenged by reformers who called themselves the Young Turks (Chapter 23). For centuries, the Ottoman Empire had been a multiethnic state where Muslims, Armenians, Greeks, Catholics, Protestants, Assyrians, and Jews lived alongside one another. In the nineteenth century, the loss of territories in the Balkans made the Ottoman state more homogeneous, and more identified with the Turkic-Muslim majority. These circumstances produced a new vision of the Turkish nation, which increasingly saw its sovereignty in terms of an ethnically homogeneous population bound to a homeland that needed to be defended both against the presence of non-Turkish minorities and the encroachments of European imperial powers. When the Young Turks came to power in 1913, their leadership sought an alliance with one of the European blocs as a way to gain support while they rebuilt their state along newly nationalist lines. Long-standing rivalries with Russia over the Balkans and Black Sea region precluded a treaty with the Triple Entente, so the government signed an agreement with Germany on August 2, 1914.

The Ottoman Empire threatened Russia's supply lines and endangered Britain's control of the Suez Canal. To defeat Turkey quickly, the British first lord of the admiralty, Winston Churchill, argued for a naval offensive in the Dardanelles, the narrow strait separating Europe and Asia Minor also known as the Gallipoli Peninsula. In April 1915, the Allies attempted a land invasion of the **Gallipoli Peninsula** with a combined force of French, British, Australian, and New Zealand troops. The Turks defended the narrow coast from positions high on fortified cliffs, and the shores were covered with nearly impenetrable barbed wire. After a disastrous landing, the casualties mounted for seven months before the Allied commanders admitted defeat and ordered a withdrawal in December. The defeat cost the Allies 200,000 soldiers and did little to shift the war's focus away from the deadlocked Western Front.

Attacked by the Allies at Gallipoli and at war with the Russians to the north, the Turkish government turned on its Armenian subjects, believing them to be a security risk. Approximately 2 million Armenians lived in the Ottoman Empire in 1914, comprising a sizeable Orthodox Christian minority. They were primarily an urban population whose relative prosperity and higher levels of education made them targets for resentment. As Turkish nationalism rose in the nineteenth century, Armenians faced attacks resulting in hundreds of thousands of deaths. The First World War escalated the violence against Armenians, and in April 1915, the Ottoman government executed several hundred Armenian intellectuals. This act proved to be the beginning of the **Armenian Genocide**. Throughout Anatolia, and along the Aegean and Black Sea coasts, Ottoman troops drove Armenians from their homes and forced them into death marches southward into the Syrian desert

Ottoman Turkey A state that ruled over the Anatolian peninsula, portions of southeastern Europe, the Middle East, and North Africa from the fourteenth century until 1919.

Gallipoli During the First World War, a combined force of French, British, Australian, and New Zealand troops tried to invade the Gallipoli Peninsula, and seize it from the Turks.

Armenian Genocide The Ottoman government's attempt to exterminate the Armenian people within the Ottoman Empire during the First World War, resulting in the deaths of 1.5 million Armenians between 1914 and 1923.

without food or water; thousands were robbed, raped, and beaten to death along the way. Between 1915 and 1923, about 1.5 million Armenians were killed. By the mid-1920s, fewer than 300,000 Armenians survived in Anatolia; a further 600,000 survived deportation and took up residence primarily in Europe and North America.

TOTAL WAR, ECONOMIC BLOCKADE, AND POPULATION DISPLACEMENT

After the failure of the Schlieffen Plan, all sides realized that a prolonged war between modern industrialized powers would require mobilizing their entire resources. The numbers of men in arms and the new technologies of warfare created logistical needs that placed enormous burdens on the civilian population, who were pressed both to work for the war effort and to limit their own consumption of food, fuel, and consumer goods. This was "total war"—in which the line between civilian and military targets became blurred, and maintaining the morale of the home front was just as important as keeping soldiers fed and supplied in the trenches.

The Allies realized that Germany's great vulnerability lay in its reliance on imports for one-third of its food supply. They accordingly established a naval blockade of Germany in order to limit access to global markets for food and raw materials. Germany responded with a submarine blockade of Britain, threatening to attack ships headed to British ports. On May 7, 1915, a German submarine torpedoed the passenger liner *Lusitania*, which also carried war supplies, killing 1,198 people, including 128 Americans. The attack provoked the animosity of the United States, forcing Germany to promise that it would no longer fire without warning. When Germany again declared unrestricted submarine warfare in 1917, the United States was drawn into the war.

The logic of "total war" produced massive displacements of civilian populations. Some, such as the Armenians in the Ottoman Empire, were specifically targeted and killed as enemies. Others were caught in territories overtaken by foreign armies and

In "total war," both military and civilian forces are drawn into all-consuming war effort

THE NEW TECHNOLOGIES OF WAR IN THE AIR AND AT SEA. The use of airplanes and submarines, both produced in large numbers during the First World War, changed the nature of warfare. The air war helped dissolve the boundaries between the front line and the home front, as civilian populations were brought within range of the enemy's destructive power, while submarine warfare could not easily distinguish between ships carrying passengers or supplies for the war effort. The photo on the left shows the German submarine base in Kiel, on the Baltic coast. The photo on the right shows a German plane attacking an English tank.

forced to flee. The German invasion of France through Belgium, for example, produced 1.5 million Belgian refugees who sought safety in France, the Netherlands, and Britain alongside 735,000 internally displaced French refugees. The Jews of central Europe were particularly vulnerable: Russian commanders deported tens of thousands of Galician Jews to the east, and hundreds of thousands more from the same region were uprooted. Within the Russian Empire, the number of civilians on the move may have reached 7 million by the time Russia pulled out of the war in 1917. These population movements, the product of panic, fear of persecution, and forced resettlement by military commanders, created enormous hardship and suffering. Unlike prewar migrations, where people made a conscious choice to seek lives elsewhere, the population movements caused by war were beset with uncertainty and fear.

TRENCH WARFARE ON THE WESTERN FRONT

Machine guns and barbed wire gave well-supplied and entrenched defenders an enormous advantage. Eventually, 25,000 miles of trenches snaked along the Western Front, typically in three lines on each side of No Man's Land. The front line was the attack trench, lying anywhere from fifty yards to a mile away from the enemy. Behind the front lay a maze of connecting trenches and lines, leading to a complex of supply centers, field hospitals, and command posts. These bases were intended to allow an army to project its power forward, but just as often, they acted as a tether, making it difficult to advance.

Squalid conditions in the trenches ❯

Rain turned the trenches into squalid mud pits and flooded the floors up to waist level. Soldiers lived with lice and large black rats, which fed on dead soldiers and horses. Cadavers could go unburied for months and were often embedded in the trench walls. Soldiers were rotated out of the front lines frequently—after only three to seven days. The threat of enemy fire was constant, with thousands of men killed or wounded daily. This "wastage," as it was called, was part of the routine, along with the inspections, rotations, and mundane duties of life on the Western Front. Despite this danger, the trenches were a relatively reliable means of protection, especially compared with the casualty rates of going on the offensive.

New weapons—exploding bullets, liquid fire, and poison gas—added to the frightening dimensions of daily warfare. Gas, in particular, transformed the battlefront, as the deadly clouds frequently hung over the trenches. First used effectively by the Germans in April 1915 at the Second Battle of Ypres, poison gas was not only physically devastating—especially in its later forms—but also psychologically disturbing, although the quick adoption of gas masks limited its effectiveness. Like other new weapons, poison gas solidified the lines and took more lives but could not end the stalemate.

<New technologies transform the nature of warfare>

THE EASTERN FRONT IN 1915

Germany's ally Austria struggled with a two-front war of its own in 1915, against Serbia in the south and the Russians to the east. Italy's entry into the war created a new threat to Austria's southern flank. Germany came to its assistance, and German and Austrian armies succeeded in pushing the undersupplied Russians out of Galicia and deep into their own lands. By the time the Eastern Front stabilized once more, 15 percent of Russia's prewar territory, including much of Poland and Lithuania, was in German and Austrian hands. Russian casualties during the difficult retreat were 1 million soldiers killed, wounded, or missing, and 750,000 taken prisoner.

Austrian and German successes convinced Bulgaria—which also sought to gain territory from Serbia—to enter the war on the side of the Dual Alliance in September 1915. The arrival of the Bulgarians tipped the balance heavily to the side of the Austrians on the Serbian front. The ensuing struggle brought terrible punishment to the Serbian people for their government's role in the assassination of Franz Ferdinand the previous year. One-sixth of the Serbian population died of hunger

POISON GAS. Poison gases (mustard gas, chlorine gas, and phosgene were the most commonly used) caused thousands of casualties in the First World War, and were greatly feared by the troops. Although such weapons led to offensive breakthroughs when first used, gas was difficult to control, and they did not change the balance of forces in the war, especially once both sides developed gas masks to protect their troops. The environmental damage was severe, however, as concentrations of gas residue were intense enough to cause injury to farmers decades after the war ended, and unexploded gas shells are still occasionally found in former battlefields.

War Propaganda

Poster art was a leading form of propaganda used by all belligerents in the First World War to enlist men, sell war bonds, and sustain morale on the home front. Posters demonized the enemy and glorified the sacrifices of soldiers to better rationalize the unprecedented loss of life and national wealth. The posters shown here are from a wide range of combatant nations during the war, but they all share a desire to link the war effort with a set of assumptions about the different roles of men and women in the national struggle.

A. British Poster: "Women of Britain Say—'Go!'"

B. Russian Poster: "Women Workers! Take Up the Rifle!"

Questions for Analysis

1. Why would nationalists resort to such gendered images in a time of crisis?

2. What do these images tell us about the ways that feelings of national belonging are created and sustained in times of urgency?

3. How might the changes brought about by war, such as an increase in the number of women working in industry or outside the home, and greater autonomy for women regarding their wages or management of their household affairs, have affected the way individuals responded to such images?

C. German Poster: "Collect women's hair that has been combed out. Our industry needs it for drive belts."

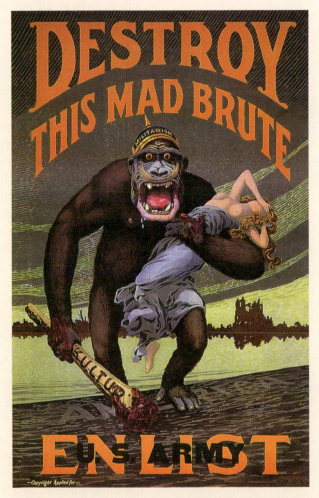

D. American Poster: "Destroy This Mad Brute. Enlist." The mad beast with *MILITARISM* inscribed on his helmet, meant to represent Germany, threatens American civilization with a club of *Kultur* (culture).

and disease. Some 200,000 Serbian troops sought to escape through the Albanian mountains to the Adriatic coast, but fewer than 140,000 survived the journey to be picked up by Italian ships in Albanian ports.

The Failed Offensives of 1916–1917

The bloodiest battles of all occurred in the **offensives of 1916–1917** on the Western Front, when first the Germans and later the British and French launched major attacks to end the stalemate. Massive campaigns in the war of attrition, these assaults produced hundreds of thousands of casualties but only minor territorial gains. These battles encapsulated the military strategy of soldiers in cloth uniforms marching against machine guns, resulting in enormous numbers of casualties. The common response to these staggering losses was to replace the generals in charge, but the strategy did not change. The "cult of the offensive" insisted that with enough troops and weapons, a breakthrough was possible.

Germany attempts to break the stalemate on Western Front at Verdun

>

VERDUN

The first of these offensives began with a German attack on the French stronghold of **Verdun** in February 1916. Verdun had little strategic importance, but it quickly became a symbol of France's strength and was defended at all costs. Germany's goal was to break French morale by inflicting unimaginable losses. As the German general Erich von Falkenhayn said, the offensive would "compel the French to throw in every man they have. If they do so the forces of France will bleed to death."

One million shells were fired on the first day of battle, inaugurating a ten-month struggle of intense ferocity. Led by General Philippe Pétain, the French pounded the Germans with artillery and received heavy bombardment in return. The French moved supplies and troops into Verdun continuously: 259 out of 330 regiments in the French forces served at Verdun. Neither side could gain a real advantage—one small village on the front changed hands thirteen times in one month alone. By the end of June, more than 400,000 French and German soldiers were dead. In the end, the advantage fell to the French, who survived and bled the Germans as badly as they themselves had suffered.

THE SOMME

The British opened their own offensive against Germany, beginning the Battle of the **Somme** on June 24, 1916. The Allied attack began with a fierce bombardment, blasting the German lines with 1,400 guns. The British assumed that this attack would break German barbed wire, obliterate their trenches, and clear the way for an Allied advance. They were tragically wrong. The wire and trenches withstood the bombardment, and when the British soldiers advanced toward enemy lines, they found themselves facing fully operational German machine guns. On the first day of battle alone, a stunning 21,000 British soldiers died, and another 30,000 were wounded. The carnage continued from July until mid-November, resulting in massive casualties on both sides: 600,000 German, 400,000 British, and 200,000 French. For all their sacrifices, neither side made any real gains. The futility of offensive war was not lost on the soldiers, but mutinies and desertions were rare before

offensives of 1916–1917
A series of costly but unsuccessful offensive operations initiated by the Allies and the Germans to break the stalemate on the Western Front, including the battles of Verdun, the Somme, and Passchendaele (also known as the Third Battle of Ypres).

Verdun This battle between German and French forces lasted for ten months during the First World War.

Somme (1916) During this battle in the First World War, Allied forces attempted to take entrenched German positions from July to mid-November of 1916.

1917, and surrenders became an important factor only in the final months of the war.

Again in 1917, the French general Robert Nivelle promised to break through the German lines with overwhelming manpower, but the "Nivelle Offensive" (April–May 1917) failed immediately, with first-day casualties matching those at the Somme. The British also reprised the Somme at the Third Battle of Ypres (also known as Passchendaele, July–November 1917), in which a half-million casualties earned Great Britain only insignificant gains, and no breakthrough. The one weapon with the potential to break the stalemate—the tank—was first introduced into battle in 1916, but with such reluctance by tradition-bound commanders that its deployment made almost no difference. Other innovations were equally ineffectual: airplanes were used almost exclusively for reconnaissance, though occasional "dogfights" did occur between German and Allied pilots. The Germans sent zeppelins to raid London, but they did little significant damage.

THE FAILURE OF OFFENSIVE WAR IN THE EAST

On the Eastern Front, equally indecisive offensives marked the year 1916. In May, the Austrians inflicted 147,000 casualties on the Italians at Trentino, but the Italian line did not break. Russia counterattacked farther to the east, calling up its massive reserves. A Russian offensive in March 1916 gained no territory, but in June the Russians had more success, taking 400,000 prisoners and inflicting losses of 600,000 on the Austrians. The cost, however, was high, with 1 million Russian casualties. Perhaps the most significant consequence of this Russian "victory" was that it convinced Romania to join the war on the side of the Entente in August 1916; France and Russia agreed to reward Romania with significant territories in Transylvania in the event of a victory. This proved a disastrous miscalculation for Romania, which lost 310,000 men by the end of 1916. The year ended with growing disillusionment on all sides. Not even the well-organized Germans had the mobility or fast-paced communications to win the ground war. Increasingly, the Allied forces hoped to use the vast resources of their empires to win the conflict in Europe.

THE LINES OF BATTLE ON THE WESTERN FRONT. A British reconnaissance photo showing three lines of German trenches (on the right), No Man's Land (black strip in the center), and the British trenches (partially visible on the left). The upper right-hand quadrant of the photo shows communications trenches linking the front to the safe area. **› What technologies gave these defenses such decisive advantages?**

War of Empires

Coming as it did at the height of European imperialism, the Great War quickly became a war of empires. As the demands of warfare rose, Europe's colonies provided soldiers and material support. Britain, in particular, benefited from its vast network of colonial dominions and dependencies, bringing in soldiers from Canada, Australia, New Zealand, India, and South Africa. Nearly 1.5 million Indian troops served in the British forces, some on the Western Front but many more in the

1914–1915

— Fronts, end of 1914

---- Fronts, end of 1915

NORWAY

SWEDEN

NORTH SEA

BALTIC SEA

Moscow

Riga

KURLAND

DENMARK

British Blockade, Nov. 1914

Kiel

Hamburg

× Masurian Lakes Sept. 1914

Tannenberg Aug. 27–30, 1914 ×

POLAND

GREAT BRITAIN (Aug. 4, 1914)

London

NETH. The Hague

Warsaw

Brest-Litovsk

Kyiv

GERMANY (Aug. 1, 1914)

Berlin

R U S S I A (Aug. 1, 1914)

ATLANTIC OCEAN

Limit of German Advance, 1915

BEL. (Aug. 4, 1914)

Invasion, Aug. 1914

Prague

GALICIA

Battle of the Marne Sept. 1914

LUX.

× Paris

Allied Offensive Sept.–Nov. 1915

Munich

Vienna

AUSTRIA-HUNGARY (July 28, 1914)

Budapest

JAPAN (Aug. 23, 1914)

FRANCE (Aug. 3, 1914)

SWITZER-LAND

Bucharest

ROMANIA

BLACK SEA

Bordeaux

Milan

SAN MARINO (June 3, 1915)

Belgrade

SERBIA (July 28, 1914)

BULGARIA (Oct. 14, 1914)

Marseilles

ADRIATIC SEA

Sarajevo

Sofia

Constantinople

PORTUGAL

SPAIN

ITALY (May 23, 1915)

Rome

Gallipoli

OTTOMAN EMPIRE (Nov. 2, 1914)

MONTENEGRO (Aug. 5, 1914)

ALBANIA

Salonika

Dardanelles

GREECE

Allied Offensive Feb. 1915– Jan. 1916

0   125   250 Miles

0 125   250 Kilometers

THE FIRST WORLD WAR

■ Allied Powers   ■ Central Powers

■ Neutral nations

Dates of entry into the war: (Aug. 1, 1914)

NORWAY

SWEDEN

Jutland May–June 1916 ×

Moscow

Riga

KURLAND

DENMARK

NORTH SEA

BALTIC SEA

R U S S I A

Kiel

Hamburg

POLAND Independent, Nov. 5, 1916

GREAT BRITAIN

The Hague

NETH.

Berlin

Warsaw

Brest-Litovsk

Russian Offensive June–Dec. 1916

ATLANTIC OCEAN

London

Somme, June–Nov. 1916

BEL.

GERMANY

LUX.

Paris

Verdun July–Dec. 1916

Prague

GALICIA

CARPATHIAN MTS.

Munich

Vienna

AUSTRIA-HUNGARY

Budapest

ROMANIA (Aug. 27, 1916)

BLACK SEA

FRANCE

SWITZER-LAND

Milan

Bucharest

Belgrade

ADRIATIC SEA

MONTENEGRO Surrender, Jan. 1916

SERBIA

BULGARIA

Sofia

Marseilles

PORTUGAL (Mar. 9, 1916)

SPAIN

ITALY

Rome

ALBANIA

Salonika

Constantinople

OTTOMAN EMPIRE

GREECE (Oct. 18, 1916)

M E D I T E R R A N E A N   S E A

1916

— Fronts, Aug. 31, 1916

---- Fronts, Dec. 31, 1916

0   125   250 Miles

0 125   250 Kilometers

THE GREAT WAR, 1914–1916. ❯ What were the farthest points of German expansion on both fronts? ❯ Why did the British blockade have such a large impact on the war? ❯ Why did the war become stalemated?

THE GREAT WAR, 1917–1918. › What were the key events of 1917? › How did they change the course of the war? › Considering the map of 1918, why might German people have believed that they nearly won the war? › Why were developments in the Middle East significant in the aftermath of the war?

A GLOBAL WAR. The effects of the First World War were immediately felt in other parts of the world. Japan entered the war in August 1914 on the side of France, Russia, and Britain to secure German territory in the Pacific and extend its influence over China. (The image at the bottom shows Japanese troops landing in China at Tsingtao in 1915.) The same month, Turkey joined Germany and Austria-Hungary's alliance. (The top left image shows an Islamic cleric reading the proclamation of war before a mosque in the Turkish capital of Constantinople in 1914.) Meanwhile, all the European colonial powers recruited laborers and soldiers from their imperial territories. (The top right image shows colonial troops marching in German East Africa during the war.)

Middle East. And France sent 607,000 soldiers, especially from North and West Africa, to fight with the Allies, 31,000 of whom died in Europe. Colonial recruits were also employed in industry.

As the war stalled in Europe, colonial territories also became strategically important theaters of conflict. The campaign against Turkey began poorly for Britain at Gallipoli, but after 1916, Allied forces pushed the Turks out of Egypt and captured Baghdad, Jerusalem, Beirut, and other cities throughout the Middle East. Britain encouraged Arab nationalism for strategic purposes, offering a qualified acknowledgment of Arab political aspirations. At the same time, for similar but conflicting strategic reasons, the British declared their support of "the establishment in Palestine of a national home for the Jewish people," a pledge made by Arthur Balfour, Britain's foreign secretary. European Zionists, who were seeking a Jewish homeland, took the Balfour Declaration very seriously. These conflicting pledges to Bedouin leaders and Zionists sowed the seeds of the future Arab-Israeli conflict. First the war and then the promise of oil drew Europe more deeply into the Middle East, where conflicting dependencies and commitments created numerous postwar problems.

IRISH REVOLT

The demands of war strained the British Empire to the breaking point in Ireland. Before the war, long-standing tensions between Irish Catholics and the Protestant

British government had reached fever pitch. The Sinn Féin (We Ourselves) party had formed in 1900 to fight for Irish independence, and a home rule bill had passed Parliament in 1912. In 1914, however, the "Irish question" was tabled, and 200,000 Irishmen volunteered for the British army. On Easter Sunday 1916, a group of Irish nationalists revolted against British rule in Dublin. The insurgents' plan to smuggle in arms from Germany failed, and they had few illusions of achieving victory. The British army arrived with artillery and machine guns and crushed the uprising within a week.

The revolt was a military disaster but a striking political success. Britain shocked the Irish public by executing the rebel leaders, and the martyrdom of the "Easter Rebels" seriously damaged Britain's relationship with its Irish Catholic subjects. The deaths galvanized the cause of Irish nationalism and touched off guerrilla violence that kept Ireland in turmoil for years. The leaders of the so-called Dáil Éireann (Irish Assembly) proclaimed an Irish Republic in 1918, only to see themselves outlawed by the British. In 1920, a new home rule bill was enacted, establishing separate parliaments for the Catholic south of Ireland and for Ulster, the northeastern counties where the majority population was Protestant. In 1921, Catholic Ireland was granted dominion status, but civil war broke out almost immediately over the status of Ulster and continued connections to Britain. The conflict eventually ended in an uneasy compromise. The Irish Free State was established in 1922, and British sovereignty was partially abolished in 1937. Full status as a republic came in 1945, after some American pressure and Britain's exhausted indifference.

> *Moderate goal of Irish self-governance, known as "home rule," turns to outright fight for independence*

The Home Front

The belligerent governments were unprepared for the burdens of sustained and total war. The costs of war—in both money and manpower—were staggering. By 1918, the cost of the German war effort had skyrocketed to 146 million marks per day.

Great Britain had estimated it would need 100,000 soldiers but ended up mobilizing 3 million. The enormous task of feeding, clothing, and equipping the armies became as much of a challenge as breaking through enemy lines, and civilian populations were increasingly asked—or forced—to support these efforts. Bureaucrats and industrialists led the effort to mobilize the home front, focusing all parts of society on the single goal of military victory. Civilians—as workers, taxpayers, and consumers—were vital parts of the war economy, and they produced munitions, purchased war bonds, and shouldered the burden of tax hikes, inflation, and material privations.

The demands of industrial warfare led to increased state control of all aspects of production and distribution. The governments of Britain and France managed to direct the economy without serious detriment to their standard of living. Germany, meanwhile, put its economy in the hands of the army and industry. Under the Hindenburg Plan, named for Paul von Hindenburg, the chief of the imperial staff of the German army, pricing and profit margins were set by individual industrialists. Germany's systems of war finance and commodity distribution were not decisively worse than those of Britain or France, but they could not overcome the disadvantage caused by the naval blockade and a lack of access to global markets.

WOMEN IN THE WAR

As women become increasingly crucial to war effort, they gain new freedoms

As Europe's adult men left farms and factories to become soldiers, the composition of the workforce changed. Thousands of women were recruited into fields from which they had previously been excluded; young people, foreigners, and colonial workers were also pressed into supporting the war effort. The employment of women was nevertheless the most visible sign of the changes brought by the Great War. In Germany, one-third of the labor force in heavy industry was female by 1918. In France, 684,000 women worked in the munitions industry alone. In England, the "munitionettes," as they were dubbed, numbered nearly 1 million. Women also entered the clerical and service sectors, and hundreds of thousands of women worked with the army near the front lines as nurses and ambulance drivers. Under squalid and dangerous conditions, they worked to save lives and patch bodies back together.

Middle-class women often said that the war broke down the restrictions on their lives. They could now ride the train, walk on the street alone, or go out to dinner without an older woman present to chaperone them. A gulf seemed to separate the gender expectations of the wartime world from those of prewar society. In a famous autobiography of her war experience, Vera Brittain (1896–1970) wrote: "As a generation of women we were now sophisticated to an extent which was revolutionary when compared with the romantic ignorance of 1914. Where we had once spoken with polite evasion of 'a certain condition,' or 'a certain profession,' we now unblushingly used the words 'pregnancy' and 'prostitution.'" For every Vera Brittain who celebrated the changes, however, journalists, novelists, and other observers grumbled that women were now smoking, refusing to wear restrictive corsets, and cutting their hair into the newly fashionable and boyish bobs. The "new woman" became a symbol of profound and disconcerting cultural transformation.

How long-lasting were these changes? After the war, governments and employers sent women workers home, in order to give jobs to veterans and to answer male workers' complaints that women were undercutting their wages. Efforts to demobilize women faced real barriers, however. Many women—widowed, charged with caring for relatives, or faced with inflation and soaring costs—needed their earnings more than ever. It was also difficult to persuade women workers who had grown accustomed to the relatively higher wages in heavy industry to return to their poorly paid traditional sectors of employment: textile and garment industries, and domestic service. The demobilization of women after the war created as many dilemmas as had their mobilization during the war. Governments passed "natalist" policies to encourage women to go home, marry, and—most important—have children. These policies made maternity benefits available to women for the first time, including time off, medical care, and some allowances for the poor. Nonetheless, birth rates had been falling across Europe by the early twentieth century, and they continued to do so after the war. One upshot of the war was the increased availability of birth control, and a combination of economic hardship, increased knowledge, and the demand for freedom made both men and women more likely to use it.

Before the war, universal suffrage and the vote for all adult men and women, and for women in particular, had been one of the most controversial issues in European politics. At the end of the war, women's suffrage was harder to oppose. Britain was first off the mark, granting the vote to all men and women over thirty with the Representation of the People Act in 1918. The United States gave women the vote with the Nineteenth Amendment the following year. And Germany's new republic and the Soviet Union did likewise. France, however, did not grant women the vote until 1945, after the Second World War.

WOMEN AT WORK. The total war effort combined with a manpower shortage at home brought women into factories across Europe in unparalleled numbers. This image shows German women assembling military equipment. › **How might the participation of women in the industrial workforce have changed attitudes toward women's labor?** › **What tensions might this have created within families or between male and female workers?**

Though not all wartime freedoms endure, women successfully push for suffrage in Britain and the United States

MOBILIZING RESOURCES

In addition to mobilizing labor, the wartime governments had to mobilize soldiers and money. All the belligerent countries had conscription laws before the war, except Great Britain. Millions of young Europeans went to recruitment offices in 1914, bolstered by a widespread public support for the war. The French began the war with about 4.5 million trained soldiers, but by the end of 1914—just four months into the war—300,000 were dead and 600,000 injured. Eventually, France called up 8 million citizens, almost two-thirds of Frenchmen aged eighteen to forty. In 1916, the British finally introduced conscription, dealing a serious blow to civilian morale. By the summer of 1918, half the army was under the age of nineteen.

Government propaganda, while part of a larger effort to sustain both soldier and civilian morale, was important to the recruitment effort. From the outset, the war had been sold to the people on all sides of the conflict as a moral crusade (see *Interpreting Visual Evidence* on pages 858–59). In 1914, the French president Raymond Poincaré (in office, 1913–1920) assured his fellow citizens that France had no other purpose than to stand "before the universe for Liberty, Justice and Reason." Germans were presented with the task of defending their superior *Kultur* (culture) against the wicked encirclement policy of the Allied nations. By the middle of the war, massive propaganda campaigns were under way. All forms of media—films, posters, post-cards, newspapers—proclaimed the strength of the cause, the evil of the enemy, and the absolute necessity of total victory. The success of these campaigns is difficult to determine, but they had at least one painful effect: they made it more difficult for any country to accept a fair, nonpunitive peace settlement.

Financing the war was another heavy obstacle. Before 1914, military spending accounted for 3 to 5 percent of government expenditure in the combatant countries, but it soared to perhaps half of each nation's budget during the war. Governments had to borrow money or print more money. The Allied nations borrowed heavily from the British, who borrowed even more from the United States. Economic aid from the United States was a decisive factor in the Allied victory, but it left Britain with a $4.2 billion debt that hobbled the economy after the war. The situation was far worse for Germany, which faced a total blockade. Lacking an outside source of cash, the German government funded its war effort largely by increasing the money supply. Paper money in circulation increased by over 1,000 percent during the war, triggering a rise in prices of 400 percent, double the inflation in Britain and France. Inflation pushed middle-class people living on pensions or fixed incomes into poverty.

THE STRAINS OF WAR, 1917

The demands of total war worsened in 1917. After the debacle of the Nivelle Offensive, the French army recorded acts of mutiny in two-thirds of its divisions; similar resistance arose in nearly all major armies in 1917. Most mutinies were nonpolitical. As one soldier put it: "All we wanted was to call the government's attention to us, make it see that we are men, and not beasts for the slaughterhouse." More than 6,000 cases of "war neuroses" were reported among German troops—an indication, if not of intentional disobedience, then of the severe physical and psychological trauma that caused the mutinies.

The war's toll also mounted for civilians, who often suffered from shortages of basic supplies. In 1916–1917, the lack of clothing, food, and fuel was aggravated by abnormally cold weather in central Europe. These strains provoked rising discontent on the home front. Governments attempted to solve the problem with tighter controls on the economy, but their policies often provoked further hostilities from civilians. In urban areas, people stood in lines for hours to get rations that scarcely met their most basic needs. The price of bread and potatoes—still the staples of working-class meals—soared; prices were even higher in the thriving black market. Consumers worried aloud that speculators were hoarding supplies and creating artificial shortages, selling tainted goods, and profiting from others' misery. Governments faced difficult decisions about who needed supplies the most: soldiers on the front, workers in the munitions industry, or hungry and cold families.

DESPERATION ON THE GERMAN HOME FRONT, 1918. A photograph of German women digging through garbage in search of food. The last year of the war brought starvation to cities in Germany and Austria-Hungary, sending many people into the countryside to forage for provisions. **›** **Foraging was often illegal, a violation of rationing rules. How might the need to break the law in this way have affected support for the war effort and the state?**

Like other nations, Germany moved from merely encouraging citizens to restrain their consumption to direct control—issuing ration cards in 1915. Britain was the last to institute control, rationing bread only in 1917, when Germany's submarines brought British food reserves to within two weeks of starvation level. But rations indicated only what was allowed, not what was available; and hunger continued throughout despite mass bureaucratic control.

Governments also regulated working hours and wages, and unhappy workers directed their anger at the state, adding a political dimension to labor disputes. The breadlines, filled mainly by women, were flash points of political dissent, petty violence, and even large-scale riots. In this context, the class conflicts of prewar Europe reemerged with new intensity, undermining morale. Thousands of strikes erupted throughout Europe, involving millions of frustrated workers. In April 1917, in Berlin, 300,000 went on strike to protest ration cuts. In May, a strike of Parisian seamstresses touched off a massive work stoppage that included white-collar employees and munitions workers. Shipbuilders and steelworkers in Glasgow went on strike, and the British government responded by sending armored cars to "Red Glasgow." The strains of total war produced social upheavals that threatened regimes throughout Europe. The Russian Revolution, which resulted in the overthrow of the tsar, was the most dramatic response to the widespread social problems.

Anger over wartime shortages fuels renewed class and labor disputes

The Russian Revolutions of 1917

The outbreak of war temporarily united Russian society, but the military effort quickly turned sour. All levels of Russian society became disillusioned with **Tsar Nicholas II**, who was unable to provide leadership. The strain of war brought two revolutions in 1917. The first revolution, in February, according to the Julian calendar used in Russia at the time (or March, according to the Gregorian calendar used today), overthrew the tsar and established a transitional government. The second revolution, in October (or November, according to the Gregorian calendar), was a communist revolution that marked the emergence of the Soviet Union.

THE FIRST WORLD WAR AND RUSSIA'S FEBRUARY REVOLUTION

Like the other participants in the First World War, Russia entered the war with the assumption that it would be over quickly. Autocratic Russia, plagued by internal difficulties before 1914 (Chapter 23), could not sustain the demands of extended warfare. Success depended on the government's ability to maintain social and political cooperation. Nicholas's authority had been undermined by his unpopular actions following the Russian Revolution of 1905 and his efforts to erode the political power he had grudgingly granted to the Duma (Russia's parliament). Corruption in the royal court further tarnished his image. In 1915, Nicholas insisted on personally commanding Russian troops, leaving the government in the hands of his court, especially his wife, Alexandra, and her eccentric spiritual mentor and faith healer, Grigori Rasputin (1869–1916). Rasputin won Alexandra's sympathy by treating her hemophiliac son, and used his influence to operate corrupt and self-aggrandizing schemes. His presence added to the image of an incompetent court mired in decadence.

In 1914 and 1915, Russia suffered terrible defeats. All of Poland and substantial territory in the Baltics fell to the Germans at the cost of 1 million Russian casualties. The Russian army was the largest in Europe, but it was poorly trained and inadequately equipped. Generals sent soldiers to the front without rifles or shoes, instructing them to scavenge supplies from fallen comrades. By 1915, to the surprise of many, Russia was producing enough food, clothing, and ammunition, but political problems blocked the supply effort, as tsarist officials made crucial decisions about the allocation of resources without consultation. When word came that the government was requisitioning grain from the countryside to feed the cities, peasant soldiers began to desert en masse, returning to their farms to guard their families' holdings. By the end of 1916, a combination of political ineptitude and military defeat brought the Russian state to the verge of collapse.

As the war dragged on, the government faced not only liberal opposition in the Duma, soldiers unwilling to fight, and an increasingly militant labor movement but also a rebellious urban population that was becoming impatient with inflation and shortages of food and fuel. In February 1917, these forces came together in Petrograd (now St. Petersburg). The revolt began on International Women's Day, February 23 by the Julian calendar (or March 8), an occasion for a loosely organized march of women who demanded food, fuel, and political reform. Within a few days, the unrest spiraled into a mass strike of 300,000 people. Nicholas sent police and military forces to quell the disorder, but nearly 60,000 troops in Petrograd mutinied and joined the revolt. What was left of the tsar's power evaporated, and Nicholas abdicated the throne on March 2 (or March 15 by the Gregorian calendar). This abrupt decision brought a century-long struggle over Russian autocracy to a sudden end.

After the collapse of the monarchy, two parallel centers of power emerged, each with its own objectives and policies. The first was the **provisional government**, dominated by middle-class liberals in the Duma. This new government hoped to establish a democratic system under constitutional rule. Its main task was to set up a national election for a constituent assembly, and it also acted to grant and secure civil liberties, release political prisoners, and redirect power into the hands of local officials. The second center of power lay with the *soviets*, a Russian term for local councils elected by workers and soldiers. Since 1905, socialists had been active in organizing these councils, which claimed to be the true democratic representatives of the people. The Petrograd Soviet, organized during the 1905 revolution and led by the well-known socialist Leon Trotsky, reemerged after February 1917 and pressed for social reform, redistribution of land, and a negotiated settlement with Germany and Austria. The provisional government, however, refused to concede military defeat. Its decision to continue the war effort made domestic reforms impossible and cost valuable popular support. By autumn, desertion in the army was rampant, making administering the country nearly impossible.

THE BOLSHEVIKS AND THE OCTOBER REVOLUTION

The chain of events leading to the October Revolution surprised most contemporary observers. Because peasants constituted 80 to 85 percent of the Russian population, most Russian socialists reasoned that a proletarian revolution was premature and that Russia needed first to complete its capitalist development. But the **Bolsheviks**, under the leadership of Vladimir Ilyich Ulyanov, who took the pseudonym **Lenin**, believed otherwise (Chapter 23). Lenin saw the crisis of 1917 as an opportunity to create a revolution that could achieve socialism even without a large urban working class in Russia.

Lenin argued that the Bolsheviks needed to organize their party to act on behalf of Russia's growing working class. The Bolsheviks remained a minority among Social Democrats well into 1917, and industrial workers remained a small part of the population, but the Bolsheviks' dedication and their tight, conspiratorial organization gave them tactical advantages over the larger and more loosely organized opposition parties (see *Analyzing Primary Sources* on page 873). The Bolsheviks merged a uniquely Russian tradition of revolutionary zeal with Western Marxism, and created a party capable of seizing the moment when the tsar left the scene.

Throughout 1917, the Bolsheviks consistently demanded an end to the war, improvement in working and living conditions for workers, and redistribution of aristocratic land to the peasantry. Even most Bolsheviks considered Lenin's approach too radical, but, as conditions in Russia deteriorated, his uncompromising

When Nicholas abdicates throne amid widespread protests, autocracy suddenly comes to an end

Russian provisional government After the collapse of the Russian monarchy in February 1917, leaders in the Duma organized a government and hoped to establish a democratic system under constitutional rule.

soviets Local councils organized by socialists beginning in 1905 and elected by workers and soldiers in Russia.

Bolsheviks Former members of the Russian Social Democratic Party who advocated the destruction of capitalist political and economic institutions, and started the Russian Revolution.

Lenin (1870–1924) Leader of the Bolshevik Revolution in Russia (1917) and the first leader of the Soviet Union.

VLADIMIR ILYICH LENIN. Lenin speaking in Moscow in 1918, at the first anniversary of the October Revolution. A forceful speaker and personality, Lenin was the single most powerful politician in Russia from October 1917 to his death in 1924.

calls for "Peace, Land, and Bread, Now" and "All Power to the Soviets" won support from workers, soldiers, and peasants. As many ordinary people saw it, the other parties could not govern, win the war, or achieve an honorable peace. As unemployment continued to climb and starvation and chaos reigned in the cities, the Bolsheviks' credibility rose quickly.

In October 1917, Lenin convinced his party to act. He goaded Leon Trotsky, who was better known among the workers, into organizing a Bolshevik attack on the provisional government on October 24–25 (November 6–7), 1917. During the revolt, Lenin appeared from hiding to announce at a meeting of stunned soviet representatives that "all power has passed to the soviets." The head of the provisional government fled to rally support at the front lines, and the Bolsheviks took over the Winter Palace, the seat of the provisional government. The initial stage of the revolution was quick and relatively bloodless.

The Bolsheviks rapidly consolidated their position. First, they moved against all political competition, beginning with the soviets. They expelled parties that disagreed with their actions, and created a new government composed entirely of Bolsheviks. They followed through with the provisional government's promise to elect a constituent assembly, but when they did not win a majority in the elections, they refused to let the assembly reconvene. From that point on, the Bolsheviks ruled as a one-party dictatorship. As the country fell into civil war, Lenin created a militarized state security service known as the Cheka, a form of political police for suppressing dissent in both rural areas and in the cities, as well as in the army.

When peasant soldiers at the front heard that a revolution had occurred, they streamed home to take the land they had worked for generations and believed to be rightfully theirs. The provisional government had set up commissions to deal with the legal issues surrounding the redistribution of land, but the Bolsheviks simply approved the spontaneous redistribution of the nobles' land to peasants without compensation to the former owners. They also nationalized banks and gave workers control of the factories.

The Bolsheviks negotiated a separate treaty with Germany, signed at Brest-Litovsk in March 1918. The revolutionaries surrendered vast Russian territories, much of which were already in German hands: the rich agricultural region of Ukraine, Georgia, Finland, Russia's Polish territories, the Baltic states, and more. Though humiliating, the treaty ended Russia's role in the fighting and saved the fledgling communist regime from almost certain military defeat at the hands of the Germans. It enraged Lenin's political enemies, who were prepared to wage a civil war rather than accept the revolution. Russia's withdrawal from war thus plunged the country into a vicious civil conflict (see Chapter 25). Later, in 1918–1919, when the German army collapsed, the Soviet army pushed westward again. In these conflicts, which occurred after the armistice, Russia retook territories in Latvia, Lithuania, Belarus, and Ukraine, but failed to reconquer Estonia and Poland, after meeting resistance from their newly created independent governments.

The Russian autocracy had fended off opposition for the better part of a century, but in 1917, the Russian state collapsed with little resistance. Building the

Lenin's View of a Revolutionary Party

At the turn of the century, Russian revolutionaries debated political strategy. How could they defeat Russian autocracy? Should revolutionaries follow the programs of their counterparts in the West? Or did the Russian situation require different tactics? In What Is to Be Done? *(1902), Lenin (Vladimir Ilyich Ulyanov; 1870–1924) argued that Russian socialists must revise the traditional Marxist view, which states that a large and politically conscious working class is needed to make revolution. In Russia, Lenin argued, revolution required only a small but dedicated group of revolutionaries to lead the working class. Lenin's vision was important in shaping the tactics and strategies of the Bolsheviks in 1917 and beyond.*

The national tasks of Russian Social-Democracy are such as have never confronted any other socialist party in the world. We shall have occasion further on to deal with the political and organisational duties which the task of emancipating the whole people from the yoke of autocracy imposes upon us. At this point, we wish to state only that the *role of vanguard fighter can be fulfilled only by a party that is guided by the most advanced theory.* . . .

I assert: (1) that no revolutionary movement can endure without a stable organisation of leaders maintaining continuity; (2) that the broader the popular mass drawn spontaneously into the struggle, which forms the basis of the movement and participates in it, the more urgent the need for such an organisation, and the more solid this organisation must be (for it is much easier for all sorts of demagogues to side-track the more backward sections of the masses); (3) that such an organisation must consist chiefly of people professionally engaged in revolutionary activity; (4) that in an autocratic state, the more we *confine* the membership of such an organisation to people who are professionally engaged in revolutionary activity and who have been professionally trained in the art of combating the political police, the more difficult will it be to unearth the organisation; and (5) the *greater* will be the number of people from the working class and from the other social classes who will be able to join the movement and perform active work in it. . . .

Social-Democracy leads the struggle of the working class, not only for better terms for the sale of labour-power, but for the abolition of the social system that compels the propertyless to sell themselves to the rich. Social-Democracy represents the working class, not in its relation to a given group of employers alone, but in its relation to all classes of modern society and to the state as an organised political force. Hence, it follows that not only must Social-Democrats not confine themselves exclusively to the economic struggle. . . . We must take up actively the political education of the working class and the development of its political consciousness.

Source: Vladimir Lenin, "What Is to Be Done?" in *Collected Works of V. I. Lenin*, vol. 5 (Moscow: 1964; original work published 1902), pp. 369–70, 373, 375.

Questions for Analysis

1. What were the key features of Lenin's thought?

2. Lenin more or less sets down the rules for the revolutionary vanguard. What historical experiences and political theories shaped his thinking? In what ways was the Russian experience unique?

new state proved vastly more difficult. John Reed, an American journalist covering the Russian Revolution, called the events of October "ten days that shook the world." What had been shaken? First, the Allies, because the revolution allowed the Germans to win the war on the Eastern Front. Second, the conservative governments, which in the aftermath of the war worried about a wave of revolution sweeping away other regimes. Third, the expectations of many socialists, who were startled to see a socialist regime gain and hold power in what many considered a backward country. Over the long run, 1917 was to the twentieth century what 1789 had been to the nineteenth century. It was a year of political transformation that set the stage for the bitter political struggles that would shape successive generations.

The Road to German Defeat, 1918

Russian withdrawal dealt an immediate strategic and psychological blow to the Allies. Germany claimed victory on the Eastern Front, and could now concentrate its entire army to the west. The Allies feared that Germany might win the war before the United States, which entered the conflict in April 1917, could make a difference—which almost happened. On March 21, Germany initiated a major assault on the west and quickly broke through the Allied lines. The British were hit hardest: some units, surrounded, fought to the death with bayonets and grenades, but most recognized their plight and surrendered, putting tens of thousands of prisoners in German hands. The Germans advanced to within fifty miles of Paris by early April, but the British—and especially troops from the overseas empire—did just as they were asked and stemmed the tide. As German forces turned southeast, the French, who had refused to participate in the foolish attacks over the top, showed stubborn courage on the defensive and slowed the German advance.

The Allied counterattack, which came in July and August, was devastating. The Allies improved their use of tanks and the "creeping barrage," in which infantry marched close behind a rolling wall of shells that overwhelmed their targets. In another of the war's ironies, these new tactics were pioneered by the conservative British, who launched their own crushing offensive in July, relying on the survivors of the armies of the Somme and reinforced by troops from Australia, Canada, and India. The French made use of American troops, whose generals attacked the Germans with the same harrowing indifference to casualties shown in 1914. Despite their lack of experience, the American troops were tough and resilient, and combined with French and Australian forces, they punched several large holes through German lines, crossing into the "lost provinces" of Alsace and Lorraine by October.

The Allies finally brought their material advantage to bear on the Germans, who were suffering acutely by the spring of 1918, not only because of the Allied blockade but also because of growing domestic conflict. German soldiers were exhausted, and many surrendered. Facing one

CASUALTY OF WAR.
A German soldier killed during the Allies' October 1917 offensive.

shattering blow after another, the German army was pushed deep into Belgium. Moreover, popular discontent mounted, and the government, which was now largely in the hands of the military, seemed unable either to win the war or to meet the basic needs of the home front.

By the end of September, the Central Powers were headed for defeat. In the Middle East, a British army that combined Bedouin guerrillas, Indian sepoys, Scottish highlanders, and Australian light cavalry, defeated Ottoman forces in Syria and Iraq. In the Balkans, a three-week offensive in September by Greek and Allied forces knocked Bulgaria out of the war. Meanwhile, Austria-Hungary faced disaster on all sides, collapsing in Italy as well as in the Balkans. Czech and Polish representatives in the Austrian government began pressing for self-government, and Croat and Serb politicians proposed a "kingdom of Southern Slavs" (soon known as Yugoslavia). When Hungary joined the chorus for independence, Emperor Karl I accepted reality and sued for peace; the Habsburg Empire surrendered on November 3, 1918, and disintegrated soon after.

Germany was now left with the impossible task of carrying on the struggle alone. By the fall of 1918, the country was starving and on the verge of civil war. At the start of November, a plan to use the German surface fleet to attack the combined British and American navies only produced a mutiny among German sailors, and on November 8, a revolutionary republic was proclaimed in Bavaria. The next day, nearly all of Germany was in the throes of revolution. On November 9, the kaiser's abdication was announced in Berlin, and he fled to Holland. Control of the German government fell to a provisional council headed by Friedrich Ebert (1871–1925), the socialist leader in the Reichstag. Ebert and his colleagues immediately took steps to negotiate an armistice. The Germans could do nothing but accept the Allies' terms, so at five o'clock in the morning of November 11, 1918, two German delegates met with the Allied army commander in the Compiègne Forest and signed papers officially ending the war. Six hours later, the order to cease fire was given across the Western Front, and that night, thousands of people danced through the streets of London, Paris, and Rome, engulfed in a different delirium from that of four years earlier, a joyous burst of exhausted relief.

THE UNITED STATES AS A WORLD POWER

A turning point of the war had been the entry of the United States in April 1917. Although the United States had supported the Allies financially throughout the war, President **Woodrow Wilson** (in office, 1913–1921) had been reluctant to send troops. He changed his mind after the Russian Revolution began. Wilson's decision to join the Entente powers undeniably tipped the scales. The United States created a fast and efficient wartime bureaucracy, instituting conscription in May 1917: about 10 million men were registered and, by the following year, 300,000 soldiers a month were being shipped "over there." Large amounts of food and supplies also crossed the Atlantic, under the protection of the U.S. Navy. This system of convoys effectively neutralized the threat of German submarines to Allied merchant ships: the number of ships sunk fell from 25 percent to 4 percent. The United States' entry—though not immediately decisive—gave a quick, colossal boost to British and French morale at a crucial moment after the Russian Revolution had already begun.

An important cause of the United States' entry into the war was the German U-boat. Germany had gambled that unrestricted submarine warfare would cripple Britain's supply lines and win the war. But by attacking neutral and unarmed American ships, Germany only provoked an opponent it could not afford to fight. Germany correctly suspected that the British were clandestinely receiving war supplies via U.S. passenger ships; and on February 1, 1917, the kaiser's ministers announced that they would sink all ships on sight, without warning. The American public was further outraged by an intercepted telegram from German foreign minister Arthur Zimmermann (in office, 1916–1917), stating that Germany would support a Mexican attempt to capture American territory if the United States entered the war. The United States cut off diplomatic relations with Berlin, and on April 6, President Wilson requested and received a declaration of war from Congress.

The United States' primary interest was maintaining the international balance of power. For years, U.S. diplomats and military leaders believed that American security depended on the equilibrium of strength in Europe, that as long as Britain could prevent any one nation from achieving supremacy on the Continent, the United States was safe. But now Germany threatened not only the British navy—which had come to be seen as the shield of American security—but also the international balance of power. In 1918, American involvement stemmed those threats, but the monumental task of establishing peace still lay ahead.

THE PEACE SETTLEMENT

U.S. president Woodrow Wilson plays a strong role at the Paris Peace Conference of 1919

The Paris Peace Conference, which opened in January 1919, was an extraordinary moment, one that dramatized just how much the world had been transformed by the war and the decades that preceded it. Gone were the Russian, Austro-Hungarian, and German Empires, and the prominent role of the American president Woodrow Wilson marked the rise of the United States as a world power. The United States' new status was rooted in the economic development of the second industrial revolution during the nineteenth century. Before the war, the United States had rivaled the largest European powers (Britain and Germany) in mass production and technological innovation. During the war, its intervention (although it came late) had decisively broken the military-economic deadlock. And in the war's aftermath, its industrial culture, engineering, and financial networks loomed very large on the European continent.

Some thirty nations sent delegates to the peace conference, a reflection of three factors: the scope of the war, heightened national sentiment and aspirations, and the tightening of international communication and economic ties in the latter part of the nineteenth century. The world in 1900 was vastly more globalized than it had been fifty years earlier. Many more countries had political, economic, and human investments in the war and its settlement. A belief that peace would secure and be secured by free peoples in sovereign nations represented the full flowering of nineteenth-century liberal nationalism. Delegates came to work for Irish home rule; for a Jewish state in Palestine; and for the recognition of independent nations in Poland, Ukraine, and Yugoslavia. Europe's colonies, which had been vital to the war effort and increasingly impatient with their status, sent delegates to negotiate for self-determination. They discovered, however, that the western European leaders' commitment to the principle of national self-determination was hedged by a widely shared imperial racism, which held that colonized peoples in Africa and Asia should not be allowed to assert their own sovereignty. Also present at the conference were Nongovernment organizations—international groups asking for women's suffrage, civil rights, minimum wages, or maximum work hours. Last, correspondents from all over the world wired news home from Paris, a sign of vastly improved communications, transatlantic cables, and the mushrooming of the mass press.

Although many attended, the conference was largely controlled by the so-called Big Four: the U.S. president Woodrow Wilson, the British prime minister David Lloyd George (in office, 1916–1922), the French premier Georges Clemenceau (in office, 1917–1920), and the Italian premier Vittorio Orlando (in office, 1917–1919). In total, five separate treaties were signed, one with each of the defeated nations: Germany, Austria, Hungary, Turkey, and Bulgaria. The settlement with Germany was called the **Treaty of Versailles**, after the town in which it was signed.

Wilson had proposed his widely publicized program known as the "**Fourteen Points**" before the war ended, intending it to be the foundation for a permanent peace and the basis for a new international order. Based on the principle of "open covenants of peace, openly arrived at," the Fourteen Points called for an end to secret diplomacy, freedom of the seas, removal of international tariffs, and reduction of national armaments "to the lowest point consistent with safety." Most troubling for Britain and France, however, Wilson's program also called for a system of adjusting colonial claims that gave equal weight to the interests of the colonized populations alongside the interests of European colonial powers. Regarding eastern Europe, Wilson went much further, calling for the "self-determination of peoples" in the diverse territories that were now claiming national independence after the collapse of the German, Austrian, and Russian Empires. Finally, Wilson called for the establishment of a League of Nations to settle international conflicts. Thousands

VERSAILLES PEACE TREATY. Representatives of the Allied Powers working on the agreement in Versailles, 1919.

of copies of the Fourteen Points were scattered by Allied planes over the German trenches and behind the lines in an attempt to convince both soldiers and civilians that the Allied nations were striving for a just and durable peace, and they shaped the expectations that Germans brought to the peace talks.

Throughout the war, however, Allied propaganda led soldiers and civilians to believe that their sacrifices to the war effort would be compensated by payments extracted from the enemy—total war demanded total victory. Lloyd George had campaigned during the British election of 1918 on the slogan "Hang the Kaiser!" Clemenceau had twice in his long lifetime seen France invaded and its existence imperiled, and now with the tables turned, he believed that the French should take full advantage of their opportunity to place Germany under strict control. The settlement with Germany was shaped as much by the desire for punishment as by Wilson's hopes for a new international order under the League of Nations.

The Treaty of Versailles required Germany to surrender the "lost provinces" of Alsace and Lorraine to France, and other territories to Denmark and the new state of Poland. The treaty gave Germany's coal mines in the Saar Basin to France for fifteen years, at which point the German government could buy them back. Germany's province of East Prussia was cut off from the rest of its territory. The Polish port of Gdansk (German: Danzig), where the majority of the population was German, was put under the administrative control of the League of Nations and the economic domination of Poland. The treaty also disarmed Germany, forbade a German air force, and reduced its navy to a token force to match an army capped at 100,000 volunteers. To protect France and Belgium, all German soldiers and fortifications were to be removed from the Rhine Valley.

The Versailles treaty's language on German responsibility causes controversy

The most controversial part of the Versailles treaty, seemingly at odds with Wilson's original plan, was the so-called "war-guilt" provision in Article 231. The provision held Germany and its allies responsible for the damages suffered by the Allied governments and their citizens "as a consequence of the war imposed upon them by the aggression of Germany and her allies." This legal statement of responsibility for damages caused by the Germans beyond their borders was interpreted by many Germans as a statement of responsibility for the war itself. When the Reparations Commission set the total reparations owed by Germany at $33 billion in 1921, the German public deeply resented the payments. In *The Economic Consequences of the Peace*, the noted British economist John Maynard Keynes (1883–1946) argued that reparations would undermine the urgent task of repairing the world economy.

new nation-states After the collapse of the Russian and Austrian Empires in eastern Europe during the First World War, the negotiators of the postwar settlement created new states in Poland, Hungary, Czechoslovakia, and Yugoslavia. The Baltic nations of Estonia, Latvia, and Lithuania were also granted independence.

The other treaties at the Paris Peace Conference were based partly on the Allies' strategic interests and partly on the principle of national self-determination. The experience of the prewar years convinced leaders that they should draw nations' boundaries to conform to the ethnic, linguistic, and historical traditions of the people they were to contain. Wilson's support for national self-determination confirmed these aims. Representatives of Yugoslavia were granted a state, Czechoslovakia was created, Poland reestablished, Hungary separated from Austria, and the Baltic states were made independent (see the map on page 879). These national boundaries did not, and indeed in most cases could not, follow ethnic divisions. They were instead created according to the facts on the ground, the result of armed confrontation, hasty compromises, and political dictates—such as insulating western Europe from the communist threat of the Soviet Union. The peacemakers carved these **new nation-states** from older, multiethnic empires, especially the

The following is the text within the image:

GREENLAND *(Denmark)*

A R C T I C
O C E A N

ICELAND

FAROE IS.
(Denmark)

SHETLAND IS.

HEBRIDES   ORKNEY IS.

UNITED
KINGDOM

NORTH
SEA

Dublin

London

NETHERLANDS

Brussels
BELGIUM
Paris
LORRAINE
ALSACE
Bern

FRANCE

SWITZ.

PORTUGAL

Lisbon

SPAIN

Madrid

CORSICA
(Fr.)
Rome

SARDINIA
(It.)

BALEARIC
IS. *(Sp.)*

Tangier

Rabat

Algiers

MOROCCO

TUNISIA

FRENCH
ALGERIA

Tripoli

LIBYA

NORWAY

SWEDEN

Christiania

DENMARK

Copenhagen

Berlin

GERMANY

Prague

LUX.

Amsterdam

Rhine R.

Vienna

AUSTRIA

ITALY

MONTENEGRO

Tirana

SICILY
(It.)

ALBANIA

Tunis

M E D I T E R R A N E A N   S E A

CRETE *(Gr.)*

FINLAND

Helsinki

Leningrad

Tallinn

Stockholm

ESTONIA

GOTLAND
ÖLAND

BALTIC SEA

Riga

LATVIA

Kaunas

LITHUANIA

Danzig

EAST
PRUSSIA
(Ger.)

Warsaw

POLAND

Brest-Litovsk

CZECHOSLOVAKIA

Budapest

HUNGARY

YUGOSLAVIA

Belgrade

SERBIA

Danube R.

Sofia

BULGARIA

ROMANIA

Bucharest

Odessa

BLACK SEA

Constantinople

Ankara

GREECE

Athens

DODECANESE
IS. *(It.)*

CYPRUS
(U.K.)

Beirut

LEBANON
Damascus

PALESTINE
Jerusalem

TRANS-
JORDAN

Alexandria

Suez
Canal

E G Y P T

Nile R.

RED SEA

Lake Ladoga

Archangel

Moscow

Kazan

Volga R.

SOVIET RUSSIA

Kyiv

Samara

Stalingrad

ARAL
SEA

CASPIAN SEA

Tiflis

ARMENIA

TURKEY

Mosul

SYRIA

Tigris R.

Euphrates R.

IRAQ

KUWAIT

Persian Gulf

PERSIA

ARABIA

Legend:

— 1914 boundaries
— New boundaries as a result of postwar treaties
To United Kingdom
To France
To Italy
To Romania
To Denmark
To Yugoslavia (Serbia and Montenegro)
To Belgium
To Greece
Became independent

Scale: 0   250   500 Miles
0   250   500 Kilometers

TERRITORIAL CHANGES IN EUROPE AND THE NEAR EAST AFTER THE FIRST WORLD WAR. Note the changes in geography as a result of the First World War. › **Which areas were most affected by the changes within Europe, and why?** › **Can you see any obvious difficulties created by the redrawing of the map of Europe?** › **What historical circumstances and/or new threats guided the victors to create such geopolitical anomalies?**

Austro-Hungarian Empire, whose fragility had helped spark the war and whose structure had collapsed with the conflict. Creating nation-states, however, almost invariably created new minorities, posing enormous challenges for the newly created democratic institutions and complicating the task of establishing more representative forms of government. The architects of the new Europe briefly wrestled with the problem of minorities but did not resolve it; this issue would return and undermine European stability in the 1930s.

The Ottoman Empire, which allied with Germany, was initially partitioned by the postwar Treaty of Sèvres (1920). Before the treaty could be ratified by a new Turkish government, however, a war broke out between Turkish nationalists led by General Mustafa Kemal Atatürk against Greece, Armenia, and the Allied Powers. The Turkish War of Independence ended in 1923 with the Treaty of Lausanne, which set the boundaries of the new and secular Turkish Republic—with Atatürk's Turkey much reduced in size. Former Ottoman territories in the Middle East were placed under French and British control, as part of what became known as the colonial "mandate system," which legitimized Europe's dominance over territories in the Middle East, Africa, and the Pacific. Territories were divided into groups on the basis of their location and their "level of development"; that is, how far, in European eyes, they would have to progress to earn self-government. Choice pieces of land became mandates held by the League of Nations, in principle, but administered by Britain (Transjordan, Iraq, and Palestine) and France (Lebanon and Syria). The British and French Empires, therefore, expanded after the war, although these territories held troubles ahead. The British faced revolt in Iraq and escalating tensions in Palestine, where they tried to juggle conflicting promises made to Zionist settlers and Indigenous Arab communities. These circumstances made the end of the First World War a great disappointment for Arab leaders in Lebanon, Syria, Palestine, and Iraq, some of whom had cooperated with Britain during the war in exchange for the promise of independence at war's end.

The peoples of the Allies' existing colonies were also disappointed. Ho Chi Minh, a future revolutionary leader in Vietnam, was one of many activists who attended the conference to protest conditions in the colonies and to ask that the rights of nations be extended to their homelands. Well-organized delegations from French West Africa and the Congress Party of India, which favored dominion status in return for the wartime efforts of millions of Indian soldiers who had fought for the British Empire, were also snubbed. The peacemakers' belief in democracy and self-determination collided with their baseline assumptions about Western superiority, inherited from the nineteenth century, that justified imperial rule. Although the European powers spoke about reforming colonialism, little was done, leaving many nationalists in the colonies, who had favored moderate legislative change, to decide that active struggle might be the only answer to the injustices of colonialism.

Each of the five peace treaties incorporated the Covenant of the League of Nations, an organization envisioned as the arbiter of world peace, but it never achieved the idealistic aims of its founders. The League was handicapped from the start by the number of changes to its original design. The arms-reduction requirement was watered down, and the League's power to enforce it was rendered almost nonexistent. Japan did not join until it was allowed to keep former German concessions in China. France demanded that both Germany and Soviet Russia be excluded from the League, and neither the Bolsheviks nor the defeated Central Powers were allowed in the talks. The League received an even more debilitating blow when the U.S. Congress, citing a long-standing national preference for isolation, refused to approve U.S. membership in the League. Hobbled from the start, the international organization had little potential to avert conflicts.

Mandate system in former Ottoman territories extends European control in Middle East

Conclusion

Europe fought the First World War on every front possible—military, political, social, and economic. Consequently, the war's effects extended far beyond the devastated landscapes of the Western Front, and statistics can only hint at the enormous loss of human life: of the 70 million men mobilized, nearly 9 million were killed. Although Russia, Germany, France, and Hungary recorded the highest number of deaths, the smaller countries of southeast Europe had the highest percentages of soldiers killed. Almost 40 percent of Serbia's soldiers died in battle, and with the addition of war-related deaths caused by privation and disease, Serbia lost 15 percent of its population; in comparison, Britain, France, and Germany lost 2 to 3 percent of their populations. But the percentages are much more telling if we look at the young men of the war generation, known as the "lost generation." During 1914–1918, 13 percent of German men born between 1880 and 1899 were killed. In France, the figure was 17 percent, nearly one out of every six.

The breakdown of the prewar treaty system and the scale of the diplomatic failure that produced the war discredited the political classes in many countries. Meanwhile, the war itself planted seeds of political and social discontent around the globe. Relations between Russia and western Europe had grown sour and suspicious, ever since the Allies had attempted to overthrow the Bolsheviks during the war and had excluded them from negotiations afterward. These actions instilled in the Soviets a mistrust of the West that lasted for generations. The Allied nations, in turn, feared that Russia would dominate the new states of eastern Europe, building a "Red Bridge" across the continent. Elsewhere, the conflicting demands of colonialism and nationalism struck only a temporary balance, while the redrawn maps left ethnic and linguistic minorities in every country. The fires of discontent raged most fiercely in Germany, where the Treaty of Versailles was decried as outrageously unjust, and nearly all national governments agreed that it would eventually have to be revised. In the end, neither war nor peace had ended the rivalries that caused the Great War.

The war also had powerful and permanent economic consequences. Beset by inflation, debt, and the difficult task of industrial rebuilding, Europe found itself displaced from the center of the world economy. The war had accelerated the decentralization of money and markets, which financially benefited many Asian, African, and South American nations as their economies became less dependent on Europe and so were better able to profit from Europe's need for their natural resources. The United States and Japan reaped the biggest gains and emerged as leaders in the new world economy.

The war's most powerful cultural legacy was disillusionment, as a generation of men had been sacrificed to no apparent end. Surviving soldiers—many of them permanently injured, both physically and psychologically—were sickened by their participation in such useless slaughter. Women and other civilians who had made extraordinary sacrifices on the home front were also disappointed by their little apparent gain. Both veterans and civilians were disgusted by the greedy abandonment of principles by the politicians at Versailles. In the postwar period, many younger men and women mistrusted the "old men" who had dragged the world into war. These feelings of loss and alienation were voiced in the vastly popular genre of war literature—memoirs and fiction that commemorated the experience of soldiers on the front lines. In his novel *All Quiet on the Western Front*, the German writer and ex-soldier Erich Maria Remarque captured the disillusion of the generation: "Through the years our business has been killing;—it was our first calling in life. Our knowledge of life is limited to death. What will happen afterwards? And what shall come out of us?"

That was the main question facing postwar Europe. The German novelist Thomas Mann recognized that 1918 had brought "an end of an epoch, revolution and the dawn of a new age," and that he and his fellow Germans were "living in a new and unfamiliar world." The struggle to define this new world would increasingly be

AFTER YOU READ THIS CHAPTER ⌄

CHRONOLOGY

1879	The Dual Alliance (Germany and Austria-Hungary)
1907	The Triple Entente (France, Russia, and Britain)
June 1914	Assassination of Archduke Franz Ferdinand in Sarajevo
September 1914	Battle of the Marne
April 1915	Gallipoli campaign begins
May 1915	Italy enters the war against Austria-Hungary
February 1916	Battle of Verdun begins
July 1916	British offensive on the Somme begins
January 1917	Germany begins unrestricted submarine warfare
April 1917	United States enters the war
November 1917	Russian Revolution
March 1918	Treaty of Brest-Litovsk
November 1918	Armistice
June 1919	Treaty of Versailles signed

REVIEWING THE OBJECTIVES

❯ The First World War broke out as a result of conflicts in the Balkans. Why?

❯ The Western Front was seen by all sides as a crucial theater of the conflict. What measures did the French, British, and Germans take to break the stalemate? Why did they fail?

❯ How did European governments intervene in the economy to ensure the production of matériel for the war effort and to remedy the social crises caused by mobilization?

❯ The war led European nations to mobilize people and resources from their colonies. How did colonial subjects participate in the war effort? What did many of them expect in return?

❯ Russia was devastated by the war, and the population lost confidence in the tsar's government. What circumstances allowed the Bolsheviks to seize power in 1917? What were their goals?

❯ The Treaty of Versailles blamed Germany for the war. Who were the most important participants in the peace conference? Who did the most to shape the terms of the treaty?

conceived of in terms of rival ideologies—democracy, communism, and fascism—competing for the future of Europe. The eastern autocracies had fallen with the war, but liberal democracy was on the decline as well. Although militarism and nationalism remained strong, calls for major social reforms gained force during a worldwide depression. Entire populations had been mobilized during the war, and they would remain so afterward, as active participants in the age of mass politics. Europe was about to embark on two turbulent decades of rejecting and reinventing its social and political institutions. As Tomáš Masaryk, the first president of the newly formed Czechoslovakia, described it, postwar Europe was a "laboratory atop a graveyard."

Go to **INQUIZITIVE** to see what you've learned—and learn what you've missed—with personalized feedback along the way.

PEOPLE, IDEAS, AND EVENTS IN CONTEXT

❯ Why was **FRANZ FERDINAND** assassinated? How did his death contribute to the outbreak of the war?

❯ What was the **SCHLIEFFEN PLAN**? How was it connected to the outbreak of the war?

❯ What was the significance of the **BATTLE OF THE MARNE** and the **BATTLE OF TANNENBERG** in 1914?

❯ Why did the British attempt to attack the Ottoman Empire at **GALLIPOLI**?

❯ Why did **OTTOMAN TURKEY** enter the war on the side of Germany? What circumstances led to the **ARMENIAN GENOCIDE**?

❯ Why did **ITALY, BULGARIA**, and **ROMANIA** enter the war? What were the consequences of their participation?

❯ What was the goal of the attacking forces at **VERDUN** and the **SOMME** in 1916? What was accomplished by the **OFFENSIVES OF 1916–1917**?

❯ Why did many people in Russia, and especially soldiers in the Russian army, lose faith in **TSAR NICHOLAS II** of Russia?

❯ How did **LENIN** make use of the **SOVIETS** in challenging the **PROVISIONAL GOVERNMENT** in Russia after the fall of the tsar?

❯ What policies did the **BOLSHEVIKS** follow after seizing power in Russia?

❯ What were **WOODROW WILSON'S FOURTEEN POINTS**?

❯ What kind of treatment did Germany receive under the terms of the **TREATY OF VERSAILLES**? What **NEW NATION-STATES** were created in central and eastern Europe as a result of the treaty?

THINKING ABOUT CONNECTIONS

❯ What made the First World War different from previous military conflicts in Europe that had involved large numbers of states, such as the Napoleonic Wars of the early nineteenth century (Chapter 18) or the Thirty Years' War of the seventeenth century (see Chapter 15)?

❯ In what ways might the effects and consequences of the First World War have shaped the lives of Europeans in the decades to come? How did it change the lives of various peoples from other parts of the world who were drawn into the conflict?

Turmoil between the Wars

KÄTHE KOLLWITZ, a Berlin artist, understood the costs of the First World War; her son, Peter, was killed on October 22, 1914. Her diary recorded the last moments she spent with him before his departure for the front: "It was dark, and we went arm in arm through the wood. He pointed out constellations to me, as he had done so often before." Her entry for October 30 was more succinct, quoting a postcard she had received from his commanding officer: "Your son has fallen." Kollwitz's later work explored in naked terms the grief and powerlessness that she felt during the war years. Her suffering found expression, too, in socialism, a political ideology that provided an antidote to the nationalism. Kollwitz's socialism drew the attention of the Gestapo (state police) after the Nazis came to power in 1933, and she was fired from her position at the Academy of Art. She put up with house searches and harassment but refused to go into exile. She died in 1945, surviving long enough to see her cherished grandson, also named Peter, killed in the Second World War in 1942 while fighting on the Eastern Front in Russia.

The story of Käthe Kollwitz and her family between 1914 and 1945 was not unusual. Their suffering was all too familiar to many others, as was the search for new political ideologies that might save Europeans from their past. The Great War had left 9 million dead, shattered the confidence that had been so characteristic of nineteenth-century European culture, and led to another world war even more horrific.

> With the exception of Bolshevik Russia, European states attempted to find stability in the traumatic aftermath of the First World War by reinforcing democratic institutions and focusing on an orderly transition from wartime production to a peacetime economy.

> The Bolsheviks won the civil war that followed the Russian Revolution in 1917, and by the late 1920s, Joseph Stalin had embarked on an unprecedented revolution from above, industrializing the nation and transforming rural life through the collectivization of agriculture. The human costs were enormous; millions died of hunger, and millions more were arrested and deported to labor camps in the east.

> The Great Depression undermined political support for Europe's democracies in the 1930s, and the decade saw the consolidation of fascist regimes in Italy and Germany and an anticapitalist communist regime in the Soviet Union.

CORE OBJECTIVES

> **UNDERSTAND** the direction taken by the Russian Revolution after 1917 and the consequences of Stalin's revolution from above in the 1930s.

> **DEFINE** *fascism* and **EXPLAIN** Mussolini's rise to power in Italy in the 1920s.

> **DESCRIBE** the challenges faced by the Weimar Republic and other democracies in Britain, France, and the United States after the First World War.

> **EXPLAIN** Hitler's rise to power in Germany in 1933 and the reasons for the broad support for Nazis among many Germans.

> **DESCRIBE** the circumstances that led to the Great Depression and the responses of European governments to this economic crisis.

> **UNDERSTAND** the ways that the interwar atmosphere of social and political crisis was reflected in the world of the arts, literature, and popular culture.

Many in the interwar years shared Kollwitz's hope for a socialist or communist future, while many others turned to extremisms of the right. The result in the 1920s was a near collapse of democracy. By the late 1930s, few Western democracies remained, and even in those that did—most notably Britain, France, and the United States—regimes were frayed by the same pressures that wrecked democratic governments elsewhere.

The foremost cause of democracy's decline was the disruptions in the world economy following the First World War and the Great Depression of 1929–1939; a second source lay in increased social conflict. Many hoped that these conflicts would be resolved by peace and a renewed commitment to democracy, but the opposite occurred. Broad swaths of the electorate rallied to extremist movements that promised radical transformations of nations and their cultures. Nationalism, sharpened by the war, proved a key source of discontent in its aftermath, and frustrated nationalist sentiment turned citizens against their governments in Italy and Germany.

The most dramatic instance of democracy's decline came with the rise of new authoritarian dictatorships, especially in Russia, Italy, and Germany. The experiences of these three nations differed significantly, but in each case, many citizens were persuaded that only drastic measures could bring order from chaos. Those measures, including the elimination of parliamentary government, strict restrictions on political freedom, and increasingly virulent repression of "enemies" of the state, were implemented with a combination of violence, intimidation, and propaganda. That so many citizens seemed willing to sacrifice their freedoms—or those of others—was a measure of their alienation and desperation.

THE SURVIVORS, BY KÄTHE KOLLWITZ (1923). Kollwitz (1867–1945), a German artist and socialist activist in Berlin, lost her son in the First World War and her grandson in the Second World War. Her work poignantly illustrates the effects of poverty and war on the lives of ordinary people.

The Soviet Union under Lenin and Stalin

THE RUSSIAN CIVIL WAR

The Bolsheviks seized power in October 1917. They signed a separate peace treaty with Germany in March 1918 (the Treaty of Brest-Litovsk), but Russia collapsed into civil war soon after. Fury at the terms of Brest-Litovsk mobilized the Bolsheviks' enemies, known collectively as "Whites," against the "Reds" in power. The "Whites" included supporters of the old regime, the former nobility, and liberals; they were later joined by anti-Bolshevik dissident groups and anarchist peasant bands that opposed all central state power. The Bolsheviks also faced insurrections from nationalist movements in Ukraine, Georgia, and the north Caucasus. Several foreign powers, including the United States, Great Britain, and Japan, landed troops on the periphery of the old empire. These interventions proved to be an insignificant threat to the revolutionary government, but they heightened the Bolsheviks' mistrust of the capitalist world.

THE SOVIET UNION, 1918–1945. › What were the areas lost by Russia in the Treaty of Brest-Litovsk? › How did the possession of Moscow and Leningrad (St. Petersburg) aid the Bolsheviks in their victory over the Whites? › How did the civil war of 1917–1920 affect the new Soviet state?

The Bolsheviks won the civil war because they gained the support—or at least the tacit acceptance—of the majority of the population and because they were better organized for the war effort. Leon Trotsky, the revolutionary hero of 1905 and 1917, became the commissar of war and created a disciplined military machine that grew to 5 million men. By the end of 1920, Trotsky's Red Army triumphed over the White Armies, although fighting continued into 1922. The Bolsheviks also invaded Poland and nearly reached Warsaw before being thrown back. The Polish victory outside Warsaw in August of 1920 prevented the Bolsheviks from pursuing their plan to connect with communists in Germany and spread their revolution to western Europe.

When the civil war was over, the Soviet Union had suffered 1 million combat casualties, several million deaths from hunger and disease caused by the war, and 100,000 to 300,000 executions of noncombatants as part of Red and White terror. The barbarism of the war engendered lasting hatreds within the emerging Soviet nation, especially among ethnic minorities, and brutalized the fledgling society that came into existence under the newly militarized Bolshevik regime. The Bolsheviks created a new political police force during the civil war, which institutionalized a system of terror, executing and sending opponents of the regime to detention camps.

The civil war also shaped the Bolsheviks' approach to the economy. Lenin at first attempted to create a state-capitalist system that resembled the successful European wartime economies. The new government took control of large-scale industry, banking, and all other major capitalist concerns, while allowing small-scale private economic activity, including agriculture, to continue. But the civil war pushed the new government toward a more radical economic stance known as "**war communism**." The Bolsheviks requisitioned grain from the peasantry, and outlawed private trade in consumer goods as "speculation," militarized industry, and abolished money.

War communism sustained the Bolshevik military effort but disrupted the war-ravaged economy. Cities were emptied of their populations—the population of Moscow fell by 50 percent between 1917 and 1920. Urban workers, who had supported the Bolshevik Revolution, melted back into the countryside. Industrial output fell to 20 percent of prewar levels. The situation in rural areas proved even worse. The peasants had initially benefited from the revolution when they spontaneously seized and redistributed noble lands. But the agricultural system was severely disrupted by the civil war, the grain requisitioning of war communism, and the outlawing of all private trade in grain. In 1921, wide-scale famine claimed some 5 million lives.

As the civil war ended, urban workers and soldiers became increasingly impatient with the Bolshevik regime, which had promised socialism and workers' control but delivered something more akin to a military dictatorship. In late 1920, large-scale strikes and protests broke out, but the Bolsheviks moved swiftly and effectively to subdue these "popular revolts." The Bolshevik regime that emerged from the civil war would not tolerate public opposition.

THE NEW ECONOMIC POLICY

After winning the civil war, the Bolsheviks formalized their new regime in 1922 by creating the Union of Soviet Socialist Republics (USSR or Soviet Union), a union of national Soviet republics governed by a strongly centralized state controlled by

Bolsheviks, with broader support base and better organization than "White" dissidents, win the civil war

War communism leads to widespread economic disruption and contributes to famine in countryside

war communism The Russian civil war forced the Bolsheviks to take a more radical economic stance. They requisitioned grain from the peasantry and outlawed private trade in consumer goods as "speculation."

the Communist Party. On the economic front, the government had already abandoned war communism in 1921 and embarked on a radically different course known as the **New Economic Policy (NEP)**. The new goal was a mixed economy that contained elements of socialist central planning, while also allowing some capitalist entrepreneurship, particularly in agriculture. The state continued to own all major industry and financial concerns, but individuals were allowed to own private property, trade within limits, and—most important—farm land for their own benefit. Grain requisitioning was replaced by fixed taxes. The Bolshevik most identified with the NEP was Nikolai Bukharin (1888–1938), a young and brilliant Marxist theoretician who argued that the Bolsheviks could best industrialize the Soviet Union by taxing private peasant economic activity.

The NEP allowed Soviet agriculture to recover from the civil war. By 1924, harvests had returned to prewar levels. Peasants redistributed land among themselves to level wealth discrepancies between rich and poor, and reasserted the power of the peasant commune in the countryside. Under the NEP, the peasantry produced enough grain to feed the country. The NEP was less successful, however, in encouraging peasants to sell grain to urban areas. The result was a series of food shortages, a situation that prompted many Bolsheviks to call for revival of the radical economic practices of war communism. The fate of these radical proposals was tied to the fate of the man who replaced Lenin as the leader of the USSR and became one of the most notorious dictators of all time: Joseph Stalin.

STALIN AND THE "REVOLUTION FROM ABOVE"

Stalin's rise was swift and unpredicted. His political success was rooted in intraparty conflicts in the 1920s, but it was also closely tied to the abrupt end of the NEP and the beginning of a massive program of social and economic modernization in the late 1920s. This "revolution from above" was the most rapid social and economic transformation any nation has seen in modern history, and it was carried out at unprecedented human cost.

Joseph Stalin (1878–1953), the son of a poor shoemaker, was a Bolshevik from the Caucasus nation of Georgia. Educated in an Orthodox seminary, he participated in revolutionary activity in the Caucasus and spent many years in Siberian exile before the revolution. Although an important member of the Bolshevik party in 1917, he was not one of the central figures. After Lenin's death in 1924, the civil war hero Leon Trotsky was widely assumed to be the best candidate to succeed him.

Stalin was not a brilliant orator like Trotsky or a respected Marxist theoretician like Bukharin, but he was a master political strategist. He sidelined his opponents within the Bolshevik party and expelled each of them successively. Trotsky was the first to go, driven out by a coalition of Stalin and others who, ironically, feared Trotsky's desire to take control of the party

LENIN AND STALIN. During Stalin's regime, this picture was used to show his close relationship with Lenin; but the photograph, in fact, had been doctored.
› What opportunities for propaganda and manipulation were offered by new technologies of photography and film?

collectivization Stalin's plan for nationalizing agricultural production, which began in 1929. Twenty-five million peasants were forced to give up their land and join 250,000 large collective farms.

Stalin revives a new version of war communism in a sudden and forceful push to state-run agriculture

himself. Stalin then turned on his former allies and removed them in turn, culminating in the removal of Bukharin from the Politburo (short for political bureau, which governed the Communist party and state) in 1928–1929.

Stalin's campaign against Bukharin aimed at eliminating a rival who was closely associated with the NEP. Stalin believed that the Soviet Union could not industrialize by relying on taxes generated from small-scale peasant agriculture. He pushed for an increase in the tempo of industrialization as early as 1927, prompted by fears of falling behind the West and the threat of another world war. Few anticipated what happened next under Stalin's growing dictatorship: an abrupt turn toward forced industrialization and the collectivization of agriculture.

Collectivization

In early 1928, Stalin ordered officials in the distant Urals and Siberian areas to begin requisitioning grain, and then soon applied this revival of war communism to the entire country. **Collectivization**—the abolition of private farming and the creation of state-run agricultural establishments—was initially expected to be a gradual process, but in late 1929, the Politburo issued orders to use force against peasants who resisted. The process that ensued was brutal and chaotic. Local party and police officials forced peasants to give up their land, farming implements, and livestock, and to join collective farms; the peasants resisted, often violently. There were some 1,600 large-scale rebellions in the Soviet Union between 1929 and 1933; some involved several thousand people. Quelling them required military intervention, including the use of artillery. Peasants resisted by slaughtering their livestock instead of turning their animals over to the farms, a loss that hampered agricultural production for years. By 1935, collectivization of agriculture was complete in most areas of the Soviet Union.

Stalin launched an all-out attack on peasants by calling them *kulaks* ("tight-fisted ones"), a derogatory term for well-to-do farmers. Between 1929 and 1933, some 1.5 million peasants were uprooted, dispossessed of their property, and resettled either to distant Soviet camps in the north or to poor farmland closer to their

WINTER DEPORTATIONS, 1929–1930. Ukrainian families, charged with being kulaks, were deported from their homes after refusing to join Stalin's collective farming plan. Many of the evicted families were shipped north by train to the Arctic, where they perished, owing to the lack of adequate food and shelter.

original homes. Peasants forced into collective farms had little incentive to produce extra food, and exiling many of the most productive peasants weakened the agricultural system. The result was one of the most devastating famines in modern European history, spreading in 1932–1933 throughout central Russia, Ukraine, and the northern Caucasus, the country's most productive agricultural areas. The famine took 5 to 7 million lives across the entire Soviet Union and was most devastating for Ukrainians and the Kazakhs of Soviet central Asia. The Bolsheviks maintained substantial grain reserves in other parts of the country, but they refused to send the grain to the affected areas, preferring instead to seal off famine-stricken regions and allow people to starve. Grain reserves were sold overseas for hard currency and stockpiled in case of war. After 1935, there would never again be any large-scale resistance to Soviet power in the countryside.

THE FIVE-YEAR PLANS

Collectivization provided the resources for the other major aspect of Stalin's revolution from above: a rapid campaign of forced industrialization. Stalin's first Five-Year Plan (1928–1932) called for truly herculean industrialization efforts, and resulted in one of the most stunning periods of economic growth the modern world has ever seen. Soviet statistics boasted of annual growth rates of 20 percent a year, but even the more cautious Western estimates of 14 percent annual growth were remarkable, given the worldwide depression elsewhere. The Bolsheviks built entirely new industries in entirely new cities. In 1926, only one-fifth of the population lived in towns; but fifteen years later, in 1939, roughly one-third did. The urban population had grown from 26 to 56 million in under fifteen years. The Soviet Union was well on its way to becoming an urban, industrial society.

This rapid industrialization came at enormous human cost. Many large-scale projects were carried out with prison labor, especially in the timber and mining industries. The labor-camp system, known as the *gulag*, became a central part of the Stalinist economic system. People were arrested and sent to camps on a bewildering array of charges: petty crimes, contact with foreigners, or simply having the ill fortune to be born of bourgeois or kulak parents. By the end of the decade, the regime had incarcerated roughly 3.6 million people. This army of prisoners was used to complete the most arduous and dangerous tasks in Stalin's modernization plan.

The economic system created during this period was fraught with problems that would plague the Soviet Union throughout its history. The command economy, with each year's production levels planned in advance in Moscow, never functioned in a rational way. Heavy industry was always favored, and the emphasis on quantity made quality practically meaningless. A factory that was charged with producing a certain number of pairs of shoes, for example, could

Stalin forces a surge in industrial output at enormous human cost

"IMPERIALISTS CANNOT STOP THE SUCCESS OF THE FIVE-YEAR PLAN!"
> Did propaganda such as this appeal to Russian nationalist pride?

Stalin's Industrialization of the Soviet Union

How did the Soviet people experience Stalin's industrialization drive? Archives opened after the fall of the Soviet Union in 1991 helped historians glimpse what the common people lived through and how they responded. The first document is an excerpt from a speech Stalin gave at the First All-Union Conference of Managers of Socialist Industry in 1931. In his usual style, he invoked Russian nationalism and fears of Soviet backwardness while summoning all to take up the task of industrial production.

The letters in the second selection come from several hundred that workers and peasants sent to Soviet newspapers and authorities, recounting their experiences and offering their opinions. Both printed here were sent to the Soviet paper Pravda.

"The Tasks of Business Executives"

It is sometimes asked whether it is not possible to slow down the tempo somewhat, to put a check on the movement. No, comrades, it is not possible! The tempo must not be reduced! On the contrary, we must increase it as much as is within our powers and possibilities. This is dictated to us by our obligations to the workers and peasants of the USSR. This is dictated to us by our obligations to the working class of the whole world.

To slacken the tempo would mean falling behind. And those who fall behind get beaten. But we do not want to be beaten. No, we refuse to be beaten. One feature of the history of old Russia was the continual beatings she suffered because of her backwardness. She was beaten by the Mongol khans. She was beaten by the Turkish beys. . . . She was beaten by the British and French capitalists. She was beaten by the Japanese barons. All beat her—for her backwardness: for military backwardness, for cultural backwardness, for political backwardness, for industrial backwardness, for agricultural backwardness. . . .

We are fifty or a hundred years behind the advanced countries. We must make good this distance in ten years. Either we do it, or we shall be crushed. . . .

In ten years at most we must make good the distance which separates us from the advanced capitalist countries. We have all the "objective" possibilities for this. The only thing lacking is the ability to take proper advantage of these possibilities. And that depends on us. *Only* on us! . . . It is time to put an end to the rotten policy of non-interference in production. It is time to adopt a new policy, a policy adapted to the present times—the policy of interfering in everything. If you are a factory manager, then interfere in all the affairs of the factory, look into everything, let nothing escape you, learn and learn again. Bolsheviks must master technique. It is time Bolsheviks themselves became experts. . . .

cut costs by producing all one style and size; the consumer would be left with useless goods, but the producer would have fulfilled the plan. Stalin's industrialization drive transformed the country from an agrarian nation into a world industrial power in the space of a few short years. In the long term, however, the system would become an economic disaster.

Stalin's revolution altered the face of Soviet cities and the working class populating them. New cities were largely made up of first-generation peasants who brought their rural traditions to the cities, changing the fragile urban culture that had

There are no fortresses which Bolsheviks cannot capture. We have assumed power. We have built up a huge socialist industry. We have swung the middle peasants to the path of socialism. . . . What remains to be done is not so much: to study technique, to master science. And when we have done that we will develop a tempo of which we dare not even dream at present.

Source: Joseph Stalin, "The Tasks of Business Executives" (speech given at the First All-Union Conference of Managers of Socialist Industry, February 4, 1931), as cited in Richard Sakwa, *The Rise and Fall of the Soviet Union, 1917–1991* (New York: 1999), pp. 187–88.

Stalin's Industrial Development: The View from Below

It should not be forgotten that many millions of workers are participating in the building of socialism. A horse with its own strength can drag seventy-five poods,* but its owner has loaded it with a hundred poods, and in addition he's fed it poorly. No matter how much he uses the whip, it still won't be able to move the cart.

This is also true for the working class. They've loaded it with socialist competition, shock work, over-fulfilling the industrial and financial plan, and so forth. A worker toils seven hours, not ever leaving his post, and this is not all he does. Afterward he sits in meetings or else attends classes for an hour and a half or two in order to increase his skill level, and if he doesn't do these things, then he's doing things at home. And what does he live on? One hundred fifty grams of salted mutton, he will make soup without any of the usual additives, neither carrots, beets, flour, nor salt pork. What kind of soup do you get from this? Mere "dishwater."

—B. N. Kniazev, Tula, September 1930

Comrade Editor, Please give me an answer. Do the local authorities have the right to forcibly take away the only cow of industrial and office workers? What is more, they demand a receipt showing that the cow was handed over voluntarily and they threaten you by saying if you don't do this, they will put you in prison for failure to fulfill the meat procurement. How can you live when the cooperative distributes only black bread, and at the market goods have the prices of 1919 and 1920? Lice have eaten us to death, and soap is given only to railroad workers. From hunger and filth we have a massive outbreak of spotted fever.

—Anonymous, from Aktyubinsk, Kazakhstan

* A *pood* is a Russian unit of weight, equal to 36.11 pounds.

Source: Lewis Siegelbaum and Andrei Sokolov, *Stalinism as a Way of Life: A Narrative in Documents* (New Haven, CT: 2000), pp. 39–41.

Questions for Analysis

1. What are Stalin's priorities?

2. What images does Stalin use to capture his audience's attention?

3. How did the Soviet people experience Stalin's industrialization drive?

developed during the 1920s. Women, too, entered the urban workforce in increasing numbers in the 1930s: women went from 20 to almost 40 percent of the workforce in one decade.

At the same time, Stalin promoted a sharply conservative shift in all areas of culture and society. In art, the radical modernism of the 1920s was crushed by socialist realism, a deadening aesthetic that celebrated the drive toward socialism and left no room for experimentation. Also crushed were earlier Bolsheviks' utopian attempts to rebuild one of the basic structures of prerevolutionary society—the family—and to create a genuinely new proletarian social structure. During the 1920s, the Bolsheviks had legalized divorce, banned the Orthodox Church from performing marriage ceremonies, and legalized abortion. Stalin abandoned these reforms in favor of traditional family ties: divorce became more difficult, abortion was outlawed in 1936 except in cases that threatened the life of the mother, and homosexuality was declared a criminal offense. State subsidies and support for mothers could not change the reality that Soviet women were increasingly forced to carry the double burden of familial and wage labor to support Stalin's version of Soviet society.

THE GREAT TERROR

The apogee of Stalinist repression came with the "**Great Terror**" of 1936–1938, which left nearly 1 million people dead and as many as 1.5 million more in labor camps. As Stalin consolidated his personal dictatorship, he eliminated enemies—real and imagined—whom he considered superfluous to the new Soviet society.

The Terror was aimed at various categories of internal "enemies," from the top to the very bottom of Soviet society. The top level of the Bolshevik party itself was purged almost completely; some 100,000 party members were removed, including the "Old Bolsheviks," most facing prison sentences or execution. The purge also struck nonparty elites, industrial managers, and intellectuals. Stalin purged the military, which he feared as a threat to his power: between 35,000 and 41,000 officers were killed, including 90 percent of the highest-ranking army officers. Whole ethnic groups were purged as a national security threat, including Poles, Ukrainians, Lithuanians, Latvians, and Koreans. From the bottom, some 200,000 to 300,000 "dekulakized" peasants, petty criminals, and other social misfits were arrested, and many were shot. The purges disrupted the government, the military, and the economy, but they also enabled Stalin to promote a new, young cadre of officials who owed their careers, if not their lives, to Stalin personally. The Great Terror solidified Stalin's personal control over social and political life in the Soviet Union, but it did so by destroying the most talented elements in Soviet society.

The results of the Soviet revolution were profound. No other regime in the history of Europe had ever attempted to reorder completely the politics, economy, and society of a major nation, as the Soviets had done in a mere twenty years. By 1939, private manufacturing and trade had been almost entirely abolished. Factories, mines, railroads, and public utilities were exclusively owned by the state, and agriculture had been almost completely collectivized. The society that emerged was industrial, more urban than rural, and more modern than traditional. Russian society was badly brutalized in the process, and the USSR that emerged from this tumultuous period would barely be able to withstand the immense strains placed on it when the Germans struck less than three years after the end of the Terror.

The Emergence of Fascism in Italy

Italy emerged from the First World War as a democracy in distress. The war had cost nearly 700,000 thousand Italian lives and over $15 billion. Moreover, Italy had received secret promises of territorial gains, only to see those promises withdrawn at the Versailles peace conference. At first the nationalists blamed the "mutilated victory" on President Wilson, but soon they turned on their own rulers and blamed what they saw as the weaknesses of parliamentary democracy.

Since unification, the Italian nation had been divided between a prosperous industrialized north and a poor agrarian south. Social conflict over land, wages, and local power caused friction in the countryside as well as in urban centers. These tensions were aggravated by the war and the period of inflation and unemployment that followed. Inflation produced high prices, speculation, and profiteering, and wages were kept low by the return of veterans seeking jobs. Business elites were shaken by strikes, which became increasingly large and frequent, and by the closing of foreign markets.

Italians wanted drastic reforms. For the working class, this meant social-ism, and in 1919, the socialists won about a third of the seats in the Chamber of Deputies. In 1920, the socialist and anarchist workers seized scores of factories, most in the metallurgy sector, and tried to run them for the benefit of the workers. In some rural areas, so-called Red Leagues tried to break up large estates and force landlords to reduce their rents. In all these actions, the model of the Russian Revolution, although it was only vaguely understood, encouraged the development of local radicalism.

The rising radical tide, especially seen against the backdrop of the Bolshevik rev-olution, worried other social groups. Industrialists and landowners feared for their property, and small shopkeepers and white-collar workers—social groups that did not think the working-class movement supported their interests—found themselves alienated by both business elites and the revolutionary radicals. The threat from the left provoked a strong surge to the right, as fascist vigilante groups fought with workers in the streets and with the Red Leagues in the countryside.

THE RISE OF MUSSOLINI

Benito Mussolini's (1883–1945) father was a socialist blacksmith and his mother was a schoolteacher. He became a schoolteacher himself as a young man, but was restless and dissatisfied. He soon left Italy for Switzerland, where he began to write articles for socialist newspapers. He returned to Italy and became a journalist, and eventually the editor of *Avanti*, the leading socialist daily.

After war broke out in August 1914, Mussolini became a nationalist. He founded a new paper, *Il Popolo d'Italia* ("The People of Italy"), and dedicated its columns to arousing enthusiasm for war. As early as October 1914, Mussolini had organized groups, called *fasci*—made up of young idealists and fanatical national-ists—to help drum up support for the war. After the war, these groups formed the base of Mussolini's **fascist** movement. Mussolini's original platform for the Fascist party from 1919 called for universal suffrage (including for women), an eight-hour workday, and a tax on inheritances. But a new platform, adopted in 1920, aban-doned all references to economic reforms. Neither platform, however, earned the fascists much electoral success.

What the fascists lacked in political support, they made up in aggressive deter-mination. They gained the respect of the middle class and landowners by violently attacking leftist industrial workers and peasants. They attacked socialists, often physically, and succeeded in taking over some local governments. As the national

Benito Mussolini (1883–1945) The Italian founder of the Fascist party who came to power in Italy in 1922 and allied himself with Hitler and the Nazis during the Second World War.

fascist Derived from the Latin *fasces,* an ax surrounded by a bundle of sticks that represented the authority of the Roman state, the Italian *fascio* means "group" or "band."

EUROPE IN 1923. › Which countries and empires lost territories after the First World War? › What were the consequences for those countries and empires? › How did the Russian Revolution change European politics? › What problems arose in the central and eastern European nations that were created after the First World War?

Areas lost by Germany
Areas lost by Russia
Areas lost by Ottoman Empire
Areas lost by Austro-Hungarian Empire

regime weakened, Mussolini's coercive politics made him look like a solution to the absence of leadership. In September 1922, he began to negotiate with other parties and with the king for fascist participation in government. In the last week of October, Mussolini called for a demonstration of fascist popular support to strengthen his hand, bringing several tens of thousands of fascist militia members to the outskirts of the capital. The government attempted to implement emergency powers to counter the threat of a fascist coup, but King Victor Emmanuel III refused to allow the army to be used against Mussolini's supporters. Instead, the king invited Mussolini to form a new government. Mussolini arrived in Rome by train and organized a parade of his supporters after he became prime minister. The fascist myth of the "March on Rome" held that power had been taken by force, but, in fact, Mussolini's accession to the head of the government conformed to the provisions of the Italian constitution.

The "March on Rome" was later mythologized as fascist seizure of power

The parliamentary system folded under pressure, and though Mussolini had "legally" been granted his power, he immediately began to establish a one-party dictatorship. The doctrines of Italian fascism had three components. The first was statism, in which the state incorporated every interest and demanded unquestioning loyalty from all members of the nation. The second was nationalism, in which nationhood was the highest form of society, with a life and a soul of its own, transcending the individuals who composed it. The third was militarism. Fascists believed that war was ennobling, and that nations that did not expand aggressively would wither and die.

Mussolini began to rebuild Italy in accordance with these principles. The first steps were to change the electoral laws to give his party solid parliamentary majorities and to intimidate the opposition. He then moved to close down parliamentary government and other political parties entirely. He abolished the cabinet system and all but extinguished the powers of Parliament. He made the Fascist party an integral part of the Italian constitution. He assumed the dual position of prime minister and party leader (*duce*), and used the party's militia to eliminate his enemies through intimidation and violence. Mussolini's government also controlled the police, muzzled the press, and censored academic activity.

Despite constitutional rise to power, Mussolini radically reworks nature of Italian state

Mussolini preached the end of class conflict while attacking Italy's independent labor unions. The Italian economy was placed under the management of twenty-two corporations, each responsible for a major industrial enterprise. In each corporation were representatives of official trade unions, whose members were organized by the Fascist party, the employers, and the government. The decisions of these bodies were closely supervised by the government and favored the positions of management. Indeed, the government quickly aligned with big business, creating more of a corrupt bureaucracy than a revolutionary economy.

Mussolini secured some working-class assent with state-sponsored programs, such as massive public-works projects, library building, paid vacations, and social security. In 1929, he settled Italy's sixty-year-old conflict with the Roman Catholic Church by signing a treaty that granted independence to the papal residence in Vatican City and established Roman Catholicism as the official religion of the state. The treaty also guaranteed religious education in the nation's schools and made religious marriage ceremonies mandatory. The Italian dictator boasted that fascism had pulled the country back from economic chaos, and, like other European economies, the Italian economy did improve during the late 1920s. Fascism did little, however, to improve Italy's plight during the worldwide economic depression of the 1930s.

Fascism had contradictory elements. It sought to restore traditional authority and, at the same time, mobilize all of Italian society for economic and nationalist purposes—a process that inevitably undercut traditional elites. It created new authoritarian organizations and activities: youth camps to make young people fit

Fascism's contradictions

for service, awards to mothers of large families, political rallies, and parades in small towns in the countryside. Activities like these offered people a feeling of political involvement, even as they no longer enjoyed political rights. This mobilized, yet essentially passive, citizenship was a hallmark of fascism.

Weimar Germany

On November 9, 1918—two days before the armistice ending the First World War—a massive uprising in Berlin resulted in the kaiser's abdication and the birth of a new German republic. The leader of the new government was Friedrich Ebert, a member of the Social Democratic party (SPD) in Parliament. The revolution spread quickly, and by the end of the month, councils of workers and soldiers controlled hundreds of German cities. The "November Revolution" was not as revolutionary as many middle- and upper-class conservatives feared. The majority of socialists wanted democratic reforms but were willing to leave much of the existing imperial bureaucracy intact. Above all, they wanted a popularly elected national assembly to draft a constitution for the new republic.

Two months passed, however, before elections could be held—a period of crisis that verged on civil war. The revolutionary movement that had brought the SPD to power now threatened it. Independent socialists and a nascent Communist party wanted radical reforms, and in December 1918 and January 1919, they staged armed uprisings in the streets of Berlin. Fearful of a Bolshevik-style revolution, the Social Democratic government turned against its former allies and sent troops to crush the uprisings. During the conflict, the government's fighters murdered Rosa Luxemburg and Karl Liebknecht, two German communist leaders who became instant martyrs. Violence continued into 1920, creating a lasting bitterness among groups on the left.

The revolutionary aftermath of the war also gave rise to bands of militant counter-revolutionaries. Veterans and other young nationalists joined the so-called *Freikorps* ("free corps"); such groups developed throughout the country, drawing as many as several hundred thousand members. Former army officers who led these militias applied their war experience to fighting the Bolsheviks, Poles, and communists. The politics of the Freikorps were fiercely right wing. Anti-Marxist, antisemitic, and antiliberal, they openly opposed the new German republic and its parliamentary democracy. Many of the early Nazi leaders fought in the First World War and participated in Freikorps units.

Germany's new government, known as the Weimar (*VY-mahr*) Republic for the city in which its constitution was drafted, rested on a fragile electoral majority formed by a coalition of socialists, Catholic centrists, and liberal democrats. The Weimar constitution of 1919 established universal suffrage (for both women and men) and a bill of rights that guaranteed not only civil liberties but also a range of social entitlements. On paper, at least, the revolutionary movement had succeeded in establishing a framework for German democracy.

By 1930, however, the Weimar Republic was in crisis, and in 1933, it collapsed. What happened? Many of Weimar's problems were born from Germany's defeat in the First World War. Many Germans soon latched on to rumors that the army hadn't actually been defeated in battle but had been "stabbed in the back" by socialists and Jewish leaders in the German government. Army officers cultivated this story even before the war was over; though untrue, it helped salve the wounded pride of German patriots. In the next decade, those in search of a scapegoat also blamed the republican regime, which had signed the Treaty of Versailles.

In fact, contemporaries exaggerated the harshness of the Versailles treaty, which was much less punitive than the Treaty of Brest-Litovsk that Germany had forced on Bolshevik Russia in 1917. The Versailles treaty demanded that Germany cede a tenth of its territory, but a great deal of this land, including the French territories of Alsace and Lorraine, had only recently become German. The so-called "war guilt clause" was not a statement of culpability for the war itself but a declaration of legal responsibility for damages caused by the German military beyond their borders. The reparations, seen as punitive by the Germans, were soon adjusted downward, though they did cause hardships for the German public.

Much of the reputation for the harshness of the Versailles treaty came from an international crisis about reparation payments in January 1923. When the Germans fell behind on their allotted deliveries of coal that were a part of the Versailles arrangements, the French marched their army into the Ruhr valley, a key German industrial region. The demands for reparations forced the Weimar government to make payments by simply printing more money. The result was a period of bewildering hyperinflation that peaked in late 1923. A pound of potatoes that cost 9 marks in January cost 40 million marks by October. For those on fixed incomes, such as pensioners and stockholders, savings and security were wiped out. The government finally took drastic measures to stabilize the currency in 1924, but by then millions of Germans had already been financially ruined. Many blamed the Versailles treaty and the intransigence of the French government for their losses.

> *After harsh reparations are enforced, Weimar government responds by printing more money—triggering hyperinflation*

HYPERINFLATION. German children use stacks of money as toys. In July 1922, the American dollar was worth 670 German marks; in November 1923, it was worth 4,210,500,000,000 marks. ›**How might hyperinflation have affected German attitudes toward the Weimar Republic's government?**

In 1924, Germany accepted a new schedule of reparations designed by an international committee headed by the American financier Charles G. Dawes. The Dawes Plan included loans from the United States that helped to stabilize the economy. At the same time, taking advantage of a change in government in France, the German chancellor Gustav Stresemann moved Germany toward a foreign policy of cooperation that lasted throughout the 1920s. The result was a new international framework, known as the Locarno Treaties (1925), which recognized the legitimacy of the French-German border, but left open the question of Germany's eastern frontiers with Poland and Czechoslovakia.

In the late 1920s, the German economy seemed to stabilize. By borrowing money under the Dawes Plan, the Weimar government was able to make its reparation payments. But this stability was misleading, because the German economy remained dependent on capital from the United States. When the U.S. stock market crashed in 1929, setting off the Great Depression, capital flow to Germany virtually stopped.

The **Great Depression** pushed Weimar's political system to the breaking point. In 1929, there were 2 million unemployed; and in 1932, there were 6 million. In those three years, production dropped by 44 percent. The depression meant lower salaries, poor working conditions, and a constant threat of unemployment. Tax revenues plummeted, and the government repeatedly cut welfare benefits, further demoralizing the electorate. The crisis created an opportunity for Weimar's opponents. Many leading industrialists and equally conservative landowners supported a return to authoritarian government. These conservative forces wielded considerable power in Germany. So, too, did the army and the civil service, which were staffed with opponents of the republic—men who rejected the principles of parliamentary democracy and the international cooperation that Weimar represented.

Great Depression reveals fragility of German economy and its dependence on outside capital

Hitler and the National Socialists

National socialism in Germany emerged out of the bitterness of defeat in the First World War, but Adolf Hitler's political party did not gain mass support until after the unemployment crisis caused by the depression that began in 1929.

Adolf Hitler was born in Austria in 1889. The son of a petty customs official, he hoped to become an artist, but he was rejected by the academy. Forced to eke out a dismal existence doing manual labor and painting cheap watercolors, he developed violent antisemitic and Pan-German political beliefs while living in inexpensive rooming houses. When war broke out in 1914, Hitler enlisted in the German army, where he claimed to have finally found meaning in life. After the war, he joined the newly formed German Workers' party, whose name changed in 1920 to the National Socialist German Workers' party (abbreviated in popular usage to

Great Depression Global economic crisis following the U.S. stock market crash on October 29, 1929, and ending with the onset of the Second World War.

Nazi). The Nazis were a small, militant group of disaffected Germans who refused to accept the defeat that brought the Weimar Republic to power. They blamed Germany's misfortune on socialists and Jews.

Hitler quickly moved up the rather short ladder of party leadership. In November 1923, during the worst days of the inflation crisis, the Nazis made a failed attempt (the Beer Hall Putsch in Munich) at overthrowing the state government of Bavaria. Hitler spent the next seven months in prison, where he wrote his autobiography and political manifesto *Mein Kampf* (*myn KAHMPF*; "My Struggle") in 1924. Combining antisemitism with anticommunism, the book set out at great length the popular theory that Germany had been betrayed by its enemies and that the country needed strong leadership to regain international prominence. After being released from prison in 1924, he resumed leadership of the party. For the next five years, he consolidated his control over a growing movement of ardent supporters. Actively cultivating the image of the Nazi movement as a crusade against Marxism, capitalism, and Jews, Hitler portrayed himself as the heroic savior of the German people.

In the "inflation election" of 1924, the Nazis polled 6.6 percent of the vote as a protest party at the radical fringe. During the economic stabilization of the mid-1920s, their meager share dropped to below 3 percent. During this time of seeming decline, the Nazis were building an extensive organization of party activists to help lay the foundation for the party's later electoral gains.

After 1928, political polarization between the right and the left worked to Hitler's advantage. Alienated voters, especially in rural areas, deserted the traditional political parties. The Nazis stepped up their efforts to attract members of the rural and urban middle classes. Guided by its chief propagandist, Joseph Goebbels, the Nazi party hammered home a critique of Weimar society and culture. They criticized parliament, the power of the left, and the labor movement. They pointed to women wearing "decadent" flapper fashions, and "cosmopolitan" (Jewish or insufficiently nationalist) movies such as the 1930 Best Picture Oscar winner *All Quiet on the Western Front*. Presenting themselves as young and dynamic, the Nazis built a national profile as an alternative to the parties of middle-class conservatives.

By 1930, they were better funded and better organized than ever, winning 18.3 percent of the vote and 107 of 577 seats in the Reichstag, second only to the Social Democrats. No party could gain a majority, and no governing coalition was possible without Nazi support. The Nazis also refused to join any cabinet that was not headed by Hitler. The chancellor, Heinrich Brüning of the Catholic Center party, continued to govern by emergency decrees, but his deflationary economic policies were disastrous: industrial production continued to crash and unemployment continued to climb. In 1932, Hitler ran for president and received 37 percent of the vote against the victorious incumbent Paul von Hindenburg, a retired general and a hero of the First World War. When another parliamentary election was called in July 1932, the Nazis won 37.4 percent of the vote.

In January 1933, Hitler was appointed chancellor by President Hindenburg, who hoped to create a conservative coalition government with Nazi support. But Hindenburg underestimated the Nazis' power and popularity. When a Dutch anarchist with links to the Communist party set fire to the Reichstag on the night of February 27, Hitler seized the opportunity to suspend civil rights "as a defensive

Adolf Hitler (1889–1945) The author of *Mein Kampf* and leader of the Nazis, who became chancellor of Germany in 1933. Hitler and his Nazi regime started the Second World War and orchestrated the systematic murder of over 6 million Jews, hundreds of thousands of people with disabilities, tens of thousands of Roma, and thousands of homosexuals.

Hitler and the Nazis present themselves as a racially pure alternative to a radical left and inept traditional elites

measure against communist acts of violence." He then convinced Hindenburg to dissolve the Reichstag and to order a new election on March 5, 1933. Under Hitler's sway, the new parliament legally granted him unlimited powers for four years, allowing Hitler to proclaim his new government the Third Reich. (*Reich* means "empire" or "realm" in German; the First Reich was the German Empire of the Middle Ages, and the Second Reich was that of the kaisers from 1871 to 1918.)

NAZI GERMANY

By the fall of 1933, Germany was a one-party state. The socialist and communist left was crushed by the new regime and almost all non-Nazi organizations had been abolished or absorbed into the Nazi system. Party propaganda touted the regime's "monolithic efficiency," but the Nazi government was a tangled bureaucratic maze, with both agencies and individuals vying fiercely for Hitler's favor.

In 1934, the most serious challenges to Hitler came from within the party. Hitler's paramilitary Nazi storm troopers (the *Sturmabteilung*, or SA) had been formed to maintain discipline and impose order. In 1933, SA membership soared to 2 million, and many in the SA hailed Hitler's appointment as the beginning of a genuine Nazi revolution. Such radicalism alarmed the more traditional conservative groups that had helped make Hitler chancellor. If Hitler was to maintain power, he needed to tame the SA. On the night of June 30, 1934, hundreds of Nazi SA officials, including several of Hitler's oldest associates, were executed in a bloody purge known as the Night of the Long Knives.

Hitler's purge was accomplished by a second paramilitary organization, the *Schutzstaffel* ("bodyguard"), or SS. Headed by the fanatical Heinrich Himmler, the SS became the most dreaded arm of Nazi terror. The mission of the SS was to fight political and racial enemies of the regime, a by-product of which included building the system of concentration camps (the first camp opened in March 1933 at Dachau). The secret state police, known as the Gestapo, were responsible for the arrest, incarceration in camps, and murder of thousands of Germans.

Hitler and the Nazis enjoyed a sizable amount of popular support. Many Germans approved of Hitler's use of violence against the left, as the Nazis played on deep-seated fears of communism and presented Hitler as a symbol of a strong, revitalized Germany, But Hitler's appeal also rested on his ability to give the German people what they wanted: jobs for workers, a productive economy for industrialists, a bulwark against communism for those who feared the wave of revolution, and, finally, the power to lead Germany back to national greatness and "overthrow" the Versailles treaty.

For most Germans, Hitler represents a promise of a strong Germany, including state and economy ⟩

Hitler called for full rearmament and economic self-sufficiency, but Germany depended on imports for its agriculture, textile, mining, steel, and automobile industries. In 1934, Hitler repudiated all of Germany's debts and called for new bilateral negotiations with Britain, France, and the U.S. He established authoritarian controls over the economy, increasing military spending and imposing price and wage controls. In the short term, Hitler's policies had public support as unemployment fell from a high of over 30 percent in 1933. But this growth could not be maintained indefinitely and required an atmosphere of permanent national emergency to justify the sacrifices it asked of the German public. These policies contributed to the drive toward political extremism while making the seizure of territory in the east more attractive to Hitler's supporters.

Like Mussolini, Hitler outlawed trade unions and strikes, froze wages, and organized workers and employers into a National Labor Front. At the same time, he increased workers' welfare benefits, generally in line with other Western nations. Class distinctions were blurred somewhat by the regime's attempts to infuse a new national "spirit" into the entire society. The Hitler Youth, a club modeled in part on the international scouting movement, was highly successful at teaching German children the values of Hitler's Reich, especially the dogmas of racial purity and mass mobilization. Government policy encouraged women to withdraw from the labor force, both to ease unemployment and to conform to Nazi notions of a woman's proper role as mothers of the next generation.

Nazi Racism

At the core of Nazi ideology lay a particularly virulent form of racism. Hitler and the Nazis drew on an aggressive version of social Darwinism, according to which nations and races struggled to survive, with superior peoples strengthening themselves in the process. This form of racial thinking was not unique to Germany. By the early twentieth century, the rise of the social sciences had taken nineteenth-century prejudices and racial thinking into new terrain in Europe and North America. Scientists and intellectuals worked to purify the body politic, improve the human race, and eliminate the "unfit" through eugenics, a "racial" engineering program to improve the health and well-being of national populations that was the subject of wide consensus. In Western democracies these programs were used to determine racial quotas for immigration and to justify the sterilization of people—often without their knowledge—who were determined to be unfit to reproduce. In Nazi Germany, racial science and eugenics became an important part of state policy, beginning with a law for the compulsory sterilization of "innumerable inferior and hereditarily tainted" people in 1933. The Nazis later used this "social-hygienic racism" to justify the systematic murder of mentally and physically ill patients. Social policy was governed by a basic division between those who were seen to possess biological "value" and those who did not, with the aim of creating a racial utopia.

> In Germany and elsewhere, evolutionary theory was used to justify programs of racial eugenics

The first principle of Nazi racism was that human populations could be divided into separate races defined by blood and descent, and presumed some races were "superior" to others. Hitler argued in *Mein Kampf* that the Slavic peoples of central and eastern Europe were fit only to be slaves of the superior German "Aryans," and he decried the tendency of populations in the modern world to become "mixed" and "degenerate" through migration and intermarriage. His racial theories always reserved a special place for **antisemitism**. Hitler's hatred of Jews was built on older European traditions of religious antisemitism that had long been accepted within Christian communities. He also benefited from the anti-Jewish writings of nineteenth-century nationalists who saw Jews as permanent outsiders who could become citizens only if they denied their Jewish identity. There were also examples of modern antisemitic movements before Hitler: the Dreyfus Affair in France (Chapter 23) generated a barrage of propaganda against Jews, and the late nineteenth century also saw a wave of pogroms (violent assaults on Jewish communities), especially in Russia. But Hitler's antisemitism emphasized newer forms of racial thinking: he and his Nazi followers assumed—erroneously—that Jews were biologically different. They would not accept Jews who converted to Christianity or

antisemitism Hostility toward Jewish people. Sometimes expressed in religious terms, or accompanied by accusations of alleged political or economic corruption. In the late nineteenth and twentieth centuries, antisemitism was increasingly rooted in presumed—and spurious—racial differences.

NAZI BOYCOTT OF JEWISH SHOPS IN BERLIN, 1933. Nazis stand in front of a Jewish-owned clothing store. The sign reads: "Germans! Defend yourselves! Buy nothing from the Jews!"

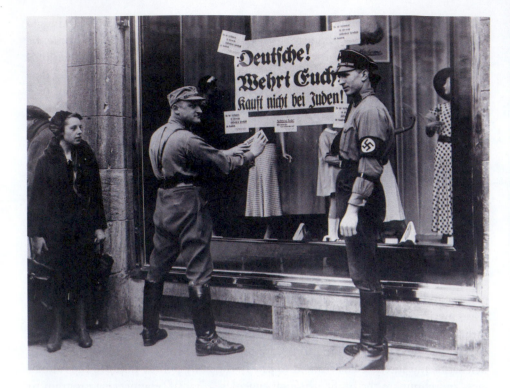

who assimilated to the larger culture. They needed to be removed completely from the body of the nation. Hitler gave this antisemitism an especially murderous twist by tying it to the doctrines of war and the racism of eugenics.

Although the "Jewish Question" was clearly Hitler's primary obsession during the early 1920s, he made it less central as the Nazi movement entered mainstream politics, shifting his attacks instead to Marxism and the Weimar Republic. Before 1933, antisemitic beliefs did not distinguish the Nazi party from other parties on the right; it was likely of only secondary importance to most people's opinions of the Nazis. After Hitler came to power, however, German Jews faced discrimination and escalating violence. Racial laws excluded Jews from public office as early as April 1933. The Nazis encouraged boycotts of Jewish merchants, and SA street attacks on Jews created a constant threat of random violence. In 1935, the Nuremberg Decrees deprived Jews (defined by bloodline) of their German citizenship and prohibited marriage between Jews and other Germans. In November 1938, the SA ransacked some 7,5000 Jewish stores, burned nearly 200 synagogues, murdered 91 Jews, and beat up thousands more in a nationwide campaign of terror known as *Kristallnacht* ("Crystal Night"; also referred to as the Night of Broken Glass). Although violence like this raised some opposition from ordinary Germans, legal persecution met only silent acquiescence. For Jewish people, Kristallnacht made it plain that there was no safe place for them in Germany, but unfortunately, only one year remained before the outbreak of war made it impossible for them to escape.

What did national socialism and Italian fascism have in common? Both arose during the interwar period as responses to the First World War and the Russian Revolution. Both were violently antisocialist and anticommunist, determined to "rescue" their nations from the threat of Bolshevism. Both were intensely nationalistic, believing that national solidarity came before all other allegiances and superseded

Kristallnacht ("Crystal Night") Organized attack by Nazis and their supporters on the Jews of Germany following the assassination of a German diplomat by a Jewish man in Paris.

all other rights. Both opposed parliamentary government and democracy as cumbersome and divisive. Both found power in mass-based authoritarian politics. Similar movements existed in all the countries of the West, but only in a few cases did they actually take power. Nazism, however, distinguished itself by making a racially pure state central to its vision, a vision that would lead to global struggle and mass murder.

◀ Commonalities between national socialism in Germany and fascism in Italy

The Interwar Years in Europe's Major Democracies

The three major Allied Powers—Great Britain, France, and the United States—emerged from the First World War confident in the legitimacy of their democratic institutions. The extension of the vote to women in the United States and Britain (French women would have to wait until 1945) was proof of the sincerity of these democratic commitments, but the persistence of legal racism and threat of race-based violence showed the limits of western democracies' commitment to civil rights. In 1896, in *Plessy v. Ferguson*, the Supreme Court had upheld the right of individual states to provide separate facilities for people of different races under the doctrine of "separate but equal." Nearly six decades of legal discrimination ensued under "Jim Crow" laws, which excluded Black people from many public facilities. When Black Americans organized politically to fight this system of discrimination, they were vulnerable to attack by vigilantes defending **white supremacy**. Moreover, Britain, France, and the United States remained imperial powers after the First World War, and the principle of national self-determination or citizenship rights did not extend to the colonized peoples of the world after 1918—a fact that would lead to the development of anticolonial nationalist movements in many parts of the world, culminating ultimately in a wave of decolonization after the Second World War (see Chapter 27).

In fact, the post–World War I treaties allowed both Britain and France to expand the size of their empires as they absorbed former German colonies in Africa and took control of a large part of the Middle East under the mandate system set up by the League of Nations (Chapter 24). In the 1920s, France claimed Syria and Lebanon, while Britain ruled over Palestine and Iraq. The United States, which had already shown interest in Central America and the Caribbean during the Spanish-American War of 1898, occupied Cuba (four times between 1898 and 1922), Haiti (1915–1934), the Dominican Republic (1916 and 1924), and Nicaragua (1912–1925 and 1926–1933). It also intervened during the same years in Panama, Honduras, and Mexico to defend strategic and commercial interests in the region, and to support authoritarian—and undemocratic—governments that cooperated with U.S. companies.

The Western democracies were shaped by the broader context of imperial rule. The French used colonial troops and labor extensively during the First World War, and in the 1920s, French industry depended in part on immigrant laborers. In Britain, the population of port cities reflected the arrival of colonial laborers, and migration to the United States from Latin America, especially Mexico, increased substantially during the same period. These population movements were small compared with the large numbers of Europeans who immigrated to the United States or Australia and New Zealand in the nineteenth century, but they were the beginnings of a pattern of migration to Europe and the United States that would take on greater significance after World War II.

white supremacy A belief that white people constitute a superior race that is entitled to control a given nation's institutions and laws in order to preserve their dominance over other people.

Propaganda in Mussolini's Italy and Hitler's Germany

Fascism in Italy and Germany promised many things to many people. Mussolini's rhetoric focused on the ideas of national greatness in the aftermath of the First World War, and the need to counter the imperialism of other powers when they threatened Italian interests. The Nazis blended antisemitism, racial nationalism, vaguely defined (and anti-Marxist) socialism, and disgust with the state of German culture and politics into their propaganda, as the document by Joseph Goebbels shows. Goebbels, one of the early members of the Nazi party, later became head of the National Ministry for Public Enlightenment and Propaganda.

Benito Mussolini, *My Rise and Fall*

It was at this time, right after the spirit of exhilaration of victory, that I observed strange tendencies in the Italian political world. Evil activity was at hand. It needed to be exposed and suppressed. It was cloaked under the appearance of humanitarianism. It was planning to give a series of national rights to peoples who never had the consciousness and the dignity of nations—to peoples who had been for more than a century instruments of oppressing the Italian elements under Austria, under the instigation of the despotic empire. The sun of our victory was rising, but to be a complete victory, a victory that would carry our soldiers on the road to Vienna, it must not falter through false sentimentality. . . .

I felt that we were left without any cohesive force, any suggestive heroism, any remembrance, any political philosophy, sufficient to overcome and stop the factors of dissolution. I sensed the chills and heats of decay and destruction. . . .

I knew those who whipped up our degeneration. They were German and Austrian spies, Russian agitators, mysterious subventions. In a few months they had led the Italian people into a state of marasmus. The economic crisis existing in every corner of the world could not be expected to spare Italy. The soldiers, like myself, returning from the war, rushed to their families. Who can describe our feelings? Such an imposing phenomenon as the demobilization of millions of men took place in the dark, without noise, in an atmosphere of throwing discipline to the winds. There were, for us, the troubles of winter and the difficulties of finding new garments and adjustments for peace. . . .

Those who came to the meeting for the constitution of the Italian Fascisti of Combat used few words. They did not exhaust themselves by laying out dreams. Their aim seemed clear and straight-lined. It was to defend the victory at any price, to maintain intact the sacred memory of the dead, and the admiration not only for those who fell and for the families of those who were dead but for the mutilated, for the invalids, for all those who had fought. The prevalent note, however, was of anti-socialist character, and as a political aspiration, it was hoped a new Italy would be created that would know how to give value to the victory and to fight with all its strength against treason and corruption, against decay within and intrigue and avarice from without.

I was certain at the time that it was necessary to fix, without any possibility of equivocation, the essential brand of the new movement. For this reason I made three planks for our platform. The first was the following:

The meeting of the twenty-third of March sends its first greeting and reverent thought to the sons of Italy who died for the greatness of their country and for the freedom of the world; to the mutilated and to the invalids, to all those who fought, to the ex-prisoners who fulfilled their duty. It declares itself ready to uphold with all its energy the material and moral claims that will be put forward by the associations of those who fought.

The second declaration pledged the Fascisti of Combat to oppose themselves to the imperialism of any other countries damaging to Italy. It accepted the supreme postulates of the League of Nations regarding Italy. It affirmed the necessity to complete the stability of our frontiers between the Alps and the Adriatic with the claim of annexation of Fiume and of Dalmatia.

The third declaration spoke of the elections that were announced for the near future. In this motion the Fasci di Combattimento pledged themselves to fight with all their means the candidates that were milk-and-water Italians, to whatever party they belonged.

Finally we talked of organization—the organization that would be adapted to the new movement. I did not favor any bureaucratic cut-and-dried organization. It was thought wise that in every big town the correspondent of the *Popolo d'Italia* should be the organizer of a section of the Fasci di Combattimento, with the idea that each group should become a centre of Fascist ideas, work and action.

Source: Benito Mussolini, *My Rise and Fall* (New York: 1998), pp. 54, 60–61, 71–72.

Joseph Goebbels, *"Why Are We Enemies of the Jews?"*

We are NATIONALISTS because we see in the NATION the only possibility for the protection and the furtherance of our existence.

The NATION is the organic bond of a people for the protection and defense of their lives. He is nationally minded who understands this IN WORD AND IN DEED. . . .

Young nationalism has its unconditional demands, BELIEF IN THE NATION is a matter of all the people, not for individuals of rank, a class, or an industrial clique. The eternal must be separated from the contemporary. The maintenance of a rotten industrial system has nothing to do with nationalism. I can love Germany and hate capitalism; not only CAN I do it, I also MUST do it. The germ of the rebirth of our people LIES ONLY IN THE DESTRUCTION OF THE SYSTEM OF PLUNDERING THE HEALTHY POWER OF THE PEOPLE.

WE ARE NATIONALISTS BECAUSE WE, AS GERMANS, LOVE GERMANY. And because we love Germany, we demand the protection of its national spirit and we battle against its destroyers.

WHY ARE WE SOCIALISTS?

We are SOCIALISTS because we see in SOCIALISM the only possibility for maintaining our racial existence and through it the reconquest of our political freedom and the rebirth of the German state. SOCIALISM has its peculiar form first of all through its comradeship in arms with the forward-driving energy of a newly awakened nationalism. Without nationalism it is nothing, a phantom, a theory, a vision of air, a book. With it, it is everything, THE FUTURE, FREEDOM, FATHERLAND! . . .

WHY DO WE OPPOSE THE JEWS?

We are ENEMIES OF THE JEWS, because we are fighters for the freedom of the German people. THE JEW IS THE CAUSE AND THE BENEFICIARY OF OUR MISERY. He has used the social difficulties of the broad masses of our people to deepen the unholy split between Right and Left among our people. He has made two halves of Germany. He is the real cause for our loss of the Great War.

The Jew has no interest in the solution of Germany's fateful problems. He CANNOT have any. FOR HE LIVES ON THE FACT THAT THERE HAS BEEN NO SOLUTION. If we would make the German people a unified community and give them freedom before the world, then the Jew can have no place among us. He has the best trumps in his hands when a people lives in inner and outer slavery. THE JEW IS RESPONSIBLE FOR OUR MISERY AND HE LIVES ON IT.

That is the reason why we, AS NATIONALISTS and AS SOCIALISTS, oppose the Jew. HE HAS CORRUPTED OUR RACE, FOULED OUR MORALS, UNDERMINED OUR CUSTOMS, AND BROKEN OUR POWER.

Source: Anton Kaes, Martin Jay, and Edward Dimendberg, *The Weimar Republic Sourcebook* (Los Angeles: 1994), pp. 137–38, 142.

Questions for Analysis

1. How did Mussolini and Goebbels use metaphors of good and evil, illness and health, growth and degeneration? Do the metaphors by Goebbels suggest what the Nazis would try to do to cure the ills of Germany if they took power?

2. Mussolini and Goebbels both emphasize their nationalism, but their attitudes toward socialism are different. How do you explain this difference?

3. Where does Goebbels place antisemitism in his version of German nationalism? Whom does Mussolini identify as the enemies of fascism?

Britain, France, and the United States weathered the upheavals of the interwar years, but not easily. In France and Britain worker discontent boiled just below the surface, as successive governments refused to raise taxes to pay for social reforms. Workers' resentment helped elect the first Labour party government in Britain in 1924, and again in 1929. In France, as the period of strikes immediately after the war subsided, it was followed by a period in which employers refused to bargain with labor unions. The United States, meanwhile, was a bastion of conservatism. Presidents Warren G. Harding, Calvin Coolidge, and Herbert Hoover held a social philosophy formulated by the barons of big businesses during the nineteenth century. And the U.S. Supreme Court used its power of judicial review to nullify progressive legislation enacted by state governments and, occasionally, by Congress.

The conservative economic and social policies of the prewar period were dealt their deathblow by the Great Depression of 1929. This worldwide depression peaked during the years 1929–1933, but its effects lasted a decade. The depression was an important factor in the rise of Nazism, but it also forced every country to forge new economic policies to deal with the unprecedented economic turmoil.

THE ORIGINS OF THE GREAT DEPRESSION

Loss of confidence in U.S. stock markets leads to economic crash, bank closures, failure of manufacturing firms, and rising unemployment

What caused the Great Depression? The Dawes Plan of 1924 and the Young Plan of 1928 had put an end to the reparations crisis that led to hyperinflation in post–World War I Germany by providing American loans to the German government. The Germans, in turn, used these funds to pay back the reparations demanded by France and Britain. This spirit of multilateral cooperation succeeded in stabilizing the European economy in the late 1920s, but it also made Europe dependent on the strength of American economic institutions. When crisis hit the United States in September 1929, its effects were quickly transmitted to Europe. The postwar U.S. stock market boom peaked that month after a period in which investors bid prices to unprecedented levels using borrowed money. A catastrophic sell-off in October produced a decline that lasted until July 1932, by which time the market was down 90 percent from its 1929 high. Private investors on both sides of the Atlantic pulled their money out of the market in an attempt to wait out the crisis. Banks found themselves short of capital and were forced to close, wiping out their depositors' savings. Manufacturers laid off virtually their entire workforces and bank closures made it impossible to get credit. In 1930, 4 million Americans were unemployed; in 1933, it was 13 million—nearly a third of the workforce. By then, per capita income in the United States had fallen 48 percent, and production had dropped 47 percent. In Germany, too, the drop was brutal. In 1929, some 2 million were unemployed; in 1932, it was 6 million.

The U.S. and European governments worsened the crisis by refusing to rescue the banks with infusions of cash—that is, acting as "lenders of last resort." Governments feared inflation and assumed that the capital for economic recovery could only come from the private sector. This assumption overestimated the ability of the banks to produce stability on their own. The depth of the crisis led Britain to abandon the gold standard in 1931; the United States followed suit in 1933. By no longer pegging their currencies to the price of gold, both countries hoped to make money cheaper and thus more available for economic recovery programs. This action was the forerunner of a broad currency management program, an important element in monetary policy after the Second World War. But monetary policy alone could not end the hardships of ordinary families, and governments were increasingly forced to address their concerns with a wide range of social reforms.

Britain was cautious in its relief efforts, but France adopted an ambitious set of policies to combat the effects of the depression. In 1936, responding to a threat from ultraconservatives to overthrow the republic, a Popular Front coalition under the leadership of socialist Léon Blum formed a majority in Parliament that lasted for two years. The Popular Front nationalized the munitions industry and reorganized the Bank of France to allow for an expansion of credit. It also decreed a forty-hour week for all urban workers and initiated a program of public works. Although the Popular Front temporarily quelled the threat from the political right, conservatives were uncooperative with attempts to aid the French working class. Both a socialist and Jewish, Blum faced fierce antisemitism in France. Fearing that Blum was the forerunner of a French Lenin, conservatives declared, "Better Hitler than Blum." They got their wish before the decade was out.

The most dramatic response to the depression came in the United States. The United States had clung longest to the nineteenth-century policy of "laissez-faire" while European nations had accepted a greater degree of government intervention in economic affairs during the First World War. Before the depression, American industrialists insisted on their right to form monopolies, and they used the government as a tool to frustrate the demands of both workers and consumers. When President Herbert Hoover persisted in a hands-off approach to the depression, the crisis quickly became more severe in the United States than in European democracies. America had survived the First World War unscathed—and, indeed, had benefited enormously—but now, its economy was ravaged even more than that of Europe. In 1933, Franklin D. Roosevelt succeeded Herbert Hoover as president and announced the New Deal, a program of reform and reconstruction to rescue the country.

The **New Deal** aimed to get the country back on its feet without destroying the capitalist system. The government would manage the economy, sponsor relief programs, and fund public-works projects to increase purchasing power. These policies were shaped by the theories of the British economist John Maynard Keynes. Keynes argued that capitalism could create a just and efficient society if governments played a part in its management. Keynes reasoned that the government could temporarily operate in the red—deficit spending—during recessions when demand fell. Keynes also favored the creation of large amounts of venture capital—money for high-risk, high-reward investments—which he saw as the only socially productive form of capital. Finally, he recommended monetary control to promote prosperity and full employment.

The New Deal helped individuals and the country recover, but it left the crucial problem of unemployment unsolved. In 1939, after six years of the New Deal, the United States still had more than 9 million jobless workers—a figure that exceeded the combined unemployment rate of the rest of the world. Only with the outbreak of a new world war, which required millions of soldiers and armament workers, did the United States reach a full recovery.

New Deal President Franklin D. Roosevelt's package of government reforms that were enacted during the Great Depression and provided jobs, social welfare programs, and security to the financial markets.

THE DUST BOWL AND THE ARAL SEA BASIN IN THE INTERWAR YEARS AND AFTER

During the twentieth century, parallel environmental crises of comparable scale unfolded in the southwestern United States and Soviet central Asia. In the American Dust Bowl of the 1930s, severe drought and man-made changes to the environment resulted in vast dust storms, which affected a 100 million acres of grassland and dispersed the region's topsoil over thousands of miles. In Soviet central Asia, the acceleration of water use during and after the collectivization of agriculture in the 1930s resulted in the disappearance of the fourth-largest lake in the world. In both cases, the delicate balance of complex ecosystems was disrupted by efforts to increase the productivity of agricultural land.

The Dust Bowl was centered in Kansas, Colorado, New Mexico, Oklahoma, and Texas, a region that had been put to use by cattle ranchers in the nineteenth century, after the resident Native American peoples had been killed or driven away and the bison herds depleted. After 1890, farmers with iron plows settled in the region. Nicknamed "sodbusters," they developed a system of row-crop agriculture whose profitability depended on mechanization. This system expanded through World War I, when demand for wheat pushed prices higher, and into the 1920s, when new mechanical tractors enhanced productivity. But the plows that broke the ground destroyed the landscape's natural ability to retain moisture. When a multiyear drought began in 1930, the dislodged earth became vulnerable to erosion and wind. Crops died in the field, and the soil dried up and blew away. Dust storms repeatedly rolled across the United States, blowing millions of tons of earth into the atmosphere, eventually falling like snow on eastern cities. By 1936, farm losses in the United States were at $25 million a day, exacerbating the economic effects of the Great Depression. The rains did not return until 1941. Agriculture continues to be profitable in the region but only because of intensive fertilization, new crop breeds, and deep-well irrigation

THE DUST BOWL. A "black roller" dust storm descends on Clayton, New Mexico, in 1937. Within minutes, the city was engulfed—first by dust, and then by rain. The fine dust penetrated the interiors of houses and left the streets covered in mud.

from the increasingly depleted Ogallala Aquifer. This large but finite source of underground water lies deep beneath the plains, stretching from South Dakota to Texas. Scientists estimate that once emptied, it will take 6,000 years for it to refill through rainfall.

The story of the Aral Sea is also about water and agriculture. Before the twentieth century, the Aral Sea covered 66,000 square kilometers, making it larger than Lake Michigan. It was fed by two major rivers that carried rain and ice melt from the Hindu Kush mountains. Large delta regions supported fisheries that survived off many species, including the Aral sturgeon, a source of caviar. The Aral Sea itself was surrounded by a dry landscape that previously supported only a small nomadic population. Starting in the late nineteenth century, the tsarist government invested in irrigation to encourage cotton production. The Bolsheviks pursued this project further after 1917, drastically enlarging the area of irrigation. When the nomadic population of Kazakhs in the Aral Sea region protested, Stalin persecuted them: over 1 million Kazakhs died or fled the region during the years of collectivization. Stalin's successors were equally enthusiastic about irrigation for cotton production and built broad canals to bring more land into cultivation. By the end of the 1960s, more than 90 percent of the water flowing toward the Aral Sea had been diverted, causing the Aral Sea to shrink while the water that remained increased in salinity. Within twenty years, the world's fourth largest inland lake had been reduced to a toxic salt plain incapable of sustaining plant life. Its eastern basin is now known as the Aralkum Desert.

The Dust Bowl in the United States and the disappearance of the Aral Sea in central Asia demonstrated that human activity could result in large-scale environmental changes over a relatively short span of time. Neither the capitalist economy of the United States nor the planned socialist economy of the Soviet Union encouraged people to think about the long term when making decisions about

THE DISAPPEARING ARAL SEA. The Aral Sea began to shrink in 1960, after several decades during which the Soviet Union began to divert the rivers that fed it to irrigate their cotton production. The satellite images show the Aral Sea in 1989 (left) and in 2016 (right).

natural resources. Both systems emphasized increased production, at the risk of upsetting the ecological balance of the landscape. Ultimately, neither system was able to anticipate long-term changes in the environment until after the crisis had already begun.

Interwar Culture: Artists and Intellectuals

The interwar period brought dramatic upheavals in the arts and sciences. Artists, writers, architects, and composers brought revolutionary artistic forms into the mainstream, experimenting with new forms of expression. Scientists and psychologists challenged established beliefs about the universe and human nature. Finally, radio, movies, and advertising created a new kind of mass culture that fed off the atmosphere of crisis in politics and contributed to the anxieties of the age.

INTERWAR INTELLECTUALS

Interwar literature reflects themes of disillusionment ❯

Novelists, poets, and dramatists were disillusioned by the war. Literature in the interwar period reflected themes of frustration and disenchantment that emerged when victory failed to fulfill its promises. The mood of the era is captured in the early work of the American author Ernest Hemingway, who wrote about a "lost generation" in his novel *The Sun Also Rises* (1926). The poetry of the Anglo-American T. S. Eliot explored a peculiarly modern form of despair: life as a living death, to be endured as boredom and frustration. In Germany, Bertolt Brecht depicted the cynical corruption of social elites in plays written for working-class audiences.

Writers experimented with new forms of prose. In *Ulysses* (1922), the Irish writer James Joyce perfected a style that became known as "stream of consciousness," a technique also associated with French author Marcel Proust. In the same vein, the British author Virginia Woolf offered an eloquent and biting critique of Britain's elite institutions, from the universities that isolated women in separate, underfunded colleges to the suffocating decorum of middle-class families and relationships.

The depression of the 1930s fostered a second wave of more politicized literature, as a new generation felt called on to indict injustice and point the way to a better society. In *The Grapes of Wrath* (1939), the American writer John Steinbeck depicts the plight of impoverished farmers fleeing from the Dust Bowl to California only to find the land monopolized by companies that exploited their workers. Younger British authors such as W. H. Auden, Stephen Spender, and Christopher Isherwood were communist sympathizers, who believed it was their duty as artists to support the revolution.

INTERWAR ARTISTS

The innovations of the prewar avant-garde thrived during the interwar period, as the visual arts responded to the rapid transformations of twentieth-century society: new technologies, scientific discoveries, the abandonment of traditional beliefs, and the influence of non-Western cultures. Like the writers of the period, visual artists pushed the boundaries, moving far beyond the conventional tastes of average men and women.

Pablo Picasso pursued his experiments in "cubist" paintings that refused to offer a single perspective, depicting his subjects in angular broken forms. The "expressionists" argued that color and line expressed inherent psychological qualities, eliminating the need for a representational subject in paintings. A second group of expressionists claimed that their goal was "objectivity," by which they meant a candid appraisal of the state of humanity. Chief among this group was German George Grosz (*Grohz*; 1893–1959), whose scathing cartoon-like images became the most popular portraits of the despised Weimar government.

The "dadaists" went further, rebelling against the very idea of aesthetic principles. Pulling their name at random from a dictionary, the dadaists rejected formal artistic conventions, preferring random juxtapositions of cutouts and collages, and bizarre assemblages of wood, glass, and metal. The leading dadaist artists—the Frenchman Marcel Duchamp, the German Max Ernst, and the Alsatian Jean (Hans) Arp—claimed their works were meaningless and playful, but critics saw them as expressions of the subconscious. In Germany, dadaism took on political undertones as the dadaists' anarchistic social critique challenged the very basis of national culture.

Other artists found inspiration for their work in social and political conflict. Many writers were veterans of World War I and sought to depict their experiences in realistic fiction. The French novelist Henri Barbusse published his combat story, *Under Fire*, in 1916, before the war was over; after the war, he joined the Communist party and became an outspoken pacifist. Erich Maria Remarque told a story about an ordinary German soldier in *All Quiet on the Western Front* (1928), a bestseller that was banned by the Nazis. Mexican muralists Diego Rivera and José Clemente Orozco and the Americans Thomas Hart Benton and Reginald Marsh sought to depict the social conditions of the modern world, presenting in graphic detail the lives of ordinary working people. These artists avoided the experimentalism of the dadaists and the expressionists, and aimed instead to create an intelligible art that was accessible to all.

Architects, too, rejected tradition, seeking a style that was more in harmony with the needs of modern civilization. Charles Édouard Jeanneret (known as Le Corbusier) in France, and Louis Sullivan and Frank Lloyd Wright in the United States pioneered a style known as functionalism. The functionalists believed that the appearance of a building should proclaim its use and purpose, and ornaments should be designed to reflect an age of science and machines. The German functionalist Walter Gropius established a school in 1919—the Bauhaus—as a center for the development of modern architecture. The Bauhaus design aesthetic, the so-called international style, explored the use of new materials, such as chromium, glass, steel, and concrete, becoming familiar after World War II as the "glass boxes" that populate the skylines of the world's major cities.

A REVOLUTION IN PHYSICS

The first decades of the twentieth century witnessed a scientific revolution in physics. Already in 1900, the German physicist Max Planck (1858–1947) had proved that light emerged from heated gases in specific "energy packets." A Danish physicist, Niels Bohr (1885–1962), proved that this phenomenon was related to the structure of each gas's atoms, and that each "quanta" of energy corresponded to electrons that occupied specific orbits around an atomic nucleus. By 1925, the German physicist Werner von Heisenberg (1879–1955) elaborated a theory of quantum mechanics to explain the physical properties of subatomic particles.

These remarkable breakthroughs were understood at the time by only a few specialists, but the pioneering work of German-born Albert Einstein (1879–1955) became much more well-known. Einstein wrote a series of articles that proposed an entirely new theory for thinking about space, matter, time, and gravity: the theory of general relativity. Ultimately, Einstein proved that light was not immune to gravity's effects as it moved through space, that massive objects could "bend" or "curve" space and time, and that time itself would be experienced differently by two observers moving at different speeds. Along with quantum mechanics, Einstein's theory of relativity became a central foundation for research in physics and astronomy in subsequent decades.

A practical application for these theoretical breakthroughs came in 1932 when the English physicist James Chadwick showed scientists how to split an atom by bombarding it with a newly discovered particle known as a neutron. In 1939, two German physicists, Otto Hahn and Fritz Strassmann, successfully split atoms of uranium and discovered that the initial collision produced a chain of reactions: each atom that was split shot off more neutrons, which split even more atoms, releasing extraordinary amounts of energy. Scientists in Germany, Great Britain, and the United States were spurred on by governments anxious to turn these discoveries into weapons during World War II, and American scientists eventually prepared an atomic bomb, the most destructive weapon ever created.

MASS CULTURE AND ITS POSSIBILITIES

Cultural change extended far beyond circles of artistic and intellectual elites. The explosive rise of mass media during the interwar years transformed popular culture and the lives of ordinary people. New media, especially radio and films, reached audiences of unprecedented size. Politicians used these new media, setting off worries that the common people—increasingly referred to as the "masses"—could be manipulated by demagogues and propaganda. In 1918, mass politics was rapidly becoming a fact of life, because of universal suffrage (varying by country), well-organized parties reaching out to voters, and increased participation in political life. Mass politics was accompanied by the rise of mass culture. Books, newspapers, films, and fashions were produced in large numbers and in standardized formats, which were less expensive and more accessible, appealing to many different kinds of people. Mass culture, at least in principle, cut across lines of class and ethnicity, and even nationality. The term *mass culture* can be misleading; the world of culture did not suddenly become homogeneous. No more than half the population read newspapers regularly; not everyone listened to the radio; and those who did, did not believe everything they heard. The pace of cultural change, however, quickened perceptibly. During the interwar years, mass culture showed that it held both democratic and authoritarian potential.

The expansion of mass culture rested on the widespread applications of existing technologies. Wireless communication was invented before the turn of the twentieth century, but the radio industry did not boom until the 1920s, after major financial

Popular media forms grow increasingly inexpensive and accessible, producing so-called "mass culture"

***VOICE OF THE PEOPLE, VOICE OF GOD*, BY GEORGE GROSZ (1920).** Industrialization, the First World War, and political change combined to make early twentieth-century Berlin a center of mass culture and communication. In this drawing, the radical artist and social critic George Grosz deplores the newspapers' power over public opinion. That public opinion could be manipulated was a common theme for many who wrote about early twentieth-century democracy. **> How does this cynicism about the public sphere compare with the attitudes of earlier defenders of free speech, such as John Stuart Mill?**

The Fascist Spectacle of Mass Participation

Like other revolutionary movements, fascism in Italy and national socialism in Germany needed to project an image of popular support for their political programs. As far back as the French Revolution of 1789, representations of "the people" as political actors took on special significance in revolutionary propaganda (see *Interpreting Visual Evidence* on pages 634–35). Both Hitler and Mussolini understood how to use such images to create the impression of an organic and seamless connection between the party's leadership and the rank and file who made up the movement.

Representations of the people in nineteenth-century liberal revolutionary movements emphasized an activist definition of political participation, as citizens came together to constitute a national body that reflected the will of the movements. Both Italian fascism and German

A. Benito Mussolini visits a youth camp, where recruits to his Blackshirts were in training, 1935.

B. Image from Leni Riefenstahl's *Triumph of the Will* (1935), a film about a Nazi party rally in Nuremberg, Germany, in 1934.

investments. Three out of four British families had a radio by the end of the 1930s; in Germany, the ratio was even higher. In Europe, broadcasting rights were controlled by the governments, but in the United States radio was managed by corporations. The radio broadcast soon became the national soapbox for politicians, and it played no small role in creating new kinds of political language. President Franklin Roosevelt's reassuring "fireside chats" took advantage of the way radio bridged the public world of politics and the private world of the home. Hitler cultivated a different kind of radio personality, barking his fierce invectives on the air; he made some fifty addresses in 1933 alone. In Germany, Nazi propagandists beamed their messages into homes or blared them through loudspeakers in town squares, constant and repetitive. Broadcasting created new rituals of political life, and new means of communication and persuasion.

C. Women of the British Union of Fascists model their uniforms.

national socialism defined themselves in opposition to democratic or parliamentary regimes, explicitly rejecting the individualism that was the basis for liberal citizenship. In their orchestration of public celebrations for their programs, both fascists and national socialists emphasized images of obedience and subordination to the leader (image A) and to the national movement (image B). Although the pageantry of fascism and national socialism typically emphasized an aggressively masculine image of enthusiastic devotion, most fascist movements also organized special female sections within their movements. In these groups, women would clothe themselves in uniforms (image C), as did their male counterparts, and express their own allegiance to the spirit of self-sacrifice that was at the heart of such collective movements.

Questions for Analysis

1. Each of these images was carefully staged and orchestrated to project a specific message. What are the messages implied in these images? What details are important?

2. What do these images tell us about the place of the individual in a fascist society?

3. What sense of belonging do you think these images are designed to produce? What made such images attractive to so many people?

So did advertising. Advertising was not new, but it was newly prominent. Businesses spent vastly more on advertising than before. Hard-hitting visual images replaced older ones that simply announced products, prices, and brand names. Many observers considered advertising the most "modern" of art forms because its efficient communication—streamlined and standardized—produced images that appealed to all. It also drew on modern psychology: advertising agencies used social science to influence the behavior of consumers. In a world remade by mass politics, and at a moment when the purchasing power of the common people was beginning to rise, the stakes in advertising (as in much of mass culture) were high.

The most dramatic changes came to movie screens. The technology of moving pictures had arrived earlier. The 1890s were the era of nickelodeons and short action pictures, and film was further popularized by news shorts during the war. When sound was added to movies in 1927, costs soared, competition intensified, and audiences grew rapidly. By the 1930s, an estimated 40 percent of British adults went to the movies once a week, a strikingly high figure, and many went more often. The U.S. film industry gained a competitive edge in Europe, buoyed by the size of its home market, huge investments in equipment and distribution, aggressive marketing, and Hollywood's star system of long-term contracts with well-known actors.

Germany, too, was home to a particularly talented group of directors, writers, and actors, and a major production company, UFA (Universum Film AG), which ran the largest and best-equipped studios in Europe. The history of UFA paralleled that of the country: it was run by the government during the First World War, devastated by the economic crisis of the early 1920s, rescued by wealthy German nationalists in the late 1920s, and finally taken over by the Nazis. During the Weimar years, UFA produced some of the most remarkable films of the period, including *Der letzte Mann* ("The Last Man"; released as *The Last Laugh* in English), a universally acclaimed film directed by F. W. Murnau, one of the two great masters of German expressionism. Fritz Lang was the other, directing such masterpieces as the science-fiction film *Metropolis* (1927) and his most famous German film, *M* (1931). After Hitler's rise to power, the Nazis took control of UFA and placed it under the control of Joseph Goebbels and the Ministry of Propaganda. Though production continued unabated during the Third Reich, many of the industry's most talented members fled from the oppressive regime, ending the golden age of German cinema.

Many Europeans found the new mass culture disturbing. Some perceived the United States, which deluged Europe with cultural exports after the war, as a threat. Hollywood westerns, cheap dime novels, and jazz music—which became increasingly popular in the 1920s—introduced Europe to new ways of life. Advertising, comedies, and romances disseminated new and often disconcerting images of femininity; with bobbed haircuts and short dresses, "new women" seemed assertive, flirtatious, capricious, and materialistic. The Wild West genre was popular with teenage boys, much to the dismay of their parents and teachers who saw westerns as an inappropriate, low-class form of entertainment. In Europe, the cross-class appeal of American popular culture grated against long-standing social hierarchies. American critics expressed many of the same concerns, but the United States enjoyed more social and political stability than Europe. War and revolution had shaken Europe's economies and cultures, and, in that context, "Americanization" seemed a handy shorthand for economic as well as cultural change.

Authoritarian governments decried these developments as decadent threats to national culture. Fascist, communist, and Nazi governments tried to control both elite and popular culture. In the early years of the Soviet Union, Russian filmmakers had been enormously innovative. Sergei Eisenstein (1898–1948) is often credited with developing the *montage*, a technique for creating visual narration in film through effective editing and quick cuts from different perspectives. His films from the 1920s, including *Strike* (1925), *Battleship Potemkin* (1925), and *October* (1928), were hugely influential, revealing new possibilities for the medium with their dramatic use of camera angles and startling juxtapositions of images. Stalin, however, preferred a more conservative socialist realism to the new Soviet avant-garde, and so Eisenstein was forced to make more conventional films in the 1930s.

Mussolini had a penchant for classical kitsch, though he was far more accepting of modern art than Hitler, who despised its supposed decadence. Nazism had its own cultural aesthetic, which promoted "Aryan" art and architecture and rejected the modern, international style that the Nazis associated with the "international Jewish conspiracy." Modernism, functionalism, and atonality were banned; thus the hallmarks of Weimar Germany's cultural preeminence were replaced by a state-sponsored revival of an alleged mystical and heroic past. Walter Gropius's acclaimed experiments in modernist architecture, for example, stood as monuments to everything the Nazis hated. The Bauhaus school was closed in 1933, and Hitler hired Albert Speer as his personal architect, commissioning him to design grandiose neoclassical buildings, including an extravagant plan to rebuild the entire city of Berlin.

The Nazis, like other authoritarian governments, used mass media as an efficient means of indoctrination and control. Movies became part of the Nazis' pioneering use of "spectacular politics": media campaigns, mass rallies, parades, and ceremonies were all designed to display the strength and glory of the Reich as well as to impress and intimidate spectators. In 1934, Hitler commissioned filmmaker Leni Riefenstahl to record a political rally staged by herself and Albert Speer in Nuremberg. The film, *Triumph of the Will*, was a visual hymn to the Nordic race and the Nazi regime. Everything in it was on a grand scale—masses of bodies stood in parade formation, and flags rose and fell in unison—inviting viewers to surrender to the power of the stately ritual and symbolism. The comedian Charlie Chaplin riposted this film in his celebrated lampoon *The Great Dictator* (1940), an enormously successful parody of Nazi pomposities.

Regarding culture, the Nazis were forced to strike a balance between party propaganda and popular entertainment. The Nazis tried to eliminate the influences of American popular culture, which they had decried as an example of biological and cultural degeneracy even before 1933. Critics, for instance, associated American dances and jazz—both increasingly popular in German cities—with what the Nazis deemed "racially inferior" Blacks and Jews. The regime, however, allowed many cultural imports, including Hollywood films, to continue while consciously cultivating German alternatives to American cinema, music, fashion, and even dances. Joseph Goebbels, the minister of propaganda who controlled most film production, placed a high value on economic viability. During the Third Reich, the German film industry turned out comedies, escapist fantasies, and sentimental romances; developed its own star system; and tried to keep audiences happy, while becoming a major competitor internationally. For domestic consumption, the industry also produced vicious antisemitic films, such as *The Eternal Jew* (1940) and *Jew Süss* (1940), a fictional tale of a Jewish moneylender who brings the city of Württemberg to ruin in the eighteenth century. In the final scene of the film, the town expels the entire Jewish community from its midst, asking that "posterity honor this law." Goebbels reported that the entire Reich cabinet had viewed the film and considered it "an incredible success."

Authoritarian governments use new forms of mass media for indoctrination and social control

Conclusion

The strains of the First World War created a world that few recognized—transformed by revolution, mass mobilization, and loss. In retrospect, it is hard not to see the period that followed as a succession of failures: capitalism foundered in the Great Depression, democracies collapsed in the face of authoritarianism, and the Treaty of Versailles proved hollow. Stalin's Soviet Union paid a terrible price for the creation of a modern industrial economy, with years of famine, political repression, and state terror. Hitler's Germany and Mussolini's Italy offered a vision of the future that held no comfort for those committed to basic human freedoms and equality under the law. We can better understand the experiences

AFTER YOU READ THIS CHAPTER ⌄

CHRONOLOGY

1918	The November Revolution establishes the Weimar Republic in Germany
1918–1920	Russian civil war
1920	National Socialist German Workers' party founded in Germany
1922	Mussolini comes to power in Italy
1923	Hitler's Beer Hall Putsch in Munich
1928	First Soviet Five-Year Plan
1928–1929	Stalin gains power in Russia
1929–1933	Collectivization and famine in Soviet Union
1933	Hitler becomes chancellor of Germany
1936–1938	The Great Terror in the Soviet Union

REVIEWING THE OBJECTIVES

❯ After 1917, the Bolsheviks in Russia debated how fast they should move to reorganize society along the lines demanded by their revolutionary ideology. What circumstances determined the outcome of this debate? What were the consequences of Stalin's revolution from above in the 1930s?

❯ Mussolini's Fascist party offered an alternative to Italian voters who were disappointed with their government in the aftermath of the First World War. What was fascism? How did Mussolini come to power?

❯ The Weimar Republic failed in its attempt to establish a stable democracy in Germany, while other democracies in France, Britain, and the United States underwent severe strain. What challenges did democratic regimes face during the interwar period?

❯ Hitler came to power legally in 1933 through the German electoral system. What did he stand for? Why did so many Germans support his cause?

❯ The Great Depression forced European and North American nations to reassess their assumptions about the how governments should react to economic crises. What challenges did the depression create for the United States, France, Britain, and Germany, and what policies did these governments pursue?

❯ Artists, writers, and other intellectuals of the interwar period could not help but reflect the atmosphere of social and political crisis in their work. How did artists and writers react to the crisis of the interwar period?

and outlooks of ordinary people if we do not treat the failures of the interwar period as inevitable. By the late 1920s, many were cautiously optimistic that the Great War's legacy could be overcome and that problems were being solved. The Great Depression, however, wrecked these hopes, bringing economic chaos and political paralysis. Paralysis and chaos, in turn, created new audiences for political leaders offering authoritarian solutions, attracting more voters to their political parties. Finally, economic troubles and political turmoil made contending with rising international tensions, to which we now turn, vastly more difficult. By the 1930s, even cautious optimism about international relations had given way to apprehension and dread.

Go to **INQUIZITIVE** to see what you've learned—and learn what you've missed—with personalized feedback along the way.

PEOPLE, IDEAS, AND EVENTS IN CONTEXT

> What was the difference between the Bolshevik policies of **WAR COMMUNISM** and the **NEW ECONOMIC POLICY (NEP)**?

> What were **JOSEPH STALIN**'s goals in implementing his catastrophic plan for **COLLECTIVIZATION** of agriculture? What did he hope to accomplish with his purging of an entire generation of Bolshevik leaders, along with millions of other Soviet citizens, in the **GREAT TERROR**?

> What was the basis of **BENITO MUSSOLINI**'s rejection of liberal democracy? What kinds of changes followed in Italian society after the adoption of **FASCISM** as the official state ideology?

> How did **ADOLF HITLER**'s economic policy contribute to a drive toward political extremism?

> How important was **ANTISEMITISM** to Hitler's political career? What do events such as *KRISTALLNACHT* tell us about the depth of German antisemitism?

> How did the principle of **WHITE SUPREMACY** perpetuate discrimination and violence toward Black Americans during the interwar years?

> How did the **NEW DEAL** in the United States or the popular front in France attempt to respond to the economic crisis of the **GREAT DEPRESSION**?

THINKING ABOUT CONNECTIONS

> What did Soviet communism, German national socialism, and Italian fascism have in common during the years 1919–1939? What made them different from each other?

> How much of the crisis of the interwar period can be attributed to the effects of the First World War or the economic upheaval of the Great Depression? How might one understand the ideological conflicts of these years as the result of a much longer history?

26

The Second World War

IN 1939, ADOLF HITLER WANTED WAR. By March of that year, he revealed to the world the weakness of the French and British governments, which had stood by while he dismantled Czechoslovakia, a democratic nation created at the end of World War I. He turned next to Poland, confident that Britain and France could do little to prevent him from fulfilling his pledge to conquer territories for the German people. Before he could invade Poland, however, he needed an understanding with another long-standing enemy: the Soviet Union of Joseph Stalin. Since 1934, Stalin had participated in a broad-based antifascist coalition in Europe, the Popular Front. This alliance had brought the Soviets to side with the "bourgeois democracies" that were their sworn enemies. The Popular Front also led the Soviets to support the republican side in the Spanish Civil War; the Nationalists were backed by Hitler's Germany and Mussolini's Italian fascists. Hitler's propaganda campaign against the Soviets was relentless. He portrayed the Soviet regime as a cabal run by Jewish communists, and constantly referred to Stalin's commissar for foreign affairs, Maxim Litvinov, whose brother was a rabbi, as "Finkelstein." Given this history, what possible understanding could Hitler hope to achieve with Stalin?

By 1939, Stalin had been forced to recalculate his alliances in Europe. The Republicans' loss in the Spanish Civil War and the failure of France and Britain to uphold their obligations to preserve the international order

BEFORE
YOU
READ
THIS
CHAPTER

> In the 1930s, Hitler's Germany and Mussolini's Italy allied with imperial Japan to form the Axis. The Axis eventually provoked the Second World War against a group of Allied powers that included Britain, the United States, Canada, Australia, and the Soviet Union.

> The Nazi regime's military successes in 1939–1941 brought almost all of Europe under German control. The Russian victory at Stalingrad in 1942 proved to be a turning point, and from 1942 to 1945, the Allies progressively rolled back the German and Japanese armies, leading to Allied victory in 1945.

> The Nazi state embarked on a genocidal project of mass murder to exterminate its perceived racial and ideological enemies: Europe's Jews, homosexuals, the Roma, and the Slavic populations of Russia and eastern Europe were targets for conquest and subjugation

> Attacks on civilian populations and the plundering of resources by occupying armies made the Second World War a "total war," in which the distinction between military and home front meant little for many Europeans.

CORE OBJECTIVES

> **IDENTIFY** the broader political and economic causes of the Second World War.

> **EXPLAIN** the reasons for the British and French policy of "appeasement" when faced with Hitler's violations of international law.

> **UNDERSTAND** the consequences of German conquest and occupation on European nations and their populations, and the challenges met by those who chose to resist.

> **DESCRIBE** how the Holocaust became possible after Germany's conquest of territory in eastern Europe during the invasion of the Soviet Union.

> **UNDERSTAND** the military operations that led to the defeat of the Nazi regime and their allies in Europe.

> **EXPLAIN** the main areas of conflict in Asia and the Pacific, and the circumstances that led to the Japanese surrender in 1945.

guaranteed by the Versailles peace treaty led the Soviet leader to believe that his regime had no choice but to come to an agreement with Hitler, in an attempt to gain time to prepare for a war that now seemed inevitable. His hope was that the other European powers—France, Britain, Italy, and Germany—would weaken themselves in a general war, thus benefiting the Soviet Union. To show his willingness to talk, he fired Litvinov on May 3 and replaced him with his closest adviser, Vyacheslav Molotov (1890–1986), an ethnic Russian. In August, Hitler responded by sending his own foreign minister, Joachim von Ribbentrop (1893–1946), to Moscow to meet with Stalin. When the German envoy arrived, the Moscow airport was decorated with swastikas. The two sides cynically agreed to carve up Poland between them, and announced the agreement on August 23, 1939. The world was shocked to discover that these two powers, sworn ideological enemies, had made common cause to destroy Poland. On September 1, 1939, Hitler invaded Poland from the west and two weeks later, Soviet troops entered Poland from the east. The Second World War had begun.

The **Second World War** was a conflict among nations, whole populations, and fiercely opposing ideals. Adolf Hitler, and his supporters in Germany and abroad, cast the conflict as a racial war against the twin enemies of national socialism: the democracies in western Europe and the United States on the one hand, and the communist order of the Soviet Union on the other. Hitler's opponents in the West and the East believed just as fervently that they were defending a way of life and a vision of justice that was bigger than the narrow definitions of national interest.

Belief that the world was now characterized by ideologies and world-views that were in mortal combat with one another meant that the scale of the killing overtook even that of the First World War. In 1914, military firepower outmatched mobility, resulting in four years of static, mud-soaked slaughter. In 1939, firepower and mobility were joined on a massive scale, with terrifying results. On the battlefield, the tactics of high-speed armored warfare, aircraft carriers sinking ships far below the horizon, and submarines deployed in vast numbers to dominate shipping lanes changed the scope and the pace of combat. This was not a war of trenches and barbed wire but a war of motion, dramatic conquests, and terrible destructive power. The devastation of 1914–1918 paled in comparison to this new, global conflict.

The other great change involved targets, not tactics. Much of the unprecedented killing power now available was aimed directly at civilians. Cities were laid waste by artillery and aerial bombing, whole regions were put to the torch, and towns and villages were systematically cordoned off and leveled. Whole populations were targeted as well, in ways that continue to appall. The Nazi regime's systematic murder of Roma, homosexuals, and other "deviants," along with the effort to exterminate the Jewish people completely, drove the combatants in the Second World War to unprecedented levels of destruction. So did the United States' use of a weapon whose existence would dominate politics and society for the next fifty years: the atomic bomb.

The naive enthusiasm that had marked the outbreak of the Great War was absent from the start, as terrible memories of the first conflict still lingered. Yet those who fought against the Axis powers (and many who fought for them) found that their determination to fight and win grew as the war went on. Unlike the seemingly meaningless killing of the Great War, the Second World War was cast as a war of absolutes, of good versus evil, of national and global survival. Nevertheless, the scale of destruction brought with it a profound weariness. It also provoked deep-seated questions about the value of Western "civilization," weakened Europe's imperial powers, and raised for the first time the possibility of destructive wars capable of destroying human society altogether.

The Causes of the War: Unsettled Quarrels, Economic Fallout, and Nationalism

The obvious cause of the outbreak of the Second World War in Europe in 1939 was the aggressively expansionist policy of Hitler's Germany. Beyond these immediate circumstances, historians have isolated three long-term causes, which set the stage for the confrontation between 1939 and 1945: the failure to create international guarantees for peace and security after 1918, the successive economic crises of the interwar years, and the violent forms of nationalism that emerged in Europe during the 1930s.

The Versailles treaty of 1919–1920 created new nations out of the ruins of the eastern European empires: Austria, Czechoslovakia, Poland, Hungary, Yugoslavia, as well as Finland and the Baltic states of Estonia, Latvia, and Lithuania. Some peoples in this region—the Poles especially—welcomed this as a recognition of their long-standing claims for independence from empires that they viewed as foreign powers. At the same time, however, the borders of the new states crossed ethnic boundaries and created new minorities without protecting them. These borders also depended on the willingness of other powers—especially France and Britain—to defend them. Ultimately, these boundaries would be redrawn by force in the 1930s, after Hitler had rearmed Germany.

Diplomats spent the decade after 1919 trying to establish standards for peace and security in Europe. In 1925, the Locarno Accords secured the German-French frontier in order to reassure the French against any resurgence of German expansionism. In 1928, the Kellogg-Briand Pact made war an international crime. But these pacts carried no real weight, and they revealed the unwillingness on the part of France and Britain to actively defend the borders of central Europe's new nation-states. Had the League of Nations been better organized, it might have relieved some of the tensions. But the League was never a league of all nations: essential members were absent, Germany and the Soviet Union were excluded for most of the interwar period, and the United States never joined.

Long-term causes of World War II: (1) Demands for redrawing national boundaries in Europe after World War I

Economic conditions were an additional important cause of the renewed conflict. The reparations imposed on the Germans and France's occupation of much of Germany's industrial heartland slowed Germany's recovery. German and French stubbornness about the pace of repayments combined disastrously to bring on the German inflation of the early 1920s. The spiraling inflation made German money nearly worthless, damaging the stability and credibility of Germany's young republic almost beyond repair (Chapter 25).

(2) Effects of the Great Depression on European economies and politics

The depression of the 1930s contributed to the coming of the war by intensifying economic nationalism and weakening democratic governments when they were under siege by political extremists. Baffled by problems of unemployment and

Long-term causes
of World War II:
(3) Polarizing collision
between violent
nationalisms and
class-based political
movements

>

business stagnation, governments imposed high tariffs in an effort to preserve their home markets for their own producers. The collapse of investment and soaring domestic unemployment brought the Nazis to power in Germany, exacerbated political battles between left and right in France, and caused the United States to withdraw from world affairs. Britain turned to its empire, raising tariffs for the first time and guarding its financial investments jealously.

The decisive factor in the outbreak of another world war lay in a blend of violent nationalism and polarizing ideologies that glorified violent struggle against enemies. Despite the misgivings of many in the governments of Britain and France, Germany was allowed to ignore the terms of the peace treaties and rearm. Large-scale armaments expansion first began in Germany under Hitler in 1935, which reduced unemployment and eased the effects of the depression. Other nations followed the German example, not only to boost their economies but also in response to growing Nazi power.

Imperial success served as consolation when economic methods failed. As the depression dragged on in fascist Italy, Mussolini tried to distract his public with conquests overseas, culminating in the invasion of Ethiopia in 1935. Hitler, too, argued that Germany's dynamically superior "race" needed "room for living" (*Lebensraum*) in the east. The expansionist policies of Italy and Germany incentivized them to challenge the international order set up after the First World War, leading to a separate treaty between the two fascist nations in 1936, known as the "Rome-Berlin Axis." In the Pacific, meanwhile, the effects of the depression encouraged Japanese imperialism. Japanese leaders, convinced of the cultural inferiority of the Chinese, invaded China in order to take control over the East Asian economy. They began in 1931 with the invasion of Manchuria, and then moved to create a "Greater Pacific Co-Prosperity Sphere" by seizing other territories as Japanese colonies. The common imperial goals of Germany, Italy, and Japan culminated in the enlargement of the Axis, which formally became a military alliance among the three nations in 1939.

The 1930s: Challenges to the Peace and Appeasement

The 1930s witnessed simultaneous economic and political crises at a global scale. Fascist and nationalist governments flouted the League of Nations by launching new conquests and efforts at nationalist expansion. Each new conflict seemed to warn of another, much wider war to come unless it could somehow be averted. Ordinary people—particularly in Britain, France, and the United States—were divided; some argued that aggressors had to be met with force, while others hoped to avoid premature or unnecessary conflict. Their governments, meanwhile, tried to negotiate with the fascists at several points in the hopes that they could maintain the peace through "appeasement."

Appeasement was grounded in several deeply held assumptions. The first, widely shared, was that provoking another war was unthinkable. The 1914–1918 slaughter and its aftermath left many in the West embracing pacifism, and the democratically elected officials in France and Britain believed that an aggressive

appeasement The policy pursued by Western governments, which attempted to accommodate and negotiate peace in the face of German, Italian, and Japanese aggression leading up to the Second World War.

response to Hitler's provocations might result in diminished support for their governments. Second, many appeasers were staunch anticommunists. They believed that the fascist states in Germany and Italy were an essential bulwark against the advance of Soviet communism, and that division among the major European states only played into the hands of the Soviet Union. Even those who believed that the Nazis posed the greater threat argued that appeasement was the only option until Britain and France finished rearming, at which point they hoped their greater military power would deter Hitler or Mussolini from risking a general European war. It took most of the 1930s for the debate among appeasers to come to a head.

The 1930s brought three crucial challenges to the international order: crises in China, Ethiopia, and Spain. In China, the Japanese invasion of Manchuria in 1931 turned into an invasion of the whole country. Chinese forces were routed before the Japanese advance, and the Japanese deliberately targeted civilians to break their will to fight. In 1937, the Japanese laid siege to the strategic city of Nanjing. Their orders on taking the city were simple: "kill all, burn all, destroy all." More than 200,000 Chinese citizens were killed in what came to be known as the "Rape of Nanjing." The League of Nations voiced shock and disapproval but did nothing. In 1935, Mussolini began his efforts to build an Italian empire by returning to Ethiopia to avenge the defeat of 1896. The Ethiopians fought bravely but hopelessly, because this time, the Italians came with tanks, bombers, and poison gas. This imperial massacre also aroused world denunciation but little practical response. Enforcing sanctions on Italy or Japan would require military or naval action, and neither France nor Britain was ready to undertake such an effort.

THE SPANISH CIVIL WAR

A new challenge arose in Europe in 1936, when civil war broke out in Spain. Right-wing military officers under General Francisco Franco (who ruled after the civil war in 1939 until his death in 1975) attempted to overthrow the Spanish Republic and seize power. Although Hitler and Mussolini had signed a pact of nonintervention with the other Western powers, both leaders sent troops and equipment to assist Franco's Nationalist forces. The Soviet Union then countered with aid to communist troops serving under the banner of the Spanish Republic. Thousands of volunteers from all over Europe and North America who saw the war as a test of Europe's determination to resist fascism and military dictatorship also took up arms as private soldiers for the Republican government, including many working-class socialists and writers

THE SPANISH CIVIL WAR. › Why did thousands of foreign fighters join the war? › How did the strategies and weapons used in the war anticipate those used in the Second World War? › What were the consequences of Franco's victory?

ANTIFASCIST PROPAGANDA, SPANISH CIVIL WAR. This poster, produced by a left-wing labor organization affiliated with the international anarchist movement, shows a worker delivering a killing blow to a fascist snake.

such as George Orwell of Britain and Ernest Hemingway of the United States.

The United States, France, and Britain remained neutral in the Spanish Civil War. For the British, Franco was useful as an anticommunist, just like Mussolini and the Japanese. But the French prime minister Léon Blum stood at the head of a Popular Front government—an alliance of socialists, communists, and republicans—which had been elected on a program of social reform and opposition to fascism in France and abroad. Blum feared that intervening in Spain would further polarize his country, and bring down his government. Without allies, the Republican camp in Spain degenerated into a hornet's nest of competing factions among republican, socialist, communist, and anarchist groups.

The Spanish Civil War resulted in more than half a million deaths over three years and ended in victory for Franco in 1939. Both the German and the Soviet "advisers" saw it as a "dress rehearsal" for a later war between the two powers, and each deployed their newest weapons and practiced their skills in destroying civilian targets from the air. In April 1937, a raid by German dive bombers utterly destroyed the town of Guernica in northern Spain. The raid was commemorated by Pablo Picasso in one of the most famous paintings of the twentieth century. The Republican loyalists responded with a punishing violence of their own, focusing especially on the Catholic Church, which they identified as a supporter of General Franco's Nationalist movement. Attacks on priests and monasteries were frequent, and tens of thousands of people were executed behind the front lines.

Hitler drew two lessons from Spain. The first was that if Britain, France, and the Soviet Union ever tried to contain fascism, they would have a hard time coordinating their efforts. The second was that Britain and France were deeply averse to fighting another European war, which meant that the Nazis could use every means short of war to achieve their goals.

GERMAN REARMAMENT AND THE POLITICS OF APPEASEMENT

In 1933, Hitler removed Germany from the League of Nations, to which it had finally been admitted in 1926. In 1935, he revived conscription and military training, ignoring the disarmament provisions in the Versailles treaty. In 1936, Germany reoccupied the Rhineland, along the border with France, a move that risked a war with the much more powerful French army. But France and Britain did not mount a military response. In retrospect, this was an important turning point, where the balance of power tipped in Germany's favor.

In March 1938, Hitler annexed Austria, reaffirming his intention to bring all Germans into his Reich. Once more, no official reaction came from the

***GUERNICA*, BY PABLO PICASSO (1937).** *Guernica*, one of Picasso's most influential works, was painted as a mural for the Spanish Republican government during its fight for survival in the Spanish Civil War; the Basque town of Guernica had been bombed by German fighters just a few months earlier, in April 1937. Near the center, a horse writhes in agony; to the right a distraught woman holds her dead child. **› Compare this mural with the antifascist propaganda poster on the left. What is different about the way the two images deliver their political messages? › Does Picasso's rejection of realism diminish the power of his political message? › Does the antifascist poster seek any outcome other than the annihilation of the enemy?**

West. The Nazis' next target was the Sudetenland in Czechoslovakia, a region with a large ethnic German population. With Austria now a part of Germany, Czechoslovakia was almost entirely surrounded by its hostile neighbor. Hitler declared that the Sudetenland was a natural part of the Reich and that he intended to occupy it.

Hitler's generals were wary of this gamble, because Czechoslovakia had a strong, well-equipped army and a line of fortifications along the border. Some in the French government argued in favor of coming to the aid of the Czechs, but Poland and Hungary actively supported Hitler's claims against Czechoslovakia, hoping to gain from an eventual partition or at least to strengthen their positions before Hitler turned his attention on them. In the end, Hitler pushed his claim on the Sudetenland, and the British prime minister Neville Chamberlain (1937–1940) ultimately agreed to Hitler's terms. Chamberlain's logic was that if Hitler were allowed to unify all Germans in one state, then German ambitions would be satisfied. Chamberlain also believed that defending eastern European boundaries against Germany ranked low on Great Britain's list of priorities, at least in comparison to ensuring free trade in western Europe and protecting the strategic centers of the British Empire.

On September 29, 1938, Hitler met with Chamberlain, Premier Édouard Daladier (1938–1940) of France, and Mussolini in the four-power **Munich Conference.**

Munich Conference (1938)
Hitler met with the leaders of Britain, France, and Italy and negotiated an agreement that gave Germany a major slice of Czechoslovakia.

GERMAN SOLDIERS ENTER COLOGNE IN THE RHINELAND, 1936. Hitler's reoccupation of the Rhineland—an area bordering France, Belgium, and the Netherlands—was a direct violation of the Treaty of Versailles, but it was difficult for the French and British governments to respond effectively, because voters in these nations were reluctant to go to war over Hitler's decision to move troops into what was, after all, German territory.

The four negotiators bargained away a major slice of Czechoslovakia while Czech representatives were left to await their fate outside the conference room. Chamberlain returned to London, proclaiming "peace in our time," but Hitler soon proved that boast hollow. In March 1939, Germany invaded what was left of Czechoslovakia, annexed Bohemia and Moravia, and established a puppet regime in Slovakia. This was Germany's first conquest of territory that did not have a significant German population, and it sent shock waves across Europe, revealing the futility of appeasement. The British and the French strived to speed up their rearmament dramatically. Together with France, Britain guaranteed the sovereignty of the two states now directly in Hitler's path: Poland and Romania.

Hitler perceived an opportunity in this impasse and secretly promised Stalin a share of Poland, Finland, the Baltic states, and Bessarabia (a part of Romania bordering Ukraine) if the Soviet Union remained neutral in the event of war between Germany and Poland. Stalin seized his chance. An agreement with the Nazis offered the possibility of immediate Soviet expansion into Poland and the Baltic region, and no war with Germany. The alternative was less palatable: an alliance with faraway Britain and France, ideological opponents of his regime, and an obligation to protect Poland in the event of a German attack. In August 1939, the world was shocked to hear that the Soviets had reversed their long-standing anti-Nazi position and signed a nonaggression pact with Hitler. With the **Hitler-Stalin Pact**, sometimes known as the Molotov-Ribbentrop Pact after the Soviet and Nazi diplomats who signed it, Stalin bought himself some time and a promise of significant territory along the Soviet Union's western frontier. For the Poles and the peoples of the Baltic nations, however, the Nazi-Soviet Pact placed them squarely between two hostile and expansionist powers, making them more dependent than ever on the support of their distant allies.

Hitler-Stalin Pact (1939) Treaty between Stalin and Hitler that promised Stalin a share of Poland, Finland, the Baltic states, and Bessarabia in the event of a German invasion of Poland.

Map legend:

GERMANY
- Reoccupied Rhineland, March 1936
- Annexed Austria, March 1938
- Annexed Sudetenland, October 1938
- Annexed Bohemia and Moravia, March 1939
- Annexed Memel, March 1939

ITALY
- Annexed Albania, April 1939

POLAND AND HUNGARY
- Annexed Czech territory, 1938 and 1939

( ) Former independent nations: Albania, Austria, and Czechoslovakia

GERMAN AND ITALIAN EXPANSION, 1936–1939. › What were Hitler's first steps in unifying all the ethnic Germans in Europe? › How did Hitler use these initial gains to annex territory from the Czechs? › After winning Czechoslovakia, why did Hitler choose to invade Poland?

The Beginning of the War in Europe

Poland invaded by both Nazi Germany and the Soviet Union, with devastating consequences for the Polish population

With the Soviets now in his camp, Hitler believed that Poland had no choice but to acquiesce to the annexation and that the Western allies would back down once again. Poland, however, stood firm, and Hitler attacked. On September 1, 1939, German troops crossed the western Polish border, and Britain and France declared war on Germany two days later. The Second World War had begun.

The conquest of Poland took four weeks, and the results were devastating. Germany committed nearly all of its combat troops and planes to the invasion. Well-coordinated attacks by German *panzers* (tanks) and armored vehicles, supported by air power, cut the Polish army to pieces. The Poles fought doggedly but with little hope of mounting an effective defense against a well-equipped and larger force. The **Blitzkrieg** (*blitz-kreeg*; "lightning war") for which the German officer corps had trained for so long was a complete success. Within three weeks, German troops were laying siege to Warsaw. German terror bombing, designed to destroy the heart of Warsaw from the air and frighten the population into surrender, was successful. Historians have pointed out that the Polish military never expected to win this war. Their goal was to hold out for two weeks, enough time for the Western allies to fulfill their treaty obligations by launching an attack across the Rhine in Germany. The Polish army succeeded in this, but the Allied attack never came.

Instead, in accordance with its secret agreement with Nazi Germany, the Soviet Union moved its troops into eastern Poland after September 17. For the nearly two years that the Molotov-Ribbentrop Pact remained in effect (from August 1939 until the Nazi invasion of the Soviet Union in June 1941), Poland found itself divided in two, occupied by two hostile powers. The character of the respective occupations reflected the priorities of each regime. In Warsaw, the Germans immediately separated the Jews from the rest of the population, and the gates of the Jewish quarter were closed in November 1939. Close to 50,000 Poles were shot by German security police and soldiers in the fall of 1939. German-occupied Poland was subdivided in two parts, with the north and west absorbed into the German Reich, and the central and southern areas placed under a separate military administration, the General Government. The Germans instituted martial law with only two punishments: death or deportation to a concentration camp.

On the Russian side of occupied Poland, the Soviet army used Stalin's signature methods to deal with the enemy—deportations, imprisonments, and executions. The goal was to prevent the establishment of an independent Poland at war's end. Nearly 22,000 people—Polish military officers and police officials along with a number of arrested professionals and intellectuals, some Jewish—were executed. Mass deportations—in many ways a continuation of the Soviet purges of the late 1930s—sent more than 600,000 Poles, in locked railway cars without adequate food or heat, thousands of miles to the east to forced labor camps in central Asia and Siberia. During the same period, the Soviets invaded Finland, eking out a precarious victory in a four-month "Winter War" of 1939–1940.

After the fall of Poland, the war between the Western allies and Germany became an ominous "phony war," as Britain and France struggled to ready themselves. In the spring of 1940, the Germans struck in Scandinavia, taking Denmark in a day and invading Norway. On May 10, German forces invaded Belgium and the Netherlands on their way to France, conquering both nations in short order. In the weeks that followed, the French army was carved up by the Blitzkrieg. Its divisions

Blitzkrieg The German "lightning war" strategy used during the Second World War; the Germans invaded Poland, France, Russia, and other countries with fast-moving and well-coordinated attacks.

were isolated, outflanked, and overwhelmed by German aircraft and armored columns working according to an exacting plan. French units fought fierce battles until they were hopelessly surrounded or simply collapsed. In the face of rapid German maneuvers, the French defeat quickly turned into a rout. Hundreds of thousands of civilians fled south, where they were joined by thousands of Allied soldiers without weapons. These columns of refugees were attacked constantly by German dive bombers. British soldiers supporting the French made a desperate retreat to the port of Dunkirk on the English Channel. Despite heavy German air attacks, Britain's Royal Navy evacuated more than 300,000 British and French troops, with the help of commercial and pleasure boats that had been pressed into emergency service.

After Dunkirk, the outcome was inevitable. French reservists fought "to the last cartridge," but could not stop the Germans from reaching Paris in mid-June 1940. The French army faced enormous losses with 100,000 soldiers killed, nearly 2 million imprisoned, and 3,000 African soldiers, fighting for the French, who were executed by the German army. The political will of France's government collapsed along with its armies, and the French surrendered on June 22. The armistice cut the country in two. The Germans occupied all of northern France, including Paris and the Channel ports. The south and the French territories in North Africa lay under the jurisdiction of a conservative government formed at the spa town of Vichy (*VIH-shee*), under the leadership of an elderly First World War hero, Marshal Philippe Pétain. A small Free French force was simultaneously founded in London under General Charles de Gaulle, but this movement was condemned by Pétain's government. De Gaulle eventually found the first supporters of his resistance movement in the French colonial territories west and central Africa, which remained far from German control.

The penalties exacted on France did not end with its defeat. Supporters of the republic within France and de Gaulle's Free French movement soon felt they had two enemies to fight: Germany and Pétain's regime. The Vichy government collaborated

France's Vichy regime, formed after military defeat and German occupation, seeks collaboration with Hitler in bid to preserve sovereignty

with the Germans in return for a small measure of sovereignty, but this hope was ultimately misplaced. The Vichy Regime instituted its own National Revolution, which came very close to fascism, and repudiated France's republican institutions. The state reorganized French society, passed antisemitic legislation, cultivated allies within the French Catholic hierarchy, and helped the Germans crush any resistance. "Work, Family, and Fatherland" was Vichy's call to order.

Not Alone: The Battle of Britain and the Beginnings of a Global War

From July to November 1940, in the Battle of Britain, thousands of German planes dropped millions of tons of bombs on British targets, in preparation for an invasion across the English Channel. By the end of 1940, the British had effectively contested the German attempt to establish control of the skies, but German bombing raids continued until June 1941. More than 40,000 British civilians died. After a daring British bombing raid on Berlin, Hitler angrily told his generals to concentrate on civilian targets, which spared the Royal Air Force (RAF), whose bases had been steadily devastated up to that point. Given the chance to keep fighting, the RAF forced a costly stalemate in the air. Hitler then scrapped the invasion plans and turned his attention east toward Russia.

Britain's determined resistance was reinforced by a change in political leadership. In May 1940, Chamberlain's government was replaced by a coalition that brought together Conservative, Liberal, and Labour politicians for the sake of national unity. The new prime minister was Winston Churchill (1940–1945 and 1951–1955), a political maverick. Extremely talented and arrogant, he had a sharp temper, but he

LONDON DURING THE BATTLE OF BRITAIN. German air raids that lasted from July 1940 to June 1941 wrought destruction, but they did not achieve Hitler's goal of breaking the British. The Holland House Library in London lost its roof but still managed to engage in business as usual.

had an ability to inspire the British public with extraordinary words of courage and defiance when they needed it most.

Churchill also had a gift for personal diplomacy. He convinced the American president Franklin D. Roosevelt (1933–1945) to end American neutrality and send massive amounts of aid and weapons to Britain free of charge. Churchill also allowed the new government coalition to work: the ablest Conservative ministers stayed, and Labour politicians were allowed to take positions of genuine power. Most of the Labour representatives turned out to be excellent administrators and were directly in touch with Britain's huge working class, which now felt fully included in the war effort.

With Britain's survival, the war moved into different theaters: the Atlantic (a battle over sea-lanes and supplies), North Africa (strategically important for the Suez Canal and access to oil), the Pacific (the war with Japan), and the Soviet Union (where Hitler's determination to annihilate Stalin merged with his murderous campaign against the Jewish populations of Europe).

THE ATLANTIC AND NORTH AFRICA

Learning from the First World War, the Germans sent hundreds of submarines (U-boats) out in "wolf packs" to stalk the major sea-lanes to Britain. The ensuing Battle of the Atlantic was a dire threat to the Allies. Britain's supplies of weapons, raw materials, and food hung in the balance as German submarines sank millions of tons of merchant shipping. The British used technical resourcefulness to save their convoys, developing modern sonar and new systems of aerial reconnaissance. With help from a group of Polish mathematicians, the British cracked the German codes for communicating with submarines. These efforts kept the supplies coming until the United States entered the war in December 1941, and by late 1942, the threat to the major sea-lanes receded.

The war in North Africa stemmed from British efforts to protect the Suez Canal. Indian, South African, and West African troops, fighting for the British, drove the Italians from Ethiopia in May 1941. The Soviets and the British invaded Iran to keep the shah (ruler) from making a deal with Germany over Iranian oil, and held the country until 1946. A small British army in Egypt humiliated a much larger Italian invasion force, forcing Germany to intervene. Erwin Rommel's Afrika Korps drove the British back in the spring of 1941, starting a two-year war in the desert that pitted Australians, Indians, New Zealanders, Britons, and Poles against the Germans and the Italians. Despite heavy losses from German planes and submarines, the British eventually took control of the Mediterranean, and established domination in the air over North Africa. When Rommel tried to invade Egypt in July, his forces were badly defeated near the town of El Alamein, and driven back toward Tunisia later that fall.

The United States intervened in November 1942, landing in the French territories of Algeria and Morocco. An Allied conference was held at Casablanca, Morocco, to discuss the future course of the war and the fate of French territories in North Africa. French administrators in Algeria and Morocco, who had supported Vichy in public, surrendered peacefully or joined the Allied side. Rommel continued to defend Tunisia against the Allies for four months, but a joint offensive broke the German lines in March 1943, putting an end to the fighting. The Allied takeover of French Algeria weakened the Vichy Regime's territorial claims in North Africa, while at the same time an Algerian nationalist movement developed that would eventually seek independence from France after the war.

THE SECOND WORLD WAR IN EUROPE. › Which parts of Europe were controlled by the Allies and the Axis? › Which countries were neutral in 1941? › In what parts of Europe did the major Axis and Allied campaigns occur? › What was Germany's greatest geographical challenge during the Second World War?

THE ALLIES AND JAPAN IN THE PACIFIC

The war became truly global when Japan attacked the American naval base at Pearl Harbor, Hawaii, on the morning of December 7, 1941. To establish a Japanese Empire throughout Asia, Japan needed to destroy the U.S. Pacific Fleet and seize British, French, and Dutch colonies in the region. The surprise attack on Pearl Harbor devastated the American fleet and shocked the American public. More than 2,000 American lives were lost, but much of the American

0   1000   2000 Miles
0   1000   2000 Kilometers

Japanese Empire, 1936
Japanese control, August 1942
Allies
Neutral nations
Allied offenses
Major battles
Atomic bomb targets

THE SECOND WORLD WAR IN THE PACIFIC. › What areas did the Japanese and Allies each control in the Pacific during World War II? › Trace the route of the Allied offense. What did the main Allied strategy appear to be? › What factors led the Americans to decide that dropping the atomic bombs on Hiroshima and Nagasaki, rather than invading Japan, was the most expeditious way to end the war?

fleet—including its aircraft carriers, submarines, and many smaller ships—were safely at sea on the day of the strike. The attack galvanized American public opinion in a way the war in Europe had not. When Germany rashly declared war on the United States as well, America declared itself ready to take on all comers and joined the Allies.

For the European colonial powers, Japan's entry into the war was a catastrophe. Japanese troops swept through the British protectorate of Malaya in weeks, sinking the Pacific squadrons of both the British and Dutch navies in swift attacks. Britain's fortified island port at Singapore, the keystone of British defenses in the Pacific, fell at the end of December 1941, and American soldiers and marines were forced to surrender on the island of Corregidor. Thousands of Allied troops were captured and sent off to four years of torture, forced labor, and starvation in Japanese prison camps. Meanwhile, the Japanese invaded the Philippines, and the Dutch East Indies also fell. It seemed that there would be no stopping the Japanese before they reached Australia.

The Allies redoubled their efforts in 1942. An obscure British Indian army officer, William Slim, reorganized the imperial defenses of Burma (present-day Myanmar), and a joint force of British and Indian troops defeated an attempted Japanese invasion of India at the end of 1942. In New Guinea, Australian troops, fresh from North Africa, were the first to defeat the Japanese on land in bitter hand-to-hand combat.

America's navy benefited from a rapidly increased production schedule that turned out new ships and planes that outnumbered the Japanese fleet. In 1942, the United States won crucial victories in the Coral Sea and at Midway, a battle fought at sea and in the air by aircraft flown from carriers. American marines landed on the island of Guadalcanal in August 1942 and captured this strategic Japanese base after months of bitter fighting. Their success began a campaign of island hopping as the marines destroyed Japan's network of island bases throughout the Pacific. This was brutal warfare, often settled with grenades and bayonets, with each side considering the other racially inferior. The Japanese often refused to surrender, and the Americans and Australians took few prisoners. By 1943, the Japanese victories halted, and with the Japanese navy severely weakened, the Allies began a slow march toward Singapore and the Philippines.

"A DATE WHICH WILL LIVE IN INFAMY," DECEMBER 7, 1941. The U.S.S. *West Virginia* was one of eight battleships sunk during the Japanese surprise attack targeting Battleship Row at the American naval base at Pearl Harbor. More than 2,000 people were killed, but most of the American fleet, en route to or from other locations in the Pacific, was spared.

The Rise and Ruin of Nations: Germany's War in the East and the Occupation of Europe

Operation Barbarossa The code name for Hitler's invasion of the Soviet Union in 1941.

While battles ebbed and flowed in the Atlantic and the North African desert, Germany moved southeast into the Balkans. In 1941, Germany took over Yugoslavia almost without a fight. The Germans split Yugoslavia's ethnic patchwork by establishing a Croatian puppet state, pitting Croats against their Serb neighbors, who were ruled directly by the Nazis. Romania, Hungary, and Bulgaria joined the Nazis' cause as allies. The Greeks, who had dealt a crushing defeat to an Italian invasion, were suddenly confronted with a massive German force that overran the country. The Greeks stubbornly refused to surrender, and an unexpected combination of Greek, British, and New Zealand troops nearly defeated the German paratroopers sent to capture the island of Crete in June 1941; but in the end, the country fell. By the summer of 1941—with the exceptions of Spain, Portugal, Sweden, and Switzerland—the whole European continent was either allied with the Nazis or subject to their rule. These victories, and the economy of plunder that enriched Germany with forced labor and other nations' money, won Hitler considerable popularity at home.

Much of the European continent is brought under German control

Hitler's ultimate goal lay to the east. He had always seen the nonaggression pact with the Soviet Union as an act of convenience, and by the summer of 1941, Germany was prepared to move against Stalin. On June 22, 1941, Hitler began **Operation Barbarossa**, the invasion of the Soviet Union. The elite of the German army led the way, defeating all the forces the Russians could put in front of them. Stalin's purges of the 1930s had exiled or executed many of his most capable army officers, and the effects showed in Russian disorganization and disaffection in the face of the panzers. Hundreds of thousands of prisoners were taken as German forces pressed deep into Belorussia (modern Belarus), the Baltic states, and Ukraine. The Germans led a multinational army, which included Italians, Hungarians, most of the Romanian army, and freelance soldiers from the Baltics and Ukraine who bore grudges against Stalin's authoritarian regime. During the fall of 1941, the Nazis destroyed much of the Red Army's fighting strength and vigorously pursued their two goals: the destruction of communism and racial purification.

The German war against the Soviets was a war of ideologies and racial hatred. The advancing Nazi forces left burning fields and towns in their wake and methodically wiped the occupied territories clean of "undesirable elements." When Russian guerrillas counterattacked, German forces shot or hanged hundreds of innocent hostages in reprisal, often first torturing their victims. The Russian guerrillas delivered the same punishment to any captured Germans. By the end of 1941, it was clear that the war in the East was a war of destruction, and both sides believed that only one would survive. It seemed then that the Germans would be the victors, their forces on the march toward Moscow. On orders from Berlin, however, some of the German forces were diverted south to attack Russia's industrial heartland. Moscow was never taken, giving the Russian population, its leaders, and its armies time to organize a determined resistance.

Hitler nonetheless managed to piece together an empire that stretched across the entire continent of Europe. He compared his rule to a "new Indian empire," and claimed to have studied British imperial techniques. In fact, much of Hitler's

KULTUR-TERROR

"CULTURAL TERROR," 1944. Produced in Nazi-occupied Holland, this poster of a cultural Frankenstein's monster warns of the looming destruction of European identity with the advance of American troops, who will bring American culture with them. The terror of this culture is embodied in a long list of visual references: aerial bombardment, the Ku Klux Klan and its violence of lynching, African American jazz, Jewish racial threats, sexual license, common criminality, and financial manipulation. › **What image of European culture was this image designed to defend?**

"New Order" rested on a patchwork of improvised regimes: military occupation in Poland and Ukraine, collaborators in France, allied fascists in Hungary, and so on. The clearest principle was German supremacy. The empire was meant to feed German citizens and maintain their morale, preventing the "stab in the back" Hitler believed had thwarted a German victory in 1914–1918. Occupied countries paid inflated "occupation costs" in taxes, food, industrial production, and manpower. In total, more than 6 million foreign workers were brought into Germany in 1942–1943 from throughout occupied Europe, with those from Poland, France, and the Soviet Union accounting for 75 percent. The treatment of conscript laborers followed the "racial" logic of official Nazi policy: people considered to be of "Nordic" races (Scandinavians and the Dutch) fared much better than the Slavs of central and eastern Europe, whose treatment was extremely harsh.

The German occupations raised political and moral questions about collaboration and resistance across Europe. Both Norway and the Netherlands were deeply divided by the occupation's puppet regimes; in both countries, a relatively small but dedicated party of Nazis governed in the name of the Germans, while determined resistance movements gathered information for the Allies and carried out acts of sabotage. In Denmark, the population engaged in regular acts of passive resistance that infuriated German administrators. They also banded together as private citizens to smuggle most of the country's Jewish population out to safety in neutral Sweden.

Elsewhere, the relationship among collaboration, resistance, and self-interested indifference was more complex. In France, collaboration ranged from simple survival tactics—keeping silent or looking the other way—to active support for Nazi ideals and goals. The worst example of such support was the French Vichy regime's active antisemitism: French authorities helped the Germans by arresting and deporting Jews in France to German concentration camps. Living with the German conquerors forced citizens in France (and elsewhere) to make choices. Many chose to protect their own interests by sacrificing "undesirables" such as Jews and communists. At the same time, communist activists, some members of the military, and many ordinary citizens—such as the people of France's central mountains, who had a long tradition of smuggling and resisting government—became active guerrillas and saboteurs. They established links with the Free French movement in London, led by General Charles de Gaulle, and supplied important intelligence to the Allies. The Poles also had a government-in-exile in London, led by Władysław Sikorski, who helped coordinate the Polish resistance.

In eastern Europe, resistance movements had less room to maneuver, but perhaps more reason to engage in direct action, because quiet submission did not guarantee safety under the harsh German military occupation. The result of such

MAP LABELS:

FINLAND

NORWAY

SWEDEN

- Leningrad

NORTH SEA

IRELAND

DENMARK

ESTONIA

- Moscow

UNITED KINGDOM

NETHERLANDS

MEMELAND
Danzig

LATVIA

LITHUANIA

- Vilna

SOVIET UNION

- London

GREATER GERMANY

- Berlin

EAST PRUSSIA

BIALYSTOK

POSEN

- Warsaw

ATLANTIC OCEAN

BELGIUM

EUPEN LUX.

BOHEMIA

GOVERNMENT GENERAL OF POLAND

EASTERN POLAND

- Kyiv

Occupied

- Paris

SUDETEN-LAND

MORAVIA

- Lemberg

NORTHERN BUKOVINA

LORRAINE
ALSACE

SLOVAKIA

F R A N C E

SWITZ.

AUSTRIA

- Budapest

- Vichy

HUNGARY

BESSARABIA

VICHY FRANCE
Unoccupied until November 1942

- Milan

CROATIA

YUGOSLAVIA
Partitioned April, 1941

- Belgrade

ROMANIA

- Bucharest

BLACK SEA

PORTUGAL

- Toulon

ITALY

SERBIA

- Sofia

SPAIN

CORSICA (Vichy)

- Rome

CATTARO (It.)

ALBANIA (It.)

BULGARIA

- Istanbul

- Ankara

BALEARIC ISLANDS

SARDINIA (It.)

ADRIATIC SEA

GREECE

T U R K E Y

- Athens

CYPRUS

LEBANON

MOROCCO

ALGERIA (Fr.)

SICILY

CRETE

MEDITERRANEAN SEA

TUNISIA (Fr.)

LIBYA (It.)

EGYPT

PALESTINE

SCALE:
0   250   500 Miles
0   250   500 Kilometers

INSET: EUROPE / Area of detail / AFRICA

LEGEND:
- Axis states and annexed areas
- Axis occupied
- Axis allies
- Sudetenland

AXIS EUROPE, 1941. › How had Hitler and Mussolini come to dominate the bulk of mainland Europe by the eve of the German invasion of the Soviet Union? › Why did Hitler choose to annex certain territories to Germany but settle for occupation in others? › As you look at this map, do you think a German victory seems inevitable? Why or why not?

The Nazis and the "Gypsy Question"

Historians do not know the exact numbers of Roma (commonly known as "Gypsies" among non-Roma speakers, though this is now considered an offensive term) killed by the Nazis in their quest for a racially pure society. The U.S. Holocaust Museum estimates that 220,000 of the slightly fewer than 1 million Roma living in Europe were killed, either by the Germans or their allies. The Ustasha militia of Croatia, for example, was responsible for killing between 15,000 and 20,000 Roma. At Auschwitz, where 19,000 of the 23,000 Roma inmates died, Josef Mengele conducted pseudoscientific medical experiments on many Roma individuals. The documents reproduced here show the evolution of German policy toward the Roma people from 1938 to 1943, and provide a clear example of the way the German racial laws were applied to an entire population.

Circular Directive of December 8, 1938, by the Reichsführer-SS and Chief of German Police, Pertaining to the "Settlement of the Gypsy Question"

A. General Directives

I. Domestic Gypsies

1. (1) The experiences collected so far in combating the Gypsy plague, and the knowledge gained from racial-biological research would make it seem advisable to tackle the settlement of the Gypsy Question with the nature of this race in mind. According to experience, individuals of mixed race contribute the largest share to Gypsy criminality. Conversely, it has been shown that all attempts to settle Gypsies in a permanent place of residence failed in particular with pure-blooded Gypsies because of their strong urge to roam. Thus, it will be necessary to deal separately with the pure-blooded Gypsies and those of mixed blood when it comes to the final solution of the Gypsy Question.

* * *

(3) I therefore direct that all Gypsies, whether sedentary or not, as well as all persons roaming in Gypsy fashion must be rounded up [*erfaßt*] by the Reich Criminal Police Office—Central Reich Administration for Combating Gypsy Malefaction.

* * *

3. (1) The ultimate determination as to whether one deals with a Gypsy, a Gypsy of mixed blood, or some person roaming in Gypsy fashion will be made by the Reich Criminal Police Office based on the testimony of an expert.

(2) I therefore direct . . . that all Gypsies, Gypsies of mixed blood, and persons roaming in Gypsy fashion be compelled to submit to a racial-biological examination required for the presentation of a testimony by an expert, and to provide the necessary information about their descent. The implementation of this directive is to be ensured by means of forceful police measures.

* * *

II. Foreign Gypsies

1. Foreign Gypsies must be prevented from entering German territory. Refusal to grant entry permits and to move them back is required procedure even if foreign Gypsies are in possession of passports entitling them to immigrate, of substitute documents in lieu of passports, or of visa.

* * *

Express Letter of August 17, 1939 from the Reich Security Main Office, pertaining to the "rounding up" [*Erfassung*] of Gypsies

Berlin, October 10, 1939

Reich Security Main Office
Tgb. No. RKPA. 149/1939-g
Express Letter

To the State Criminal Police—Regional and Local Commands of the Criminal Police . . .

Subject: Rounding Up of Gypsies

By order of the *Reichsführer-SS* and Chief of German Police the Gypsy Question will be fundamentally settled before long within the entire German territory by a uniform standard applied throughout the Reich. I therefore ask you to initiate the following measures at once:

1. The local police stations and the Rural Police must be instructed immediately to notify all Gypsies and Gypsies of mixed blood within their respective districts that effective immediately they may not leave their residence or their present whereabouts until further notice. Anybody in violation of this injunction will be threatened with dispatch to a concentration camp.

* * *

Express Letter of January 29, 1943 from the Reich Security Main Office, Pertaining to the Confinement of "Gypsies of Mixed Blood," "Romany Gypsies," and "Balkan Gypsies" to a Concentration Camp

Berlin, January 29, 1943

Reich Security Main Office
VA No. 59/43 g
Express Letter

* * *

Subject: Confinement of Gypsies of mixed blood, Romany Gypsies and Balkan Gypsies in a concentration camp

* * *

I. By order of the *Reichsführer-SS* dated December 16, 1942 . . . , Gypsies of mixed blood, Romany Gypsies and members of Gypsy clans of non-German blood and of Balkan origins are to be selected according to fixed

guidelines, and in the course of an operation lasting only a few weeks are to be confined in a concentration camp. People affected [*Personenkreis*] will henceforth briefly be referred to as "Persons of Gypsy origin."

Confinement will take place by families, regardless of the degree of mixed blood, in Concentration Camp (Gypsy Camp) Auschwitz.

* * *

(III) 1. Attempts should be made to obtain consent for sterilization from persons of Gypsy origin above 12 years of age and not yet sterilized;

* * *

4. In case of refusal, the Reich Criminal Police Office, after having ascertained the reasons, will decide what steps are to be taken.

Source: Reinhard Rürup, ed., *Topography of Terror: Gestapo, SS, and Reichssicherheitshauptamt on the "Prinz-Albrecht-Terrain": A Documentation*, trans. Werner T. Angress (Berlin: 1989).

Questions for Analysis

1. How was the language of racial science used to justify discriminatory practices against the Roma in the 1938 document? Why was it necessary to differentiate among "Gypsies, Gypsies of mixed blood, and persons roaming in Gypsy fashion"?

2. What was the significance of the 1939 document's statement that the "Gypsy Question will be fundamentally settled before long within the entire German territory by a uniform standard applied throughout the Reich"? If the goal was extermination, why use such bureaucratic language? If the goal was other than extermination, why was it necessary to "round up" the Roma?

3. By 1943, the extermination policy was already under way. Why, then, was it necessary to continue to speak in vague terms of "Gypsies of mixed blood, Romany Gypsies and members of Gypsy clans of non-German blood and of Balkan origins"?

circumstances ranged from open warfare against the fascists to civil wars between those who supported the Germans and those who fought them. Organized resistance groups formed immediately in 1939 in Poland, where collaboration was never an option because the Germans never considered it. By 1942, the Polish Home Army was the largest underground resistance movement in Europe. Harassing the Nazis through acts of sabotage and attacks on military convoys, the Polish resistance circulated legal guidelines on how Poles should conduct themselves under the occupation, established clandestine courts, and built an underground education system that reached 1 million children. They also kept university classes, meeting in secret after all institutions of higher learning had been banned. By the fall of 1943, the Home Army was already engaging the Germans directly.

The Germans' system of occupation in Yugoslavia led to violent civil conflict. In Croatia, a fascist regime allied with the Germans fought against the Serbs who resisted. The Croatian fascist guard, the Ustasha, massacred hundreds of thousands of Orthodox Christian Serbs. Josip Broz (Tito), born in Croatia to a Croatian father and a Slovene mother, emerged as the leader of the most powerful Yugoslavian resistance movement. Tito's communist partisans were the only resistance group in eastern Europe to succeed in liberating its country without the presence of Soviet troops, fighting Germans, Italians, as well as Croat fascists, and gained support and supplies from the Allies.

Perhaps the most important moral issue facing citizens of occupied Europe was not their national allegiance but rather their personal attitudes toward the fate of the Nazis' sworn enemies: Jews, communists, Roma, homosexuals, and political "undesirables." Popular journalists in France called for the deportation of Jewish children and celebrated their collaborationist government when it carried out the plan. Some French Jews along the Riviera found that the Italian Catholic army officers who occupied the area were more willing to save them from deportation than were their fellow Frenchmen. The Germans executed at least 700 Poles for sheltering Jews, and in spite of the great danger, tens of thousands of non-Jewish residents of Warsaw did what they could to aid the Jews in their city, in large or small ways. In 1941, however, Polish villagers in Jedwabne massacred their Jewish neighbors at the instigation of the Gestapo. These consequences of wartime choices—to risk family, friends, and careers to aid the deportees; to put one's head down and look the other way; or to actively aid and abet mass murder—deeply scarred the generation of Europeans who survived the war.

Nazi persecutions of Jews, Roma, homosexuals, and political dissidents found fervent support from local populations as well as determined resistance

Racial War, Ethnic Cleansing, and the Holocaust

The Nazis saw the conflict as a racial war from the beginning. In *Mein Kampf* (1925), Hitler outlined his view that a war against the *Untermenschen* ("subhumans")—Jews, Roma, and Slavs—was natural and necessary (see **Analyzing Primary Sources** on pages 942–43). As soon as the war broke out, the Nazis implemented ambitious plans for redrawing the racial map of the Reich, through terror, deportation, and murder. In the fall of 1939, with Poland conquered, Heinrich Himmler directed the *Schutzstaffel* ("bodyguard"), or SS, to begin massive population transfers. Ethnic Germans who lived in territories conquered by the Nazi armies were brought to the German Reich, while Poles and Jews were deported to the east, in a brutal campaign of terror as the Nazis sought to root out all sources of potential resistance. Professors at the University of Kraków, considered dangerous intellectuals, were deported to concentration camps, where they died. Ordinary Poles were deported to forced labor camps. Jews by the thousands were transported to the region of Lublin, south of Warsaw. Special death squads shot Jews in the streets and in front of synagogues. These German campaigns in Poland took 100,000 Jewish lives in 1940.

The elimination of European Jewry stood at the center of the Nazis' *Rassenkampf* ("racial conflict"). We have seen the role of antisemitism in Hitler's rise to power and the escalating campaign of terror against the Jewish community inside Germany in the 1930s, including the Night of Broken Glass (Chapter 25). Most historians now agree that although Hitler and other Nazis verbally announced "war" against the Jews early on, such a policy was not possible until after 1941, when the conquest of territory in the east suddenly brought millions of Jews under Nazi control. During the organized pogroms of 1938, the Nazis' anti-Jewish policy aimed not at extermination but forced emigration, and until 1941, the Nazi leadership continued to consider plans to deport Europe's Jews to Madagascar, at that time a French colony off the coast of Africa. These schemes took shape against the background of daily terror and frequent massacres, especially in Poland.

The invasion of the Soviet Union turned these atrocities into something much deadlier. Operation Barbarossa was animated by the Nazis' intense ideological and racial hatred of Slavs, Jews, and Marxists. Goebbels, for example, called the Russians "not a people but an agglomeration of animals." The invasion of the Soviet Union was thus openly a "war of extermination." The campaign's initial success also created pressing practical problems for the German army in the newly conquered territories, as they debated on how to control the millions of people—including military prisoners,

WHERE WERE THE CAMPS? In 2013, historians compiled a list of more than 42,000 separate extermination camps, detention centers, ghettos, and slave-labor sites in German-controlled Europe during the war years. Their conclusion that virtually every population center was close to such a site has caused historians to revise upward their estimates of who in Europe had knowledge of the extermination policy.

eastern European Jews, and other civilians—who had now fallen into Nazi hands. Although Hitler had certainly prepared the way for what followed in his long-nurtured campaigns against the Jews, historians now believe that a significant part of the driving force for the Holocaust came from rivalries within the Nazi bureaucracy, which led to a radicalization of persecution and murder on a scale few could have imagined.

As the Nazi army swept into the Soviet Union in 1941, captured communist officials, political agitators, and hostile civilians were imprisoned, tortured, or shot. Most Poles, Ukrainians, and Russians in the region were deported to Germany as slave labor. About 5.5 million Soviet military prisoners were marched into camps,

THE LIBERATION OF THE CONCENTRATION CAMPS. Many Allied soldiers documented the liberation of the concentration camps at the end of the war, taking photographs and films of the appalling scenes they encountered. In many cases, German civilians were brought into the camps and compelled to witness the countless bodies of camp prisoners that remained unburied, before being conscripted to help with the disposal of the corpses to prevent the spread of disease. In this photograph, local residents view the victims of Nazi crimes at the Landsberg camp near Dachau, Germany, in 1945.
› What complications did the Allies face in the task of assigning responsibility for these crimes?

where over half of them died of starvation or were executed. On the heels of the advancing German army came special battalions of *Einsatzgruppen* ("task forces"), or death squads, who stormed through Jewish villages and towns. The men of the villages were shot; the women and children were either deported to labor camps or massacred along with the men. By September 1941, the Einsatzgruppen reported that they had killed 85,000 people, most of them Jews; by April 1942, the number was half a million. These killings began before the gas chambers had gone into operation and continued through the campaigns on the Eastern Front. By 1943, the death squads had killed roughly 2.2 million Jews.

As Operation Barbarossa progressed, German administrations in occupied areas herded local Jewish populations even more tightly into walled ghettos. Warsaw and Łódź in Poland were the largest. The ghettos became centers of starvation and disease. Those who left the ghettos were shot rather than returned. A German doctor summarized the regime's logic about killing this way: "One must, I can say it quite openly in this circle, be clear about it. There are only two ways. We sentence the Jews in the

NORWAY
1,300

FINLAND

SWEDEN

ESTONIA
"Free of Jews"

SOVIET
UNION
5 MILLION

NORTH
SEA

DENMARK
5,600

LATVIA
3,500

LITHUANIA
34,000

WHITE
RUSSIA
446,484

IRELAND

UNITED
KINGDOM

NETHLERANDS
160,800

GERMANY
131,800   Berlin
          Wannsee

BIALYSTOK
DISTRICT
400,000

EASTERN
TERRITORIES
420,000

BELGIUM
43,000

BOHEMIA and
MORAVIA
74,200

GENERAL
GOVERNMENT
2,284,000

FRANCE
Occupied Zone
165,000

LUX.

SLOVAKIA
88,000

UKRAINE
2,994,684

FRANCE
Unoccupied Zone
700,000
(including
French North Africa)

SWITZ.

AUSTRIA
43,700

HUNGARY
742,800

SPAIN

CORSICA

CROATIA
40,000

SERBIA
10,000

ROMANIA
342,000

BLACK SEA

ITALY
58,000

BULGARIA
48,000

SARDINIA

ALBANIA
200

MEDITERRANEAN SEA

SICILY

GREECE
69,600

RHODES

CRETE

CYPRUS

Area of
detail

EUROPE

AFRICA

0   250   500 Miles
0   250   500 Kilometers

HITLER'S "FINAL SOLUTION": JEWS MARKED FOR DEATH. On January 20, 1942, German officials met at Wannsee, just outside Berlin, to discuss the "Final Solution" to the "Jewish problem." They also discussed what they believed to be the remaining number of Jewish people in territories they controlled or soon hoped to control. **› Examine the figures closely. How many millions of innocent people did the Nazis propose to slaughter? › Based on your reading, what percentage of Jews did they actually kill? › Which two countries were set for the most executions?**

ghetto to death by hunger or we shoot them. Even if the end result is the same, the latter is more intimidating." In other words, the point was not simply death but terror.

Through the late summer and fall of 1941, Nazi officials discussed plans for mass killings in death camps. That summer, the Nazis had experimented with vans equipped with poison gas that could kill thirty to fifty people at a time. Those experiments and the gas chambers were designed with the help of scientists from the T-4 euthanasia program, which had already killed 80,000 racially, mentally, or physically "unfit" individuals in Germany. By October 1941, the SS was building camps with gas chambers and deporting people to them. Auschwitz-Birkenau (*OWSH-vihts BIHR-kuh-now*), originally intended to hold Polish prisoners, was the largest of the camps. It eventually held many different types of prisoners—"undesirables" such as Jehovah's Witnesses and homosexuals, Poles, Russians, and even some British prisoners of war (POWs). Jews and Roma were singled out for systematic annihilation. Between the spring of 1942 and the fall of 1944, more than 1 million people were killed at Auschwitz-Birkenau alone. Freight cars hauled Jewish people to the camps, first from the ghettos of Poland, then from France, Holland, Belgium, Austria, and the Balkans, and later from Hungary and Greece. Bodies were buried in pits dug by prisoners or burned in crematoria.

The death camps have come to symbolize the horrors of Nazism as a system of modern mass murder. Yet it is worth emphasizing that much of the slaughter was not anonymous, industrialized, or routine, but took place in face-to-face encounters outside the camps. Jews and other victims were not simply killed, but tortured, beaten, and executed publicly while soldiers and other onlookers recorded the executions with cameras—and sent photos home to their families. During the last phases of the war, inmates still in the concentration camps were taken on death marches whose sole purpose was suffering and death. And the killings were not done only by the specially indoctrinated SS and Einsatzgruppen. The Nazi regime called up groups of conscripts, such as Reserve Police Battalion 101, from duty in their home city of Hamburg and sent them into occupied territories, and once there, the unit of middle-aged policemen received and obeyed orders to kill 1,500 Jewish men, women, and children in one village in one day. When the commander offered to excuse men who did not feel they could carry out the assignment, only a few asked for a different task.

How many people knew of the extent of the Holocaust? No operation of this scale could be carried out without the cooperation or knowledge of many: the Nazi hierarchy, architects who helped design and build the camps, engineers who designed the gas chambers and crematoria, municipal officials of cities from which people were deported, train drivers, residents of villages near the camps who reported the smell of bodies burning, and so on. Recent research has shown that the number of extermination camps, ghettos, slave-labor sites, and detention centers in Nazi-controlled Europe was greater than 42,000. Given the difficulty of hiding sites that required guards, logistical support, and access to transportation networks, it is now clear that many more people must have been aware of what was happening. It is not surprising that most who suspected the worst were terrified and powerless. But it is also clear that many people did not want to know and did their best to ignore evidence and carry on with their lives. Moreover, there were reasons many continued to support the Nazis, such as personal opportunism or because they opposed communism and wanted order restored. Yet mere popular indifference, fear, or approval does not provide a satisfactory explanation for the Nazis' ability to accomplish the murder of so many people. Indeed, many Europeans—German, French, Dutch, Polish, Swiss, and Russian—had come to believe that there was a "Jewish problem" that had to be "solved."

The Nazis tried to conceal the death camps. Nevertheless, in July 1943, the Polish government-in-exile sent an envoy, Jan Karski, to the United States to present a report on Germany's plan to murder Europe's Jews. Karski, a member of the Polish underground, had been in the Warsaw ghetto and witnessed Jews being transported to the extermination center at Belzec. He met with President Franklin D. Roosevelt to plead for an intervention that would stop the killing, but neither Roosevelt nor

Despite Nazi attempts to conceal the existence of the death camps, the Holocaust could only have been accomplished with the support of many people throughout Europe

The Architecture of Mass Murder

The camp at Auschwitz-Birkenau was the largest of the German concentration camps. Its central purpose was the murder of Europe's Jews: nearly 1.1 million people, of whom 1 million were Jews, were murdered there.

Auschwitz-Birkenau was a complex of three camps: an extermination center, a prisoner-of-war camp, and a labor camp built with the cooperation of German industrial firms such as IG Farben. Forty other smaller installations and work camps in the surrounding area were also run by the camp's administration. The construction of the Auschwitz-Birkenau complex occupied thousands of workers and continued throughout the war. When the Soviet army arrived in January 1945, they found that the Germans had burned the camp archives before fleeing, but they had not burned the construction archive, which was kept separately. Hundreds of technical drawings were found in this archive, and they became accessible to historians after the collapse of the Soviet Union in 1991;

A. Blueprint for Crematorium II, Birkenau, dated November 1941. The five shaded squares in the lower drawing are the gas ovens in the structure's underground level, and the area to the right is labeled "Corpses Room."

the other Allied leaders were willing to commit the necessary resources, either because they did not believe Karski's story or because they were preoccupied with the enormity of the crisis facing them. The Nazis, however, could count on vocal support throughout Europe for persecuting Jews. For reasons that had to do with both traditional Christian antisemitism and modern, racialized nationalism, many Europeans had come to see Jewish Europeans as "foreign," and no longer members of their national communities.

another cache of such documents was discovered in an abandoned building in Berlin in 2008. The drawings are now held by Yad Vashem, the Holocaust archive in Jerusalem, Israel.

The discovery of these drawings does not add substantially to what was already known about the murder of Jews and other prisoners at Auschwitz, but it provides an arresting example of the bureaucratic apparatus—and the chilling coldness of the planning—that went into the Nazi extermination policy.

Questions for Analysis

1. Who would have seen these plans and been aware of their purpose?

2. What do these images tell us about the nature of the effort that went into the Nazi extermination policy?

3. Is there a way to understand the relationship between the careful renderings, with precise measurements and rectilinear lines, and the ultimate purpose of the buildings?

B. Blueprint for the "Delousing Facility" at Auschwitz-Birkenau, showing a room of 11.6 by 11.2 meters marked *Gaskammer* ("gas chamber").

Other governments' cooperation with Nazi policies varied. The French Vichy regime, on its own initiative, passed laws that required Jews to wear identifying stars and strictly limited their movements and activities. Although 75 percent of the Jews in France survived the war, only about 2,500 of the approximately 75,000 Jews deported to German death camps survived. The vast majority of those deported were arrested not by the Germans but by Vichy authorities seeking to prove that France could be Germany's partner in Hitler's New Order. The Hungarian government

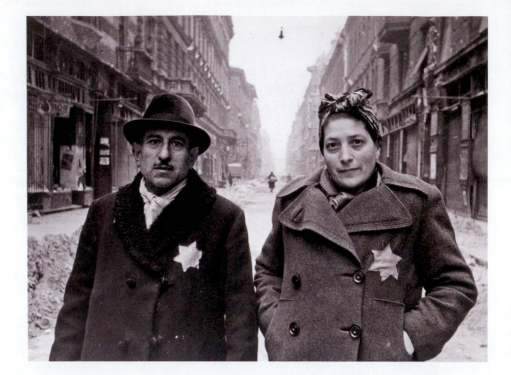

JEWISH COUPLE IN BUDAPEST, BY YEVGENY KHALDEI (1945). Khaldei, a Soviet photographer and journalist who traveled with the Red Army, recounts his remarkable and moving encounter with this couple: "There was a Jewish couple wearing Stars of David. They were afraid of me. There was still fighting going on in the city, and they thought I might be an SS soldier. So I said *Sholem Aleichem* [hello] to them, and the woman began to cry. After I'd taken the picture, I pulled their stars off and said, 'The fascists are beaten. It's terrible to be marked like that.'"

also allied with the Nazis and persecuted Jews, but dragged its heels about deportations. The Hungarian Jewish community survived until March 1944, when the Germans took direct control and began mass deportations. So determined were the Nazis to carry out their "final solution" that in May 1944, they killed up to 12,000 Hungarian Jews a day at Auschwitz, contributing to a total death toll of 600,000. Italy, though a fascist country, participated less actively; not until 1943, when the Germans occupied the north of Italy, were drastic antisemitic measures implemented.

In the face of Nazi determination, little resistance was possible. The concentration camps were designed to numb and incapacitate the inmates, making them acquiesce in their own slow deaths, if they were not killed right away. In his famous account, the survivor Primo Levi writes: "Our language lacks words to express this offence, the demolition of a man. . . . It is not possible to sink lower than this; no human condition is more miserable than this, nor could it conceivably be so. Nothing belongs to us any more; they have taken away our clothes, our shoes, even our hair; if we speak, they will not listen to us, and if they listen, they will not understand." The few rebellions in Auschwitz and Treblinka were repressed with savage efficiency. In the villages of Poland, Ukraine, and elsewhere, people rounded up to be deported or shot had to make split-second decisions to escape, and saving oneself nearly always meant abandoning one's children or parents, which very few could—or would—do. The countryside offered no shelter, as local populations were usually either hostile or too terrified to help. Nothing could have prepared these populations for the kind of violence that overwhelmed them.

The largest Jewish resistance movement was in the Warsaw ghetto, in the spring of 1943. The previous summer, the Nazis had deported 80 percent of the ghetto's

Area of detail

EUROPE

AFRICA

NORTH SEA

BALTIC SEA

Line of furthest German advance

Bergen

Oslo

Narva

Kovno

Vilna

Grodno

Hamburg

Amsterdam

Westerbork

Sachsenhausen

Berlin

Bialystok

Wolkowysk

Vught

Plonsk

Pruzana

Malines

Brussels

Buchenwald

Leipzig

Lodz

Radom

Lille

Breslau

Lublin

Rouen

Caen

Paris

Nancy

Theresienstadt

Auschwitz

Munkacs

Angers

Nantes

Orléans

Tours

Kosice

Beregszasz

Dijon

Munich

Vienna

Maramrossziget

Eger

Debrecen

Beszterce

Budapest

Cluj

Szaszregen

Lyon

Merano

Szeged

Mako

Bordeaux

Milan

Turin

Padua

Venice

Trieste

Zagreb

Pecs

Sepsiszentgyorgy

Gurs

Toulouse

Avignon

Marseilles

Genoa

Pisa

Florence

RAB

ADRIATIC SEA

Rivesaltes

Rome

Pristina

Skopje

Veles

Xanthi

Nea Orestea

BLACK SEA

MEDITERRANEAN SEA

Florina

Salonica

CORFU

Arta

Patras

Athens

KOS

RHODES

0   100   200   300 Miles

0   100   200   300 Kilometers

— Deportation railroads

DEPORTATION RAILWAYS. Between March 1942 and November 1944, Jews are known to have been deported from every location on this map, as well as from other numerous locales. Note the effort the Nazis made to transport Jews from the very frontiers of the empire at the height of a two-front war. **› According to the map, to which site were most Jews deported? › Look back at Hitler's "Final Solution" map on page 948. Why was Auschwitz in Poland chosen as the main deportation site? › What does the map say about the Nazi regime in particular and the other nations willing to collaborate with the Nazis?**

residents to the camps, making it clear that those left behind had little hope of survival. Those in the ghetto had virtually no resources, yet when deportations started again, a small Jewish underground movement—1,000 fighters, perhaps, in a community of 70,000—took on the Nazis with a tiny arsenal of gasoline bombs, pistols, and ten rifles. The Nazis responded by burning the ghetto to the ground and executing and deporting nearly everyone who was left. In the end, some 56,000 Jews died, and the SS commander reported, "The Warsaw Ghetto is no more." Word of the rising spread, but the repression made it clear that the targets of Nazi extermination could choose only between death in the streets or death in the camps.

The Holocaust claimed nearly 6 million Jewish lives, more than one-third of the world's Jewish population, 2.9 million of whom were Polish. To realize their racial utopia, the Nazis also killed more than 200,000 Roma and 250,000 people with disabilities, as well as 2.7 million non-Jewish Poles, 5.7 million non-Jewish Soviet civilians, and 3 million Soviet prisoners of war. These enormous numbers cannot capture the nearly total destruction of some communities and their cultures. Well over 80 percent of the long-established Jewish communities were annihilated in the Baltic states (Latvia, Estonia, and Lithuania), Germany, Czechoslovakia, Yugoslavia, and Poland; elsewhere, the figures were closer to 50 percent. The Holocaust was part of an even longer period of ethnically and racially motivated mass murder. Through both world wars and afterward, ethnic and religious groups—Jews, Armenians, Poles, Serbian Orthodox—were hunted, massacred, and legally deported en masse. Hitler's government had planned to build a "new Europe," safe for ethnic Germans and their allies and secure against communism, on the graveyards of whole cultures. At war's end, however, the ethnic Germans of eastern Europe themselves were expelled and sometimes killed in retaliation for Nazi crimes.

Total War: Home Fronts, the War of Production, Bombing, and the Bomb

> *Total war required the complete mobilization of every nation's military, political, and economic resources*

The Second World War was a "total war," even more so than the First World War. It involved the combined efforts of whole populations and the mobilization of entire economies, changing standards of living around the world. In the neutral nations of Latin America, which supplied raw materials to the Allies, wartime profits led to a wave of prosperity. In the lands occupied by Germany or Japan, forced extraction robbed local areas of resources, workers, and food. In East Asia, deprivation created resentment against the Japanese, who had been seen initially as liberators ending the rule of European colonial powers. Work schedules were grueling, as women and the elderly pressed back into wage work or working for the first time put in long shifts. This was especially taxing on women, who would return home to care for families and neighbors affected by wartime shortages. Almost everywhere, food, gasoline, and basic household goods were rationed. In occupied Europe and the Soviet Union, rations were close to starvation level.

Production—churning out tanks, planes, bombs, and supplies—was essential to winning the war. Britain, the Soviet Union, and the United States launched well-designed propaganda campaigns to encourage the production of war equipment.

Appeals to patriotism struck a chord, and the Allied populations committed themselves to the effort. Despite strikes and disputes with government officials, the Allied powers devoted more of their economies to war production than any nations in history, swamping the enemy with constant reinforcements and superior firepower. Japan had invested heavily in its military in the 1930s, but during the war its production levels declined, as Allied advances on land and American submarines cut off overseas sources of vital supplies. Germany was less efficient in its use of workers and materials than the Allied nations. Germany's ability to produce devastatingly successful weapons led to a damaging side effect: vast amounts of money and time spent developing pet projects of high-ranking Nazi officials. The Allies, meanwhile, developed functional designs and produced them in overwhelming numbers, rather than losing time and resources pursuing perfection.

Industrial centers became vital military targets. The Allies began bombing German ports and factories early in the war. American and British planners made a major commitment to strategic bombing, developing new planes and technology that put thousands of bombers in the air over occupied Europe night and day. As the war wore on the Allies expanded their campaign, from pinpoint bombing of the military and industry to attacks on Germany's civilian populations. Despite a public debate about the morality of the bombings, for the British, it was a war of retribution; for the Americans, it was an effort to grind the Germans down without sacrificing too many Allied lives. The Allies killed tens of thousands of German civilians as they struck Berlin, Hamburg, and the industrial cities of the Ruhr—but German war production persisted and its fighter planes shot down hundreds of Allied bombers. After the Allied invasion of Europe in 1944, bombing expanded well beyond targets of military value. The German city of Dresden, a center of culture and education without heavy industry, was firebombed on February 13–15, 1945, killing at least 35,000 people in a city that held uncounted refugees who had fled the war in the East. German industry slowly degraded, but the Germans' will to keep fighting, like that of the British and the Soviets, remained intact.

> In total war, the line between "civilians" and "combatants" is blurred as both groups become legitimate targets

THE RACE TO BUILD THE BOMB

Allied scientists in the United States developed the world's first nuclear weapon during the war: an atomic bomb that released tremendous explosive energy in a nuclear chain reaction. Physicists in Britain and Germany first suggested that such a weapon might be possible, but only the United States had the resources to build such a bomb before the end of the war. A group of physicists led by Enrico Fermi at the University of Chicago, including many refugees from fascist regimes in Europe, built the world's first nuclear reactor. Fearful that the Germans would develop a bomb of their own, the U.S. government built a laboratory at Los Alamos, New Mexico, and charged the physicists with building an atomic bomb. Physicist J. Robert Oppenheimer directed the top-secret plan, known to researchers as the **Manhattan Project**. The goal was to perfect a bomb that could be dropped by plane and detonated above the target. The physicists successfully tested a device on July 16, 1945, in New Mexico, vaporizing the test tower in a wave of heat and fire that rose in a mushroom shape overhead. The United States now possessed the most destructive weapon ever devised.

Manhattan Project The secret U.S. government research project to develop the first nuclear bomb.

The Allied Counterattack and the Dropping of the Atomic Bomb

Hitler had invaded the Soviet Union in June 1941, but the war in the east became his undoing.

Nearly 90 percent of the Soviet Union's tanks, most of their aircraft, and huge stores of supplies were destroyed in the initial invasion. Nazi forces penetrated deep into European Russia, laying siege to Leningrad (St. Petersburg). The city held out for 844 days—through three winters, massive destruction by artillery and aircraft, and periods of starvation—until a large relief force broke the siege.

THE EASTERN FRONT

On the Eastern front, successive winters took a heavy toll on the Germans, and at the same time, Soviet industry also made an astonishing recovery. Whole industries were rebuilt behind the safety of the Ural Mountains, and entire urban populations were sent to work in them, turning out tanks, fighter planes, machine guns, and ammunition. Finally, the Germans were the victims of the success of their own Blitzkrieg tactics; their lines extended deep into Russian territory, opening them up to counterattacks.

The turning point came in 1942–1943, when the Germans attempted to take **Stalingrad** in an effort to break the back of Soviet industry. The Russians drew the invading army into the city, where the Germans became bogged down in house-to-house fighting that neutralized their tanks and gave the outnumbered Soviet forces greater chances of success. In November 1942, large Russian armies encircled the city and besieged the invaders in a battle that continued through a cruel winter. By the end of January 1943, when the German commander defied his orders and surrendered, more than half a million German, Italian, and Romanian soldiers had died; Russian casualties numbered more than 1 million, including a 100,000 civilians.

After Stalingrad, a series of Soviet attacks drove the Germans back toward the frontier and beyond. In what may have been the largest battle ever fought—with more than 6,000 tanks and 2 million men—Soviet armies destroyed a German force at Kursk in the summer of 1943. The Russians then launched a major offensive into Ukraine, which was back in Soviet hands by the spring of 1944. In the summer of 1944, the Soviet army's Operation Bagration cleared the Nazis entirely from Soviet territory. The Soviets then moved south to secure control of the Balkans, taking Romania, Bulgaria, and Hungary out of the war. In August 1944, elements of the Polish Home Army organized an insurrection against the Germans in Warsaw in an attempt to liberate the Polish capital before the arrival of the Soviet army. The uprising

PRISONERS OF WAR. More than 90,000 captured German troops were forced to march through the streets of Stalingrad after their defeat by the Soviet forces. The combination of the battle and the Russian winter resulted in the loss of more than 300,000 German soldiers.

lasted for more than two months and was cruelly suppressed by the Germans, while the Soviets observed from the other side of the Vistula River, abstaining from sending assistance. Meanwhile, as Tito's Serbian guerrilla force moved against the German armies in Yugoslavia, the Soviets retook large parts of Czechoslovakia. In the first weeks of 1945, the Soviet army closed in on Berlin.

THE WESTERN FRONT

When the Nazis invaded Russia, Stalin called on the Allies to open a second front in the West. In response, the United States led an attack on Italy in 1943, beginning with an invasion of Sicily in July. Italy's government deposed Mussolini and surrendered in the summer of 1943, and the nation collapsed into civil war, with Italian partisans, especially the communists, siding with the Americans. The Germans occupied Italy with more than a dozen elite divisions, and the bitter campaign against American and British forces lasted eighteen months.

The most important second front opened on June 6, 1944, with massive Allied landings in Normandy on the French coast. Casualties were high, but careful planning allowed the Allied invasion to gain a foothold in northern Europe, eventually breaking through the German lines. A second landing in southern France also succeeded, aided by the Resistance. By August, Allied armies liberated Paris and pushed into Belgium. In the fall, however, the Germans managed to defeat a British airborne invasion in the Netherlands before mounting a devastating counterattack in December 1944, in the Battle of the Bulge. The Allied lines nearly broke, but the American forces held. In April 1945, the Allies crossed the Rhine into Germany, swiftly overwhelming the last defenders of the German Reich.

By late April, Soviets reached the suburbs of Berlin. In the savage ten-day battle for the German capital, more than 100,000 Russians and Germans died. On April 30, Adolf Hitler killed himself in a bunker beneath the Chancellery. On May 2, the heart of the city was captured, and the Soviets' red banner flew from the Brandenburg Gate. On May 7, the German high command signed a document of unconditional surrender. The war in Europe was over.

STORMING HITLER'S "FORTRESS EUROPE." American troops landing on Omaha Beach on D-Day, June 6, 1944. In the three months that followed, the Allies poured more than 2 million men, almost a half million vehicles, and 4 million tons of supplies onto the Continent—a measure of how firmly the Germans were established.

THE WAR IN THE PACIFIC

The war in the Pacific ended four months later. The British pushed the Japanese out of Burma while the Germans were surrendering in the West, and Australian forces recaptured the Dutch East Indies. By late 1944, the U.S. Navy had destroyed most of Japan's surface ships in the Philippine Islands, and American troops took Manila in bloody house-to-house fighting. A series of hard-fought amphibious assaults on Pacific islands that had begun after the Battle of Midway in 1941 brought U.S. troops closer to the Japanese mainland. When Okinawa fell to the Americans after

RAISING THE RED FLAG OVER THE REICHSTAG, BY YEVGENY KHALDEI (1945). Khaldei was one of several Soviet Jewish photographers to document Nazi atrocities and Soviet heroism (in this case) on the Eastern Front. In this photograph, which became the best-known image of Soviet victory, a Soviet soldier raises a flag over the Reichstag in Berlin. › **How was the Soviet occupation of the German capital seen from the perspective of the other Allied governments?**

eighty-two days of desperate fighting, the United States had a foothold less than 500 miles from Japan. Japanese pilots mounted suicide attacks on American ships, as American marines and Japanese soldiers fought over every inch of the shell-blasted rocks in the Pacific.

On July 26, the governments of the United States, Britain, and China jointly called on Japan to surrender or be destroyed. The United States had already been using long-range B-29 bombers in systematic attacks on Japanese cities, killing hundreds of thousands of Japanese civilians in firestorms produced by the incendiary bombs. When the Japanese government refused to surrender, the United States decided to use its atomic bomb.

Many senior military and naval officers argued that the use of the bomb was not necessary, on the assumption that Japan was already beaten. Some of the scientists involved believed that using the bomb for political ends would set a deadly precedent. Harry Truman, who became U.S. president when Roosevelt died in April 1945, decided otherwise. On August 6, a single American plane dropped an atomic bomb on Hiroshima, obliterating 60 percent of the city. Three days later, on August 9, the United States dropped a second bomb on Nagasaki. On August 14, Japan surrendered unconditionally.

The decision to use the bomb was extraordinary (see **Competing Viewpoints** on pages 960–61). It did not greatly alter the American plans for the destruction of Japan, since more Japanese died in earlier fire bombings than in the two atomic blasts—but the bomb was an entirely new kind of weapon. The instantaneous, total devastation of the blasts—and the lingering effects of cancerous radiation that would claim victims decades later—were a new kind of threat with unpredictable consequences for the future. The world now had a weapon that could destroy not just cities and peoples, but humanity itself.

Conclusion

After the Second World War, Europeans confronted a world they no longer recognized. In 1945, Europeans emerged from shelters or began long trips back to their homes, traumatized by their experiences and uncertain of the future. The products of industry (tanks, submarines, and strategic bombings) had destroyed the structures of industrial society (factories, ports, and railroads). The tools of mass culture—fascist and communist appeals, patriotism proclaimed via radios and movie screens, mobilization of mass armies and industry—had been put to full use. In the aftermath, much of Europe lay destroyed and, as we will see, vulnerable to the rivalry of the postwar superpowers: the United States and the Soviet Union.

THE ATOM BOMB. A mushroom cloud hovers over Nagasaki after the city was bombed. Hiroshima had been bombed three days earlier.

The two world wars profoundly affected Western empires. Nineteenth-century imperialism had made twentieth-century war a global matter. In both conflicts, warring nations used the resources of their empires to the fullest. Key campaigns in North Africa, Burma, Ethiopia, and the Pacific were fought in and over colonial territories. Hundreds of thousands of colonial troops—sepoys and Gurkhas from India and Nepal, Britain's King's African Rifles, French from Algeria and West Africa—served in armies on both sides of the conflict. After two massive mobilizations, many anticolonial leaders found renewed confidence in their peoples' courage and resourcefulness, and seized the opportunity of European weakness to press for independence. In many areas that had been under European or Japanese imperial control—from sections of China to Korea, Indochina, Indonesia, and Palestine—the end of the Second World War only paved the way for a new round of conflict. This time, the issue was when imperial control would end, and by whom.

The Second World War also carried on the Great War's legacy of massive killing. Historians estimate that between 62 million to 78 million people died across the world, two-thirds of them civilians, with about 20 percent dying of starvation or disease directly caused by the war. In Europe, the killing fields of the east, where the extermination of the Jews took place, suffered the highest tolls. At least 23 million Soviet citizens died: 8.8 million soldiers and 15 million civilians. Nearly

The Atomic Bomb and Its Implications

In July 1945, scientists associated with the Manhattan Project became involved in debates about how the atomic bomb should be deployed. Members of the Scientific Panel of the secretary of war's Interim Advisory Committee agreed that a bomb could be used for military purposes but disagreed about whether it could be used without prior warning and demonstration. Other groups of scientists secretly began circulating petitions, such as the one reprinted here, in which they set out their views. The petitions never reached the president, but they raised issues that emerged in the postwar period.

In the section of his memoirs reprinted here, President Harry S. Truman sets out the views of other scientists on the secretary of war's Advisory Committee, and explains the logic of his decision to use the atomic bomb on Hiroshima (August 6, 1945) and Nagasaki (August 9, 1945) and the events as they unfolded.

A Petition to the President of the United States

July 17, 1945

A PETITION TO THE PRESIDENT OF THE UNITED STATES

We, the undersigned scientists, have been working in the field of atomic power. Until recently we have had to fear that the United States might be attacked by atomic bombs during this war and that her only defense might lie in a counterattack by the same means. Today, with the defeat of Germany, this danger is averted and we feel impelled to say what follows:

The war has to be brought speedily to a successful conclusion and attacks by atomic bombs may very well be an effective method of warfare. We feel, however, that such attacks on Japan could not be justified, at least not unless the terms which will be imposed after the war on Japan were made public in detail and Japan were given an opportunity to surrender. . . .

[I]f Japan still refused to surrender our nation might then, in certain circumstances, find itself forced to resort to the use of atomic bombs. Such a step, however, ought not to be made at any time without seriously considering the moral responsibilities which are involved.

The development of atomic power will provide the nations with new means of destruction. The atomic bombs at our disposal represent only the first step in this direction, and there is almost no limit to the destructive power which will become available in the course of their future development. Thus a nation which sets the precedent of using these newly liberated forces of nature for purposes of destruction may have to bear the responsibility of opening the door to an era of devastation on an unimaginable scale.

If after this war a situation is allowed to develop in the world which permits rival powers to be in uncontrolled possession of these new means of destruction, the cities of the United States as well as the cities of other nations will be in continuous danger of sudden annihilation. . . .

The added material strength which this lead [in the field of atomic power] gives to the United States brings with it the obligation of restraint and if we were to violate this obligation our moral position would be weakened in the eyes of the world and in our own eyes. It would then be more difficult for us to live up to our responsibility of bringing the unloosened forces of destruction under control.

In view of the foregoing, we, the undersigned, respectfully petition: first, that you exercise your power as Commander-in-Chief, to rule that the United States shall not resort to the use of atomic bombs in this war unless the terms which will be imposed upon Japan have been made public in detail and Japan knowing these terms has refused to surrender; second, that in such an event the question of whether or not to use atomic bombs be decided by you in the light of the consider-ations presented in this petition as well as all the other moral responsibilities which are involved.

Source: Michael B. Stoff, Jonathan F. Fanton, and R. Hal Williams, eds., *The Manhattan Project: A Documentary Introduction to the Atomic Age* (New York: 2000), p. 173.

President Truman's Memoirs

I had realized, of course, that an atomic bomb explosion would inflict damage and casualties beyond imagination. On the other hand, the scientific advisers of the committee reported, "We can propose no technical demonstration likely to bring an end to the war; we see no acceptable alternative to direct military use." It was their conclusion that no technical demonstration they might propose, such as over a deserted island, would be likely to bring the war to an end. It had to be used against an enemy target.

The final decision of where and when to use the atomic bomb was up to me. Let there be no mistake about it. I regarded the bomb as a military weapon and never had any doubt that it should be used. The top military advisers to the President recommended its use, and when I talked to Churchill he unhesitatingly told me that he favored the use of the atomic bomb if it might aid to end the war.

In deciding to use this bomb I wanted to make sure that it would be used as a weapon of war in the manner prescribed by the laws of war. That meant that I wanted it dropped on a military target. I had told Stimson that the bomb should be dropped as nearly as possibly upon a war production center of prime military importance.

Stimson's staff had prepared a list of cities in Japan that might serve as targets. Kyoto, though favored by General Arnold as a center of military activity, was eliminated when Secretary Stimson pointed out that it was a cultural and religious shrine of the Japanese.

Four cities were finally recommended as targets: Hiroshima, Kokura, Niigata, and Nagasaki. They were listed in that order as targets for the first attack. The order of selection was in accordance with the military importance of these cities, but allowance would be given for weather conditions at the time of the bombing. Before the selected targets were approved as proper for military purposes, I personally went over them in detail with Stimson, Marshall, and Arnold, and we discussed the matter of timing and the final choice of the first target. . . .

On August 6, the fourth day of the journey home from Potsdam, came the historic news that shook the world. I was eating lunch with members of the *Augusta*'s crew when Captain Frank Graham, White House Map Room watch officer, handed me the following message:

To the President from the Secretary of War

Big bomb dropped on Hiroshima August 5 at 7:15 P.M. Washington time. First reports indicate complete success which was even more conspicuous than earlier test.

I was greatly moved. I telephoned Byrnes aboard ship to give him the news and then said to the group of sailors around me, "This is the greatest thing in history. It's time for us to get home."

Source: Harry S. Truman, *Memoirs*, vol. 1, *Year of Decisions* (Garden City, NY: 1955), pp. 419–21.

Questions for Analysis

1. Scientists circulated petitions to express their fears about how the atomic bomb would be used. Examine the outcomes the scientists proposed. Which came closest to subsequent events? Which was the most prudent? The most honest?

2. Is it appropriate for scientists to propose how new weapons should be used? Are they overreaching in trying to give advice in foreign affairs and military strategy, or are they obligated to voice moral qualms?

20 percent of the Polish population died, nearly 6 million people. Also killed were 1 million Yugoslavs, including militias of all sides; and 3.5 million German soldiers and 700,000 German civilians, not including the hundreds of thousands of ethnic Germans who died while being deported west at the end of the war. The United States, shielded from the full horrors of total war by two vast oceans, lost 292,000 soldiers in battle and more to accidents or disease.

Why was the war so murderous? The advanced technology of modern industrial war and the openly genocidal ambitions of the Nazis offer a part of the answer,

AFTER YOU READ THIS CHAPTER ⌄

CHRONOLOGY

1931	Japanese invasion of Manchuria
1936–1939	Spanish Civil War
September 1938	Sudeten Crisis and Munich Conference
August 1939	Nazi-Soviet Pact
September 1939	German invasion of Poland
May 1940	German invasion of the Low Countries and France
June 1941	German invasion of the Soviet Union
December 1941	Japanese attack on Pearl Harbor
September 1942–January 1943	Battle of Stalingrad
June 1944	D-Day invasion
May 1945	German surrender
August 1945	The United States drops atomic bombs on Hiroshima and Nagasaki
August 1945	Japanese surrender

REVIEWING THE OBJECTIVES

❯ The Second World War stemmed from the political and economic crises of the 1930s. What were the causes of the war?

❯ British and French leaders in the 1930s hoped to avoid another war in Europe through diplomatic negotiation with Hitler. What were the consequences of these negotiations?

❯ The populations of nations occupied by the Germans faced a difficult set of choices. What were the consequences of the occupation for European nations? What possibilities existed for resistance?

❯ The mass murder of European Jews, homosexuals, Roma, and the Slavic populations of Russia and eastern Europe reached a climax during the invasion of the Soviet Union, though the victims came from every corner of Europe. How did this enormous project come about? What efforts did it entail?

❯ The Nazi regime and its allies eventually collapsed after costly defeats in both eastern and western Europe. Where and when did these major defeats take place? What was their human cost?

❯ The Japanese government surrendered in August 1945 after the United States dropped atomic bombs on Hiroshima and Nagasaki. What events led to the decision to drop these bombs? What were the consequences?

and the global reach of the conflict offers another. Finally, the Second World War overlapped with, and eventually devolved into, a series of smaller, but no less bitter, conflicts: overlapping attempts by the Germans and Soviets to wipe out Poland's political leaders and professional classes; a civil war in Greece; conflicts among Orthodox Christians, Catholics, and Muslims in Yugoslavia; and political battles for control of the French Resistance. These struggles left deep political scars, as did memories of the war. Also, Hitler's empire could not have lasted as long as it did without the active collaboration or passive acquiescence of many, a fact that produced bitterness and recrimination for years.

Go to INQUIZITIVE to see what you've learned—and learn what you've missed—with personalized feedback along the way.

PEOPLE, IDEAS, AND EVENTS IN CONTEXT

❯ What was Hitler asking for at the **MUNICH CONFERENCE** of 1938? What made many people in Europe think that **APPEASEMENT** was their best option?

❯ What was the **HITLER-STALIN PACT** of 1939?

❯ What was **BLITZKRIEG**? What effect did it have on those who faced German invasions?

❯ What were Hitler's goals in **OPERATION BARBAROSSA**, the invasion of the Soviet Union in 1941? What were the consequences of the German defeat at **STALINGRAD**?

❯ What made the **SECOND WORLD WAR** a global war? Where outside of Europe were the main consequences of the war felt most keenly?

❯ What was the **MANHATTAN PROJECT**? How did it affect the outcome of the Second World War?

THINKING ABOUT CONNECTIONS

❯ What long-term causes, going back to the history of Europe in the nineteenth century, might you point to in order to understand the outbreak of the Second World War? Can you link the story of this war with the history of European imperialism in the nineteenth century or with the successes and failures of the German national unification movements?

❯ What circumstances made the Second World War a global conflict?

27

The Cold War World:

GLOBAL POLITICS, ECONOMIC RECOVERY, AND CULTURAL CHANGE

BEFORE YOU READ THIS CHAPTER ❯

THE WAR ENDED THE WAY a passage through a tunnel ends," wrote Heda Kovály, a Czech woman who survived the concentration camps. "From far away you could see the light ahead, a gleam that kept growing, and its brilliance seemed ever more dazzling to you huddled there in the dark the longer it took to reach it. But when at last the train burst out into the glorious sunshine, all you saw was a wasteland." The war left Europe a land of wreckage and confusion. Millions of refugees trekked hundreds or thousands of miles on foot to return to their homes, while others were forcibly displaced from their lands. In some areas, housing was practically nonexistent, with no available means to build anew. Food remained in dangerously short supply: a year after the war, roughly 100 million people in Europe still lived on fewer than 1,500 calories a day. Families scraped vegetables from their gardens or traded smuggled goods on the black market. Governments continued to ration food and coal. Meanwhile, the brutality of war and occupation had divided countries from within, shredding relations among ethnic groups and fellow citizens. Intense relief at liberation often went hand in hand with recriminations over their neighbors' wartime betrayal, collaboration, or simple opportunism.

How does a nation, region, or civilization recover from a catastrophe on the scale of the Second World War? Nations had to do much more than deliver food and rebuild economic infrastructures; they had to restore—or create—government authority, functioning bureaucracies, and

> Postwar Europeans looked to rebuild their shattered continent in the shadow of a cold war between the United States and the Soviet Union. The new international order sharply curtailed the ability of European nations to act independently.

> After 1945, European imperial powers faced challenges from movements for national independence in Africa, the Middle East, and Asia. By the early 1960s, almost all the colonies of Britain and France had gained their independence.

> Western European nations increasingly turned toward political and economic cooperation, leading to unprecedented economic growth in the 1950s and the 1960s. In Eastern Europe, the socialist regimes of the Eastern bloc sought to chart a different path under Soviet sponsorship, achieving modest growth in economies that emphasized heavy industries more than the manufacture of consumer goods.

CORE OBJECTIVES

> **UNDERSTAND** the origins of the Cold War and the ways that the United States and the Soviet Union sought to influence the political and economic restructuring of Europe in the postwar period.

> **IDENTIFY** the policies that led to the economic integration of Western European nations in the postwar decades and the reasons for the subsequent rapid economic growth.

> **DESCRIBE** the process of decolonization that brought the colonial era in Africa and Asia to an end.

> **EXPLAIN** the developments in European postwar culture, as intellectuals, writers, and artists reacted to the loss of European influence in the world and the ideological conflicts of the Cold War.

THE REMAINS OF DRESDEN, 1947. Dresden was devastated by a controversial Allied bombing in February 1945. Kurt Vonnegut dramatically portrayed its destruction and the aftermath in his novel *Slaughterhouse-Five*.
›How did the war's new strategies of aerial bombardment—culminating in the use of atomic weapons—change the customary division between combatants and noncombatant civilians?

legal systems. They had to rebuild bonds of trust and civility among citizens, steering a course between demands for justice on the one hand, and the overwhelming desire to bury memories of the past on the other. Rebuilding entailed a commitment to renewing democratic institutions that could withstand threats such as those the West had experienced in the 1930s. Some aspects of this process were successful, more than even the most optimistic forecaster might have thought possible in 1945. But others failed or were deferred until later in the century.

The war's devastating effects brought two dramatic changes in the international balance of power. The first change was the emergence of the so-called superpowers—the United States and the Soviet Union—and the swift development of a "cold war" between them. The Cold War divided Europe, with Eastern Europe occupied by Soviet troops and Western Europe dominated by the military and economic presence of the United States (see *Interpreting Visual Evidence* on pages 970–71). In both Western and Eastern Europe, the Cold War led to increased political and economic integration, resulting in the emergence of the European Common Market in the West and the socialist bloc dominated by the Soviet Union in the East.

The second great change came with the dismantling of the European empires that had once stretched worldwide. Between 1945 and the 1960s most of the colonies established by European nations in the previous century gained their political independence in an unprecedented—and at times violent—process known as **decolonization**. The collapse of empires and the creation of newly emancipated nations challenged the West's vision of itself as the motor of modernity. It also raised

decolonization A complex process by which an empire relinquishes formal political control over colonial territory while the formerly colonized peoples assert their independence and create institutions for self-rule.

the stakes of the Cold War and brought superpower rivalry to far-flung regions of the globe. These twin fractures—the split between the Soviet Union and the United States, and the global confrontation between European imperial powers and anticolonial independent movements—intersected in unpredictable ways. The threat of nuclear confrontation and the need for economic rebuilding after the Second World War meant that neither the United States nor the Soviet Union could back away from global affairs, just as formerly colonized nations in Africa, Asia, and the Middle East asserted themselves against European and U.S. power and influence.

The Cold War and a Divided Continent

No peace treaty ended the Second World War. As the war drew to a close, relations between the Allies began to fray over issues of power and influence in Central and Eastern Europe. After the war, mistrust became open conflict. The United States and the Soviet Union rapidly formed two opposing imperial blocs. Their rivalry, which came to be known as the **Cold War**, pitted the two military powers—and their different ideologies, capitalism and communism—against one another. The Cold War's repercussions reached well beyond Europe, as anticolonial movements turned to the Soviets for help in their struggles for independence. The Cold War thus structured the peace on a global scale.

THE DISPLACED

In 1945, an unprecedented number of people were on the move in Europe, Asia, and the Middle East. These mass migrations were a response to, and often a continuation of, wartime deportations and expulsions. After the invasion of Poland in 1939, Soviet Russia deported hundreds of thousands of Poles, Jews, and Ukrainians to camps in Siberia. After the Nazi invasion in 1941, the Soviets followed up by sending similar numbers of ethnic Germans, Crimean Tatars, and Chechens residing in Soviet territory to central Asia.

Some 3 million refugees from Central and Eastern Europe fled westward in 1945, fleeing territory controlled by the Soviet Union. Between 1944 and 1946, transfers between Poland and the Soviet Union alone involved 1.3 million people, while simultaneously 2 million Russians and 450,000 Poles held in Germany were repatriated from areas controlled by the Allies. A further 7 million ethnic Germans were expelled from Czechoslovakia, Poland, Hungary, and Yugoslavia. During the same period, Bulgaria expelled a quarter million Turks, and Romania deported thousands of Armenian refugees to an unwilling Turkey. Overseeing these migrations was a new organization, the Relief and Rehabilitation Administration (UNRRA), founded in 1943 and put under United Nations control in 1945. For four years, the UNRRA administered nearly 800 Displaced Persons Camps, reaching some 7 million people. In 1947, its activities were replaced by the UN's International Refugee Organization and the economic assistance offered by the Marshall Plan (see pages 972–73).

THE IRON CURTAIN

The Soviet Union insisted during wartime negotiations at Tehran (1943) and the **Yalta Conference** (1945) that it had a legitimate claim to control Eastern Europe, a claim that Western leaders accepted as the price of defeating Hitler. The

SURVIVORS AT BERGEN-BELSEN EXCHANGE CAMP, 1945. This photograph was taken after the liberation of the concentration camp complex at Bergen-Belsen by British and Canadian soldiers in April 1945. The Germans used the exchange camp to detain Jewish women and children, whom they hoped to exchange for German prisoners or cash. These survivors, and countless others like them across Europe, needed shelter, food, and medical attention from the Allies in the aftermath of the war.

Joseph Stalin (1878–1953) The Bolshevik leader who succeeded Lenin as leader of the Soviet Union and ruled until his death in 1953.

Across Eastern Europe, the Soviet Union installs "people's republics" sympathetic to Moscow ❯

Soviets respond to Western anticommunist efforts with alliances and programs that consolidate so-called Eastern bloc ❯

Declaration of Liberated Europe issued at the Yalta Conference guaranteed free elections, but **Joseph Stalin** believed that the framework of Allied cooperation gave him a free hand in Eastern Europe. Stalin's authoritarian regime cast nearly everyone at home or abroad as a potential threat or enemy of the state. Yet Soviet policy did not rest on Stalin's personal paranoia alone. The country's catastrophic wartime losses made the Soviets determined to control the lands they had liberated from Nazi rule. When their former allies resisted their demands, the Soviets became suspicious and defensive.

The Soviet Union used diplomatic pressure, political infiltration, and military power to create "people's republics" in Eastern Europe. Despite different local political contexts, in country after country the same process unfolded. First, the Central and Eastern European states set up coalition governments that excluded former Nazi sympathizers. Next came coalitions dominated by communists. Finally, the Communist party took hold of all the key positions of power. This progression prompted Winston Churchill to say that an "Iron Curtain" had "descended across Europe." In 1948, the Soviets crushed a Czechoslovakian coalition government—a break from Yalta's guarantee of democratic elections that shocked many Europeans. That year, governments dependent on Moscow had been established in Poland, Hungary, Romania, and Bulgaria, creating a Soviet-dominated "Eastern bloc."

Soviet efforts to control Eastern Europe did not go unchallenged. The Yugoslavian communist leader Marshal Tito (Josip Broz; 1892–1980) fought to keep his government independent of Moscow. Tito came to power without Soviet help during the war, and thanks to his wartime record he was able to draw support from Serbs, Croats, and Muslims in Yugoslavia. Moscow charged that Yugoslavia had become a

NORWAY
Oslo
SWEDEN
Stockholm
FINLAND
Helsinki
Leningrad

From Finland, 1940–1956

NORTH SEA

DENMARK
Copenhagen

BALTIC SEA

ESTONIA
To U.S.S.R., 1940

LATVIA
To U.S.S.R., 1940

LITHUANIA
To U.S.S.R., 1940

NETHERLANDS
Amsterdam
U.S. Zone
Bremen
Soviet Zone
Berlin

Incorporated into U.S.S.R., 1945
Gdansk (Danzig)

Incorporated into Poland, 1945

WHITE RUSSIA
Brest

Brussels
British Zone
EAST GERMANY (1949)

BELGIUM
Bonn

WEST GERMANY
U.S. Zone

LUXEMBOURG

Warsaw

POLAND (1947)

From Poland, 1940–1947

UKRAINE

Prague
CZECHOSLOVAKIA (1948)

From Czechoslovakia, 1945–1947

SWITZERLAND
Bern
French Zone
Munich
U.S. Zone
French Zone
Vienna
Soviet Zone
AUSTRIA
British Zone

SOVIET UNION (1917)

BESSARABIA

From Romania, 1940–1947

Milan

From Italy, 1945

Budapest
HUNGARY (1949)

ROMANIA (1947)

CRIMEA

Yalta

YUGOSLAVIA (1945)

ITALY
Rome

Bucharest

BLACK SEA

Danube R.

From Romania, 1940–1947

ADRIATIC SEA

CORSICA (Fr.)

SARDINIA (It.)

BULGARIA (1946)
Sofia

Tirane

ALBANIA (1944)

GREECE

Istanbul

TURKEY

SICILY (It.)

Athens

CRETE

CYPRUS

MEDITERRANEAN SEA

Legend:
- Allied occupation of Germany and Austria, 1945–1955
- Territory regained by Poland from Germany
- Territory gained by Soviet Union
- Postwar national boundaries, to 1989
- "Iron Curtain" to 1989
- (19—) Year communist control of government was gained

Inset: EAST GERMANY
French Sector
WEST British Sector
BERLIN U.S. Sector
EAST Soviet Sector
BERLIN
Potsdam
Berlin Wall (1961–1989)
0 10 Miles
0 10 Kilometers

Inset: Area of detail
EUROPE
AFRICA

Scale: 0 200 400 Miles / 0 200 400 Kilometers

TERRITORIAL CHANGES IN EUROPE AFTER THE SECOND WORLD WAR. At the end of the Second World War, the Soviet Union annexed territory in Eastern Europe to create a buffer between it and Western Europe. At the same time, the United States established a series of military alliances in Western Europe to stifle the spread of communism in Europe. › **Which Eastern European countries fell under Soviet control?** › **Where is Berlin located?** › **Why did the location and control of Germany cause so much tension?** › **How did these new territorial boundaries aggravate tensions between the Soviet Union and the United States?**

The End of the Second World War and the Onset of the Cold War

The need to defeat Nazi Germany brought the United States and the Soviet Union together in a common struggle, despite their contrasting political systems. Both nations emerged from the Second World War with a renewed sense of purpose, and both tried to use the victory against fascism to promote their claims for legitimacy and leadership in Europe. These circumstances placed a special burden on European nations and their postwar governments, as they were forced to take sides in this global confrontation at a moment of weakness and uncertainty.

The images shown here, all from May 1945 in Czechoslovakia, an Eastern European country, display

A. Czech propaganda poster celebrating German defeat, May 1945.

B. Czech propaganda poster, May 1945.

"colony of the imperialist nations," and expelled the country from the economic and military pacts of communist countries.

Determined to reassert control elsewhere, the Soviets purged the parties and administrations of various satellite governments, beginning in the Balkans. The fact that democratic institutions had been broken in many places before the war made it easier to establish dictatorships in its aftermath. The purges succeeded by playing on fears and festering hatreds. In particular antisemitism, far from being crushed, remained a potent political force, and it became common to blame Jews for bringing several different possibilities for representing the German defeat. Image A shows a Czech civilian rending the Nazi flag, with the Prague skyline in the background and the flags of the major Allied Powers and Czechoslovakia overhead. Image B shows a triumphant Czech laborer wielding a rifle and a socialist red flag, while standing over the corpse of a German soldier. Image C shows portraits of Stalin and the Czech president Edvard Beneš above two columns of Soviet and Czech soldiers marching together under their respective flags. Beneš, who had been president of Czechoslovakia before the war, was returned to office in October 1945, only to be forced to resign in 1948 after a successful coup by the Soviet-backed Communist party.

Questions for Analysis

1. How do these images portray the victory over the Germans?

2. How do these images deal with the question of Czechoslovakian nationalism?

3. Which of the three images most coincides with the Soviet view of the Czech situation?

C. Czech propaganda card, May 1945.

the horrors of war to Europe. These purges were accompanied by broad economic changes, as states seized private property for public use and mobilized the population for reconstruction and industrial development. All public life—and even culture—was strictly controlled by the regime.

The end of war did not mean peace. In Greece, as in Yugoslavia and through much of the Balkans, the war's end brought a local communist-led resistance close to seizing power; the bloody civil war, which lasted until 1949, took a higher toll than the wartime occupation. The British and the Americans aimed to keep Greece in their

Legend:
- American zone
- British zone
- French zone
- Soviet zone
- Eastern bloc countries
- Berlin airlift 1948–1949

sphere of influence and sent large infusions of aid to the anticommunist monarchy. Greece's bloodletting became one of the first crises of the Cold War and a touchstone for the United States' escalating fear of communist expansion.

Defeated Germany became the front line of the Cold War. The Western Allies divided Germany into four zones of occupation; the capital, Berlin, was in Soviet territory, but it too was divided. The occupation zones were intended to be temporary, but the Soviets and the other Allies quarreled over reparations and economic development in Germany. Conflicts among the French, British, and United States were almost as intense as their disagreements with the Soviets, but the quickening Cold War put those arguments on hold, and in 1948 the three Western Allies began to create a single government for their territories. They introduced a new currency—a powerful symbol of economic unity. The Soviets retaliated by cutting all access from the Western Zone to West Berlin. The Western Allies refused to cede control of the capital, and for eleven months, they airlifted 12,000 tons of supplies a day over Soviet territory to the besieged Western Zone of Berlin. The Berlin blockade, which lasted from June 1948 to May 1949, ended with the creation of two Germanies: the Federal Republic in the west and the German Democratic Republic in the east. Within a few short years, both Germanies looked strikingly like armed camps.

GERMANY DIVIDED AND THE BERLIN AIRLIFT.
In the summer of 1948, the Soviet Union blocked routes through the German Democratic Republic to the Allies' Western Zone of Berlin. The blockade forced the Allies to airlift supplies to West Berlin and exacerbated tensions between the Soviet Union and the United States. At one point, planes landed in Berlin every three minutes. › **Why were the Western Allies able to airlift so much food so frequently?** › **How did this event lead to the eventual division of Germany into two nations?** › **What were the consequences of this division for the German people?**

THE MARSHALL PLAN

The United States countered Soviet expansion with economic and military aid to Western Europe. President Harry Truman, in a 1947 speech to Congress, set out the **Truman Doctrine**: a pledge to support the resistance of "free peoples" against communism. The American president declared the Soviet–American conflict to be a choice between "two ways of life," and tied the contest for political power to economics. A few months later, Secretary of State George Marshall outlined an ambitious plan of economic aid to Europe— the European Recovery Program (ERP)—including, initially, the Eastern European states. Stalin, however, prohibited the communist governments of Central and Eastern Europe from accepting American aid.

The ERP, also known as the **Marshall Plan**, provided $13 billion over four years, beginning in 1948, targeting industrial redevelopment. The plan supplied American tractors, locomotive engines, food, technical equipment, and capital to

Truman Doctrine (1947)
Declaration promising U.S. economic and military intervention to counter any attempt by the Soviet Union to expand its influence.

GERMAN COMMUNISTS PROTEST IN BERLIN AGAINST THE MARSHALL PLAN, 1952. Cold War tensions between the United States and the Soviet Union divided Europeans against one another. The signs in this protest read: "Strength and Labor through Trade with the East!" and "Against the Marshall Plan [which] brings unemployment and poverty." › **What made the question of U.S. economic assistance so controversial for Germans?**

participating states. Unlike a relief plan, however, it encouraged the participating states to diagnose their own economic problems and develop their own solutions. With a series of other economic agreements, the Marshall Plan became one of the building blocks of European economic unity. The plan, however, required decontrol of prices, restraints on wages, and balanced budgets. The Americans encouraged opposition to left-leaning politicians and movements sympathetic to communism. The pressure to confront the Soviet Union also led the United States to abandon its plan to purge former Nazi party members from positions of influence in West Germany. The most prominent surviving Nazi leaders were tried at Nuremberg in 1945–1946, and twelve were executed. Subsequent trials lasted until 1949, but many of the millions of Nazi party members simply resumed their lives.

The Cold War led the United States to shore up military defenses in Western Europe. In April 1949, Canada, the United States, and representatives of Western European states established the **North Atlantic Treaty Organization** (**NATO**); Greece, Turkey, and West Germany were later added as members. An armed attack against any NATO member would now be regarded as an attack against all and would bring a united military response. NATO's ground forces grew to sixty divisions by 1953—including a dozen divisions from the young state of West Germany. Among the most striking aspects of the war's aftermath was how rapidly Germany was reintegrated into Europe. In the new Cold War world, *the West* quickly came to mean anticommunism, and all potentially reliable allies, whatever their past, were not to be punished or excluded.

Marshall Plan Economic aid package given to Europe by the United States after the Second World War to promote reconstruction and economic development and to secure European countries from a feared communist takeover.

North Atlantic Treaty Organization (NATO) A 1949 military agreement among the United States, Canada, Great Britain, and eight Western European nations, which declared that an armed attack against any one of the members would be regarded as an attack against all.

TWO WORLDS AND THE RACE FOR THE BOMB

The Soviets viewed NATO, the Marshall Plan, and the United States' involvement in Europe's affairs with mounting alarm. They responded by establishing an Eastern European version of the plan: the Council for Mutual Economic Assistance (or Comecon). In 1947, the Soviets organized an international political arm, the Communist Information Bureau (or Cominform), to coordinate international communist programs. They responded to NATO with their own military alliance, the Warsaw Pact of 1955. This agreement set up a joint command among the states of Albania, Bulgaria, Czechoslovakia, Hungary, Poland, Romania, and East Germany, and guaranteed the continued presence of Soviet troops in all those countries.

These conflicts were overshadowed by the nuclear arms race. In 1949, the Soviet Union tested its first **atomic bomb**, modeled on the plutonium bomb that Americans had used in 1945. By 1953, both superpowers possessed hydrogen bombs, weapons that were 1,000 times more powerful than the bomb dropped on Hiroshima. Within a few years, both countries developed intercontinental missiles that could carry several nuclear warheads. These weapons could be fired from land or from nuclear-powered submarines that roamed the seas at all times. J. Robert Oppenheimer, who oversaw the development of the first atomic bomb, warned that the H-bomb's dramatic power could make it a "weapon of genocide."

The H-bomb quickly took on enormous cultural significance as a symbol of the age, confirming both humanity's power and its vulnerability. Beyond the grim warnings that nuclear war would wipe out human civilization, the bomb had more specific strategic consequences. The nuclearization of warfare fed into the polarizing effect of the Cold War because countries without nuclear arms found it difficult to avoid joining either the Soviet or the American pact. The threat of nuclear war divided the world in a new way: superpowers, with their enormous military budgets, on the one hand, and the nations that came to rely on agreements and international law on the other. It changed the nature of face-to-face warfare as well, encouraging "proxy wars" between clients of superpowers and raising fears that local conflicts might trigger a general war.

Was the Cold War inevitable? Could the Americans and the Soviets have negotiated an agreement? On the Soviet side, Stalin's personal suspiciousness, ruthlessness, and autocratic ambitions combined with genuine security concerns to fuel a Cold War mentality. U.S. leaders feared Soviet influence in Eastern Europe made it impossible for Western European nations to respond to postwar crises in Germany, Greece, and elsewhere. The United States was unwilling to give up the power it had acquired during the war. Turning away from its traditional isolationism, the United States articulated new strategic interests with global consequences, including access to European industry and far-flung military bases. These interests played into Soviet fears, and trust became all but impossible.

A new strategy to "contain" Soviet threat

The new international balance of power required new strategies. In 1946, diplomat George Kennan argued that the United States needed to make containing the Soviet threat a priority. According to Kennan, the Soviets had not embarked on world revolution and were not necessarily expansionist. Against this opponent, displays of toughness or threats were counterproductive. The United States needed to respond with "the adroit and vigilant application of counterforce at a series of constantly shifting geographical and political points." This policy of containment became the point of reference for U.S. foreign policy for the next forty years (see *Competing Viewpoints* on pages 978–79).

U.S. AND SOVIET VIEWS OF THE ARMS RACE. From 1946 to 1958, the United States detonated multiple nuclear weapons as tests at the Bikini Atoll in the Pacific Ocean; the Soviet Union's first successful nuclear test came in 1949. These posters, both apparently depicting the Pacific site of the U.S. nuclear testing, demonstrate the use of nuclear warfare images by both governments to communicate with their populations. The U.S. civil defense poster (left) seeks to convince the American population that "it *can* happen here"; the Soviet poster (right) states simply: *Het!* ("No!") › **Coming so soon after the destruction left by the Second World War, how might such images have been received by the populations of the United States and the Soviet Union?**

At its height, the Cold War had a chilling effect on domestic politics in both countries. In the Soviet Union, writers and artists were attacked for deviating from the party line. The party disciplined economists for suggesting that Western European industry might recover from wartime destruction. Soviet radio blared news that Czech or Hungarian reformist leaders had been exposed as traitors. In the United States, congressional committees launched campaigns to root out alleged "communists." On both sides of the Iron Curtain, the Cold War intensified everyday anxiety, provoked by repeated warnings that a way of life was at stake and appeals to defend family and home against the menacing "other."

KHRUSHCHEV AND THE THAW

After Stalin died in 1953, **Nikita Khrushchev**'s slow accession to power, not secure until 1956, signaled a change of direction. Whereas Stalin had secluded himself in the Kremlin, Khrushchev traveled throughout the world. He visited the United States in 1959, meeting with Iowa farmers and spending a day at Disneyland. Khrushchev was a shrewd politician, and he soon agreed to a summit meeting with British, French, and

Nikita Khrushchev
(1894–1971) Leader of the Soviet Union during the Cuban missile crisis, Khrushchev came to power after Stalin's death in 1953.

NIKITA KHRUSHCHEV. Khrushchev, premier (1958–1964) and first secretary of the Communist party (1953–1964) of the Soviet Union, visited the United States in 1959. Here, he is shown joking with an Iowa farmer. › **Why was it important for Khrushchev to engage a foreign audience in this way?**

American leaders. This summit eased frictions in Europe, and led to a ban on testing nuclear weapons above ground.

Khrushchev's famous "secret speech" to communist party leaders in 1956 acknowledged the excesses of Stalin's era. Though the speech was not public, his accusations were widely discussed. Stalin's regime had generated popular discontent, and Soviet leaders faced demands for more consumer goods, more freedom in the arts, and for an end to police repression. The ensuing Soviet "thaw" unleashed forces that proved difficult to control. Between 1956 and 1958, the Soviet prison camps released thousands of prisoners, and Soviet citizens besieged the regime with requests to rehabilitate relatives of those who had been executed or imprisoned under Stalin. In the new cultural climate, private life—family issues, the shortage of men after the war, and the problem of orphans—became a legitimate subject of concern and discussion. During this period, many foreigners in prison and labor camps, including Germans, Poles, Czechs, and Hungarians, were allowed to leave the Soviet Union.

The thaw provided a brief window of opportunity for some of the Soviet Union's most important writers. In 1957, Boris Pasternak's novel *Doctor Zhivago* could not be published in the Soviet Union, and Pasternak was barred from receiving his Nobel Prize. In 1962, Aleksandr Solzhenitsyn's (*suhl-zhih-NYEE-tsihn*) first novel, *One Day in the Life of Ivan Denisovich*, marked the relative cultural freedom of the thaw. *Ivan Denisovich* was based on Solzhenitsyn's own experiences in the camps, where he had spent eight years for criticizing Stalin in a letter. By 1964, Khrushchev had fallen and the thaw ended, driving criticism and writers underground. Solzhenitsyn kept working in secret on what would become *The Gulag Archipelago*, a massive historical and literary study of the Stalinist camps (gulags).

AFTER STALIN IN EASTERN EUROPE

By the year of Stalin's death in 1953, tensions had exploded in Eastern Europe. The East German government, burdened by reparation payments to the Soviet Union, faced an economic crisis. The illegal exodus of East German citizens to the West rose sharply: 58,000 left in March 1953 alone. In June, strikes broke out in East Berlin, and the unrest spread throughout the country. The Soviet army put down the uprising, and hundreds were executed in the subsequent purge. In the aftermath, the East German government, under the leadership of Walter Ulbricht, used fears of disorder to solidify one-party rule.

In 1956, Khrushchev's policy of de-Stalinization and the "thaw" brought about a sense of relief for many in the Soviet sphere. Perceiving an opening, Poles and Hungarians demanded more independence in the management of their domestic affairs. In Poland, the movement began in June 1956 with a rebellion by Polish workers in Poznań that was soon crushed by the military. By October, the leading Polish Stalinists were forced to resign, replaced by the anti-Stalinist Polish leader Władysław Gomułka. By pledging Poland's loyalty to the Warsaw Pact, Gomułka won Soviet permission for his country to pursue its own "ways of Socialist development." A few years of liberalization followed, but Gomułka became more conservative and resistant to political reform in the 1960s.

Events in Hungary turned out very differently. The charismatic leader of Hungary's communist government, Imre Nagy (*EEM-re NOD-yuh*), was as much a Hungarian nationalist as a communist. Under his government, protests against Moscow's policies developed into a much broader anticommunist struggle. He announced that he would dismantle Hungary's political police and withdraw from the Warsaw Pact. Khrushchev's thaw never envisioned such a consequence, and on November 4, 1956, Soviet troops occupied Budapest, arresting and executing leaders of the Hungarian rebellion. The Hungarians took up arms, and street fighting continued for several weeks. They had hoped for Western aid, but President Dwight D. Eisenhower steered clear of giving them support. Soviet forces installed a new government under the staunchly communist János Kádár, and tens of thousands of Hungarian refugees fled to the West. Khrushchev's efforts at presenting a gentler, more conciliatory Soviet Union to the West had been shattered by revolt and repression.

When Nagy's government threatens to secede from Warsaw Pact, Soviets under Khrushchev occupy Hungary and install new government

Furthermore, East Germans continued to flee the country via West Berlin. Between 1949 and 1961, some 2.7 million East Germans left—stark evidence of the unpopularity of the regime. Attempting to stem the tide, Khrushchev demanded that the West recognize the permanent division of Germany with an undivided Berlin. When that demand was refused, the East German government built a ten-foot wall separating the two sectors of the city in 1961. For almost thirty years, until 1989, the Berlin Wall remained a monument to how far the war had gone cold, darkly mirroring the division of Germany, and Europe as a whole.

THE BERLIN WALL, 1961 AND 1989. By 1960, the East German economy was in severe trouble, and many people, especially educated professionals, were fleeing to the West: 200,000 in 1960 and 103,000 in the first six months of 1961. On August 13, 1961, the East German government placed armed guards and barbed wire around West Berlin to stop the flow (see photo on the left). This bold move allowed the East German nation to survive, but it also created a powerful symbol of the regime's repressive character. In 1989, the breach in the wall was the final sign of the East German government's collapse, and the freedom to enter West Berlin marked a turning point after nearly three decades of enforced isolation. In the photo on the right, Chancellor Helmut Kohl of West Germany (center, looking up), shakes hands with East Germans on top of the wall in December 1989.

The Cold War: Soviet and American Views

The first excerpt is from a speech titled "The Sinews of Peace," delivered by Winston Churchill at Westminster College in Fulton, Missouri, in early 1946. Warning of the rising power of the Soviet Union in Eastern Europe, he coined the phrase "iron curtain."

The second excerpt is from an address by Nikita Khrushchev, who became first secretary of the Communist party in 1953. Three years later, his power secure, he began publicly to repudiate the crimes of Joseph Stalin. Khrushchev presided over a short-lived thaw in Soviet–American relations. Yet, as can be seen in his address, Khrushchev shared Churchill's conception of the world as divided into two mutually antagonistic camps.

Winston Churchill's "Iron Curtain" Speech

A shadow has fallen upon the scenes so lately lighted by the Allied victory. Nobody knows what Soviet Russia and its Communist international organization intend to do in the immediate future, or what are the limits, if any, to their expansive and proselytizing tendencies. I have a strong admiration and regard for the valiant Russian people and for my wartime comrade, Marshal [sic] Stalin. There is deep sympathy and goodwill in Britain . . . towards the people of all the Russias and a resolve to persevere through many differences and rebuffs in establishing lasting friendships. We understand the Russian need to be secure on her western frontiers by the removal of all possibility of German aggression. We welcome Russia to her rightful place among the leading nations of the world. We welcome her flag upon the seas. Above all, we welcome constant, frequent and growing contacts between the Russian people and our own people on both sides of the Atlantic. It is my duty however . . . to place before you certain facts about the present position in Europe.

From Stettin in the Baltic to Trieste in the Adriatic, an iron curtain has descended across the Continent. Behind that line lie all the capitals of the ancient states of Central and Eastern Europe. Warsaw, Berlin, Prague, Vienna, Budapest, Belgrade, Bucharest and Sofia, all these famous cities and the populations around them lie in what I must call the Soviet sphere, and all are subject in one form or another, not only to Soviet influence but to a very high and, in many cases, increasing measure of control from Moscow. . . .

From what I have seen of our Russian friends and allies during the war, I am convinced that there is nothing they admire so much as strength, and there is nothing for which they have less respect than for weakness, especially military weakness. For that reason the old doctrine of a balance of power is unsound. We cannot afford, if we can help it, to work on narrow margins, offering temptations to a triad of strength. If the Western Democracies stand together in strict

Economic Renaissance

Despite the ongoing tensions of global superpower rivalry, the postwar period brought an economic "miracle" in Western Europe. The war had encouraged technological innovations that could be applied in peacetime: improved communications, the development of synthetic materials, increasing use of aluminum and alloy steels, and advances in prefabrication. Wartime manufacturing had added significantly to adherence to the principles of the United Nations Charter, their influences for furthering those principles will be immense and no one is likely to molest them. If however they become divided or falter in their duty and if these all-important years are allowed to slip away then indeed catastrophe may overwhelm us all.

Source: Winston Churchill, *Winston S. Churchill: His Complete Speeches, 1897-1963*, vol. 7, *1943-1949*, ed. Robert Rhodes James (New York: 1983), pp. 7290-91.

Nikita Khrushchev, Report to the Communist Party Congress (1961)

Comrades! The competition of the two world social systems, the socialist and the capitalist, has been the chief content of the period since the 20th party Congress. It has become the pivot, the foundation of world development at the present historical stage. Two lines, two historical trends, have manifested themselves more and more clearly in social development. One is the line of social progress, peace and constructive activity. The other is the line of reaction, oppression and war.

In the course of the peaceful competition of the two systems capitalism has suffered a profound moral defeat in the eyes of all peoples. The common people are daily convinced that capitalism is incapable of solving a single one of the urgent problems confronting mankind. It becomes more and more obvious that only on the paths to socialism can a solution to these problems be found. Faith in the capitalist system and the capitalist path of development is dwindling. Monopoly capital, losing its influence, resorts more and more to intimidating and suppressing the masses of the people, to methods of open dictatorship in carrying out its domestic policy and to aggressive acts against other countries. But the masses of the people offer increasing resistance to reaction's acts.

It is no secret to anyone that the methods of intimidation and threat are not a sign of strength but evidence of the weakening of capitalism, the deepening of its general crisis. As the saying goes, if you can't hang on by the mane, you won't hang on by the tail! Reaction is still capable of dissolving parliaments in some countries in violation of their constitutions, of casting the best representatives of the people into prison, of sending cruisers and marines to subdue the "unruly." All this can put off for a time the approach of the fatal hour for the rule of capitalism. The imperialists are sawing away at the branch on which they sit. There is no force in the world capable of stopping man's advance along the road of progress.

Source: *Current Soviet Policies IV: The Documentary Record of the 22nd Congress of the Communist Party of the Soviet Union*, ed. Charlotte Saikowski and Leo Gruliow, from the translations of the *Current Digest of the Soviet Press*, Joint Committee on Slavic Studies (New York: 1962), pp. 42-45.

Questions for Analysis

1. Whom did Churchill blame for building the Iron Curtain between the Soviet sphere and the Western sphere?

2. How was the Soviet Union actively trying to create international communism? How was the United States trying to spread its way of life globally?

nations' productive capacities. The Marshall Plan seems to have been less central than many claimed at the time, but it solved immediate problems with the balance of payments and a shortage of American dollars to buy American goods. The boom was further fueled by high consumer demand and very high levels of employment throughout the 1950s and the 1960s. Rising demand for Europe's goods hastened agreements that encouraged the free flow of international trade and currencies (discussed on pages 981–82).

EUROPE DURING THE COLD WAR. Examine the membership of NATO and the Warsaw Pact, respectively. › Which nations were the member states of NATO? › Which nations were members of the Warsaw Pact? › Why do you think some countries did not join NATO? › Why did the membership of each alliance stay relatively stable for nearly a half century?

Western European political leaders assumed that states should manage the economy: directing investment, making decisions about what to modernize, and coordinating policies between industries and countries. This, too, was a legacy of wartime deprivation. The result was a series of "mixed" economies combining public and private ownership. France and Britain nationalized a wide range of industries including energy, utilities, transportation, and banking. Nationalization was less common in West Germany, though railways, and portions of the automotive, electrical, chemical, and metallurgical sectors remained in state hands.

These government policies and programs contributed to astonishing growth rates. Between 1945 and 1963, the average yearly growth of West Germany's gross domestic product—gross national product (GNP) minus income received from abroad—was 7.6 percent. Growth in Austria, Italy, France, and the Netherlands was also high. The recovery actually reversed prewar economic patterns of overproduction and insufficient investment, leaving factories hard-pressed to keep up with the soaring demand.

West Germany's recovery was spectacular, and important to the rest of Europe. Production increased sixfold between 1948 and 1964 and unemployment fell to record lows: in 1965 there were six jobs for every unemployed person. In the 1950s, the state and private industry built a half million new housing units each year, to accommodate citizens whose homes had been destroyed, as well as refugees from East Germany and Eastern Europe, and transient workers from Italy, Spain, Greece, and elsewhere drawn in by West Germany's high demand for labor. German mechanical goods, optics, and chemicals led world markets. West German women were included in the process as well: during the 1950s, German politicians encouraged women to take up a role as "citizen consumers," as active but prudent buyers of goods that would keep the German economy humming.

Western European nations all shared in the general prosperity. Economic growth, however, did not eliminate differences among and within states: in southern Italy, illiteracy remained high, and land continued to be held by a few rich families; and the per capita GNP in Sweden was almost ten times that of Turkey. Britain remained a special case. British growth was respectable when compared with past performance, yet the British economy remained sluggish. The country was burdened with obsolete factories and methods and an unwillingness to invest in new industries.

Western European governments opt for mixed economies that combined public and private ownership in postwar decades

EUROPEAN ECONOMIC INTEGRATION

The Western European renaissance was a collective effort. Aided by Marshall Plan support from the United States, Western European leaders sought to foster economic interdependence among their nations, an "ever closer union" that could become the basis for a common European identity. The process of European integration began with a project to create a common market for the most essential primary materials: coal and steel. The European Coal and Steel Community (ECSC) was founded in 1951 to coordinate trade between West Germany's coal mines and France's steel mills. The next crucial step came in 1957, when the Treaty of Rome created the European Economic Community (EEC), or Common Market, which aimed to abolish trade barriers among its members: France, West Germany, Italy, Belgium, the Netherlands, and Luxembourg. The organization pledged itself to

European Economic Community eliminates trade barriers among member states in Western Europe common external tariffs, free movement of labor and capital among member nations, and uniform wage structures and social security systems to ensure similar working conditions throughout the Common Market.

Integration did not proceed smoothly. Great Britain stayed away, fearing the effects of the ECSC on its declining coal industry. Instead, Britain continued to rely on its economic relations with the empire and commonwealth. In the other countries, domestic opposition to EEC provisions on wages or agricultural prices often threatened to scuttle agreements. France and other countries, sensitive to the importance of the peasantry to political stability, insisted on protecting agriculture.

The seismic shifts that began to make oil and nuclear power more important than coal (see Chapter 28) made the ECSC less effective, but the EEC was a remarkable success. By 1963, the EEC had become the world's largest importer. Its steel production was second only to that of the United States, and its total industrial production was over 70 percent higher than it had been in 1950. And it established a new long-term political trend: individual countries sought European solutions to their problems.

Postwar efforts to manage global trade reflected and reinforced the United States' position as world's most powerful economy

Agreements reached in July 1944 in Bretton Woods, New Hampshire, aimed to coordinate the movements of the global economy and internationalize solutions to economic crises to avoid disasters like the Great Depression. The United States and Britain struggled to reach a consensus over currency exchange rates. The resulting compromise, elucidated in the Bretton Woods Accords, created the International Monetary Fund (IMF) and the World Bank, which oversaw new currency arrangements and limited the amount of investment capital that was allowed to move across national borders. The currencies of participating nations were pegged to the dollar, which provided stability while also enhancing the United States' role as the West's foremost financial power. The new international system was formed with the American–European sphere in mind, but these organizations soon began to play a role in the economic development of other global regions in Africa, Asia, and Latin America. The postwar period, then, quickened global economic integration, largely on American terms.

ECONOMIC DEVELOPMENT IN THE EAST

Economic development also occurred in Eastern Europe, though growth was not as dramatic as in the West. The communist governments undertook ambitious reconstruction and development projects by mobilizing the entire population, with initially impressive results. The culmination of communist engineering was the Soviet launch of Sputnik, the first orbiting satellite, in 1957.

Eastern European economies also grew after the Second World War under agreements that reflect Soviet power

Under these state-directed programs, national incomes rose and output increased in Eastern Europe. Poland and Hungary strengthened their economic connections with the West, primarily with France and West Germany. By the late 1970s, about 30 percent of Eastern Europe's trade was conducted outside the Soviet bloc. Nevertheless, the Soviet Union required its satellite countries to serve more than their own national interests. Regulations governing Comecon, the Eastern European equivalent of the Common Market, ensured that the Soviet Union could sell its exports at prices well above the world level and compelled other members to trade with the Soviet Union to their disadvantage.

Eastern European economic development focused initially on heavy industry and collectivized agriculture, but political tensions forced the Soviets to permit the manufacture of more consumer goods and the development of trade with the West.

This transition revealed the weakness of the planned economies of these countries. Managers of factories would receive production quotas, but the inability to balance supply and demand created shortages of consumer products and raw materials. Consumers waited for hours in queues when a long-desired product was suddenly available, and producers hoarded raw materials in anticipation of the next production cycle, exacerbating shortages elsewhere. In the long term, the economy was weakened by rising costs and lack of innovation.

THE WELFARE STATE

Economic growth became a watchword of the postwar era; *social welfare* was another. The roots of the new legislation extended back to the late 1880s, when Otto von Bismarck had introduced insurance plans for old age, sickness, and disability in Germany. Postwar economic expansion allowed European states to fund more comprehensive social programs, and commitments to put democracy on a stronger footing provided the political motivation. Clement Attlee, a leader of the British Labour party, coined the term *welfare state*. His government, in power until 1951, passed legislation that provided free medical care to all through the National Health Service, assistance to families, and guaranteed secondary education. Welfare states also assumed that governments should support popular purchasing power, generate demand, and provide unemployment insurance. Although the British Labour party and Continental socialist parties pressed these measures, welfare was a consensus issue, backed by the moderate coalitions that governed most postwar Western European states. Understood in this way, welfare was not poor relief but a social right. It thus marked a break with centuries-old ways of thinking about poverty and citizenship.

Welfare state policies in Western Europe seek to strengthen democratic tendencies in Europe by supporting purchase power and new social programs

EUROPEAN POLITICS

Postwar political leaders were pragmatic. Konrad Adenauer, the West German chancellor from 1949 to 1963, blamed German militarism for Hitler's rise to power but was apprehensive about German parliamentary democracy. His determination to end the long-held hostility between France and Germany contributed significantly to the movement toward European integration. Alcide De Gasperi, the Italian premier from 1948 to 1953, was also a centrist. Among postwar French leaders, the most colorful was the Resistance hero General Charles de Gaulle. De Gaulle had retired from politics in 1946 when French voters refused to accept his proposals for strengthening the executive branch of the government. But in 1958, he was invited to return when, faced with civil turmoil caused by the Algerian war and an abortive coup attempt by a group of right-wing army officers, the government collapsed. De Gaulle accepted but insisted on a new constitution. That constitution, which created the Fifth Republic in 1958, strengthened the executive branch of the government and weakened the power of Parliament. De Gaulle used his new authority to restore France's power and prestige, pivoting from France's imperial past to influencing the process of European integration. In 1966, he pulled French forces out of NATO, and cultivated better relations with the Soviet Union and West Germany. Finally, he accelerated French economic and industrial expansion by building a modern military establishment, complete with atomic weapons. De Gaulle steered a centrist course, and was committed to combating the radicalisms of the right and the left. Most other Western European nations did the same.

Revolution, Anticolonialism, and the Cold War

In the colonial world, the end of war unleashed new conflicts that complicated Cold War relations and Europe's political and economic recovery. The Cold War, as we have seen, created two powerful centers of gravity in world politics. But the wave of anticolonial independence movements that swept through postwar Asia and Africa created a new group of nations that attempted to avoid aligning with either bloc. These nations came to be known as the "Third World."

THE CHINESE REVOLUTION

The Chinese Revolution was the single most radical global development after the Second World War. A civil war had raged in China since 1926, with Mao Zedong's (*mow zeh-DOONG*; 1893–1976) communist insurgents in the north in revolt against the Nationalist forces of Jiang Jieshi (Chiang Kai-shek; 1887–1975). Though they agreed on a truce to face the Japanese during the war years, the civil war resumed after the Japanese defeat. In 1949, Mao's insurgents took control of the Chinese government and drove the Nationalists into exile on the island of Formosa (Taiwan).

The Chinese Revolution was above all a peasant revolution, even more so than the Russian Revolution. Mao adapted Marxism to conditions very different from those imagined by Marx himself, emphasizing radical reform in the countryside—reducing rents, providing health care and education, and reforming marriage—and autonomy from Western colonial powers. The leaders of the revolution set about turning China into a modern industrial nation within a generation, at an enormous human cost and with very mixed results.

To anticolonial activists in many parts of the world, the Chinese Revolution stood as a model; to colonial powers, it represented the dangers inherent in decolonization. The "loss of China" provoked fear and consternation and intensified Western anxiety about governments in Asia. Although Mao and Stalin distrusted one another and relations between the two regimes were extremely difficult, the United States considered both nations a communist bloc until the early 1970s.

THE KOREAN WAR

China's revolution helped turn Korea into a Cold War confrontation. A Japanese colony since the 1890s, Korea had been brutally exploited by the occupiers. At the end of the Second World War, the peninsula was divided into two states: North Korea, run by the Soviet client and communist Kim Il-Sung; and South Korea, led by the anticommunist autocrat Syngman Rhee, backed by the United States. When North Korean troops attacked the South in 1950, the United Nations Security Council gave permission for the United States to defend South Korea.

U.S. General Douglas MacArthur, drove the Korean communists to the Chinese border, but was relieved of his command by President Harry Truman after calling for attacks on Chinese territory. More than 1 million Chinese troops flooded across the border in support of the North Koreans, forcing the international troops

A RED GUARD DEMONSTRATION. Middle-school students display their solidarity with Mao Zedong's revolution by waving copies of a book of his quotations. The slogan proclaims, "Not only are we able to destroy the old world, we are able to build a new world instead—Mao Zedong." › **What made the Chinese Revolution different from the Bolshevik Revolution of 1917?**

into a bloody retreat. The war became a stalemate, pitting Chinese and North Korean troops against UN troops composed of American and South Korean forces backed by contingents from Britain, Australia, Ethiopia, the Netherlands, Turkey, and elsewhere. The war ended inconclusively in 1953, with Korea divided roughly along the original line. South Korea had not been "lost," but with more than 53,000 Americans and over 1 million Koreans and Chinese killed, neither side could claim a decisive victory.

DECOLONIZATION

Between 1947 and 1960, the sprawling European empires built during the nineteenth century disintegrated. Opposition to colonial rule stiffened after the First World War, forcing war-weakened European states to renegotiate the terms of empire. After the Second World War, the continuation of imperial rule quickly became untenable. In some regions, European states simply cut their losses and withdrew. In others, well-organized and tenacious nationalist movements successfully demanded new constitutional arrangements and independence. In a third set of cases, European powers were drawn into complicated and violent struggles between indigenous peoples and European settler communities.

THE BRITISH EMPIRE UNRAVELS

India was the first and largest colony to win self-government after the war. Early in the Second World War, the umbrella party of India's independence movement, the Indian National Congress, called on Britain to "quit India." The extraordinary Indian nationalist Mohandas K. (Mahatma) Gandhi (1869–1948) had been at work in India since the 1920s (see *Analyzing Primary Sources* on page 987). Gandhi advocated not violence but *swaraj* ("self-rule"), urging Indians to develop their own resources and withdraw from the imperial economy—by going on strike, refusing to pay taxes, and boycotting imported textiles and wearing homespun clothes. By 1947, Gandhi and his fellow nationalist Jawaharlal Nehru (1889–1964; prime minister 1947–1964) had gained such widespread support that the British found it impossible to remain in power.

Gandhi's "self-rule" calls for collective resistance and withdrawal from imperial economy

Even as talks proceeded, however, India was torn by ethnic and religious conflict. The Muslim League, led by Mohammed Ali Jinnah (1876–1948), feared the predominantly Hindu Congress party's authority over a single united state. Cycles of rioting broke out between Muslims and Hindus, and in June 1947, British India was partitioned into two nations: India (majority Hindu) and Pakistan (majority Muslim). The process of partition brought religious and ethnic warfare: more than 1 million Hindus and Muslims died, and an estimated 12 million became refugees. Throughout the chaos, Gandhi continued to protest violence and focus his attention on overcoming the legacy of colonialism. In January 1948, he was assassinated by a Hindu zealot. Jawaharlal Nehru, who became the first prime minister of India, embarked on a program of industrialization and modernization—not at all what Gandhi would have counseled. Nehru proved particularly adept at maneuvering in the Cold War world, steering a course of nonalignment with either of the blocs, while getting aid for industry from the Soviet Union and food imports from the United States.

PALESTINE The year 1948 brought more crises for the British Empire, including an end to the British mandate in Palestine. During the First World War, British diplomats encouraged Arab nationalist revolts against the Ottoman Empire. At the same time, with the 1917 Balfour Declaration, they also promised a "Jewish homeland" in Palestine for European Zionists. These contradictory promises and the flight of European Jews from Nazi Germany contributed to a rising conflict between Jewish settlers and Arabs in Palestine during the 1930s, provoking an Arab revolt that was bloodily suppressed by the British. During this time, the newly important oil concessions in the Middle East were multiplying Britain's strategic interests in the Suez Canal region. Mediating local conflicts and balancing its own interests proved an impossible task for Britain.

In 1939, the British limited further Jewish immigration to Palestine. They tried to maintain that limit after the war, but faced pressure from tens of thousands of Jewish refugees from Europe. The conflict quickly became a three-way war among Palestinian Arabs fighting for their land and independence; Jewish settlers and Zionist militants determined to defy British restrictions; and British administrators with divided sympathies. Britain responded to these conflicts with military force, and by 1947, there was one British soldier for every eighteen inhabitants of the Mandate. The years of fighting, however, with terrorist tactics on all sides, persuaded the British to leave.

Mohandas K. Gandhi and Nonviolent Anticolonialism

After leading a campaign for Indian rights in South Africa between 1894 and 1914, Mohandas K. Gandhi (1869–1948), known as Mahatma ("great-souled") Gandhi, became a leader in the long battle for home rule in India. This battle was finally won in 1947 with the partition of India and the creation of Pakistan. Gandhi's insistence on the power of nonviolent noncooperation brought him to the forefront of Indian politics, and provided a model for many later liberation struggles, including the American civil rights movement. Gandhi argued that only nonviolent resistance, which dramatized the injustice of colonial rule and colonial law, had the spiritual force to unite a community and end colonialism.

Passive resistance is a method of securing rights by personal suffering; it is the reverse of resistance by arms. When I refuse to do a thing that is repugnant to my conscience, I use soul-force. For instance, the Government of the day has passed a law which is applicable to me. I do not like it. If by using violence I force the Government to repeal the law, I am employing what may be termed body-force. If I do not obey the law and accept the penalty for its breach, I use soul-force. It involves sacrifice of self.

Everybody admits that sacrifice of self is infinitely superior to sacrifice of others. Moreover, if this kind of force is used in a cause that is unjust, only the person using it suffers. He does not make others suffer for his mistakes. Men have before now done many things which were subsequently found to have been wrong. . . . It is therefore meet that he should not do that which he knows to be wrong, and suffer the consequence whatever it may be. This is the key to the use of soul-force. . . .

It is contrary to our manhood if we obey laws repugnant to our conscience. Such teaching is opposed to religion and means slavery. If the Government were to ask us to go about without any clothing, should we do so? If I were a passive resister, I would say to them that I would have nothing to do with their law. But we have so forgotten ourselves and become so compliant that we do not mind any degrading law.

A man who has realized his manhood, who fears only God, will fear no one else. Man-made laws are not necessarily binding on him. Even the Government does not expect any such thing from us. They do not say: "You must do such and such a thing." But they say: "If you do not do it, we will punish you." We are sunk so low that we fancy that it is our duty and our religion to do what the law lays down. If man will only realize that it is unmanly to obey laws that are unjust, no man's tyranny will enslave him. This is the key to self-rule or home-rule.

Source: M. K. Gandhi, "Indian Home Rule (1909)," in *The Gandhi Reader: A Source Book of His Life and Writings*, ed. Homer A. Jack (Bloomington, IN: 1956), pp. 104–21.

Questions for Analysis

1. Why did Gandhi believe that "sacrifice of self" was superior to "sacrifice of others"?

2. What did Gandhi mean when he said, "it is contrary to our manhood if we obey laws repugnant to our conscience"?

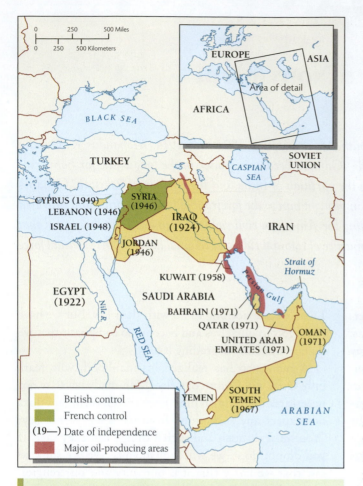

DECOLONIZATION IN THE MIDDLE EAST.
> Which countries were the colonial possessions of the British and of the French in the Middle East? > What were the three stages of decolonization in the Middle East? > Why did the British hold on to the small states bordering the Persian Gulf and the Arabian Sea until 1971?

The United Nations then voted (by a narrow margin) to partition the territory into two states. Neither Jewish settlers nor Palestinian Arabs found the partition satisfactory, and both began to fight for territory even before British troops withdrew. When Israel declared its independence in May 1948, five neighboring states invaded. The new but well-organized Israeli nation survived the war and extended its boundaries. On the losing side, 1 million Palestinian Arabs who fled or were expelled found themselves clustered in refugee camps in the Gaza Strip and on the West Bank of the Jordan River, which the armistice granted to an enlarged state of Jordan. Both the Soviets and the Americans recognized Israel for their own reasons. The creation of this new nation, however, marked a permanent change to the culture and balance of power in the region.

AFRICA A number of West African colonies had established independence movements by the 1950s, and the British government moved hesitantly to meet their demands. By the middle of the 1950s, Britain agreed to a variety of terms for independence in these territories, leaving them with written constitutions and a British legal system but little else in terms of modern infrastructure or economic support. Defenders of British colonialism claimed that these formal institutions would give advantages to the independent states, but without other resources, even the most promising foundered. In the early 1960s, Ghana, known formerly as the Gold Coast and the first of these colonies to gain independence, was seen as a model for free African nations. But its politics soon became conflictual, and its president, Kwame Nkrumah, became the first of several African leaders driven from office for corruption and autocratic behavior.

Belgium and France also withdrew from their colonies in Africa. By 1965, virtually all of the former African colonies had become independent, and virtually none possessed the means to redress the losses from colonialism to make that independence work. As Belgian authorities raced out of the Congo in 1960, they left crumbling railways and fewer than two dozen Indigenous people with college educations. Post-independence governments could not forego the revenue from industries developed under colonialism like mining, timber, and agriculture, making it difficult to reform economies shaped by generations of colonialism.

The process of decolonization was most violent where large populations of European settlers complicated European withdrawal. Settler resistance made the French exit from Algeria wrenching and complex (discussed on pages 992–94). In Kenya, the majority Kikuyu population revolted against the British in an uprising that came to be known as the Mau Mau rebellion. British troops fired freely at targets in rebel-occupied areas, sometimes killing civilians; and internment camps set up by colonial security forces became sites of atrocities that drew public investigations and condemnation. In 1963, a decade after the rebellion began, the British conceded Kenyan independence.

In the late 1950s, the British prime minister Harold Macmillan endorsed independence for a number of Britain's African colonies. But in southern Africa, the exceptionally large and wealthy population of European settlers resisted decolonization for decades. These settlers, a mixture of English migrants and the Franco-Dutch Afrikaners, who traced their arrival to the eighteenth century, controlled huge tracts of fertile farmland, along with the most lucrative gold and diamond mines on earth. During the late 1940s, Britain's Labour government made a fateful political bargain with South Africa's settler government: in return for guarantees that South African gold would be used to support Britain's global financial power, Britain tolerated the introduction of racial apartheid in South Africa. Even by other standards of racial segregation, **apartheid** was especially harsh. Africans, Indians, and colored persons of mixed descent lost all political rights. All the institutions of social life, including marriage and schools, were segregated. The apartheid system forced Africans to live in designated "homelands," forbade them from traveling without specific permits, and created elaborate government bureaus to manage the labor essential to the economy. The government also banned any political protest. These measures made Western powers uncomfortable with the apartheid regime, but white South Africans held on to American support by presenting themselves as a bulwark against communism.

In Rhodesia, the British government encouraged a large federation, controlled by white settlers but with the opportunity for majority rule in the future. By the early 1960s, however, the federation was on the verge of collapse. In 1964, the majority-rule state of Malawi was allowed to exit the federation, and Rhodesia split in two. In the north, an African populist leader, Kenneth Kaunda, established an independent government representing the majority population. In the south, angry Afrikaners backed by 200,000 right-wing English migrants who had arrived since 1945 refused to accept majority rule. When the British government attempted to force their hand, the settlers unilaterally declared independence in 1965 and began a bloody civil war against southern Rhodesia's Black population that lasted a half generation.

CRISIS IN SUEZ AND THE END OF AN ERA Under pressure from Egyptian nationalists, the British agreed in 1951 to withdraw their troops from Egyptian territory within three years. In 1952, a group of nationalist army officers deposed King Farouk, who had close ties to Britain, and proclaimed a republic. Shortly after the final British withdrawal, an Egyptian colonel, Gamal Abdel Nasser (1918–1970), became president of the country (1956–1970). His first major public act as president was to nationalize the Suez Canal Company, which would help finance the construction of the Aswan Dam on the Nile. Nasser also adopted the anticolonial ideology of Pan-Arabism, proposing that Arab nationalists throughout the Islamic world create an alliance of modern nations, no longer beholden to the West. To achieve that goal, he accepted support from the Soviet Union, and this made the Suez Canal a Cold War issue.

apartheid The racial segregation policy of the Afrikaner-dominated South African government. Legislated in 1948 by the Afrikaner National Party, it existed in South Africa for many decades.

Pan-Arabism calls for new alliance of Islamic world nations, separate from West

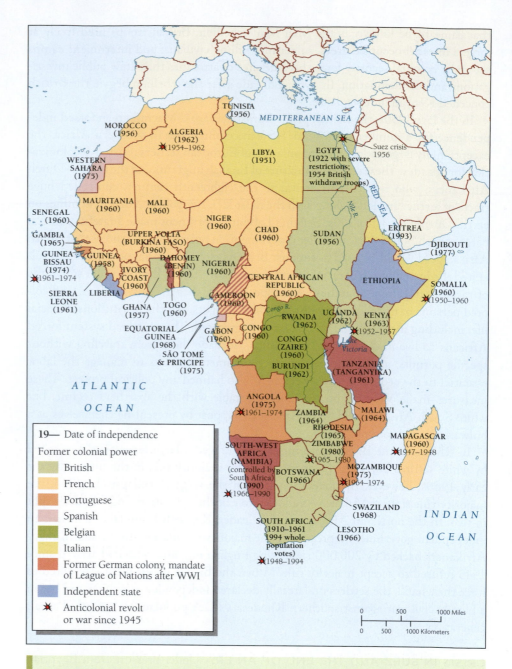

19— Date of independence

Former colonial power

- British
- French
- Portuguese
- Spanish
- Belgian
- Italian
- Former German colony, mandate of League of Nations after WWI
- Independent state
- ✷ Anticolonial revolt or war since 1945

MOROCCO (1956)
TUNISIA (1956)
ALGERIA (1962) 1954–1962
WESTERN SAHARA (1975)
LIBYA (1951)
EGYPT (1922 with severe restrictions; 1954 British withdraw troops)
Suez crisis 1956
MAURITANIA (1960)
MALI (1960)
SENEGAL (1960)
GAMBIA (1965)
GUINEA BISSAU (1974) 1961–1974
GUINEA (1958)
UPPER VOLTA (BURKINA FASO) (1960)
NIGER (1960)
CHAD (1960)
SUDAN (1956)
ERITREA (1993)
DJIBOUTI (1977)
IVORY COAST (1960)
DAHOMEY (BENIN) (1960)
NIGERIA (1960)
CENTRAL AFRICAN REPUBLIC (1960)
ETHIOPIA
SOMALIA (1960) 1950–1960
SIERRA LEONE (1961)
LIBERIA
GHANA (1957)
TOGO (1960)
EQUATORIAL GUINEA (1968)
GABON (1960)
CAMEROON (1960)
SÃO TOMÉ & PRINCIPE (1975)
CONGO (1960)
CONGO (ZAIRE) (1960)
RWANDA (1962)
BURUNDI (1962)
UGANDA (1962)
KENYA (1963) 1952–1957
TANZANIA (TANGANYIKA) (1961)
ANGOLA (1975) 1961–1974
ZAMBIA (1964)
RHODESIA (1965)
ZIMBABWE (1980) 1965–1980
MALAWI (1964)
MADAGASCAR (1960) 1947–1948
SOUTH-WEST AFRICA (NAMIBIA) (controlled by South Africa) (1990) 1966–1990
BOTSWANA (1966)
MOZAMBIQUE (1975) 1964–1974
SWAZILAND (1968)
SOUTH AFRICA (1910–1961 1994 whole population votes) 1948–1994
LESOTHO (1966)

MEDITERRANEAN SEA
RED SEA
Nile R.
Congo R.
Lake Victoria
ATLANTIC OCEAN
INDIAN OCEAN

0   500   1000 Miles
0   500   1000 Kilometers

DECOLONIZATION IN AFRICA. › What were the forces behind decolonization in Africa? › Who were the biggest imperial losers in the decolonization of Africa? › By what decade had most African countries achieved their independence?

Three nations were threatened by Nasser and his pan-Arab ideals: Israel, France, and Britain. Israel sought an opportunity to seize the strategic Sinai Peninsula and create a buffer against Egypt. France, already fighting a war against Algerian nationalists, hoped to counter Arab nationalism in Egypt. Britain depended on the canal as a route to its strategic bases. The three nations colluded in an attack on Egypt in 1956. Israel occupied the Sinai while British and French jets destroyed Egypt's air force on the ground. The former colonial powers landed troops at the mouth of the canal but lacked the resources to push on toward Cairo. The final blow came when the United States refused to support the attack on Egypt. The war left Nasser in power and made him a hero to the Egyptian public for holding the imperialists at bay. The attack was condemned around the world, and the United States imposed financial penalties on Britain and France, forcing both countries to withdraw their expeditions. The failure at Suez marked the end of the imperial era.

FRENCH DECOLONIZATION

In two particular cases, France's experience of decolonization was especially violent for the populations that had lived under French rule for several generations. The first was Indochina, where French efforts to restore imperial authority after the Second World War resulted in military defeat and further humiliation. The second was French Algeria, where a determined nationalist movement fought a bitter and ultimately successful war of independence, leading to a profound domestic political crisis.

THE FIRST VIETNAM WAR, 1946–1954 The two world wars had galvanized nationalist and then, also, communist independence movements in French Indochina. The communist resistance became particularly effective under the leadership of Ho Chi Minh (1890–1969). Ho was French educated and had hoped his country would win independence at Versailles in 1919 (Chapter 24). He read Marx and Lenin, and absorbed the Chinese communists' lessons about organizing peasants around a social and agrarian issues. During the Second World War, Ho's movement fought first the French Vichy government and later the Japanese occupiers, while providing intelligence reports for the Allies. In 1945, however, the United States and Britain allowed the French to reclaim their colonies throughout Southeast Asia. In response, the Vietnamese communists renewed their guerrilla war against the French.

The French government could have decolonized on favorable terms after one of its most capable generals, Jean de Lattre de Tassigny, finally achieved a military advantage against the rebels in 1951. But instead, the French decided to press on for total victory, sending troops deep into Vietnamese territory. One major outpost, Dien Bien Phu, was established in a valley bordering modern Laos, manned by thousands of French paratroopers and colonial soldiers from Algeria and West Africa. Vietnamese nationalist fighters hauled heavy artillery up the mountainsides by hand and besieged the fortress for months, provoking a national crisis in France.

When Dien Bien Phu fell in May 1954, the French government began peace talks with the Vietnamese in Geneva. The Geneva Accords created three new states out of Indochina: Laos, Cambodia, and Vietnam. Vietnam was provisionally partitioned into two zones, a North Vietnam taken over by Ho Chi Minh's party, and a South Vietnam that was led by a succession of Western-supported politicians. Corruption, repression, and instability in the south, coupled with Ho Chi Minh's nationalist desire to unite Vietnam, guaranteed that the war would continue. The U.S. government, which had provided military and financial aid to the French, began to send aid to the South Vietnamese regime. The Americans saw the conflict through the prism of the Cold War; their project was not to restore colonialism but to contain

DECOLONIZATION IN ASIA. › Among colonial powers, who were the biggest losers after World War II?
› What was the single most important geopolitical change in Asia during this period? › What role did the
Soviet Union and the United States play in Asia?

communism and prevent it from spreading through Southeast Asia. The limits of
this policy would not become clear until the mid-1960s.

ALGERIA Still reeling from the humiliation of Dien Bien Phu, France faced a complex colonial problem in Algeria. Since the 1830s, the colony had evolved into a
settler society as Europeans migrated to North Africa looking for economic opportunity. By the mid-twentieth century, the settlers constituted about 10 percent of
the population and controlled 80 percent of Algeria's economic wealth, while the
Muslim colonial subjects constituted 90 percent of the population but controlled
20 percent of the wealth. Settlers enjoyed full citizenship and representation in
French parliament. The majority population of Muslims was denied the right to

vote, though some Amazigh (called Berbers by the French) were favored by the French administration as part of its divide and rule policy. The French government offered small reforms to increase the rights of Muslim colonial subjects, but the reforms came too late and they were also undercut by European settlers anxious to maintain their privileges.

In 1945, Algerian nationalists called on the Allies to recognize Algeria's independence in return for service during the war. When celebrations of the German defeat in May 1945 flared into violence against settlers in the town of Sétif, French security forces and settler vigilantes killed several thousand Algerians. After the war, the French government approved a provincial assembly for all of Algeria, elected by two pools of voters, dominated by settlers and the other by Muslim colonial subjects. This very limited enfranchisement gave non-European Algerians little political power.

In 1954, a younger generation of Algerian nationalists had taken charge of a movement now dedicated to achieving independence by force. The activists organized the National Liberation Front (FLN), which included Arabs as well as Amazigh, and secular socialists as well as religious activists. The war in Algeria was fought on several fronts. The first was a guerrilla war between the regular French army and the FLN, fought in the mountains and deserts of the country. The French conscripted Algerian Muslims to serve in the French army against the FLN, producing bitter divisions in Algerian society. This war continued for years, a clear-cut victory eluding the French. The second front, fought in the cities, began with an FLN campaign of bombing and terrorism, killing European civilians. French paratroopers hunted down and destroyed the networks of FLN bombers. The information that allowed the French to break the FLN network was extracted through systematic torture conducted by French security forces. The torture became an international scandal, bringing waves of protest in France. These tactics divided the French electorate and eventually led to a government crisis that brought Charles de Gaulle back into power in 1958.

De Gaulle at first declared that Algeria would always be French, but after another year of violence, he and his advisers changed their minds. By 1962, talks had produced a formula for independence: a referendum would be held, voted on by the whole population of Algeria. On July 1, 1962, the referendum passed by a landslide vote. Guerrillas from the FLN entered Algiers in triumph. Settlers and those Algerians who had fought for the French army fled to France by the hundreds of thousands. Later, these refugees were joined in France by another influx of Algerian economic migrants.

Algeria illustrated the dramatic domestic impact of decolonization, cutting deep divides through French society. Withdrawing from Algeria meant reorienting French views of what it meant to be a modern power. To France and to the other imperial powers, the conclusions seemed clear: traditional forms of colonial rule could not withstand the demands of postwar

THE STRUGGLE FOR NATIONAL INDEPENDENCE IN ALGERIA. Ahmed Bencherif, a commander in the FLN, handcuffed in 1961. › How might the Algerian struggle for independence against the French have shaped the generation of political leaders who took power after decolonization?

politics and culture, and the leading European nations, once distinguished by their empires, would have to look for new forms of influence. The domestic transformation of which de Gaulle spoke—recovery from the war, economic restructuring, and political renewal—had to take place on a radically changed global stage.

Postwar Culture and Thought

The postwar period brought a remarkable burst of cultural production. Writers and artists did not hesitate to take up big issues: freedom, civilization, and the human condition itself. The search for democratic renewal gave this literature urgency, whereas the moral dilemmas of war, occupation, and resistance gave it resonance and popular appeal. The process of decolonization, too, forced the issues of race, culture, and colonialism to center stage in Western debates.

THE BLACK PRESENCE

The journal *Présence Africaine* ("African Presence"), founded in Paris in 1947, was only one in a chorus of new cultural voices. *Présence Africaine* published such writers as Aimé Césaire (1913–2008), the surrealist poet from Martinique, and Léopold Senghor of Senegal (1906–2001). Césaire and Senghor were educated in the most elite French universities and elected to the French National Assembly. Césaire became an important political figure in Martinique, a French Caribbean colony that became a department of France in 1946. In 1960, Senghor was elected the first president of Senegal. Both men, models of Frenchness in important respects, became the most influential exponents of *Négritude*, which could be translated as "Black consciousness" or "Black pride." Senghor wrote

> Assimilation was a failure. We could assimilate mathematics or the French language, but we could never strip off our black skins or root out our black souls. And so we set out on a fervent quest for . . . our collective soul. Negritude is the whole complex of civilized values—cultural, economic, social and political—which characterize the black people.

Césaire's *Discourse on Colonialism* (1950), meanwhile, argued that colonialism not only dehumanized colonial subjects but degraded the colonizers themselves.

Césaire's student Frantz Fanon (1925–1961), also from Martinique, went further. He argued that withdrawing into an insular Black culture was not an effective response to racism. He believed that people of color needed a theory of radical social change. Fanon's views on race came from close observation of the colonial situation in Algeria where he treated patients for mental illness. Observing the ways that the French settler regime had segregated the populations in North Africa, he concluded that the racism of colonialism could only be confronted by dismantling its fundamental structures of social organization, a position that led him to join the FLN and embrace their revolutionary movement for national liberation. His *The Wretched of the Earth* (1961) became one of the most influential revolutionary manifestos of the period (see *Analyzing Primary Sources* on page 995). More than Césaire, Fanon argued that the colonial system was rooted in violence and could only be defeated by violent anticolonial movements. He bluntly rejected Gandhi's theories and practice of nonviolent resistance. Fanon also believed that many anticolonial leaders would

Frantz Fanon calls upon colonized peoples to overcome the dehumanizing violence of imperialism through a liberating violence of their own

Anticolonialism and Violence

Born in the French Caribbean colony of Martinique, Frantz Fanon (1925–1961) studied psychiatry in France before working in Algeria during the early 1950s. Fanon became a member of the Algerian revolutionary National Liberation Front (FLN), and an ardent advocate of decolonization. His Black Skin, White Masks, *published in 1952 with a preface by Jean-Paul Sartre, is a study of the psychological effects of colonialism and racism on Black culture and individuals; and* The Wretched of the Earth *(1961) is a revolutionary manifesto, one of the most influential of the period. Fanon attacked nationalist leaders for their ambition and corruption, and believed that revolutionary change could come only from poor peasants, or those who "have found no bone to gnaw in the colonial system." Diagnosed with leukemia, Fanon sought treatment in the Soviet Union, and then in Washington, DC, where he died.*

In decolonization, there is therefore the need of a complete calling in question of the colonial situation. If we wish to describe it precisely, we might find it in the well-known words: "The last shall be first and the first last." Decolonization is the putting into practice of this sentence. . . .

The naked truth of decolonization evokes for us the searing bullets and bloodstained knives which emanate from it. For if the last shall be first, this will only come to pass after a murderous and decisive struggle between the two protagonists. That affirmed intention to place the last at the head of things, and to make them climb at a pace (too quickly, some say) the well-known steps which characterize an organized society, can only triumph if we use all means to turn the scale, including, of course, that of violence.

You do not turn any society, however primitive it may be, upside down with such a program if you have not decided from the very beginning, that is to say from the actual formation of that program, to overcome all the obstacles that you will come across in so doing. The native who decides to put the program into practice, and to become its moving force, is ready for violence at all times. From birth it is clear to him that this narrow world, strewn with prohibitions, can only be called in question by absolute violence.

Source: Frantz Fanon, *The Wretched of the Earth*, trans. Constance Farrington (New York: 1963), pp. 35–37.

Questions for Analysis

1. Why did Fanon believe that violence lay at the heart of both the colonial relationship and anticolonial movements?

2. What arguments would Fanon offer to counter Gandhi?

be corrupted by their ambition and collaboration with former colonial powers. Revolutionary change, he believed, could come only from poor peasants, those who "have found no bone to gnaw in the colonial system."

How did these writers fit into postwar culture? Western intellectuals sought to revive humanism and democratic values after the atrocities of the Second World War. Fanon and Césaire pointed out that the struggles over colonialism made that project more difficult, as the violent repression of anticolonial movements in Kenya, South Africa, or Algeria seemed to be a relapse into brutality. They pointed to the ironies of Europe's "civilizing mission" and demanded a reevaluation of Blackness as a central concept in Western culture. The West's postwar recovery would eventually entail facing this challenge to the universal claims of its culture.

SIMONE DE BEAUVOIR (1908–1986). A philosopher, novelist, memoirist, and pathbreaking theorist of sex and gender, de Beauvoir's work challenged widespread beliefs about femininity and womanhood.

EXISTENTIALISM, AMNESIA, AND THE AFTERMATH OF WAR

The French existentialist writers, most prominently Jean-Paul Sartre (*SAHR-truh*; 1905–1980) and Albert Camus (*KAM-oo*; 1913–1960), put the themes of individuality, commitment, and choice at center stage. The existentialists took themes from Nietzsche, Heidegger, and Kierkegaard, and reworked them in the new context of war-torn Europe. The starting point for **existentialism** was that "existence precedes essence." In other words, meaning in life is not given but created by humans. Individuals were "condemned to be free," to give meaning to their lives by making choices and accepting responsibility. To deny one's freedom or responsibility was to act in "bad faith." War, collaboration and resistance, genocide, and the development of weapons of mass destruction gave these abstractions new meaning—how should responsibility for these collective horrors be determined?

Existentialist insights opened other doors. The existentialist approach to race, influenced by Frantz Fanon, emphasized that no necessary meaning inhered in skin color; instead, race derived meaning from a lived experience or situation. This view was a powerful critique of eugenics and the racial sciences that had reached their apogee in Nazi genocide. The racial sciences asserted that skin color and outward appearance were visible signs of a biological essence. Existentialists rejected this view and accepted Fanon's claim that white and Black exist "only insofar as they create one another."

Simone de Beauvoir (*duh bohv-WAHR*; 1908–1986) made a similar claim about gender, arguing that "One is not born a woman, one becomes one." In *The Second Sex* (1949), de Beauvoir questioned why women seemed to accept a subordinate status in society, insisting that they should become the authors of their own lives rather than accept unquestioningly the roles of wife or mother that society had prepared for them.

The theme of individual helplessness in the face of state power runs through countless works of the period, beginning, most famously, with George Orwell's *Animal Farm* (1946) and *1984* (1949). The American Joseph Heller's wildly popular *Catch-22* (1961) embodied a form of popular existentialism, concerned with the absurdity of war and offering a biting commentary on regimentation and its toll on individual freedom. The Czech author Milan Kundera, who fled the repressive Czech government to live in Paris, eloquently captured the bittersweet efforts to resist senseless bureaucracy. Some writers expressed their despair by escaping into the absurd and fantastic. In Irishman Samuel Beckett's deeply pessimistic *Waiting for Godot* (1953; writing in French) and in the Briton Harold Pinter's *Caretaker* (1960) and *Homecoming* (1965), nothing happens; characters speak in banalities, paralyzed by the absurdity of modern times.

Questions of terror and dictatorship haunted social and political thought of the postwar era, especially in the works of émigrés from Europe. Members of the Frankfurt School, an institute founded for the study of Marxism, who became wartime refugees in the United States, sought to understand how fascism and Nazism had taken root in Western culture and politics. Theodor Adorno joined Max Horkheimer in a series of essays, *Dialectic of Enlightenment* (1947), the best known of which indicted the "culture industry" for depoliticizing the masses and crippling democracy. Adorno also coauthored *The Authoritarian Personality* (1950), which used social surveys in an effort to discover how people become receptive to racism, prejudice, and dictatorship. Whatever the specific roots of German Nazism, the Frankfurt School suggested that there are more general tendencies in modern societies, which should give cause for concern.

Hannah Arendt (1906–1975), a Jewish refugee from Germany, in *The Origins of Totalitarianism* (1951), was the first to propose that both Nazism and Stalinism be understood as forms of a distinctive, twentieth-century type of government: totalitarianism. Unlike earlier forms of tyranny or despotism, totalitarianism works by mobilizing mass support. It uses terror to crush resistance, break down political and social institutions, destroy the relations between individuals that sustain human communities. Totalitarianism, Arendt argued, also forges new ideologies. Totalitarian regimes do not concern themselves with whether killing is justified by law; instead, they justify camps and extermination by pointing to the objective laws of history or racial struggle. By unleashing destruction and eliminating entire populations, totalitarian politics makes collective resistance virtually impossible. Arendt returned to the same theme in a provocative and disturbing essay on the trial of a Nazi leader, *Eichmann in Jerusalem* (1963). To the distress of many readers, she pointedly refused to demonize Nazism, exploring instead what she termed the "banality of evil": how the rise of new forms of state power and terror created a world in which Nazis, such as Adolf Eichmann, could implement genocide as simply one more policy. The crisis of totalitarianism, Arendt argued, was the moral collapse of society, for it destroyed human feeling and the power of resistance in both executioners and victims—"tormentors and the tormented"—alike.

Discussions of the war and its legacy, however, were limited, although some memoirs and novels dealing directly with the war and its brutal aftermath did reach a large public. Tadeusz Borowski's stories based on his experience in Auschwitz were widely read in postwar Poland. Czesław Miłosz's (*CHES-swaf MEE-wosh*) memoir, *The Captive Mind* (1953), about intellectual collaboration in Eastern Europe, was translated quickly into other languages and read internationally. Of all the memoirs, *The Diary of a Young Girl* by Anne Frank, published in 1947, was undoubtedly the most widely read. Yet the main current in postwar culture ran in a different direction, toward repressing painful issues and bad memories.

Postwar governments could not or would not purge all those implicated in war crimes. In France, the courts sentenced 2,640 to death and executed 791; in Austria, 13,000 were convicted of war crimes and 30 were executed. Those who called for justice grew demoralized and cynical; others responded by mythologizing the Resistance and exaggerating their participation in it or by avoiding discussion of collaboration. Most Jewish survivors, wherever they lived, found that few editors were interested in publishing their stories. In 1947, only a small publishing house

> Postwar intellectuals grappled with the question: Was Nazism an aberration, or an ever-present danger within modern democratic societies?

THE SOVIET UNION AS DEFENDER OF THE THIRD WORLD. This billboard from the Soviet Union's 1968 annual May Day parade depicts Soviet bombs raining down on a monstrous image of Uncle Sam, a symbol of the United States. The caption reads "U.S. out of Vietnam!" **› How did the Soviet Union attempt to take advantage of the wars of decolonization to advance its influence in other parts of the world? › Who was the audience for this kind of imagery? › How might have this billboard have been perceived in Europe or in Vietnam?**

would take on the Italian survivor Primo Levi's *Survival in Auschwitz*; this book and Levi's other writings did not find a wide audience until later.

The Cold War was an important factor in burying and distorting memories. West of the Iron Curtain, the eagerness to embrace West Germany as an ally, the single-minded emphasis on economic development, and the ardent anticommunism blurred views of the past. One example involved Klaus Barbie, an agent for the Gestapo in occupied France who arrested and personally tortured members of the Resistance and deported thousands, including Jewish children, to concentration camps. After the war, American intelligence services recruited Barbie for his anticommunist experience and paid to smuggle him out of Europe, beyond the reach of those who wanted to prosecute him for war crimes. He was finally extradited from Bolivia in 1983, tried in France for crimes against humanity, and convicted. In the Eastern bloc, regimes declared fascism a thing of the past and did not scrutinize that past or seek out the many who had collaborated with the Nazis. Thus, reckoning with history was postponed until the fall of the Soviet Union. On both sides of the Iron Curtain, the vast majority of people turned inward, cherishing their domestic lives, relieved to have privacy.

The Cuban Missile Crisis

One of the last serious confrontations of the Cold War came in 1962, in Cuba. A revolution in 1958 had brought the charismatic communist Fidel Castro to power. Immediately after, the United States began working with exiled Cubans, supporting, among other ventures, a bungled attempt to invade Cuba via the Bay of Pigs in 1961. Castro not only aligned himself with the Soviets but also invited them to base nuclear missiles on Cuban soil, which was only a few minutes' flying time from Florida. When American spy planes identified the missiles and related military equipment in 1962, President Kennedy confronted Khrushchev. After deliberating about the repercussions of an air strike, Kennedy ordered a naval blockade of Cuba. On October 22, he appeared on television, visibly tired and without makeup, and announced the grave situation to the public, and challenged Khrushchev to withdraw the weapons and "move the world back from the abyss of destruction." Terrified of the looming threat of nuclear war, Americans fled urban areas, prepared for a cramped and uncomfortable existence in fallout shelters, and bought firearms and canned foods. After thirteen days, the Soviets agreed to withdraw and remove the bombers and missiles already on Cuban soil. But citizens of both countries spent many anxious hours in their bomb shelters, and onlookers the world over wrestled with their rising fears that a nuclear Armageddon was upon them.

Conclusion

The Cold War reached deep into postwar culture and dominated postwar politics. It decisively shaped the development of both the Soviet Union and the United States. Fearful of losing control of territory they had conquered at such high cost in the Second World War, the Soviets intervened repeatedly in the politics of their Eastern European allied states in the 1940s and 1950s, ensuring the creation of hard-line governments in East Germany, Czechoslovakia, Poland, Hungary, and elsewhere in the Eastern bloc. In the United States, anticommunism became a powerful political force, shaping foreign policy and preparing the military for confrontation with the Soviet Union, to such an extent that President Dwight D. Eisenhower warned in his farewell address that a "military-industrial complex" had taken shape in the United States, one in which its "total influence—economic, political, even spiritual—is felt in every city, every statehouse, every office of the federal government."

In Western Europe, rebuilding the economy and creating a new political order in the aftermath of the Second World War meant accepting the new power and influence of the United States. But Europeans also searched for ways to create and express a European identity that would preserve some independence and freedom of action. Led by the efforts of France and Germany, Western Europeans eventually found elements of this freedom in increasing integration and economic cooperation. In Eastern Europe, however, the political leadership found fewer opportunities for independent action, and the threat of military intervention by the Soviet Union made any innovations or experimentation difficult, if not impossible.

The sense that Europeans were no longer in a position to act independently, or exert their influence in other parts of the world, was compounded by the loss of their colonies abroad, as former European colonies in Africa and Asia became independent nations. This loss of influence may have further encouraged the former European imperial powers to lay the groundwork for a more integrated Europe. The consensus in the West about the new role that the state should take in economic planning, education, and ensuring social welfare helped lay the groundwork for a Europe that was dedicated to ensuring equal opportunities for its

AFTER YOU READ THIS CHAPTER

CHRONOLOGY

1946–1964	Twenty French colonies, eleven British colonies, the Belgian Congo, and Dutch Indonesia become independent nations
1947	Truman Doctrine
1948	Soviets create the Eastern bloc
1948	Marshall Plan
1949	Chinese Revolution
1949	Formation of NATO
1950–1953	Korean War
1953–1956	Revolts in East Germany, Poland, and Hungary
1955	Formation of Warsaw Pact
1957	Treaty of Rome creates the European Economic Community (EEC), or the Common Market
1961	Building of the Berlin Wall
1964	U.S. Vietnam War begins

REVIEWING THE OBJECTIVES

❯ The Cold War between the United States and the Soviet Union began as the Second World War ended. How did these two nations seek to influence the postwar political order in Europe?

❯ Postwar economic growth was accompanied by greater economic integration among Western European nations. What were the goals of those who sought to create a unified European market? Which nations played key roles in its development?

❯ Between the late 1940s and the mid-1960s, almost all the European colonies in Asia and Africa demanded and received their independence, either peacefully or through armed conflict. What combination of events made Europeans less able to defend their colonial empires against the nationalists who sought independence from Europe?

❯ Decolonization and the Cold War reinforced a sense that Europeans needed to rethink their place in the world. How did intellectuals, writers, and artists react to the loss of European influence in the world?

citizens. These commitments were driven by the search for stable forms of democratic government. The achievement of an integrated Western Europe (under U.S. sponsorship) on the hinge of Franco-German cooperation, while memories of the violent ideological conflicts of the 1920s and the 1930s were still fresh, must be seen as one of the major victories of the postwar decades. The hard-won stability of this period was to be temporary, however, as a new series of political conflicts and economic crises, beginning in the 1960s, would test the limits of consensus in Cold War Europe.

Go to **INQUIZITIVE** to see what you've learned—and learn what you've missed—with personalized feedback along the way.

PEOPLE, IDEAS, AND EVENTS IN CONTEXT

❯ When Allied leaders met to discuss the postwar order at the **YALTA CONFERENCE** and Potsdam in 1945, what were the major issues discussed?

❯ What were the goals of the U.S. **MARSHALL PLAN**? How did **JOSEPH STALIN** react to its implementation?

❯ What was the **TRUMAN DOCTRINE**? How was it related to the creation of **NATO**?

❯ How did the successful detonation of an **ATOMIC BOMB** by the Soviet Union in 1949 change the dynamic of the **COLD WAR**?

❯ How did the political climate in the Soviet Union and Eastern Europe change under **NIKITA KHRUSHCHEV** and during the "thaw" that followed Stalin's death?

❯ Which nations were key to the plans for the European Union?

❯ Why was the **DECOLONIZATION** of settler colonies in Africa, such as Algeria, Kenya, and Rhodesia, more violent than in other colonies on the continent?

❯ What was **APARTHEID**? Why did the settler government in South Africa adopt it?

❯ What was **EXISTENTIALISM** and how did it challenge prevailing conceptions of race, gender, and human freedom?

THINKING ABOUT CONNECTIONS

❯ Compare the United States' role in Western European affairs during the Cold War with the United States' and Europe's reaction to the Russian invasion of Ukraine in 2022. What has changed since the 1950s?

❯ What challenges did the process of decolonization pose to those who believed that European traditions of democratic rule and individual rights—ideas associated with the Enlightenment and the French Revolution— were universal?

28

Red Flags and Velvet Revolutions:

THE END OF THE COLD WAR, 1960–1990

BEFORE YOU READ THIS CHAPTER

❯

IN 1964, A PHOTOGRAPH of a Portuguese laborer, Armando Rodriguez, appeared on the cover of the German news magazine *Der Spiegel*. As the 1 millionth "guest worker" to arrive in Germany, he had been met at the border by an official delegation and given a motorcycle as a prize. This moment reflected the confidence of the West German government that its postwar economic recovery would continue, and that material prosperity would bring a new stability to Europe. The early 1960s, in fact, seemed golden and full of promise for many in Western Europe. Despite nearly constant international tension, everyday life seemed to be improving. Full employment drove increases in living standards, the mass availability of consumer items and modern appliances transformed daily life, and a life of relative prosperity and ample leisure seemed accessible to many. As television, radio, and film promoted images of American middle-class life, Europeans looked across the Atlantic and saw their own aspirations reflected back at them. Even amid the uncertainties of the Cold War, a new spirit of cooperation animated European governments; party divisions had given way to a broad consensus in favor of an expanded welfare state, and the future looked good.

By the 1990s, however, most of that confidence was gone. Western Europeans were no longer certain of their prosperity or of their leaders' ability to provide the sort of life they took for granted. Already in the late 1960s, movements of social protest, especially among young people, shattered the postwar consensus. Bitter disagreements about persistent

STORY LINES

> The postwar economy in Western Europe saw record growth that lasted until the 1970s. Labor shortages led many nations to recruit workers from abroad, causing tensions when unemployment rates rose as the boom came to an end.

> Radio, television, and film combined to create a new kind of global mass culture that contributed to a spirit of novelty and rebellion among young people. More open discussion of sexual matters and an end to restrictions on contraception led some to speak of a "sexual revolution."

> Movements for national independence in the colonial world found an echo in the civil rights movement in the United States, and in the student protests in Europe and the Americas in the 1960s. These protest movements peaked in 1968, provoking a conservative backlash in the 1970s and the 1980s.

> Support for the Soviet Union waned in the 1980s, as its economy stagnated and its political system failed to adapt. The Eastern bloc collapsed suddenly in 1989, ending the Cold War.

CORE OBJECTIVES

> **DESCRIBE** postwar changes in employment and consumption, and their effects on daily life and mass culture in Europe.

> **UNDERSTAND** the shift in attitudes toward sexuality, reproduction, and conceptions of male and female social roles that took place in the postwar decades, and the consequences of this shift for women in Europe.

> **IDENTIFY** the motives and goals of the social and political movements that climaxed in 1968 in both Western and Eastern Europe.

> **EXPLAIN** the reasons for the economic downturn that began in the 1970s, and its consequences for governments and populations in Europe.

> **UNDERSTAND** the events that led to the collapse of the Soviet bloc in 1989.

> **EXPLAIN** the reasons for the uncertainty and violence that followed the conclusion of the Cold War in Europe in the 1990s.

racial inequality and the legacy of slavery and colonialism in Europe and North America fed calls for reform and protest movements demanding more rapid change. At the same time, the material comforts of a consumer society proved less satisfying than they had once seemed, and environmentalists, feminists, and other cultural critics criticized the assumptions of the older generation. In the 1970s, these problems were compounded by a continuing economic crisis that threatened the security the postwar generation had labored so hard to achieve. European societies began to fragment in unexpected ways, well before the end of the Cold War in the 1990s.

The challenges in the Soviet sphere proved even more fundamental. Economic decay combined with political stagnation to produce another wave of revolt. The year 1989 marked the beginning of communist collapse in Eastern Europe. Hopes for peace were soon replaced by fears of conflict from unexpected quarters. Immigrants were no longer celebrated in Germany and elsewhere, and instead became targets of suspicion or even violence. Shortly after the reunification of Germany in 1991, a wave of attacks against immigrants and refugees in Eastern Germany by right-wing extremists took the lives of seventeen foreigners, including two Turkish women and a Turkish girl who died in an arson attack by neo-Nazi skinheads in Schleswig-Holstein; similar attacks took place in France, Britain, Italy, and other nations. When post-socialist Yugoslavia collapsed into brutal civil war in the early 1990s, Europeans faced once again the spectacle of political movements motivated by hatred and fear, leading to ethnic violence and mass murder on European land.

The startlingly sudden dissolution of the Soviet bloc brought an end to the postwar era of superpower confrontation, and observers of European society were forced to confront the uncomfortable fact that the Cold War had provided its own form of stability. Seen from the early 1990s, the future looked much less certain. Could the emerging institutions of an integrated Europe absorb nations of the former Soviet sphere that wished to join? What would such a Europe look like? Who would determine its larger boundaries? What these changes meant for the future of democracy, the stability of the European economy, and the definitions of European identity remained an open question.

Social Change and Cultural Dynamism, 1945–1968

The prosperity of the 1950s had profound and far-reaching effects on social life in Western Europe. Demand for labor increased so rapidly that both West Germany and France found it necessary to import workers. Most came from the south, particularly from the agrarian areas of southern Italy, where unemployment remained high. These migrations, in addition to the influx of political and ethnic refugees during and after the war, contributed to the breakdown of national barriers, and were accelerated by the creation of the Common Market. Workers from former colonies emigrated to Britain, often to take low-paid, menial jobs, and encountered pervasive discrimination at work and in the community. Such patterns of discrimination revealed that assumptions about race that had become entrenched in European societies during the colonial period persisted after decolonization.

Rural Europe was transformed by changes in land holding and agriculture. Agricultural productivity had barely changed over the first half of the twentieth century, but after midcentury, it soared. Common Market policy, state-sponsored programs of modernization, new agricultural machinery, and new kinds of fertilizer, seed, and animal feed helped produce the transformation. In Western Europe, lower food prices enabled families to spend less on food and freed up money for other forms of consumption, which, in turn, fueled economic growth. The percentage of the labor force employed in agriculture fell, leading to an expansion in industry, especially in the service sector. In the 1960s, the French spoke of an "end of the peasantry," as 100,000 moved from the countryside to cities each year. These changes sparked continuous protests as farmers tried to protect their standard of living, and the Common Market responded with policies that protected prices for some agricultural goods.

Change also came to the workplace. The number of middle-class, white-collar employees grew rapidly—the result, in part, of the dramatic bureaucratic expansion of the state. By 1964, in most European states, the total number of men and women employed in government service exceeded 40 percent of the labor force, significantly higher than during the prewar decades. In business and industry, the number of middle-management and salaried employees also grew. As manufacturing tasks became more specialized, based on technological expertise rather than custom and routine, *skill* came to mean the ability to monitor automatic controls, to interpret abstract signals, and to make precise, mathematically calculated adjustments. More women entered the workforce, meeting less resistance than they had in the past, and their jobs were less starkly differentiated from those of men.

Nineteenth-century society had been marked by clearly defined class cultures. The working class lived a "life apart" from the middle class, and in 1900 no one would have mistaken a peasant for a worker. Economic changes after 1950 chipped away at those distinctive cultures. Trade unions remained powerful institutions, but union membership was variable across Europe in the postwar boom, though they now included many more women than in the past. Communist parties retained electoral clout, but class had a less rigidly defined meaning as the economy developed.

The expansion of education also helped shift social hierarchies. All Western nations passed laws providing for the extension of compulsory secondary education. This legislation, combined with rising birthrates, dramatically boosted school populations. Education did not automatically guarantee social mobility, but when combined with economic prosperity, new structures of labor, and the consumerist boom, it began to lay the foundation for what would be called a "postindustrial" society, where the proportion of the population working in industry declined and the proportion in technical occupations, the professions, and service jobs increased.

What about the Eastern bloc? In the socialist regimes of the Soviet satellites, small peasant holdings were increasingly replaced by large-scale collective agriculture, and industry was nationalized, though not always at the same pace. The collective farms did not significantly increase agricultural productivity, however, meaning that industrial growth had to be paid for by keeping rates of consumption low.

In general, economic development in the Eastern bloc was determined by the requirements of the Soviet economy. The Soviet Union purchased manufactured goods from Eastern Europe at advantageous prices, while charging more for the raw materials exported from the Soviet Union. This imbalance of trade amounted to a net extraction of wealth from Eastern Europe, hampering economic growth and providing a stark contrast with the economic boom of Western Europe.

Subsidized education, increases in the number of civil service jobs, and the growth of salaried management positions fuel growth in middle classes

MORNING CALISTHENICS AT A RUSSIAN FACTORY, 1961. This image from a Russian factory illustrates the growing number of industrial workers and women in the workforce in the latter half of the twentieth century. The workers' state, however, still bestowed little status on its workers—a factor that contributed to the weakened Russian economy.

While Western Europeans experienced increasing social mobility and an expanding middle class, two world wars and Stalin's rule had liquidated the traditional middle classes and their culture throughout Eastern Europe. In their place, the Soviet Union and its satellites created new forms of privilege and status through positions within the party and the bureaucracy. Educational reforms instituted by Nikita Khrushchev in 1958 encouraged bright children to pursue a course of study that led to managerial positions for those who did not challenge the ideology of the regime.

Soviet education also aimed to unify a nation that remained culturally heterogeneous. The Soviet Union included not only Russians, but also Ukrainians, Latvians, Lithuanians, Estonians, Azerbaijanis, Armenians, Chechens, Turkmen, Uzbeks, and Kazakhs, to name only a few of the most notable groups. Ethnic or religious differences were a persistent threat to the "union" of the Soviet regime. Party bureaucracies throughout the Soviet Union demanded adherence to the official communist ideology in all realms of life—including the press, television, radio, literature, and the arts.

Surging demand for household appliances leads to rising expectations for female labor at home

MASS CONSUMPTION

In Western Europe, rising employment, higher earnings, and lower agricultural prices gave individuals more purchasing power. Household appliances and cars became the most striking emblems of what was virtually a new world of everyday objects. Vacuum cleaners, refrigerators, washing machines, and telephones all became common features of everyday life. They did not save labor or create free time, however, because household appliances came packaged with more demanding standards of housekeeping and new investments in domesticity, creating work that fell disproportionately on women in households.

In 1948, an estimated 5 million Western Europeans had cars; in 1965, that became 40 million. Cars captured imaginations throughout the world; in magazines, advertisements, and countless films, the car was central to new images of romance, movement, freedom, and vacation. Of course, automobiles alone did not allow workers to take inexpensive holidays; reducing the workweek from forty-eight hours to about forty-two was more important, as was the institution of annual vacations (in most countries, workers received more than thirty days of paid vacation per year).

These changes marked a new culture of mass consumption, boosted by new industries devoted to marketing and credit payment. Consumer culture also entailed shifts in values. In the nineteenth century, a responsible middle-class family did not go into debt, and thrift was a hallmark of respectability. By the second half of the twentieth century, banks and retailers persuaded middle- and working-class people alike not to be ashamed of debt. Terms such as *abundance, credit, consumer spending,* and *standards of living* all became part of the vocabulary of everyday economic life, reshaping how citizens thought about their needs and measured themselves against others. As a result, politicians, economists, and marketing experts paid closer attention to the spending habits of ordinary people.

In Eastern Europe and the Soviet Union, consumption was organized differently. Governments, rather than markets, determined the distribution of consumer goods and economic policy channeled resources into heavy industry at the expense of consumer durables. This resulted in shortages of even basic necessities, and often poor-quality goods. Women, in particular, frequently waited for hours in store lines after finishing a full day of wage work. The inefficiencies of Soviet consumption made women's double burden of wage work and housework especially heavy. Citizens' unhappiness with scarcities and the failure of policies to provide consumer goods contributed to the downfall of communist regimes.

A CAR FOR THE PEOPLE. Originally designed in Hitler's Germany as a car for the people (*das Volk*), the Volkswagen "Beetle" was produced in large numbers after 1945, and sold in many countries.

MASS CULTURE

New patterns of consumption spurred wide-ranging changes in **mass culture**. The origins of "mass" culture lay in the 1890s with the expansion of the popular press, music halls, organized sports, and "nickelodeons," all of which started the long process of displacing traditional, class-based forms of entertainment: village dances, street fairs, boulevard theater, and middle-class concerts. Mass culture quickened in the 1920s, its importance heightened by mass politics (Chapter 25). The social transformations of the 1950s meant that families had both more spending money and more leisure time. This combination created a golden opportunity for the growing culture industry. The result can fairly be called a cultural revolution: a transformation of culture and its role in the lives of ordinary men and women, and of the power wielded by the media, especially film, radio, and television.

mass culture The spread of literacy and public education in the nineteenth century created a new audience for print entertainment and a new class of media entrepreneurs to cater to this audience. The invention of radio, film, and television in the twentieth century carried this development to another level, as millions of consumers were now accessible to the producers of news, information, and entertainment.

PICCADILLY CIRCUS, LONDON. In the 1960s and the 1970s, a growing consumer culture led to the expansion of marketing and advertising industries. › **Why did Europeans associate this kind of commercial culture with the United States?**

MUSIC AND YOUTH CULTURE Much of the mass culture of the 1960s depended on the spending habits and desires of the new generation. Young people stayed in school longer, prolonging the adolescent years. They had more distance from their parents and the workforce and more time to spend with each other. In the countryside especially, schools began to break down the barriers that had separated the activities of boys and girls, creating one factor in the "sexual revolution" (discussed on pages 1014–16). From the late 1950s on, music became *the* cultural expression of this new generation. Wider distribution of portable transistor radios, first sold in the United States and Europe in the mid-1950s, gave birth to new musical radio programming and, later, to magazines reporting on popular singers and movie stars. Radio programs shaped the tastes of adolescents, and musicians tailored their songs with themes and lyrics aimed at the young. Technological changes made long-playing records less expensive; and the number of buyers multiplied. Music was no longer confined to the concert hall or cafe, but reverberated through people's homes, cars, and teenagers' rooms—providing a sound track for everyday life.

Postwar youth culture owed much to rock and roll, a hybrid musical style that drew from the blues tradition of African Americans, Appalachian country string bands, and western swing (itself a fusion of country and jazz). After the Second World War, Black rhythm and blues musicians as well as white Southern rockabilly performers found much wider audiences through the use

Portable radios enable popular music culture to flourish, especially among the young

of new technology: electric guitars, better equipment for studio recording, and wideband radio stations in large cities. The blend of styles and sounds and the increasing willingness of white teenagers to listen to what recording studios marketed as "race music"—that is, for African American audiences—came together to create rock and roll. The music was exciting, sometimes aggressive, and full of energy.

In Europe, rock and roll found its way into working-class neighborhoods, particularly in Britain and Ireland. There, local youths took American sounds, echoed the inflections of poverty and defiance, and added touches of music-hall showmanship to produce successful artists and bands, collectively referred to as the "British invasion." During the 1960s, British sounds and stars blended with their American counterparts, and as the music's popularity spread, music culture came loose from its national moorings. The Beatles managed to get their music on the hit lists in France, Germany, and the United States. By the time of the Woodstock festival (1969), youth music culture was international. Rock became the sound of young people worldwide, eventually absorbing musical motifs from South Asia—think of the Beatles' use of the sitar—and the rhythms of North Africa.

Rock also provided a bridge across the Cold War divide. Despite Eastern bloc prohibitions of "capitalist" music, pirated songs circulated. In Prague, one month after Soviet tanks entered Czechoslovakia to overthrow the government of Alexander Dubček (see pages 1022–25), a rock band known as the Plastic People of the Universe took a stand of cultural defiance. Such cultural protest movements had a different political significance in the Soviet bloc: they were more pointedly a challenge to the official culture of the regime and its attempts to censor expressions of dissidence.

Rock music also became an expression of political dissidence in Soviet-dominated Eastern Europe

ART AND PAINTING

High culture was also changed by the rise of consumer culture. The power of the dollar helped make New York a center of modern art, one of the most striking developments of the period. Immigration was another: New York proved hospitable to European artists, and a stream of immigrants from Europe nourished American art and literature as well as its social and political thought (Chapter 27). Finally, the creative work of the school of abstract expressionism sealed New York's postwar reputation. The abstract expressionists—Willem de Kooning (from the Netherlands), Mark Rothko (from Russia), Franz Kline, Jackson Pollock, Helen Frankenthaler, and Robert Motherwell—followed trends established by the cubists and surrealists, experimenting with color, texture, and technique to find new forms of expression. Pollock poured and threw paint on the canvas, creating powerful images of physical expressiveness; critics dubbed this process "action painting."

Abstract expressionism also produced its opposite, sometimes called pop art. Pop artists distanced themselves from the elusive meditations of abstract expressionism. They refused to distinguish between avant-garde and popular art, or between the artistic and the commercial. They lavished attention on instantly recognizable—often commercial—images; borrowed techniques from graphic design; and were interested in the immediacy of everyday art and ordinary people's visual experience. Jasper Johns's paintings of the American flag formed part of this trend. So did the work of Andy Warhol and Roy Lichtenstein, who took objects such as soup cans and images of comic-strip heroes as their subjects. Warhol did not see his work as a protest against the banality of commercial culture and argued that he was continuing to experiment with abstractions. Treating popular culture with this tongue-in-cheek seriousness became a central theme of 1960s art.

ACTION PAINTING. Photographer Martha Holmes reveals the dynamic technique of the abstract expressionist Jackson Pollock in this photo, taken while he paints, 1950.

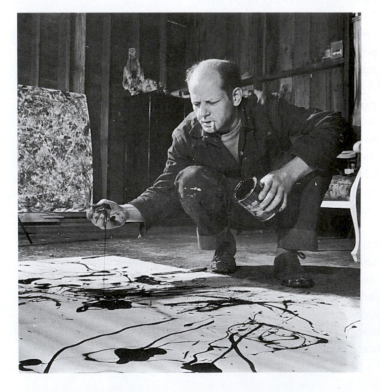

FILM

Mass culture made its most powerful impact through film. Film flourished after the Second World War, developing in several different directions. The Italian neorealists of the late 1940s and the 1950s, antifascists and socialists, set out to capture authenticity, or "life as it was lived," especially working-class existence. They shot on location, using natural light and little-known actors, deliberately steering away from the production values they associated with the tainted cinema of fascist and wartime Europe. Not strictly realists, they played with nonlinear plots and unpredictable characters and motivations. Roberto Rossellini's *Rome: Open City* (1945) is a loving portrait of Rome under Nazi occupation. Vittorio De Sica's *Bicycle Thief* (1948) tells the story of a man struggling against poverty, who desperately needs a bicycle to keep his job as a poster hanger. Federico Fellini's breakout film, *La Dolce Vita* (1959; starring Marcello Mastroianni), took Italian film to screens throughout Europe and the United States. It also marked Fellini's transition to his signature surrealist and carnivalesque style, developed in *8½* (1963).

The French directors of the new wave developed an unsentimental social vision in films that encouraged improvisation and experimental storytelling. Made with small budgets, and shot using portable equipment away from the studios, the films of the new wave inspired later generations of independent filmmakers. François Truffaut's (1932–1984) *400 Blows* (1959) and *The Wild Child* (1970), and Jean-Luc Godard's (1930–) *Breathless* (1960) and *Contempt* (1963; starring Brigitte Bardot), are leading examples. France made other contributions to international film by sponsoring the Cannes Film Festival. The first Cannes festival was held before the Second World War, but the city opened its gates again in 1946, under the banner of artistic internationalism. Placing itself at the center of an international film industry became part of France's ongoing recovery from the war, and Cannes became one of the world's largest markets for film.

In Eastern Europe, film also became an important means of creative expression in the postwar decades, and the Cannes festival introduced many of the films from the east to Western audiences. Polish director Andrzej Wajda's trilogy about the war years—*A Generation* (1954), *Kanal* (1956), and *Ashes and Diamonds* (1958)—portrayed young Poles confronted with the German occupation, the Warsaw uprisings in 1943 and 1944, and the politics of anticommunism in the aftermath of the war. Jiří Menzel of Czechoslovakia (1938–) directed *Closely Watched Trains* (1966), which won the Academy Award for Best Foreign Language Film in 1968. Like the films of Godard and Truffaut, Menzel's films raised the creative status of the director by insisting that a film's camera work and vision constituted the real art—another part of the new value accorded to the visual.

HOLLYWOOD'S GLOBAL INFLUENCE The American film industry, based in Hollywood, increasingly reached a global audience. The huge domestic market for film in the United States gave Hollywood a big advantage. By the 1950s, Hollywood was making 500 films a year, and accounted for between 40 and 75 percent of films shown in Europe. The same period brought the conversion to color and new optical formats, including widescreen. Hollywood's expanding influence was but one instance of the "Americanization" of Western culture.

The domestic politics of the Cold War weighed heavily on filmmaking in the United States. Between 1947 and 1951, members of the House Un-American Activities Committee (HUAC) investigated hundreds of actors, directors, and writers for alleged sympathies with communism, causing many in the film industry to be blacklisted by the studios. At the same time, paradoxically, American censorship was breaking down, with dramatic consequences on-screen. Since the early 1930s, the Motion Picture Production Code had refused to approve "scenes of passion" (including married couples sharing a bed), immorality, realistic violence, and profanity. In 1952, the U.S. Supreme Court ruled that films were protected by the

Success of American film in Western Europe an example of "Americanization"

Race and American Popular Culture in the Second Half of the Twentieth Century

Trends in American popular music in the postwar decades and their reception by audiences at home and abroad were the product of a complicated set of historical circumstances: new technologies for rapidly disseminating film and music to millions, the prosperity of the postwar boom, which allowed people to have more money to spend on leisure; the migration of Black Americans from the rural South to urban cities in the north; and the emergence of adolescence as a distinct life stage that was targeted as an important demographic by marketers of fashion, style, and clothing. When this potent mix produced new trends—rock and roll in the 1950s, protest music in the 1960s, disco and rap in the 1970s and 1980s—commentators were quick to both celebrate and castigate each of these developments as either creative expressions of a new generation or as symptoms of larger social problems. These two examples—one by a German journalist describing a concert given by a Black musician in California (Fats Domino) in a German newsmagazine, and the second, an essay by a Black American critic about sexism in gangsta rap—show the different ways that contemporaries deciphered and interpreted the apparent connections between music, sexuality, and race in their perspective decades.

"The Master Rhythm," *Der Spiegel* (1956).

Downstairs in the auditorium where 5000 young people sit it is getting warm. They can no longer stay in their seats—the spastic movements of [the performers] on the stage spread like a wave through the rows of seats in the hall. The movement in the room becomes ever more hypnotic, ever more hectic. Here and there the boys leap to their feet and tear their shirts from their bodies; their glazed eyes giving no sign that they are aware of their surroundings. Only the master-rhythm seems to drive them onward. [...]

As if in a trance, the half-grown people in the great hall dance alone like possessed medicine men of a jungle tribe, completely taken over by a music that has held America's youth in its thrall for several months. The international market for music has created a new kind of hit, after the Mambo, while at the same time generating protests from teachers, parents, and the police. The new kind of hit music that has produced all these reactions is called "Rock 'n' Roll" (actually: "Rock and Roll"). [...]

At a large Rock 'n' Roll gathering in the small California city of San Jose, the battle began shortly after midnight. A beer bottle sailed through the dancehall where 2500 young people were listening to the beats of Fats Domino, billed as the "King of Rock 'n' Roll." The panting adolescents fell upon one another, glass splintered, chairs were smashed, and the stage barriers were ripped from their posts. Fats Domino and his horn players fled, sixteen police patrol cars arrived from every district, and 40 police officers stormed a neighboring building where the crowd had gathered. It took them an hour to clear the hall. Similar scenes unfolded in many other American cities where the magic Rock 'n' Roll rhythm has liberated the destructive impulses of young people. [...]

The history of Rock 'n' Roll has unfolded following the same process as almost every other dance fad and hit music in the white world in the last fifty years. In the 1870s, for example, Ragtime emerged from the black workers who built railroads of North America, and over forty years later—between 1910 and 1925—Ragtime burst forth in a modified form as a hit in American dance halls.

Like Ragtime, the Charleston, Foxtrot, Boogie, Swing and Jitterbug, Rumba, and the Mambo, and even Rock 'n' Roll, forms of black folk music in North or South America, were removed from their original expression and finally transformed into white dance and popular music. Black music appears to be an inexhaustible reservoir for the white popular music market, which has taken nothing from the old continent of Europe beyond its orchestra instruments and conventional harmonies.

Source: "Der Über-Rhythmus," *Der Spiegel* (September 26, 1956).

bell hooks, "Gangsta Culture—Sexism and Misogyny: Who Will Take the Rap?" (1994)

To the white-dominated mass media, the controversy over gangsta rap makes great spectacle. Besides the exploitation of these issues to attract audiences, a central motivation for highlighting gangsta rap continues to be the sensationalist drama of demonizing black youth culture in general and the contributions of young black men in particular. It's a contemporary remake of *Birth of a Nation*—only this time we are encouraged to believe it is not just vulnerable white womanhood that risks destruction by black hands, but everyone. When I counter this demonization of black males by insisting that gangsta rap does not appear in a cultural vacuum, that it is not a product created in isolation within a segregated black world but is rather expressive of the cultural crossing, mixings, and engagement of black youth culture with the values, attitudes, and concerns of the white majority, some folks stop listening.

The sexist, misogynist, patriarchal ways of thinking and behaving that are glorified in gangsta rap are a reflection of the prevailing values in our society, values created and sustained by white supremacist capitalist patriarchy. As the crudest and most brutal expression of sexism, misogynistic attitudes tend to be portrayed by the dominant culture as always an expression of male deviance. In reality, they are part of a sexist continuum, necessary for the maintenance of patriarchal social order. [...] It is useful to think of misogyny as a field that must be labored in and maintained both to sustain patriarchy but also to nourish an antifeminist backlash. And what better group to labor on this "plantation" than young black men?

To see gangsta rap as a reflection of dominant values in our culture rather than as an aberrant pathological standpoint does not mean that a rigorous feminist critique and interrogation of the sexist and misogyny expressed in this music is not needed. Without a doubt black males, young and old, must be held politically accountable for their sexism. Yet this critique must always be contextualized or we risk making it appear that the problems of misogyny, sexism, and all the behaviors this thinking supports and condones, including rape, male violence against women, is a black male thing. And this is what is happening. Young black males are forced to take the heat for encouraging via their music the hatred of and violence against women that is a central core of patriarchy.

Source: bell hooks, "Gangsta Culture—Sexism and Misogyny: Who Will Take the Rap?" *Outlaw Culture: Resisting Representations* (New York: Routledge, 1994), pp. 134–137.

Questions for Analysis

1. What assumptions does the German journalist make about Black American musical traditions and the behavior of Fats Domino's white audience? What value judgements does he invite by his choice of language, and what is his implied judgement about the scene that he observed?

2. How does bell hooks view those who suggest that Black rappers should be criticized for perpetuating attitudes that are demeaning to women in their music? What value judgements does she insist on, when considering these examples of popular music in their broader social context?

3. Both authors seem to agree that these genres of music—rock and roll in the 1950s, gangsta rap in the 1990s—need to be understood in their historical context. What is different about their two approaches?

JAMES DEAN IN REBEL WITHOUT A CAUSE (1955). Films from the 1950s and the 1960s contributed to the romanticization of automobiles, sexuality, and youthful rebellion.

First Amendment, and films such as *Rebel without a Cause* (1955)—about juvenile delinquency—challenged these Production Code standards. By the 1960s, the code had been scuttled, and the extremely graphic violence at the end of Arthur Penn's *Bonnie and Clyde* (1967) marked the scope of the transformation.

GENDER ROLES AND SEXUAL REVOLUTION

The so-called sexual revolution of the 1960s had several aspects. The first was less censorship and fewer taboos regarding public discussion of sexuality. In the United States, the notorious Kinsey Reports on male and female sexuality (published in 1948 and 1953, respectively) made morality and sexual behavior front-page news. Alfred Kinsey was a zoologist turned social scientist, and the way in which he applied science and statistics to sex attracted considerable attention. Kinsey's research showed that moral codes and private behaviors did not line up neatly; although 80 to 90 percent of the women he interviewed disapproved of premarital sex, 50 percent of them had engaged in it. *Time* magazine warned that publicizing disparities between beliefs and behavior might prove subversive—that is, women and men would decide there was "morality in numbers."

> *Aspects of the "sexual revolution": (1) Loosening of taboos on sexual practices* ❯

Was the family crumbling? Transformations in agriculture and life in the European countryside did mean that the peasant family was no longer the institution that governed birth, work, courtship, marriage, and death. Yet the family became newly important as the center of consumption, spending, and leisure time, for television took people (usually men) out of bars, cafés, and music halls. Meanwhile, the family became the focus of government attention in the form of family allowances, health care, and Cold War appeals to family values. People brought higher expectations to marriage, which raised divorce rates; and paid more attention to children, which resulted in smaller families. Despite a postwar spike in the birth rate that produced the "baby boom," fertility declined over the long term, even in countries that outlawed contraception. The family assumed new meanings as its traditional structures of authority—namely paternal control over wives and children—eroded under the pressure of social change.

> *(2) An openness toward representations of sexuality* ❯

The second aspect of the revolution was the centrality of sex and eroticism to mass consumer culture. Magazines, which flourished in this period, offered advice on how to be attractive and succeed in love. Cultivating one's looks, including sexual attractiveness, fitted with the new accent on consumption: health and personal hygiene was the fastest-rising category of family spending. Advertising, advice columns, TV, and film blurred the boundaries on buying consumer goods, seeking personal fulfillment, and satisfying sexual desire. There was nothing new about appeals to eroticism, but the fact that sexuality was now widely considered a form of self-expression—perhaps even the core of oneself—was new to the twentieth century. These developments helped propel change, and they also made the sexual revolution prominent in the politics of the time.

The third aspect of the revolution came with the legal and medical or scientific changes in contraception. Oral contraceptives, first approved for development in 1960, became mainstream in the next decade. The **birth control pill** did not have revolutionary effects on the birth rate, which was already falling, but it marked a dramatic change because it was simple (though expensive) and could be used by women themselves. By 1975, two-thirds of British women between the ages of fifteen and forty-four said they were taking the Pill. Numbers like these marked a long, drawn-out end to centuries-old views that discussing birth control was pornographic, an affront to religion, and an invitation to indulgence and promiscuity. By and large, Western countries legalized contraception in the 1960s, and abortion in the 1970s. In 1965, the U.S. Supreme Court struck down laws banning the use of contraception, though selling contraceptives remained illegal in Massachusetts until 1972. The Soviet Union legalized abortion in 1950, after banning it during most of Stalin's regime. Throughout Eastern Europe, abortion rates were extremely high, because contraceptives proved as difficult to obtain as other consumer goods, men often refused to use them, and women—doubly burdened with long hours of wage work and housework and facing, in addition, chronic housing shortages—had little choice but to resort to abortion.

Legal changes would not have occurred without the women's movements of the time. For nineteenth-century feminists, winning the right to vote was the most difficult practical and symbolic struggle (Chapter 23). For the revived feminism of the 1960s and the 1970s, family, work, and sexuality—all put on the agenda by the social changes of the period—were central. Since the Second World War, the assumption that middle-class women belonged in the home had been challenged by the steadily rising demand for workers, especially in education and the service sector. Thus, many more married women and mothers became part of the labor force. Moreover, across the West, young middle-class women, like men, were part of the rising number of university students. But in the United States, to take just one example, only 37 percent of women who enrolled in college in the 1950s finished their degrees. They believed they should marry instead, because they found it difficult to get non-secretarial jobs, received less pay for the same work, and, even when employed, had to rely on their husbands to establish credit.

The tension between rising expectations stemming from abundance, growth, and the emphasis on self-expression on the one hand, and the reality of limited opportunity on the other, created quiet waves of discontent. Betty Friedan's book *The Feminine Mystique* (1963) brought much of this discontent into the open, contrasting the cultural myths of the fulfilled and happy housewife with the realities of economic inequality, hard work, and narrowed horizons. In 1949, Simone de Beauvoir had described how Western culture (myth, literature, and psychology) had created an image of woman as the second, and lesser sex. In 1963, Friedan, using a more journalistic style and writing at a time when social change had made readers more receptive to her ideas, showed how the media, the social sciences, and advertising at once exalted femininity and lowered women's expectations and possibilities. Friedan cofounded the National Organization for Women (NOW) in 1966; and smaller, often more radical, women's movements multiplied across Europe in the following decades. For this generation of feminists, reproductive

(3) Increased understanding and availability of contraception

birth control pill This oral contraceptive became widely available in the mid-1960s. For the first time, women had a simple method of birth control that they could take themselves.

freedom was both a private matter and a basic right—a key to women's control over their lives. Outlawing contraception and abortion, they argued, made women alone bear responsibility for the consequences of sweeping changes in Western sexual life, and such measures were ineffective as well as unjust. Mass consumption, mass culture, and startlingly rapid transformations in public and private life were all intimately related.

Social Movements during the 1960s

The social unrest of the 1960s was connected to the global political struggles and social transformations of the postwar period. Of these, the most important were anticolonial and civil rights movements. Anticolonial movements (Chapter 27) reflected a growing awareness that assumptions about race underlay definitions of citizenship and national belonging, as well as the way that resources were distributed in the postwar world. In the West, particularly in the United States, many people of color identified with the social and economic grievances of colonized peoples elsewhere. Newly independent African and Caribbean nations remained wary of neocolonial attitudes and the continuing economic hegemony of Western Europe and North America.

THE CIVIL RIGHTS MOVEMENT

The emergence of new Black nations in Africa and the Caribbean was paralleled by a growing African American **civil rights movement**. The Second World War increased African American migration from the American South to northern cities, intensifying a drive for rights, dignity, and independence led earlier by the National Association for the Advancement of Colored People (NAACP), founded in 1909. By 1960, civil rights groups, led by the Congress of Racial Equality (CORE), organized boycotts and demonstrations directed at private businesses and public services that discriminated against Blacks in the South.

Martin Luther King Jr. (1929–1968), a Baptist minister who embraced the philosophy of nonviolence promoted by the Indian social and political activist Mohandas K. Gandhi (Chapter 27), emerged as the most visible and effective leader of the movement until his assassination in 1968.

King, the Southern Christian Leadership Conference (SCLC), and organizations such as CORE aspired to a fully integrated United States, believing that the liberal principle of equality could be realized in society that disavowed racial hierarchy and discrimination. Other Black leaders, such as Malcolm X (1925–1965), sought independence from white society and embraced Black nationalism, fearing that the long history of white supremacy in the U.S. made integration impossible. Although

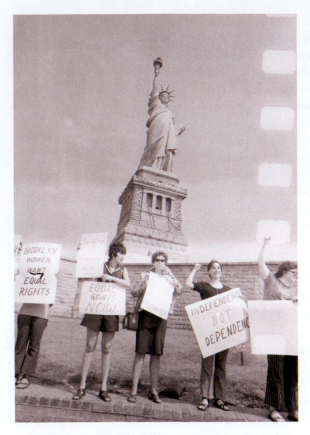

SECOND WAVE FEMINISM.
U.S. women, standing beneath the Statue of Liberty, celebrate the passage of the Equal Rights Amendment by the House of Representatives in 1970; the bill, however, did not pass the Senate and never became law. The feminists of the "second wave" distinguished themselves from the "first wave," who had focused on gaining voting rights in Europe and the Americas in the nineteenth and early twentieth centuries, by arguing that votes for women did not end pervasive gender discrimination. They demanded equal pay for equal work and challenged widespread expectations about women's roles in families and the workplace.

MARTIN LUTHER KING JR., 1964. The African American civil rights leader is welcomed in Oslo, Norway, on a trip to accept the Nobel Peace Prize. He would be assassinated four years later. › **How might have Europeans viewed King's campaign?** › **How might have their views affected their vision of the United States?**

the civil rights movement in the United States could point to real successes—voting rights and school desegregation among them—the visible and violent resistance to civil rights organizers in the South and persistent racism in housing and employment hurt the image of the United States in Europe.

These problems were not confined to the United States. Indian, West Indian, and Pakistani immigrants in Britain faced discrimination in jobs, housing, and everyday interaction with the authorities, producing frequent racial disturbances in major British cities. France witnessed hostility toward immigration from France's former colonies, and Germany toward the importation of Turkish labor. In Western Europe, as in the United States, struggles for racial and ethnic integration complicated government economic policies aimed at reducing social inequality.

The U.S. civil rights movement had enormous significance for the twentieth century, and it galvanized other movements. It dramatized, as perhaps no other movement could, the chasm between the egalitarian promises of American democracy and the real inequalities at the core of American social and political life—a chasm that could be found in other Western nations as well. Black Americans' demands for equality were morally and politically compelling, as were their critiques of the United States' claims to defend liberty during the Cold War.

civil rights movement
Movement by African Americans and their supporters against racial segregation and discrimination in the United States in the decades after the Second World War. Community organizing, boycotts, and demonstrations led to the passage of civil rights legislation in the 1960s to protect voting rights and target racial segregation in schools.

The "Woman Question" on Both Sides of the Atlantic

How did Western culture define femininity? Did women internalize those definitions? These questions were central to postwar feminist thought, and they were sharply posed in two classic texts: Simone de Beauvoir's The Second Sex *(1949) and Betty Friedan's* The Feminine Mystique *(1963). De Beauvoir (1908–1986) started from the existentialist premise that humans were "condemned to be free" and to give their own lives meaning. Why, then, did women accept the limitations imposed on them and, in de Beauvoir's words, "dream the dreams of men"? Although dense and philosophical,* The Second Sex *was read throughout the world.*

Betty Friedan's equally influential bestseller drew heavily on de Beauvoir. Friedan (1921–2006) sought the origins of the feminine mystique, her term for the model of femininity promoted by experts, advertised in women's magazines, and seemingly accepted by middle-class housewives in postwar United States. As Friedan points out in the excerpt here, the new postwar mystique was in many ways more conservative than prewar ideals had been, despite continuing social change, the greater range of careers opening up to women, the expansion of women's education, and so on. She cofounded the National Organization for Women (NOW) in 1966, and served as its president until 1970.

Simone de Beauvoir, *The Second Sex* (1949)

But first, what is a woman? . . . Everyone agrees there are females in the human species; today, as in the past, they make up about half of humanity; and yet we are told that "femininity is in jeopardy"; we are urged, "Be women, stay women, become women." . . . Although some women zealously strive to embody it, the model has never been patented. It is typically described in vague and shimmering terms borrowed from a clairvoyant's vocabulary. . . .

If the female function is not enough to define woman, and if we also reject the explanation of the "eternal feminine," but if we accept, even temporarily, that there are women on the earth, we then have to ask: what is a woman?

Merely stating the problem suggests an immediate answer to me. It is significant that I pose it. It would never occur to a man to write a book on the singular situation of males in humanity. If I want to define myself, I first have to say, "I am a woman"; all other assertions will

arise from this basic truth. A man never begins by positing himself as an individual of a certain sex: that he is a man is obvious. The categories "masculine" and "feminine" appear as symmetrical in a formal way on town hall records or identification papers. The relation of the two sexes is not that of two electrical poles: the man represents both the positive and the neuter. . . . Woman is the negative, to such a point that any determination is imputed to her as a limitation, without reciprocity. . . . [A] man is in his right by virtue of being man; it is the woman who is in the wrong. . . . Woman has ovaries and a uterus; such are the particular conditions that lock her in her subjectivity; some even say she thinks with her hormones. Man vainly forgets that his anatomy also includes hormones and testicles. He grasps his body as a direct and normal link with the world that he believes he apprehends in all objectivity whereas he considers woman's body an obstacle, a prison, burdened by everything that particularises it. "The female is female by virtue of a certain *lack* of qualities," Aristotle said. "We should regard women's nature as suffering from natural defectiveness." And St. Thomas in his turn decreed that woman was an "incomplete man," an "incidental" being. This is what the Genesis story symbolises, where Eve appears as if drawn from Adam's "supernumerary" bone, in Bossuet's words. Humanity is male, and man defines woman, not in herself, but in relation to himself; she is not considered an autonomous being. . . . And she is nothing other than what man decides; she is thus called "the sex," meaning that the male sees her essentially as a sexed being; for him she is sex, so she is it in the absolute. She determines and differentiates herself in relation to man, and he does not in relation to her; she is the inessential in front of the essential. He is the Subject, he is the Absolute. She is the Other.

Source: Simone de Beauvoir, *The Second Sex*, trans. Constance Borde and Sheila Malovany-Chevallier (London: 2009), pp. 3-6.

Betty Friedan, *The Feminine Mystique* (1963)

In 1939, the heroines of women's magazine stories were not always young, but in a certain sense they were younger than their fictional counterparts today. They were young in the same way that the American hero has always been young: they were New Women, creating with a gay determined spirit a new identity for women—a life of their own. There was an aura about them of becoming, of moving into a future that was going to be different from the past. . . .

These stories may not have been great literature. But the identity of their heroines seemed to say something about the housewives who, then as now, read the women's magazines. These magazines were not written for career women. The New Woman heroines were the ideal of yesterday's housewives; they reflected the dreams, mirrored the yearning for identity and the sense of possibility that existed for women then. . . .

In 1949 . . . the feminine mystique began to spread through the land. . . .

The feminine mystique says that the highest value and the only commitment for women is the fulfillment of their own femininity. It says that the great mistake of Western culture, through most of its history, has been the undervaluation of this femininity. . . . The mistake, says the mystique, the root of women's troubles in the past, is that women envied men, women tried to be like men, instead of accepting their own nature, which can find fulfillment only in sexual passivity, male domination, and nurturing maternal love.

But the new image this mystique gives to American women is the old image: "Occupation: housewife." The new mystique makes the housewife-mothers, who never had a chance to be anything else, the model for all women; it presupposes that history has reached a final and glorious end in the here and now, as far as women are concerned. . . .

It is more than a strange paradox that as all professions are finally open to women in America, "career woman" has become a dirty word; that as higher education becomes available to any woman with the capacity for it, education for women has become so suspect that more and more drop out of high school and college to marry and have babies; that as so many roles in modern society become theirs for the taking, women so insistently confine themselves to one role. Why. . . should she accept this new image which insists she is not a person but a "woman," by definition barred from the freedom of human existence and a voice in human destiny?

Source: Betty Friedan, *The Feminine Mystique* (New York: 2001; first publication, 1963), pp. 38, 40, 42-43, 67-68.

Questions for Analysis

1. Why does de Beauvoir ask, "What is a woman?"

2. Why does Friedan think that a "feminine mystique" emerged after the Second World War?

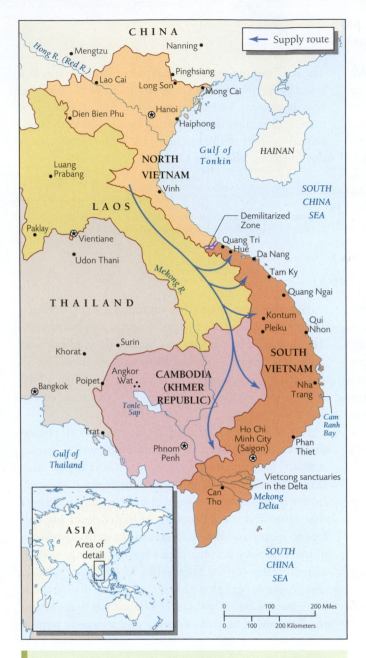

THE ANTIWAR MOVEMENT

The United States' escalating war in Vietnam also became a focus for discontent. In 1961, President John F. Kennedy (1917–1963) promised that the United States would "bear any burden" to fight communism, and to ensure the victory of American models of representative government and free-market economics in developing nations. Kennedy's plan entailed massive increases in foreign and military aid and provided the impetus for humanitarian institutions such as the Peace Corps, intended to show Americans' good intentions by supporting local development projects. Bearing burdens also meant fighting guerrillas who turned to the Soviets for aid. This led to covert American interventions in Latin America, the Congo, and Vietnam.

By the time of Kennedy's assassination in 1963, nearly 15,000 American "advisers" were in South Vietnam. Kennedy's successor, Lyndon Johnson, began the strategic bombing of North Vietnam and sent hundreds of thousands of American troops to Vietnam. The rebels in the south, known as the Viet Cong, were highly experienced guerrilla fighters backed by the well-equipped and Soviet-supported North Vietnamese army under Ho Chi Minh. The South Vietnamese government, meanwhile, resisted reform and lacked popular support. The U.S. escalation produced only stalemate, mounting American casualties, and rising discontent.

The debate over Vietnam exacerbated the political turmoil of the 1960s in the United States. As Martin Luther King Jr. pointed out, the war—which relied on a disproportionate number of Black soldiers to conduct a fight against a small nation of color—echoed and magnified racial inequality at home. Exasperated by troubles in the field, American planners continued to increase troop levels and the military draft of young men polarized the public. In 1968, criticism of his Vietnam policy forced President Johnson to abandon his plans to run for a second term. His successor, Richard M. Nixon (1913–1994), who campaigned on promises to end the war, expanded it instead. Student protests against the war frequently ended in violence. Avoiding the draft became so widespread that the system was changed in 1970. Seen from abroad, the

THE WAR IN VIETNAM AND SOUTHEAST ASIA.
The 1954 Geneva Accords divided Vietnam at the seventeenth parallel: the north went to Ho Chi Minh, the communist leader; and the south was controlled by Ngo Dinh Diem, an ally of the United States. In 1956, South Vietnam refused to hold the elections mandated by the Geneva Accords. In response, Ho Chi Minh mobilized a guerrilla army, the Viet Cong, and the Vietnam War began. **› Which other countries in this region were drawn into the war? › How did the Viet Cong use the proximity of Cambodia and Laos to their strategic advantage? › Why did the United States choose to get involved?**

Vietnam War became a spectacle, in which the most powerful nation in the world seemed intent on destroying a country of poor peasants in the name of anticommunism, democracy, and freedom.

THE STUDENT MOVEMENT IN 1968

The year 1968 brought a sudden wave of revolution that eventually reached every continent. The possibility of a global youth culture fostered a sense of collective identity. The news media relayed images of civil rights protests in the United States to Europe, and broadcast news footage of the Vietnam War on television screens from West Virginia to West Germany. The wave of unrest shook both the Eastern and Western blocs and unsettled societies in Africa, Asia, and Latin America.

The student movement can be seen as a consequence of postwar developments: a growing cohort of young people possessing more time and wealth than in the past; generational consciousness heightened by the marketing of mass youth culture; and educational institutions unable to deal with rising numbers and expectations. Universities, founded to educate a small elite, were overwhelmed by the new generation. Lecture halls were packed, thousands of students took exams simultaneously, and university bureaucracies did not respond to student demands for input into university governance. More philosophically, students raised questions about the role and meaning of elite education in a democratic society, and about the relationship between universities and the broader political establishment. On American campuses, student demands for fewer restrictions on personal life—for instance, permission to have a member of the opposite sex in a dormitory room—provoked

"THE PRESS IS POISON. READ OUR TRACTS AND POSTERS, THE NEWSPAPERS ON THE WALL." Criticizing the official media was central to the politics of May 1968.

authoritarian reactions from university representatives. Waves of student protest were not confined to the United States and Western Europe; they also swept across Poland and Czechoslovakia, where students protested one-party bureaucratic rule, stifling intellectual life, and authoritarianism; they also helped sustain networks of dissidents. By the mid-1960s, simmering anger in Eastern Europe had once again reached a dangerous point.

MAY 1968 IN PARIS The most serious outbreak of student unrest in Europe came in Paris in the spring of 1968. The French Republic had been shaken by conflicts over the Algerian war in the early 1960s. The unrest began when French students at the University of Paris demanded reforms to modernize their university. Protest first peaked at Nanterre, a new branch of the university built in a poorly served neighborhood, starved for funds, and overcrowded with students. Petitions, demonstrations, and confrontations with university authorities traveled quickly from Nanterre to the Sorbonne, in central Paris.

Protests in French universities, met with repression by de Gaulle's government, spread into many other industries

In the face of growing disorder, the University of Paris shut down, sending students into the streets and into uglier confrontations with the police. The violence of the police response startled onlookers and television audiences and backfired on the authorities. Sympathy with the students' cause expanded rapidly, bringing in opponents of President Charles de Gaulle's government. Massive trade union strikes broke out as workers in industry, and public-sector employees went on strike. By mid-May, an astonishing 10 million French workers had walked off their jobs. The government seemed poised to fall, but it satisfied strikers with wage increases and appeals to public demand for order. The student protests gradually petered out and the government recovered. The events of 1968 nevertheless weakened de Gaulle's position; he retired from office the following year.

Paris was not the only city to explode in 1968. Student protests also broke out in West Berlin, targeting the government's close ties to the autocratic shah of Iran and the power of media corporations; clashes with the police here also turned violent. In Italian cities, undergraduates staged demonstrations to draw attention to university overcrowding; twenty-six universities closed. The London School of Economics was nearly shut down by protests. In the United States, antiwar demonstrations and student rebellions spread across the country after the North Vietnamese and Viet Cong launched the Tet Offensive. In the United States, President Johnson chose not to run for reelection. The year 1968 also saw trauma and damage to the country's political future with the assassinations of Martin Luther King Jr. (April 4) and the presidential candidate Robert F. Kennedy (June 5). King's assassination was followed by a wave of rioting in more than fifty cities across the United States. In late summer, street battles raged between police and student protesters at the Democratic National Convention in Chicago. Some saw the flowering of protests as another "springtime of peoples," but others saw it as a long nightmare.

Prague Spring A period of political liberalization in Czechoslovakia between January and August 1968 that was initiated by Alexander Dubček, the Czech leader.

PRAGUE The student movement in the United States and Western Europe took inspiration from one of the most significant challenges to Soviet authority since the Hungarian revolt of 1956 (see Chapter 27): the "**Prague Spring**" of 1968. The

A RUSSIAN TANK ATTACKED DURING THE PRAGUE SPRING, 1968.
The Soviet-led invasion of Czechoslovakia on August 20–21, 1968, put an end to
Alexander Dubček's experiment in creating "socialism with a human face."

events began with the emergence of a liberal communist government in Czechoslovakia, led by the Slovak **Alexander Dubček** (*DOOB-chehk*; 1921–1992). Dubček
had outmaneuvered the more traditional, authoritarian party leaders, and advocated
"socialism with a human face." He encouraged debates within the party, academic
and artistic freedom, and less censorship. As was often the case, party members
were divided between proponents of reform and those fearful that reform would
unleash a revolution, but the reformers gained the upper hand with support from
outside the party: student organizations, the press, and networks of dissidents. As
in Western Europe and the United States, the protest movement overflowed into
traditional party politics.

In the Soviet Union, Khrushchev had fallen in 1964, and the reins of Soviet power
had passed to Leonid Brezhnev as secretary of the Communist party. Brezhnev was
more conservative than Khrushchev, less inclined to bargain with the West, and
prone to defensive actions to safeguard the Soviet sphere of influence. Initially, the
Soviets tolerated Dubček, but the events of 1968 raised their fears. Most Eastern
European communist leaders denounced Czech reformism, but student demonstrations of support broke out in Poland and Yugoslavia, calling for an end to one-
party rule, less censorship, and reform of the judicial system. In addition, Josip Broz
Tito of Yugoslavia and Nicolae Ceauşescu (*chow-SHEHS-koo*) of Romania—two of
the more stubbornly independent communist leaders in Eastern Europe—visited
Dubček. To Soviet eyes, these activities looked like an affront to Warsaw Pact and
Soviet security.

Alexander Dubček (1921–
1992) Communist leader
of the Czechoslovakian
government who advocated
for "socialism with a human
face."

Ludvík Vaculík, "Two Thousand Words" (1968)

During the Prague Spring of 1968, a group of Czech intellectuals published a document titled "Two Thousand Words That Belong to Workers, Farmers, Officials, Scientists, Artists, and Everybody," known simply as "Two Thousand Words." The author of the document, Ludvík Vaculík, was a member of the Czech Communist party who hoped to encourage the people of Czechoslovakia to implement democratic reforms, including freedom of the press. Seen as a direct affront by Moscow, this manifesto heightened Soviet–Czech tensions. In August 1968, Warsaw Pact tanks rolled into Prague, overthrowing the reformist government of Alexander Dubček.

Most of the nation welcomed the socialist program with high hopes. But it fell into the hands of the wrong people. It would not have mattered so much that they lacked adequate experience in affairs of state, factual knowledge, or philosophical education, if only they had enough common prudence and decency to listen to the opinion of others and agree to being gradually replaced by more able people. . . .

The chief sin and deception of these rulers was to have explained their own whims as the "will of the workers." Were we to accept this pretense, we would have to blame the workers today for the decline of our economy, for crimes committed against the innocent, and for the introduction of censorship to prevent anyone writing about these things. The workers would be to blame for misconceived investments, for losses suffered in foreign trade, and for the housing shortage. Obviously no sensible person will hold the working class responsible for such things. We all know, and every worker knows especially, that they had virtually no say in deciding anything. . . .

Since the beginning of this year we have been experiencing a regenerative process of democratization. . . .

Let us demand the departure of people who abused their power, damaged public property, and acted dishonorably or brutally. Ways must be found to compel them to resign. To mention a few: public criticism, resolutions, demonstrations, demonstrative work brigades, collections to buy presents for them on their retirement, strikes, and picketing at their front doors. But we should reject any illegal, indecent, or boorish methods. . . . Let us convert the district and local newspapers, which have mostly degenerated to the level of official mouthpieces, into a platform for all the forward-looking elements in politics; let us demand that editorial boards be formed of National Front representatives, or else let us start new papers. Let us form committees for the defense of free speech. . . .

There has been great alarm recently over the possibility that foreign forces will intervene in our development. Whatever superior forces may face us, all we can do is stick to our own positions, behave decently, and initiate nothing ourselves. We can show our government that we will stand by it, with weapons if need be, if it will do what we give it a mandate to do. . . .

The spring is over and will never return. By winter we will know all.

Source: Jaromír Navrátil, ed., *The Prague Spring 1968: A National Security Archive Documents Reader*, trans. Mark Kramer, Joy Moss, and Ruth Tosek (Budapest: 1998), pp. 177–81.

Questions for Analysis

1. According to Vaculík, where did socialism go wrong?

2. What specific reforms did Vaculík demand?

In August 1968, after Dubček attempted to democratize the Communist party and did not attend a meeting of the Warsaw Pact, the Soviets sent tanks and troops into Prague in August 1968. Again, the world watched as streams of Czech refugees left the country and a repressive government, picked by Soviet security forces, took charge. Dubček and his allies were imprisoned or sent into "internal exile." Purges expelled 20 percent of the members of the Czech Communist party. Following the destruction of the Prague Spring, Soviet diplomats announced the new Brezhnev Doctrine, which stated that no socialist state could adopt policies endangering the interests of international socialism, and that the Soviet Union could intervene in the domestic affairs of any Soviet bloc nation if communist rule was threatened. The repressive rules applied to Hungary in 1956 remained unchanged.

When Czech leader Dubček pushes for liberal reforms, Soviets invade Prague

In the short term, the consequences of 1968 seemed limited. De Gaulle's government recovered and the Republican Richard M. Nixon won the U.S. presidential election that year. From 1972 to 1975, the United States withdrew from Vietnam; and in the wake of that war came a refugee crisis and a new series of horrific regional conflicts. In Prague, Warsaw Pact tanks put down the uprising and the Brezhnev Doctrine reasserted the Soviet Union's right to control its satellites.

Over the long term, however, the protesters' and dissidents' demands proved more difficult to contain. In Eastern Europe and the Soviet Union, dissent was defeated but not eliminated. The Czech rebellion of 1968 prefigured the collapse of Soviet control in 1989. In Western Europe and the United States, the student movement subsided, but the issues and the kinds of politics that it pioneered proved more enduring. After 1968, the antiwar movement took up the issue of nuclear weapons—a particularly volatile issue in Europe. The environmental movement took hold, concerned not only with pollution and the world's dwindling resources but also with mushrooming urbanization and the excesses of a consumer society. Finally, feminism came into its own after 1968, as its numbers expanded with women a generation younger than Simone de Beauvoir and Betty Friedan. These feminists had been in student political organizations in the 1960s, and their impatience with traditional political parties and, often, with their male student allies sent them into separate groups, where they championed equality in sexual relationships and in the family. In a phrase that captured some of the changes of the 1950s and the 1960s, they insisted that "the personal is political," meaning that true equality required an analysis of sexuality, women's health, child care, cultural images of women, and so on. In this way, the social movements of the 1960s eventually became part of a broader shift in attitudes that persisted long after the decade was over.

Economic Stagnation: The Price of Success

Economic as well as social problems plagued Europe during the 1970s and 1980s. Already by the mid-1960s the West German growth rate had slowed and the country suffered its first postwar recession. In France, a persistent housing shortage raised the cost of living. Though new industries continued to prosper, the basic industries—coal, steel, and railways—struggled. The Common Market—expanded in 1973 to include Britain, Ireland, and Denmark; and again in the early 1980s to admit Greece, Spain, and Portugal—struggled to overcome problems stemming from the conflict between domestic economic regulations and the free-market policies that prevailed within what would become the European Economic Community (EEC) countries.

Oil prices spiked for the first time in the early 1970s, compounding these difficulties. In 1973, the Arab-dominated **Organization of the Petroleum Exporting Countries (OPEC)** instituted an **oil embargo** against the Western powers, causing a rapid price increase. This increase produced an inflationary spiral: interest rates rose, and with them the price of almost everything else Western consumers were used to buying—and rising costs produced wage demands and strikes. The calm industrial relations of the 1950s and the early 1960s were a thing of the past. At the same time, European manufacturers encountered serious competition, not only from such highly developed countries as Japan but also from the increasingly active economies of Asia and Africa. By 1980, Japan had captured 10 percent of the automobile market in West Germany and 25 percent in Belgium. In 1984, unemployment in Western Europe reached about 19 million—the lean years had arrived.

Economies in the Soviet bloc also stalled. The expansion of heavy industry had helped recovery in the postwar period, but by the 1970s, those sectors no longer provided growth or innovation. The Soviet Communist party proclaimed in 1961 that, by 1970, the USSR would exceed the United States in per capita production. By the end of the 1970s, however, Soviet per capita production was not much higher than in the less industrialized countries of southern Europe. The Soviets were also overcommitted to military defense industries that had become inefficient, though lucrative for the party members who ran them. The Soviet economy did get a boost from the OPEC oil price hikes of 1973 and 1979. (The Soviet Union did not belong to OPEC, but as the world's largest producer of oil, it benefited from rising prices.) Without this boost, the situation would have been far grimmer.

Western governments struggled for effective reactions to the abrupt change in their economic circumstances. The new leader of the British Conservative party, Margaret Thatcher (elected prime minister in 1979, and reelected in 1983 and 1987), established a program of curbing trade union power, cutting taxes, and privatizing publicly owned enterprises, but the economy remained weak and unemployment high. In West Germany, a series of Social Democratic governments attempted to combat economic recession with job-training programs and tax incentives. These programs, however, did little to assist economic recovery, and the country shifted to the right.

The fact that governments of the right and the left were unable to re-create Europe's unprecedented postwar prosperity suggests the degree to which economic forces remain outside the control of individual states. The continuing economic malaise renewed efforts to Europeanize common problems. By the end of the 1980s, the EEC embarked on an ambitious program of integration. Long-term goals, agreed on when the European Union (EU) was formed in 1991, included a monetary union—with a Central European bank and a single currency—and unified social policies to reduce poverty and unemployment. The goal was to develop the economic and political strength to counter the global domination of the United States, but uncertainty remained about the relationship between this new European "federal" state and the individual member states, who did not all share the same economic interests or challenges.

SOLIDARITY IN POLAND

In 1980, a wave of strikes rolled throughout Poland, shocking the government. The strikes began as protests over the cost of basic foodstuffs, but quickly spiraled into something much larger. The credit for the unrest was attributed to a visit by the new pope, John Paul II (Karol Józef Wojtyła; 1920–2005) to Poland in 1979. The new pope, a Pole who had been Archbishop of Kraków before becoming a cardinal, voiced criticisms of the Polish political system, which were interpreted by many as an invitation to disobey. During the unrest, the Catholic Church in Poland endorsed the strikers and gave them its support.

Polish workers took control of the shipyards in Gdansk and formed an independent trade union, **Solidarity**, led by an electrician named **Lech Wałęsa** (1943–). The workers formulated several key demands. First, they objected to the working conditions imposed by the government to combat the economic crisis. Second, they protested high prices and shortages, which had roots in government policy and priorities. Above all, the Polish workers in Solidarity demanded truly independent labor unions, instead of labor organizations sponsored by the government. Their belief that society had the right to organize itself and, by implication, create its own government, stood at the core of the movement. For a period of fifteen months the world was transfixed by this attempt to confront the Communist party's authority in Poland.

In December 1981, General Wojciech Jaruzelski, the head of the Polish Communist party and prime minister, decided to put an end to the movement by force and declared martial law. More than 5,000 Solidarity members were arrested and jailed, including Lech Wałęsa, and army checkpoints were set up throughout Polish cities. A few protests were quickly put down with overwhelming force, and several people were killed, but Solidarity explicitly came out against armed resistance, a decision that undoubtedly saved many lives. Many journalists and teachers were prohibited from returning to their jobs. Jaruzelski later claimed that his action had prevented the Soviets from invading, as they had done in Hungary in 1956 and in Czechoslovakia in 1968. Nevertheless, the experience of martial law left Solidarity's millions of sympathizers embittered, and many in the Polish army were demoralized by their participation in the repression.

THE POPE KNEELS BEFORE THE AUSCHWITZ MEMORIAL, 1979. Pope John Paul II's visit to his native Poland in June 1979 included a pilgrimage to Auschwitz, the largest of the Nazi death camps during World War II. In the context of ongoing controversy over the persistence of antisemitism in Europe after the war, his public statements were scrutinized closely. He invoked his own personal experience of living under the Nazi occupation, and the memory of people he had known as a child who had been killed.

Europe Recast: The Collapse of Communism and the End of the Soviet Union

Did the Soviet Union intend to invade Poland in 1981? Perhaps not. There is some evidence that Soviet leaders were hesitant, though the plans were in place. With uncertainty at the top about political succession (Leonid Brezhnev would die less than a year later, in 1982) and being bogged down in a costly and difficult war in Afghanistan after 1979, it is possible that the Soviets would have let Poland go its own way, preoccupied as they were with their own growing economic and political problems. Only a few short years later, the Soviets embarked on their own program of reform, a decision that led to the astonishing collapse of the Soviet Union's power over the Eastern bloc countries in 1989, and the end of the Soviet Union itself in 1991.

GORBACHEV AND SOVIET REFORM

The Soviet reforms began in 1985, when a new generation of officials began taking charge and **Mikhail Gorbachev** (1931–2022) became leader of the Communist party. In his midfifties, Gorbachev was significantly younger than his immediate predecessors, and thus less prey to the habits of mind that had shaped Soviet domestic and foreign affairs. He was critical of the repressive aspects of communist society as well as its sluggish economy, and did not hesitate to voice those criticisms openly. His twin policies of *glasnost* (intellectual openness) and *perestroika* (economic restructuring) held out hope for a freer, more prosperous Soviet Union.

The policies of glasnost took aim at the privileges of the political elite and the immobility of the state bureaucracy by allowing greater freedom of speech, instituting competitive elections to official positions, and limiting terms of office. Gorbachev's program of perestroika called for a shift from the centrally planned economy instituted by Stalin to a mixed economy, combining planning with the operation of market forces. In agriculture, perestroika accelerated the move away from cooperative production and instituted incentives for the achievement of production targets. Gorbachev planned to integrate the Soviet Union into the international economy by participating in organizations such as the International Monetary Fund (IMF).

Even these dramatic reforms, however, were too little, too late. Ethnic unrest, a legacy of Russia's nineteenth-century imperialism, threatened to split the Soviet Union apart, while secession movements gathered steam in the Baltic republics and elsewhere. From 1988 onward, fighting between Armenians and Azerbaijanis over an ethnically Azerbaijani region located inside Armenia threatened to escalate into a border dispute with Iran. Only Soviet troops patrolling the border and Gorbachev's willingness to suppress a separatist revolt in Azerbaijan by force temporarily quelled the conflict.

Spurred on by these events, the countries of Eastern Europe began to agitate for independence from Moscow.

GORBACHEV IN POLAND AT THE HEIGHT OF HIS POWER IN 1986. Gorbachev's policy of perestroika was aimed at the privileges of the political elite, and would eventually lead to his fall from power.

Gorbachev encouraged open discussion (glasnost) not only in his own country but also in the satellite nations. He revoked the Brezhnev Doctrine, with its insistence on single-party socialist governments, and made frequent and inspiring trips to the capitals of neighboring satellites.

The consequences of this political shift were first realized in Poland, where Solidarity had been defeated but not destroyed by martial law in 1981, as the union launched a new series of strikes in 1988. These disturbances culminated in an agreement between the government and Solidarity that legalized the union and permitted its members to run for office in the June 1989 elections. The results astonished the world: in parliament, Solidarity won all the seats that it was allowed to contest, and in the newly created Senate, it won 99 out of 100 seats. The Communist party and its allies were still guaranteed 65 percent of the seats, but its reputation and prestige had been shattered. By 1991, Poland was holding free parliamentary elections, and the transition to democracy had been largely accomplished.

Hungary was next. János Kádár, the Hungarian leader since the Soviet crackdown of 1956, resigned in the face of continuing demonstrations in May 1988, and was replaced by the reformist government of the Hungarian Socialist Workers' party. By the spring of 1989, the Hungarian regime had been purged of Communist party supporters. The government also began to dismantle its security fences along the Austrian border—the first legal breach in the Iron Curtain. A year later, the Hungarian Democratic Forum, pledging it would reinstate full civil rights and restructure the economy, secured a plurality of seats in the National Assembly.

The Czechs, too, staged demonstrations against Soviet domination in late 1988. Brutal beatings of student demonstrators by the police in 1989 radicalized the nation's workers and provoked mass demonstrations. Civic Forum, an opposition coalition, called for the installation of a coalition government to include noncommunists, the resignation of the country's communist leadership, and free elections. It reinforced its demands with continuing mass demonstrations and threats of a general strike, resulting in the toppling of the old regime and the election of the playwright and Civic Forum leader Václav Havel as president in December 1989.

THE FALL OF THE BERLIN WALL

The most significant political changes in Europe during the late 1980s were the collapse of communism in East Germany and the unification of East and West Germany. Though considered the most prosperous of the Soviet satellite countries, East Germany suffered from severe economic stagnation and environmental degradation. When Hungary opened its border with Austria in May 1989, waves of East Germans registered their discontent with the worsening conditions by way of massive illegal emigration to the West. This exodus combined with evidence of widespread official corruption to force the resignation of East Germany's longtime hard-line premier, Erich Honecker.

On November 4, 1989, the government opened its border with Czechoslovakia, a move that effectively freed East Germans to travel to the West legally. In a matter of days, the Berlin Wall—the embodiment of the Cold War, the Iron Curtain, and the division of East from West—was demolished, first by groups of ordinary citizens and, later, by the East German government. Jubilant men, women, and children from both sides of the wall walked through the gaping holes that now permitted

glasnost Introduced by the Soviet leader Mikhail Gorbachev in June 1987, it called for transparency in Soviet government and institutional activities by reducing censorship in mass media and lifting significant bans on the political, intellectual, and cultural lives of Soviet civilians.

perestroika Introduced by Soviet leader Mikhail Gorbachev in June 1987, *perestroika* was the name given to economic and political reforms begun earlier in his tenure.

REAGAN AT THE BERLIN WALL. On June 12, 1987, in a speech given before the Brandenburg Gate in Berlin, President Ronald Reagan challenged Mikhail Gorbachev to "tear down this wall."

> In series of "velvet" revolutions, one-party rule dismantled peacefully—with notable exception of Romania

them to take the few steps that symbolized the return to freedom and a chance for national unity. Free elections were held throughout Germany in March 1990, resulting in a victory for the Alliance for Germany, a coalition allied with the West German chancellor Helmut Kohl's Christian Democratic Union. With heavy emigration continuing, reunification talks quickly culminated in the formal proclamation of a united Germany on October 3, 1990.

The public mood in Eastern Europe, and perhaps worldwide, was swept up with the jubilation of these peaceful "velvet revolutions" during the autumn of 1989. Yet the end of one-party rule in Eastern Europe was accomplished not without violence. The most repressive government in the old Eastern bloc, Nicolae Ceaușescu's outright dictatorship in Romania, came apart with much bloodshed. By December, faced with the wave of popular revolts in surrounding countries and riots by ethnic Hungarians, a number of party officials and army officers in Romania tried to hold on to their positions by deposing Ceaușescu. His extensive secret police resisted the coup, resulting in nearly two weeks of bloody street fighting in Bucharest. Ceaușescu and his wife were ultimately seized by populist army units and executed; images of their bloody bodies were flashed worldwide by satellite television.

Throughout the rest of Eastern Europe, single-party governments in the countries behind what was left of the tattered Iron Curtain—Albania, Bulgaria, and Yugoslavia—collapsed in the face of democratic pressure for change. Within the Soviet Union itself, the Baltic republics of Lithuania and Latvia unilaterally proclaimed their independence from the Soviet Union in 1990, throwing into sharp relief the tension between "union" and "republics." Gorbachev reacted with an uncertain mixture of armed intervention and promises of greater local autonomy. In the fall of 1991, Lithuania and Latvia, along with the third Baltic state of Estonia, won international recognition as independent nations.

THE COLLAPSE OF THE SOVIET UNION

While Soviet influence eroded in Eastern Europe, the unproductive Soviet economy continued to fuel widespread ire. The failure of perestroika was followed by the rise of a powerful political rival to Gorbachev: his former ally Boris Yeltsin. In 1990, Yeltsin, the reforming mayor of Moscow, was elected president of the Russian Federation—the largest Soviet republic—on an anti-Gorbachev platform. Pressure from the Yeltsin camp weakened Gorbachev's ability to maneuver independently of reactionary factions in the Politburo and the military, undermining his reform program and his ability to remain in power.

Gorbachev's policies failed to improve—and indeed lowered—the living standard of the Soviet people, leading to mounting protests in 1991. Sensing their political lives to be in jeopardy, a group of highly placed hard-line Communist party officials staged an abortive coup against Gorbachev in August 1991. The Soviet citizenry, especially in large cities like Moscow and Leningrad, defied these self-proclaimed saviors. Protesters led by Boris Yeltsin, who at one point mounted a tank in a Moscow street to rally the people, successfully called the plotters' bluff. Within two weeks, Gorbachev was back in power and the coup leaders were in prison.

This counterrevolution returned Gorbachev to office, but at the same time it destroyed the power of the Soviet state he had led. Throughout the fall of 1991, as Gorbachev struggled to hold the Soviet Union together, Yeltsin joined the presidents of the other large republics to capitalize on the discontent. On December 8, 1991, the presidents of the republics of Russia, Ukraine, and Byelorussia (now Belarus) declared that the Soviet Union was no more: "The USSR as a subject of international law and geopolitical reality is ceasing to exist." Though the prose was flat, the message was momentous. The once-mighty Soviet Union, founded seventy-five years before in a burst of revolutionary fervor and violence, had evaporated nearly

RUSSIAN TANKS IN RED SQUARE NEAR THE KREMLIN. Boris Yeltsin convinced many in the military not to support the coup of August 1991, ensuring the failure of the plot and hastening the collapse of the Soviet Union.

The collapse of the Soviet Union creates political disorder and economic hardship within its former borders

overnight, leaving in its wake a collection of eleven far-from-powerful nations loosely joined together as the Commonwealth of Independent States. On December 25, 1991, Gorbachev resigned and left political life. The Soviet flag—the hammer and sickle symbolizing a nation that had kept half of Europe in thrall for fifty years—was lowered for the last time over the Kremlin.

The mighty fall left mighty problems in its wake. Food shortages worsened during the winter of 1992, the value of the ruble plummeted, and the republics could not agree on common military policies or resolve the difficult and dangerous questions concerning the control of nuclear warheads. Yeltsin's pleas for economic assistance from the West resulted in massive infusions of private and public capital, which nevertheless failed to prevent serious economic hardship and dislocation. Free enterprise brought with it unemployment and profiteering through crime. When parliament balked at Yeltsin's economic proposals in September 1993, he dissolved it, which helped provoke an attempted coup two months later, staged by conservative politicians and army officers. Officials loyal to Yeltsin put the revolt down with far more force than against the 1991 coup attempt. After Parliament was restored, the 1995 elections became a benchmark of discontent: the resurgent communists claimed roughly one-third of the seats; while xenophobic nationalists, led by Vladimir Zhirinovsky, also took a notable bloc of the vote, thanks to the steady blame he heaped on the West for Russia's troubles.

Meanwhile, ethnic and religious conflict plagued the former Soviet republics. Warfare flared in Georgia, Armenia, and Azerbaijan. The most serious conflict arose in the predominantly Muslim area of Chechnya, bordering Georgia in the Caucasus, which had declared its independence from Russia in late 1991. In 1994, the Russian government, weary of this continuing challenge to its authority, launched a concerted effort to quash the resistance. As Russian forces moved into the Chechen capital, Grozny, they were ambushed with firepower largely stolen from disused Soviet armories. The result was a massacre of the invading Russians, followed by a long and bloody guerrilla war between Russian and Chechen forces, marked by repeated atrocities on both sides. After brief pauses in 1995 and 1997, the Chechen war dragged on into the new century, echoing Russia's conflict in Afghanistan, but on a scale that was more destructive and closer to home.

The Iron Curtain had established one of the most rigid borders in European history. The collapse of the Soviet Union not only dismantled these borders—it also opened up Russia, destabilized its former imperial dominions, and brought the Cold War to an end. In addition, it created a host of unforeseen problems, such as ethnic conflict and diplomatic uncertainty about the new Russian government. Moreover, it left a single superpower in the world: the United States. Within the Russian and several of the former Soviet republics a new era emerged, which some called the Russian "Wild West." Capitalist market relations began to develop without clearly defined property laws or a stable legal framework to enforce them. Corruption ran rampant, as former government officials profited from their positions of power to take over whole sectors of the economy; and organized crime controlled industries, stock exchanges, a thriving trade in illegal drugs, and even some local governments. Even the most energetic central governments in the large republics, such as Russia, Ukraine, and Kazakhstan, found themselves facing enormous problems. Post-Soviet openness could lay the groundwork for a new democratic Russia, or it could set in motion the resurgence of older forms of tyranny.

POSTREVOLUTIONARY TROUBLES: EASTERN EUROPE AFTER 1989

The **velvet revolutions** of Central and Eastern Europe raised high hopes: local hopes that an end to authoritarian government would lead to economic prosperity and cultural pluralism, and Western hopes that these countries would join them as capitalist partners in an enlarged European Economic Community. The reality, however, was slower and harder than any of the optimists of 1989 foresaw. Though it enjoyed great support among Germans, the reunification of Germany was controversial, and France, in particular, needed to be convinced that a bigger and more populous Germany was a good idea. The euphoria of reunification masked uncertainty even among Germans themselves, because the foundering East German economy meant that integrating the two Germanies would be a costly project. Piled onto other economic difficulties in the former West Germany during the 1990s, it produced resentment in the West of the need to "rescue" the East.

Adapting to change was challenging throughout Eastern Europe. Czechoslovakia's velvet revolution collapsed into a "velvet divorce," as Slovakia declared itself independent from the Czech Republic. Poland enjoyed an upswing in its economy during the 1990s, after many years of hardship, but most of the rest of Eastern Europe continued to find transformation rough going. Attempts to create free-market economies brought inflation, unemployment, and, in their wake, anti-capitalist demonstrations. Inefficient industries, a workforce resistant to change, energy shortages, a lack of venture capital, and a severely polluted environment combined to hinder progress and dash hopes. Racial and ethnic conflicts continued to divide these newly liberated democracies, recalling the divisions that led to the First World War and have plagued Eastern Europe throughout its history. Minorities waged campaigns for autonomous rights or outright secession that often descended into violence.

The most extreme example of these conflicts came with the implosion of the state of Yugoslavia. After the death of Tito in 1980, the government that had held Yugoslavia's federalist ethnic patchwork together came undone. The 1960s and the 1970s brought uneven economic growth, benefiting the capital, Belgrade, and the provinces of Croatia and Slovenia the most, while other areas in Serbia, Bosnia and Herzegovina, and the tiny district of Kosovo lagged far behind. A number of Serb politicians, most notably **Slobodan Milošević**, began to redirect their frustration with economic hardship toward subjects of national pride and sovereignty.

Serbian and Croatian nationalism had long dogged Yugoslavia's firmly federal political system. Feelings ran especially deep among Serbs, whose national myths reach back to the Middle Ages. Milošević, and the Serb nationalists who gathered around him, ignited those political flashpoints in ways that both

velvet revolutions The peaceful political revolutions against the Soviet Union throughout Eastern Europe in 1989.

Slobodan Milošević (1941–2006) The Serbian nationalist politician who became president of Serbia and whose policies during the Balkan wars of the early 1990s led to the deaths of thousands of Croatians, Bosnian Muslims, Albanians, and Kosovars.

nationalism Movement to unify a country under one government, based on perceptions of the population's common history, customs, and social traditions.

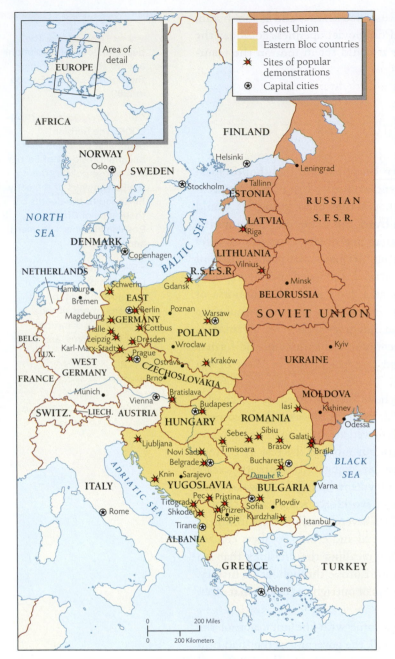

EASTERN EUROPE IN 1989. › What political changes in the Soviet Union allowed for the spread of demonstrations throughout Eastern Europe? **›** Why did the first political upheavals of 1989 occur in Poland and Hungary? **›** In what countries were demonstrations the most widespread? Why?

Map legend:
- Soviet Union
- Eastern Bloc countries
- ✳ Sites of popular demonstrations
- ✪ Capital cities

catapulted him into crucial positions of authority while also alienating people from non-Serb Yugoslavian republics. Representatives of the small Yugoslavian province of Slovenia declared that they had been denied adequate representation and economic support inside the republic; and in 1991, on a tide of nationalism and reform, the Slovenes seceded from Yugoslavia. The newly reunited Germany was quick to recognize the new nation. After a brief attempt to hold the union together by force, the Yugoslav government relented and let Slovenia claim its independence, beginning a process of disintegration that would eventually lead to civil war.

When the larger republic of Croatia declared independence soon after, a war broke out between federal Yugoslav forces and well-armed Croatian militias. The conflict was exacerbated by religious differences between Catholic Croats and Orthodox Serbs, and the legacies of fighting between these communities in the Second World War led to atrocities. Towns and villages where Serbs and Croats had lived together since the 1940s were torn apart as each ethnic group rounded up and massacred members of the other.

Slovenia's independence was relatively easily obtained, as the population of this northern Yugoslavian republic was relatively homogeneous. Croatia's independence was more difficult because it contained regions where Hungarians and Serbs were numerous. For the neighboring republic of Bosnia and Herzegovina, however, independence meant disaster. Bosnia was the most ethnically diverse republic in Yugoslavia, and its population was nearly 50 percent Muslim. Its capital, Sarajevo, was home to several major ethnic groups and had been often praised as an example of peaceful coexistence. Left alone in a "rump" Yugoslavia, dominated by Milosevic's Serbian nationalists, Bosnia had little choice but to seek independence as well. But its tradition of ethnic coexistence did not survive the transition. Armed bands equipped by the governments of a now Serb-dominated Yugoslavia and Croatia were soon battling each other in Bosnia, and the improvised army that Bosnia hastily created quickly became a target of both Croats and Serbs.

The Serbs and Croats, both of whom disliked the Muslim Bosnians, were especially well equipped and organized. They rained shells and bullets on towns and villages, burned houses with families inside, imprisoned and starved Muslim men in detention camps, and raped thousands of Bosnian women. Bosnian Serbs besieged Sarajevo for almost four years, killing nearly 14,000 residents in the process. All sides committed atrocities, but the Serbs orchestrated and carried out the worst crimes, including what came to be called ethnic cleansing. This involved sending irregular troops on campaigns of murder and terror through Muslim and Croat territories to encourage the much larger populations to flee the area. During the first eighteen months of fighting, as many as a 100,000 people were killed, including 80,000 civilians, mostly Bosnian Muslims.

The United Nations sent a peacekeeping force, but their orders were to treat all groups equally, and so did not recognize that Serbia was often the aggressor. This situation benefited the Serbs, who occupied most of Bosnia and a large portion of Croatia by 1994. In July 1994, Serbs in Bosnia attacked a village called Srebrenica, which the United Nations had designated as a "safe zone." Using United Nations equipment, the Serbs encouraged a group of about 10,000 Bosnian Muslim men who had sought shelter in Srebrenica to surrender; but over the next few days, the Serb units massacred 7,000 Bosnians and buried them in mass graves.

In 1995, the United States began a campaign of air strikes against Serbian positions, and these actions brought the Bosnian Serbs to peace talks held at Dayton, Ohio. The agreement divided Bosnia into two countries: "Bosnia and Herzegovina," with the majority of land in the hands of Muslims and Croats, and a small, autonomous "Serb Republic" in areas that included land ethnically "cleansed" in 1992. Stability was restored, but three years of war had killed more than 200,000 people. The International Criminal Tribunal for the former Yugoslavia, established to prosecute the conduct of military groups during the conflict, later concluded that the killings at Srebrenica and the ethnic cleansing of Bosnian Muslims constituted genocide, a crime against humanity.

The legacy of Bosnia flared into conflict again over Kosovo, the medieval homeland of the Orthodox Christian Serbs, now occupied by a largely Albanian Muslim population. In the name of a "greater Serbia," Serb soldiers fought Albanian separatists, and a new round of ethnic cleansing drove hundreds of thousands of Albanians from their homes. When talks brokered by NATO failed to end the fighting, another wave of American-led bombings hit Serbia itself, concentrating on bridges, power plants, factories, and Serbian military bases. The Russian government was troubled by this unilateral attack on fellow Slavs, but nonetheless played an important part in brokering a cease-fire. Eventually, warfare and corruption destroyed Milošević's credentials as a nationalist and populist. After he attempted to reject the results of a democratic election in 2000, his government fell to popular protests. He died in 2006 while being tried by a UN tribunal for war crimes.

As we gain perspective on the twentieth century, it is clear that the Yugoslavian wars of the 1990s were not an isolated instance of Balkan violence. The issues were thoroughly European. The Balkans form one of Europe's borderlands, where

Emergence of nationalism in Yugoslavia was particularly dangerous for the multi-ethnic society of Bosnia and Herzegovina

Representing the People in Eastern Europe, 1989

The enthusiasm of the mass demonstrations, preceding the revolutionary changes in Eastern Europe in 1989, gave these events a sense of immediate drama. Images of Eastern Europeans massed together in protest, crossing boundaries that had been closed to them, and celebrating the downfall of their repressive governments spread quickly around the world. The symbolism of these images was stark, resonating a triumphant story about the progress of democratic ideals in an increasingly unified and integrated Europe. In the East, the people's desire to join with the West, long denied, had finally been realized.

The unity of these early days, nevertheless, obscured a basic uncertainty about the aspirations of the populations of the newly independent nations in Eastern Europe. Many East Germans expressed reservations about the rapid pace of German reunification; and people from the West and the East continued to talk about "the wall in the head" long after the Berlin Wall had been torn down. The unity of Czechoslovakia's peaceful velvet revolution in 1989 led quickly to the "velvet divorce" that produced the dissolution of Czechoslovakia into the Czech Republic and Slovakia in 1993. Throughout the region, many commentators continued to speak of a persistent *Ostalgia*: nostalgia for an alternative Eastern European past that had been lost in the abrupt transition.

A. Crowd during Czechoslovakia's velvet revolution in November 1989.

We have seen in earlier chapters how representations of the people gave meaning to moments of rapid social and political change, such as in the French Revolution or the unification of Germany. The images here, from media coverage in 1989, also frame the interpretations that contemporaries gave to the unfolding events. Image A shows a crowd in Prague waving the Czechoslovakian flag in November 1989. Image B shows East Germans gathering in front of a Woolworth market in West Berlin on November 12, 1989, days after the fall of the Berlin Wall. Image C shows a demonstrator bearing a sign that reads "WE ARE ONE PEOPLE" in East Berlin on December 12, 1989.

"We are the people" was the slogan of the weekly demonstrations in Leipzig in 1989, and it was used to discredit the East German government in the months before the fall of the Berlin Wall. "We are one people" became the slogan of the West German chancellor Helmut Kohl as he pushed for rapid reunification of the two Germanies.

Questions for Analysis

1. How should one interpret the wave of nationalist enthusiasm that engulfed Czechoslovakia in 1989 (image A), in light of what we know of the subsequent failure to keep Czechoslovakia together as a unified nation?

2. Photographs showing East Berliners shopping in Western stores, such as image B, were extremely common in the media in 1989. What do such images suggest about how the East's previous isolation was interpreted in the West? What does it say about how both sides may have viewed the consequences of the East's newfound freedom?

3. What is the difference between "We are the people" and "We are one people" as political slogans?

B. East Germans gather in front of a Woolworth market in West Berlin on November 12, 1989.

C. "We are one people" poster during a demonstration on December 12, 1989.

MASS FUNERAL IN KOSOVO, 1999. Ethnic Albanians bury victims of a Serbian massacre toward the end of Yugoslavia's ten years of fighting.
› **Although the nature of war has changed radically in the last 100 years, "ethnic cleansing" has remained remarkably constant and frequent in the modern period. What keeps states from taking effective action to prevent it?**

cultures influenced by Roman Catholicism, Eastern Orthodoxy, and Islam meet, overlap, and contend for political domination and influence. Since the nineteenth century, this region of enormous religious, cultural, and ethnic diversity has struggled with the implications of nationalism. We have seen how the conflicts over the creation of new national states in Central Europe, drawn mostly on ethnic lines, were worked out with many instances of tragic violence. The failure to prevent these wars or to limit their effects on vulnerable populations was a deep blow to the international community, and revealed the limits of the power exercised by the United States and other European nations in the years after the end of the Cold War.

Conclusion

The protest movements of the 1960s and the 1970s revealed that postwar hopes for stability in Western Europe through economic development alone were short-sighted, and, in any case, the astounding rates of growth from 1945 to 1968 could not be sustained forever. The great successes of these first postwar decades were the establishment of the European Common Market and the spirit of cooperation between Western European nations that, only a few years before, had been locked in a deadly conflict.

Map legend:

- Soviet Union to 1991
- Soviet-dominated Eastern Europe to 1989
- Other communist states before 1991
- German Democratic Republic (GDR) united with Federal Republic of Germany 1990
- Czechoslovakia to December 1992
- Yugoslavia to 1991
- **1990** Date of first free election

Area of detail

EUROPE

AFRICA

RUSSIAN FEDERATION 1993

NORTH SEA

BALTIC SEA

ESTONIA 1992

LATVIA 1993

LITHUANIA 1990

RUS. FED.

BELARUS 1995

EAST GERMANY 1990

POLAND 1989

CZECH REPUBLIC 1992

SLOVAKIA 1992

HUNGARY 1990

SLOVENIA 1992

CROATIA 1992

YUGOSLAVIA 1992

ROMANIA 1990

BOSNIA AND HERZEGOVINA 1992

ALBANIA 1991

BULGARIA 1990

MACEDONIA 1990

UKRAINE

MOLDAVIA 1994

KAZAKHSTAN
1991: President Nazarbayev runs in election unopposed
1995: Nationwide referendum extends his term to 2000

KYRGYZSTAN

TAJIKISTAN

UZBEKISTAN

TURKMENISTAN

1992: Tensions between Russia and Ukraine over whether Black Sea Fleet is part of strategic forces controlled by Commonwealth of Independent States

1993: Joins the CIS to secure Russian military support against ousted President Gamsakhurdia

GEORGIA 1991

ARMENIA 1995

AZERBAIJAN 1995

to AZERBAIJAN

0   250   500 Miles
0   250   500 Kilometers

RUSSIA AND EASTERN EUROPE AFTER THE COLD WAR. Examine closely the geography of southeastern and Central Europe. › **How were political boundaries reorganized?** › **How did the collapse of the Soviet Union and the end of the Cold War allow for the reemergence of certain forces in the political landscape of Europe?** › **How were the boundaries of the Soviet Union reorganized after 1991?**

The Eastern European revolutions of 1989 and the subsequent collapse of the Soviet Union were major turning points, and posed challenging questions to those who sought to guarantee stability by continuing down the path of further integration among European nations. Like the French Revolution of 1789, the 1989 revolutions brought down not only a regime but also an empire. They also gave way to violence, providing no easy consensus for the peoples who were left to construct some form of political and social stability in their wake. In the former Yugoslavia, Slovakia, and Russia itself, the uncertainty of the post-1989 years gave fresh impetus to energetic nationalist movements. Although militant nationalism might be a useful short-term political strategy for certain politicians, it is unlikely to create stability in Europe, because the broad population movements of the postwar years have continued unabated and there is no part of Europe that possesses the ethnic or cultural homogeneity demanded by hard-line nationalists. Europe's long history is one of heterogeneity, and there is no reason to think that the future will be different in this respect.

Profound differences in wealth and economic capacity between Western and Eastern Europe were the most challenging hurdle to a stable integration of the newly independent nations of the former Soviet Empire. In the 1980s, it was possible to imagine that a relatively wealthy country, such as the Netherlands or Belgium, might be willing to subsidize the integration of a less wealthy, small country, such as Portugal, into Europe.

AFTER YOU READ THIS CHAPTER ⌄

CHRONOLOGY

1957	Creation of European Common Market
1961	Berlin Wall built
1963	Betty Friedan, *The Feminine Mystique*
1964–1975	Vietnam War
mid-1960s	Birth control pill becomes available
1968	Czech revolt, Prague Spring
1968	Student protests in Europe and the Americas
1970s	Détente between Soviet Union and Western powers
1973–1980s	Rising oil prices and worldwide recession
1980	Polish Solidarity workers' movement
1989	Berlin Wall falls
1990	Reunification of Germany
1991–1995	Yugoslavian civil wars
1992	Soviet Union dissolved
1993	European Union

REVIEWING THE OBJECTIVES

❯ The success of economic rebuilding after the Second World War produced a new prosperity in Western Europe. What contributed to this success? What were its effects on the daily life and mass culture in Europe?

❯ The postwar decades witnessed an important shift in attitudes about women and their place in society. What caused this shift? What were its consequences for European women?

❯ In Europe and the United States, significant movements of social and political protest emerged in the 1960s. What were the goals of these movements? What did they accomplish?

❯ The postwar economic boom ended in the 1970s, leading to a prolonged period of economic contraction. What were the consequences of this recession for both governments and populations in Europe?

❯ In the 1980s, Mikhail Gorbachev proposed reforms for the Soviet Union, which failed to prevent the collapse of the Soviet bloc in Eastern Europe. What combination of events led to this collapse?

❯ The first post-Soviet decade in Europe was marked by political uncertainty, economic dislocation, and violence, with war in Yugoslavia and Chechnya. What circumstances made these years so difficult for Europeans?

But it has proved quite another task to convince the Dutch, the Belgians, or the Danes to help shoulder the burden of bringing large countries, such as Ukraine or Turkey, into the European fold. Given this difficulty, can anyone say with confidence where Europe's outermost borders now lie? In the broader context of the global conflicts that emerged in the aftermath of the Cold War, Europe's boundaries and future remain both uncertain and linked to developments elsewhere in the world. This broader context and global linkages are the subject of the last chapter of this book.

Go to **INQUIZITIVE** to see what you've learned—and learn what you've missed—with personalized feedback along the way.

PEOPLE, IDEAS, AND EVENTS IN CONTEXT

❯ How did the wide availability of the **BIRTH CONTROL PILL** change public attitudes toward sex and sexuality in the 1960s?

❯ What made the **MASS CULTURE** of the postwar decades different from popular culture in previous historical eras?

❯ How did the struggles of the **CIVIL RIGHTS MOVEMENT** in the United States affect American efforts to promote democracy in Europe during the Cold War?

❯ What were the goals of **ALEXANDER DUBČEK**'s government in Czechoslovakia during the **PRAGUE SPRING**?

❯ How did the 1973 **OPEC OIL EMBARGO** affect the economies of Eastern and Western Europe?

❯ How did **LECH WAŁĘSA** and the **SOLIDARITY** movement challenge the Polish government in the early 1980s?

❯ How did **MIKHAIL GORBACHEV** envision reforming the Soviet Union? What did he mean by *PERESTROIKA* and *GLASNOST*?

❯ What were the **VELVET REVOLUTIONS** of Central and Eastern Europe in 1989?

❯ What made Serbian and Croatian **NATIONALISM** such a powerful force in Yugoslavia in the early 1990s? What role did **SLOBODAN MILOŠEVIĆ** play in the breakup of the Yugoslavian federation?

THINKING ABOUT CONNECTIONS

❯ The wave of protests and cultural discontent that spread throughout Europe in the 1960s encompassed both Western and Eastern Europe, in spite of the divisions imposed by the Cold War. Can you detect an echo of the 1848 revolutions in the 1968 protests? What common concerns can you detect? What is different?

❯ Many observers were surprised by the resurgence of nationalism in Eastern Europe in the aftermath of the collapse of the Soviet Union. Can you compare the situation in Yugoslavia after 1989 with the circumstances in that part of the world in the late nineteenth century, as Ottoman power waned and the Russian and Austrian Empires competed for influence in the region?

A World without Walls? Globalization and the West

IN THE TWENTY-FIRST CENTURY, basic assumptions about the stability of nation-states, the roots of prosperity, and the boundaries of cultures are changing fast. This is not new—a disconcerting sense of seismic and confusing change has been central to Western culture during several previous historical periods, including the Industrial Revolution of the nineteenth century or decolonization after 1945. Just as the term *industrial revolution*, coined in the early nineteenth century, captured contemporaries' perceptions of changes in their own time, *globalization* captures ours. Globalization itself is not new, but our acute consciousness of its effects on our lives is constantly reinforced by the pace with which information circulates through modern technology.

Some aspects of globalization are relatively easy to name, though their interconnections are not always obvious: the internet, protests against the World Trade Organization (WTO), outsourcing of jobs and services, Walmart in Mexico, the dismantling of the Berlin Wall, Beyoncé selling out shows in China, and so on. These are powerful images of enormously significant developments. The internet has transformed global communication, the media, and forms of knowledge. The fall of the Berlin Wall, the symbol of a divided Cold War world, marked a dramatic reconfiguration of international relations, an end to capitalism's struggle with communism, and the creation of new alliances, markets, and communities.

BEFORE YOU READ THIS CHAPTER

>

Globalization also had its costs. Outsourcing of jobs and services showed globalization could have negative effects on local economies. Most strikingly, the attacks on the World Trade Center and the Pentagon in 2001 gave the term *globalization* a frightening and new meaning. In the early 2000s, the perceived costs of globalization generated a nationalist backlash against the project of a more interconnected world. More recently, the COVID-19 pandemic brought global supply chains to a halt, and Russia's 2022 invasion of Ukraine precipitated unprecedented international sanctions that caused companies to reevaluate their foreign investments and entire nations to reconsider their dependence on foreign sources of energy and food. In the 1990s, globalization was often celebrated as a source of optimism and prosperity. Thirty years later, globalization is just as likely to be associated with a sense of vulnerability and fear.

What, precisely, does the term mean? Most simply, globalization means integration. It is the process of creating networks—political, social, economic, and cultural—that connect different regions of the world. New technologies have combined with changing laws to make global exchange faster and more intense. Information, goods, and people now move easily and rapidly across national boundaries. Yet *globalization* is not synonymous with *internationalization*. International relations are established between nation-states, while global exchanges can happen independent of national control.

Globalization radically altered the distribution of industry and patterns of trade around the world. Supranational economic institutions such as the **International Monetary Fund (IMF)** are examples of globalization, and they work to quicken its pace. Likewise, the International Criminal Court (ICC) represents an important trend in law: the globalization of judicial power. New and surprisingly intimate forms of mass communication—blogs, social media, internet-based political campaigns, and so on—have spawned new forms of politics. Such globalizing trends seem to be threatening the sovereignty of nation-states.

Are these developments new? For centuries, religion, empire, commerce, and industry have had globalizing effects. European economic development was enmeshed in global networks that supplied raw materials, markets, and labor. Since the fifteenth century, the "West" has been inseparable from its global dimensions, from the slave trade to European industrialization.

Consider migration and immigration. The contemporary world has witnessed vast movements of people, but mass migration—from Europe to the Americas, from east Asia throughout the Pacific and the Indian Oceans, to name only the largest flows—peaked during the nineteenth century. Faster long-distance transportation, via railways and steamships, made these long journeys possible, and the industrialization of the receiving regions provided the economic dynamics. The demographic, social, economic, and cultural effects of these migrations were transformative (Chapter 22). However, after the First World War, governments set out to close their gates. Since the 1920s, laborers (and refugees) found it harder to move, and this remains so in the present, even in the face of periodic refugee crises produced by the Syrian civil war after 2011 or the Russian invasion of Ukraine in 2022. If migration is a measure of globalization, our world has become less "globalized" than it was a century ago.

Equating globalization with integration may also be misleading. The effects of globalizing trends are difficult to predict, and do not necessarily lead to peace or

Globalization refers to the increasing integration of political, social, economic, and cultural networks throughout the world

International Monetary Fund (IMF) Established in 1945 to ensure international cooperation regarding currency exchange and monetary policy, the IMF is a specialized agency of the United Nations.

stability. Many Europeans firmly believed in the 1990s that the world was becoming more harmonious, that Western culture could be exported, and that Western standards were universal. History has defied those expectations. Some scholars argue that the term *globalization* should be jettisoned, because it suggests a uniform, leveling process that operates similarly everywhere. In reality, its local effects can be very different because they are shaped by increasing inequality in power and wealth among nations or regions. At the level of everyday human contact, globalization has hastened new kinds of cultural blending and sociability, but it has also produced a reaction against that blending.

In this chapter, we explore three aspects of globalization, as it relates to the post–Cold War world of the twenty-first century. First is the set of changes that accelerated the free flow of money, people, products, and ideas across the globe. Second is what we call postcolonial politics: the varied trajectories that mark the contemporary experience of former colonies. Third, we will consider in greater depth the complex and important role of Middle Eastern politics in contemporary global affairs.

Liquid Modernity? The Flow of Money, Ideas, and Peoples

In the late twentieth century, the world economy was transformed by the rapid integration of markets after 1970. In that decade, the international agreements that had regulated the movement of people, goods, and money since the Second World War were overturned. The postwar Bretton Woods Accords (Chapter 27) eroded in the late 1960s, as Western industrial nations faced a double burden of inflation and economic stagnation. In 1971, the United States abandoned the postwar gold standard and allowed the value of the dollar—the keystone of the system—to float freely against other currencies. As a result, formal state regulations of currencies and international banking were replaced by an informal network of large private lenders, state officials, and independent financial agencies such as the IMF and the World Bank. The economists and administrators who dominated these networks steered away from the interventionist policies of Bretton Woods and relied instead on market-driven models that sought to make the economy less subject to state regulation. This stance, called "**neoliberalism**" because of its allegiance to classic liberal economics, emphasized free markets, profit incentives, and sharp restraints on state spending, especially social welfare programs. The new system had mixed results: it allowed greater flows of capital across borders, which created opportunities for rapid growth in some global regions but also the risk of catastrophic collapse when international investors decided to put their money elsewhere. Industrial development in the globalized economy created jarring juxtapositions of development and deterioration across entire continents and even within single cities.

At the same time, local and national economies became more connected and interdependent. Export trade flourished and, with the rapid development of electronics after the 1960s, came to include an increasing proportion of high-technology goods. The boom in export commerce was tied to changes

neoliberalism Ideology emphasizing free markets, profit incentives, and restraints on both budget deficits and social welfare programs as the best guarantee of individual liberties.

The Meaning of the "Third World"

Alfred Sauvy, a French demographer, coined the term Third World in a famous 1952 article about the effects of the Cold War on international relations and economic development: the First World was the West, a world of democratic political institutions and capitalist economies; the Second World was the Soviet sphere, committed to socialist institutions; and the Third World was everybody else—the world of European colonies and former colonies, marked by the history of imperialism.

Though commonly used between the 1950s and the 1980s, the term Third World is less frequently encountered in the present. B. R. Tomlinson, a British economic historian, examines the ways in which the concept was rooted in the ideological world of the Cold War, as he looks for new vocabulary to tell the history of globalization in the contemporary world.

Alfred Sauvy, "Three Worlds, One Planet" (1952)

We speak voluntarily about two worlds today, about the possibility of war between them, about their coexistence, etc., forgetting too often that there is a third world . . . the collectivity called, in the style of the United Nations, the under-developed countries. . . .

* * *

Unfortunately, the struggle for the possession of the third world does not allow the two others to simply pursue their own path, believing it to be obviously the best, the "true" way. The Cold War has curious consequences: over there, a morbid fear of espionage has pushed them to the most ferocious isolation. With us, it has caused a halt in social evolution. What good is it to trouble ourselves or deprive ourselves, at a moment when the fear of communism is holding back those who would like to go further [on the path to equality]? Why should we consider any social reforms at all when the progressive majority is split? . . . Why worry about it, since there is no opposition?

In this way, any evolution toward the distant future has been halted in both camps, and this obstacle has one cause: the costs of war.

Meanwhile . . . the under-developed nations, the third world, have entered into a new phase. Certain medical techniques have now been introduced suddenly for a simple reason: they are cheap. . . . For a few pennies the life of a man can be prolonged for several years. Because of this, these countries now have the mortality that we had in 1914 and the birthrate that

we had in the eighteenth century. Certainly, this has resulted in economic improvement, lower infant mortality, better productivity of adults, etc. Nevertheless, it is easy to see how this demographic increase must be accompanied by important investments in order to adapt the container to what it must contain. Now, these vital investments cost much more than 68 francs per person. They crash right into the financial wall imposed by the Cold War. The result is eloquent: the millennial cycle of life and death continues to turn, but it is a cycle of poverty.

* * *

Since the preparation for war is priority number 1, secondary concerns such as world hunger will only occupy our attention enough to avoid an explosion that might compromise our first priority. But when one remembers the enormous errors that conservatives have committed so many times, we can only have a mediocre confidence in the ability of the Americans to play with the fire of popular anger. . . . They have not clearly perceived that under-developed nations of a feudal type might evolve more readily towards a communist regime than toward democratic capitalism. One might console oneself, if one were so inclined, by pointing to the greater advance of capitalism, but the fact remains undeniable. And maybe, in the glare of its own vitality, the first world, even in the absence of any human solidarity, might notice this slow, irresistible, humble and ferocious, push toward life. Because in the end, this ignored, exploited Third World, as despised as the Third Estate [in the French Revolution], wants to be something.

Source: Alfred Sauvy, "Trois Mondes, Une Planète," *L'Observateur* 14 (August 1952): 5. This translation, by Joshua Cole, comes from a French reprint in *Vingtième Siècle*, no. 12 (October–December 1986): 81–83.

B. R. Tomlinson, "What Was the Third World?" (2003)

The term "Third World" was used frequently in histories of the societies, economies and cultures of many parts of the world in the second half of the twentieth century. . . . Like other collective descriptions of Africa, Asia, the Middle East, the Pacific islands and Latin America—such as the "South," the "developing world," or the "less-developed world"—the designation "Third World" was more about what such places were not than what they were.

* * *

Those who developed a concept of the Third World around a set of measurable criteria usually relied on identifying material circumstances. . . . However, all such attempts to establish a standard measurement of relative poverty that can distinguish various parts of the world from each other run into considerable difficulties. It has often been argued that the various countries of Asia, Africa and Latin America (not to mention the Pacific islands and elsewhere) differ greatly in their size, political ideologies, social structures, economic performance, cultural backgrounds and historical experiences. These differences exist not simply between Third World countries, but within them as well. There are rich and poor people, empowered and disempowered citizens, to be found inside all states and societies in the world.

It was over broad issues of economic development that the fiercest battles for the concept of the Third World were fought. Orthodox development economists in the 1950s and 1960s had suggested that the poverty of non-Western economies was the result of low levels of savings and investment, and that these problems could best be resolved by increasing external influence over them to help local élites modernize their societies (in other words, make them more like those of the West) by providing technology and education to increase productivity and output.

* * *

To many radical critics, these ideas, and the U.S. government's development policies that flowed from them, seemed to mask a narrow political agenda that sought to justify the dominance of free-market capitalism as a model and mechanism for economic, social and cultural development. One powerful reaction to this agenda was to argue that dependence on the West had distorted the economic and social conditions of non-Western societies, leading to a common process of historical change in the periphery of the world economy brought about by "a situation in which the economy of certain countries [and hence their social and political structures] is conditioned by the development and expansion of another economy to which the former is subjected."

* * *

The history of imperialism has been immensely important in shaping our view of the modern world, both from the top down and from the bottom up, but the phenomenon was also historically specific, and represents only one stage in the process of understanding the interaction between the local and the global. To write the history of the "Rest," as well as of the West, we need now to move on, and to construct new narratives of global history that go beyond the models of coherent and distinct communities, nations and states, arranged into hierarchies of material achievement and cultural power, and underpinned by universal institutional ideals of participatory democracy and free markets, that dominated thinking about international and local systems in the world for much of the nineteenth and twentieth centuries.

Source: B. R. Tomlinson, "What Was the Third World?" *Journal of Contemporary History* 38, no. 2 (April 2003): 307–21.

Questions for Analysis

1. In Sauvy's argument, what do the "under-developed nations" have in common? Does Tomlinson agree?

2. Sauvy calls for the First World to invest in the Third World to prevent an explosion of anger. What possible difficulties with this solution does Tomlinson identify?

3. How do Sauvy and Tomlinson see the relationship between the Cold War and the problem of understanding the "Third World?"

"CHECKERBOARD OF POVERTY AND AFFLUENCE." Scenes of slums confronting towering skylines, such as this one from São Paulo, Brazil, in 2014, are visible around the world as one of the side effects of development and deterioration.

in the division of labor worldwide: industrial jobs emerged in the postcolonial world, not just among the Asian "tigers," but also in India, Latin America, and elsewhere. Skilled industrial jobs started to disappear in Western nations—often replaced by lower-paying menial work—and financial and service sector employment expanded. Trade also became much more complex: industrial goods could be designed in one country, using components manufactured in another, and shipped across borders before being sold and consumed. These global economic changes became the source of painful debates about the nature of citizenship, the power and accountability of transnational corporations, and the human and environmental costs of global capitalism.

Another crucial change involved the new commercial and cultural importance attached to information itself. Electronic devices designed to create, store, and share information multiplied, becoming staggeringly more powerful and accessible; none has had greater impact than the personal computer. By the early 1990s, sophisticated computers brought people into instant communication with each other across continents. The internet revolution shared features of earlier print revolutions. Pioneered by entrepreneurs with utopian ambitions, the growth of the internet was driven by the new network's ability to deliver personal or commercial messages as well as culturally illicit and politically scandalous material that could be published easily and informally. It also offered new possibilities for individuals to connect with one another and form social and political groups, constituting new "publics."

What was new about the internet revolution was the scale of information generated about consumer behavior. Corporations and governments realized that information about consumers' online activity—what they read, listened to, and watched—could now be stored in databases, digitally analyzed, and bought and sold by companies interested in influencing the decisions made by millions of people. Companies such as Sony now produce entertainment content as well as the electronic equipment to play that content. Bill Gates's Microsoft emerged as the world's major producer of computer software—with a corporate profit margin that at one point surpassed Spain's gross domestic product. At the level of production, marketing, and management, information industries are global; their corporate headquarters, however, typically remain in the West and support neoliberal politics. The international media, news, and entertainment conglomerates run by, for example, the Australian-born Rupert Murdoch or Time Warner (now Spectrum), are firmly allied to U.S. institutions and worldviews, edging aside state-run media companies in other parts of the world.

Like the movement of money, goods, and ideas, the flow of labor has become a central aspect of globalization. Since 1945, migration, particularly between former colonies and imperial powers, has changed everyday life around the world. Immigrant workers have filled the lower rungs of expanding economies in Europe and in oil-rich Arab states, where they attract Asian and Filipino laborers. In the United States, both permanent and seasonal migrations from Mexico and other Latin American nations have spread across the continent. This mobility has produced striking new blends of popular culture, influencing language use, music, food, sport, and other forms of sociability. Such fusion has also created conflicts over the definition of citizenship and the boundaries of national communities—familiar themes in modern history. Cycles of violent xenophobia, bigotry, and political extremism have arisen in host countries and regions as a result, but so, too, have new conceptions of civil rights and cultural belonging.

Globalization's sharp divides between wealthy nations and disadvantaged postcolonial societies also shaped the development of illicit global commerce. The production of illegal drugs—especially opium, heroin, and cocaine—is a thriving industry in countries such as Colombia, Myanmar (formerly Burma), Pakistan, Afghanistan, and Malaysia. Though the drug trade is banned, public and private powers turn a blind eye to their production and trafficking because of the revenue it generates or because they are involved in some way for their own profit. Other forms of illegal commerce have grown beyond the label of "organized crime" in their scope and political importance. Human trafficking, corrupt financial transactions, trade in illicit animals and animal products, and "conflict" diamonds from brutal postcolonial civil wars are all indicative of this trend. The organizations behind this criminal commerce have exploited cracks, loopholes, and unsupervised opportunities in the less regulated system of global trade, carving out centers of power not directly subject to the laws of any single state.

Increased population mobility has reinforced economic integration between global regions, produced new forms of hybrid culture, and generated both backlash and new definitions of human rights

DEMOGRAPHICS AND GLOBAL HEALTH

Globalization is tied in complex ways to the health and size of the world's population. Between 1800 and the mid-twentieth century, the worldwide population roughly tripled, rising from 1 to 3 billion; between 1960 and 2012, the population more than doubled again to 7 billion. Improvements in basic health and nutrition, particularly for young children and childbearing women, contributed to the increase. Asia's population has increased nearly fourfold since 1900, to nearly two-thirds of the world's present population. Such growth has strained social services, and urban infrastructures, increasing the potential for epidemic diseases, as well as for ethnic and political violence nursed by poverty and dislocation.

A different type of demographic crisis confronts parts of the West, where aging populations and rising health care costs contribute to the challenge. Populations in the United States and Great Britain have been stable or have slowly expanded by immigration; in Italy, Scandinavia, and, recently, Russia, sharp drops in the birthrate have led to population decline. These declining birthrates have been accompanied by growing populations of older adults, whose health and vitality resulted from improved medical standards and state-run entitlement programs. Maintaining the long-term solvency of such programs poses difficult choices for European countries because they depend on a shrinking population of earners to support the older generation through taxes.

Globalization has also created public health threats as well as promising treatments. Better health care has accompanied other kinds of prosperity and has been more accessible in the West. In Africa, Latin America, and parts of Asia and the Middle East, political chaos, imbalances of trade, and practices of some pharmaceutical companies have resulted in shortages of medicine and an undeveloped medical infrastructure, making it difficult to combat deadly new waves of disease. The risk of epidemic diseases is a new reality of globalization, a product of increased cultural interaction, exposure of new ecosystems to human development, and the speed of intercontinental transportation. The **HIV-AIDS epidemic** became a global health crisis in the 1980s—particularly in Africa, where the disease spread catastrophically. In 2003, the successful containment of an outbreak of severe acute respiratory syndrome (SARS) demonstrated the effectiveness of advanced response planning, but the Ebola outbreaks of 2014 and 2019, the spread of the mosquito-borne Zika virus after 2015, and eventually the **COVID-19 pandemic** in 2019 and beyond proved that response planning is an ongoing struggle.

Earlier epidemiological studies had shown that it was only a matter of time before a new airborne virus spread globally. Governments were nevertheless caught off guard with COVID-19, and nobody was ready for the social and political effects of simultaneous lockdowns that ultimately affected 95 percent of the world's economies. By the end of 2021 global excess deaths associated with the pandemic had reached 14.9 million. Billions of people across the world transitioned to remote work, lost their jobs, or faced heightened risk by continuing to work despite the threat of infection. An entire generation of students found their education interrupted as schools struggled to respond to the needs of a global public health crisis. The world's scientific community responded quickly with effective vaccines in the first year. The pandemic proved to be a revealing stress test for governments everywhere—in nations where political life was already polarized, public health measures such as mask-wearing or vaccination became subject to polarized political debate, complicating efforts to protect the most vulnerable populations and slow the spread of the disease.

The rapid development of COVID vaccines was made possible by genetic engineering, after the monumental discovery of the DNA molecule's structure in the 1950s. By 2003, scientists had successfully mapped the human genome, revealing the entire architecture of chromosomes and genes contained in human DNA. Genetic engineering is now routine, allowing scientists to alter biology of living beings. Infertile couples can now conceive through medical procedures. It is now possible to determine the genetic makeup of any individual human being and measure their risk of developing

HIV-AIDS epidemic The first cases of HIV (human immunodeficiency virus) infection appeared in the late 1970s. It swiftly became a global crisis as those infected passed away from its late stages, AIDS, or acquired immunodeficiency syndrome.

COVID-19 pandemic The airborne novel coronavirus that allegedly emerged in Wuhan, China, in December 2019 and rapidly spread around the world, causing the deaths of more than 6 million people and economic disruption worldwide.

GOVERNMENT EFFORTS TO CURTAIL THE SPREAD OF INFECTIOUS DISEASES. In May 2003, to combat the SARS outbreak, migrant workers at a Beijing railway station line up to have their temperatures checked before boarding trains. In March 2020, a worker disinfects a museum gallery against the novel coronavirus in Naples, Italy.

cancers or other life-threatening conditions. These developments raise provocative questions about the relationship between individual responsibility and public health, how scientists should understand biological "defects" or diversions from genetic norms. The debate continues about who should establish the ground rules for dealing with the consequences of this new knowledge—should it be nations, international bodies, or local cultural and religious communities? Once again, scientific progress has raised fundamental questions about ethics, citizenship, and the measure of humanity.

SPOTLIGHT ON THE ENVIRONMENT: CLIMATE CHANGE

Perhaps no issue raises thornier questions about the relationships between economic development and public welfare than the matter of climate change. Scientists now agree that the average temperature of the planet is rising steadily as a result of atmospheric increases of "greenhouse gases": carbon dioxide, methane, nitrous oxide, and ozone. Since 1981, this warming has accelerated, and ocean temperatures have increased even more rapidly. The year 2021 was the forty-fifth consecutive year where the average annual temperature was above the average in the twentieth century. And eighteen of the nineteen warmest years on record have occurred since 2000.

Scientists have concluded that climate change is caused by human activity, primarily by the burning of fossil fuels, which has contributed to a worldwide rise in average temperatures. The consequences of global warming will be substantial: a rise in sea levels as polar ice caps melt; an increase in the frequency of heat waves, droughts, wildfires, rainfall intensity, and coastal flooding; and a greater incidence and severity of storms, tornadoes, and tropical cyclones. Scientists now believe that these developments are already observable in the increased frequency of extreme weather events though there is still hope that the worst consequences might be mitigated by limiting further emissions. The long-term risks of inaction for human society are severe. A rapid rise in sea levels would destroy many of the earth's major cities and render them

Climate change, caused by the burning of fossil fuels, has already led to increases in extreme weather patterns and a rise in sea levels that threaten coastal cities

Media Representations of Globalization

Because the effects of *globalization* are so often experienced as disruptions of well-entrenched habits or ways of life, debates about globalization are particularly open to manipulation through the presentation of charged imagery. Since the end of the Cold War, provocative images that capture the world's new interconnectedness have become ubiquitous in the media. The movement of peoples and goods are variously defined as necessary to maintain standards of living or a threat to local jobs and local production. Globalization is defended as good for the economy, the consumer, and competition, but it is also blamed for hurting workers, destroying local cultures, and eroding long-standing definitions of national identity.

Image A shows ships waiting to be loaded and unloaded at one of the largest container terminals in the world, in Hong Kong, where most Chinese shipping comes through this terminal. Image B shows a temporary refugee camp in Turkey occupied by Kurds, who had fled from Islamic State violence in Syria, where they are an ethnic minority. From 2014 to 2019 Syrians fleeing violence and civil war settled in neighboring countries such as Turkey and Lebanon, but also migrated into countries in western Europe (see map on page 1059). Image C shows a Labor Day protester (medical mask is a reference to the SARS epidemic) at a demonstration in the Philippine capital, Manila, in which globalization was blamed for labor code amendments favorable to employers, such as a ban on strikes, and antiterrorist measures that were perceived to be an infringement on personal liberties.

A. Cargo ships in Kowloon Bay, Hong Kong, 2002.

uninhabitable. An agricultural crisis in one region could create starvation and chaos in another. Governments could collapse, as massive flows of refugees would strain even wealthy nations. The worst-case scenario would be mass extinctions of plants and animals, which the earth has already experienced on multiple occasions.

Governments first sounded the alarm about climate change in the early 1990s, but a coordinated policy proved difficult, because individual nations worried about compromising their economic competitiveness. Energy producers resisted pollution limits and the adoption of expensive "clean" technologies, and it has proved difficult to change the habits of consumers dependent on automobiles, cheap air travel, and manufactured goods from distant places. Finding policy solutions is doubly difficult because those parts of the globe closely associated with pollution caused by the burning of fossil fuels—industrialized societies in Europe and North America—are not necessarily those that will feel its effects acutely in the near term: poorer countries in the global south with few resources to cope with the effects of climate change.

Since the 1990s, international efforts to coordinate a response to climate change focused on a United Nations–sponsored agreement known as the Kyoto Protocol.

Questions for Analysis

1. Image A is typical of images emphasizing the economic consequences of globalization. Does globalization appear to be a force that is subject to human control in this image? How do such images shape perceptions of China's place in the global economy?

2. Compare image A with image B. Is there a connection between the accelerating flows of money and goods and restrictions on the movements of people?

3. In image C, the woman's medical mask names globalization as the enemy of Filipino workers. Who is the target of this protest? What does this say about the local conflict over the conditions of labor in the Philippines?

B. This refugee camp in Suruç, Turkey, held Kurds who had fled northern Syria after it was besieged by the Islamic State in 2014.

C. Filipino protester on Labor Day in Manila, the Philippines, 2003.

The United States never joined the Kyoto agreement, claiming that it could not participate in an accord that did not include China (the United States and China are both leading producers of greenhouse gases). In 2015, however, 195 nations—including both the United States and China—came to a landmark agreement in Paris that committed nearly every nation on the planet to limiting greenhouse gas emissions.

Recently, the international effort represented by the Paris Accords has been rendered uncertain by events in the United States. After twenty-nine states sued, the Supreme Court halted adoption of Paris Agreement policies in the United States, and in 2017, President Donald Trump pulled out of the agreement altogether. In 2020, President Biden reentered the agreement. But even assuming all nations followed through, scientists agree that the emissions limits promised in the Paris Accords would cut only about half of what is necessary to prevent irreversibly disastrous effects. To prevent this from happening, scientists believe that the transition to clean energy sources will need to be completed by 2050. These hotly debated issues about climate change clearly illustrate the necessity for global thinking in the contemporary world.

After Empire: Postcolonial Politics in the Global Era

After the end of the Cold War, one legacy of the postwar era continued to shape international relations: postcolonial relationships between former colonies and Western powers. (See decolonization struggles detailed in Chapter 27.) Former colonies gained formal independence; but, in some respects, very little changed for people in these new nations because colonialism's legacies endured even after independence. Some former colonizers retained so much power that formal independence actually meant very little. In other nations, bloody independence struggles poisoned the political culture, exacerbated by decades of colonial policies. The results thus ranged from extraordinary industrial success to ethnic slaughter, or from democratization to new local models of autocratic rule. During the Cold War, these postcolonial regions were often the turf on which the superpower struggle was waged. They benefited from superpower patronage, but also became the staging ground for proxy wars funded by the West in its fight against communism. Their various trajectories since 1989 point to the complex legacy of the imperial past.

EMANCIPATION AND ETHNIC CONFLICT IN AFRICA

Colonialism's legacies weighed heavily on sub-Saharan Africa. Most of the continent's former colonies became independent after the Second World War with their basic infrastructures deteriorating after decades of imperial negligence. The Cold War decades brought scant improvement, as African governments were plagued by both homegrown and externally imposed corruption, poverty, and civil war. Two very different trends began to emerge around 1989, shaped by the end of the Cold War.

A trend toward democracy could be seen in South Africa, where the white minority government's brutal racial policies of apartheid were challenged by **Nelson Mandela**, a member of the African National Congress (ANC) who had been imprisoned since 1962. In the following years, the South African government pursued a policy of intense repression. In the 1990, with the nation on the verge of open civil war, the South African government released Mandela from prison. Mandela resumed leadership of the ANC and turned the party away from violence and toward renewed public demonstrations. Negotiation with the Afrikaner-dominated white regime became possible when F. W. de Klerk succeeded P. W. Botha as prime minister. A pragmatist who feared civil war and national collapse over apartheid, de Klerk was well matched with Mandela. In March 1992, the two men began direct talks to establish majority rule. Legal and constitutional reforms followed, and, in May 1994, during elections in which all South Africans took part, Nelson Mandela was chosen as the country's first Black president. Mandela defused the climate of organized racial violence and gained tremendous personal popularity as a living symbol of a new political culture in South Africa and worldwide. In a number of smaller postcolonial states such as Benin, Malawi, and Mozambique, the early 1990s also brought political reforms that ended one-party or one-man rule in favor of parliamentary democracy and economic reform.

> The end of apartheid in South Africa marks an advance for democracy but other former colonies struggle with ethnic conflicts, refugee crises, and civil war

Nelson Mandela (1918–2013) The South African opponent of apartheid who led the African National Congress and was imprisoned from 1962 until 1990. After his release from prison, he worked with Prime Minister Frederik Willem de Klerk to establish majority rule.

The other major trend ran in a less encouraging direction, as other former colonies across the continent collapsed into ruthless ethnic conflict. In Rwanda, a former Belgian colony, conflicts between the Hutu and Tutsi populations erupted into a highly organized campaign of genocide against the Tutsi after the country's Hutu president was assassinated. Carried out by ordinary Hutus of all backgrounds, the ethnic slaughter left over 800,000 Tutsi dead in a matter of weeks. French and United Nations troops were present, but failed to intervene or provide safe areas. The United Nations and the governments of the United States and France were widely criticized in the aftermath for failing to do more to stop the killing, only using the word *genocide* when it was too late.

When a Tutsi-led force captured the Rwandan capital of Kigali, the Hutu government collapsed, and many of the perpetrators of the genocide fled to neighboring Zaire. Once in Zaire, they became hired mercenaries in that country's many-sided civil war. Mobutu Sese Seko, the country's long-time dictator, was infamous for diverting billions of dollars in foreign aid into his personal bank accounts. Neighboring countries intervened, hoping to secure some of Zaire's valuable resources. Fighting continued into the new century and was dubbed "Africa's world war" by many observers. Public services, normal trade, even basic health and safety inside Zaire—later renamed the Democratic Republic of Congo by an ineffective government in the capital—collapsed. By 2008, an estimated 5.4 million people had died in the war and its aftermath, the equivalent of losing the entire population of Denmark in a single decade. As of 2022, fighting still continues in the eastern regions of the Congo.

NELSON MANDELA VOTES IN SOUTH AFRICA'S FIRST DEMOCRATIC ELECTIONS, 1994. Mandela was elected the country's first Black president.

ECONOMIC POWER ON THE PACIFIC RIM

By 2000, east Asia had become a global industrial powerhouse. China, after beginning trade with the West in the 1970s, became the world's leading heavy industrial producer by the year 2000. Its state-owned companies contracted with Western firms to produce goods at moderate prices for sale to the United States and Europe. Beijing established semicapitalist commercial zones around major port cities such as Shanghai and reclaimed Hong Kong from Britain in 1997. Hong Kong worked to preserve its position as an economic and cultural middle ground with the rest of the world, but attempts by the Chinese to assert greater control over Hong Kong continue to threaten Hong Kong's special status.

Other Asian nations also emerged as global commercial powers. After the Second World War, industry flourished in Japan, South Korea, Taiwan, and other east Asian states. By the 1980s, their robust industrial expansion earned them the collective nickname of the "tigers," taken from the ambitious, forward-looking tiger in Chinese mythology. These Pacific rim states formed the most important industrial region in the world outside the United States and Europe. Japan led the way, becoming an influential model, with a postwar revival that surpassed the West German economic miracle (Chapter 28). Other east Asian nations tried to mimic Japan's success. Some, such as South Korea and the Chinese Nationalist stronghold of Taiwan, treated the creation of prosperity as a fundamental patriotic duty. In Malaysia and Indonesia, postcolonial governments parlayed their natural resources and expansive local labor pools (which had made them attractive to imperial powers in earlier times) into investment for industrialization.

The Pacific rim's boom, however, also produced a "bust." During the 1990s, a confluence of factors resulted in an economic slowdown. Japan experienced rising production costs, overvalued stocks, and uncontrolled speculation in its high-priced real estate market. When the bubble burst in 1991, Japan entered a "lost decade" of economic stagnation. Responses to the economic downturn varied. In South Korea, an older generation that remembered economic catastrophe after the Korean War invested their own savings to prop up ailing companies. Japan launched austerity programs to cope with its first serious spike in unemployment in two generations. In Indonesia, inflation and unemployment reignited sharp ethnic conflicts. This predominantly Muslim country, with a long tradition of tolerance and pluralism inside the faith, also saw outbursts of violent religious fundamentalism associated with another region: the Middle East.

Postwar economic and industrial development make Pacific rim states into global powerhouses by the 1980s, but the 1990s see retrenchment as growth stalls

A New Center of Gravity: The Middle East

Perhaps no other region has drawn more attention from the West in the age of globalization than the Middle East, where a combination of Western political and economic interests converged with regional conflicts and transnational Islamic politics. Here we consider three important aspects of recent history in the region: the **Arab-Israeli conflict**, the region's emergence as a global center of oil production, and the development of a specific, modern brand of Islamic radicalism that challenged the legacies of imperialism and promised revolutionary changes in postcolonial nations. The most violent elements of this radicalism have pushed for direct conflict with Western governments.

THE ARAB-ISRAELI CONFLICT

Arab-Israeli conflict A series of wars fought between Israel and neighboring Arab nations since the founding of the state of Israel.

Arab nationalism During the period of decolonization, secular forms of Arab nationalism, or Pan-Arabism, found a wide following in many countries throughout the Middle East.

Israel was a battleground from the start (Chapter 27). The aspirations of European Jewish immigrants fleeing the Holocaust clashed with the goals of pan-Arabists— secular, anticolonial nationalists who championed **Arab nationalism** and self-reliance. By the late 1970s, after two Arab-Israeli wars, it appeared that a generation of fighting might come to an end. American mediators sponsored talks to prevent further conflict, while Soviet leaders remained neutral. The Egyptian president Anwar Sadat, who authorized the 1973 war against Israel, decided that coexistence was the long-term answer to regional conflict. In 1978, aided by the American president Jimmy Carter, Sadat brokered a peace between Egypt and Israel's staunchly conservative leader, Menachem Begin.

Hopes for a lasting peace were soon dashed. Agreement on a two-state solution—one for Palestinians and one for Jews—proved impossible. Palestinians insisted on the right to return to land they lost in 1948, when the state of Israel was created. Meanwhile, Israelis had begun to settle—in violation of international law, according to the United Nations—in territories occupied by Israel after the 1967 war: the Golan Heights, the Gaza Strip, the West Bank, and East Jerusalem, a territory that includes religious sites sacred to both Jews and Muslims. On each side of the Israeli-Palestinian conflict, a potent blend of ethnic and religious nationalism drove both debate and action. Conservatives in Israel played to a public sentiment that put security ahead of other priorities, particularly among the most recent Jewish immigrants, often from the United States and the former Soviet Union. On the other side, younger Palestinians—embittered by their lives in the occupied territories—turned against the secular radicalism of the Palestinian Liberation Organization (PLO) and moved toward radical Islam.

In 1987, in this combustible political environment, the Palestinians living on the West Bank and in the desperately overcrowded Gaza Strip revolted in an outburst of street rioting. This rebellion, called the *intifada* (literally, a "throwing off," or uprising), continued for years in daily battles between stone-throwing Palestinian youths and armed Israeli security forces. Street fights escalated into cycles of Palestinian terrorism, particularly suicide bombings of civilian targets, and reprisals from the Israeli military. International efforts to broker a peace produced the Oslo Accords of 1993, which established an autonomous Palestinian Authority led by the PLO chief, Yasser Arafat. The peace was weakened by continued attacks by Islamist terrorists, and the Accords suffered fatal damage when Israel's reformist prime minister Yitzhak Rabin was assassinated by a reactionary Israeli in 1995.

In the twenty-first century, the cycle of violence has continued. Palestinians launched a second intifada in 2000, which ended only with Yasser Arafat's death in 2004. Arafat's successor, Mahmoud Abbas, was challenged by a more militant Palestinian organization, Hamas, which was labeled a terrorist organization by the United States and the European Union. Hamas' victory in Palestinian parliamentary elections in 2006 limited Abbas's power to negotiate with Israel and diplomatic efforts could not prevent the resumption of conflict in Gaza in 2008–2009, 2012, and 2014. In 2013, the UN General Assembly recognized the state of Palestine, granting it nonmember observer status, but bitter divisions between Hamas and the Palestinian Authority persist. Egypt helped to broker a ceasefire in 2018, when violence in Gaza flared again, renewed conflict in 2021 led to thousands of rocket attacks from Gaza and hundreds of Israeli airstrikes against Palestinians. A permanent end to the conflict is not in sight.

> Hopes for a two-state solution fades as Israeli settlements grow in territories occupied after the 1967 war and as Palestinians challenge Israeli soldiers in the intifada of 1987 and 2004

OIL, POWER, AND ECONOMICS

The struggles between the state of Israel and its neighbors have been important in their own right. Yet one of the most compelling reasons that this conflict mattered to outside powers was material: oil. Global demand for oil skyrocketed after the Second World War. During the consumer boom in the West, ordinary citizens bought cars and other petroleum-powered consumer durables, while industrial plastics made from petroleum by-products were used to manufacture basic household items. The demand for these goods, and the profit and power that went with them, drew Western corporations and governments toward the oil-rich states of the Middle East, whose vast reserves were discovered in the 1930s and the 1940s. Large corporations conducted joint diplomacy with Middle Eastern states and their home governments to design concessions for drilling, refining, and shipping the oil, while pipelines were laid by contractors based around the world, from California to Rome to Russia.

The enormous economic value of Middle Eastern oil reserves made energy a fundamental tool in the new struggles over political power. Producer states sought to turn their resources into leverage with the West's former imperial powers. In 1960, leading Middle Eastern, African, and Latin American producers banded together in a cartel, the Organization of the Petroleum Exporting Countries (OPEC), to regulate the production and pricing of crude oil. During the 1970s, OPEC played a leading role in the global economy. Its policies reflected not only the desire to draw maximum profits out of bottlenecks in oil production, but also the militant politics of some OPEC leaders who wanted to use oil as a weapon against the West's support for Israel in the Arab-Israeli conflict. After the 1973 Arab-Israeli war, an OPEC **oil embargo** sparked spiraling inflation in Western nations, triggering a recession that lasted nearly a decade.

In response, Western governments treated the Middle Eastern oil regions as a vital strategic center of gravity. If conflict directly threatened oil production or friendly governments, Western powers were prepared to intervene by force, as demonstrated by the 1991 Gulf War. By the 1990s, another new front of competition and potential conflict emerged, as the energy demands of other nations grew. The new industrial giants, China and India, in particular, eyed the Middle Eastern oil reserves with the same nervousness as the West. The oil boom also generated violent conflict within some Middle Eastern producer states, as oil revenues were distributed unevenly. The inequalities within Middle Eastern societies created by the oil economy caused resentments, corruption, and a new wave of radical politics. As pan-Arab nationalists faded from the scene, a rising revolutionary force gathered around modern readings of Islamic fundamentalism, now tied to postcolonial politics.

THE RISE OF POLITICAL ISLAM

In North Africa and the Middle East, modernization and globalization produced tremendous discontents. The new nations that emerged from decolonization south of the Sahara often shared the characteristics of the "kleptocracies": corrupt state agencies, cronyism based on ethnic or family kinship, decaying public services, rapid increases in population, and constant state repression of dissent. Disappointment with these conditions was especially high in the seat of Pan-Arabism, **Gamal Abdel Nasser**'s Egypt. During the 1960s, an Egyptian opposition movement emerged that denounced Egypt's nationalist government as greedy, brutal, and corrupt. The government's critics offered modern interpretations of certain legal and political currents in Islamic thought, ideas that linked loosely across centuries with revolts against foreign interference and official corruption.

> The economic importance of Middle East oil reserves drive U.S. and European foreign policy in the region, and create incentives to intervene when the flow of oil is interrupted

oil embargo In 1973, Arab members of the Organization of the Petroleum Exporting Countries (OPEC) declared an embargo on oil sales to the United States in protest against U.S. support for Israel.

Gamal Abdel Nasser (1918–1970) President of Egypt and the most prominent spokesman for secular Pan-Arabism. He became a target for Islamist critics because of his use of Western-inspired policies during his regime.

Map legend (left map):

Proposed by UN in 1947:
- Jewish state
- Arab state
- International zone
- Boundary of Israel 1949

LEBANON · Damascus · SYRIA · Haifa · Nazareth · MEDITERRANEAN SEA · Jordan R. · Tel Aviv · Jericho · Amman · Jerusalem · Dead Sea · Gaza · Beer Sheva · ISRAEL · TRANSJORDAN · EGYPT · Al Aqabah · SAUDI ARABIA · RED SEA

Map legend (right map):

- Israel before 1967 war
- Territory occupied by Israel June 1967
- Territory occupied by Israel October 1973
- Territory occupied by Egypt October 1973

LEBANON · Beirut · Sidon · Damascus · SYRIA · Golan Heights · Haifa · Nazareth · MEDITERRANEAN SEA · Jordan R. · Tel Aviv · Jericho · Amman · Jerusalem · Dead Sea · Gaza · Beer Sheva · ISRAEL · JORDAN · Port Said · Cairo · EGYPT · Suez · SINAI · Gulf of Suez · Gulf of Aqaba · Al Aqabah · SAUDI ARABIA · RED SEA

EUROPE · ASIA · AFRICA · Area of detail

THE ARAB-ISRAELI WARS OF 1967 AND 1973. › What were the major changes in the political geography of the Middle East as a result of the Arab-Israeli war of 1967? › At the end of the 1967 war, why did the Israelis wish to occupy the Sinai and the West Bank regions? › What problems did this occupation create, and how might it have led to the war of 1973?

The most influential of these Islamist critics, Sayyid Qutb (*Kutb*; 1906–1966), argued that the Arab world's moral failure lay in centuries of colonial contact with the West. Qutb was arrested several times by Egyptian authorities, and ultimately executed. Qutb accused the ruling elites of Arab states of pursuing foreign-influenced policies that frayed local and family bonds and deepened economic divides. To remain in power, he claimed, these elites lived in the pockets of Western imperial and corporate powers, and this collaboration not only caused cultural impurity but also eroded authentic Muslim faith. This harsh judgment of Arab societies—that they were poisoned from without as well as within—required an equally drastic solution. Qutb believed Arab societies should reject not only oppressive postcolonial

EGYPTIAN PRESIDENT GAMAL ABDEL NASSER AND SOVIET MINISTER ALEKSEY KOSYGIN, 1966. As the most prominent spokesman for secular Pan-Arabism, Nasser became a target of Islamist critics, such as Sayyid Qutb and the Muslim Brotherhood, who were angered by the Western-influenced policies of his regime.

governments but also all the political and cultural ideas that traveled with them, especially those that could be labeled "Western." After popular revolts, the Arab autocracies would be replaced by an idealized Islamic government—a system in which a rigid form of Islam would link law, government, and culture.

Qutb's Islamist movement combined popular anger, intellectual opposition to "foreign" influences, and a highly idealized vision of the past. By the 1970s, Qutb's ideas were put into practice by Egypt's Muslim Brotherhood, a secretive organization rooted in anticolonial politics, local charity, and fundamentalist Islam. Similar organizations were organized in other urbanized Arab countries and leading Islamic universities, which were historically centers of debate on political theory and religious law. Radical Islam emerged as a driving force in criticism of autocratic Arab regimes, while more liberal Islamists and secular critics, who called for open elections and a free press, were more fragmented and thus easier to silence. The new wave of fundamentalists also gained concessions that allowed them to preach and publish in public as long as they did not launch actual revolts. Despite the movement's steady rise throughout the Middle East, radical Islam's defining moment as a political force came in an unexpected place: Iran.

IRAN'S ISLAMIC REVOLUTION Despite tremendous economic growth in the 1960s and the 1970s, Iranians labored with legacies of foreign intervention and corrupt rule at the hands of the shah, **Mohammad Reza Pahlavi**, a West-friendly leader installed during a 1953 military coup supported by Britain and the United States. In exchange for the shah's support for the West during the Cold War and for providing reasonably priced oil, the Iranian government received vast sums in oil contracts, weapons, and development aid. Thousands of Westerners,

Mohammad Reza Pahlavi (1919–1980) The Western-friendly shah of Iran who was installed during a 1953 coup supported by Britain and the United States.

especially Americans, came to Iran, introducing foreign influences that challenged traditional values. The shah denied democratic representation to Iranians and governed, instead, through a small aristocracy, while also relying on brutal campaigns of repression by the army and the secret police. Despite all this, the United States embraced the shah as a strategically vital ally: a key to anti-Soviet alliances and a safe source of oil.

The shah retired under popular pressure in February 1979, after a lengthy period of public unrest. Most Westerners fled the country and the provisional government appointed by the shah collapsed. Into the vacuum surged a broad Islamist movement led by **Ayatollah Ruhollah Khomeini** (1902–1989), Iran's senior Shī'ite cleric and theologian, who returned from exile in France. The country's large population of unemployed, and deeply religious university students provided the movement's energy. The new Iranian government was committed to strict interpretations of Islamic law, restrictions on women's public life, and the prohibition of ideas or activities linked to Western influence. The regime also defined itself against its enemies: the Sunni religious establishment of neighboring states, "atheistic" Soviet communism, and, especially, Israel and the United States. Fearing that the United States would try to overthrow Khomeini, militant students stormed the American embassy in November 1979, taking fifty-two hostages. The act quickly became an international crisis that heralded a new kind of confrontation between Western powers and postcolonial Islamic radicals. The Democratic president Jimmy Carter's administration ultimately gained the release of the hostages, but the crisis contributed to the election of Republican Ronald Reagan.

THE SHAH'S DOWNFALL. In 1979, two Iranians symbolically replace a picture of the shah with one of Ayatollah Khomeini after the Iranian revolution. **› What did the Iranian revolutionaries who overthrew the shah have in common with the anticolonial nationalists in former European colonies and client states?**

IRAN, IRAQ, AND UNINTENDED CONSEQUENCES OF THE COLD WAR

In 1980, Iran's Arab neighbor and traditional rival Iraq invaded, hoping to seize Iran's southern oil fields. Iran counterattacked, resulting in a murderous eight-year conflict marked by the use of chemical weapons and tremendous loss of life. The war ended with Iran's defeat, but not the collapse of its theocratic regime. Ultimately, the strongest threats to the Iranian regime came from within, as a new generation of young students and disenfranchised service workers found that their prospects for prosperity and active citizenship had not changed much since the days of the shah.

The Iran-Iraq conflict created another problem for Western interests and the governments of leading OPEC states: Iraq. When Hussein invaded oil-rich

Ayatollah Ruhollah Khomeini (1902–1989) Iranian Shī'ite religious leader who led the revolution in Iran that resulted in the abdication of the shah in 1979, and whose government rejected Western influence.

Kuwait in 1990, Western nations led by the United States reacted forcefully. Within months, Iraq faced the full weight of the United States military along with forces from several OPEC states, French troops, and armored divisions from Britain, Egypt, and Syria. This coalition retook Kuwait in a brief ground campaign. This changed the tenor of relations between the United States and Arab oil producers, encouraging closeness between governments, but also generating a new anti-Americanism among radical groups in the Middle East. Hussein remained in power after his 1991 defeat, and pursued a confrontational policy to develop nuclear and biological weapons.

The conflicts in the Middle East also brought the Soviet Union into conflict with Islamic radicalism after the **Soviet invasion of Afghanistan.** In 1979, the socialist government of Afghanistan turned against its Soviet patrons. Fearing a spread of fundamentalism into the Muslim regions of Soviet central Asia, Moscow responded by installing a pro-Soviet government in Afghanistan. The new government found itself immediately at war with fighters who combined local conservatism with militant Islam, including volunteers from radical Islamic movements elsewhere. These fighters, who called themselves *mujahidin*, viewed the conflict as a holy war. They benefited from weapons and training given by the United States, which saw the conflict as a chance to undermine the Soviet Union. The Soviet invasion of Afghanistan in 1979 produced a war that dragged on for nearly ten years, taking thousands of Russian lives and resulting in Soviet withdrawal in 1989. After five years of warfare, hard-line Islamic factions tied to foreign elements in the mujahidin took over the country. Their experiment in theocracy made Iran's seem mild by comparison.

War and Terrorism in the Twenty-First Century

Global networks of communication, finance, and mobility gave radical political violence a disturbing new character at the end of the twentieth century. In the 1960s, organized terrorism had become a significant part of political conflict in the Middle East, Europe, and Latin America. The Irish Republican Army, the Italian Red Brigades, and the various Palestinian revolutionary organizations had specific goals, such as national independence or the establishment of revolutionary governments. Beginning in the 1980s, a different kind of terrorist organization emerged that ranged freely across territory and national boundaries. These newer terrorist groups called for decisive conflict to eliminate their enemies and grant themselves martyrdom. They often separated themselves from the local crises that first spurred their anger, roaming widely among countries in search of recruits for their cause.

FROM AL QAEDA TO THE IRAQ WAR

An example was the radical Islamist umbrella organization **al Qaeda**, created by leaders of the foreign mujahidin who fought against the Soviet Union in Afghanistan, among them the Saudi-born multimillionaire Osama bin Laden.

Soviet invasion of Afghanistan In 1979, to combat rising fundamentalism in the region, the Soviet Union directed soldiers to overthrow the Afghan president and installed a Soviet government.

al Qaeda The radical Islamic organization founded in the late 1980s by former mujahidin (Islamist guerrilla fighters) who had fought against the Soviet Union in Afghanistan. al Qaeda carried out the 9/11 terrorist attacks and is responsible as well for attacks in Africa, Southeast Asia, Europe, and the Middle East.

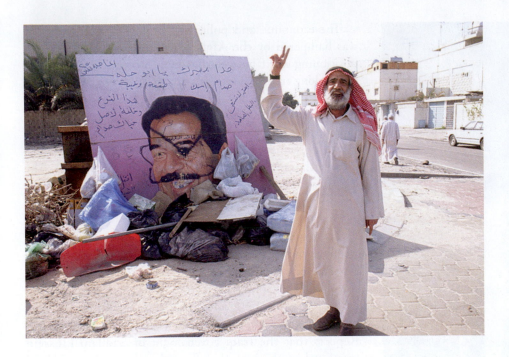

Another was the Egyptian radical Ayman al-Zawahiri, whose political career linked him directly to Sayyid Qutb and other founding thinkers of modern revolutionary Islam. These leaders organized networks of largely self-contained terrorist cells around the world—from the Islamic regions of Southeast Asia to Europe, East Africa, and the United States. Their goals, which were not to negotiate for territory or change the government of a specific state. Instead, they spoke of the destruction of the state of Israel and the American, European, and other non-Islamic systems of government worldwide, and called for a united, apocalyptic revolt by fundamentalist Muslims to create an Islamic community bounded only by faith.

In 2001, al Qaeda attacked the United States. Small teams of suicidal militants, aided by al Qaeda's organization, planned to hijack airliners and use them as flying bombs to strike the most strategically important symbols of America's global power. On September 11, 2001, hijacked planes struck the Pentagon, the U.S. military headquarters, and both of the World Trade Center towers in New York City. A fourth plane, possibly aimed at the U.S. Capitol, crashed in open farmland in Pennsylvania, its attack thwarted when the passengers fought back against their captors. The World Trade Center towers collapse was watched on television and the internet by hundreds of millions of viewers. Nearly 3,000 people died.

The immediate American response was to take action against al Qaeda's central haven in Afghanistan, a state in total collapse after the warfare of the previous thirty years. American soldiers, along with armed Afghan militias angry at the country's disarray, quickly routed al Qaeda's Taliban sponsors and scattered the terrorists. The search for Osama bin Laden took a decade, during which time the United States and its allies faced a renewed insurrection by the Taliban in Afghanistan, beginning in 2003. U.S. forces killed Osama bin Laden in nearby Pakistan in 2011.

The economic and political rebuilding of Afghanistan was hampered by the Afghan government's difficulties in positioning itself between its U.S. ally and a population with a long tradition of mistrusting foreign powers. Many U.S. forces departed Afghanistan in 2013–2014, but continued Taliban attacks prolonged the U.S. presence until Donald Trump's administration negotiated a final withdrawal agreement and President Joe Biden ordered a complete withdrawal of U.S. troops in the spring of 2021. The twenty-year conflict came to a chaotic end as the Taliban retook control of the country and the U.S.-supported government collapsed.

Groups such as al Qaeda are feared because of the weapons they might use: chemical and biological agents or portable nuclear weapons that could kill millions. With the end of the Cold War, technologies that the superpowers employed to maintain their balance of power became potentially accessible to displaced groups on the margins. Reports that the Iraqi government of Saddam Hussein was reaching biological and nuclear capabilities helped propel the Gulf War of 1991, and active international efforts to disarm Iraq thereafter. Later, fear that states such as Iraq might transfer such weapons to apocalyptic terrorists, a concern given new life after the attacks in New York and Washington, provided the rationale for an American-led invasion of Iraq in the spring of 2003. The

TWENTY-FIRST-CENTURY TERRORISM.
World Trade Center towers in New York City under attack on September 11, 2001.

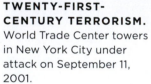

campaign, which used a remarkably small force, both on the ground and in the air, quickly took over Iraq and deposed Hussein. No evidence of recent, active weapons development programs was found, and, in the process, the United States inherited the complex reconstruction of a broken state, fractured by guerrilla violence and anti-Western terrorism. In 2011, after a long struggle against a shifting insurgency that fought the new Iraqi government and the U.S.-led forces that supported it, U.S. troops left Iraq. A small number of troops have returned in recent years to help the Iraqi government deal with a new threat: the so-called Islamic State, known in the Middle East by its Arabic acronym, Daesh (see page 1065).

FROM THE ARAB SPRING TO THE ISLAMIC STATE

In December 2010, an unexpected protest movement, which began in Tunisia, resulted in a wave of protest and popular insurrection in much of the Arab Middle East and North Africa. Just over a year later, powerful authoritarian rulers who had been in command for decades were overthrown, including Zine al-Abidine Ben Ali of Tunisia, Hosni Mubarak of Egypt, and Muammar Gaddafi of Libya. The speed of these momentous changes surprised people living in these countries as much as they astonished foreign observers—many had long assumed that political change, when it came to these regimes, would proceed at a glacial pace. Did this mean that a wave of democratic revolution was sweeping through the Middle East?

A transition to more democratic forms of government in the Middle East has not happened. Protest movements in Bahrain were brutally repressed. In Yemen and Syria, opposition to the government led to long and violent civil conflicts that have continued into the present. Tunisia's regime change was the most successful. Democratic elections brought a moderate Islamist party to power in 2011, and a former human rights activist became president soon after. In 2014, however, a new president with strong ties to the old regime was elected. In Egypt, a brief period where Islamist parties held a majority in parliament was followed by the election of Abdel Fattah el-Sisi, who did not hesitate to use the army to violently suppress protests against his accession.

The **Syrian civil war** may be the most intractable conflict to emerge directly from the protests of the Arab Spring. Syria's current president, Bashar al-Assad, is a member of a family that has controlled the country in a dictatorial fashion since 1971. In 2011, protests calling for reform turned into violent confrontation with the army and civil war, complicated by the presence of local militias and foreign religious extremists. European nations and the United States have provided some military support, but Russia actively supported Assad's government. Civilians have been the major victims of the fighting, with some estimating the number of deaths at about half a million between 2011 and 2021. People fleeing the violence created the worst refugee crisis the world has known since the Second World War.

The Syrian civil war and the invasion of Iraq by the United States created a large space between the eastern Mediterranean coast and Iran that was only loosely governed by recognizably functioning states. It was in this space that the so-called **Islamic State** emerged. A Muslim millenarian group, Daesh seized and imposed its rule in territory in Syria and Iraq in 2014, declaring itself to be a new caliphate—the sole legitimate steward of Islam on earth. Unlike other militant terrorist groups such as al Qaeda, the Islamic State insisted that it must hold territory and subject the population to its vision of religion.

The Islamic State embraced violence—including against other Muslims—and its terror tactics and narrow interpretations of Islam repulsed people elsewhere in the world. Many Muslim leaders condemned the movement. Others were inspired by their militancy, however, and more than 27,000 foreigners traveled to join the Islamic State, including people from Europe, North Africa, Asia, Australia, and North America. Daesh lost most of its territory in 2017, and by the time U.S. forces killed the Islamic State's leader, Abu-Bakr al-Baghdadi, in 2019, the Islamic State's last remaining enclave had been defeated.

U.S. president Donald Trump's sudden decision to withdraw support from the United States' Kurdish allies in October 2019 led immediately to a Turkish invasion of northeastern Syria in order to seize territory controlled by the Kurds. At the same time, President Assad of Syria, backed by Russia, moved into the power vacuum left by the departure of U.S. troops, reestablishing control over large portions of the country that had opposed him since the beginning of the civil war.

Syrian civil war (2011–) Sparked when protesters called for reform to Syria's dictatorial government in 2011, the conflict has since escalated, with two chief camps: Assad's government backed by Russia and Iran, and rebel groups backed by the United States, Turkey, Saudi Arabia, and other powers in the region.

Islamic State (Daesh) In 2014 a militant group of Muslim fundamentalists seized territory in northeastern Syria and northwestern Iraq and proclaimed themselves a new *caliphate*, the authority over all Muslims. Known as the Islamic State of Iraq and Syria (ISIS) or the Islamic State of Iraq and the Levant (ISIL), they are also called Daesh by Arabic-speaking critics of their violence and brutality.

CRISIS IN SYRIA AND THE MIDDLE EAST, 2014–2019. The smaller map shows the extent of Islamic State territory at its height in 2014 and in 2017. In the larger map, shaded in red are the nine most common resettlement countries for Syrians fleeing the intense civil war. Most were internally displaced within Syria or settled in neighboring countries such as Turkey, which has been a member of the Council of Europe since 1949 and has been negotiating to become a full member of the European Union since 2005. These negotiations are now on hold due to a lack of support for Turkey's membership in other European nations. › **How does Turkey's geographical and political position connect Europe to the Middle East?**

The simultaneous crises created by terrorism and the arrival of hundreds of thousands of refugees fleeing Syria created a dilemma for European societies and a deep political crisis. Multiple terrorist attacks—such as those in Paris in 2015 and in Brussels and Nice in 2016—were conducted by militants who claimed loyalty to the Islamic State. Unlike the 9/11 attacks, however, these terrorist incidents were undertaken by citizens of European states who became radicalized on their own. These attacks nevertheless fed an atmosphere of fear that created opposition to Europe's tradition of offering sanctuary to people who face persecution or violence at home. With mainstream political parties in Europe already seeing declines in support after the financial crisis of 2008 and the eurozone crisis that began in 2009, the political consequences have been far-reaching, leading to a surge in support for right-wing parties that have embraced a xenophobic nationalism. Europe's commitment to its own tradition of human rights is under extreme pressure.

Transformations: Human Rights

Our conception of citizenship, rights, and law has been transformed over time by long-term processes of globalization. High school halls and college walkways are crammed with the tables of international organizations, such as Amnesty International, that promote universal human rights. How has this notion of human rights become so familiar? What older traditions has it built on or replaced?

The contemporary language of human rights took its present form in response to the atrocities of the First and Second World Wars. The concern for human rights did not lead automatically to institutions dedicated to upholding them, however. Enforcing *universal* human rights challenges the sovereignty of nation-states, and an individual nation-state's power over its citizens. International courts and human rights organizations thus require what political thinkers call the globalization of judicial power.

The belief that rights were embedded in "nature," "natural order," or "natural law" formed a powerful strain of early modern political thought. John Locke understood natural law as the law of reason (Chapter 15); others understood it to be the law of God. Both ideas referred to a higher authority to which men owed their obedience. The English Bill of Rights of 1689, accepted by William and Mary after the Glorious Revolution, insisted on "the true, ancient, and indubitable rights and liberties of the people of this kingdom." A century later, the American Declaration of

> *The idea of universal human rights implies a global agreement to challenge nation-states that do not protect their own citizens*

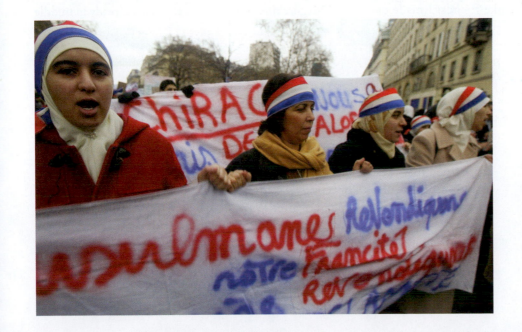

THE FRENCH HEADSCARF CONTROVERSY. In 2004, more than 10,000 demonstrators, mostly women, marched in Paris to voice their opposition to a proposed law banning the Islamic headscarf in public schools. The choice of the red, white, and blue headbands on their scarves underlines their claim for a French identity that they saw as compatible with their religious faith. Their banner states: "Muslim women, let's proclaim our Frenchness."

Islamic Headscarves in France

Beginning in the late 1980s, France faced a bitter debate about young Muslim women wearing a Islamic headscarves in public schools. After a long history of conflict between secularists and Catholics, public schools traditionally have been defined as a secular space in France. In defense of this principle, many girls were expelled from school for wearing an Islamic headscarf, sometimes referred to as a foulard, *or* voile *(veil); and in 2004, headscarves were banned from schools.*

The young women and their defenders framed the issue in terms of fundamental individual freedoms, and claim that the exclusion of the girls' freedom is the result of anti-Muslim racism. In the early 2000s, an American anthropologist interviewed young women in France to hear their stories of living through this controversy. Souad is a young woman in her midtwenties, born in France to Algerian immigrant parents. She did not have a religious upbringing, and describes her childhood as a "zigzag" between two cultures.

At middle and high school people sort themselves by group, as Maghrebins [North Africans] or as French. Already in the *sixième* [eleven years old] we felt the difference between those whose parents had money and the others. They put me in the advanced section because I had received a 20 in math the previous year [an unusually high grade]; they thought they perhaps had an intellectual. It traumatized me that they put me with the others [French]. There was one girl who said: "you, you're an Arab, don't get close to me." I was the "Arab of the classroom." It was really a shock. I was the only one, and I found it very hard to make friends; I made one.

You find yourself with people; you do not know their culture; you feel very bad, feel still more that you are not well integrated: "we don't want anything to do with you, you are Arab, dirty." They were taught this from their parents, the racism.

So the following year (*cinquième*) I came down to the ordinary level and was with people like me, of Maghrebin origin, and it was easier to get along, without the racism. And I really feel that the school system contributes to that because it is they who make the difference from the beginning, with only French people at one level and all Maghrebins and others in the other already in middle

Independence and the French Declaration of the Rights of Man more broadly proclaimed the "natural, inalienable and sacred rights of man." In fact, of course, those bold declarations of rights were not universal. Women, enslaved people, people of color, and people of different religions were excluded, wholly or partially. Many nineteenth-century political theorists and scientists dedicated countless volumes to the proposition that these groups were *not* created equal. Which human beings might receive the "rights of man" was bitterly contested, and a more inclusive conception of human rights did not develop until after 1945.

The rise of nationalism and nation-states in the nineteenth century meant that rights, and political movements claiming them, became increasingly inseparable from nationhood. "What is a country . . . but the place in which our demands for individual rights are most secure?" asked the Italian nationalist Giuseppe Mazzini. For nineteenth-century Italians, Germans, Serbs, and Poles, and for twentieth-century Indians, Vietnamese, and Algerians—to name just a few—fighting for national school, so it's normal that later on the racism will grow in people's minds. So the schools have a responsibility.

* * *

Once I got to high school, friends told me about my religion. I discovered an aspect I did not know, I studied, I read books, I found that enriching.

It was clear to me that the headscarf was an obligation, and I felt the need to please our Creator, it was in that spirit that I wanted to wear it, but the social conditions at high school presented problems. I had to prepare to be rejected by others. I studied for my bac [the all-important school finishing exam] and practiced my religion but the voile was another thing. I always did my prayer, that's something very important for Muslims, and I am proud of myself there. But there was always that desire to go higher in faith, to go closer to the Creator, to please him. So I put on a small hair band so that people would get used to it, because before I wore mini skirts, long hair, but never drank alcohol. In effect I was a bit of a tomboy and hung out with guys, who considered me their little sister and made sure I did not veer toward drugs and night clubs.

One day I decided to become a woman, not a boy, and I changed my behavior, because I had been very aggressive in my gestures and words. I realized that it is hard to live in society as a woman, because there is a lot of sexism, in French society as well. So, to return to the zigzag, my

behavior as a woman, the fact that God asked me to do certain things, so I decided to go in that direction while adapting myself to the society where I live, and I succeed at this, for, when I am at work I wear the scarf not like I have it now but on top, swirled around like the Africans [makes gesture around her head]. That seems to work. I began wearing it as an intern and it worked. This shows that there are still people who are very tolerant. They knew me before and after the foulard, and their attitude did not change. They saw that my work did not change, even got better, and one said, if anyone criticizes you let me know and I will take care of it. I found that touching.

Source: John R. Bowen, *Why the French Don't Like Headscarves: Islam, the State, and Public Space* (Princeton: 2007), pp. 75–77.

Questions for Analysis

1. How does Souad describe the way her primary school contributed to a sense of otherness, or separation between people whose families came from North Africa and those whose culture was "French"?

2. How does Souad describe the thinking that led her to wear a headscarf? Was it simply a religious decision? Does she cite other factors?

3. What experiences did Souad have as a result of wearing the headscarf to work?

independence was a way to secure the rights of citizens. Note, however, the tension that is built into the history of human rights: on the one hand, the tradition of rights as an aspect of "natural law" was built on a foundation of Enlightenment universalism that assumed that liberty and personal autonomy belonged to everybody. The actual enjoyment of such rights depended on the existence of nation-states that were committed only to protect the rights of their own citizens. What recourse would people have if their nation-state restricted civil rights to people of one race, one religion, or one gender? The world wars marked a turning point. The Paris Peace Conference of 1919 aimed for more than a territorial settlement. With the League of Nations, it tried, tentatively, to establish an organization that would transcend the power of individual nations and uphold the (ill-defined) principles of "civilization." (Despite this commitment, the League bowed to British and American objections to a statement condemning racial discrimination.) The League was swept aside by a surge of extreme nationalism in the 1930s, but revulsion at the atrocities of the war that followed brought forth more decisive efforts. The United Nations, the International Court of Justice at the Hague (Netherlands), and the United Nation's Commission on Human Rights were all established after 1945. Unlike anything attempted after the First World War, the Commission on Human Rights set out to establish the rights of individuals—even against the nation-state.

This **Universal Declaration of Human Rights**, published by the Commission in 1948, became the touchstone of our modern notion of human rights. The Commission argued that the war and the "barbarous acts which have outraged the conscience of mankind" showed that no state should have absolute power over its citizens. The Universal Declaration prohibited torture, cruel punishment, and slavery. It built on earlier declarations that universalized the right to legal equality, freedom of religion and speech, and the right to participate in government. Finally, it reflected the postwar period's effort to put democracy on a more solid footing, by establishing *social* rights to education, work, "just and favorable remuneration," an adequate "standard of living," and social security, among others. A separate convention, also passed in 1948, dealt with the newly defined crime of genocide.

Few nations were willing to ratify the Universal Declaration of Human Rights. For decades after the war, its idealistic principles could not be reconciled with British and French colonialism, American racial segregation, or Soviet dictatorship. As long as the wars to end colonialism continued, declarations of universal principles rang hollow. As long as the Cold War persisted, human rights seemed only a weapon in the sparring between the superpowers. Decolonization and, later, the end of the Cold War made human rights seem more legitimate. International institutions set up after the Second World War gained expertise and stature. Global communications and media dramatically expanded the membership and influence of organizations that, like Amnesty International (founded in 1961), operated outside the economic or political boundaries of the nation-state. Memories of the Second World War helped drive the creation of the International Criminal Tribunals for Yugoslavia and Rwanda in 1993. Finally, human rights offer a way of talking about rights, goods, and environmental protections in a globalized world that nation-states cannot provide on their own.

The troubled era that began with the 9/11 attacks on the United States in 2001 has seen many challenges to the notion of universal human rights. Terrorism, no matter the ideology of the perpetrator, is a fundamental violation of every human's right to safety and security. In their zeal to punish terrorists, meanwhile, many nations tacitly turned away from the emerging international legal structures that attempted to defend the rights of all individuals everywhere. The tactics that the United States and its allies used against al Qaeda and the Taliban, which included torture, indefinite detention without trial, and the use of pilotless drones to kill suspected militant leaders, have raised troubling questions. Drone technologies make it easier to avoid U.S. casualties in operations against a dangerous enemy, but many in the United States and abroad have expressed concerns about the government's right to identify, target, and execute individuals, including, in some cases, U.S. citizens, on the basis of criteria that are never subject to independent legal review.

As Western governments pursue their interests abroad, debates about the use of military power in other parts of the world, and the form that this power takes, have become pressing concerns. These issues raise questions that have been a central part of the liberal democratic political tradition since it emerged in opposition to monarchist forms of government in the seventeenth century. How should a nation determine the balance between individual freedoms and national security? What forms of force or violence can a state legitimately use against its enemies at home or abroad? What kinds of information about its citizenry should a government be allowed to keep? Are the terrorist threats that democratic regimes routinely face today so serious that they justify the suspension of internationally recognized human rights? There are no easy answers to these questions, but the answers that self-proclaimed democratic governments and societies give will shape how people everywhere will perceive the legitimacy of the political institutions and values that they claim to represent.

Europe and the United States in the Twenty-First Century

The confidence that Europeans felt after 1989 was badly shaken by the time the second decade of the twenty-first century approached its end. European integration, an engine of economic growth and political stability in the decades after the Second World War, reached its apparent limits in the east and become a source of bitter political disagreements even in nations that had long been members of the European Union. In the 2000s, the idea of an integrated "Europe" was challenged by populist politicians from the right, who saw European institutions as an infringement on national sovereignty, and also from leftists who feared that European guidelines on financial institutions and on state spending threatened the social protections of the welfare state. In both Europe and the United States, the development of a highly polarized political atmosphere revealed deep divisions in the most prosperous nations of the developed world.

Some of this bitterness can be traced to the global financial crisis of 2007–2008, which began with a classic bubble in the United States housing market. Rising home prices encouraged buyers to "flip" homes for quick profit. This speculation was abetted by banks, who issued ever riskier loans to homebuyers. Since the local banks that issued individual mortgages resold these loans almost immediately, they had little incentive to worry about nonpayment. In turn, the larger banks that bought these mortgages repackaged them as complicated financial products known as mortgage-backed securities, which they sold to large institutional investors, including pension funds and other banks elsewhere in the world. During the run-up to the crash, global investment banks flooded international markets with trillions of dollars of risky mortgage-backed securities—often aided by the ratings agencies that were supposed to be independent arbiters of risk.

When housing prices fell, the crisis became inevitable. Homeowners could no longer cover their mortgages and mortgage-backed securities became "toxic assets," impossible to sell and of little value. Confidence in the banking sector plummeted. Banks stopped lending, businesses failed, and trillions of dollars of consumer savings were wiped out. Millions of people lost their jobs. Unprecedented government bailouts of banks with taxpayer money were required to stabilize the banking system. The severity of this crisis led many in Europe and North America to rethink the central assumptions of late twentieth-century economic policy, especially the belief that markets were by definition self-regulating. Popular resentment against

The United Nations on the Protection of Refugees, 1951

The United Nations' Universal Declaration of Human Rights, adopted in 1948, declared that "everyone has the right to seek and to enjoy in other countries asylum from persecution." In order to establish a basis in international law for guaranteeing this right, the United Nations established the 1951 Convention Relating to the Status of Refugees. Originally intended to deal with refugee movements produced by the end of the Second World War, the 1951 Convention was amended in 1967 to provide universal coverage for the protection of refugees throughout the world. The Convention defined the term refugee and established the minimum level of protection that all states who were members of the United Nations were obligated to maintain for refugees who sought asylum on their territory.

Article 1: Definition of the Term "Refugee"

For the purposes of the present Convention, the term "refugee" shall apply to any person who:

[. . .] As a result of events occurring before 1 January 1951 and owing to well-founded fear of being persecuted for reasons of race, religion, nationality, membership of a particular social group or political opinion, is outside the country of his nationality and is unable or, owing to such fear, is unwilling to avail himself of the protection of that country; or who, not having a nationality and being outside the country of his former habitual residence as a result of such events, is unable or, owing to such fear, is unwilling to return to it. [. . .]

Article 2: General Obligations

Every refugee has duties to the country in which he finds himself, which require in particular that he conform to its laws and regulations as well as to measures taken for the maintenance of public order.

Article 3: Non-Discrimination

The Contracting States shall apply the provisions of this Convention to refugees without discrimination to race, religion, or country of origin.

Article 4: Religion

The Contracting States shall accord to refugees within their territories treatment at least as favourable as that accorded to their nationals with respect to freedom to practice their religion and freedom as regards the religious education of their children. [. . .]

Article 12: Personal Status

[. . .] Rights previously acquired by a refugee and dependent on personal status, more particularly rights attaching to marriage, shall be respected by a Contracting State, subject to compliance, if this be necessary, with the formalities required by the law of that State, provided that the right in question is one which would have been recognized by the law of that State had he not become a refugee. [. . .]

Article 16: Access to Courts

A refugee shall have free access to the courts of law on the territory of all Contracting States. [. . .]

Article 17: Wage-Earning Employment

The Contracting State shall accord to refugees lawfully staying in their territory the most favourable treatment accorded to nationals of a foreign country in the same circumstances, as regards the right to engage in wage-earning employment.

In any case, restrictive measures imposed on aliens or the employment of aliens for the protection of the national labor market shall not be applied to a refugee who was already exempt from them [. . .] or who fulfils one of the following conditions:

a) He has completed three years' residence in the country
b) He has a spouse possessing the nationality of the country of residence. A refugee may not invoke the benefits of this provision if he has abandoned his spouse.
c) He has one or more children possessing the nationality of the country of residence. [. . .]

Article 22: Public Education

The Contracting States shall accord to refugees the same treatment as is accorded to nationals with respect to elementary education. [. . .]

Article 23: Public Relief

The Contracting States shall accord to refugees lawfully staying in their territory the same treatment with respect to public relief and assistance as is accorded to their nationals.

Article 26: Freedom of Movement

Each Contracting State shall accord to refugees lawfully in its territory the right to choose their place of residence and to move freely within its territory, subject to any regulations applicable to aliens generally in the same circumstances. [. . .]

Article 31: Refugees Unlawfully in the Country of Refuge

The Contracting States shall not impose penalties, on account of their illegal entry or presence, on refugees who, coming directly from a territory where their life or freedom was threatened in the sense of article 1, enter or are present in their territory without authorization, provided they present themselves without delay to the authorities and show good cause for their illegal entry or presence. [. . .]

Article 32: Expulsion

The Contracting States shall not expel a refugee lawfully in their territory save on grounds of national security or public order.

The expulsion of such a refugee shall be only in pursuance of a decision reached in accordance with due process of law. Except where compelling reasons of national security otherwise require, the refugee shall be allowed to submit evidence to clear himself, and to appeal to and be represented for the purpose before competent authority or a person or persons specially designated by the competent authority. [. . .]

Article 33: Prohibition of Expulsion or Return ("Refoulement")

No Contracting State shall expel or return ("refouler") a refugee in any manner whatsoever to the frontiers of territories where his life or freedom would be threatened on account of his race, religion, nationality, membership of a particular social group or political opinion.

The benefit of the present provision may not, however, be claimed by a refugee whom there are reasonable grounds for regarding as a danger to the security of the country in which he is, or who, having been convicted by a final judgment of a particularly serious crime, constitutes a danger to the community of that country.

Source: Office of the United Nations High Commissioner for Refugees (UNHCR; UN Refugee Agency). Convention and Protocol Relating to the Status of Refugees. Available from: https://www.unhcr.org/3b66c2aa10. Accessed September 10, 2019.

Questions for Analysis

1. What are the most important rights that the 1951 Convention guarantees for refugees?

2. What forms of discrimination did the authors of the Convention appear to be most concerned about?

3. What language did the authors of the Convention include that allowed contracting states to limit the rights of refugees to claim asylum?

the financial industry inspired many nations to consider widespread reform and government regulation of banks.

Contemporary debates about political integration in Europe or the benefits of free-market capitalism can be seen as a continuation of debates within the traditions of political and economic liberalism that go back to the eighteenth century. In the classic formulation of Enlightenment liberals such as Adam Smith, political and economic liberties were best defended in a nation with a small and limited government. By the end of the nineteenth century, this assumption was challenged by an alternative model, that of social democracy, which argued that liberalism's ideal of small governments could not do enough to remedy the social and economic inequalities produced within modern industrial societies. After the devastation of the Second World War, Western European governments were much more willing to use the power of the state to assist the unemployed or the aged, to support families, and to provide subsidies for education, public transportation, and national programs for health care. This consensus emerged in part from a belief that the depression of the 1930s was not an anomaly but a sign that a market economy needed guardrails to prevent the emergence of destabilizing and antidemocratic political movements such as fascism or Bolshevism. In the United States, enthusiasm for such government programs was not shared by all. President Lyndon Johnson's administration used the power of the federal government to challenge racial segregation and address broad problems such as urban poverty or environmental pollution in the 1960s, but a conservative backlash in the 1980s and 1990s led to an end to welfare programs, the repeal of environmental regulations, and the dismantling of government regulations on business.

By the end of the first decade of the twenty-first century, both Europe and the United States faced serious challenges. European democracies witnessed an intensifying political polarization during these years. The success of the European welfare state in the decades after the Second World War, depended on a combination of factors that are impossible to reproduce today: Marshall Plan investment from the United States; the benefits of the first stages of European integration; and cooperation among representatives of labor, employers, and the state.

This system worked well as long as the economy kept growing. When the economy flattened out beginning in the 1970s, however, businesses reduced their investments, unemployment went up, workers expressed discontent with their wage restraints, and European states had less revenue for social protection. In the 1980s and the 1990s, European governments resorted to deficit spending to protect their welfare programs. This fix worked well enough as long as the banks lending the governments money were confident that they would be repaid. Faith in this system led to the creation of the euro as the single currency of a new "eurozone" in 1999, and notes and coins denominated in euros began to circulate in 2002. At the moment of its creation, there were eleven member nations; in 2019, the eurozone included nineteen of the twenty-eight members of the European Union.

But monetary union created a new set of unanticipated challenges. The establishment of a single currency led many European banks to underestimate the risks of lending money to developing economies on the periphery of the eurozone, especially Portugal, Ireland, Greece, and Spain. Easy credit fueled a construction boom in these countries, but when the risks became apparent, the money dried up, and the bubble collapsed. Many banks in these regions were so indebted that their governments were forced to bail them out. Thus, the bank debt transformed into government debt, reducing the credibility of officials managing the crisis and hindering their ability to raise new funds for essential services, such as pensions or health care.

The crisis revealed a fatal flaw in the plan for monetary union. Normally, when a country runs into trouble with its economy it can devalue its currency, making its goods cheaper for foreign buyers, and hence, stimulating the economy. But this option was unavailable for member nations of the eurozone that found themselves under stress after 2009, because they shared their currency with many other nations. Instead, the financially stressed governments were humiliatingly dependent on decision makers in other countries to provide the financing they needed to stay afloat. At its most extreme, such situations might cause nations to leave the eurozone, raising troubling questions about the founding assumptions of the European Union—that it would lead to "an ever closer union."

The eurozone crisis exposed deeper fissures that had opened up in Europe since the end of the Cold War. From the outset, European integration was premised on the assumption that a new equilibrium could be found between national sovereignty and supranational bodies at the European level. At the same time, supporters of integration believed that Europe could commit itself to capitalist growth while also remaining true to the promises of the postwar welfare state. In both instances, the balance was hard to find. Anti-European political parties blamed "Europe" for a wide range of policies, including environmental regulations, migration policy, and restrictions on state spending. The bitter aftermath of the eurozone debacle and the financial crisis of 2008 gave new life to nationalist parties in all corners of Europe. Nationalist parties in Europe regularly invoke xenophobic—and at times openly antisemitic or anti-Muslim—language, leading some to fear that the hatreds of the first half of the twentieth century have been reawakened.

No issue has focused more attention on the possibility of breaking up the European Union than "Brexit." In 2016, Prime Minister David Cameron of the Conservative party in Britain called for a referendum on British membership in the European Union (EU). The initial debate about **Brexit** (Britain + Exit) was largely an argument about immigration from the European continent, with supporters of Brexit demanding a strong assertion of national identity, an end to immigration, and a rejection of membership in the European Union. Britain was never part of the eurozone, but EU membership gave it access to Europe's common market, and this connection was an important part of British economic growth, fueling the rise of London as a global financial center. In exchange for access to Europe's markets, however, the European Union asked Britain to accept the principle of freedom of movement within EU countries. To the surprise of many, a slight majority favored leaving Europe, under the belief that there would be little cost to a reassertion of British independence.

Brexit became official on January 31, 2020, when Britain formally withdrew from the European Union. The consequences were more severe than Brexit's supporters had promised. British businesses that depended on European imports and manufacturers who relied on European suppliers were forced to confront new rules that caused persistent delays and long-standing shortages. The long-term economic effects of Brexit are nevertheless difficult to disentangle from the effects of the pandemic shutdowns that coincided with British withdrawal from the EU, and may take years to fully understand.

The United States experienced intense polarization in these years as well. The U.S. model of economic development had generated extraordinary wealth for the

Brexit A public referendum in June 2016 in which the population of the United Kingdom, by a slim majority, voted to leave the European Union.

financial industry but also widened the gap between the rich and the poor. The financial crisis of 2008 and the bailout of the banking industry that followed proved that this model relied on taxpayer money to shore up the system when markets failed. Widespread dissatisfaction with this outcome was an important factor in a turn away from centrist leadership in both the Democratic and Republican parties in subsequent years. Since both Republicans and Democrats had extolled the virtues of the globalized economy since the 1990s and underestimated its risks, neither party was well-positioned to defend their economic record after 2009. Donald Trump's populist campaign of 2016 took advantage of this frustration, and his messaging focused on those aspects of globalization that appeared to be most threatening to many voters, including the outsourcing of jobs, the danger of terrorism, and both legal and clandestine migration. The general mistrust of mainstream political leadership also left an opening for Trump and his supporters to distinguish themselves from their opponents by staking out extreme positions on divisive cultural issues such as gender and gay rights, abortion, and the United States' unresolved and bitter history of racial violence. Political campaigns that centered on these hot-button and emotional issues also lent themselves easily to the new media environment offered by Facebook, Twitter, and other platforms that were capable of spreading political messages—and disinformation—with an intensity that quickly overwhelmed the ability of older news organizations to fact check and verify.

Brexit seemed to indicate that the dream of a "United States of Europe" was as remote as ever, while Donald Trump's refusal to accept the election results in 2020 raised real questions about the solidity of democracy in the United States. Nevertheless, the surprisingly unified response of European nations and the United States to **Russia's invasion of Ukraine** in February 2022 may be giving new life to European and American solidarity. The unprecedented economic sanctions announced against Russia by Europe and the United States isolated Russia from

ANTI-EUROPEAN SENTIMENT IN THE UK. On the left, a pro-Brexit protester in London calls on the then prime minister Theresa May to begin the negotiations that would conclude with a British withdrawal from the European Union (EU). **THE RISE OF DONALD TRUMP.** On the right, supporters of Donald Trump wait for his arrival at a Florida airport during his 2016 presidential campaign.

the global economy, confirmed Putin's ongoing break with the West, and created the conditions for an emerging new Cold War that might easily become hot. At the same time, the desire to defend Ukraine in its existential struggle against Russia galvanized European nations and reinvigorated the security ties between Europe and the United States, which had been weakened during four years of Donald Trump's presidency. It is impossible to predict the outcome of the war in Ukraine but is likely that Putin's disastrous invasion of Ukraine will mark a significant break in the nearly eighty years of continuous global economic integration that began after the Second World War.

Conclusion

Globalization, defined loosely as the process by which the economies, societies, and cultures of different parts of the world have become increasingly interconnected, was hailed as a solution to old problems, even as it was criticized as a source of new ones. Many hoped that the end of the Cold War in 1989 meant that economic liberalism—that is, a global free-market capitalist system unfettered by government regulations—had triumphed for good in the world, but continued political instability in many parts of the globe, the global economic crisis of 2008, and the Russian invasion of Ukraine have called into question such optimistic interpretations of world events. In the economic realm, nation-states have looked for ways to reassert their control over the flow of currencies and goods, and to protect their populations against decisions made elsewhere by financial speculators and investors. Overreaching by superpowers—the United States in Iraq, Russia in Ukraine—has made it difficult to argue with nations in every global region who seek to develop their own nuclear arsenal to defend against foreign attack. Meanwhile, the danger of radical forms of terrorism, both foreign and domestic, has caused even strong democratic governments in the West to create new and pervasive surveillance bureaucracies, demonstrating that global threats can have real and seemingly permanent local effects on definitions of citizenship, the permeability of borders, and extensions of state power.

In such uncertain times, it is difficult to remain consistent or to determine national priorities. How can democracies—in which legitimate leadership is seen as coming from the consent of the "people"—cope with political movements that seek to exclude significant portions of the population from voting or running for office? How can societies protect themselves from destructive disinformation—and the technologies that make such disinformation so cheap—while also protecting the freedom of expression? Is the threat of terrorism greater than the threat of loss of liberty stemming from extensions in government power? Is it fair of the International

Legend:
- European Union member, 2022
- European Union Eurozone
- Left EU in 2020 (Brexit)
- Candidate for EU membership

EUROPEAN UNION AND EUROZONE, 2022. The Brexit controversy raised for the first time the possibility of a member nation leaving the EU. Although anti-European nationalist parties gained ground in European parliamentary elections in 2019, the Russia-Ukraine War has encouraged more cooperation among European nations. **› What do these trends say about the future of the European integration?**

Monetary Fund to ask developing nations to adhere to austere cuts to their social welfare spending, when wealthy investment banks receive billion-dollar bailouts after making bad bets in the financial markets because they are "too big to fail"? The complexity of the world's interconnections makes it difficult to find definitive answers to such questions. Interconnections between global regions and the mobility of peoples have been a part of human history since the beginning. The anxieties of the present are bound up in a sense of accelerating political and technological changes at a moment when the scale of looming global problems—climate change is only the most obvious—is just now coming into focus. The loss of familiar moorings makes fundamental questions about human behavior and political community

AFTER YOU READ THIS CHAPTER ⌄

CHRONOLOGY

1948	State of Israel formed
1948–1949	Arab-Israeli War
1967	Arab-Israeli conflict: The Six-Day War
1973	Arab-Israeli War
1979	Soviet invasion of Afghanistan
	Islamic revolution in Iran
1980–1988	Iran-Iraq War
1991	Persian Gulf War
1994	Genocide against Tutsis in Rwanda
2001	9/11 terrorist attacks
	U.S. invasion of Afghanistan
2003	U.S. invasion of Iraq
2004–2005	Terrorist attacks in Madrid and London
2008	Global financial crisis
2011	Arab Spring
	Beginning of Syrian civil war
2015–2016	Terrorist attacks in Europe
2020	Britain withdraws from European Union ("Brexit")
2022	Russia invades Ukraine

REVIEWING THE OBJECTIVES

> Globalization in the second half of the twentieth century was not new. What does globalization mean? What was similar or different about the most recent phase of globalization compared with others in the past?

> The burden of the colonial past continued to weigh heavily on many former colonies after the 1960s. What accounts for the success of some former colonies in the global economy and the continued social and political challenges facing others?

> Since the end of the Second World War, conflicts and events in the Middle East have taken on a global significance far beyond the region's borders. What crucial conflicts have occupied the attention of other nations? What events have proved to be crucial turning points in the emergence of the Middle East as a region that drives developments elsewhere?

difficult to answer, and the study of history offers no quick solutions. The untidy and contradictory evidence that historians find in the archives rarely yields unblemished heroes, unvarnished villains, or easy lessons that can be applied to the present. Good history reveals the complex processes and dynamics of change over time. It helps us understand the many layers of the past that have formed our present world. It shows again and again that the past does not preordain what happens next. Globalization, in this sense, is not the final destination of history. It is merely the constantly renewed reality of human existence, and the context for future struggles about the goals of political association, the meanings of liberty or equality, and the possibility of shared values.

Go to **INQUIZITIVE** to see what you've learned—and learn what you've missed—with personalized feedback along the way.

PEOPLE, IDEAS, AND EVENTS IN CONTEXT

❯ What were the policy goals of **NEOLIBERALISM** after the 1970s, as exemplified by the activities of institutions such as the **INTERNATIONAL MONETARY FUND** and the World Bank?

❯ How do the **HIV-AIDS EPIDEMIC** of the 1980s and **COVID-19 PANDEMIC** illustrate the new realities of public health in a globalized world?

❯ What was the significance of **NELSON MANDELA**'s election as president of South Africa in 1994?

❯ How was the 1973 **OIL EMBARGO** related to the **ARAB-ISRAELI CONFLICT**? What were its effects on the global economy?

❯ What did radical critics dislike about secular forms of **ARAB NATIONALISM** such as that espoused by **GAMAL ABDEL NASSER** in Egypt?

❯ What led the United States and Britain to support the regime of **MOHAMMAD REZA PAHLAVI** in Iran? What events brought **AYATOLLAH RUHOLLAH KHOMEINI** to power in 1979?

❯ What circumstances link the **SOVIET INVASION OF AFGHANISTAN** in 1979 with the origins of **AL QAEDA**? How is the rise of the so-called **ISLAMIC STATE** linked to the **SYRIAN CIVIL WAR** or the American-led invasion of Iraq in 2003?

❯ What made it difficult for European and North American governments to sign the United Nation's **UNIVERSAL DECLARATION OF HUMAN RIGHTS** in 1948? What events have occurred since 1948, when the Universal Declaration of Human Rights was signed, that indicate that at least some nations might agree to international treaties guaranteeing human rights?

❯ What was at issue in the **BREXIT** debate?

❯ How might **RUSSIA'S INVASION OF UKRAINE** have affected the recent trend toward greater economic integration?

THINKING ABOUT CONNECTIONS

❯ Many of the global linkages between Europe and the United States on the one hand, and the independent nations of Asia, Africa, and Latin America on the other, were first forged during earlier periods of imperial expansion. How is this history still felt in the present?

❯ Global networks of transport, trade, and communication have long been significant vectors for cultural change by bringing different peoples into contact and conversation with one another. How have recent developments in technology changed the nature of this global conversation?

Appendix

Rulers of Principal States

THE CAROLINGIAN DYNASTY

Pepin of Heristal, mayor of the palace, 687–714
Charles Martel, mayor of the palace, 715–741
Pepin III, mayor of the palace, 741–751; king, 751–768
Charlemagne, king, 768–814; emperor, 800–814
Louis the Pious, emperor, 814–840

West Francia

Charles the Bald, king, 840–877; emperor, 875–877
Louis II, king, 877–879
Louis III, king, 879–882
Carloman, king, 879–884

Middle Kingdoms

Lothair, emperor, 840–855
Louis (Italy), emperor, 855–875
Charles (Provence), king, 855–863
Lothair II (Lorraine), king, 855–869

East Francia

Ludwig, king, 840–876
Carloman, king, 876–880
Ludwig, king, 876–882
Charles the Fat, emperor, 876–887

HOLY ROMAN EMPERORS

Saxon Dynasty

Otto I, 962–973
Otto II, 973–983
Otto III, 983–1002
Henry II, 1002–1024

Franconian Dynasty

Conrad II, 1024–1039
Henry III, 1039–1056
Henry IV, 1056–1106
Henry V, 1106–1125
Lothair II (Saxony), 1125–1137

Hohenstaufen Dynasty

Conrad III, 1138–1152
Frederick I (Barbarossa), 1152–1190
Henry VI, 1190–1197
Philip of Swabia, 1198–1208 } Rivals
Otto IV (Welf), 1198–1215

Frederick II, 1220–1250
Conrad IV, 1250–1254

Interregnum, 1254–1273

Emperors from Various Dynasties

Rudolf I (Habsburg), 1273–1291
Adolf (Nassau), 1292–1298
Albert I (Habsburg), 1298–1308
Henry VII (Luxemburg), 1308–1313
Ludwig IV (Wittelsbach), 1314–1347
Charles IV (Luxemburg), 1347–1378
Wenceslas (Luxemburg), 1378–1400
Rupert (Wittelsbach), 1400–1410
Sigismund (Luxemburg), 1410–1437

Habsburg Dynasty

Albert II, 1438–1439
Frederick III, 1440–1493

Maximilian I, 1493–1519
Charles V, 1519–1556
Ferdinand I, 1556–1564
Maximilian II, 1564–1576
Rudolf II, 1576–1612
Matthias, 1612–1619
Ferdinand II, 1619–1637
Ferdinand III, 1637–1657

Leopold I, 1658–1705
Joseph I, 1705–1711
Charles VI, 1711–1740
Charles VII (not a Habsburg), 1742–1745
Francis I, 1745–1765
Joseph II, 1765–1790
Leopold II, 1790–1792
Francis II, 1792–1806

RULERS OF FRANCE FROM HUGH CAPET

Capetian Dynasty

Hugh Capet, 987–996
Robert II, 996–1031
Henry I, 1031–1060
Philip I, 1060–1108
Louis VI, 1108–1137
Louis VII, 1137–1180
Philip II (Augustus), 1180–1223
Louis VIII, 1223–1226
Louis IX (Saint Louis), 1226–1270
Philip III, 1270–1285
Philip IV, 1285–1314
Louis X, 1314–1316
Philip V, 1316–1322
Charles IV, 1322–1328

Valois Dynasty

Philip VI, 1328–1350
John, 1350–1364
Charles V, 1364–1380
Charles VI, 1380–1422
Charles VII, 1422–1461
Louis XI, 1461–1483
Charles VIII, 1483–1498
Louis XII, 1498–1515
Francis I, 1515–1547

Henry II, 1547–1559
Francis II, 1559–1560
Charles IX, 1560–1574
Henry III, 1574–1589

Bourbon Dynasty

Henry IV, 1589–1610
Louis XIII, 1610–1643
Louis XIV, 1643–1715
Louis XV, 1715–1774
Louis XVI, 1774–1792

After 1792

First Republic, 1792–1799
Napoleon Bonaparte, first consul, 1799–1804
Napoleon I, emperor, 1804–1814
Louis XVIII (Bourbon dynasty), 1814–1824
Charles X (Bourbon dynasty), 1824–1830
Louis Philippe, 1830–1848
Second Republic, 1848–1852
Napoleon III, emperor, 1852–1870
Third Republic, 1870–1940
Pétain regime, 1940–1944
Provisional government, 1944–1946
Fourth Republic, 1946–1958
Fifth Republic, 1958–

RULERS OF ENGLAND

Anglo-Saxon Dynasty

Alfred the Great, 871–899
Edward the Elder, 899–924
Ethelstan, 924–939
Edmund I, 939–946
Edred, 946–955
Edwy, 955–959
Edgar, 959–975

Edward the Martyr, 975–978
Ethelred the Unready, 978–1016
Canute, 1016–1035 (king of Denmark)
Harold I, 1035–1040
Hardicanute, 1040–1042
Edward the Confessor,
   1042–1066
Harold II, 1066

House of Normandy

William I (the Conqueror), 1066–1087
William II, 1087–1100
Henry I, 1100–1135
Stephen, 1135–1154

House of Plantagenet

Henry II, 1154–1189
Richard I, 1189–1199
John, 1199–1216
Henry III, 1216–1272
Edward I, 1272–1307
Edward II, 1307–1327
Edward III, 1327–1377
Richard II, 1377–1399

House of Lancaster

Henry IV, 1399–1413
Henry V, 1413–1422
Henry VI, 1422–1461

House of York

Edward IV, 1461–1483
Edward V, 1483
Richard III, 1483–1485

House of Tudor

Henry VII, 1485–1509
Henry VIII, 1509–1547
Edward VI, 1547–1553
Mary I, 1553–1558
Elizabeth I, 1558–1603

House of Stuart

James I, 1603–1625
Charles I, 1625–1649

Commonwealth and Protectorate, 1649–1659

Oliver Cromwell, Lord protector, 1653–1658

House of Stuart Restored

Charles II, 1660–1685
James II, 1685–1688
William III and Mary II, 1689–1694
William III alone, 1694–1702
Anne, 1702–1714

House of Hanover

George I, 1714–1727
George II, 1727–1760
George III, 1760–1820
George IV, 1820–1830
William IV, 1830–1837
Victoria, 1837–1901

House of Saxe-Coburg-Gotha

Edward VII, 1901–1910
George V, 1910–1917

House of Windsor

George V, 1917–1936
Edward VIII, 1936
George VI, 1936–1952
Elizabeth II, 1952–2022
Charles III, 2022–

RULERS OF AUSTRIA AND AUSTRIA-HUNGARY

*Maximilian I (archduke), 1493–1519
*Charles V, 1519–1556
*Ferdinand I, 1556–1564
*Maximilian II, 1564–1576
*Rudolf II, 1576–1612
*Matthias, 1612–1619
*Ferdinand II, 1619–1637
*Ferdinand III, 1637–1657
*Leopold I, 1658–1705
*Joseph I, 1705–1711
*Charles VI, 1711–1740
Maria Theresa, 1740–1780

*Joseph II, 1780–1790
*Leopold II, 1790–1792
*Francis II, 1792–1835 (emperor of Austria as Francis I after 1804)
Ferdinand I, 1835–1848
Francis Joseph, 1848–1916 (after 1867 emperor of Austria and king of Hungary)
Charles I, 1916–1918 (emperor of Austria and king of Hungary)
Republic of Austria, 1918–1938 (dictatorship after 1934)
Republic restored, under Allied occupation, 1945–1956
Free Republic, 1956–

*Also bore title of Holy Roman emperor

RULERS OF PRUSSIA AND GERMANY

*Frederick I, 1701–1713
*Frederick William I, 1713–1740
*Frederick II (the Great), 1740–1786
*Frederick William II, 1786–1797
*Frederick William III, 1797–1840
*Frederick William IV, 1840–1861
*William I, 1861–1888 (German emperor after 1871)
Frederick III, 1888

*kings of Prussia

*William II, 1888–1918
Weimar Republic, 1918–1933
Third Reich (Nazi dictatorship), 1933–1945
Allied occupation, 1945–1952
Division into Federal Republic of Germany in west and German Democratic Republic in east, 1949–1991
Federal Republic of Germany (united), 1991–

RULERS OF RUSSIA

Ivan III, 1462–1505
Vasily III, 1505–1533
Ivan IV, 1533–1584
Theodore I, 1584–1598
Boris Godunov, 1598–1605
Theodore II, 1605
Vasily IV, 1606–1610
Michael, 1613–1645
Alexius, 1645–1676
Theodore III, 1676–1682
Ivan V and Peter I, 1682–1689
Peter I (the Great), 1682–1725
Catherine I, 1725–1727
Peter II, 1727–1730

Anna, 1730–1740
Ivan VI, 1740–1741
Elizabeth, 1741–1762
Peter III, 1762
Catherine II (the Great), 1762–1796
Paul, 1796–1801
Alexander I, 1801–1825
Nicholas I, 1825–1855
Alexander II, 1855–1881
Alexander III, 1881–1894
Nicholas II, 1894–1917
Russian Revolution and Civil War, 1917–1922
Union of Soviet Socialist Republics, 1922–1991
Russian Federation, 1991–

RULERS OF UNIFIED SPAIN

Ferdinand {
 and Isabella, 1479–1504
 and Philip I, 1504–1506
 and Charles I, 1506–1516
}

Charles I (Holy Roman Emperor Charles V), 1516–1556
Philip II, 1556–1598
Philip III, 1598–1621
Philip IV, 1621–1665
Charles II, 1665–1700
Philip V, 1700–1746
Ferdinand VI, 1746–1759
Charles III, 1759–1788
Charles IV, 1788–1808
Ferdinand VII, 1808

Joseph Bonaparte, 1808–1813
Ferdinand VII (restored), 1814–1833
Isabella II, 1833–1868
Republic, 1868–1870
Amadeo, 1870–1873
Republic, 1873–1874
Alfonso XII, 1874–1885
Alfonso XIII, 1886–1931
Republic, 1931–1939
Authoritarian nationalist dictatorship under Francisco Franco, 1939–1975
Juan Carlos I, 1975–2014
Felipe VI, 2014–

RULERS OF ITALY

Victor Emmanuel II, 1861–1878
Humbert I, 1878–1900
Victor Emmanuel III, 1900–1946

Fascist dictatorship under Benito Mussolini, 1922–1943
   (maintained in northern Italy until 1945)
Humbert II, May 9–June 13, 1946
Republic, 1946–

PROMINENT AND RECENT POPES

Silvester I, 314–335
Leo I, 440–461
Gelasius I, 492–496
Gregory I, 590–604
Nicholas I, 858–867
Silvester II, 999–1003
Leo IX, 1049–1054
Nicholas II, 1058–1061
Gregory VII, 1073–1085
Urban II, 1088–1099
Paschal II, 1099–1118
Alexander III, 1159–1181
Innocent III, 1198–1216
Gregory IX, 1227–1241
Innocent IV, 1243–1254
Boniface VIII, 1294–1303
John XXII, 1316–1334
Nicholas V, 1447–1455
Pius II, 1458–1464
Alexander VI, 1492–1503

Julius II, 1503–1513
Leo X, 1513–1521
Paul III, 1534–1549
Paul IV, 1555–1559
Sixtus V, 1585–1590
Urban VIII, 1623–1644
Gregory XVI, 1831–1846
Pius IX, 1846–1878
Leo XIII, 1878–1903
Pius X, 1903–1914
Benedict XV, 1914–1922
Pius XI, 1922–1939
Pius XII, 1939–1958
John XXIII, 1958–1963
Paul VI, 1963–1978
John Paul I, 1978
John Paul II, 1978–2005
Benedict XVI, 2005–2013
Francis, 2013–

Further Readings

CHAPTER 10

Abu-Lughod, Janet L. *Before European Hegemony: The World System A.D. 1250–1350.* Oxford and New York, 1989. A now classic study of the trading links among Europe, the Middle East, India, and China, with special attention to the role of the Mongol Empire; extensive bibliography.

Allsen, Thomas T. *Culture and Conquest in Mongol Eurasia.* Cambridge and New York, 2001. A synthesis of the author's earlier studies, emphasizing Mongol involvement in the cultural and commercial exchanges that linked China, Central Asia, and Europe.

Barker, *Hannah. That Most Precious Merchandise: The Mediterranean Trade in Black Sea Slaves, 1260–1500.* Cambridge, 2021. A path-breaking new book that combines Arabic, Latin, and Italian sources to describe every aspect of the medieval slave trade during the centuries before the shift to a new transatlantic system.

Cole, Bruce. *Giotto and Florentine Painting, 1280–1375.* New York, 1976. A clear and stimulating introduction.

Crummey, Robert O. *The Formation of Muscovy, 1304–1613.* New York, 1987. The standard account.

Dante Alighieri. *The Divine Comedy.* Trans. Mark Musa. 3 vols. Baltimore, 1984–1986.

Dunn, Ross E. *The Adventures of Ibn Battuta: A Muslim Traveler of the Fourteenth Century.* Rev. ed. Berkeley, 2005. Places the writings and experiences of this far-reaching Muslim traveler in their historical and geographical contexts.

Fancy, Hussein. *The Mercenary Mediterranean: Sovereignty, Religion, and Violence in the Medieval Crown of Aragon.* Chicago, 2018. An acclaimed archival study of the complicated relationship between religion and politics in medieval Spain.

Foltz, Richard. *Religions of the Silk Road: Premodern Patterns of Globalization.* 2nd ed. New York, 2010. A compelling and thought-provoking study of the varieties of religious experience and cross-cultural interaction in medieval Eurasia.

Green, Monica, ed. *Pandemic Disease in the Medieval World: Rethinking the Black Death.* Special inaugural issue, *The Medieval Globe,* 1, no. 1 (2014). Available online in an open-access format: http://scholarworks.wmich.edu/tmg/vol1/iss1/. A pathbreaking collection of articles synthesizing the most recent research in the history, epidemiology, microbiology, and archaeology of the plague.

Horrox, Rosemary, ed. *The Black Death.* New York, 1994. A fine collection of documents reflecting the impact of the Black Death, especially in England.

Jackson, Peter. *The Mongols and the West, 1221–1410.* Harlow, UK, 2005. A well-written survey that emphasizes the interactions among the Mongol, Latin Christian, and Muslim worlds.

Jordan, William Chester. *The Great Famine: Northern Europe in the Early Fourteenth Century.* Princeton, NJ, 1996. An outstanding social and economic study.

Keen, Maurice, ed. *Medieval Warfare: A History.* Oxford and New York, 1999. The most attractive introduction to this important subject, lively and well illustrated.

Kitsikopoulos, Harry, ed. *Agrarian Change and Crisis in Europe, 1200–1500.* London, 2011. An up-to-date collection of scholarly essays that addresses a classic and complicated set of historical questions.

Komaroff, Linda, and Stefano Carboni, eds. *The Legacy of Ghenghis Khan: Courtly Art and Culture in Western Asia, 1256–1353.* New York, 2002. An informative and lavishly illustrated catalog of an acclaimed exhibition.

Larner, John. *Marco Polo and the Discovery of the World.* New Haven, 1999. A study of the influence of Marco Polo's *Travels* on Europeans.

Memoirs of a Renaissance Pope: The Commentaries of Pius II. Abridged ed. Trans. Florence A. Gragg, ed. Leona C. Gabel. New York, 1959. Remarkable insights into the mind of a particularly well-educated mid-fifteenth-century pope.

Morgan, David. *The Mongols.* 2nd ed. Oxford, 2007. An accessible introduction to Mongol history and its sources, written by a noted expert on medieval Persia.

Onon, Urgunge, trans. *The History and the Life of Chinggis Khan: The Secret History of the Mongols.* Leiden, 1997. A newer version of *The Secret History,* now the standard English version of this important Mongol source.

Polo, Marco. *The Description of the World.* Trans. Sharon Kinoshita. Indianapolis, 2016. A faithful and accessible new translation of the text, with authoritative notes and commentary.

Rossabi, Morris. *Khubilai Khan: His Life and Times.* Berkeley, 1988. The standard English biography.

Seymour, M. C., ed. *Mandeville's Travels*. Oxford, 1968. An edition of the *Book of Marvels* based on the Middle English version popular in the fifteenth century.

Swanson, R. N. *Religion and Devotion in Europe, c. 1215–c. 1515*. Cambridge and New York, 1995. An excellent study of late-medieval popular piety; an excellent complement to Oakley.

Vaughan, Richard. *Valois Burgundy*. London, 1975. A summation of the author's four-volume study of the Burgundian dukes.

CHAPTER 11

Alberti, Leon Battista. *The Family in Renaissance Florence (Della Famiglia)*. Trans. Renée Neu Watkins. Columbia, SC, 1969.

Allmand, Christopher T., ed. *Society at War: The Experience of England and France during the Hundred Years' War*. Edinburgh, 1973. An outstanding collection of documents.

Boccaccio, Giovanni. *The Decameron*. Trans. Mark Musa and P. E. Bondanella. New York, 1977.

Brucker, Gene. *Florence: The Golden Age, 1138–1737*. Berkeley and Los Angeles, 1998. A classic account of the city at the height of its influence.

Bruni, Leonardo. *The Humanism of Leonardo Bruni: Selected Texts*. Trans. Gordon Griffiths, James Hankins, and David Thompson. Binghamton, NY, 1987. Excellent translations, with introductions, to the Latin works of a key Renaissance humanist.

Cassirer, Ernst, et al., eds. *The Renaissance Philosophy of Man*. Chicago, 1948. Excerpts from important original works by Petrarch, Ficino, and Pico della Mirandola, among others.

Castor, Helen. *Joan of Arc: A History*. London, 2015. An accessible and highly readable account of the ways that Joan was understood in her own time, and her changing reputation up to the present day.

Chaucer, Geoffrey. *The Canterbury Tales*. Trans. Nevill Coghill. New York, 1951. A modern English verse translation, lightly annotated.

Cohn, Samuel K., Jr. *Lust for Liberty: The Politics of Social Revolt in Medieval Europe, 1200–1425. Italy, France, and Flanders*. Cambridge, MA, 2006. An important and provocative study of social movements before and after the Black Death.

Coles, Paul. *The Ottoman Impact on Europe*. London, 1968. An excellent introductory text, still valuable despite its age.

Dobson, R. Barrie. *The Peasants' Revolt of 1381*. 2nd ed. London, 1983. A comprehensive source collection, with excellent introductions to the documents.

Fernández-Armesto, Felipe. *Before Columbus: Exploration and Colonisation from the Mediterranean to the Atlantic, 1229–1492*. London, 1987. An indispensable study of the medieval background to the sixteenth-century European colonial empires.

Froissart, Jean. *Chronicles*. Trans. Geoffrey Brereton. Baltimore, 1968. A selection from the most famous contemporary account of the Hundred Years' War to about 1400.

Frost, Robert. *The Oxford History of Poland-Lithuania. Volume One: The Making of the Polish-Lithuanian Union, 1385–1569*. Oxford, 2018. A magisterial study of this powerful medieval state.

Goffman, Daniel. *The Ottoman Empire and Early Modern Europe*. Cambridge and New York, 2002. A revisionist account that presents the Ottoman Empire as a European state.

Green, Monica. "The Four Black Deaths," *The American Historical Review* 125.5 (2020): 1601–1631. A summary of the state of research on the Black Death based on recent genetic evidence.

Hankins, James. *Plato in the Italian Renaissance*. Leiden and New York, 1990. A definitive study of the reception and influence of Plato on Renaissance intellectuals.

———, ed. *Renaissance Civic Humanism: Reappraisals and Reflections*. Cambridge and New York, 2000. An excellent collection of scholarly essays reassessing republicanism in the Renaissance.

Hobbins, Daniel, ed. and trans. *The Trial of Joan of Arc*. Cambridge, MA, 2007. An excellent translation of the transcripts of Joan's trial.

Inalcik, Halil. *The Ottoman Empire: The Classical Age, 1300–1600*. London, 1973. The standard history by the dean of Turkish historians.

———, ed. *An Economic and Social History of the Ottoman Empire, 1300–1914*. Cambridge, 1994. An important collection of essays, spanning the full range of Ottoman history.

John Hus at the Council of Constance. Trans. M. Spinka, New York, 1965. The translation of a Czech chronicle with an expert introduction and appended documents.

Kafadar, Cemal. *Between Two Worlds: The Construction of the Ottoman State*. Berkeley and Los Angeles, 1995. An important study of Ottoman origins in the border regions between Byzantium, the Seljuk Turks, and the Mongols.

Kaldellis, Anthony. *A New Herodotos: Laonikos Chalkokondyles on the Ottoman Empire, the Fall of Byzantium, and the Emergence of the West*. Washington, DC, 2014. This volume is the first full-length study of Laonikos Chalkokondyles, a historian from Athens who wrote a classical Greek history of his own times, tracing the fall of Constantinople.

Kempe, Margery. *The Book of Margery Kempe*. Trans. Barry Windeatt. New York, 1985. A fascinating personal narrative by an early fifteenth-century Englishwoman who hoped she might be a saint.

Lane, Frederic C. *Venice: A Maritime Republic*. Baltimore, 1973. An authoritative account.

Ormrod, W. Mark. *Edward III*. New Haven, 2012. A new biography of this English monarch by a leading social historian.

Normore, Christina. *A Feast for the Eyes: Art, Performance, and the Late Medieval Banquet*. Chicago, 2015. A fascinating study of the aristocratic feast and its meanings.

Shirley, Janet, trans. *A Parisian Journal, 1405–1449.* Oxford, 1968. A marvelous panorama of Parisian life recorded by an eyewitness.

Sumption, Jonathan. *The Hundred Years' War.* Vol. 1, *Trial by Battle.* Vol. 2, *Trial by Fire.* Philadelphia, 1999. The first two volumes of a massive narrative history of the war, carrying the story up to 1369.

CHAPTER 12

Baxandall, Michael. *Painting and Experience in Fifteenth-Century Italy.* Oxford, 1972. A classic study of the perceptual world of the Renaissance.

Carballo, David M. *Collision of World: A Deep History of the Fall of Aztec Mexico and the Forging of New Spain.* Oxford, 2020. This is a thorough and nuanced study of Mesoamerican and European histories over a millennium, culminating in the arrival of the first conquistadors and the fall of the Aztec capital.

Castiglione, Baldassare. *The Book of the Courtier.* Many editions. The translations by C. S. Singleton (New York, 1959) and by George Bull (New York, 1967) are both excellent.

Cellini, Benvenuto. *Autobiography.* Trans. George Bull. Baltimore, 1956. This Florentine goldsmith (1500–1571) is the source for many of the most famous stories about the artists of the Florentine Renaissance.

Columbus, Christopher. *The Four Voyages of Christopher Columbus.* Trans. J. M. Cohen. New York, 1992. Columbus's own self-serving account of his expeditions to the Indies.

Cover, R. Allan. *Inca Apocalypse: The Spanish Conquest and the Transformation of the Andean World.* Oxford, 2020. A new account, based on archaeological and ethnographic evidence, of the Incas' conquest but prolonged resistance to Spanish colonial rule.

Erasmus, Desiderius. *The Praise of Folly.* Trans. J. Wilson. Ann Arbor, MI, 1958.

Fernández-Armesto, Felipe. *1492: The Year the World Began.* London, 2010. A panoramic view of the world in a pivotal year, putting the voyage of Columbus in a broad historical perspective.

Flint, Valerie I. J. *The Imaginative Landscape of Christopher Columbus.* Princeton, NJ, 1992. A short, suggestive analysis of the intellectual influences that shaped Columbus's geographical ideas.

Grafton, Anthony, and Lisa Jardine. *From Humanism to the Humanities: Education and the Liberal Arts in Fifteenth- and Sixteenth-Century Europe.* London, 1986. An account that presents Renaissance humanism as the elitist cultural program of a self-interested group of pedagogues.

Grendler, Paul, ed. *Encyclopedia of the Renaissance.* New York, 1999. A valuable reference work.

Jardine, Lisa. *Worldly Goods.* London, 1996. A revisionist account that emphasizes the acquisitive materialism of Italian Renaissance society and culture.

Kanter, Laurence, Hilliard T. Goldfarb, and James Hankins. *Botticelli's Witness: Changing Style in a Changing Florence.* Boston, 1997. This catalog for an exhibition of Botticelli's works, at the Gardner Museum in Boston, offers an excellent introduction to the painter and his world.

King, Margaret L. *Women of the Renaissance.* Chicago, 1991. Deals with women in all walks of life and in a variety of roles.

Machiavelli, Niccolò. *The Discourses* and *The Prince.* Many editions. These two books must be read together if one is to understand Machiavelli's political ideas properly.

Mallett, Michael, and Christine Shaw. *The Italian Wars, 1494–1559: War, State, and Society in Early Modern Europe.* Boston, 2012. Argues that the endemic warfare of this period within Italy revolutionized European military tactics and technologies.

Mann, Charles. C. *1491: New Revelations of the Americas before Columbus.* New York, 2006.

———. *1493: Uncovering the New World Columbus Created.* New York, 2012. Written for a popular audience, these are also engaging and well-informed syntheses of historical research.

Martines, Lauro. *Power and Imagination: City-States in Renaissance Italy.* New York, 1979. Insightful account of the connections among politics, society, culture, and art.

More, Thomas. *Utopia.* Many editions.

Olson, Roberta. *Italian Renaissance Sculpture.* New York, 1992. The most accessible introduction to the subject.

Parker, Geoffrey. *The Military Revolution: Military Innovation and the Rise of the West (1500–1800).* 2nd ed. Cambridge and New York, 1996. A work of fundamental importance for understanding the global dominance achieved by early modern Europeans.

Perkins, Leeman L. *Music in the Age of the Renaissance.* New York, 1999. A massive study that needs to be read in conjunction with Reese.

Phillips, J. R. S. *The Medieval Expansion of Europe.* 2nd ed. Oxford, 1998. An outstanding study of the thirteenth- and fourteenth-century background to the fifteenth-century expansion of Europe. Important synthetic treatment of European relations with the Mongols, China, Africa, and North America. The second edition includes a new introduction and a bibliographical essay; the text is the same as in the first edition (1988).

Phillips, William D., Jr., and Carla R. Phillips. *The Worlds of Christopher Columbus.* Cambridge and New York, 1991. The first book to read on Columbus: accessible, engaging, and scholarly. Then read Fernández-Armesto's biography.

Rabelais, François. *Gargantua and Pantagruel.* Trans. J. M. Cohen. Baltimore, 1955. A robust modern translation.

Reese, Gustave. *Music in the Renaissance*. Rev. ed. New York, 1959. A great book; still authoritative, despite the more recent work by Perkins, which supplements but does not replace it.

Rice, Eugene F., Jr., and Anthony Grafton. *The Foundations of Early Modern Europe, 1460–1559*. 2nd ed. New York, 1994. The best textbook account of its period.

Rowland, Ingrid D. *The Culture of the High Renaissance: Ancients and Moderns in Sixteenth-Century Rome*. Cambridge and New York, 2000. Beautifully written examination of the social, intellectual, and economic foundations of the Renaissance in Rome.

Russell, Peter. *Prince Henry "The Navigator": A Life*. New Haven, 2000. A masterly biography by a great historian who has spent a lifetime on the subject. The only book one now needs to read on Prince Henry.

Scammell, Geoffrey V. *The First Imperial Age: European Overseas Expansion, 1400–1715*. London, 1989. A useful introductory survey, with a particular focus on English and French colonization.

Waltom, Nicholas. *Genoa, "La Superba": The Rise and Fall of a Merchant Pirate Superpower*. London, 2015. A history of the maritime city-state that shaped the career of Columbus and other adventurers.

CHAPTER 13

Bainton, Roland. *Erasmus of Christendom*. New York, 1969. A classic biography in English of the Dutch reformer and intellectual.

Benedict, Philip. *Christ's Churches Purely Reformed: A Social History of Calvinism*. New Haven, 2002. A wide-ranging recent survey of Calvinism in both western and eastern Europe.

Bouwsma, William J. *John Calvin: A Sixteenth-Century Portrait*. Oxford and New York, 1988. The best biography of this magisterial reformer.

Duffy, Eamon. *The Stripping of the Altars: Traditional Religion in England, c. 1400–c. 1550*. A brilliant study of religious exchange at the parish level.

————. *The Voices of Morebath: Reformation and Rebellion in an English Village*. New Haven, 2003. How the crises of this period affected and are reflected in the history of a single parish.

Hart, D. G. *Calvinism: A History*. New Haven, 2013. A new survey of this leading Protestant movement from its beginnings to the present day.

John Calvin: Selections from His Writings. Ed. John Dillenberger. Garden City, NY, 1971. A judicious selection, drawn mainly from Calvin's *Institutes*.

Jouanna, Arlette. *The St. Bartholomew's Day Massacre: The Mysteries of a Crime of State*. Translated from the French by Joseph Bergin. Manchester, 2015. A new interpretation of the events and motives surrounding the slaughter of Protestants in Paris on August 24, 1572.

Koslofksy, Craig. *The Reformation of the Dead: Death and Ritual in Early Modern Germany*. Basingstoke, UK, 2000. How essential rituals and responses to death were reshaped during this period.

Loyola, Ignatius. *Personal Writings*. Trans. by Joseph A. Munitiz and Philip Endean. London and New York, 1996. An excellent collection that includes Loyola's autobiography, his spiritual diary, and some of his letters, as well as his *Spiritual Exercises*.

MacCulloch, Diarmaid. *Reformation: Europe's House Divided, 1490–1700*. London and New York, 2003. A definitive new survey; the best single-volume history of its subject in a generation.

Marshall, Peter, ed. *The Oxford Illustrated History of the Reformation*. Oxford, 2015. A compendium of new perspectives on the religious upheavals of the sixteenth century.

Martin Luther: Selections from His Writings, ed. John Dillenberger. Garden City, NY, 1961. The standard selection, especially good on Luther's theological ideas.

McGrath, Alister E. *Reformation Thought: An Introduction*. Oxford, 1993. A useful explanation, accessible to non-Christians, of the theological ideas of the major Protestant reformers.

Mikhail, Alan. *God's Shadow: Sultan Selim, His Ottoman Empire, and the Making of the Modern World*. Norton, 2020. A fascinating history that places the rise of the Ottoman Empire in a global context.

Mullett, Michael A. *The Catholic Reformation*. London, 2000. A sympathetic survey of Catholicism from the mid-sixteenth to the eighteenth century that presents the mid-sixteenth-century Council of Trent as a continuation of earlier reform efforts.

Murray, Linda. *High Renaissance and Mannerism*. London, 1985. The place to begin a study of fifteenth- and sixteenth-century Italian art.

O'Malley, John W. *The First Jesuits*. Cambridge, MA, 1993. A scholarly account of the origins and early years of the Society of Jesus.

————. *Trent: What Happened at the Council*. Cambridge, MA, 2012. A clear and comprehensive narrative of the Church council that gave birth to the modern Catholic Church.

Pettegree, Andrew. *Brand Luther: How an Unheralded Monk Turned His Small Town into a Center of Publishing, Made Himself the Most Famous Man in Europe—and Started the Protestant Reformation*. Penguin, 2016. The title says it all.

Pelikan, Jaroslav. *Reformation of Church and Dogma, 1300–1700*. Vol. 4 of *A History of Christian Dogma*. Chicago, 1984. A masterful synthesis of Reformation theology in its late-medieval context.

Roper, Lyndal. *The Holy Household: Women and Morals in Reformation Augsburg*. Oxford, 1989. A pathbreaking study of Protestantism's effects on a single town, with special attention to its impact on attitudes toward women, the family, and marriage.

Ryrie, Alex. *Being Protestant in Reformation Britain*. Oxford, 2015. A vivid portrait of daily life in a turbulent time.

Shagan, Ethan H. *Popular Politics and the English Reformation*. Cambridge, 2002. Argues that the English Reformation reflects an ongoing process of negotiation, resistance, and response.

Tracy, James D. *Europe's Reformations, 1450–1650*. 2nd ed. Lanham, MD, 2006. An outstanding survey, especially strong on Dutch and Swiss developments, but excellent throughout.

White, Eric Marshall. *Editio Princeps: A History of the Gutenberg Bible*. Harvey Miller Publishers, 2017. The first comprehensive account of the first book printed in the West.

Williams, George H. *The Radical Reformation*. 3rd ed. Kirksville, MO, 1992. Originally published in 1962, this is still the best book on Anabaptism and its offshoots.

CHAPTER 14

Bonney, Richard. *The European Dynastic States, 1494–1660*. Oxford and New York, 1991. An excellent survey of continental Europe during the "long" sixteenth century.

Briggs, Robin. *Witches and Neighbors: The Social and Cultural Context of European Witchcraft*. New York, 1996. An influential recent account of Continental witchcraft.

Cervantes, Miguel de. *Don Quixote*. Trans. Edith Grossman. New York, 2003. A splendid new translation.

Clarke, Stuart. *Thinking with Demons: The Idea of Witchcraft in Early Modern Europe*. Oxford and New York, 1999. By placing demonology into the context of sixteenth- and seventeenth-century intellectual history, Clarke makes sense of it in new and exciting ways.

Cochrane, Eric, Charles M. Gray, and Mark A. Kishlansky. *Early Modern Europe: Crisis of Authority*. Chicago, 1987. An outstanding source collection from the University of Chicago Readings in Western Civilization series.

Cook Harold. *The Young Descartes: Nobility, Rumor, and War*. Chicago, 2018. A new biography that firmly embeds the philosopher in his historical context.

Elliot, J. H. *The Old World and the New, 1492–1650*. Repr. ed. Cambridge, 1992. A brilliant and brief set of essays on the ways that the discovery of the Americas challenged European perspectives on the world and themselves.

———. *Empires of the Atlantic World: Britain and Spain in America, 1492–1830*. An illuminating comparative study. New Haven, 2007.

Geschwend, Annemarie Jordan, and K. J. P. Lowe, eds. *The Global City: On the Streets of Renaissance Lisbon*. London, 2015. A beautifully illustrated collection of essays by leading scholars.

Hibbard, Howard. *Bernini*. Baltimore, 1965. The basic study in English of this central figure of Baroque artistic activity.

Hirst, Derek. *England in Conflict, 1603–1660: Kingdom, Community, Commonwealth*. Oxford and New York, 1999. A complete revision of the author's *Authority and Conflict* (1986), this is an up-to-date and balanced account of a period that has been a historical battleground over the past twenty years.

Hobbes, Thomas. *Leviathan*. Ed. Richard Tuck. 2nd ed. Cambridge and New York, 1996. The most recent edition, containing the entirety of *Leviathan*, not just the first two parts.

Holt, Mack P. *The French Wars of Religion, 1562–1629*. Cambridge and New York, 1995. A clear account of a confusing time.

Ipsen, Pernille. *Daughters of the Trade: Atlantic Slavers and Interracial Marriage on the Gold Coast*. Philadelphia, 2014. A study that puts women and families at the heart of the story of African slavery.

Kors, Alan Charles, and Edward Peters. *Witchcraft in Europe, 400–1700: A Documentary History*. 2nd ed. Philadelphia, 2000. A superb collection of documents, significantly expanded in the second edition, with up-to-date commentary.

Kochanowski, Jan. *Laments*. Translated by Stanislaw Baranczak and Seamus Heaney. New York, 1995. A moving rendition of works by the great poet of Renaissance Poland.

Levack, Brian P. *The Witch-Hunt in Early Modern Europe*, 2nd ed. London and New York, 1995. The best account of the persecution of suspected witches; coverage extends from Europe in 1450 to America in 1750.

Levin, Carole. *The Heart and Stomach of a King: Elizabeth I and the Politics of Sex and Power*. Philadelphia, 1994. A provocative argument for the importance of Elizabeth's gender for understanding her reign.

Limm, Peter, ed. *The Thirty Years' War*. London, 1984. An outstanding short survey, followed by a selection of primary-source documents.

Lynch, John. *Spain, 1516–1598: From Nation-State to World Empire*. Oxford and Cambridge, MA, 1991. The best book in English on Spain at the pinnacle of its sixteenth-century power.

MacCaffrey, Wallace. *Elizabeth I*. New York, 1993. An outstanding traditional biography by an excellent scholar.

Martin, Colin, and Geoffrey Parker. *The Spanish Armada*. London, 1988. Incorporates recent discoveries from undersea archaeology with more traditional historical sources.

Mattingly, Garrett. *The Armada*. Boston, 1959. A great narrative history that reads like a novel; for more recent work, however, see Martin and Parker.

McGregor, Neil. *Shakespeare's Restless World*. London, 2013. Based on an acclaimed BBC Radio program, this book illuminates Shakespeare's life, times, and plays with reference to specific objects in the British Museum.

Newson, Linda A., and Susie Minchin. *From Capture to Sale: The Portuguese Slave Trade to Spanish South America in the Early Seventeenth Century*. London, 2007. Makes use of slave traders' own rich archives to track the process of human trafficking.

Parker, Geoffrey. *The Dutch Revolt*. 2nd ed. Ithaca, NY, 1989. The standard survey in English.

―――――. *Emperor: A New Life of Charles V*. Yale, 2019. An acclaimed new biography of the man who controlled large swathes of Europe and its American colonies.

Pascal, Blaise. *Pensées* (French-English edition). Ed. H. F. Stewart. London, 1950.

Pestana, Carla. *Protestant Empire: Religion and the Making of the British Atlantic World*. Philadelphia, 2010. How the Reformation helped to drive British imperial expansion.

Roberts, Michael. *Gustavus Adolphus and the Rise of Sweden*. London, 1973. Still the authoritative English-language account.

Russell, Conrad. *The Causes of the English Civil War*. Oxford, 1990. A penetrating and provocative analysis by one of the leading "revisionist" historians of the period.

Schmidt, Benjamin. *Innocence Abroad: The Dutch Imagination and the New World, 1570–1670*. Cambridge, 2006. A cultural history of Europeans' encounter with the Americas that highlights the perspective and experience of Dutch merchants, colonists, and artists.

Strum, Daniel. *The Sugar Trade: Brazil, Portugal, and the Netherlands (1595–1630)*. Translated by Colin Foulkes, Roopanjali Roy, and H. Sabrina Gledhill. Stanford, CA, 2013. A close examination of the merchants, seafarers, and slaves who drove the economy of the Atlantic world.

CHAPTER 15

Beik, William. *A Social and Cultural History of Early Modern France*. Cambridge, 2009. A broad synthesis of French history from the end of the Middle Ages to the French Revolution, by one of the world's foremost authorities on absolutism.

Berlin, Ira. *Many Thousands Gone: The First Two Centuries of Slavery in North America*. Cambridge, MA, 1998. Award-winning account of the evolution of Black society in America, emphasizing the contributions of enslaved peoples to the building of the American nation.

Clark, Christopher. *Iron Kingdom: The Rise and Downfall of Prussia, 1600–1947*. Cambridge, MA, 2009. A definitive account of Prussian history over nearly four centuries.

Dubois, Laurent and Julius S. Scott. *Origins of the Black Atlantic: Rewriting Histories*. New York, 2010. Field-changing collection of essays on the central place of African peoples in the creation of the culture and economy of the Atlantic world.

Jones, Colin. *The Great Nation: France From Louis XV to Napoleon*. New York, 2002. An excellent and readable scholarly account that argues that the France of Louis XV in the eighteenth century was even more dominant than the kingdom of Louis XIV in the preceding century.

Kishlansky, Mark A. *A Monarchy Transformed: Britain, 1603–1714*. London, 1996. An excellent survey that takes seriously its claim to be a "British" rather than merely an "English" history.

Lewis, William Roger, gen. ed. *The Oxford History of the British Empire*. Vol. I: *The Origins of Empire: British Overseas Enterprise to the Close of the Seventeenth Century*, ed. Nicholas Canny. Vol. II: *The Eighteenth Century*, ed. Peter J. Marshall. Oxford and New York, 1998. A definitive, multiauthor account.

Monod, Paul K. *The Power of Kings: Monarchy and Religion in Europe, 1589–1715*. New Haven, 1999. A study of the seventeenth century's declining confidence in the divinity of kings.

Page Moch, Leslie. *Moving Europeans: Migration in Western Europe since 1650*. Bloomington, Indiana, 2003.

Patterson, Orlando. *Slavery and Social Death: A Comparative Study*. Cambridge, MA, 1982. Transformative work of comparative history, examining the condition of slavery in dozens of societies in the ancient, medieval, and modern world.

Quataert, Donald. *The Ottoman Empire, 1700–1822*. Cambridge and New York, 2000. Well balanced and intended to be read by students.

Riasanovsky, Nicholas V., and Steinberg, Mark D. *A History of Russia*. 7th ed. Oxford and New York, 2005. Far and away the best single-volume textbook on Russian history: balanced, comprehensive, and intelligent, with full bibliographies.

Smallwood, Stephanie. *Saltwater Slavery: A Middle Passage from Africa to American Diaspora*. Cambridge, MA, 2007. Innovative book that traces the slave system from Africa, through horrors of the Middle Passage to the history of the African American diaspora, emphasizing the experience of the men and women who struggled against the forces that sought to redefine them as laboring commodities.

Snyder, Timothy. *The Reconstruction of Nations: Poland, Ukraine, Lithuania, Belarus, 1569–1999*. New Haven, 2004. Essential account of nation building and state collapse in eastern Europe with significant relevance to the region's contemporary situation.

Thomas, Hugh. *The Slave Trade: The History of the Atlantic Slave Trade, 1440–1870*. London and New York, 1997. A survey notable for its breadth and depth of coverage and for its attractive prose style.

Tracy, James D. *The Rise of Merchant Empires: Long-Distance Trade in the Early Modern World, 1350–1750*. Cambridge and New York, 1990. Important collection of essays by leading authorities.

White, Richard. *The Middle Ground: Indians, Empires and Republics in the Great Lakes Region, 1650–1815*. Cambridge, 1991. A path-breaking account of interactions between Europeans and Native Americans during the colonial period.

CHAPTER 16

Biagioli, Mario. *Galileo, Courtier*. Chicago, 1993. Emphasizes the importance of patronage and court politics in Galileo's science and career.

Cohen, I. B. *The Birth of a New Physics*. New York, 1985. Emphasizes the mathematical nature of the revolution; unmatched at making the mathematics understandable.

Daston, Lorraine, and Elizabeth Lunbeck, eds. *Histories of Scientific Observation*. Chicago, IL, 2011. Field-defining collection of essays on the history of scientific observation from the seventeenth to the twentieth centuries.

Daston, Lorraine. *Wonders and the Order of Nature, 1150–1750*. Cambridge, MA, 2001. Erudite, sweeping account of the history of science in the early modern period, emphasizing the natural philosopher's awe and wonder at the marvelous, the unfamiliar, and the counterintuitive.

Dear, Peter. *Revolutionizing the Sciences: European Knowledge and Its Ambitions, 1500–1700*. Princeton, NJ, 2001. Among the best short histories.

Drake, Stillman. *Discoveries and Opinions of Galileo*. Garden City, NY, 1957. The classic translation of Galileo's most important papers by his most admiring modern biographer.

Feingold, Mardechai. *The Newtonian Moment: Isaac Newton and the Making of Modern Culture*. New York, 2004. An engaging essay on the dissemination of Newton's thought, with excellent visual material.

Gaukroger, Stephen. *Descartes: An Intellectual Biography*. Oxford, 1995. Detailed and sympathetic study of the philosopher.

Gleick, James. *Isaac Newton*. New York, 2003. A vivid and well-documented brief biography.

Grafton, Anthony. *New Worlds, Ancient Texts: The Power of Tradition and the Shock of Discovery*. Cambridge, MA, 1992. Accessible essay by one of the leading scholars of early modern European thought.

Jacob, Margaret. *Scientific Culture and the Making of the Industrial West*. Oxford, 1997. A concise examination of the connections between developments in science and the Industrial Revolution.

Kuhn, Thomas. *The Structure of Scientific Revolutions*. Chicago, 1962. A classic and much-debated study of how scientific thought changes.

Pagden, Anthony. *European Encounters with the New World*. New Haven and London, 1993. Subtle and detailed on how European intellectuals thought about the lands they saw for the first time.

Rudwick, Martin J. S. *Earth's Deep History: How It Was Discovered and Why It Matters* (Chicago, 2014). A fascinating account of the origins of the geological sciences and awareness of the earth's long history before the advent of human civilizations.

Scheibinger, Londa. *The Mind Has No Sex? Women in the Origins of Modern Science*. Cambridge, MA, 1989. A lively and important recovery of the lost role played by women mathematicians and experimenters.

Shapin, Steven. *The Scientific Revolution*. Chicago, 1996. Engaging, accessible, and brief—organized thematically.

Shapin, Steven, and Simon Schaffer. *Leviathan and the Air Pump*. Princeton, NJ, 1985. A modern classic, on one of the most famous philosophical conflicts in seventeenth-century science.

Stephenson, Bruce. *The Music of the Heavens: Kepler's Harmonic Astronomy*. Princeton, NJ, 1994. An engaging and important explanation of Kepler's otherworldly perspective.

Thoren, Victor. *The Lord of Uranibourg: A Biography of Tycho Brahe*. Cambridge, 1990. A vivid reconstruction of the scientific revolution's most flamboyant astronomer.

Westfall, Richard. *The Construction of Modern Science*. Cambridge, 1977.

———. *Never at Rest: A Biography of Isaac Newton*. Cambridge, 1980. The standard work.

Wilson, Catherine. *The Invisible World: Early Modern Philosophy and the Invention of the Microscope*. Princeton, NJ, 1995. An important study of how the "microcosmic" world revealed by technology reshaped scientific philosophy and practice.

Zinsser, Judith P. *La Dame d'Esprit: A Biography of the Marquise Du Châtelet*. New York, 2006. An excellent cultural history. Issued in paperback as *Emilie du Châtelet: Daring Genius of the Enlightenment* (2007).

CHAPTER 17

Bade, Klaus J. *Migration in European History*. Oxford, 2003.

Baker, Keith. *Condorcet: From Natural Philosophy to Social Mathematics*. Chicago, 1975. An important reinterpretation of Condorcet as a social scientist.

Blum, Carol. *Rousseau and the Republic of Virtue: The Language of Politics in the French Revolution*. Ithaca, NY, and London, 1986. Fascinating account of how eighteenth-century readers interpreted Rousseau.

Buchan, James. *The Authentic Adam Smith: His Life and Ideas*. New York, 2006.

Calhoun, Craig, ed. *Habermas and the Public Sphere*. Cambridge, MA, 1992. Calhoun's introduction is a good starting point for Habermas's argument.

Chartier, Roger. *The Cultural Origins of the French Revolution.* Durham, NC, 1991. Looks at topics from religion to violence in everyday life and culture.

Chukwudi Eze, Emmanuel, ed. *Race and the Englightenment: A Reader.* Malden, MA, 1997. A compendium of writings on race by influential Englightenment thinkers, including Buffon, Hume, Kant, Herder, Blumenbach, Jefferson, and Hegel.

Darnton, Robert. *The Business of Enlightenment: A Publishing History of the* Encyclopédie, *1775–1800.* Cambridge, MA, 1979. Darnton's work on the Enlightenment offers a fascinating blend of intellectual, social, and economic history. See his other books as well: *The Literary Underground of the Old Regime* (Cambridge, MA, 1982); *The Great Cat Massacre and Other Episodes in French Cultural History* (New York, 1984); and *The Forbidden Best-Sellers of Revolutionary France* (New York and London, 1996).

Davis, David Brion. *The Problem of Slavery in Western Culture.* New York, 1988. A Pulitzer Prize–winning examination of a central issue as well as a brilliant analysis of different strands of Enlightenment thought.

Gay, Peter. *The Enlightenment: An Interpretation.* Vol. 1, *The Rise of Modern Paganism.* Vol. 2, *The Science of Freedom.* New York, 1966–1969. Combines an overview with an interpretation. Emphasizes the *philosophes'* sense of identification with the classical world and takes a generally positive view of their accomplishments. Includes extensive annotated bibliographies.

Goodman, Dena. *The Republic of Letters: A Cultural History of the French Enlightenment.* Ithaca, NY, 1994. Important in its attention to the role of literary women.

Hunt, Lynn, Margaret C. Jacob, and Wijnand Mijnhardt. *The Book That Changed Europe: Picart and Bernard's Religious Ceremonies of the World.* Cambridge, MA, 2010. Lively study of a book on global religions that came out of the fertile world of the Dutch Enlightenment in the eighteenth century.

Israel, Jonathan Irvine. *Radical Enlightenment: Philosophy and the Making of Modernity, 1650–1750.* New York, 2001. Massive and erudite, a fresh look at the international movement of ideas.

———. *Enlightenment Contested: Philosophy, Modernity, and the Emancipation of Man, 1670–1752.* New York, 2006. An encyclopedic account of Enlightenment debates, focusing on the contest between supporters and opponents of democratic ideals.

Morgan, Edmund S. *American Slavery, American Freedom: The Ordeal of Colonial Virginia.* New York, 1975. Influential account of the ways that Virginians, including George Washington, dealt with the contradiction between their embrace of slavery and their defense of freedom.

Outram, Dorinda. *The Enlightenment.* Cambridge, 1995. An excellent short introduction and a good example of new historical approaches.

Pagden, Anthony. *The Enlightenment: And Why It Still Matters.* New York, 2013. Spirited history of the Enlightenment and a defense of its continued relevance.

Porter, Roy. *The Creation of the Modern World: The Untold Story of the British Enlightenment.* New York, 2000.

Sapiro, Virginia. *A Vindication of Political Virtue: The Political Theory of Mary Wollstonecraft.* Chicago, 1992. A subtle and intelligent analysis for more advanced readers.

Schama, Simon. *Rough Crossings: Britain, the Slaves, and the American Revolution.* New York, 2006. A moving account of the experience of enslaved people in the American Revolution and the contested definitions of liberty associated with this moment.

Sewell, William H. *Capitalism and the Emergence of Civic Equality in Eighteenth-Century France.* Chicago, 2021. Powerful synthetic account of the ways that commercial capitalism made the idea of civic equality possible in the century before the French Revolution.

Shklar, Judith. *Men and Citizens: A Study of Rousseau's Social Theory.* London, 1969.

———. *Montesquieu.* Oxford, 1987. Shklar's studies are brilliant and accessible.

Taylor, Barbara. *Mary Wollstonecraft and the Feminist Imagination.* Cambridge and New York, 2003. Fascinating study that sets Wollstonecraft in the radical circles of eighteenth-century England.

Taylor, Barbara, and Sarah Knott, eds. *Women, Gender, and Enlightenment.* New York, 2007. Multiauthor collection examining the significance of sex, gender, and politics across a wide swath of the Enlightenment world, from Europe to the American colonies.

Valls, Andrew, ed. *Race and Racism in Modern Philosophy.* Ithaca, 2005. A collection of thoughtful essays on the salience of race for the evolution of the European philosophical canon, with particular attention to the Enlightenment tradition and its critics.

Venturi, Franco. *The End of the Old Regime in Europe, 1768–1776: The First Crisis.* Trans. R. Burr Litchfield. Princeton, NJ, 1989.

———. *The End of the Old Regime in Europe, 1776–1789.* Princeton, NJ, 1991. Both detailed and wide-ranging, particularly important on international developments.

Wolff, Larry. *Inventing Eastern Europe: The Map of Civilization on the Mind of the Enlightenment.* Stanford, CA, 1994. The place of eastern Europe in the imagination of Enlightenment thinkers interested in the origins and destiny of the civilizing process.

CHAPTER 18

Applewhite, Harriet B., and Darline G. Levy, eds. *Women and Politics in the Age of the Democratic Revolution.* Ann Arbor, MI, 1990. Essays on France, Britain, the Netherlands, and the United States.

Bell, David A. *The First Total War: Napoleon's Europe and the Birth of Warfare as We Know It*. Boston and New York, 2007. Lively and concise study of the "cataclysmic intensification" of warfare.

Blackburn, Robin. *The Overthrow of Colonial Slavery*. London and New York, 1988. A longer view of slavery and its abolition.

Blanning, T. C. W. *The French Revolutionary Wars, 1787–1802*. Oxford, 1996. On the revolution and war.

Blum, Carol. *Rousseau and the Republic of Virtue: The Language of Politics in the French Revolution*. Ithaca, NY, 1986. Excellent on how Rousseau was read by the revolutionaries.

Cobb, Richard. *The People's Armies*. New Haven, 1987. Brilliant and detailed analysis of the French popular militias.

Cole, Juan. *Napoleon's Egypt: Invading the Middle East*. New York, 2007. Readable history by a scholar familiar with sources in Arabic as well as European languages.

Desan, Suzanne. *The Family on Trial in Revolutionary France*. Berkeley, 2006. Persuasive study of the ways that women in France were able to take advantage of the revolution and defend their interests in debates about marriage, divorce, parenthood, and the care of children.

Desan, Suzanne, Lynn Hunt, and William Max Nelson, eds. *The French Revolution in Global Perspective*. Ithaca, NY, 2013. Multiauthor exploration of the French Revolution's global resonance.

Doyle, William. *Origins of the French Revolution*. New York, 1988. A revisionist historian surveys recent research on the political and social origins of the revolution and identifies a new consensus.

———. *Oxford History of the French Revolution*. New York, 1989.

Dubois, Laurent. *Avengers of the New World. The Story of the Haitian Revolution*. Cambridge, MA, 2004. Now the best and most accessible study.

———, and John D. Garrigus. *Slave Revolution in the Caribbean, 1789–1804: A Brief History with Documents*. New York, 2006. A particularly good collection.

Englund, Steven. *Napoleon: A Political Life*. Cambridge, MA, 2004. Prize-winning biography, both dramatic and insightful.

Forrest, Alan. *The French Revolution and the Poor*. New York, 1981. A moving and detailed social history of the poor, who fared little better under revolutionary governments than under the Old Regime.

Furet, François. *Revolutionary France, 1770–1880*. Trans. Antonia Nerill. Cambridge, MA, 1992. Overview by the leading revisionist.

Hunt, Lynn. *Politics, Culture, and Class in the French Revolution*. Berkeley, 1984. An analysis of the new culture of democracy and republicanism.

Hunt, Lynn, and Jack R. Censer. *Liberty, Equality, Fraternity: Exploring the French Revolution*. University Park, PA, 2001. A lively, accessible study by two leading historians of the revolution, with excellent documents and visual materials.

Jarvis, Katie. *Politics in the Marketplace: Work, Gender, and Citizenship in Revolutionary France*. New York, 2019. This compelling account of the radical market women of Paris during the French Revolutions combines an economist's understanding of markets with a political historian's awareness of the stakes of revolutionary change.

Landes, Joan B. *Women and the Public Sphere in the Age of the French Revolution*. Ithaca, NY, 1988. On gender and politics.

Lefebvre, Georges. *The Coming of the French Revolution*. Princeton, NJ, 1947. The classic Marxist analysis.

Lewis, Gwynne, and Colin Lucas. *Beyond the Terror: Essays in French Regional and Social History, 1794–1815*. New York, 1983. Shifts focus to the understudied period after the Terror.

O'Brien, Connor Cruise. *The Great Melody: A Thematic Biography of Edmund Burke*. Chicago, 1992. Passionate, partisan, and brilliant study of Burke's thoughts about Ireland, India, America, and France.

Palmer, R.R. and Isser Woloch. *Twelve Who Ruled: The Year of the Terror in the French Revolution*. Princeton, NJ, 2005. The terrific collective biography of the Committee of Public Safety, now updated.

Schama, Simon. *Citizens: A Chronicle of the French Revolution*. New York, 1989. Particularly good on art, culture, and politics.

Scott, Joan. *Only Paradoxes to Offer: French Feminists and the Rights of Man*. Cambridge, MA, 1997. A history of feminist engagement with a revolutionary ideology that promised universal liberties while simultaneously excluding women from citizenship.

Scott, Julius. *The Common Wind: Afro-American Currents in the Age of the Haitian Revolution*. London, 2018. Field-defining work on the ways that Afro-American peoples of the Atlantic World shaped and made manifest the contested definitions of liberty that were at play in the revolutions of the late 18th and early 19th century in the Americas, the Caribbean, and Europe.

Soboul, Albert. *The Sans-Culottes: The Popular Movement and Revolutionary Government, 1793–1794*. Garden City, NY, 1972. Dated, but a classic.

Sutherland, D. M. G. *France, 1789–1815: Revolution and Counterrevolution*. Oxford, 1986. An important synthesis of work on the revolution, especially in social history.

Tackett, Timothy. *The Coming of the Terror in the French Revolution*. Cambridge, 2015. A richly detailed explanation of why the French Revolution took such a violent turn.

Tocqueville, Alexis de. *The Old Regime and the French Revolution*. Garden City, NY, 1955. Originally written in 1856, this remains a provocative analysis of the revolution's legacy.

Trouillot, Michel Rolph. *Silencing the Past*. Boston, 1995. Essays on the Haitian revolution.

Woloch, Isser. *The New Regime: Transformations of the French Civic Order, 1789–1820*. New York, 1994. The fate of revolutionary civic reform.

CHAPTER 19

Bridenthal, Renate, Claudia Koonz, and Susan Stuard, eds. *Becoming Visible: Women in European History*. 2nd ed. Boston, 1987. Excellent, wide-ranging introduction.

Briggs, Asa. *Victorian Cities*. New York, 1963. A survey of British cities, stressing middle-class attitudes toward the new urban environment.

Chevalier, Louis. *Laboring Classes and Dangerous Classes during the First Half of the Nineteenth Century*. New York, 1973. An important, though controversial, account of crime, class, and middle-class perceptions of life in Paris.

Clark, Anna. *The Struggle for the Breeches: Gender and the Making of the British Working Class*. Berkeley, CA, 1997. Examines the process of class formation during the industrial revolution in Britain through the lens of gender.

Cott, Nancy. *The Bonds of Womanhood: "Woman's Sphere" in New England, 1780–1935*. New Haven and London, 1977. One of the most influential studies of the paradoxes of domesticity.

Davidoff, Leonore, and Catherine Hall. *Family Fortunes: Men and Women of the English Middle Class, 1780–1850*. Chicago, 1985. A brilliant and detailed study of the lives and ambitions of several English families.

Ferguson, Niall. "The European Economy, 1815–1914." In *The Nineteenth Century*, ed. T. C. W. Blanning. Oxford and New York, 2000. A very useful short essay.

Gay, Peter. *The Bourgeois Experience: Victoria to Freud*. New York, 1984. A multivolume, path-breaking study of middle-class life in all its dimensions.

———. *Schnitzler's Century: The Making of Middle-Class Culture, 1815–1914*. New York and London, 2002. A synthesis of some of the arguments presented in *The Bourgeois Experience*.

Harzig, Christiane, Dirk Hoerder, and Donna Gabaccia. *What Is Migration History?* Cambridge, UK, 2013.

Hellerstein, Erna, Leslie Hume, and Karen Offen, eds. *Victorian Women: A Documentary Account*. Stanford, CA, 1981. Good collection of documents, with excellent introductory essays.

Hobsbawm, Eric J. *The Age of Revolution, 1789–1848*. London, 1962.

———, and George Rudé. *Captain Swing: A Social History of the Great English Agricultural Uprising of 1830*. New York, 1975. Analyzes rural protest and politics.

Horn, Jeff. *The Path Not Taken: French Industrialization in the Age of Revolution, 1750–1830*. Cambridge, 2006. Argues that industrialization in France succeeded in ways that other historians have not appreciated, and was much more than a failed attempt to imitate the British model.

Jones, Eric. *The European Miracle: Environments, Economies and Geopolitics in the History of Europe and Asia*. Cambridge, 2003. Argues that the Industrial Revolution is best understood as a European phenomenon.

Kemp, Tom. *Industrialization in Nineteenth-Century Europe*. London, 1985. Good general study.

Kindelberger, Charles. *A Financial History of Western Europe*. London, 1984. Emphasis on finance.

Landes, David S. *The Unbound Prometheus: Technological Change and Industrial Development in Western Europe from 1750 to the Present*. London, 1969. Excellent and thorough on technological change and its social and economic context.

Livi-Bacci, Massimo. *A Short History of Migration*. Cambridge, UK, 2012.

McNeill, J. R. *Something New under the Sun: An Environmental History of the Twentieth-Century World*. New York and London, 2000. Short section on the nineteenth century.

Mokyr, Joel. *The Lever of Riches: Technological Creativity and Economic Progress*. New York, 1992. A world history, from antiquity through the nineteenth century.

O'Gráda, Cormac. *Black '47 and Beyond: The Great Irish Famine*. Princeton, NJ, 1999.

———. *The Great Irish Famine*. Cambridge, 1989. A fascinating and recent assessment of scholarship on the famine.

Osterhammel, Jürgen. *The Transformation of the World: A Global History of the Nineteenth Century*. Princeton, 2014. Pioneering global account of this revolutionary century of industrialization and commercial expansion, which convincingly charts the interconnections between the world's regions and the forces that drove historical change.

Pomeranz, Kenneth. *The Great Divergence: China, Europe, and the Making of the Modern World Economy*. Princeton, NJ, 2000. Path-breaking global history of the Industrial Revolution that argues that Europe was not so different from other parts of the world as scholars have previously thought.

Rendall, Jane. *The Origins of Modern Feminism: Women in Britain, France and the United States, 1780–1860*. New York, 1984. Helpful overview.

Rose, Sonya O. *Limited Livelihoods: Gender and Class in Nineteenth-Century England*. Berkeley, 1992. On the intersection of culture and economics.

Sabean, David Warren. *Property, Production, and Family Neckarhausen, 1700–1870*. New York, 1990. Brilliant and very detailed study of gender roles and family.

Sabel, Charles, and Jonathan Zeitlin. "Historical Alternatives to Mass Production." *Past and Present* 108 (August 1985): 133–76. On the many forms of modern industry.

Schivelbusch, Wolfgang. *Disenchanted Night: The Industrialization of Light in the Nineteenth Century*. Berkeley, 1988.

———. *The Railway Journey*. Berkeley, 1986. Schivelbusch's imaginative studies are among the best ways to understand how the transformations of the nineteenth century changed daily experiences.

Thompson, E. P. *The Making of the English Working Class*. London, 1963. Shows how the French and Industrial Revolutions fostered the growth of working-class consciousness. A brilliant and important work.

Tilly, Louise, and Joan Scott. *Women, Work and the Family*. New York, 1978. Now the classic study.

Valenze, Deborah. *The First Industrial Woman*. New York, 1995. Excellent and readable on industrialization and economic change in general.

Williams, Raymond. *Keywords: A Vocabulary of Culture and Society*. New York, 1976. Brilliant and indispensable for students of culture. Now updated as *New Keywords: A Revised Vocabulary of Culture and Society* (2005), ed. Tony Bennett, Lawrence Grossberg, and Meaghan Morris.

Zeldin, Theodore. *France, 1848–1945*. 2 vols. Oxford, 1973–1977. Eclectic and wide-ranging social history.

CHAPTER 20

Anderson, Benedict. *Imagined Communities: Reflections on the Origin and Spread of Nationalism*. London, 1983. The most influential recent study of the subject; highly recommended for further reading.

Barzun, Jacques. *Classic, Romantic, and Modern*. Chicago, 1943. An enduring and penetrating mid-twentieth-century defense of the Romantic sensibility by a humane and influential cultural historian.

Berlin, Isaiah. *Karl Marx: His Life and Environment*. 4th ed. New York, 1996. An excellent short account.

Blackbourn, David. *The Conquest of Nature: Water, Landscape and the Making of Modern Germany* (New York, 2007). A noted historian turns his attention to the importance of ecology and environmental change for the emergence of modern Germany.

Briggs, Asa. *The Age of Improvement, 1783–1867*. New York, 1979. A survey of England from 1780 to 1870, particularly strong on Victorian attitudes.

Colley, Linda. *Britons: Forging the Nation, 1707–1837*. New Haven, 1992. An important analysis of Britain's emerging national consciousness in the eighteenth and early nineteenth centuries.

Furet, François. *Revolutionary France, 1770–1880*. New York, 1970. An excellent and fresh overview by one of the preeminent historians of the revolution of 1789.

Gilbert, Sandra M., and Susan Gubar. *The Madwoman in the Attic: The Woman Writer and the Nineteenth-Century Literary Imagination*. New Haven and London, 1970. A study of the history of women writers and an examination of women writers as historians of their time.

Hannaford, Ivan. *Race: The History of an Idea in the West*. Washington, DC, 1996. Encyclopedic account of the evolution of racial thinking in the West since antiquity, with particular attention to the importance of race in Enlightenment thought and its connection to modern notions of national identity.

Kramer, Lloyd. *Nationalism: Political Cultures in Europe and America, 1775–1865*. London, 1998. Excellent recent overview.

Langer, William. *Political and Social Upheaval, 1832–1851*. New York, 1969. Long the standard and still the most comprehensive survey.

Laven, David, and Lucy Riall. *Napoleon's Legacy: Problems of Government in Restoration Europe*. London, 2002. A recent collection of essays.

Levinger, Matthew. *Enlightened Nationalism: The Transformation of Prussian Political Culture, 1806–1848*. New York, 2000. A nuanced study of Prussian conservatism, with implications for the rest of Europe.

Macfie, A. L. *Orientalism*. London, 2002. Introductory but very clear.

Merriman, John M., ed. *1830 in France*. New York, 1975. Seminal collection of essays examining the 1830 Revolution, its social origins, and its impact on the French nation.

Porter, Roy, and Mikulas Teich, eds. *Romanticism in National Context*. Cambridge, 1988.

Raeff, Marc. *The Decembrist Movement*. New York, 1966. A study of the Russian uprising with documents.

Sahlins, Peter. *Forest Rites: The War of the Demoiselles in Nineteenth-Century France*. Cambridge, MA, 1994. A fascinating study of relations among peasant communities, the forests, and the state.

Said, Edward W. *Orientalism*. New York, 1979. A brilliant and biting study of the imaginative hold of the Orient on European intellectuals.

Saville, John. *1848: The British State and the Chartist Movement*. New York, 1987. A detailed account of the movement's limited successes and ultimate failure.

Schroeder, Paul. *The Transformation of European Politics, 1763–1848*. Oxford and New York, 1994. For those interested in international relations and diplomacy; massively researched and a fresh look at the period. Especially good on the Congress of Vienna.

Sewell, William H. *Work and Revolution in France: The Language of Labor from the Old Regime to 1848*. Cambridge, 1980. A very influential study of French radicalism and its larger implications.

Smith, Bonnie. *The Gender of History: Men, Women, and Historical Practice*. Cambridge, MA, 1998. On Romanticism and the historical imagination.

Sperber, Jonathan. *Karl Marx: A Nineteenth-Century Life*. New York, 2013. A detailed biography examining Marx's public and private engagements, setting him in the context of his time.

Stovall, Tyler. *White Freedom: The Racial History of an Idea*. Princeton, 2021. Original and path-breaking examination of European and North American liberalism, arguing that modern democratic nations have always linked their ideas about liberty to assumptions about race.

Wordsworth, Jonathan, Michael C. Jaye, and Robert Woof. *William Wordsworth and the Age of English Romanticism.* New Brunswick, NJ, 1987. Wide ranging and beautifully illustrated, a good picture of the age.

CHAPTER 21

Agulhon, Maurice. *The Republican Experiment, 1848–1852.* New York, 1983. A full treatment of the revolution in France.

Beales, Derek. *The Risorgimento and the Unification of Italy.* New York, 1971. Objective, concise survey of Italian unification.

Blackbourn, David. *The Long Nineteenth Century: A History of Germany, 1780–1918.* New York, 1998.

Blackbourn, David, and Geoff Eley. *The Peculiarities of German History: Bourgeois Society and Politics in Nineteenth-Century Germany.* Oxford, 1984. Critical essays on the course of German history during the age of national unification and after.

Blackburn, Robin. *The Overthrow of Colonial Slavery.* London, 1988. Brilliant and detailed overview of the social history of slavery and antislavery movements.

Brophy, James M. *Capitalism, Politics, and Railroads in Prussia, 1830–1870.* Columbus, OH, 1998. Important, clear, and helpful.

Coppa, Frank. *The Origins of the Italian Wars of Independence.* London, 1992. Lively narrative.

Craig, Gordon. *Germany, 1866–1945.* New York, 1978. An excellent and thorough synthesis.

Davis, David Brian. *Inhuman Bondage: The Rise and Fall of Slavery in the New World.* New York, 2006. As one reviewer aptly puts it, "A gracefully fashioned masterpiece."

Deak, Istvan. *The Lawful Revolution: Louis Kossuth and the Hungarians, 1848–1849.* New York, 1979. The best on the subject.

Eyck, Erich. *Bismarck and the German Empire.* 3rd ed. London, 1968. The best one-volume study of Bismarck.

Hamerow, Theodore S. *The Birth of a New Europe: State and Society in the Nineteenth Century.* Chapel Hill, NC, 1983. A discussion of political and social change, and their relationship to industrialization and the increase in state power.

———. *The Social Foundations of German Unification, 1858–1871.* 2 vols. Princeton, NJ, 1969–1972. Concentrates on economic factors that determined the solution to the unification question. An impressive synthesis.

Higonnet, Patrice. *Paris: Capital of the World.* London, 2002. Fascinating and imaginative study of Paris as "capital of the nineteenth century."

Hobsbawm, Eric J. *The Age of Capital, 1848–1875.* London, 1975. Among the best introductions.

———. *Nations and Nationalism since 1870: Programme, Myth, Reality.* 2nd ed. Cambridge, 1992. A clear, concise analysis of the historical and cultural manifestations of nationalism.

Hutchinson, John, and Anthony Smith, eds. *Nationalism.* New York, 1994. A collection of articles, not particularly historical, but with the merit of discussing non-European nationalisms.

Johnson, Susan. *Roaring Camp.* New York, 2000. A history of one mining camp in California and a microhistory of the larger forces changing the West and the world.

Kolchin, Peter. *Unfree Labor: American Slavery and Russian Serfdom.* Cambridge, MA, 1987. Pioneering comparative study.

Mack Smith, Denis. *Cavour and Garibaldi.* New York, 1968.

———. *The Making of Italy, 1796–1870.* New York, 1968. A narrative with documents.

McPherson, James. *Battle Cry of Freedom: The Civil War Era.* New York, 1988. Universally acclaimed and prize-winning book on the politics of slavery and the conflicts entailed in nation building in the mid-nineteenth-century United States.

Pflanze, Otto. *Bismarck and the Development of Germany.* 2nd ed. 3 vols. Princeton, NJ, 1990. Extremely detailed analysis of Bismarck's aims and policies.

Pinkney, David. *Napoleon III and the Rebuilding of Paris.* Princeton, NJ, 1972. An interesting account of the creation of modern Paris during the Second Empire.

Robertson, Priscilla. *Revolutions of 1848: A Social History.* Princeton, NJ, 1952. Old-fashioned narrative, but very readable.

Sammons, Jeffrey L. *Heinrich Heine: A Modern Biography.* Princeton, NJ, 1979. An excellent historical biography as well as a study of culture and politics.

Saunt, Claudio. *Unworthy Republic: The Dispossession of Native Americans and the Road to Indian Territory.* New York, 2020. Powerful and widely praised account of the deportation of Native American peoples from the southeastern United States in the nineteenth century.

Scott, Rebecca J. *Degrees of Freedom: Louisiana and Cuba after Slavery.* Cambridge, MA, 2008. Brings the lives of slaves and their owners to life during the era of emancipation in a comparative history that places the southern United States in the context of the Atlantic world.

Sheehan, James J. *German Liberalism in the Nineteenth Century.* Chicago, 1978. Fresh and important synthesis.

Snyder, Timothy. *The Reconstruction of Nations: Poland, Ukraine, Lithuania, Belarus.* New Haven, 2003. An indispensable account of the emergence of national cultures and nation-states in central and eastern Europe from the early modern period to the present.

Sperber, Jonathan. *The European Revolutions, 1848–1851.* Cambridge, 2005. An excellent synthesis and the best one-volume treatment of the 1848 revolutions, describing the reasons for their failure.

_____. *Rhineland Radicals: The Democratic Movement and the Revolution of 1848–1849*. Princeton, NJ, 1993. A detailed study of Germany by the author of an overview of the revolutions of 1848.

Stearns, Peter N. *1848: The Revolutionary Tide in Europe*. New York, 1974. Stresses the social background of the revolutions.

Zeldin, Theodore. *The Political System of Napoleon III*. New York, 1958. Compact and readable, by one of the major scholars of the period.

CHAPTER 22

Achebe, Chinua. *Things Fall Apart*. Expanded edition with notes. Portsmouth, NH, 1996. An annotated edition of the now classic novel about colonial Africa.

Adas, Michael. *Machines as the Measure of Man: Science, Technology, and Ideologies of Western Dominance*. Ithaca, NY, and London, 1989. An important study of Europeans' changing perceptions of themselves and others during the period of industrialization.

Bayly, C. A. *Indian Society and the Making of the British Empire*. Cambridge, 1988. A good introduction, and one that bridges eighteenth- and nineteenth-century imperialisms.

Burbank, Jane, and Frederick Cooper. *Empires in World History: Power and the Politics of Difference*. Princeton, NJ, 2010. Powerful synthesis that sets European empires in the broader context of world history.

Burton, Antoinette. *Burdens of History: British Feminists, Indian Women, and Imperial Culture, 1865–1915*. Chapel Hill, NC, 1994. On the ways in which women and feminists came to support British imperialism.

Cain, P. J., and A. G. Hopkins. *British Imperialism, 1688–2000*. London, 2002. One of the most influential studies. Excellent overview and exceptionally good on economics.

Chakrabarty, Dipesh. *Provincializing Europe: Postcolonial Thought and Historical Difference*. Princeton, NJ, 2000. Sophisticated theoretical challenge to European narratives of social and political progress.

Clancy Smith, Julia, and Frances Gouda. *Domesticating the Empire: Race, Gender, and Family Life in French and Dutch Colonialism*. Charlottesville, VA, and London, 1998. A particularly good collection of essays that both breaks new historical ground and is accessible to nonspecialists. Essays cover daily life and private life in new colonial cultures.

Cohn, Bernard S. *Colonialism and Its Forms of Knowledge*. Princeton, NJ, 1996. Argues that new forms of cultural knowledge were essential to the project of British imperialism in India.

Conklin, Alice. *A Mission to Civilize: The Republican Idea of Empire in France and West Africa, 1895–1930*. Stanford, CA, 1997. One of the best studies of how the French reconciled imperialism with their vision of the Republic.

Cooper, Frederick. *Colonialism in Question: Theory, Knowledge, History*. Berkeley, 2005. Crucial collection of path-breaking essays on the history of colonialism.

Darwin, John. *After Tamerlane: The Rise and Fall of Global Empires*. New York, 2008. A comprehensive global account of the phenomenon of empire and empire building that begins with the Mongol conquests and takes the story up to the present.

_____. *The Empire Project: The Rise and Fall of the British World System*. Cambridge, 2009.

Elkins, Caroline. *Legacy of Violence: A History of the British Empire*. New York, 2022. Definitive synthesis of British imperial history in the nineteenth and twentieth centuries.

Fredrickson, George M. *Racism: A Short History*. Princeton, 2002. Concise account emphasizing the difference between earlier religious conceptions of racial difference and modern notions of white supremacy and antisemitism.

Goody, Jack. *Islam in Europe*. Cambridge, 2004. A broad overview of the different ways in which Islam and Muslims helped to shape European history.

Headrick, Daniel R. *The Tools of Empire: Technology and European Imperialism in the Nineteenth Century*. Oxford, 1981. A study of the relationship between technological innovation and imperialism.

Hobsbawm, Eric. *The Age of Empire, 1875–1914*. New York, 1987. Surveys the European scene at a time of apparent stability and real decline.

Hochschild, Adam. *King Leopold's Ghost: A Story of Greed, Terror, and Heroism in Colonial Africa*. Boston, 1998. Reads like a great novel.

Hull, Isabell. *Absolute Destruction: Military Culture and the Practices of War in Imperial Germany*. Ithaca, NY, 2005. A study of the German military and its role in imperial expansion in Africa; argues that the experience was crucial in shaping this institution as it entered the twentieth century.

Lorcin, Patricia. *Imperial Identities: Stereotyping, Prejudice and Race in Colonial Algeria*. New York, 1999.

Louis, William Roger. *The Oxford History of the British Empire*. 5 vols. Oxford, 1998. Excellent and wide-ranging collection of the latest research.

Manning, Patrick. *Navigating World History*. New York, 2003.

Metcalf, Thomas. *Ideologies of the Raj*. Cambridge, 1995.

Prochaska, David. *Making Algeria French: Colonialism in Bône, 1870–1920*. Cambridge, 1990. One of the few social histories in English of European settlement in Algeria.

Robinson, Ronald, and J. Gallagher. *Africa and the Victorians: The Official Mind of Imperialism*. London, 1961. A classic.

Said, Edward. *Culture and Imperialism*. New York, 1993. A collection of brilliant, sometimes controversial, essays.

Sangari, Kumkum, and Sudesh Vaid. *Recasting Women: Essays in Colonial History*. New Delhi, 1989. A collection of essays on women in India.

Schneer, Jonathan. *London 1900: The Imperial Metropolis.* New Haven, 1999. Excellent study of the empire—and opposition to empire—in the metropole.

Sonn, Tamara. *Islam: History, Religion, and Politics.* Chichester, 2016. A brief but helpful introduction to the history of Islam in its broad social and political context.

Spence, Jonathan. *The Search for Modern China.* New York, 1990. An excellent and readable introduction to modern Chinese history.

CHAPTER 23

Berghahn, Volker. *Imperial Germany, 1871–1914: Economy, Society, Culture, and Politics.* Providence, RI, 1994. Inclusive history that seeks to go beyond standard political accounts.

Berlanstein, Lenard. *The Working People of Paris, 1871–1914.* Baltimore, 1984. A social history of the workplace and its impact on working men and women.

Blackbourn, David. *The Long Nineteenth Century: A History of Germany, 1780–1918.* New York, 1998. Among the best surveys of German society and politics.

Bowler, Peter J. *Evolution: The History of an Idea.* Berkeley, 1984. One of this author's several excellent studies of the evolution of Darwinism.

Burns, Michael. *Dreyfus: A Family Affair.* New York, 1992. Follows the story of Dreyfus through the next generations.

Clancy-Smith, Julia. *Mediterraneans: North Africa and Europe in an Age of Migration, c. 1800–1900.* Berkeley, 2011. Students interested in contemporary debates about migration in Europe will find helpful historical context in this rich study of population movements in the Mediterranean world during the nineteenth century.

Clark, T. J. *The Painting of Modern Life: Paris in the Art of Manet and His Followers.* New York, 1985. Argues for seeing impressionism as a critique of French society.

Crosby, Alfred. *Ecological Imperialism: The Biological Expansion of Europe, 900–1900.* Cambridge, 1986. A foremost environmental historian follows up on his earlier work on the Columbian exchange with a broad-reaching account of the movement of people, animals, and plants from Europe to other parts of the globe across the last millennium.

Cox Richardson, Heather. *The Death of Reconstruction: Race, Labor, and Politics in the Post-Civil War North, 1865–1901.* Cambridge, MA, 2001. Influential account of the ways that the failure of Reconstruction after the Civil War transformed the situation of Black laborers and drove migration of formerly enslaved people to northern cities.

Engelstein, Laura. *Slavophile Empire: Imperial Russia's Illiberal Path.* Ithaca, NY, 2009. An examination of Russia's political culture before World War I, with an eye toward later evolution during the twentieth century.

Foner, Eric. *The Second Founding: How the Civil War and Reconstruction Remade the Constitution.* New York, 2019. Prize-winning book on the ways that the Civil War, Emancipation, and Reconstruction shaped notions of citizenship and racial exclusion in the United States.

Frank, Stephen. *Crime, Cultural Conflict, and Justice in Rural Russia, 1856–1914.* Berkeley, 1999. A revealing study of social relations from the ground up.

Gay, Peter. *The Bourgeois Experience: Victoria to Freud.* 5 vols. New York, 1984–2000. Imaginative, brilliant study of private life and middle-class culture.

————. *Freud: A Life of Our Time.* New York, 1988. Beautifully written and lucid about difficult concepts; now the best biography.

Harris, Ruth. *Dreyfus: Politics, Emotion, and the Scandal of the Century.* London, 2011. A reassessment of the politics of the Dreyfus affair, with an eye toward its resonance in French culture as a whole.

Herbert, Robert L. *Impressionism: Art, Leisure, and Parisian Society.* New Haven, 1988. An accessible and important study of the impressionists and the world they painted.

Hughes, H. Stuart. *Consciousness and Society.* New York, 1958. A classic study on late-nineteenth-century European thought.

Jones, Gareth Stedman. *Outcast London.* Oxford, 1971. Studies the breakdown in class relationships during the second half of the nineteenth century.

Joyce, Patrick. *Visions of the People: Industrial England and the Question of Class, 1848–1914.* New York, 1991. A social history of the workplace.

Kelly, Alfred. *The German Worker: Autobiographies from the Age of Industrialization.* Berkeley, 1987. Excerpts from workers' autobiographies provide fresh perspective on labor history.

Kern, Stephen. *The Culture of Time and Space.* Cambridge, MA, 1983. A cultural history of the late nineteenth century.

Lidtke, Vernon. *The Alternative Culture: Socialist Labor in Imperial Germany.* New York, 1985. A probing study of working-class culture.

Micale, Mark S. *Approaching Hysteria: Disease and Its Interpretations.* Princeton, NJ, 1995. Important study of the history of psychiatry before Freud.

Rupp, Leila J. *Worlds of Women: The Making of an International Women's Movement.* Princeton, NJ, 1997.

Roediger, David R. *The Wages of Whiteness: Race and the Making of the American Working Class.* New York, 1991. Influential account of the intersection of race and class in American history, arguing that racial identities have served both psychological as well as material interests.

Schivelbusch, Wolfgang. *Disenchanted Night: The Industrialization of Light in the Nineteenth Century.* Berkeley, 1995. Imaginative study of how electricity transformed everyday life.

Schorske, Carl E. *Fin-de-Siècle Vienna: Politics and Culture.* New York, 1980. Classic account of avant-garde art, music, and intellectual culture set against the background of mass politics in the Austrian capital.

Schwartz, Vanessa. *Spectacular Realities: Early Mass Culture in Fin-de-Siècle Paris*. Berkeley, 1998. Innovative approach to the emergence of mass culture in modern France.

Showalter, Elaine. *The Female Malady: Women, Madness, and English Culture, 1890–1980*. New York, 1985. Brilliant and readable on Darwin, Freud, gender, and the First World War.

Silverman, Deborah L. *Art Nouveau in Fin-de-Siècle France: Politics, Psychology, and Style*. Berkeley, CA, 1989. A study of the relationship between psychological and artistic change.

Smith, Bonnie. *Changing Lives: Women in European History since 1700*. New York, 1988. A useful overview of European women's history.

Stern, Fritz. *The Politics of Cultural Despair: A Study of the Rise of the Germanic Ideology*. Berkeley, 1974. Classic account of the rise of nationalist and populist politics in German-speaking lands of central Europe before World War I.

Tickner, Lisa. *The Spectacle of Women: Imagery of the Suffrage Campaign, 1907–14*. Chicago, 1988. A very engaging study of British suffragism.

Vital, David. *A People Apart: A Political History of the Jews in Europe, 1789–1939*. Oxford and New York, 1999. Comprehensive and extremely helpful.

Walkowitz, Judith. *City of Dreadful Delight: Narratives of Sexual Danger in Late-Victorian London*. Chicago, 1992. Cultural history of the English capital at the end of the nineteenth century.

Weber, Eugen. *Peasants into Frenchmen: The Modernization of Rural France, 1870–1914*. Stanford, CA, 1976. A study of how France's peasantry was assimilated into the Third Republic.

Wehler, Hans-Ulrich. *The German Empire, 1871–1918*. Dover, 1997. Standard account by a respected German historian.

CHAPTER 24

Aksakal, Mustapha. *The Ottoman Road to War in 1914: The Ottoman Empire and the First World War*. Cambridge, 2009. A compelling look at Ottoman involvement in the First World War.

Bourke, Joanna. *Dismembering the Male: Men's Bodies, Britain, and the Great War*. Chicago, 1996. A cultural history of the war's effects on male bodies and codes of masculinity.

Chickering, Roger. *Imperial Germany and the Great War, 1914–1918*. New York, 1998. An excellent synthesis.

Clark, Christopher. *The Sleepwalkers: How Europe Went to War in 1914*. New York, 2013. Comprehensive reassessment of the war's origins.

Eksteins, Modris. *Rites of Spring: The Great War and the Birth of the Modern Age*. New York, 1989. Fascinating, though impressionistic, on war, art, and culture.

Ferguson, Niall. *The Pity of War*. London, 1998. A fresh look at the war, including strategic issues, international relations, and economics.

Ferro, Marc. *The Great War, 1914–1918*. London, 1973. Very concise overview.

Figes, Orlando. *A People's Tragedy: A History of the Russian Revolution*. New York, 1997. Excellent, detailed narrative.

Fischer, Fritz. *War of Illusions*. New York, 1975. Deals with Germany within the context of internal social and economic trends.

Fitzpatrick, Sheila. *The Russian Revolution, 1917–1932*. New York and Oxford, 1982. Concise overview.

Fussell, Paul. *The Great War and Modern Memory*. New York, 1975. A brilliant examination of British intellectuals' attitudes toward the war.

Hynes, Samuel. *A War Imagined: The First World War and English Culture*. New York, 1991. The war as perceived on the home front.

Jelavich, Barbara. *History of the Balkans: Twentieth Century*. New York, 1983. Useful for an understanding of the continuing conflict in eastern Europe.

Joll, James. *The Origins of the First World War*. London, 1984. Comprehensive and very useful.

Keegan, John. *The First World War*. London, 1998. The best overall military history.

Kershaw, Ian. *To Hell and Back: Europe 1914–1949*. New York, 2015. A thorough introduction to the history of Europe during the First and Second World Wars, by the world's foremost biographer of Adolf Hitler.

Macmillan, Margaret, and Richard Holbrooke. *Paris 1919: Six Months That Changed the World*. New York, 2003. Fascinating fresh look at the peace conference.

Mazower, Mark. *Dark Continent: Europe's Twentieth Century*. New York, 1999. An excellent survey, particularly good on nations and minorities in the Balkans and eastern Europe.

Rabinowitch, Alexander. *The Bolsheviks Come to Power*. New York, 1976. A well-researched and carefully documented account.

Roberts, Mary Louise. *Civilization without Sexes: Reconstructing Gender in Postwar France, 1917–1927*. Chicago, 1994. A prize-winning study of the issues raised by the "new woman."

Schivelbusch, Wolfgang. *The Culture of Defeat: On National Trauma, Mourning, and Recovery*. New York, 2001. Fascinating if impressionistic comparative study.

Smith, Leonard. *Between Mutiny and Obedience: The Case of the French Fifth Infantry Division during World War I*. Princeton, NJ, 1994. An account of mutiny and the reasons behind it.

Stevenson, David. *Cataclysm: The First World War as Political Tragedy*. New York, 2003. Detailed and comprehensive, now one of the best single-volume studies.

Stites, Richard. *Revolutionary Dreams: Utopian Visions and Experimental Life in the Russian Revolution*. New York, 1989. The influence of utopian thinking on the revolution.

Suny, Ronald Grigor, Fatma Muge Gocek, and Norman Naimark, eds. *A Question of Genocide: Armenians and Turks at the End of the Ottoman Empire*. Oxford, 2011. Multiauthor work offering a comprehensive summary of research on the Armenian genocide.

Williams, John. *The Home Fronts: Britain, France and Germany, 1914–1918*. London, 1972. A survey of life away from the battlefield and the impact of the war on domestic life.

Winter, Jay. *Sites of Memory, Sites of Mourning: The Great War in European Cultural History*. Cambridge, 1998. An essential reference on the legacy of World War I in European cultural history.

Winter, Jay, and Jean-Louis Robert. *Capital Cities at War: Paris, London, Berlin, 1914–1919*. Cambridge, 1997 (vol. 1), 2007 (vol. 2). Multiauthor work on the demographic, social, and cultural effects of the war on civilian populations of three European capitals.

CHAPTER 25

Bosworth, R. J. B. *Mussolini's Italy: Life under the Fascist Dictatorship, 1915–1945*. New York, 2007. Comprehensive account of "everyday" fascism in Italy.

Conquest, Robert. *The Great Terror: A Reassessment*. New York, 1990. One of the first histories of the Terror; should be read in conjunction with others in this list.

Crew, David F., ed. *Nazism and German Society, 1933–1945*. New York, 1994. An excellent and accessible collection of essays.

de Grazia, Victoria. *How Fascism Ruled Women: Italy, 1922–1945*. Berkeley, 1993. The contradictions between fascism's vision of modernity and its commitment to patriarchal institutions, seen from the point of view of Italian women.

Figes, Orlando. *Peasant Russia, Civil War: The Volga Countryside in Revolution, 1917–1921*. Oxford, 1989. Detailed and sophisticated but readable. Study of the region from the eve of the revolution through the civil war.

Fitzpatrick, Shelia. *Everyday Stalinism: Ordinary Life in Extraordinary Times; Soviet Russia in the 1930s*. Oxford and New York, 1999. Gripping on how ordinary people dealt with famine, repression, and chaos.

Friedlander, Saul. *Nazi Germany and the Jews: The Years of Persecution. 1933–1939*. Rev. ed. New York, 2007. Excellent; the first of a two-volume study.

Gay, Peter. *Weimar Culture*. New York, 1968. Concise and elegant overview.

Getty, J. Arch, and Oleg V. Naumov. *The Road to Terror: Stalin and the Self-Destruction of the Bolsheviks, 1932–1939*. New Haven, 1999. Combines analysis with documents made public for the first time.

Goldman, Wendy Z. *Women, the State, and Revolution: Soviet Family Policy and Social Life, 1917–1936*. New York, 1993. On the Bolshevik attempts to transform gender and family.

Kershaw, Ian. *Hitler*. 2 vols: *1889–1936 Hubris*, New York, 1999; *1936–1945: Nemesis*, New York, 2001. The best biography: insightful about politics, culture, and society as well as the man.

———. *The Hitler Myth: Image and Reality in the Third Reich*. New York, 1987. Brilliant study of how Nazi propagandists sold the myth of the Fuhrer and why many Germans bought it.

Klemperer, Victor. *I Will Bear Witness: A Diary of the Nazi Years, 1933–1941*. New York, 1999.

———. *I Will Bear Witness: A Diary of the Nazi Years, 1942–1945*. New York, 2001. Certain to be a classic.

Kotkin, Stephen. *Stalin*. Vol. 1, *Paradoxes of Power, 1878–1928*. New York, 2015. The first volume of a new comprehensive biography of the Russian leader, based on deep familiarity with archival sources.

Lewin, Moshe. *The Making of the Soviet System: Essays in the Social History of Interwar Russia*. New York, 1985. One of the best to offer a view from below.

Maier, Charles. *Recasting Bourgeois Europe*. Princeton, NJ, 1975. Now classic account of the political and social adjustments made between state and society during the interwar years throughout Europe.

McDermott, Kevin. *Stalin: Revolutionary in an Era of War*. Basingstoke, UK, and New York, 2006. Useful, short, and recent.

Montefior, Simon Sebag. *Stalin: The Court of the Red Tsar*. London, 2004. On the relations among the top Bolsheviks, an interesting personal portrait. Takes you inside the inner circle.

Orwell, George. *The Road to Wigan Pier*. London, 1937. On unemployment and life in the coal-mining districts of England, by one of the great British writers of the twentieth century.

———. *Homage to Catalonia*. London, 1938. A firsthand account of the Spanish Civil War.

Paxton, Robert O. *The Anatomy of Fascism*. New York, 2004. Excellent introduction to a complex subject by a foremost historian of twentieth century Europe.

Payne, Stanley G. *A History of Fascism, 1914–1945*. Madison, WI, 1996. Thorough account of the origins and evolution of fascism in Europe through the end of World War II.

Peukert, Detlev. *The Weimar Republic*. New York, 1993. Useful and concise history of Weimar by a respected German historian of the period.

Schumpeter, Joseph A. *Capitalism, Socialism and Democracy*. New York, 1942. Classic account of twentieth-century capitalism's "creative destruction"—by an influential Austrian economist.

Suny, Ronald Grigor. *The Revenge of the Past: Nationalism, Revolution, and the Collapse of the Soviet Union*. Stanford, CA, 1993. Path-breaking study of the issues of nationalism and ethnicity from the revolution to the end of the Soviet Union.

Tooze, Adam. *The Deluge: The Great War, America, and the Remaking of the Global Order, 1916–1931*. New York, 2014. Original argument about the ways that the United

States' entry into the First World War dramatically changed the calculations of European powers during the years that culminated in the Great Depression of the 1930s.

Tucker, Robert C. *Stalin as Revolutionary, 1879–1929*. New York, 1973.

———. *Stalin in Power: The Revolution from Above, 1928–1941*. New York, 1990. With *Stalin as Revolutionary*, emphasizes Stalin's purpose and method and sets him in the tradition of Russian dictators.

Weitz, Eric D. *Weimar Germany: Promise and Tragedy*. Princeton, NJ, 2009. A valuable and thorough account that ties together the complex connections between Weimar culture and politics in this transformational period.

Worster, Donald. *The Dust Bowl: The Southern Plains in the 1930s*. Oxford, 1979, 2004. A pioneering work of U.S. environmental history that changed the way people understood the history of the Depression and economic change in United States.

CHAPTER 26

The U.S. Holocaust Memorial Museum has an extraordinary collection of articles, photographs, and maps. See www. ushmm.org.

Bartov, Omer. *Hitler's Army: Soldiers, Nazis, and War in the Third Reich*. New York, 1991. A study of the radicalization of the German army on the Russian front.

Braithwaite, Rodric. *Moscow 1941: A City and Its People at War*. London, 2006. Readable account of one of the turning points of the war.

Browning, Christopher R. *The Path to Genocide: Essays on Launching the Final Solution*. Cambridge, 1992. Discusses changing interpretations and case studies. See also this author's *Ordinary Men: Reserve Police Battalion 101 and the Final Solution in Poland*.

Burrin, Philippe. *France under the Germans: Collaboration and Compromise*. New York, 1996. Comprehensive on occupation and collaboration.

Cesarani, David. *The Final Solution: The Fate of the Jews, 1933–1949*. New York, 2016. A powerful synthesis of decades of research that challenges understandings of the "efficiency" of the Nazi state and argues that the genocide was produced by a muddled and chaotic regime that lacked basic coherence.

Davies, Norman. *Heart of Europe: The Past in Poland's Present*. Oxford, 2001. Revised edition of a classic account of Poland's place in European history, with special attention to the second half of the twentieth century.

Dawidowicz, Lucy S. *The War against the Jews, 1933–1945*. New York, 1975. A full account of the Holocaust.

Djilas, Milovan. *Wartime*. New York, 1977. An insider's account of the partisans' fighting in Yugoslavia and a good example of civil war within the war.

Fritzsche, Peter. *Life and Death in the Third Reich*. Cambridge, MA, 2009. A compelling account of the appeal of Nazi ideology and the extent to which it was embraced by ordinary people in Germany.

Gellately, Robert, and Ben Kiernan, eds. *The Specter of Genocide: Mass Murder in Historical Perspective*. New York, 2003. A particularly thoughtful collection of essays.

Graham, Helen. *The Spanish Civil War: A Very Short Introduction*. Oxford and New York, 2005. Excellent and very concise, based on the author's new interpretation in the more detailed *The Spanish Republic at War, 1936–1939*. Cambridge, 2002.

Hilberg, Raul. *The Destruction of the European Jews*. 2nd ed. 3 vols. New York, 1985. An excellent treatment of the Holocaust, its origins, and its consequences.

Hitchcock, William I. *The Bitter Road to Freedom: A New History of the Liberation of Europe*. New York, 2008. The story of Europe's liberation from Hitler's control, seen from the point of view of civilian populations.

Kedward, Roderick. *In Search of the Maquis: Rural Resistance in Southern France, 1942–1944*. Oxford, 1993. An engaging study of French guerrilla resistance.

Keegan, John. *The Second World War*. New York, 1990. By one of the great military historians of our time.

Krach, Helge. *Quantum Generations: A History of Physics in the Twentieth Century*. Princeton, 1999. Knowledgeable and thorough account of the scientific breakthroughs that brought about modern physics, written in a form that will satisfy both the demands of the specialist and the needs of a general reader.

Marrus, Michael R. *The Holocaust in History*. Hanover, NH, 1987. Thoughtful analysis of central issues.

Mawdsley, Evan. *Thunder in the East: The Nazi-Soviet War, 1941–1945*. New York, 2005.

Megargee, Geoffrey. *War of Annihilation: Combat and Genocide on the Eastern Front, 1941*. Lanham, MD, 2006. Represents some of the new historical work on the Eastern Front.

Merridale, Catherine. *Ivan's War: Life and Death in the Red Army, 1939–1945*. New York, 2006. Raises many questions and insights.

Michel, Henri. *The Shadow War: The European Resistance, 1939–1945*. New York, 1972. Compelling reading.

Milward, Alan S. *War, Economy, and Society, 1939–1945*. Berkeley, 1977. On the economic impact of the war and the strategic impact of the economy.

Overy, Richard. *Russia's War*. New York, 1998. A very readable account that accompanies the PBS series of the same title.

———. *Why the Allies Won*. New York, 1995. Excellent analysis; succinct.

Paxton, Robert O. *Vichy France: Old Guard and New Order, 1940–1944.* New York, 1982. Brilliant on collaboration and Vichy's National Revolution.

Roberts, Mary Louise. *What Soldiers Do: Sex and the American GI in World War II France.* Chicago, 2013. Critical reappraisal of how sex between GIs and civilians became an issue for French and U.S. military personnel after the D-Day invasion.

Snyder, Timothy. *Bloodlands: Europe between Hitler and Stalin.* New York, 2010. Thorough and penetrating account of the methods and motives of Hitler's and Stalin's regimes.

Stoff, Michael B. *The Manhattan Project: A Documentary Introduction to the Atomic Age.* New York, 1991. Political, scientific, and historical; excellent documents and commentary.

Tooze, Adam. *The Wages of Destruction: The Making and Breaking of the Nazi Economy.* New York, 2006. Persuasive explanation of the ways that decisions about the German economy drove the radicalization of Nazi policy, contributing to the catastrophic decision to invade the Soviet Union and ultimately, the Holocaust.

Weinberg, Gerhard L. *A World at Arms: A Global History of World War II.* Cambridge, 2005. Second edition of a comprehensive and respected global account of the Second World War.

Wilkinson, James D. *The Intellectual Resistance in Europe.* Cambridge, MA, 1981. A comparative study of the movement throughout Europe.

CHAPTER 27

Carter, Erica. *How German Is She? Postwar West German Reconstruction and the Consuming Woman.* Ann Arbor, MI, 1997. A thoughtful examination of gender and the reconstruction of the family in West Germany during the 1950s.

Clayton, Anthony. *The Wars of French Decolonization.* London, 1994. Good survey.

Connelly, Matthew. *A Diplomatic Revolution: Algeria's Fight for Independence and the Origins of the Post–Cold War Era.* New York and Oxford, 2003. An international history.

Cooper, Frederick. *Citizenship between Empire and Nation: Remaking France and French Africa, 1945–1960.* Broadly cast synthetic account of the many possibilities that were considered by African peoples as they sought independence from France in the decades after the Second World War.

Cooper, Frederick, and Ann Laura Stoler, eds. *Tensions of Empire: Colonial Cultures in a Bourgeois World.* Berkeley, CA, 1997. Collection of new essays, among the best.

Darwin, John. *Britain and Decolonization: The Retreat from Empire in the Postwar World.* New York, 1988. Best overall survey.

Deák, István, Jan T. Gross, and Tony Judt, eds. *The Politics of Retribution in Europe: World War II and Its Aftermath.* Princeton, NJ, 2000. Collection focusing on the attempt to come to terms with the Second World War in Eastern and Western Europe.

Farmer, Sarah. *Martyred Village: Commemorating the 1944 Massacre at Oradour-sur-Glane.* Berkeley, CA, 1999. Gripping story of French attempts to come to terms with collaboration and complicity in atrocities.

Jarausch, Konrad Hugo, ed. *Dictatorship as Experience: Towards a Socio-Cultural History of the GDR.* Trans. Eve Duffy. New York, 1999. Surveys recent research on the former East Germany.

Judt, Tony. *The Burden of Responsibility: Blum, Camus, and the French Twentieth Century.* Chicago and London, 1998. Also on French intellectuals.

————. *A Grand Illusion? An Essay on Europe.* New York, 1996. Short and brilliant.

————. *Past Imperfect: French Intellectuals, 1944–1956.* Berkeley, 1992. Very readable, on French intellectuals, who loomed large during this period.

————. *Postwar: A History of Europe since 1945.* London, 2005. Detailed, comprehensive, and groundbreaking, this single volume surpasses any other account of the entire postwar period.

Koven, Seth, and Sonya Michel. *Mothers of a New World: Maternalist Politics and the Origins of Welfare States.* New York, 1993. Excellent essays on the long history of welfare politics.

LaFeber, Walter. *America, Russia, and the Cold War.* New York, 1967. A classic, now in its ninth edition.

Leffler, Melvyn P. *A Preponderance of Power: National Security, the Truman Administration, and the Cold War.* Stanford, 1992. Solid political study.

Louis, William Roger. *The Ends of British Imperialism: The Scramble for Empire, Suez, and Decolonization.* London, 2006. Comprehensive and wide ranging.

Macey, David. *Frantz Fanon.* New York, 2000. Comprehensive recent biography.

Medvedev, Roy. *Khrushchev.* New York, 1983. A perceptive biography of the Soviet leader by a Soviet historian.

Milward, Alan S. *The Reconstruction of Western Europe, 1945–1951.* Berkeley, 1984. A good discussion of the "economic miracle."

Moeller, Robert G. *War Stories: The Search for a Usable Past in the Federal Republic of Germany.* Berkeley, 2001. Revealing analyses of postwar culture and politics.

Reynolds, David. *One World Divisible: A Global History Since 1945.* New York, 2000. Fresh approach, comprehensive, and very readable survey.

Rousso, Henri. *The Vichy Syndrome: History and Memory in France since 1944.* Cambridge, MA, 1991. First in a series of books by one of the preeminent French historians.

Schissler, Hanna, ed. *The Miracle Years: A Cultural History of West Germany, 1949–1968.* Princeton, NJ, 2001. The cultural effects of the "economic miracle."

Schneider, Peter. *The Wall Jumper: A Berlin Story.* Chicago, 1998. A fascinating novel about life in divided Berlin.

Shepard, Todd. *The Invention of Decolonization: The Algerian War and the Remaking of France.* Ithaca, NY, 2006. Excellent and original: a study of the deeply wrenching war's many ramifications.

Shipway, Martin. *Decolonization and Its Impact: A Comparative Approach to the End of the Colonial Empires.* Malden, MA, 2008. Accessible account emphasizing the unintended consequences of decolonization.

Stedman Jones, Daniel. *Masters of the Universe: Hayek, Friedman, and the Birth of Neoliberal Politics.* Princeton, 2012. A compelling history of the ideas behind the economic policies associated with Margaret Thatcher and Ronald Reagan in the twentieth century.

Trachtenberg, Mark. *A Constructed Peace: The Making of the European Settlement, 1945–1963.* Princeton, NJ, 1999. A detailed study of international relations that moves beyond the Cold War framework.

Tessler, Mark. *A History of the Israeli-Palestinian Conflict.* 2nd ed. Bloomington, 2009. Updated edition of the definitive account from the 1990s.

Westad, Odd Arne. *The Global Cold War.* New York, 2005. An international history that sees the roots of the world's present conflict in the history of the Cold War.

Wilder, Gary. *Freedom Time: Negritude, Decolonization, and the Future of the World.* Durham, NC, 2015. An intellectual history of decolonization told through the perspectives of Léopold Segnhor (Senegal) and Aimé Césaire (Martinique), who each sought a federal solution to the problem of European empires, reflecting critically on the consequences of national sovereignty for former European colonies.

Yergin, Daniel. *Shattered Peace: The Origins of the Cold War.* New York, 1977. Rev. ed., 1990. Dramatic and readable.

Young, Marilyn B. *The Vietnam Wars, 1945–1990.* New York, 1991. Excellent account of the different stages of the war and its repercussions.

CHAPTER 28

Alexander, Michelle. *The New Jim Crow: Mass Incarceration in the Age of Colorblindness.* New York, 2010. Influential account of the ways that policing and crime policy in the United States have served to perpetuate deep racial and economic divisions in American society.

Bailey, Beth. *From Front Porch to Back Seat: Courtship in Twentieth-Century America.* Baltimore, 1988. Good historical perspective on the sexual revolution.

Berman, Sheri. *Democracy and Dictatorship in Europe: From the Ancien Régime to the Present Day.* New York, 2019. Comprehensive historical overview of the conditions under which European democracies have succeeded—and failed—since the 18th century, with pointed relevance to the post–Cold War situation.

Beschloss, Michael, and Strobe Talbott. *At the Highest Levels: The Inside Story of the End of the Cold War.* Boston, 1993. An analysis of the relationship between presidents Gorbachev and George H. W. Bush and their determination to ignore hard-liners.

Brown, Archie. *The Gorbachev Factor.* Oxford and New York, 1996. One of the first serious studies of Gorbachev, by an Oxford scholar of politics.

Caute, David. *The Year of the Barricades: A Journey through 1968.* New York, 1988. A well-written global history of 1968.

Charney, Leo, and Vanessa R. Schwartz, eds. *Cinema and the Invention of Modern Life.* Berkeley, 1995. Collection of essays.

Dallin, Alexander, and Gail Lapidus. *The Soviet System: From Crisis to Collapse.* Boulder, CO, 1995.

de Grazia, Victoria. *Irresistible Empire: America's Advance through Twentieth-Century Europe.* Cambridge, MA, 2006. Thorough exploration of the history of consumer culture in Europe and its links to relations with the United States.

Echols, Alice. *Daring to Be Bad: Radical Feminism in America, 1967–1975.* Minneapolis, 1989. Good narrative and analysis.

Eichengreen, Barry. *The European Economy Since 1945.* Princeton, 2007. Matchless synthesis of the economic history of Europe and the story of European integration in the second half of the twentieth century, emphasizing the interplay between institutions and society.

Eley, Geoff. *Forging Democracy: The History of the Left in Europe, 1850–2000.* Oxford and New York, 2002. Among its other qualities, one of the best historical perspectives on the 1960s.

Fink, Carole, Phillipp Gassert, and Detlef Junker, eds. *1968: The World Transformed.* Cambridge, 1998. A transatlantic history of 1968.

Fulbrook, Mary, ed. *Europe since 1945 (The Short Oxford History of Europe).* Oxford, 2001. Particularly good articles on economics and political economy. Structural analysis.

Garton Ash, Timothy. *In Europe's Name: Germany and the Divided Continent.* New York, 1993. An analysis of the effect of German reunification on the future of Europe.

Glenny, Misha. *The Balkans, 1804–1999: Nationalism, War and the Great Powers.* London, 1999. Good account by a journalist who covered the fighting.

Horowitz, Daniel. *Betty Friedan and the Making of the Feminine Mystique: The American Left, the Cold War, and Modern Feminism.* Amherst, MA, 1998. A reconsideration.

Hosking, Geoffrey. *The Awakening of the Soviet Union.* Cambridge, MA, 1990. The factors that led to the end of the Soviet era.

Hughes, H. Stuart. *Sophisticated Rebels: The Political Culture of European Dissent, 1968–1987*. Cambridge, MA, 1990. The nature of dissent on both sides of the disintegrating Iron Curtain in the years 1988–1989.

Hulsberg, Werner. *The German Greens: A Social and Political Profile*. New York, 1988. The origins, politics, and impact of environmental politics.

Jarausch, Konrad. *The Rush to German Unity*. New York, 1994. The problems of reunification analyzed.

Judah, Tim. *The Serbs: History, Myth, and the Destruction of Yugoslavia*. New Haven, 1997. Overview of Serbian history by journalist who covered the war.

Kotkin, Stephen. *Armageddon Averted: The Soviet Collapse, 1970–2000*. Oxford, 2001. Excellent short account.

Kurlansky, Mark. *1968: The Year that Rocked the World*. New York, 2005. An accessible introduction for nonspecialists.

Lewin, Moshe. *The Gorbachev Phenomenon*. Expanded ed. Berkeley, 1991. Written as a firsthand account, tracing the roots of Gorbachev's successes and failures.

Lieven, Anatol. *Chechnya, Tombstone of Russia Power*. New Haven and London, 1998. Longer view of the region, by a journalist.

Maier, Charles S. *Dissolution: The Crisis of Communism and the End of East Germany*. Princeton, NJ, 1997. Detailed and sophisticated.

Mann, Michael. *The Dark Side of Democracy: Explaining Ethnic Cleansing*. New York, 2005. Brilliant essay on different episodes from Armenia to Rwanda.

Marwick, Arthur. *The Sixties*. Oxford and New York, 1998. An international history.

Pells, Richard. *Not Like Us: How Europeans Have Loved, Hated, and Transformed American Culture since World War II*. New York, 1997. From the point of view of an American historian.

Poiger, Uta G. *Jazz, Rock, and Rebels: Cold War Politics and American Culture in a Divided Germany*. Berkeley, 2000. Pioneering cultural history.

Sheehan, Neil. *A Bright Shining Lie: John Paul Vann and America in Vietnam*. New York, 1988. A study of the war and its escalation through one of the U.S. Army's field advisers.

Strayer, Robert. *Why Did the Soviet Union Collapse? Understanding Historical Change*. Armonk, NY, and London, 1998. A good introduction, with bibliography.

Suri, Jeremi. *Power and Protest*. New ed. Cambridge, MA, 2005. One of the best of the new global histories of the 1960s, looking at connections between social movements and international relations.

CHAPTER 29

Bowen, John R. *Why the French Don't Like Headscarves: Islam, the State, and Public Space*. Princeton, NJ, 2008. An ethnographic account of this volatile debate in France.

Coetzee, J. M. *Waiting for the Barbarians*. London, 1980. A searing critique of apartheid-era South Africa by a leading Afrikaner novelist.

Eichengreen, Barry. *Hall of Mirrors: The Great Depression, the Great Recession, and the Uses—and Misuses—of History*. Oxford, 2015. A historical comparison of the financial crisis of 2008 with the depression of 1929 by an economist with a firm grasp on political and social history.

Epstein, Helen. *The Invisible Cure: Africa, the West, and the Fight Against AIDS*. New York, 2007. One of the best recent studies.

Esposito, John. *What Everyone Needs to Know about Islam*. Oxford, 2011. A useful general introduction to Islam, its place in world history, and contemporary Muslim societies, organized for quick reference by students.

Frieden, Jeffrey H. *Global Capitalism: Its Rise and Fall in the Twentieth Century*. New York, 2007. Broad-ranging history for the advanced student.

Geyer, Michael, and Charles Bright. "World History in a Global Age." *American Historical Review* 100, no. 4 (October 1995). An excellent short discussion.

Glendon, Mary Ann. *A World Made New: Eleanor Roosevelt and the Universal Declaration of Human Rights*. New York, 2001. A fascinating study of the High Commission in its time by a legal scholar.

Harvey, David. *A Brief History of Neoliberalism*. New York, 2007. A critical account of the history of neoliberalism that encompasses the United States, Europe, and Asia.

Hopkins, A. G., ed. *Globalization in World History*. New York, 2002. Excellent introduction, written by one of the first historians to engage the issue.

Hunt, Lynn. *Inventing Human Rights: A History*. New York, 2007. A short study of the continuities and paradoxes in the West's human rights tradition, by one of the foremost historians of the French Revolution. On 1776, 1789, and 1948.

Keddie, Nikki. *Modern Iran: Roots and Results of Revolution*. New Haven, 2003. A revised edition of her major study of Iran's 1979 revolution, with added perspective on Iran's Islamic government.

Lacqueur, Walter. *The Age of Terrorism*. Boston, 1987. An important study of the first wave of post–1960s terrorism.

Landes, David. *The Wealth and Poverty of Nations: Why Some Are So Rich and Some So Poor*. New York, 1998. Leading economic historian's account of globalization's effects on the international economy.

Lewis, Bernard. *The Crisis of Islam: Holy War and Unholy Terror*. New York, 2003. Conservative scholar of the Arab world discussing the political crises that fueled terrorism.

Mckeown, Adam. "Global Migration, 1846–1940." *Journal of World History* 15, no. 2 (2004). Includes references to more work on the subject.

McNeill, J. R. *Something New under the Sun: An Environmental History of the Twentieth-Century World.* New York and London, 2000. Fascinating new approach to environmental history.

Merlini, Cesare, and Olivier Roy, eds. *Arab Society in Revolt: The West's Mediterranean Challenge.* Washington, DC, 2012. A multiauthor attempt to understand the Arab Spring of 2011.

Novick, Peter. *The Holocaust in American Life.* Boston, 1999.

Power, Samantha. *A Problem from Hell: America and the Age of Genocide.* New York, 2013. A prize-winning survey of the entire twentieth century, its genocides, and the different human rights movements that responded to them.

Rodrik, Dani. *The Globalization Paradox: Democracy and the Future of the World Economy.* New York, 2012. A historical-minded account of the challenges faced by nation-states in the contemporary global economy.

Roy, Olivier. *Globalized Islam: The Search for a New Ummah.* New York, 2006. Examines changes in religious belief and practice as Islam has spread from its historic centers in the Middle East to other areas of the world, including Europe and North America.

Scott, Joan. *The Politics of the Veil.* Princeton, NJ, 2010. A leading feminist scholar analyzes the debate about the veil and the Islamic headscarf in Europe.

_____. *On the Judgment of History.* New York, 2020. Probing analytic essays on the complex legacies of enslavement, racial violence, and genocide in the Germany, South Africa, and the United States, which argues that any accounting for the consequences of past atrocities must include a critical approach to the potentials for exclusion which remain a part of national identities and institutions in the present.

Shlaim, Avi. *The Iron Wall: Israel and the Arab World.* New York, 2000. Leading Israeli historian on the evolution of Israel's defensive foreign policy.

Stiglitz, Joseph E. *Globalization and Its Discontents.* New York, 2002. A recent and important consideration of contemporary globalization's character and the conflicts it creates, particularly over commerce and culture.

_____. *Freefall: America, Free Markets, and the Sinking of the World Economy.* New York, 2010. Nobel Prize–winning economist's account of the financial crisis of 2008.

Tooze, Adam. *Crashed: How a Decade of Financial Crises Changed the World.* New York, 2018.

_____. *Shutdown: How Covid Shook the World's Economy.* New York, 2021. Global narrative of the coronavirus pandemic and the economic shock that followed by a prize-winning historian.

Turkle, Sherry. *Life on the Screen: Identity in the Age of the Internet.* New York, 1995. An important early study of Web culture and the fluid possibilities of electronic communication.

Winter, Jay. *Dreams of Peace and Freedom: Utopian Moments in the Twentieth Century.* New Haven, 2006. One of the leading historians of war and atrocity turns here to twentieth-century hopes for peace and human rights.

Wolf, Martin. *The Shifts and the Shocks: What We've Learned—and Have Still to Learn—From the Financial Crisis.* New York, 2014. A respected journalist offers a judgment on the financial crisis of 2008 and the subsequent European debt crisis.

Yanow, Dvora. *Constructing "Race" and "Ethnicity" in America: Category-Making in Public Policy and Administration.* Armonk, NY, 2003. An examination of ethnic and racial classification in the United States at the end of the twentieth century.

Zahra, Tara. *The Great Departure: Mass Migration from Eastern Europe and the Making of the Free World.* New York, 2017.

Glossary

1973 OPEC oil embargo Some leaders in the Arab-dominated Organization of the Petroleum Exporting Countries (OPEC) wanted to use oil as a weapon against the West in the Arab-Israeli conflict. After the 1972 Arab-Israeli war, OPEC instituted an oil embargo against Western powers. The embargo increased the price of oil and sparked spiraling inflation and economic troubles in Western nations, triggering in turn a cycle of dangerous recession that lasted nearly a decade. In response, Western governments began viewing the Middle Eastern oil regions as areas of strategic importance.

Abbasid caliphate (750–930) The Abbasid family claimed to be descendants of Muḥammad, and in 750 they successfully led a rebellion against the Umayyads, seizing control of Muslim territories in Arabia, Persia, North Africa, and the Near East. The Abbasids modeled their behavior and administration on those of the Persian princes and their rule on that of the Persian Empire, establishing a new capital at Baghdad.

Peter Abelard (1079–1142) Highly influential philosopher, theologian, and teacher, often considered the founder of the University of Paris.

absolutism Form of government in which one person or body, usually the monarch, controls the right to make war, tax, judge, and coin money. The term was often used to refer to the state monarchies in seventeenth- and eighteenth-century Europe.

abstract expressionism The mid-twentieth-century school of art based in New York that included Jackson Pollock, Willem de Kooning, Franz Kline, and Helen Frankenthaler. It emphasized form, color, gesture, and feeling instead of figurative subjects.

Academy of Sciences This French institute of scientific inquiry was founded in 1666 by Louis XIV. France's statesmen exerted control over the academy and sought to share in the rewards of any discoveries its members made.

Aeneas Mythical founder of Rome, Aeneas was a refugee from the city of Troy whose adventures were described by the poet Virgil in the *Aeneid*, which was modeled on the oral epics of Homer.

Aetolian and Achaean Leagues These two alliances among Greek poleis were formed during the Hellenistic period in opposition to the Antigonids of Macedonia. Unlike the earlier defensive alliances of the classical period, each league was a real attempt to form a political federation.

African National Congress (ANC) Multiracial organization founded in 1912 whose goal was to end racial discrimination in South Africa.

Afrikaners Descendants of the original Dutch settlers of South Africa; formerly referred to as Boers.

agricultural revolution Numerous agricultural revolutions have occurred in the history of Western civilizations. One of the most significant began in the tenth century C.E. and increased the amount of land under cultivation as well as the productivity of the land. This revolution was made possible through the use of new technology, a rise in global temperatures, and more efficient methods of cultivation.

AIDS Acquired Immunodeficiency Syndrome. The final phase of HIV, AIDS first appeared in the 1970s and has developed into a global health catastrophe; it is spreading most quickly in developing nations in Africa and Asia.

Akhenaten (r. 1352–1336 B.C.E.) Pharaoh whose attempt to promote the worship of the sun god, Aten, ultimately weakened his dynasty's position in Egypt.

Alexander the Great (356–323 B.C.E.) The Macedonian king whose conquests of the Persian Empire and Egypt created a new Hellenistic world.

Alexander II (1818–1881) After the Crimean War, Tsar Alexander embarked on a program of reform and modernization, which included the emancipation of the serfs. A radical assassin killed him in 1881.

Alexius Comnenus (1057–1118) This Byzantine emperor requested Pope Urban II's help in raising an army to recapture Anatolia from the Seljuk Turks. Instead, Pope Urban II called for knights to go to the Holy Land and liberate it from its Muslim captors, launching the First Crusade.

Algerian War (1954–1962) The war between France and Algerians seeking independence. Led by the National Liberation Front (FLN), guerrillas fought the French army in the mountains and desert of Algeria. The FLN also initiated a campaign of bombing and terrorism in Algerian cities that led French soldiers to torture many Algerians, attracting world attention and international scandal.

Dante Alighieri (c. 1265–1321) Florentine poet and intellectual whose *Divine Comedy* was a pioneering work in the Italian vernacular and a vehicle for political and religious critique.

Allied Powers The First World War coalition of Great Britain, Ireland, Belgium, France, Italy, Russia, Portugal, Greece, Serbia, Montenegro, Albania, and Romania.

al Qaeda The radical Islamic organization founded in the late 1980s by former mujahidin who had fought against the Soviet Union in Afghanistan. Al Qaeda carried out the 9/11 terrorist attacks and is responsible as well for attacks in Africa, Southeast Asia, Europe, and the Middle East.

Ambrose (c. 340–397) One of the early church fathers, he helped define the relationship between the sacred authority of bishops and other Church leaders and the secular authority of worldly rulers. He believed that secular rulers were a part of the Church and therefore subject to it.

American Revolution (1775–1783) A period of insurrection and war in which thirteen British colonies in North America won their independence from the British king and founded a new nation, the United States of America.

Americas The name given to the two great landmasses of the New World, derived from the name of the Italian geographer Amerigo Vespucci. In 1492, Christopher Columbus reached the Bahamas and the island of Hispaniola, which began an era of Spanish conquest in North and South America. Originally, the Spanish had sought a route to Asia. Instead they discovered two continents whose wealth they decided to exploit. They were especially interested in gold and silver, which they either stole from indigenous peoples or mined, using indigenous peoples as labor. Silver became Spain's most lucrative export from the New World.

Amnesty International Nongovernmental organization formed in 1961 to defend "prisoners of conscience"—those detained for their beliefs, color, sex, ethnic origin, language, or religion.

Anabaptism Protestant movement that emerged in Switzerland in 1521; its adherents insisted that only adults could be baptized Christians.

anarchism In the nineteenth century, a political movement with the aim of establishing small-scale, localized, and self-sufficient democratic communities that could guarantee a maximum of individual sovereignty. Renouncing parties, unions, and any form of modern mass organization, the anarchists fell back on the tradition of conspiratorial violence.

Anatolia A region consisting of the peninsula linking Asia to Europe and reaching northward to the Black Sea, southward to the Mediterranean, and westward to the Aegean; often called "Asia Minor."

Anthropocene A term coined by geographers, geologists, and climate scientists to describe the era when human activities began to reshape earth's environment. Although some scholars contend that this epoch dates only as far back as the Industrial Revolution of the mid-nineteenth century, others date it from the Neolithic Revolution and the emergence of the earliest civilizations.

Anti–Corn Law League This organization successfully lobbied Parliament to repeal Britain's Corn Laws in 1846. The Corn Laws of 1815 had protected British landowners and farmers from foreign competition by establishing high tariffs, which kept bread prices artificially high for British consumers. The league saw these laws as unfair protection of the aristocracy and pushed for their repeal in the name of free trade.

antisemitism Antisemitism refers to hostility toward Jewish people. Religious forms of antisemitism have a long history in Europe, but during the nineteenth century antisemitism emerged as a potent ideology for mobilizing new constituencies in the era of mass politics. Playing on popular conspiracy theories about alleged Jewish influence in society, antisemites effectively rallied large bodies of supporters in France during the Dreyfus Affair, and then again during the rise of National Socialism in Germany after the First World War. The Holocaust would not have been possible without the acquiescence or cooperation of many thousands of people who shared antisemitic views.

apartheid The racial segregation policy of the Afrikaner-dominated South African government. Legislated in 1948 by the Afrikaner National Party, it existed in South Africa for many decades.

appeasement The policy pursued by Western governments in the face of German, Italian, and Japanese aggression leading up to the Second World War. The policy, which attempted to accommodate and negotiate peace with the aggressive nations, was based on the belief that another global war like the First World War was unimaginable, a belief that Germany and its allies had been mistreated by the terms of the Treaty of Versailles, and a fear that fascist Germany and its allies protected the West from the spread of Soviet communism.

Thomas Aquinas (1225–1274) Dominican friar and theologian whose systematic approach to Christian doctrine was influenced by Aristotle.

Arab-Israeli conflict Between the founding of the state of Israel in 1948 and the present, a series of wars has been fought between Israel and neighboring Arab nations: the war of 1948 when Israel defeated attempts by Egypt, Jordan, Iraq, Syria, and Lebanon to prevent the creation of the new state; the 1956 war between Israel and Egypt over the Sinai Peninsula; the 1967 war, when Israel gained control of additional land in the Golan Heights, the West Bank, the Gaza strip, and the Sinai; and the Yom Kippur War of 1973, when Israel once again fought with forces from Egypt and Syria. A particularly difficult issue in all of these conflicts has been the situation of the 950,000 Palestinian refugees made homeless by the first war in 1948 and the movement of Israeli settlers into the occupied territories (outside of Israel's original borders). In the late 1970s, peace talks between Israel and Egypt inspired some hope of peace, but an ongoing cycle of violence between Palestinians and the Israeli military has made a final settlement elusive.

Arab nationalism During the period of decolonization, secular forms of Arab nationalism, or pan-Arabism, found a wide following in many countries of the Middle East, especially in Egypt, Syria, and Iraq.

Arianism A variety of Christianity condemned as a heresy by the Roman Church, it derives from the teaching of a fourth-century priest named Arius, who rejected the idea that Jesus could be the divine equal of God.

aristocracy From the Greek word meaning "rule of the best." By 1000 B.C.E., the accumulated wealth of successful traders in Greece had created a new type of social class, which was based on wealth rather than warfare or birth. These men saw their wealth as a reflection of their superior qualities and aspired to emulate the heroes of old.

Aristotle (384–322 B.C.E.) A student of Plato, he based his philosophy on rational analysis of the material world. In contrast to his teacher, he stressed the rigorous investigation of real phenomena, rather than the development of universal ethics. He was, in turn, the teacher of Alexander the Great.

Armenian genocide The Ottoman government's attempt to exterminate the Armenian people with the Ottoman Empire during the First World War, resulting in the deaths of 1.5 million Armenians between 1914 and 1923.

Assyrians A Semitic-speaking people that moved into northern Mesopotamia around 2400 B.C.E.

Athens Athens emerged as the Greek polis with the most markedly democratic form of government through a series of political struggles during the sixth century B.C.E. After its key role in the defeat of two invading Persian forces, Athens became the preeminent naval power of ancient Greece and the exemplar of Greek culture. But it antagonized many other poleis, and became embroiled in a war with Sparta and its allies in 431 B.C.E. Called the Peloponnesian War, this bloody conflict lasted until Athens was defeated in 404 B.C.E.

atomic bomb In 1945, the United States dropped atomic bombs on Hiroshima and Nagasaki in Japan, ending the Second World War. In 1949, the Soviet Union tested its first atomic bomb, and in 1953 both superpowers demonstrated their new hydrogen bombs. Strategically, the nuclearization of warfare polarized the world. Countries without nuclear weapons found it difficult to avoid joining either the Soviet or American military pacts. Over time, countries split into two groups: the superpowers with enormous military budgets and those countries that relied on agreements and international law. The nuclearization of warfare also encouraged "proxy wars" between clients of superpowers. Culturally, the hydrogen bomb came to symbolize the age as well as both humanity's power and its vulnerability.

Augustine (c. 354–397) One of the most influential theologians of all time, Augustine described his conversion to Christianity in his autobiographical *Confessions* and articulated a new Christian worldview in *The City of God*, among other works.

Augustus (63 B.C.E.–14 C.E.) Born Gaius Octavius, this grandnephew and adopted son of Julius Caesar came to power in 27 B.C.E. His reign signals the end of the Roman Republic and the beginning of the Principate, the period when Rome was dominated by autocratic emperors.

Auschwitz-Birkenau The Nazi concentration camp in Poland that was designed for the systematic murder of Jews and Gypsies. Between 1942 and 1944 over one million people were killed in Auschwitz-Birkenau.

Austro-Hungarian Empire The dual monarchy established by the Habsburg family in 1867; it collapsed at the end of the First World War.

authoritarianism A centralized and dictatorial form of government, proclaimed by its adherents to be superior to parliamentary democracy. Authoritarian governments claim to be above the law, do not respect individual rights, and do not tolerate political opposition. Authoritarian regimes that have developed a central ideology such as fascism or communism are sometimes termed "totalitarian."

Avignon A city in southeastern France that became the seat of the papacy between 1305 and 1377, a period known as the "Babylonian Captivity" of the Roman Church.

Aztecs An indigenous people of central Mexico; their empire was conquered by Spanish conquistadors in the sixteenth century.

baby boom (1950s) The post–Second World War upswing in U.S. birth rates; it reversed a century of decline.

Babylon An ancient city between the Tigris and Euphrates Rivers, which became the capital of Hammurabi's empire in the eighteenth century B.C.E. and continued to be an important administrative and commercial capital under many subsequent imperial powers, including the Neo-Assyrians, Chaldeans, Persians, and Romans. It was here that Alexander the Great died in 323 B.C.E.

Babylonian captivity Refers both to the Jews' exile in Babylon during the sixth century B.C.E. and the period from 1309 to 1378, when papal authority was subjugated to the French crown and the papal court was moved from Rome to the French city of Avignon.

Francis Bacon (1561–1626) British philosopher and scientist who pioneered the scientific method and inductive reasoning. In other words, he argued that thinkers should amass many observations and then draw general conclusions or propose theories on the basis of these data.

balance of powers The principle that no one country should be powerful enough to destabilize international relations. Starting in the seventeenth century, this goal of maintaining balance influenced diplomacy in western and central Europe for two centuries until the system collapsed with the onset of the First World War.

Balfour Declaration A letter dated November 2, 1917, by Lord Arthur J. Balfour, the British foreign secretary, that promised a homeland for the Jews in Palestine.

Laura Bassi (1711–1778) She was accepted into the Academy of Science in Bologna for her work in mathematics, which made her one of the few women to be accepted into a scientific academy in the seventeenth century.

Bastille The Bastille was a royal fortress and prison in Paris. In June 1789, a revolutionary crowd attacked the Bastille to show support for the newly created National Assembly. The fall of the Bastille was the first instance of the people's role in revolutionary change in France.

Bay of Pigs invasion (1961) The unsuccessful invasion of Cuba by Cuban exiles, supported by the U.S. government. The rebels intended to incite an insurrection in Cuba and overthrow the communist regime of Fidel Castro.

Cesare Beccaria (1738–1794) An influential writer during the Enlightenment who advocated for legal reforms. He believed that the only legitimate rationale for punishments was to maintain social order and to prevent other crimes. He argued for the greatest possible leniency compatible with deterrence and opposed torture and the death penalty.

Thomas Becket (1118–1170) Archbishop of Canterbury whose opposition to King Henry II's innovations to the court system led to his exile and later assassination by the king's knights. Becket was later proclaimed a martyr and saint, and his tomb at Canterbury became one of the most important pilgrimage sites in Europe.

Beer Hall Putsch (1923) An early attempt by the Nazi party to seize power in Munich; Adolf Hitler was imprisoned for a year after the incident.

Benedict of Nursia (c. 480–c. 547) Benedict's rule for monks formed the basis of Western monasticism and is still observed in monasteries all over the world.

Benedictine monasticism This form of monasticism was developed by Benedict of Nursia. Its followers adhere to a defined cycle of daily prayers, lessons, communal worship, and manual labor.

Jeremy Bentham (1748–1832) Influential British liberal philosopher who proposed in his major work, *The Principles of Morals and Legislation* (1789), that society adopt the organizing principle of utilitarianism.

Berlin airlift The transport in 1948 of vital supplies to West Berlin by air, primarily under U.S. auspices, in response to a blockade of the city that had been instituted by the Soviet Union to force the Allies to abandon West Berlin.

Berlin Conference At this conference in 1884, the leading colonial powers met and established ground rules for the partition of Africa by European nations. By 1914, 90 percent of African territory was under European control. The Berlin Conference ceded control of the Congo region to a private company run by King Leopold II of Belgium. The company agreed to make the Congo valleys open to free trade and commerce, to end the slave trade in the region, and to establish a Congo Free State. In reality, King Leopold II's company established a regime that was so brutal in its treatment of local populations that an international scandal forced the Belgian state to take over the colony in 1908.

Berlin Wall The wall built in 1961 by the East German Communists to prevent citizens of East Germany from fleeing to West Germany; it was torn down in 1989.

birth control pill This oral contraceptive became widely available in the mid-1960s. For the first time, women had a simple method of birth control that they could take themselves.

Otto von Bismarck (1815–1898) The prime minister of Prussia and later the first chancellor of a unified Germany, Bismarck was the architect of German unification and helped to consolidate the new nation's economic and military power.

Black Death The epidemic of bubonic plague that ravaged Europe, Asia, and North Africa during the fourteenth century, killing one third to one half of the population.

William Blake (1757–1827) Romantic writer who criticized industrial society and factories. He championed the imagination and poetic vision, seeing both as transcending the limits of the material world.

Blitzkrieg The German "lightning war" strategy used during the Second World War; the Germans invaded Poland, France, Russia, and other countries with fast-moving and well-coordinated attacks using aircraft, tanks, and other armored vehicles, followed by infantry.

Bloody Sunday On January 22, 1905, the Russian tsar's guards killed 130 demonstrators who were protesting the tsar's mistreatment of workers and the middle class.

Jean Bodin (1530–1596) A French political philosopher whose *Six Books of the Commonwealth* advanced a theory of absolute sovereignty, on the grounds that the state's paramount duty is to maintain order and that monarchs should therefore exercise unlimited power.

Giovanni Boccaccio (1313–1375) Florentine author best known for his *Decameron*, a collection of prose tales about sex, adventure, and trickery written in the Italian vernacular after the Black Death.

Boer War (1898–1902) Conflict between British and ethnically European Afrikaners in South Africa, with terrible casualties on both sides.

Boethius (c. 480–524) A member of a prominent Roman family, he sought to preserve aspects of ancient learning by compiling a series of handbooks and anthologies appropriate for Christian readers. His translations of Greek philosophy provided a crucial link between classical Greek thought and the early intellectual culture of Christianity.

Bolsheviks Former members of the Russian Social Democratic Party who advocated the destruction of capitalist political and economic institutions and started the Russian Revolution. In 1918, the Bolsheviks changed their name to the Russian Communist Party. Prominent Bolsheviks included Vladimir Lenin and Joseph Stalin. Leon Trotsky joined the Bolsheviks late but became a prominent leader in the early years of the Russian Revolution.

Napoleon Bonaparte (1769–1821) Corsican-born French general who seized power and ruled as dictator and emperor from 1799 to 1814. After the successful conquest of much of Europe, he was defeated by Russian and Prussian forces and died in exile.

Boniface VIII During his pontificate (1294–1303), repeated claims to papal authority were challenged by King Philip IV of France. When Boniface died in 1309 (at the hands of Philip's thugs), the French king moved the papal court from Rome to the French city of Avignon, where it remained until 1378.

Sandro Botticelli (1445–1510) An Italian painter devoted to the blending of classical and Christian motifs by using ideas associated with the pagan past to illuminate sacred stories.

bourgeoisie Term for the middle class, derived from the French word for a town dweller, *bourgeois*.

Boxer Rebellion (1899–1900) Chinese peasant movement that opposed foreign influence, especially that of Christian missionaries; it was finally put down after the Boxers were defeated by a foreign army composed mostly of Japanese, Russian, British, French, and American soldiers.

Tycho Brahe (1546–1601) Danish astronomer who believed that the careful study of the heavens would unlock the secrets of the universe. For over twenty years, he charted the movements of significant objects in the night sky, compiling the finest set of astronomical data in Europe.

Brexit A public referendum in June 2016 in which the population of the United Kingdom, by a slim majority, voted to leave the European Union (EU). This marked the first time that a member nation chose to retreat from the goal of increased integration with other members of the EU. The Brexit vote was controversial in Scotland and Northern Ireland, because in these areas of the United Kingdom, a majority expressed a wish to remain in the EU.

Bronze Age (3200–1200 B.C.E.) The name given to the era characterized by the discovery of techniques for smelting bronze (an alloy of copper and tin), which was then the strongest known metal.

Edmund Burke (1729–1797) Conservative Anglo-Irish writer and member of the British Parliament who was critical of the French Revolution and its goal of radical political change.

George Gordon, Lord Byron (1788–1824) Writer and poet whose life helped give the Romantics their reputation as rebels against conformity. He was known for his love affairs, his defense of working-class movements, and his passionate engagement in politics, which led to his death in the war for Greek independence.

Byzantium A small settlement located at the mouth of the Black Sea and at the crossroads between Europe and Asia, it was chosen by Constantine as the site for his new imperial capital of Constantinople in 324. Modern historians use this name to refer to the eastern Roman Empire, which lasted in this region until 1453, but the inhabitants of that empire referred to themselves as Romans.

Julius Caesar (100–44 B.C.E.) The Roman general who conquered the Gauls, invaded Britain, and expanded Rome's territory in Asia Minor. He became the dictator of Rome in 46 B.C.E. His assassination led to the rise of his grand-nephew and adopted son, Gaius Octavius Caesar, who ruled the Roman Empire as Caesar Augustus.

caliphs Muslim rulers who claim descent from the prophet Muḥammad.

John Calvin (1509–1564) French-born theologian and reformer whose radical form of Protestantism was adopted in many Swiss cities, notably Geneva.

Canary Islands Islands off the western coast of Africa that were colonized by Portugal and Spain in the mid-fifteenth century, after which they became bases for further expeditions around the African coast and across the Atlantic.

Carbonari An underground organization that opposed the Concert of Europe's restoration of monarchies. They held influence in southern Europe during the 1820s, especially in Italy.

Carolingian Derived from the Latin name Carolus (Charles), this term refers to the Frankish dynasty that began with the rise to power of Charlemagne's grandfather, Charles Martel (688–741). At its height under Charlemagne (Charles "the Great"), this dynasty controlled what are now France, Germany, northern Italy, Catalonia, and portions of central Europe. The Carolingian Empire collapsed under the combined weight of Viking raids, economic disintegration, and the growing power of local lords.

Carolingian Renaissance A cultural and intellectual flowering that took place around the court of Charlemagne in the late eighth and early ninth centuries.

Carthage The great maritime empire that grew out of Phoenician trading colonies in North Africa and rivaled the power of Rome. Its wars with Rome, collectively known as the Punic Wars, ended in its destruction in 146 B.C.E.

Cassiodorus (c. 490–c. 583) Member of an old senatorial family, he was largely responsible for introducing classical learning into the monastic curriculum and for turning monasteries into centers for the collection, preservation, and transmission of knowledge. His *Institutes*, an influential handbook of classical literature for Christian readers, was intended as a preface to more intensive study of theology and the Bible.

Catalonia Maritime region in northeastern Spain; during the thirteenth century, Catalan adventurers conquered and colonized a series of western Mediterranean islands.

Catholic Church The "universal" (catholic) church based in Rome, which was redefined in the sixteenth century, when the Counter-Reformation resulted in the rebirth of the Catholic faith at the Council of Trent.

Margaret Cavendish (1623–1673) English natural philosopher who developed her own speculative natural philosophy. She used this philosophy to critique those who excluded her from scientific debate.

Camillo Benso di Cavour (1810–1861) Prime minister of Piedmont-Sardinia and founder of the Italian Liberal party; he played a key role in the movement for Italian unification under the Piedmontese king, Victor Emmanuel II.

Central Powers The First World War alliance between Germany, Austria-Hungary, Bulgaria, and Turkey.

Charlemagne (742–814) As king of the Franks (767–813), Charles "the Great" consolidated much of western Europe under his rule. In 800, he was crowned emperor by the pope in Rome, establishing a problematic precedent that would have wide-ranging consequences for western Europe's relationship with the eastern Roman Empire in Byzantium and for the relationship between the papacy and secular rulers.

Charles I (r. 1625–1649) The second Stuart king of England, Ireland, and Scotland, Charles attempted to rule without the support of Parliament, sparking a controversy that erupted into civil war in 1642. The king's forces were ultimately defeated and Charles himself was executed by an act of Parliament, the first time in history that a ruling king was legally deposed and executed by his own government.

Charles II Nominally king of England, Ireland, and Scotland after his father Charles I's execution in 1649, Charles II lived in exile until he was restored to the throne in 1660. Influenced by his cousin, King Louis XIV of France, he presided over an opulent royal court until his death in 1685.

Chartism A working-class movement in Britain that called for reform of the British political system during the 1840s. The Chartists were supporters of the "People's Charter," which had six demands: universal white male suffrage, secret ballots, an end to property qualifications as a condition of public office, annual parliamentary elections, salaries for members of the House of Commons, and equal electoral districts.

Geoffrey Chaucer (1340–1400) English poet whose collection of versified stories, *The Canterbury Tales*, features characters from a variety of classes.

Christendom A term used to denote an ideal vision of Christian unity—political and cultural, as well as spiritual—promoted by powerful Christian rulers, beginning with Charlemagne. The "Holy Roman Empire," a term coined by Frederick I Barbarossa, was an outgrowth of this idea. Christendom was never a united entity, but it was a powerful vision.

Christine de Pizan (c. 1364–c. 1431) Born in Italy, Christine spent her adult life attached to the French court and, after her husband's death, became the first laywoman to earn her living by writing. She was the author of treatises on warfare and chivalry as well as of books and pamphlets that challenged long-standing misogynistic claims.

Church of England Founded by Henry VIII in the 1530s, as a consequence of his break with the authority of the Roman pope.

Winston Churchill (1874–1965) British prime minister who led the country during the Second World War. He also coined the phrase "Iron Curtain" in a speech at Westminster College in 1946.

Marcus Tullius Cicero (106–43 B.C.E.) Influential Roman senator, orator, Stoic philosopher, and prose stylist. His published writings still form the basis of instruction in classical Latin grammar and usage.

Lucius Quinctius Cincinnatus (519–c. 430 B.C.E.) A legendary citizen-farmer of Rome who reluctantly accepted an appointment as dictator. After defeating Rome's enemies, he allegedly left his political office and returned to his farm.

Civil Constitution of the Clergy Issued by the French National Assembly in 1790, the Civil Constitution of the Clergy decreed that all bishops and priests should be subject to the authority of the state. Their salaries were to be paid out of the public treasury, and they were required to swear allegiance to the new state, making it clear that they served France rather than Rome. The Assembly's aim was to make the Catholic Church of France a truly national and civil institution.

civilizing mission The basis of an argument made by Europeans to justify colonial expansion in the nineteenth century. Supporters of this idea believed that Europeans had a duty to impose Western ideas of economic and political progress on the indigenous peoples they ruled over in their colonies. In practice, the colonial powers often found that ambitious plans to impose European practices on colonial subjects led to unrest that threatened the stability of colonial rule. By the early twentieth century most colonial powers were more cautious in their plans for political or cultural transformation.

civil rights movement The Second World War increased African American migration from the American South to northern cities, intensifying a drive for rights, dignity, and independence. By 1960, civil rights groups had started organizing boycotts and demonstrations directed at discrimination against blacks in the South. During the 1960s, civil rights laws passed under President Lyndon B. Johnson did bring African Americans some equality with regard to voting rights and, to a much lesser degree, school desegregation. However, racism continued in areas such as housing, job opportunities, and the economic development of African American communities.

Civil War (1861–1865) Conflict between the northern and southern states of America that cost over 600,000 lives; this struggle led to the abolition of slavery in the United States.

classical learning The study of ancient Greek and Latin texts. After Christianity became the only legal religion of the Roman Empire, scholars needed to find a way to make classical learning applicable to a Christian way of life. Christian monks played a significant role in resolving this problem by reinterpreting the classics for a Christian audience.

Cluny A powerful Benedictine monastery founded in 910 whose enormous wealth and prestige derived its independence from secular authorities as well as from its wide network of daughter houses (priories).

Cold War (1945–1991) Ideological, political, and economic conflict in which the USSR and Eastern Europe opposed the United States and Western Europe in the decades after the Second World War. The Cold War's origins lay in the breakup of the wartime alliance between the United States and the Soviet Union in 1945 and resulted in a division of Europe into two spheres: the West, committed to market capitalism; and the East, which sought to build socialist republics in areas under Soviet control. The Cold War ended with the collapse of the Soviet Union in 1991.

collectivization Stalin's plan for nationalizing agricultural production, begun in 1929. Twenty-five million peasants were forced to give up their land and join 250,000 large collective farms. Many who resisted were deported to labor camps in the Far East, and Stalin's government cut off food rations to those areas most marked by resistance to collectivization. In the ensuing human-caused famines, millions of people starved to death.

Columbian exchange The widespread exchange of peoples, plants, animals, diseases, goods, and culture between the African and Eurasian landmass (on the one hand) and the region that encompasses the Americas, Australia, and the Pacific Islands (on the other); precipitated by Christopher Columbus's voyage in 1492.

Christopher Columbus (1451–1506) A Genoese sailor who persuaded King Ferdinand and Queen Isabella of Spain to fund his expedition across the Atlantic, with the purpose of discovering a new trade route to Asia. His miscalculations landed him in the Bahamas and the island of Hispaniola in 1492.

commercial revolution A period of economic development in Europe lasting from c. 1500 to c. 1800. Advances in agriculture and handicraft production, combined with the expansion of trade networks in the Atlantic world, brought new wealth and new kinds of commercial activity to Europe. The commercial revolution prepared the way for the Industrial Revolution of the 1800s.

Committee of Public Safety Political body during the French Revolution that was controlled by the Jacobins, who defended the revolution by executing thousands during the Reign of Terror (September 1793–July 1794).

commune A community of individuals who have banded together in a sworn association, with the aim of establishing their independence and setting up their own form of representative government. Many medieval towns originally founded by lords or monasteries gained their independence through such methods.

The Communist Manifesto Radical pamphlet by Karl Marx (1818–1883) that predicted the downfall of the capitalist system and its replacement by a classless, egalitarian society. Marx believed that this revolution would be accomplished by the workers (the proletariat).

Concert of Europe (1814–1815) The body of diplomatic agreements designed primarily by the Austrian minister Klemens von Metternich between 1814 and 1848 and supported by other European powers until 1914. Its goal was to maintain a balance of power on the Continent and to prevent destabilizing social and political change in Europe.

conciliarism A doctrine developed in the thirteenth and fourteenth centuries to counter the growing power of the papacy, conciliarism holds that papal authority should be subject to a council of the Church at large. Conciliarists emerged as a dominant force after the Council of Constance (1414–1418) but were eventually outmatched by a rejuvenated papacy.

Congress of Vienna (1814–1815) International conference to reorganize Europe after the downfall of Napoleon and the French Revolution. European monarchies restored the Bourbon family to the French throne and agreed to respect each other's borders and to cooperate in guarding against future revolutions and war.

conquistador Spanish term for "conqueror," applied to the mercenaries and adventurers who campaigned against indigenous peoples in central and South America.

conservatives In the nineteenth century, conservatives aimed to legitimize and solidify the monarchy's authority and the hierarchical social order. They believed that change had to be slow, incremental, and managed so that the structures of authority were strengthened and not weakened.

Constantine (275–337 c.e.) The first emperor of Rome to convert to Christianity, Constantine came to power in 312 c.e. In 324 c.e., he founded a new imperial capital, Constantinople, on the site of a maritime settlement known as Byzantium.

Constantinople Founded by the emperor Constantine on the site of a village called Byzantium, Constantinople became the new capital of the Roman Empire in 324 c.e. and continued to be the seat of imperial power after its capture by the Ottoman Turks in 1453. It is now known as Istanbul.

contract theory of government A theory of government written by Englishman John Locke (1632–1704) that posits that government authority is both contractual and conditional; therefore, if a government has abused its given authority, society has the right to dissolve it and create another.

Nicolaus Copernicus (1473–1543) Polish astronomer who advanced the idea that the earth revolves around the sun.

cosmopolitanism Stemming from the Greek word meaning "universal city," the culture characteristic of the Hellenistic world challenged and transformed the narrower worldview of the Greek polis.

cotton gin Invented by Eli Whitney in 1793, this device mechanized the process of separating cotton seeds from cotton fibers, which sped up the production of cotton and reduced its price. This change made slavery profitable in the United States.

Council of Constance (1417–1420) A meeting of clergy and theologians in an effort to resolve the Great Schism within the Roman Church. The council deposed all rival papal candidates and elected a new pope, Martin V, but it also adopted the doctrine of conciliarism, which holds that the supreme authority within the Church rests with a representative general council and not with the pope. However, Martin V himself was an opponent of this doctrine and refused to be bound by it.

Council of Trent The name given to a series of meetings held in the Italian city of Trent (Trento) between 1545 and 1563, when leaders of the Roman Church reaffirmed Catholic doctrine and instituted internal reforms.

Counter-Reformation The movement to counter the Protestant Reformation, initiated by the Catholic Church at the Council of Trent in 1545.

coup d'état French term for the overthrow of an established government by a group of conspirators, usually with military support.

COVID-19 pandemic The airborne novel coronavirus that allegedly emerged in Wuhan, China, in December 2019 and rapidly spread around the world, causing the deaths of more than 6 million people and economic disruption worldwide.

Crimean War (1854–1856) War waged by Russia against Great Britain and France. Spurred by Russia's encroachment on Ottoman territories, the conflict revealed Russia's military weakness when Russian forces fell to British and French troops.

Crusader States The four fragile European principalities established on the eastern coast of the Mediterranean after the First Crusade (1096–1099): the county of Edessa (which effectively disappeared by 1150), the principality of Antioch (until 1268), the county of Tripoli (until 1291), and the kingdom of Jerusalem (which lost control of Jerusalem itself in 1187 and fell in 1291).

Cuban missile crisis (1962) Diplomatic standoff between the United States and the Soviet Union that was provoked by the Soviet Union's attempt to base nuclear missiles in Cuba; it brought the world closer to nuclear war than ever before or since.

cuius regio, eius religio A Latin phrase meaning "as the ruler, so the religion." Adopted as a part of the settlement of the Peace of Augsburg in 1555, it meant that those principalities ruled by Lutherans would have Lutheranism as their official religion and those ruled by Catholics must practice Catholicism.

cult of domesticity Concept associated with Victorian England that idealized women as nurturing wives and mothers.

cult of the Blessed Virgin The beliefs and practices associated with the veneration of Mary, the mother of Jesus, which became increasingly popular in the twelfth century.

cuneiform An early writing system that began to develop in Mesopotamia during the fourth millennium B.C.E. By 3100 B.C.E., its distinctive markings were impressed on clay tablets using a wedge-shaped stylus.

Cyrus the Great (c. 585–529 B.C.E.) As architect of the Persian Empire, Cyrus extended his dominion over a vast territory stretching from the Persian Gulf to the Mediterranean and incorporating the ancient civilizations of Mesopotamia. His successors ruled this Persian Empire as "Great Kings."

Darius (521–486 B.C.E.) The Persian emperor whose conflict with Aristagoras, the Greek ruler of Miletus, ignited the Persian Wars. In 490 B.C.E., Darius sent a large army to punish the Athenians for their intervention in Persian imperial affairs, but this force was defeated by Athenian hoplites on the plain of Marathon.

Charles Darwin (1809–1882) British naturalist who wrote *On the Origin of Species* and developed the theory of natural selection to explain the evolution of organisms.

D-Day (June 6, 1944) Date of the Allied invasion of Normandy, under General Dwight Eisenhower, to liberate Western Europe from German occupation.

Decembrists Nineteenth-century Russian army officers who were influenced by events in France and formed secret societies that espoused liberal governance. They were put down by Nicholas I in December 1825.

Declaration of Independence (1776) Historic document stating the principles of government on which the United States was founded.

Declaration of the Rights of Man and of the Citizen (1789) French charter of liberties formulated by the National Assembly during the French Revolution. The seventeen articles later became the preamble to the new constitution, which the assembly finished in 1791.

decolonization A complex process by which an empire relinquishes formal political control over colonial territory while the formerly colonized peoples assert their independence and create institutions for self-rule.

democracy In ancient Greece, this form of government allowed a class of propertied male citizens to participate in the governance of their polis; but it excluded women, slaves, and citizens without property from the political process. As a result, the ruling class amounted to only a small percentage of the entire population.

René Descartes (1596–1650) French philosopher and mathematician who emphasized the use of deductive reasoning.

Denis Diderot (1713–1784) French philosophe and author who was the guiding force behind the publication of the first encyclopedia. His *Encyclopedia* showed how reason could be applied to nearly all realms of thought and aimed to be a compendium of all human knowledge.

Dien Bien Phu (1954) Defining battle in the war between French colonialists and the Viet Minh that secured North Vietnam for Ho Chi Minh and his army and left the south to form its own government, which was supported by France and the United States.

Diet of Worms The select council of the Church that convened in the German city of Worms and condemned Martin Luther on a charge of heresy in 1521.

Diocletian (245–316 C.E.) As emperor of Rome from 284 to 305 C.E., Diocletian recognized that the empire could not be governed by one man in one place. His solution was to divide the empire into four parts, each with its own imperial ruler, but he himself remained the dominant ruler of the resulting tetrarchy ("rule of four"). He also initiated the Great Persecution, a time when many Christians became martyrs to their faith.

Directory (1795–1799) Executive committee that governed after the fall of Robespierre and held control until the coup of Napoleon Bonaparte.

Discourse on Method Philosophical treatise by René Descartes (1596–1650) proposing that the path to knowledge was through logical deduction, beginning with one's own self: "I think, therefore I am."

Dominican order Also called the Order of Preachers, it was founded by Dominic of Osma (1170–1221), a Castilian preacher and theologian, and approved by Innocent III in 1216. The order was dedicated to the rooting out of heresy and the conversion of Jews and Muslims. Many of its members held teaching positions in European universities and contributed to the development of medieval philosophy and theology. Others became the leading administrators of the Inquisition.

Dreyfus Affair The 1894 French scandal surrounding accusations that a Jewish captain, Alfred Dreyfus, sold military secrets to the Germans. Convicted, Dreyfus was sentenced to solitary confinement for life. However, after a public outcry, it was revealed that the trial documents were forgeries, and Dreyfus was pardoned after a second trial in 1899. In 1906, he was fully exonerated and reinstated in the army. The affair revealed the depths of popular anti-semitism in France.

Alexander Dubček (1921–1992) Communist leader of the Czechoslovakian government who advocated for "socialism with a human face." He encouraged debate within the party, academic and artistic freedom, and less censorship, which led to the "Prague spring" of 1968. People in other parts of Eastern Europe began to demonstrate in support of Dubček and demanded their own reforms. When Dubček tried to democratize the Communist party and did not attend a meeting of the Warsaw Pact, the Soviets sent tanks and troops into Prague and ousted Dubček and his allies.

Duma The Russian parliament, created in response to the revolution of 1905.

Dunkirk The French port on the English Channel where British and French forces retreated after sustaining heavy losses against the German military. Between May 27 and June 4, 1940, the Royal Navy evacuated over 300,000 troops in commercial and pleasure boats.

Eastern Front Battlefront between Berlin and Moscow during the First and Second World Wars.

East India Company (1600–1858) British charter company created to outperform Portuguese and Spanish traders in the Far East; in the eighteenth century the company became, in effect, the ruler of a large part of India. There was also a Dutch East India Company.

Edict of Nantes (1598) Issued by Henry IV of France in an effort to end religious violence. The edict declared France to be a Catholic country but tolerated some forms of Protestant worship.

Edward I King of England from 1272 to his death in 1307, Edward presided over the creation of new legal and bureaucratic institutions in his realm, violently subjugated the Welsh, and attempted to colonize Scotland. He expelled English Jews from his domain in 1290.

Eleanor of Aquitaine (1122–1204) Ruler of the wealthy province of Aquitaine and wife of Louis VII of France, Eleanor had her marriage annulled in order to marry the young count of Anjou, Henry Plantagenet, who became King Henry II of England a year later. The mother of two future kings of England, she was an important patron of the arts.

Elizabeth I (1533–1603) The Protestant daughter of Henry VIII and his second wife, Anne Boleyn, Elizabeth succeeded her sister Mary as the second queen regnant of England (1558–1603).

emancipation of the serfs (1861) The abolition of serfdom was central to Tsar Alexander II's program of modernization and reform, but it produced a limited amount of change. Former serfs now had legal rights. However, farmland was granted to village communes instead of to individuals. The land was of poor quality, and the former serfs had to pay installments for it to the village commune.

emperor Originally the term for any conquering commander of the Roman army whose victories merited celebration in an official triumph. After Augustus seized power in 27 B.C.E., it was the title borne by the sole ruler of the Roman Empire.

empire A centralized political entity consolidated through the conquest and colonization of other nations or peoples in order to benefit the ruler and/or his homeland.

enclosure Long process of privatizing what had been public agricultural land in eighteenth-century Britain; it helped to stimulate the development of commercial agriculture and forced many people in rural areas to seek work in cities during the early stages of industrialization.

Encyclopedia Joint venture of French philosophe writers, led by Denis Diderot (1713–1784), which proposed to summarize all modern knowledge in a multivolume illustrated work with over 70,000 articles.

Friedrich Engels (1820–1895) German social and political philosopher who collaborated with Karl Marx on many publications.

English Civil War (1642–1649) Conflicts between the English Parliament and King Charles I erupted into civil war, which ended in the defeat of the royalists and the execution of Charles on charges of treason against the crown. A short time later, Parliament's hereditary House of Lords was abolished and England was declared a Commonwealth.

English Peasants' Revolt Violent 1381 uprising in London, during which thousands of people marched on London to demand an end to serfdom and called for the redistribution of property. It ended with the arrest and execution of the ringleaders.

Enlightenment Intellectual movement in eighteenth-century Europe with a belief in human betterment through the application of reason to solve social, economic, and political problems.

Epicureanism A philosophical position articulated by Epicurus of Athens (c. 342–270 B.C.E.), who rejected the idea of an ordered universe governed by divine forces; instead, he emphasized individual agency and proposed that the highest good is the pursuit of pleasure.

Desiderius Erasmus (c. 1469–1536) Dutch-born scholar, social commentator, and Catholic humanist whose new translation of the Bible influenced the theology of Martin Luther.

Estates General The representative body of the three estates in France. In 1789, King Louis XVI summoned the Estates General to meet for the first time since 1614 because it seemed to be the only solution to France's worsening economic crisis and financial chaos.

Etruscans Settlers of the Italian peninsula who dominated the region from the late Bronze Age until the rise of the Roman Republic in the sixth century B.C.E.

Euclid Hellenistic mathematician whose *Elements of Geometry* (c. 300 B.C.E.) forms the basis of modern geometry.

eugenics A Greek term, meaning "good birth," referring to the project of "breeding" a superior human race. It was popularly championed by scientists, politicians, and social critics in the late nineteenth and early twentieth centuries.

Eurasia The preferred term for the geographical expanse that encompasses both Europe and Asia.

European Common Market (1957) The Treaty of Rome established the European Economic Community (EEC), or Common Market. The original members were France, West Germany, Italy, Belgium, Holland, and Luxembourg. The EEC sought to abolish trade barriers between its members and it pledged itself to common external tariffs, the free movement of labor and capital among the member nations, and uniform wage structures and social security systems to create similar working conditions in all member countries.

European Union (EU) Successor organization to the European Economic Community or European Common Market, formed by the Maastricht Treaty, which took effect in 1993. Currently twenty-eight member states compose the EU, which has a governing council, an international court, and a parliament. Over time, member states of the EU have relinquished some of their sovereignty, and cooperation has evolved into a community with a single currency, the euro.

Exclusion Act of 1882 U.S. law prohibiting nearly all immigration from China to the United States; fueled by animosity toward Chinese workers in the American West.

existentialism Philosophical movement that arose out of the Second World War and emphasized the absurdity of human condition. Led by Jean-Paul Sartre and Albert Camus, existentialists encouraged humans to take responsibility for their own decisions and dilemmas.

expulsion of the Jews European rulers began to expel their Jewish subjects from their kingdoms beginning in the 1280s, mostly due to their inability to repay the money they had extorted from Jewish moneylenders but also as a result of escalating antisemitism in the wake of the Crusades. Jews were also expelled from the Rhineland during the fourteenth century and from Spain in 1492.

fascism The doctrine formulated by Benito Mussolini, which emphasized three main ideas: statism ("nothing above the state, nothing outside the state, nothing against the state"), nationalism, and militarism. Its name derives from the Latin *fasces*, a symbol of Roman imperial power adopted by Mussolini.

Fashoda incident (1898) Disagreements between the French and the British over land claims in North Africa led to a standoff between armies of the two nations at the Sudanese town of Fashoda. The crisis was solved diplomatically. France ceded southern Sudan to Britain in exchange for a stop to further expansion by the British.

Federal Republic of Germany Nation founded from the Allied zones of occupation of Germany after the Second World War; also known as West Germany.

The Feminine Mystique Groundbreaking book by the feminist Betty Friedan (1921–2006), who tried to define *femininity* and explored how women internalized those definitions.

Franz Ferdinand (1863–1914) Archduke of Austria and heir to the Austro-Hungarian Empire; his assassination led to the beginning of the First World War.

Ferdinand (1452–1516) **and Isabella** (1451–1504) In 1469, Ferdinand of Aragon married the heiress to Castile, Isabella. Their union allowed them to pursue several ambitious policies, including the conquest of Granada, the last Muslim principality in Spain, and the expulsion of Spain's large Jewish community. In 1492, Isabella granted three ships to Christopher Columbus of Genoa (Italy), who went on to claim portions of the New World for Spain.

Fertile Crescent An area of fertile land comprising what are now Syria, Israel, Turkey, eastern Iraq, and western Iran that was able to sustain settlements due to its wetter climate and abundant natural food resources. Some of the earliest known civilizations emerged there between 9000 and 4500 B.C.E.

feudalism A problematic modern term that attempts to explain the diffusion of power in medieval Europe and the many different kinds of political, social, and economic relationships that were forged through the giving and receiving of fiefs (*feoda*). But because it is anachronistic and inadequate, this term has been rejected by most historians of the medieval period.

financial crisis of 2008 A global economic crisis following the sudden collapse of real estate prices in many parts of the world in 2008. The effects of this crisis were magnified by the increased level of globalization in the world economy, particularly in banking and the financial industry. In order to prevent a complete collapse of the global economy, governments in the United States and in Europe provided bailouts to cash-strapped banks and financial institutions, funded by taxpayers.

First Crusade (1095–1099) Launched by Pope Urban II in response to a request from the Byzantine emperor Alexius Comnenus. Alexius had asked for a small contingent of knights to assist him in fighting Turkish forces in Anatolia, but Urban instead directed the crusaders' energies toward the Holy Land and the recapture of Jerusalem, promising those who took the cross (*crux*) that they would merit eternal salvation if they died in the attempt. This crusade prompted attacks against Jews throughout Europe and resulted in six subsequent—and unsuccessful—military campaigns.

First World War A total war from August 1914 to November 1918, involving the armies of Britain, France, and Russia (the Allies) against Germany, Austria-Hungary, and the Ottoman Empire (the Central Powers). Italy joined the Allies in 1915, and the United States joined them in 1917, helping to tip the balance in favor of the Allies, who also drew on the populations and raw materials of their colonial possessions. Also known as the Great War.

Five Pillars of Islam The Muslim teaching that salvation is assured only through observance of five basic precepts: submission to God's will as described in the teachings of Muḥammad, frequent prayer, ritual fasting, the giving of alms, and an annual pilgrimage to Mecca (the Hajj).

Five-Year Plan Soviet effort launched under Stalin in 1928 to replace the market with a state-owned and state-managed economy in order to promote rapid economic development over a five-year period and thereby "catch and overtake" the leading capitalist countries. The First Five-Year Plan was followed by the Second Five-Year Plan (1933–1937) and so on, until the collapse of the Soviet Union in 1991.

fly shuttle Invented by John Kay in 1733, this device sped up the process of weaving.

Charles Fourier (1772–1837) French philosopher and thinker who sought to organize utopian societies.

Fourteen Points President Woodrow Wilson proposed these points as the foundation on which to build peace in the world after the First World War. They called for an end to secret treaties, "open covenants, openly arrived at," freedom of the seas, the removal of international tariffs, the reduction of arms, the "self-determination of peoples," and the establishment of a League of Nations to settle international conflicts.

Franciscan order Also known as the Order of the Friars Minor. The earliest Franciscans were followers of Francis of Assisi (1182–1226) and strove, like him, to imitate the life and example of Jesus. The order was formally established by Pope Innocent III in 1209. Its special mission was the care and instruction of the urban poor.

Frankfurt Assembly (1848–1849) Failed attempt to create a unified Germany under constitutional principles. In 1849, the assembly offered the crown of the new German nation to Frederick William IV of Prussia, but he refused the offer and suppressed a brief protest. The delegates went home disillusioned.

Frederick I "Barbarossa" ("Red Beard"; r. 1155–1190) was the first of Charlemagne's successors to call his realm the Holy Roman Empire, thereby claiming its spiritual and political independence from Rome. He spent his long reign struggling with the papacy and the rebellious towns of northern Italy. He died during the Third Crusade.

Frederick the Great (1712–1786) Prussian ruler (1740–1786) who engaged the nobility in maintaining a strong military and bureaucracy and led Prussian armies to notable military victories. He also encouraged Enlightenment rationalism and artistic endeavors.

French Revolution of 1789 In 1788, a severe financial crisis forced the French monarchy to convene the Estates General, an assembly representing the three estates of the realm: the clergy, the nobility, and the commons (known as the Third Estate). When the Estates General met in 1789, representatives of the Third Estate demanded major constitutional changes. When the king and his government proved uncooperative, the Third Estate broke with the other two estates and renamed itself the National Assembly, demanding a written constitution. The position of the National Assembly was confirmed by a popular uprising in Paris, forcing the king to accept the transformation of France into a constitutional monarchy. This constitutional phase of the revolution lasted until 1792, when the pressures of foreign invasion and the emergence of a more radical revolutionary movement caused the collapse of the monarchy and the establishment of a Republic in France.

French Revolution of 1830 The French popular revolt against Charles X's July Ordinances of 1830, which dissolved the French Chamber of Deputies and restricted suffrage to exclude almost everyone except the nobility. After several days of violence, Charles abdicated the throne and was replaced by a constitutional monarch, Louis Philippe.

French Revolution of 1848 Revolution overthrowing Louis Philippe in February 1848, leading to the formation of the Second Republic (1848–1852). Initially enjoying broad support from both the middle classes and laborers in Paris, the new government became more conservative after elections in which the French peasantry participated for the first time. A workers' revolt was violently repressed in June 1848. In December 1848, Napoleon Bonaparte's nephew, Louis-Napoleon Bonaparte, was elected president. In 1852, Louis-Napoleon declared himself emperor and abolished the republic.

Sigmund Freud (1856–1939) Austrian physician who founded the discipline of psychoanalysis and suggested that human behavior was largely motivated by unconscious and irrational forces.

Galileo Galilei (1564–1642) Italian physicist and inventor; the implications of his ideas raised the ire of the Catholic Church, and he was forced to retract most of his findings.

Gallipoli (1915) During the First World War, a combined force of French, British, Australian and New Zealand troops tried to invade the Gallipoli Peninsula, in the first large-scale amphibious attack in history, and seize it from the Turks. After seven months of fighting, the Allies had lost 200,000 soldiers. Defeated, they withdrew.

Mohandas K. (Mahatma) Gandhi (1869–1948) The Indian leader who advocated nonviolent noncooperation to protest colonial rule and helped win home rule for India in 1947.

Giuseppe Garibaldi (1807–1882) Italian revolutionary leader who led the fight to free Sicily and Naples from the Habsburg Empire; those lands were then peaceably annexed by Sardinia to produce a unified Italy.

Gaul The region of the Roman Empire that was home to the Celtic people of that name, comprising modern France, Belgium, and western Germany.

Geneva Peace Conference (1954) International conference to restore peace in Korea and Indochina. The chief participants were the United States, the Soviet Union, Great Britain, France, the People's Republic of China, North

Korea, South Korea, Vietnam, the Viet Minh party, Laos, and Cambodia. The conference resulted in the division of North and South Vietnam.

Genoa Maritime city on Italy's northwestern coast. The Genoese were active in trading ventures along the Silk Road and in the establishment of trading colonies in the Mediterranean. They were also involved in the world of finance and backed the commercial ventures of other powers, especially Spain.

German Democratic Republic Nation founded from the Soviet zone of occupation of Germany after the Second World War; also known as East Germany.

German Social Democratic party Founded in 1875, it was the most powerful socialist party in Europe before 1917.

Gilgamesh Sumerian ruler of the city of Uruk around 2700 B.C.E., Gilgamesh became the hero of one of the world's oldest epics, which circulated orally for nearly a millennium before being written down.

Giotto (c. 1266–1337) Florentine painter and architect who is often considered a forerunner of the Renaissance.

glasnost Introduced by the Soviet leader Mikhail Gorbachev in June 1987, *glasnost* was one of the five major policies that constituted *perestroika* ("reform" or "restructuring"). Often translated into English as "openness," it called for transparency in Soviet government and institutional activities by reducing censorship in mass media and lifting significant bans on the political, intellectual, and cultural lives of Soviet civilians.

globalization The term used to describe political, social, and economic networks that span the globe. These global exchanges are not limited by nation-states and in recent decades have become associated with new technologies, such as the Internet. Globalization is not new, however; human cultures and economies have been in contact with each other for centuries.

Glorious Revolution The overthrow of King James II of England and the installation of his Protestant daughter, Mary Stuart, and her husband, William of Orange, to the throne in 1688 and 1689. It is widely regarded as the founding moment in the development of a constitutional monarchy in Britain. It also established a more favorable climate for the economic and political growth of the English commercial classes.

Mikhail Gorbachev (1931–2022) Soviet leader who attempted to reform the Soviet Union through his programs of glasnost and perestroika in the late 1980s. He encouraged open discussions in other countries of the Soviet bloc, which helped inspire the velvet revolutions throughout Eastern Europe. Eventually the political, social, and economic upheaval he had unleashed led to the breakup of the Soviet Union.

Gothic style A type of graceful architecture emerging in twelfth- and thirteenth-century England and France. This style is characterized by pointed arches, delicate decoration, and large windows.

Great Depression Global economic crisis following the U.S. stock market crash on October 29, 1929, and ending with the onset of the Second World War.

Great Famine A period of terrible hunger and deprivation in Europe that peaked between 1315 and 1317, caused by a cooling of the climate and by soil exhaustion due to over-farming. It is estimated to have reduced the population of Europe by 10 to 15 percent.

Great Fear (1789) Following the outbreak of revolution in Paris, fear spread throughout the French countryside, as rumors circulated that armies of brigands or royal troops were coming. Some peasants and villagers organized into militias; others attacked and burned the manor houses in order to destroy the records of manorial dues.

Great Schism (1378–1417) Also known as the Great Western Schism, to distinguish it from the long-standing rupture between the churches of the Greek East and the Latin West. During the Great Schism, the Roman Church was divided between two (and, ultimately, three) competing popes. Each pope claimed to be legitimate, and each denounced the heresy of the others.

Great Terror (1936–1938) The systematic murder of nearly a million people and the deportation of another million and a half to labor camps by Stalin's regime in an attempt to consolidate power and remove perceived enemies.

Greek East After the founding of Constantinople, the eastern Greek-speaking half of the Roman Empire grew more populous, prosperous, and central to imperial policy. Its inhabitants considered themselves to be the true heirs of Rome and their own Orthodox Church to be the true manifestation of Jesus's ministry.

Greek independence Nationalists in Greece revolted against the Ottoman Empire and fought a war that ended in Greek independence in 1827. They received crucial help from British, French, and Russian troops as well as widespread sympathy throughout Europe.

Pope Gregory I (r. 590–604) Also known as Gregory the Great, he was the first bishop of Rome to successfully negotiate a more universal role for the papacy. His political and theological agenda widened the rift between the western Latin (Catholic) Church and the eastern Greek (Orthodox) Church in Byzantium. He also articulated the Church's official position on the status of Jews, promoted effective approaches to religious worship, encouraged the Benedictine monastic movement, and sponsored missionary expeditions.

guilds Professional organizations in commercial towns that regulated business and safeguarded the privileges of those practicing a particular craft. Often identical to confraternities ("brotherhoods").

Gulag The vast system of forced labor camps under the Soviet regime. It originated in 1919 in a small monastery near the Arctic Circle and spread throughout the Soviet Union. Penal labor was required of both ordinary criminals and those accused of political crimes. Tens of millions of people were sent to the camps between 1928 and 1953; the exact figure is unknown.

Gulf War (1991) Armed conflict between Iraq and a coalition of thirty-two nations, including the United States, Britain, Egypt, France, and Saudi Arabia. The seeds of the war were planted with Iraq's invasion of Kuwait on August 2, 1990.

Johannes Gutenberg European inventor of the printing press. His shop in Mainz produced the first printed book—a Bible—between the years 1453 and 1455.

Habsburg Dynasty A powerful European dynasty that came to power in the eleventh century in a region now part of Switzerland. Early generations of Habsburgs consolidated their control over neighboring German-speaking lands. Through strategic marriages with other royal lines, later rulers eventually controlled a substantial part of Europe— including much of central Europe, the Netherlands, and even Spain and all its colonies for a time. In practice, the Holy Roman Emperor was chosen from a member of the Habsburg lineage. By the latter half of the seventeenth century, the Austrian Habsburg Empire was made up of nearly 300 nominally autonomous dynastic kingdoms, principalities, duchies, and archbishoprics.

Hagia Sophia The enormous church dedicated to "Holy Wisdom," built in Constantinople at the behest of the emperor Justinian in the sixth century C.E. When Constantinople fell to Ottoman forces in 1453, it became an important mosque.

Haitian Revolution (1791–1804) In 1802, Napoleon sought to reassert French control of Saint-Domingue, but stiff resistance and yellow fever crushed the French army. In 1804, Jean-Jacques Dessalines, a general in the army of former slaves, declared the independent state of Haiti (see slave revolt in Saint-Domingue).

Hajj The annual pilgrimage to Mecca; an obligation for Muslims.

Hammurabi Ruler of Babylon from 1792 to 1750 B.C.E., Hammurabi issued a collection of laws that were greatly influential in the Near East and that constitute the world's oldest surviving law code.

Hatshepsut (1479–1458 C.E.) As a pharaoh during the New Kingdom, she launched several successful military campaigns and extended trade and diplomacy. She was an ambitious builder who probably constructed the first tomb in the Valley of the Kings. Though she never pretended to be a man, she was routinely portrayed with a masculine figure and a ceremonial beard.

Hebrews Originally a pastoral people divided among several tribes, they were briefly united under the rule of David and his son, Solomon, who promoted the worship of a single god, Yahweh, and constructed the first temple at the new capital city of Jerusalem. After Solomon's death, the Hebrew tribes were divided between the two kingdoms of Israel and Judah, which were eventually conquered by the Neo-Assyrian and Chaldean empires. It was in captivity that the Hebrews came to define themselves through worship of Yahweh and to develop a religion, Judaism, that could exist outside of Judea. They were liberated by the Persian king Cyrus the Great in 539 B.C.E.

Hellenistic art The art of the Hellenistic period bridged the tastes, ideals, and customs of classical Greece and those that became more characteristic of Rome. The Romans strove to emulate Hellenistic city planning and civic culture, thereby exporting Hellenistic culture to their own far-flung colonies in western Europe.

Hellenistic culture The "Greek-like" culture that dominated the ancient world in the wake of Alexander's conquests.

Hellenistic kingdoms Following the death of Alexander the Great, his vast empire was divided into three separate states: Ptolemaic Egypt, under the rule of the general Ptolemy and his successors; Seleucid Asia, ruled by the general Seleucus and his heirs; and Antigonid Greece, governed by Antigonus of Macedonia. Each state maintained its independence, but the shared characteristics of Greco-Macedonian rule and a shared Greek culture and heritage bound them together in a united cosmopolitan world.

Hellenistic world The various Western civilizations of antiquity that were loosely united by shared Greek language and culture, especially around the eastern Mediterranean.

Heloise (c. 1090–1164) One of the foremost scholars of her time, she became the pupil and the wife of the philosopher and teacher Peter Abelard. In later life, she was the founder of a new religious order for women.

Henry II (1133–1189) Also known as Henry of Anjou, he was king of England from 1154 to 1189. Thanks to his marriage to Eleanor of Aquitaine, who had annulled her first marriage to the French king Louis VII in order to marry him, he was also able to control the Aquitaine.

Henry IV King of Germany and Holy Roman Emperor from 1056—when he ascended the throne at the age of six—until his death in 1106. Henry's reign first was weakened by conflict with the Saxon nobility and later was marked by the Investiture Controversy with Pope Gregory VII.

Henry VIII (1491–1547) King of England from 1509 until his death, Henry rejected the authority of the Roman Church in 1534 when the pope refused to annul his marriage to his queen, Catherine of Aragon; Henry became the founder of the Church of England.

Henry of Navarre (1553–1610) Crowned King Henry IV of France, he renounced his Protestantism but granted limited toleration to Huguenots (French Protestants) through the Edict of Nantes in 1598.

Prince Henry the Navigator (1394–1460) A member of the Portuguese royal family, Henry encouraged the exploration and conquest of western Africa and the trade in gold and slaves.

hieroglyphs The writing system of ancient Egypt, based on a complicated series of pictorial symbols. It fell out of use when Egypt was absorbed into the Roman Empire and was deciphered only after the discovery of the Rosetta Stone in the early nineteenth century.

Hildegard of Bingen (1098–1179) A powerful abbess, theologian, scientist, musician, and visionary who claimed to receive regular revelations from God. Although highly influential in her own day, she was never officially canonized by the Church, in part because her strong personality no longer matched the changing ideal of female piety.

Hiroshima Japanese port devastated by an atomic bomb on August 6, 1945.

Adolf Hitler (1889–1945) The author of *Mein Kampf* and leader of the Nazis who became chancellor of Germany in 1933. Hitler and his Nazi regime started the Second World War and orchestrated the systematic murder of over 6 million Jews, hundreds of thousands of people with disabilities living in institutions, tens of thousands of Roma, and thousands of homosexuals.

Hitler-Stalin Pact (1939) Treaty between Stalin and Hitler that promised Stalin a share of Poland, Finland, the Baltic states, and Bessarabia in the event of a German invasion of Poland, which began shortly thereafter, on September 1, 1939.

HIV-AIDS epidemic The first cases of HIV (human immunodeficiency virus) infection appeared in the late 1970s. It swiftly became a global crisis as those infected passed away from its late stages, AIDS, or acquired immunodeficiency syndrome.

Thomas Hobbes (1588–1679) English political philosopher whose *Leviathan* argued that any form of government capable of protecting its subjects' lives and property might act as an all-powerful sovereign. This government should be allowed to trample over both liberty and property for the sake of its own survival and that of its subjects. Hobbes argued that in his natural state, man was like "a wolf" toward other men.

Holy Roman Empire The loosely allied collection of lands in central and eastern Europe ruled by German kings from the twelfth century until 1806. Its origins are usually identified with the empire of Charlemagne, the Frankish king who was crowned emperor of Rome by the pope in 800. The term itself was promoted by Frederick I "Barbarossa" in the mid-twelfth century.

homage A ceremony in which an individual becomes the "man" (French: *homme*) of a lord.

Homer (fl. eighth century B.C.E.) A Greek rhapsode ("weaver" of stories) credited with merging centuries of poetic tradition in the epics known as the *Iliad* and the *Odyssey*.

hoplite A Greek foot-soldier armed with a spear or short sword and protected by a large round shield (*hoplon*). In battle, hoplites stood shoulder to shoulder in a close formation called a phalanx.

Huguenots French Protestants who endured severe persecution in the sixteenth and seventeenth centuries.

humanism A program of study associated with the movement known as the Renaissance, humanism aimed to replace the scholastic emphasis on logic and philosophy with the study of ancient languages, literature, history, and ethics.

human rights The rights of all people to legal equality, freedom of religion and speech, and the right to participate in government. Human rights laws prohibit torture, cruel punishment, and slavery.

David Hume (1711–1776) Scottish writer who applied Newton's method of scientific inquiry and skepticism to the study of morality, the mind, and government.

Hundred Years' War (1337–1453) A series of wars between England and France, fought mostly on French soil and prompted by the territorial and political claims of English monarchs.

Jan Hus (c. 1373–1415) A Czech reformer who adopted many of the teachings of the English theologian John Wycliffe, and who also demanded that the laity be allowed to receive both the consecrated bread and wine of the Eucharist. The Council of Constance burned him at the stake for heresy. In response, his supporters, the Hussites, revolted against the Church.

Saddam Hussein (1937–2006) The dictator of Iraq who invaded Iran in 1980 and started the eight-year-long Iran-Iraq war; invaded Kuwait in 1990, which led to the Gulf War of 1991; and was overthrown when the United States invaded Iraq in 2003. Involved in Iraqi politics since the mid-1960s, Hussein became the official head of state in 1979.

Iconoclast Controversy (717–787) A serious and often violent theological debate that raged in Byzantium after Emperor Leo III ordered the destruction of religious art on the grounds that any image representing a divine or holy personage was likely to promote idol worship and blasphemy. *Iconoclast* means "breaker of icons." Those who supported the veneration of icons were called iconodules, "adherents of icons."

Inca Empire The highly centralized South American empire that was toppled by the Spanish conquistador Francisco Pizarro in 1533.

Indian National Congress Formed in 1885, this Indian political party worked to achieve Indian independence from British colonial control. The Congress was led by Gandhi during the 1920s and 1930s.

Indian Rebellion of 1857 This uprising began near Delhi, when the military disciplined a regiment of Indian soldiers employed by the British for refusing to use rifle cartridges greased with pork fat—unacceptable to both Hindus and Muslims. Rebels attacked law courts and burned tax rolls, protesting debt and corruption. The mutiny spread through large areas of northwest India before being violently suppressed by British troops.

Indo-Europeans A group of people speaking variations of the same language and who moved into the Near East and Mediterranean region shortly after 2000 B.C.E.

indulgences Grants exempting Catholic Christians from the performance of penance, either in life or after death.

The abusive trade in indulgences was a major catalyst of the Protestant Reformation.

Innocent III (1160/61–1216) As pope, he wanted to unify all of Christendom under papal hegemony. He furthered this goal at the Fourth Lateran Council of 1215, which defined one of the Church's dogmas as the acknowledgment of papal supremacy. The council also took an unprecedented interest in the religious education and habits of every Christian.

Inquisition Formalized in the thirteenth century, this tribunal of the Roman Church aims to enforce religious orthodoxy and conformity.

International Monetary Fund (IMF) Established in 1945 to ensure international cooperation regarding currency exchange and monetary policy, the IMF is a specialized agency of the United Nations.

Investiture Controversy The name given to a series of debates over the limitations of spiritual and secular power in Europe during the eleventh and early twelfth centuries, it came to a head when Pope Gregory VII and Emperor Henry IV of Germany both claimed the right to appoint and invest bishops with the regalia of office. After years of diplomatic and military hostility, it was partially settled by the Concordat of Worms in 1122.

Irish potato famine Period of agricultural blight from 1845 to 1849 whose devastating results produced widespread starvation and led to mass immigration to the United States.

Iron Curtain Term coined by Winston Churchill in 1946 to refer to the borders of Eastern European nations that lay within the zone of Soviet control.

Islamic learning and culture The Crusades brought the Latin West in contact with the Islamic world, which influenced European culture in myriad ways. Europeans adapted Arabic numerals and mathematical concepts as well as Arabic and Persian words. Through Arabic translations, Western scholars gained access to Greek learning, which had a profound influence on Christian theology. European scholars also learned from the Islamic world's accomplishments in medicine and science.

Islamic State (Daesh) In 2014, following the outbreak of the civil war in Syria, a militant group of Muslim fundamentalists seized territory in northeastern Syria and northwestern Iraq and proclaimed themselves a new *caliphate*, the authority over all Muslims. Known as the Islamic State of Iraq and Syria (ISIS) or the Islamic State of Iraq and the Levant (ISIL), they are also called Daesh by Arabic-speaking critics of their violence and brutality. ("Daesh" is an Arabic acronym for the group's name, but it also sounds like a word that means to trample or crush something.) They have been designated a terrorist organization by the United Nations and many countries of the world, both for their actions in the Middle East and for their encouragement of terrorist acts in Europe, Africa, and North and South America.

Islamicate world The regions influenced by the social, cultural, and political norms associated with Islam.

Italian invasion of Ethiopia (1896) Italy invaded Ethiopia, the last major independent African kingdom. Menelik II, the Ethiopian emperor, soundly defeated the Italian forces.

Ivan III, the Great (1440–1505) Russian ruler who annexed neighboring territories and consolidated his empire's position as a European power.

Jacobins Radical French political group during the French Revolution that took power after 1792, executed the French king, and sought to remake French culture.

Jacquerie Violent 1358 peasant uprising in northern France, incited by disease, war, and taxes.

James I (1566–1625) Monarch who ruled Scotland as James VI and who succeeded Elizabeth I as king of England in 1603. He supervised the English vernacular translation of the Bible known by his name.

James II King of England, Ireland, and Scotland from 1685 to 1688 whose commitment to absolutism and Catholic zealotry led to his exile to France after the Glorious Revolution of 1688.

Janissaries Corps of enslaved soldiers recruited as children from the Christian provinces of the Ottoman Empire and trained to display intense personal loyalty to the Ottoman sultans, who used these forces to curb local autonomy and as their personal bodyguards.

January Rising Failed attempt by Polish nationalists to reestablish the Polish-Lithuanian Commonwealth in 1863–1864.

Jerome (c. 340–420 c.e.) One of the early church fathers, he translated the Bible from Hebrew and Greek into a popular form of Latin—hence the name by which this translation is known: the Vulgate, or "vulgar" (popular), Bible.

Jesuits The religious order formally known as the Society of Jesus, founded in 1540 by Ignatius Loyola to combat the spread of Protestantism. The Jesuits became active in politics, education, and missionary work.

Jesus (c. 4 b.c.e.–c. 30 c.e.) A Jewish preacher and teacher in the rural areas of Galilee and Judea who was arrested for seditious political activity, tried, and crucified by the Romans. After his execution, his followers claimed that he had been resurrected from the dead and taken up into heaven. They began to teach that Jesus had been the divine representative of God, the Messiah foretold by ancient Hebrew prophets, and that he had suffered for the sins of humanity and would return to judge all the world's inhabitants at the end of time.

Joan of Arc (c. 1412–1431) A peasant girl from the province of Lorraine who claimed to have been commanded by God to lead French forces against the English occupying army during the Hundred Years' War. Successful in her efforts, she was betrayed by the French king and handed over to the English, who condemned her to death for heresy. Her reputation underwent a process of rehabilitation, but she was not officially canonized as a saint until 1920.

Judaism The religion of the Hebrews as it developed in the centuries after the establishment of the Hebrew kingdoms under David and Solomon, especially during the period of Babylonian Captivity.

June Days Uprising of workers in Paris against the Second Republic in June 1848, over the government's decision to curtail economic support for the unemployed.

Justinian (527–565) Emperor of Rome who unsuccessfully attempted to reunite the eastern and western portions of the empire. Also known for his important codification of Roman law, in the *Corpus Juris Civilis*.

Justinian's Code of Roman Law Formally known as the *Corpus Juris Civilis*, or "Body of Civil Law," this compendium consisted of a systematic compilation of imperial statutes, the writings of Rome's great legal authorities, a textbook of legal principles, and the legislation of Justinian and his immediate successors. As the most authoritative collection of Roman law, it formed the basis of canon law (the legal system of the Roman Church) and became essential to the developing legal traditions of every European state as well as of many countries around the world.

Das Kapital ("Capital") The 1867 book by Karl Marx that outlined the theory behind historical materialism and attacked the socioeconomic inequities of capitalism.

Johannes Kepler (1571–1630) Mathematician and astronomer who elaborated on and corrected Copernicus's theory and is chiefly remembered for his discovery of the three laws of planetary motion that bear his name.

Keynesian Revolution Postdepression economic ideas developed by the British economist John Maynard Keynes, whereby the state took a greater role in managing the market economy through monetary policy in order to maintain levels of unemployment during periods of economic downturn.

Genghis Khan (c. 1167–1227) "Oceanic Ruler," the title adopted by the Mongol chieftain Temujin, founder of a dynasty that conquered much of southern Asia.

Khanate The major political unit of the vast Mongol Empire. There were four Khanates, including the Yuan Empire in China, forged by Chingiz Khan's grandson Kubilai in the thirteenth century.

Ruhollah Khomeini (1902–1989) Iranian Shi'ite religious leader who led the revolution in Iran that resulted in the abdication of the shah in 1979. His government allowed some limited economic and political populism combined with strict constructions of Islamic law, restrictions on women's public life, and the prohibition of ideas or activities linked to Western influence.

Nikita Khrushchev (1894–1971) Leader of the Soviet Union during the Cuban missile crisis, Khrushchev came to power after Stalin's death in 1953. His reforms and criticisms of the excesses of the Stalin regime led to his fall from power in 1964.

Kremlin Once synonymous with the Soviet government, this word refers to Moscow's walled city center and the palace originally built by Ivan the Great.

Kristallnacht Organized attack by Nazis and their supporters on the Jews of Germany following the assassination of a German embassy official by a Jewish man in Paris. Throughout Germany, thousands of stores, schools, cemeteries, and synagogues were attacked on November 9, 1938. Dozens of people were killed, and tens of thousands of Jews were arrested and held in camps, where many were tortured and killed in the ensuing months.

Labour party Founded in Britain in 1900, this party represented workers and was based on socialist principles.

Latin West After the founding of Constantinople, the western Latin-speaking half of the Roman Empire became poorer and more peripheral, but it also fostered the emergence of new barbarian kingdoms. At the same time, the Roman pope claimed to have inherited both the authority of Jesus and the essential elements of Roman imperial authority.

League of Nations International organization founded after the First World War to solve international disputes through arbitration; it was dissolved in 1946 and its assets were transferred to the United Nations.

Leonardo da Vinci (1452–1519) Florentine inventor, sculptor, architect, and painter whose breadth of interests typifies the ideal of the "Renaissance man."

Vladimir Lenin (1870–1924) Leader of the Bolshevik Revolution in Russia (1917) and the first leader of the Soviet Union.

Leviathan A book by Thomas Hobbes (1588–1679) that recommended a ruler have unrestricted power.

liberalism Political and social theory that judges the effectiveness of a government in terms of its ability to protect individual rights. Liberals support representative forms of government, free trade, and freedom of speech and religion. In the economic realm, liberals believe that individuals should be free to engage in commercial or business activities without interference from the state or their community.

lithograph Art form that involves drawing or writing on stone and producing printed impressions.

John Locke (1632–1704) English philosopher and political theorist known for his contributions to liberalism. Locke had great faith in human reason and believed that just societies were those that infringed the least on the natural rights and freedoms of individuals. This led him to assert that a government's legitimacy depended on the consent of the governed, a view that had a profound effect on the authors of the United States' Declaration of Independence.

Louis IX King of France from 1226 to his death on crusade in 1270, Louis was famous for his piety and for his close attention to the administration of law and justice in his realm. He was officially canonized as Saint Louis in 1297.

Louis XIV (1638–1715) Called the "Sun King," he was known for his success at strengthening the institutions of the French absolutist state.

Louis XVI (1754–1793) Well-meaning but ineffectual king of France, finally deposed and executed during the French Revolution.

Louis Philippe (1773–1850) King of France from 1830 to 1848, during a period known as the July Monarchy, after the July Revolution of 1830 that brought him to the throne. Abdicated during the Revolution of 1848.

Toussaint L'Ouverture (1743–1803) A former slave who, after 1791, led the slaves of the French colony of Saint-Domingue in the largest and most successful slave insurrection in world history. After his capture and death in 1803, his followers succeeded in establishing an independent Haiti in 1804.

Ignatius Loyola (1491–1556) Founder of the Society of Jesus (commonly known as the Jesuits), whose members vowed to serve God through poverty, chastity, and missionary work. He abandoned his first career as a mercenary after reading an account of Christ's life written in his native Spanish.

Lucretia According to Roman legend, Lucretia was a virtuous Roman wife who was raped by the son of Rome's last king and who virtuously committed suicide in order to avoid bringing shame on her family.

Lusitania The British passenger liner that was sunk by a German U-boat (submarine) on May 7, 1915. Public outrage over the sinking contributed to the United States' decision to enter the First World War.

Martin Luther (1483–1546) A German monk and professor of theology whose critique of the papacy launched the Protestant Reformation.

ma'at The Egyptian term for the serene order of the universe, with which the individual soul (*ka*) must remain in harmony. The power of the pharaoh was linked to *ma'at*, insofar as it ensured the prosperity of the kingdom. After the upheavals of the First Intermediate Period, the perception of the pharaoh's relationship with *ma'at* was revealed to be conditional, something that had to be earned.

Niccolò Machiavelli (1469–1527) As the author of *The Prince* and the *Discourses on Livy*, he looked to the Roman past for paradigms of greatness, at the same time hoping to win the patronage of contemporary rulers who would restore Italy's political independence.

Magna Carta The "Great Charter" of 1215, enacted during the reign of King John of England and designed to limit his powers. It is regarded now as a landmark in the development of constitutional government. In its own time, its purpose was to restore the power of great lords.

Magyar nationalism Lajos Kossuth led this national movement in the Hungarian region of the Habsburg Empire, calling for national independence for Hungary in 1848. With the support of Russia, the Habsburg army crushed the movement and all other revolutionary activities in the empire. Kossuth fled into exile.

Moses Maimonides (c. 1137–1204) Jewish scholar, physician, and scriptural commentator whose *Mishneh Torah* is a fundamental exposition of Jewish law.

Thomas Malthus (1766–1834) British political economist who believed that populations inevitably grew faster than the available food supply. Societies that could not control their population growth would be checked only by famine, disease, poverty, and infant malnutrition. He argued that governments could not alleviate poverty. Instead, the poor had to exercise "moral restraint," postpone marriage, and have fewer children.

Nelson Mandela (1918–2013) The South African opponent of apartheid who led the African National Congress and was imprisoned from 1962 until 1990. After his release from prison, he worked with Prime Minister Frederik Willem De Klerk to establish majority rule. Mandela became the first black president of South Africa in 1994.

Manhattan Project The secret U.S. government research project to develop the first nuclear bomb. The vast project involved dozens of sites across the United States, including New Mexico, Tennessee, Illinois, California, Utah, and Washington. The first test of a nuclear bomb was near Alamogordo, New Mexico, on July 16, 1945.

manors Common farmland worked collectively by the inhabitants of entire villages, sometimes on their own initiative, sometimes at the behest of a lord.

Mao Zedong (1893–1976) The leader of the Chinese Revolution who defeated the Nationalists in 1949 and established the Communist regime in China.

Battle of the Marne A major battle of the First World War in September 1914; halted the German invasion of France and led to protracted trench warfare on the Western Front.

Marshall Plan Economic aid package given to Europe by the United States after the Second World War to promote reconstruction and economic development and to secure European countries from a feared communist takeover.

Karl Marx (1818–1883) German philosopher and economist who believed that a revolution of the working classes would overthrow the capitalist order and create a classless society. Author of *Das Kapital* and *The Communist Manifesto*.

Marxists Followers of the socialist political economist Karl Marx, who called for workers everywhere to unite and create an independent political force. Marxists believed that industrialization brought about an inevitable struggle between laborers and the class of capitalist property owners. This struggle would culminate in a revolution that would abolish private property and establish a society committed to social equality.

Mary See **cult of the Virgin**.

Mary I (1516–1558) Catholic daughter of Henry VIII and his first wife, Catherine of Aragon, Mary Tudor was the first queen regnant of England. Her attempts to reinstitute Catholicism in England met with limited success. After her early death, she was labeled "Bloody Mary" by the Protestant supporters of her half sister and successor, Elizabeth I.

mass culture The spread of literacy and public education in the nineteenth century created a new audience for print entertainment and a new class of media entrepreneurs to cater to this audience. The invention of radio, film, and television in the twentieth century carried this development to another level, as millions of consumers were now accessible to the producers of news, information, and entertainment. The rise of this "mass culture" has been celebrated as an expression of popular tastes but also criticized as a vehicle for the manipulation of populations through clever and seductive propaganda.

Maya Native American people whose culturally and politically sophisticated empire encompassed lands in present-day Mexico and Guatemala.

Giuseppe Mazzini (1805–1872) Founder of Young Italy and an ideological leader of the Italian nationalist movement.

Mecca Center of an important commercial network of the Arabian Peninsula and birthplace of the prophet Muḥammad. It is now considered the holiest site in the Islamic world.

Medici A powerful dynasty of Florentine bankers and politicians whose ancestors were originally apothecaries ("medics").

Mensheviks Within the Russian Social Democratic Party, the Mensheviks advocated slow changes and a gradual move toward socialism, in contrast to the Bolsheviks, who wanted to push for a proletarian revolution. The Mensheviks believed that a proletarian revolution in Russia was premature and that the country needed to complete its capitalist development first.

mercantilism A theory and policy for directing the economy of monarchical states between 1600 and 1800 based on the assumption that wealth and power depended on a favorable balance of trade (more exports and fewer imports) and the accumulation of precious metals. Mercantilists advocated forms of economic protectionism to promote domestic production.

Maria Sibylla Merian (1647–1717) A scientific illustrator and an important early entomologist. She conducted research on two continents and published the well-received *Metamorphosis of the Insects of Surinam*.

Merovingian dynasty A Frankish dynasty that claimed descent from a legendary ancestor called Merovic, the Merovingians were the only powerful family to establish a lasting kingdom in western Europe during the fifth and sixth centuries.

Mesopotamia The "land between the Tigris and the Euphrates rivers," where the civilization of Sumer, the first urban society, flourished.

Klemens von Metternich (1773–1859) Austrian foreign minister whose primary goals were to bolster the legitimacy of monarchies and, after the defeat of Napoleon, to prevent another large-scale war in Europe. At the Congress of Vienna, he opposed social and political change and wanted to check Russian and French expansion.

Michelangelo Buonarroti (1475–1564) A virtuoso Florentine sculptor, painter, and poet who spent much of his career in the service of the papacy. He is best known for the decoration of the Sistine Chapel and for his monumental sculptures.

Middle East Like "Near East," this term was invented in the nineteenth century. It usually describes a region stretching from North Africa and Egypt to the Arabian Peninsula and Anatolia.

Middle Kingdom of Egypt (2055–1650 B.C.E.) The period following the First Intermediate Period of dynastic warfare, which ended with the reassertion of pharaonic rule under Mentuhotep II.

Miletus A Greek polis and Persian colony on the Ionian coast of Asia Minor. Influenced by the cultures of Mesopotamia, Egypt, and Lydia, it produced several of the ancient world's first scientists and sophists. Thereafter, a political conflict between the ruler of Miletus, Aristagoras, and the Persian emperor, Darius, sparked the Persian Wars with Greece.

John Stuart Mill (1806–1873) English liberal philosopher whose faith in human reason led him to support a broad variety of civic and political freedoms for men and women, including the right to vote and the right to free speech.

Slobodan Milošević (1941–2006) The Serbian nationalist politician who became president of Serbia and whose policies during the Balkan wars of the early 1990s led to the deaths of thousands of Croatians, Bosnian Muslims, Albanians, and Kosovars. After leaving office in 2000, he was arrested and tried for war crimes at the International

Court in The Hague. The trial ended before a verdict with his death in 2006.

Minoan Crete A sea empire based at Knossos on the Greek island of Crete and named for the legendary King Minos. The Minoans dominated the Aegean for much of the second millennium B.C.E.

modernism There were several different modernist movements in art and literature, but they shared three key characteristics. First, modernists believed that the world had radically changed and that this change should be embraced. Second, they believed that traditional aesthetic values and assumptions about creativity were ill suited to the present. Third, they developed a new conception of what art could do that emphasized expression over representation and insisted on the value of novelty, experimentation, and creative freedom.

Mongol people A nomadic people from the steppes of Central Asia who were united under the ruler Genghis Khan. His conquest of China was continued by his grandson Kubilai and his great-grandson Ogedei, whose army also seized southern Russia and then moved through Hungary and Poland toward eastern Germany. The Mongol armies withdrew from eastern Europe after the death of Ogedei, but his descendants continued to rule his vast empire for another half century.

Michel de Montaigne (1533–1592) French philosopher and social commentator, best known for his *Essays*.

Baron de Montesquieu (1689–1755) An Enlightenment philosophe whose most influential work was *The Spirit of Laws*. In this work, he analyzed the structures that shaped law and categorized governments into three types: republics, monarchies, and despotisms. His ideas about the separation of powers among the executive, the legislative, and the judicial branches of government influenced the authors of the U.S. Constitution.

Thomas More (1478–1535) Christian humanist, English statesman, and author of *Utopia*. In 1529, he was appointed lord chancellor of England but resigned because he opposed King Henry VIII's plans to establish a national church under royal control. He was eventually executed for refusing to take an oath acknowledging Henry to be the head of the Church of England and has since been canonized by the Catholic Church.

mos maiorum Literally translated as the "code of the elders" or the "custom of ancestors." This unwritten code governed the lives of Romans under the Republic and stressed the importance of showing reverence to ancestral tradition. It was sacrosanct and essential to Roman

identity and an important influence on Roman culture, law, and religion.

Wolfgang Amadeus Mozart (1756–1791) Austrian composer, famous at a young age as a concert musician and later celebrated as a prolific composer of instrumental music and operas that are seen as the apogee of the Classical style in music.

Muḥammad (570–632 C.E.) The founder of Islam, regarded by his followers as God's last and greatest prophet.

Munich Conference (1938) Hitler met with the leaders of Britain, France, and Italy and negotiated an agreement that gave Germany a major slice of Czechoslovakia. The British prime minister Neville Chamberlain believed that the agreement would bring peace to Europe, but instead Germany invaded and seized the rest of Czechoslovakia.

Muscovy The duchy centered on Moscow whose dukes saw themselves as heirs to the Roman Empire. In the early fourteenth century, Moscow was under the control of the Mongol Khanate. After the collapse of the Khanate, the Muscovite grand duke, Ivan III, conquered all the Russian principalities between Moscow and the border of Poland-Lithuania, and then Lithuania itself. By the time of his death, Ivan had established Muscovy as a dominant power.

Benito Mussolini (1883–1945) The Italian founder of the Fascist party who came to power in Italy in 1922 and allied himself with Hitler and the Nazis during the Second World War.

Mycenaean Greece (1600–1200 B.C.E.) The term used to describe the civilization of Greece during the late Bronze Age, when territorial kingdoms such as Mycenae formed around a king, a warrior caste, and a palace bureaucracy.

Nagasaki Second Japanese city on which the United States dropped an atomic bomb. The attack took place on August 9, 1945; the Japanese surrendered shortly thereafter, ending the Second World War.

Napoleon III (1808–1873) The nephew of Napoleon Bonaparte, Napoleon III was elected president of the French Second Republic in 1848 and made himself emperor of France in 1852. During his reign (1852–1870), he rebuilt the French capital of Paris. Defeated in the France-Prussian War of 1870, he went into exile.

Napoleonic Code Legal code drafted by Napoleon in 1804 and based on Justinian's *Corpus Iuris Civilis*. It distilled different legal traditions to create one uniform law. The code confirmed the abolition of feudal privileges of all kinds and set the conditions for exercising property rights.

Gamal Abdel Nasser (1918–1970) President of Egypt and the most prominent spokesman for secular pan-Arabism. He became a target for Islamist critics, such as Sayyid Qutb and the Muslim Brotherhood, angered by the Western-influenced policies of his regime.

National Assembly Governing body of France that succeeded the Estates General in 1789 during the French Revolution. It was composed of, and defined by, the delegates of the Third Estate.

National Association for the Advancement of Colored People (NAACP) Founded in 1910, this U.S. civil rights organization is dedicated to ending inequality and segregation for Black Americans.

National Convention The governing body of France from September 1792 to October 1795. It declared France a republic and then tried and executed King Louis XVI. The Convention also confiscated the property of the enemies of the revolution, instituted a policy of de-Christianization, changed marriage and inheritance laws, abolished slavery in its colonies, placed a cap on the price of necessities, and ended the compensation of nobles for their lost privileges.

nationalism Movement to unify a country under one government based on perceptions of the population's common history, customs, and social traditions.

nationalism in Yugoslavia In the 1990s, Slobodan Milošević and his allies reignited Serbian nationalism in the former Yugoslavia, which led non-Serb republics in Croatia and Slovenia to seek independence. The country erupted into war, with the worst violence taking place in Bosnia, a multiethnic region with Serb, Croatian, and Bosnian Muslim populations. European diplomats proved powerless to stop attempts by Croatian and Serbian military and paramilitary forces to claim territory through ethnic cleansing and violent intimidation. Atrocities were committed on all sides, but pro-Serb forces were responsible for the most deaths.

NATO The North Atlantic Treaty Organization, a 1949 military agreement among the United States, Canada, Great Britain, and eight Western European nations, which declared that an armed attack against any one of the members would be regarded as an attack against all. Created during the Cold War in the face of the Soviet Union's control of Eastern Europe, NATO continues to exist today. Its thirty countries include former members of the Warsaw Pact as well as Albania and Turkey.

Nazi party Founded in the early 1920s, the National Socialist German Workers' Party (NSDAP) gained control over Germany under the leadership of Adolf Hitler in 1933 and continued in power until Germany was defeated in 1945.

Nazism The political movement in Germany led by Adolf Hitler that advocated a violent antisemitic, anti-Marxist, pan-German ideology.

Near East Like "Middle East," a geographical term coined during the nineteenth century to describe western Asia and the eastern Mediterranean—that is, the parts of Asia nearest to Europe.

Neo-Assyrian Empire (883–859 B.C.E. to 612–605 B.C.E.) Assurnasirpal II laid the foundations of the Neo-Assyrian Empire through military campaigns against neighboring peoples. Eventually, the empire stretched from the Mediterranean Sea to western Iran. A military dictatorship governed the empire through its army, which it used to frighten and oppress both its subjects and its enemies. The empire's ideology was based on waging holy war in the name of its principal god, Assur, and the exaction of tribute through terror.

neoliberalism Neoliberals believe that free markets, profit incentives, and restraints on both budget deficits and social welfare programs are the best guarantee of individual liberties. Beginning in the 1980s, neoliberal theory was used to structure the policy of financial institutions such as the International Monetary Fund and the World Bank, which turned away from interventionist policies in favor of market-driven models of economic development.

Neolithic Revolution The "New" Stone Age, which began around 11,000 B.C.E., saw new technological and social developments, including managed food production, the beginnings of permanent settlements, and the rapid intensification of trade.

Neoplatonism A school of thought based on the teachings of Plato. Prevalent in the Roman Empire, it had a profound effect on the formation of Christian theology. Neoplatonists argued that nature is a book written by its creator to reveal the ways of God to humanity. Convinced that God's perfection must be reflected in nature, the Neoplatonists searched for the ideal and perfect structures that they believed must lie behind the "shadows" of the everyday world.

New Deal President Franklin D. Roosevelt's package of government reforms that were enacted during the depression of the 1930s to provide jobs for the unemployed, social welfare programs for the poor, and security to the financial markets.

New Economic Policy In 1921, the Bolsheviks abandoned war communism in favor of the New Economic Policy (NEP). Under the NEP, the state still controlled all major industry and financial concerns, while individuals could own private property, trade freely within limits, and farm their own land for their own benefit. Fixed taxes replaced grain requisition. The policy successfully helped Soviet agriculture recover from the civil war but was later abandoned in favor of collectivization.

Isaac Newton (1642–1727) One of the foremost scientists of all time, Newton was an English mathematician and physicist; he is noted for his development of calculus, work on the properties of light, and theory of gravitation.

Nicholas II (1868–1918) The last Russian tsar, who abdicated the throne in 1917. He and his family were executed by the Bolsheviks on July 17, 1918.

Friedrich Nietzsche (1844–1900) The German philosopher who denied the possibility of knowing absolute "truth" or "reality," since all knowledge comes filtered through linguistic, scientific, or artistic systems of representation. He also criticized Judeo-Christian morality for instilling a repressive conformity that drained civilization of its vitality.

nongovernmental organizations (NGOs) Private organizations such as the Red Cross that play a large role in international affairs.

novel A fictional work typically written in narrative prose, that recounts the actions and circumstances of individuals and their social lives. The novel as a literary form first emerged in the eighteenth century and was particularly popular among women readers.

Novum Organum Work by the English statesman and scientist Francis Bacon (1561–1626) that advanced a philosophy of study through observation.

October Days (1789) The high price of bread and the rumor that the king was unwilling to cooperate with the assembly caused the women who worked in Paris's large central market to march to Versailles along with their supporters to address the king. Not satisfied with their initial reception, they broke through the palace gates and called for the king to return to Paris from Versailles, which he did the following day.

offensives of 1916–1917 A series of costly but unsuccessful offensive operations initiated by the Allies and the Germans to break the stalemate on the western front, including the battles of Verdun, the Somme, and Passchendaele (also known as the Third Battle of Ypres).

Old Kingdom of Egypt (c. 2686–2160 B.C.E.) During this period, the pharaohs controlled a powerful and centralized bureaucratic state whose vast human and material resources are exemplified by the pyramids of Giza. This period came to an end as the pharaoh's authority collapsed, leading to a period of dynastic warfare and localized rule.

OPEC (Organization of the Petroleum Exporting Countries) Organization created in 1960 by oil-producing countries in the Middle East, South America, and Africa to regulate the production and pricing of crude oil.

Operation Barbarossa The code name for Hitler's invasion of the Soviet Union in 1941.

Opium Wars (1839–1842, 1856–1860) Wars fought between the British and Qing China to protect the British trade in opium; resulted in the ceding of Hong Kong to the British.

Oracle at Delphi The most important shrine in ancient Greece. The priestess of Apollo who attended the shrine was believed to have the power to predict the future.

Orthodox Refers to an adherence to traditional or conservative practice as it related to doctrinal decisions and disputes in the eastern Roman empire.

Ottoman Empire (c.1300–1923) During the thirteenth century, the Ottoman dynasty established itself as leader of the Turks. From the fourteenth to sixteenth centuries, the Ottomans conquered Anatolia, Armenia, Syria, and North Africa as well as parts of southeastern Europe, the Crimea, and areas along the Red Sea. Portions of the Ottoman Empire persisted up to the time of the First World War, but it was dismantled in the years following the war.

Robert Owen (1771–1858) Welsh industrialist and reformer who made efforts to improve factory conditions for workers in Scotland.

Mohammad Reza Pahlavi (1919–1980) The West-friendly shah of Iran who was installed during a 1953 coup supported by Britain and the United States. After a lengthy economic downturn, public unrest, and personal illness, he retired from public life under popular pressure in 1979.

Pan-African Conference A 1900 assembly in London that sought to draw attention to the sovereignty of African people and their mistreatment by colonial powers.

Panhellenism The "all-Greek" culture that allowed ancient Greek colonies to maintain a connection to their homeland and to each other through their shared language and heritage. These colonies also exported their culture into new areas and created new Greek-speaking enclaves, which permanently changed the cultural geography of the Mediterranean world.

pan-Slavism Cultural movement that sought to unite native Slavic peoples within the Russian and Habsburg Empires under Russian leadership.

Partition of India (1947) At independence, British India was partitioned into the nations of India and Pakistan. The majority of the population in India was Hindu, and the majority of the population in Pakistan was Muslim. The process of partition brought brutal religious and ethnic warfare. More than 1 million Hindus and Muslims died, and 12 million became refugees.

Blaise Pascal (1623–1662) A Catholic philosopher who wanted to establish the truth of Christianity by appealing simultaneously to intellect and emotion. In his *Pensées*, he argued that faith alone can resolve the world's contradictions and that his own awe in the face of evil and uncertainty must be evidence of God's existence.

Paul of Tarsus Originally known as Saul, Paul was a Greek-speaking Jew and Roman citizen who underwent a miraculous conversion experience and became the most important proponent of Christianity in the 50s and 60s C.E.

Pax Mongolica In imitation of the *Pax Romana* ("The Roman Peace"), this is the phrase used to describe the relatively peaceful century after the Mongol conquests, which enabled an intensified period of trade, travel, and communication within the Eurasian landmass.

Pax Romana (27 B.C.E.–180 C.E.) Literally translated as the "Roman Peace." During this time, the Roman world enjoyed an unprecedented period of peace and political stability.

Peace of Augsburg A settlement negotiated in 1555 among factions within the Holy Roman Empire, it formulated the principle *cuius regio, eius religio* ("he who rules, his religion"): the inhabitants of any given territory should follow the religion of its ruler, whether Catholic or Protestant.

Peace of Paris The 1919 Paris Peace Conference established the terms to end the First World War. Great Britain, France, Italy, and the United States signed five treaties with each of the defeated nations: Germany, Austria, Hungary, Turkey, and Bulgaria. The settlement is notable for the territory that Germany had to give up, including large parts of Prussia to the new state of Poland, and Alsace and Lorraine to France; the disarming of Germany; and the "war-guilt" provision, which required Germany and its allies to pay massive reparations to the victors.

Peace of Westphalia (1648) An agreement reached at the end of the Thirty Years' War that altered the political map of Europe. France emerged as the predominant power on the Continent. The Austrian Habsburgs had to surrender all the territories they had gained and could no longer use the office of the Holy Roman Emperor to dominate central Europe.

Spain was marginalized, and Germany became a volatile combination of Protestant and Catholic principalities.

Pearl Harbor The American naval base in Hawaii that was bombed by the Japanese on December 7, 1941, bringing the United States into the Second World War.

peasantry Term used in continental Europe to refer to rural populations that lived from agriculture. Some peasants were free and could own land. Serfs were peasants who were legally bound to the land and subject to the authority of the local lord.

Peloponnesian War The name given to the series of wars fought between Sparta (on the Greek Peloponnesus) and Athens from 431 B.C.E. to 404 B.C.E., which ended in the defeat of Athens and the loss of its imperial power.

perestroika Introduced by Soviet leader Mikhail Gorbachev in June 1987, *perestroika* was the name given to economic and political reforms begun earlier in his tenure. It restructured the state bureaucracy, reduced the privileges of the political elite, and instituted a shift from the centrally planned economy to a mixed economy, combining planning with the operation of market forces.

Periclean Athens Following his election as strategos in 461 B.C.E., Pericles pushed through political reforms in Athens that gave poorer citizens greater influence in politics. He promoted the Athenians' sense of superiority through ambitious public works projects and lavish festivals to honor the gods, thus ensuring his continual reelection. But eventually, Athens' growing arrogance and aggression alienated it from the rest of the Greek world.

Pericles (c. 495–429) Athenian politician who occupied the office of strategos for thirty years and who presided over a series of civic reforms, building campaigns, and imperialist initiatives.

Persian Empire Consolidated by Cyrus the Great in 559, this empire eventually stretched from the Persian Gulf to the Mediterranean and also encompassed Egypt. Persian rulers were able to hold their empire together through a policy of tolerance and a mixture of local and centralized governance. This imperial model of government was adopted by many future empires.

Persian Wars (490–479 B.C.E.) In 501 B.C.E., a political conflict between the Greek ruler of Miletus, Aristagoras, and the Persian emperor, Darius, sparked the first of the Persian Wars when Darius sent an army to punish Athens for its intervention on the side of the Greeks. Despite being heavily outnumbered, Athenian hoplites defeated the Persian army at the plain of Marathon. In 480 B.C.E.,

Darius's son Xerxes invaded Greece but was defeated at sea and on land by combined Greek forces under the leadership of Athens and Sparta.

Peter the Great (1682–1725) Energetic tsar who transformed Russia into a leading European country by centralizing government, modernizing the army, creating a navy, and reforming education and the economy.

Francesco Petrarca (Petrarch) (1304–1374) Italian scholar who revived interest in classical writing styles and was famed for his vernacular love sonnets.

pharaoh A term meaning "household," which became the title borne by the rulers of ancient Egypt. The pharaoh was regarded as the divine representative of the gods and the embodiment of Egypt itself. The powerful and centralized bureaucratic state ruled by the pharaohs was more stable and long lived than any other civilization in world history, lasting (with few interruptions) for approximately 3,000 years.

Pharisees A group of Jewish teachers and preachers who emerged in the third century B.C.E. They insisted that all of Yahweh's (God's) commandments were binding on all Jews.

Philip II (382–336 B.C.E.) King of Macedonia and father of Alexander, he consolidated the southern Balkans and the Greek city-states under Macedonian domination.

Philip II King of Spain from 1556 to 1598 and briefly king of England and Ireland during his marriage to Queen Mary I of England. As a staunch Catholic, Philip responded with military might to the desecration of Catholic churches in the Spanish Netherlands in the 1560s. When commercial conflict with England escalated, Philip sent the Spanish Armada to conquer England in 1588, but it was largely destroyed by stormy weather.

Philip II Augustus (1165–1223) The first French ruler to use the title "king of France" rather than "king of the French." After he captured Normandy and its adjacent territories from the English, he built an effective system of local administration, which recognized regional diversity while promoting centralized royal control. This administrative pattern would characterize French government until the French Revolution.

Philip IV (1268–1314) King of France from 1285 until his death. Philip's conflict with Pope Boniface VIII led to the transfer of the papal court to Avignon from 1309 to 1378.

Philistines Descendants of the Sea Peoples who fled to the region that now bears their name, Palestine, after their defeat at the hands of the pharaoh Ramses III. They dominated their neighbors the Hebrews, who used writing as an effective means of discrediting them. (The Philistines themselves did not leave a written record to contest the Hebrews' views.)

philosophe During the Enlightenment, this word referred to a person whose reflections were unhampered by the constraints of religion or dogma.

Phoenicians A Semitic people known for their trade in exotic purple dyes and other luxury goods, they originally settled in present-day Lebanon around 1200 B.C.E. and from there established commercial colonies throughout the Mediterranean, notably Carthage.

Plato (429–349 B.C.E.) A student of Socrates, Plato dedicated his life to transmitting his teacher's legacy through the writing of dialogues on philosophical subjects in which Socrates himself plays the major role. The longest and most famous of these, known as the *Republic*, describes an idealized polis governed by a superior group of individuals chosen for their natural attributes of intelligence and character, and who rule as philosopher-kings.

Plotinus (204–270 C.E.) A Neoplatonist philosopher who taught that everything in existence has its ultimate source in the divine and that the highest goal of life should be the mystic reunion of the soul with this divine source, something that can be achieved through contemplation and asceticism. This outlook blended with that of early Christianity and was instrumental in the spread of that religion within the Roman Empire.

polis One of the major political innovations of the ancient Greeks was the *polis*, or city-state (plural *poleis*). These independent social and political entities began to emerge in the ninth century B.C.E., organized around an urban center and fostering markets, meeting places, and religious worship. Frequently, poleis also controlled some surrounding territory.

Polish nationalism Movement to reestablish an independent Polish nation after the partitions of the late eighteenth century divided the former Polish-Lithuanian Commonwealth between the Prussian, Austrian, and Russian empires.

Marco Polo (1254–1324) Venetian merchant who traveled throughout Asia for twenty years and published his observations in a widely read memoir.

population growth In the nineteenth century, Europe experienced a dramatic increase in population. During this period, the spread of rural manufacturing allowed men and women to marry younger and raise families earlier, which increased the size of the average family. As the population increased, the proportion of young and fertile people also increased, which reinforced population growth. By 1900, population growth was strongest in Britain and Germany and slower in France.

portolan charts Also known as *portolani*, these special charts were invented by medieval mariners during the fourteenth century and were used to map locations of ports and sea routes, while also taking note of prevailing winds and other conditions at sea.

Potsdam Conference (1945) At this conference, Truman, Churchill, and Stalin met to discuss their options at the conclusion of the Second World War, including making territorial changes to Germany and its allies and the question of war reparations.

Prague spring A period of political liberalization in Czechoslovakia between January and August 1968 that was initiated by Alexander Dubček, the Czech leader. This period of expanding freedom and openness in this Eastern-bloc nation ended on August 20, when the USSR and Warsaw Pact countries invaded with 200,000 troops and 5,000 tanks.

pre-Socratics A group of philosophers in the Greek city of Miletus who raised questions about humans' relationship with the natural world and the gods and who formulated rational theories to explain the physical universe they observed. Their name reflects the fact that they flourished prior to the lifetime of Socrates.

Price Revolution An unprecedented inflation in prices during the latter half of the sixteenth century, resulting in part from the enormous influx of silver bullion from Spanish America.

Principate Modern term for the centuries of autocratic rule by the successors of Augustus, who seized power in 27 B.C.E. and styled himself Rome's *princeps* (or "first man"). See Roman Republic.

printing press Developed in Europe by Johannes Gutenberg of Mainz in 1453–1455, this new technology quickly revolutionized communication and played a significant role in political, religious, and intellectual movements.

Protestantism The name given to the many dissenting varieties of Christianity that emerged during the Reformation in sixteenth-century western Europe. Although Protestant beliefs and practices differed widely, all were united in their rejection of papal authority and the dogmas of the Roman Catholic Church.

provisional government After the collapse of the Russian monarchy in February 1917, leaders in the Duma organized a government and hoped to establish a democratic system under constitutional rule. They also refused to concede military defeat in the First World War. It was impossible to institute domestic reforms and fight a war at the same time. As conditions worsened, the Bolsheviks gained support. In October 1917, they attacked the provisional government and seized control.

Claudius Ptolomeus, called Ptolemy (c. 100–170 C.E.) A Greek-speaking geographer and astronomer active in Roman Alexandria, he rejected the findings of previous Hellenistic scientists in favor of the erroneous theories of Aristotle, publishing highly influential treatises that promulgated these errors and suppressed, for example, the accurate findings of Aristarchus, who had discovered the heliocentric universe, and Erathosthenes, who had calculated the circumference of the earth.

Ptolemaic system Ptolemy of Alexandria promoted Aristotle's understanding of cosmology. In this system, the heavens orbit the earth in an organized hierarchy of spheres, and the earth and the heavens are made of different matter and subject to different laws of motion. A prime mover produces the motion of the celestial bodies.

Ptolemy (c. 367–c. 284 B.C.E.) One of Alexander the Great's trusted generals (and possibly his half brother), he became pharaoh of Egypt and founded a new dynasty that lasted until that kingdom's absorption into the Roman Empire in 30 B.C.E.

public sphere Between the official realm of state activities and the private realm of the household and individual lies the public sphere. The public sphere has a political dimension—it is the space of debate, discussion, and expressions of popular opinion. It also has an economic dimension—it is where business is conducted, where commercial transactions take place, where people enter into contracts, search for work, or hire employees.

Punic Wars (264–146 B.C.E.) Three periods of warfare between Rome and Carthage, two maritime empires that struggled for dominance of the Mediterranean. Rome emerged as the victor, destroyed the city of Carthage, and took control of Sicily, North Africa, and Hispania (Spain).

pyramid Constructed during the third millennium B.C.E., the pyramids were monuments to the power and divinity of the pharaohs entombed inside them.

Qur'ān (often Koran) Islam's holy scriptures, comprising the prophecies revealed to Muḥammad and redacted during his life and after his death.

Raphael (Raffaelo Sanzio) (1483–1520) Italian painter active in Rome. His works include *The School of Athens*.

realism Artistic and literary style that sought to portray common situations as they would appear in reality.

Realpolitik Political strategy based on advancing power for its own sake.

reason The human capacity to solve problems and discover truth in ways that can be verified intellectually. Philosophers distinguish the knowledge gained from reason from the teachings of instinct, imagination, and faith, which are verified according to different criteria.

reconquista The process during which Christian rulers in Spain were beginning to forge effective alliances, in order to counter the power of their wealthy and well-governed Muslim neighbors.

Reformation Religious and political movement in sixteenth-century Europe that led to a break between dissenting forms of Christianity and the Roman Catholic Church; notable figures include Martin Luther and John Calvin.

Reich A term for the German state. The First Reich corresponded to the Holy Roman Empire (ninth century to 1806), the Second Reich lasted from 1871 to 1919, and the Third Reich lasted from 1933 through May 1945.

Reign of Terror (1793–1794) Campaign at the height of the French Revolution in which violence, including systematic executions of opponents of the revolution, was used to purge France of its "enemies" and to extend the revolution beyond its borders. Radicals executed as many as 40,000 people who were judged enemies of the state.

Renaissance From the French word meaning "rebirth," this term came to be used during the nineteenth century to describe the artistic, intellectual, and cultural movement that emerged in Italy after 1300 and that sought to recover and emulate the heritage of the classical past.

Renaissance humanism An intellectual movement that stressed the study and debate of ancient Greek and Roman texts.

Restoration (1815–1848) European movement after the defeat of Napoleon to restore Europe to its pre–French Revolution status and to prevent the spread of revolutionary or liberal political movements.

Cardinal Richelieu (1585–1642) First minister to King Louis XIII, he is considered by many to have ruled France in all but name, centralizing political power and suppressing dissent.

Roman army Under the Republic, the Roman army was made up of citizen-soldiers who were required to serve in wartime. As Rome's empire grew, the need for more fighting men led to the extension of citizenship rights and, eventually, to the development of a vast, professional, standing army that numbered as many as 300,000 by the middle of the third century B.C.E. By that time, however, citizens were not themselves required to serve, and many legions were made up of paid conscripts and foreign mercenaries.

Roman citizenship The rights and responsibilities of Rome's citizens were gradually extended to the free (male) inhabitants of other Italian provinces and later to most provinces in the Roman world. In contrast to slaves and non-Romans, Romans had the right to be tried in an imperial court and could not be legally subjected to torture.

Roman Republic The Romans traced the founding of their republic to the overthrow of their last king and the establishment of a unique form of constitutional government, in which the power of the aristocracy (embodied by the Senate) was checked by the executive rule of two elected consuls and the collective will of the people. For hundreds of years, this balance of power provided the Republic with a measure of political stability and prevented any single individual or clique from gaining too much power.

Romanticism Beginning in Germany and England in the late eighteenth century and continuing until the end of the nineteenth century, Romanticism was a movement in art, music, and literature that countered the rationalism of the Enlightenment by placing greater value on human emotions and the power of nature to stimulate creativity.

Jean-Jacques Rousseau (1712–1778) Philosopher and radical political theorist whose *Social Contract* attacked privilege and inequality. One of the primary principles of Rousseau's political philosophy is that politics and morality should not be separated.

Royal Society The goal of this British society, founded in 1660, is to pursue collective research. Members would conduct experiments, record the results, and share them with their peers, who would study the methods, reproduce the experiment, and assess the results. This arrangement gave English scientists a sense of common purpose as well as a system for reaching a consensus on facts.

Russia's invasion of Ukraine, 2022 Conflict between Russia and Ukraine began in 2014, when pro-European protesters in Ukraine's capital forced a change of government. In response, Russia annexed Crimea, and Russian-supported paramilitary groups seized territory in southeast Ukraine. In February 2022, Russia invaded Ukraine but were unable to defeat the much smaller Ukrainian army. The European Union and the United

States supported Ukraine with weaponry and announced severe economic sanctions against Russia.

Russian Revolution of 1905 After Russia's defeat in the Russo-Japanese War, Russians began clamoring for political reforms. Protests grew over the course of 1905, and the autocracy lost control of entire towns and regions as workers went on strike, soldiers mutinied, and peasants revolted. Forced to yield, Tsar Nicholas II issued the October Manifesto, which pledged individual liberties and provided for the election of a parliament (called the Duma). The most radical of the revolutionary groups were put down with force, and the pace of political change remained very slow in the aftermath of the revolution.

Russo-Japanese War (1904–1905) Japanese and Russian expansionist goals collided in Manchuria and Korea. Russia was humiliated after the Japanese navy sank its fleet, which helped provoke a revolt in Russia and led to an American-brokered peace treaty.

sacrament A sacred rite. In the Catholic tradition, the administration of the sacraments is considered necessary for salvation.

Saint Bartholomew's Day Massacre The mass murder of French Protestants (Huguenots) instigated by Queen Catherine de' Medici of France and carried out by Catholics. It began in Paris on August 24, 1572 (Saint Bartholomew's day) and spread to other parts of France, continuing into October of that year. More than 70,000 people were killed.

salon Informal gathering of intellectuals and aristocrats that allowed discourse about Enlightenment ideas.

Sappho (c. 620–c. 550 B.C.E.) One of the most celebrated Greek poets, she was revered as the "Tenth Muse" and emulated by many male poets. Ironically, though, only two of her poems survive intact, and the rest must be pieced together from fragments quoted by later poets.

Sargon the Great (r. 2334–2279 B.C.E.) The Akkadian ruler who consolidated power in Mesopotamia.

SARS epidemic (2003) The successful containment of severe acute respiratory syndrome (SARS) is an example of how international health organizations can effectively work together to recognize and respond to a disease outbreak. The disease itself, however, is a reminder of the dangers that exist in a globalized economy with a high degree of mobility of both populations and goods.

Schlieffen Plan Devised by the German general Alfred von Schlieffen in 1905 to avoid the dilemma of a two-front war against France and Russia. The Schlieffen Plan required that Germany attack France first through Belgium and secure a quick victory before wheeling to the east to meet the slower armies of the Russians on the Eastern Front. The Schlieffen Plan was put into operation on August 2, 1914, at the outset of the First World War.

scholasticism The methods for resolving complex theological and philosophical problems that were born from the educational revolution that began in the eleventh century.

scientific revolution of antiquity The Hellenistic period was the most brilliant age in the history of science before the seventeenth century C.E. Aristarchus of Samos posited the existence of a heliocentric universe. Eratosthenes of Alexandria accurately calculated the circumference of the earth. Archimedes turned physics into its own branch of experimental science. Hellenistic anatomists became the first to practice human dissection, which improved their understanding of human physiology. Ironically, most of these discoveries were suppressed by pseudoscientists who flourished under the Roman Empire during the second century C.E., notably Claudus Ptolomeus (Ptolemy) and Aelius Galenus (Galen).

second industrial revolution The technological developments in the last third of the nineteenth century, which included new techniques for refining and producing steel; increased availability of electricity for industrial, commercial, and domestic use; advances in chemical manufacturing; and the creation of the internal combustion engine.

Second World War Worldwide war that began in September 1939 in Europe, and even earlier in Asia (the Japanese invasion of Manchuria began in 1931), pitting Britain, the United States, and the Soviet Union (the Allies) against Nazi Germany, Italy, and Japan (the Axis). The war ended in 1945 with Germany and Japan's defeat.

Seleucus (d. 280 B.C.E.) The Macedonian general who ruled the Persian heartland of Alexander the Great's empire.

Semitic language The Semitic language family has the longest recorded history of any linguistic group and is the root of most languages of the Middle and Near East. Ancient Semitic languages include those of the ancient Babylonians and Assyrians, Phoenician, the classical form of Hebrew, early dialects of Aramaic, and the classical Arabic of the Qur'ān.

Sepoy Mutiny of 1857 See **Indian Rebellion of 1857.**

serfdom Peasant labor. Unlike slaves, serfs are "attached" to the land they work and are not supposed to be sold apart from that land.

William Shakespeare (1564–1616) An English playwright who flourished during the reigns of Elizabeth I and James I. Shakespeare received a basic education in his hometown of Stratford-upon-Avon and worked in London as an actor before achieving success as a dramatist and poet.

Shi'ites An often-persecuted minority within Islam, Shi'ites, from the Arabic word *shi'a* ("faction"), believe that only descendants of Muḥammad's successor Ali and his wife Fatima, Muḥammad's daughter, can have any authority over the Muslim community. Today, Shi'ites constitute the ruling party in Iran and are numerous in Iraq but otherwise comprise only 10 percent of Muslims worldwide.

Abbé Sieyès (1748–1836) In 1789, he wrote the pamphlet "What Is the Third Estate?" in which he posed fundamental questions about the rights of the Third Estate and helped provoke its secession from the Estates General. He was a leader at the Tennis Court Oath, but he later helped Napoleon seize power.

Sinn Féin The Irish revolutionary organization that formed in 1900 to fight for Irish independence.

Sino-Japanese War (1894–1895) Conflict over the control of Korea; China was forced to cede the province of Taiwan to Japan.

slave revolt in Saint-Domingue (1791–1804) In September of 1791, the largest slave rebellion in history broke out in Saint-Domingue, an important French colony in the Caribbean. In 1794, the revolutionary government in France abolished slavery in the colonies, though this act essentially only recognized the liberty that the slaves had seized by their own actions. Napoleon reestablished slavery in the French Caribbean in 1802 but failed in his attempt to reconquer Saint-Domingue. Armies commanded by former slaves succeeded in winning independence for a new nation, Haiti, in 1804, making the revolt in Saint-Domingue the first successful slave revolt in history.

slavery The practice of subjugating people to a life of bondage and of selling or trading these unfree people. For most of human history, slavery had no racial or ethnic basis and was widely practiced by all cultures and civilizations. Anyone could become a slave, for example, by being captured in war or by being sold for the payment of a debt. It was only in the fifteenth century, with the growth of the African slave trade, that slavery came to be associated with particular races and peoples.

Adam Smith (1723–1790) Scottish economist and liberal philosopher who proposed that competition between self-interested individuals led naturally to a healthy economy. He became famous for his influential book *The Wealth of Nations* (1776).

Social Darwinism Belief that Charles Darwin's theory of natural selection (evolution) was applicable to human societies and justified the right of the ruling classes or countries to dominate the weak.

social democracy The belief that democracy and social welfare go hand in hand and that diminishing the sharp inequalities of class society is crucial to fortifying democratic culture.

socialism Political ideology that calls for a classless society with collective ownership of all property.

Society of Jesus See **Jesuits**.

Socrates (469–399 B.C.E.) The Athenian philosopher and teacher who promoted the careful examination of all inherited opinions and assumptions on the grounds that "the unexamined life is not worth living." A veteran of the Peloponnesian War, he was tried and condemned by his fellow citizens for engaging in allegedly seditious activities and was executed in 399 B.C.E. His most influential pupils were the philosopher Plato and the historian and social commentator Xenophon.

Solidarity Polish trade union that organized a series of strikes across Poland in 1980.

Solon (d. 559 B.C.E.) Elected archon in 594 B.C.E., this Athenian aristocrat enacted a series of political and economic reforms that formed the basis of Athenian democracy.

Somme (1916) During this battle of the First World War, Allied forces attempted to take entrenched German positions from July to mid-November of 1916. Neither side was able to make any real gains despite massive casualties: 500,000 Germans, 400,000 British, and 200,000 French.

sovereignty An inviolable authority over a defined territory.

Soviet bloc International alliance that included the East European countries of the Warsaw Pact as well as the Soviet Union; it also came to include Cuba.

Soviet invasion of Afghanistan In 1979, to combat rising fundamentalism in the region, the Soviet Union directed soldiers to overthrow the Afghan president and installed a Soviet government.

soviets Local councils elected by workers and soldiers in Russia. Socialists started organizing these councils in 1905, and the Petrograd soviet in the capital emerged as one of the centers of power after the Russian monarchy collapsed in 1917 in the midst of World War I. The soviets became increasingly powerful, pressing for social reform and the redistribution of land, and calling for Russian withdrawal from the war effort.

Spanish-American War (1898) War between the United States and Spain in Cuba, Puerto Rico, and the Philippines. It ended with a treaty whereby the United States took over the Philippines, Guam, and Puerto Rico; Cuba won partial independence.

Spanish Armada The supposedly invincible fleet of warships sent against England by Philip II of Spain in 1588 but vanquished by the English fleet and bad weather in the English Channel.

Sparta Around 650 B.C.E., after the suppression of a slave revolt, Spartan rulers militarized their society in order to prevent future rebellions and to protect Sparta's superior position in Greece, orienting their society toward the maintenance of their army. Sparta briefly joined forces with Athens and other poleis in the second war with Persia in 480–479 B.C.E., but these two rivals ultimately fell out again in 431 B.C.E. when Sparta and its Peloponnesian allies went to war against Athens and its allies. This bloody conflict lasted until Athens was defeated in 404 B.C.E., after Sparta received military aid from the Persians.

Spartiate A full citizen of Sparta, hence a professional soldier of the hoplite phalanx.

spinning jenny Invention of James Hargreaves (c. 1720–1774) that revolutionized the British textile industry by allowing a worker to spin much more thread than was possible on a hand spinner.

SS (Schutzstaffel) Formed in 1925 to serve as Hitler's personal security force and to guard Nazi party (NSDAP) meetings, the SS grew into a large militarized organization that became notorious for its participation in carrying out Nazi policies.

Joseph Stalin (1879–1953) The Bolshevik leader who succeeded Lenin as leader of the Soviet Union and ruled until his death in 1953.

Stalingrad (1942–1943) The turning point on the Eastern Front during the Second World War came when the German army tried to take the city of Stalingrad in an effort to break the back of Soviet industry. The German and Soviet armies fought a bitter battle, in which more than a half million German, Italian, and Romanian soldiers were killed and the Soviets suffered over a million casualties. The German army surrendered after over five months of fighting. After Stalingrad, the Soviet army launched a series of attacks that pushed the Germans back.

Nicolas Steno (1638–1686) Danish scientist whose studies of rock layers and fossils were foundational to the development of geological sciences.

Stoicism An ancient philosophy derived from the teachings of Zeno of Athens (fl. c. 300) and widely influential within the Roman Empire; it also influenced the development of Christianity. Stoics believe in the essential orderliness of the cosmos and that everything that occurs happens for the best. Since everything is determined in accordance with rational purpose, no individual is master of his or her fate, and the only agency that human beings have consists in their response to good fortune or adversity.

Sumerians The ancient inhabitants of southern Mesopotamia (modern Iraq and Kuwait) whose sophisticated civilization emerged around 4000 B.C.E.

Sunnis Proponents of Islam's customary religious practices (*sunna*) as they developed under the first two caliphs to succeed Muḥammad: his father-in-law Abu-Bakr and his disciple Umar. Sunni orthodoxy is dominant within Islam but is opposed by the Shi'ites.

syndicalism A nineteenth-century political movement that embraced a strategy of strikes and sabotage by workers. The syndicalists hoped that a general strike of all workers would bring down the capitalist state and replace it with workers' syndicates, or trade associations. Their refusal to participate in politics limited their ability to command a wide influence.

Syrian civil war (2011–) Sparked when protesters called for reform to Syria's dictatorial government in 2011, the conflict has since escalated, with two chief camps: Assad's government backed by Russia and Iran, and rebel groups backed by the United States, Turkey, Saudi Arabia, and other powers in the region.

tabula rasa Latin for "clean slate." Term used by John Locke (1632–1704) to describe people's minds before they acquired ideas as a result of experience.

Battle of Tannenberg German victory over Russian armies in August 1914, leading to the almost complete destruction of Russia's offensive capacity in the first months of the war.

Tennis Court Oath (1789) Oath taken by representatives of the Third Estate in June 1789, pledging to form a National Assembly and write a constitution limiting the powers of the king.

tetrarchy The result of Diocletian's political reforms of the late third century C.E., which divided the Roman Empire into four quadrants.

Theban Hegemony The term describing the period when the polis of Thebes dominated the Greek mainland, which reached its height after 371 B.C.E., under leadership of the Theban general Epaminondas. It was in Thebes that the future King Philip II of Macedon spent his youth. Macedonian hegemony was forcefully asserted in the defeat of Thebes and Athens at the hands of Philip and Alexander at the Battle of Chaeronea in 338.

theory of evolution Darwin's theory linking biology to history. Darwin believed that competition among different organisms and their struggle with the environment were fundamental and unavoidable facts of life. In this struggle, those individuals who were better adapted to their environment survived, whereas the weak perished. This produced a "natural selection," or the favoring of certain adaptive traits over time, leading to a gradual evolution of different species.

Third Estate The population of France under the Old Regime was divided into three estates, corporate bodies that determined an individual's rights or obligations under royal law. The nobility constituted the First Estate, the clergy the Second, and the commoners (the vast majority of the population) made up the Third Estate.

Third Reich The German state from 1933 to 1945 under Adolf Hitler and the Nazi party.

Third World Those nations—mostly in Asia, Latin America, and Africa—that are not highly industrialized.

Thirty Years' War (1618–1648) Beginning as a conflict between Protestants and Catholics in Germany, this series of skirmishes escalated into a general European war fought on German soil by armies from Sweden, France, and the Holy Roman Empire.

Timur the Lame (1336–1405) Also known as Tamerlane, he was the last ruler of the Mongol Khans' Asian empire.

Josip Broz Tito (1892–1980) This Yugoslavian communist and resistance leader became the leader of Yugoslavia and fought to keep his government independent of the Soviet Union. In response, the Soviet Union expelled Yugoslavia from the communist countries' economic and military pacts.

town A center for markets and administration. Towns existed in a symbiotic relationship with the countryside. They provided markets for surplus food from outlying farms as well as produced manufactured goods. In the Middle Ages, towns tended to grow up around a castle or monastery that afforded protection.

transatlantic triangle The trading of African slaves by European colonists to address labor shortages in the Americas and the Caribbean. Slaves were treated like cargo, loaded onto ships and sold in exchange for molasses, tobacco, rum, and other precious commodities.

Treaty of Brest-Litovsk (1918) Separate peace between imperial Germany and the new Bolshevik regime in Russia. This treaty acknowledged the German victory on the Eastern Front and withdrew Russia from the war.

Treaty of Utrecht (1713) Resolution to the War of Spanish Succession that reestablished a balance of power in Europe, to the benefit of Britain and in ways that disadvantaged Spain, Holland, and France.

Treaty of Versailles Signed on June 28, 1919, this peace settlement ended the First World War and required Germany to surrender a large part of its most valuable territories and to pay huge reparations to the Allies.

trench warfare Weapons such as barbed wire and the machine gun gave tremendous advantages to defensive positions in the First World War, leading to prolonged battles between entrenched armies in fixed positions. The trenches eventually consisted of 25,000 miles of tunnels and ditches that stretched across the Western Front in northern France, from the Atlantic coast to the Swiss border. On the Eastern Front, the large expanse of territories made trench warfare less significant.

triangular trade The eighteenth-century commercial Atlantic shipping pattern that took rum from New England to Africa, traded it for slaves taken to the West Indies, and brought sugar back to New England to be processed into rum.

Triple Entente Alliance developed before the First World War that eventually included Britain, France, and Russia.

Truman Doctrine (1947) Declaration promising U.S. economic and military intervention to counter any attempt by the Soviet Union to expand its influence. Often cited as a key moment in the origins of the Cold War.

tsar Russian word for "emperor," derived from the Latin *caesar* and similar to the German *kaiser*. This was the title claimed by the rulers of medieval Muscovy and of the later Russian Empire.

Ubaid culture An early civilization that flourished in Mesopotamia between 5500 and 4000 B.C.E., it was characterized by large village settlements and temple complexes: a precursor to the more urban civilization of the Sumerians.

Umayyad caliphate (661–930) The Umayyad family resisted the authority of the first two caliphs who succeeded Muḥammad but eventually placed a member of their own family in that position of power. The Umayyad caliphate ruled the Islamic world from 661 to 750, modeling its administration on that of the Roman Empire. But after a rebellion led by the rival Abbasid family, the power of the Umayyad caliphate was confined to its territories in al-Andalus (Spain).

Universal Declaration of Human Rights (1948) United Nations declaration that laid out the rights to which all human beings are entitled.

University of Paris The reputation of Peter Abelard and his students attracted many intellectuals to Paris during the twelfth century. Some of them began offering instruction to aspiring scholars. By 1200, this loose association of teachers had formed itself into a *universitas*, or corporation. The teachers began collaborating in the higher academic study of the liberal arts, with a special emphasis on theology.

Urban II (1042?–1099) Instigator of the First Crusade (1096–1099), this pope promised that anyone who fought or died in the service of the Church would receive absolution from sin.

urban population During the nineteenth century, urban populations in Europe increased sixfold. For the most part, urban areas had medieval infrastructures, which new populations and industries overwhelmed. As a result, many European cities became overcrowded and unhealthy.

James Ussher (1581–1656) An Irish archbishop who attempted to reconcile natural and biblical events in a later discredited chronology of the world.

Utilitarianism Theory based on the idea that social institutions and laws should be measured according to their social usefulness, which is equated to the amount of happiness it produced.

Utopia A semisatirical social critique by the English statesman Sir Thomas More (1478–1535); the title derives from the Greek "best place" or "no place."

Utopian Socialists A body of writers and intellectuals in western Europe who supported social reforms and economic planning that would mitigate what they saw as the devastating effects of industrialization on European society.

Lorenzo Valla (1407–1457) One of the first practitioners of scientific philology (the historical study of language). Valla's analysis of the so-called Donation of Constantine showed that this document could not possibly have been written in the fourth century c.e. but must have been forged centuries later.

vassal A person who pledges to be loyal and subservient to a lord in exchange for land, income, or protection.

velvet revolutions The peaceful political revolutions against the Soviet Union throughout Eastern Europe in 1989.

Verdun (1916) This battle between German and French forces lasted for ten months during the First World War. The Germans saw the battle as a chance to break French morale through a war of attrition, and the French believed the battle to be a symbol of France's strength. In the end, over 400,000 lives were lost, and the German offensive failed.

Versailles Conference (1919) Peace conference of the victors of the First World War, it resulted in the Treaty of Versailles, which forced Germany to pay reparations and to give up its colonies to the victors.

Victoria (1819–1901) Influential queen of Great Britain, who reigned from 1837 until her death. Victoria presided over the expansion of the British Empire as well as the evolution of English politics and social and economic reforms.

Viet Cong Vietnamese communist group formed in 1954; committed to overthrowing the government of South Vietnam and reunifying North and South Vietnam.

Vikings (800–1000) The collapse of the Abbasid caliphate disrupted Scandinavian commercial networks and turned traders into raiders. (The word *viking* describes the activity of raiding.) These raids often escalated into invasions that contributed to the collapse of the Carolingian Empire, resulted in the devastation of settled territories, and ended with the establishment of Viking colonies. By the tenth century, Vikings controlled areas of eastern England; Scotland; the islands of Ireland, Iceland, and Greenland; and parts of northern France. They had also established the beginnings of the kingdom that became Russia and made exploratory voyages to North America, founding a settlement in Newfoundland (Canada).

Virgil (70–19 b.c.e.) An influential Roman poet who wrote under the patronage of the emperor Augustus. His *Aeneid* was modeled on the ancient Greek epics of Homer and told the mythical tale of Rome's founding by the Trojan refugee Aeneas.

Visigoths The tribes of "west" Goths who sacked Rome in 410 c.e. and later established a kingdom in the Roman province of Hispania (Spain).

Voltaire Pseudonym of French philosopher and satirist François Marie Arouet (1694–1778), who championed the cause of human dignity against state and Church oppression. Noted deist and author of *Candide*.

Lech Wałęsa (1943–) Leader of the Polish labor movement Solidarity, which organized a series of strikes across Poland in 1980. The strikers protested working conditions, shortages, and high prices. Above all, they demanded an independent labor union. Solidarity's leaders were imprisoned and the union banned, but they launched a new series of strikes in 1988 that led to the legalization of Solidarity and open elections.

war communism The Russian civil war forced the Bolsheviks to take a more radical economic stance. They requisitioned grain from the peasantry and outlawed private trade in consumer goods as "speculation." They also militarized production facilities and abolished money.

Wars of the Roses Fifteenth-century civil conflict between the English dynastic houses of Lancaster and York, each of which was symbolized by the heraldic device of a rose (red and white, respectively). It was ultimately resolved by the accession of the Lancastrian king Henry VII, who married Elizabeth of York.

Warsaw Pact (1955–1991) Military alliance between the USSR and other communist states that was established in response to the creation of the NATO alliance.

The Wealth of Nations 1776 treatise by Adam Smith, whose laissez-faire ideas predicted the economic boom of the Industrial Revolution.

Weimar Republic The government of Germany between 1919 and the rise of Hitler and the Nazi party in 1933.

West Africa The western coastal region of the African continent which had long been linked to Western civilization by trading networks, but which became, in the fifteenth century, a source of enslaved humans for trafficking.

Western Front During the First World War, the military front that stretched from the English Channel through Belgium and France to the Alps.

white supremacy A belief that white people constitute a superior race that is entitled to control a given nation's institutions and laws in order to preserve their dominance over other people.

Whites Refers to the "counterrevolutionaries" of the Bolshevik Revolution (1918–1921) who fought the Bolsheviks (the "Reds"); included former supporters of the tsar, Social Democrats, and large independent peasant armies.

William the Conqueror (1027–1087) Duke of Normandy who laid claim to the throne of England in 1066, defeating the Anglo-Saxon king Harold at the Battle of Hastings. William and his Norman followers imposed imperial rule in England through a brutal campaign of military conquest, surveillance, and the suppression of the indigenous Anglo-Saxon language.

William of Ockham (d. 1349) An English philosopher and Franciscan friar, he denied that human reason could prove fundamental theological truths, such as the existence of God. Instead, William argued that there is no necessary connection between the observable laws of nature and the unknowable essence of divinity. His theories, derived from the work of earlier scholastics, form the basis of the scientific method.

Woodrow Wilson (1856–1924) U.S. president who requested and received a declaration of war from Congress so that America could enter the First World War. After the war, his prominent role at the Paris Peace Conference signaled the rise of the United States as a world power. He also proposed the Fourteen Points, which influenced the peace negotiations.

Maria Winkelmann (1670–1720) German astronomer who worked with her husband in his observatory. Although she discovered a comet and prepared calendars for the Berlin Academy of Sciences, the academy would not let her take her husband's place within the body after he died.

witch craze The rash of persecutions that took place in both Catholic and Protestant countries of early modern Europe and their colonies, facilitated by secular governments and religious authorities.

women's suffrage movement Nineteenth- and early twentieth-century campaigns led by women to gain the right to vote and run for office.

William Wordsworth (1770–1850) Romantic poet whose central themes were nature, simplicity, and feeling. He considered nature to be the most trustworthy teacher and the source of sublime power that nourished the human soul.

World Bank International agency established in 1944 to provide economic assistance to war-torn nations and countries in need of economic development.

John Wycliffe (c. 1330–1384) A professor of theology at the University of Oxford, Wycliffe urged the English king to confiscate ecclesiastical wealth and to replace corrupt priests and bishops with men who would live according to the apostolic standards of poverty and piety. He advocated direct access to the scriptures and promoted an English translation of the Bible. His teachings played an important role in the Peasants' Revolt of 1381 and inspired the still more radical initiatives of a group known as Lollards.

Xerxes (519?–465 B.C.E.) Xerxes succeeded his father, Darius, as Great King of Persia. Seeking to avenge his father's shame and eradicate any future threats to Persian hegemony, he launched his own invasion of Greece in 480 B.C.E. An allied Greek army defeated his forces in 479 B.C.E.

Yalta conference Meeting among U.S. president Franklin D. Roosevelt, British prime minister Winston Churchill, and Soviet premier Joseph Stalin that occurred in the Crimea in 1945 shortly before the end of the Second World War in which the three leaders planned for the postwar order.

Young Turks The 1908 Turkish reformist movement that aimed to modernize the Ottoman Empire, restore parliamentary rule, and depose Sultan Abdul Hamid II.

ziggurats Temples constructed under the Dynasty of Ur in what is now Iraq, beginning around 2100 B.C.E.

Zionism A political movement dating to the end of the nineteenth century holding that the Jewish people constitute a nation and are entitled to a national homeland. Zionists rejected a policy of Jewish assimilation and advocated the reestablishment of a Jewish homeland in Palestine.

Zollverein In 1834, Prussia started a customs union, which established free trade among the German states and a uniform tariff against the rest of the world. By the 1840s, the union included almost all of the German states except German Austria. It is considered an important precedent for the political unification of Germany, which was completed in 1870 under Prussian leadership.

Zoroastrianism One of the three major universal faiths of the ancient world, alongside Judaism and Christianity, it was derived from the teachings of the Persian Zoroaster around 600 B.C.E. Zoroaster redefined religion as an ethical practice common to all, rather than as a set of rituals and superstitions that cause divisions among people. Zoroastrianism teaches that there is one supreme god in the universe, Ahura-Mazda (Wise Lord), but that his goodness will be constantly assailed by the forces of evil until the arrival of a final "judgment day." Proponents of this faith should therefore help good to triumph over evil by leading a good life and by performing acts of compassion and charity. Zoroastrianism exercised a profound influence over many early Christians, including Augustine.

Ulrich Zwingli (1484–1531) A former priest from the Swiss city of Zurich, Zwingli joined Luther and Calvin in attacking the authority of the Roman Catholic Church.

Text Credits

CHAPTER 10

Walter Bower: "A Declaration of Scottish Independence," from *Scotichronicon*, Volume 7, by Walter Bower. Edited by B. Scott and D. E. R. Watt. Copyright © University of St. Andrews 1996. Reproduced with permission of Birlinn Ltd. through PLSclear.

Anna Colet, et. al.: "The Black Death and Its Consequences for the Jewish Community In Tàrrega: Lessons from History and Archeology." *Pandemic Disease in the Medieval World: Rethinking the Black Death*, edited by MONICA H. GREEN, Arc Humanities Press, 2015, pp. 63–96. Reprinted with permission.

Rosemary Horrox (ed.): Excerpts from *The Black Death*, translated and edited by Rosemary Horrox. © Rosemary Horrox 1994. Reproduced with permission of Manchester University Press through PLSclear.

M. C. Seymour (ed.): "The Legend of Prester John" from *Mandeville's Travels*, pp. 195–199. Copyright © 1967 Clarendon Press. Reproduced with permission of Oxford University Press through PLSclear.

CHAPTER 11

John H. Chandler (ed.): Translated by Carol Symes from University of Rochester, Middle English Texts Series, Robbins Library Digital Projects, *The King of Tars* (Medieval Institute Publications, Kalamazoo, MI, 2015)

Gabriel Biel: "Execrabilis." Reprinted by permission of the publisher from *Defensorium Obedientiae Apostolicae et alia Documenta* by Gabriel Biel, edited and translated by Heiko A. Oberman, Daniel E. Zerfoss and William J. Courtenay, pp. 224–227, Cambridge, Mass.: The Belknap Press of Harvard University Press, Copyright © 1968 by the President and Fellows of Harvard College.

Christine de Pisan: Excerpt from pages 11–13, in *The Book of the Deeds of Arms and of Chivalry*, edited by Charity Cannon Willard and translated by Sumner Willard, 1999. Copyright © 1999 by The Pennsylvania State University Press. Reprinted by Permission of The Pennsylvania State University Press.

Carolyne Larrington (trans.): "The Condemnation of Joan of Arc by the University of Paris" from *Women and Writing in Medieval Europe: A Sourcebook*, by Carolyne Larrington, Copyright © 1995 Routledge. Reproduced with permission of Taylor & Francis Books UK.

CHAPTER 12

Bartolome de las Casas: Excerpts from *A Short Account of the Destruction of the Indies* by Bartolome de las Casas, edited and translated by Nigel Griffin, introduction by Anthony Pagden (Penguin Classics, 1992). Translation and Notes copyright © Nigel Griffin, 1992. Introduction copyright © Anthony Pagden 1992. Reproduced by permission of Penguin Books Ltd.

Niccoló Machiavelli: From *The Prince* by Niccoló Machiavelli, translated and edited by Thomas G. Bergin, pp. 75–76, 78. Copyright © 1947 by F. S. Crofts & Co., Inc., copyright © renewed 1975 by Thomas G. Bergin. Reprinted by permission of John Wiley & Sons, Inc.

CHAPTER 13

Henry Bettenson (ed.): 'Rules for Thinking with the Church' and 'Obedience of the Jesuits' from *Documents of the Christian Church*, 2nd Edition (1967). Reproduced with permission of Oxford University Press through PLSclear.

E. M. Plass (ed.): From *What Luther Says, Vol. II*, (pgs. 888–889) © 1959, 1987 Concordia Publishing House. Used with permission of CPH. All rights reserved. cph.org

CHAPTER 14

Michel de Montaigne: Excerpts from *Montaigne: Essays* by Michel de Montaigne, translated by J. M. Cohen (Penguin Classics, 1958). Copyright © J. M. Cohen, 1958. Reproduced by permission of Penguin Books Ltd.

Habtamu Mengistie Tegegne: Excerpt from "The Edict of King Gälawdéwos Against the Illegal Slave Trade in Christians: Ethiopia, 1548." *Legal Encounters on the Medieval Globe*, edited by ELIZABETH LAMBOURN, Arc Humanities Press, 2017, pp. 73–11. Reprinted with permission.

CHAPTER 16

René Descartes: From *A Discourse on the Method*, translated by Ian Maclean. Copyright © Ian Maclean 2006. Reproduced with permission of Oxford University Press through PLSclear.

Galileo Galilei: Excerpts from *Discoveries and Opinions of Galileo* by Galileo, translated by Stillman Drake, copyright © 1957 by

Nikita Khrushchev: "Report to the Communist Party Congress (1961)" from *Current Soviet Policies IV*, 1962, pp. 42–45, from the translations of the Current Digest of the Soviet Press. Copyright East View Information Services, Inc. All rights reserved. Reproduced by permission.

CHAPTER 28

Simone de Beauvoir: From *The Second Sex* by Simone de Beauvoir, translated by Constance Borde & Sheila Malovany-Chevallier, translation copyright © 2009 by Constance Borde and Sheila Malovany-Chevallier. Used by permission of Alfred A. Knopf, an imprint of the Knopf Doubleday Publishing Group, a division of Penguin Random House LLC. All rights reserved. And by permission of Random House Ltd.

Der Spiegel: Translation by Joshua Cole from "Der Über-Rhythmus", DER SPIEGEL 39/1956, pages 51–54. Translation made by permission of SPIEGEL-Verlag Rudolf Augstein GmbH & Co. KG.

Betty Friedan: From *The Feminine Mystique* by Betty Friedan. Copyright © 1963 by Betty Friedan. Reprinted by permission of Curtis Brown, Ltd. All rights reserved.

bell hooks: From "Gangsta Culture—Sexism and Misogyny: Who will take the rap?," *Outlaw Culture: Resisting Representations* (New York: Routledge, 1994) © 1994 by Gloria Watkins. Reprinted by permission of Taylor & Francis.

Ludvík Vaculík: "Two Thousand Words" originally published as "Dva Tisice Slov," *Literarny Listy* (Prague) June 27, 1968. Translated by Mark Kramer, Joy Moss, and Ruth Tosek. From *The Prague Spring 1968*, edited by Jaromir Navrátil. Budapest-New York: Central European University Press, 1998, pp. 177–181. Reprinted by permission.

CHAPTER 29

John R. Bowen: Excerpt from *Why the French Don't Like Headscarves: Islam, the State, and Public Space* by John R. Bowen. © 2007 by Princeton University Press. Reprinted by permission of Princeton University Press.

Alfred Sauvy: Excerpt from "Trois Mondes, Une Planéta," originally published in *L'Observateur*, No. 118, 14 April 1952. Translated into English for this edition and reprinted by permission of Le Nouvel Observateur.

B. R. Tomlinson: Reproduced by permission of SAGE Publications Ltd., London, Los Angeles, New Delhi, Singapore and Washington DC, from B. R. Tomlinson, "What was the Third World?" *Journal of Contemporary History*, Vol. 38, No. 2 (April 2003), pp. 307–321. Copyright © SAGE Publications, 2003.

United Nations: Excerpts from the Text of the 1951 Convention Relating to the Status of Refugees, UNHCR. Reprinted with permission.

Photo Credits

Author photos throughout: W. W. Norton & Company, Inc.

FRONT MATTER

ii–iii: National Geographic; xv: The Picture Art Collection/Alamy Stock Photo; xvi: Album/Alamy Stock Photo; Juice Images/Alamy Stock Photo; xvii: The Picture Art Collection/Alamy Stock Photo; Archivart/Alamy Stock Photo; xviii: IanDagnall Computing/Alamy Stock Photo; Bridgeman Images; xix: The Picture Art Collection/Alamy Stock Photo; Album/Alamy Stock Photo; xx: The Picture Art Collection/Alamy Stock Photo; Niday Picture Library/Alamy Stock Photo; xxi: Chronicle/Alamy Stock Photo; © Leonard de Selva/Bridgeman Images; xxii: akg-images; Imperial War Museum/Bridgeman Images; xxiii: Keystone-France/Gamma-Keystone via Getty Images; The Print Collector/Alamy Stock Photo/© 2022 Estate of Pablo Picasso/Artists Rights Society (ARS), New York; xxiv: Military Collection/Alamy Stock Photo; imageBROKER/Alamy Stock Photo; xxv: Sandy Huffaker/Corbis/Getty Images

CHAPTER 10

334: The Picture Art Collection/Alamy Stock Photo; 339: CPA Media Pte Ltd/Alamy Stock Photo; 341: Bridgeman Images; 345: The Picture Art Collection/Alamy Stock Photo; 347: Album/Alamy Stock Photo; 348: Sueddeutsche Zeitung Photo/Alamy Stock Photo; 350 (both): Granger; 351: Album/Alamy Stock Photo; 352: Angelo Hornak/Corbis via Getty Images; 353: Interfoto/Alamy Stock Photo; 356: incamerastock/Alamy Stock Photo; 357: Brian Lawrence/Alamy Stock Photo

CHAPTER 11

370: Album/Alamy Stock Photo; 373: Album/British Library/Alamy Stock Photo; 376: Pictorial Press Ltd/Alamy Stock Photo; 378: © Veneranda Biblioteca Ambrosiana/Gianni Cigolini/Mondadori Portfolio/Bridgeman Images; 381 (left): Bildarchiv Preussischer Kulturbesitz/Art Resource, NY; (right): Scala/Art Resource, NY; 385: The Picture Art Collection/Alamy Stock Photo; 392: Réunion des Musées Nationaux/Art Resource, NY; 396: Hemis/Alamy Stock Photo; 402: World History Archive/Alamy Stock Photo; 403: Pictorial Press Ltd/Alamy Stock Photo

CHAPTER 12

406: Juice Images/Alamy Stock Photo; 414: Peter Barritt/Alamy Stock Photo; 415: Ian Dagnall/Alamy Stock Photo; 416 (top): Public Domain via Wikipedia; (bottom): Juice Images/Alamy Stock Photo; 418 (left): Nimatallah/Art Resource, NY; (center): Classic Image/Alamy Stock Photo; (right): Erich Lessing/Art Resource, NY; 420: Ian G Dagnall/Alamy Stock Photo; 421: Universal Images Group North America LLC/Alamy Stock Photo; 423: classicpaintings/Alamy Stock Photo; 426: Aleksey Stemmer/Shutterstock; 428: Album/Art Resource, NY; 435: Bridgeman Images; 437: akg-images

CHAPTER 13

442: The Picture Art Collection/Alamy Stock Photo; 444: PRISMA ARCHIVO/Alamy Stock Photo; 445: Bildarchiv Preussischer Kulturbesitz/Art Resource, NY; 446: lucky-photographer/Alamy Stock Photo; 448 (left): Bridgeman Images; (right): Bpk, Berlin/Art Resource, NY; 449 (left): PRISMA ARCHIVO/Alamy Stock Photo; (right): Ivy Close Images/Alamy Stock Photo; 450: The Picture Art Collection/Alamy Stock Photo; 454: akg-images; 454: Erich Lessing/Art Resource, NY; 456 (both): Erich Lessing/Art Resource, NY; 462: PRISMA ARCHIVO/Alamy Stock Photo; 465 (left): Niday Picture Library/Alamy Stock Photo; (right): Archivart/Alamy Stock Photo; 467: Peter Horree/Alamy Stock Photo

CHAPTER 14

474: Archivart/Alamy Stock Photo; 477: Virginia Historical Society, Richmond/Bridgeman Images; 486: agefotostock/Alamy Stock Photo; 488: ART Collection/Alamy Stock Photo; 490: Archivart/Alamy Stock Photo; 491: Andreas Juergensmeier/Shutterstock; 497: Granger; 499: The National Trust Photolibrary/Alamy Stock Photo; 500: Military History Collection/Alamy Stock Photo; 505 (left): Pictorial Press Ltd/Alamy Stock Photo; (right): Interfoto/Alamy Stock Photo; 507: Heritage Image Partnership Ltd/Alamy Stock Photo; 509: PAINTING/Alamy Stock Photo; 510: Peter Horree/Alamy Stock Photo; 511 (top): classicpaintings/Alamy Stock Photo; (left): IanDagnall Computing/Alamy Stock Photo; (right): The Artchives/Alamy Stock Photo

CHAPTER 15

514: IanDagnall Computing/Alamy Stock Photo; 517: Courtesy of Rijksmuseum, Amsterdam; 520 (left): FORGET Patrick/SAGAPHOTO.COM/Alamy Stock Photo; (right): The Picture Art Collection/Alamy Stock Photo; 521 (top): Edinburgh University Library, Scotland/With kind permission of the University of Edinburgh/Bridgeman Images; (bottom): Erich Lessing/Art Resource, NY; 525: IanDagnall Computing/Alamy Stock Photo; 526: Pictorial Press Ltd/Alamy Stock Photo; 530: Gianni Dagli Orti/Shutterstock; 533: Bpk, Berlin/Jörg P. Anders. Stiftung Preussische Schlösser und Gärten/Art Resource, NY; 537: World History Archive/Alamy Stock Photo

CHAPTER 16

544: Bridgeman Images; **548:** Jeffrey Coolidge/Getty Images RF; **549:** Album/Alamy Stock Photo; **550:** Science History Images/Alamy Stock Photo; **552 (left):** Granger; **(right):** Science History Images/Alamy Stock Photo; **553 (left):** Universal History Archive/UIG/Bridgeman Images; **(right):** Royal Astronomical Society/Science Source; **557:** Photos 12/Alamy Stock Photo; **560:** Public Domain via Wikimedia Commons; **564:** Courtesy of Historical Collections & Services, Claude Moore Health Sciences Library, University of Virginia; **565:** Universal History Archive/ UIG/Bridgeman Images; **566:** Historic Images/Alamy Stock Photo; **568:** Bridgeman Images

CHAPTER 17

572: The Picture Art Collection/Alamy Stock Photo; **574:** "The Cruel Death of Calas" courtesy of the Elizabeth Nesbitt Room Chapbook Collection/Hillman Library Special Collections, University of Pittsburgh; **577:** Heritage Image Partnership Ltd/Alamy Stock Photo; **578:** Pictorial Press Ltd/Alamy Stock Photo; **580:** Bridgeman Images; **582:** Bridgeman Images; **583 (left):** Charles Walker Collection/Alamy Stock Photo; **(right):** FL Historical 36/ Alamy Stock Photo; **584:** Art Collection 2/Alamy Stock Photo; **588 (left):** Courtesy of the National Library of Australia; **(right):** History and Art Collection/Alamy Stock Photo; **589:** Courtesy of the National Library of Australia; **590:** Historical Picture Archive/CORBIS/via Getty Image; **592:** The Picture Art Collection/Alamy Stock Photo; **594:** Courtesy of the National Gallery of Art, Washington. Gift of Mrs. Mellon Bruce in memory of her father, Andrew W. Mellon; **599:** The Picture Art Collection/ Alamy Stock Photo; **600:** Bettmann/Getty Images; **604:** Scala/ Art Resource, NY; **605:** Granger

CHAPTER 18

610: Album/Alamy Stock Photo; **615 (left):** akg-images; **(right):** Cci/Shutterstock; **616:** Godong/Alamy Stock Photo; **618:** The Picture Art Collection/Alamy Stock Photo; **619:** Bridgeman Images; **625:** Photo 12/Alamy Stock Photo; **629:** The Artchives/ Alamy Stock Photo; **634 (left):** Risma Archivo/Alamy Stock Photo; **(right):** Dagli Orti/REX/Shutterstock; **635 (left):** Courtesy of Museo Carnavalet - Historia de París; **(right):** Historical Images Archive/Alamy Stock Photo; **638 (left):** Courtesy of Château de Versailles, France; **(right):** ART Collection/Alamy Stock Photo; **640:** Heritage Image Partnership Ltd/Alamy Stock Photo; **643:** Chris Hellier/Alamy Stock Photo

CHAPTER 19

646: The Picture Art Collection/Alamy Stock Photo; **649:** Courtesy of Peak District National Park Authority; **652:** Stefano Bianchetti/Corbis via Getty Images; **653 (left):** The National Archives of the UK; **(right):** Granger; **654:** Photo 12/Alamy Stock Photo; **662:** Album/Alamy Stock Photo; **663:** The Cartoon Collector/Heritage-Images/TopFoto; **664:** FLHC 33/Alamy

Stock Photo; **665:** Bridgeman Images/TopFoto; **670:** Archives Charmet/Bridgeman Images; **672:** Geoffrey Clements/Corbis/ VCG via Getty Images; **674:** Heritage Image Partnership Ltd/ Alamy Stock Photo; **678:** Granger; **680:** Granger

CHAPTER 20

684: Niday Picture Library/Alamy Stock Photo; **693:** Niday Picture Library/Alamy Stock Photo; **695:** ART Collection/ Alamy Stock Photo; **699:** ©The Trustees of the British Museum/ Art Resource, NY; **705:** Pictorial Press Ltd/Alamy Stock Photo; **714:** Lebrecht Music & Arts/Alamy Stock Photo; **715 (left):** ©Russell-Cotes Art Gallery/Bridgeman Images; **(right):** Chronicle/Alamy Stock Photo; **718:** The Picture Art Collection/Alamy Stock Photo; **719 (left):** GL Archive/Alamy Stock Photo; **(right):** Album/Alamy Stock Photo

CHAPTER 21

722: Chronicle/Alamy Stock Photo; **727:** Gibson Green/Alamy Stock Photo; **730:** Album/Alamy Stock Photo; **732:** Bildarchiv Preussischer Kulturbesitz/Art Resource, NY; **733:** Bpk, Berlin/ Geheimes Staatsarchiv, Preussischer Kulturbesitz/Thommen/Art Resource, NY; **735:** Album/Alamy Stock Photo; **739:** Rischgitz/ Getty Images; **740:** Scala/Art Resource, NY; **742:** Hulton Archive/Getty Images; **743:** Scala/Art Resource, NY; **744:** World History Archive/Alamy Stock Photo; **750:** Bpk, Berlin/Deutsches Historiches Museum/Arne Psille/Art Resource, NY; **751 (left):** Bildarchiv Preussischer Kulturbesitz/Dietmar Katz/Art Resource, NY; **(right):** Bildarchiv Preussischer Kulturbesitz/Art Resource, NY; **754:** MPI/Getty Images

CHAPTER 22

764: © Leonard de Selva/Bridgeman Images; **766:** © Leonard de Selva/Bridgeman Images; **770 (left):** Ken and Jenny Jacobson Orientalist Photography Collection/Research Library, The Getty Research Institute, Los Angeles (2008.R.3); **(right):** Hulton Archive/Getty Images; **774:** British Library Board/Robana/Art Resource, NY; **780:** Niday Picture Library/Alamy Stock Photo; **782:** Hulton Archive/Springer/Getty Images; **785:** Chronicle/ Alamy Stock Photo; **786:** North Wind Picture Archives/Alamy Stock Photo; **788:** Sarin Images/Granger; **792–93 (all):** Department of Image Collections, National Gallery of Art Library, Washington, DC; **794:** Bettmann/Getty Images; **795:** Chronicle/ Alamy Stock Photo; **796:** Courtesy of The Ohio State University Billy Ireland Cartoon Library & Museum

CHAPTER 23

800: akg-images; **803:** akg-images; **807:** Lordprice Collection/ Alamy Stock Photo; **811:** bpk Bildagentur/Art Resource, NY; **812:** Look and Learn/Bridgeman Images; **813 (left):** PA Images/Alamy Stock Photo; **(right):** Topical Press Agency/ Hulton/Getty Images; **814 (left):** Geogphotos/Alamy Stock

Photo; **(right):** Bettmann/Getty Images; **815:** Hulton-Deutsch Collection/Corbis via Getty Images; **821 (left):** Granger; **(middle):** Zip Lexing/Alamy Stock Photo; **(right):** Rue des Archives/Granger; **823:** Heritage Image Partnership Ltd/Alamy Stock Photo; **825:** Pictorial Press Ltd/Alamy Stock Photo; **834:** Science History Images/Alamy Stock Photo; **835:** Bettmann/Getty Images; **837:** Bettmann/Getty Images; **839:** Heritage Image Partnership Ltd/Alamy Stock Photo; **840:** Album/Alamy Stock Photo; **841:** Album/Alamy Stock Photo/© 2022 Estate of Pablo Picasso/Artists Rights Society (ARS), New York

CHAPTER 24

844: Imperial War Museum/Bridgeman Images; **848:** Classic Image/Alamy Stock Photo; **855:** Everett Collection Historical/Alamy Stock Photo; **856 (left):** © SZ Photo/Scherl/Bridgeman Images; **(right):** Bettmann Archive/Getty Images; **857 (left):** Hulton-Deutsch Collection/Corbis via Getty Images; **(right):** Bettman/Getty Images; **858 (left):** Album/Alamy Stock Photo; **(right):** Swim Ink 2, LLC/Corbis/via Getty Images; **859 (left):** Courtesy of the Poster Collection, Poster ID #GE 189, Hoover Institution Archives, Stanford University; **(right):** Pictures Now/Alamy Stock Photo; **861:** Universal History Archive/UIG/Bridgeman Images; **864 (left):** Everett Collection Historical/Alamy Stock Photo; **(right):** © SZ Photo/Scherl/Bridgeman Images; **(bottom):** © Sueddeutsche Zeitung Photo/Alamy Stock Photo; **865:** Bettmann/Getty Images; **867:** © Archives Charmet/Bridgeman Images; **869:** Bpk, Berlin/Art Resource, NY; **872:** Akademie/Alamy Stock Photo; **874:** Bettmann/Getty Images; **877:** Library of Congress

CHAPTER 25

884: Keystone-France/Gamma-Keystone via Getty Images; **886:** DeAgostini/Getty Images/© 2022 Artists Rights Society (ARS), New York; **889:** Science History Images/Alamy Stock Photo; **890:** Sputnik/Alamy Stock Photo; **891:** Heritage Image Partnership Ltd/Alamy Stock Photo; **899:** George Rinhart/Corbis via Getty Images; **900:** Hulton-Deutsch Collection/Corbis via Getty Images; **904:** Hulton-Deutsch Collection/Corbis via Getty Images; **910:** Everett Collection Inc/Alamy Stock Photo; **911 (left):** University of Maryland Global Land Cover Facility; **(right):** World History Archive/Alamy Stock Photo; **913:** Sueddeutsche Zeitung Photo/Alamy Stock Photo; **915:** CNAC/MNAM, Dist. RMN-Grand Palais/Art Resource, NY/Art Resource, NY/© 2022 Estate of George Grosz/Licensed by VAGA at Artists Rights Society (ARS), NY; **916 (left):** TopFoto; **(right):** Album/Alamy Stock Photo; **917:** William Vanderson/Fox Photos/Getty Images

CHAPTER 26

922: The Print Collector/Alamy Stock Photo/© 2022 Este of Pablo Picasso/Artists Rights Society (ARS), New York; **928:** Courtesy of The Southworth Collection, The Mandeville

Special Collections Library of UC San Diego; **929:** The Print Collector/Alamy Stock Photo/© 2022 Estate of Pablo Picasso/Artists Rights Society (ARS), New York; **930:** Hulton-Deutsch Collection/Corbis via Getty Images; **933:** akg-images/Alamy Stock Photo; **934:** Archive PL/Alamy Stock Photo; **938:** RGB Ventures/SuperStock/Alamy Stock Photo; **940:** Pictures from History/Bridgeman Images; **945:** AP Photo; **947:** akg-images/Ullstein Bild; **950–51:** Yad Vashem Photo Archive, Jerusalem; **952:** Ullstein Bild/Granger; **956:** Sovfoto/UIG via Getty Images; **957:** National Archives/Franklin D. Roosevelt Library Public Domain Photographs; **958:** Shawshots/Alamy Stock Photo; **959:** Library of Congress

CHAPTER 27

964: Military Collection/Alamy Stock Photo; **966:** Corbis via Getty Images; **968:** Everett Collection Historical/Alamy Stock Photo; **970 (left):** Lebrecht Music & Arts/Alamy Stock Photo; **(right):** Michael Nicholson/Corbis via Getty Images; **971:** Michael Nicholson/Corbis via Getty Images; **973:** Everett Collection Historical/Alamy Stock Photo; **975 (left):** The Protected Art Archive/Alamy Stock Photo; **(right):** Granger; **976:** AP Photo; **977 (left):** Giehr/picture-alliance/dpa/Newscom; **(right):** dpa picture alliance/Alamy Stock Photo; **985:** ©Sovfoto/UNIVERSAL IMAGES GROUP/agefotostock; **993:** Marc Garanger/Corbis/via Getty Images; **996:** Uber Bilder/Alamy Stock Photo; **998:** Sovfoto/UIG/Bridgeman Images

CHAPTER 28

1002: imageBROKER/Alamy Stock Photo; **1006;** Bettmann/Getty Images; **1007:** Heritage Image Partnership Ltd/Alamy Stock Photo; **1008:** David Scott/Alamy Stock Photo; **1009:** MARKA/Alamy Stock Photo; **1010:** Martha Holmes/The LIFE Picture Collection/Shutterstock; **1014:** Bettmann/Getty Images; **1016:** Bettmann/Getty Images; **1017:** AP Photo; **1021:** API/Gamma-Rapho/Getty Images; **1023:** Bettmann/Getty Images; **1027:** Bettmann/Getty Images; **1028:** Peter Turnley/Corbis/VCG via Getty Images; **1030:** Wally McNamee/Corbis/via Getty Images; **1031:** AFP/Getty Images; **1036:** Justin Leighton/Alamy Stock Photo; **1037 (left):** Oliver Ruether/Laif/Redux; **(right):** AP Photo; **1038:** Patrick Robert/Sygma/Corbis via Getty Images

CHAPTER 29

1042: Sandy Huffaker/Corbis via Getty Images; **1048:** Pulsar Imagens/Alamy Stock Photo; **1051 (left):** Guang Niu/Reuters/Newscom; **(right):** Alessandro Pone/LaPresse via AP; **1052:** xPACIFICA/Getty Images; **1053 (left):** Joerg Boethling/Alamy Stock Photo; **(right):** REUTERS/Alamy Stock Photo; **1055:** David Turnley/Corbis/VCG via Getty Images; **1060:** Rolls Press/Popperfoto via Getty Images; **1061:** Jacques Dejean/Sygma via Getty Images; **1063:** Peter Turnley/Corbis/VCG via Getty Images; **1064:** REUTERS/Alamy Stock Photo; **1067:** Pascal Le Segretain/Getty Images; **1076 (left):** Jeff Gilbert/Alamy Stock Photo; **(right):** Spencer Platt/Getty Images

Index

Note: Page numbers in *italics* refer to illustrations, maps, and tables.

colonialism (*Continued*)
  European colonialism and conflict, overview, 484
  European poverty and, 484–486
  social hierarchies of New Spain, 479
colonialism (1870–1914), 764–799. *see also* colonialism (twentieth century)
  chronology, 798
  Columbian exchange and environmental effects, 797
  crises at turn of twentieth century, 794, *794–798, 795, 796*
  ecological consequences of European migrations, 796–798
  French colonialism, 769, 779–781, *780*
  imperial culture, 785–793, *786, 788, 792–793*
  imperialism, defined, 767
  imperialism, overview, 767–769, *768*
  imperialism in China, 659, 774–777, *776*
  imperialism in South Asia, 769–773, *770, 776*
  "scramble for Africa," 767, 781–785
  Suez Canal inauguration and, 764–765, *766*
colonialism (twentieth century)
  decolonization during Cold War, 983, 984–995, *988, 990, 992, 993, 995,* 1070
  postcolonial politics in global era, 1054–1056, *1055*
  World War I and "mandate system," 880, 905, 986
  World War I/II interwar years in Europe's major democracies, 905
color spectrum, Newton on, 567
Columbian exchange, 477–478, *478,* 797
Columbus, Christopher
  Canary Islands, 346, 433
  Ferdinand and Isabella and, 427, 429, 434
  printing presses and, 408
  traditions of reconquest and crusading and, 429
  travel books carried on voyage, 334, 342–343
  voyages, 346, 433–434, 547
Comedy (Dante), 348–349, 375
commerce. *see also* economic issues; factories; globalization; Industrial Revolution; trade
  during Enlightenment, 575–578
  Enlightenment and, 584–585

European economic integration, post–World War II, 981–982, 1074–1077
extension of European commerce and settlement, Late Middle Ages, 344–346
globalization and illegal commerce, 1040
Ottoman Empire, 387
commercial revolution during Enlightenment, 576–578
Committee of Public Safety (France), 628–629, 630
Common Market, or European Economic Community (EEC), 966, 981–982, 1004, 1026, 1033
Commonwealth of Independent States, 1032
communism. *see also* Cold War; communism collapse; socialism; Soviet Union
  Berlin Wall, fall of, *977,* 1029–1030, *1030,* 1037, 1042
  Berlin Wall symbol of Cold War repression, 977, *977,* 1029, 1042
  Chinese Revolution, 984, *985*
  Cuban missile crisis, 999
  fear of, in 1930s, 927
  first Vietnam War (1946–1954), 991–992
  Iron Curtain, 967–972, 978–979, 998, 1029, 1030, 1032
  Korean War, 984–985
  war communism, 888, 889, 890
communism collapse
  chronology, 1040
  collapse of Soviet Union, *1031,* 1031–1033
  Eastern European troubles, 1033–1038, *1036*
  fall of Berlin Wall, *977,* 1029–1030, *1030,* 1037, 1042
  German reunification, 1004, 1029–1030, 1033, 1034, 1037, *1037*
  Gorbachev and Soviet reform, *1028,* 1028–1029, 1030, *1030,* 1031–1033
  maps, 1989 and after Cold War, *1034, 1039*
  overview, 1004, 1027
  Solidarity movement (Poland), 1027, 1029
  Soviet Union plans to invade Poland (1981), 1028
  "velvet revolutions" of Eastern Europe, 1030, 1033, 1036, *1036*

Yugoslavia wars, 1004, 1033–1035, *1038*
Communist Information Bureau (Cominform), 974
Communist Manifesto, The (Marx, Engels), 707, 708–709, 712, 722
compass, magnetic, 347, 431, 546
Compendium of Chronicles (al-Din), 339
Compiègne Forest, World War I cease fire in, 875
Complaint of Peace (Erasmus), 421
concentration camps
  Auschwitz-Birkenau, 942, 943, 950–951, *950–951,* 952, 997, *1027*
  Belzec, 950
  Bergen-Belsen, *968*
  blueprints and construction, 902, 950–951, *950–951*
  Boer War, 795, *795*
  Dachau, 902, 947
  deportation railways, map, *953*
  deportation to, 940, 942–943, 944–945, *945,* 946–947, 949, 951–952
  description of, 950–951, *952*
  Holocaust death toll from, 954
  liberation of, *947, 968*
  map, *946*
  number of camps, *946,* 949
  Treblinka, *945,* 952
Concert of Europe
  Congress of Vienna and, 688
  Metternich and, 688, 689, 722
  resistance to, 689, 692–694
conciliarism, 398–399, 400, 425–426, 468
concordats, 426, 450, 633, 636
Condition of the Working Class in England, The (Engels), 656, 657, 707
Condorcet, Marquis de, 621
confession of sins, 353
confraternities, 378
Congo Free State, 781–782, 791
Congress of Racial Equality (CORE), 1016
Congress of Vienna
  balance of power and, 688
  German Confederation, 688, 731
  politics of enslavement and, 699
  Restoration, 686–688, 692, 700–701
  revolts following, 689, *690*
conquistadors, 436–438, *437*
Conrad, Joseph, 782, 788

iron, Industrial Revolution and, 652–653, 656, 671, 672
Iron Curtain, 967–972, 978–979, 998, 1029, 1030, 1032
Isabella (queen of Aragon and Castile), 427, *428*, 428–429, 433
Isabella (queen of France), 362
Isherwood, Christopher, 912
ISIS (Islamic State of Iraq and Syria). *see* Islamic State (Daesh)
Islam. *see also* Abbasid dynasty; Shi'ite Muslims; Sunni Muslims
    Arab-Israeli conflict, 1056–1057, *1059*
    end of Muslim rule in Spain, 427
    enslaved people trade and, 782
    European imperialism and, 792
    headscarf controversy, *1067*, 1068–1069
    Islamic fundamentalism, 1058, 1060, 1062, 1063, 1065
    Mongol Empire and, 340, 384
    radical Islam, 1057, 1060, 1062
    rise of political Islam, 1058–1061
Islamic State (Daesh), *1053*, 1064, 1065, 1066, *1067*
Israel
    Arab-Israeli conflict, 1056–1057, *1059*
    Balfour Declaration, 864, 986
    establishment of modern-day Israel, 986, 988
    Sinai Peninsula and, 990
Israel, ancient. *see* Judaism
Istanbul, 385. *see also* Constantinople
Italy
    art, seventeenth century, 507–509
    Black Death impact on, 373, 380, 382
    Carbonari and resistance to Concert of Europe, 689
    Cold War economics, 981
    emergence of fascism, 894–898, 906–907
    Ethiopia and, 794–795, 926, 927, 935
    expansion (1936–1939), *931*
    expulsion of Jews, 516
    films/film industry (1945–1968), 1010–1011
    French Revolution and, 628, 631
    imperialism, 783, 794–795, 826
    Industrial Revolution and, 659
    Italian unification, Cavour and Garibaldi, *739*, *743*, 743–745, *744*, *745*
    Italian unification, early stages (1848), 738–740, *739*, 757
    Late Middle Ages conflict in, 394–395

    medieval drama in, 378
    Napoleon and, 631, 638
    papal power, Middle Ages, 349
    population growth, at turn of twentieth century, *804*
    rebellion by guilds in 1378, 374
    Renaissance beginning in, 378–383, 408
    Renaissance politics of, and philosophy of Machiavelli, 408–413
    social change and cultural dynamism (1945–1968), 1010–1011
    states of Italy (c. 1494), 412, *412*
    student movements (1960s), 1022
    women scientists of scientific revolution in, 566
    World War I, 848–849, 853–854, 857, 861, 875, 894–895
    World War I aftermath, 894–898
    World War II, Allied counterattack, 957
    World War II, German occupation of, 952, 957
Ivan I (Grand Prince of Rus'), 338
Ivan III (the Great; tsar of Russia), 424–425, *426*
Ivory Coast, 780

Jackson, Andrew, 755
Jacobins, 624, 628, 630, 631, 705
Jacquerie Rebellion, 374
Jadwiga (female king of Poland), 396
Jagiello (grand duke of Lithuania), 396, *396*
Jagiellonian dynasty, 396
Jagiellonian University (Kraków), 395, 401
Jamaica, 700
James, William, 834
James I (king of England), 498, 507, 560
James II (king of England), 525, 526, *526*, 527
Jansen, Cornelius, 506, 519
Jansenism, 506, 519
January Rising, 753
Japan
    economic growth in 1970s and 1980s, 1026
    globalization effects on, 1055–1056
    imperialism, in China, 776, 777, 926, 927
    Russo-Japanese War of 1904, 779, 824
    Sino-Japanese War, 776
    war with China, 926, 927
    World War I, 848, 864, 880

    World War II
        Allied counterattack, 957–959, *959*, 960–961
        atomic bombing of Nagasaki and Hiroshima, 958–959, *959*, 960–961, 974
        outbreak, 926, 927
        Pearl Harbor attack, 936–937, *938*
        resources needed for production, 954–955
        war in the Pacific, 936–937, *937*, 957–959, *959*, 960–961
Jaruzelski, Wojciech, 1027
Java, 342
Jeanneret, Charles Édouard, 914
Jefferson, Thomas, 579, 586, 598, 643, 754–755
Jerome, Saint, 383, 423, *423*, 467
Jesuit order (Society of Jesus), 468–470, 519
Jesus of Nazareth
    crucifixion, 356
Jew Süss (film), 919
"Jewish Question" (Hitler), 904
Jiang Jieshi (Chiang Kai-shek), 984
Jiménez de Cisneros, Francisco, 467
Jinnah, Mohammed Ali, 986
Joan of Arc, 376, 392, 393, 399
Joao I (king of Portugal), 429
Joao II (king of Portugal), 430
Joffre, Jules, 852
John Bull, 662, 663
John II Casimir (king of Poland), 495
John III Sobieski (king of Poland), 532, 534
John (king of England), 357
John of Leyden, 455
John Paul II (pope), 450, 1027, *1027*
John XXII (pope), 360
Johns, Jasper, 1010
Johnson, Lyndon B., 1020, 1022, 1074
joint-stock companies, 488, 490, 658, 806
Jonson, Ben, 507
Jordan, 988
Joseph II (emperor of Austria), 603, 605
Josephine, Empress of France (Josephine de Beauharnais), 639
Joyce, James, 912
Judaism. *see also* antisemitism; Hebrew Bible; Holocaust
    Arab-Israeli conflict, 1056–1057, *1059*
    Babylonian Captivity and, 352
    Black Death blamed on Jews, 366
    conversion of Jews to Christianity, Middle Ages, 428

Ludd, Ned, *653*

Luddites, *653*

Ludwig I (king of Bavaria), *732*

Lusiads (Portuguese epic), *430*

Lusitania (passenger liner), *855*

Luther, Martin, *449*

    on accused witches, *504*

    Augustine's effect on, *445*

    biographical information, *444–445*

    break with Rome, *447–450, 456*

    Calvinism and, *455, 456*

    Charles V and condemnation at Worms, *450–451, 468*

    German princes and Lutheran Church, *451–452*

    justification by faith doctrine of, *445, 447*

    on marriage and celibacy, *447, 459, 460, 461*

    Ninety-Five Theses of, *442, 446*

    pamphlet publication and effect of printing press, *445, 447, 448–449, 452*

    portrait, *444*

    primary premises, *447*

    on religious education, *459*

    translation of the bible, *445*

Luxemburg, Rosa, *898*

Lyrical Ballads (Wordsworth), *713*

M (movie), *918*

MacArthur, Douglas, *984*

Macbeth (Shakespeare), *507*

Macedonia. *see* Alexander the Great

Machaut, Guillaume de, *423*

Machiavelli, Niccolò, *408–412*

Macmillan, Harold, *989*

Madagascar, *945*

Madame Bovary (Flaubert), *836*

Madeira, *429, 433*

Magdeburg Law, *395*

Magellan, Ferdinand, *434*

Magna Carta, *357, 525*

Magyar nationalism, *734, 736–737, 748, 749*

Mahdi, war against, *794*

Mahler, Gustav, *750*

Maids of Honor, The (Las Meniñas) (Velázquez), *509, 509*

Maistre, Joseph de, *701*

Malawi, *785, 989, 1054*

Malaya, *777, 937*

Malaysia, *777, 792, 1040, 1056*

Mali, *344, 345*

Malinche, La, *436*

Malory, Thomas, *410*

Malthus, Thomas, *664, 828*

Mamluk Sultanate of Egypt, *338*

Man Farthest Down, The (Washington), *808–809*

Manchuria, *926, 927*

Mandela, Nelson, *1054, 1055*

Mandeville, John de, *334, 342–343*

Manhattan Project, *955, 960*

Manifesto of Futurism, The (Marinetti), *841*

Mann, Thomas, *882*

Mannerism, *507–508*

Mansa Musa, *344, 345*

Mao Zedong, *984, 985*

Maoris, *588, 590, 797*

Maoris in a War Canoe near Lookout Point, 590

Marat, Jean Paul, *628*

Maria Theresa (empress of Austria), *603, 604, 616*

Marie Antoinette (queen of France), *604, 616, 624*

Marie Louise (second wife of Napoleon Bonaparte), *639*

Marinetti, Filippo Tommaso, *800, 841*

Mark (Gospel), *402*

Marlowe, Christopher, *507*

Marne, battle of the, *852*

marriage. *see also* divorce; family life

    French Revolution and, *621*

    Henry VIII and Protestant Reformation, *462–463*

    inequities in the Enlightenment, *594*

    intermarriage of Muslims and Christians, *387, 388*

    Luther and, *447, 459, 460, 461*

    Napoleonic Code, *633*

    Protestant Reformation and Council of Trent on, *460*

    Protestant Reformation and patriarchy, *459, 461–462*

    Renaissance in Italy, *382–383*

    as sacrament, *353, 460, 461*

Marsh, Reginald, *913*

Marshall, George, *972*

Marshall Plan, *967, 972–973, 973, 979, 981, 1074*

Martin, John, *718, 718*

Martin V (pope), *399*

Martineau, Harriet, *698*

Martini, Simone, *353, 378*

Martinique, *496, 641, 698, 994*

Marx, Karl

    Capital, *810*

    class struggle, *708–709, 728–729*

    Communist Manifesto, The, *707, 708–709, 712, 722*

    feudalism concept and, *708*

    French Revolution and theories of, *614*

    on June Days, *728–729*

Marxism in late nineteenth century, *695, 707–710, 810–811, 812, 871*

    on the Paris Commune, *817*

    Russian Marxism in early twentieth century, *823–824*

Marxists, *712, 810, 812, 823–824*

Mary I (Bloody Mary, Mary Tudor, queen of England), *462, 464–465, 465, 466, 488–489*

Mary Magdalene, *381*

Mary Stuart (queen of England), *525, 526, 527, 529, 1067*

Masaryk, Tomáš, *883*

Masonic lodges, *598*

Mass

    doctrine of transubstantiation, *353, 353–354*

    Middle Ages, *353–354*

mass culture

    late nineteenth and early twentieth centuries, *804, 835–836, 1007*

    post–World War II era (1945–1968), *1007–1009, 1008, 1009, 1012–1013*

    radio and, *915–916, 1008*

    World War I/II interwar years, *914–917, 916, 917*

mass politics (1870–1914). *see also* modern industry and mass politics (1870–1914)

    Dreyfus Affair and antisemitism as politics, *817, 821, 903*

    French Third Republic and Paris Commune, *816–817*

    Germany's search for imperial unity, *818–820*

    Great Britain, moderation to militancy, *820–822*

    labor politics and mass movements, *809–812, 811, 812*

    liberalism and its discontents, *816–827*

    Ottoman Empire, nationalism and imperial politics, *826–827, 827*

    Russian Revolution, events leading to, *822–824, 869*

    Russian Revolution of 1905, *824–825, 825, 870*

printing during, 408, *409*, 410–411, 546

reading ancient texts during, 379, 380, 383, 547, 548

"Renaissance man" ideal, 413

scientific revolution and, 547

sculpture, 416, *418*, 418–419

Reni, Guido, *467*

Renoir, Pierre-Auguste, 840

Reparations Commission (Treaty of Versailles), 878

reparations (Treaty of Versailles), 878, 899–900, 925

"Report to the Communist Party Congress (1961)" (Khrushchev), 978, 979

Representation of the People Act (1918), 867

republic, defined, 581

Republic of San Marco, 739

republicanism, nineteenth-century ideology, 686, 705–706, 728, 730

resistance movements during World War II, 940, 944, 952–953, 954, 957

revisionists, 812

revolutions of 1848. *see also* nation building (nineteenth century)
causes and goals, 669, 725, 727
French Revolution of 1848, 727, 727–730
"German question" and, 730–732, *732*
"Hungry Forties" and, 725
Italian unification, early stages, 738–740, *739*
nationalist movements in Austrian Empire, 735–738
overview, 725, 727
"springtime of peoples," 735–738

Reynolds, Joshua, *588*, 589

Rhine Palatinate, League of Augsburg, 529

Rhine River, Industrial Revolution and, 671, 672–673

Rhineland, 628, 657, 925, *930*

Rhineland Gazette, 707

Rhodes, Cecil, 772, 784–785, *785*, 794, 795

"Rhodes Colossus, The" (cartoon), *785*

Rhodesia, 772, 785, 989

Ribbentrop, Joachim von, 924

Ricardo, David, 704

Richard II (king of England), 374, 390, 394

Richardson, Samuel, 600

Richelieu, Cardinal (Armand Jean du Plessis), 497

Riefenstahl, Leni, *916*, 919

Rigaud, Hyacinthe, 520, *520*

Rights of Man, The (Paine), 626, 627

Río de la Plata, 689

Rire, Le, 821, *821*

risorgimento, 740

Rivera, Diego, 913

Roanoke Island (North Carolina), 476

Robert the Bruce, 360

Robespierre, Maximilien, 628, 630, 642

Robinson Crusoe (Defoe), 600

rock and roll, 1008–1009, 1012–1013

Rodriguez, Armando, 1002

Roma (gypsies), 924, 942–943, 944, 949, 954

Roman Catholic Church. *see also* Catholicism; papacy
absolutism and, 518
Catholic reforms at time of Protestant Reformation, 467–468
Council of Trent, 460, 466, 467–468
Counter-Reformation, 466–471, 519
1830 Revolution in France, 693
Galileo and, 470, 551–552, 554–555, 556
Grotto of Lourdes, *835*
Ignatius Loyola and Society of Jesus, 468–470
Index of Prohibited Books, 468
Jansenism, 505, 519
Louis Napoleon Bonaparte and, 730
Louis XIV (king of France) and, 519
on marriage as sacrament, 353, 460, 461
Mussolini and, 897
Napoleon and, 633, 636, 638–639
National Assembly (France) and, 623
Protestant Reformation and rebirth of, 466–471
reformed Catholic Church of seventeenth and eighteenth centuries, 470–471
sacraments, 353–354, 445, 447
Syllabus of Errors (Pius IX), 834
witchcraft accusations and, 504

Roman de Silence, 358–359

Roman Empire. *see also* Byzantine Empire; Holy Roman Empire
end of eastern Roman Empire, 383–387

Roman Republic. *see* Roman Empire

Romanesque architecture, 419

Romania
Armenian refugees expelled from, 967
Cold War in, 967
independence from Ottoman Empire, 826
Industrial Revolution, 659
violence and collapse of communism, 1030
World War I, 861
World War II, 930, 939, 956

Romanticism
as cultural revolt, overview, 686, 713
literature, 713–716, *715*
painting, 716, *718*, 718–720, *719*
politics of, 716–717
Romantic nationalism, 717, 739, 750
women writers, gender, and, *715*, 715–716

Rome. *see also* Roman Empire
Renaissance art in, 415–419

Rome: Open City (film), 1010

Rome-Berlin Axis, 926, *941*

Romeo and Juliet (Shakespeare), 507

Rommel, Edwin, 935

Roosevelt, Franklin D., 909, 916, 935, 949, 958

Roosevelt, Theodore, 830

Rossellini, Roberto, 1010

Rossini, Gioacchino, 717

Rothko, Mark, 1010

Rothschild, Jakob, 821, *821*

Rougon-Macquart (Zola), 836

Roundheads, 499

Rousseau, Jean-Jacques, 591–593, *592*, 594, 596–597, 598, 599, 600, 622

Royal Air Force (RAF), 934

Royal Exchange (London), *807*

Royal Prussian Academy of Sciences, 598

Royal Society of London, 565, 567, 569, 598

Rubens, Peter Paul, 510–511, *511*

Rudolf II (Holy Roman Emperor), 550

Ruhr valley crisis in Weimar Germany, 899

"Ruined Cottage, The" (Wordsworth), 713

Rule of Saint Benedict, 469

Rûm, sultanate of, 338, 384

Rus', 336, 338

Russia. *see also* Moscow; Soviet Union
absolutism and, 516, 536–541, *537*
assassination of Alexander II, 811, 822
Balkan crisis and, 848, 849
Civil War, following World War I, 872, 887–888
code of law, 691

United States (*Continued*)
    U.S. troops at the front, 874
    as world power, 875–876
    World War II
        aid sent to Britain, 935
        Allied counterattack, *957, 957–959, 959*
        entry into war, 935, 937
        intervention in North Africa, 935
        in the Pacific, 936–938, *937, 938,* 957–959, *959*
        Pearl Harbor attack, 936–937, *938*
        and resources needed for production, 954–955
Universal Declaration of Human Rights, 1070
universities
    establishment in central and eastern Europe, 395
    in northern Europe and Italy, contrasted, 419
University of Bologna, 566
University of Chicago, 955
University of Paris, 393, 420, 1022
Untermenschen, 944
Urban VI (pope), 397
Urban VIII (pope), 554
urbanization
    Black Death impact on, 373, 380, 382
    in Eastern Europe, Late Middle Ages, 395
    during Enlightenment, 575–576
    during Industrial Revolution, 668–669, *669*
    Industrial Revolution and environmental issues, *672,* 672–673
Ure, Andrew, 656
Ursulines, 470
U.S.S. West Virginia, *938*
Ussher, James, 555, 557
usury, 658
utilitarianism, 704–705, 742
Utopia (More), 421
utopian socialists, 706
Uzbekistan, 752

Vaculík, Ludvík, 1024
Valla, Lorenzo, 383, 421
Valois dynasty, 362
van der Meulen, Adam Frans, 521
van der Straet, Jan, 435, *435*
van der Weyden, Rogier, 376, 381
van Gogh, Vincent, 840
Vashem, Yad, 951

Velázquez, Diego, 509, *509*
"velvet revolutions"
    of Central and Eastern Europe, 1030, 1033, 1036, *1036*
    fall of Berlin Wall and, 1029–1030, *1030,* 1037, 1042
    Yugoslavia wars and, 1033
Venice
    Black Death impact on, 373
    commerce and settlement, Middle Ages, 345
    oligarchy in, 395, 524
    siege of, 739, *740*
    trading empire, 345
Venus (Roman goddess), 590
Verdi, Giuseppe, 670
Verdun, battle of, 860
Versailles
    absolutism and, 518, 520, 522
    Hall of Mirrors, 748
    October Days of 1789 (popular revolt), 619
    Peter the Great's emulation of, 539
Vespucci, Amerigo, 434, 547
Vichy government, 933–934, 935, 940, 951, 991
Victor Emmanuel II (king of Piedmont-Sardinia), *744,* 744–745
Victor Emmanuel III (king of Italy), 897
Victoria (queen of England), 675, 678
Vienna, siege of, 532, 534–535
Viennese Secession movement, 751
Viet Cong, 1020, *1020,* 1022
Vietnam
    first war, 1946–1954 (First Indochina War), 991–992
    French imperialism in, 780, 991
    Tet offensive, 1022
    Vietnam War and antiwar movement, *1020,* 1020–1021, 1022, 1025
    World War I and Treaty of Versailles, 880, 991
View of London with Saint Paul's Cathedral in the Distance (Crome), 672
View of the Inside of a House in the Island of Ulietea, 589
View of Toledo (El Greco), *507,* 509
Vikings
    Greenland and, 346, 434
    Iceland and, 434
    in North America, 346, 433–434
    Rus', 336
Vindication of the Rights of Women, A (Wollstonecraft), 593, 621

Vinland (Newfoundland), 346
Virgil (Publius Virgilius Maro; Roman poet)
    in Dante's *Comedy,* 348
    Petrarch and, 378, 379
Virgin of the Rocks, The (Leonardo da Vinci), 414, *414*
Virginia
    colonization of, 476, 490, 491
    enslaved people rebellion in 1800, 700
Vitruvius, 419
Vladimiri, Paulus, 401
Voice of the People, Voice of God (Grosz), 915
Volard, Ambroise, *841*
Volkswagen, *1007*
Voltaire (François-Marie Arouet)
    on the Calas case, 572, 574, 580, 582
    deism, 583
    on enslavement, 587
    imprisonment and exiles, 580
    Newton and, 568–569, 578, 580
    on noble privileges, 614
    writing of, 574–575, 578, *580,* 580–581, 583, 600
von Bora, Katharina, 447
Vonnegut, Kurt, 966
voting rights
    civil rights movement, 1016–1017
    in fascist Italy, 895
    of men, in France, 630, 632, 727, 741, 812
    of men, in Germany, 748, 812
    of men, in Great Britain, 743, 812, 820
    Nineteenth Amendment (U.S. Constitution), 867, 905
    of women, in France, 905
    of women, in Great Britain, 905
    women's suffrage and Second Reform Bill (Great Britain), 742, 742–743
    women's suffrage and women's movement, turn of twentieth century, 812–816, *813, 814,* 867, *1016*
Vulgate, 467, 468

Waiting for Godot (Beckett), 996
Wajda, Andrzej, 1011
Walachia, 759
Wales, 357
Wałęsa, Lech, 1027
War and Peace (Tolstoy), 837–838
war communism, 888, 889, 890
War of the Austrian Succession, 602
War of the Spanish Succession, 529–530, *530*

Young Turks, 826, 854
youth culture, 1008–1009, *1009*, 1021
Ypres, battles of, 857, 861, 862
Yugoslavia
    collapse of communism, 1004, 1030,
        1033–1035, *1038*
    end of World War II and, 967,
        968–970
    International Criminal Tribunal, 1070
    student movements (1960s), 1023

Treaty of Versailles and creation of
    nation-state of, 925
wars of 1990s, 1033–1035, *1038*, 1039
World War I and, 875, 878
World War II, 939, 944, 957

Zaire, 1055
Zaleski, Marcin, *695*
Zambia, 785
Zawahiri, Ayman al-, 1063

Zetkin, Clara, 813
Zhirinovsky, Vladimir, 1032
Zika virus, 1050
Zimbabwe, 785
Zimmerman, Arthur, 876
Zionism, 818, *819*, 864, 880, 986
Zola, Émile, 836
Zollverein, 731
Zwingli, Ulrich, 454
Zwinglianism, 454